Kerrie Meyle
Cameron
John Joy

with Jonathan Alm, Alex Fedotyev,
Scott Moss, Oskar Landman,
Marnix Wolf, and Pete Zerger

System Center 2012 Operations Manager

UNLEASHED

SAMS | 800 East 96th Street, Indianapolis, Indiana 46240 USA

System Center 2012 Operations Manager Unleashed

ISBN-10: 0-672-33591-3
ISBN-13: 978-0-672-33591-4

Library of Congress Cataloging-in-Publication Data is on file

Printed in the United States of America

First Printing: February 2013

Trademarks

All terms mentioned in this book that are known to be trademarks or service marks have been appropriately capitalized. Pearson Education, Inc. cannot attest to the accuracy of this information. Use of a term in this book should not be regarded as affecting the validity of any trademark or service mark.

Warning and Disclaimer

Every effort has been made to make this book as complete and as accurate as possible, but no warranty or fitness is implied. The information provided is on an "as is" basis. The author and the publisher shall have neither liability nor responsibility to any person or entity with respect to any loss or damages arising from the information contained in this book.

Bulk Sales

Pearson offers excellent discounts on this book when ordered in quantity for bulk purchases or special sales. For more information, please contact:

U.S. Corporate and Government Sales
1-800-382-3419
corpsales@pearsontechgroup.com

For sales outside of the U.S., please contact:

International Sales
+1-317-581-3793
international@pearsontechgroup.com

Editor-in-Chief
Greg Wiegand

Executive Editor
Neil Rowe

Development Editor
Mark Renfrow

Managing Editor
Kristy Hart

Project Editor
Andy Beaster

Copy Editor
Geneil Breeze

Indexer
Heather McNeill

Proofreader
Debbie Williams

Technical Editor
Kevin Holman

Publishing Coordinator
Cindy Teeters

Cover Designer
Mark Shirar

Compositor
Gloria Schurick

Contents at a Glance

Table of Contents

About the Authors

Kerrie Meyler, System Center MVP for Cloud and Datacenter Management, is the lead author of numerous System Center books in the Unleashed series. This includes *System Center Operations Manager 2007 Unleashed* (2008), *System Center Configuration Manager 2007 Unleashed* (2009), *System Center Operations Manager 2007 R2 Unleashed* (2010), *System Center Opalis Integration Server 6.3 Unleashed* (2011), *System Center Service Manager 2010 Unleashed* (2011), and *System Center 2012 Configuration Manager Unleashed* (2012). She is an independent consultant and trainer with more than 15 years of Information Technology experience. Kerrie was responsible for evangelizing SMS while a Sr. Technology Specialist at Microsoft and has presented on System Center technologies at TechEd and MMS.

Cameron Fuller, System Center MVP for Cloud and Datacenter Management, is a principal consultant for Catapult Systems and serves as their Corporate Practice Lead for System Center. With 20 years of infrastructure experience, he focuses on management solutions. Cameron coauthored *Microsoft Operations Manager 2005 Unleashed* (Sams, 2006), *System Center Operations Manager 2007 Unleashed* (Sams, 2008), and *System Center Operations Manager 2007 R2 Unleashed* (Sams, 2010), and was a contributor to *System Center Configuration Manager 2007 Unleashed* (Sams, 2009). Cameron has written for *Windows IT Professional* and *TechNet* magazines and blogs on System Center related topics. Cameron has presented at numerous Microsoft conferences, including TechEd and MMS.

John Joyner, System Center MVP for Cloud and Datacenter Management, is Director of Product Development at ClearPointe, a provider of remote network management and cloud-based Network Operations Center (NOC) services to customers and partners around the world since 2001. John is a coauthor of *System Center Operations Manager 2007 Unleashed* (Sams, 2008) and *System Center Operations Manager 2007 R2 Unleashed* (Sams, 2010). He is also a syndicated technology columnist for CBS-Interactive, covering the Enterprise Cloud and Datacenter beats weekly for TechRepublic since April 2011. John has taught at the University of Arkansas at Little Rock as an adjunct professor for an IT course on cloud infrastructure management.

About the Contributors

Jonathan Almquist has been working in the information technology industry since 1999, focusing primarily on Operations Manager. During his tenure at Microsoft as a Premier Field Engineer, he assisted several top 10 Fortune 500 companies in implementing and managing large-scale OpsMgr 2007 environments. Currently he provides an array of consulting services and delivers training events in System Center Operations Manager through his business, SCOMskills, LLC (http://scomskills.com).

Alex Fedotyev is a seasoned APM professional with experience in development, architecture, product management, and customer implementations. He spent seven years at AVIcode building the product and driving enterprise implementations; after the acquisition, he spent about six months at Microsoft working on integration with System Center Operations Manager. Alex then worked with several organizations as a senior consultant to implement AVIcode for enterprise customers. He currently works at AppDynamics to bring his expertise of monitoring applications based on Microsoft .NET technologies, and improve sales and product quality of the AppDynamics APM solution.

Scott Moss, Service Center Cloud and Datacenter Management MVP, is a senior consultant for 1E. He has worked in the IT industry for 17 years, the majority of that time working for numerous telecommunications companies. Scott first worked the PC help desk and worked his way up to the position of server administrator, administering servers in multiple datacenters across the country, and has monitored servers since MOM 2000. Today he is an active member of the community contributing to the Operations Manager TechNet forums and SystemCenterCentral.com.

Oskar Landman, System Center Cloud and Datacenter Management MVP, is a consultant at inovativ in The Netherlands, with more than 10 years of IT consulting experience. Oskar focuses on Operations Manager and Service Manager, designing complex monitoring solutions and writing management packs and reports.

Marnix Wolf, System Center Cloud and Datacenter Management MVP, is a senior consultant for PQR, an IT consulting company and Microsoft Gold Certified Partner. He focuses on private cloud solutions, based on the System Center 2012 product and Windows Server 2012, with 13 years of infrastructure experience. Marnix is the owner and author of Thoughts on OpsMgr, which has become one of the leading blogs on OpsMgr. With the shift to the private cloud, this blog is also shifting its focus in the same direction and has been retitled Thoughts on OpsMgr and System Center 2012.

Pete Zerger, System Center Cloud and Datacenter Management MVP, is a consultant, author, and speaker focusing on Microsoft System Center technologies, virtualization, and cloud computing. Pete also speaks at user group meetings and technical conferences such as the Microsoft Management Summit. He has contributed to multiple whitepapers and technical books, including *System Center Operations Manager 2007 R2 Unleashed* and *System Center Opalis 6.3 Unleashed*, and is a coauthor to the upcoming *System Center 2012 Orchestrator Unleashed*. In his scant spare time, Pete can be found blogging on SystemCenterCentral.com, an online community focusing on Microsoft System Center technologies.

Dedication

To our readers:

Dedicated to those who have read our previous books and used them to build OpsMgr environments, those who have read their copy to the point where it is falling apart, and those who email words of encouragement.

Writing a book is a tremendous undertaking, but knowing it makes a difference makes it all worthwhile.

Acknowledgments

Writing a book is an all-encompassing and time-consuming project, and this book certainly meets that description. Operations Manager is a far-reaching topic, and this book benefited from the input of many individuals. The authors and contributors would like to offer their sincere appreciation to all those who helped with *System Center 2012 Operations Manager Unleashed*. This long list includes Daniele Muscetta, Neil Harrison, Rob Kuehfus, Daniel Savage, Joseph Chan, and Victor Mushkatin of Microsoft; Chris Dugas and Ambers Ferrara of Transplace; Neale Browne, Graham Davies, Anders Bengtsson, and Paul Johnson; Scott Weisler for his recommendations on cross-platform security; Trevor Langston for his assistance with Exchange and its integration with OpsMgr; and Gary Farris for his assistance with PerformancePoint and Power View. Thank you also to Andreas Zuckerhut, Björn Axell, Walter Chomak, Jonathan Cowan, Matt Hester, Marco Shaw, Simon Skinner, and Pete Zerger, along with thanks to Kevin Garner for his assistance with the Configuration Manager 2012 management pack for Appendix A, and to Kevin Holman for being a great technical editor.

We would also like to thank our spouses and significant others for their patience and understanding during the many hours spent on this book, including production edits during the holiday season.

Thanks also go to the staff at Pearson, in particular to Neil Rowe, who has worked with us since *Microsoft Operations Manager 2005 Unleashed* (Sams, 2006).

We Want to Hear from You!

As the reader of this book, you are our most important critic and commentator. We value your opinion and want to know what we're doing right, what we could do better, what areas you'd like to see us publish in, and any other words of wisdom you're willing to pass our way.

As an executive editor for Sams Publishing, I welcome your comments. You can email or write me directly to let me know what you did or didn't like about this book—as well as what we can do to make our books better.

Please note that I cannot help you with technical problems related to the topic of this book. We do have a User Services group, however, where I will forward specific technical questions related to the book.

When you write, please be sure to include this book's title and author as well as your name, email address, and phone number. I will carefully review your comments and share them with the author and editors who worked on the book.

Email: feedback@samspublishing.com

Mail: Neil Rowe
Associate Publisher
Sams Publishing
800 East 96th Street
Indianapolis, IN 46240 USA

Reader Services

Visit our website and register this book at informit.com/register for convenient access to any updates, downloads, or errata that might be available for this book.

Foreword

System Center 2012 – Operations Manager: not just a monitoring platform

"In 2000, Microsoft acquired a technology license for the software that became Microsoft Operations Manager (MOM) 2000 and later MOM 2005. In ten years, things have changed." This is how our colleague Justin Incarnato began the foreword to *System Center Operations Manager 2007 R2 Unleashed.*

Operations Manager 2007 was certainly a revolutionary release, introducing service modeling and breaking from the previous codebase. Building upon that foundation, Operations Manager 2007 R2 was an evolutionary release, as it expanded its reach cross-platform and added stability and credibility, introducing concepts such as service level tracking while essentially maintaining the same architecture.

Things don't stop at Microsoft: Our products keep changing. This time around, the 2012 release is both evolutionary and revolutionary at the same time. 2012 has also been a transformational moment in the marketplace: the moment that all System Center components started being shipped as a single product, offering integrated scenarios that allow you to create, operate, and monitor your private and hybrid clouds.

When looking at the Operations Manager component (the topic of this book), we redesigned the topology and architecture to reduce your TCO while increasing scalability and high availability through resource pools for load distribution and automatic failover, and bringing to the table phenomenal value with many new features.

Infrastructure monitoring has always been the main focus of Operations Manager, but with the 2012 release the capabilities go well beyond monitoring servers and their operating systems (albeit here the list grew by supporting Windows Server 2012 as well as additional Linux distributions with Service Pack 1!). Operations Manager now supports monitoring thousands of different network devices, and can show the relationships and connections between network devices and servers. As infrastructure more and more evolves from physical hardware into a virtual cloud "fabric," concepts of "vicinity" on the network are achieved through tight integration with Virtual Machine Manager (another System Center 2012 component).

In addition, Operations Manager provides rich insights into the behavior of your applications: We always envisioned providing 360 degrees of visibility into your environment's health, walking up the stack from the network to the OS and up into the applications, down to code-level visibility. In this release, we think we have reached unprecedented breadth as well as depth in application insights we can provide, both for .NET applications as well as for Java, for the first time. These application performance monitoring (APM) capabilities will be augmented with an attached Software-as-a-Service offering such as Global Service Monitoring, which allows you to extend your monitoring system to run synthetic transactions from Microsoft data centers in the cloud.

As if this wasn't enough, the 2012 release of Operations Manager brings visibility, communication, and collaboration features such as a new dashboard infrastructure that allows you to build a dashboard once and make it available in multiple locations such as the Operations Manager console, the Web console, as well as through Microsoft SharePoint 2010. We also introduced the Team Foundation Server Synchronization management pack that allows you to escalate code-level problems identified by APM quickly to the developers of the application, with rich traces and insights about issues seen in production.

With all of this, it is our hope that System Center will bridge the gap between the Operations and Developer teams in your organization, allowing them to troubleshoot issues in production and quickly narrow down where problems have occurred—was it the network, the operating system, the application's code that caused downtime, or a bad user experience? This will help you reduce mean time to resolution.

Written by a team of experts—many of whom are personally known and who are the best heralds of our vibrant System Center community—this book should be a great help to you for learning and experiencing System Center 2012 Operations Manager.

System Center 2012 - Operations Manager Program Managers, including
Daniele Muscetta, Daniel Savage, Joseph Chan, and Victor Mushkatin
Microsoft Corporation

Introduction

In January 2012, Microsoft announced its shift in focus with System Center—no longer a suite of products, but a single product. System Center 2012 is a collection of components designed to help IT Pros configure and manage applications, services, computers, virtual machines (VMs), and the cloud; with each component designed to let you manage more of these than before. System Center provides a degree of interoperability between components through connectors and System Center Orchestrator; this will increase over time. System Center 2012 also includes a unified installer to install all eight components, although the installer currently is rather limited in scope.

Operations Manager (OpsMgr), one of the more popular System Center components and the topic of this book, has been Microsoft's monitoring solution for over a decade. OpsMgr monitors the operation and performance of applications, services, systems, and network devices. Beginning with Operations Manager 2007 R2, monitoring was extended beyond the Windows platform to encompass UNIX and Linux systems. Operations Manager generates alerts when a particular condition occurs, and depending on how that alert was generated, can even auto close the alert when the situation is resolved. Alerts can be viewed in a console, or configured to notify targeted individuals when there is a problem. Built-in data warehousing capability enables you to view historical data and statistics.

Operations Manager has come a long way from its early days after Microsoft's licensing of the technology from NetIQ in 2000. Operations Manager 2007 R2 was in the Gartner Group's "magic quadrant" for IT Event Correlation and Analysis. Each version has seen enhancements in scalability, performance, and capabilities.

Operations Manager is all about monitoring application health. This is defined and measured by the health of the components that make up that application. In today's environment, monitoring health typically includes network devices and the various pieces of a distributed application. Monitoring at the component level means that if a database used by an application has a problem, Operations Manager knows which application is affected. This is more useful than simply knowing that a database is down! New features in OpsMgr 2012 include increased reliability through implementation of management server pools, enhanced monitoring of network devices, improved dashboard capabilities, and deep monitoring of .NET and JEE applications through Microsoft's integration of AVIcode (acquired in 2010). These add to existing capabilities such as end-to-end monitoring encompassing Windows, UNIX, and Linux systems, using synthetic transactions, managing security and audit data, and defining distributed applications for monitoring.

Successfully implementing Operations Manager requires planning, design, and a thorough understanding of how to utilize its many capabilities. This complete guide for using Operations Manager 2012 from the authors of *System Center Operations Manager 2007 Unleashed* gives system administrators the information they need to know about Operations Manager and what it can do for their operations. This includes an overview of why operations management is important; planning, installing, and implementing Operations Manager 2012; and its integration with System Center. *System Center 2012 Operations Manager Unleashed* provides a comprehensive guide to this newest version of Microsoft's premier management software.

As always, the authors have a disclaimer: Management packs and technical information are constantly evolving. Sometimes it seemed that even before we finished a chapter, the information was changing. This has been particularly challenging as Microsoft is close to releasing its first service pack for System Center 2012 as we complete this book. We have done our best to present the information as it relates to both the released version and the service pack, even as that continues to take shape. The information in the book is current as of the time it was written, and the authors have done their best to keep up with the constant barrage of changing management packs, utilities, URLs, and knowledge base articles.

Fast Track: A Quick Look at What's New

Many of the chapters of this book include a "Fast Track" section. Fast Track is an aid to OpsMgr 2007 administrators that are familiar with *System Center Operations Manager 2007 Unleashed* and the *System Center Operations Manager 2007 R2 Unleashed* supplement. This section provides a quick overview of what has changed from the previous version. Some features have major enhancements, others relatively few, and some are completely new. Chapters covering new features and topics such as installation and upgrade do not include a Fast Track.

Part I: Operations Management Overview and Concepts

System Center 2012 Operations Manager Unleashed begins with an introduction to configuration management including initiatives and methodology. This includes Dynamic System Initiative (DSI), the IT Infrastructure Library (ITIL), and Microsoft Operations Framework (MOF). Although some consider this to be more of an alphabet soup of frameworks than constructive information, these strategies and approaches give structure to managing one's environment—and have special relevance in that the objective of System Center 2012 is to optimize, automate, and provide process agility and maturity in IT operations. More importantly, implementing Operations Manager is a project, and as such, it should include a structured approach with its own deployment. It's more than just running a setup program!

- Chapter 1, "Operations Management Basics," starts with the big picture and brings it down to the pain points that system administrators deal with on a daily basis, showing how System Center plans to address these challenges.
- Chapter 2, "What's New in System Center 2012 Operations Manager," appropriately tells you just that. It also covers the history of Operations Manager, compares this version with the previous releases, and introduces terminology and key concepts.
- In Chapter 3, "Looking Inside OpsMgr," the book begins to peel back the layers of the onion to discuss the design concepts behind System Center 2012 Operations Manager, the major OpsMgr components, health modeling, management group mechanics, management pack schema, and more.

Part II: Planning and Installation

Before diving into OpsMgr's setup program, it is best to take a step back to map out the requirements for your management environment and plan your server topology.

- Chapter 4, "Planning an Operations Manager Deployment," discusses the steps required for successfully planning an Operations Manager deployment.
- Once it is time to implement your design, Chapter 5, "Installing System Center 2012 Operations Manager," discusses installation prerequisites before going through the steps to install the various server components in a management group.
- Chapter 6, "Upgrading to System Center 2012 Operations Manager," discusses how to move from an Operations Manager 2007 to 2012 environment.

Part III: Moving Toward Application-Centered Management

With OpsMgr installed, how does one start using it? The third part of this book focuses on Operations Manager operations in your environment, which is where you will spend the bulk of your time, moving beyond setup to post-installation activities and potential adjustments to your initial configuration.

- Chapter 7, "Configuring and Using System Center 2012 Operations Manager," discusses what you need to know to get started with OpsMgr. It provides an overview of the Operations console and a drill-down into its functionality.
- Chapter 8, "Installing and Configuring Agents," goes through the details of computer discovery, the different techniques for implementing agents, and managing agents.
- Chapter 9, "Complex Configurations," discusses high availability, resource pools, the root management server emulator, using gateway servers, multi-homed agents, designing for distributed environments, and more.

- Chapter 10, "Security and Compliance," discusses role-based security, Run As profiles and accounts, required accounts, mutual authentication, cross platform security considerations, firewall considerations, and communications security. It also discusses Audit Collection Services, an optional but highly recommended part of your OpsMgr implementation.

- Chapter 11, "Dashboards, Trending, and Forecasting," covers the built-in dashboard functionality of Operations Manager 2012. It discusses prebuilt dashboards, creating your own dashboards, and enhancing dashboards using third-party options. The chapter also covers reporting, trending, and capacity planning.

Part IV: Administering System Center 2012 Operations Manager

All applications require administration, and Operations Manager is no exception.

- Chapter 12, "Backup and Recovery," discusses the components required for a complete backup and recovery plan, and steps for designing a disaster recovery plan. It also introduces System Center Data Protection Manager as a tool for managing your backups.

- Chapter 13, "Administering Management Packs," covers the components of a management pack, how to troubleshoot, deploy, and manage management packs, and the details of importing and exporting management packs into your OpsMgr environment.

- Chapter 14, "Monitoring with System Center 2012 Operations Manager," discusses the different monitors and rule types in Operations Manager and their functionality, creating alerts, overrides, and resolution sates, notification workflow, approaches for tuning monitors and rules and managing alerts, and maintenance mode.

Part V: Service-Oriented Monitoring

This section of the book gets into what Operations Manager is really about—using it to ease the pain of monitoring and managing your environment from end-to-end. It discusses using OpsMgr to manage different aspects of your environment.

- Chapter 15, "Monitoring .NET Applications," is a deep dive into .NET application monitoring, including information not yet documented by Microsoft. This new feature in OpsMgr 2012 lets you monitor web applications to get details about application performance and reliability. Using the Application Advisor console, you can identify problem areas, and then use the Application Diagnostics console to investigate and troubleshoot specific events.

- Chapter 16, "Network Monitoring," discusses the new network monitoring capabilities that provide the long-awaited pieces required for effective end-to-end monitoring. You can get detailed port, interface, and peripheral monitoring of your network devices, as well as virtual local area networks (vLANs), and hot standby router protocol (HSRP) groups. OpsMgr 2012 now includes monitoring of all types of devices, including firewalls and load balancers.

- ▶ Chapter 17, "Using Synthetic Transactions," talks about simulating connections into applications to verify their performance.
- ▶ Chapter 18, "Distributed Applications," discusses OpsMgr's capability to monitor the various pieces and components that make up the distributed applications commonly used in today's multi-system computing environment.
- ▶ Chapter 19, "Client Monitoring," covers the capabilities in OpsMgr for client monitoring, and managing crash errors using the Agentless Exception Monitoring functionality.

These chapters talk about the issues faced by administrators in each of these areas, and show how Operations Manager 2012 helps to monitor operational issues and maintain application health and stability.

Part VI: Beyond Operations Manager

The book now looks at extending one's use of Operations Manager through cross platform monitoring, authoring management packs and reports, and PowerShell. It also discusses integration with System Center and provides a glimpse of using OpsMgr as a hosted service and as a tool to deliver other managed services by leveraging multi-tenant cloud implementations of OpsMgr.

- ▶ Chapter 20, "Interoperability and Cross Platform," provides an update to the cross platform extensions first introduced in OpsMgr 2007 R2. This capability enables you not only to monitor UNIX/Linux platforms but also application workloads on non-Windows operating systems such as Java enterprise applications.
- ▶ Chapter 21, "System Center 2012 Integration," discusses Operations Manager's integration with other System Center components. These integration capabilities enable you to support private and hybrid cloud scenarios in enterprise environments.
- ▶ Chapter 22, "Authoring Management Packs and Reports," includes best practices around authoring and building custom management packs. It provides the means for you to design your own management pack complete with classes, monitors, rules, views, and reports, using the tools provided by Microsoft.
- ▶ Chapter 23, "PowerShell and Operations Manager," includes an introduction to PowerShell and then dives into practical examples of using PowerShell to administer your Operations Manager environment.
- ▶ Chapter 24, "Operations Manager for the Service Provider," explores various ways to deliver hosted and managed services, including an introduction to the new service provider foundation in Service Pack 1.

Part VII: Appendixes

By this time, you should have at your disposal all the tools necessary to unleash yourself as an Operations Manager expert. The last part of the book includes five appendixes:

- Appendix A, "OpsMgr By Example: Configuring and Tuning Management Packs," is a compilation of the authors' experiences with implementing some of the management packs available for Operations Manager 2012.
- Appendix B, "Performance Counters," discusses the performance counters specific to Operations Manager.
- Appendix C, "Registry Settings," discusses some of the more significant registry settings used by Operations Manager 2012.
- Appendix D, "Reference URLs," incorporates useful references you can access for further information about Operations Manager and System Center. The references are also included as live links available for download under the Downloads tab at Pearson's InformIT website at http://www.informit.com/store/system-center-2012-operations-manager-unleashed-9780672335914.
- Appendix E, "Available Online," discusses value-added content also available at the InformIT page.

Throughout, this book provides in-depth reference and technical information about System Center 2012 Operations Manager, as well as information about the other products and technologies on which OpsMgr features depend.

Disclaimers and Fine Print

There are several disclaimers. Microsoft is continually improving and enhancing its products. This means the information provided is probably outdated the moment the book goes to print.

In addition, the moment Microsoft considers code development on any product complete, it begins working on a service pack or future release; as the authors continue to work with the product, it is likely yet another one or two wrinkles will be discovered! The authors and contributors of *System Center 2012 Operations Manager Unleashed* have made every attempt to present information that is accurate and current as known at the time. Updates and corrections will be provided as errata on the InformIT website.

Thank you for purchasing *System Center 2012 Operations Manager Unleashed*. The authors hope it is worth your while (and their effort). Enjoy the ride!

PART I

Operations Management Overview and Concepts

IN THIS PART

CHAPTER 1

Operations Management Basics

IN THIS CHAPTER

- Ten Reasons to Use Operations Manager
- The Problem with Today's Systems
- Operations Management Defined
- Microsoft's Strategy for Operations Management
- Managing System Health
- Bridging the Operations Management Gap
- Overview of Microsoft System Center
- The Value Proposition of Operations Manager

With System Center 2012 Operations Manager (OpsMgr), Microsoft offers a management tool that consolidates information about Windows servers, UNIX/ Linux servers, and network devices to provide end-to-end monitoring of your applications and services and centralized administration. Operations Manager 2012 gives you the resources you need to get and stay in control of your environment and helps with managing, tuning, and securing applications. For example, this version of Operations Manager includes the following capabilities:

- **Architectural changes for improved stability and ease of maintenance:** System Center 2012 Operations Manager introduces resource pools for increased availability and eliminates the root management server (RMS), a potential single point of failure in OpsMgr 2007.
- **Enhanced network monitoring capabilities:** The newest version of Operations Manager now incorporates EMC Smarts network discovery and health monitoring technology.
- **Application performance monitoring:** System Center 2012 Operations Manager integrates Microsoft's acquisition of AVIcode for deep .NET application monitoring.
- **New and improved dashboards:** This version of Operations Manager contains significant enhancements in the ability to display data through use of its new dashboard technologies, enabling you to view operational and historical data in a single pane of glass.

This chapter serves as an introduction to System Center 2012 Operations Manager. To avoid constantly repeating that very long name, this book utilizes the Microsoft-approved abbreviation of this name, Operations Manager, or simply OpsMgr. System Center 2012 Operations Manager, the fifth version of Microsoft's operations management platform, includes numerous additions in functionality and scalability improvements over its predecessors. In doing so, it has a high standard to meet, as its predecessor, Operations Manager 2007 R2, was placed by Gartner Group in their Magic Quadrant for IT Event Correlation and Analysis in 2010; see https://h10078.www1.hp.com/bto/download/Gartner_Magic_Quadrant_IT_Event_Corr_Analysis.pdf. (Gartner retired this quadrant in 2011.)

The chapter discusses the Microsoft approach to Information Technology (IT) operations and systems management. This includes an explanation and comparison of the Microsoft Operations Framework (MOF), which incorporates and expands on the concepts contained in the Information Technology Infrastructure Library (ITIL) standard. It also examines the Microsoft Infrastructure Optimization Model (IO Model) used in the assessment of the maturity of organizations' IT operations. The IO Model is a component of Microsoft's Dynamic Systems Initiative (DSI), which aims at increasing the dynamic capabilities of organizations' IT operations.

These discussions have special relevance in that the objective of System Center is optimization, automation, process agility, and maturity in IT operations.

Ten Reasons to Use Operations Manager

Why should you use Operations Manager in the first place? How does this make your daily life as a systems administrator easier? Although this book covers the features and benefits of Operations Manager in detail, it definitely helps to have some quick ideas to illustrate why OpsMgr is worth a look!

Let's look at 10 compelling reasons why you might want to use Operations Manager:

1. The bulk of your department's budget goes towards maintaining current systems and services, rather than using the bucks to hire people to manage those assets or develop new systems.

2. You realize system monitoring would be much easier if you had a single view of the health of your environment, including the applications and services running in production.

3. You feel stuck in the IT version of the movie *Groundhog Day*—you solve the same problems over and over again every day in exactly the same way, except unlike in the movie, you and your systems can really die. Plus, this is not a particularly efficient way to maintain operations.

4. You don't have enough internal manpower (or brainpower) to solve problems as they come up, and consultants aren't cheap.

5. You find out there are problems when users (or upper management) start calling you. Although this mechanism is actually quite effective in getting your attention, it is somewhat stress inducing and definitely not proactive.

6. You realize that even though your servers are humming along just fine, you have no idea how your client applications are actually performing against what is running on those servers. This makes it tough to know whether latency issues exist.
7. Demonstrating that your organization is compliant with regulations such as Sarbanes-Oxley (SOX), the Health Insurance Portability and Accountability Act (HIPAA), the Federal Information Security Management Act (FISMA), or *<insert your own favorite compliance acronym here>* has become your new full-time job.
8. You would be more productive if you weren't monitoring your production environment all day...and night. And during lunch and vacation.
9. Your production environment is so diverse and widespread that when a problem arises, you don't even know where to start looking.
10. You don't have the time to write down all the troubleshooting information that is in your brain, and your boss is concerned you might be hit by a truck (or want to take that vacation). This probably is not the best way to run a production environment.

Although these 10 points contain some humor and a bit of satire, they represent real issues. If any of these themes resonate with you, you really owe it to yourself to investigate Operations Manager. These pain points are common to almost all users (even those using Microsoft technologies!), and System Center 2012 Operations Manager resolves them to a great degree.

However, the biggest reasons of all for using OpsMgr is the confidence and peace of mind it can bring you, knowing you have visibility and control of your IT systems. Deploying Operations Manager allows you to relax; you can feel comfortable knowing that with OpsMgr watching your back, your systems will be in good shape.

The Problem with Today's Systems

Microsoft describes System Center 2012 Operations Manager as a software solution that provides deep application diagnostics and infrastructure monitoring, helping you ensure the predictable performance and availability of vital applications, and offering a comprehensive view of your datacenter, private, and public clouds. What exactly does this mean? Operations Manager provides an easy-to-use monitoring environment, integrating information from Microsoft and non-Microsoft systems, applications, and devices, and providing a single view of the health of your operations environment—be that in a cloud or your own data center.

These capabilities are significant because today's IT systems are prone to a number of problems from the perspective of operations management, including the following:

- System isolation
- Lack of notification
- Lack of historical information
- Not enough expertise

- Lack of methodology
- Missing information
- False alarms
- Proliferation of virtualization and cloud computing

This list should not be surprising, because these problems manifest themselves in all IT shops with varying degrees of severity. In fact, Forrester Research estimates that 82% of larger shops are pursuing service management, and 67% are planning to increase Windows management. Let's look at what the issues are.

Why Do Systems Go Down?

Let's start with examining reasons why systems go down. Figure 1.1 illustrates reasons for system outages, based on the authors' personal experiences and observations.

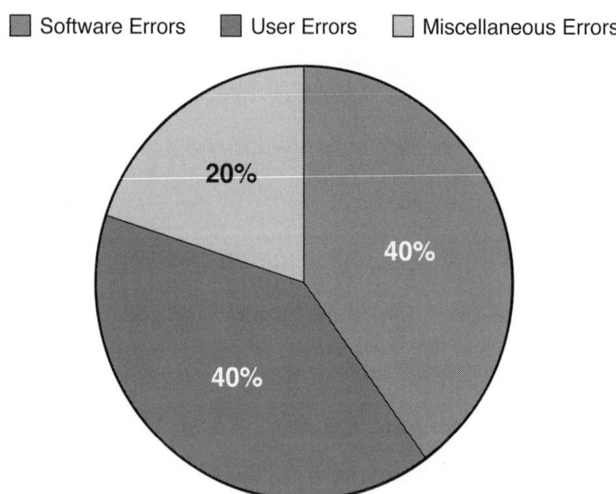

FIGURE 1.1 Causes of system outages. D. Scott, in a May 2002 presentation titled *Operation Zero Downtime*, discussed similar statistics at a Gartner Group Security Conference.

Here are some of the reasons for these outages:

- **Software errors:** Software is responsible for somewhat less than half the errors. These errors include software coding errors, software integration errors, data corruption, and such.

- **User errors:** End users and operators cause just fewer than half the errors. This includes incorrectly configuring systems, failing to catch warning messages that turn into errors, accidents, unplugging the power cord, and so on.
- **Miscellaneous errors:** This last category is fairly small. Causes of problems here include disk crashes, power outages, viruses, natural disasters, and so on.

As Figure 1.1 demonstrates, the vast majority of failures result from software-level errors and user errors. It is surprising to note that hardware failures account for only a small percentage of problems, which is a tribute to modern systems such as redundant arrays of independent disks (RAID), clustering, and other mechanisms deployed to provide server and application redundancy.

The numbers show that to reduce system downtime, you need to attack the software and user error components of the equation. That is where you will get the most "bang for the buck."

No System Is an Island

Microsoft Windows Server and the applications that run on it, such as Microsoft Exchange and Microsoft SQL Server, expose a wealth of information with event logs, performance counters, and application-specific logs. However, this data is isolated and typically server-centric, making it difficult to determine where the problem really is. To get a handle on your operations, you need to take actions to prevent the situation shown in Figure 1.2, where applications and system components are isolated islands of information.

FIGURE 1.2 Multiple islands of information.

You can find isolated information in a number of locations:

- **Event logs:** Events are generated by operating systems, components, and applications. The logs include errors, warnings, information, and security auditing events. Event logs are stored locally on each server.
- **Log files:** File-based logs contain information related to system and software component installations, and they can include ongoing information related to the status of an application. For example, a web server maintains log files listing every request made to the server, and Microsoft SQL Server maintains a series of log files capturing events related to its operation. Operations Manager uses log files as well.
- **Performance counters:** The Windows operating system and multiple applications expose detailed performance information through performance counters. The data includes processor utilization, memory utilization, network statistics, disk free space, and thousands of other pieces of operational information.
- **Windows Management Instrumentation (WMI):** WMI provides access to an incredible amount of information, ranging from high-level status of services to detailed hardware information.
- **Expertise:** Consultants, engineers, and subject matter experts have information locked up in their heads or written down on whiteboards and paper napkins. This is as much an island of information as the statistics and data stored on any computer!

Although system information is captured through event logs, performance counters, file-based logs, and experiences, it is typically lost over time. Most logs roll over, are erased to clear space, or eventually overwritten. Even if the information is not ultimately lost or forgotten, it typically is not reviewed on a regular basis.

Most application information is also server-centric, typically stored on the server, and specific to the server where the application resides. There is no built-in, systemwide, cross-system view of critical information or system health.

Having islands of information, where operational data is stranded on any given island, makes it difficult to get to needed information in a timely or effective manner.

Lack of Notification

In your typical unmanaged IT environment, often no one knows when noteworthy events occur. Going to each server and reviewing its event logs regularly is a massive undertaking for the typical system administrator. Although the event logs capture a tremendous amount of information, they will eventually roll over and be overwritten without being looked at; that information is lost.

You may be familiar with an old philosophical saying: If a tree falls in a forest and no one is around to hear it, does it make a sound?

Here's the operations management equivalent: If an event is logged on a system and no one knows, does logging it make a difference?

The answer to this question is definitely "no;" if no one knows, the event may as well not be logged. This loss of information can affect the long-term health of the system—if you knew about its occurrence you could avert potential outages.

As an example, there was a situation where an Exchange server at a large manufacturing organization was receiving 1018 errors in the Application Event log for several months, but the administrators never checked the logs to catch it. Error 1018 indicates an Exchange database problem; it is a severe error requiring immediate action. The server eventually crashed and the backups were unusable—the backed up databases were corrupt. Restoring the mail system necessitated an expensive disaster recovery scenario using outside consultants, resulting in the loss of critical messaging data and the jobs of the staff held responsible.

In the end, information is only informative if you are aware of it, and it is only as good as what you do with it. To put this another way, most IT shops have many trees falling without someone hearing them...until it is too late.

Lack of Historical Information

Sometimes you may capture information about a system problem, but are not able to look back in time to see whether this is an isolated instance or part of a recurring pattern. An incident can be a one-time blip or may indicate an underlying issue. Without a historical context, it is difficult to understand the significance of any particular incident. This is especially true with performance data.

Here's an example: An IT shop brings in a technical consultant to review a system's performance problems. As evidence, the in-house IT staff points out there are complaints about performance but that memory and CPU are only 50% utilized. However, this does not indicate anything by itself. It could be that memory and the CPU are normally 65% utilized and the problem is really a network utilization problem, which in turn reduces the load on the other resources. The problem could even be a newly implemented but poorly written application! A historical context could provide useful information.

As a technical expert, the consultant develops a hypothesis and tests it, which takes time and costs money. Instead of trying to solve a problem, many IT shops just throw more hardware at it—only to find that this does not necessarily improve performance. With historical records, they would see that system utilization actually dropped at the same time users started complaining, and they could look elsewhere to find the network problems. Ideally, you would have historical information for troubleshooting and detecting trends.

Lack of Expertise

Do you lack the in-house expertise necessary to diagnose some of the messages or trends appearing on your servers and applications? Do you pay an arm and a leg to call in consultants, only to find that those messages are actually not severe? On the other hand, do you ignore messages you don't think are significant—only to later discover that they are important and possibly critical?

If the expertise you need is not available when you need it, you can miss diagnostic opportunities or incur higher operational costs from downtime. Missed diagnostics opportunities can translate to system outages and ultimately higher operational expenses should emergency measures be required to resolve problems.

Lack of Methodology

Many IT organizations still "fly by the seat of their pants" when it comes to identifying and resolving problems. Using standard procedures and a methodology helps you minimize risk and solve issues faster.

A *methodology* is a body of practices, procedures, and rules used by those who work in a discipline or engage in an inquiry. It can also refer to a set of working methods. You can look at a methodology as a structured process that defines the who, what, where, when, and why of your operations, and the procedures to use when defining problems, solutions, and courses of action.

Consistently using a methodology gives you the tools to help measure or compare where you are to where you were. A methodology also includes identifying and using standards, policies, and rules of operation.

With IT's continually increased role in running successful business operations, having a structured and standard way to define IT operations can increase your business decision-makers' confidence that IT is a significant and ongoing business concern. In addition, that increased level of confidence may translate to higher job satisfaction.

Missing Information

Sometimes problems are detected by what occurred elsewhere, or by what did not occur rather than what actually happened. A classic example of this is data backups. Regardless of whether the backup is successful or fails, it generates an event and some type of notification.

However, what happens when the backup doesn't fail or succeed, but just doesn't occur? If you are not looking closely at your event logs, you will likely not discover this fact until later. To cite an example, a large educational institution doing backups missed one server during an initial configuration. Eventually the server crashed and they attempted to restore to an earlier point in time, only then discovering there were no backups. Even though all their backup jobs were configured to generate success notices and notify of failures, that particular server was not generating these notifications and was missed—with severe consequences impacting management, faculty, staff, and students.

Sometimes when you do not receive a notification or event, it is a signal to take action. The bottom line is you need to be able to test whether something has failed to happen.

False Alarms

Even when you are notified of events, it may be difficult to tell whether you actually have a problem. Windows Server and the services and applications running under it are good about generating errors, warnings, and informational messages. The challenge is that there is so much information that it can be difficult to tell which of these thousands of messages are normal operating events, rather than errors that require remedial action.

False alarms are typically due to a lack of knowledge or inadequate filtering. Sometimes a benign message may look ominous to the untrained eye. One example would be event 11 from w32time in the System Event log, which is a warning indicating an unreachable Network Time Protocol (NTP) server. This actually is a normal occurrence and is not a problem (although several of these errors may indicate a problem that needs action).

Proliferation of Virtualization and Cloud Computing

Here's an old saying: *If you fail to plan, you plan to fail.* In no area of IT operations is this truer than when considering virtualization technologies. Managing operations in an increasingly "virtual" world, where boundaries between systems and applications are not always clear, will require considering new elements of management not present in a purely physical environment.

Virtualization as a concept is very exciting to IT operations. Whether talking about virtualization of servers or applications, the potential for dramatic increases in process automation and efficiency and reduction in deployment costs is very real. New servers and applications can be provisioned in a matter of minutes. With this newfound agility comes a potential downside, which is the reality that virtualization can increase the velocity of change in your environment. The tools used to manage operations often fail to address new dynamics that come when virtualization is introduced into a computing environment.

Many organizations make the mistake of taking on new tools and technologies in an ad-hoc fashion, without first reviewing them in the context of the process controls used to manage the introduction of change into the environment. These big gains in efficiency can lead to a completely new problem—inconsistencies in processes not designed to address the new dynamics that come with the virtual territory.

The Bottom Line

The issues described so far generally occur in an unmanaged environment, with "unmanaged" meaning an environment that is not using a disciplined approach for managing its operational information. By not correlating operational data across systems, being aware of potential issues, maintaining a history of past performance and problems, and so on, IT shops open themselves up to fighting time bombs and putting out fires (see Figure 1.3) that could be prevented by using a more systematic approach to operations management, which is described in the next section.

FIGURE 1.3 Fighting fires.

Operations Management Defined

Operations management is not something you achieve at a point in time. Rather, it is a process aimed at improving the reliability and availability of computer applications and services through addressing the problems discussed in the previous sections of this chapter. It consists of the care and feeding of an IT asset, as well as managing, maintaining, and supporting the needs and events (including dependencies) of an operation.

This means that you do not attain operations management bliss merely by running a setup program to install a "management application." Achieving this calls for coordination between technology, processes, and people, resulting in improved quality and productivity, as depicted in the IT service triangle shown in Figure 1.4.

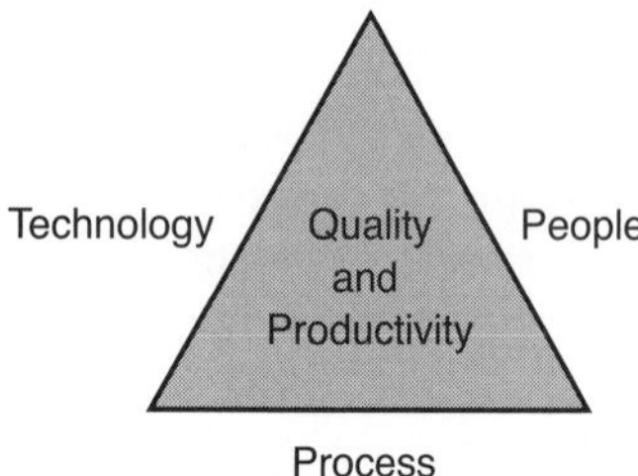

FIGURE 1.4 The IT service triangle.

At a more granular level, operations management is about correlating what may appear to be seemingly unrelated events and data across machines to determine what information is significant to your operational environment versus what is not. Operations management is also about managing the ongoing activities that Information Technology personnel perform on various IT components with the goal of improving the performance of one's business organization. It results in higher reliability, greater availability, better asset allocation, and a more predictable IT environment.

How does operations management accomplish this? As IT operations grow in size and impact, it quickly becomes apparent that effectively managing complex production environments requires the use of standardized methodologies and approaches to manage servers. Once a business relies on IT to maintain daily operations, having a disciplined and informative methodology is necessary to help ensure IT is supporting the organization's business goals and objectives. These goals typically include reducing costs, increasing productivity, and providing information security.

Reducing costs and increasing productivity are important because, in addition to taking up a significant part of the IT budget, the business impact of failed systems or performance degradation can be devastating to the entire enterprise, resulting in increased operational costs, decreased quality of service, and lost revenue and profit. Time, after all, is money! Information security is also imperative because the price tag of compromised systems and data recovery from security exposures can be large, and those costs continue to rise each year.

THE COST OF DOWNTIME

CIO Insight (http://www.cioinsight.com/c/a/Infrastructure/IT-Downtime-Carries-a-High-Pricetag-448122/) reports that IT downtime costs businesses, collectively, more than 127 million hours per year (an average of 545 hours per company) in employee productivity, according to an online survey of IT and business executives sponsored by CA Technologies and conducted by research firm Coleman Parkes in November 2010.

This loss is equivalent to 63,500 people being unable to work for an entire year. The survey of 2,000 organizations in North America and Europe also found that IT outages are frequent and lengthy, and can substantially damage company reputation, staff morale, and customer loyalty; 50% of respondents say IT outages can damage a company's reputation, and 18% think outages can be very damaging.

Let's look at some direct costs. Consider a simplified example of the impact of temporarily disrupting an ecommerce site normally available 7×24. The site generates an average of $4,000 per hour in revenue from customer orders, for an annual value in sales revenue of $35,040,000. If the website were unavailable for 6 hours due to a security vulnerability, the directly attributable losses for the outage would be $24,000.

This number is only an average cost; most ecommerce sites generate revenue at a wide range of rates based on the time of day, day of week, time of year, marketing campaigns, and so on. Typically the outage occurs during peak times when the system is already stressed, thus greatly increasing the cost of that 6-hour loss. Adding indirect costs, (loss of customers and reputation) brings this sample 6-hour outage far higher than the simple hourly proportion of time applied to an average revenue stream.

Another case in point would be a large-sized credit card–processing company that estimates it would stand to lose nearly $400,000 in direct revenue if it experienced a 1–hour operational outage affecting its ability to process credit card transactions. This number assumes an estimated cost of just over $1.00 per missed transaction and does not include the inevitable decline in revenues due to a loss of confidence from clients if such an outage were to happen.

As part of an operations management plan, any company with more than nontrivial IT requirements stands to benefit by using software tools to automate tasks such as managing server networks and the help desk, tracking desktop systems, and enforcing security policies. Microsoft software addresses these areas with System Center. System Center solutions help you manage your physical and virtual IT environments across datacenters, desktops, and devices. These integrated and automated management solutions can help you be a more productive service provider for your business. System Center captures and aggregates knowledge about systems, policies, processes, and best practices so that you can optimize your infrastructure to reduce costs, improve application availability, and enhance service delivery.

Keep in mind, however, that the System Center components are merely tools; they enable you to meet objectives by incorporating software that automates the process.

Microsoft's Strategy for Operations Management

Microsoft utilizes a multipronged approach to operations management. This strategy includes the following areas:

- Continuing to make Windows easier to manage by providing core management infrastructure and capabilities in the Windows platform itself. This allows business and management application developers to improve their infrastructures and capabilities. Microsoft believes that improving the manageability of solutions built on Windows Server System will be a key driver in shaping the future of Windows management.
- Building complete management solutions on this infrastructure, either through making them available in the operating system or by using management tools such as Operations Manager, Service Manager, Virtual Machine Manager, Configuration Manager, and other System Center components.
- Integrating infrastructure and management, exposing services and interfaces that applications can utilize.
- Supporting a standard web services specification for system management. WS-Management is a specification of a Simple Object Access Protocol (SOAP)-based protocol, based on web services, used to manage servers, devices, and applications. The intent is to provide a universal language that all types of devices can use to share data about themselves, which in turn makes them more easily managed. Microsoft has included support for WS-Management beginning with Windows

Vista and Windows Server 2008, and it is leveraged by multiple System Center components.

- Using an Infrastructure Optimization (IO) Model as a framework for aligning IT with business needs. The "Optimizing Your Infrastructure" section later in this chapter discusses the IO Model further. The IO Model describes your IT infrastructure in terms of cost, security risk, and operational agility.
- Adopting a model-based management strategy (a component of the Dynamic Systems Initiative, discussed in "Microsoft's Dynamic Systems Initiative," the next section of this chapter) to implement synthetic transaction technology. Operations Manager is intended to deliver a service-based monitoring set of scenarios, enabling you to define models of services to deliver to end users.

Microsoft's Dynamic Systems Initiative

A large percentage of IT departments' budgets and resources typically focuses on mundane maintenance tasks such as applying software patches or monitoring the health of a network, without leaving the staff with the time or energy to focus on more exhilarating (and more productive) strategic initiatives.

DSI is a Microsoft and industry strategy intended to enhance the Windows platform, delivering a coordinated set of solutions that simplifies and automates how businesses design, deploy, and operate their distributed systems. Using DSI helps IT and developers create operationally aware platforms. By designing systems that are more manageable and automating operations, organizations can reduce costs and proactively address their priorities.

DSI is about building software that enables knowledge of an IT system to be created, modified, transferred, and operated on throughout the life cycle of that system. It is a commitment from Microsoft and its partners to help IT teams capture and use knowledge to design systems that are more manageable and to automate operations, which in turn reduces costs and gives organizations additional time to focus proactively on what is most important. By innovating across applications, development tools, the platform, and management solutions, DSI will result in

- Increased productivity and reduced costs across all aspects of IT,
- Increased responsiveness to changing business needs, and
- Reduced time and effort required to develop, deploy, and manage applications.

Microsoft is positioning DSI as the connector of the entire system and service life cycles.

Microsoft Product Integration

DSI focuses on automating datacenter operational jobs and reducing associated labor through self-managing systems. Here are several examples where Microsoft products and tools integrate with DSI:

- Operations Manager uses the application knowledge captured in management packs to simplify identifying issues and their root causes, facilitating resolution and restoring services or preventing potential outages, and providing intelligent management at the system level.
- Configuration Manager uses model-based configuration baseline templates in its Compliance Management feature to automate identification of undesired shifts in system configurations.
- Service Manager uses model-based management packs. You can easily add new models describing your own configuration items or work items to track their life cycle. Each data model is stored in one or more management packs that make up the model.
- Visual Studio is a model-based development tool that leverages Service Modeling Language (SML), enabling operations managers and application architects to collaborate early in the development phase and ensure applications are modeled with operational requirements in mind.
- Windows Server Update Services (WSUS) enables greater and more efficient administrative control through modeling technology that enables downstream systems to construct accurate models representing their current state, available updates, and installed software.

SDM AND SML: WHAT'S THE DIFFERENCE?

Microsoft originally used the System Definition Model (SDM) as its standard schema with DSI. SDM was a proprietary specification put forward by Microsoft. The company later decided to implement SML, which is an industrywide published specification used in heterogeneous environments. Using SML helps DSI adoption by incorporating a standard that Microsoft's partners can understand and apply across mixed platforms. SML is discussed later in the section "The Role of Service Modeling Language in IT Operations."

DSI focuses on automating datacenter operations and reducing total cost of ownership (TCO) through self-managing systems. Can logic be implemented in management software such that it can identify system or application issues in real time and then dynamically take actions to mitigate the problem? Consider the scenario where, without operator intervention, a management system moves a virtual machine running a line-of-business application because the existing host is experiencing an extended spike in resource utilization. This is now a reality, delivered in the live migration feature of Virtual Machine Manager. DSI aims to extend this type of self-healing and self-management to other areas of operations.

In support of DSI, Microsoft has invested heavily in three major areas:

- **Systems designed for management:** Microsoft is delivering development and authoring tools, such as Visual Studio, that enable businesses to capture the knowledge of everyone from business users and project managers to the architects, developers, testers, and operations staff using models. By capturing and embedding this knowledge into the infrastructure, organizations can reduce support complexity and cost.

- **An operationally aware platform:** The core Windows operating system and its related technologies are critical when solving everyday operational and service challenges. This requires designing the operating system services for manageability. In addition, the operating system and server products must provide rich instrumentation and hardware resource virtualization support.
- **Virtualized applications and server infrastructure:** Virtualization of servers and applications improves the agility of the organization by simplifying the effort involved in modifying, adding, or removing the resources a service utilizes in performing work.

THE MICROSOFT APPROACH TO SYSTEMS MANAGEMENT

End-to-end automation could include update management, availability and performance monitoring, change and configuration management, service management, provisioning, and rich reporting services. Microsoft's System Center is a set of system management tools and solutions that focus on providing you with the knowledge and tools to manage and support your IT infrastructure. The objective of System Center is to create integrated systems management tools and technologies, thus helping to ease operations, reduce troubleshooting time, and improve planning capabilities.

The Importance of DSI

There are three architectural elements behind the DSI initiative:

- That developers have tools (such as Visual Studio) to design applications in a way that makes them easier for administrators to manage after those applications are in production
- That Microsoft products can be secured and updated in a uniform way
- That Microsoft server applications are optimized for management, to take advantage of System Center Operations Manager

DSI represents a departure from the traditional approach to systems management. DSI focuses on designing for operations from the application development stage, rather than a more customary operations perspective that concentrates on automating task-based processes. This strategy highlights the fact that Microsoft's Dynamic Systems Initiative is about building software that enables knowledge of an IT system to be created, modified, transferred, and used throughout the life cycle of a system. DSI's core principles of knowledge, models, and the life cycle are key in addressing the challenges of complexity and manageability faced by IT organizations. By capturing knowledge and incorporating health models, DSI can facilitate easier troubleshooting and maintenance, and thus lower TCO.

The Role of Service Modeling Language in IT Operations

A key underlying component of DSI is the eXtended Markup Language (XML)-based specification called the Service Modeling Language. SML is a standard developed by several leading information technology companies that defines a consistent way for infrastructure and application architects to define how applications, infrastructure, and services are modeled in a consistent way.

SML facilitates modeling systems from a development, deployment, and support perspective with modular, reusable building blocks that eliminate the need to reinvent the wheel when describing and defining a new service. The end result is systems that are easier to develop, implement, manage, and maintain, resulting in reduced TCO to the organization. SML is a core technology that will continue to play a prominent role in future products developed to support the ongoing objectives of DSI.

NOTE: SML RESOURCES ON THE WEB

SML functionality and configuration management within Configuration Manager are implemented using compliance settings. For more information about SML, view the latest draft of the SML standard at http://www.w3.org/TR/sml/. For additional technical information about SML from Microsoft, see http://www.microsoft.com/download/en/details.aspx?displaylang=en&id=24838.

IT Infrastructure Library and Microsoft Operations Framework

ITIL is widely accepted as an international standard of best practices for operations management. MOF is closely related to ITIL, and both describe best practices for IT service management processes. The next sections introduce you to ITIL and MOF. Warning: Fasten your seatbelt, because this is where the fun really begins!

What Is ITIL?

As part of Microsoft's management approach, the company relied on an international standards-setting body as its basis for developing an operational framework. The British Office of Government Commerce (OGC) provides best practices advice and guidance on using IT in service management and operations. The OGC also publishes the IT Infrastructure Library, commonly known as ITIL.

ITIL provides a cohesive set of best practices for IT Service Management (ITSM). These best practices include a series of books giving direction and guidance on provisioning quality IT services and facilities needed to support IT. The documents are maintained by the OGC and supported by publications, qualifications, and an international users group.

Started in the 1980s, ITIL is under constant development by a consortium of industry IT leaders. The ITIL covers a number of areas and is primarily focused on ITSM; its ITIL is considered to be the most consistent and comprehensive documentation of best practices for ITSM worldwide.

ITSM is a business-driven, customer-centric approach to managing IT. It specifically addresses the strategic business value generated by IT and the need to deliver high quality IT services to one's business organization. Here are the key objectives of ITSM:

- Align IT services with current and future needs of the business and its customers.
- Improve the quality of IT services delivered.
- Reduce long-term costs of providing services.

1

MORE ABOUT ITIL

The core books for version 3 (ITIL v3) were published on June 30, 2007. With v3, ITIL has adopted an integrated service life cycle approach to ITSM, as opposed to organizing itself around the concepts of IT service delivery and support.

ITIL v2 was a targeted product, explicitly designed to bridge the gap between technology and business, with a strong process focus on effective service support and delivery. The v3 documents recognize the service management challenges brought about by advancements in technology, such as virtualization and outsourcing, and emerging challenges for service providers. The v3 framework emphasizes managing the life cycle of the services provided by IT and the importance of creating business value, rather than just executing processes.

There are five core volumes of ITIL v3:

- **Service Strategy:** This volume identifies market opportunities for which services could be developed to meet a requirement on the part of internal or external customers. Key areas here are service portfolio management and financial management.
- **Service Design:** This volume focuses on the activities that take place to develop the strategy into a design document that addresses all aspects of the proposed service and the processes intended to support it. Key areas of this volume are availability management, capacity management, continuity management, and security management.
- **Service Transition:** This volume centers on implementing the output of service design activities and creating a production service (or modifying an existing service). There is some overlap between Service Transition and Service Operation, the next volume. Key areas of the Service Transition volume are change management, release management, configuration management, and service knowledge management.
- **Service Operation:** This volume involves the activities required to operate the services and maintain their functionality as defined in service level agreements (SLAs) with one's customers. Key areas here are incident management, problem management, and request fulfillment.
- **Continual Service Improvement:** This volume focuses on the ability to deliver continual improvement to the quality of the services that the IT organization delivers to the business. Key areas include service reporting, service measurement, and service level management.

A 2011 update, currently referred to as ITIL 2011, updated the core v3 publications to address errors and inconsistencies. The update also simplified concepts, principles, and process flows. The Service Strategy publication saw significant revisions defining new processes for strategy management and business relationship management. For additional information, see http://www.itilnews.com/ITIL_v4_Simply_CSI_for_ITIL_v3.html.

Philosophically speaking, ITSM focuses on the customer's perspective of IT's contribution to the business, which is analogous to the objectives of other frameworks in terms of their consideration of alignment of IT service support and delivery with business goals in mind.

While ITIL describes the what, when, and why of IT operations, it stops short of describing how a specific activity should be carried out. A driving force behind its development was the recognition that organizations are increasingly dependent on IT for satisfying their corporate objectives relating to both internal and external customers, which increases the requirement for high quality IT services. Many large IT organizations realize that the road to a customer-centric service organization runs along an ITIL framework.

ITIL also specifies keeping measurements or metrics to assess performance over time. Measurements can include a variety of statistics, such as the number and severity of service outages, along with the amount of time it takes to restore service. These metrics or key performance indicators (KPIs) can be used to quantify to management how well IT is performing. This information can prove particularly useful for justifying resources during the next budget process!

MANAGING SYSTEMS IS LIKE MANAGING A BASEBALL TEAM

Baseball is replete with metrics on its KPIs. Some statistics are more than a century old, which is the context for an often-quoted statement by the legend of malapropisms, baseball's Most Valuable Player Yogi Berra: "I knew the record would stand until it was broken."

IT organizations can learn a valuable lesson from Major League Baseball by publishing its own "application management box score." For every critical transaction or process, IT should be able to report the AVR (average response time), the AAR (aggregate adoption rate), and RTQA (run time quality average)!

By adopting clear, undisputed metrics, IT could provide a common language on the level of service delivered for critical business applications, fundamental for IT and business alignment. This is the goal driving the estimated $26 billion invested in IT management tools annually (http://www.cio.com/article/685035/).

Major League Baseball knows that you can have the best players on your team, but without monitoring their health and performance, you won't optimize the team's performance. How do you plan to optimize IT performance? As Yogi also said, "If you don't know where you're going, you might not get there."

What Is MOF?

ITIL is generally accepted as the "best practices" for the industry. Being technology agnostic, it is a foundation that can be adopted and adapted to meet the specific needs of various IT organizations. Although Microsoft chose to adopt ITIL as a standard for its own IT operations for its descriptive guidance, Microsoft designed MOF to provide prescriptive guidance for effective design, implementation, and support of Microsoft technologies.

MOF is a set of publications providing both descriptive (what to do, when, and why) and prescriptive (how to do) guidance on ITSM. The key focus in developing MOF was providing a framework specifically geared toward managing Microsoft technologies. Microsoft created the first version of the MOF in 1999. The latest iteration of MOF (version 4) is designed to further

- ▶ Update MOF to include the full end-to-end IT service life cycle.
- ▶ Let IT governance serve as the foundation of the life cycle.
- ▶ Provide useful, easily consumable best practice-based guidance.
- ▶ Simplify and consolidate service management functions (SMFs), emphasizing workflows, decisions, outcomes, and roles.

MOF v4 now incorporates Microsoft's previously existing Microsoft Solutions Framework (MSF), providing guidance for application development solutions. The combined framework provides guidance throughout the IT life cycle, as shown in Figure 1.5.

At its core, the MOF is a collection of best practices, principles, and models. It provides direction to achieve reliability, availability, supportability, and manageability of mission-critical production systems, focusing on solutions and services using Microsoft products and technologies. MOF extends ITIL by including guidance and best practices derived from the experience of Microsoft's internal operations groups, partners, and customers worldwide. MOF aligns with and builds on the ITSM practices documented within ITIL, thus enhancing the supportability built on Microsoft's products and technologies.

MOF uses a model that describes Microsoft's approach to IT operations and the service management life cycle. The model organizes the ITIL volumes of service strategy, service design, service transition, service operation, and continual service improvement, and includes additional MOF processes in the MOF components, which are illustrated in Figure 1.6.

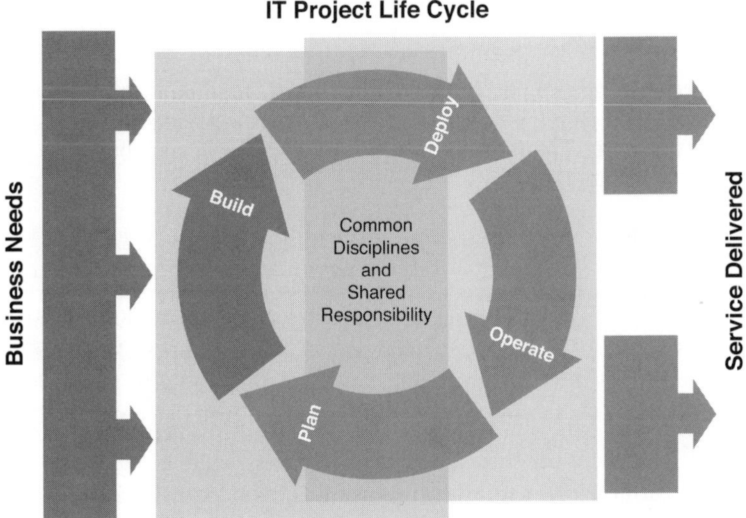

FIGURE 1.5 The IT life cycle.

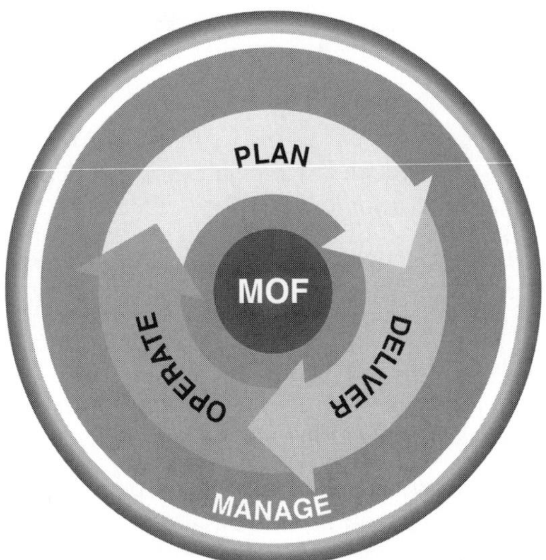

FIGURE 1.6 The IT life cycle, as described in MOF v4, has three life cycle phases and the Manage functional layer operating throughout all the other phases.

TIP: USING MOF FOR OPERATIONS MANAGER DEPLOYMENT

Microsoft uses MOF to describe IT operations and uses System Center as a tool to put that framework into practice. However, components such as Operations Manager are also applications and, as such, best deployed using a disciplined approach. Although the MOF Deliver Phase is geared toward application development, it can be adapted to support infrastructure solution design and deployment, as discussed in Chapter 4, "Planning an Operations Manager Deployment."

It is important to note that the activities pictured in Figure 1.6 can occur simultaneously within an IT organization. Each area has a specific focus and tasks, and within each area are policies, procedures, standards, and best practices that support specific service management-focused tasks.

Operations Manager can be employed to support tasks in the different top-level MOF components. Look briefly at each of these areas and see how one can use System Center 2012 Operations Manager to support MOF:

- **Plan:** This phase covers activities related to IT strategy, standards, policies, and finances. This is where the business and IT collaborate, to determine how IT can most effectively deliver services enabling the overall organization to succeed.

  Operations Manager delivers services that support the business, enabling IT to change to meet business strategy and support the business in becoming more efficient.

- **Deliver:** This phase represents activities related to envisioning, planning, building, testing, and deploying IT service solutions. It takes a service solution from vision through deployment, ensuring you have a stable solution inline with business requirements and customer specifications.

  Using a connector, Operations Manager provides incident information about alerts to Service Manager, enabling that information to be used in the Service Manager configuration management database (CMDB).

  Operations Manager enables configuration of service level objectives (SLOs) to define the availability and performance goals for an application.

- **Operate:** This phase focuses on activities related to operating, monitoring, supporting, and addressing issues with IT services. It ensures that IT services function in line with SLA targets.

  You can use Operations Manager to create a health model for an application that can be used to accurately measure the health of each class in the service model.

- **Manage:** This layer, operating continuously through the three phases, covers activities related to managing governance, risk, compliance, changes, configurations, and organizations. It promotes consistency and accountability in planning and delivering IT services, providing the basis for developing and operating a flexible and durable IT environment.

  The Manage layer establishes an approach to ITSM activities, which helps to coordinate the work of the SMFs in the three life cycle phases.

  Organizations can audit and report IT security–related events when complying to regulations such as SOX, FISMA, HIPAA, and the Gramm-Leach-Bliley Act (GLBA) using tools such as Operations Manager and SQL Server Reporting Services, combined with third-party applications like Enterprise Certified Corporation's Enterprise Compliance Auditing and Reporting (ECC ECAR).

You can find additional information about the MOF at http://go.microsoft.com/fwlink/?LinkId=50015.

MOF Does Not Replace ITIL

Microsoft believes that ITIL is the leading body of knowledge of best practices. For that reason, it uses ITIL as the foundation for MOF. Instead of replacing ITIL, MOF complements it and is similar to ITIL in several ways:

- MOF (now incorporating MSF) spans the entire IT life cycle.
- Both MOF and ITIL are based on best practices for IT management, drawing on the expertise of practitioners worldwide.
- The MOF body of knowledge is applicable across the business community (from small businesses to large enterprises). MOF also is not limited only to those using the Microsoft platform in a homogenous environment.

- As is the case with ITIL, MOF has expanded to be more than just a documentation set. In fact, MOF is now intertwined thoroughly with several System Center components, Configuration Manager, Service Manager, and Operations Manager!

In addition, Microsoft and its partners provide a variety of resources to support MOF principles and guidance, including self-assessments, IT management tools that incorporate MOF terminology and features, training programs and certification, and consulting services.

ISO 20000

You can think of ITIL and ITSM as providing a framework for IT to rethink the ways in which it contributes to and aligns with the business. ISO 20000, which is the first international standard for ITSM, institutionalizes these processes. The ISO 20000 helps companies to align IT services and business strategy and create a formal framework for continual service improvement and provides benchmarks for comparison to best practices.

Published in December 2005, ISO 20000 was developed to reflect the best practice guidance contained within ITIL. The standard also supports other ITSM frameworks and approaches, including MOF, CMMI, and Six Sigma. ISO 20000 consists of two major areas:

- Part 1 promotes adopting an integrated process approach to deliver managed services effectively that meet business and customer requirements.
- Part 2 is a "code of practice" describing the best practices for service management within the scope of ISO 20000-1.

These two areas—what to do and how to do it—have similarities to the approach taken by the other standards, including MOF.

ISO 20000 goes beyond ITIL, MOF, and other frameworks in providing organizational or corporate certification for organizations that effectively adopt and implement the ISO 20000 code of practice.

Optimizing Your Infrastructure

According to Microsoft, analysts estimate that more than 70% of the typical IT budget is spent on infrastructure—managing servers, operating systems, storage, and networking. Add to that the challenge of refreshing and managing desktop and mobile devices, and there's not much left over for anything else. Microsoft describes an Infrastructure Optimization Model that categorizes the state of one's IT infrastructure, describing the impacts on cost, security risks, and the ability to respond to changes. Using the model shown in Figure 1.7, you can identify where your organization is and where you want to be:

- **Basic:** Reactionary, with much time spent fighting fires
- **Standardized:** Gaining control

- **Rationalized:** Enabling the business
- **Dynamic:** Being a strategic asset

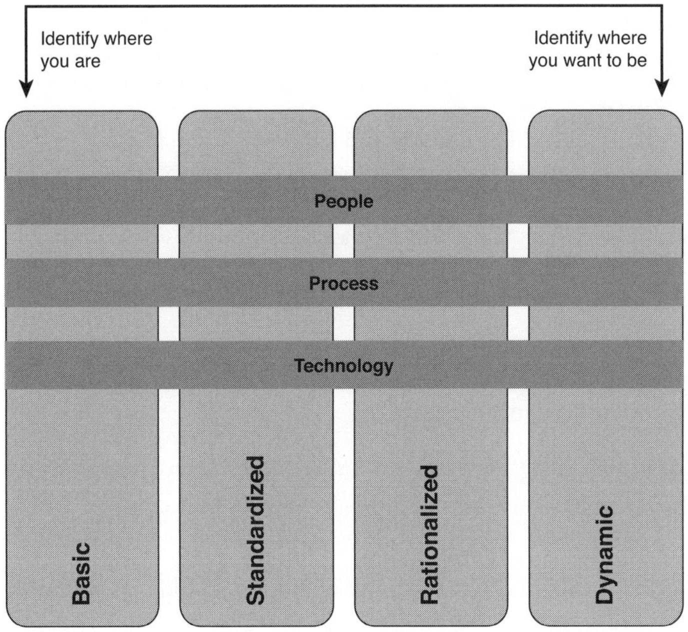

FIGURE 1.7 The Infrastructure Optimization Model.

Although most organizations are somewhere between the basic and standardized levels in this model, typically one would prefer to be a strategic asset rather than fighting fires. Once you know where you are in the model, you can use best practices from ITIL and guidance from MOF to develop a plan to progress to a higher level. The IO Model describes the technologies and steps organizations can take to move forward, whereas the MOF explains the people and processes required to improve that infrastructure. Similar to ITSM, the IO Model is a combination of people, processes, and technology.

You can find more information about infrastructure optimization at http://www.microsoft.com/technet/infrastructure.

ABOUT THE IO MODEL

Not all IT shops want or need to be dynamic. Some choose, for all the right business reasons, to be less than dynamic! The IO Model includes a three-part goal:

- Communicate that there are levels.
- Target the desired levels.
- Provide reference on how to get to the desired levels.

Realize that infrastructure optimization can be by application or by function, rather than a single ranking for the entire IT department.

Items that factor into an IT organization's adoption of the IO Model include cost, ability, and whether the organization fits into the business model as a cost center versus being an asset, along with a commitment to move from being reactive to proactive.

From Fighting Fires to Gaining Control

At the basic level, your infrastructure is hard to control and expensive to manage. Processes are manual, IT policies and standards are either nonexistent or not enforced, and you don't have the tools and resources (or time and energy) to determine the overall health of your applications and IT services. Not only are your desktop and server management costs out of control, but you are also in reactive mode when it comes to security threats and user support. In addition, you tend to use manual rather than automated methods for applying software deployments and patches.

Does this sound familiar? If you can gain control of your environment, you may be more effective at work! Here are some steps to consider:

- Develop standards, policies, and controls.
- Alleviate security risks by developing a security approach throughout your IT organization.
- Adopt best practices, such as those found in ITIL, and operational guidance found in the MOF.
- Build IT to become a strategic asset.

If you can achieve operational nirvana, this will go a long way toward your job satisfaction and IT becoming a constructive part of your business.

From Gaining Control to Enabling the Business

A standardized infrastructure introduces control by using standards and policies to manage desktops and servers. These standards control how you introduce machines into your network. For example, you could use directory services to manage resources, security policies, and access to resources. Shops in a standardized state realize the value of basic standards and some policies but still tend to be reactive. Although you now have a managed IT infrastructure and are inventorying your hardware and software assets and starting to manage licenses, your patches, software deployments, and desktop services are not yet automated. In terms of security, the perimeter is now under control, although internal security may still be a bit loose. Service management becomes a recognized concept and your organization is taking steps to implement it.

To move from a standardized state to the rationalized level, you need to gain more control over your infrastructure and implement proactive policies and procedures. You might also begin to look at implementing service management. At this stage, IT can also move more toward becoming a business asset and ally, rather than a burden.

From Enabling the Business to Becoming a Strategic Asset

At the rationalized level, you have achieved firm control of desktop and service management costs. Processes and policies are in place and beginning to play a large role in supporting and expanding the business. Security is now proactive, and you are responding to threats and challenges in a rapid and controlled manner.

Using technologies such as lite-touch and zero-touch operating system deployment helps you to minimize costs, deployment time, and technical challenges for system rollouts. Because your inventory is now under control, you have minimized the number of images to manage, and desktop management is now largely automated. You also are purchasing only the software licenses and new computers the business requires, giving you a handle on costs. Security is proactive with policies and control in place for desktops, servers, firewalls, and extranets. You have implemented service management in several areas and are taking steps to implement it more broadly across IT.

Mission Accomplished: IT as a Strategic Asset

At the dynamic level, your infrastructure is helping run the business efficiently and stay ahead of competitors. Your costs are now fully controlled. You have also achieved integration between users and data, desktops and servers, and the different departments and functions throughout your organization.

Your IT processes are automated and often incorporated into the technology itself, allowing IT to be aligned and managed according to business needs. New technology investments are able to yield specific, rapid, and measurable business benefits. Measurement is good—it helps you justify the next round of investments!

Using self-provisioning software and quarantine-like systems to ensure patch management and compliance with security policies allows you to automate your processes, which in turn improves reliability, lowers costs, and increases your service levels. Service management is implemented for all critical services with SLAs and operational reviews.

According to IDC Research (October 2006), very few organizations achieve the dynamic level of the Infrastructure Optimization Model—due to the lack of availability of a single toolset from a single vendor to meet all requirements. Through execution on its vision in DSI, Microsoft aims to change this. To read more about this study, visit http://download.microsoft.com/download/a/4/4/a4474b0c-57d8-41a2-afe6-32037fa93ea6/IDC_windesktop_IO_whitepaper.pdf.

MICROSOFT INFRASTRUCTURE OPTIMIZATION HELPS REDUCE COSTS

The April 21, 2009, issue of *BizTech* magazine includes an article by Russell Smith about Microsoft's Infrastructure Optimization Model. Russell makes the following points:

Although dynamic or fully automated systems that are strategic assets to a company sometimes seem like a far-off dream, infrastructure optimization models and products can help get you closer to making IT a valuable business asset.

Microsoft's Infrastructure Optimization is based on Gartner's Infrastructure Maturity Model and provides a simple structure to evaluate the efficiency of core IT services, business productivity, and application platforms.

Though the ultimate goal is to make IT a business enabler across all three areas, you will need to concentrate on standardizing core services: moving your organization from a basic infrastructure (in which most IT tasks are carried out manually) to a managed infrastructure with some automation and knowledge capture.

A 2006 IDC study of 141 enterprises with 1,000 to 20,000 users found that PC standardization and security management could save up to $430 per user annually; standardizing systems management servers could save another $46 per user.

For additional information and the complete article, see http://www.biztechmagazine.com/article.asp?item_id=569.

Managing System Health

ITIL and MOF are utilized to define management approaches, and the IO Model prescribes actions to become a strategic asset. However, the day-to-day operations, strategies, and solutions in today's world are at a different level of granularity. Typically, computing environments consist of distributed systems where work is performed utilizing dispersed servers—because distributed computing often requires using numerous machines that may be in multiple locations. Having an overall management strategy is necessary for preventing chaos and gaining control, but daily management of production server environments also requires being thoroughly aware of the operational health and security of those systems—are they performing the tasks they are meant to, are they the focus of a hacker, or are they even reachable across the network?

Operations management, in addition to introducing an alphabet soup of acronyms of management concepts, is concerned with monitoring your servers to ensure they maintain a required level of performance. Looking specifically at the Windows platform, Microsoft provides a number of basic monitoring utilities with the Windows Server product. These tools incorporate core event monitoring, performance monitoring, and management components such as the Event Viewer and Performance/System Monitor.

However, as mentioned in the section "The Problem with Today's Systems," understanding the significance of the information that is available with such utilities can be daunting, particularly with a large number of servers and a complex environment. Although these basic tools are included with Windows Server, they provide a view of the trees without the ability to see the entire forest. In other words, they give a detailed view of a single server and do not scale or give easy diagnoses of information to resolve problems that occur across multiple systems.

Because these utilities only provide raw data, effectively using that data requires personnel with the knowledge to select, understand, filter, interpret, and correlate the information. These tools typically show only pieces and parts of the overall picture, and additional data may be required from different sources.

The information spewing from these systems consists of thousands of events and other types of operational data that can be captured from a single server, which brings to mind the phrase "drinking water from a fire hose," as shown in Figure 1.8. You are inundated with a gushing stream of facts and figures coming at you with tremendous built-up pressure. Making sense of all that data, or "taming the fire hose," is a challenge facing IT shops of all sizes, and one that OpsMgr is designed to address.

FIGURE 1.8 Drinking water from a fire hose.

Unlike scenes from the movie *The Matrix*, numbers are not just pouring vertically down the screen—and you don't need the ability to jump from roof to roof or dodge bullets to be able to decipher them. You only need the tools and products available to mere mortals.

Bridging the Operations Management Gap

System Center 2012 Operations Manager is Microsoft's software tool for solving operations management issues and is a key component in Microsoft's management strategy and System Center. Operations Manager is a comprehensive operations management solution, using an agent-based centralized management model to localize data collection while centralizing collected data and agent configuration information. As discussed at the beginning of this chapter, OpsMgr now incorporates the following benefits:

- **Architectural changes for improved stability and ease of maintenance:** When you install Operations Manager, three resource pools are created automatically:
    - All Management Servers Resource Pool
    - Notifications Resource Pool
    - AD Assignment Resource Pool

Resource pools ensure continuity of monitoring by providing multiple management servers as a pool that can distribute monitoring workflows should any of the other management servers in that pool become unavailable.

- **Enhanced network monitoring capabilities:** The newest version of Operations Manager now incorporates EMC Smarts network discovery and health monitoring technology.

  System Center 2012 Operations Manager can monitor devices using Simple Network Monitoring Protocol (SNMP) v1, v2c, and v3. The benefit from monitoring network devices is when a server appears to be down you can actually determine whether the problem is a switch or router port connected to that server. More importantly, it also allows for quicker root cause analysis of availability issues with servers, services, and applications that are related to network performance problems or outages. The new Network Vicinity view provides a network topology diagram. Here is what you can monitor:

  - Connection health between connected network devices and between monitored servers and the network device
  - Virtual local area network (VLAN) health based on health state of switches participating in a VLAN
  - Hot standby router protocol (HSRP) group health based on health state of individual HSRP end points
  - Port/Interface monitoring such as Up/Down, and Inbound/Outbound volume traffic
  - Port/Interface utilization, packets dropped and broadcasted
  - Processor utilization for certified devices
  - Memory utilization for certified devices

- **Application performance monitoring (APM):** System Center 2012 Operations Manager integrates Microsoft's acquisition of AVIcode to provide deep .NET application monitoring from an end user's perspective.

  In addition to server-side monitoring, APM includes a client-side monitoring option that inserts JavaScript snippets into the web pages, which are used for extensive performance and exception monitoring.

- **New and improved dashboards:** This version of Operations Manager contains significant enhancements in the ability to display data through use of its new dashboard technologies, enabling you to view operational and historical data in a single pane of glass.

  Dashboards enable quick access to data where you can view critical metrics for specific situations. They can be hosted as a SharePoint web part, enabling IT managers and business owners to access data using a user interface with which they are already familiar.

Management packs, which are models based on the SML schema, continue to be the brain behind Operations Manager, providing the knowledge to monitor applications, systems, and services. Using a service-centric view, OpsMgr can understand service and application structures and monitor the overall health of services and applications by viewing the state of any object.

To put Operations Manager's capabilities in a clearer context, the next sections discuss key technical features as they relate to the issues identified earlier in the section "The Problem with Today's Systems."

Connecting Systems

System Center 2012 Operations Manager solves the isolated systems problem with end-to-end monitoring and collecting information from your different islands of information. It monitors event logs, performance monitor counters, application programming interfaces, WMI information, and network devices, gathering the data from each monitored agent, storing it centrally, and taking action as appropriate. OpsMgr also provides a centralized console to monitor the operational status of your entire network. Figure 1.9 shows the health state of computers in a monitored organization. Looking at the view, you can see there is a problem on the Apollo computer, and it shows the affected area is the Windows operating system.

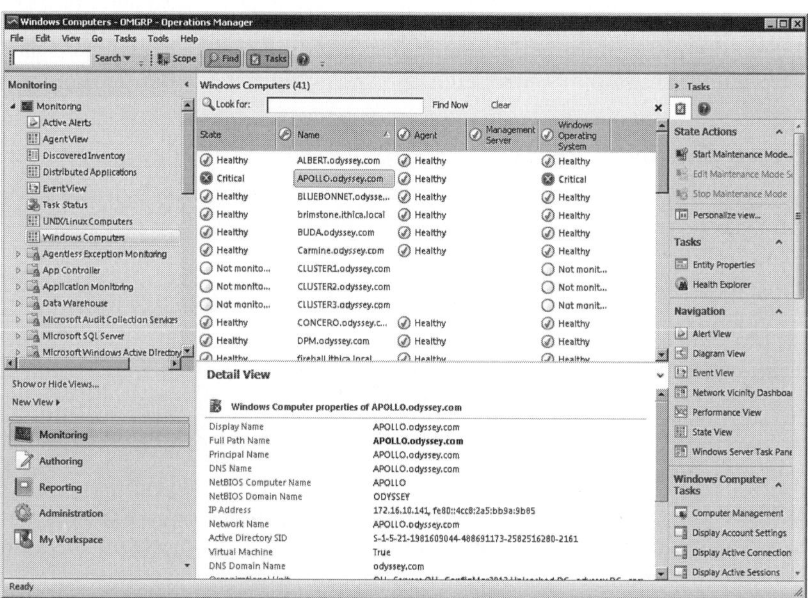

FIGURE 1.9 Viewing computer health in the OpsMgr Operations console.

These views enable you to see which systems and components are healthy and which are not. Health is based on rolling up information from each monitored object.

OpsMgr's centralized databases also address the islands of information issue by using local agents to collect information enabling consolidated views, dashboards, and reports of the many different "islands" across multiple servers, operating systems, and devices. For example, an administrator can generate a report comparing error events, CPU performance, the length of message queues, and network interface performance on Exchange servers in different parts of the network at one time. Without using OpsMgr, providing this information could require multiple interfaces and tools. Having a holistic view of the information allows the system to respond to complex conditions where several events viewed independently would not constitute a problem, but taken together demand immediate action.

This book uses a fictitious company named Odyssey to illustrate examples. Odyssey has 2,000 Windows and Linux servers spread throughout two locations. Let's say Odyssey has a network load-balanced farm with four web servers that provide web services. By using a web farm, the failure of any one system does not jeopardize the overall service. Arguably, that is the purpose for having load-balanced servers! However, the failure of two or three of these web servers would constitute a critical condition requiring immediate attention. OpsMgr can detect the difference and generate an error alert if any individual server fails, yet create a critical alert if two or more servers fail. Through integration with other System Center 2012 components, a new virtual server could be provisioned using Virtual Machine Manager and Orchestrator—either automatically as a response to the alert if that was desired, or as a user request using App Controller.

Notification: Errors and Availability

If you right-click a system in the Results pane shown in Figure 1.9, you can open the alert, diagram event, performance, and state views associated with this object. You can also open the Health Explorer from the Tasks pane. Figure 1.10 displays the Health Explorer. You can see how OpsMgr shows the various monitored components, known as *monitors*, and the rollup for these monitors.

Figure 1.10 quickly shows the amount of physical memory available for applications and processes has become critically low. By using the Health Explorer, you can quickly isolate the target area. You can even customize the view to show which applications are impacted.

System Center 2012 Operations Manager solves the notification problem by automatically detecting and responding to changes in state, informing you of alerts using its notification flow engine. As it collects information, responses to conditions, changes, and state can be triggered at each collection point in the OpsMgr architecture.

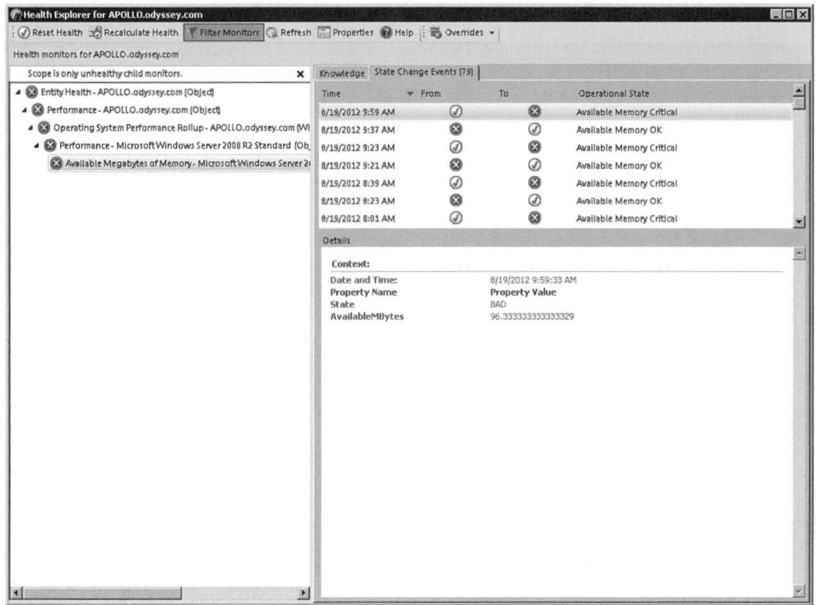

FIGURE 1.10 The Operations Manager Health Explorer.

The agent on the local machine processes data and analyzes it using the business logic in the management packs, making a decision whether to pass the information to a management server. This approach incorporates the best of all possible worlds, as agents on the monitored servers collect and initially process the information based on logic in management packs, reducing the load on the management server and network bandwidth as information is acted on centrally only as necessary. The design also allows the local agents to continue to respond to alerts should communication with the management server be disrupted. This preprocessing minimizes the traffic flow from the agents, and lightens the database storage footprint.

Even so, to avoid being deluged with information, administrators would prefer not to be notified of all the myriad of data collected by Operations Manager. Accordingly, OpsMgr detects changes in state and incorporates self-tuning thresholds, enabling it to be selective about the alerts it raises.

Using the Knowledge tab of the Health Explorer shown in Figure 1.10, you can pivot to the performance view to see a graphical representation of available memory. You can also use the Active Alerts pane to view all outstanding alerts. The example displayed in Figure 1.11 shows available memory over an eight-hour period, and Figure 1.12 shows knowledge for the alert that caused the state change.

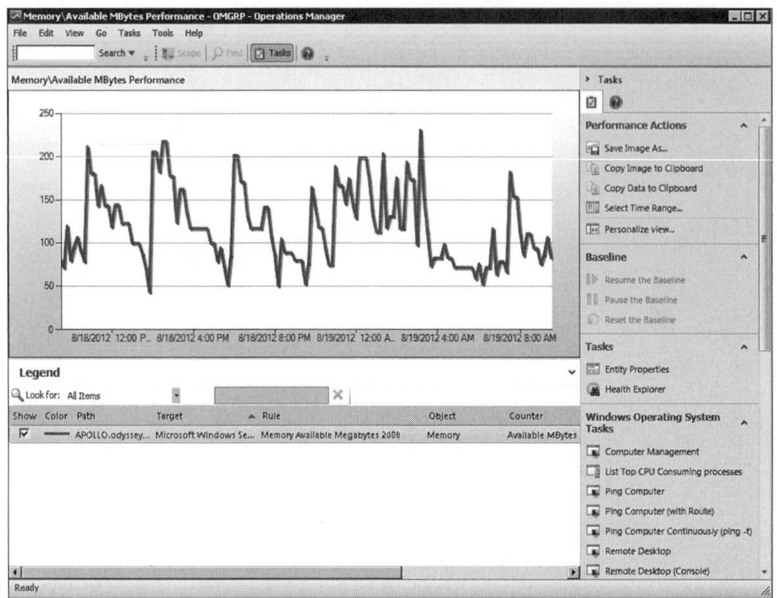

FIGURE 1.11 Performance view of available megabytes.

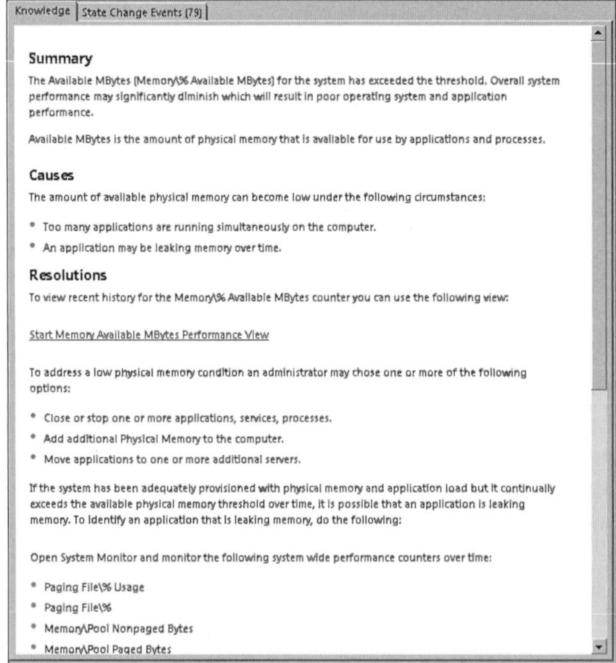
Knowledge | State Change Events (79)

Summary

The Available MBytes (Memory\% Available MBytes) for the system has exceeded the threshold. Overall system performance may significantly diminish which will result in poor operating system and application performance.

Available MBytes is the amount of physical memory that is available for use by applications and processes.

Causes

The amount of available physical memory can become low under the following circumstances:

- Too many applications are running simultaneously on the computer.
- An application may be leaking memory over time.

Resolutions

To view recent history for the Memory\% Available MBytes counter you can use the following view:

Start Memory Available MBytes Performance View

To address a low physical memory condition an administrator may chose one or more of the following options:

- Close or stop one or more applications, services, processes.
- Add additional Physical Memory to the computer.
- Move applications to one or more additional servers.

If the system has been adequately provisioned with physical memory and application load but it continually exceeds the available physical memory threshold over time, it is possible that an application is leaking memory. To identify an application that is leaking memory, do the following:

Open System Monitor and monitor the following system wide performance counters over time:

- Paging File\% Usage
- Paging File\%
- Memory\Pool Nonpaged Bytes
- Memory\Pool Paged Bytes

FIGURE 1.12 Knowledge view in the Health Explorer.

You can highlight any alert in the Active Alerts pane to view the detail behind that alert in the Alerts Detail view. Figure 1.13 has a specific error highlighted, showing the cause of the error and additional knowledge.

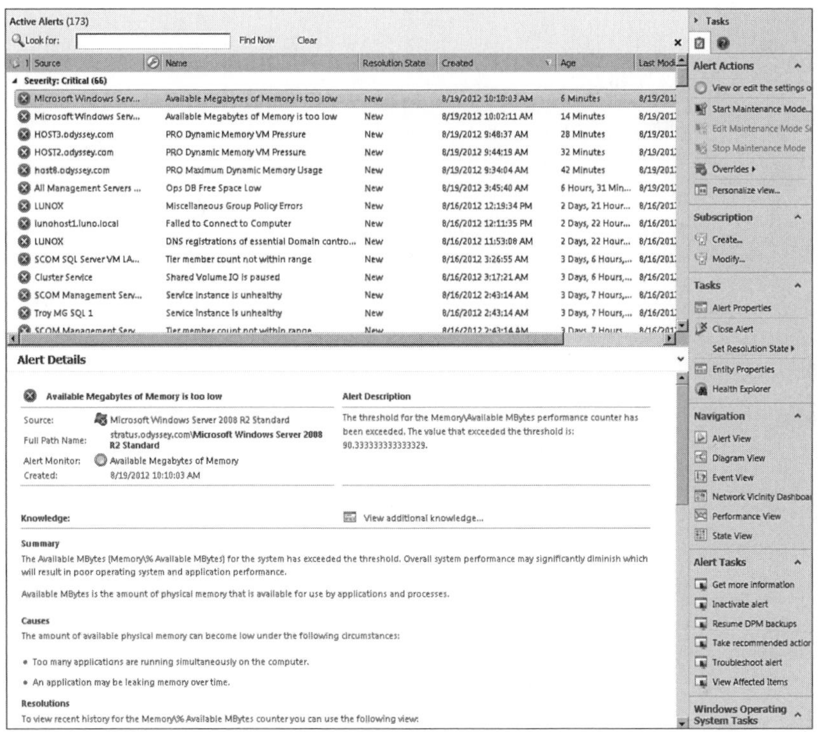

FIGURE 1.13 The Active Alerts pane in the Operations console.

You can also click on the **Alert Properties** task to bring up the specific properties behind that alert. Note that in Figure 1.14 the information is broken into six areas or tabs:

- **General:** This tab provides general information, including a description and the capability to change the alert status.
- **Product Knowledge:** Provides information collected by the vendor (Microsoft in this case) about the conditions related to the alert, including causes and potential resolutions.
- **Company Knowledge:** Use this area to add information specific to this condition at your particular organization.
- **History:** Shows the history of this alert.
- **Alert Context:** Shows the context of the alert. This may contain additional or deeper information about the condition that caused the alert to be raised.
- **Custom Fields:** Lets you add up to 10 custom fields pertaining to this alert.

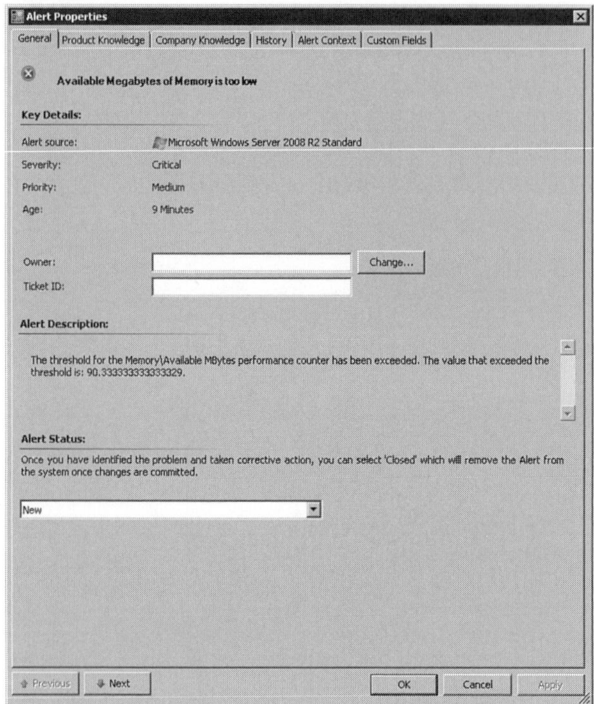

FIGURE 1.14 Alert properties.

In addition to generating alerts, Operations Manager can send notifications based on the severity or age of a particular alert. Using the notification workflow engine, you can define subscriptions where alerts are sent to targeted recipients in a variety of ways:

- Via a network message, email message, instant message, or short message service (text messaging).
- By generating an SNMP trap via a command piped to an external SNMP generator to integrate with another management system.
- By launching a script for complex processing. This ensures that even when alerts are generated, they do not intrusively notify you unless necessary. Scripts are also useful for sending alerts to other systems, logging, and so on.

You can use the Operations console to view the state of your organization as a whole or to drill down into detail about any particular alert.

TIP: MORE ABOUT ALERTS

Alerts can be generated by rules or monitors. The types of properties displayed for the alert vary depending how the alert is generated. See Chapter 14, "Monitoring with System Center 2012 Operations Manager," for additional information on rules and monitors.

Historical Information

Operations Manager lets you view the information it gathers quickly and effectively, presenting it in ways that make it easy to view, print, or publish. OpsMgr generates reports both automatically and in an ad-hoc fashion, and includes an easy-to-use report designer integrated into the Operations Manager console. The reporting capabilities allow you to generate substantial reports complete with titles, numeric information, text information, graphics, and charts.

You can use views to display performance information. Figure 1.15 shows some performance spikes for the Hector computer. This particular view actually displays several performance counters: percent processor time, processor queue length, pages per second, and percent memory used. Using views gives you immediate access to information as it is collected, and you can adjust the view of that information quickly, perhaps to compare it with another system or examine other performance aspects, as in this view.

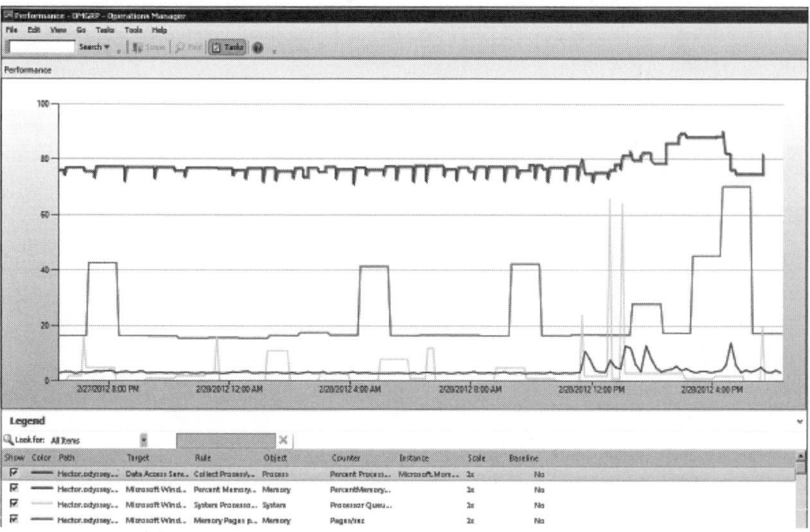

FIGURE 1.15 CPU performance analysis view.

However, the display in Figure 1.15 does not indicate whether what is seen is normal performance for the computer, as it shows less than two full days of activity. You can visually put the CPU utilization spike in context by seeing what a longer-term CPU utilization looks like for that system. OpsMgr reporting lets you access the long-term view of historical data. The Performance report shown in Figure 1.16 shows performance for the top five systems in terms of processor queue length, and identifies Hector as having the most activity.

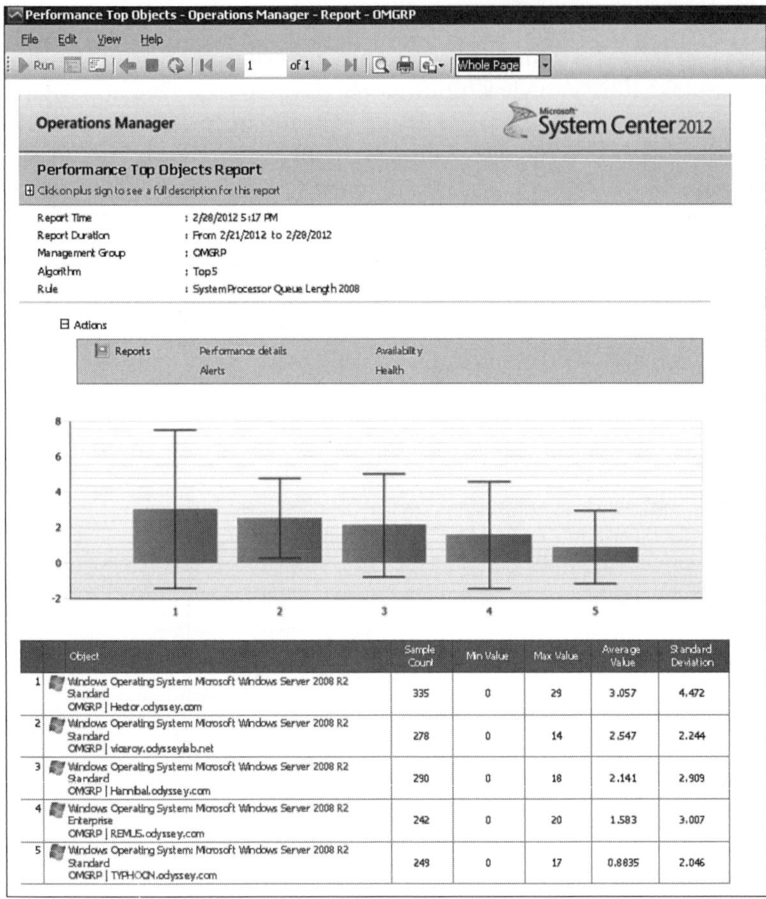

FIGURE 1.16 Performance Top Objects Report.

You may notice an Actions section in the middle of the report that allows you to open or pivot to other reports of interest. For example, selecting **Performance details** opens a Performance Detail report for Hector, displayed in Figure 1.17. This report presents a graphic drill-down on the minimum, maximum, and average values for the week, along with the standard deviation, which is the degree of variation for those numbers. You can expand the Actions section on this report as well to see additional reports or views. With only several mouse clicks, you now know that the average length for the processor queue is 3. Knowing what is normal can be half the battle when troubleshooting.

Reports are static once generated, whereas views and dashboards are interactive and will update as the underlying data changes. You can export reports as XML, saved in CSV, TIF, Excel, or PDF format or published as HTML (MHTML) files using the Web archive option. The HTML option is quite powerful, as it allows you to generate reports to publish for general viewing in a browser. You can use PDF format to email reports to specified recipients.

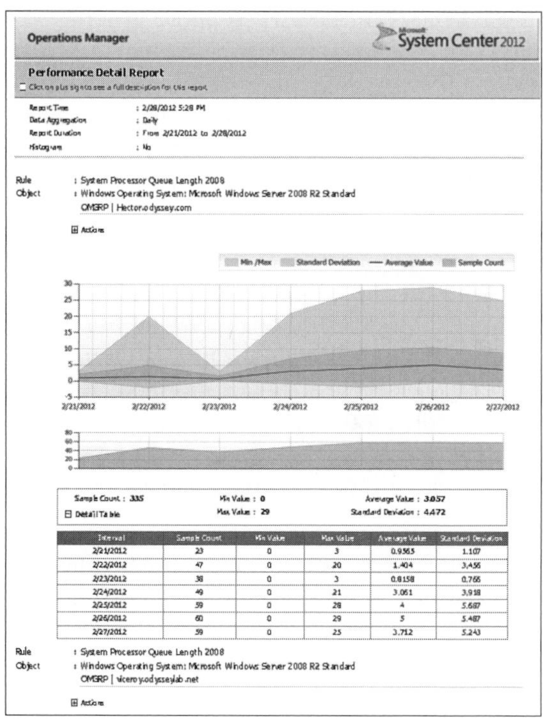

Interval	Sample Count	Min Value	Max Value	Average Value	Standard Deviation
2/21/2012	23	0	3	0.9565	1.107
2/22/2012	47	0	20	1.404	3.456
2/23/2012	38	0	3	0.8158	0.766
2/24/2012	49	0	21	3.061	3.918
2/25/2012	59	0	28	4	5.687
2/26/2012	60	0	29	5	5.487
2/27/2012	59	0	25	3.712	5.243

FIGURE 1.17 Performance Detail Report for the Hector computer.

You can generate historical reports of what has happened over any period the data is collected to use with long-term trending and capacity planning. Using views, you can also look at the information as it is collected in real time for a snapshot view of what is occurring, drilling down into specific details as needed.

Access to a long-term view of information can help detect trends and patterns otherwise hidden in a snapshot view. Recall the example in the "Lack of Historical Information" section of this chapter, where the IT staff called out that CPU utilization was 50%. Operations Manager lets you look at the historical information and see that this was actually a normal condition. Using the same process, you can detect increases in network utilization and diagnose the problem appropriately. With OpsMgr at work, the IT staff might not even need those outside consulting services!

Built-in Expertise

As soon as you install System Center 2012 Operations Manager, it begins to use its built-in expertise. Management packs, which are models containing a comprehensive set of predefined rules that form an expert system, focus on the health of your systems and alert you to significant events, suppress unimportant data, and correlate seemingly unimportant information to identify potential underlying problems. Rather than just collecting a ton of information for the administrator to sort out, OpsMgr uses its knowledge to determine what is important, what is not, and will escalate as necessary. When OpsMgr determines a downgraded change in state has occurred, it alerts appropriate personnel that you have previously identified. Prior to escalating to a live person, Operations Manager can automatically respond to various conditions, such as restarting stopped services. These actions are accomplished with the knowledge encapsulated in management packs.

Management packs are the brains of Operations Manager. They contain the knowledge from Microsoft's best people, including the product support teams, developers, and TechNet resources. This expertise is enhanced with the local expertise of your own organization. Knowledge is added as alerts are generated, troubleshooting performed, and problems resolved, enhancing the system. Similar to a human expert, OpsMgr improves its skills and capabilities over time. OpsMgr looks for changes in state of a monitored object. After alerting appropriate personnel, it assists in resolving the problem—by providing detailed knowledge including historical performance and event information, suggestions for fixes, direct links to tasks to resolve the problems, and pointers for where to research further.

As shown earlier in the Alert Details pane in the lower part of Figure 1.13, the highlighted alert contains concrete and specific guidance on what it means, its possible causes, possible resolutions, and where to get additional information. In some cases, the Alert Details pane does not show the entire contents of the knowledge for a particular alert, so the authors have duplicated the full text of the Product Knowledge tab in the Alert Properties sidebar. While in the console, you could click the **View additional knowledge** link in the Alert Details pane in Figure 1.13 to launch the alert properties page with the product knowledge in it.

ALERT PROPERTIES: PRODUCT KNOWLEDGE

Summary

The Available MBytes (Memory\% Available MBytes) for the system has exceeded the threshold. Overall system performance may significantly diminish, which results in poor operating system and application performance.

Available MBytes is the amount of physical memory available for use by applications and processes.

Causes

The amount of available physical memory can become low under the following circumstances:

- Too many applications are running simultaneously on the computer.
- An application may be leaking memory over time.

Resolutions

To view recent history for the Memory\% Available MBytes counter you can use the following view:

Start Memory Available MBytes Performance View

To address a low physical memory condition an administrator may choose one or more of the following options:

- Close or stop one or more applications, services, processes.
- Add additional physical memory to the computer.
- Move applications to one or more additional servers.

If the system has been adequately provisioned with physical memory and application load but it continually exceeds the available physical memory threshold over time, it is possible that an application is leaking memory. To identify an application that is leaking memory, do the following:

Open System Monitor and monitor the following systemwide performance counters over time:

- Paging File\% Usage
- Paging File\%
- Memory\Pool Nonpaged Bytes
- Memory\Pool Paged Bytes

If any one of these counters continually increases over time, it is possible that an application may be leaking memory.

If the system appears to be leaking memory, the specific application can be identified by monitoring the following counters for each running process:

- Process\Page File Bytes
- Process\Pool Nonpaged Bytes
- Process\Pool Paged Bytes
- Process\Private Bytes
- Process\Thread Count

If you observe a consistent and significant increase in any of these counters, it may be necessary to contact the application vendor for support.

Using a Methodology

Operations Manager includes monitors and rules in management packs that keep tabs on your services and applications. OpsMgr focuses on the health of an application. Management packs are containers that include what are called service models, which use the SMLs discussed earlier in the "Microsoft's Dynamic Systems Initiative" section of this chapter and are formal definitions of types of objects. OpsMgr captures knowledge through models, putting knowledge in a structure the software can act on.

Management packs describe *classes*. You won't see classes anywhere in the Operations console, and that is by design. Classes are a concept; you can describe things about them. A class is a type of object. A database is an object, and it has common types of properties, regardless of the server it runs on. Properties give us a common way to describe a database—it has a name, an owner, and other assorted attributes.

You can describe what makes up a database, and you can describe a relationship between other objects. A Microsoft SQL database must exist on a SQL Server database engine—so it has to have some type of relationship with the SQL Server. The SQL Server runs on a Windows machine—so it has some relationship with the Windows machine. These relationships come into play when building management packs.

By incorporating models and methods for monitoring in its management packs, OpsMgr uses a structured approach to determine whether there are situations requiring attention.

Catching Missed Information

OpsMgr continually monitors, helping ensure there are no missed events. The system also understands that certain events should take place and can generate an alert if those events do not occur. A special type of rule checks for a condition to occur within a defined period, such as every day between midnight and 5:00 a.m. If the specified condition does not occur within that time frame, that information is caught and an alert is generated, helping you to catch and take action on problems such as missed backups—one of the more useful items to check for in terms of a job not executing. Still, OpsMgr needs to be told to watch for the event; it still is not quite smart enough to do what you're thinking or to catch what it isn't looking for.

Reducing False Alarms

OpsMgr uses its built-in knowledge and self-tuning capability to correlate different types of information and changes in state, ensuring it will alert only when needed, and typically reducing the number of alerts to a fraction of the underlying data. This capability reduces the flood of information typical management systems generate; enabling you to focus on what is important to keep your system up with optimal performance.

This occurs easily and automatically. OpsMgr supports a number of ways to install its agent on computers, including automatic computer discovery of all systems in the domain. Management packs are distributed automatically, helping you deploy your management infrastructure quickly and effectively. With its central console, OpsMgr allows you to implement a consistent systems monitoring and alerting policy to all your systems. Agents perform monitoring and apply the specific business logic and models for each monitored computer, automatically updating each system with the appropriate logic. Operations Manager also automatically removes business logic rules from the distributed systems, once the specified conditions no longer apply.

OpsMgr is scalable to all sizes of organizations, performing well even as it scales. The same tool and basic architecture can be used to support medium, large, and enterprise-sized organizations with their varied requirements:

- It works well for small to medium-sized organizations, where you would have a single AD forest and less than 500 servers to monitor.

- It works for large organizations, where fault tolerance and performance might be critical factors in the requirements. In this case, OpsMgr supports redundant and load-balanced components to ensure that it can monitor up to 3,000 systems per management server with no loss of performance or service.
- It also works well for enterprise organizations, where fault tolerance, performance, and organizational boundaries must be accommodated. OpsMgr supports communication between connected management groups, capable of using an architecture of connected management groups to handle a large organization's requirements, in addition to its redundant and load-balancing needs. Moreover, while scaling, Operations Manager still provides the cohesive view needed for a centralized management model.

Operations can be monitored through an installed console application or a web interface. The console has views into the collected information—be it state, events, diagrams, alerts, or performance. You can also view reports. You can even view the status of your IT systems in a graphical diagram view that rapidly shows you the status of all systems, as in Figure 1.18, which shows the current Active Directory status. The highest-level state is shown in the state of the group, found at the top of Figure 1.18. In this particular example, the highest-level state is Healthy, meaning directory services are functioning properly in the Odyssey.com domain. As Figure 1.18 shows, you can also drill down into more detailed status of any particular component that has a plus sign (+) next to the diagram, indicating the view can be expanded.

Operations Manager's flexibility lets you start small, managing a specific group of servers or a department. Once you are comfortable with the management platform, you can then scale it up to the rest of your organization.

With OpsMgr handling your monitoring needs, you as an operations manager can relax (somewhat!) knowing that you will be alerted when there is a problem and have help in resolving it. It is like having your own IT genie on the job 24×7! But it won't take your job, not if you read this book.

Managing Virtualization and the Cloud

It seems like everyone, including Microsoft, is jumping into cloud computing. But like any other technology, if you don't plan proactively, you can create more of a problem than the one you were trying to solve. Between public clouds, private clouds, and hybrid environments, it's easy to get caught up in the excitement of the cloud bandwagon without considering the ability to manage what you are implementing.

What it comes down to is identifying what you want to monitor and having the tools available to do so. For example, using the Virtual Machine Manager (VMM) management pack and Veeam's VMware management pack, you can manage your virtual machines from the Operations Manager console, having a complete view of the IT infrastructure to identify and escalate issues to the correct team to speed problem resolution and minimize user impact. Performance and Resource Optimization (PRO) ties specific alerts from Operations Manager to remediation actions in VMM or VMware. For example, you might perform load-balancing of virtual machines between physical hosts when specific thresholds are exceeded, such as transactions per second, CPU utilization, email message delivery SLA, and so on. Alternatively, you may want to migrate virtual machines when a hardware failure is detected (for example, a fan failure). The integration available lets you do this and more.

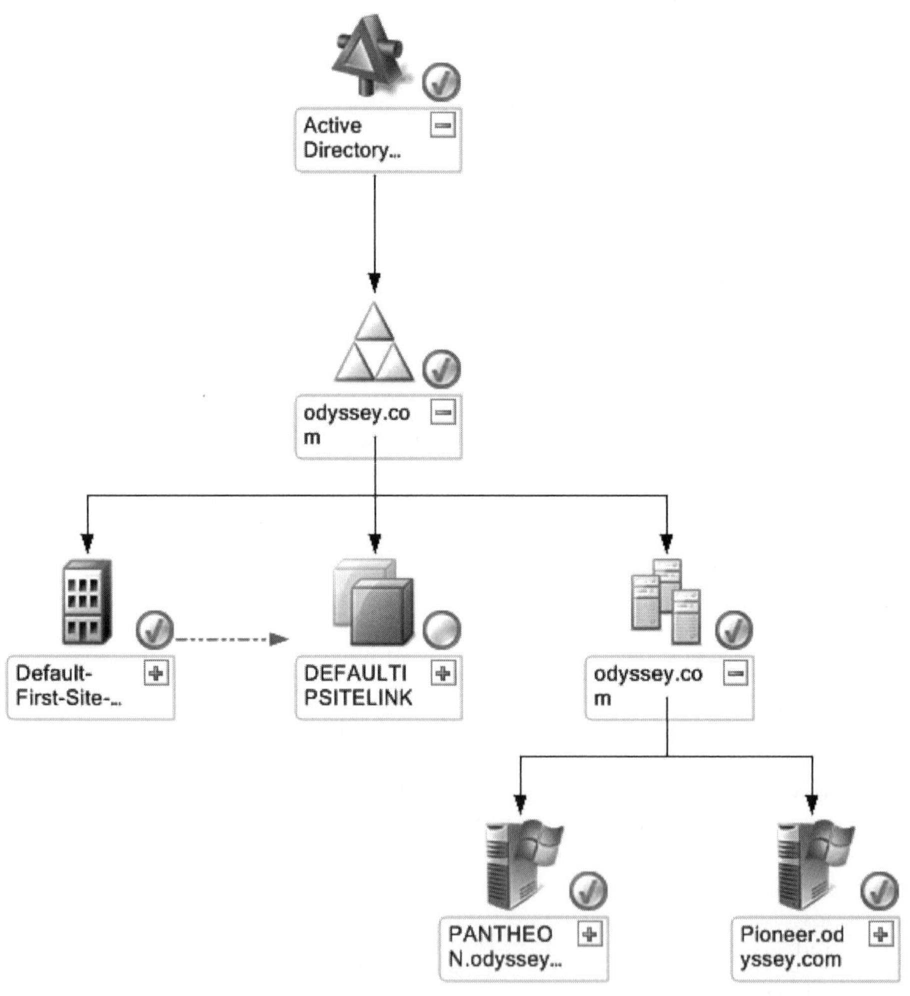

FIGURE 1.18 Active Directory topology diagram view.

Overview of Microsoft System Center

Microsoft first announced System Center at the Microsoft Management Summit (MMS) in 2003, envisioning a future solution to provide customers with complete application and system management for enterprises of all sizes. (See http://www.microsoft.com/presspass/press/2003/mar03/03-18mssystemcenterpr.mspx for the original press release.) The first phase was anticipated to include Microsoft Operations Manager (MOM) 2004—later released as MOM 2005—and Systems Management Server (SMS) 2003.

WHAT IS SYSTEM CENTER?

System Center is a brand name for Microsoft's management platform, and as such has new components added over time. System Center represents a means to integrate system management tools and technologies to help you with systems operations, troubleshooting, and planning.

Different from the releases of Microsoft Office (another Microsoft product with multiple components), Microsoft has historically released System Center in "waves;" the components were not released simultaneously. The first wave initially included SMS 2003, MOM 2005, and System Center Data Protection Manager 2006; 2006 additions included System Center Reporting Manager 2006 and System Center Capacity Planner 2006.

The second wave included Operations Manager 2007, Configuration Manager 2007, System Center Essentials 2007, Virtual Machine Manager 2007, and new releases of Data Protection Manager and Capacity Planner. Next released were updates to Virtual Machine Manager (version 2008), Operations Manager 2007 R2, Configuration Manager 2007 R2 and R3, DPM 2010, System Center Essentials 2010, and Service Manager 2010. Think of these as rounding out the second wave.

Microsoft also widened System Center with its acquisitions of Opalis (rebranded for System Center 2012 as Orchestrator) and AVIcode. With System Center 2012, Microsoft is moving from the wave approach and making the various components available at the same time. System Center 2012 also includes the first version of a common installer.

The System Center 2012 product includes Operations Manager, Configuration Manager, Virtual Machine Manager, Service Manager, Data Protection Manager, Orchestrator, Endpoint Protection, App Controller, and Advisor. System Center Advisor, separately licensed and previously code-named Atlanta, promises to offer configuration-monitoring cloud service for Microsoft SQL Server and Windows Server deployments; expect the list of monitored products to grow over time. Microsoft's System Center 2012 cloud and datacenter solutions provide a common management toolset for your private and public cloud applications and services to help you deliver IT as a service to your business.

System Center builds on Microsoft's DSI, introduced in the "Microsoft's Dynamic Systems Initiative" section, which is designed to deliver simplicity, automation, and flexibility in the data center across the IT environment. Microsoft System Center components share the following DSI-based characteristics:

- Ease of use and deployment
- Based on industry and customer knowledge
- Scalability (both up to the largest enterprises and down to the smallest organizations)

Figure 1.19 illustrates the relationship between the System Center 2012 components and MOF.

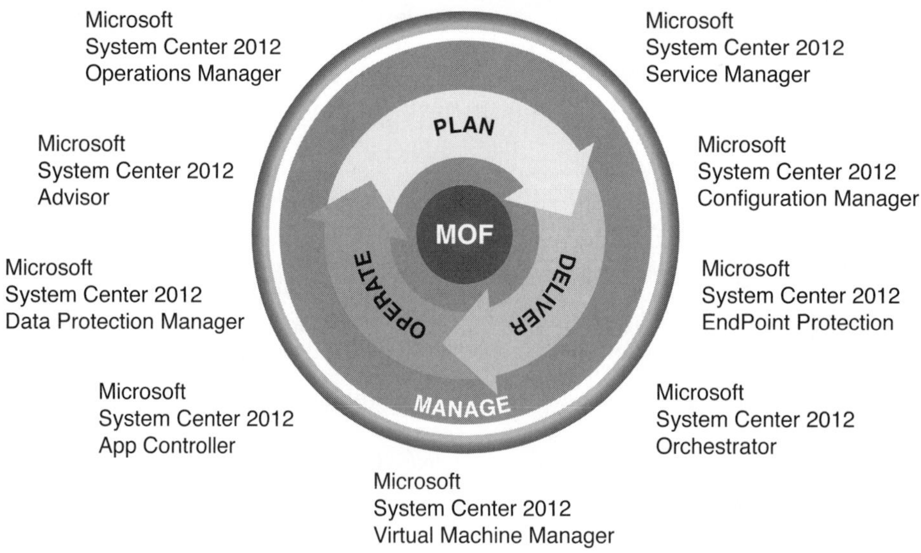

FIGURE 1.19 MOF with System Center components.

NOTE: MORE ABOUT SYSTEM CENTER COMPONENTS

System Center Endpoint Protection is integrated with Configuration Manager, but requires a separate license. System Center Advisor also has separate licensing; it is a software assurance benefit for Windows Server and specific workloads.

Reporting in System Center

The data gathered by Operations Manager is collected in a self-maintaining SQL Server database and comes with numerous reports available using Microsoft SQL Server Reporting Services (SSRS). Using the native functionality of SSRS, you can export report output to a variety of formats, including a Report Server file share, web archive format, Excel, and PDF. You can schedule and email reports, enabling users to open these reports independent of the tool.

System Center 2012 introduces the concept of integrated reporting for System Center, available with the data warehouse shipping with Service Manager. This data warehouse utilizes SQL Server Analysis Services and incorporates consolidated reporting for Service Manager, Configuration Manager, and Operations Manager. Operations Manager data includes alerts and inventory information. Data for the individual components is available in separate data marts.

Service Management

Using Service Manager implements a single point of contact for all service requests, knowledge, and workflow. System Center 2012 Service Manager incorporates processes such as incident, problem, change, and release management.

Service Manager's CMDB includes population from Configuration Manager, Operations Manager, Virtual Machine Manager, and Orchestrator via connectors, enabling it to consolidate information throughout System Center. As an example, Service Manager fills a gap in Operations Manager: What occurs when OpsMgr detects a condition that requires human intervention and tracking for resolution? Until Service Manager, the answer was to create a ticket or incident in one's help desk application. Now, within the System Center framework, OpsMgr can hand off incident management to Service Manager. The Configuration Manager connector enables Service Manager to incorporate the inventory information captured by ConfigMgr.

Enhancements to the 2012 version include a service catalog, release management, and the System Center data warehouse.

Protecting Data

System Center 2012 Data Protection Manager (DPM) is a disk-based backup solution for continuous data protection supporting Windows servers such as SQL Server, Exchange, SharePoint, virtualization, and file servers—as well as Windows desktops and laptops. DPM provides block-level backup as changes occur, utilizing Microsoft's Virtual Disk Service and Shadow Copy technologies.

This version of DPM incorporates a number of enhancements over the previous version, including:

- Centralized management
- Centralized monitoring
- Remote administration
- Remote recovery
- Role-based management
- Remote corrective actions
- Scoped troubleshooting

- Push to resume backups
- SLA-based alerting
- Consolidated alerts
- Alert categorization
- PowerShell

Virtual Machine Management

Virtual Machine Manager is Microsoft's management platform for heterogeneous virtualization infrastructures. VMM provides centralized management of virtual machines across several popular hypervisor platforms, specifically Windows Server 2008 and 2008 R2 Hyper-V (Windows Server 2012 when using System Center 2012 Service Pack 1), VMware ESX, and Citrix XenServer. VMM enables increased utilization of physical servers, centralized management of a virtual infrastructure, delegation of administration in distributed environments, and rapid provisioning of new virtual machines by system administrators and users via a self-service portal.

System Center 2012 Virtual Machine Manager includes the ability to build both Hyper-V hosts and host clusters as it moves to being a private cloud tool in terms of management and provisioning rather than just a virtualization management solution. This provisioning will involve deploying services using service templates, in addition to simply configuring storage and networking.

VMM enables you to

- Deliver flexible and cost-effective Infrastructure as a Service (IaaS). You can pool and dynamically allocate virtualized datacenter resources (compute, network, and storage) enabling a self-service infrastructure, with flexible role-based delegation and access control.
- Apply cloud principles to provisioning and servicing your datacenter applications with techniques like service modeling, service configuration, and image-based management. You can also state-separate your applications and services from the underlying infrastructure using server application virtualization. This results in a "service-centric" approach to management where you manage the application or service life cycle and not just datacenter infrastructure or virtual machines.
- Optimize your existing investments by managing multihypervisor environments such as Hyper-V, Citrix XenServer, and VMware using a single pane of glass.
- Dynamically optimize your datacenter resources based on workload demands, while ensuring reliable service delivery with features like high availability.
- Achieve best-of-breed virtualization-management for Microsoft workloads such as Exchange and SharePoint.

Deploy and Manage in the Cloud

System Center 2012 App Controller, previously code-named Concero, is a self-service portal built on Silverlight, allowing IT managers to more easily deploy and manage applications in cloud infrastructures. App Controller provides a single console for managing multiple private and public clouds while provisioning virtual machines and services to individual business units. Using App Controller with VMM, data center administrators will be able to provision not only virtual machine OS deployments but also, leveraging Server App-V, deploy and manage down to the application level, minimizing the number of virtual hard disk (VHD) templates necessary to maintain.

Orchestration and Automation

System Center 2012 Orchestrator is based on Opalis Integration Server (OIS), acquired by Microsoft in December 2009. It provides an automation platform for orchestrating and integrating IT tools to drive down the cost of one's datacenter operations while improving the reliability of IT processes. Orchestrator enables organizations to automate best practices, such as those found in MOF and ITIL, by using workflow processes that coordinate the System Center platform and other management tools to automate incident response, change and compliance, and service life cycle management processes.

The IT process automation software reduces operational costs and improves IT efficiency by delivering services faster and with fewer errors. Orchestrator replaces manual, resource-intensive, and potentially error-prone activities with standardized, automated processes. This System Center component can orchestrate tasks between Configuration Manager, Operations Manager, Service Manager, Virtual Machine Manager, Data Protection Manager, and third-party management tools. This positions it to automate any IT process across a heterogeneous environment, providing full solutions for incident management, change and configuration management, and provisioning and service management.

Cloud-Based Configuration Monitoring

System Center Advisor promises to offer configuration-monitoring cloud service for Microsoft Windows Server, SQL Server, Exchange, and SharePoint deployments. Microsoft servers in the Advisor cloud analyze the uploaded data, and then provide feedback to the customer in the Advisor console in the form of alerts about detected configuration issues. System Center Advisor's mission statement is to be a proactive tool to help Microsoft customers avoid configuration problems, reduce downtime, improve performance, and resolve issues faster. The web-based console itself is written with Silverlight and is similar to the look and feel of the Microsoft Intune console, Microsoft's cloud-based management service for PCs and other devices.

Configuration Management

Microsoft's most recent release of its flagship configuration management tool, System Center 2012 Configuration Manager delivers the functionality to detect "shift and drift" in system configuration. Configuration Manager consolidates information about clients and servers, hardware, and software into a single console for centralized management and control. This version of Configuration Manager includes the following features:

- New look for the console, replacing the Microsoft Management Console (MMC) with the standard System Center Outlook-style interface
- Targeting management to the user, not the device; delivering the right application in the right way to the right user under the right condition
- Redesign of the software distribution process
- Architectural changes to simplify the site server hierarchy

Endpoint Protection

Previously known as Forefront Endpoint Protection, Microsoft's enterprise antimalware suite is getting a name change and moving into System Center. Its integration with Configuration Manager enables administrators to better deploy, monitor, and maintain antimalware software and updates, and provides a single infrastructure for client management and security.

Configuration Manager integration enables System Center 2012 Endpoint Protection to provide a single infrastructure for deploying and managing endpoint protection. You have a single view into the compliance and security of client systems through antimalware, patching, inventory, and usage information.

The Value Proposition of Operations Manager

The value of Operations Manager lies in three areas:

- Increasing the quality of service that IT departments deliver to their business units
- Reducing the operational cost to deliver that service
- Delivering a best-of-breed management tool

As a management tool monitoring system health, Operations Manager is designed as a best-of-breed monitoring solution, providing enterprise scale and operations management. By incorporating a rich application and service monitoring environment using its management packs, OpsMgr provides a high level of automation.

As an enterprise-ready solution, OpsMgr provides redundant support and high availability with an open architecture—a requirement for computing enterprises that encompass multiple environments that include non-Microsoft platforms. System Center 2012 Operations Manager can monitor, manage, and secure a wide range of resources, including computers, applications, server farms, ecommerce sites, network devices, cross-platform systems, and corporate servers. It supports networked systems scaling up to thousands of computers on the network. OpsMgr can continuously monitor user actions, application software, servers, and desktop computers.

The goal for the IT manager considering OpsMgr is to lower the cost of deploying and managing Windows solutions. This goal includes the "time to resolution"—or how rapidly the IT manager can get an understanding of what is happening in the operating environment and then automatically (or as quickly as possible) achieve a resolution. Operations Manager—when correctly tuned—is positioned to help you tame the fire hose (as shown in Figure 1.20) and control the deluge of system and operational information pouring at you from across your operating environment. It is a key component of DSI.

FIGURE 1.20 Taming the fire hose.

Summary

This chapter introduced you to operations management. You learned that operations management is a process to enhance the supportability of a production environment. The chapter illustrated how Operations Manager can solve a horde of problems. System Center 2012 Operations Manager works to eliminate the isolated islands of information in your shop, notifies you of problems, and maintains a historical database of what happened and how issues were resolved.

The chapter discussed ITIL, which is an international set of best practices for IT Service Management. ITIL describes at a high level what should be accomplished, although not actually how to accomplish it. In furtherance of that process, Microsoft chose ITIL as the foundation for its own operations framework. With the MOF, Microsoft provides both descriptive (what to do and why) as well as prescriptive (how to do it) guidance for IT service management.

Microsoft's management approach, which encompasses MOF and also DSI, is a strategy or blueprint intended to automate data center operations. Microsoft's investment in DSI includes building systems designed for operations, developing an operationally aware platform, and establishing a commitment to intelligent management software.

Operations Manager is a tool to increase the quality of service IT delivers while reducing the operational cost of delivering that service. Together with the other System Center components, OpsMgr is a crucial player in Microsoft's approach to system management.

Management software is a key element in Microsoft's strategy to convince corporate customers that Redmond is serious about proactive management of Windows systems. As you step through the different areas of this book, you will become aware of just how powerful Operations Manager is, and how serious Microsoft is about operations management.

CHAPTER 2

What's New in System Center 2012 Operations Manager

IN THIS CHAPTER

- ▶ The History of Operations Manager
- ▶ Introducing System Center 2012 Operations Manager
- ▶ Terminology and Concepts

The newest version of Operations Manager (OpsMgr), System Center 2012 Operations Manager, builds on the capabilities introduced in OpsMgr 2007. In its fourth major release by Microsoft, the product team takes the best of OpsMgr 2007 and adds a number of enhancements, including resource pools for redundancy and high availability, significant changes in network and application monitoring, and new dashboard capabilities. This chapter takes a brief look at the history of Operations Manager and then highlights the changes in this release.

The History of Operations Manager

Let's spend a moment reviewing the history of Microsoft's presence in the server monitoring space. Microsoft first included server health and monitoring functionality with applications such as Application Center 2000, Systems Management Server (SMS) 2.0, and BackOffice Server 2000. The monitoring capability in these products enabled a system administrator to have a centralized view of information pertaining to functional health, performance, and the event log data of servers within that specific application environment; monitoring was limited to the servers used by the application.

The Early Years: MOM 2000 and MOM 2005

Beginning with its very first version, Operations Manager went beyond examining the health of servers in a single application to examine one's entire environment. The product was originally based on technology developed by Mission Critical Software for its OnePoint Operations Manager product, which Microsoft licensed in 2000 from

NetIQ shortly after that company acquired Mission Critical. Microsoft's first release, Microsoft Operations Manager (MOM) 2000, addressed scalability and performance issues in the OnePoint product, and added significant improvements to management packs for monitoring Microsoft applications software. Microsoft positioned MOM 2000 as an enterprise monitoring solution with comprehensive event management, monitoring and alerting, reporting, a built-in knowledge base, and trend analysis capabilities. However, the architecture remained largely unchanged from the Mission Critical product.

Microsoft released one service pack (SP) for MOM 2000. SP 1 included globalization, failover cluster support for the MOM database, performance improvements to the event management infrastructure, enhancements to most of its management packs with particular emphasis on those for Microsoft Exchange Server and Active Directory, and several new management packs.

In 2003, Microsoft began work on the next version of MOM. Microsoft Operations Manager 2005 was released in August 2004. It sported an improved user interface, additional management packs, enhanced reporting, and improved performance and scalability. SP 1 released in July 2005 with support for Windows 2003 SP 1 and SQL Server 2000 SP 4. SP 1 was also required to support SQL Server 2005 for the operational and reporting database components after that product's release later that year.

Operations Manager 2007

Development for the next version, code named "MOM V3," began in 2005. In 2006, Microsoft officially announced the product's rebranding as System Center Operations Manager 2007. Microsoft completed work on Operations Manager 2007, which was a total rewrite of the product, in March 2007—a list of what was new would be longer than listing what was unchanged! OpsMgr 2007 provided best-of-breed end-to-end service management for the Microsoft Windows platform, helping you to increase efficiency and achieve greater control over your Information Technology (IT) environment. The focus moved from monitoring events and generating alerts to monitoring a server's health and holistically monitoring server and client environments.

OpsMgr 2007 uses model-based management, where an IT environment is defined as a model. Using models allows granular discovery of service components and presents the ability to monitor not only the server but also the entire end-to-end service as a unique object. These models, represented in eXtensible Markup Language (XML), are stored in management packs; beginning with OpsMgr 2007, Microsoft moved away from the proprietary management pack format used by MOM 2000 and MOM 2005.

OpsMgr 2007 also includes Agentless Exception Monitoring (AEM), which provides information on application crashes; it introduces client monitoring, PowerShell support, role-based security, an Authoring console, the Health Explorer, Active Directory Integration, Audit Collection Services (ACS), changes in capturing and collecting data for the OpsMgr data warehouse, and more. A list of features introduced is available at www.microsoft.com/en-us/download/details.aspx?id=2353. Most importantly, the architecture introduced with Operations Manager 2007 forms the base of the technology and architecture found today in System Center 2012 Operations Manager.

Operations Manager 2007 SP 1 released in February 2008. SP 1 addressed bugs from the original release including a rollup of all hot-fixes, and added enhancements in performance and reliability, setup and recovery, user interface and experience, reporting, the Web console, and more. (A complete list of what was new in the service pack is available at http://technet.microsoft.com/en-us/library/bb821996.aspx, and a list of bug fixes is at http://support.microsoft.com/kb/944443/.)

Operations Manager 2007 R2 and Beyond

Operations Manager 2007 had an "R2" release in May 2009. Release 2's most publicized enhancement was cross platform support for UNIX and Linux servers. Here are some of the more notable improvements in this release:

- Cross platform monitoring
- Integration with System Center Virtual Machine Manager (VMM) 2008, which enabled maximizing availability of virtual workloads
- Large scale monitoring of URLs
- Service level monitoring
- Performance enhancements
- Updated Authoring console, which shipped with the installation bits

A full list of features is available at http://technet.microsoft.com/en-us/library/dd362653.aspx.

OpsMgr 2007 R2 built upon the base release of the 2007 product, enabling it to be firmly placed in Gartner Group's challenger's quadrant for IT Event Correlation and Analysis in July 2009 and then the highly sought "magic" or leader's quadrant in December 2010, as shown in Figure 2.1. Gartner's magic quadrant indicates superiority in completeness of vision and ability to execute. (In 2011, Gartner retired the IT Event Correlation and Analysis magic quadrant. For information, see http://www.gartner.com/id=1749715.)

Rather than releasing service packs, bug fixes to the product after OpsMgr 2007 R2 were released in the form of cumulative updates (CUs). The most recent CU, released just before this book was printed, is CU7 (January 8, 2013). Meanwhile, Microsoft was working on what was variously code-named MOM V4, OM 10, and most widely known as the "vNext" release of the product, publicly released in April 2012 as System Center 2012 Operations Manager. Figure 2.2 illustrates Operations Manager's life cycle.

NOTE: CUMULATIVE UPDATES BECOME UPDATE ROLLUPS

With the release of System Center 2012, cumulative updates have been renamed to update rollups (URs), which are released for all System Center components (including Configuration Manager). Microsoft released UR4 January 9, 2013. Beginning with UR3, Operations Manager updates are installable with Windows Update.

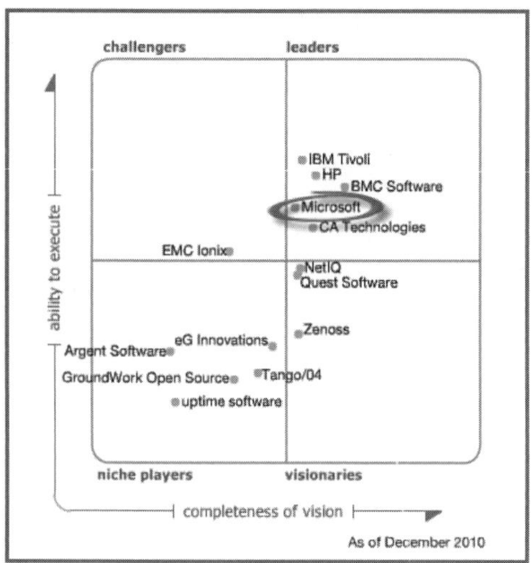

FIGURE 2.1 Operations Manager 2007 R2 in the Gartner magic quadrant (source: http://www.gartner.com/technology/media-products/reprints/microsoft/vol2/article5/article5.html).

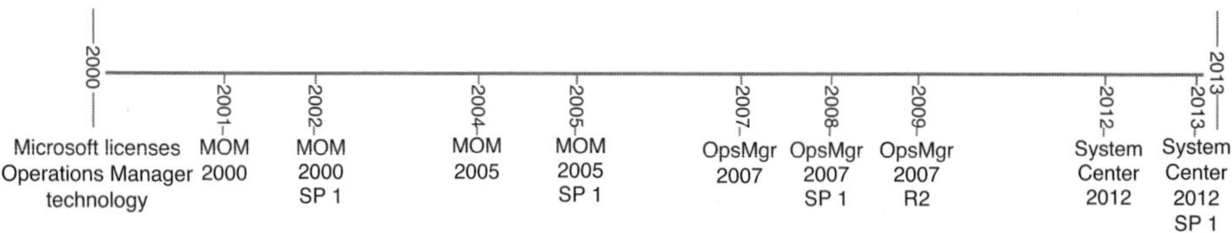

FIGURE 2.2 Operations Manager development timeline.

Introducing System Center 2012 Operations Manager

System Center Operations Manager 2007 Unleashed (Sams, 2008) discussed how the nomenclature change from Microsoft Operations Manager 2005 to System Center Operations Manager 2007 suggested OpsMgr had a facelift with that release. The same is true with System Center 2012 Operations Manager. While the core architecture has not undergone the vast changes introduced with the OpsMgr 2007 product and changes for the most part are evolutionary, the name change emphasizes System Center is the actual product, with the latest release being System Center 2012, with the component of interest being Operations Manager.

Beginning with System Center 2012, Microsoft is releasing System Center as a single product, rather than in waves of individual components. Corresponding with this are significant licensing changes for System Center, discussed in Chapter 4, "Planning an Operations Manager Deployment." System Center 2012 also includes a higher level of integration and cohesion between its components, along with a common installer, although the first version of the installer is far from the robust installer available in products such as Microsoft Office. This is not to say that System Center 2012 is the ultimate vision of integration between its components. Rather, it is a first release of a single System Center product, first announced at the Microsoft Management Summit (MMS) in 2003, and then consisting of two technically unrelated products: MOM 2000 and SMS 2003. System Center, you've come a long way, but the journey isn't over yet!

The System Center 2012 Operations Manager component includes a number of new features and capabilities; some key improvements being changes in management server architecture to eliminate single points of failure, new capabilities for network monitoring, and application performance monitoring, just to name a few. The next sections discuss the changes in this release, which Microsoft documents at http://technet.microsoft.com/en-US/library/jj656648.aspx. Additional information is available at http://www.windows-networking.com/articles_tutorials/Introduction-System-Center-Operations-Manager-2012-Part1.html, although this was written during the beta timeframe.

THE SYSTEM CENTER 2012 SERVICE PACK 1 RELEASE

This book was written while System Center 2012 SP 1 was in development. While the contents of the service pack are subject to change with its final release, here is what is anticipated for Operations Manager with this service pack:

- **Full support for Windows Server 2012:** Support for the OS on System Center (and OpsMgr) 2012 servers; management packs for Windows Server 2012.
- **Full support for SQL Server 2012:** Support for the database engine on System Center (and OpsMgr) servers, including support for AlwaysOn; management packs for SQL Server 2012.
- **Storage functionality enhancements:** SP 1 adds hypervisor support for storage monitoring alerting based on provisioning thresholds as defined by Windows Server 2012.
- **Virtual network support:** This will be available for Hyper-V systems only. VMware support is unchanged from System Center 2012 RTM.
- **Enhanced network monitoring:** Additional network device support.
- **Global Service Monitor (GSM):** This is a new cloud-enabled capability that extends application monitoring, enabling you to add outside-in testing to incorporate your users' experience of your website or web application.
- **APM enhancements:** Support for Windows Foundation Classes (WFC), ASP.NET model-view controller (MVC), .NET Windows services, Azure SDK (storage and SQL Azure support), and Internet Information Services (IIS) 8.
- **Resolution States:** With Service Pack 1 for Operations Manager 2012, Microsoft is adding several new resolution states.

- **360 dashboards:** The term "360" refers to an out of the box capability. These dashboards are a .NET application that is immediately functional out of the box. A new Applications dashboard will be available under Application Monitoring in the Operations console.
- **Team Foundation Server (TFS) synchronization:** Two-way communication between OpsMgr and TFS, such that changes a developer makes are communicated to the OpsMgr administrator.

Microsoft also documents the changes to OpsMgr 2012 in SP 1 at http://technet.microsoft.com/en-US/library/jj656650.aspx.

Supported Configurations

System Center 2012 Operations Manager continues to build on the robustness of OpsMgr 2007 R2. Table 2.1 lists supported configurations for agents, applications, consoles, and network devices. "Supported" means Microsoft has tested these configurations and will support them; these are not necessarily the outer limits of what will run. In some cases, the load on individual agents may affect what will perform well. For additional information on monitored item capacity, see http://technet.microsoft.com/en-us/library/hh205990.aspx#BKMK_MonitoredItem.

TABLE 2.1 Supported configurations for agents, applications, consoles, and network devices

Monitored Item	Recommended Limit
Open Operations consoles	50
Agent-monitored computers reporting to a management server	3,000
Agent-monitored computers reporting to a gateway server	2,000
Agents in a single management group	15,000
Collective client monitored computers per management server	2,500
Agentless Exception Monitored (AEM) computers per dedicated management server	25,000
AEM computers per management group	100,000
Management servers per agent for multi-homing	4
Agentless-managed computers per management server	10
Agentless-managed computers per management group	60
Agent-managed and UNIX or Linux computers per management group	6,000 (with 50 open consoles); 15,000 (with 25 open consoles)

Monitored Item	Recommended Limit
UNIX or Linux computers per dedicated management server	500
UNIX or Linux computers monitored per dedicated gateway server	100
Network devices managed by a resource pool with three or more management servers	1,000
Network devices managed by two resource pools	2,000
Application performance monitoring (APM) agents	700
APM applications	400
URLs monitored per dedicated management server	3,000
URLs monitored per dedicated management group	12,000
URLs monitored per agent	50

Root Management Server and Root Management Server Emulator

Sometimes an area of angst with the management server architecture introduced in OpsMgr 2007 was the root management server (RMS). The RMS, often referred to as the product's "Achilles' heel," was a single point of failure, as it ran workflows and services that did not run on other management servers. When the RMS was unavailable, these functions would not run. Here's what the RMS was solely responsible for providing:

- Console access
- Role based access control
- Distribution of configurations to agents
- Connectors to other management systems
- Alert notifications
- Health aggregation
- Group calculations
- Availability
- Dependency monitoring
- Database grooming
- Enabling model-based management

In addition, there were two Windows services that started only on the RMS and were disabled on other management servers: the SDK and Config services. A third service, the Health Service—renamed in OpsMgr 2007 R2 to System Center Management but often referred to by its previous name—runs on all management servers (and agent-monitored systems), but had a unique role on the RMS, running workloads for the entire management group.

With all these responsibilities, the RMS often was a performance and scalability bottleneck, in addition to being a single point of failure. Making the RMS highly available required clustering—not necessarily for the faint of heart—or having a secondary management server available to be promoted to the RMS role. If the RMS became unavailable, those functions the RMS was responsible for were also unavailable until another management server could take over that role.

System Center 2012 Operations Manager removes the RMS role. The SDK service (renamed to the System Center Data Access Service or DAS) now starts automatically on every management server, and the Config service (now the System Center Management Configuration service), rewritten and renamed from OMCG to CSHOST, is federated among management servers. Rather than using data stored in memory on the RMS as was the case in OpsMgr 2007, the configuration service uses a new set of tables in the Operations Manager database (known as the Configuration Store and identified as CS.*) to persist the instance space.

NOTE: DEVELOPMENT TRIVIA ON THE CONFIGURATION STORE

During early test releases of System Center 2012 Operations Manager, the Configuration Store was in a separate database. It was later incorporated into the operational database once it was determined that this would not affect performance, giving OpsMgr administrators one less database to maintain and back up.

To distribute the RMS-specific workloads to all management servers, Microsoft developed the concept of resource pools, discussed in depth in the "Resource Pools" section. Three resource pools distribute the RMS-specific workloads:

- **All Management Servers Resource Pool:** This pool has most RMS-specific instances and workflows. Exceptions are the AD Integration workflows and Alert Subscription Service.
- **Notifications Resource Pool:** The Alert Subscription Service instance is targeted to this pool. Using a separate pool allows you to easily remove management servers from the pool that should not be participating in notifications.
- **AD Assignment Resource Pool:** AD Integration workflows are targeted to this pool so you can more easily control the location where the AD assignment workflows are running.

The RMS emulator (RMSE) is a special role added to one of the management servers, by default the first installed management server. The RMS emulator is for backwards compatibility to legacy management packs; it is not actually required for the management group to function correctly. To determine which management server has the role of RMS emulator, open the OpsMgr Operations console and navigate to **Administration -> Management Servers**. Figure 2.3 shows that Helios is currently acting as the RMS emulator in the Odyssey OMGRP management group. Should you need to move the RMS emulator role, Microsoft provides the `Get-SCOMRMSEmulator`, `Set-SCOMRMSEmulator`, and `Remove-SCOMRMSEmulator` PowerShell cmdlets to identify, move, and delete the RMSE; these scripts are discussed in Chapter 23, "PowerShell and Operations Manager."

TIP: INFORMATION ABOUT RMS EMULATOR

For additional information on the RMS emulator, see these posts:

- http://blogs.catapultsystems.com/cfuller/archive/2012/01/11/what-does-the-root-management-server-emulator-rmse-actually-do-in-opsmgr-scom.aspx
- http://scug.be/blogs/christopher/archive/2012/01/09/scom-2012-move-rms-emulator-role.aspx
- http://blogs.technet.com/b/momteam/archive/2011/08/22/topology-changes-in-system-center-2012-operations-manager-overview.aspx.

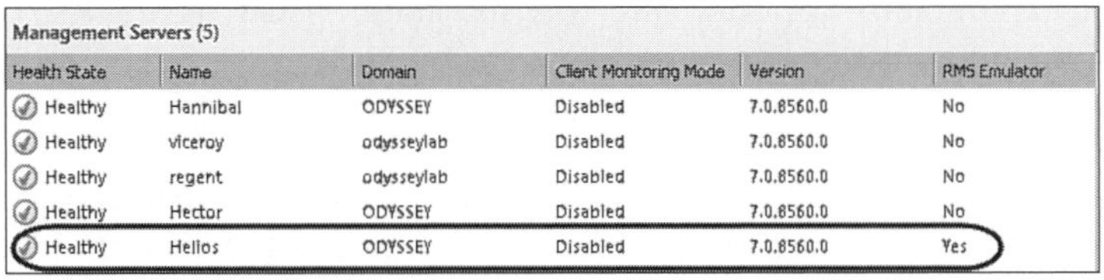

Management Servers (5)

Health State	Name	Domain	Client Monitoring Mode	Version	RMS Emulator
Healthy	Hannibal	ODYSSEY	Disabled	7.0.8560.0	No
Healthy	viceroy	odysseylab	Disabled	7.0.8560.0	No
Healthy	regent	odysseylab	Disabled	7.0.8560.0	No
Healthy	Hector	ODYSSEY	Disabled	7.0.8560.0	No
Healthy	Helios	ODYSSEY	Disabled	7.0.8560.0	Yes

FIGURE 2.3 The Management Servers view identifies the current RMS emulator.

NOTE: GATEWAY SERVERS DISPLAY IN THE MANAGEMENT SERVERS LIST IN OPERATIONS CONSOLE

Figure 2.3 shows three management servers in the ODYSSEY domain and two in odysseylab. The viceroy and regent servers are actually gateway servers.

High Availability with Resource Pools

Resource pools are a collection of management or gateway servers that can take on monitoring workflows if one of the management/gateway servers becomes unavailable. Several resource pools are installed with the OpsMgr 2012, and you can create your own for specific purposes. As an example, you could create a resource pool of management servers located in the same geographic area that provide network device monitoring. Using resource pools helps your management group to be highly available.

The management servers in any given resource pool are treated as having equal capacity; differences in processors and memory are not considered; different workloads are not taken into account and are distributed among available servers in the pool. The authors recommend you plan for all management servers to have similar configurations.

By default, all management servers are members of the resource pools created when OpsMgr is installed, and management servers added to the management group are automatically added to any resource pool with a membership type of Automatic. Removing a management server from a pool changes the membership type of that pool to Manual. Figure 2.4 shows the resource pools created by default. To see the current list of resource pools, navigate in the Operations console to **Administration** -> **Resource Pools**.

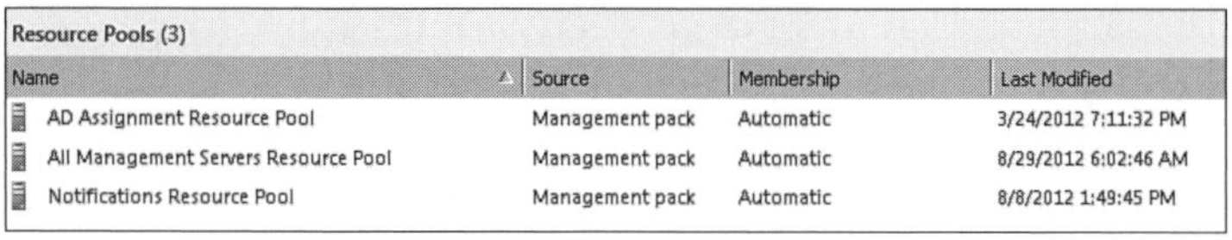

Resource Pools (3)

Name	Source	Membership	Last Modified
AD Assignment Resource Pool	Management pack	Automatic	3/24/2012 7:11:32 PM
All Management Servers Resource Pool	Management pack	Automatic	8/29/2012 6:02:46 AM
Notifications Resource Pool	Management pack	Automatic	8/8/2012 1:49:45 PM

FIGURE 2.4 Resource pools created by OpsMgr management group installation.

Here are several caveats to keep in mind:

- Windows agents do not use resource pools for failover; they continue to function as in OpsMgr 2007. You can implement Active Directory Integration (ADI) as discussed in Chapter 8, "Installing and Configuring Agents."
- Resource pools only cover health service functionality. The workflows targeted to the instances are loaded by the health service in the pool that is managing that instance. Should one of the health services in the resource pool fail, the other health services pick up the work the failed member was running. For failover of the SDK service, consider Network Load Balancing, covered in Chapter 9, "Complex Configurations."

Viewing Resource Pool Health

You can view the health of resource pool members in the Administration pane of the Operations console. Navigate to the Resource Pool node, select the pool you want to work with and then select **View Resource Pool Members** in the Tasks pane to view the health of the members of the selected resource pool.

Resource Pool Events

A number of events provide feedback regarding the state of each member of the pool. These events, listed in Table 2.2, are not collected or stored by Operations Manager; you must connect to each pool member's event log to view the events. If there is a problem with the health of a pool, start your investigation by looking at the event log. All resource pool events are logged under the Pool Manager category.

TABLE 2.2 Resource pool events

Event ID	Name	Severity	Explanation	Description
15000	Pool Member Initialized Event	Informational	Indicates a member of a pool has received configuration and started the failover process.	The pool member has initialized.
15001	Operations Manager Resource Pool Member Initial Check Ack Quorum	Informational	More than half the pool members must be able to communicate with each other for a pool to perform work. Once the initial check ack quorum is achieved, a lease request can be sent out.	More than half of the members of the pool have acknowledged the most recent initialization check request. The pool member will send a lease request to acquire ownership of managed objects assigned to the pool.
15002	Operations Manager Resource Pool Member Quorum Failure	Error	This is the only event that can occur repeatedly without intermediate events, so it is throttled to once every 10 minutes per pool if no other changes in the pool occur. It indicates a majority of pool members has not acknowledged the initial check request.	The pool member cannot send a lease request to acquire ownership of managed objects because half or fewer members of the pool acknowledged the most recent initialization check request. The pool member will continue to send an initialization check request.
15003	Operations Manager Resource Pool Member Failover	Informational	This event is the result of a check ack message that influenced the logic used to determine if a pool member is available.	Availability of one or more members of the pool has changed. Ownership for all managed objects assigned to the pool will be redistributed between pool members.

Event ID	Name	Severity	Explanation	Description
15004	Operations Manager resource pool member not allowed to perform work	Error	This event is logged if a majority of pool members do not respond to the last lease request before the previous lease expired.	The pool member no longer owns any managed objects assigned to the pool because half or fewer members did not acknowledge the most recent lease request. The pool member has unloaded the workflows for managed objects it previously owned.

Network Monitoring Enhancements

OpsMgr 2012 provides physical network monitoring of routers and switches, extending to their interfaces and ports. This and other functionality is made available by Microsoft's licensing of EMC's SMARTS. The SMARTS technology provides root-cause analysis capability across an enterprise by looking at network connections and interpreting events by looking at the symptoms those events spawn. Here's what is included in networking monitoring:

- Network device discovery, monitoring and reporting
- SNMP v3 support; previous versions supported SNMP v1 and v2c
- IPv4 and IPv6 support
- Port/interface monitoring; this includes, along other monitors:
    - Up/down monitoring
    - Traffic volume
    - Utilization
    - Dropped packet rate
    - Broadcast traffic statistics
- Virtual Local Area Network (VLAN) health monitoring
- Overall connection health
- Hot Standby Router Protocol (HSRP) group health
- New visualization/dashboards

- **Overall network summary:** Shows the health of the network.
- **Network node:** Shows health of a device on the network. Figure 2.5 is an example of this dashboard.
- **Network interface:** Displays interface-level statistics.
- **Vicinity:** Shows a device, its neighbors, and connected Window servers.

See Chapter 16, "Network Monitoring," for a detailed discussion of network monitoring.

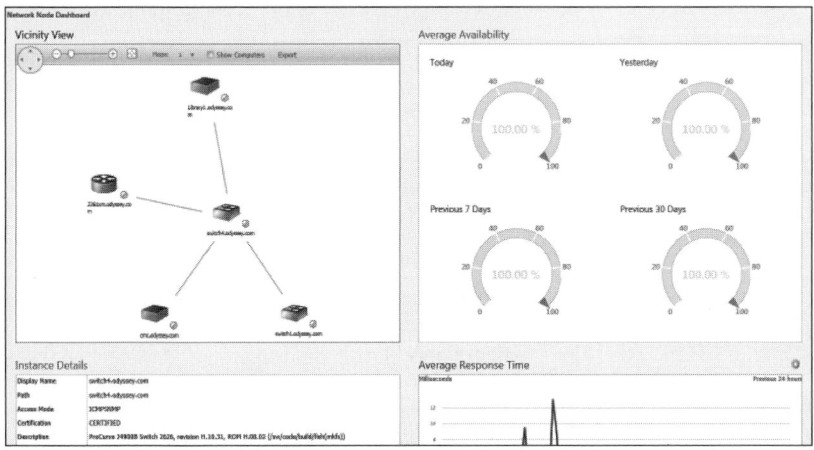

FIGURE 2.5 The Network Node Dashboard.

Monitoring .NET Applications

Also known as application performance monitoring, APM is Microsoft's integration of AVIcode into OpsMgr. APM has the ability to drill into an application performance alert down to the code level to see exactly what is going on and where the issues are, giving you a single tool to monitor both applications and your infrastructure. As APM is configured using templates, it does not require authoring management packs or code modifications. Interfaces include the Application Advisor (shown in Figure 2.6) and Applications Diagnostics Web consoles, with the Web Application Availability Monitoring Wizard added to the Monitoring space of the Operations console.

This feature, discussed in Chapter 15, "Monitoring .NET Applications," is available for .NET web applications and web services running IIS 7.x in OpsMgr 2012 RTM; SP 1 adds support for WFC, ASP.NET MVC, .NET Windows Services, Azure SDK, and IIS 8.

APM is the Gartner Group 2012 Challenger's quadrant for Application Performance monitoring, as discussed at http://www.gartner.com/technology/reprints.do?ct=120820&id=1-1BRNFO0&st=sg and http://innetworktech.com/wp-content/uploads/2012/08/2012-Magic-Quadrant-for-Application-Performance-Monitoring.pdf.

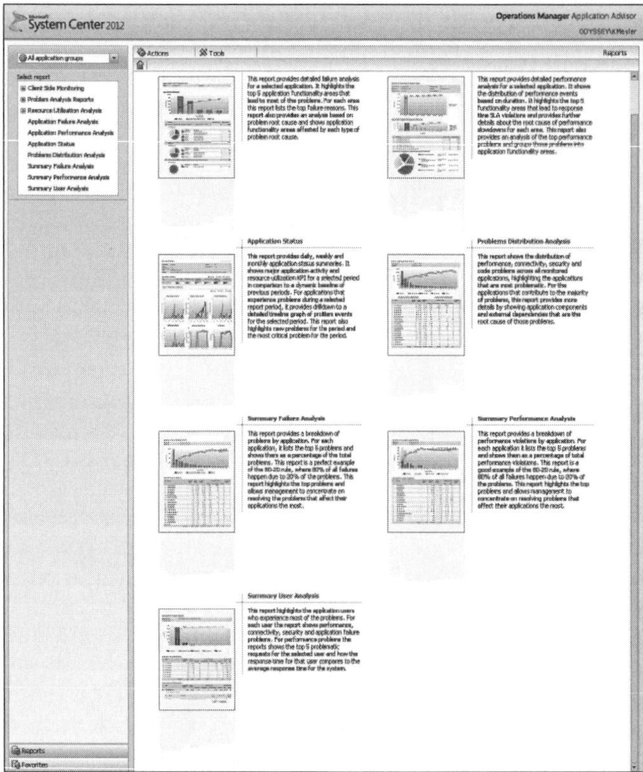

FIGURE 2.6 APM Application Advisor.

Using PowerShell

System Center 2012 Operations Manager incorporates about 30 new PowerShell cmdlets, enabling support of anything performed in the console via a cmdlet. Previous OpsMgr 2007 cmdlets are renamed to have a SCOM prefix in the name and now have new parameters; the OpsMgr 2007 cmdlets, although depreciated, still work in this version by loading the OpsMgr 2007 snap-in. PowerShell capabilities are discussed in Chapter 23.

Saving Overrides

A welcome change is that the Default management pack is no longer the default location for saving overrides or creating new management packs. Figure 2.7 shows where the drop-down now prompts you to select a management pack.

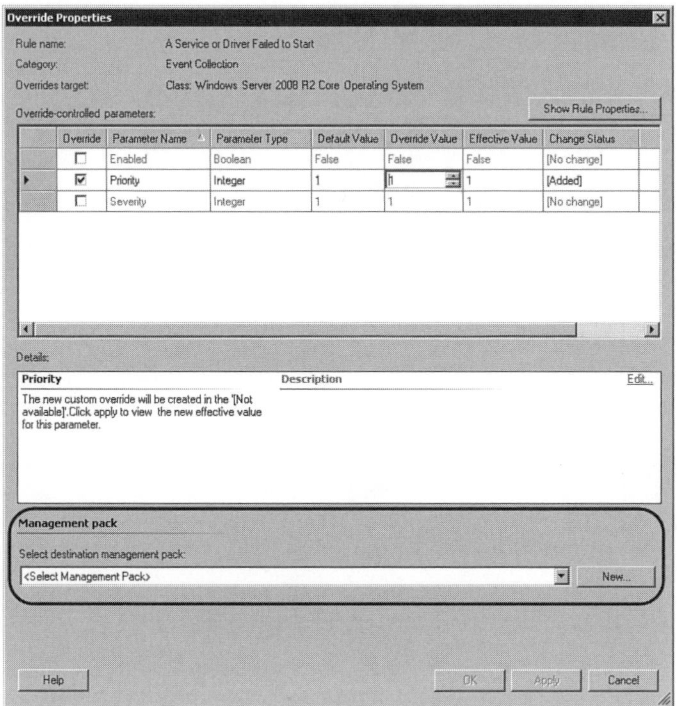

FIGURE 2.7 Overrides are no longer saved in the Default management pack by default.

Using the Console

The Operations Manager "full" console remains largely unchanged in OpsMgr 2012. Unlike consoles in some of the other System Center 2012 components, the Operations console does not include the ribbon bar (some may consider this an advantage). One change is the Actions pane is renamed to the Tasks pane. For an in-depth discussion of the console, see Chapter 7, "Configuring and Using System Center 2012 Operations Manager." Figure 2.8 shows the Operations console.

Web Console Updates

The OpsMgr 2012 Web console is completely redesigned and based on Silverlight. All monitoring capabilities in the full console are now available in the Web console, along with access to the My Workspace node. Figure 2.9 shows the Monitoring space in the Web console.

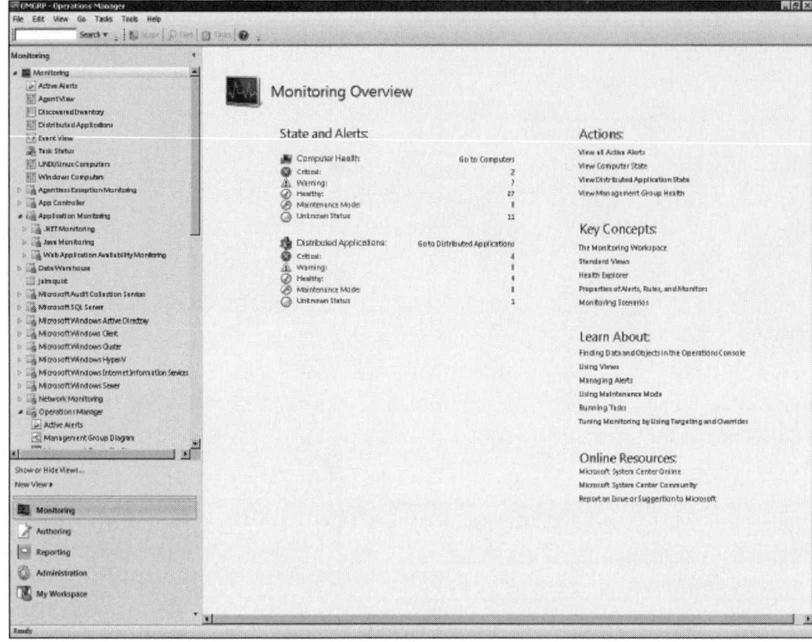

FIGURE 2.8 Initial view of the Operations console opens to the Monitoring Overview in the Monitoring space.

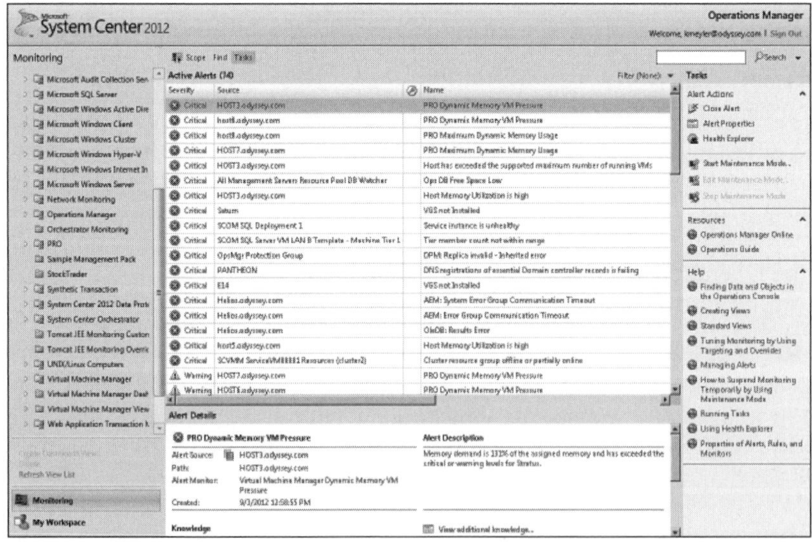

FIGURE 2.9 Active Alerts view in the Monitoring space of the Web console.

Maintenance Mode on Management Servers

Operations Manager does not block placing management servers into maintenance mode. However, the way management servers behave when placed into maintenance mode has changed:

- When you place a management server in maintenance mode, the System Center Management Configuration Service changes the agent assignment to force the agents to fail over to another management server, ensuring data loss does not occur.
- In OpsMgr 2007, a management server was unable to take itself out of maintenance mode. This was because maintenance mode unloaded all workflows, including the End Maintenance Mode workflow! This now changes with the assignment of the End Maintenance Mode workflow to the All Management Servers resource pool. By being in the resource pool, the workflow fails over to another management server and reloads to be able to exit maintenance on the management server that is placed in maintenance mode. (By definition, having a resource pool requires at least two management servers, so if you only have a single management server it will never come out of maintenance mode because there is no other management server available for workflow failover.)

Dashboards

OpsMgr contains significant enhancements in its capability to display data through use of dashboard technologies. Discussed in Chapter 11, "Dashboards, Trending, and Forecasting," here are some of the highlights:

- Dashboards are distributed in management packs.
- Authoring dashboards does not require coding.
- You can access dashboards via the Operations console, the Web console, and a SharePoint Web Part.

What's New in Security

In OpsMgr 2012, the local Administrators group is used to populate the Operations Manager Administrator role. This differs from OpsMgr 2007, where you could configure the group in that role; if you specified an incorrect group, you ran the risk of being unable to start the Operations console to be able to change that group without editing MomAuth.xml.

Operations Manager 2007 R2 simplified the original presentation of Run As accounts and profiles by adding distribution and targeting features. When you associate a Run As account with a particular Run As profile, you can target the profile to any class available in Operations Manager and see the logical relationship between the two. Both Run As account distribution and Run As account targeting must be correctly configured for the Run As profile to work properly.

Connector Functionality Replaced by System Center 2012 Orchestrator

Previous versions of Operations Manager used connectors to connect to other systems. In System Center 2012 Operations Manager, this functionality is replaced by Orchestrator integration packs. For information on Orchestrator, see Chapter 21, "System Center Integration," and *System Center 2012 Orchestrator Unleashed* (Sams, 2013).

Changes in Capacity

With the most recent version of Operations Manager, Microsoft has increased capacity in several areas to extend the product's monitoring capabilities. Table 2.3 compares management features across the different versions.

TABLE 2.3 Comparison of Operations Manager capabilities across versions

Feature	MOM 2000	MOM 2000 SP 1	MOM 2005	MOM 2005 SP 1	OpsMgr 2007	OpsMgr 2007 SP 1	OpsMgr 2007 R2	OpsMgr 2012
Managed computers per management group	1,000	2,000	3,500	4,000	5,000	6,000	6,000	15,000
Managed computers per management server	700	1,000	1,200	2,000	2,000	2,000	2,000 UNIX/ Linux: 200	3,000 UNIX/ Linux:500
Management servers per management group	4	10	10	10	10	No defined limit	No defined limit	No defined limit
Agentless managed computers per management group	n/a	n/a	60	60	60	60	60	60
Agentless managed computers per management server	n/a	n/a	10	10	10	10	10	10
Agents per gateway server	n/a	n/a	n/a	n/a	200	800	1,500	2,000 UNIX/ Linux: 100

Terminology and Concepts

Microsoft has added some terms in Operations Manager 2012 with which you need to become familiar. Before beginning how to deploy and operate OpsMgr, familiarize yourself with the terminology and concepts that define System Center 2012 Operations Manager, discussed in the following sections. Microsoft provides a glossary of terms for System Center 2012 Operations Manager at http://technet.microsoft.com/en-us/library/hh710011.aspx.

AEM: Capturing Application Crash Information

Agentless exception monitoring provides data on application crashes, resulting in information your organization can analyze for patterns. A management server can optionally forward AEM data to Microsoft for analysis rather than having each individual client forward the data.

Operations Manager Agent

An OpsMgr agent is the feature installed on a computer that performs management. Based on the management packs associated with the computer, the agent collects data, compares sampled data to predefined values, creates alerts, and runs responses. Computers can be agent-managed, or agentless. An agentless-monitored computer does not run the OpsMgr agent. The agent feature on a management server (or another OpsMgr agent) gathers data from the agentless managed computer through remote calls to that system.

Audit Collection

ACS is a secure and efficient way to gather Security event logs from systems and consolidate them for analysis and reporting. These events are stored in an audit database. Deploying ACS involves ACS forwarders, the ACS collector, and the ACS audit database. The ACS agent is included in the OpsMgr agent deployment.

Post OpsMgr 2007 R2, Microsoft extended ACS to include cross platform support. ACS capabilities are largely unchanged in System Center 2012 Operations Manager. ACS is discussed further in Chapter 10, "Security and Compliance."

Classes: Templates for Objects

A class is an item that is targeted for all operations. Think of a class as a template defining a set of objects of a certain type and the properties of those objects. Classes can exist in a parent-child relationship where the child class inherits properties from the parent class.

Features Versus Components

Components in OpsMgr 2007 are now called product *features*, as the previous products in the System Center suite are now components of System Center 2012. As an example, the OpsMgr agent is now a feature, rather than a component.

Gateways

The gateway server plays two roles in Operations Manager:

- Operations Manager requires mutual authentication between the management server and the agent. A gateway server enables monitoring of computers that lie outside the Kerberos trust boundaries (Kerberos realm) of the management group. When an agent belongs to an untrusted domain, is outside the corporate firewall, in a demilitarized zone (DMZ, also known as a *perimeter network*), or in a workgroup, it is not able to use mutual authentication as a secure channel to communicate with a management server. Gateway servers use certificates to communicate with those agents that cannot otherwise communicate with a management server. The gateway acts as a proxy server to take data from these agents and forward it to a management server inside the firewall.
- An additional use of gateway servers is their implementation in distributed environments where remote sites are located at the end of a long-distance wide area network (WAN) link. The gateway server aggregates communications from agents and minimizes traffic between the remote site and a management server. The data transmitted between the agent and a management server (or gateway server) is both encrypted and compressed. By compressing at the gateway before sending it across the WAN, you can take advantage of a compression ratio ranging from approximately 4:1 to 6:1. More information on using gateways is in Chapter 4.

Heartbeats: Checking the Health of the Agent

A heartbeat is a message sent by an agent to its management server that tells the management server the agent is functioning. The heartbeat also informs Operations Manager of the current rules evaluated by the agent and requests updates if necessary.

Management Group

A management group is the basic functional unit of an Operations Manager implementation that can perform monitoring. It must contain a SQL Server database server, one or more management servers, one or more Operations consoles, and one or more agents. It can also contain a SQL Server reporting server, a gateway server, and an ACS server and database.

Management Pack

The heart of Operations Manager is its management packs, which are collections of objects including monitors, rules, alerts, performance events, and reports for a specific application or product feature set. Management packs use XML. Management packs are the brains of Operations Manager; they provide the logic and reports used for monitoring.

Management Server

Management servers are those components of an Operations Manager management group that are responsible for communication with agents, databases, and the consoles. Each management group must have at least one management server, which is installed during OpsMgr setup.

Models

Models are software representations of hardware, software, services, and other logical components that are in your environment. The model captures the nature of those components and the relationships between them.

Resource Pool

A resource pool is a collection of management or gateway servers that automatically distribute Operations Manager workflows between the management servers in that collection. If one or more servers in the pool become unavailable, the workflows are automatically redistributed.

RMS Emulator

The RMS emulator is a management server designated to run management pack functions specifically targeted to the `Root Management Server` class. These tend to be older (legacy) management packs, as newer management packs do not target this class. The RMS emulator role was created to not break existing management packs that specifically target the RMS. Here are two articles with additional information:

- http://blogs.technet.com/b/momteam/archive/2011/08/22/topology-changes-in-system-center-2012-operations-manager-overview.aspx
- http://www.systemcentercentral.com/BlogDetails/tabid/143/IndexID/91085/Default.aspx

Run As Account

This is a Windows account that can be associated with a Run As profile, and can use Windows Authentication, NTLM, Basic, Digest, Simple, or Binary methods of authentication.

Run As Profile

A Run As profile is a profile that associates a credential with a workflow so it can run using those credentials.

When a workflow requires credentials that cannot be provided by the default action account, it can be written to use a Run As profile. The Run As profile can have multiple Run As accounts associated with it, each specifying the necessary credentials for specific computers. Multiple workflows can use the same Run As profile, as shown in Figure 2.10.

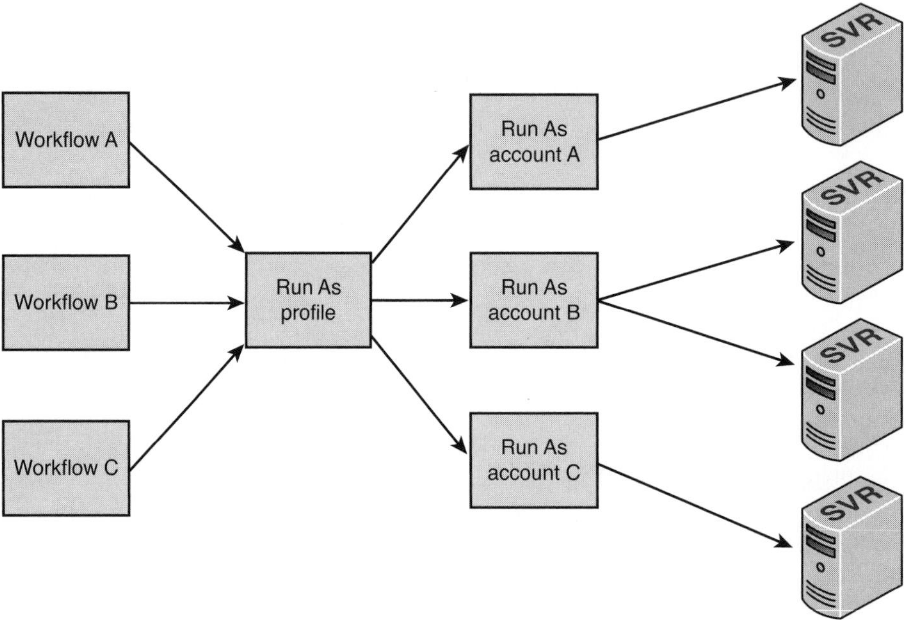

FIGURE 2.10 Using a Run As profile.

User Role

A user role is a combination of a profile that combines actions users can take (such as an OpsMgr Administrator or OpsMgr Operator) and a scope, which are the objects the users can take those actions on, such as all SQL Servers. A user role is also a security boundary. The OpsMgr administrator can utilize user roles to control access to views and tasks to those OpsMgr users assigned to that role.

Summary

This chapter covered the history of Operations Manager and highlighted the changes in the System Center 2012 Operations Manager release. It also discussed Service Pack 1, in prerelease at the time of writing this chapter. The next chapter discusses how OpsMgr actually works, giving you a look at the internals of this System Center component.

CHAPTER 3

Looking Inside OpsMgr

IN THIS CHAPTER

System Center 2012 Operations Manager (OpsMgr) is the monitoring and operations management component in System Center 2012. OpsMgr is implemented using one or more computers that perform their assigned roles as components of a management group. The components cooperate over several secure communications channels to achieve management information workflow, ultimately delivering status and decision-making information to operators and administrators. The most important data collected is the health of the managed objects; this health status is arrived at using models that derive their intelligence through tactically selected and placed probes called *monitors*.

This chapter will make these terms and relationships clear, enabling the job of deploying and supporting OpsMgr 2012 to be easier and the deliverables from OpsMgr more valuable. For those OpsMgr administrators who really want to understand what is happening "under the hood," this chapter is for you. The Authoring space in the Operations console as well as the OpsMgr Authoring console will be a focus during much of this chapter.

Without overcomplicating the architecture, two practical goals of this chapter are

- To enable you to understand the product well enough to extend it through simple custom management packs
- To equip you with the concepts and terminology to communicate accurately with fellow OpsMgr professionals in Microsoft's systems management community

For those not seeking deep knowledge on OpsMgr internals, the authors recommend reading at least the "System Center 2012 Integration" and "Management Group Defined" sections of this chapter.

Architectural Overview

This chapter looks at OpsMgr design and internals at three levels:

- **The integration story:** How OpsMgr supports and powers other components in System Center 2012
- **The macro level:** Computer roles that comprise a management group and how management groups interact
- **The micro level:** Examination of the elements that constitute a management pack, in particular the workflow and presentation of data to the operator

As an OpsMgr administrator, you have no influence over product and server component characteristics—these are hard coded features of the System Center software architecture. On the other hand, administrators can enjoy almost complete flexibility regarding the manner in which management packs are utilized and the deliverables desired from the management packs. As far as System Center 2012 components, you can deploy just OpsMgr, all the components, or any combination of components as fits your business needs.

OpsMgr administrators of the smallest and simplest environments—where all OpsMgr components are installed on a single server and all managed computers are in a trusted domain environment—are generally less concerned about OpsMgr architecture. However, even these simpler networks may be running several System Center components such as Data Protection Manager (DPM) or Configuration Manager (ConfigMgr). To get the most out of System Center 2012, you need to know how to set up the attach points between the components; these take the form of management packs, connectors, and integration packs.

Most OpsMgr administrators will need to distribute multiple features across different servers. This scale-out is necessary to manage more than a small number of computers and to achieve any level of redundancy in your OpsMgr infrastructure. For example, to monitor service delivery at a branch office where there is no virtual private network (VPN) connectivity, you would want to deploy one or more OpsMgr gateway servers. While a seemingly simple activity, deploying gateway servers requires an understanding of OpsMgr management group architecture.

System Center 2012 Integration

With the OpsMgr and System Center 2012 release, OpsMgr administrators have a unique opportunity to extend the value of Information Technology (IT) management services in their organizations. In earlier releases, each component such as OpsMgr or ConfigMgr was licensed separately; with System Center 2012, you own one or more comprehensive

System Center 2012 management license(s) per physical host. These licenses also cover your guest computers, with all System Center components included. This development presents opportunities for two types of organizations:

- **Previously using only OpsMgr:** These OpsMgr administrators can extend the value of System Center into areas such as backup and security, by adding components such as Data Protection Manager and ConfigMgr with Endpoint Protection.
- **Previously using other System Center products:** By implementing Operations Manager, administrators of other System Center components can extend the value of System Center—enabling their organizations to run better and making their own jobs easier.

Installing multiple System Center 2012 components at once is beyond the scope of this book. However, if you plan to deploy multiple components, you need to be aware of their dependences and relationships. If OpsMgr is the first System Center 2012 component you install and you intend to deploy additional components, you will want to keep your design options open. Figure 3.1 demonstrates the depth of interaction between the System Center 2012 components.

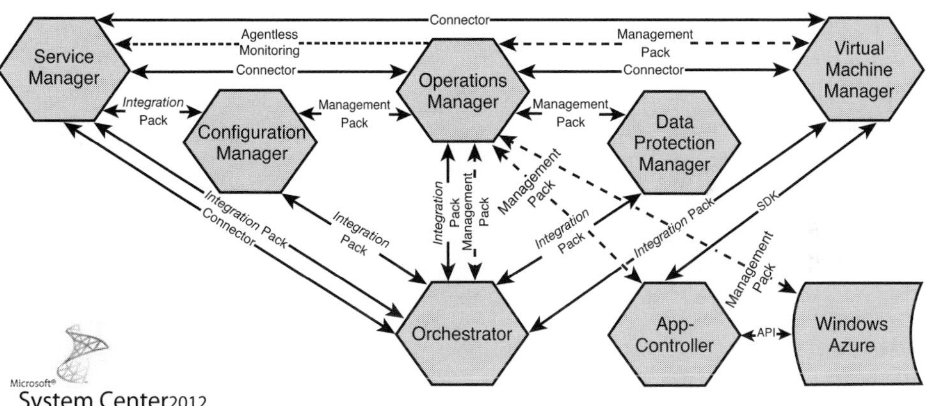

FIGURE 3.1 OpsMgr (center, top) and component relationships in System Center 2012.

Observe in Figure 3.1 that OpsMgr is the most connected component in System Center 2012! (Orchestrator is the second-most connected component.) That makes OpsMgr a logical choice as the first component to install in a complete System Center 2012 deployment project that will include some or all System Center components. When you install multiple System Center 2012 components on your network, Microsoft and third parties provide management packs, integration packs, and connectors to provide workflow and automation between components.

There are two directions where OpsMgr interoperates within System Center, as a monitor and as a data source:

- To cover the monitoring aspect, know that in the released version of OpsMgr 2012, every System Center component has a corresponding OpsMgr management pack. OpsMgr management packs generally provide two main operational services:
  - Monitoring the System Center component's health.
  - Extending the Operations console with tasks that remotely control the component using remediation and maintenance tasks.

  Figure 3.2 is an example of this interoperability; observe the DPM Tape Library Tasks panel added to the OpsMgr Tasks pane by the DPM management pack. These tasks allow the OpsMgr operator to remotely control backup and tape library operations from the Operations console. The consolidation of monitoring view and backup operations functions across hundreds of computers makes OpsMgr the single pane of glass for backup operations that it is capable of being.

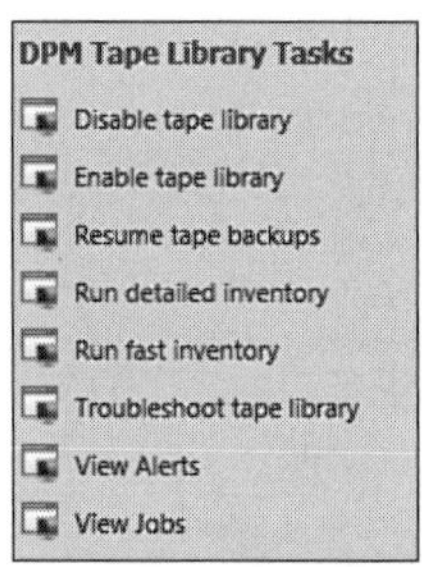

FIGURE 3.2 DPM Tape Library Tasks panel added to OpsMgr Tasks pane by DPM management pack.

- OpsMgr also interoperates within System Center as a data source. A great example is the connector with Service Manager. In this connector, OpsMgr is the source of alerts that can be turned into Service Manager incidents and trouble tickets. OpsMgr provides the data on the alert condition to populate the ticket in Service Manager. Another example is the Orchestrator integration pack for OpsMgr. After registering and deploying this integration pack, the runbook designer includes an OpsMgr ribbon bar (seen in Figure 3.3) to create workflows based on OpsMgr alerts and monitor state changes.

FIGURE 3.3 OpsMgr workflow elements added to Orchestrator runbook designer by integration pack for OpsMgr.

If you plan to deploy multiple System Center components, be aware that every component (such as OpsMgr, ConfigMgr, Service Manager, and the others) could require from one to several computers in distributed roles. While there is little you can do other than consume a good number of server computers when building out a System Center 2012 implementation, you can consolidate on the SQL back ends for each component. Table 3.1 summarizes the shared and unique SQL requirements for System Center 2012 and OpsMgr components.

TABLE 3.1 Shared SQL services across System Center 2012 components

SQL Component	Cross-Component Requirements
SQL Version	SQL 2008 R2 Service Pack 1 with Full Text Search enabled
SQL Instance	Single instance possible depending on scale (> 1,000 agents, high performance SQL TempDB with 8GB data and 2GB log)
SQL Collation	SQL_Latin1_General_CP1_CI_AS
SQL Reporting Services	OpsMgr must have separate instance

Management Group Defined

A *management group* is an instance of Microsoft's end-to-end service management solution named System Center 2012 Operations Manager. The central pieces of a management group are the operational database and the first installed management server. Additional OpsMgr features such as agents and consoles interact with the database through management servers. Adding management servers and gateway servers scales out and extends the capacity of the management group. Adding a report server and web consoles extends the features of OpsMgr.

Organizations may host several management groups (instances of OpsMgr on their networks) if appropriate for their business needs. Likewise, any managed computer or device can participate in two or more instances (management groups) of OpsMgr if appropriate. Most organizations of all sizes deploy a single management group, which is analogous to a single Active Directory (AD) forest or a single Exchange organization. Just as many large organizations are well served by a single AD forest and Exchange organization, you should strive to deploy only one production management group unless you are required by capacity or other reasons to deploy more than one.

Figure 3.4 illustrates a default, single-server management group in the smallest organization and contrasts that with a more complex implementation you might encounter in a very large organization. In the simple, all-in-one example on the left side of Figure 3.4, all OpsMgr features are installed on one server, which is the only OpsMgr server in the single-server management group monitoring the managed computers (agents) in the organization. If running on a robust machine (16GB or more of memory, four or more CPU cores, and fast SQL storage), several hundred computers can be monitored with an all-in-one deployment of OpsMgr 2012.

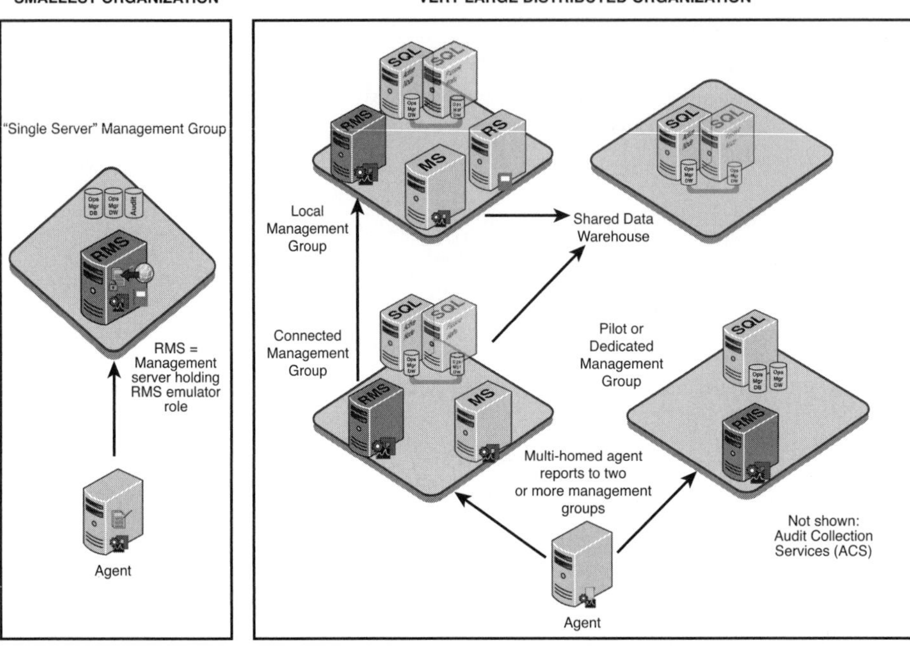

FIGURE 3.4 Contrasting the smallest and very large OpsMgr deployment model.

In the complex large organization on the right side of Figure 3.4, a single computer agent (known as a *multi-homed* agent) is reporting simultaneously to two management groups, a production and a pilot management group. The production management group is itself *connected* to a central management group (known as the *local group*). In this scenario, the connected management group and the local management group share a data warehouse database. By connecting additional management groups to the local group, this creates an architecture capable of monitoring tens of thousands of widely distributed computers and devices.

You seldom need multiple management groups to get the most out of OpsMgr 2012, as the product's design provides full functionality to all but the largest of organizations while still using a single management group. For the very large organization (over 6,000 computers, 2,000 devices, or 100 remote sites), deploying several OpsMgr 2012 management groups can distribute the workload. In this scenario, the local management group provides limited functionality—only alerts and tasks are surfaced from the connected management groups. To investigate alerts appearing in the local management group you may want to consult the performance and state views of those computers that are the source of the alerts. This requires retargeting the Operations console to the connected management group, or opening additional consoles, targeted at the source connected management group(s).

Introducing connected management group architecture does present administrative overhead; do not do this without first considering the impact to the operator workflow. Both having more than one instance of OpsMgr in your organization and having a computer or device report to more than one management group are advanced configurations to accomplish particular business goals. Learn more about these situations in Chapter 9, "Complex Configurations."

TIP: MANAGEMENT GROUP NAMES

A management group name is a unique alphanumeric name specified by the administrator when installing the first management server. The management group name cannot be changed after installation, so it is a good idea to select a name that is easy to remember and that makes sense given the organization's geographic or administrative needs. Management group names are case-insensitive and cannot begin with or contain a space.

Server Features

More than a dozen possible computer features, or roles, can be deployed in an OpsMgr 2012 management group. Focusing on the features that constitute a single OpsMgr 2012 management group, this section first describes the most basic features constituting every OpsMgr management group: the databases, the first management server, one or more agents, and one or more consoles. These four core features must be included in an OpsMgr 2012 deployment for minimum functionality.

These basic features, diagrammed in Figure 3.5, are installed in every management group, including the single-server OpsMgr environment:

- **Operations Manager operational and data warehouse databases:** These two databases, in particular the operational database, are at the heart of the OpsMgr management group. Every management group must have a dedicated operational database (default name: OperationsManager) and access to either a dedicated or a shared data warehouse database (default name: OperationsManagerDW). The operational database contains the configuration store of what objects are managed, operational data about the managed objects, and all customizations to the OpsMgr environment. All OpsMgr 2012 management groups must have a data warehouse database, which stores historical reporting data, even if you do not install the reporting server component.

  The operational database is the central repository and processing point for all data in a management group, and is created when you install your first management server. The data warehouse database is also created at this time; optionally, you can specify an existing data warehouse database repository. The operational and data warehouse databases should run on clustered SQL Server instances for high availability of the OpsMgr management group.

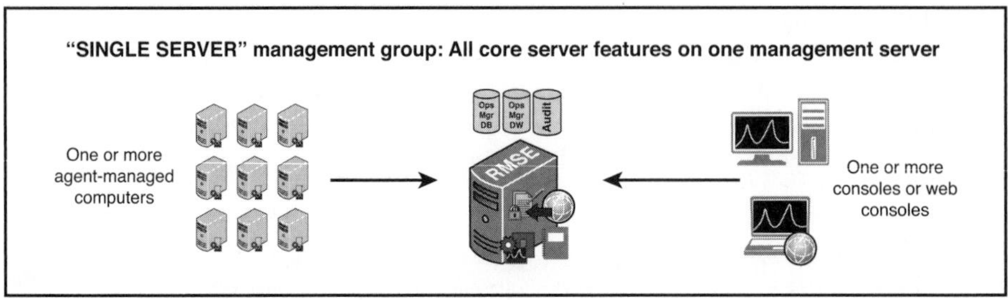

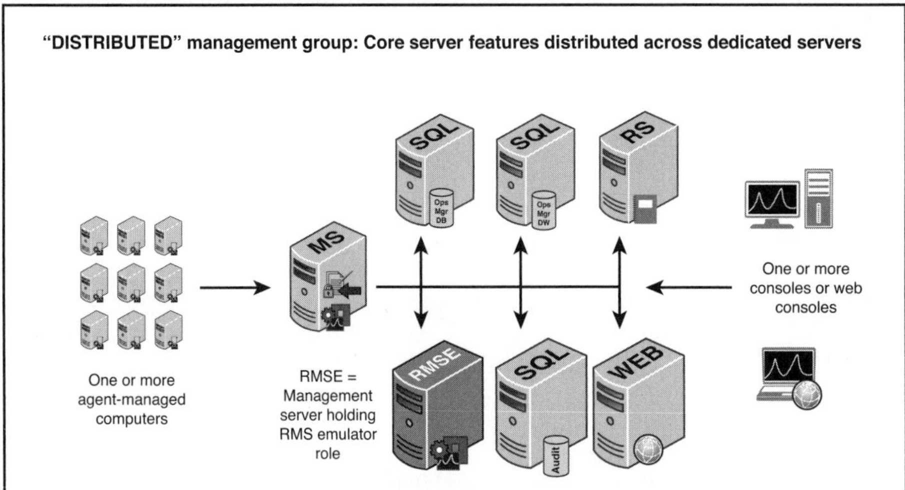

FIGURE 3.5 OpsMgr core features in a single-server scenario (above), and distributed across dedicated servers (below).

- **First management server:** The first management server is initially the only member of the All Management Servers Resource Pool. The first management server also automatically holds the root management server emulator (RMSE) role. Any additional management servers you install will join the All Management Servers Resource Pool. Here are several important things to understand about the All Management Servers Resource Pool and RMSE functionality:
  - These management workloads are distributed across members of the All Management Servers Resource Pool: Group calculation, availability, distributed monitor health roll up, and database grooming. Only the RMS performed these tasks in OpsMgr 2007, and this was a primary reason the RMS needed to be clustered for high availability. In OpsMgr 2012, these tasks automatically fail over to other management servers as needed.
  - How many additional management workloads run only on the RMSE is dependent on the legacy and third-party management packs you are running that target the `root management server` class. This class is depreciated in OpsMgr

2012, but supported for backward compatibility. Workloads targeted to the OpsMgr 2007 RMS class will run only on the RMSE in OpsMgr 2012. Failover of the RMSE role to any surviving additional management server is performed simply but manually in OpsMgr 2012 using a PowerShell cmdlet.

In addition to the management group and RMSE tasks running on the first management server, this server, like all management servers, is the intermediary between the agents and gateways and the OpsMgr databases. Management servers read configuration data from the operational database, send configuration data to managed computers, receive data from agents and network device monitoring pools, and write data to the operational and the data warehouse databases simultaneously.

Windows computer agents have assigned primary and failover management servers, in the same manner as OpsMgr 2007. Agent-managed Windows computers are not involved in the All Management Servers Resource Pool failover mechanism. (Management and gateway servers performing UNIX/Linux agent and network device monitoring do respect the new resource pool concept, and monitoring automatically fails over to surviving members of monitoring pools.)

An optional Audit Forwarder feature is installed with every OpsMgr server feature, the same forwarder installed with every OpsMgr agent. The audit forwarder feature on a management server or gateway server is activated by a task in the Operations console.

Unlike the RMS in OpsMgr 2007, you cannot cluster management servers in OpsMgr 2012. Therefore, Microsoft recommends a minimum of two management servers be deployed in all management groups monitoring mission-critical highly available infrastructures. This populates the All Management Servers Resource Pool with multiple management servers and achieves the goal of a highly available and disaster tolerant management group (assuming you also configure all gateways and agent-managed computers to fail over to an additional management server).

- **Agents:** The agent is used to monitor server and client computers. Windows and UNIX/Linux agents can be push-installed from either management servers or gateway servers. You can install agents manually on both Windows and UNIX/Linux computers. In the case of Windows computers, the agent can be staged in computer images, and the agent can discover its configuration from Active Directory.
    - The agent is a service on Windows computers that communicates outbound to specific management and/or gateway servers.
    - On UNIX/Linux computers, the agent takes the form of an open source daemon that is actively polled by a pool of one or more management and/or gateway servers.

An optional Audit Forwarder feature is installed with every OpsMgr agent. This feature on an agent-managed computer is activated by a task in the Operations console.

You might create a special purpose, single-server management group that only monitors network devices; in this scenario, there would be no agents. OpsMgr also has a capacity-limited and rudimentary agentless monitoring feature for Windows computers, but you would not deploy OpsMgr 2012 just to perform agentless monitoring. For most every OpsMgr management group, deploying core features is not complete until one or more computers are selected for management and the agent feature is installed.

As described in the "Management Group Defined" section earlier in the chapter, an OpsMgr 2012 agent can report to more than one management group simultaneously (multi-homing). The process of multi-homing an agent occurs automatically by discovering the computer and pushing agents from two management groups—the first discovery installs the agent; the second discovery multi-homes the agent. Manually multi-homing an agent becomes simple in OpsMgr 2012 with the addition of a new Windows control panel applet, shown in Figure 3.6.

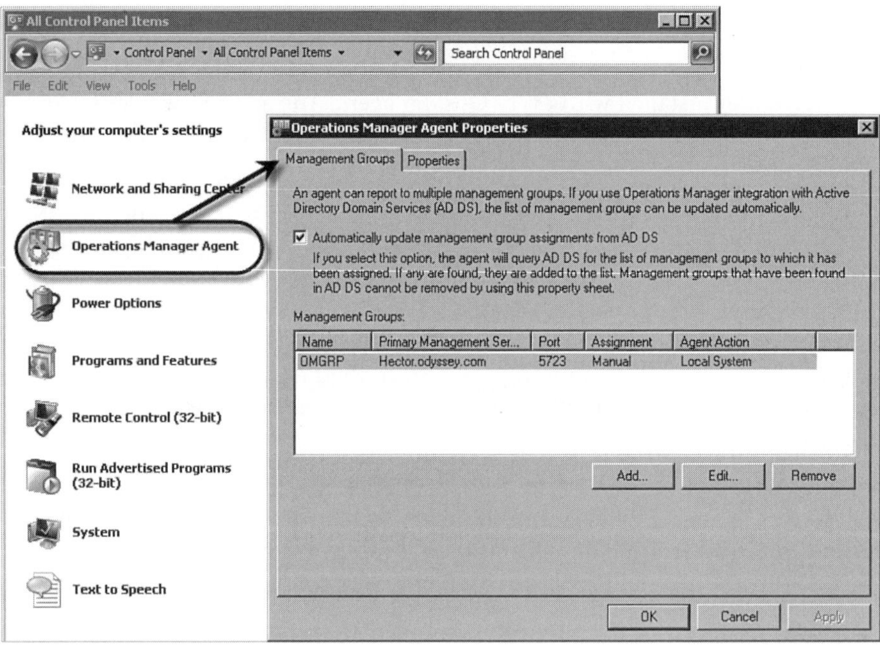

FIGURE 3.6 The Operations Manager Agent control panel applet, new in OpsMgr 2012.

- **Consoles:** The Operations console is the primary means of interacting with the management group and the only component required to perform OpsMgr operator role monitoring duties. (OpsMgr administrators will also utilize PowerShell and command line utilities for administration.) OpsMgr 2012 includes role-based security to ensure an optimized experience for all users. A web-based console has a subset of the Operations console features, which mirrors the role-based security of the full console.

Each console connects to a particular management server or to the DNS alias of the highly available Data Access Service (DAS) pool, should you deploy this new OpsMgr 2012 feature using a network load balancing solution. If you do not deploy a highly available DAS pool, consoles connect to the management server you specify, which does not need to be the RMSE. Each open console adds a processing burden to the management group, and too many open consoles can constrain the maximum capacity of a management group, so only install and use consoles as needed for operational purposes.

Figure 3.7 shows the Connect To Server dialog box, launched by the console on first startup or on demand from the console menu. After connecting, the console shows the server name and management group name for future logins.

FIGURE 3.7 The Connect To Server dialog box displays the management groups and servers you have connected to.

The four basic features just described are mandatory for any OpsMgr management group with agent-managed computers to function. The optimal features include the reporting-server feature, which most OpsMgr administrators will install regardless of their environment size, and nine additional features. Computers are deployed with these features or they are enabled in existing computers. Add these features as needed or desired to increase capacity or add functionality to the management group:

- **Reporting server:** Installing this feature activates reporting functions throughout the Operations console, including making the reporting space visible and adding context-relevant report tasks to the Tasks panel in the Monitoring space. All OpsMgr 2012 management groups have a dedicated or shared data warehouse database. However, you must install the reporting feature, which queries and displays historical data from the data warehouse database, to be able to utilize the reporting capability in OpsMgr.

  The reporting server is installed on a server running SQL Server Reporting Services (SSRS). Because of the integration between the OpsMgr 2012 console and Web console and the SSRS instance where the OpsMgr reporting server is installed, it is transparent to the console user that report data is arriving from SSRS.

You can install the reporting server feature on the same SQL Server hosting the data warehouse database in a small environment. In large and high-availability environments, SSRS typically runs on a dedicated server. While the OpsMgr reporting server itself cannot be made highly available, it is a simple task to redeploy OpsMgr reporting on a new SSRS instance in a disaster recovery scenario.

- **Additional management servers:** This feature refers to management servers installed after the first management server. The primary reason to deploy the *first* additional management server is to achieve fault tolerance on the management group, as there now are two management servers. Beyond the first two management servers, deploying additional management servers enables agent failover at scale and managing a large number of objects. At scale refers to should large numbers of agents fail over, the surviving failover management server(s) need the capacity to manage both their normal and failover load.

  All management servers are members of the All Management Servers Resource Pool unless they are expressly removed using a PowerShell cmdlet. One management server holds the RMSE role, and you can manually promote any additional management server to RMSE if the first management server (the default RMSE holder) needs to be replaced.

  Since management servers automatically share core management group workflows, Microsoft recommends all management servers have no more than 5ms latency between them. Place all management servers in the same datacenter, using gateways to connect to other datacenters and branch or field offices.

- **Highly available Data Access Service:** This feature appeals to a large organization with multiple management servers and service delivery objectives to be able to tolerate change without interrupting operations. If you have two or more management servers, deploy a network load balancer solution in front of the management servers and then assign a DNS alias to the load-balanced address. This removes the need for your reporting server, web consoles, and consoles to have fixed assignment to a particular management server, and eliminates disconnection when a particular management server is down.

- **Web consoles:** Any Windows server running a supported version of Internet Information Services (IIS) can host a web-based version of the Operations console. With functionality similar to using a thin client much like Outlook Web Access (OWA), operators can view topology diagrams, open the health explorer of an object, run tasks and reports, and even create custom dashboard views in the Web console. Based on a Silverlight engine, this console is a responsive full-function operations workspace that can replace the complete Operations console in some scenarios.

In small environments, install the Web console on a management server. In heavy use and high-availability scenarios, you can load balance one or more dedicated Web console servers. Web console sessions, similar to open Operations consoles, can drain management group resources, so don't over-extend access to the Web console, or leave Web console sessions open indiscriminately. The client for the Web console is a web browser with Silverlight extensions installed.

- **Gateway servers:** The primary role of the gateway is a communications conduit to monitoring agents in untrusted or remote networks without routed network connectivity. The gateway server resides in an external environment and uses certificates (rather than AD-based Kerberos) to secure communication back to the other features in the management group.

  An optional audit forwarder feature is installed with every gateway server, the same forwarder installed with every OpsMgr agent. The audit forwarder feature on a gateway server is activated by a task in the Operations console.

  The gateway has two subordinate roles:

  - Serving as a communications nexus in large wide area networks, because gateway servers compress agent to management server traffic by as much as 50%. In a fully trusted domain scenario, the gateway does not require a certificate.
  - Being a member of a dedicated resource pool, such as for monitoring a large number of network devices.

TIP: MANAGEMENT SERVER VERSUS GATEWAY SERVER RESOURCE POOLS

All management servers are by default members of three resource pools: the AD Assignment, the All Management Servers, and the Notifications resource pools. Given that every management server may have those extra duties, there may be a preference to creating pools of gateway servers to perform dedicated functions such as UNIX/Linux computer monitoring, network device monitoring, or notification pool duties such as instant message integration. Gateways remain fully available for specific purposes, while management servers may have a portion of their resources reserved for management group workflows, the RMSE even more so.

- **Audit database:** While "just a database" to the ACS collector and "just a data source" to the reporting server, Microsoft requires the version of SQL Server for the audit database match the SQL Server version of the operational database. You can cluster the SQL instance hosting the ACS database for high availability, although you are always limited to a single ACS collector per ACS database.

  The audit database stores audit event information from managed computer event logs, forwarded by agents to the ACS collector, which writes events to the audit database. Reports are run against the audit database to enforce security policies.

- **Audit collector:** This server function collects events from audit collection-enabled agents and writes them to the audit database. The audit collector function is added to an existing OpsMgr management server. You enable audit collection on OpsMgr servers and agents by running a task in the Operations console. There is a one-to-one relationship between ACS collectors and ACS databases, so you will generally have only one ACS collector per management group.
- **Client monitoring server:** The Client Monitoring Configuration Wizard in the Administration space of the Operations console is used to configure this feature on one or more management servers (gateway servers cannot perform the client monitoring role). The Agentless Exception Monitoring (AEM) client feature is activated by a group policy object (GPO) applied to computers. AEM centralizes the crash and bug information collected by Dr. Watson and Windows Error Reporting (WER) in your organization.
- **Network device monitoring:** OpsMgr 2012 includes a new network device monitoring feature with location awareness and information-rich dashboards. You activate the feature by discovering one or more network devices to monitor. Except in the smallest environments, you will want to create a network device monitoring pool with specific management servers or gateway servers as members. Monitoring large numbers of network devices is resource-intensive for a management server or gateway server, so you should only include those management servers or gateway servers in network device monitoring pools that are not already heavily loaded with agent management traffic.
- **Application performance monitoring (APM):** Like network device monitoring in OpsMgr 2012, APM is a new feature that can be optionally enabled. APM is activated by importing the APM Web IIS 7 (or IIS 8 if running Windows Server 2008 with System Center SP 1) management pack and running the Add Monitoring Wizard in the Authoring space. To view APM performance monitoring event details, you must install the OpsMgr Web console in your management group.

Figure 3.8 illustrates a management group with all components on distributed servers and with many high-availability features deployed. This large enterprise management group could provide end-to-end monitoring of thousands of managed computers and network devices with a high degree of reliability.

TIP: SHARING RESOURCES BETWEEN MANAGEMENT GROUPS

A multi-homed OpsMgr agent by definition is a member of two or more management groups. There are other ways to leverage computer resources across management groups, particularly at the database server layer:

- **Share SQL servers:** Because the operations database can be assigned any user-selectable name during installation, a single SQL server or cluster can provide database backend services to multiple management groups.
- **Share data warehouse databases:** During management server installation, you can select to use an existing OpsMgr 2012 data warehouse database for a new OpsMgr 2012 management group. Create a new data warehouse database when installing

the first management group, then point to the same data warehouse database when installing subsequent management groups. Note that sharing the data warehouse database does not permit you to exceed the maximum capacity of a non-shared management group data warehouse.

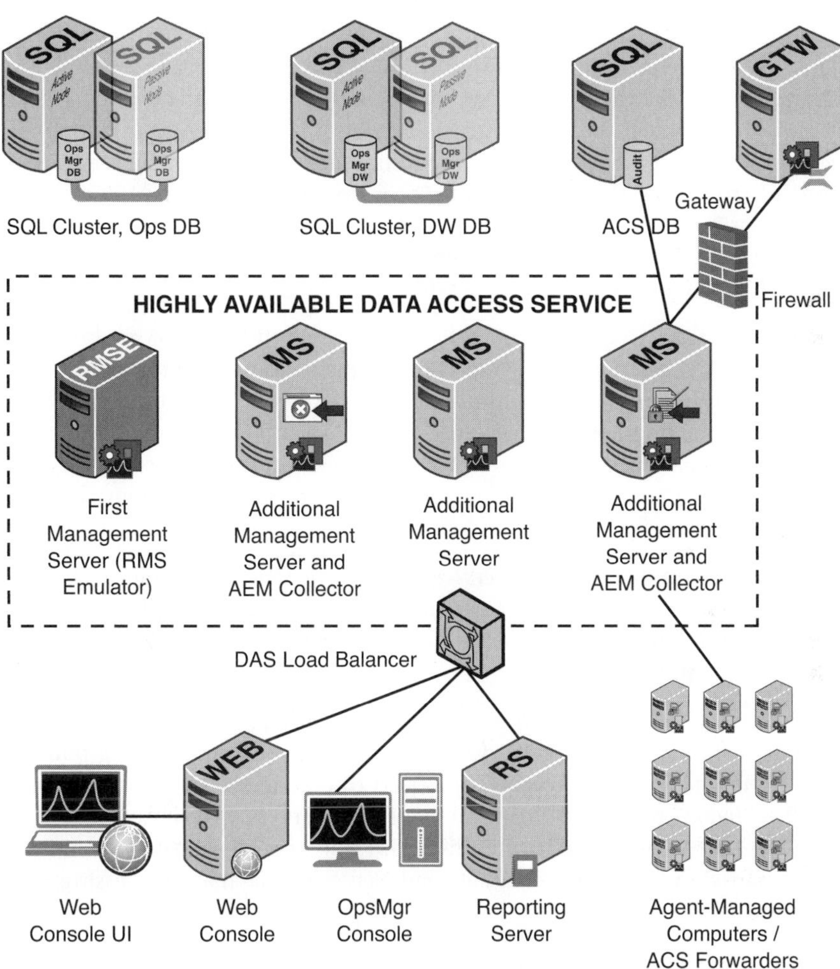

FIGURE 3.8 All OpsMgr features deployed on dedicated servers.

Windows Services

Computers running OpsMgr features also host particular Windows services in specific configurations depending on their functions. The presence of the System Center Management service (HealthService.exe) is universal to all computers participating in an

OpsMgr 2012 management group. How the service functions, as a management server, gateway server, or agent, depends on the OpsMgr function installed. The next sections describe the System Center Management service as well as the other services that exist in a management group.

System Center Management Service

Also known by its service name, *health service*, the System Center Management service provides a general execution environment for monitoring modules that read, probe, detect, and write data. These modules form different workflows, enabling end-to-end monitoring scenarios. Installing and configuring management packs extend the options available for the health service running on all computers in the management group. The health service usually runs under the local system account on all computers.

System Center Management Service Implementations

There are actually three "flavors" of the health service:

- The first implementation, the agent health service, runs on monitored Windows computers. The service executes tasks, collects performance data, and performs other functions on the managed computer. The System Center Management service continues to run, collecting data and performing tasks, even when the agent is disconnected from a management or gateway server. Data and events accumulate in a disk-based queue, and are reported when the connection to the management or gateway server is restored.
- Another implementation of the health service runs on management servers. The functionality of the System Center Management service on management servers is highly variable and depends on the setup of the management group and the management packs installed.
- The third implementation is found on gateway servers. Similar to management servers, gateway servers can push agents to computers and serve as reporting points for agents and other gateways. Gateways can report to management servers or other gateways (called *chained gateways*). Unlike management servers, gateways cannot access the OpsMgr databases directly; they can only store, compress, and forward the OpsMgr agent traffic on its way to a management server for database processing.

System Center Management Service Security

Another important feature of the health service is that it provides credential management services to other OpsMgr processes, supporting execution of modules running as different users. The OpsMgr agent to management or gateway server connection is encrypted by a public-private key pair created on each instance of the health service (agent, management server, and gateway server), after being authenticated by Kerberos or certificate. The public key is automatically regenerated during health service startup, when the key expires, and when there is a failure to decrypt a message. TCP port 5723 in OpsMgr is associated with the health service.

System Center Data Access Service

All management servers run the System Center Data Access Service, previously known as the SDK service (Microsoft.Mom.Sdk.ServiceHost.exe). OpsMgr agents and gateways report to management servers, and the DAS service reads and writes data to the OpsMgr databases on behalf of the management pack workflows running on the agents and gateways. TCP port 5724 in OpsMgr is associated with the System Center Data Access Service; this port is published by a load balancer for a highly available DAS because consoles, web consoles, and report servers connect to the System Center Data Access Service.

The System Center Data Access Service owns a symmetric encryption key for the management group that accesses the Run As account information stored in the OpsMgr database—the master key to all credentials. This key was manually exported and imported in OpsMgr 2007 for RMS backup and recovery scenarios. In OpsMgr 2012, this key is automatically and securely staged on all management servers.

In OpsMgr 2007, the SDK service ran only on the RMS, while in OpsMgr 2012 the SDK service runs on all management servers. The DAS typically runs under a domain service account on management servers.

System Center Management Configuration Service

Similar to the DAS service on management servers, the System Center Management Configuration service (cshost.exe) runs on all management servers. The configuration service is responsible for providing the monitoring configuration to each agent's health service, which may include sensitive information such as Run As account credentials. The service acts as an intermediary for delivering sensitive information in an encrypted format from the OpsMgr database to the target health service on a managed computer.

In OpsMgr 2007, the configuration service ran only on the RMS (Microsoft.Mom.ConfigServiceHost.exe), while in OpsMgr 2012 the configuration service runs on all management servers. Like the DAS, the configuration service almost always runs under a domain service account on management servers.

OpsMgrVSSWriter Service

The VSS Writer service (OpsMgrVssWriterService.exe) is responsible for backing up and restoring System Center data on management servers. The VSS writer enables you to create shadow copies that include point in time recovery options.

System Center Audit Forwarding Service

The System Center Audit Forwarding service (AdtAgent.exe) sends security log events to an ACS collector for storage in a SQL Server database. The audit forwarding service is automatically installed (but not configured) on every OpsMgr management server, gateway server, and agent. After you install the ACS collector and database, you can remotely enable the audit forwarding service on multiple agents through the Operations console by running the Enable Audit Collection task.

Audit Collection Service Collector Service

The Operations Manager Audit Collection service (AdtServer.exe) is responsible for receiving audit events over the network from Audit Collection Service (ACS) forwarders and writing them to the audit database. Each management server in the organization that runs the ACS collector feature requires a dedicated audit database, so most organizations will only install one ACS collector. The service is installed and the database is created during setup of the ACS service on the selected management server.

TIP: BEWARE MULTIPLE ACS COLLECTORS

Several times this chapter discusses most organizations having only one ACS collector. This recommendation is based on avoiding two common undesirable scenarios involving more than one ACS collector:

- **Uncertainty about ACS database location for a given ACS forwarder:** It is possible to assign primary and failover ACS collectors to the same forwarder. However, this results in audit data from the same computer with multiple authoritative report sources, less desirable than having a single repository.
- **Collector and database malfunction when sharing an ACS database:** Setup of the ACS collector feature does not check that the ACS database is not already in use by another ACS collector. If two ACS collectors report to the same database, the collector service will probably stop on one or both collectors and the database might experience corruption.

If you elect to deploy multiple collector and database pairs due to geographic regions, network connectivity, or other reasons, ensure you avoid these situations, as expected audit data may be unreliable or missing.

Application Performance Monitoring Service

The System Center Management APM service (InterceptSvc.exe) monitors the health of .NET applications when the APM feature is enabled. Similar to the audit forwarder feature, the APM service is automatically installed (but not configured) on every OpsMgr management server, gateway server, and agent.

OpsMgr Communications Channels

System Center 2012 Operations Manager uses a variety of communications methods optimized for security and efficiency. Communication between management servers and the three OpsMgr databases (operational, data warehouse, and audit) is always via standard SQL client/server protocols, specifically OLE DB (Object Linking and Embedding Database).

Communication with the databases is via management servers (and in the case of the audit database, specifically the management server running the ACS collector feature). The reporting server also accesses the data warehouse database directly. Agents, gateways, consoles, and Web consoles (without APM) do not directly interact with the SQL database servers. An exception is the Web console when using the optional APM feature—this scenario requires the Web console to access the operational and data warehouse databases directly.

Between agents, as well as management and gateway servers, the primary Transmission Control Protocol (TCP) port is 5723, which is the only outbound firewall exception needed to manage a computer in a minimal configuration once the agent is installed. Additional outbound ports are used when enabling ACS and AEM features. A complete list of communications protocols and default ports used in an OpsMgr environment is provided in Table 3.2.

TABLE 3.2 Communication paths and ports

From Component	To Component	TCP or UDP Port
Management server	Databases	1433
Operational database	Management servers	1434 UDP[1]
Management server	Management server	5723, 5724[2]
Operations console	Management server	5724
Operations console	Reporting server	80
Gateway server	Management or gateway server	5723
Agent	Management or gateway server	5723
Reporting server	Management server	5723, 5723[2]
Reporting server	Data warehouse database	1433
Web console server	Management server	443 (or other selected website port)
Web console server	Operational and data warehouse databases (when using APM)	1433
Web console client	Web console server	443 (or other selected web site port)
Connector framework source	Management server	51905
AEM and CEIP data from client	Management server	51906, 51907
ACS forwarder	ACS collector	51909
Management server or gateway server	Network device	161 UDP, 162 UDP (both bidirectional)
Management server or gateway server	UNIX or Linux computer	22, 1270

[1] *If the operational database is installed on a named instance of SQL, such as in a cluster, 1434 UDP inbound to the management server is required.*

[2] *Port 5724 outbound on management and reporting servers is required to install the feature. After the feature is installed, this access can be removed.*

The logic in Table 3.2 is diagrammed in Figure 3.9, which also illustrates management server pool concepts. A quick study of the communications paths highlights the importance of the pool of management servers at the heart of the diagram and the management group. The management servers are both participating in the All Management Servers Resource Pool and in a highly available Data Access Server load-balanced pool.

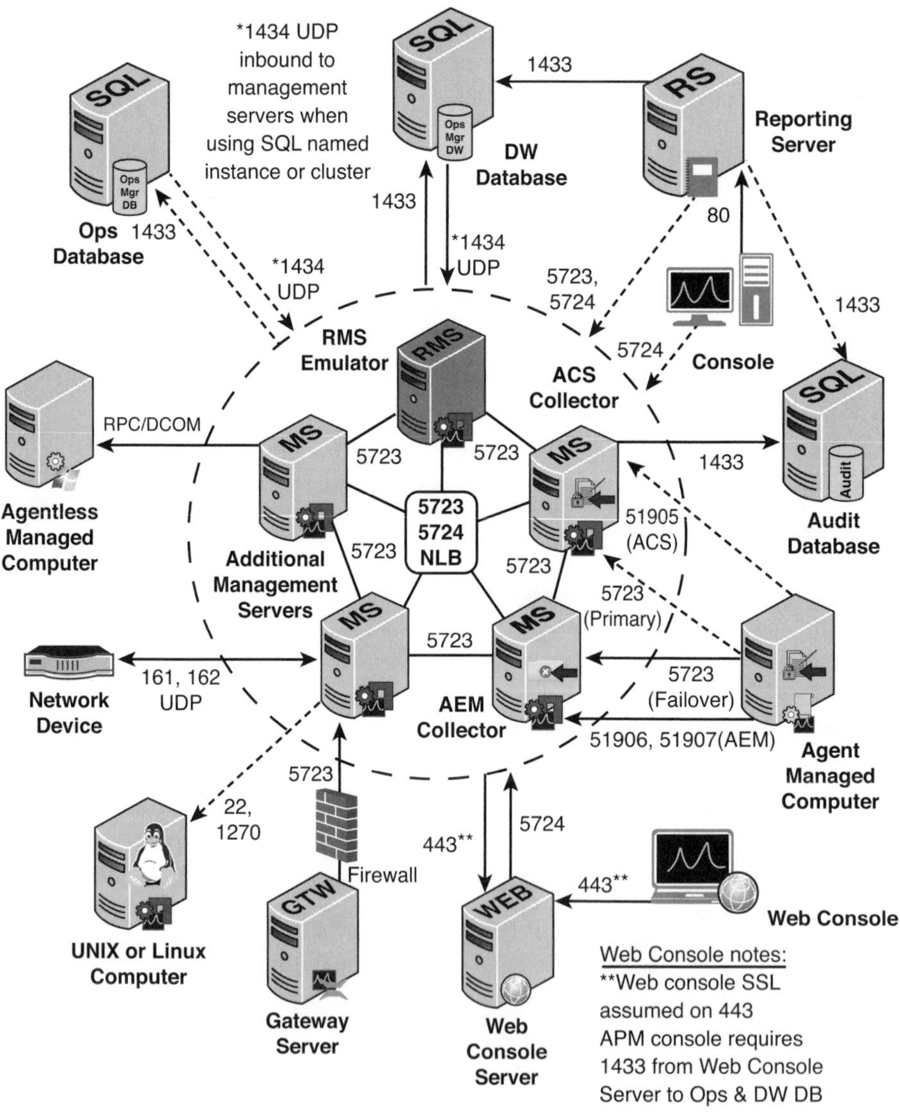

FIGURE 3.9 Communication paths and firewall considerations for OpsMgr 2012.

Clustered operational and data warehouse databases, along with the additional and load-balanced management servers, make this a highly available management group. Both databases and at least one management server must be running for the management group to function normally. Two management servers provide primary and failover coverage to agents and gateways. On remote networks with gateways, two gateways on the remote segment can also provide primary and failover service to agents and even other gateways.

The diagram in Figure 3.9 does not illustrate the need for RPC/DCOM communication between a management or gateway server and a managed computer to push the agent. Details on this, as well as how to configure the Windows Firewall on a managed computer to perform push installation of the agent from a management or gateway server are covered in Chapter 8, "Installing and Configuring Agents."

How Does OpsMgr Do It?

The chapter has covered how OpsMgr relates to the rest of System Center 2012, what a management group is, and how the features of a management group communicate with one another—the macro view. Now the focus shifts to the micro view of the management pack, and to how monitoring work occurs. The management group and the communications paths are the framework within which management packs do the work. The contents of management packs completely determine what traffic traverses the OpsMgr communications paths, the work the management and gateway servers perform, and what workflows run on agent-managed computers.

Management Group Mechanics

The primary OpsMgr agent-management server connection, TCP port 5723, is protected with a unique digital key and is essentially a secure sockets layer (SSL) connection, an encrypted tunnel. Looking inside, you will observe files being transferred. The files in the tunnel exchanged between management servers and agents include the form of compressed XML (eXtensible Markup Language) text-based documents that communicate management pack configuration. These XML files contain instructions for the server or agent, such as scripts to run. Data is returned from the agent to the management server for processing and storage in the databases.

All OpsMgr management servers, gateway servers, and agent-managed computers have a Health Service State folder in their OpsMgr program files folder structure, such as *%ProgramFiles%*\System Center Operations Manager\Agent\Health Service State. Figure 3.10 shows this folder and the XML documents that are the contents of the Management Packs subfolder. As an example of how management packs influence the behavior of workflows on an agent, the circled portion of the XML document where the word "true" appears is a setting that enables a workflow that would otherwise be disabled.

The contents of the Health Service State folder are transient; they constantly change and are replaceable. This folder is a temporary working and data storage area for the Health Service, where files are saved that are unique to the management groups in which the agent participates. A good way to observe the intersection between the management group and management packs is a quick study of the events that occur on an agent-managed computer when you delete the Health Service State folder.

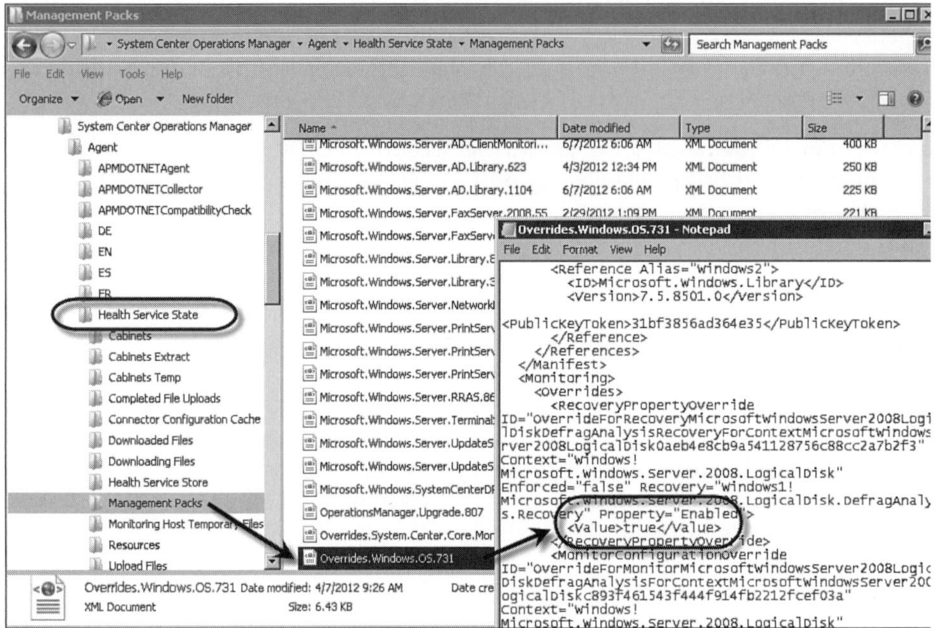

FIGURE 3.10 Viewing the contents of an override management pack on an agent.

Stopping the health service (the System Center Management Service) and deleting the Health Service State folder is a safe and standard procedure to troubleshoot many OpsMgr server and agent issues. Upon restarting, the health service performs the same steps as when the agent was first installed—the Health Service State folder is recreated and a complete fresh set of management pack XML documents is again downloaded.

Here are the expected events that occur, as seen from the Operations Manager event log of the agent-managed computer when starting an agent after deleting the Health Service State folder:

1. If a certificate is installed for authentication with computers that are not members of trusted domains, that certificate is loaded.
2. The health service starts a new instance of the database engine and checks Active Directory for optional agent configuration settings.
3. The health service publishes the public key used to encrypt the connection to the management server or gateway.
4. A TCP socket on port 5723 is opened, encrypted with the key for that health service.

5. Authentication occurs with the selected management server or gateway server, using either Kerberos for domain-joined computers in the same and trusted domains, or certificate-based authentication.
6. The agent requests that the management server provide configuration data.
7. The management server provides the configuration, the agent loads that configuration and requests that the management server download management packs.
8. One by one, an XML version of each management pack targeted to the agent is downloaded to the Health Service State folder on the agent, and an event is logged similar to that seen in Figure 3.11.

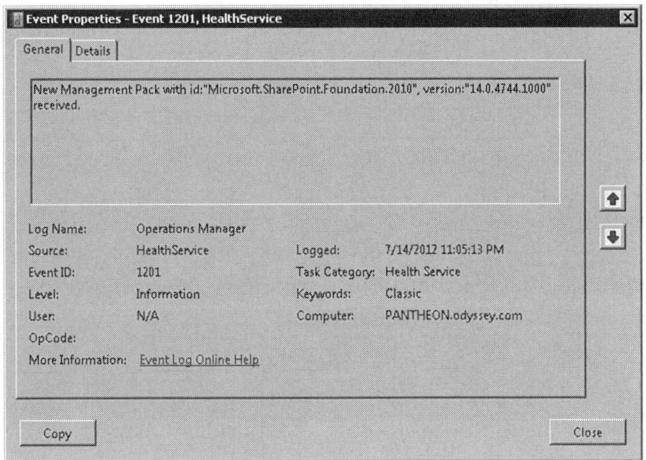

FIGURE 3.11 Management packs download to each agent from the management group.

9. Monitoring begins when the agent has downloaded all management packs in the configuration.

Service Modeling

Operations Manager is a System Center 2012 component established on the concept of model-based management. The abstraction of services into *models* is a prerequisite mental exercise for acting on physical entities such as routers and logical entities such as websites. Using models in this context is a way to transform human knowledge and experience into something with which machines can operate. Models capture knowledge and make it redistributable. In OpsMgr, service models live inside management packs.

Service modeling in OpsMgr 2012 is rooted in the well-known Service Modeling Language (SML) used by developers in the .NET development environment and introduced in Chapter 1, "Operations Management Basics." SML provides a way to think about computer systems, operating systems, applications, and datacenter and cloud infrastructure—particularly defining how they interact, are combined, connected, deployed and managed. Just as XML is a standard model for exchange of formatted text data, SML is used to create models of complex IT services and systems.

The management pack author should understand several basic concepts, covered in this section:

- **Class inheritance of objects:** Classes are defined as having certain attributes. An object is an instance of a class. The attributes an object has are inherited from the class.
- **Accounting for relationships between objects:** Relationships between objects usually take the form of a dependence on another object, or of a container of another object.
- **The taxonomy of SML:** OpsMgr describes objects and management pack elements using a hierarchical system of descriptors that are increasingly specific.

OpsMgr 2012 operates on a class-based structure. When a management pack discovery workflow acts on a new *object* (or *entity*), it assigns a set of logical classes to the object. These classes describe the object when the attributes are populated with data. The first thing a management pack author does is list and describe the classes of objects defined by the management pack and the attributes included with the object definitions. After the objects are defined, the relationships between objects are described.

Classes, objects, and relationships are how OpsMgr recognizes something, understands it, and knows how to act on it. SML nomenclature comes into play when the management pack author wants to describe the attributes of a particular object. Just as you more precisely describe a particular body part by adding the descriptor "left" to the object "hand," OpsMgr adds classification terms in a particular way to narrow down and eventually recognize any managed object. Observe the SML layer concept in action to describe a particular object, a website running on a Windows computer. Notice the *entity* in the upper-left portion of the description in the diagram in Figure 3.12. This is another word for "object" in OpsMgr, and it is like a placeholder for the object's root.

Proceeding down and to the right in the hierarchy shown in Figure 3.12, you see descriptors added to successively narrow, or focus, the description of the particular managed object. As depicted, the Windows Computer Role is a subordinate descriptor to Computer Role. Likewise, the Internet Information Services (IIS) service is a particular Windows Computer Role in OpsMgr, and the monitored website is a particular feature of the IIS service.

Also illustrated in this figure are relationships between objects, such as the Windows OS *containing* (or *hosting*) the IIS service, and a particular disk drive hosting the monitored website—which is the object of interest in this description. The capability of management packs to define relationships between objects is critical to technological innovations in System Center. Examples of capabilities made possible via SML and its layered approach to describing objects include monitoring a distributed application with containment relationships, using a diagram view for cross-platform fault isolation, and maintenance mode on individual computer components.

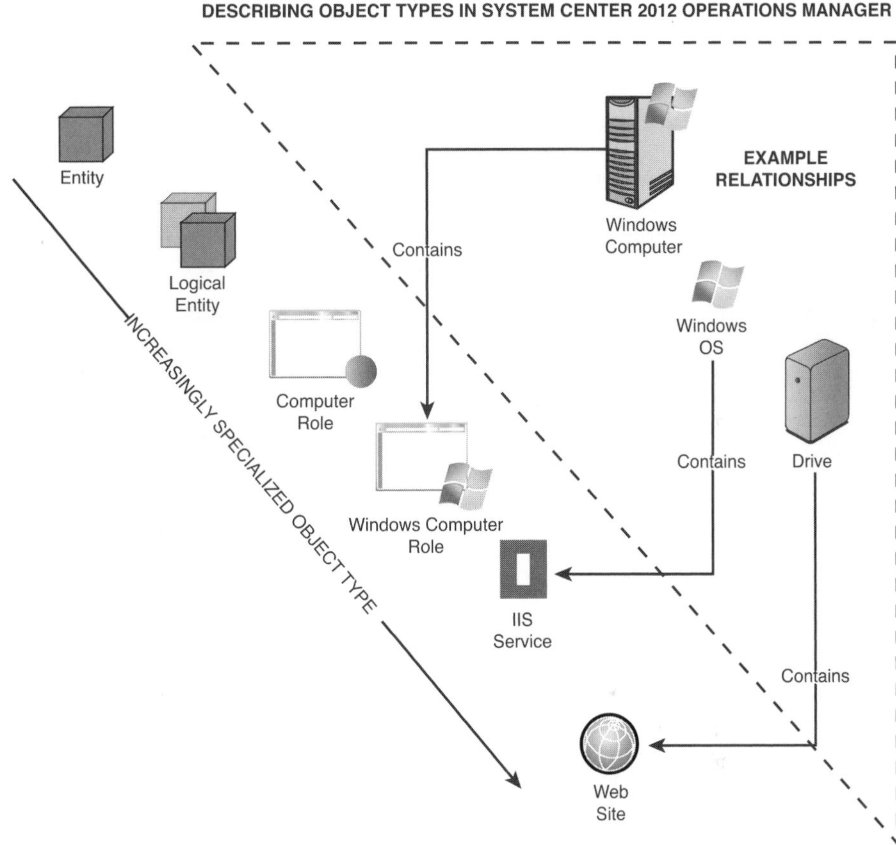

FIGURE 3.12 Objects are described by increasingly specialized types.

A fundamental management pack design concept is that objects (or entities) are not added (that is, instantiated) to the OpsMgr database directly; they are discovered using an *object discovery rule*, and the new object instance is created by the discovery rule. A discovery rule is a workflow that occurs on a scheduled or on-demand basis, as defined by the author of the management pack. A discovery runs against a class (or type) of object; this is known as the discovery *target*. Managing something with OpsMgr is all about defining—in fact creating—the class of the object you want to monitor.

The first question a management pack author is going to answer is *How can I identify a computer or application that would contain the object(s) I want to manage?* The discovery rule process is usually accomplished by authoring a probe, targeted to the class that contains the class being discovered. The discovery rule examines computer registries using

Windows Management Instrument (WMI) queries, or scripts, database queries (OLE DB), the Lightweight Directory Access Protocol (LDAP), and other methods as defined in the management pack.

In addition to creating the new object, the discovery rule may also collect one or more attributes that describe the object. The attributes provide descriptive data about the object that help operators identify and manage the object. Figure 3.13 is an introduction to the Authoring space of the Operations console and is focused on the discovery rule for Windows Logical Disks. This rule was added to OpsMgr by importing the Windows Server 2008 OS Discovery management pack. The target class of the discovery rule is the `Windows Server 2008 Operating System`. Logical disks discovered by this rule will have a containment relationship with the OS.

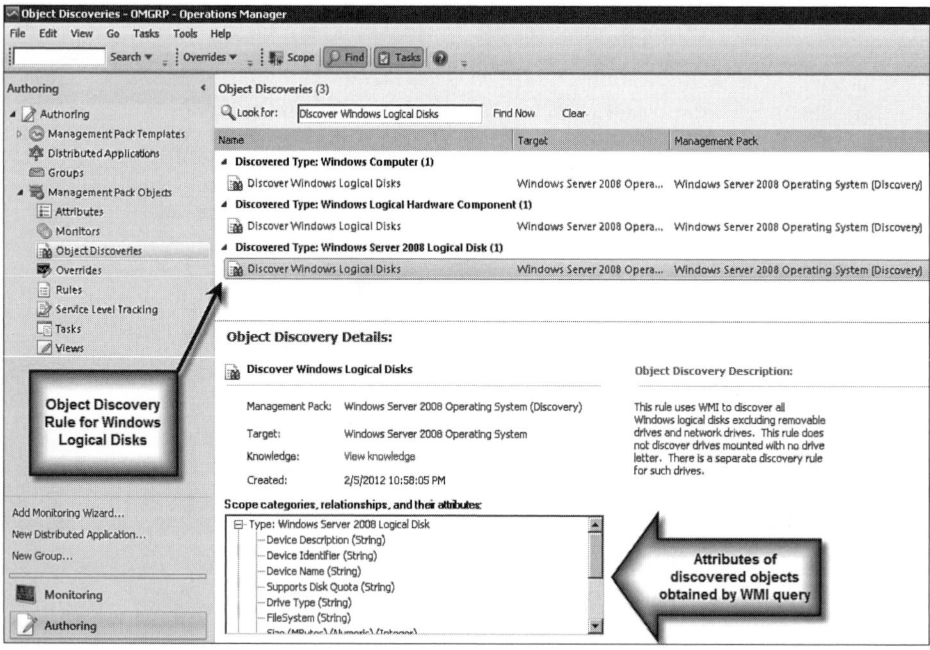

FIGURE 3.13 Object discovery rule for Windows Logical Disks.

Management packs are often distributed with separate discovery and monitoring management packs (two or more physical management pack files). The discovery management pack typically targets a broad class (such as `Windows Server OS`) that contains the new, more narrowly defined class (such as `Windows Logical Disk`). The monitoring management pack has rules and monitors targeted to the narrower class.

An annotated arrow at the bottom of Figure 3.13 points to the attributes, in this case those of logical disks discovered by this rule, which will be collected and stored in the database and associated with the discovered object. Logical disk attributes include data like the file system type, such as NTFS or FAT32, the size of the volume in megabytes, and the disk label name.

Relationship discovery rules operate in addition to object discovery rules. Object discovery rules use WMI or other probes to locate managed objects and populate the OpsMgr databases with actionable object attributes. This enables relationship discovery rules to look at object properties for particular discovered attributes that indicate dependence, hosting, or containing a relationship. Figure 3.14 focuses on the relationship discovery rule that finds physical disk partitions associated with discovered logical disks.

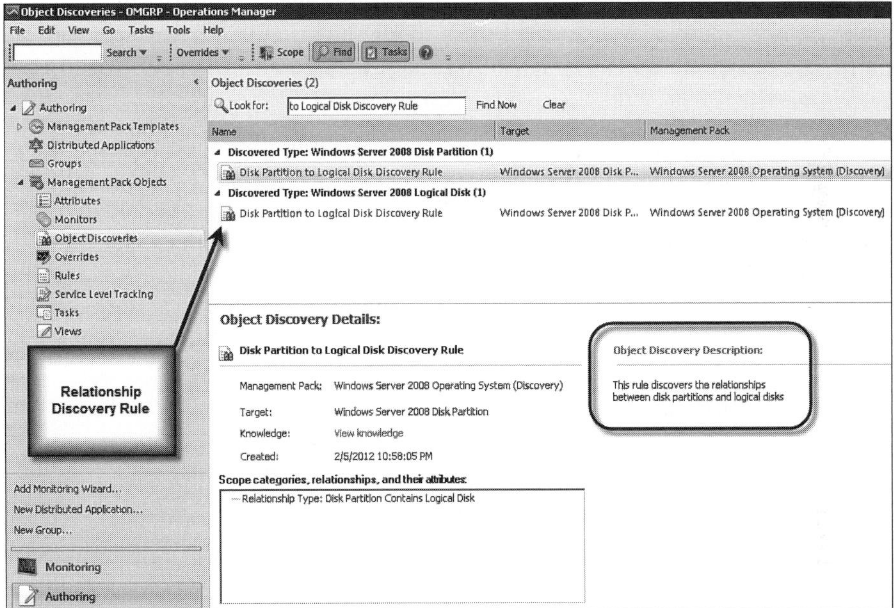

FIGURE 3.14 Relationship discovery rule: Disk partition to logical disk.

After the Windows Server 2008 OS discovery rule creates an object for discovered logical disks as shown in Figure 3.13, a second discovery as shown in Figure 3.14 occurs. The disk partition to logical disk discovery rule creates containment relationships that are themselves objects in the OpsMgr databases. Notice the relationship discovery rule is targeted to the *physical* disk partition, yet it discovers the association of the *logical* disk.

How Health Models Work

After object relationship discovery is complete, the OpsMgr databases are populated with unique objects that have names, that are members of well-defined classes, and that may have additional descriptive data (attributes). Now OpsMgr can begin performing the primary work of the management pack—managing the state of the objects' health models.

Every class, or object type, has a health model. A health model represents the status, or health, of even the simplest managed object. A *model* is a collection of monitors. Monitors are covered in detail later in the "Populating the Health Model with Monitors" section. As you add monitors to a health model, you enrich the fidelity, accuracy, and value of the health model of that object.

Monitors are arranged in a tree structure that is as deep or shallow as required to convey management information. The status of the health model represents the current state of the object. A pop-up tool in the Operations console, the Health Explorer shows a live view of an object's health model. The health explorer tool can be launched against any managed object from all views in the Monitoring pane of the Operations console and Web console.

A key monitoring concept in OpsMgr is the *rollup*. This term refers to the way health status "bubbles up" from lower levels in the health model hierarchy, or tree, to higher-level monitors. The top-level monitor in a health model, located at the root Entity object layer, is the rollup, which represents the overall health state of the object.

Figure 3.15 diagrams, on the left side, the class hierarchy of a service on a computer, and on the right side a corresponding health model for the same service. Notice the *unit* monitors located at the lower right of the diagram, the *aggregate* monitor in the center right, and the *rollup* monitor at the top right. Unit monitors do the work to collect data, and aggregate monitors are parent containers of multiple child unit monitors. Round "pearl" shapes represent monitors in each of the four basic categories (Availability, Performance, Configuration, and Security).

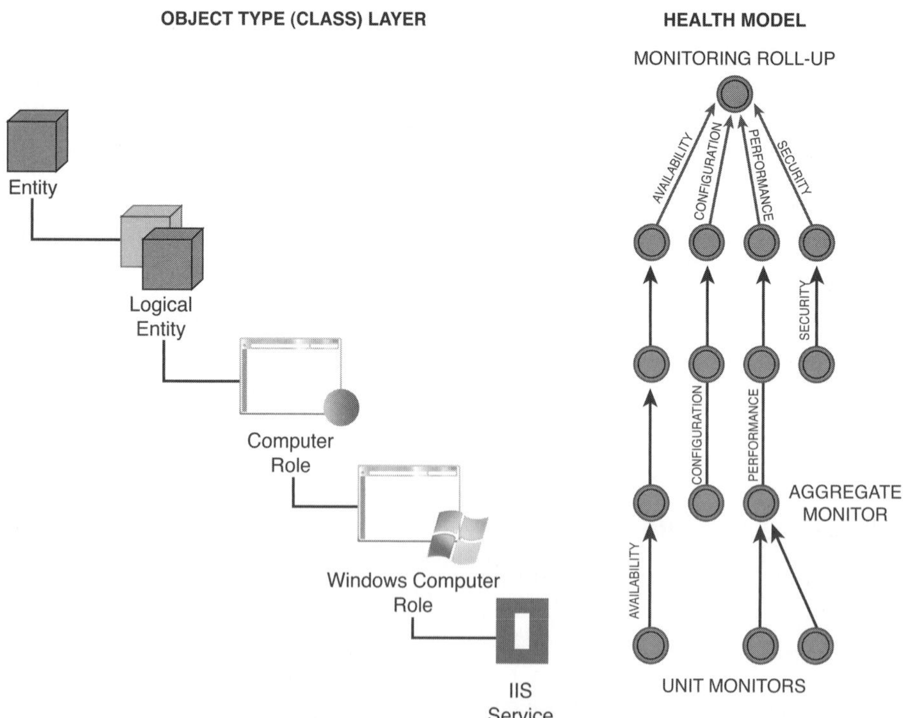

FIGURE 3.15 The object model side-by-side with a health model.

Lower-layer monitor status is propagated by the health model to monitors in successively higher levels of the class layer. For any given health model, monitors are not necessarily located at every layer, or within every monitor category. The management pack author determines what monitors are targeted against which class layers.

Finally notice in Figure 3.15 the uppermost, triangular arrangement of four monitors rolling up into the health state of the managed object. This is a universal feature of OpsMgr health models, even if no monitors are located in any categories.

About State-Based Monitoring

A key theme first introduced with OpsMgr 2007, object-oriented *state-based management* remains a distinguishing feature of Microsoft System Center compared to other network monitoring tools that are exclusively alert-based. Every monitored object has a health model that includes a top-level rollup monitor representing the health of the object. There are effectively two primary "lenses" through which to process live operational status in the Operations console: alert views and state views. When evaluating the status of a monitored object, there will always be these differing aspects to consider.

A list of new and unacknowledged alerts is indispensable for a monitoring team to review to be aware of specific problems as soon as possible. However, there are limits to the effectiveness of a flat chronological list of alerts that impede rapidly correlating and triaging issues at scale.

Here is how OpsMgr implements a parallel system of alerts and health monitors: OpsMgr watches for a condition, raises an alert, and optionally changes the state of the object's health due to generation of the alert. Even after manually closing the alert, the unhealthy condition in the health model remains as a second-level reminder that something is still wrong and needs attention. The OpsMgr implementation of state-based management applies the following workflow sequence:

1. A unit monitor watches for a condition, such as low disk space.
2. When the unit monitor detects the condition, it changes the state of the unit monitor, such as the logical disk object in the case of low disk space.
3. Unit monitor states are rolled up as required to higher-level aggregate and parent monitors in the object's health model.
4. Rules optionally generate an alert or initiate a notification event.

Management Pack Schema

A management pack is an XML document that provides the structure to monitor specific hardware and software. In software terminology, a *schema* describes how real world entities are modeled in a database. The schema of an OpsMgr management pack consists of one mandatory section and several optional sections. A sealed management pack is a read-only, encrypted version of the XML document.

The mandatory section to the XML document is the *manifest*, which specifies the identity, name, and references for the management pack. *References* are management packs that this management pack depends on, and only sealed management packs can be references.

Figure 3.16 shows the XML for the "Empty Management Pack"; this is the simplest possible management pack and contains only the manifest section. Observe the child sections (or *elements*) of the manifest section: Identity, Name, and References. The Manifest section is the only mandatory element; there are 10 total possible management pack elements as listed in Table 3.3. All other elements are optional, and few management packs contain all 10. Sections are added as needed as the management pack is being authored.

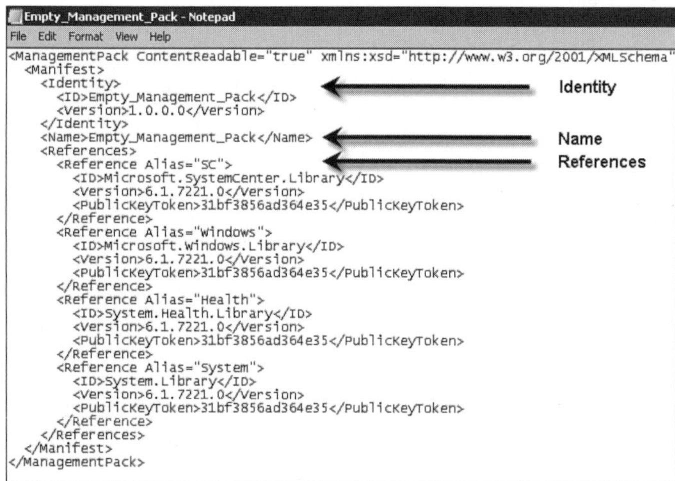


```
<ManagementPack ContentReadable="true" xmlns:xsd="http://www.w3.org/2001/XMLSchema"
  <Manifest>
    <Identity>
      <ID>Empty_Management_Pack</ID>
      <Version>1.0.0.0</Version>
    </Identity>
    <Name>Empty_Management_Pack</Name>
    <References>
      <Reference Alias="SC">
        <ID>Microsoft.SystemCenter.Library</ID>
        <Version>6.1.7221.0</Version>
        <PublicKeyToken>31bf3856ad364e35</PublicKeyToken>
      </Reference>
      <Reference Alias="Windows">
        <ID>Microsoft.Windows.Library</ID>
        <Version>6.1.7221.0</Version>
        <PublicKeyToken>31bf3856ad364e35</PublicKeyToken>
      </Reference>
      <Reference Alias="Health">
        <ID>System.Health.Library</ID>
        <Version>6.1.7221.0</Version>
        <PublicKeyToken>31bf3856ad364e35</PublicKeyToken>
      </Reference>
      <Reference Alias="System">
        <ID>System.Library</ID>
        <Version>6.1.7221.0</Version>
        <PublicKeyToken>31bf3856ad364e35</PublicKeyToken>
      </Reference>
    </References>
  </Manifest>
</ManagementPack>
```

FIGURE 3.16 "Empty Management Pack" consists only of the manifest section.

TABLE 3.3 Management Pack schema elements

Element (Schema Section)	Function and Child Elements
Manifest	Contains the Identity, Name, and References of the management pack.
TypeDefinitions	Contains all types defined in the management pack: EntityTypes, DataTypes, SchemaTypes, SecureReferences, ModuleTypes, MonitorTypes.
Monitoring	Contains all monitoring workflows defined in the management pack: Discoveries, Rules, Tasks, Monitors, Diagnostics, Recoveries, and Overrides.
ConfigurationGroups	Contains each ConfigurationGroup defined in the management pack.
Templates	Contains each Template defined in the management pack.

Element (Schema Section)	Function and Child Elements
PresentationTypes	Contains all defined user interface-related types defined in the management pack: ViewTypes, Images, UIPages, and UIPageSets.
Presentation	Contains all user interface-related elements defined in the management pack: ConsoleTasks, Views, Folders, FolderItems, ImageReferences, and StringResources.
Reporting	Contains all reporting-related elements: DataWarehouseScripts, DataWarehouseDataSets, ReportResources, Reports, LinkedReports, and ReportParameterControls.
LanguagePacks	Contains a LanguagePack element for each language supported by the management pack. Each language pack contains DisplayStrings and KnowledgeArticles elements.
Resources	Contains all the resources of a management pack: Resource, Assembly, ReportResource, Image).

Looking inside the schema of the management pack, you can appreciate how management pack construction aligns with the health model of an object. Figure 3.17 introduces the OpsMgr Authoring console, focused on the Health Model pane. The navigation panes in the Authoring console (the lower half of Figure 3.17) correspond to equivalent sections of the management pack schema listed in Table 3.3. The Health Model node of the Authoring console in the upper half of Figure 3.17 corresponds to the Monitoring element of the schema.

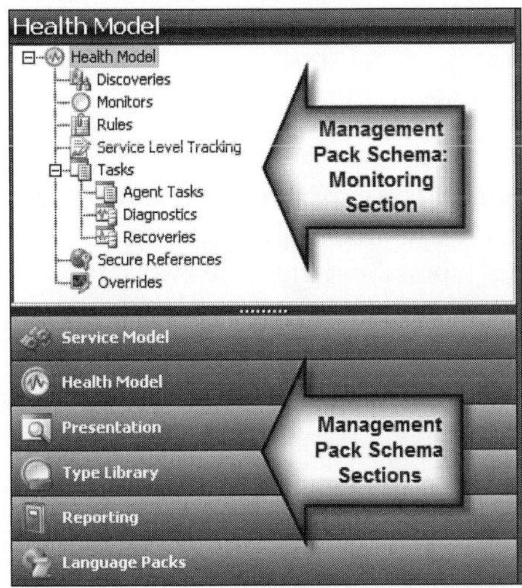

FIGURE 3.17 Health Model in the Authoring console exposes the Monitoring section.

The Monitoring section of the management pack is where most of the action taking place in OpsMgr comes from; correspondingly, this chapter is primarily about the Monitoring management pack element. The following list summarizes the purpose of relevant child elements in the Monitoring section:

- **Discoveries:** A *discovery* is a workflow that discovers one or more objects of a particular class. A discovery can discover objects of multiple classes at one time. As introduced in the "Service Modeling" section, there are both object discoveries and relationship discoveries.
- **Monitors:** A *monitor* is a state machine and ultimately contributes to the state of some object that is monitored by OpsMgr. The unit monitor is the simplest monitor. This monitor type detects a condition, changes its state, and propagates that state to parent monitors in the health model that roll up the status as appropriate. Monitors are covered in more detail in the next section.
- **Rules:** A *rule* is a generic workflow that can do many different things. For example, rules can collect a data item, alert on a specific condition, or run a scheduled task at some specified frequency. Rules are primarily used to collect data to present in the console or in reports, and to generate alerts.
- **Agent tasks:** A *task* is a workflow executed on demand; usually initiated by a user of the console or Web console. OpsMgr does not load tasks until required.
- **Diagnostics:** A *diagnostic* is an on-demand workflow attached to a specific monitor. Diagnostic workflows are initialized automatically, either when a monitor enters a particular state or on demand by a console user. A diagnostic does not change the object health state; it gathers additional information to help resolve the issue.
- **Recoveries:** A *recovery* is also an on-demand workflow attached to a specific monitor. Similar to a diagnostic workflow, a recovery is initialized automatically either when a monitor enters a particular state or on demand by a console user. A recovery can change the object health state, for example, by running a task that fixes the root cause.
- **Overrides:** An *override* is used to change monitoring behavior in some way. OpsMgr administrators make extensive use of overrides to customize management pack behavior for local network environments. Many types of overrides are available, including overrides of specific monitoring features such as discovery, performance, and recoveries. (Figure 3.10 exposed the XML of a management pack containing only overrides.)

Populating the Health Model with Monitors

It all starts with monitors in Operations Manager. If you were to author a management pack that discovers a new class of object, each discovered instance creates a new object that has its own four-category health model as previously described in the "How Health

Models Work" section. If you did not populate the health model with monitors, the object's rollup would always consist of an empty pearl icon that conveys no information. It is up to you to select one or more aspects of the object's behavior to monitor that represent the health of the object.

Adding Monitors to the Health Model

When adding a monitor, the first thing you might do is create a unit monitor that alerts when the single most critical factor in determining that particular object's health is found to be in a failure state. Then, add just sufficient additional monitors to reach a happy medium between too little and too much monitoring.

A health model for the human body would start adequately with the single unit monitor being a two-state "Heartbeat present = True or False." More advanced monitors that compare a value to a desirable range such as "Blood Pressure > x and < y" add fidelity and depth to the health model. Many body characteristics such as eye color have no bearing on health. Obviously, you want to avoid over-monitoring a human because medical tests are time consuming and many have their own side effects and consequences!

Likewise, the health model for a service or application should be as simple as necessary to get the job done, but also not so shallow or monitor meaningless data as to give a false impression that everything is OK. Collecting and processing data in OpsMgr is expensive from the point of view that you increase the size of your OpsMgr databases, potentially reducing the overall capacity and processing speed of your management group if you add new monitors indiscriminately. You might also want to create monitors in OpsMgr to establish relationships between objects that speed troubleshooting. Sufficient monitors in a health model create relationship connection points for other managed objects that host, contain, depend on, or reference the object.

Figure 3.18 is a chart showing the monitor icon images and their operational meaning. A functioning monitor displays exactly one of three states: Success (green), Warning (yellow), or Critical (red). A newly created, empty, or nonfunctional monitor shows the blank pearl icon. A grey maintenance mode wrench icon appears in all monitoring views that contain the object placed in maintenance mode. The final type of state icon you will encounter is the greyed state icon, which indicates OpsMgr has lost contact with the monitored object. This icon can be either a success, warning, or critical icon depending on the health state of the object at the time contact was lost.

Management pack authors can create three types of monitors: aggregate monitors, dependency monitors, and unit monitors; these are discussed in the following sections. Figure 3.19 is the **New -> Monitor** menu in the OpsMgr authoring console. Each of the eight folders expands with specific types of unit monitors, and you can also select the Custom Unit Monitor—these are all unit monitors. The aggregate monitor and dependency monitor items are at the bottom of the menu.

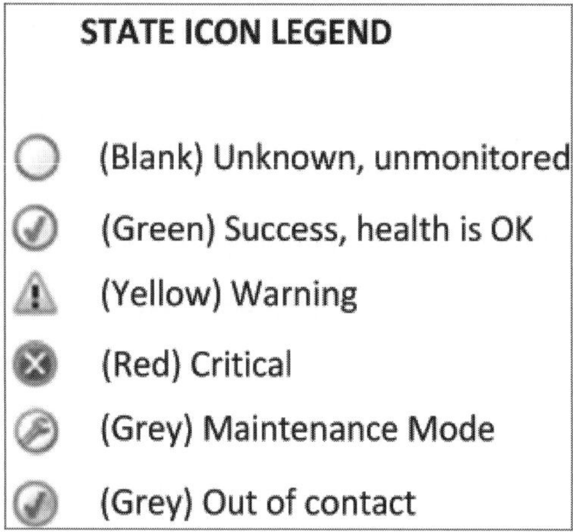

STATE ICON LEGEND
(Blank) Unknown, unmonitored
(Green) Success, health is OK
(Yellow) Warning
(Red) Critical
(Grey) Maintenance Mode
(Grey) Out of contact

FIGURE 3.18 State icons take six principal forms.

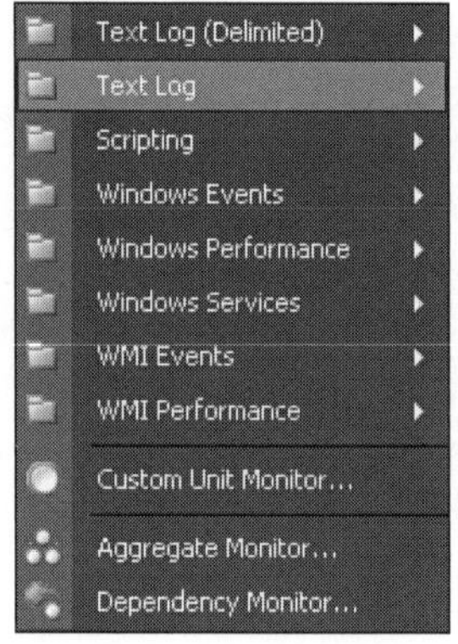

FIGURE 3.19 New Monitor options in the OpsMgr authoring console.

Aggregate Monitors

Returning to the Figure 3.15 view of a monitoring rollup, notice the four categories of monitors that appear immediately below the entity object. The top-level monitor in each category is essentially an aggregate monitor, which is by definition a monitor that doesn't monitor anything itself directly, but rather rolls up the state of one or more subordinate monitors. Figure 3.20 shows the health rollup settings of an aggregate monitor.

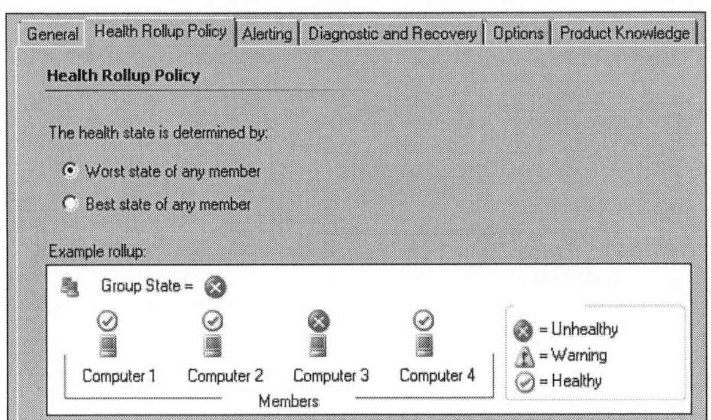

FIGURE 3.20 An aggregate monitor only rolls up the health of subordinate monitors.

While somewhat arbitrary, Microsoft selected four categories during OpsMgr development as a framework that limits the scope of the top-level rollup. Here are the four categories of aggregate monitors in a state monitor:

- **Availability:** Examples include checking that services are running, that modules within the OpsMgr health service are loaded, and basic node up/down tracking.
- **Performance:** Examples include thresholds for available memory, process utilization, and network response time.
- **Configuration:** Examples include confirming the Windows activation state and that website logging is enabled.
- **Security:** Monitors related to security that are not included in the other aggregate monitors.

Dependency Monitors

The second category of monitor is the dependency monitor. This type of monitor rolls up health from targets linked to one another by either a hosting or a membership relationship. Dependency rollup monitors function similarly to aggregate monitors, but are located at the intermediate layer of the SML hierarchy. Dependency monitors have more options for determining rollup health, as shown in Figure 3.21.

Earlier the "Service Modeling" section explained how objects such as disk partitions, logical disks, and physical disks have numerous relationships. Figure 3.22 shows a sample dependency monitor involving disk systems created in the Operations console Authoring space.

The monitor created in Figure 3.22 is targeted against the `Windows Server 2008 Disk Partition` class. OpsMgr knows that disk partitions contain logical disks, so when you create a new dependency monitor targeting this class, OpsMgr offers existing monitors to select from (to be the source, or connection point for the dependency) that are targeted already to the `Windows Server 2008 Logical Disk` class.

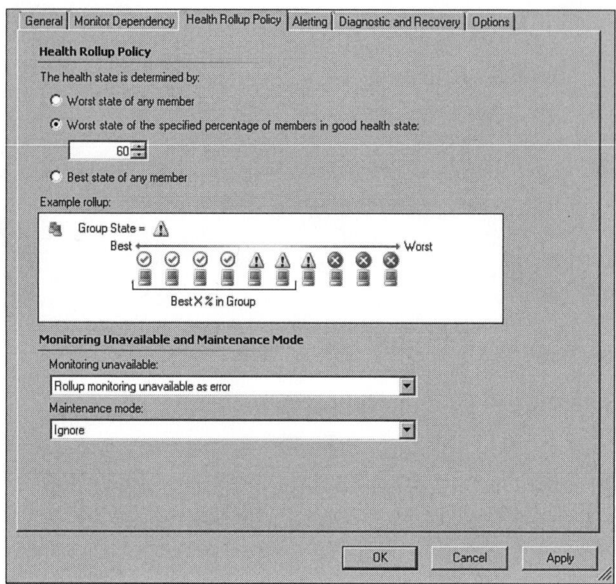

FIGURE 3.21 A dependency monitor configuration includes advanced rollup options.

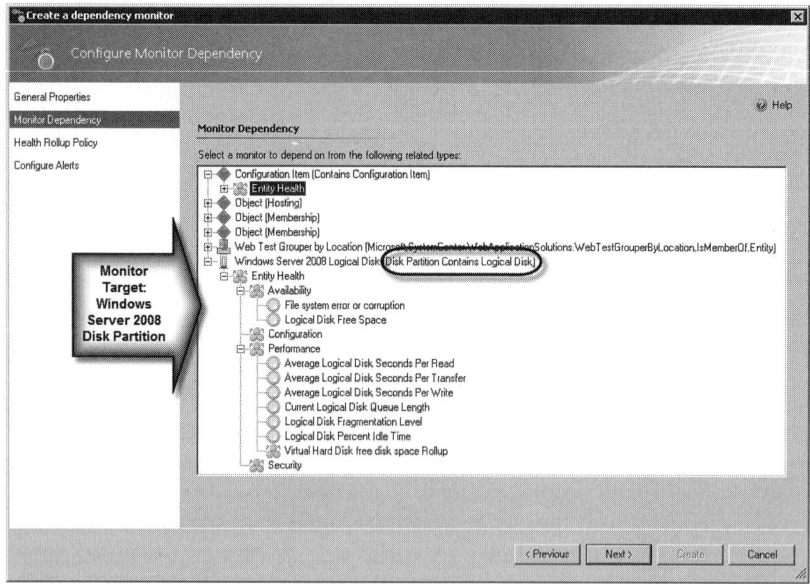

FIGURE 3.22 Creating a dependency monitor when the target is a disk partition.

Unit Monitors

A unit monitor is an active instrumentation that makes a high-level decision on the state of something. Think of taking someone's pulse using a finger on the wrist or the neck—this would be a two-state unit monitor, healthy state (pulse present and in normal range) or critical state (such as absent), with an optional intermediate/third warning state (such as present, but outside normal range). A unit monitor allows management pack authors to define a list of states, and determine how to detect those states.

A simple unit monitor is the Basic Service Monitor. This monitor raises state changes when a Windows service stops and starts running. It is a two-state monitor because the service is either running or not running. More complex unit monitors can run scripts, examine text files, and perform Simple Network Management Protocol (SNMP) queries. Monitors can watch for either a condition or the absence of a condition; and they can wait a certain amount of time before checking a condition.

Figure 3.23 presents a montage screenshot that includes all possible types of unit monitors available in the Authoring space of the Operations console. In other words, when you select **Create a Monitor -> Unit Monitor** in the Authoring space, you can create any of the monitor types in Figure 3.23. More than 50 unit monitors are available to place as software instrumentation in the SML framework. The placement of a monitor in the SML is determined by the class of object the monitor targets, the containing (or parent) monitor, any referencing or dependent monitors, and the monitoring category.

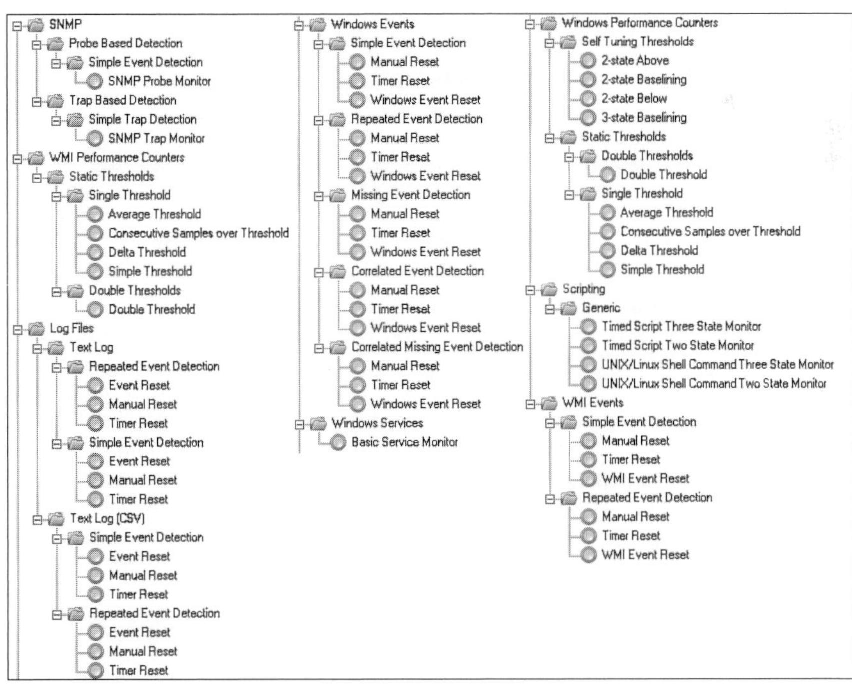

FIGURE 3.23 Possible unit monitor types that can be authored.

Remember that unit monitors roll up into aggregate monitors in four categories (Availability, Performance, Configuration, and Security), sometimes via dependency monitors. Table 3.4 provides an explanation of some of the unit monitor types found on the menu shown in Figure 3.23.

TABLE 3.4 Common monitor types and their descriptions

Monitor Type	Description
Average Threshold	Average value over a number of samples.
Consecutive Samples over Threshold	Value that remains above or below a threshold for a consecutive number of minutes.
Delta Threshold	Change in value.
Simple Threshold	Single-value threshold.
Double Threshold	Two thresholds (monitors whether values are between a given pair of thresholds).
Event Reset	Clearing condition occurs and resets the state automatically.
Manual Reset	Event based, wait for operator to clear.
Timer Reset	Event based, automatically clear after certain time.
Basic Service Monitor	Uses WMI to check the state of the specified Windows service. The monitor will be unhealthy when the service is not running or has not been set to start automatically.
Two State Monitor	Monitor has two states: Healthy and Critical.
Three-State Monitor	Monitor has three states: Healthy, Warning, and Critical.

Figure 3.24 overlays the SML of the IIS service on computer Typhoon with the Health Explorer view of the health model. The SML hierarchy on the left is the same health model used in Figure 3.15 when introducing Service Modeling Language. The health model on the right includes relevant monitors when the web management service is not running on an IIS computer.

Observe the red "X" (unhealthy) state icon in a unit monitor at the lowest SML layer echoes up through the SML layers to the top-level rollup monitor. Since the default view in the Health Explorer efficiently exposes only those monitors that are not healthy, even a complex and deep health model can quickly convey meaningful status to Operations console users when something goes wrong.

The center top portion of Figure 3.24 is a view of the actual OpsMgr Health Explorer for the Typhoon Windows computer object, when the same web management service critical state is encountered. Arrows in the health explorer view in the top of Figure 3.24 refer to the same two unit monitors appearing in the lower right of the figure at the base of the health model.

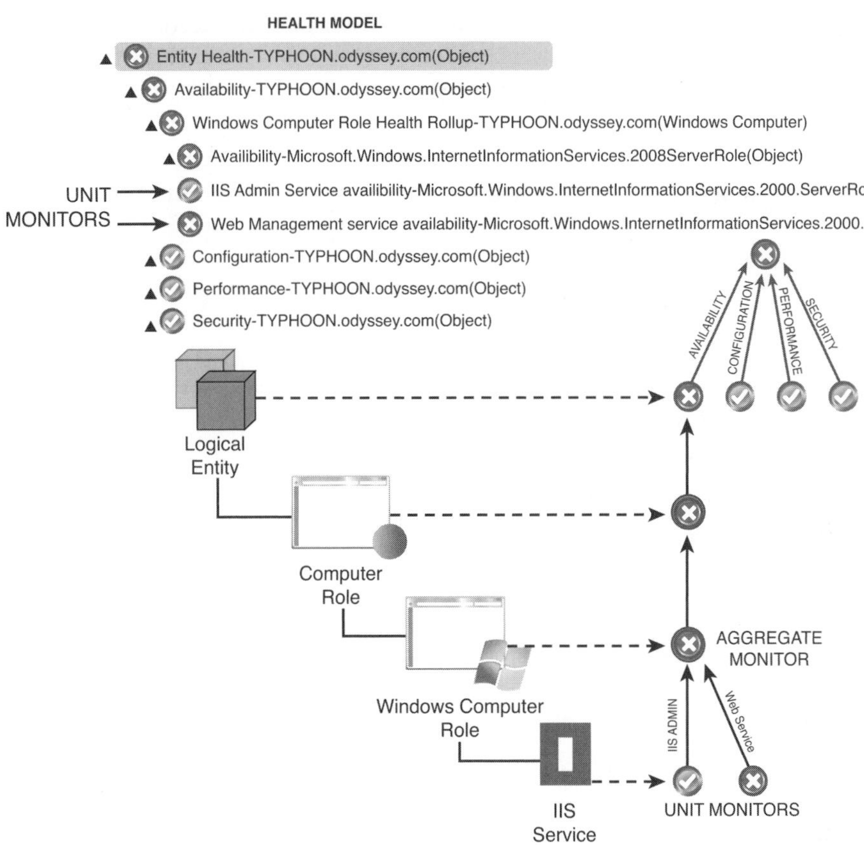

FIGURE 3.24 How the Health Explorer view aligns with SML and the health model.

How Rules Differ from Monitors

An overview of Operations Manager features would not be complete without including *rules*, even if monitors are more interesting! Rules are still the backbone of many management packs and are the source of most OpsMgr alerts. Among the questions expected from anyone learning about OpsMgr for the first time is *what's the difference between a monitor and a rule?* Here are some broad guidelines:

- **Monitors:** Since only monitors are seen in the Health Explorer, when you think of *health state*, think monitors (remembering that an alert is often, but optionally, generated from a monitor's unhealthy state change). Also, think of monitors when you create a new class of object, because doing so automatically creates a rollup monitor waiting for unit monitors to be deployed. A management pack may include one or more health models (one for each class added by the management pack), and each health model may contain from one to dozens of monitors.
- **Rules:** Rules raise alerts (not necessarily associated with a monitor), collect performance data used for charts and reports, and run timed commands to do just about

anything. When you think about alerts—*that don't automatically change a health state*—think rules. Also think of rules when you want to extend monitoring for an existing class and don't want to or need to extend the health model for the class. A management pack may include a large number of event-based rules, often hundreds.

Figure 3.25 presents a montage screenshot that includes all possible types of rules available in the Authoring space of the Operations console. This means when you select **Create a new rule** in the Authoring space, you can create any of the rule types in Figure 3.25. More than 20 rule types are available to add to a management pack. The three main categories of rules are alert-generating rules, collection rules, and timed command rules. These are covered in more detail in Chapter 14, "Monitoring with System Center 2012 Operations Manager."

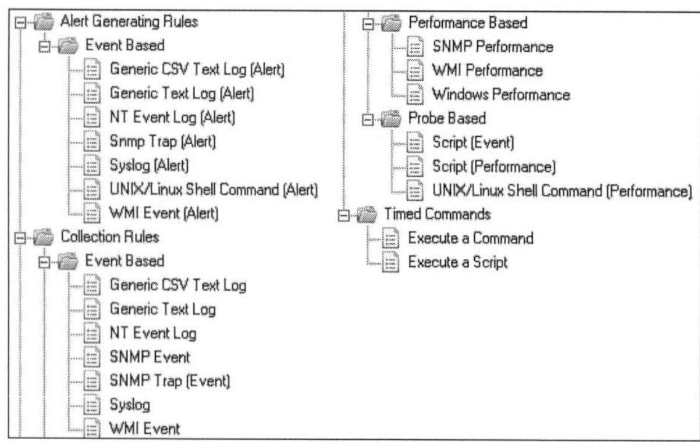

FIGURE 3.25 Possible rule types that can be authored.

OpsMgr as a Workflow Engine

It is accurate to describe Operations Manager as a colossal workflow engine. In fact, at the application layer OpsMgr is based on the concept of workflows. A workflow is an instruction to do some work, such as "read this data" and then "make this decision." Well-defined rules enable smooth interchange of work inputs and outputs and prevent a system breakdown. Workflow occurs as Windows MonitoringHost.exe executes processes in instruction blocks called *modules*, and data is exchanged between modules using defined *data types*.

Recall from the "Management Group Mechanics" section that management pack instructions and overrides are delivered in the form of XML documents through encrypted connections. Once a management pack is loaded on an agent and begins functioning, the action shifts to the workflows. Figure 3.26 captures the Windows task manager processes running on an OpsMgr 2012 management server.

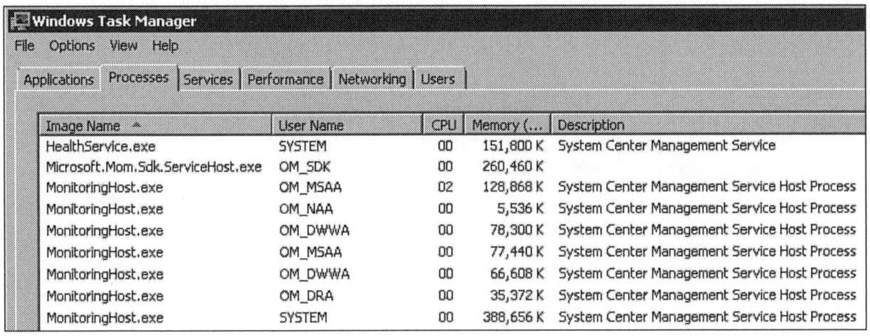

Windows Task Manager

File Options View Help

Applications | Processes | Services | Performance | Networking | Users

Image Name	User Name	CPU	Memory (...	Description
HealthService.exe	SYSTEM	00	151,800 K	System Center Management Service
Microsoft.Mom.Sdk.ServiceHost.exe	OM_SDK	00	260,460 K	
MonitoringHost.exe	OM_MSAA	02	128,868 K	System Center Management Service Host Process
MonitoringHost.exe	OM_NAA	00	5,536 K	System Center Management Service Host Process
MonitoringHost.exe	OM_DWWA	00	78,300 K	System Center Management Service Host Process
MonitoringHost.exe	OM_MSAA	00	77,440 K	System Center Management Service Host Process
MonitoringHost.exe	OM_DWWA	00	66,608 K	System Center Management Service Host Process
MonitoringHost.exe	OM_DRA	00	35,372 K	System Center Management Service Host Process
MonitoringHost.exe	SYSTEM	00	388,656 K	System Center Management Service Host Process

FIGURE 3.26 The MonitoringHost.exe processes run workflows.

Some details to notice in Figure 3.26 include that there is one instance each of the HealthService.exe and the Microsoft.Mom.Sdk.ServiceHost.exe processes. These correspond to the System Center Management and the System Center Data Access Service services previously described in the "Windows Services" section.

Also, notice in Figure 3.26 multiple instances of the MonitoringHost.exe process. It is normal for any OpsMgr management server, gateway server, or agent-managed computer to run several MonitoringHost.exe processes simultaneously. When OpsMgr needs to do work, that is, execute a workflow, it spawns an instance of MonitoringHost.exe to run the workflow module.

On a management server, instances run for the various data warehouse, management server, and notification action account workflows because each workflow runs under a different security context. On an agent-managed computer, workflows will generally all run under the Local System account of the agent-managed computer. Specific workflows that require authenticated login by domain accounts, such as synthetic transaction monitors, can have Run As accounts for those workflows.

Managing Workflows

On all OpsMgr servers and agent-managed computers, work such as running a script supplied by a monitor or rule (like checking free disk space) occurs in a temporary process viewed by Windows as a MonitoringHost.exe process. Since at any given time, a number of semi-random scripts or timed events might be taking place, the quantity of instances will vary.

Rules, monitors, and discoveries launch workflows, and one way to view what workflows are loaded on a management server is to run the Workflow Analyzer tool from the OpsMgr resource kit. This tool provides a list in a simple GUI of all workflows that are running or have run on the computer. The Type column in Figure 3.27 demonstrates the three types of workflow sources running on an example server: Rule, Monitor, and Discovery types.

Workflow Analyzer

Workflow Trace

Filter

*

Status	Display Name	Type	Category	Target Type
Running	Collect Maintenance Mode Events	Rule	EventCollection	Health Service
Running	Data Access Service SPN Registration	Rule	Alert	Data Access Service
Running	Snapshot synchronization state	Monitor	StateCollection	Management Configuration Service
Running	Cluster Node Roles Discovery	Discovery	Discovery	Cluster Roles

FIGURE 3.27 Workflow Analyzer resource kit tool showing running workflows.

Most workflows run quickly and a MonitoringHost.exe process lifetime is of short duration, perhaps just several seconds. Some scripts do run longer by design. All scripts have a default timeout value as a safety feature to avoid allowing idle or dormant monitoring threads to stack up and overload the system. Figure 3.28 shows a common Health Service Modules event in the Operations Manager log that occurs when a script (circled in the figure) exceeds its timeout value and is terminated as a "housekeeping" function.

Notice in Figure 3.28 that the file system location from where the script runs is the Health Service State folder, previously introduced in the "Management Group Mechanics" section as the working directory for the health service. These types of module failure events indicate something is wrong with the management pack or the agent computer, or at least there is some unexpected condition. In any case, any time a management pack workflow fails, some discovery or monitoring process expected to happen is not happening, and merits investigation and resolution.

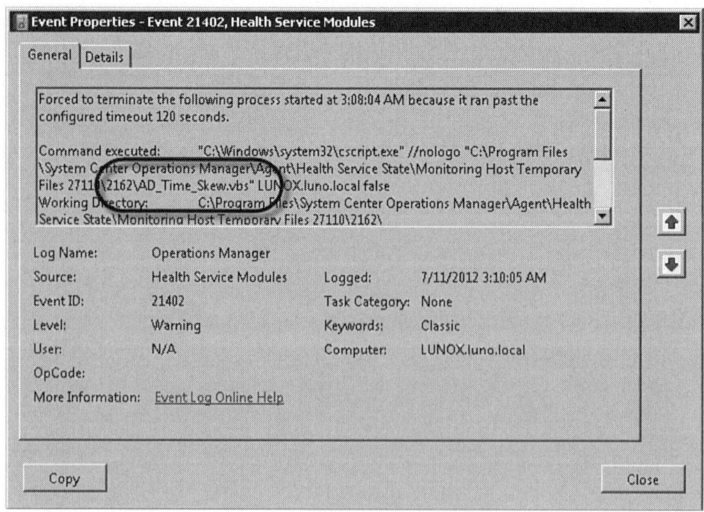

FIGURE 3.28 A workflow being terminated due to script timeout.

Module Types

The unit of activity that runs in a workflow is the *module*. For programming purposes, Microsoft defined four module types. Modules are the fundamental building blocks of management pack activity. The four different module types are data source, condition detection, probe action, and write action. Table 3.5 provides descriptive comments about each type of module.

TABLE 3.5 Monitoring workflow module types

Data Source	Condition Detection	Probe Action	Write Action
Does not take inputs, generates output based on external sources. Does not change object state.	One or more input streams, one output. No external sources and no state changes.	One input and one output; when triggered, generates output from external sources.	One input and zero or one output streams. Changes object state. Always the last module.

There are already many workflow modules defined by default with System Center management packs, such as generic workflows to read event logs or scan text files. It is only necessary to create new modules when authoring a custom management pack and extending the functionality of OpsMgr. Figure 3.29 shows the Type Library pane of the Authoring console, again showing the four types of modules you can create in OpsMgr. The figure is showing the modules included with the Exchange 2010 management pack.

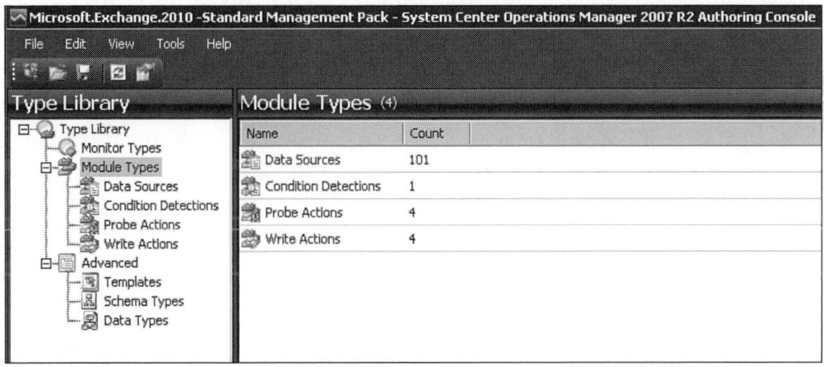

FIGURE 3.29 Module types included in the Exchange 2010 management pack.

TIP: MANAGEMENT PACK AUTHORS MUST LEARN AND OBEY MODULE RULES

It is up to the management pack author to adhere to the module type definition guidance. Microsoft publishes a module types reference at http://msdn.microsoft.com/en-us/library/ee533869.aspx. For example, consider that OpsMgr cannot determine if a probe action is being used to change an object's state in some way. Changes to object states should only occur in response to write action modules. If you run a script that is part of a probe action module, you could change object state in some way with your script, perhaps because this appeared to be easier to author. However, if you are changing an object's state, you should always use a write action module. Failure to use the correct module types can lead to unintended state changes.

Managing Workloads with "Cookdown"

If the quantity of MonitoringHost.exe processes becomes excessive, system performance can suffer. In addition, the combined processor or memory load of all MonitoringHost.exe processes can be a processing burden. This condition can indicate an agent or server malfunction, management pack overload, or one or more poorly written management packs. Management pack authors must take care not to spawn processes that consume excessive resources and/or fail to release resources. Rather, management pack authors should consider the principle of *cookdown* when defining and using modules.

It is easy to degrade a monitored system through too much monitoring. A direct consequence of running too many instances of MonitoringHost.exe can be 100% processor utilization of the monitored computer—the monitoring actually causing, rather than preventing, a service outage! OpsMgr designers included the concept of cookdown as a way to scale the monitoring engine, efficiently reusing code pieces (modules). To help in understanding, consider the following two rules that will cook down:

- **Collect application log event source MsiInstaller ID 11724:** This event indicates successful application removal.
- **Collect application log event source MsiInstaller ID 1005:** This event indicates a system restart is required to complete or continue application configuration.

The key to these rules cooking down (that is, the checking for both rules being performed by the same MonitoringHost.exe process, or workflow), is that OpsMgr sees the event log provider data source module (application log events) is the same for both rules. Only one instance of the data source module will run and OpsMgr will feed the output to all the condition detection, probe, and write action workflows.

In this example, the two MsiInstaller event ID rules, or *expression filters*, can take input data from the output of one condition detection module (the application log provider). In the case of event log providers, there normally is only one module executing for each log that is monitored, thanks to cookdown.

Cookdown becomes important when you are writing custom scripts that are probe actions to collect and process data. If you don't think about cookdown and design a reusable module structure, you could end up with too many scripts running, each in their own MonitoringHost.exe process, and degrading system performance.

Data Types

OpsMgr must pass data between modules. The format of this data varies depending on the module that output the data. Here are some examples:

- A threshold-based condition detection module expects the output of a data source module to be performance data.
- A data source module that reads data from an event log will output different data than a data source module that reads data from a text log.

Data types are a standard mechanism to identify those types of modules that are compatible with others.

Figure 3.30 shows the Type Library pane of the Authoring console, with the Exchange 2010 management pack loaded. The **Data Source** module type is selected on the left. Since this is a list of data source modules, and it is known from Table 3.5 that data source modules always create output, you should understand why (at the Data Types tab) a list of output data types appears in the properties of the data source module. Also appreciate that the data source module has no input data; it only outputs data to the other module types, which do all receive input data.

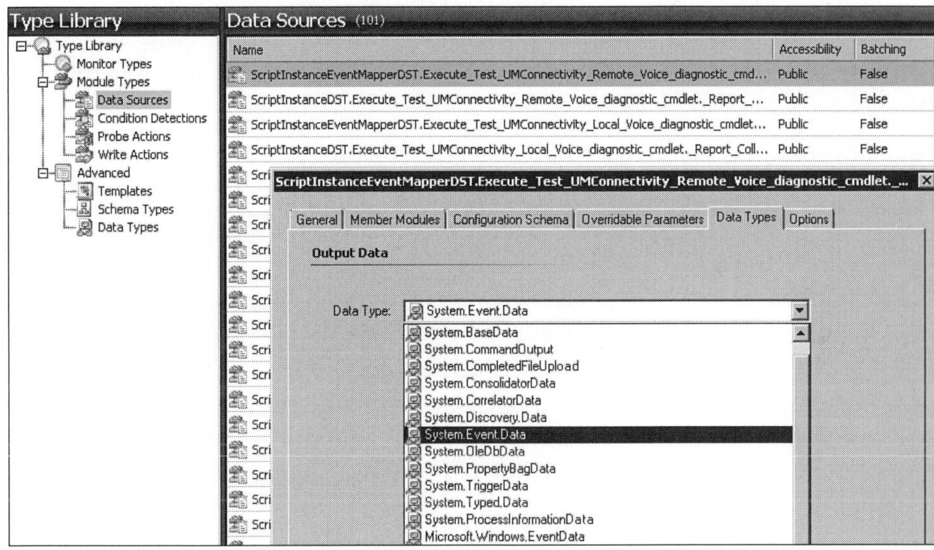

FIGURE 3.30 Data types exposed as output formats for data sources.

When extending System Center to monitor new applications and devices, recall that the "Populate the Health Model with Monitors," "How Rules Differ from Monitors," and "OpsMgr as a Workflow Engine" sections of this chapter have covered:

- How to create new classes of objects,
- New rules and monitors relevant to the new objects, and
- New modules that run custom workflows relevant to the line of business of your organization.

If you define a new module, you must specify the input and output data types it accepts and provides. These must be valid data types, defined in the same management pack or a referenced management pack. When a module is used in a workflow, the data types the module accepts and provides must be compatible with the other modules in the workflow.

Presentation Layer Scenarios

The job of any application's presentation layer is to deliver and format relevant and interesting information to the user or operator. An important concept with OpsMgr is that you don't usually interact directly with the operational SQL Server database when performing monitoring operations; interaction is via the System Center Data Access Service, also known as the SDK, or via SQL Server Reporting Services when running reports. (An exception is when you run the dedicated APM Web consoles; in this case, you read data directly from a SQL Server database server.)

The primary presentation layer scenario for OpsMgr is to receive a new alert, then investigate and resolve the alert using information in the alert and other views, monitors, and tasks in the console. The console connects to the DAS service on a management server and uses the DAS to populate the views with alerts, states, health models, performance charts, diagrams, and dashboards. The operator uses the console, which uses the DAS, which talks to SQL.

The Operations console is the primary and only necessary presentation layer scenario if you will either watch the console 24x7 and act on alerts as they appear, and/or if you will review the console periodically, checking alert and state views and investigating issues as needed. Additional presentation layer use scenarios enabled in OpsMgr 2012 are

- **Notification:** If you want to be alerted remotely via some means such as email or text message of alerts, you create a subscription and receive notifications on your choice of device.
- **Web console access:** If you want to be able to investigate alerts remotely, including opening health explorers and running remediation tasks, securely publish the OpsMgr Web console much as you would Outlook Web Access (OWA or Outlook WebApp).
- **Reporting products:** For offline or historical access to performance data or configuration lists, use the scheduled publishing and emailing features of OpsMgr reporting. This is a great solution for compliance reporting.

CAUTION: DO NOT EDIT DATABASE DIRECTLY EXCEPT WHEN MICROSOFT INSTRUCTS

There are occasions when an official Microsoft reference, such as TechNet or a Knowledge Base article, will explicitly instruct you to execute a SQL query directly on the SQL Server. Such a query can modify data in the OpsMgr databases. In the past, OpsMgr cumulative updates have sometimes contained one or more .SQL query files to execute on the SQL database servers. Outside these very rare cases, never attempt manual edits directly to an OpsMgr database, especially with SQL Management Studio's table editing tools. A rule of thumb is that any manual edits to the OpsMgr database will always result in loss of the management group.

Using the Operations Console

The Operations Manager console is a sophisticated "fat client" application; it is not a Microsoft Management Console (MMC) snap-in. The console connects to the DAS (SDK) service on a management server (or the highly available DAS pool if using a load balancer), and the DAS pulls data from the OpsMgr databases to populate views in the console. The console is generally installed on every OpsMgr management server and is optionally installed on any supported Windows computer you will use for monitoring or OpsMgr administration.

The console in OpsMgr 2012 is little changed from that in OpsMgr 2007, a testament to the efficiency of its design. The console packs a lot of function into an accessible and usable interface that includes scoping and filtering features necessary to work in high capacity environments. Figure 3.31 is the Operations console, with labels to indicate the names of the respective panes and sections of the interface.

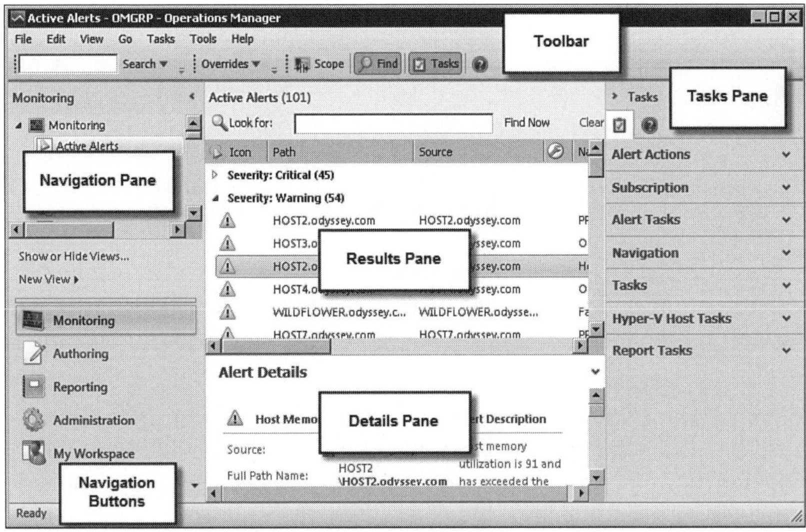

FIGURE 3.31 Operations console layout.

The Navigation pane in the upper left of the console is a changeable hierarchy of folders. Navigation pane folders contain child folders, views, and "nodes" where you change administration settings. Below the Navigation pane, observe the five navigation buttons regulating which of five possible panes are selected as the focus of the console:

Monitoring, Authoring, Reporting, Administration, and My Workspace. (The reporting pane is only visible if you install a reporting server in your management group.)

When you click on a navigation button, the Navigation pane switches to a folder and view hierarchy appropriate for that pane. Simultaneously, the Results, Detail, and Tasks panes switch to displaying data about the folder, view, or node selected in the Navigation pane. A text-sensitive filter is quickly available by typing text in the **Look for** box above the Results pane. Clicking the **Scope** button above the Results pane lets you focus the entire console on a particular group or class of objects.

If you are an OpsMgr operator, you will spend most of your time in the Monitoring space, where management packs add view folders filled with child folders and the following types of views: Alert, Event, State, Performance, Diagram, Task Status, Web Page, and Dashboard. Looking at data in the views is how an operator does work with the Operations console. Figure 3.32 shows these types of views to select from when clicking **New View** in the Monitoring space.

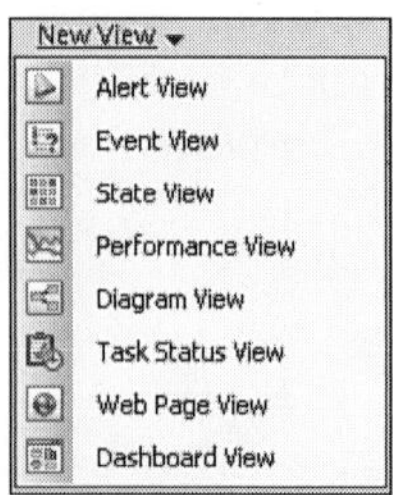

FIGURE 3.32 View type choices when clicking New View in the Monitoring space.

The most commonly used views are the alert and state views. Monitoring duty with the Operations console consists of periodically scanning the Active Alerts alert view and the Windows Computer (and/or UNIX/Linux Computer) state views. Issues discovered, by the appearance of new alerts and/or unhealthy state changes, can be immediately investigated by right-clicking the alert (in the Alert view) or the object (in the State view) and *pivoting* to another view.

An example of a common use of this feature is to investigate a low disk warning alert by pivoting to the performance view for the disk and seeing how quickly the disk has been filling up to assess the urgency of the issue. You don't need to consult a second console or shift the focus of the console to another view to follow up on the issue you are interested in. Another very common activity is pivoting to the Health Explorer for an object in an alert—this lets you assess the alert in the context of the overall health state of the object, not just the information in the alert you are focusing on.

An innovative feature of the OpsMgr 2012 Health Explorer is that only unhealthy monitors appear when you first open an object's health model. As shown in Figure 3.33, the resolution to the issue detected by the management pack is easy to find on the Knowledge tab of the unit monitor. The automatic filter that only displays unhealthy monitors also makes the Health Explorer open quickly, even for an object with many otherwise healthy monitors.

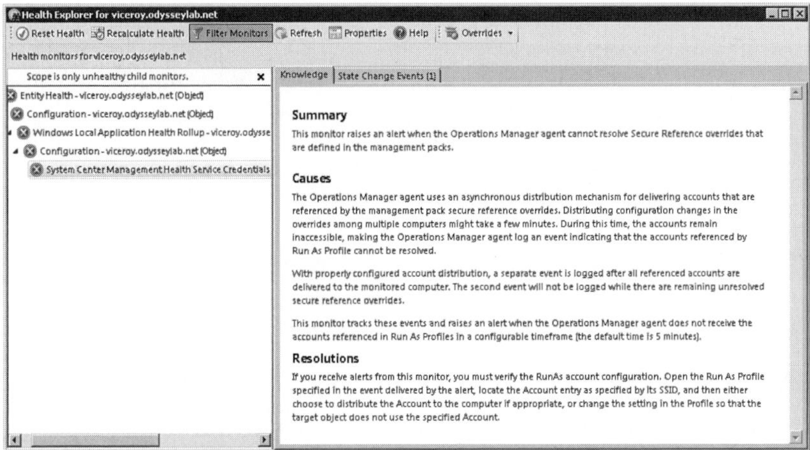

FIGURE 3.33 The Health Explorer is automatically scoped to unhealthy monitors.

Improvements to the Web Console

Among the most complex Silverlight-based web applications out there, Microsoft released an all-new Web console with OpsMgr 2012. The mission of the Web console is to extend most of the monitoring features of the Operations console to operators anywhere in the world using a web browser running Silverlight extensions. Microsoft did an excellent job of mimicking nearly all the normal console monitoring features in the Silverlight-based Web console, including right-click and pivot. Figure 3.34 presents the Web console open to a favorite view in the My Workspace pane.

Notice in the lower right of the Web console seen in Figure 3.34 that a variety of context-sensitive tasks are available, just as they are from the regular Operations console. Consider that you can stage any scriptable activity for remote, on-demand execution on any computer in your organization, from anywhere you can access the Web console—that is a lot a power that is always just a few clicks away. Limitations of the Web console include that it does not contain an Authoring or Administration pane, has limited access to reports, and does not expose event views.

Portals into APM

In addition to the completely new Web console debuting with OpsMgr 2012, there are also two new web portals associated with the APM feature. An Application Advisor website is basically a portal for generating detailed APM-specific reports, and the Application Diagnostics website exists to help review and analyze APM event data. Figure 3.35 shows some application failure events in the Application Diagnostics portal.

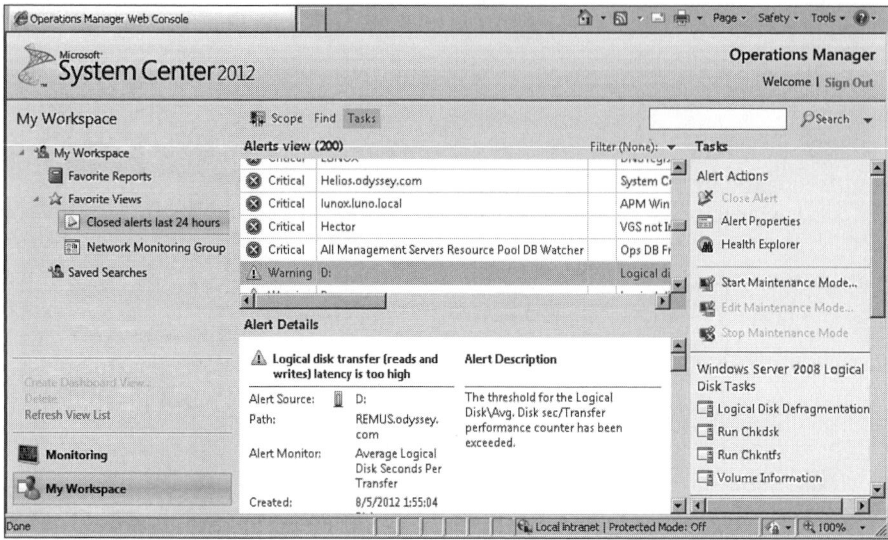

FIGURE 3.34 The Web console extends access to favorite views and tasks.

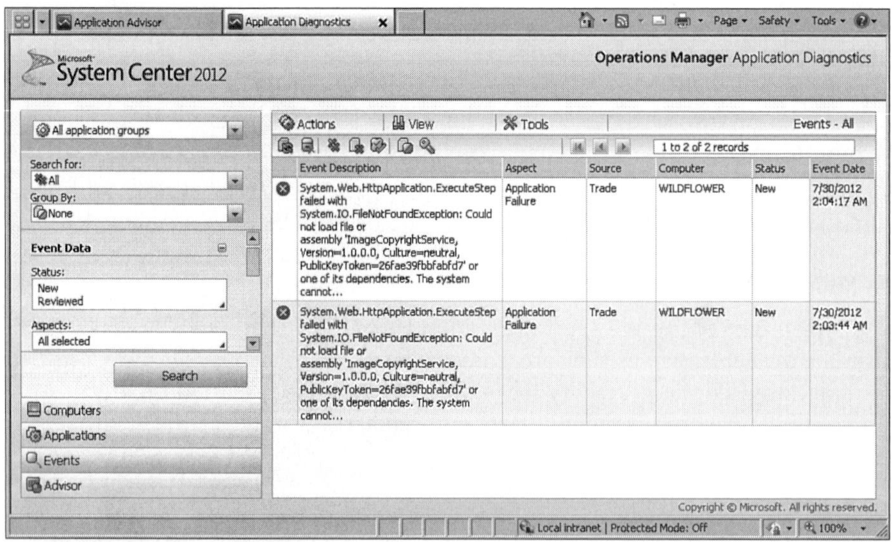

FIGURE 3.35 APM includes Application Advisor and Application Diagnostics sites.

The idea behind the dedicated portals for APM is that an organization will extend access to one or both web portals to their application development team over the local network. This lets the developers that can understand and act on detailed application data use APM without having to open the OpsMgr Operations console, or to learn how to use the full console.

OpsMgr Reporting

Under the covers, the Operations console coexists with a parallel report server infrastructure. This provides a fairly seamless experience for the console operator when you want to generate reports containing historical data. Since the performance views in the Operations console only contain several days' or at most a week's worth of data, you must run reports to learn about trends over weekly and monthly time spans. Figure 3.36 shows a simple report on the alerts per day seen by the management group.

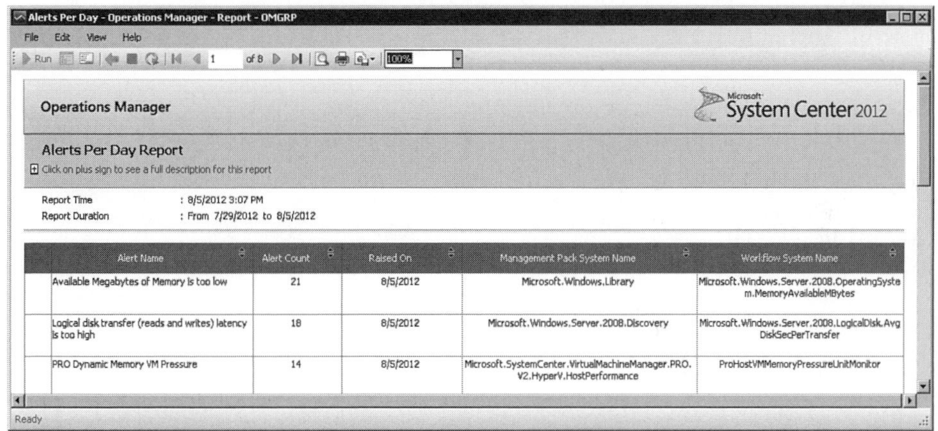

FIGURE 3.36 Reports can be flexibly viewed in SSRS, emailed, and published.

Another valuable feature of reports is you can easily extend access to OpsMgr reports to people outside your monitoring organization. Favorite reports can be scheduled for publication to file shares, posted to intranet sites, and even emailed directly to report consumers such as auditors and regulators.

PowerShell as a Presentation Layer

Although it is unlikely you would use PowerShell as an operator to perform monitoring duties, PowerShell is your primary tool anytime you need to script the use of OpsMgr data. PowerShell can also look at Operations console data on your behalf, and take action with the speed and tireless precision of a machine. PowerShell enables the IT Pro and the developer to extend the OpsMgr presentation layer in new ways and to other systems.

Here's a simple example: Say your enterprise portal dashboard administrator wants to know the quantity of active critical alerts in your management group. They need a number, updated every few minutes, to move the needle on a gauge. As demonstrated in Figure 3.37, there are two PowerShell commands you can run, then sum the numeric outputs mathematically, to arrive at the same number of active alerts that appear in the Operations console.

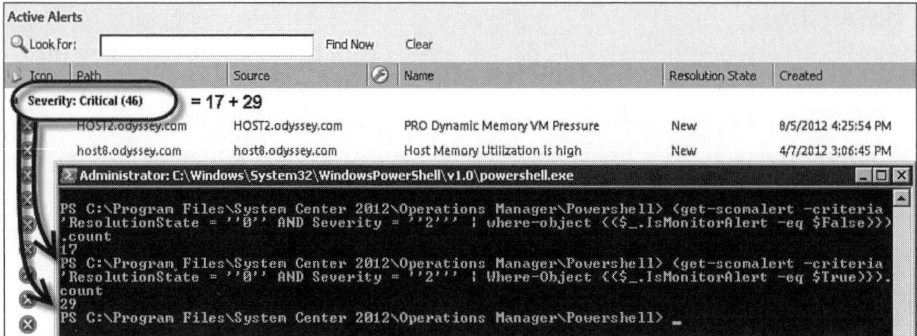

FIGURE 3.37 Command-line interaction with the SDK using PowerShell.

The scripts are included here for your convenience:

```
(Get-SCOMAlert -criteria 'ResolutionState = ''0'' AND Severity = ''2''' |
➥Where-Object {($_.IsMonitorAlert -eq $False)}).count

(Get-SCOMAlert -criteria 'ResolutionState = ''0'' AND Severity = ''2''' |
➥Where-Object {($_.IsMonitorAlert -eq $True)}).count
```

Notification Channels

You can define four types of notification channels in OpsMgr: E-mail (SMTP), Instant Message (IM), Text Message (SMS or Short Message Service), and command line. Notifications are sent to recipients on their selected channel(s) through *subscriptions* to specific alert criteria. It is not a good idea to attempt to receive every alert through a notification channel; you could be flooded with unimportant alerts that mask an important one. Create subscriptions for the subset of alerts you know merit your immediate attention. Figure 3.38 shows an email notification of a Linux security alert as seen in the Outlook client.

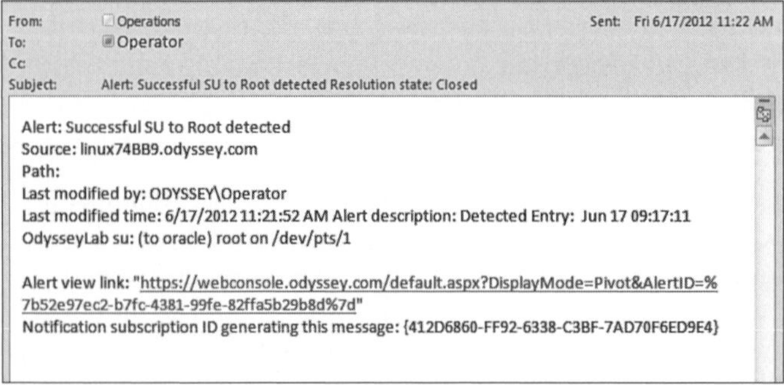
From: Operations Sent: Fri 6/17/2012 11:22 AM
To: Operator
Cc:
Subject: Alert: Successful SU to Root detected Resolution state: Closed

Alert: Successful SU to Root detected
Source: linux74BB9.odyssey.com
Path:
Last modified by: ODYSSEY\Operator
Last modified time: 6/17/2012 11:21:52 AM Alert description: Detected Entry: Jun 17 09:17:11
OdysseyLab su: (to oracle) root on /dev/pts/1

Alert view link: "https://webconsole.odyssey.com/default.aspx?DisplayMode=Pivot&AlertID=%7b52e97ec2-b7fc-4381-99fe-82ffa5b29b8d%7d"
Notification subscription ID generating this message: {412D6860-FF92-6338-C3BF-7AD70F6ED9E4}

FIGURE 3.38 An emailed notification in the Outlook client.

Notice in Figure 3.38 that the emailed alert summary contains an Alert view link to the OpsMgr Web console, where you can consult a detailed view of the alert as well as pivot to other views to learn more. That view could contain explanatory information to help understand the alert and even in-line tasks that launch a recovery action to fix the issue.

An even more minimalist notification is possible with the Instant Message channel, which in OpsMgr 2012 is Microsoft Lync. (Lync can in turn operate with public messenger networks such as Google, Yahoo, and MSN/Live.) Figure 3.39 shows a loss of heartbeat alert as it appears from the desktop of a Lync user. On the left is the popup "toast" notification from the OpsMgr Notification Action account, and on the right is the text of the notification.

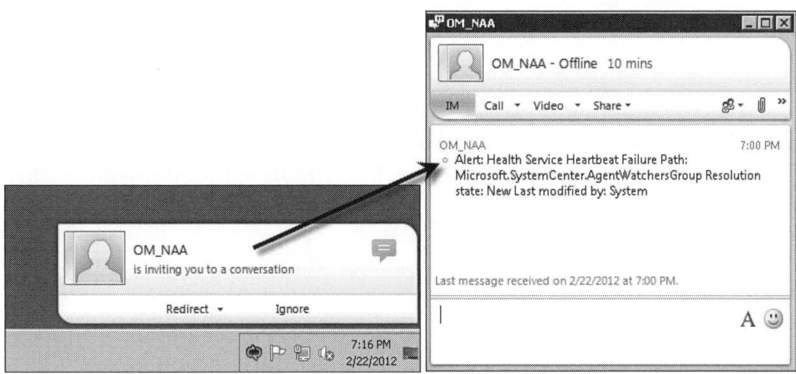

FIGURE 3.39 Notification of an alert via the Lync messenger client.

Fast Track

The presentation layer and monitoring/workflow aspects of OpsMgr 2012 are visually and architecturally little changed from OpsMgr 2007. As OpsMgr 2012 does not implement a new management pack schema, OpsMgr 2007 management packs can run in OpsMgr 2012. There are, however, some significant changes in the management group structure. This chapter concludes with a summary of changes, looking inside OpsMgr, provided especially for those developers and IT pros already familiar with OpsMgr 2007:

- OpsMgr 2012 is now delivered as a component in the System Center 2012 product. There are integration packs, management packs, and connectors between every System Center 2012 component and OpsMgr. There is also a new license model for System Center 2012 that bundles eight formerly separate software products—if you own one System Center component, you own them all.
- Data warehouse sharing is now possible out of the box. During installation of the data warehouse database, you can either use a new one, dedicated to the local management group, or an existing database, essentially establishing a central data warehouse repository. New is a requirement that all OpsMgr 2012 management

groups have a data warehouse database assigned, even if reporting is not installed in the management group.

- The RMS is replaced by a management server pool concept. The management group workflows previously run only on the RMS are now distributed among one or more peer management servers in a pool. One OpsMgr 2012 management server in the management group still holds the RMS emulator role. The RMSE role exists only to support legacy management packs that explicitly target the OpsMgr 2007 RMS role.
- The Data Access Service (DAS), also known as the SDK, runs on every management server, and is used to interface with the OpsMgr database. Optionally, you can establish a DNS name that maps to a load-balanced IP address that publishes a highly available DAS. Consoles, web consoles, and report servers can connect to the DNS name of the highly available DAS rather than be hard coded to use a specific management server name.
- The OpsMgr 2012 agent component now includes a control panel applet. This makes verifying and modifying the list of management groups easier. In previous versions of OpsMgr, it was necessary to use the Add/Remove Programs applet (now Programs and Features) to modify the agent.

Summary

This chapter looked inside OpsMgr from a System Center 2012 integration aspect, from the macro aspect of the management group, and from the micro aspect of the management pack and workflows. OpsMgr provides data to other System Center 2012 components and is used by other components to perform work. The OpsMgr features are deployed on a single server or across many servers in large organizations. Management packs encapsulate and distribute knowledge about objects and classes of objects, including relationships between objects. Management packs use workflows composed of modules that exchange specific data types. The chapter also listed and compared the consoles and other deliverables of the OpsMgr presentation layer.

PART II

Planning and Installation

IN THIS PART

CHAPTER 4

Planning an Operations Manager Deployment

IN THIS CHAPTER

If you are an Operations Manager (OpsMgr) 2007 or 2007 Release 2 (R2) administrator, the good news is that planning your Operations Manager deployment has not changed significantly since the 2007 releases of the product. The "bad" news is that proper planning is still crucial for a successful Operations Manager deployment. The majority of technical product deployments that fail do so because of ineffective planning.

Too often for Information Technology (IT) organizations, the thought process is to deploy new products as quickly as possible; however, this approach frequently results in not gaining full benefit from those tools. This can be referred to as the RSA approach: Ready, Shoot, Aim. Using RSA results in technology deployments that are not properly designed, which then require changes, or potentially a complete redeployment to resolve issues identified after the fact. The authors' recommended technique is RAS (or if you prefer, measure twice, cut once):

- **Ready:** Are you ready to deploy Operations Manager? Assess your environment to understand how to deploy Operations Manager to meet your unique requirements.
- **Aim:** What is the target you are trying to hit? Based on your assessment, create a design for your proof of concept, pilot, or production implementation.
- **Shoot:** Implement the solution you designed!

Start by creating a single high-level design and planning document. This approach is essential because Operations Manager affects all IT operations throughout the enterprise.

Many projects fail due to missed expectations, finger pointing, or the "not invented here" syndrome, which occurs when some IT staff members have stakes in preexisting or competitive solutions. Avoid these types of problems by developing a comprehensive plan and receiving backing from the appropriate sponsors within your organization. A properly planned environment helps answer questions such as the number of OpsMgr management servers you will have, how many management groups to use, the management packs you will deploy, and so forth.

Proper technical deployments require a disciplined approach to implement the solution. Microsoft's recommended approach for IT deployments historically has been the Microsoft Solutions Framework (MSF), which is now incorporated into version 4 of the Microsoft Operations Framework (MOF). Microsoft has designed MOF to provide practical guidance for the entire IT life cycle. The primary focus areas for MOF include

- Processes for planning, delivering, operating, and managing IT driven by the community
- Compliance, governance, risks
- Management reviews
- Best practices from MSF

Online documentation on MOF 4.0 is available at http://technet.microsoft.com/en-us/library/cc506049.aspx. For additional information on MOF, see Chapter 1, "Operations Management Basics."

The IT life cycle, as described by MOF v4, has three life cycle phases (Plan, Deliver, and Operate), with a Manage functional layer operating throughout all the phases. MOF organizes IT activities and processes into service management functions (SMFs) specific to each phase. The MOF Deliver phase includes SMFs that this chapter focuses on:

- **Envisioning:** Development of the vision and scope information
- **Planning:** Development of the design specification and master project plan
- **Developing:** Development and optimization of the solution
- **Stabilization:** Deployment to pilot systems, tuning and testing
- **Deployment:** Product rollout and completion

The goal of this chapter is not to teach MOF but to provide an example of how you can apply the framework to a System Center 2012 Operations Manager implementation. Information on the MOF Deliver phase is available at http://technet.microsoft.com/en-us/library/cc543223.aspx and http://technet.microsoft.com/en-us/library/cc506047.aspx. For this chapter, the authors use the Envisioning and Planning SMFs to provide an example of how you could use MOF to plan an OpsMgr deployment.

Envisioning Operations Manager

During the Envisioning phase, you should seek to understand the history and requirements for System Center 2012 Operations Manager. With these understood, you can develop the vision for the project, identify what is in scope, and determine any potential risks to the success of the project.

Understanding History, Requirements, and Goals

The first step when envisioning for a System Center 2012 Operations Manager solution is to understand from a monitoring perspective the current environment and history, how the organization reached where they are today. The reason for needing to understand a company's history to design a solution is well summarized by a quote from George Santayana's "Life of Reason I":

Those who cannot remember the past are condemned to repeat it.

An organization's history of monitoring will show where previous pitfalls existed so they can be avoided in the future. The history also shows successes that you can focus on and repeat for a System Center 2012 Operations Manager solution.

Here are some areas to concentrate on when gathering information:

- **History of monitoring solutions:** Was a previous version of Operations Manager or other related monitoring solution deployed in the past? If so, what happened and is this still in use today? If not, why?
- **Current monitoring solutions:** These products may include server, network, or hardware monitoring products (including earlier versions of Operations Manager such as OpsMgr 2007 and Microsoft Operations Manager/MOM 2005). Gather information regarding the following areas:
  - The products that are monitoring your production environment
  - The server(s) the product is running on
  - The devices and applications being monitored
  - Who the users of the product are
  - What the product is doing well
  - What the product currently is not doing well

  Options for your existing monitoring solutions include integration with Operations Manager, replacement by Operations Manager, and no impact by Operations Manager.
- **OpsMgr 2007 upgrade/replacement:** This is applicable for environments currently using Operations Manager 2007. An in-depth analysis of the functionality OpsMgr 2007 provides is critical to present a System Center 2012 Operations Manager design that replaces and enhances that functionality.

- **Current service level agreements:** A service level agreement (SLA) is a formal written agreement designed to provide the level of support expected (in this case, the SLA is from the IT organization to the business itself). For example, your SLA for web servers may be 99.9% uptime during business hours. Organizations could have official or unofficial SLAs. Some organizations will have defined these within Operations Manager 2007 or in System Center Service Manager.

  Unofficial SLAs are actually the most common type in the industry. An example of an unofficial SLA might be that email cannot go offline during business hours at all. You should document the existence and nonexistence of SLAs as part of your assessment, to take full advantage of Operations Manager's capability to increase system uptime.

- **Administrative model:** Organizations are either centralized, decentralized, or a combination of the two. The current administrative model and plans for the administrative model help determine where the OpsMgr features might best be located within the organization.

- **Integration:** You can integrate Operations Manager using a variety of solutions, including help desk/problem management solutions and existing monitoring solutions, using OpsMgr connectors or through System Center Orchestrator. Chapter 21, "System Center Integration," discusses connectors in OpsMgr and methods to integrate solutions within System Center. If OpsMgr requires integration with existing solutions, you should gather details including the product name, version, and type of integration necessary.

- **Service dependencies:** New functionality in this version of Operations Manager (particularly network monitoring) makes it even more important to be aware of any services on which OpsMgr may have dependencies. These include but are not limited to local area network (LAN)/wide area network (WAN) connections and speeds, routers, switches, firewalls, Domain Name Server (DNS), Active Directory (AD), instant messaging, and Exchange. Having a solid understanding of these services and documenting them will improve the design and planning for your System Center 2012 Operations Manager deployment.

- **Functionality requirements:** You will also use the Envisioning phase to gather information specific to the functionality OpsMgr will require. This includes determining which servers Operations Manager will be monitoring (including domain/[s] workgroup they are in), applications on these servers that need to be monitored, and how long to retain alert, event, and performance information.

  While gathering information for your functionality requirements, concentrate on the applications OpsMgr will manage. Identifying these applications and mapping out their dependencies will provide information important to your Operations Manager design.

- **Business and technical requirements:** What technical and financial benefits does OpsMgr need to bring to the organization? The business and technical requirements you gather are critical because they determine the design you ultimately create.

For example, if high server availability is a central requirement, this will significantly affect your Operations Manager design (discussed in Chapter 9, "Complex Configurations"). If customized dashboards or reports are required, these will require additional assessment to determine the time required to develop these solutions. It is also important to determine what optional features are required for your Operations Manager monitoring, audit collection, and reporting environments. Identify, prioritize, and document your requirements; you can then discuss and revise them until you finalize your requirements.

Vision

A vision statement identifies a long-term vision to resolve current problems that achieve the requirements for the project. Here are some simple examples of a vision statement for Operations Manager:

- To provide proactive monitoring for our customers both internally and externally and to more quickly resolve issues when they occur.
- To assist the company's efforts to achieve high availability for our line of business applications and websites through effective proactive monitoring.

The vision for your OpsMgr deployment might be completely different. A vision statement should provide an unrestricted view of what OpsMgr can provide for the organization and provides direction for the project.

Scope

During the Envisioning phase, you also need to focus on what will be the scope of the project and solution. If a consulting organization is involved, the scope is usually defined as part of the statement of work (SOW) that is provided before the engagement begins. If you are deploying OpsMgr without a consulting organization, it is still important that you identify what is and is not in scope for the project. Examples of this may include breaking down the deployment of System Center 2012 Operations Manager into different phases. As an example, a first phase deployment for OpsMgr 2007 often did not include monitoring for non-Windows operating systems or devices, Audit Collection Services (ACS), or Agentless Exception Monitoring (AEM), but those could be added to a later phase. A typical first phase deployment of System Center 2012 Operations Manager will include design of the OpsMgr environment, deployment of OpsMgr, and tuning OpsMgr.

Risks

Any project could have risks associated with its success. While risks will vary between projects, common risks include

- **Staff and subject matter expert (SME) availability:** Personnel should have time committed to the OpsMgr deployment project both from an OpsMgr deployment SME perspective and from a business SME perspective, enabling your OpsMgr deployment to meet the organization's requirements.

- **Scope creep:** After a project begins, additional items are often identified that would appear to be logical to add to the project. These items, which can affect the duration of the project, are often referred to as *scope creep*.

Develop mitigation and contingency plans for any risks identified. As an example, the mitigation for a scope creep risk might be to provide documentation explaining that the item is not in scope but could be delivered in a later phase. A contingency plan for the same situation might involve the creation of a change control to alter the project's scope to include the additional item.

Gather the information you collect into a single document, called an *envisioning document*. Have this document reviewed and discussed by those personnel in your organization most capable of validating that the information is correct and comprehensive. These reviews often result in, and generally should result in, revisions to the document; do not expect that a centrally written document will get everything right from the get-go. Examine the content of the document, particularly the business and technical requirements, to validate they are correct and properly prioritized. After reaching agreement on the document content, move the project to the next step: planning your OpsMgr solution.

Planning Operations Manager

During the Planning phase, you will focus on designing the System Center 2012 Operations Manager solution and then creating a plan to deploy the solution as designed. These tasks are discussed in the next sections.

Designing

Here are several key tenets to remember when designing an Operations Manager environment:

- **Keep it simple:** Only add complexity to a design to meet identified requirements.
- **Virtualization:** Any OpsMgr server role can be virtualized. There is still debate on virtualizing highly disk intensive applications such as SQL Server, but that will depend upon how many input/output operations per second (IOPS) are necessary for your environment.

As you design your environment, consider management groups, the OpsMgr features you will install, server locations, management servers, gateway servers, database servers, reporting servers, ACS, AEM, consoles, and agents.

Management Groups

As introduced in Chapter 3, "Looking Inside OpsMgr," an Operations Manager management group consists of the following:

- Operational database
- At least one management server

- Operations Manager consoles (Operations, Web, and Authoring)
- Data warehouse database
- Optional features (additional management servers, reporting servers, ACS, database servers, gateway servers), and up to 15,000 managed computers (with 25 open consoles; with 50 open consoles the number of supported managed computers decreases to 6,000).

Start with one management group and add additional management groups only if necessary. In most cases, a single management group is the simplest configuration to implement, support, and maintain. Here are some considerations that may affect the number of management groups you establish:

- **Exceeding management group support limits:** One reason to add an additional management group is if you need to monitor more than the 15,000 managed computers supported in a single management group (with 25 open consoles). The type of servers monitored directly affects the 15,000 managed computers limit; there is nothing magical or hard-coded about this number. For example, monitoring many Exchange backend servers has a far more dramatic impact on a management server's performance than monitoring the same number of Windows Vista or Windows 7 workstations.

  If the load on the management servers is excessive, (servers are reporting excessive OpsMgr queue errors or high CPU, memory, disk, or network utilization) consider adding another management group to split the load.

- **Separating administrative control:** A reason for establishing multiple or standalone management groups is to separate control of computer systems between multiple support teams. Consider an example where the Applications support team is responsible for all application servers and the Web Technologies team is responsible for all web servers; each group configures those management packs applicable to the servers it supports.

  With a single Operations Manager management group, the two groups may be configuring the same management packs. In this particular scenario, the Applications support team and Web Technologies team are both responsible for supporting Internet Information Services (IIS) web servers. If these servers are within the same management group, the rules in the management packs are accessible to each of the two support groups. If either team changes the rules within the IIS management pack, it may affect the functionality required by the other team.

  While there are approaches to minimize the impact by using techniques such as overrides, in situations such as this you may decide to implement multiple management groups. In a multiple management group solution, each set of servers has its own management group and can have rules customized as required for the particular support organization.

- **Security model:** In most situations, the OpsMgr security model provides sufficient granularity by using roles when the user is not in the Administrator role. An Operations Manager role consists of a profile and a scope. A profile, such as the Operations Manager Operator or Operations Manager Read-Only Operator, defines the actions one can perform; the scope defines the objects against which one can perform those actions. This means that roles limit the access users have. Although versions of Operations Manager prior to OpsMgr 2007 often required multiple management groups to separate different groups from performing actions outside their area of responsibility, roles limit who can monitor and respond to alerts generated by different management packs—and could eliminate the need to partition management groups for security purposes. (Security is discussed in more detail in Chapter 10, "Security and Compliance.")

  Even with this security model, it may be necessary to implement multiple management groups to meet your organization's security requirements. While OpsMgr provides a granular security model, it does not provide the ability to restrict the Administrator role. The Administrator role can perform any action, including altering rules or monitors, creating and changing groups, deploying agents, and more. If it is required that an administrator be unable to perform these actions on specific systems, you would need to create an additional management group.

- **Dedicated ACS management group:** Although ACS does not require a separate management group to function, splitting the audit functionality into its own management group may be necessary to meet your company's security requirements. Using a separate management group may be required should your auditors or company mandate state that the ACS functionality be administered by a separate group of individuals.

- **Production and test environments:** The authors recommend creating at least one separate test environment for Operations Manager; there could be situations where you need two, so you can test and tune management packs before deploying them into the production environment. This approach minimizes unexpected changes on production systems and permits extensive testing since it will not affect the functionality of your production systems.

- **Geographic locations:** Physical location is also a factor when considering multiple management groups. If many servers exist at a single location with localized management personnel, it may make sense to create a management group at that location. Let's look at a situation where a company—Odyssey—based in Plano, Texas, has 1,500 servers that will be monitored by Operations Manager; an additional location in Berlin has 500 servers that also will be monitored. If each location has local IT personnel responsible for managing its own systems, it might make sense to maintain separate management groups at each location.

NOTE: MANAGEMENT GROUP NAMING CONVENTIONS

When you are naming your management groups, the following characters cannot be used: ( ) ^ ~ : ; . ! ? ", ' ` @ # % \ / * + = $ | & [ ] <>{}

Management groups cannot have a leading or trailing space in their name. Additionally, do not choose an existing management group name used for Operations Manager or Service Manager. To avoid confusion, the authors recommend creating management group names that are unique within your organization. Remember that the management group name is case sensitive.

- **Network environment:** If you have a server location with minimal bandwidth or an unstable network connection, consider adding a management group locally to reduce WAN traffic. The data transmitted between the agent and a management server (or gateway server) is both encrypted and compressed. The compression ratio ranges from approximately 4:1 to 6:1. The authors have determined an average client will use 3Kbps of network traffic between itself and the management server, and typically recommend installing a gateway server at network sites with between 30 and 100 local systems. Operations Manager can support approximately 30 agent-managed computers on a 128KB network connection (agent-managed systems use less bandwidth than agentless-managed systems).

TIP: WHY NOT TO INSTALL A MANAGEMENT SERVER AT A REMOTE NETWORK SITE

Install management servers in the same physical location as the database servers and on the same subnet if possible. OpsMgr requires high bandwidth and low latency between the management server and the database server.

The authors have seen situations where management servers reside across a WAN link from the database. This configuration resulted in database locking that occurred when the remote management servers were writing to the database. These locks in turn caused console non-responsiveness while the database was locked.

Table 4.1 lists the minimum network connectivity speeds between the various OpsMgr features, based on the System Center 2012 Operations Manager Supported Configurations documentation available at http://technet.microsoft.com/en-us/library/hh205990.aspx.

TABLE 4.1 Minimum network connectivity

Feature A	Feature B	Minimum Requirement
Management server	Agent	64Kbps
Management server	Agentless	1024Kbps
Management server	Operational database	256Kbps
Management server	Console	768Kbps
Management server	Management server	64Kbps
Management server	Data warehouse database	768Kbps
Management server	Reporting server	256Kbps

Feature A	Feature B	Minimum Requirement
Management server	Gateway server	64Kbps
Web console server	Web console	128Kbps
Reporting data warehouse	Reporting server	1024Kbps
Console	Reporting server	768Kbps
Audit collector	Audit database	768Kbps

MORE INFORMATION ON BANDWIDTH UTILIZATION

Satya Vel's article, "Network Bandwidth Utilization for the Various OpsMgr 2007 Roles" (http://blogs.technet.com/momteam/archive/2007/10/22/network-bandwidth-utilization-for-the-various-opsmgr-2007-roles.aspx), has a good discussion on bandwidth utilization by the various OpsMgr features. While written for OpsMgr 2007, the information in the article also applies to this version. There are three major areas of discussion, summarized here:

- **Agent communication to management servers and gateway servers:** The amount of data sent by the agent depends on the management packs installed on each agent, the type of activity generated, how those management packs are tuned, and conditions in your environment. The good news is that data between agents and the management server/gateway server is compressed. Satya's tests determined about 200Kbps is sent for 200 agents in an environment with the AD, Windows Base OS, DNS, and OpsMgr management packs.

  Gateway servers: These are basically proxy agents that send data from multiple agents to a management server. Satya noted bandwidth utilization of about 22Kbps received by gateway servers from agents.

- **Management server communication to the operational and data warehouse databases:** OpsMgr 2012 management servers write directly to the operational database and the data warehouse. Data sent from the management servers to the databases is not compressed.

  The best practice here is to place your management servers close to your databases with fast network links between them. It is better for agents to report to a remote management server (compressed data) than have management servers in remote locations writing to the OpsMgr databases (uncompressed data) over slower links.

- **Audit Collection Systems (forwarder to collector):** Security events are sent in near real time rather than being batched together. If there is a loss of network connectivity, the forwarder re-sends all security events not yet confirmed by the collector as written to the audit database. The forwarder sends heartbeats to the collector every 60 seconds by default to try to re-send the data. If three heartbeats are missed, the collector drops the connection and the forwarder (if alive) automatically reinitiates it.

  Security events sent from the agent to the collector are typically less than 100 bytes, and the event in the database is under .05KB. Typical CPU and memory utilization used by the agent is generally less than 1%, with memory overhead approximately 4MB to 6MB.

The heartbeat interval default is set on the collector. You can change the default in the registry at `HKEY_LOCAL_MACHINE\SYSTEM\CurrentControlSet\Services\AdtServer\Parameters\HeartBeatInterval`. For additional information, see Appendix C, "Registry Settings."

- **Installed languages:** Each feature installed in your Operations Manager management group must use the same language. As an example, you cannot install the first management server in a management group using the English version of Operations Manager and deploy the Operations console in a different language, such as Spanish or German. If these features must be available in different languages, you must deploy additional management groups to provide this functionality.
- **Multiple management group architectures:** Implementing multiple management groups introduces two different architectures for management groups:
  - **Connected management groups:** A connected management group provides the capability for the user interface in one management group to query data from another management group.
  - **Multi-tiered management groups:** Multi-tiered architectures exist when there are multiple management groups where one or more management groups report information to another management group.

  The major difference between a multi-tiered environment and a connected management group is that in a connected management group data exists in only one location; connected management groups do not forward alert information to each other.

  For an example of a connected management group design, consider the Odyssey organization used throughout this book. Odyssey has locations in Plano and Berlin. For Odyssey, the administrators in Berlin need the autonomy to manage their own systems and Operations Manager environment. The Plano location needs to manage its own servers and be aware of the alerts occurring in Berlin. In this situation, you can configure the Berlin management group as a connected management group to the Plano management group.

  As an example of a multi-tiered management group design, consider a hybrid service provider architecture. In one such architecture, a master management group is created that rolls up connected management groups and customer owned management groups connect via the Microsoft Connector Framework (MCF). Scenarios around service providers and Operations Manager are discussed in Chapter 24, "Operations Manager for the Service Provider."
- **Multi-homed architectures:** A multi-homed architecture exists when a system belongs to multiple management groups, reporting information to each management group.

  As an example, Eclipse (Odyssey's sister company) has a single location based in Frisco, Texas. Eclipse also has multiple support teams organized by function. The Operating Systems management team is responsible for monitoring the health of all server operating systems within Eclipse, and the Applications management team oversees the business critical applications. Each team has its own OpsMgr management group for monitoring servers. In this scenario, a single server running Windows 2008 R2 and IIS is configured as multi-homed and reports information to both the Operating Systems management group and the Applications management group.

Another example of where multi-homed architectures are useful is when testing or prototyping Operations Manager management groups. Using multi-homed architectures, your OpsMgr 2007 agents (upgraded to System Center 2012 Operations Manager) continue to report to your production OpsMgr 2007 R2 management group while also reporting to a new or preproduction 2012 management group. This allows testing of the new management group without affecting your existing production monitoring (see Figure 4.1 for details).

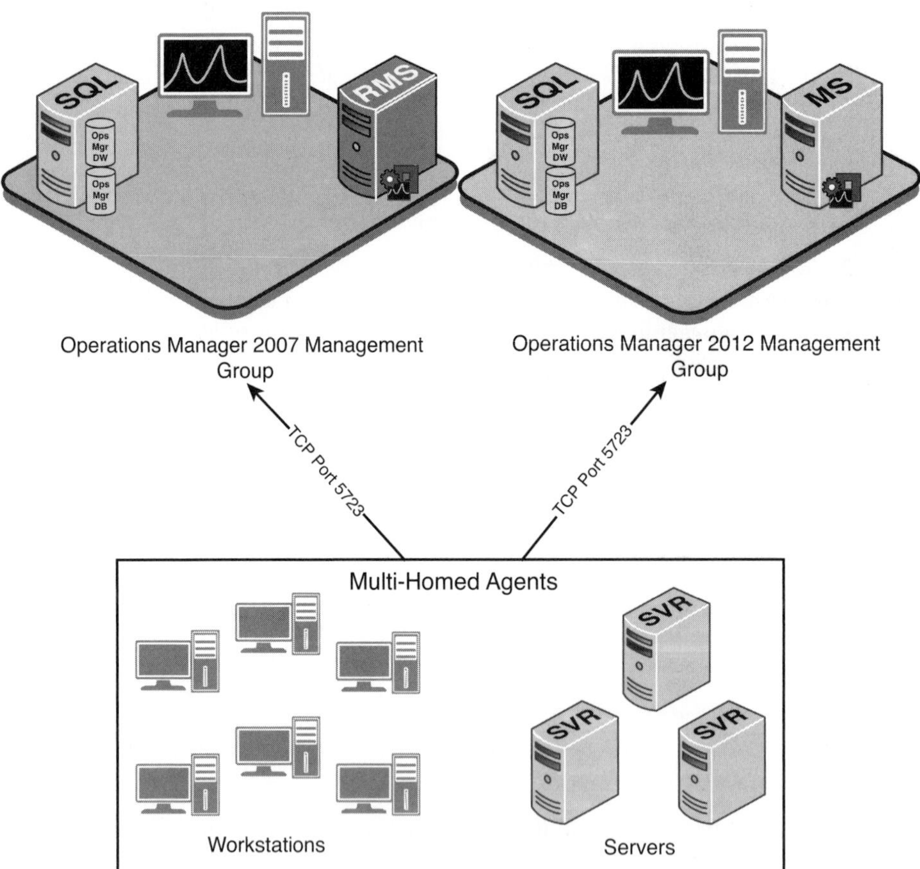

FIGURE 4.1 Multi-homed 2007 R2 and 2012 architecture.

Operations Manager Features

The number of management groups directly affects the number and location of your OpsMgr servers. The server features in a management group include at a minimum one management server, an Operations Manager operational database server, an Operations Manager data warehouse server, and Operations consoles. Various additional server features are also available within Operations Manager, depending on your business requirements.

Optional server features within a management group include additional management servers, a Web console server, reporting servers, ACS database servers, and gateway servers. The next sections discuss the following features and the hardware and software required for those features:

- Management servers
- Gateway servers
- Operations database server
- Reporting servers
- Data warehouse server
- ACS database servers
- ACS collectors
- ACS forwarders
- Agentless Exception Monitoring
- Operations consoles
- Web console servers
- Operations Manager agents

As discussed in Chapter 3, these are all part of a management group. In a small environment, you can install the required features on a single server with sufficient hardware resources. As with management groups, it is best to keep things simple by keeping the number of Operations Manager servers as low as possible while still meeting your business requirements.

With the System Center 2012 Operations Manager features, the hardware requirements vary depending on the role each feature provides. The next sections discuss where OpsMgr servers should be located, break down each of the different features, and discuss hardware requirements.

Operations Manager Server Locations

Select the most appropriate site to host the majority of the OpsMgr infrastructure. The majority of the OpsMgr infrastructure is nearly always hosted in a single site. OpsMgr without the ACS feature consists of two databases, a number of management servers and gateways, plus an optional dedicated web console and reporting server. How you locate these features in relation to each other is critical to ensure that your OpsMgr infrastructure functions correctly and performs well. If planning a distributed OpsMgr environment, there are several simple rules to remember. These include the following:

- **Physical location of servers:** For a distributed OpsMgr implementation, consider the location of the majority of the systems you will be managing. This generally is where you deploy the bulk of your OpsMgr environment, and should be the first thing to consider during planning. Here's why:
  - You can usually assume that if the majority of your servers are in a single data center or location, it will be easier to provision additional hardware in that location, minimizing deployment and configuration costs.
  - Storage Area Network (SAN) equipment for hosting large and heavily utilized OpsMgr databases is often found in data centers.
  - From an agent point of view, it makes sense to host the majority of the OpsMgr infrastructure close to the majority of intended agents.
- **Primary user location:** Consider where your primary OpsMgr users are located. Although technology such as Terminal Services and Citrix allow access to the Operations console from anywhere, these technologies have some inherent issues, discussed in the "Real World: Terminal Services Access Issues" sidebar. It also makes logical sense to host the OpsMgr environment close to where your primary users (and hopefully administrators) are.
- **Supporting multiple time zones (following the sun):** Following the sun refers to spanning international time zones. If your business has a sizeable presence in several locations spanning international time zones, you should plan management and maintenance to ensure coverage of working hours in all relevant time zones; that is, following the sun. Plan to support the OpsMgr infrastructure and monitored environment adequately during all hours users may be accessing the servers.

  Depending on the time zones spanned and hours of operation of your servers, you may need to provide 24-hour server support from one or multiple locations; in this case, consider access to the OpsMgr environment for users supporting OpsMgr from a site other than where the OpsMgr servers are located.

REAL WORLD: TERMINAL SERVICES ACCESS ISSUES

While Terminal Services and Citrix enable you to run the Operations console from a remote location, using these technologies introduces some inherent issues. The most prevalent of these concerns console tasks. OpsMgr has two forms of tasks—agent-based tasks and console tasks:

- Agent-based tasks do not cause any issues; regardless of where they are initiated from, they filter down to an agent's primary management server, and then to the agent where the task is run locally. Results are passed back the same way—through the agent's primary management server, and then displayed in the Operations console. An example of an agent-based task would be ipconfig, which you cannot execute remotely and therefore runs on the agent.

- Console tasks are a different story, as these are initiated and run within the console. An example of a console task is the Microsoft Management Console (MMC) Computer Management application, which is loaded on the local machine and connects remotely to the target machine. This may not initially appear to be an issue when using Terminal Services, as the management server and the console are both on the same LAN. However, consider this scenario:

  You are monitoring machines in both Plano and Berlin. Your OpsMgr environment is located in Plano, with monitored servers in both Plano and Berlin. Your user accesses OpsMgr via Citrix in Berlin. The admin wants to stop a service on a server located in Plano (about 20 feet from where he is sitting), so he runs the Computer Management task from OpsMgr. As a console task, the task is executed from the console in Berlin, targeted at a server on the other side of the world in Plano! In addition, the Computer Management console performs best on a high-speed LAN connection; hence, it can be expected to run exceptionally slowly across the WAN link.

  Running more intensive snap-ins such as Exchange System Manager only intensifies the problem. Unfortunately, there is no easy way around this issue if your environment is configured as described here, other than training and setting expectations.

  It is important to educate your users that should they run tasks such as launching Computer Management from a remote location to expect slow performance and time delays; this typically cannot be avoided.

Management Servers

Management servers provide the communication path between OpsMgr agents and gateway servers and the Operations database and OpsMgr data warehouse. Additional management servers (MS) within the management group can provide increased scalability and redundancy for your Operations Manager solution.

While there is no longer a root management server (RMS) in OpsMgr (see Chapter 2, "What's New in System Center 2012 Operations Manager"), there is an *RMS emulator* role that by default is configured on the first management server installed in the management group. This is for backward compatibility only.

The number of management servers required depends on the business requirements identified during the Envisioning phase:

- Unless the environment you are designing is to monitor a small lab environment, plan for a minimum of two management servers per management group. Each management server can handle up to 3,000 agent-managed computers. OpsMgr 2012 has a limit of 10 agentless monitored systems per management server. Each additional agentless monitored system increases the processing overhead on the management server. For details on agentless monitoring, see Chapter 8, "Installing and Configuring Agents."

- If a management group will monitor more than 3,000 computers, install multiple management servers in the management group. If you need to monitor agentless systems, a good practice is to split the load of the agentless monitoring between management servers in the environment.

- Add management servers to provide monitoring for up to 500 UNIX and Linux servers monitored by OpsMgr and to provide redundancy for these functions.
- Add management servers to provide monitoring for network devices monitored by OpsMgr and to provide redundancy for those functions.
- Each management group must have at least one management server (the first MS, which has the RMS emulator role).

Given a sample design of 1,000 monitored computers, you would plan for multiple management servers to provide redundancy. Each management server needs to support one-half the load during normal operation and the full load during failover situations. Although each management server does not store any major amounts of data, it does rely on the processor, memory, and network throughput of the system to perform effectively.

When you design for redundancy, plan for each server to have the capacity to handle not only the agents it is responsible for but also the agents it will be responsible for in a failover situation. For example, with a configuration using two management servers, should either management server fail, the second needs to have sufficient resources to handle the entire agent load.

The location of your management servers also depends on the business requirements identified during the Envisioning phase:

- Management servers should be separate from the Operations database in anything but an all-in-one OpsMgr management group configuration. In an all-in-one configuration, one server encompasses all the applicable Operations Manager features, including the management server, the operational database, and the Operations Manager data warehouse.
- Management servers should be within the same network segment where there are large numbers of systems to monitor with Operations Manager. The exception to this rule is across WAN links where gateways are preferred (additional information is provided in the "Gateway Servers" section later in this chapter).

If the MS and operational database are on the same server, the authors recommend monitoring no more than 200 agents with that server because it can degrade the performance of your OpsMgr solution. If monitoring more than 200 agents, you should split these two features onto separate servers, or use an existing SQL Server (even a SQL cluster!) for the operational database, thus lowering your hardware cost and increasing scalability.

NOTE: USING EXISTING SQL SYSTEMS FOR THE OPSMGR DATABASES

The question often arises if you could leverage an existing SQL Server database server by using it for the OpsMgr databases. Using existing hardware can lower hardware costs and increase scalability.

As a rule, the authors do not recommend this because there are high processing requirements on both the operational database and data warehouse, and they perform better with their own server. However, in small environments or if you want to add a significant amount of memory to an existing system (or if you have unused processing and memory resources), you may consider installing the OpsMgr databases on an existing SQL system.

Management Server Operating System Requirements and Prerequisites

Here are operating systems requirements and prerequisites you will want to know about:

- **Disk space:** Minimum of 1,024MB free disk space on *%SystemDrive%*.
- **Server operating system:** Windows Server 2008 R2 Service Pack (SP) 1. System Center 2012 SP 1 adds support for Windows Server 2012, including Server Core installations.
- **Processor architecture:** x64.
- **Windows PowerShell version:** Windows PowerShell 2.0.
- **Windows Remote Management:** Windows Remote Management must be enabled.
- **Microsoft Core XML Services (MSXML) version:** Microsoft Core XML Services 6.0 required.
- **.NET Framework:** .NET Framework 3.5 SP 1 and .NET Framework 4 (4.5 for Windows Server 2012 installations) required.

TIP: FINDING WHAT IS OFFICIALLY SUPPORTED FOR OPSMGR 2012 WITH AND WITHOUT SP 1

You can find the official support documentation for OpsMgr 2012 in the following locations:

- **OpsMgr 2012 RTM:** http://technet.microsoft.com/en-us/library/jj656649.aspx.
- **OpsMgr 2012 Service Pack 1:** http://technet.microsoft.com/en-us/library/jj656654.aspx.

Management Server Hardware Requirements

Microsoft provides an Excel spreadsheet for System Center 2012 Operations Manager to assist with determining hardware requirements for OpsMgr environments. This spreadsheet, the Operations Manager Sizing Helper, is available for download at the Microsoft Download Center at http://go.microsoft.com/fwlink/?LinkId=231853. The tool is designed to provide supported configuration information, hardware, and server requirements based upon the number of agents as well as gateway and UNIX/Linux monitoring. It also provides sizing for the operational database and data warehouse based upon IOPS, along with Microsoft's recommendations for determining the number of servers and hardware requirements. Here are the hardware requirements for management servers, based upon the number of agents you have:

- **500 agents:** 4 Disk RAID 10, 8GB of memory, 4 Cores.
- **1,000 agents:** 4 Disk RAID 10, 16GB of memory, 4 Cores.

- **1,000+ agents:** 4 Disk RAID 10, 16GB of memory, 8 Cores. This will vary based on your specific environment (number of agents, network devices, monitored URLs, UNIX/Linux systems, and so on)

In the Odyssey lab environment with fewer than 50 servers, the authors are running a virtualized Operations Manager MS with a shared 5 Disk RAID 5 currently using approximately 30GB of space, 6GB of dynamic memory, and 4 Cores.

Management Server High Availability/Redundancy

Installing additional management servers into the All Management Servers Resource Pool provides redundancy for the Operations Manager management servers. Resource pools were introduced in Chapter 2. Resource pools provide additional scalability and redundancy for Operations Manager by gathering collections of health services working together into a pool that can perform various functions. As an example, you could have a Network Monitoring Resource Pool monitor network devices so if a single management server in the pool is offline another server in the pool would continue to monitor the network devices.

An additional option to provide redundancy (or to supplement the use of multiple management servers) is to use a highly available virtualization solution that migrates the management server(s) upon loss of a host system.

NOTE: RESOURCE POOLS AND AD INTEGRATION

Creating resource pools can be useful when monitoring network devices or UNIX/Linux systems. A pool of servers can be assigned to monitor the network devices or UNIX/Linux systems. However, this is not available for all functions, as resource pool functionality does not replace AD integration—OpsMgr Windows agents are NOT assigned to report to a pool, but to a specific management server.

After identifying how many management servers will be required and their placement, you can now consider gateway servers and their impact on your OpsMgr design.

Gateway Servers

The number of gateway servers needed depends on the business requirements identified during the Envisioning phase:

- Unlike management servers, with gateways you start from zero and add as you determine they are necessary. Here are several primary reasons to consider gateway servers:
    - To provide mutual authentication capabilities outside of the forest
    - To provide monitoring for firewall connected environments where there is a business requirement to limit the connections through the firewall
    - To provide monitoring from WAN-connected locations

- Add additional gateway servers if a management group in your organization needs to monitor more than 2,000 agents reporting to a gateway.
- Additional gateway servers can be added to provide redundancy.

Gateway Servers and Mutual Authentication

Operations Manager 2007 introduced gateway servers to provide the ability to monitor agents within untrusted domains or workgroups and maintain mutual authentication, within the same management group. Mutual authentication, provided by Kerberos and certificate authentication, was first required with OpsMgr 2007. Using gateway servers makes this viable in demilitarized zones (DMZs, also known as *perimeter networks*), untrusted domains, and workgroup environments.

A gateway server gathers communications from agents and forwards them to a management server on the other side of the firewall using port 5723. In most configurations, a gateway server will report to a management server.

TIP: GATEWAY SERVERS REPORTING TO GATEWAY SERVERS

A gateway server can report to another gateway server rather than reporting to a management server. This is useful in configurations where a data center does not have direct connectivity to the data center with the Operations Manager databases.

As an example, consider an organization with a data center in the United States where the management servers and databases reside. The same organization has two data centers in Australia; the first data center is networked directly to the data center in the United States, but the second data center routes through the first Australian data center. With this configuration, a gateway server in the second Australian data center could be configured to report to a gateway server in the first Australian data center. This approach provides a way to use gateways to route data based upon network topology and has the benefit of requiring minimal changes to the firewalls to route the traffic. For more details, see the blog post on chaining gateways at http://blogs.technet.com/b/momteam/archive/2009/12/08/how-to-link-multiple-gateway-servers-together.aspx.

The authors recommend that the specified management server handle only gateway server communication; because of load issues, it is best that agents do not report directly to the same management server as a gateway server. However, you can configure multiple gateway servers to report to a single management server, as long as you do not exceed the maximum number of 3,000 total agents reporting to the management server. You will also want to spread agents as equally as possible across multiple gateways reporting to a single management server.

USING DEDICATED MANAGEMENT SERVERS WITH YOUR GATEWAY SERVERS

In terms of priority, a management server does not distinguish between the agents and gateway servers it is hosting. This means data from a gateway is assigned the same level of priority as that from a standard agent. While this may seem reasonable, if 100 agents report to the gateway, the priority for each agent at the gateway is 1/100. If the management server hosting the gateway server also has 100 agents with each receiving 1/100 of the total priority on the management server, the agents reporting to the gateway ultimately receive only 1/100 of that 1/100 slice of priority on the management server (1/10,000 of the priority).

From a design perspective, you will want to plan for additional hardware for those management servers to which your gateway servers will report. This will require at least one dedicated management server with which the gateway server(s) will communicate. Additional management servers may be required to provide a redundant communication option for the gateway server(s). Refer to the "Management Servers" section earlier in this chapter for details on hardware specifications for the management servers. Figure 4.2 shows a sample architecture using a gateway server.

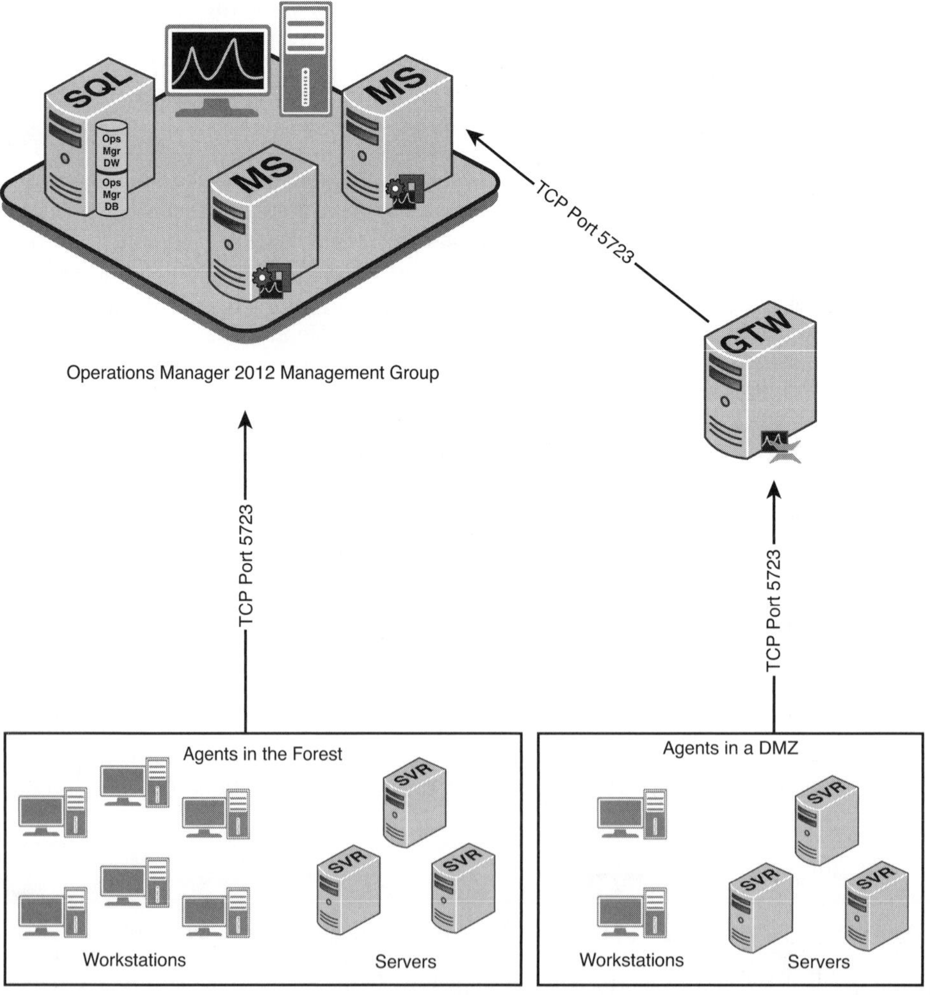

FIGURE 4.2 System Center 2012 Operations Manager architecture using a gateway server.

NOTE: REDUCED TRAFFIC WHEN DEPLOYING AGENTS WITH A GATEWAY SERVER CONFIGURATION

If you are deploying agents and using a gateway server to communicate with the other domain, know that while the management server sends the command to deploy the agents to the gateway server, the gateway server does the actual agent deployment. This means there is minimal traffic on the link between the management server and the gateway server.

Gateway Servers and WAN-Connected Locations

While Microsoft designed gateway servers to provide monitoring for agents in untrusted domains or workgroups, a second major benefit is available when monitoring agents across WAN links.

Companies that maintain multiple offices typically have a number of long-distance WAN links. In some cases, these organizations require multiple OpsMgr management groups to monitor their environment, although they often favor a single pane of glass. As using connected management groups significantly reduces the depth of the monitoring data one can display in a single console, the discussion in this chapter primarily considers a single management group scenario.

TIP: DEFINITION OF A LONG-DISTANCE WAN

The authors consider a long-distance WAN link to be either a link that spans continents or links that experience greater than expected latency, although it should be noted that a latency of less than 100ms is desired.

Typically, when monitoring servers in a number of locations, you simply add additional OpsMgr management servers to the remote locations to monitor local servers in that site. However, when these remote sites are located at the end of a long-distance WAN link, deploying management servers may not work as expected and can significantly reduce management group performance, resulting in alert delays and data loss. Here's why:

- **Management servers and long-distance WAN links:** In a traditional OpsMgr deployment, agents report to management servers that update the OpsMgr databases. However, this approach is not viable when facing data transmission over long-distance WAN links. To understand this, look at how a management server transfers data to and from the databases. A traditional management server uses a simple SQL OLEDB connection to connect the databases. The connection works (in simple terms) as shown in Figure 4.3 and listed here:

    1. Request to establish connection sent from management server to database server(s).
    2. Request received by database server and request for credentials sent to management server.
    3. Credentials sent from management server to database server.

4. Credentials verified.
5. Connection established.
6. Data transmitted.
7. Connection terminated. (The common term for this is *torn down,* meaning that no part of the connection is left intact.)

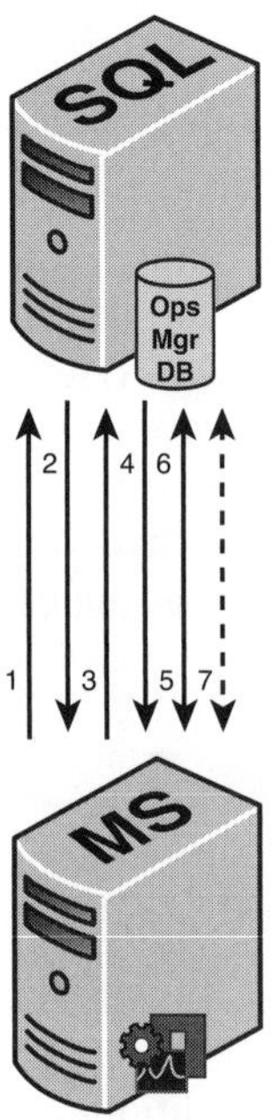

FIGURE 4.3 Management server communications with the database server.

This type of connection is appropriate when a management server is on the same local network to the database server, but not when transferring data over long-distance WAN links. This is due to physics, not technology. The physics of "Speed of Light" refers to the speed at which data is able to travel across a fiber link. The traffic associated with the SQL connection shows that the connection is very active or "chatty." While this is acceptable over a good, high-speed LAN link, it is less so when transferring data this way over a long-distance WAN link—as each step of the process is affected by latency caused by speed of light delay.

Additional latency on the connection can manifest as severe delays in updating alert and health service data, and even cause loss of agent data if the cache fills up and is overwritten. You can address this by using gateway servers in place of management servers in remote locations. Gateway servers service agents the same way as a management server, but differ in how they forward that data to the database:

- Unlike management servers, gateways do not directly connect to the database. Instead, they forward (proxy) data to another management server for transmission to the database.
- Differing from the very active OLEDB connection used by management servers, gateways establish a Transmission Control Protocol (TCP) connection with the assigned management server, maintaining this connection in an open state until the connection fails with an error or the management server is no longer available.
- Data sent from the gateway server is consolidated, resulting in an estimated 20%-30% reduction of total data sent to the database compared to individual agents reporting directly to a management server across the WAN link.

  Note that this reduction in data that is sent applies when there are approximately 50 or more agents reporting to the gateway. With smaller numbers of agents, there will be very little benefit in terms of bandwidth savings from implementing a gateway server.

  Given these characteristics, the gateway offers a much more efficient method of monitoring large numbers of agents at the end of a long-distance WAN link.

- **Using gateways across WAN links or to monitor large numbers of agents:** There are many factors to consider when using a gateway for any purpose other than monitoring agents in a DMZ. Typically, when you monitor DMZs, the number of machines monitored is relatively small when compared to the bulk of the corporate network. For that reason, Microsoft initially engineered gateways to monitor fewer agents, supporting a maximum of 200 agents with the OpsMgr 2007 release and making them unsuitable for any other purpose than monitoring DMZs and small untrusted networks. However, beginning with OpsMgr 2007 SP 1 and then R2, gateways were tested to 1,500 agents, and depending on hardware configuration and WAN link specifics could theoretically support many more than this. Documentation for System Center 2012 Operations Manager states that gateways now support up to 2,000 agents. Gateway servers provide a welcome alternative to management servers in complex, distributed environments.

  As previously discussed in the "Gateway Servers and Mutual Authentication" section, the authors and Microsoft recommend assigning a dedicated management server with no traditional agents reporting to it (even in a failover scenario), for the sole purpose of collecting data from your gateway server(s).

  When planning for failover, consider the number of gateways reporting to a management server and ensure you do not fail over gateway servers to a management server already hosting a large number of gateways. This means you typically will want to host no more than three or four gateways per management server during normal operation, and control failover such that no more than six report to a single management server at any time. Microsoft has not documented a maximum number of management servers and gateways for a management group. While there is no official limit for gateway servers, the maximum number the authors have experimented with is 16 per management group.

When a single management server hosts multiple gateways, remember not to exceed the maximum number of 3,000 total agents reporting to the management server. That means if you have three gateways reporting to a management server, each with 1,100 agents, you will exceed the supported limit of agents reporting to a management server, as that management server will have 3,300 agents reporting to it.

When planning to use gateway servers this way, ensure the management server hardware is sufficiently powerful to handle the excess load. Historically RAM was most critical for management servers, followed by CPU and finally disk I/O (which was largely unimportant). This has changed with Operations Manager 2012, as management servers are more often CPU-bound due to monitoring for a variety of devices (including UNIX, Linux, URLs, and network monitoring). Disk I/O requirements have also increased for large environments with UNIX/Linux and network devices. In these environments, the management server requires eight disks in a RAID 10 configuration to provide the required IOPS (according to the Microsoft sizer). Finally, RAM is still important but would be the third of the hardware priorities to consider.

Gateways differ as they cache far more data to disk than management servers do, so the order of importance of resources shifts. In the case of gateways, disk I/O is the priority, followed directly by RAM and then CPU. With sufficient disk I/O, gateway servers can be and are commonly virtualized.

Gateway Server Operating System Requirements and Prerequisites

Here are requirements and prerequisites for installing System Center 2012 Operations Manager gateway servers:

- **Disk space:** Minimum of 1,024MB free disk space on *%SystemDrive%*.
- **Server operating system:** Windows Server 2008 R2 SP 1; System Center 2012 SP 1 supports Windows Server 2012 including Server Core installations.
- **Processor architecture:** x64.
- **Windows PowerShell version:** Windows PowerShell 2.0.
- **Microsoft Core XML Services version:** Microsoft Core XML Services 6.0 required.

Gateway Server Hardware Requirements

The Operations Manager Sizing Helper, introduced in the "Management Server Hardware Requirements" section of this chapter, provides hardware requirements for 1-2,000 agents of a four disk RAID 10 with 8GB of memory, and 4 Cores.

Gateway Server High Availability/Redundancy

Installing additional gateway servers provides redundancy for this feature. An additional option to provide redundancy (or supplement the use of multiple gateway servers) is to use a highly available virtualization solution that would migrate the gateway server(s) upon loss of a host system.

Now that you have identified how many gateway servers are required for your environment, you can move on to designing Operations database servers.

Operations Database and Data Warehouse Servers

The operational database stores all the configuration data for the management group and all data generated by the systems in the management group.

Place the operational database on either a single server or a cluster; the authors recommend clustering if your business requirements for OpsMgr include high-availability and redundancy capabilities. Each management group must have an operational database. The operational database (by default named OperationsManager) is critical to the operation of your management group—if it is not running, the entire management group has very limited functionality. When the operational database is down, agents are still monitoring issues, but the database cannot receive that information. In addition, consoles do not function and eventually the queues on the agent and the management server completely fill.

As a rule of thumb, trim the SQL Server instance to use only what memory is available on the server, leaving 1GB per CPU socket for operating system (OS) operations. This approach provides SQL with as much memory as possible without starving the OS. Using an Active/Passive clustering configuration provides redundancy for this server feature; Active/Active clustering is also supported, although not recommended by Microsoft due to potential performance issues (see http://technet.microsoft.com/en-us/library/jj656654.aspx for details). See Chapter 9 for details on supported cluster configurations.

The authors recommend that you not install the operational database on an MS in anything but a single-server Operations Manager configuration. Although these server features can coexist, this is not a recommended configuration because it may also cause contention for resources, resulting in a negative impact on your OpsMgr environment.

TIP: HOW DOES APPLICATION PERFORMANCE MONITORING (APM) IMPACT DATABASE SIZING?

The Operations Manager Sizing Helper takes into consideration how APM will affect database sizing, based on the number of APM-enabled computers. Additionally, Daniel Muscetta of the Operations Manager engineering team blogs about APM data trends in an article available at http://blogs.technet.com/b/momteam/archive/2012/06/18/event-to-alert-ratio-reviewing-problems-and-understanding-trends-for-apm-data-in-opsmgr-2012.aspx.

Disk configuration and file placement strongly affects database server performance. Configuring the Operations database server with the fastest disks available can significantly improve the performance of your management group. Microsoft's recommendations on sizing of the databases and IOPS are available as part of the Operations Manager Sizing Helper tool, discussed in the "Management Server Hardware Requirements" section of this chapter. A single server can provide the operations database feature unless Operations Manager requires high availability. If high availability was identified as a requirement during the Envisioning phase, a server cluster with two nodes for redundancy may be required rather than a single server.

Start with a minimum of one server to provide the operations database feature. A server cluster may be required depending upon the business requirements identified during the Envisioning phase.

SQL SERVER 2008 R2 EDITIONS

Microsoft SQL Server 2008 R2 comes in seven editions: Compact, Express, Workgroup, Web, Standard, Enterprise, and Developer. Of these seven, you must use either the Standard or Enterprise editions with OpsMgr. Here are the differences between the two supported editions:

- **Standard Edition:** This edition supports up to four multicore processors, memory limited by operating system, unlimited database size, failover clustering for two nodes, log shipping, and database mirroring. It is intended for large datasets and production loads.
- **Enterprise Edition:** Enterprise Edition supports an unlimited number of multicore processors (up to the operating system maximum), memory limited by operating system, unlimited database size, failover clustering up to 16 nodes, log shipping, and database mirroring. This edition is intended for the largest and most demanding online transaction processing (OLTP) environments, data analysis, and data warehousing systems.

The authors are often asked whether to use SQL Server Standard or Enterprise Edition with OpsMgr. While realizing there are significant differences in licensing costs, Enterprise Edition is strongly recommended in high-volume ACS environments as it reduces the chance of lost security events (discussed in more detail in Chapter 10). Although not as necessary for the operational database and data warehouse, there are several reasons for considering SQL Server Enterprise Edition in your environment. Here are some benefits to consider:

- Enterprise Edition supports parallel index operations, hot-add CPU and memory, parallel DBCC operations, table and index partitioning should you want to implement that, online index operations (which is not critical for the operational database but is extremely important for the data warehouse database especially in larger environments), and online page and file restores.
- Enterprise Edition is better at supporting more than 500GB of data, which can be useful for the data warehouse. Standard Edition runs on a maximum of four CPUs, while Enterprise can handle an unlimited number of CPUs (based on the version of the underlying OS). The additional hardware capabilities provide room for growth in larger shops.

The differences between SQL Standard and Enterprise can affect your OpsMgr features and OpsMgr environment in the areas of high availability and maintenance. Chapter 9 discusses high availability, and Chapter 12, "Backup and Recovery," discusses database maintenance.

In System Center 2012 Operations Manager, the data warehouse is no longer an optional feature. The best practice for database servers in OpsMgr is to place the two databases on different servers to avoid resource contention. This is not required in smaller environments or lab requirements, as you can install both OpsMgr databases on the same SQL Server system and instance without conflicts.

SQL SERVER 2012 EDITIONS

System Center 2012 SP 1 includes support for SQL Server 2012. Microsoft SQL Server 2012 comes in four editions: Express, Standard, Enterprise, and Business Intelligence. Of these four, you must use either the Standard or Enterprise editions with OpsMgr. Here are the differences between the two supported editions in SQL 2012:

- **Standard Edition:** This edition supports up to 16 multicore processors, up to 64GB RAM, unlimited database size, failover clustering for two nodes, log shipping, and database mirroring. It is intended for large datasets and production loads.
- **Enterprise Edition:** Enterprise Edition supports an unlimited number of multicore processors (up to the operating system maximum), memory limited by operating system, unlimited database size, failover clustering up to 16 nodes, log shipping, and database mirroring. This edition is intended for the largest and most demanding online transaction processing (OLTP) environments, data analysis, and data warehousing systems.

The article at http://www.microsoft.com/sqlserver/en/us/product-info/compare.aspx provides additional information on the different SQL Server 2012 editions.

Operations Database and Data Warehouse Operating System Requirements and Prerequisites

Here are operating systems requirements and prerequisites you will want to know about:

- **Disk space:** Minimum of 1,024MB free disk space on *%SystemDrive%*.
- **Server operating system:** Windows Server 2008 SP 2 or Windows Server 2008 R2 SP 1. System Center 2012 SP 1 supports Windows Server 2012 including Server Core.
- **Processor architecture:** x64.
- **Windows Installer version:** Windows Installer 3.1 or above.
- **Microsoft SQL Server:** SQL Server SQL 2008 R2 SP 1, SQL Server 2008 R2 SP 2. System Center 2012 SP 1 adds support for SQL Server 2012.
- **SQL collation:** SQL_Latin1_General_CP1_CI_AS.
- **SQL Server Full Text Search:** Required.
- **.NET Framework:** .NET Framework 3.5 SP 1 and .NET Framework 4 (4.5 for Windows Server 2012 installations) required.

Operational Database and Data Warehouse Hardware Requirements

The Operations Manager Sizing Helper, introduced in the "Management Server Hardware Requirements" section, suggests the following hardware: (Note that these recommendations were built based upon the Microsoft sizer, which is subject to change. Refer to the Microsoft sizer for the most up-to-date sizing recommendations.)

4

- **1-500 agents:** One server with 8 Disk RAID 10, 16GB of memory, 4 Cores.
- **501-1,000 agents:** As you add agents, it is recommended you split the database server and the data warehouse onto different servers.
    - **Operational database server:** 6 Disk RAID 10 (Data), 2 Disk RAID 1 (Log), 16GB of memory, 4 Cores.
    - **Data warehouse database server:** 12 Disk RAID 10 (Data), 2 disk RAID 1 (Log), 16GB of memory, 4 Cores.
- **1,000-3,000 agents:** When you have more than 1,000 agents, the hardware requirements increase for both the operational database and the data warehouse.
    - **Operational database server:** 10 Disk RAID 10 (Data), 2 Disk RAID 1 (Log), 16GB of memory, 8 Cores.
    - **Data warehouse database server:** 16 disk RAID 10 (Data), 2 disk RAID 1 (Log), 16GB of memory, 8 Cores.
- **3,000-6,000 Agents:**
    - **Operational database server:** 16 Disk RAID 10 (Data), 2 Disk RAID 1 (Log), 24GB of memory,
      8 Cores.
    - **Data warehouse database server:** 24 disk RAID 10 (Data), 2 disk RAID 1 (Log), 24GB of memory, 8 Cores.
- **6,000+ agents:** Refer to the Operations Manager Sizing Helper for larger scale environments. The version of the sizer available when this chapter was written provides hardware requirements for environments with 6,000, 10,000, and 15,000 agent configurations.

REAL WORLD: DATABASE HARDWARE BEST PRACTICES

The operational database is often a performance bottleneck. All OpsMgr data either comes from SQL Server or goes to SQL Server, which is why you need to place, size, and configure your SQL disks appropriately—the faster the disks, the better the performance. Here are some considerations for disk and file placement.

For large environments, at least three logical disks are recommended:

- One disk for OS; one disk for OpsMgr and SQL; one disk for the transaction log.
- RAID 10 is highly recommended.

Here is the ideal configuration:

- Install the operational database separate from your management servers.
- Install the operational database and data warehouse on different systems. OpsMgr writes data in almost real time to these databases, making their loads similar.
- If there are many concurrent reporting users, place the reporting server (covered in the "Reporting Servers" section) on a different system from the data warehouse.

This will enhance performance, as running reports that query large data ranges or target many objects demand additional resources.

- Configure the database server with one disk for OS, one disk for SQL, one disk for tempdb, and one disk for transaction logs. In an ideal world, these configurations would be multiple disks with the database split in equal-sized chunks to allow multiple CPU thread efficiencies. It is best to have these files on distinct logical disks, with distinct dedicated physical disks making up the LUN.
- Use multiple database files for databases. (For each CPU, you will want to dedicate from 25% of a file to the entire physical file.)
- Use multiple files for tempdb (number of files equal to number of CPUs).

Using multiple physical files for your databases can improve physical I/O operations. The more I/O SQL Server performs at a disk level, the better your database performance. If you use separate database files, verify the files have the same initial size and growth settings. If they are of different sizes, SQL Server tries to fill the physical file with the most free space first to maintain an equal amount of free space across all the files. If the files are of identical size, writes are distributed across the various database files for improved performance.

Here is a preferred drive configuration:

- Place database data files on a different drive from the operating system.
- Place transaction logs and database files on separate drives. The transaction log workload consists of mostly sequential writes; putting the transaction logs on a separate volume allows that volume to perform I/O more efficiently. A single two-spindle RAID 1 volume is sufficient for most environments when handling very high volumes of sequential writes.
- Place the tempdb database on its own drive.
- Resize tempdb and the transaction log to be 20% of the total size of the operational database and data warehouse.
- As a best practice, Microsoft suggests using a battery-backed write-caching disk controller for both the operational database and data warehouse. Testing has shown that the workload on these databases benefits from write caching on disk controllers. When configuring read caching versus write caching on disk controllers, allocate 25% to read caching and 75% of the cache to write caching. When using write-caching disk controllers with any database system, a proper battery backup system can prevent data loss in the event of an outage.

Operations Database and Data Warehouse High Availability/Redundancy

Using a SQL cluster provides high availability for database servers in Operations Manager. An additional option to provide redundancy is a highly available virtualization solution that migrates the database functionality upon loss of a host system.

With the requirements for the operational database and data warehouse servers identified, let's discuss reporting requirements.

Reporting Servers

The Operations Manager reporting server feature uses SQL Server Reporting Services (SSRS) to provide web-based reports. This feature typically runs on a single server. The server is running Windows Server 2008 R2 (or Windows Server 2012 if you have installed System Center 2012 SP 1) with SSRS, so its hardware requirements match those discussed previously for the operational database server feature.

Reporting Server Operating System Requirements and Prerequisites

Here are operating systems requirements and prerequisites you will want to know about:

- **Disk space:** Minimum of 1,024MB free disk space on *%SystemDrive%*.
- **Server operating system:** Windows Server 2008 R2 SP 1. With the release of System Center 2012 SP 1, Windows Server 2012 including Server Core is now supported.
- **Processor architecture:** x64.
- **Windows Installer version:** Windows Installer 3.1 or above.
- **Microsoft SQL Server:** SQL Server 2008 SP 1, 2, or 3, SQL Server 2008 R2, or SQL Server 2008 R2 SP 1. System Center 2012 SP 1 adds support for SQL Server 2012.
- **SQL collation:** SQL_Latin1_General_CP1_CI_AS.
- **.NET Framework:** .NET Framework 3.5 SP 1 and .NET Framework 4 (4.5 for Windows Server 2012 installations) required.

Reporting Server Hardware Requirements

SSRS is often installed on the OpsMgr data warehouse server but can be installed on a separate web server. See the "Operational Database and Data Warehouse Hardware Requirements" section for details.

Reporting Server High Availability/Redundancy

Redundancy is available for the reporting servers by implementing web farms or Network Load Balancing (NLB), but there are issues associated with this approach that lead the authors not to recommend this as a solution. Additional details are available in Chapter 9.

ACS Database Servers

Audit Collection Services provides a method to collect records generated by a Windows audit policy and to store them in a database. This centralizes the information, which you can filter and analyze using SQL Server reporting tools. The ACS database server feature provides the repository where the audit information is stored. The hardware requirements for ACS database servers vary depending upon the number of events per second that are being inserted into the database.

ACS Database Server Operating System Requirements and Prerequisites

The ACS database server requires either SQL Server 2008, or SQL Server 2008 R2. OpsMgr 2012 SP 1 supports SQL Server 2012 for ACS. Microsoft does not support using a different version of SQL Server for different Operations Manager features, so use the same SQL version for ACS as the other OpsMgr database components.

ACS Database Server Hardware Requirements

The ACS database has not significantly changed since OpsMgr 2007. For initial sizing estimates, see the ACS sizing calculator created for OpsMgr 2007 that is available at http://blogs.technet.com/b/momteam/archive/2008/07/02/audit-collection-acs-database-and-disk-sizing-calculator-for-opsmgr-2007.aspx.

ACS Database Server High Availability/Redundancy

Use a SQL cluster to provide high availability for database servers in Operations Manager. An additional option to provide redundancy is to use a highly available virtualization solution that would migrate the database server(s) upon loss of a host system.

ACS Collector Servers

The ACS collector feature is installed on an existing management server, so the hardware requirements for the collector mirror those of the management server. The forwarders send information to the ACS collector. The collector receives the events, processes them, and sends them to the audit database. For performance reasons, the authors recommend not using an ACS collector to monitor agents.

ACS Forwarder Servers

The ACS forwarder feature uses the System Center Audit Forwarding service, which is not enabled by default. After the service is enabled, the ACS collector feature captures all security events (which are also saved to the local Windows security event log). Because this feature is included within the OpsMgr agent, the hardware requirements mirror those of the agent (discussed in the "Operations Manager Agents" section).

Agentless Exception Monitoring

System Center 2012 Operations Manager includes functionality that captures, aggregates, and reports on application crashes (Dr. Watson errors). This functionality uses the OpsMgr 2012 feature called Agentless Exception Monitoring (AEM).

From a planning perspective, if there is a requirement for AEM, there must be a plan for a server that stores the crash information, and you must deploy a group policy to redirect the application crash information to the AEM server.

Clients running Windows 2000 or Windows XP use the SMB (Server Message Block) protocol to write crash information to a folder that you specify. Windows Vista and Windows 7 clients use HTTP to send crash information. From a planning viewpoint, the server you will use must be identified and have sufficient space to store crash information. (Crash information can range from very small up to 8GB.) The crash information must be stored on an NTFS partition.

NOTE: AEM AND WINDOWS 8 CLIENTS

At the time of writing this chapter, information was not yet available regarding support of Windows 8 clients for AEM in an OpsMgr 2012 SP 1 installation.

The initial reaction to gathering Dr. Watson crash information and analyzing it is often a question of why bother? The application crashes; the user restarts it. What's the big deal? The big deal is that every crash affects end-user productivity and has an effect on the company's bottom line. By collecting this information, identifying patterns, and working to resolve them, an organization can take a large step forward to becoming more proactive in situations affecting its end users, which will affect productivity.

Operations Consoles

The Operations console provides a single user interface for Operations Manager. You should install this console on all management servers, including the server with the RMS emulator role. You can also install the console on desktop systems running Windows client operating systems. Accessing these consoles on another system removes some of the workload from your management servers. Desktop access to the consoles also simplifies day-to-day administration.

The number of consoles a management group supports is an important design specification. As the number of consoles active in a management group grows, the database load also grows. This load accelerates as the number of managed computers increases because consoles, either operator or web-based, increase the number of database queries on both the operational and data warehouse databases. From a performance perspective, it is best to run the Operations consoles from administrator workstations rather than from servers installed with OpsMgr features. Running the Operations console on the management servers increases memory and processor utilization on those systems, which in turn will slow down OpsMgr.

Operations Console Operating System Requirements and Prerequisites

Here are operating systems requirements and prerequisites you will want to know about:

- **Disk space:** Minimum of 1,024MB free disk space on *%SystemDrive%*.
- **File system:** *%SystemDrive%* must be formatted with the NTFS file system.
- **Operating system:** Windows Vista, Windows 7, Windows Server 2008, Windows Server 2008 R2, or Windows Server 2008 R2 SP 1. With the release of System Center 2012 SP 1, Windows Server 2012 including Server Core is now supported for installing the console. SP 1 also adds support for Windows 8 (non RT-versions) and removes Windows Vista support.
- **Processor architecture:** x64 for servers, x64, or x86 for a client computer.
- **Windows Installer version:** Windows Installer 3.1 or above.
- **.NET Framework:** .NET Framework 3.5 SP 1 and .NET Framework 4 (4.5 for Windows Server 2012 installations) required; you must also install the Microsoft .NET Framework 3.5 SP 1 hotfix.
- **Microsoft Report Viewer:** Microsoft Report Viewer 2010 Redistributable Package.
- **Windows PowerShell version:** Windows PowerShell 2.0; PowerShell 3.0 is required for administration of UNIX/Linux systems.

Operations Console High Availability/Redundancy

Installing the console on multiple systems provides high availability for this feature. The console can also be installed into a terminal services or Citrix farm to provide high availability and redundancy.

Web Console Servers

This server feature runs IIS and uses Silverlight to provide a web-based version of the Operations console. The new Web console provides very similar functionality to what is available in the full Operations console, and should provide a usable alternative to the Operations Manager full console in many situations. However, there are several key items the Web console does not provide, which are available using the Operations console. Here are the major differences:

- The Web console does not provide authoring, administration, or reporting functionality (although favorite reports can be saved and accessed under the My Workspace pane or by adding the URL for the report as a web page view). The Web console only includes the Monitoring and My Workspace workspaces.
- Informational alerts do not appear in the Web console.
- Events and event views do not appear in the Web console.
- Tasks run from the Web console cannot prompt for credentials.
- There are no options to personalize or create views within the Web console.
- You cannot create subscriptions in the Monitoring pane.

While there are several important limitations to the OpsMgr Web console, this version should provide sufficient functionality for many users that previously needed to use the full Operations Manager console. Most non-administrator and non-authoring users of Operations Manager should be able to use the OpsMgr Web console for a majority of day-to-day operations.

Web Console Operating System Requirements and Prerequisites

Here are operating systems requirements and prerequisites you will want to know about:

- **Server operating system:** Windows Server 2008 R2 SP 1. System Center 2012 SP 1 supports Windows Server 2012.
- **Processor architecture:** x64.
- **Web browsers:** Internet Explorer 7, Internet Explorer 8, Internet Explorer 9. Operations Manager 2012 SP 1 removes support for Internet Explorer 7 but adds Internet Explorer 10 and Silverlight 5.0.
- **Internet Information Services:** IIS 7.5 and later versions, with the IIS Management console and the following role services installed: Static Content, Default Document, Directory Browsing, HTTP Errors, HTTP Logging, Request Monitor, Request Filtering, Static Content Compression, Web Server (IIS) Support, IIS 6 Metabase Compatibility, ASP.NET, and Windows Authentication.

The IIS websites require a configured http or https binding.

Microsoft does not support installing the Web console on a computer that has SharePoint installed.

- **.NET Framework:** .NET Framework 3.5 SP 1 and .NET Framework 4 (4.5 for Windows Server 2012 installations) required.

NOTE: THE OPSMGR WEB CONSOLE AND SILVERLIGHT

It is not required that you install Silverlight on the server where you are installing the OpsMgr Web console, but it is often recommended. The 2012 Web console is Silverlight-based; installing Silverlight on the OpsMgr Web console server allows the console to be tested locally to validate it is working correctly.

Web Console Hardware Requirements

The Operations Manager Sizing Helper (referenced previously in the "Management Server Hardware Requirements" section) provides the following hardware requirements:

- **1-500 agents:** In this configuration the Web console can be installed on the Operations Manager operational database server.
- **501+ agents:** 2 Disk RAID 1, 8GB of memory, 4 Cores.

Web Console High Availability/Redundancy

You can configure redundancy for this feature by installing multiple Web console servers and leveraging NLB or other load-balancing solutions.

Operations Manager Agents

The Operations Manager agent is designed for both Windows and UNIX/Linux systems. The requirements vary based on the operating system installed.

Agent Operating System Requirements and Prerequisites

Here are the system requirements and prerequisites for the Operations Manager agent on Windows operating systems:

- **File system:** *%SystemDrive%* must be formatted with the NTFS file system.
- **Operating system:** Windows Server 2003 SP 2, Windows Server 2008 SP 2, Windows Server 2008 R2, Windows Server 2008 R2 SP 1, Windows XP Professional x64 Edition SP 2, Windows XP Professional SP 3, Windows Vista SP 2, or Windows 7. System Center 2012 SP 1 adds support for Windows Server 2012 and non-RT versions of Windows 8. (For embedded systems, POSReady, Windows XP Embedded Standard, or Windows XP Embedded Enterprise, or Windows XP Embedded POSReady, Windows 7 Professional for Embedded Systems or Windows 7 Ultimate for Embedded Systems.)

- **Processor architecture:** x64, x86, or IA64.
- **Windows Installer version:** Windows Installer 3.1 or above.
- **Microsoft Core XML Services version:** Microsoft Core XML Services 6.0 required for the Operations Manager agent.
- **Windows PowerShell version:** Windows PowerShell 2.0 (required for any agents that are monitored by a management pack using PowerShell scripts or modules).

Here is the supported UNIX and Linux operating systems for the Operations Manager agent (this list is subject to change; see the most current list of supported systems at http://technet.microsoft.com/en-us/library/jj656654.aspx#BKMK_RBF_UnixAgent):

- HP-UX 11i v2 and v3 (PA-RISC and IA64).
- Oracle Solaris 9 (SPARC) and Solaris 10 and 11 (SPARC and x86).
- Red Hat Enterprise Linux 4, 5, and 6 (x86/x64).
- Novell SUSE Linux Enterprise Server 9 (x86), 10 SP 1 (x86/x64), and 11 (x86/x64).
- IBM AIX 5.3, AIX 6.1 (POWER), and AIX 7.1 (POWER).
- With Service Pack 1, Microsoft added support for CentOS 5 (x86/x64), CentOS 6 (x86/x64), Debian 5 (x86/x64), Debian 6 (x86/x64), and Ubuntu 12.04 (x86/x64).

Agent Hardware Requirements

There are no Operations Manager-specific hardware requirements for systems running the OpsMgr agent. The hardware requirements are those of the minimum hardware requirements for the operating system itself.

Now that you have planned for each of the different features of Operations Manager, let's look at the licensing requirements for your design.

Planning for Licensing

Part of your decision regarding server placement should include evaluating licensing options for System Center 2012 Operations Manager.

To determine licensing costs, understand that there are two different levels of Management Licenses (MLs) available:

- **System Center 2012 Standard ML:** Used for lightly virtualized or non-virtualized environments
- **System Center 2012 Datacenter ML:** Used for highly virtualized environments

The System Center 2012 product also has three major changes from the previous licensing model:

- **Licenses are only required for the endpoints that are being managed:** No additional licenses are required for management servers or SQL Server.
- **Licensing based on processors:** Each license is processor-based and covers up to two processors.
- **Same capabilities for both license editions:** All server management licenses include the same components and can manage private cloud workloads.

Each device managed by the Operations Manager requires an ML, whether you are monitoring it directly or indirectly. (An example of indirect monitoring would be a network device such as a switch or router.) There are two types of device MLs:

- **System Center Client Management Suite Client ML:** Devices running client operating systems require client license MLs. This client license includes components for Service Manager, Operations Manager, Data Protection Manager, and Orchestrator.
- **Server ML (SML):** Devices running server operating systems require management license MLs.

As an example of how this would work, look at how you would license System Center 2012 Operations Manager for the Eclipse Company. Eclipse is a 1,000-user corporation with one major office. The company has decided to deploy one management group with a single management server. Eclipse is interested in monitoring 100 servers and is heavily virtualized; the majority of their servers are on Windows platforms, but a small percentage run on various forms of UNIX/Linux. Of their 100 servers, they are 90% virtualized running on four hosts. Two of their hosts are dual processors in Hyper-V, and two of their hosts are quad processors in VMware. The non-virtualized 10 servers in their environment have six servers with dual processors, two with quad processors, and two with eight processors.

The servers are all located in Eclipse's primary location in Frisco, Texas. Eclipse wants to monitor the standard Windows applications including Active Directory, DNS, Exchange, SQL Server, SharePoint, and Windows Server.

Eclipse is very interested in the new functionality available in System Center 2012 Operations Manager, especially network monitoring and .NET application monitoring. They have six core .NET applications that they want to monitor with APM, and some J2EE as well. From a network monitoring perspective they are interested in monitoring five network devices; these are split at three OSI Layers 3 and below and two OSI Layers 4.

Here are the assumptions defined for this environment:

- **Assumption #1:** With the new licensing model for System Center 2012, there is no need to license management servers or gateway servers unless they will be monitored with Operations Manager.

- **Assumption #2:** Server Management Licenses: Estimates in this section are based upon pricing shown as Volume License costs in the System Center 2012 Licensing FAQ:
  - **System Center 2012 Standard:** $1,323
  - **System Center 2012 Datacenter:** $3,607

  Actual pricing for most organizations may be lower depending upon your licensing agreements with Microsoft.
- **Assumption #3:** .NET monitoring is now integrated into Operations Manager so this does not affect licensing.
- **Assumption #4:** When monitoring network devices with Operations Manager anything OSI layer 3 and below does not require an SML.

Based upon these assumptions and the Eclipse environment, from a licensing perspective, Eclipse will be purchasing the following:

- **90 virtualized servers on 4 hosts:** Dual processor hosts (2 * $3,607) and 2 quad processor hosts (2 * 2 * $3,607) = $7,214 + $5,292 = $12,506.
- **10 physical servers:** 6 dual processor physical servers (6 * $1,323) and 2 quad processor servers (2 * 2 * $1,323) and 2 eight processor servers (2 * 4 * $1,323) = $7,938 + $5,292 + $10,584 = $23,814.
- **5 network devices:** 3 OSI layer 3 do not require licensing, 2 OSI Layer 4 (2 * $1,323) = $2,646.

The total estimate for Operations Manager licensing in this configuration is $38,966. Note that this figure is a ballpark estimate only. Your specific licensing costs may be higher or lower, based on the license agreement your organization has and your specific server configuration. Under this license approach, Eclipse now is licensed for the 100 server environment for the entire System Center cloud solution including App Controller, Operations Manager, Service Manager, Orchestrator, Virtual Machine Manager, Data Protection Manager, Configuration Manager, and System Center Endpoint Protection.

Table 4.2 lists the breakdown of the Eclipse environment from a licensing perspective, comparing it with the previous System Center Server Management Suite licensing, and Table 4.3 shows license grants between the two versions. Note that System Center 2012 Datacenter covers two processors per license, whereas Server Management Suite Datacenter (SMSD) (available with OpsMgr 2007), only covered one processor per license.

TABLE 4.2 Eclipse licensing information

Eclipse Scenario	System Center Server Management Suite	System Center 2012 Licensing Recommendation
Virtual		
	8 Hosts with dual procs	Quantity of 1 license each of Datacenter MLs for each host
	22 Hosts with quad procs	Quantity of 2 licenses each of Datacenter MLs for each host
Physical		
	60 machines with dual procs	Quantity of 1 license each for the Standard ML
	20 machines with quad procs	Quantity of 2 licenses each for the Standard ML
	20 machines with 8 procs	Quantity of 4 licenses each for the Standard ML
	Processor Count	Managed OSE Count
	Each license covers up to two physical processors, so you must count the number of physical processors on the server; divide that number by two, and then round up to the nearest whole number.	Each license permits you to manage up to two OSEs, so you must count the number of OSEs you will manage on the server, divide that number by two, and round up to the nearest whole number.

TABLE 4.3 License grants

Current License	New License	Conversion Rate
Server Management Suite Datacenter	1 System Center 2012 Datacenter license	2 to 1
Server Management Suite Enterprise (SMSE)	2 System Center 2012 Standard licenses	1 to 2
Any Single Enterprise Server ML	1 System Center 2012 Standard License	1 to 1
Any Single Standard Server ML	1 System Center 2012 Standard License	1 to 1
Any Single Management Server License	1 System Center 2012 Standard License	1 to 1
Virtual Machine Manager Server ML	1 System Center 2012 Datacenter	1 to 1

For more details on System Center 2012 Operations Manager licensing, see the Microsoft Volume Licensing Brief, available for download at http://www.microsoft.com/en-us/server-cloud/buy/pricing-licensing.aspx. The System Center 2012 Licensing FAQ is available at http://download.microsoft.com/download/8/7/0/870B5D9B-ACF1-4192-BD0A-543AF551B7AE/System%20Center%202012%20Licensing%20FAQ.pdf. (For your convenience, this URL is included as a live link in Appendix D, "Reference URLs.")

Creating the Plan

Once you have completed the design documentation, reviewed it, and received acceptance on the design, you need to create a plan to deploy the solution. Depending upon the complexity of the environment and the OpsMgr design, this might be as simple as a series of technical implementation steps or it could include a full project plan for the deployment. As part of this plan, you need to determine the steps required to provide a proof of concept (POC), pilot, or full production implementation of System Center 2012 Operations Manager.

Proof of Concept

A proof of concept should emulate the production hardware as closely as possible. Use production hardware for the OpsMgr solution if it is available, as that will most closely emulate your production environment. Isolate your POC network configuration from the production environment to allow full testing of servers without affecting their production equivalents. The planning phase identifies what needs testing as part of the POC—base testing on your business requirements.

For example, the following steps may comprise a high-level POC plan for a single-server System Center 2012 Operations Manager configuration:

1. Create an isolated network for POC testing.
2. Install the domain controllers.
3. Install the application servers that OpsMgr will monitor (or copy existing virtual servers or perform a Physical-To-Virtual migration of existing servers).
4. Create any required OpsMgr service accounts and confirm rights to service accounts.
5. Install the operational database, management server, data warehouse server, and reporting server.
6. Discover and install OpsMgr agents.
7. Install and tune management packs.
8. Configure recipients, notifications, and subscriptions.
9. Configure the Operations Manager Web console and OpsMgr reports.
10. Execute tests defined for the OpsMgr environment.

The actual content of your POC plan will vary depending on your specific environment, but it is important to plan the steps that will occur during the POC. This helps you avoid a "mad scramble" of installing systems without a plan, which you can leverage in both the POC and Pilot stages.

POC Challenges

The purpose of a proof of concept is to take the design that you have created, build it, and "kick the tires." Production is not a POC environment; when you are in a production environment you are past the proof of concept stage, and any errors you encounter have much larger costs than if you had caught them in the POC.

Virtual server environments make it much easier to create an isolated proof of concept environment.

A POC is also a great opportunity to try out a variety of management packs to see how they perform and what information they provide. If possible, retain your POC environment after moving on to later phases of your OpsMgr deployment; this provides an infrastructure to test additional management packs, management pack updates, and service packs in a non-business-critical environment.

Emulating a full production environment can be difficult within the confines of a POC. A primary reason is the hardware used in the POC environment; production-level hardware is not typically accessible. If the type of hardware used within the POC does not reflect what is in production, you might be unable to assess the speed or full functionality of your solution.

There are also some challenges inherent in any POC environment. How does one effectively scale for production? For example, if you are monitoring logon and logoff events, how do you generate enough events to monitor them successfully? From the authors' perspective, there are two options:

- Use scripts to generate sample events that can provide a large amount of event data.
- Use a POC exclusion, which is a document that describes items you could not effectively test within the POC environment. You could use this document during the pilot to determine what additional testing needs to occur during that phase.

POC environments tend to be isolated from the production network, removing potential interaction between the two environments. Network isolation removes the risk of inadvertently affecting production, but also adds complications because production network resources are not available (file shares, patching mechanisms, and so on). If your POC testing is in an isolated environment, you will want to establish a separate Internet connection to be able to patch systems and access non-POC resources.

Establishing an Effective POC

With the challenges inherent within the POC environment, how do you determine what to focus on during your POC? The authors suggest focusing on basic design validation and complexities within your specific environment:

- To validate your design, test the design and determine whether there are inherent issues. This process requires deploying your design and testing OpsMgr's basic capabilities including alerts, events, notifications, and functionality using the OpsMgr consoles. Part of basic design validation testing should also include tuning alerts and documenting your processes. If you are running in an isolated environment, you will also need a domain controller, DNS, and a mail server for email notification. Basic design validation should only require a small percentage of time within your POC.
- Spend the majority of the POC time testing the complexities specific to your design or environment. Say your design includes Tivoli or OpenView integration. This represents a complexity to test during the POC; you should deploy the other management software within your POC. Although this sounds rather difficult, how would you know how the two systems would interact without any testing? The only other option is testing within the production environment, which obviously is not recommended! (Before you decide to test in production, ask yourself how your boss would respond if your testing caused an outage in your production environment. The authors doubt he or she would be impressed with your testing methodology.)

  Other examples of potential complexities are connected management groups or multi-homed environments, highly redundant configurations, third-party management packs, and any requirements to create custom management packs. Your focus during POC testing should directly relate to the business requirements identified for your OpsMgr solution.

POC testing provides a safe method to effectively assess your design and make updates as required based on the results of your tests. Do not be surprised if your design changes based on the results of your POC tests.

Using a POC environment also enables you to configure production systems as multi-homed agents, reporting to both production and POC management groups. Utilizing a subsection of types of production systems can present insights for how Operations Manager will function in your production environment. This gives you a method to test changes to management packs, which you can then export and import into production.

Pilot

In this phase, you deploy your production hardware with System Center 2012 Operations Manager and integrate it into your production environment, but with a limited scope. In this phase, you are installing your production OpsMgr hardware and implementing the architecture you have designed.

Although you are deploying your production environment design, you will limit either the number of servers to which you are deploying OpsMgr agent or the number of management packs used. This phase provides a timeframe to identify how various management packs respond to the production systems you are monitoring. Out of the box, Operations Manager generates a limited number of alerts, but additional changes are often required to "tune" it to your particular environment. Initial tuning of OpsMgr may occur now, but is also limited in scope. You should also test any POC exclusions previously identified.

Track the amount of data gathered in the Operations database to determine whether that database has sufficient space on a per-server basis. You can check the amount of free space available on the operational database using Microsoft's SQL Server Management Studio. The Operations console also provides tracking for both database free space and log free space. To access this functionality for a SQL Server 2008 installation, navigate to **Monitoring -> SQL Server 2008 (Monitoring) -> SQL Database space**.

TIP: TRACKING OPERATIONS MANAGER DATABASE SIZE AND GROWTH

The SQL Database Space Report provides the ability to track the percentage of free space for trending purposes. This report is included with the SQL management pack.

Production Implementation

Here is where you move from pilot into full production deployment. There are two major methods generally used for deploying Operations Manager during this phase:

- **Phased deployment:** Using this approach, you will add in servers and management packs over time, allowing dedicated time for each server or management pack to tune alerts and events. A phased deployment takes a significant amount of time, but you have the benefit of thoroughly understanding each management pack and the effect it has on the servers in your environment. Using a phased approach can also mitigate risk.
- **Bulk deployment:** The second approach is a bulk deployment of Operations Manager, with limited notifications to an individual or group doing the deployment. If you deploy all servers and all management packs and your notification groups are thoroughly populated, the resulting flood of alerts may annoy the recipients in the notification groups, and they may just ignore the alerts. The benefit of a bulk deployment with limited notification is that you can deploy your entire OpsMgr environment quickly.

With either deployment approach, allow time to tune Operations Manager and your monitored systems in your specific environment. Tuning within OpsMgr is the process of fixing the problems about which OpsMgr is alerting, overriding the alerts for specific servers, or filtering those alerts. Details on implementing Operations Manager are included in Chapter 5, "Installing System Center 2012 Operations Manager."

Sample Designs

This chapter contains a considerable amount of guidance and information, which can be a bit overwhelming to absorb and translate into a design. However, many OpsMgr implementations fit into the same general guidelines. Taking a closer look at several sample organizations and their Operations Manager environment designs can give you some clues into your own organization's design. Let's look at four common OpsMgr designs for examples of how OpsMgr might be designed in your environment.

All-In-One Operations Manager

One of the most common configurations used in Operations Manager is an all-in-one configuration to provide a testing or lab environment. The goal of this environment is not necessarily to provide a high performance solution but rather a solution that can run on a single virtual server and provide an environment to test or develop management packs. Due to these constraints, the Operations Manager Sizing Helper was not used for this design.

An all-in-one OpsMgr environment uses a single server installed as a domain controller, management server, and database server. Each of the OpsMgr features is installed to the server, and agents report directly to that server. This environment does not provide the ability to test gateway functionality, as you cannot install a gateway on a management server. You could install an additional server to provide gateway functionality if that is a requirement.

To create an all-in-one Operations Manager environment, you will need a virtual server customized as follows:

- Install Windows Server 2008 R2 SP 1 (or Windows Server 2012 with System Center 2012 SP 1).
- Install DNS on the server; assign a static IP address and dcpromo the server to the first domain controller for a new domain.
- Install SQL Server 2008 R2 (or SQL Server 2012 with System Center 2012 SP 1).
- Install System Center 2012 Operations Manager features including the management server, database server, data warehouse, and reporting.

Small Organization

Eclipse is a 1,000-user corporation headquartered in Frisco. A single Windows domain, eclipse.com, is set up and configured across the enterprise. Company headquarters has 100 Windows Server 2008 systems performing roles as file servers, DHCP servers, Active

Directory domain controllers, DNS servers, SQL 2008 database servers, and Exchange 2010 messaging servers.

Due to a recent spate of system failures and subsequent downtime, preventable with better systems management, Eclipse's IT group looked at System Center 2012 Operations Manager as a solution to provide much-needed systems management for its server environment.

Because Eclipse will be monitoring approximately 100 servers, IT decided to deploy a single management group. The Operations Manager Sizing Helper recommended the following servers:

- Management server (Virtual)
- Operations Manager operational database server, Operations Manager data warehouse server, SSRS, and Web console server (Physical)

Eclipse created a single management group for all its servers, and distributed OpsMgr agents throughout the server infrastructure, which are all within their single forest environment. Figure 4.4 shows the OpsMgr environment for Eclipse.

Eclipse evaluated the Operations database retention and decided to use a retention period of four days to keep the database size down to approximately 2GB, per Table 4.4. It wants to retain its reporting data for a total of one year, and requires approximately 71GB of storage.

TABLE 4.4 Small organization OpsMgr design summaries

Design Point	Decision
Monitored servers	100
Management group	1
Management server(s)	1
Operational database retention	4 days
Estimated operational database size	2GB
Data warehouse database retention	365 days
Estimated data warehouse database size	71GB

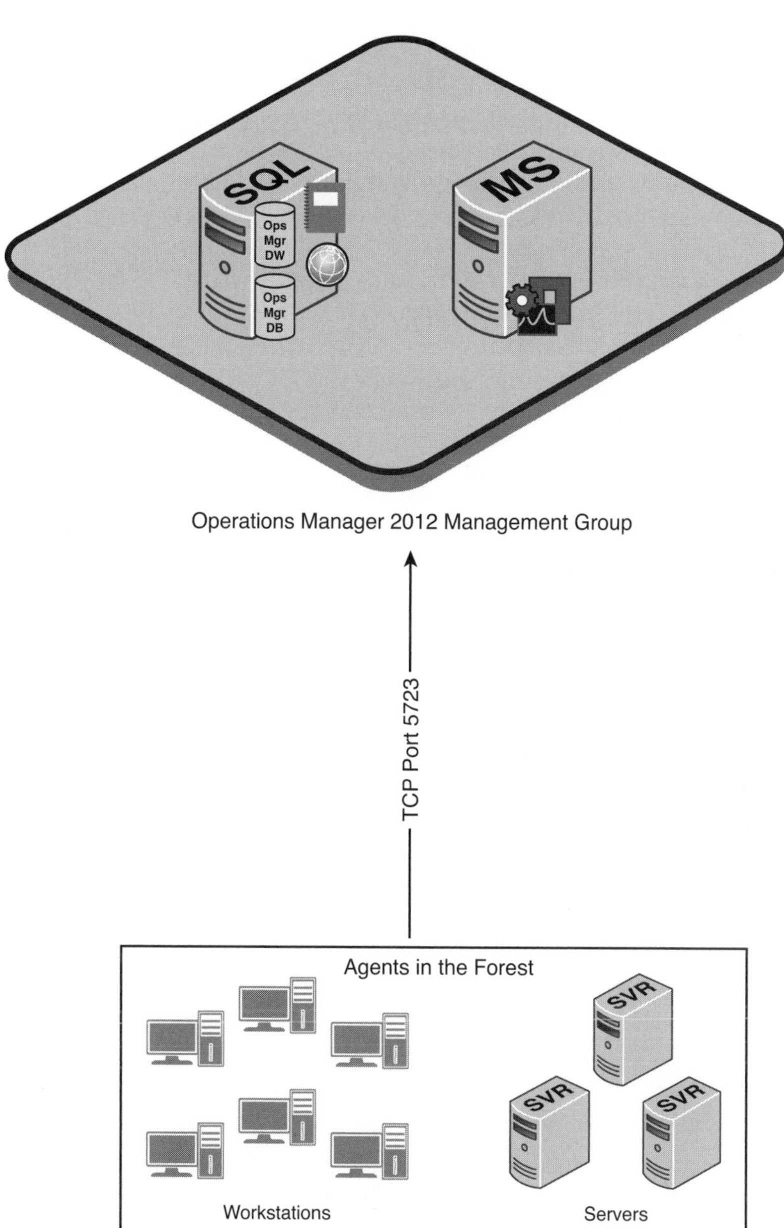

FIGURE 4.4 Small organization OpsMgr design.

4

Midsized Organization

After using OpsMgr for some amount of time, the Eclipse Corporation determined it needs redundancy and better performance for Operations Manager. The company also went through a round of acquisitions, increasing the number of managed computers to 500 servers. Eclipse re-evaluated its Operations database retention, deciding the default period of seven days better meets its requirements, giving it a database size of 12GB per Table 4.5. Eclipse still wants to retain its operations data for a total of one year, which requires approximately 356GB of storage when increasing the number of servers to 500, based on the information in the Operations Manager Sizing Helper.

TABLE 4.5 Midsized organization OpsMgr design summaries

Design Point	Decision
Monitored servers	500
Management group	1
Management server(s)	2
Operational database retention	7 days
Estimated operational database size	12GB
Data warehouse database retention	365 days
Estimated data warehouse database size	356GB

Using the Operations Manager Sizing Helper, Eclipse will have the following OpsMgr servers after the acquisition:

- Two management servers (Virtual); this includes an additional management server for high availability.
- Operations Manager operational database server (Physical).
- Operations Manager data warehouse server (Physical).
- SSRS and Web console server (Virtual).

Figure 4.5 shows the OpsMgr design for Eclipse in this scenario.

The dual-management server configuration allows Eclipse to assign 250 of its managed computers to each of the management servers. In the event of a failover, either management server could handle the load of 500 total agents. This gives Eclipse the fault tolerance it needs.

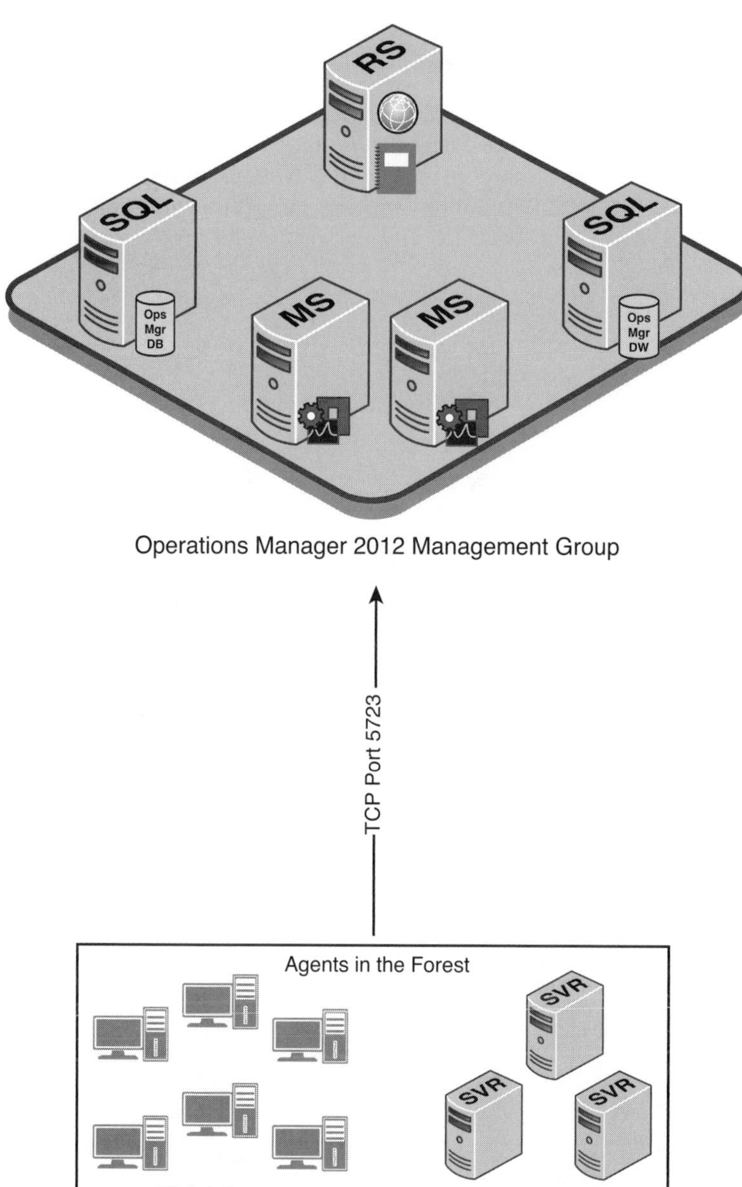

FIGURE 4.5 Medium organization OpsMgr design.

Geographically Dispersed Organization

Odyssey is a large, 10,000-user corporation with two major offices in Plano and Berlin. The Plano office hosts 1,500 servers, and the Berlin location hosts 500. Most of the servers run Windows Server 2008, but a minority is composed of Linux and Windows 2003 machines. Odyssey utilizes a single-domain Windows 2008 Active Directory.

Odyssey needs to deploy a robust server management system to increase its uptime levels and improve productivity across the enterprise. It chose System Center 2012 Operations Manager to accomplish this task.

The early design sessions indicated that a single management group could be utilized as long as the location in Germany uses a gateway server. Figure 4.6 shows Odyssey's design for OpsMgr, and Table 4.6 provides the key pieces of information for the Odyssey OpsMgr environment.

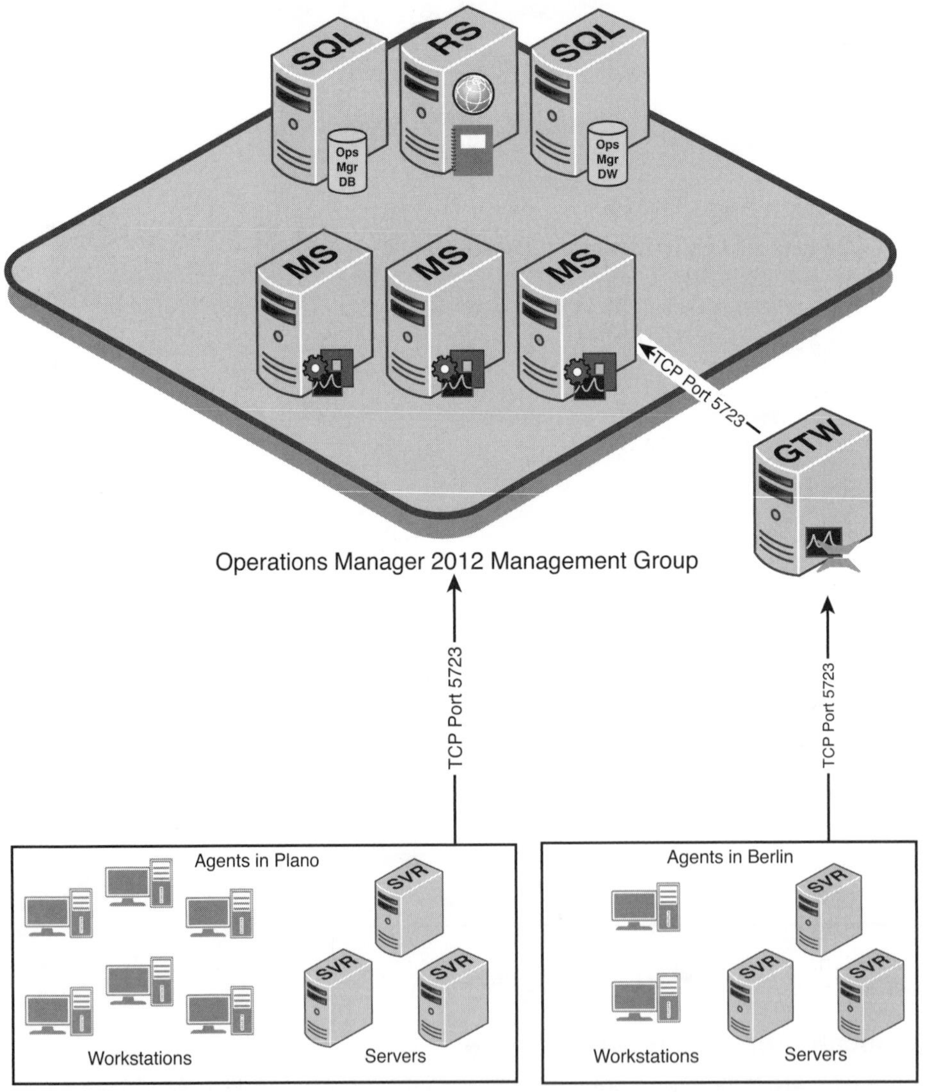

FIGURE 4.6 Geographically dispersed organization OpsMgr design.

TABLE 4.6 Geographically dispersed organization OpsMgr design summary

Design Point	Decision
Monitored servers	2,000
Management group	1
Management server(s)	3 (4 including the gateway server)
Operational database retention	7 days
Estimated operational database size	48GB
Data warehouse database retention	365 days
Estimated data warehouse database size	1.5TB

Here is the server recommendation for Odyssey, based on the Microsoft Operations Manager Sizing Helper:

- Three management servers (Virtual)

  One additional management server for high availability, one additional management server used for the gateway server to report to
- Operations Manager operational database server (Physical)
- Operations Manager data warehouse server (Physical)
- SSRS and Web console server (Virtual)
- Gateway server (Virtual)

  An additional gateway could be added in a second phase to provide additional redundancy.

This design allows the organization to have the entire organization within a single management group. Chapter 7, "Configuring and Using System Center 2012 Operations Manager," discusses groups in Operations Manager and using them to scope the Operations Manager console. Using groups in Operations Manager enables you to scope the Operations Manager console such that the Plano monitoring team sees only the Plano servers and the Berlin monitoring team sees only the servers in Berlin.

Fast Track

Planning for System Center 2012 Operations Manager is very similar to how it was in Operations Manager 2007. The following are key concepts to remember when planning OpsMgr 2012 designs compared to OpsMgr 2007 designs:

- The data warehouse is now a mandatory feature.
- There is no RMS but there is an RMS emulator role.
- Resource pools can assist with robustness and redundancy.

- Use at least two management servers unless you are building an all-in-one OpsMgr environment.
- Gateway servers are used not only for monitoring servers outside of the forest but also for monitoring across WAN links. While this is not new to Operations Manager 2012, there has been a shift in how OpsMgr gateways are used since the original release of Operations Manager 2007. (See Chapter 9 for additional information.)
- Microsoft provides an Excel hardware spreadsheet for database sizing and server specifications that is the recommended sizing tool for System Center 2012 Operations Manager. It is available at http://go.microsoft.com/fwlink/?LinkId=231853.
- Microsoft has made significant enhancements to the Web console, which makes it more usable in lieu of the Operations Manager full console.

Summary

This chapter explained why it is important to develop a plan before implementing OpsMgr into your environment. It discussed envisioning and planning and presented various sample designs. The next chapter discusses implementation of System Center 2012 Operations Manager.

CHAPTER 5

Installing System Center 2012 Operations Manager

IN THIS CHAPTER

This chapter discusses the procedures to install a new System Center 2012 Operations Manager (OpsMgr) environment on the Windows Server operating system. The goal of the chapter is to be a stand-alone reference to deploy all core OpsMgr features, enabling you to begin using OpsMgr for production as quickly as possible. Use Chapter 4, "Planning an Operations Manager Deployment," to guide your installation selections according to the architecture you have planned, and to point you to applicable sections of Chapter 9, "Complex Configurations." This chapter discusses two deployment scenarios, including pointers, tips, and potential troubleshooting areas. The scenarios encompass two types of environments:

- A single-server environment for lab, evaluation, and very small networks (with an option for a two-server variation that could support several hundred monitored computers)
- A distributed-server configuration for OpsMgr deployments that can support thousands of monitored computers

This chapter provides the information for a successful installation of each feature of an OpsMgr deployment seen on the setup wizard splash screen, except the Audit Collection Services (ACS) for UNIX/Linux option (see http://technet.microsoft.com/en-us/library/hh284670.aspx for information). Chapter 9 discusses implementations that are more complex; these include multi-location connected management groups, multi-homed deployments, and redundant configurations.

You should now be familiar with the concepts of how to plan for your deployment of System Center (SC) 2012 Operations Manager (if you still have questions, read Chapter 4). As a reminder, Chapter 4 discussed envisioning, planning, proof of concept, pilot, and implementation. The material in this chapter should be applicable during both the proof of concept and pilot phases of your OpsMgr deployment.

Planning Your Implementation

Before running the setup program, you need to determine what your Operations Manager environment will look like. As part of the planning discussions in Chapter 4, you should have answered the following questions:

- What servers will run the management server role?
- Which servers will run the database (DB) features?

  There are three databases: the operational database, data warehouse database, and the audit database used for ACS. The first two are required; the audit database is used if you implement ACS.
- What server will run the reporting feature?

  In addition to the OpsMgr data warehouse, two databases are associated with reporting: ReportServer DB and ReportServerTempDB.
- Which management server will be the ACS collector?
- Will some management servers be dedicated to resource pools?
- What servers will run the Web console feature?

In addition, if any of the following topics apply to you, you should also consult Chapter 9 on complex configurations and Chapter 24, "Operations Manager for the Service Provider," for certificate operations:

- Is redundancy for your OpsMgr solution a business requirement?
- Is your enterprise large and/or geographically distributed?
- Do you need to use a certificate authority to support gateways and agents in untrusted domains and workgroups?

Prior to installation, be sure you have completed discovery and planning for the OpsMgr server(s), database names, and the OpsMgr service accounts required to complete installation. To assist as a quick reference, this book includes a pre-installation checklist for your use as part of the online content for this book. (See Appendix E, "Available Online," for further information.) The checklist includes the major components you will be installing and information you need to have ready prior to beginning the installation.

Installation Prerequisites

The specific prerequisites for installing your OpsMgr environment depend on the components being installed. Microsoft designed System Center 2012 Operations Manager to be simple to install, with most of the OpsMgr components installed through wizards launched from the installation splash screen (Setup.exe), displayed in Figure 5.1.

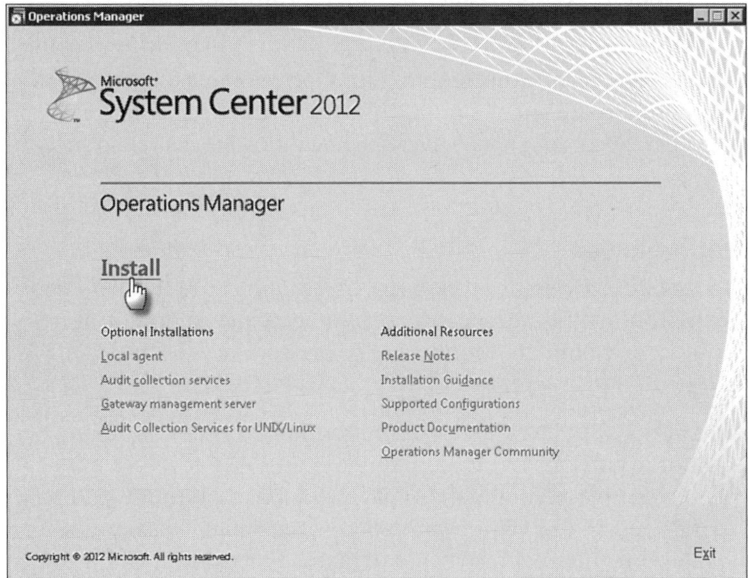

FIGURE 5.1 Setup splash screen for System Center 2012 OpsMgr.

Command line setup options exist for all procedures described using the wizards, and this chapter discusses those command line options. However, command line setup is primarily for automated and scale-out deployments of OpsMgr components. Using `Setup.exe` and the splash screen interface is the best way to ensure prerequisites are met, something not checked by the command line installer.

As shown in Figure 5.1, installation choices include the following Operations Manager components:

- System Center 2012 Operations Manager (the large Install link, which installs the server and console components)
- Local agent
- Audit collection service
- Gateway management server
- Audit Collection Services for UNIX/Linux

This chapter reviews each of these options (except ACS for UNIX/Linux, covered in Chapter 20, "Interoperability and Cross Platform"), discusses their prerequisites, and outlines a step-by-step of the installation process itself.

There are a number of prerequisites common to all OpsMgr components or that you should address prior to implementing OpsMgr. These prerequisites include server platforms (such as physical servers or virtual machines), domain and possibly certificate requirements, required Windows accounts, and the order for installing OpsMgr components.

You should have identified the server platforms required for Operations Manager components during the Planning phase. Record the names of the servers and SQL instances in your pre-installation checklist. Recommended server specifications are discussed in Chapter 4.

Windows Domain Prerequisites

You must install System Center 2012 Operations Manager in a Microsoft Active Directory (AD) and Windows server environment, but the computers to be managed do not necessarily need to be in the same, or any domain. Monitoring of network devices and UNIX/Linux computers is domain neutral by definition.

The Windows AD domain functionality level is simple: Windows 2000 native domain or higher, meaning you cannot install OpsMgr in domains running Windows NT 4.0 domain controllers (assuming you still have some!). All later versions of Windows domain functionality including Window 2003 and Windows 2008 are acceptable. OpsMgr does not have a forest functional level requirement, so other domains in the forest could be running at below Windows 2000 native domain functionality.

OpsMgr 2012 does not change the AD schema. After installation, some management packs such as the AD management pack will create containers in the domain configuration. An unusual but important requirement is you cannot install OpsMgr in an AD domain with a "flat" Domain Name System (DNS) domain space, this being an AD DNS domain with a single name and no suffix (such as *mydomain* rather than *mydomain.local* for the AD domain name).

Windows Security Accounts

Before starting the installation process, create the Windows security accounts needed for installation. Table 5.1 lists the Windows security accounts as well as the account name used for each in this book. Those that are optional are indicated as such.

TABLE 5.1 System Center 2012 OpsMgr Windows security accounts

Security Account	Name Used in This Book
Management Server Action Account	OM_MSAA
Data Access Service Account	OM_SDK
Data Warehouse Write Action Account	OM_DWWA
Data Reader Account	OM_DRA
Notification Action Account (Optional)	OM_NAA
Agent Action Account (Optional)	OM_AAA
Agent Installation Account (Optional)	(none)
Computer Discovery Account (Optional)	(none)
Gateway Server Action Account (Optional)	OM_GWAA
Global Security Group for OpsMgr Admins (Optional)	OM_Admins

These accounts are discussed in detail, including required security permissions, in Chapter 10, "Security and Compliance."

OpsMgr 2007 used a domain security group to control membership in the OpsMgr Administrators group. By default in OpsMgr 2012, the BUILTIN\Administrators group has OpsMgr administrator rights, which automatically includes Domain Admins. You can modify this setting after installation by navigating to **Administration** -> **Security** -> **User Roles** -> **Operations Manager Administrators** in the Operations console.

A common practice is to create a domain security group (such as OM_Admins) and make that domain security group a member of the local Administrators group on each management server. Since the OM_MSAA and the OM_DWWA OpsMgr service accounts must be local administrators on management servers, it is useful to have a security group that contains both accounts as well as the domain accounts of users that are OpsMgr administrators.

An additional consideration is the security status of the user performing your OpsMgr installation. The user account of this user requires sa (sysadm) rights on the SQL servers where the OpsMgr databases will be installed.

Software Requirements

Obtain all software required to deploy Operations Manager prior to installing the components. All server resources including the SQL databases must run on 64-bit (AMD64) processor architecture only. Here is the minimum software needed:

- **Operating system:** With the RTM version of OpsMgr 2012, Windows Server 2008 R2 Service Pack (SP) 1 is the only supported operating system (OS) for OpsMgr servers except the database; the OS of the SQL servers hosting the OpsMgr databases can be either Windows Server 2008 Service Pack 2 or Windows Server 2008 R2 Service Pack 1. System Center 2012 Service Pack 1 adds support for Windows Server 2012.

- **Database:** 64-bit editions of SQL Server 2008 Service Pack 1, 2, or 3, SQL Server 2008 R2, or SQL Server 2008 R2 Service Pack 1. Additionally, the SQL Server versions must be consistent for the management group, with the same version of SQL used for all databases. System Center 2012 Service Pack 1 adds support for SQL Server 2012.
- **Product setup media:** System Center 2012 Operations Manager; this is the software distribution shown in Figure 5.2.

Windows PowerShell 2.0, Windows Remote Management, and Microsoft Core XML Services (MSXML) version 6.0 are required for most components and automatically enabled in a default installation of Windows Server and OpsMgr.

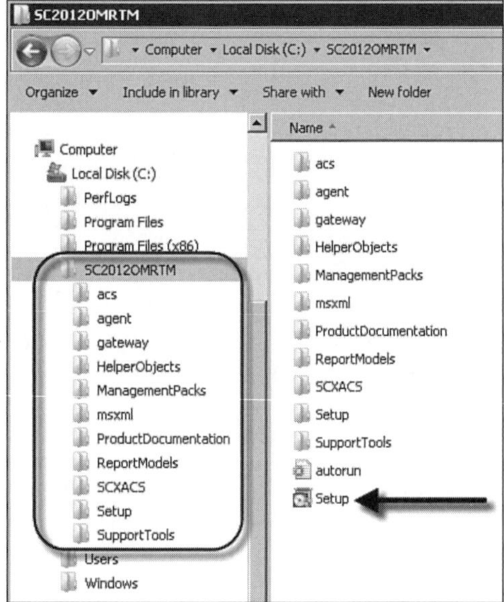

FIGURE 5.2 System Center 2012 OpsMgr software media distribution viewed in Windows Explorer.

TIP: VISIT MICROSOFT UPDATE BEFORE OPSMGR SETUP

It is a best practice to check for updates for all Microsoft products after installation, so that new features installed by setup can be immediately updated. Have your system fully updated before starting the OpsMgr installation so the number of updates required afterwards is small and identifiable.

If you attempt to install OpsMgr by running Setup (see arrow in Figure 5.2) on a Windows Server 2008 R2 SP 1 or above system that does not have both .NET 3.5 and .NET 4.0 installed (.NET 4.5 for Windows Server 2012), you get the error message similar to that seen in Figure 5.3. If one version of .NET is installed but not the other, you receive a similar error that specifies which version of .NET is missing.

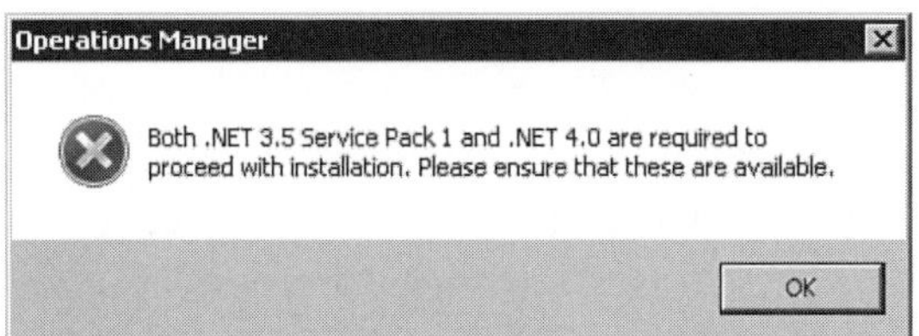

FIGURE 5.3 .NET 3.5 SP 1 and .NET 4.0 or above are required on most OpsMgr servers.

Enable .NET 3.5 Feature

All server roles except for the gateway server, including all SQL database servers, require .NET 3.5 Service Pack 1. To install .NET 3.5 Service Pack 1, add this feature in Server Manager as shown in Figure 5.4. To install this feature using the command line, type the following commands, pressing Enter after each command:

```
Import-Module ServerManager
Add-WindowsFeature as-net-framework
```

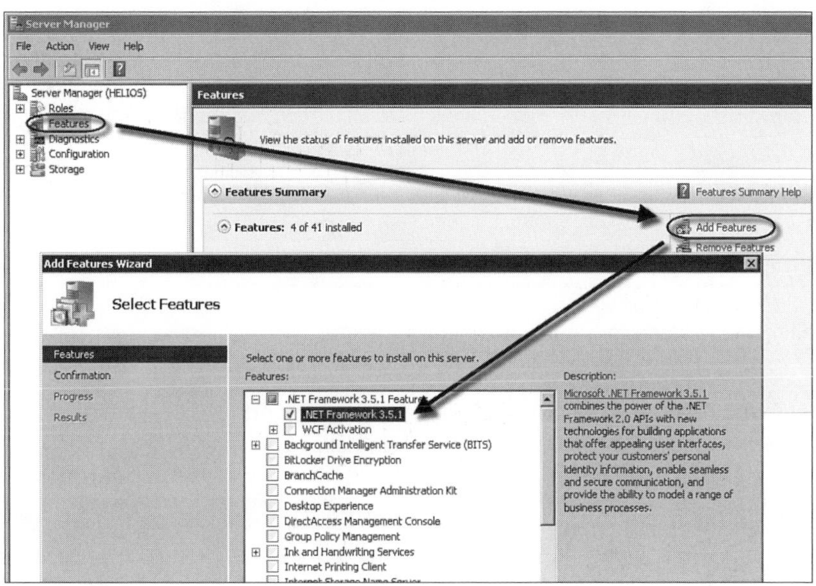

FIGURE 5.4 Enabling .NET Framework 3.5 SP1 using Server Manager.

Install .NET 4/4.5 Framework

All server roles (other than gateway servers that are not involved in monitoring network devices or UNIX/Linux computers), including the operational and data warehouse SQL database servers, require .NET Framework 4. (If running Windows Server 2012, .NET Framework 4.5 is required.) To install this software component, you can either use

Microsoft Update as displayed in Figure 5.5, or download and run an installer from the Internet.

To perform .NET Framework 4 downloads, you can use a small web installer that requires Internet access to complete, or a larger standalone download not requiring Internet access:

- **Web Installer:** Download Microsoft .NET Framework 4 (Web Installer), dotNetFx40_Full_setup.exe (869KB), from http://www.microsoft.com/download/en/details.aspx?id=17851.
- **Standalone Installer:** Download Microsoft .NET Framework 4 (Standalone Installer), dotNetFx40_Full_x86_x64.exe (48.1MB) from http://www.microsoft.com/download/en/details.aspx?id=17718.

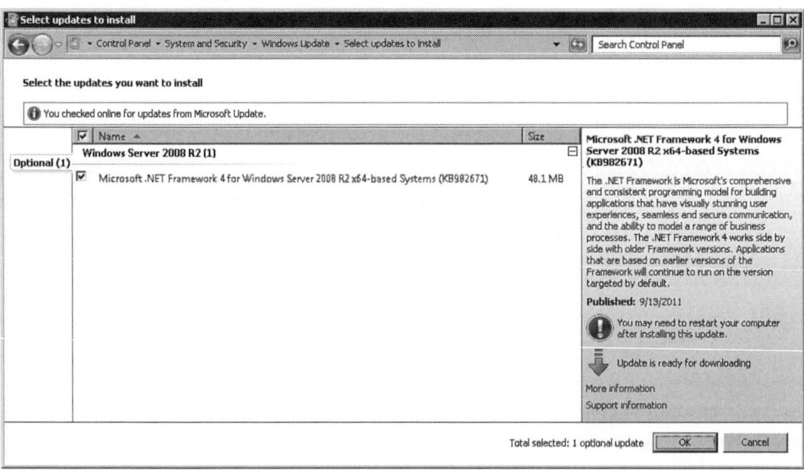

FIGURE 5.5 Installing .NET Framework 4 using Windows Update.

Be sure to select the correct language if not English. Save the file and run it locally on any prospective OpsMgr server. The .NET Framework 4 web installer is displayed in Figure 5.6.

CAUTION: INSTALL IIS FIRST IF INSTALLING THE WEB CONSOLE

If installing the Web console component, it is important the web server role (Internet Information Services) be enabled before installing .NET Framework 4. Consult the "Web Console" section later in the chapter before proceeding, in particular the Tip containing a command line to install necessary web server components. If you installed IIS after installing .NET Framework 4, you must register ASP.NET with IIS. Open a command prompt window by using the Run as Administrator option and then run the following command: **%*windir*%\Microsoft.NET\Framework64\v4.0.30139\aspnet_regiis.exe -r**.

Windows Server 2012 does not support aspnet_regiis.exe. .NET Framework 4.5 integration can only occur using the Windows Server 2012 Server Manager Add Roles and Features Wizard. If you did not install IIS and .NET Framework 4.5 at the same time, remove the IIS role, then add it and the .NET 4.5 feature at the same time.

Command line options for the .NET Framework 4 redistributable installation program are discussed at http://msdn.microsoft.com/library/ee942965(v=VS.100).aspx#command_line_options. (Information for .NET Framework 4.5, which is used with Windows Server 2012 installations, is available at http://msdn.microsoft.com/library/ee942965.aspx#command_line_options. You can download .NET Framework 4.5 for installation from http://www.microsoft.com/en-us/download/details.aspx?id=30653.)

The command line switches shown here set passive mode (meaning no prompts are displayed) and prompt if the system needs to be restarted.

```
dotNetFx40_Full_setup.exe /passive [/promptrestart]
```

After installing .NET 3.5 SP 1 and .NET Framework, the authors recommend visiting Windows Updates to check for updates. Install all critical or security updates to .NET frameworks unless otherwise indicated in your environment.

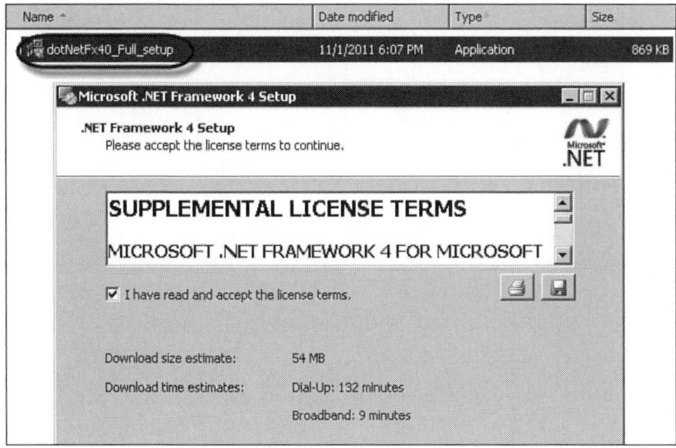

FIGURE 5.6 Installing .NET Framework 4 for Windows 2008 R2 using the web installer.

About the Enable SNMP Feature

The authors do not recommend installing this feature on management servers or gateways, unless they are physical servers that depend on SNMP-based agents for server hardware monitoring. OpsMgr 2012 does not leverage or interact with the Windows SNMP feature or service in any way. The Windows SNMP trap service is not used by OpsMgr and must not be enabled on OpsMgr servers monitoring network devices.

Install Report Viewer 2010

All console instances require Microsoft Report Viewer 2010 Redistributable Package, which you can download from http://www.microsoft.com/download/en/details.aspx?displaylang=en&id=6442. The Microsoft Report Viewer 2010 Redistributable Package includes controls for viewing reports designed using Microsoft reporting technology, including the Operations console. Preinstall Report Viewer on any server you plan to install the Operations console on, including management servers. Microsoft provides a single ReportViewer.exe file to download for all supported Windows operating systems. After downloading the file, perform these steps:

1. Run ReportViewer.exe after download. Running the installer without switches launches a GUI install as shown in Figure 5.7.
2. A second screen requires two clicks to accept the license terms and install the update.
3. Click **Finish** when setup is complete.

To avoid the four clicks required to install when using the GUI interface, here are some convenient ReportViewer.exe command line options:

- Silently install the package and create log file RV2010Setup.log in the temp folder:

```
ReportViewer.exe /q /log %temp%\RV2010Setup.log
```

- Install with no user interaction unless reboot is needed to complete the operation:

```
ReportViewer.exe /passive /promptrestart
```

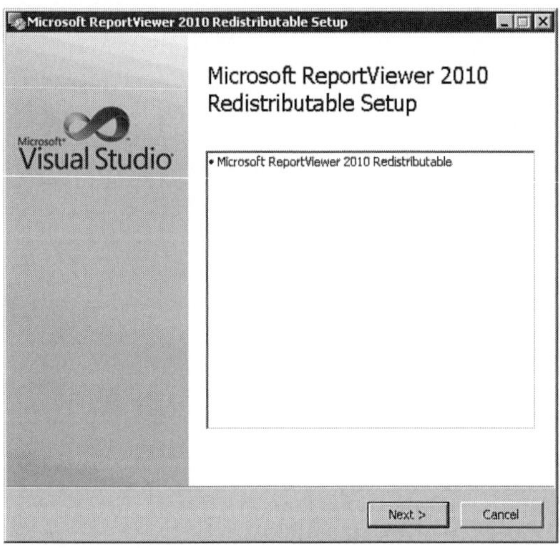

FIGURE 5.7 Installing the ReportViewer 2010 Redistributable Package.

Recommended Order of Installation

Although the recommended order for installation depends on the components you install, there are certain components you cannot install before others. For example, you cannot deploy a report server before a management server.

The list in this section is a recommended order of installation. It focuses on installing the core features first (including all features required to manage agents, view reports, and use consoles), followed by optional features such as gateway servers. Finally, you will deploy OpsMgr agents to the management group servers themselves and import core management packs to begin monitoring. Here is the list of features to install:

1. First management server
2. Additional management server(s)
3. Reporting server
4. Web console(s)
5. Gateway server(s)
6. ACS
7. Agents
8. ACS forwarders
9. Operating system management packs

Single Server Deployment

A single-server deployment is designed for training, evaluation, and very small networks; this is for monitoring several dozen computers or less. You must use a fairly robust computer to host a single-server deployment, even for evaluation purposes. Since an "all-in-one" OpsMgr management server includes the Web console, reporting, and database features, all prerequisites discussed in each of the installation sections of the "Multiple Server Deployment" section will apply. For example, you need to have Web and SQL Server services installed locally before beginning OpsMgr installation.

A minimum recommended production configuration for OpsMgr 2012 is two computers, with one computer for the OpsMgr databases, and one for the OpsMgr management server components. The "Two Server Deployment" section describes a two-server deployment model.

Capacity planning really drives your OpsMgr architecture. Consider that there are many possible OpsMgr architectures. All installation sections apply for all size deployments, except that the gateway server feature is only installed in the multiple-server model. For larger distributed deployments, add management servers and gateway servers by repeating the additional management server installation procedure in the "Additional Management Servers and Consoles" and the "Gateway Server" installation sections to scale out and/or add redundancy.

Single Server Deployment: High-level Order of Installation

Here is the recommended high-level order of installation when installing an OpsMgr 2012 single-server deployment on a new Windows Server 2008 R2 SP 1 computer (or in the case of OpsMgr 2012 SP 1, Windows Server 2012):

1. Enable the Web server role (Internet Information Services) in Server Manager.
2. Enable the .NET 3.5 feature in Server Manager and install .NET 4 Framework (.NET 4.5 Framework for Windows Server 2012).
3. Install SQL Server 2008 or 2008 R2 with database and report server features (or in the case of OpsMgr 2012 SP 1, SQL Server 2012).
4. Install Report Viewer 2010.
5. Visit Windows Updates and update all components including service packs.
6. Install Operations Manager from the setup splash screen, selecting all features: management server, management console, Web console, and reporting server.
7. Optionally, to deploy ACS, install Audit Collection Services from the setup splash screen.
8. Import operating system management packs using the Operations console.

Two Server Deployment

A common small deployment consists of two computers, a management server, and a database server. As discussed in the "Single Server Deployment" section, this is the minimum production architecture for an enterprise deployment of OpsMgr. This two-server management group model, with robust resources for SQL Server, could manage several hundred servers. Here is a recommended high-level order of installation on two servers:

1. Enable the Web server role (Internet Information Services) in Server Manager on the database computer.
2. Install SQL Server 2008 or 2008 R2 with database and report server features on the database computer. (In the case of OpsMgr 2012 SP1, you can install SQL Server 2012.)
3. Enable the .NET 3.5 feature in Server Manager and install .NET 4 Framework on both computers.
4. Install Report Viewer 2010 on both computers.
5. Visit Microsoft Updates and update all components including service packs on both computers.
6. On the management server, install Operations Manager from the setup splash screen, selecting two features: management server and Operations console.
7. On the database computer, install Operations Manager from the setup splash screen, selecting two features: Web console and reporting server.
8. Optionally, to deploy ACS, install Audit Collection Services on the management server computer from the setup splash screen; then upload the ACS reports to the SQL Server Reporting Services (SSRS) instance.

9. Use the Operations console to push an agent to the database computer.
10. Use the Operations console to import operating system management packs.

Multiple Server Deployment

At this point, the chapter has discussed a single-server and two-server deployment model. A management group can scale up to include dozens of computers dedicated to OpsMgr—management servers, gateways, consoles, and Web consoles that manage many geographically distributed data centers. The installation sections that follow deploy a 10-server management group model—with a dedicated SQL Server for each OpsMgr database—which could manage several thousand servers. Table 5.2 lists the servers used in a fictitious organization (Odyssey) and their roles. Figure 5.8 diagrams this server configuration. You can use Table 5.2 and Figure 5.8 as a reference throughout this book.

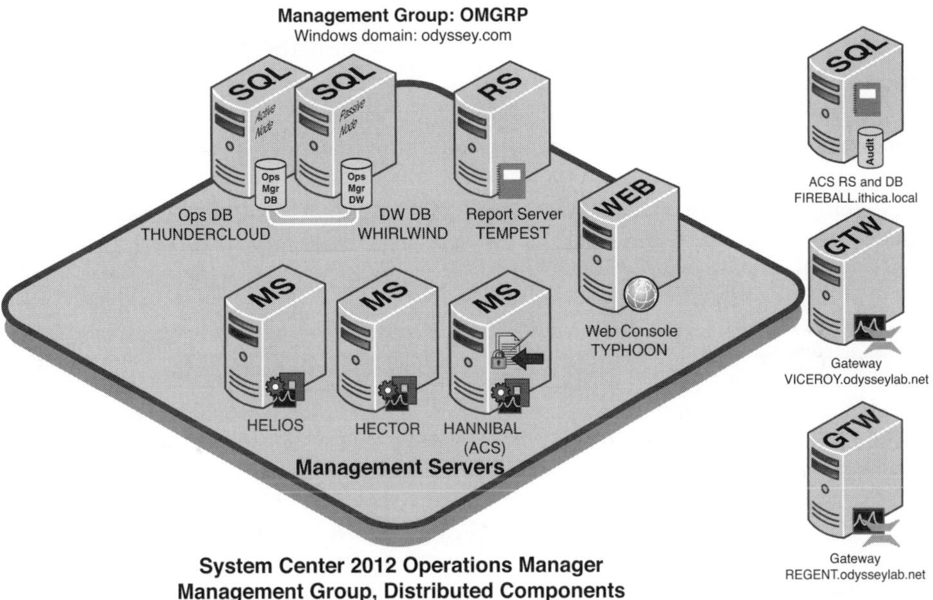

FIGURE 5.8 Multiple server System Center 2012 Operations Manager configuration.

TABLE 5.2 OpsMgr servers and their roles

Server	Operations Manager Role
Thundercloud	Operational database server
Whirlwind	Data warehouse database server
Tempest	Report server

Server	Operations Manager Role
Helios	First management server
Hector	Additional management server
Hannibal	Additional management server and ACS collector
Typhoon	Web console
Viceroy	Gateway server
Regent	Gateway server
Fireball	ACS report server and database

SQL Server

OpsMgr requires that x64-processor versions of SQL Server 2008 or 2008 R2 be installed and available at setup time (System Center 2012 SP 1 supports SQL Server 2012 as well). You must always pre-install SQL Server either locally in the case of a single server deployment, or on as many as four additional servers for a multi-server deployment (one SQL Server system each for the operations, data warehouse, and ACS databases, plus a SQL Server Reporting Services server). SQL Server installation is an independent activity that occurs before installing OpsMgr. The OpsMgr setup wizard creates and installs the database during setup of the first management server. Note that you must enable Full Text Search in SQL Server; see http://technet.microsoft.com/en-us/library/hh298609.aspx for deployment requirements.

TIP: WINDOWS FIREWALL MAY NEED INBOUND RULES ON SQL SERVERS

A default installation of SQL Server may not allow remote access to the computer. SQL needs inbound firewall rules that permit ports TCP 1433 and UDP 1434. SQL Server Reporting Services requires ports TCP 80 and TCP 443. After installing SQL Server and SSRS, check the local Windows Firewall and create rules as needed.

First Management Server

Now that you have determined your OpsMgr architecture and naming conventions, created security accounts in Active Directory, prepared your SQL server database resources, and installed the common prerequisites as described in the "Installation Prerequisites" section, you are ready to install your OpsMgr management group. Begin by installing the first management server. The first management server runs the root management server (RMS) emulator role by default, and demands the most memory and processor resources of any management server.

Like the operational database server, the first management server should be among the most powerful computers in the management group. If designing your management group for high availability and utilizing the All Management Servers Resource Pool, all management servers eligible for promotion to the RMS emulator role should have equally high performance specifications. Setup will not install with less than 2GB memory, and will issue a warning but allow installation if there is between 2GB and 4GB. In the enterprise environment, consider four processor cores and 16GB memory as a recommended minimum machine configuration for the RMS emulator role.

The System Center 2012 Operations Manager setup experience begins with performing the following steps from the OpsMgr distribution media:

1. Run Setup; from the splash screen previously seen in Figure 5.1 click the large **Install** link to start the setup wizard.
2. After the Launching Operations Manager Setup splash screen appears, you will see the dialog displayed in Figure 5.9.
3. Select **Management server** and **Operations console**. As shown in Figure 5.10, clicking the expand arrow to the right of a feature exposes a drop-down description of the feature. Click **Next**.

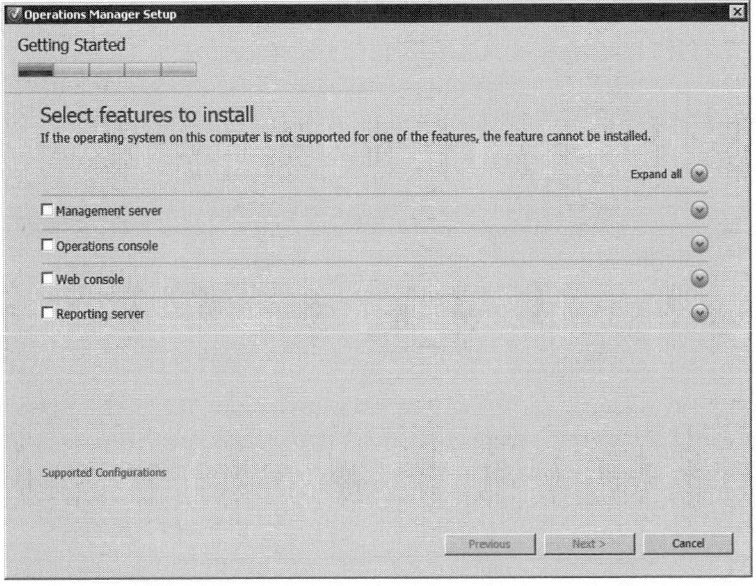

FIGURE 5.9 The first installation wizard screen after starting setup.

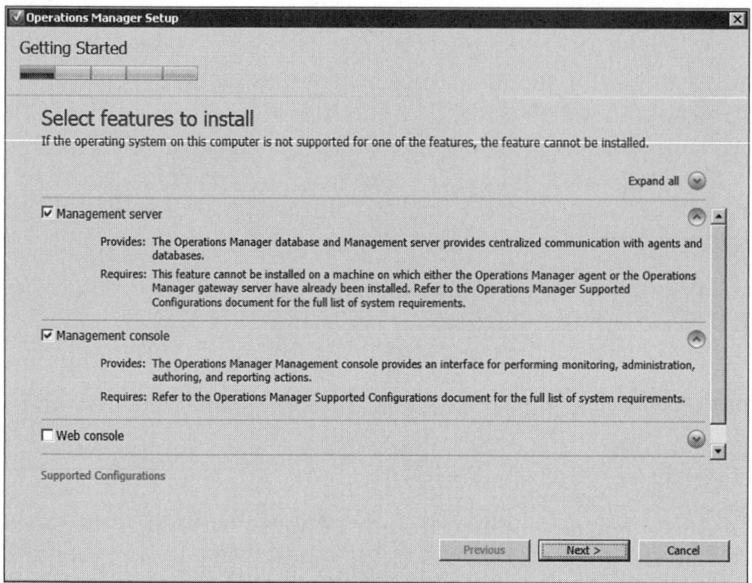

FIGURE 5.10 Installing the management server and console features.

4. On the next screen, select **Installation location**. The default location is *%ProgramFiles%*\System Center 2012\Operations Manager, where the Server and Console folders will be created. Accept the default or specify an alternative path, and click **Next**.

TIP: LEADING SPACES IN THE INSTALLATION FOLDER PATH ARE REMOVED

In Setup, when you designate the installation directory on the Installation location page, should a folder have any leading spaces, those spaces are removed. For example, "D:\ OpsMgr" will be changed to "D:\OpsMgr."

5. Setup continues with the message **Verifying that your environment has the required hardware and software.** If there are issues, the message **The Setup wizard cannot continue** appears as shown in Figure 5.11. This means additional hardware resources or software is required to continue.

TIP: SUPPORTED CONFIGURATIONS GUIDE LISTS OPSMGR PREREQUISITES

The setup wizard includes a link, displayed in Figure 5.11, **Review full system requirements**, that provides details on prerequisites. The linked document is the Supported Configurations for System Center 2012 document at http://technet.microsoft.com/en-us/library/hh205990.aspx. Consult this authoritative reference online for the most detailed descriptions of software prerequisites.

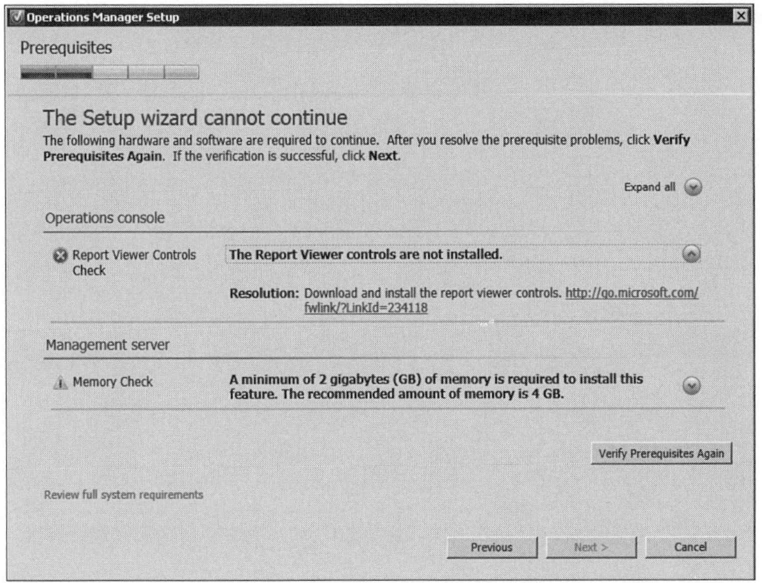

FIGURE 5.11 Prerequisite checking for minimum installation requirements.

6. After resolving any prerequisite problems, click **Verify Prerequisites Again**, shown on Figure 5.11. If the verification is successful, click **Next**.

7. At the Specify an installation option page shown in Figure 5.12, create the first management server in a new management group. Type a management group name that is unique in your organization. The name of the OpsMgr 2012 management group for the Odyssey environment used in this book is **OMGRP**. After you create a management group, you cannot change its name without reinstalling the management group. Click **Next**.

8. Accept the license agreement by selecting **I have read, understood, and agree with the license terms** and clicking **Next**.

9. Configure the operational database as demonstrated in Figure 5.13. The setup process creates and configures the database:

   - Type the server name and instance name of the SQL Server to be used for the operational database. Use the format *<ComputerName>**<instance>*. Modify the port if needed from the default 1433.

   - Click again in the server name or port number area to cause a validation process for the database server. Notice there is no option to use an existing database; you cannot install OpsMgr 2012 using a pre-created database.

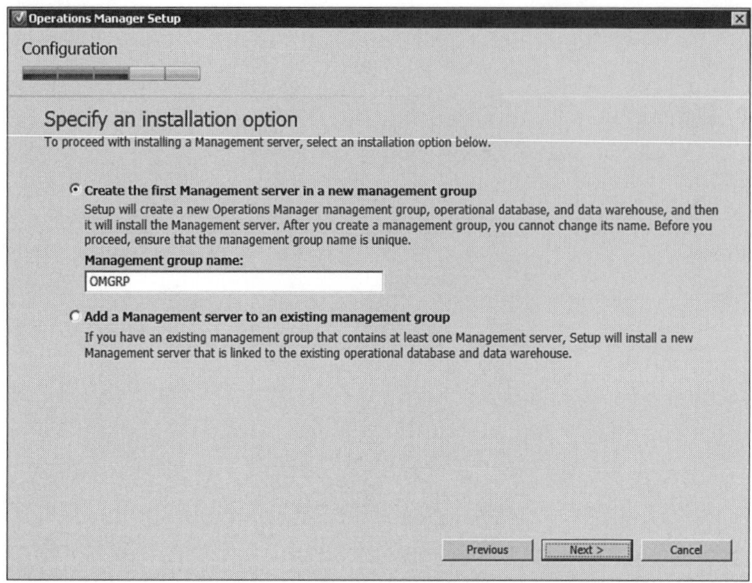

FIGURE 5.12 Create the first management server in a new management group.

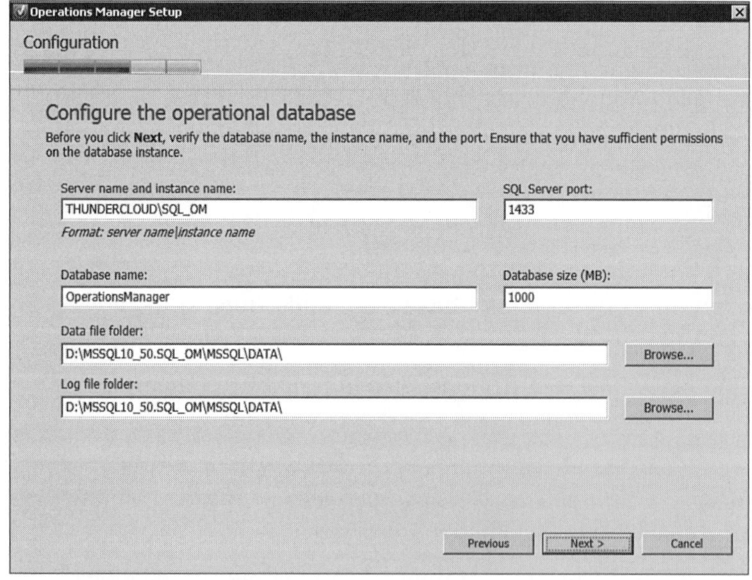

FIGURE 5.13 The operational database is created during management server setup.

- If there is an error validating the SQL Server, a red "X" icon appears to the left of the server name. Hover over the icon to read the details on the database error as shown in Figure 5.14.

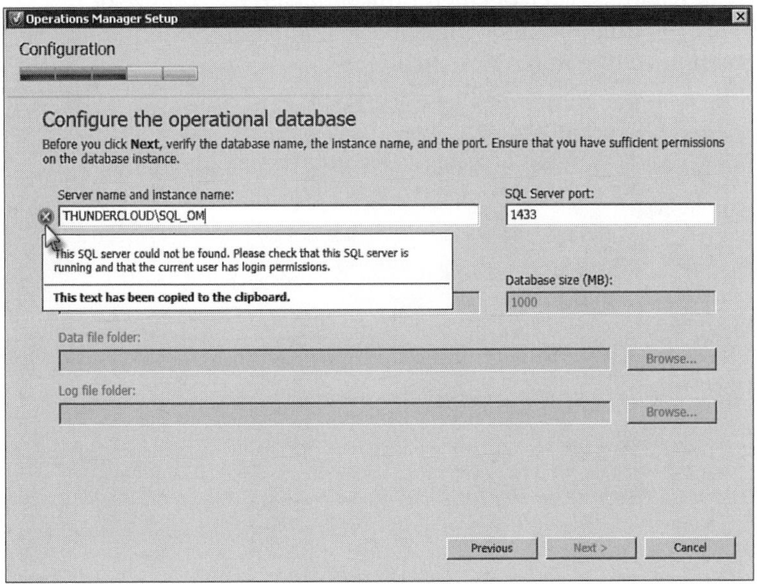

FIGURE 5.14 Hover over the error icon to read details on the database issue.

- Once Setup validates the SQL Server for the operational database, the Database name section of this page becomes modifiable. Leave the default database name of **OperationsManager** and size of 1000MB. Modify the data file and log file folders if they are different from the SQL defaults as determined by Setup. Click **Next**.

10. Configure the data warehouse database as demonstrated in Figure 5.15. Unlike the operational database installation step, there is an option to use an existing data warehouse database.

- Type the server name and instance name of the SQL Server to be used for the data warehouse database. Use the format *<ComputerName>**<instance>*. Modify the port if needed from the default 1433.
- Click again in the server name or port number area to initiate a validation process for the database server. If you have implemented a central data warehousing solution, multiple management groups are able to share a common data warehouse database.
- If there is an error validating the SQL Server, a red "X" icon appears to the left of the server name. Hover over the icon to read the details on the database error as shown previously in the example in Figure 5.14.
- Once Setup validates the SQL Server for the data warehouse database, the Database name section of the page becomes modifiable. For a new installation,

leave the default database name of **OperationsManagerDW** and size of 1000MB. Modify the data file and log file folders if different from the SQL defaults as determined by Setup. Click **Next**.

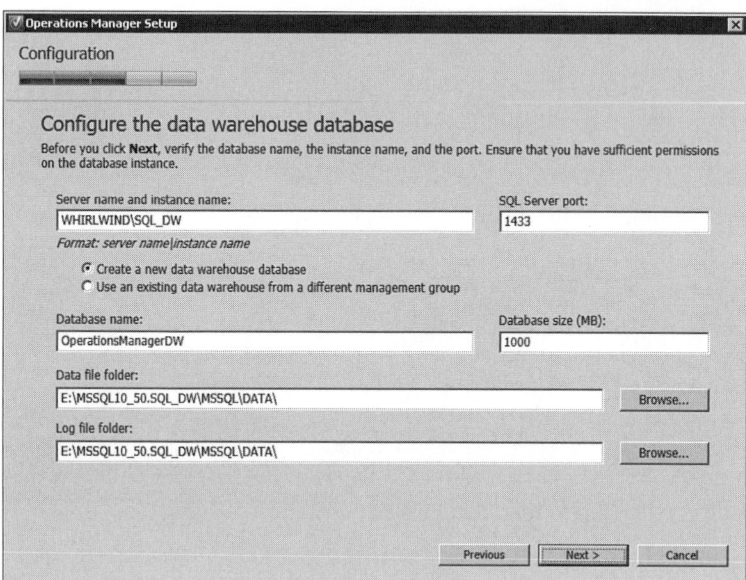

FIGURE 5.15 A data warehouse database is required for all management groups.

11. Configure the Operations Manager accounts as shown in Figure 5.16. As discussed in the "Windows Security Accounts" section, you should identify and configure each of these accounts prior to this step in the installation process.

- The management server action account is typically a named domain user account. This account is used to gather operational data from providers and perform actions such as installing and uninstalling agents on managed computers. This book uses OM_MSAA as the management server action account, which must be a member of the local Administrators group on the management server.
- The System Center Configuration service and System Center Data Access service account can run as Local System if the SQL Server for the operational and data warehouse databases is installed locally on the management server (a single server deployment). This credential reads and updates information in the operational database and is assigned the sdk_user role in this database. This book uses OM_SDK as the System Center Configuration service and System Center Data Access service account. Like the management server action account (OM_MSAA), this account must be a member of the local Administrators group on the management server.

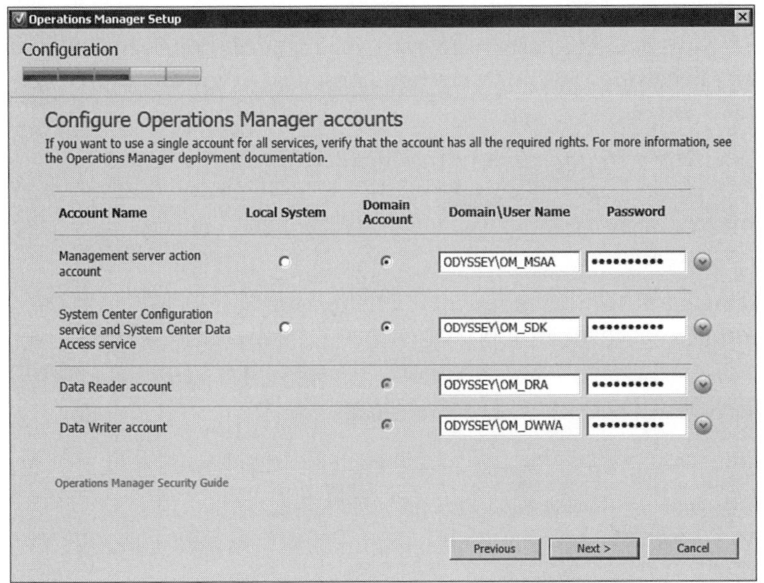

FIGURE 5.16 Specifying the management and database service accounts.

- The Data Reader and Data Writer accounts must be named domain user accounts. The Data Reader account is used to deploy reports; it is the user account SSRS uses to run queries against the data warehouse. The Data Reader account is also used as the SSRS IIS Application Pool account that connects to a management server. The Data Writer account reads data from the operational database and writes data from a management server to the data warehouse database.

After clicking **Next**, Setup verifies whether a specified action account is a domain administrator account. The warning box shown in Figure 5.17 will state this is not recommended for security reasons. The Operations Manager deployment documentation provides additional information. Click **OK** on the warning to proceed with setup if this is your intention.

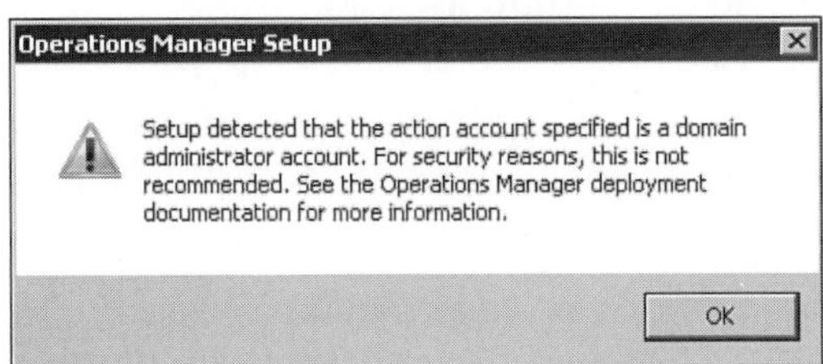

FIGURE 5.17 Specifying the management and database service accounts.

12. At the Help improve System Center 2012 Operations Manager page displayed in Figure 5.18, indicate your desire to participate in these programs. These settings can be changed after installation in the Operations console at **Administration -> Settings -> General -> Privacy**.

- **Customer Experience Improvement Program:** Participating anonymously helps Microsoft collect data about your use of OpsMgr to identify possible improvements for the product. An example is which menu items get used the most, and in what order.
- **Error Reporting:** Participating anonymously helps Microsoft identify common issues with OpsMgr when an error occurs, such as Dr. Watson.

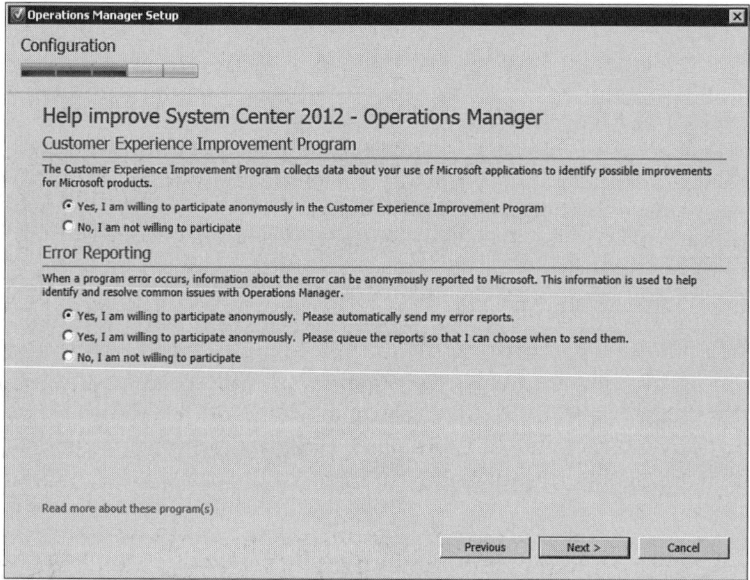

FIGURE 5.18 Anonymous participation in these programs can improve OpsMgr.

13. At the Management Server Installation Summary page shown in Figure 5.19, review your selections for the features you are installing. To continue, select **Install**. Here are the main activities that occur during setup:

- An Installation progress page provides status on components as they are installed and configured. If there is a fatal setup error, the wizard will halt after performing a rollback.
- The operational and data warehouse databases are created in their respective SQL instances. SQL security roles such as apm_datareader and sdk_users are created in the operational database, and roles OpsMgrReader and OpsMgrWriter in the data warehouse database.
- Default management packs are imported into both databases.

- The Operations console and Operations Manager Shell user applications are installed and the management server services are installed and started. Here are the new services created during management server installation, and a description of the purpose of each:

  OpsMgr VSS Writer (Manual start): This service is responsible for the backing up and restore of System Center data.

  System Center Audit Forwarding (Disabled): Sends events to an ACS collector for storage in a SQL database.

  System Center Data Access Service (Automatic start): Reads and writes to the SQL Server databases.

  System Center Management (Automatic start): The System Center Management service monitors the health of the computer and possibly other computers in addition to the computer it is running on (management servers, gateway servers, and computers running distributed applications may proxy management traffic to other computers).

  System Center Management APM (Disabled): Monitors the health of .NET applications on this computer.

  System Center Management Configuration service (Automatic start): Maintains the configuration of the management group for all management servers.

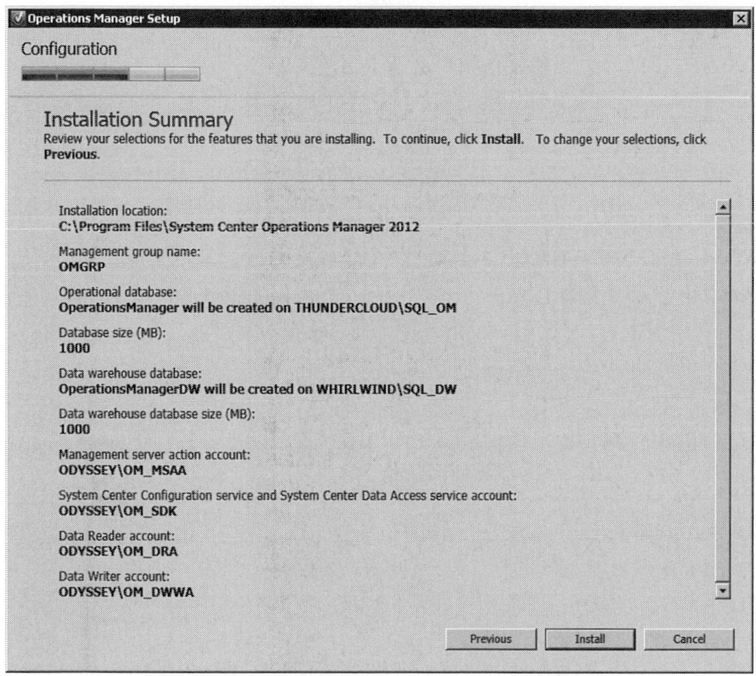

FIGURE 5.19 Summary of settings for installation of the first management server.

TIP: CHECK OUT THE ONLINE RELEASE NOTES DURING SETUP

During setup (which may take some time), click the link to review the online release notes (http://technet.microsoft.com/en-us/library/hh561709.aspx) for the latest information. The top portion of the release notes is an index of sections such as Installation and Management Servers—clicking on these links takes you to the portion of the release notes dealing with that subject.

14. Setup is complete when all green checkmarks appear in the left column as shown in Figure 5.20. Any component that failed to install is marked with a red "X."

- Click **Close** to accept the default actions to complete the wizard and start the management console without launching Microsoft Update (see the "Before Pressing the Close Button on the Setup Wizard" sidebar).
- You will also want to **Exit** the OpsMgr installer that is still open (refer to Figure 5.1), unless you wish to review the other online links such as Product Documentation.
- Figure 5.21 shows the Operations console soon after initial installation of the first management server.

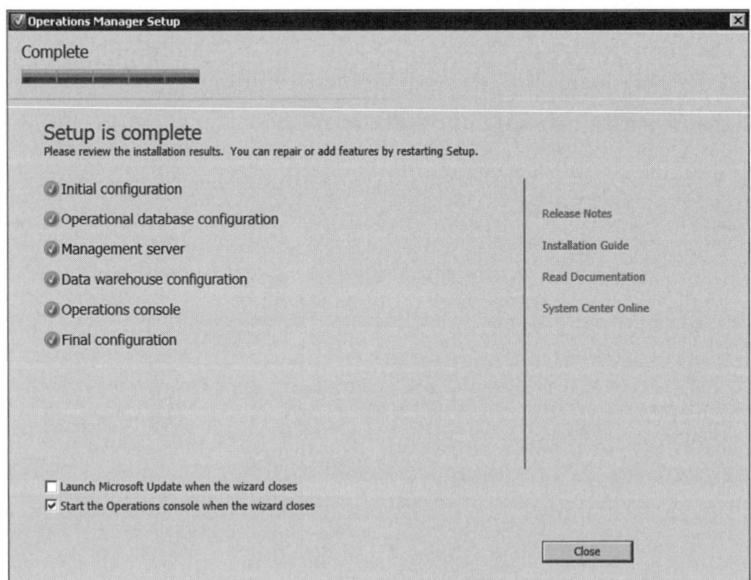

FIGURE 5.20 Successful setup of the first management server.

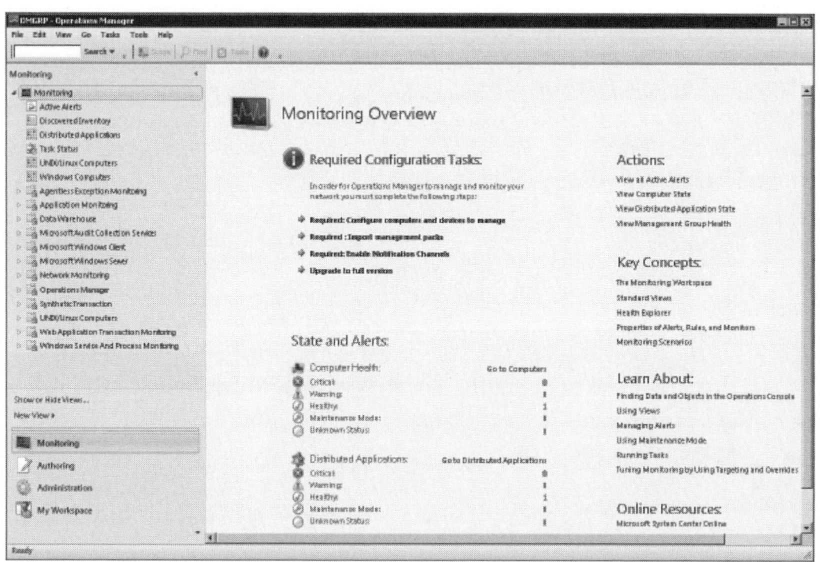

FIGURE 5.21 A new OpsMgr management group in the Operations console.

TIP: BEFORE PRESSING THE CLOSE BUTTON ON THE SETUP WIZARD

Consider reversing the default checked option boxes in the setup completion screen, that is, select **Launch Microsoft Update when the wizard closes**, and deselect **Start the Operations console when the wizard closes**. If you open the console immediately, you might see some alerts involved with initial startup of the management group that will soon close automatically. If you wait several minutes to open the console, you can avoid unnecessary evaluation of alerts. It is also a good idea to check online for updates from Microsoft Update immediately after installation if Internet connectivity is available to the server. So check for updates while you wait to open the console!

To install the first management server using the setup command line program, open an elevated command prompt, go to the folder containing the OpsMgr software media distribution, and run the command in Listing 5.1.

LISTING 5.1 Command line installation: First management server

```
setup.exe /silent /install /components:OMServer
/ManagementGroupName:"<ManagementGroupName>"
/SqlServerInstance:<ComputerName\instance>
/DatabaseName:<OperationalDatabaseName>
/DWSqlServerInstance:<ComputerName\instance>
/DWDatabaseName:<DWDatabaseName>
/DatareaderUser:<domain\UserName>
/DatareaderPassword:<password>
```

```
/DataWriterUser:<domain\UserName>
/DataWriterPassword:<password>
/EnableErrorReporting:[Never|Queued|Always]
/SendCEIPReports:[0|1]
/UseMicrosoftUpdate:[0|1]
/ActionAccountUser:<domain\UserName>
/ActionAccountPassword:<password>
/DASAccountUser:<domain\UserName>
/DASAccountPassword:<password>
/AcceptEndUserLicenseAgreement
```

If installing the first management server using the Local System account, replace the `/ActionAccountUser`, `/ActionAccountPassword`, `/DASAccountUser`, and `/DASAccountPassword` switches with these two:

```
/UseLocalSystemActionAccount
/UseLocalSystemDASAccount
```

Additional Management Servers and Consoles

Install additional management servers in the existing management group to add capacity, redundancy, and features to your management group. As mentioned in the "First Management Server" section, if you are architecting your management group for high availability (meaning you have more than one management server), all management servers in the All Management Servers Resource Pool must have equally high performance specifications.

You can install stand-alone instances of the Operations Manager console on other server and desktop operating system environments. This lets users interact with OpsMgr without logging on to a management server desktop. Install consoles on computers of OpsMgr administrators, authors, and operators. Do not install too many instances of the console, just those necessary to do the job. Each console instance creates a recurring requirement to update the console software, and the more consoles open at once, the greater the impact on overall performance and scalability of the management group. (For additional information on console performance, see Chapter 7, "Configuring and Using System Center 2012 Operations Manager.")

Prerequisites such as .NET Framework, and the steps listed next are the same for each additional management server and console. (Steps that require input on databases and service credentials are not presented during console-only installation.)

Perform the following steps from the OpsMgr distribution media:

1. Run Setup and from the Setup splash screen previously seen in Figure 5.1, click the large **Install** link to start the setup wizard.
2. After a splash screen Launching Operations Manager Setup, you will see the Select Features to install dialog previously displayed in Figure 5.9.

3. Select **Management server** and **Operations console** in the dialog previously shown in Figure 5.10. If installing the console only, select only **Operations console**. Click **Next**.

4. Select **Installation location**. The default location is *%ProgramFiles%*\System Center 2012\Operations Manager. Accept the default or specify your alternative path, and click **Next**.

5. Setup continues with the message **Verifying that your environment has the required hardware and software**. If issues are found, the message **The Setup wizard cannot continue** appears. This means additional hardware resources or software is required to continue.

6. After resolving any prerequisite problems, click **Verify Prerequisites Again**. If verification is successful, click **Next**.

7. At the Specify an installation option page shown in Figure 5.22, select **Add a management server to an existing management group**. Click **Next**.

8. Accept the license agreement by selecting **I have read, understood, and agree with the license terms** and clicking **Next**.

9. Configure the operational database as demonstrated in Figure 5.23. Specify the database previously created by the setup process on the first management server:

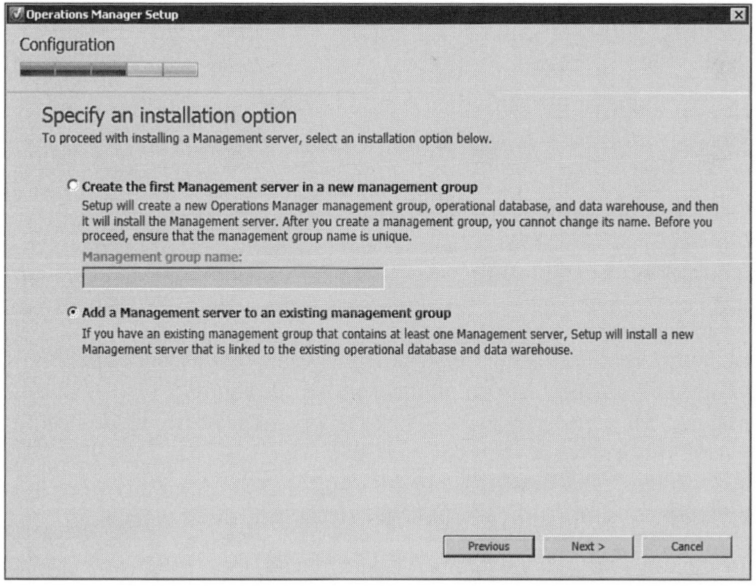

FIGURE 5.22 Add a management server to an existing management group.

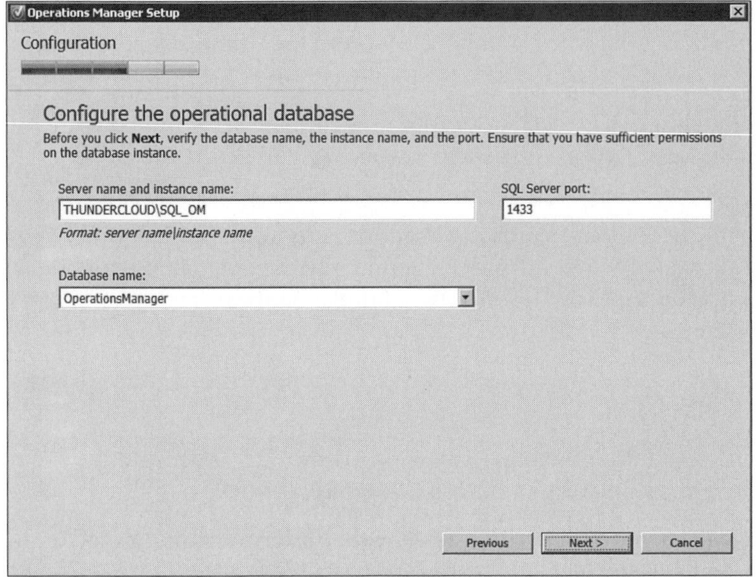

FIGURE 5.23 Specify the operations database for additional management server.

- Type the server and instance name of the SQL Server used for the operational database. Use the format *<ComputerName>**<instance>*. Modify the port if needed from the default 1433.
- Click in the server name or port number area to cause a validation process for the database server. When Setup can validate the SQL Server of the operational database, the Database name drop-down list becomes active. Select the database name, OperationsManager by default. Click **Next**.

10. Configure Operations Manager accounts as shown in Figure 5.24. Use the same accounts specified during step 11 of the installation process on the first management server.
11. After clicking **Next**, Setup verifies whether a specified action account is a domain administrator account. The warning box previously shown in Figure 5.17 will state this is not recommended for security reasons. Click **OK** on the warning to proceed with setup.

CAUTION: DO NOT GIVE SERVICE ACCOUNT DOMAIN ADMIN PRIVILEGES

While it is convenient and often seen in lab and demo environments, the authors do not recommend making OpsMgr service accounts members of the Domain Admins global security group in production scenarios. The MSAA and SDK accounts (which should not be Domain Admins in normal practice) should be made members of the local Administrators group on management servers.

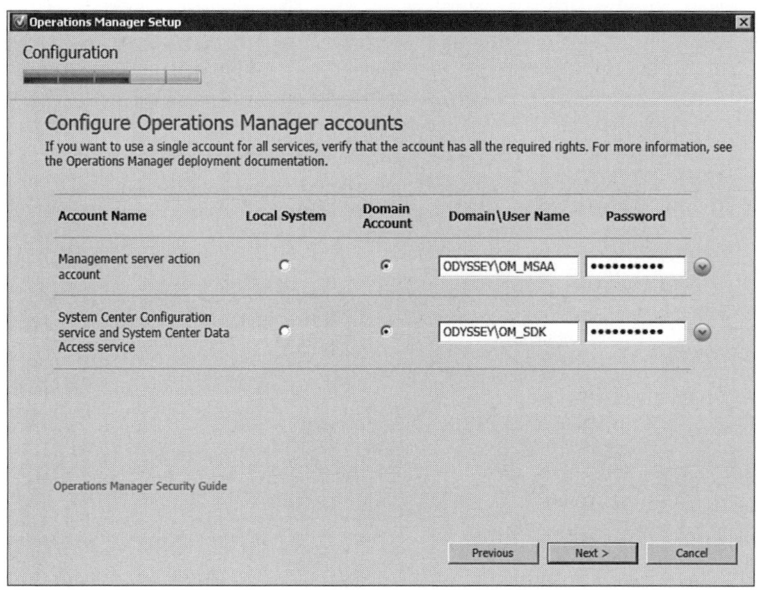

FIGURE 5.24 Management service accounts for additional management server.

12. At the Help improve System Center 2012 Operations Manager page, indicate your desire to participate in these programs. Click **Next**.

13. At the Installation Summary page, review your selections for the features you are installing as shown in Figure 5.25. To continue, press **Install**.

14. Setup is complete when all green checkmarks appear in the left column as previously shown in Figure 5.20. Any component that failed to install is marked with a red "X."

- Select **Close** to accept the default actions to complete the wizard and start the Operations console without launching Microsoft Update (see the "Before Pressing the Close Button on the Setup Wizard" sidebar).
- You will also want to **Exit** the OpsMgr installer that is still open (refer to Figure 5.1).

To install an additional management server using the setup command line, open an elevated command prompt, navigate to the folder containing the OpsMgr software media distribution, and run the command in Listing 5.2.

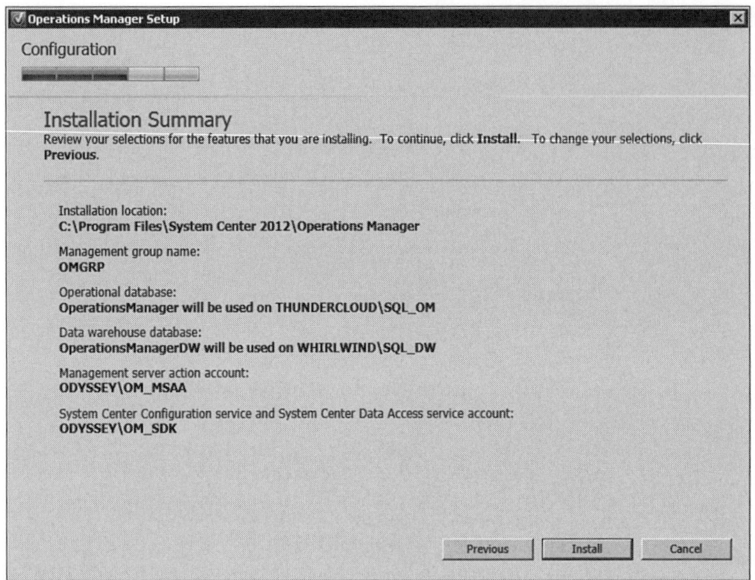

FIGURE 5.25 Summary of settings for installation of additional management server.

LISTING 5.2 Command line installation: Additional management server

```
setup.exe /silent /install /components:OMServer
/SqlServerInstance:<ComputerName\instance>
/DatabaseName:<OperationalDatabaseName>
/SendCEIPReports:[0|1]
/UseMicrosoftUpdate:[0|1] /ActionAccountUser:<domain\UserName>
/ActionAccountPassword:<password>
/DASAccountUser:<domain\UserName>
/DASAccountPassword:<password>
```

To install a stand-alone console using the setup command line, open an elevated command prompt, navigate to the folder containing the OpsMgr software media distribution, and run the command in Listing 5.3.

LISTING 5.3 Command line installation: Console

```
setup.exe /silent /install /components:OMConsole
/EnableErrorReporting:[Never|Queued|Always]
/SendCEIPReports:[0|1]
/UseMicrosoftUpdate:[0|1]
```

Reporting Server

This procedure installs the System Center 2012 Operations Manager reporting server on a dedicated server that hosts SSRS. You cannot install any other applications using SSRS on the instance of SQL Server used by OpsMgr reporting, as the Operations Manager reporting installation integrates security of the selected SSRS instance with OpsMgr role-based security; this means any reports previously installed on the SQL Server could become inaccessible. OpsMgr needs its own dedicated SSRS instance, one that is fully functional in a default SSRS configuration, before you install OpsMgr reporting.

Since each OpsMgr management group has only one reporting server, the capacity of the SSRS computer is directly dependent on the expected utilization of the reporting feature. In addition to each scheduled report, each console and Web console running reports consumes processor and memory on the SSRS computer when reports run.

TIP: CONFIRM PERMISSIONS OF ACCOUNT USED DURING INSTALLATION

Before installing OpsMgr reporting, ensure the user account you plan to use during installation has SQL sa (sysadm) permissions on all databases. The Data Warehouse Write account (OM_DWWA in this book) is granted necessary SQL Server logon rights during setup. Service accounts only require local administrative rights on the SQL servers; it is the user account performing the installation that requires elevated SQL permission. (Members of the local Administrators group have SQL logon rights by default.)

Confirming Installation Readiness of the Reporting Server

Verify that SSRS is configured correctly and running before attempting to install the OpsMgr Reporting server feature. Spending several minutes confirming readiness can save a significant amount of time recovering from a setup failure. Follow these steps to install a reporting server running SQL Server 2008 R2 Reporting Services:

1. Click **Start** -> **Programs** -> **Microsoft SQL Server 2008 R2** -> **Reporting Services Configuration Manager**. Connect to the instance on which you installed SSRS.
2. Confirm the Report Service Status is **Started** in the central pane. In the navigation pane, select **Report Manager URL**. This displays the Report Server virtual directory Uniform Resource Locator (URL) as a hyperlink in the central pane.
3. Click on the Report Manager URL hyperlink such as http://<*ComputerName*>:80/Reports. You may be prompted to enter your domain credentials again to open the Report Manager web page.
4. If you are able to view an empty but functional SSRS home page, you are ready to install the OpsMgr Reporting service role.
5. If you cannot successfully perform step 4, do not proceed with OpsMgr reporting installation. Focus first on getting the base SSRS Report Manager to work in a default configuration.

Install the Operations Manager Reporting Server

After confirming readiness of the local SSRS instance, perform the following steps from the OpsMgr distribution media:

1. Run Setup; from the splash screen previously seen in Figure 5.1, click the large **Install** link to start a setup wizard.
2. After the Launching Operations Manager Setup splash screen, you will see the Select features to install dialog previously displayed in Figure 5.9.
3. Select **Reporting server** as shown in Figure 5.26. Click **Next**.

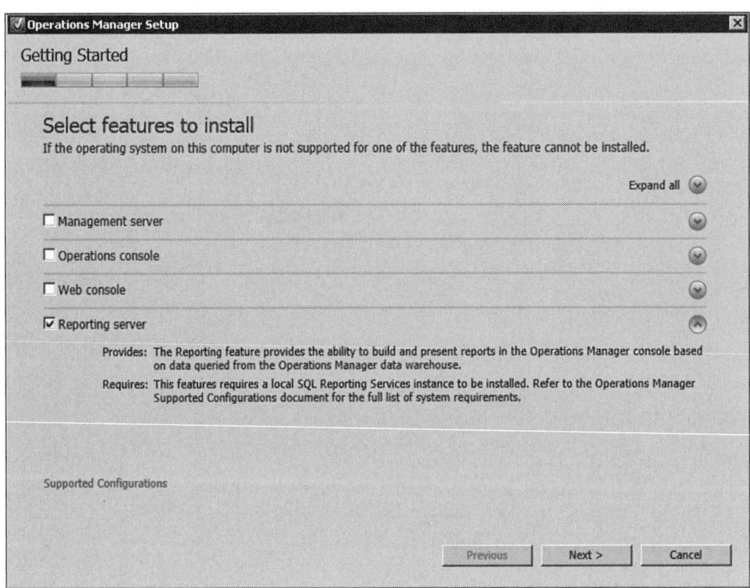

FIGURE 5.26 Selecting the Reporting server role for installation.

4. Select **Installation location**. The default location is *%Programfiles%*\System Center 2012\Operations Manager. Accept the default or specify your alternative path, and click **Next**.
5. Setup continues with the message **Verifying that your environment has the required hardware and software**. If there are issues, the message **The Setup wizard cannot continue** appears. This means additional hardware resources or software is required to continue.
6. After resolving any prerequisite problems, click **Verify Prerequisites Again**. If verification is successful, click **Next**.
7. At the Specify a Management server page, enter the name of a management server to be used by the reporting features only, shown in Figure 5.27. The specified server will handle data associated with specific management servers or management

groups. Normally, this is either the name of the first OpsMgr 2012 management server you installed, or if you are using a load-balanced management server pool, specify the virtual server name of the pool. Click **Next**.

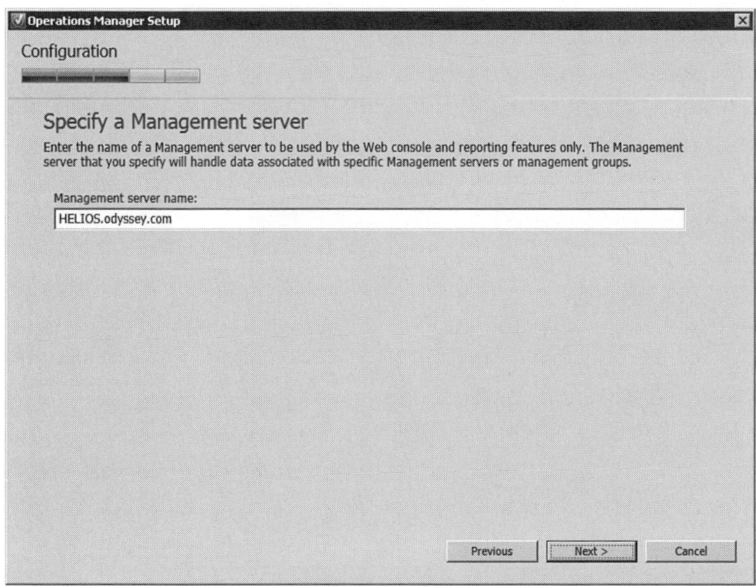

FIGURE 5.27 Specify a management server to be used by the web and reporting feature.

8. At the SQL Server instance for reporting services page, select the SQL Server instance on which you want to host SSRS. In the SQL Server instance drop-down box, select the SSRS server name, usually the server name you are installing on, as shown in Figure 5.28. Click **Next**.

9. Configure Operations Manager accounts as demonstrated in Figure 5.29:

   - Select to use a domain account for the Data Reader account. This account is used to deploy reports, is used by SSRS to run queries against the data warehouse, and is the SSRS Internet Information Services (IIS) Application Pool account that connects to a management server.

   - Use the same credential entered for the Data Reader account during installation of management servers as previously shown in Figure 5.16. Click **Next**.

10. At the Help improve System Center 2012 Operations Manager page (see Figure 5.30), indicate if you want to participate in Operational Data Reporting (ODR).

    - Operational data reports summarize how Operations Manager is running in your management group and help Microsoft determine which features its customers are using. The ODR report folder is installed automatically in every management group, even if you elect not to consent to send the data to Microsoft.

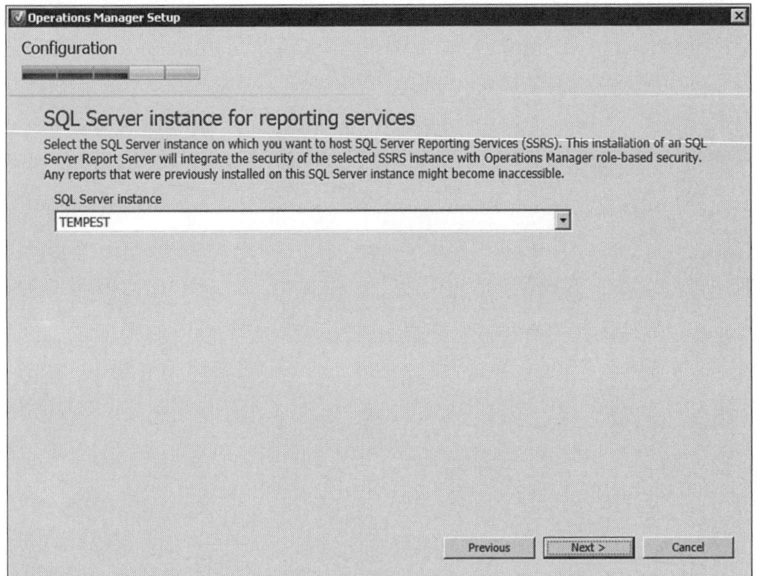

FIGURE 5.28 Specify the SQL Server instance for reporting services.

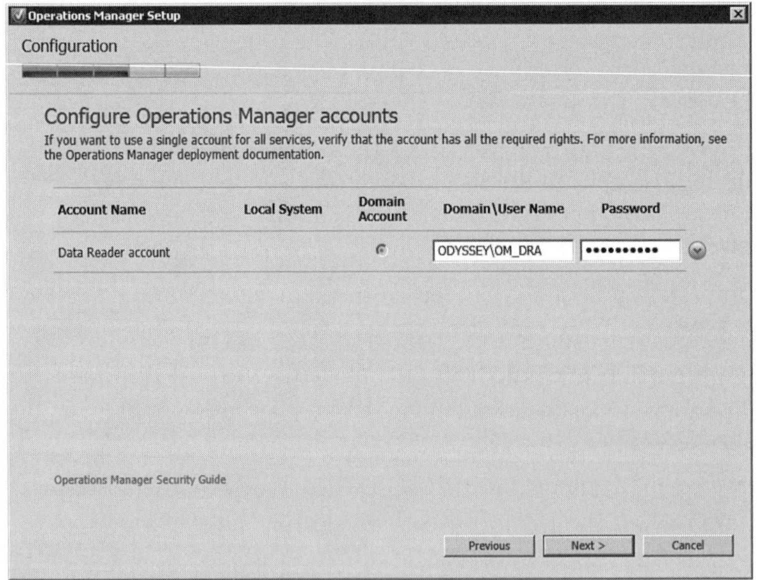

FIGURE 5.29 Data Reader account for reporting server.

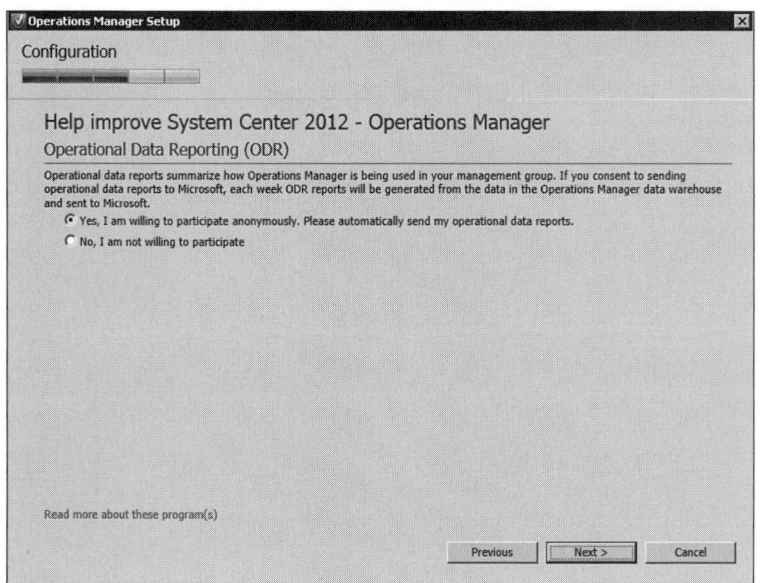

FIGURE 5.30 Enabling participation in Operational Data Reporting.

- You can preview the information Microsoft can see, such as the names of management packs and overrides loaded, by running the ODR reports manually in the Reporting space of the Operations console after installing OpsMgr reporting.
- If you agree to send operational data reports to Microsoft, ODR reports are generated weekly from the data in the Operations Manager data warehouse and the information sent to Microsoft. Select **Yes** to participate anonymously and automatically send your operational data reports, or **No** to not participate. Click **Next**.

11. At the Installation Summary page, review your selections for the feature you are installing as shown in Figure 5.31. To continue, press **Install**.

12. Setup is complete when all green checkmarks appear in the left column. Any component that failed to install is marked with a red "X."

- Optionally select to visit Microsoft Update after the wizard closes and click **Close** to complete the wizard.
- You will also want to **Exit** the OpsMgr installer that is still open (refer to Figure 5.1).

5

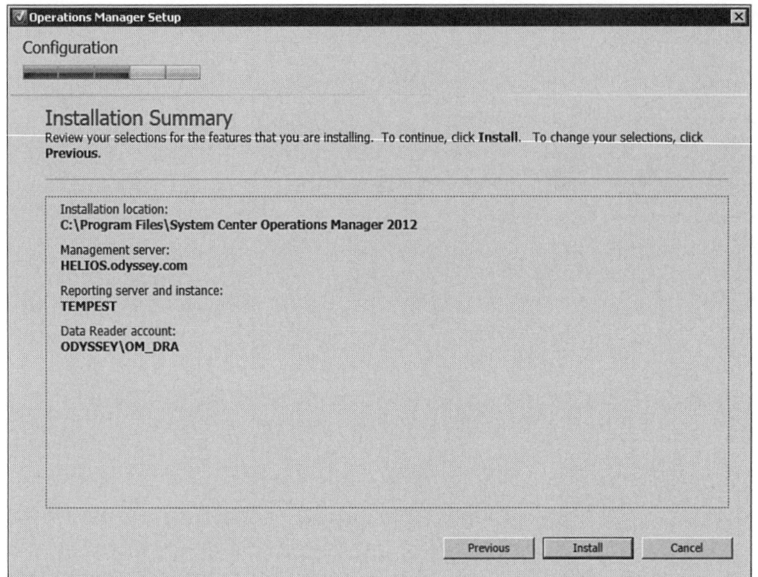

FIGURE 5.31 Summary of settings for reporting server installation.

Confirming Successful Deployment of the Reporting Server

After the reporting server is deployed, it can take up to 30 minutes for reports to appear in the Reporting space of the Operations console. You also must close and reopen each open instance of the console to expose the Reporting button in the navigation pane of the console.

After waiting a short while, close and reopen the Operations console and navigate to the Reporting space. Select the Microsoft ODR Report Library report folder in the navigation pane, and then double-click on any of the ODR reports in the central pane, such as Management Packs. The selected report is generated and displayed in a new window. Close the report window when done.

To install the reporting server using the setup command line, open an elevated command prompt, navigate to the folder containing the OpsMgr software media distribution, and run the command in Listing 5.4.

LISTING 5.4 Command line installation: Reporting server

```
setup.exe /silent /install /components:OMReporting
/ManagementServer:<ManagementServerName>
/SRSInstance:<ComputerName\instance>
/DataReaderUser:<domain\UserName>
/DataReaderPassword:<password>
/SendODRReports:[0|1]
/UseMicrosoftUpdate:[0|1]
```

Web Console

The Web console feature provides web-based access to Operations Manager for performing monitoring activities. Using a Silverlight-based client, the Web console provides a nearly equal experience to the Monitoring space of the Operations console for web users. The Web console also includes a version of the Operations console's My Workspace. It is also possible to create custom dashboard views in the Web console, which then appear in the Monitoring spaces of both consoles.

A key prerequisite for the Web console is having an existing local installation of IIS—you can ensure this by installing the web server role and related features on Windows Server. You must also install the following role services with IIS in addition to the IIS management console:

- Static Content
- Default Document
- Directory Browsing
- HTTP Errors
- HTTP Logging
- Request Monitor
- Request Filtering
- Static Content Compression
- Web Server (IIS) Support
- IIS 6 Metabase Compatibility
- ASP.NET
- Windows Authentication

As noted in the "Software Requirements" section, the authors recommend the web server role (Internet Information Services) be enabled *before* installing .NET Framework 4. If running Windows Server 2008 R2 and you install IIS after .NET Framework 4, you must register ASP.NET with IIS. Open a command prompt window using the Run as Administrator option and then run the following command:

```
%windir%\Microsoft.NET\Framework64\v4.0.30139\aspnet_regiis.exe -r
```

Windows Server 2012 does not support aspnet_regiis.exe. .NET 4.5 integration can only occur using the Windows Server 2012 Server Manager Add Roles and Features Wizard. If you did not install IIS and .NET 4.5 at the same time, remove the IIS role, and then add it and the .NET 4.5 feature at the same time.

If you want to enable an SSL connection to the Web console during installation (recommended), install a web server certificate to the default website before running the Web console setup.

TIP: INSTALL IIS ROLE AND FEATURES USING POWERSHELL

Because you must install IIS features in addition to the basic web server role, a best practice is to install the web server role using the following command line. This method meets the minimum requirements for the OpsMgr Web console without exposing unnecessary additional surface area. Open an elevated-security instance of PowerShell, type the first command, press Enter, then type the second command, and press Enter:

```
Import-Module ServerManager
Add-WindowsFeature NET-Framework-Core,Web-Static-Content,Web-Default-Doc,Web-
Dir-Browsing,Web-Http-Errors,Web-Http-Logging,Web-Request-Monitor,Web-
Filtering,Web-Stat-Compression,Web-Mgmt-Console,Web-Metabase,Web-Asp-Net,Web-
Windows-Auth
```

If you install a stand-alone Web console on a server, you will not be able to add the management server feature to this server. If you want the management server and Web console on the same server, you must either install both features simultaneously, or install the management server before you install the Web console. Follow these steps to install the Web console:

1. Installing the Web console requires ISAPI and CGI Restrictions in IIS enabled for ASP.NET 4. (If you installed the web server role using the command line in the Tip in this section, ISAPI and CGI restrictions are already enabled.) Select the web server in IIS Manager, then select the IIS -> ISAPI and CGI Restrictions feature, and click **Open Feature** in the Actions pane as demonstrated in Figure 5.32.

2. Locate ASP.NET v4.0.30319 in the Description column. You may find two entries, for 32-bit and 64-bit frameworks. Select any instances of ASP.NET v4.0.30319 in Not Allowed status, then click **Allow** in the Actions Pane as demonstrated in Figure 5.33.

3. Run Setup from the OpsMgr distribution media, and from the splash screen previously seen in Figure 5.1, click the large **Install** link to start the setup wizard. After the Launching Operations Manager Setup splash screen, you will see the Select features to install dialog previously displayed in Figure 5.9.

4. Select **Web console** as shown in Figure 5.34. Click **Next**.

5. Select **Installation location**. The default location is *%ProgramFiles%*\System Center 2012\Operations Manager. Accept the default or specify your alternative path, and click **Next**.

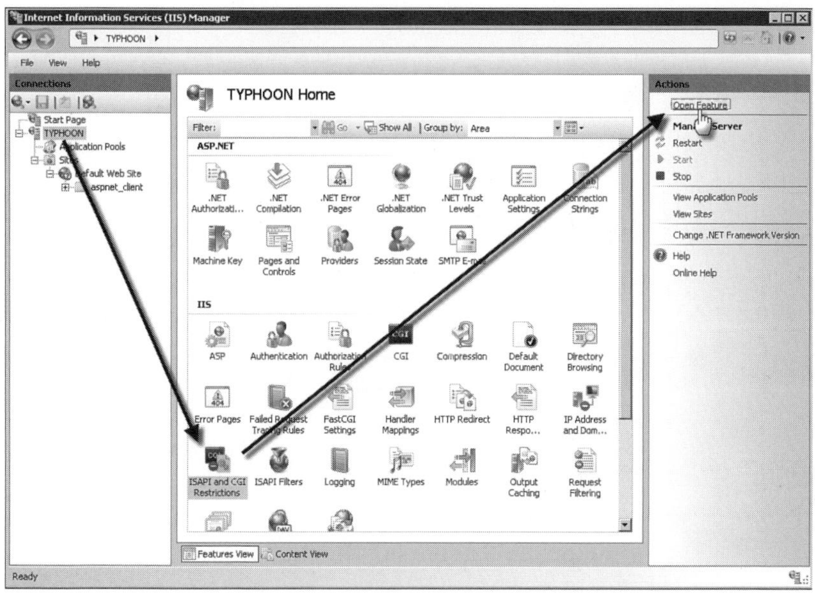

FIGURE 5.32 Opening the ISAPI and CGI Restrictions feature in IIS Manager.

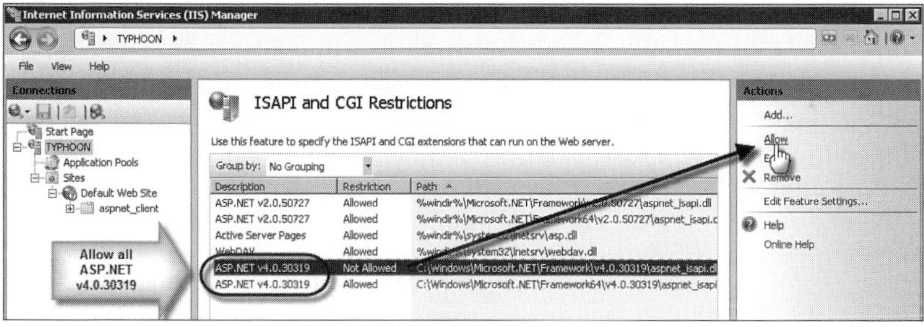

FIGURE 5.33 Allowing ASP.NET v4.0.30319 in ISAPI and CGI Restrictions.

6. Setup continues with the message **Verifying that your environment has the required hardware and software**. If issues are found, the message **The Setup wizard cannot continue** appears. This means additional hardware resources or software are required to continue.

7. After resolving any prerequisite problems, click **Verify Prerequisites Again**. If the verification is successful, click **Next**.

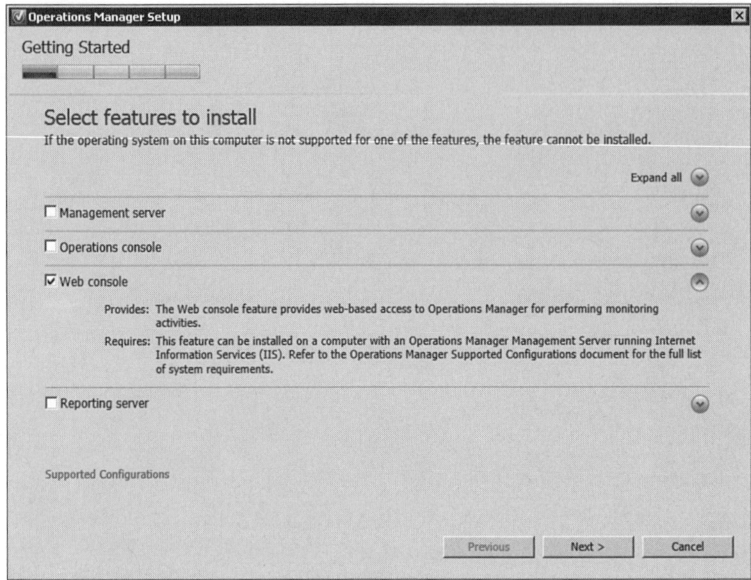

FIGURE 5.34 Selecting the Web console role for installation.

8. At the Specify a Management server page, enter the name of a management server to be used by the Web console only, as previously shown in Figure 5.27. The management server you specify will handle data associated with specific management servers or management groups. Normally, this is the name of the first installed management server, or if using a load-balanced management server pool, the virtual server name of the pool. Click **Next**.

9. At the Specify a web site for use with the Web console page, select an IIS web site to be used for the Web console. Select an existing web site from the available web sites on the local IIS server. The Default Web Site is the default setting as seen in Figure 5.35. Optionally (and recommended), if an SSL certificate is installed on the selected web site, click **Enable SSL**.

10. You may see this warning (circled in Figure 5.35): **Web console does not have sufficient access to the database. Setup can continue, but note that some components may not fully install.** If this appears and you will be using the application performance monitoring (APM) features of OpsMgr, execute the following SQL statement against the operations and data warehouse databases in SQL Server Management Studio as demonstrated in Figure 5.36.

    ```
    EXEC [apm].GrantRWPermissionsToComputer '<domain\ComputerName>$'
    ```

    After executing the SQL statement and refreshing the setup configuration (click **Previous**, then **Next** again) the warning should clear.

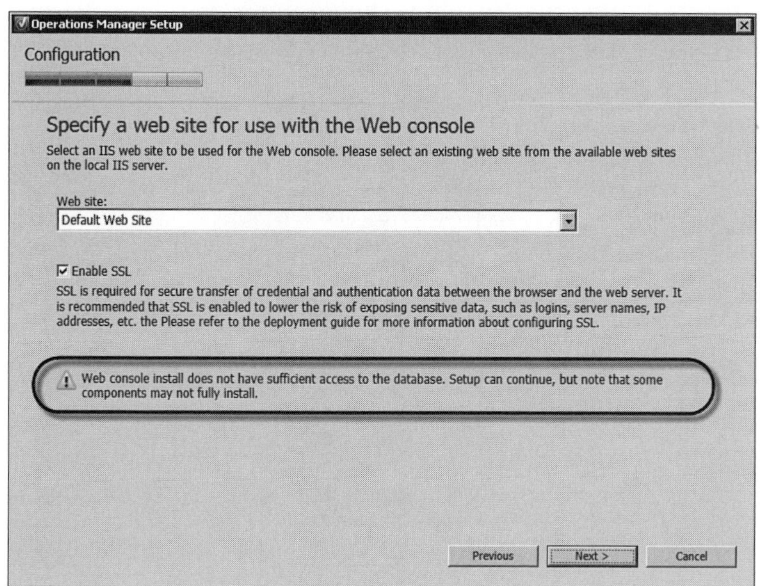

FIGURE 5.35 Specifying the default web site and to Enable SSL.

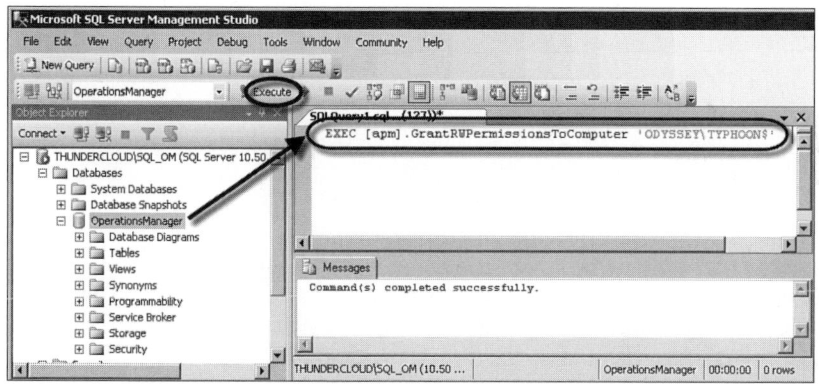

FIGURE 5.36 Executing the SQL statement that grants the web server permissions.

11. At the Select an authentication mode for use with the Web console page, select an authentication mode as seen in Figure 5.37. If you are publishing the Web console to the Internet, select **Use Network Authentication**. Use Mixed Authentication only if you are using the Web console in intranet scenarios. Click **Next**.

12. At the Web console Installation Summary page, review your selections as seen in Figure 5.38. Take note of the Uniform Resource Locators (URLs) to be used for accessing the Web console and APM features. To continue, press **Install**.

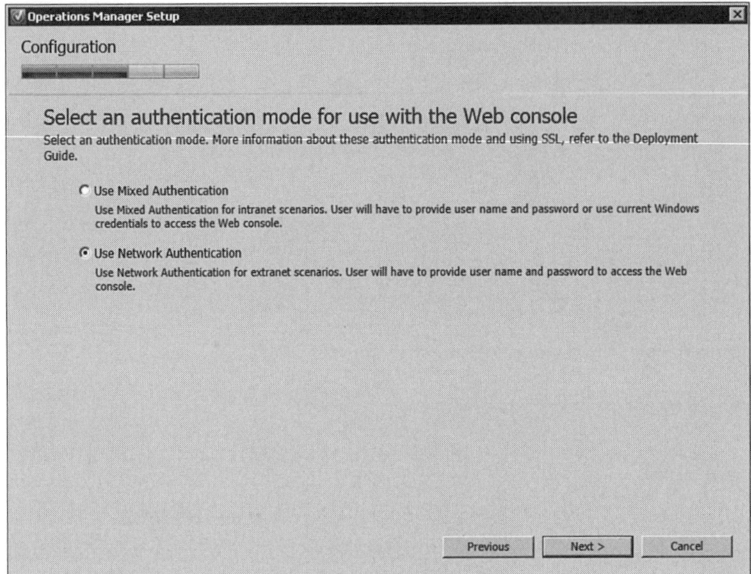

FIGURE 5.37 Network Authentication is for Internet publishing of the Web console.

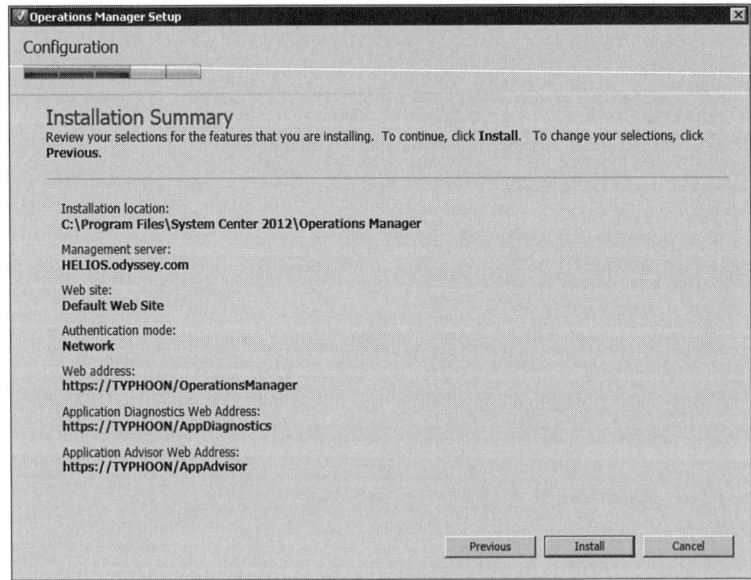

FIGURE 5.38 Web console installation summary confirms web addresses.

13. Setup is complete when all green checkmarks appear in the left column. Any component that failed to install is marked with a red "X."

- Optionally select to visit Microsoft Update after the wizard closes and select **Close** to complete the wizard.
- You will also want to **Exit** the OpsMgr installer that is still open (refer to Figure 5.1).

14. Configure permissions inheritance for the Web console:

- In Windows Explorer, navigate to the MonitoringView folder in the installation folder for the Web console (by default, *%ProgramFiles%*\System Center 2012\Operations Manager\WebConsole\MonitoringView), right-click the TempImages folder, and click **Properties**.
- On the Security tab, click **Advanced**.
- On the Permissions tab, select **Change Permissions**.
- Select the **Include inheritable permissions from this object's parent** check box.
- In Permission entries, click **Administrators**, and then click **Remove**. Repeat for the SYSTEM entry, and then click **OK**.
- Click **OK** to close Advanced Security Settings for TempImages, and then click **OK** to close TempImages Properties.

The Web console requires the latest release of Silverlight and a custom Silverlight update. The first time you access the Web console with your browser, you are prompted to install or update Silverlight if needed as shown in Figure 5.39. It may be necessary to add the website of the Web console to your browser's trusted sites list.

FIGURE 5.39 Install Silverlight to use the OpsMgr Web console.

The first time the Web console is accessed from a particular computer, a notice may be seen as shown in Figure 5.40: **Web Console Configuration Required. The Operations Manager Web console requires some additional configuration to be fully functional. Without this configuration, many types of views will not be available. Refresh this page after completing the configuration.**

FIGURE 5.40 OpsMgr Web console requires a custom Silverlight update.

To use the Web console with full functionality on a computer receiving this message, select the **Configure** button on the web page to download the update file **SilverlightClientConfiguration.exe** from the web console server to your browser. This is the custom Silverlight update needed by OpsMgr. Select the option to **Run** the update as displayed in Figure 5.41. When complete you will see the message **The Operations Manager web console was successfully configured on this computer**.

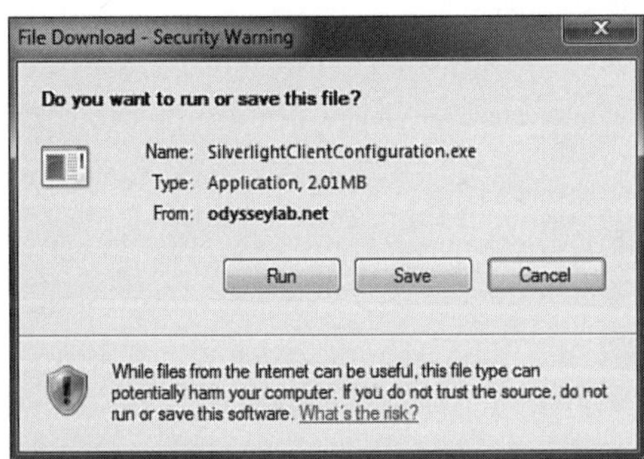

FIGURE 5.41 SilverlightClientConfiguration.exe is a custom Silverlight update.

Gateway Server

A gateway server makes OpsMgr agent to management server communication possible across security boundaries such as the Internet and to non-domain joined computers. A gateway server also serves as an agent concentrator, bundling and compressing agent to management server traffic by as much as 50%. If you are deploying a gateway across security boundaries, you must first deploy a public key infrastructure (PKI) using a public, an enterprise, or a stand-alone certificate authority (CA). See Chapter 24 for information about deploying PKI to support Operations Manager.

Preparatory work for deploying a gateway may include installing .NET Framework 4 or 4.5 and obtaining an Operations Manager client certificate with a private key. The certificate can exist either as a .PFX file or in the local computer certificate store. You must have a gateway topology planned out; in particular, you need to know the fully qualified domain name (FQDN) of the management server or gateway to which you will connect a new gateway. The management group must also be prepared for the gateway server by running the gateway approval tool.

CAUTION: RUN GATEWAY APPROVAL TOOL FIRST, BEFORE RUNNING SETUP

Always add a gateway to the management group by running the gateway approval tool on the management server *before* installing the gateway software on the target computer. If you install the gateway before running the approval tool, the management group sees the gateway as an agent rather than a gateway. If this occurs, you must delete the agent object in the management group and run the gateway approval tool before retrying the gateway installation.

Follow these steps to install a gateway server:

1. .NET Framework 4 (4.5 for Windows 2012 Server systems) is required on gateway servers to support network monitoring and UNIX/Linux computer monitoring. In Operations Manager, the gateway servers must have .NET Framework 4.x installed if using the networking monitoring feature in a management group and the devices managed are behind gateway servers. (The prerequisite checker does not check for .NET Framework 4.x when you install a gateway server.) If appropriate, install .NET Framework 4.x as described in the "Installation Prerequisites" section.

2. Run the gateway approval tool on a management server. First copy Microsoft.EnterpriseManagement.GatewayApprovalTool.exe and Microsoft.EnterpriseManagement.GatewayApprovalTool.exe.config from the \SupportTools folder on the OpsMgr installation media to the OpsMgr program files server folder, generally *%ProgramFiles%*\System Center 2012\Operations Manager\Server.

    - Open an elevated command prompt on the management server, and change directory to the OpsMgr program files server folder.

    - Run the tool with command line switches to assign the new gateway to an existing management server or gateway. The example seen in Figure 5.42 is the approval of gateway viceroy.odysseylab.net, which will report to management server hector.odyssey.com. This creates the computer object in OpsMgr for the gateway. `Microsoft.EnterpriseManagement.GatewayApprovalTool/ManagementServerName=hector.odyssey.com/GatewayName=viceroy.odysseylab.net/Action=Create`

3. On the prospective gateway server, from the OpsMgr distribution media previously shown in Figure 5.2, run Setup; at the splash screen shown in Figure 5.1, click the **Gateway management server** link in the Optional Installations section to start a setup wizard.

5

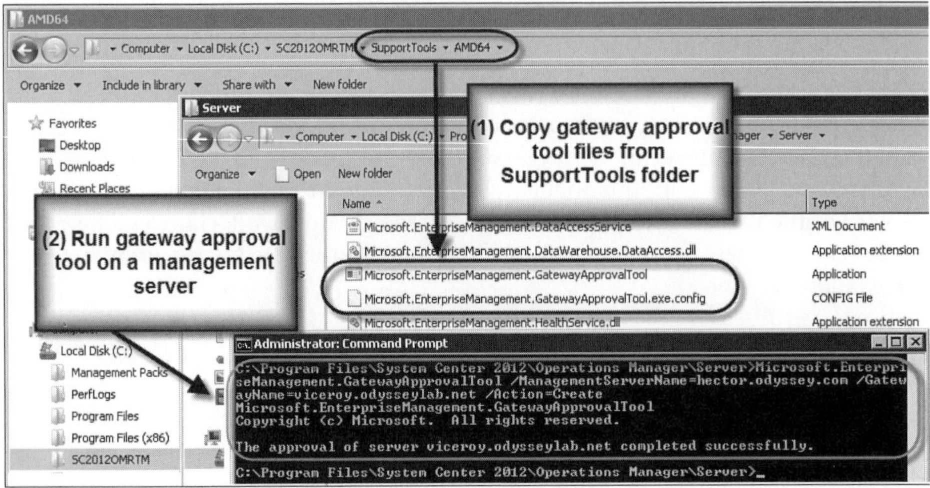

FIGURE 5.42 Copy and run gateway approval tool on the management server.

4. The Welcome to the System Center 2012 – Operations Manager Gateway Server Setup wizard appears, as shown in Figure 5.43. Click **Next**.

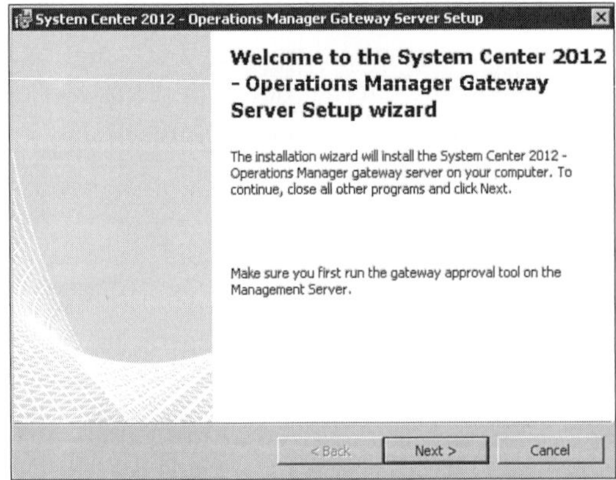

FIGURE 5.43 Setup wizard for the Operations Manager Gateway Server.

5. Select **Installation location**. The default location is *%ProgramFiles%*\System Center 2012\Operations Manager. Click **Next**.

6. At the Management Group Configuration page, enter the name of the management group and management sever name to which the gateway will report. This will be the same management server name used when running the gateway approval tool on the management server. Figure 5.44 shows this gateway (viceroy.odysseylab.net) will report to management server hector.odyssey.com. Click **Next**.

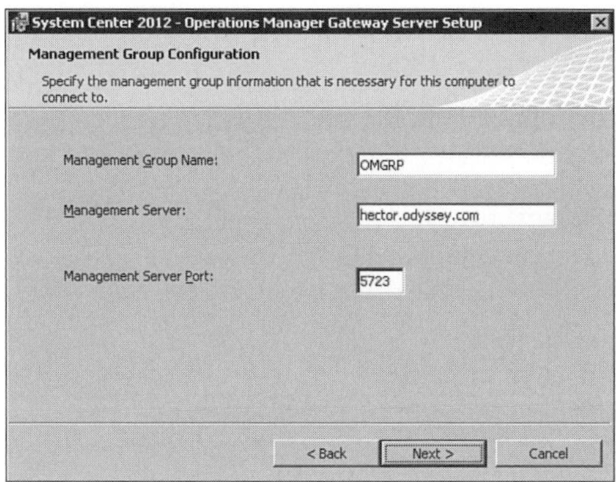

FIGURE 5.44 Pointing the gateway to a management server or another gateway.

7. At the Gateway Action Account page, select to use **Local System** if the gateway will not be pushing agents to other computers. If the gateway will push install agents, enter credential information for an administrative account in the domain of the gateway server. Since the gateway servers in the lab used in this book will not directly manage computers and will only chain to other gateways, the Local System account is used as shown in Figure 5.45. Click **Next**.

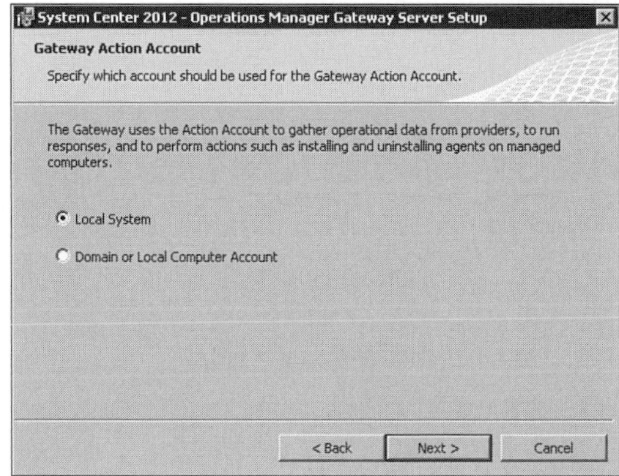

FIGURE 5.45 Installing a gateway (that won't push agents) using the Local System account.

8. At the Ready to Install page, confirm settings and click the **Install** button. When installation completes, click the **Finish** button.

9. If you are using certificates for authentication, import the Operations Manager client certificate on the gateway server as follows:

   - Copy the MOMCertImport.exe file from the \SupportTools folder on the OpsMgr installation media to the OpsMgr program files gateway folder, such as *%ProgramFiles%*\System Center Operations Manager\Gateway.

- Open an elevated command prompt on the gateway server, and change directory to the OpsMgr program files gateway folder.
- Run the tool with command line switches to import the certificate as seen in Figure 5.46.

```
MOMCertImport viceroy.odesseylab.net.pfx/Password Password1
Microsoft.EnterpriseManagement.GatewayApprovalTool/
ManagementServerName=hector.odyssey.com/GatewayName=viceroy.
odysseylab.net/Action=Create
```

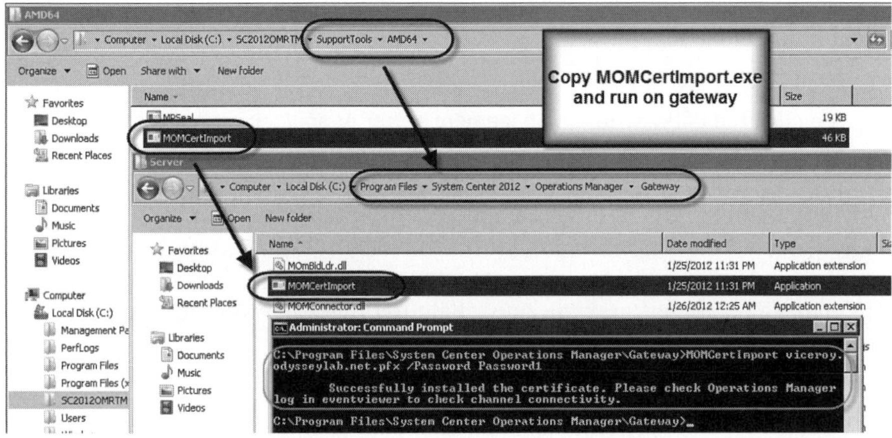

FIGURE 5.46 Copy and run MOMCertImport.exe on the gateway server.

10. You must enable the Server Proxy setting on the new gateway server. (This setting is automatically enabled for management servers but not gateways.) Navigate in the Operations console to **Administration -> Device Management -> Management Servers**, select and right-click the new gateway, and select **Properties**. On the Security tab, shown in Figure 5.47, tick the option to **Allow this server to act as a proxy and discover managed objects on other computers**. Click **OK**.
11. Within several minutes of importing the certificate on the gateway, the computer object for the gateway in the Operations console should appear as healthy.

To install a gateway server using the setup command line, open an elevated command prompt, and run the command shown in Listing 5.5.

LISTING 5.5 Command line installation: Gateway server

```
%WinDir%\System32\msiexec /i
<Path\Directory>\MOMGateway.msi /qn /l*v
<Path\Logs>\GatewayInstall.log
ADDLOCAL=MOMGateway
MANAGEMENT_GROUP="<ManagementGroupName>"
```

```
INSTALLDIR=<Path\Directory>
IS_ROOT_HEALTH_SERVER=0
ROOT_MANAGEMENT_SERVER_AD=<FQDNManagementServer>
ROOT_MANAGEMENT_SERVER_DNS=<FQDNManagementServer>
ACTIONS_USE_COMPUTER_ACCOUNT=0
ACTIONSDOMAIN=<GatewayActionAccountDomainName>
ACTIONSUSER=<GatewayActionAccountName>
ACTIONSPASSWORD=<GatewayActionAccountPassword>
ROOT_MANAGEMENT_SERVER_PORT=5723
```

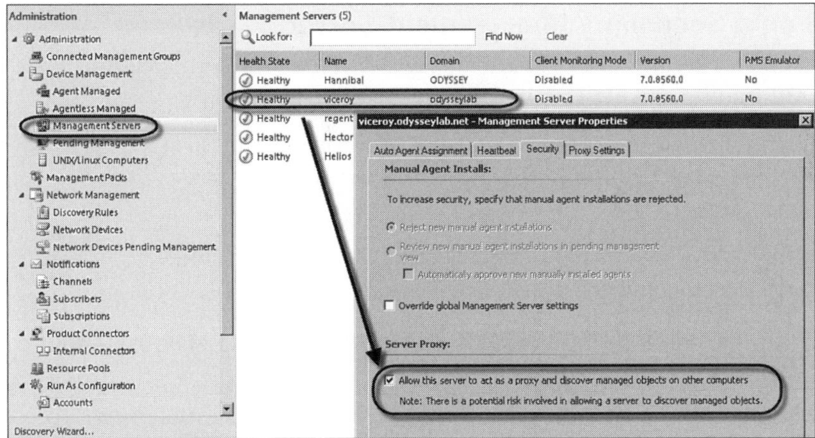

FIGURE 5.47 Allow gateway server to act as proxy and discover other computers.

Installing Audit Collection Services

ACS provides a means to collect events generated by audit policies and store them in a central database. Preparation for deploying ACS includes deciding whether you will install ACS reporting integrated with the reporting space in the Operations console, or on a separate, non-integrated, SSRS instance. Chapter 10 discusses the considerations for each mode. Regardless of the mode in which you will deploy ACS reporting, you must identify the SQL Server instance where you will create the ACS database.

Other than in a lab or demo environment, it is not a good idea to deploy the ACS collector role on the only management server in a management group. The authors recommend having two or more management servers online, one of which will assume the ACS collector role. You must install the ACS collector service on an existing management server. Although there are advanced ACS topologies and failover techniques that include more than one ACS collector (see Chapter 9 for information), generally there is a one-to-one relationship between ACS collectors and ACS databases. Unless you have created two or more ACS databases, you will only deploy one ACS collector.

There are two main activities in deploying the ACS feature:

- Installing ACS on a secondary management server, which creates the new ACS database
- Deploying ACS reporting to an SSRS instance

The following sections install the ACS collector role on management server Hannibal. odyssey.com, pointing to a SQL Server ACS database in untrusted domain ithica.local. The SSRS instance—installed on the ACS database server Fireball.ithica.local—is an example of implementing the non-integrated ACS reporting mode.

Installing ACS on a Secondary Management Server

To deploy ACS, first install ACS on a secondary management server, which creates the collector and the ACS audit database. Follow these steps:

1. Run Setup from the OpsMgr distribution media, and from the splash screen previously seen in Figure 5.1, click the **Audit collection services** link in the Optional Installations section.
2. Click **Next** at the Welcome to the Audit Collection Services Collector Setup wizard page. Accept the license agreement and click **Next**.
3. On the Database Installations Options page, select **Create a new database**. Click **Next**.
4. On the Data Source page, accept the default Open Database Connectivity (ODBC) data source name of OpsMgrAC and click **Next**.
5. On the Database page, seen in Figure 5.48, select **Remote database server** and enter the name of the SQL Server database to be used by ACS; optionally enter an instance name. Accept the default database name of OperationsManagerAC and click **Next**.

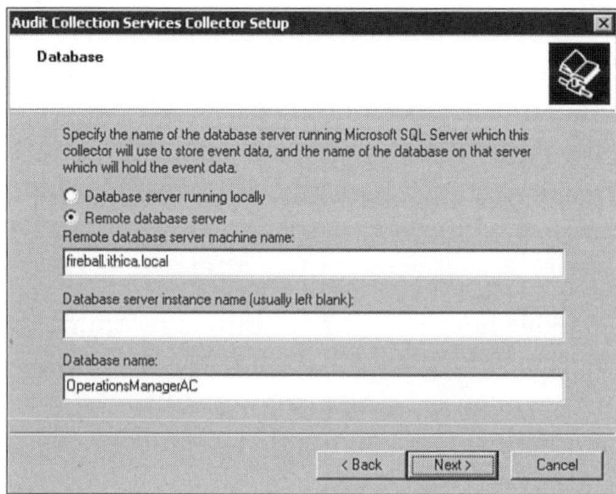

FIGURE 5.48 Selecting the database to be used by Audit Collection Services.

6. On the Database Authentication page displayed in Figure 5.49, select **SQL authentication** because you are using a SQL Server in an untrusted domain, and click **Next**.

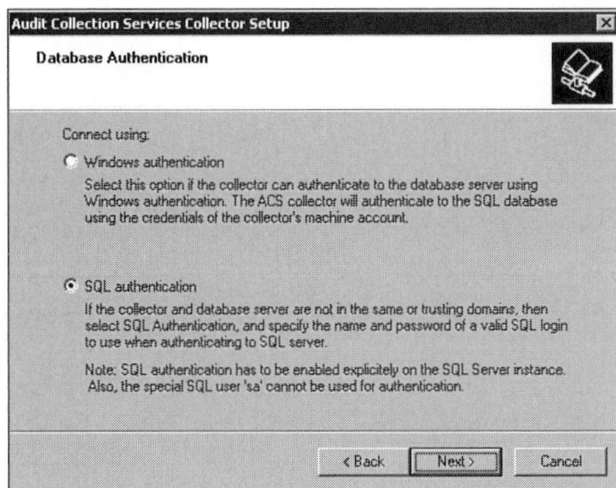

FIGURE 5.49 Selecting Windows or SQL authentication for the ACS database.

7. On the Database Credentials page, type a SQL login name to be used by the ACS collector to log in to the SQL Server, as shown in Figure 5.50. This SQL Server authentication login is created in the Security -> Logins section of SQL Server Management Studio. *The name cannot be sa*. Click **Next**.

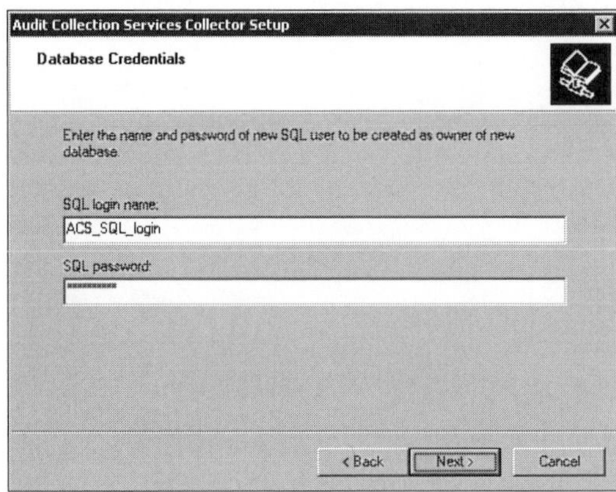

FIGURE 5.50 Entering the SQL login credentials for the ACS database.

8. On the Database Creation Options page, consider specifying unique database file locations (rather than the SQL Server default locations) as shown in Figure 5.51, and click **Next**. (Specifying unique file locations might make it easier to track database file size and perform ACS database maintenance in the future.)

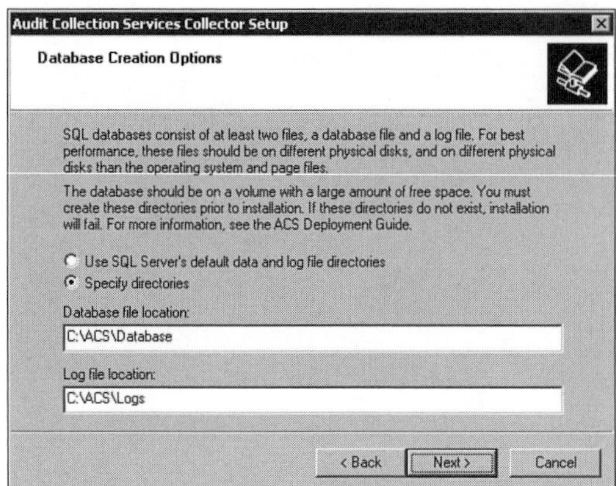

FIGURE 5.51 Specifying unique database file locations on the SQL Server.

9. On the Event Retention Schedule page, select to accept the default settings, shown in Figure 5.52, of 02:00 AM local time to perform daily database maintenance and retain 14 days of security events in the ACS audit database. Click **Next**.

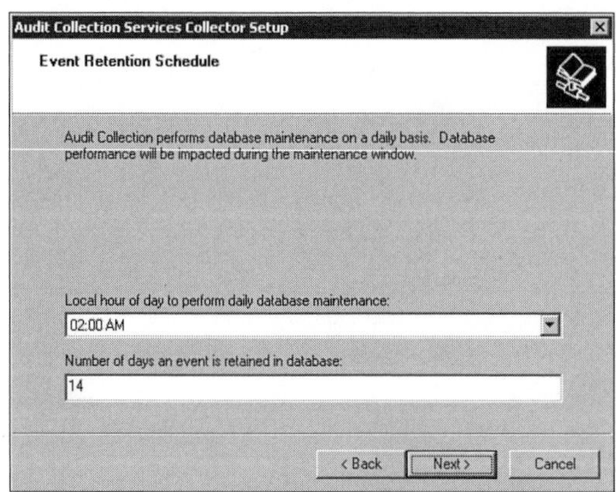

FIGURE 5.52 The ACS defaults are to retain 14 days data and roll logs at 2:00 AM.

10. On the ACS Stored Timestamp Format page, select the default to use local time zone timestamps and click **Next**.

11. On the Summary page, click **Next** to begin the installation. If prompted for SQL Authentication, enter the sa SQL authentication credential, which is used to create the SQL authentication credential in the ACS database.

12. When installation completes, look for the successful setup message displayed in Figure 5.53.

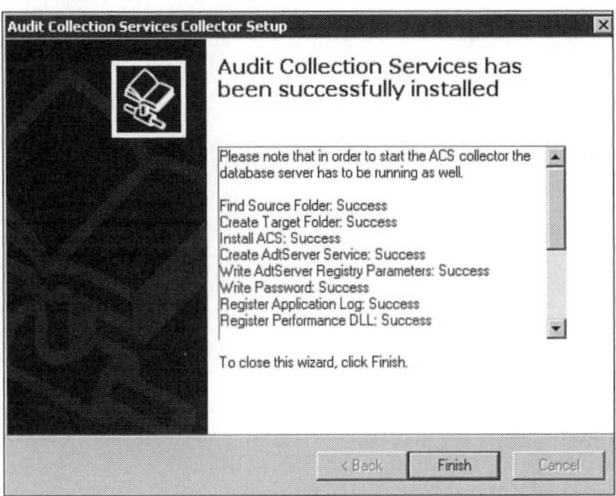

FIGURE 5.53 Checking successful installation of the ACS collector component.

13. If you will use ACS to collect security events from computers in untrusted domains or workgroups, provision the ACS collector with the same certificate used to enable management server to gateway communication. Assuming you have installed an OpsMgr client certificate on the management server, follow these steps, demonstrated in Figure 5.54, to enable certificate-based ACS authentication:

- Open an elevated command prompt and change directory to the ACS program folder, which is *%SystemRoot%*\System32\Security\AdtServer.
- Stop the ACS collector service.
- Run **`adtserver.exe -c`** and select the index number of the certificate to use.
- Start the ACS collector service.

FIGURE 5.54 Running the `adtserver -c` command to use a certificate with ACS.

Deploying ACS Reporting to an SSRS Instance

With ACS installed, your next step is deploying ACS reporting to an SSRS instance. Follow these steps:

1. Copy the acs folder shown in Figure 5.55 (and all files and subfolders) from the ReportModels folder of the System Center 2012 Operations Manager distribution media to the root of the C:\ drive of the SSRS computer that will host ACS reports. This creates a c:\acs folder with some subfolders on the SSRS computer.

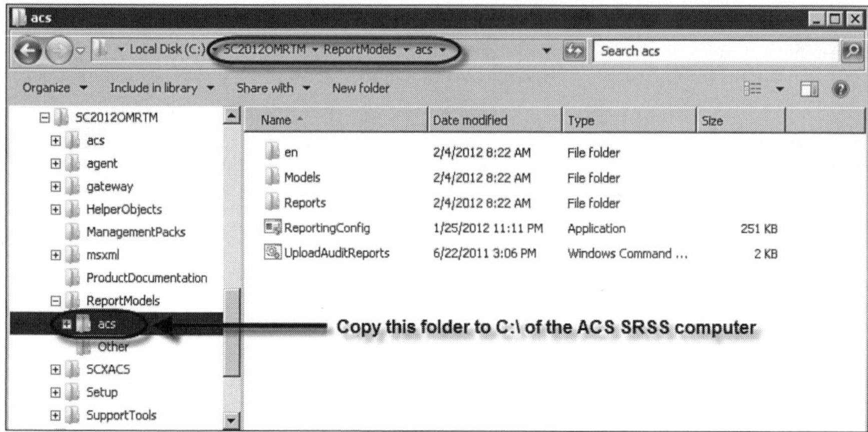

FIGURE 5.55 Copy the \ReportModels\acs folder to C:\acs on the SSRS computer.

2. Copy the ReportingConfig.exe file from the \SupportTools folder of the OpsMgr distribution media to the c:\acs folder on the SSRS computer.

3. Open an elevated command prompt on the SSRS computer and run the following command in the c:\acs folder, demonstrated in Figure 5.56:

```
UploadAuditReports "<AuditDBServer\instance>" "<Reporting Server Web Service
URL>" "<path of the copied ACS folder, such as c:\acs>"
```

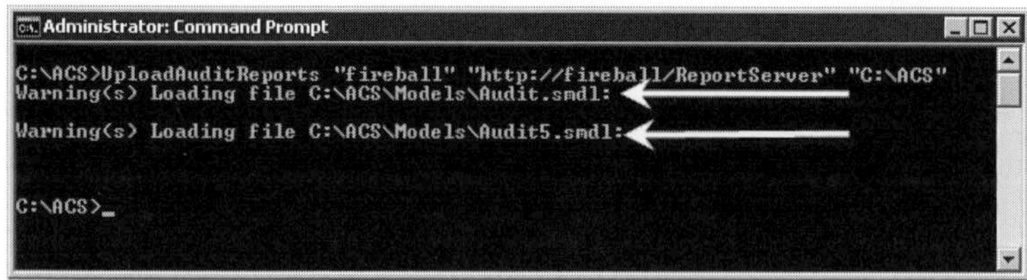

FIGURE 5.56 Run UploadAuditReports in the C:\acs folder on the SSRS computer.

4. Running this command successfully produces output similar to that seen in Figure 5.56; at first glance, these appear to be warnings, but actually are empty error lists, and this is an expected output.

5. Browse to the SSRS Report Manager URL (such as http://*<ComputerName>*/Reports) and open the Audit Reports folder. Click the Details View button on the right of the screen. Click on the DBAudit datasource and confirm Windows integrated security is selected for the connection credential type, as shown in Figure 5.57. If you make any changes, click **Apply**.

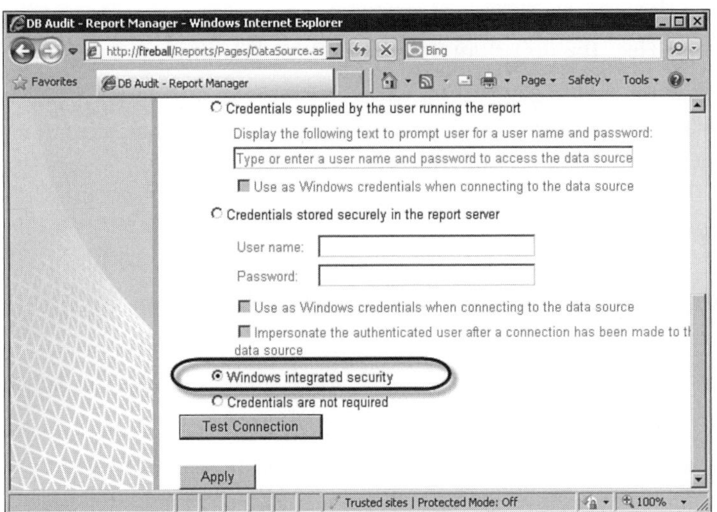

FIGURE 5.57 Confirm SSRS is using the Windows integrated security type.

NOTE: UPLOAD REPORT BANNERS IF USING ACS IN "NON-INTEGRATED" MODEL

If deploying ACS reporting in the non-integrated model that is not integrated with OpsMgr reporting but is installed on a dedicated standoff instance of SSRS, you must manually upload the report banner files to avoid a red "X" (missing graphic) at the top of your ACS reports. Open SQL Server Reporting Services in your web browser and navigate to the Home folder. (You should see the AuditReports data source folder at the same level.) Click the **Upload File** button and locate the files **banner_landscape.jpg** and **banner_portrait.jpg** in the *%ProgramFiles%*\System Center 2012\Operations Manager\Reporting\Reports folder on the SSRS computer.

Installing Agents on Servers

Chapter 8, "Installing and Configuring Agents," discusses the OpsMgr agent and the variety of ways to deploy and manage the agent. In the complete installation of an OpsMgr management group, agents should be deployed immediately to those management group infrastructure computers that are not management servers or gateways. This includes the Web console server, reporting server, SQL servers, and ACS infrastructure systems. The ACS forwarder components on each computer are also configured. These actions are described in the following sections. (This section would not apply to a single server installation; however, in a two-server model, an agent should be installed at this time on the SQL Server.)

Discovering Windows Computers in a Trusted Domain

Use this procedure to deploy agents to the SQL server(s), Web console server(s), and report server of your management group. Perform the following steps:

1. In the Operations console, navigate to the Administration space and click the **Discovery Wizard** link. Select the default option to discover **Windows computers** and click **Next**.
2. At the Auto or Advanced page, select **Advanced discovery**, select the default to discover **Servers and Clients**, and select the management server that will discover and initially manage the discovered computers. Figure 5.58 shows management server **Hector.odyssey.com** selected. Click **Next**.

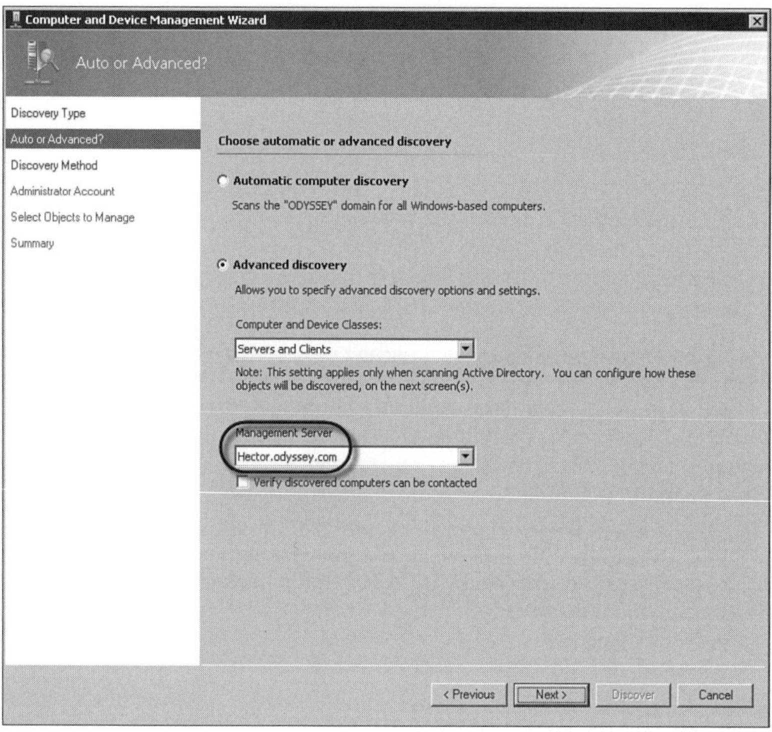

FIGURE 5.58 Select the desired management server.

3. At the Discovery Method page, select **Browse for**, or type in the computer names of your core OpsMgr infrastructure computers. Click the **Browse** button as needed to validate computer names. When all desired computers are listed, click **Next**.
4. At the Administrator Account page, select **Use selected Management Server Action Account** and click **Discover**.
5. At the Select Objects to Manage page, confirm the expected computers are listed as shown in Figure 5.59 and click **Next**.

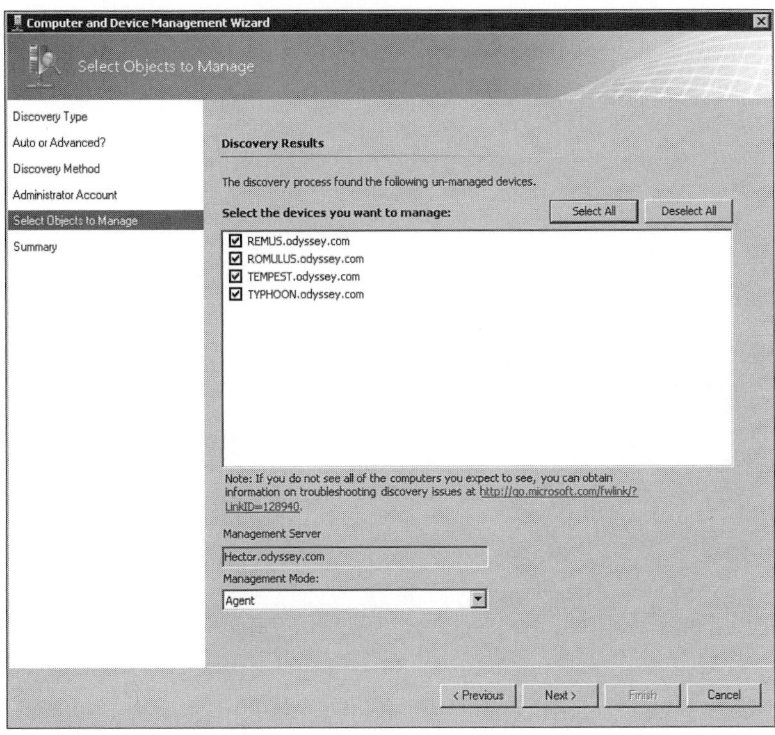

FIGURE 5.59 Confirmation of discovered computers, ready to push agents.

6. At the Summary page, click **Finish** to install the agent to the default location *%ProgramFiles%*\System Center 2012\Operations Manager with **Local System** selected as the Agent Action account.

It is often necessary to enable the Server Proxy setting on new, automatically discovered agents. (This setting is disabled for agents by default, but required for many management packs to function.) To enable this setting for an agent, navigate in the Operations console to **Administration** -> **Device Management** -> **Agent Managed**, select and right-click the new agent, and select **Properties**. On the Security tab, tick the option to **Allow this server to act as a proxy and discover managed objects on other computers**. Click **OK**.

Manually Installing Agent in an Untrusted Domain or Workgroup

This next procedure deploys agents to any computers in your core Operations Manager deployment that are not members of a trusted domain, such as a dedicated instance of SSRS in a different domain. Perform the following steps:

1. Begin with enabling manual agents to be installed in your management group. If you don't perform this step, manual agents are automatically rejected, which is the

default behavior of OpsMgr. As shown in Figure 5.60, navigate to **Administration -> Settings -> Security** in the Operations console and select **Review new manual agent installations in pending management view**. Click **OK**.

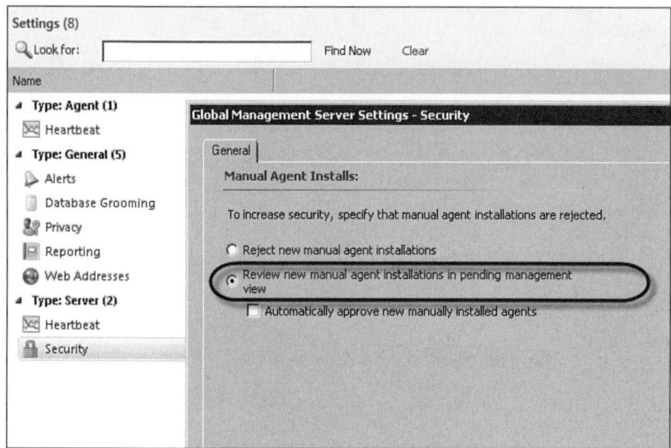

FIGURE 5.60 Enable the manual install of agents in the management group.

2. On the computer to be managed, run Setup from the OpsMgr distribution media shown in Figure 5.2. Then from the splash screen seen in Figure 5.1, click the **Local agent** link in the Optional Installations section.
3. The Welcome to the System Center 2012 – Operations Manager Agent Setup wizard appears. Click **Next**.
4. Select **Installation location**. The default location is *%ProgramFiles%*\System Center 2012\Operations Manager. Click **Next**.
5. At the Specify Management Group information page, accept the default to **Specify Management Group information** and click **Next**.
6. At the Management Group Configuration page, enter the name of the management group and management server or gateway sever name to which the agent will report. Click **Next**.
7. At the Agent Action Account page, select the default to use **Local System** and click **Next**.
8. At the Ready to Install page, confirm settings and click the **Install** button. When installation completes, click the **Finish** button.

9. Import the Operations Manager client certificate on the agent:

- Copy the MOMCertImport.exe file from the \SupportTools folder on the OpsMgr installation media to the Operations Manager program files client folder.
- Open an elevated command prompt on the agent computer, and change directory to the OpsMgr program files server folder, such as *%ProgramFiles%*\System Center 2012\Operations Manager\Agent.
- Run the tool with command line switches to import the certificate as previously seen in Figure 5.46 when installing a gateway server.

10. Within several minutes of importing the certificate on the agent, the computer object for the agent should appear in the Operations console in the Administration -> Device Management -> Pending Management view. Figure 5.61 shows manually installed agents waiting to be approved in the Operations console. Right-click and select **Approve**.

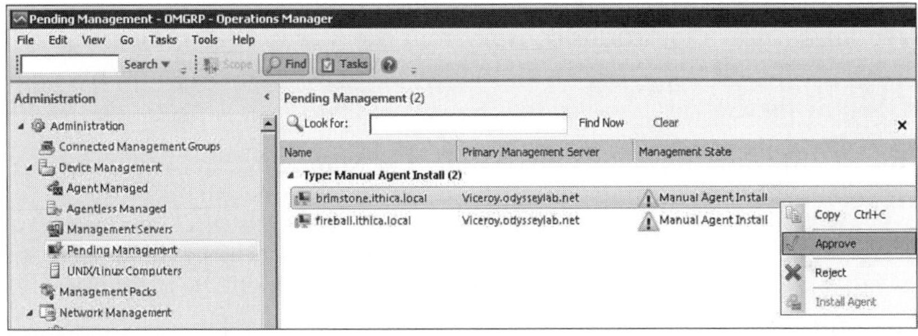

FIGURE 5.61 Manually installed agents from computers without a domain trust.

It is often necessary to enable the Server Proxy setting on new manually installed agents. (Server Proxy is disabled for agents by default, but required for many management packs to function.) Navigate in the Operations console to **Administration -> Device Management -> Agent Managed**, select and right-click each new agent and select **Properties**. On the Security tab, tick the option to **Allow this server to act as a proxy and discover managed objects on other computers**. Click **OK**.

To install the agent using the setup command line, open an elevated command prompt, navigate to the folder containing the OpsMgr software media distribution, and run the command in Listing 5.6.

LISTING 5.6 Command line installation: Agent

```
%WinDir%\System32\msiexec.exe /i
<path>\<Directory>\MOMAgent.msi /qn
USE_SETTINGS_FROM_AD={0|1}
USE_MANUALLY_SPECIFIED_SETTINGS={0|1}
```

```
MANAGEMENT_GROUP=<ManagementGroupName>
MANAGEMENT_SERVER_DNS=<ManagementServerFQDN>
MANAGEMENT_SERVER_AD_NAME=<ManagementServerFQDN>
SECURE_PORT=5723
ACTIONS_USE_COMPUTER_ACCOUNT={0|1}
ACTIONSUSER=<AgentActionAccountUserName>
ACTIONSDOMAIN=<AgentActionAccountDomainName>
ACTIONSPASSWORD=<AgentActionAccountPassword>
ACCEPTLICENSEAGREEMENT=1
```

Configuring ACS Forwarder for Certificate Operation

If you manually installed the OpsMgr agent on a computer and used certificate authentication, as for gateway servers and agents in workgroups and untrusted domains, you must also enable the ACS forwarder to use the certificate. Run **adtagent.exe –c** from an elevated command prompt and select the index number of the certificate to use.

Enabling ACS Forwarders

Audit collection is enabled in the Operations console from the Monitoring -> Operations Manager views. Enable audit collection first for all management servers and gateways, then for all agents. Follow these steps:

1. Navigate to the **Monitoring** -> **Operations Manager** -> **Management Server** -> **Management Servers** State view.
2. Select all management servers and click the **Enable Audit Collection** task as seen in the right side of Figure 5.62. This task enables and configures the Audit Collection Service on the appropriate Operations Manager Health Service.

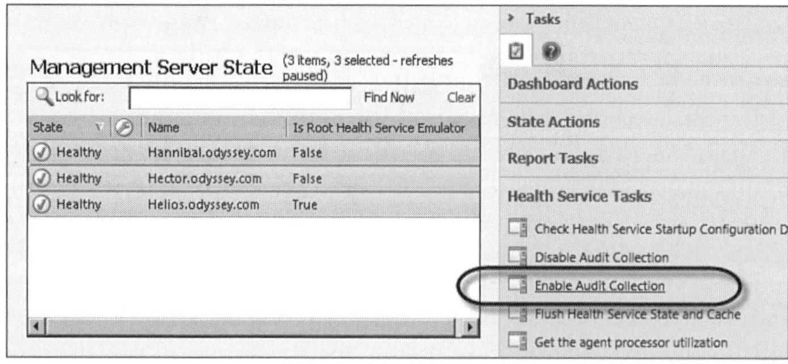

FIGURE 5.62 Running the Enable Audit Collection task for management servers.

3. Click the **Override** button, enter the name of the ACS collector to be used by the forwarders, and click **Run**.
4. Repeat steps 2 and 3, this time selecting all gateway servers and then running the Enable Audit Collection task.

5. Repeat steps 2 and 3, this time from the Operations Manager -> Agent Details -> Agents by Version view in the Monitoring space. Select all agents and run the Enable Audit Collection task.

Check Online for Update Rollups

After deploying OpsMgr 2012 components, always check for System Center updates Microsoft may have released. For any fresh deployment, deploy the latest update rollup to all management group components. To check for released updates to OpsMgr, run Microsoft Update on each server after completing the installation of OpsMgr components.

Importing Windows Server Management Packs

You should import several operating system management packs immediately. If you check the Windows Computers state view in the Operations console at this point in the installation, you will notice the Windows Operating System column on the right contains hollow green circles and all objects have Not Monitored status. This indicates the Windows Server management packs have not been imported.

Also, the new System Center 2012 Operations Manager network device monitoring feature requires the Windows Operating System management packs to be installed. To complete the core management group deployment, import these management packs:

- Windows Server Operating System Reports
- Windows Server Operating System Library
- Windows Server 2008 Operating System (Discovery)
- Windows Server 2008 Operating System (Monitoring)

If you will be monitoring the Windows Server 2012 operating system, download the management pack installer at http://www.microsoft.com/en-us/download/details.aspx?id=9296.

Figure 5.63 shows the four Windows Server 2008 management packs ready to import in the Operations console Administration space, Management Packs view. (The versions may be higher than those shown in the figure; always update to the latest version available.)

If you are using clustered OpsMgr SQL servers, consider also importing these management packs:

- Windows Cluster Management Library
- Windows Cluster Management Monitoring
- Windows Server 2008 Cluster Management Library
- Windows Server 2008 Cluster Management Monitoring
- Windows Server 2008 Cluster Shared Volume Monitoring

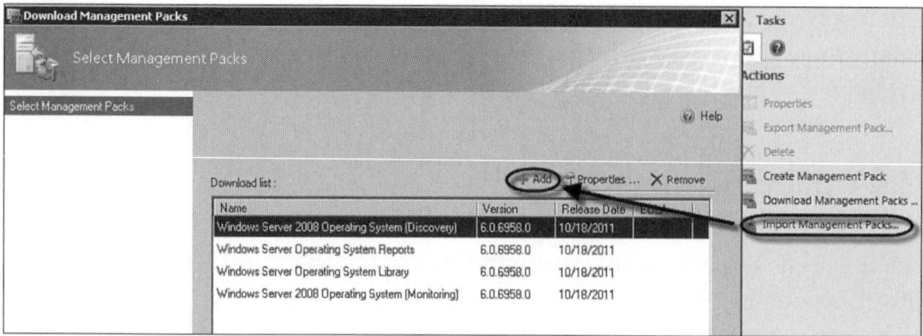

FIGURE 5.63 Importing core Windows Operating System management packs.

Removing OpsMgr

If you need to remove Operations Manager from your environment, the recommended process is the reverse order from which you installed the components. All OpsMgr installed components are manually uninstalled in a conventional manner using Control Panel -> Programs and Features. Follow this recommended outline to remove OpsMgr from your environment:

1. Disable the ACS forwarder component on all management servers, gateways, and agents using the Operations console.
2. Delete any computers monitored by agentless monitoring in the Operations console.
3. Manually uninstall all manually installed agents.
4. Remotely uninstall all automatically installed agents using the Uninstall task in the Operations console.
5. Uninstall the gateway server component from gateways and delete the gateway computer objects in the Operations console.
6. Uninstall all Web consoles and dedicated Operations console instances.
7. Uninstall the Reporting Server component.
8. Disable the ACS Collector role on any management servers running that role.
9. Uninstall each management server, uninstalling the root management server emulator last.
10. Optionally back up, and then delete the operational, data warehouse, and ACS databases from the SQL server(s) that hosted them.

Troubleshooting Your Installation

Any OpsMgr component that failed to install is marked with a red "X" in the setup wizard. A link allows you to review the setup log to learn the reason for the failure.

Clicking the link opens the log in Windows Notepad. Search on the words **FATAL ACTION**, and then examine the events that came about the same moment, to find the cause of the setup failure. See Figure 5.64 as an example of a failed installation.

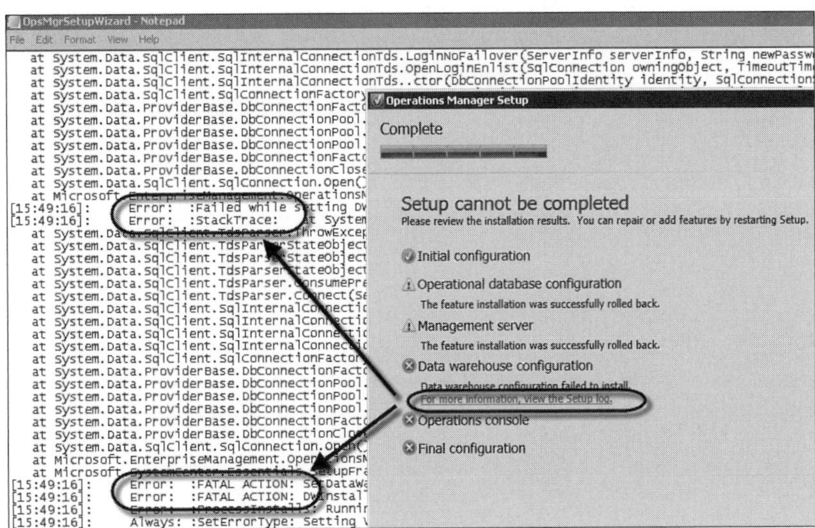

FIGURE 5.64 Searching for errors in the setup log of a failed installation.

Sometimes running setup of the first management server a second time will succeed when a first setup attempt failed, particularly when the first failure occurred during configuration of SQL security roles.

Summary

This chapter discussed the steps involved in installing a single server and a distributed System Center 2012 Operations Manager deployment. The next chapter discusses the process to upgrade an existing System Center Operations Manager 2007 R2 environment to System Center 2012 Operations Manager.

CHAPTER 6

Upgrading to System Center 2012 Operations Manager

IN THIS CHAPTER

If you are using System Center Operations Manager 2007 R2 and plan to upgrade to System Center 2012 Operations Manager, this is the chapter for you! The chapter discusses the procedures to upgrade or migrate to a System Center 2012 Operations Manager environment. If you are running an earlier version of Operations Manager (OpsMgr) than OpsMgr 2007 R2, such as OpsMgr 2007 or Microsoft Operations Manager (MOM) 2005, you must first upgrade to OpsMgr 2007 R2, as this version is required for the upgrade process.

Planning Your Upgrade

It is quite likely you will need to make some decisions upfront about the upgrade path for your OpsMgr environment. The next sections discuss how to assess your readiness to upgrade to System Center 2012 Operations Manager and the techniques available to deploy the upgrade.

Update OpsMgr 2007 R2 to Cumulative Update 4 or Later

Upgrading to System Center 2012 Operations Manager is supported from OpsMgr 2007 R2 Cumulative Update 4 (CU) or later. Before beginning any upgrade or migration process, ensure all OpsMgr 2007 R2 components, from agents to gateways to management servers, are updated to at least CU4. The latest cumulative update at publication time of this book is CU7; read more and download CU7 at http://support.microsoft.com/kb/2783850.

If you have large numbers of manually installed OpsMgr 2007 R2 agents not running a cumulative update or a version prior to CU4, you can upgrade those manually installed agents directly to OpsMgr 2012 agents after upgrading your OpsMgr 2007 R2 management and gateway servers to CU4 or a later version. Given that deploying the CU to manually installed agents is a tedious process and OpsMgr 2012 agents can report to OpsMgr 2007 R2 management servers and gateway servers running CU4 and later, this approach could save a considerable amount of time.

CAUTION: DEPLOY CUMULATIVE UPDATES CAREFULLY

If you need to update your OpsMgr 2007 R2 management group to CU4 or later, pay careful attention to the detailed instructions in the CU knowledge base article. CU rollout is a procedure with many steps, including executing SQL queries to update the operational and data warehouse databases. Hurrying your CU rollout could complicate your OpsMgr upgrade.

Strategic Upgrade Decisions

There are two categories of strategic decisions before proceeding with an upgrade or migration project:

- **Hardware/virtualization:** Decisions here involve implementing one of the following:
  - Keeping a similar architecture, in terms of physical versus virtual OpsMgr components and physical location for the management group
  - Moving to a new platform such as a private cloud, possibly in a different data center
- **OpsMgr database reuse:** A fundamental concept is that in-place upgrade of the management group occurs when (and if) the operational database is upgraded. There are two approaches to consider:
  - **Upgrade in place:** Whether to upgrade the existing database by upgrading in place the OpsMgr 2007 R2 root management server (RMS), or a secondary management server if retiring the RMS
  - **Side-by-side migration:** This approach, also known as a multi-homed migration, optionally preserves your OpsMgr 2007 R2 database and management packs but starts a clean database for OpsMgr 2012

Things have changed since the 2007 release of OpsMgr 2007. Virtualization was less widespread than now, and the concept of private clouds was just emerging. Today, factors such as the lower cost of infrastructure server virtual machines and System Center 2012 licensing (which bundles all System Center components and is discussed in Chapter 4, "Planning An Operations Manager Deployment") are likely to influence how Operations Manager upgrade projects are implemented at a business level.

OpsMgr architecture has also changed. While OpsMgr 2007 R2 included a clustered RMS architecture to achieve high availability, Operations Manager 2012 high availability does not utilize clustered management servers; this makes upgrade planning simpler if you did not deploy RMS clustering on OpsMgr 2007 R2.

System Center 2012 Operations Manager includes the new concept of a highly available management server without implementing clustering. Two or more management servers form part of a load-balanced and redundant *pool* (also known as a farm). Specifically, by deploying network load balancing (NLB) and establishing a DNS name for the NLB address of the management server pool, you can configure Operations consoles, Web consoles, and the reporting server with the DNS name for the pool. Chapter 9, "Complex Configurations," discusses the different high availability options for Operations Manager 2012.

In addition to these design concepts, here are tenants of OpsMgr 2007 R2 to Operations Manager 2012 upgrade and migration:

- **The upgrade process can include both upgrade and migration activities:** You can upgrade in place individual management server roles and gateway server roles, or migrate these roles to new computers. Remember to distinguish the concepts of upgrading a particular component (such as a single management server) from an upgrade of the entire management group. The latter is irreversible and occurs when you upgrade the operational database to System Center 2012 Operations Manager; this is generally one of the last steps of the upgrade project.
- **Upgraded components that are downstream can continue to report to legacy upstream components when rolling out an upgrade:** OpsMgr 2012 agents can report to an OpsMgr 2007 R2 gateway or management server, and OpsMgr 2012 gateways can report to OpsMgr 2007 R2 management servers.
  - Leverage this feature by multi-homing agents in side-by-side scenarios, upgrading from the edges of the OpsMgr 2007 R2 infrastructure towards your centrally located servers.
  - The key to success with your OpsMgr 2012 upgrade is the sequence of component upgrades. In a distributed upgrade, the Upgrade Helper management pack (MP) tracks the sequence of the components to upgrade. This is described in the "Performing an In-Place Upgrade" section.

  The authors define *downstream* in the upgrade scenario as agents and/or gateways that are at the edge of a distributed OpsMgr management group.
- **Operations Manager 2012 management group capacity is similar or better than OpsMgr 2007 R2:** If running a certain quantity of agents per management server on OpsMgr 2007 R2, plan on the same number or slightly higher with probably the same performance.
  - New features in OpsMgr 2012 such as network device monitoring and application performance monitoring (APM) add capacity-planning issues to consider after the upgrade if you will be using those features.

- There are no significant changes to advanced gateway and connected management group scenarios as far as architecture. There is a 25% increase in the maximum number of agents per gateway.

In-Place Upgrade Versus Multi-Homed Migration

The ability to upgrade an individual OpsMgr 2007 R2 component in place is determined by the operating system (OS) of the computer and/or version of SQL Server. Here are three points to consider about the OS and the SQL version:

- **Only Windows Server 2008 R2 with Service Pack (SP) 1 or Windows Server 2012 is supported for upgrades:** If your management servers, gateways, or database servers are running Windows Server 2008 R2 with SP 1, you can upgrade these computers to Operations Manager 2012. Otherwise, you must first upgrade the OS of that system to Window Server 2008 R2 SP 1 or migrate that OpsMgr role to a computer running Window Server 2008 R2 SP 1. Using Windows Server 2012 requires OpsMgr 2012 SP 1.
- **Only SQL Server 2008 Service Pack 1 (or later service packs) or R2 is supported when upgrading the OpsMgr databases:** Database servers running versions SQL Server 2008 SP 1 (or later service packs) or R2 can be upgraded. If using an earlier version, first upgrade the version of SQL Server on that system to SQL Server 2008 SP 1 or R2, or migrate that database role to a computer running SQL Server 2008 SP 1 or R2.

NOTE: OPSMGR 2012 SP 1 ADDS SQL 2012 AND SQL 2012 SP 1 SUPPORT

If upgrading to OpsMgr 2012 SP 1, additional SQL Server options are SQL Server 2012 and SQL Server 2012 SP 1. See http://technet.microsoft.com/en-us/library/jj628198.aspx for the list of SQL Server versions supported by SP 1.

- **SQL full-text search must be enabled:** Add this feature to any existing installation of SQL Server by running **Start** -> **SQL Server Installation Center** and selecting the **New installation or add features to an existing SQL Server installation** option.

Table 6.1 estimates the complexity of upgrade paths available in four scenarios, depending on the OS of the current management servers and gateways. The simple upgrade path is only possible if all existing OpsMgr 2007 R2 components are already running 64-bit Windows Server 2008 R2 with SP 1 and SQL Server 2008 SP 1 or R2. If you have any 32-bit operating systems or an OpsMgr 2007 R2 clustered RMS, by definition this is a complex upgrade path requiring some elements of migration. You cannot upgrade a 32-bit Windows OS to 64-bit; by definition, this is a clean install.

TABLE 6.1 Upgrade scenarios and paths

Upgrade Path	Current OpsMgr 2007 R2 = Single Server	Current OpsMgr 2007 R2 = Distributed Servers
Simple (In-place upgrade possible)	Windows Server 2008 R2 OS on the RMS	Windows Server 2008 R2 on all management servers and gateways, no clustered RMS
Complex (Some component migration needed)	32-bit OS on the RMS	32-bit OS on any management server or gateway, or clustered RMS

Upgrading your existing x64-based OpsMgr 2007 R2 database (in-place upgrade), or starting a parallel, new database (multi-homed migration) for Operations Manager 2012 is more a business decision. Here are some high-level considerations; the "Case Studies" section covers several upgrade and migration scenarios in detail.

- **In-place upgrade:** If you are satisfied with performance of your current OpsMgr 2007 R2 management group, and the new Operations Manager computers are co-located with the OpsMgr 2007 R2 management group, an upgrade and reuse of the database can save a considerable amount of time.
- **Multi-homed upgrade, clean start:** To maximize the performance and scaling potential of your new Operations Manager 2012 management group, start with a clean database and migrate custom management packs and settings from OpsMgr 2007 R2.
- **Multi-homed upgrade, new platform:** Consider using a clean database if your Operations Manager 2012 architecture is delivered from a different platform or service location than OpsMgr 2007 R2, such as part of a private cloud consolidation.

TIP: ABOUT UPGRADING THE ACS DATABASE

This chapter does not include information about upgrading the ACS database, as the ACS database version does not block an OpsMgr 2012 setup. Upgrading an ACS collector from OpsMgr 2007 R2 to OpsMgr 2012 does not perform SQL version checking; therefore, any existing ACS database will continue to be used by OpsMgr after the upgrade.

However, for support by Microsoft, all SQL servers in your management group must run the same version of SQL. If you need to upgrade or migrate the ACS database to a 64-bit OS and SQL 2008 or later because the ACS database needs to match the version of the other OpsMgr databases, upgrade or migrate the ACS database server OS and/or SQL at any convenient point during the upgrade.

RMS and Gateway Upgrade Challenges

The most common issue faced by many OpsMgr 2007 R2 administrators when considering upgrade paths to OpsMgr 2012 involves the RMS. Another common OpsMgr component requiring special planning during an upgrade is the gateway server. Here's why:

- **RMS—32-bit or clustered:** If your OpsMgr 2007 R2 RMS is running on a 32-bit OS, or is running in a clustered configuration (even a 64-bit cluster), it cannot be upgraded in place. Any OpsMgr RMS in these situations must be retired as part of the upgrade.
- **Gateway—32-bit:** If an OpsMgr 2007 R2 gateway server is running a 32-bit OS, it cannot be upgraded in place. Since you may upgrade gateways before management servers, you can deploy new gateways or redeploy gateways on new operating systems as part of your OpsMgr 2012 upgrade.

Microsoft's process flow diagram for upgrading Operations Manager is located at http://technet.microsoft.com/en-us/systemcenter/hh204732.aspx.

RMS Strategies

System Center 2012 Operations Manager achieves high management group services availability using a new resource pool concept of two or more co-equal management servers. Even after an upgrade from OpsMgr 2007 R2, one OpsMgr management server holds the root management server emulator (RMSE) role. This role is used by legacy workflows from older management packs explicitly targeting the RMS. This means the RMSE computer, as well as all OpsMgr 2012 management servers in the pool (thus eligible to succeed to the RMSE role), should be at least as powerful as the OpsMgr 2012 sizing calculator's recommendation for management servers. The OpsMgr sizing calculator includes RMSE workflows when it calculates required server capacities.

The management server initially holding the RMSE role depends on how you build your Operations Manager 2012 management group:

- **New OpsMgr 2012 management group:** Here the installed first management server holds the RMSE role.
- **OpsMgr 2007 R2 management group upgraded to OpsMgr 2012:** The RMSE is the last management server upgraded. This management server is either the RMS or a secondary OpsMgr 2007 R2 management server if you cannot upgrade the RMS in place.

Depending on the legacy management packs running in your environment, the additional workload of the RMSE can vary from negligible to significant. In smaller environments and those verified to have few if any legacy RMS-targeted workloads, it is acceptable for agents to report to the RMSE along with other management servers. Here are some RMSE and management server sizing considerations for larger environments:

- **Two management servers replace one RMS cluster for maximum scale potential:** Using two management servers provides equivalent high availability (N+1) for the management group as with the RMS cluster in OpsMgr 2007 R2. The computer running the RMSE role will have the most resources available for management group scale-out if no agents report directly to it. If no agents report to either the RMSE or an additional management server pre-selected to succeed to the RMSE role (which is seized or transferred with the `Set-SCOMRMSEmulator` cmdlet), the maximum management group scale-out capacity is possible even with an RMSE running many legacy management pack workloads.

- **Additional management servers:** Consider the number of management servers (other than the RMS) used for agent management on OpsMgr2007 R2, then plan for approximately the same number with OpsMgr 2012 dedicated to agent management. In large and complex environments, you can create special-purpose management and gateway server pools, where those management servers, if not in the All Management Servers Resource Pool, do not need to be as powerful as the server running the RMSE role.

Should your OpsMgr 2007 R2 RMS or OpsMgr 2007 R2 RMS cluster use a 32-bit OS, you must upgrade the database from a secondary management server. The database upgrade converts the management group to OpsMgr 2012, which immediately and permanently retires the former RMS/RMS cluster. The "Case Studies" section includes walkthroughs of RMS upgrade scenarios.

TIP: MANAGEMENT SERVER POOLS NOT INVOLVED WITH AGENT-MANAGED COMPUTERS

Resource pools only involve management group tasks formerly performed by the RMS, non-Windows computer monitoring, and device monitoring. Examples are group calculation tasks for the management group database, and monitoring of network devices and UNIX/Linux computers. Agent-managed Windows computers are assigned management or gateway servers using similar techniques as OpsMgr 2007 R2, including leveraging Active Directory for agent assignment. Agents are unaware of management server and gateway server pools.

9

Gateway Strategies

Gateway upgrade strategies include whether an OpsMgr 2007 R2 gateway server is running on a 32-bit OS, as you cannot upgrade these in place. Before upgrading to OpsMgr 2012, migrate the gateway server role to Windows Server 2008 R2 with SP 1 or Windows Server 2012 (with System Center 2012 SP 1) for each location requiring a gateway server. This makes the ease or difficulty in deploying (or provisioning) new infrastructure computers in those locations with existing 32-bit gateway servers an upgrade consideration.

Gateways servers are most likely in remote or untrusted network segments, while management servers typically are in or near the data center where the OpsMgr SQL Server database systems are located. The data center typically has resources that can migrate management servers to new computers running Windows Server 2008 R2 with SP 1 (or Windows Server 2012 with System Center 2012 SP 1) without much trouble.

In remote or untrusted network segments with a gateway running a 32-bit OS, you must provide a new platform that can run Windows Server 2008 R2 with SP 1 or above. If a monitoring service outage is acceptable and the hardware or virtualization permits it, you could wipe the 32-bit server, install Windows Server 2008 R2 SP 1 or above, rename the new system to match the original gateway, and install an OpsMgr 2012 gateway. Unfortunately, in an enterprise scenario the outage (and business risk of undetected problems) might be unacceptably long. The "Case Studies" section includes walkthroughs of gateway upgrade scenarios.

Using the Upgrade Helper Management Pack

Regardless of the upgrade path you select, the Upgrade Helper management pack will be useful if not required to get the job done. This MP guides you through the upgrade process when you have a distributed topology, and is located in the \ManagementPacks folder of the OpsMgr software distribution media. Follow these steps to import the management pack into your OpsMgr 2007 R2 management group before beginning your upgrade or migration:

1. Log on to a computer running the OpsMgr 2007 R2 console using an account that is a member of the Operations Manager Administrators role for the OpsMgr 2007 R2 management group.
2. In the Operations console, navigate to the Administration space, right-click the Management Packs node, and then select **Import Management Packs.**
3. In the Import Management Packs Wizard, click **Add**, and then select **Add from disk**.
4. The Select Management Packs to import dialog box opens. Browse to the \ManagementPacks folder of the System Center 2012 Operations Manager installation media. Select **OperationsManager.Upgrade.mp**, and then click **Open**.
5. The Select Management Packs page lists the management pack you selected for import. A green check mark next to the management pack indicates that it is ready to be imported. Click **Install.**
6. The Import Management Packs page appears and shows the progress for the management pack. When the import is complete as shown in Figure 6.1, click **Close**.

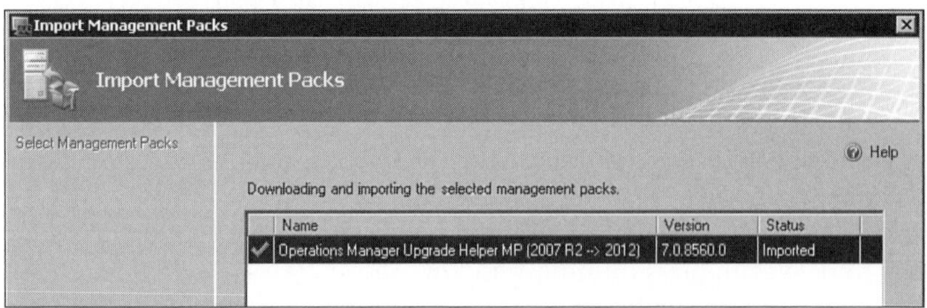

FIGURE 6.1 Importing the Upgrade Helper management pack.

The Upgrade Helper management pack is a decision and display aid for the upgrade process. It does not modify the OpsMgr database and is not required for any software process in the upgrade, so its installation is optional. However, because the status information in the console views makes your upgrade experience easier, the authors recommended you always import this management pack. Particularly in a distributed management group, it is important to upgrade the OpsMgr components in a particular sequence. In any management group with agents, you will want to know when all agents have upgraded successfully to System Center 2012 Operations Manager. The primary feature of the management pack is a series of five sequentially numbered state views in the Operations console. These views both prioritize the order of component upgrade, and provide feedback that the server and agent components have upgraded.

After you import the Upgrade Helper management pack, discovery will run within 15 minutes and populate the management pack views with unmonitored objects. It can take up to 24 hours for version status to be collected on all discovered computers (another reason to install this management pack as your first upgrade task). The left of Figure 6.2 shows a circle around the state views added by the management pack.

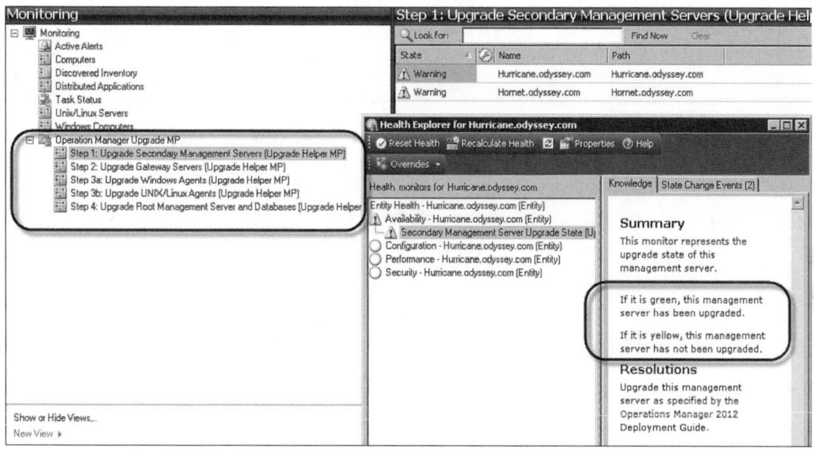

FIGURE 6.2 Step 1 view of the Upgrade Helper management pack shows the upgrade state of secondary management servers.

Figure 6.2 focuses on the Step 1 view of the Upgrade Helper MP, Upgrade Secondary Management Servers. The right side of the figure shows the Health Explorer for the upgrade status object. If green, the management server has been upgraded. If it is yellow, the management server has not been upgraded. Figure 6.3 is a similar view, this time focused on step 3a of the management pack, Upgrade Windows Agents.

The upgrade Windows and UNIX/Linux agent state views such as that shown in Figure 6.3 can be very useful to track the status of manually installed agents. You should upgrade manually installed agents to OpsMgr 2012 before upgrading the secondary management or gateway servers to which they report. Automatically installed agents are push-upgraded from the console after the management or gateway servers they report to are upgraded.

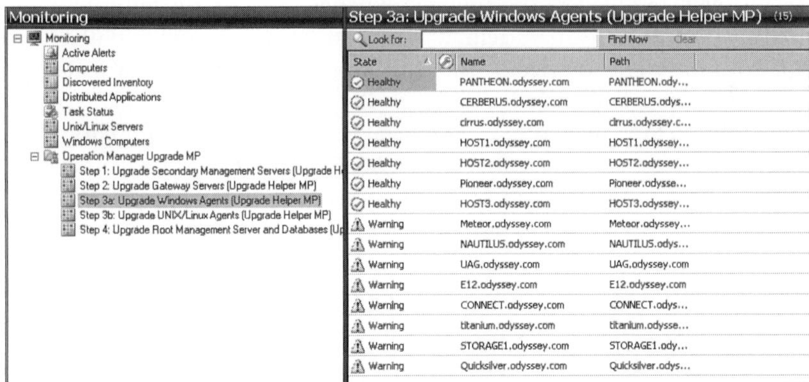

FIGURE 6.3 Step 3a view of the Upgrade Helper management pack shows the upgrade state of Windows agents.

TIP: UPGRADE MANUAL AGENTS AND GATEWAYS FIRST

The TechNet reference that discusses upgrading a distributed OpsMgr 2007 R2 environment at http://technet.microsoft.com/en-us/library/hh241304 states "When you upgrade a distributed System Center Operations Manager 2007 R2 environment to System Center 2012 – Operations Manager, you start by upgrading any manually installed agents, followed by the secondary management servers, gateways, and any push-installed agents."

Manually installed agents are your first priority. The authors recommend you then upgrade gateways that report to secondary management servers, conforming to an "outside -> inward" upgrade approach. This method is your best track to maintaining uninterrupted monitoring during migration.

The functional use of the Upgrade Helper management pack is straightforward:

1. Follow the steps in order as they appear in the Operations Manager Upgrade MP view folder in the Monitoring space of the Operations console.
2. Upgrade those computers that appear in the Results pane in Warning (yellow) status until they are all Healthy (green).
3. Once all the computers in a step view are green, move to the next higher numbered step of the management pack.
4. Upgrade the RMS and database last, after upgrading all other management group components.

When your upgrade or migration is complete, and after the database is upgraded and the OpsMgr 2007 R2 RMS is removed, you can safely uninstall the Upgrade Helper management pack. The management pack is not required by System Center 2012 Operations Manager and serves no function after the upgrade.

TIP: NEEDING TO RE-REGISTER POWERSHELL MODULE AFTER UPGRADING

If you have PowerShell (PS) scripts running in your management packs that utilize the OpsMgr 2007 snap-in PS module, verify the snap-in is still available on the upgraded servers. Run the cmdlet `Get-PSSnapin -registered`. If the output lists PSVersion: 1.0, Microsoft Operations Manager Shell Snapin, the module is registered. If the module is no longer registered, follow the instructions at http://derekhar.blogspot.de/2007/07/operation-manager-command-shell-on-any.html to register the OpsMgr 2007 modules manually.

Performing an In-Place Upgrade

The next sections cover upgrading an OpsMgr 2007 R2 management group to an OpsMgr 2012 management group using the same operational database; this preserves the management group name, settings, and performance history. If you are performing a multi-homed (side-by-side) migration that creates a new OpsMgr database, the "Performing a Multi-Homed Upgrade" section is more applicable.

If you *don't* have a clustered RMS and *are not* running a 32-bit OS on your RMS, the authors suggest an in-place upgrade of the RMS. While this is the most efficient upgrade path, it is only available for those OpsMgr 2007 R2 management groups meeting the requirements in the "Simple" row of Table 6.1 in terms of operating system and SQL Server requirements (version 2008 SP 1 or 2008 R2).

If you have an RMS that cannot be upgraded in place, the "Upgrading from a Secondary Management Server" section discusses how to upgrade the database from a secondary management server; this also allows you to preserve the OpsMgr 2007 R2 management group data. This means regardless of where you start with your OpsMgr 2007 R2 configuration, you can reuse your database and migrate to an OpsMgr 2012 configuration by following the procedures in this chapter.

TIP: DATA WAREHOUSE DATABASE UPGRADE REQUIRES 4GB RAM

Although the upgrade wizard will let you proceed (with a caution) if you have between 2GB and 4GB of memory, the data warehouse upgrade can fail with only 2GB memory installed. If using a virtual machine (VM) as your RMS or secondary management server when performing the management group upgrade, ensure that at least 4GB memory is available to the VM. If necessary, after the upgrade you could theoretically reduce the memory back to 2GB, although the authors do not recommend this.

Upgrading the Single Server Management Group

The simplest possible upgrade path to OpsMgr 2012 from OpsMgr 2007 R2 is the single (all-in-one) OpsMgr server model, where all OpsMgr and SQL components reside on the same computer. An all-in-one OpsMgr system is generally found only in the smallest of production networks and more often in lab, training, and demo environments. A candidate for this upgrade path is an OpsMgr 2007 R2 RMS on a 64-bit OS, using SQL 2008 SP 1 or R2.

When the required OS and SQL versions are present, an in-place upgrade of all components is simple. If necessary, first upgrade from an earlier 64-bit Windows Server OS to Windows Server 2008 R2 with SP 1 and/or SQL 2005 to SQL 2008 SP 1 or R2. OpsMgr 2007 R2 supports in-place upgrades of the OS and SQL versions. For instructions on upgrading SQL Server Reporting Services (SSRS) from SQL 2005 to SQL 2008 R2, see http://technet.microsoft.com/en-us/library/dd789004.aspx.

Follow these steps to upgrade a single-server management group:

1. Import the Upgrade Helper management pack as previously discussed in the "Upgrade Helper Management Pack" section.
2. Review the Operations Manager 2007 R2 event logs on the RMS to look for recurring warnings or critical events. Address any issues before proceeding. The authors do not recommend attempting to upgrade an RMS with an Operations Manager log packed with critical (red) events.
3. Reject any agents in the Device Management -> Pending Management node of the Administration space of the Operations console.
4. Back up the RMS encryption key using the SecureStorageBackup.exe utility:
   - Open a command prompt using the Run as Administrator option.
   - At the command prompt, change directory to the OpsMgr installation folder such as *%ProgramFiles%*\System Center Operations Manager 2007, and type the command **SecureStorageBackup**.
   - On the Backup or Restore page of the Encryption Key Backup or Restore Wizard, select the **Backup the Encryption Key** option and complete the wizard, providing a location and password for the key. Figure 6.4 shows the page where you specify the location and name of the backup key file.
5. Disable all notification subscriptions at Administration -> Notifications -> in the Operations console.
6. Stop all System Center Operations Manager services and disable any installed connectors. Check the Product Connectors node of the Administration space of the console to determine if your management group has any connectors.

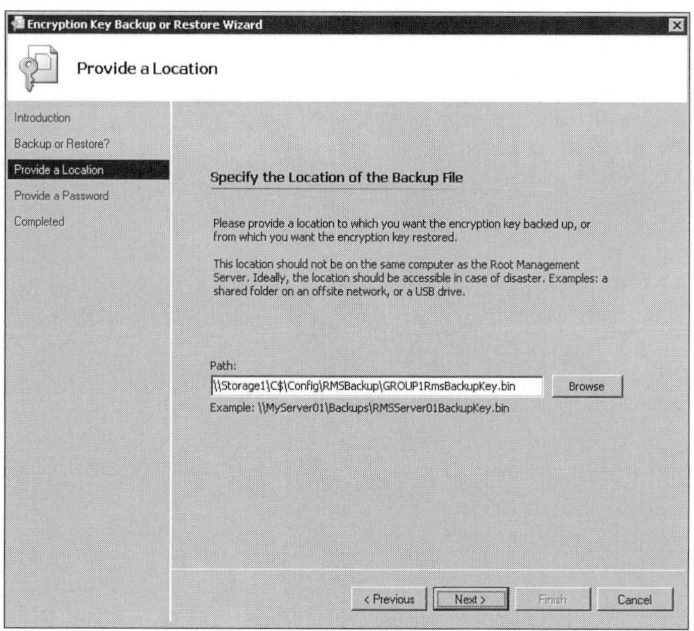

FIGURE 6.4 Back up the encryption key before upgrading the RMS.

7. Verify the operational database has at least 50% free space before upgrading the management group. The upgrade might fail if there is not enough space. Also ensure that the transaction logs are 50% of the total size of the operational database:

   - To check free space in the operational database, open SQL Server Management Studio, connect to your SQL instance, and in the Object Explorer, expand the Databases node, as shown in Figure 6.5. Right-click the operational database (such as OperationsManager), point to **Reports** -> **Standard Reports**, and then click **Disk Usage**. View the Disk Usage report to determine the percentage of free space.

   - To modify the allocated disk space, right-click the operational database and select **Properties**. In the Database Properties dialog box, under Select a page, click **Files**. In the Results pane, increase the Initial Size value for the MOM_DATA database by 50%. (This step is not required if free space already exceeds 50%.) Set the Initial Size value for the MOM_LOG to be 50% of the total size of the database. For example, if the operational database size is 100GB, the log file size should be 50GB. Click **OK**.

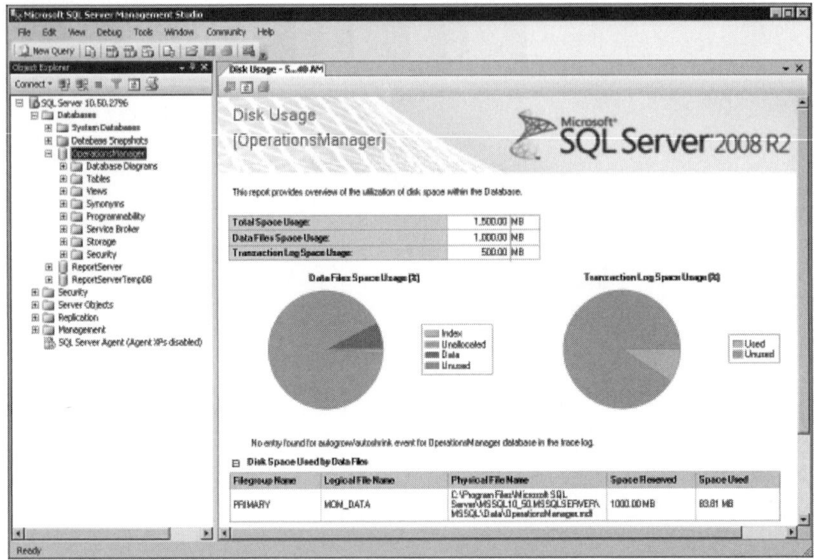

FIGURE 6.5 Confirming >50% Unallocated space in operational database.

8. Confirm you have a supported SQL Server collation on all databases and instances of databases:

   - In SQL Server Management Studio, right-click the database you want to check, and then click **Properties**. The collation is listed under Maintenance.
   - SQL Server collation for all databases and database instances must be one of those listed in Table 6.2.

TABLE 6.2 SQL Server collations supported for upgrade to System Center 2012 Operations Manager

Language	Collation
English	SQL_Latin1_General_CP1_CI_AS
French	French_CI_AS
Russian	Cyrillic_General_CI_AS
Chinese CHS	Chinese_PRC_CI_AS
Japanese	Japanese_CI_AS
Spanish	Traditional_Spanish_CI_AS
Other Languages	Latin1_General_CI_AS

9. Back up the Operations Manager databases:

   - Obtain verified recent backups of the operational database (OperationsManager by default), the data warehouse database (default OperationsManagerDW), and of the operating system and system state of the RMS computer. If your upgrade fails, these backups might be the only way to restore OpsMgr services. Follow the procedure at http://technet.microsoft.com/library/ms187510.aspx to create a full SQL database backup if you do not have a backup process in place.

- You should also create backups of databases for optional features, such as the reporting and the ACS audit databases, before upgrading them. Use Windows Backup or a third-party backup application to create the full RMS computer OS backup with system state.

10. Upgrade manually installed agents:

- Upgrade a manually installed agent by running Setup from the System Center 2012 Operations Manager distribution media on the managed computer. From the splash screen, click the **Local agent** link in the Optional Installations section. The Agent Upgrade Wizard should appear as shown in Figure 6.6. Click **Next**, **Upgrade**, and **Finish** on successive pages to complete the agent upgrade.

- To upgrade a manually installed agent using the command line, open an elevated command prompt, and navigate to the folder containing the OpsMgr software media distribution. Change directory to the \Agent folder, then to \AMD64, \i386, or \IA64 as appropriate, and run the command in Listing 6.1.

  Note: If you upgrade manually installed agents that also run the AVIcode 5.7 agent (or earlier versions of the AVIcode agent), you must include the option **NOAPM=1** in the command.

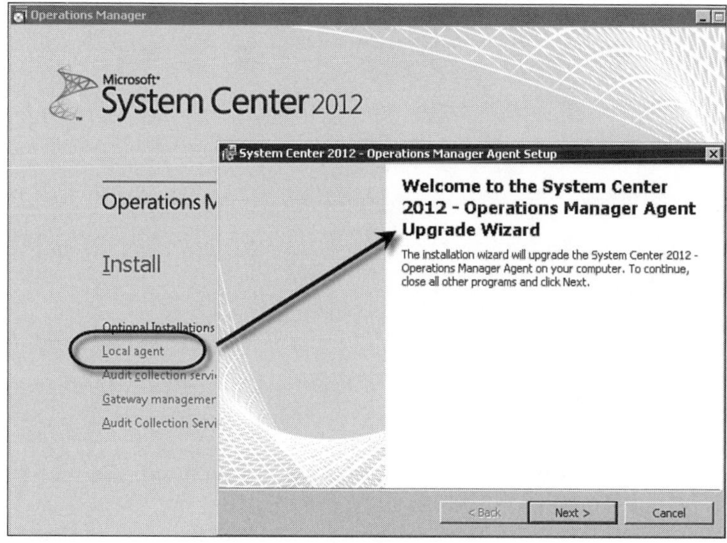

FIGURE 6.6 Manually upgrading an OpsMgr 2007 R2 agent to OpsMgr 2012.

LISTING 6.1 Command line upgrade: Agent

```
%WinDir%\System32\msiexec.exe /I MOMAgent.msi /qn [NOAPM=1]
```

11. Run the management group upgrade on the RMS.

- The same management server and database server prerequisites for a fresh install of System Center 2012 Operations Manager are required for an upgrade. Refer to Chapter 5, "Installing System Center 2012 Operations Manager," for details and procedures to install prerequisites. Prerequisites are primarily that the .NET 3.5 feature is enabled and .NET 4 Framework installed, Microsoft Report Viewer is installed, ISAPI and CGI Restrictions are enabled in web services, that SQL full text search is enabled on the OpsMgr databases, and the SQL Server Agent service is running.
- Run Setup from the System Center 2012 Operations Manager distribution media on the RMS computer. Click **Install** from the splash screen. The list of components to be upgraded is displayed as seen in Figure 6.7. Click **Next**.

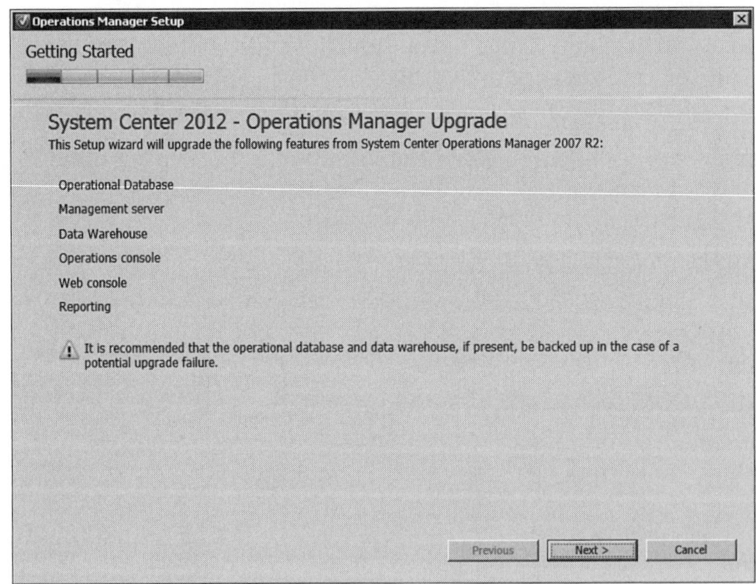

FIGURE 6.7 OpsMgr Setup ready to upgrade all components.

- Accept the license agreement by selecting **I have read, understood, and agree with the license terms** and clicking **Next**.
- On the next page, select Installation location. The default location is *%ProgramFiles%*\System Center 2012\Operations Manager. Accept the default or specify an alternative path, and click **Next**.

- Setup continues with the message **Verifying that your environment has the required hardware and software**. If there are issues, the message **The Setup wizard cannot continue** appears as shown in Figure 6.8. This means additional hardware resources or software are required to continue.

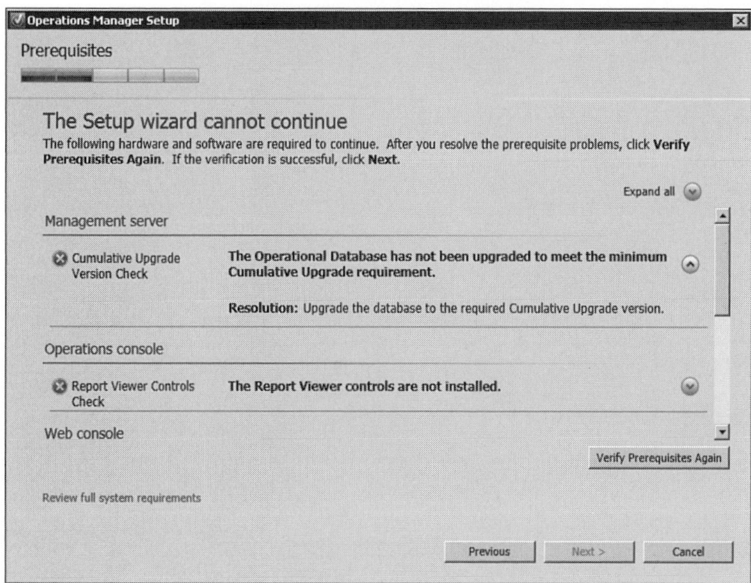

FIGURE 6.8 Setup wizard reporting issues that block upgrade.

- After resolving any prerequisite problems, click **Verify Prerequisites Again**. If verification is successful, click **Next**.
- At the Specify a web site to use with the Web console page, if you are upgrading the Web console, select the website to which to install the OpsMgr 2012 Web console. You cannot select the current Operations Manager 2007 Web console website as that site is deleted during the upgrade. Optionally select to enable Secure Sockets Layer (SSL). Click **Next**.
- At the Select an authentication mode for use with the Web console page, select **Use Network Authentication**. Click **Next**.
- At the Configure Operations Manager accounts page, specify the credentials for the System Center Configuration service and System Center Data Access service, as seen in Figure 6.9. This account must be a member of the Operations Manager Administrators role. Click **Next**.
- At the Ready to Upgrade page, review your selections for the features you are upgrading, review the web addresses (there are several new ones), and click **Upgrade** as shown in Figure 6.10.

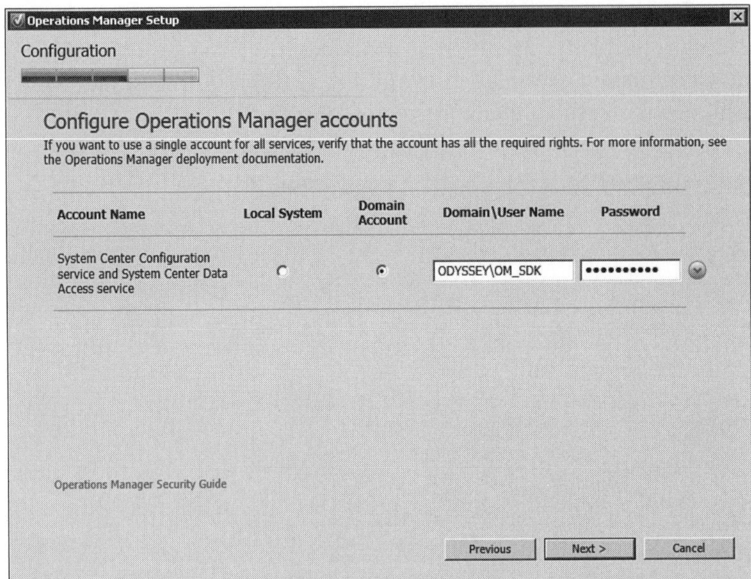

FIGURE 6.9 Specify the domain account for the Configuration and Data Access services.

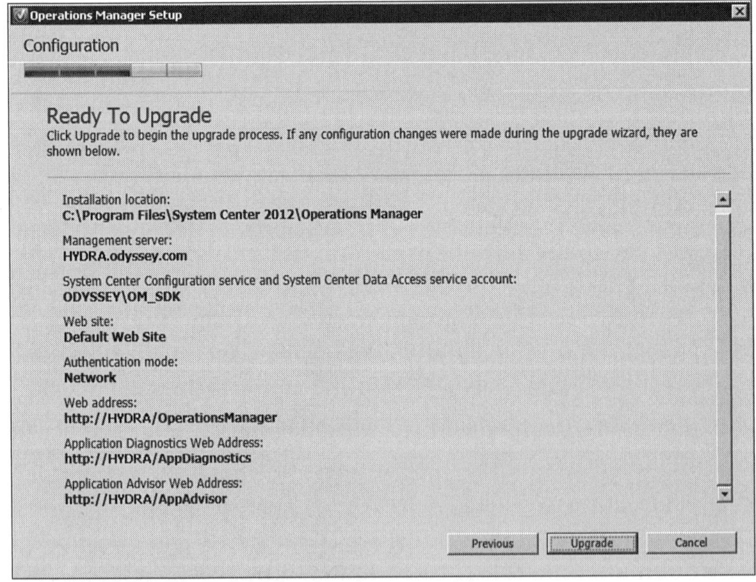

FIGURE 6.10 The final configuration page before upgrade.

- Upgrade is complete when all green check marks appear in the left column as shown in Figure 6.11. Any component that failed to install is marked with a red "X." Consider checking the option to **Launch Microsoft Update when the wizard closes**. Click **Close** to complete the wizard.

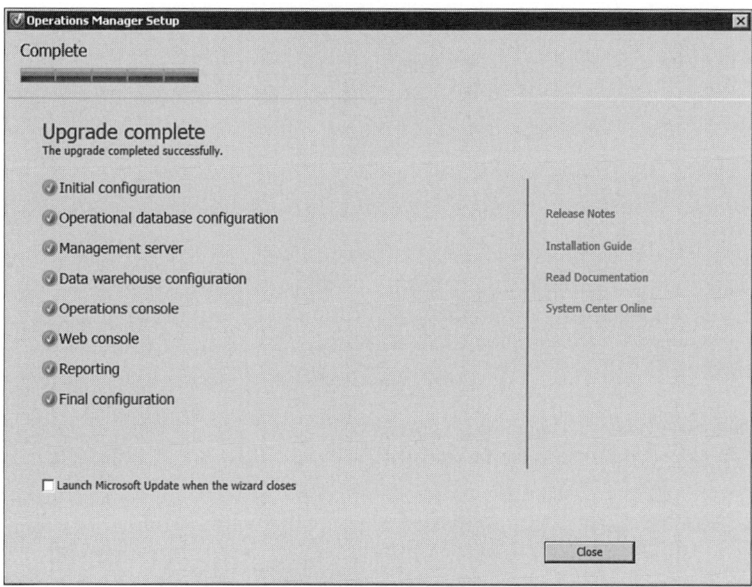

FIGURE 6.11 Upgrade complete on all OpsMgr components.

- You will want to **Exit** the OpsMgr installer that is still open, unless you wish to review the other online links such as Product Documentation, or if you need to upgrade the ACS collector, which can be performed immediately as a next step if the RMS is also an ACS collector. For details on upgrading the ACS collector, see the "Upgrading the Distributed Management Group" section.

- To upgrade a single-server management server using the command line, open an elevated command prompt, navigate to the folder containing the OpsMgr software media distribution, and run the command in Listing 6.2.

LISTING 6.2 Command line upgrade: Single-server management group

```
setup.exe /silent /upgrade
/AcceptEndUserLicenseAgreement
/DASAccountUser:<domain\UserName>
/DASAccountPassword:<password>
```

If the RMS was installed using the Local System account, replace the last two switches with this one:

```
/UseLocalSystemDASAccount
```

If a data warehouse (reporting server) is deployed in the OpsMgr 2007 R2 management group, add these switches.

```
/DWSqlServerInstance:<ComputerName\instance>
/DWDatabaseName:<DWDatabaseName>
/DatareaderUser:<domain\UserName>
/DatareaderPassword:<password>
/DataWriterUser:<domain\UserName>
/DataWriterPassword:<password>
```

If a Web console is deployed on the management server, add the switches listed below. Use the `/WebConsoleUseSSL` parameter only if your website has SSL activated. For a default web installation, specify Default Web Site for the `/WebSiteName` parameter.

```
/WebsiteName: "<WebSiteName>" [/WebConsoleUseSSL]
/WebConsoleAuthorizationMode: [Mixed|Network]
```

12. Upgrade the push-installed agents. Manually installed agents were upgraded *before* upgrading the management group; however, you can upgrade push-installed (automatically installed) agents remotely using the OpsMgr 2012 Operations console *after* upgrading the management group.

13. Upgrade push-installed agents from the Administration space of the Operations console. Navigate to **Device Management** -> **Pending Management**. OpsMgr 2007 R2 agents will be listed with the status Agent Requires Update. Select up to 200 agents at a time, right-click, and click **Approve**. From the Update Agents dialog box, confirm use of the management server action account or enter administrative credentials manually, and click **Update**.

14. Re-enable any notification subscriptions disabled for the upgrade at the **Notifications** -> **Subscriptions** node of the Administration space of the console.

15. Start or re-enable those services or connectors disabled for the upgrade at the Product Connectors node of the Administration space of the console.

16. Verify the success of the upgrade.

- Check the health state of the management server and agents in the Health Service Watcher state view in the Monitoring space of the Operations console.
- In the Administration space, ensure the management server and agents are healthy.
- In the Monitoring space, check if there are any alerts related to management group health.

- Review the event logs of the management server for new errors. (Sort alerts by the last-modified column to review the new alerts.)
- Check the CPU utilization and disk I/O on your database server(s) to ensure they are functioning normally.
- If reporting is installed, select the Reporting node, then run a generic performance report to ensure that reporting is functioning correctly.

17. Run a SQL query on the operational database to clean up the Localizedtext table and the Publishmessage table. You can copy this query from Microsoft's website at http://technet.microsoft.com/en-us/library/8c2dbaf4-2966-45e3-a72d-5de90ff4f495#BKMK_VerifyUpgrade. The authors provide this query as a convenience with the online content for this book as **SCOM-2012-Post-Upgrade-SQL-Cleanup.sql**. See Appendix E, "Available Online," for further information.

Upgrading the Distributed Management Group

This section discusses a possible upgrade scenario for mid-market and enterprise OpsMgr 2007 R2 customers running on 64-bit platforms. This procedure applies to all OpsMgr management groups with two or more Windows servers running OpsMgr server components, all meeting the required OS and SQL version requirements to upgrade. If your reporting server and/or database server(s) are not installed on the RMS, or there are dedicated Web console servers, additional management servers, or gateway servers in the management group, this procedure may apply to you. A candidate for this upgrade path has all OpsMgr 2007 R2 components running on Windows Server 2008 R2 servers, and on SQL 2008 SP 1 or R2 databases.

If necessary, consider upgrading in-place from an earlier 64-bit Windows Server OS to Windows Server 2008 R2 with SP 1 or Windows Server 2012, and/or SQL 2005 to SQL 2008 R2 or SQL Server 2012. OpsMgr 2007 R2 supports in-place upgrades of the OS and SQL Server. For instructions on upgrading SSRS from SQL 2005 to a newer release, see http://technet.microsoft.com/en-us/library/dd789004.aspx and http://msdn.microsoft.com/en-us/library/ms143747.aspx.

TIP: OPSMGR 2012 SP 1 SUPPORTS WINDOWS SERVER 2012

When considering the server OS for OpsMgr 2012 SP 1 features, you can use Windows Server 2012 as well as Windows Server 2008 R2 SP 1. OpsMgr 2012 release to manufacture (RTM) version could not install on Windows Server 2012; the ability to install on Windows Server 2012 is a new feature with SP 1. Consider upgrading to Windows Server 2012 for the longest service life on your OpsMgr server computers.

In terms of SQL Server support, OpsMgr 2012 SP 1 adds the ability to install on SQL Server 2012 and SQL Server 2012 SP 1, but OpsMgr 2012 SP 1 does not require SQL 2012. OpsMgr 2012 SP 1 still installs on SQL Server 2008 R2; although database support for earlier versions of SQL Server is dropped.

If you have the required OS and SQL versions, in-place upgrade of distributed components is fully supported; however, you must perform the upgrade steps in a particular sequence. To upgrade a distributed-server management group, follow these steps:

1. Import the Upgrade Helper management pack, previously described in the "Upgrade Helper Management Pack" section.

2. Review the event logs for Operations Manager 2007 R2 on the RMS and all management servers to look for recurring warning or critical events. Address these issues before proceeding. The authors do not recommend attempting to upgrade when any management server has an Operations Manager log packed with critical (red) events.

3. To avoid downtime of monitoring agent-managed computers, move those agents reporting to the RMS to secondary management servers. Navigate to **Administration -> Device Management -> Agent-Managed**, right-click the computers in the Agent-Managed node with agents you want to move to a secondary management server, and then click **Change Primary Management Server**. Use the same procedure to move UNIX or Linux agents.

TIP: MOVE ALL AGENTS OFF THE RMS AND UPGRADE THEM

Before upgrading the RMS, upgrade all agents from upgraded management servers, including moving agents to secondary management servers that are or will be upgraded before the RMS. While you can upgrade push-installed agents after the upgrade, there could be an extended gap in monitoring history for non-upgraded agents. For a seamless agent upgrade, push-upgrade all push-installed agents—from upgraded secondary management servers—such that no OpsMgr 2007 R2 agents remain when it is time to upgrade the RMS.

4. Reject any pending installations of agents in the **Device Management -> Pending Management** node of the Administration space of the Operations console.

5. Back up the RMS encryption key using the SecureStorageBackup.exe utility:

   - On the RMS, open a command prompt window using the Run as Administrator option.

   - At the command prompt, change directory to the OpsMgr installation folder such as *%ProgramFiles%*\System Center Operations Manager 2007 and type **SecureStorageBackup**.

   - On the Backup or Restore page of the Encryption Key Backup or Restore Wizard, select **Backup the Encryption Key** and complete the wizard, providing a location and password for the key, previously seen in Figure 6.4.

6. Confirm you have a supported SQL Server collation on all databases and instances of databases:

   - To determine the SQL Server collation of a database, check the database properties. In SQL Server Management Studio, right-click the database you want to check and select **Properties**. Database collation is listed under the Maintenance heading.

- SQL Server collation for all databases and database instances must be one of those listed in Table 6.2.

7. Upgrade manually installed agents:
   - Upgrade a manually installed agent by running Setup from the distribution media on the managed computer. On the splash screen, click the **Local agent** link in the Optional Installations section. The Agent Upgrade Wizard should appear as previously shown in Figure 6.6. Click **Next**, **Upgrade**, and **Finish** on successive pages to complete the agent upgrade.
   - To upgrade a manually installed agent using the command line, run the command in Listing 6.1.

8. Upgrade secondary management servers:
   - For each management server listed in the Upgrade Helper management pack at the Step 1 - Upgrade Secondary Management Servers view, upgrade the management server component in-place, as well as any other components installed on that server such as OpsMgr 2007 R2 consoles.
   - The same management server prerequisites for performing a fresh install of System Center 2012 Operations Manager are required for an upgrade. Chapter 5 includes details and procedures to install prerequisites. Prerequisites for management servers are primarily that the .NET 3.5 feature is enabled, .NET 4 Framework is installed, and Microsoft Report Viewer is installed.
   - Run Setup from the System Center 2012 Operations Manager distribution media on the secondary management server computer. Click **Install** on the splash screen. The list of components to be upgraded is displayed as seen in Figure 6.12. Click **Next**.
   - Accept the license agreement by selecting **I have read, understood, and agree with the license terms** and clicking **Next**.
   - On the next screen, select **Installation location**. The default location is *%ProgramFiles%*\System Center 2012\Operations Manager. Accept the default or specify an alternative path, and click **Next**.
   - Setup continues with the message **Verifying that your environment has the required hardware and software**. If there are issues, the message **The Setup wizard cannot continue** appears as previously shown in Figure 6.8; in this case additional hardware resources or software are required to continue.
   - After resolving any prerequisite issues, click **Verify Prerequisites Again**. If the verification is successful, click **Next**.

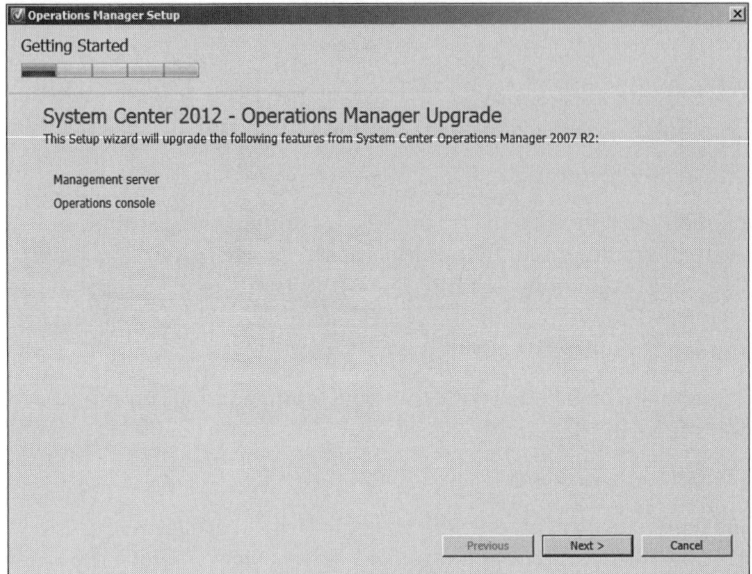

FIGURE 6.12 Upgrading a secondary management server with a console.

- At the Configure Operations Manager accounts page, specify the credentials for the System Center Configuration service and System Center Data Access service, previously shown in Figure 6.9. The account used must be a member of the Operations Manager Administrators role. Click **Next**.
- At the Ready to Upgrade page, review your selections for the features you are upgrading and click **Upgrade** as shown in Figure 6.13.
- Upgrade is complete when all green check marks appear in the left column as previously shown in Figure 6.11. Any component that failed to install is marked with a red "X." Consider selecting the option to launch Microsoft Update when the wizard closes (recommended). Click **Close** to complete the wizard.
- To upgrade a secondary management server using the command line, open an elevated command prompt, navigate to the folder containing the OpsMgr installation media, and run the command in Listing 6.3.

LISTING 6.3 Command line upgrade: Secondary management server

```
setup.exe /silent /upgrade
/DASAccountUser:<domain\UserName>
/DASAccountPassword:<password>
```

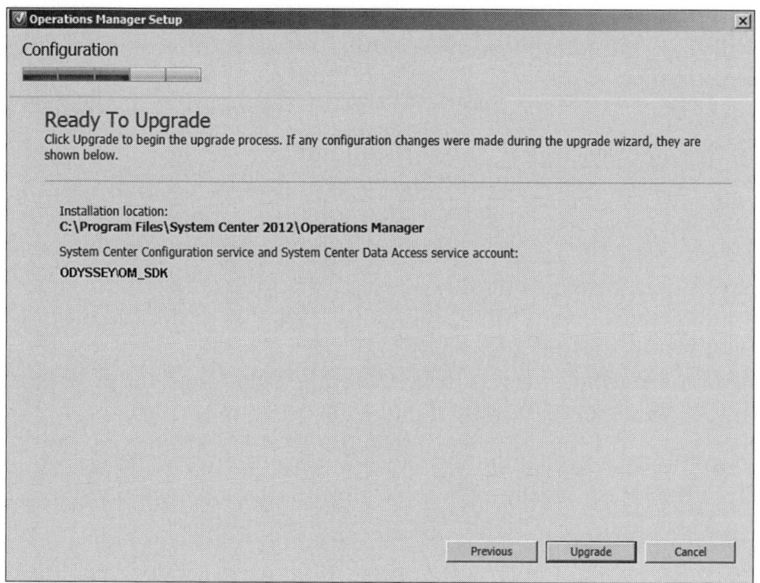

FIGURE 6.13 Ready to upgrade secondary management server with a console.

If the secondary management server was installed using the Local System account, replace the last two switches with this one:

```
/UseLocalSystemDASAccount
```

9. Upgrade gateway servers:

   - For each gateway server listed in the Upgrade Helper management pack at the Step 2 - Upgrade Secondary Management Servers view, upgrade the gateway server component in place. To confirm the management server to which each gateway reports, run the script in Listing 6.4 in PowerShell on a management server. If upgrading the management group from a secondary management server, move any gateways reporting to the RMS to another management server.

LISTING 6.4 Script to display management servers for all gateway servers

```
#Display primary and failover management servers for all gateway servers
$GWs = Get-SCOMManagementServer | where {$_.IsGateway -eq $true}
$GWs | sort | foreach {
Write-Host "";
"Gateway MS :: " + $_.Name;
"--Primary MS :: " + ($_.GetPrimaryManagementServer()).ComputerName;
$failoverServers = $_.getFailoverManagementServers();
```

```
foreach ($managementServer in $failoverServers) {
"--Failover MS :: " + ($managementServer.ComputerName);
}
}
Write-Host "";
```

- The same gateway server prerequisites for performing a fresh install of OpsMgr 2012 are required for an upgrade. Chapter 5 includes details and procedures to install prerequisites. Prerequisites for gateway servers are primarily that the .NET 3.5 feature is enabled and .NET 4 Framework installed (if network devices and/or UNIX/Linux agents are monitored), and that certificates are deployed to gateways and management servers to permit authentication. Existing (valid) certificates are automatically reused by the upgraded gateway server.
- Run Setup from the OpsMgr distribution media on the gateway server computer. From the splash screen, click the **Gateway management server** link in the Optional Installations section to start the upgrade wizard.
- The Welcome to the System Center 2012 – Operations Manager Gateway Server Upgrade Wizard appears, displayed in Figure 6.14. Click **Next**.

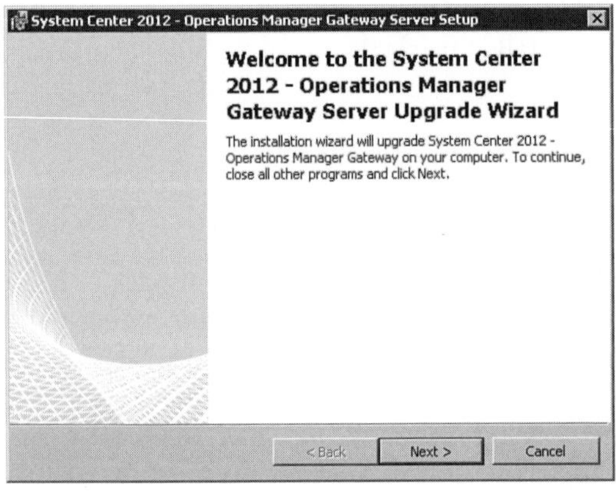

FIGURE 6.14 Upgrading the OpsMgr 2007 R2 gateway in place.

- The next page reports the wizard is ready to begin the gateway upgrade; click **Upgrade**. When upgrade completes, click **Finish**.
- Copy the MOMCertImport.exe file from the \SupportTools folder on the installation media to the OpsMgr program files gateway folder, such as *%ProgramFiles%*\System Center Operations Manager\Gateway. This will stage the correct version of the file for future use when renewing the gateway certificate.

- To upgrade a gateway server using the command line, open an elevated command prompt, navigate to the folder containing the OpsMgr software, change directory to the \Gateway\AMD64 folder, and run the command in Listing 6.5.

LISTING 6.5 Command line upgrade: Gateway server

```
%WinDir%\System32\msiexec.exe /I MOMGateway.msi /qn
```

10. Upgrade the push-installed agents:

- For each agent listed in the Upgrade Helper management pack at the Step 3a - Upgrade Windows Agents view, upgrade the agent component in place. Push-installed (automatically installed) agents can be upgraded remotely with the OpsMgr 2012 Operations console after you upgrade the management and gateways servers to which they report.
- Upgrade push-installed agents from the Administration space of the Operations console. Navigate to **Device Management** -> **Pending Management**. OpsMgr 2007 R2 agents are listed with the status Agent Requires Update. Select up to 200 agents at a time, right-click, and click **Approve**. (Selecting **Repair** also upgrades agents in the case of agents that for some reason don't appear in pending status.) Then from the Update Agents dialog box, confirm use of the management server action account or enter administrative credentials manually, and click **Update**.

11. Upgrade the Web consoles:

- For each stand-alone instance of a Web console, upgrade the Web console in place, as well as any other components installed on that server such as OpsMgr 2007 R2 consoles. If a Web console is installed on the same system as a secondary management server that was upgraded, you must reinstall the Web console. Remember that after upgrading the Web console, any customizations made to the web.config file are reset to the defaults.
- The Web console server prerequisites for performing a fresh install of System Center 2012 Operations Manager are also required for an upgrade. Refer to Chapter 5 for details and procedures to install prerequisites. Prerequisites for Web consoles are primarily that the .NET 3.5 feature is enabled and .NET Framework installed (.NET 4 having been installed *after* the Web server role was enabled). Upgrading the Web console requires ISAPI and CGI Restrictions in IIS enabled for ASP.NET.
- Run Setup from the OpsMgr 2012 distribution media on the Web console computer. Click **Install** from the splash screen. The list of components to be upgraded is displayed in Figure 6.15. Click **Next**.

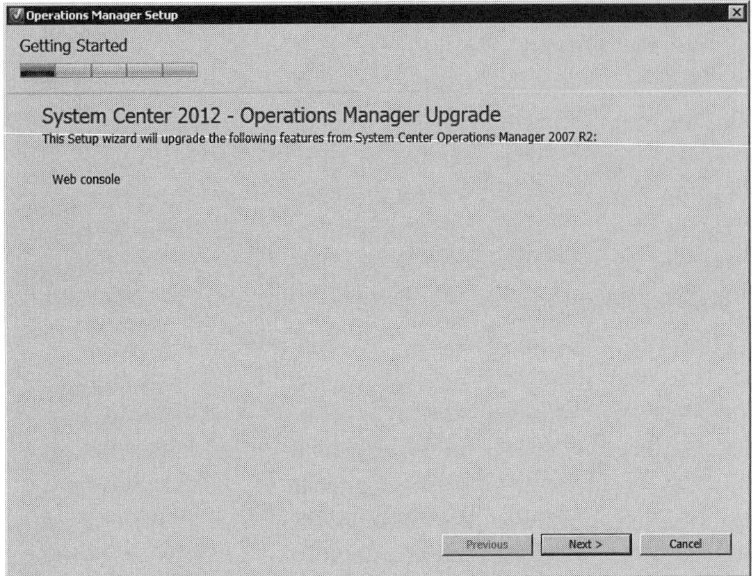

FIGURE 6.15 Upgrading the OpsMgr 2007 R2 Web console in place.

- On the next screen, select **Installation location**. The default location is *%ProgramFiles%*\System Center 2012\Operations Manager. Accept the default or specify an alternative path, and click **Next**.
- Setup continues with the message **Verifying that your environment has the required hardware and software**. If there are issues, the message **The Setup wizard cannot continue** appears. This means additional hardware resources or software is required to continue.
- After resolving any prerequisite problems, click **Verify Prerequisites Again**. If the verification is successful, click **Next**.
- At the Specify a management server page, enter the name of a management server to be used by the Web console only. The System Center 2012 Operations Manager management server you specify will handle data associated with your management group, but it cannot be the OpsMgr 2007 R2 RMS, which is not yet upgraded. Enter the name of a secondary management server already upgraded to OpsMgr 2012, or if using a load-balanced management server pool, the virtual server name of the pool. Click **Next**.
- At the Specify a web site to use with the Web console page, select the website to which to install the OpsMgr 2012 Web console. You cannot select the Operations Manager 2007 Web console website, because that site is deleted during the upgrade. Optionally select to enable SSL. Click **Next**.
- At the Select an authentication mode for use with the Web console page, select **Use Network Authentication**. Click **Next**.

- At the Ready to Upgrade page, review your selections for the features you are upgrading (see Figure 6.16), and select **Upgrade**.

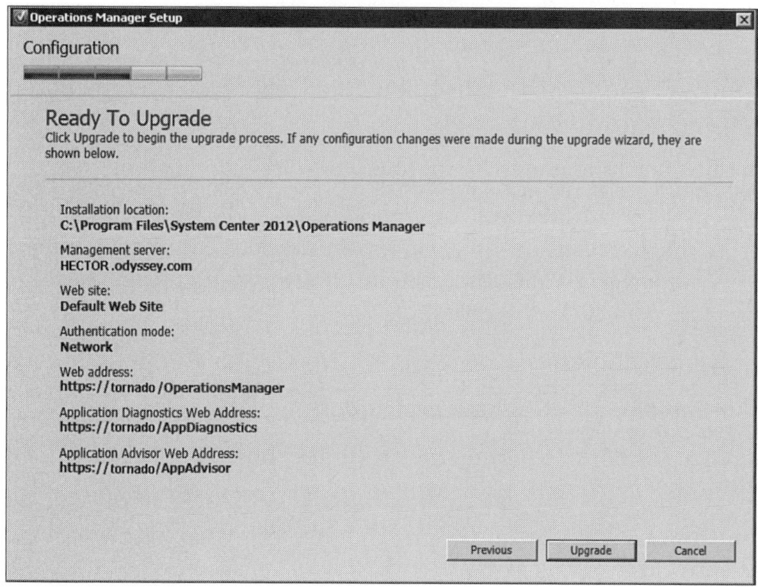

FIGURE 6.16 Ready to upgrade a Web console.

- The upgrade is complete when all green check marks appear in the left column, previously shown in Figure 6.11. Components that failed to install are marked with a red "X." Consider ticking the option to launch Microsoft Update when the wizard closes (recommended). Click **Close** to complete the wizard. You will also want to **Exit** the OpsMgr installer that is still open.

- To upgrade a stand-alone Web console with the command line, open an elevated command prompt, navigate to the folder containing the OpsMgr installation software, and run the commands in Listing 6.6.

LISTING 6.6 Command line upgrade: Stand-alone Web console

```
setup.exe /silent /upgrade
/WebsiteName: "<WebSiteName>" [/WebConsoleUseSSL]
/WebConsoleAuthorizationMode: [Mixed|Network]
```

Use the `/WebConsoleUseSSL` parameter only if your website has SSL activated. For a default web installation, specify **Default Web Site** for the `/WebSiteName` parameter.

If the Web console reports to an unsupported (that is, not yet upgraded to System Center 2012 Operations Manager) or inaccessible RMS, you must also pass the following parameter:

```
/ManagementServer:<ManagementServerName>
```

- If you want the Web console to use the current RMS, wait until after the RMS is upgraded, then upgrade the Web console.
- Configure permissions inheritance for the Web console:

  In Windows Explorer, navigate to the MonitoringView folder under the installation folder for the Web console (by default, *%ProgramFiles%*\System Center 2012\Operations Manager\WebConsole\MonitoringView), right-click the TempImages folder, and click **Properties**.

  On the Security tab, click **Advanced**.

  On the Permissions tab, click **Change Permissions**.

  Select the **Include inheritable permissions from this object's parent** check box.

  In Permission entries, click **Administrators**, and then click **Remove**. Repeat for the **SYSTEM** entry, and then click **OK**.

  Click **OK** to close Advanced Security Settings for TempImages, and then click **OK** to close TempImages Properties.

12. Disable all notification subscriptions at the **Administration** -> **Notifications** -> **Subscriptions** node of the Operations console.
13. Stop services or disable any connectors that are installed. Check the **Administration** -> **Product Connectors** node to verify if your management group has any connectors.
14. Verify the operational database has more than 50% of free space before you upgrade the management group. The upgrade could fail if there is not enough space. You should also ensure that the transaction logs are 50% of the total size of the operational database:
    - To check free space for the operational database, open SQL Server Management Studio, connect to your SQL instance, and in the Object Explorer, expand the Databases node. Right-click the operational database (such as OperationsManager), point to **Reports** -> **Standard Reports**, and select **Disk Usage**. View the Disk Usage report to determine the percentage of free space.
    - To modify disk usage, right-click the operational database, and select **Properties**. In the Database Properties dialog box, under Select a page, click **Files**. In the Results pane, increase the Initial Size value for the MOM_DATA database by 50%. (This step is not required if free space already exceeds 50%.)

Set the Initial Size value for the MOM_LOG to be 50% of the total size of the database. For example, if the operational database size is 100GB, the log file size should be 50GB. Then click **OK**.

15. Back up the Operations Manager databases:

- Obtain verified recent backups of the operational database (Operations Manager) and of the data warehouse database (OperationsManagerDW). If your upgrade fails, these backups might be the only way to restore OpsMgr services. Follow the procedure at http://technet.microsoft.com/library/ms187510.aspx to create a full SQL database backup if you do not have a backup process in place.
- You should also create backups of databases for optional features, such as the reporting and the ACS databases, before upgrading them.

CAUTION: BE PREPARED TO RESTORE THE SYSTEM STATE OF THE RMS

In addition to having fresh backups of the operational and data warehouse SQL databases in a production environment, be sure you can restore the OS and applications of the system running the RMS role. In the event of a setup failure after removing OpsMgr 2007 R2 and before the OpsMgr 2012 setup successfully completes, OpsMgr 2007 R2 services will be uninstalled and any System Center 2012 Operations Manager features are rolled-back and uninstalled. Only a full restore from backup of the RMS itself can recover from this fatal condition.

- If the RMS is a virtual machine, now is a good time for use of "snapshot" technology.
- If the RMS is a physical computer, use Windows Backup or a third-party backup solution to achieve a full, verified backup before proceeding.

---

16. Notify all co-workers to close all instances of the Operations console during the upgrade of the management group.

17. Run the management group upgrade on the RMS:

- The same management server prerequisites for performing a fresh install of System Center 2012 Operations Manager are required with an upgrade. Refer to Chapter 5 for information. For a management server upgrade, these are primarily that the .NET 3.5 feature is enabled, .NET 4 Framework is installed, SQL full text search is enabled on the OpsMgr databases, and the SQL Server Agent service is running.
- Run Setup from the System Center 2012 Operations Manager distribution media on the RMS computer. Click **Install** from the splash screen. The list of components to be upgraded is displayed as seen in Figure 6.17. Note the OpsMgr data warehouse will be added if one is not present in OpsMgr 2007 R2. Click **Next**.

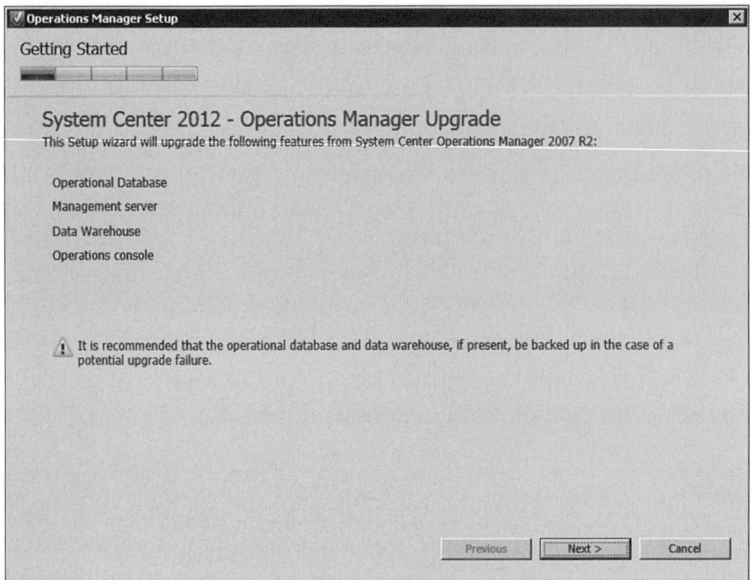

FIGURE 6.17 OpsMgr Setup ready to upgrade the distributed management group.

- Accept the license agreement by selecting **I have read, understood, and agree with the license terms** and clicking **Next**.
- On the next screen, select Installation location. The default is *%ProgramFiles%*\System Center 2012\Operations Manager. Accept the default or specify an alternative path, and click **Next**.
- Setup continues with the message **Verifying that your environment has the required hardware and software**. If there are issues, the message **The Setup wizard cannot continue** appears. This means additional hardware resources or software is required to continue.
- After resolving any prerequisite problems, click **Verify Prerequisites Again**. If the verification is successful, click **Next**.
- If you did not install the optional data warehouse feature in OpsMgr 2007 R2, a new data warehouse database is created at this time, since all OpsMgr 2012 management groups must have data warehouse databases. As shown in Figure 6.18, type the *<ComputerName>**<instance>* of the SQL Server to be used for the data warehouse database. Modify the port if needed from the default 1433. Once Setup validates the SQL Server for the data warehouse database, the Database name section of the page becomes modifiable. For a new installation, leave the default database name of **OperationsManagerDW**. Modify the data file and log file folders if different from the defaults as determined by Setup. Click **Next**.

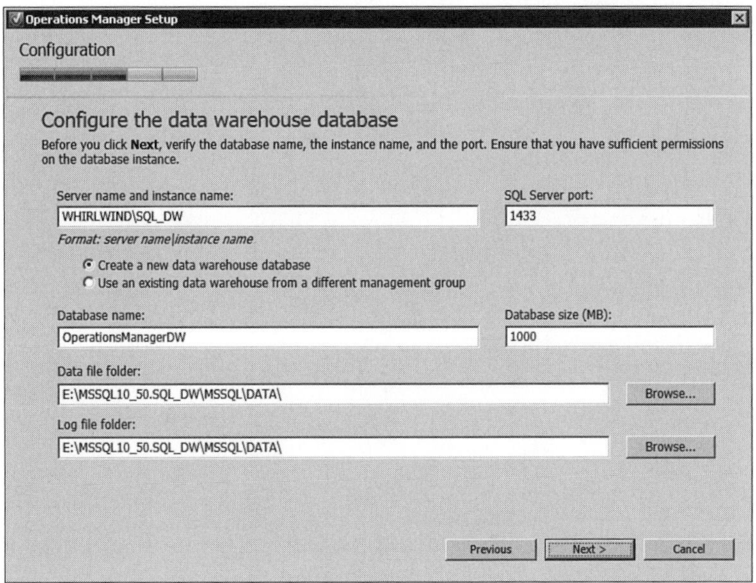

FIGURE 6.18 A data warehouse database is required for management groups.

- At the Configure Operations Manager accounts page, specify the credentials for the System Center Configuration service and the System Center Data Access service. This account must be a member of the Operations Manager Administrators role. Click **Next**.
- At the Ready to Upgrade page, review your selections for the features you are upgrading, and click **Upgrade** as shown in Figure 6.19.
- The upgrade is complete when all green check marks appear in the left column. Components that did not install are marked with a red "X." Consider ticking the option to **Launch Microsoft Update when the wizard closes**. Click **Close** to complete the wizard.
- You will also want to Exit the OpsMgr installer that is still open, unless you wish to review the other online links such as Product Documentation, or if you need to upgrade the ACS collector, which can be performed immediately as a next step if the RMS is also an ACS collector.
- To upgrade an RMS using the command line, open an elevated command prompt, navigate to the folder containing the OpsMgr software, and run the command in either Listing 6.7 or Listing 6.8, depending on whether you have a pre-existing data warehouse database.

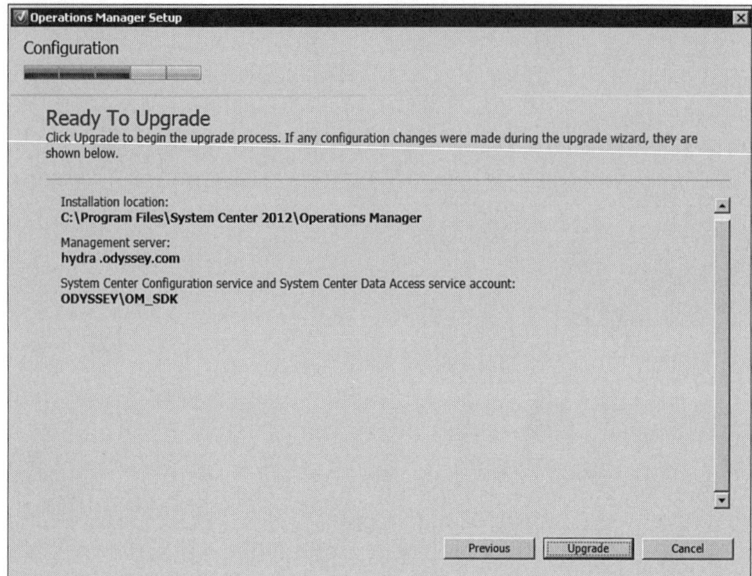

FIGURE 6.19 Ready to upgrade the management group from the RMS.

LISTING 6.7 Command line upgrade: RMS with pre-existing data warehouse database

```
setup.exe /silent /upgrade
/AcceptEndUserLicenseAgreement
/DatareaderUser:<domain\UserName>
/DatareaderPassword:<password>
/DASAccountUser:<domain\UserName>
/DASAccountPassword:<password>
```

LISTING 6.8 Command line upgrade: RMS when no data warehouse is present

```
setup.exe /silent /upgrade
/AcceptEndUserLicenseAgreement
/DWSqlServerInstance:<ComputerName\instance>
/DWDatabaseName:<DWDatabaseName>
/DatareaderUser:<domain\UserName>
/DatareaderPassword:<password>
/DataWriterUser:<domain\UserName>
/DataWriterPassword:<password>
/DASAccountUser:<domain\UserName>
/DASAccountPassword:<password>
```

If the RMS was installed using the Local System account, replace the last two switches in these listings with the following:

```
/UseLocalSystemDASAccount
```

18. Upgrade the ACS collector: On an upgraded management server that is running the ACS collector, the upgrade to the ACS collector component is a separate step and not performed during the management server upgrade.

Here's how to upgrade the ACS collector:

- Run Setup from the OpsMgr 2012 distribution media on the ACS collector computer (this splash screen may already be open on your desktop from the RMS upgrade). From the splash screen, click the **Audit Collection Services** link in the Optional Installations section.
- The Welcome to Audit Collection Services Collector Wizard should appear, click **Next**. On the ACS Collector Maintenance page, select **Update the ACS collector configuration** (see Figure 6.20). Click **Next**.

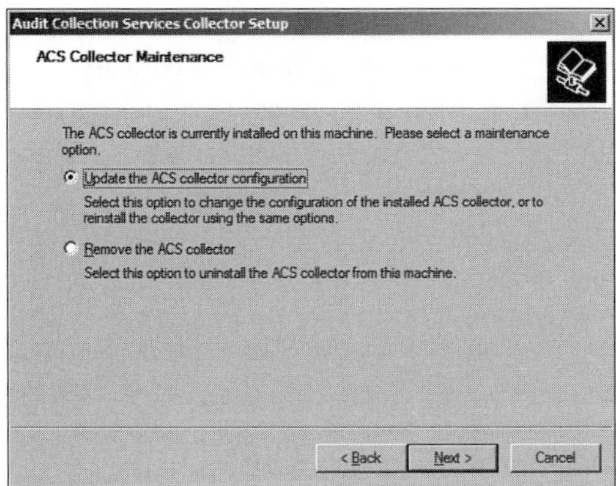

FIGURE 6.20 Upgrade the ACS collector on an upgraded management server.

- Click **Next** on each of the four successive pages in the wizard:

  Use an existing database

  Use the same ODBC data source name (default: OpsMgrAC)

  Use the same database

  Use the same database authentication

When you arrive at the Summary page shown in Figure 6.21, click **Next** to complete the upgrade of the ACS collector.

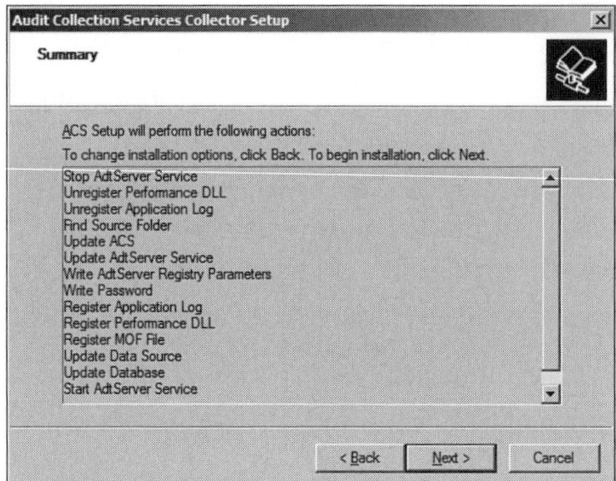

FIGURE 6.21 Confirming options for ACS collector upgrade.

19. Upgrade or reinstall the reporting server:

- A stand-alone instance of a reporting server is upgraded *after* the management group is upgraded. The data warehouse database is upgraded when the management group is upgraded, either from the RMS or from a secondary management server using the `/upgrademanagementgroup` switch. After upgrading your RMS to OpsMgr 2012, you may discover your OpsMgr 2007 R2 reporting server still works, just with the old OpsMgr 2007 R2 logo!
- The prerequisites for performing a fresh install of the System Center 2012 Operations Manager reporting server are required for an upgrade of the reporting feature; refer to Chapter 5 for details. Prerequisites for the reporting server primarily are that the .NET 3.5 feature is enabled and .NET 4 is installed, the IIS role is enabled, and the correct SQL version is installed.
- Run Setup from the OpsMgr 2012 distribution media on the reporting server. Click **Install** from the splash screen. The list of components to be upgraded is displayed, seen in Figure 6.22. Click **Next**.
- On the next screen, select **Installation location**. The default location is *%ProgramFiles%*\System Center 2012\Operations Manager. Accept the default or specify an alternative path, and click **Next**.
- Setup continues with the message **Verifying that your environment has the required hardware and software**. If there are issues, the message **The Setup wizard cannot continue** appears. This means additional hardware resources or software is required to continue.
- After resolving any prerequisite problems, click **Verify Prerequisites Again**. If the verification is successful, click **Next**.
- At the Ready to Upgrade page, in the case of a stand-alone reporting server, only an installation location is shown as seen in Figure 6.23. Click **Upgrade**.

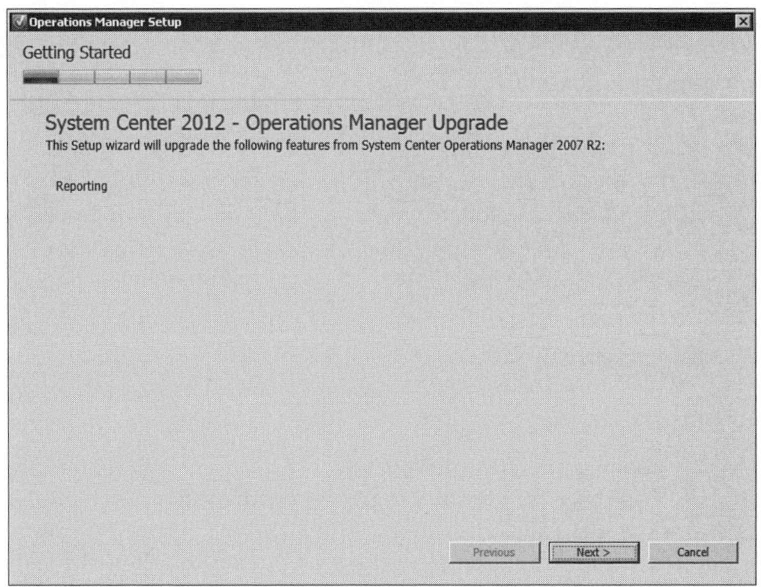

FIGURE 6.22 Upgrading the OpsMgr 2007 R2 reporting server in place.

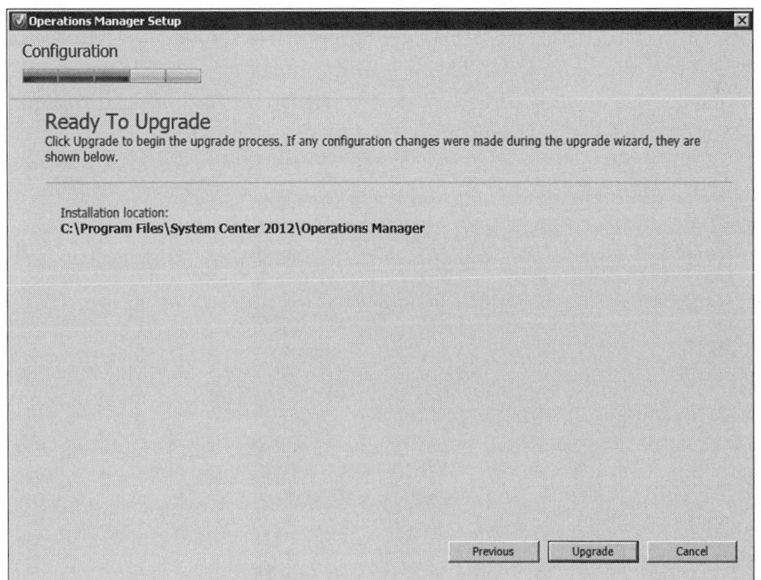

FIGURE 6.23 Ready To Upgrade indication for the OpsMgr 2007 R2 reporting server.

- To upgrade a reporting server using the command line, open an elevated command prompt, navigate to the folder containing the OpsMgr software media distribution, and run the command in Listing 6.9.

LISTING 6.9 Command line upgrade: Reporting server

```
setup.exe /silent /upgrade
```

If the reporting server reports to an unsupported or inaccessible root management server, add the following switch:

```
/ManagementServer: <ManagementServerName>
```

20. Upgrade the ACS reports.

- While OpsMgr 2012 does not include new ACS reports, half a dozen reports are updated with fixes, and there are new report graphics with System Center 2012 themes. ACS in OpsMgr 2012 SP 1 adds support for Windows Server 2012 security audit events. The easiest way to install the new reports is to follow the steps for a fresh install of ACS reports, overwriting the OpsMgr 2007 R2 versions.
- To upgrade the ACS reports, follow each of the steps in Chapter 5 to deploy ACS reporting to an SSRS instance. Copy the ACS folder over any existing C:\ACS folder on the reporting server, overwriting existing files.
- Upon running UploadAuditReports.cmd on the reporting server, you will see the errors shown in Figure 6.24, but the 2012-version reports do upload successfully. The errors about the Audit and Audit5 models being present are not a problem, because the same model files are used in both versions of OpsMgr.

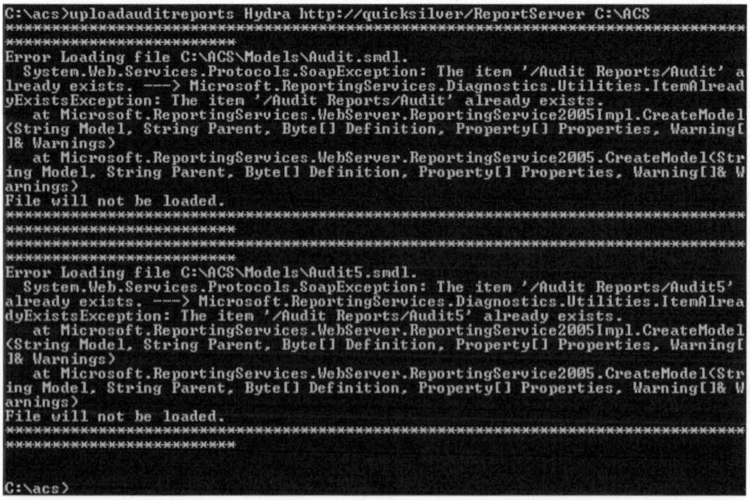

```
C:\acs>uploadauditreports Hydra http://quicksilver/ReportServer C:\ACS
********************************************************************************
*************************
Error Loading file C:\ACS\Models\Audit.smdl.
  System.Web.Services.Protocols.SoapException: The item '/Audit Reports/Audit' a
lready exists. ---> Microsoft.ReportingServices.Diagnostics.Utilities.ItemAlread
yExistsException: The item '/Audit Reports/Audit' already exists.
   at Microsoft.ReportingServices.WebServer.ReportingService2005Impl.CreateModel
(String Model, String Parent, Byte[] Definition, Property[] Properties, Warning[
]& Warnings)
   at Microsoft.ReportingServices.WebServer.ReportingService2005.CreateModel(Str
ing Model, String Parent, Byte[] Definition, Property[] Properties, Warning[]& W
arnings)
File will not be loaded.
********************************************************************************
*************************
********************************************************************************
*************************
Error Loading file C:\ACS\Models\Audit5.smdl.
  System.Web.Services.Protocols.SoapException: The item '/Audit Reports/Audit5'
already exists. ---> Microsoft.ReportingServices.Diagnostics.Utilities.ItemAlrea
dyExistsException: The item '/Audit Reports/Audit5' already exists.
   at Microsoft.ReportingServices.WebServer.ReportingService2005Impl.CreateModel
(String Model, String Parent, Byte[] Definition, Property[] Properties, Warning[
]& Warnings)
   at Microsoft.ReportingServices.WebServer.ReportingService2005.CreateModel(Str
ing Model, String Parent, Byte[] Definition, Property[] Properties, Warning[]& W
arnings)
File will not be loaded.
********************************************************************************
*************************


C:\acs>
```

FIGURE 6.24 Upgrading the OpsMgr 2007 R2 reporting server in place.

- The upgrade overwrites customizations to the security settings of the SSRS DB Audit connection, such as specifying the data reader account and the credentials stored securely in the report server option. Repeat the steps in Chapter 5 to reset SSRS security as appropriate.

21. Re-enable subscriptions and connectors at the **Administration** -> **Notifications** -> **Subscriptions** node of the Operations console. Start any services and enable any connectors disabled during the upgrade.

22. Verify the success of the upgrade:

    - Check the health state of the management servers, gateways, and agents in the Monitoring -> Health Service Watcher state view in the Operations console.
    - In the Administration space of the console, ensure that the management servers, gateways, and agents are healthy.
    - In the Monitoring space, check if there are any alerts related to management group health.
    - Review the event logs of the management servers for new errors. (Sort alerts by the last-modified column to review the new alerts.)
    - Check CPU utilization and disk I/O on your database server(s) to ensure that they are functioning normally.
    - If reporting is installed, open the Reporting space and run a generic performance report to ensure the feature is functioning correctly.
    - If ACS reports are installed, select **Reporting** -> **Audit Reports**, then run an ACS report to ensure that ACS reports were correctly uploaded and that security is working on the ACS report server.

23. Run a SQL query on the operational database to clean up the Localizedtext table and the Publishmessage table. You can copy this query from Microsoft's website at http://technet.microsoft.com/en-us/library/8c2dbaf4-2966-45e3-a72d-5de90ff4f495#BKMK_VerifyUpgrade. The SQL query, SCOM-2012-Post-Upgrade-SQL-Cleanup.sql, is available with the online content for this book; see Appendix E for information.

Upgrading from a Secondary Management Server

Many OpsMgr 2007 R2 customers will find this situation applies to them: Their current RMS is running a 32-bit OS and/or the current RMS is in a failover cluster. In these scenarios, when you elect to upgrade the management group database, you cannot upgrade the RMS in place and must upgrade from a secondary management server.

Do Not Promote Before Upgrading

There is an unofficial route to management group upgrade when you have an RMS that is unsupported for in-place upgrade: Manually promote an OpsMgr 2007 R2 secondary management server to the RMS role before starting the upgrade path to

System Center 2012 Operations Manager. Microsoft provides a supported procedure to promote an OpsMgr 2007 R2 secondary management server to the RMS role at http://technet.microsoft.com/en-us/library/cc540401(TechNet.10).aspx. This method uses `ManagementServerConfigTool.exe` with the `PromoteRMS` switch.

However, there is quite some risk in using the tool because running it can cause irreversible damage to your OpsMgr database. The "promote to RMS" feature in OpsMgr 2007 R2 mainly exists for disaster recovery purposes, and upgrading to OpsMgr 2012 from a promoted OpsMgr 2007 R2 RMS has not been extensively tested. The authors recommend if the OpsMgr 2007 R2 RMS cannot be upgraded in place because it is clustered or running a 32-bit OS, you should follow the official upgrade path and upgrade directly to OpsMgr 2012 from a secondary management server.

Overview of Upgrade from Secondary Management Server

You will run the System Center 2012 Operations Manager setup twice on the secondary management server selected for the RMSE role:

- Run setup and upgrade the secondary management server from OpsMgr 2007 R2 to OpsMgr 2012 in a conventional manner, along with all other secondary management servers. This first upgrade step should occur as early as possible in the upgrade process, after upgrading all gateway servers to OpsMgr 2012.
- When all components in the management group, including agents, are upgraded except the RMS, run setup a second time on the secondary management server, now with the `/upgrademanagementgroup` switch to upgrade the databases. If you don't yet have a data warehouse database, one is created during this second and final run of setup.

All Web consoles and any report server targeted to the RMS will no longer work after the upgrade. The authors recommend reinstalling or upgrading those components before you upgrade the management group and point them at upgraded secondary management servers, so there is no impact when you retire the RMS. Some admins may find it simpler to fully uninstall all Web consoles and the report server before the upgrade, and redeploy those components after the management group upgrade. This has little downside; you won't lose access to historical reporting data by uninstalling and reinstalling the reporting server component.

Restore the Encryption Key on the Secondary Management Server

You should have already backed up the management group encryption key on the RMS (step 5 in the "Upgrading the Distributed Management Group" section). Copy the key file to the secondary management server or make it accessible to the secondary management server over the network.

Restore the RMS encryption key to the secondary management server using the SecureStorageBackup.exe utility:

- Open a command prompt window using the Run as Administrator option.
- At the command prompt, map a network drive to the OpsMgr installation drive on the RMS, such as X: drive. Then change directory to the OpsMgr installation folder on the RMS, such as X:\Program Files\System Center Operations Manager 2007, and type the command **SecureStorageBackup**.
- On the Backup or Restore page of the Encryption Key Backup or Restore Wizard, select **Restore the Encryption Key** and complete the wizard, providing a location and password for the key. Figure 6.25 shows the page where you specify restoring the encryption key.

NOTE: ENCRYPTION KEY AND OPSMGR 2012

While the RMS encryption key is something you need to be concerned with in OpsMgr 2007, that is the last time you will need to bother with it. Once you upgrade, the encryption key is removed from the local registry of the RMS (or in the case of upgrading from a secondary management server about to become the RMSE, from the local registry of the secondary management server after you run the tool).

In OpsMgr 2012, the key is actually in the operational database and shared by the systems in the All Management Servers Resource Pool.

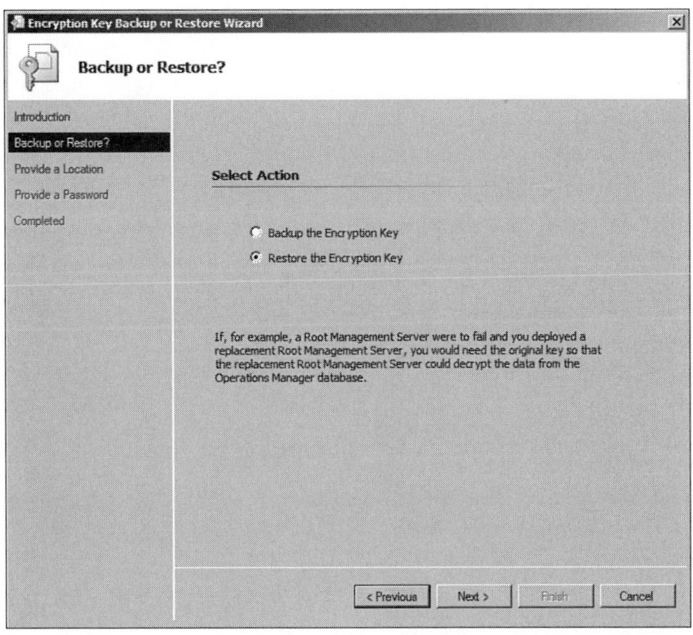

FIGURE 6.25 Restore the encryption key to the secondary management server.

Performing the Upgrade from Secondary Management Server

To upgrade the management group from a secondary management server, perform steps 1 to 16 from the "Upgrading the Distributed Management Group" section. Select the most suitable upgraded secondary management server, ideally one that is both powerful and least loaded in terms of number of agents and gateways reporting to it. Then, rather than upgrading the management group from the RMS, restore the encryption key as discussed in the "Restore the Encryption Key on the Secondary Management Server" section if you haven't already, and perform the steps in this section on the upgraded secondary management server selected to become the RMSE of the OpsMgr 2012 management group. After performing these steps, the former RMS will no longer participate in System Center 2012 Operations Manager and should be retired.

Other than upgrading the selected management server to OpsMgr 2012, restoring the encryption key, verifying SQL full text search is enabled on the OpsMgr databases and the SQL Server Agent service is running, there are no additional prerequisites for the secondary management server selected to become the RMSE. Follow these steps to upgrade the management group from the upgraded secondary management server you select:

1. Open an elevated command prompt on the selected secondary management server; navigate to the folder containing the OpsMgr software media distribution, and run **Setup.exe /upgrademanagementgroup**. (See Listing 6.10 and Listing 6.11 for complete syntax.)

2. If the upgrade wizard detects any remaining OpsMgr 2007 R2 components in the management group (other than the RMS), the Unable to Proceed message appears as seen in Figure 6.26.

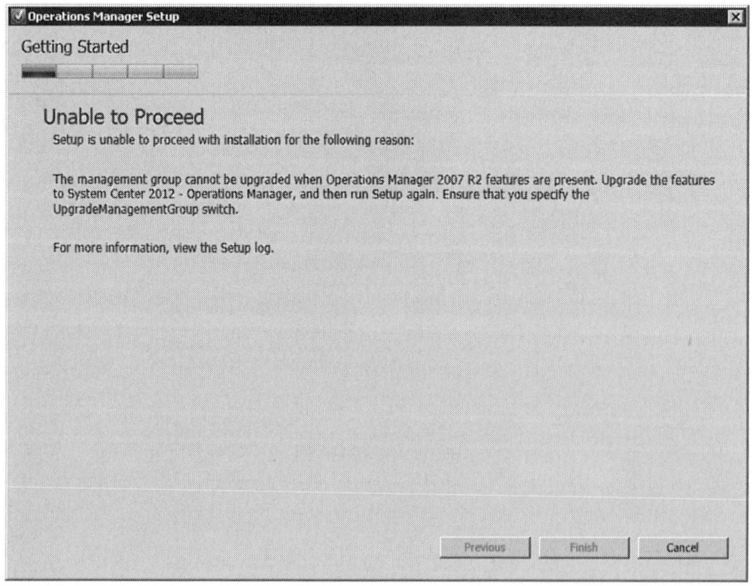

FIGURE 6.26 The presence of OpsMgr 2007 R2 components blocks upgrade.

If you have a clustered OpsMgr 2007 R2 RMS, you might receive this message even if you moved the agents to a secondary management server. To resolve this, open the Operations console, and navigate to **Administration** -> **Device Management** -> **Agentless Managed**. Right-click the agentless-managed clustered computer object representing the RMS, and then click **Delete**.

3. Figure 6.27 shows the expected wizard page when upgrading the database and adding a data warehouse database. This message is only seen when no OpsMgr 2007 R2 components were detected in the management group (other than the RMS about to be retired) and the management group is ready to be upgraded from the secondary management server.

   Take heed of the warnings to confirm your backups of the OpsMgr databases and click **Next**.

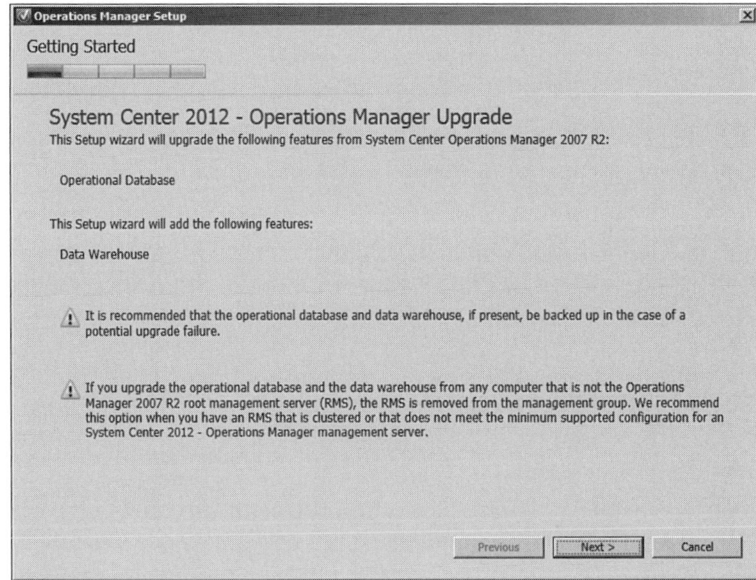

FIGURE 6.27 Upgrading the management group from a secondary management server.

4. Setup continues with the message **Verifying that your environment has the required hardware and software**. If there are issues, the message **The Setup wizard cannot continue** appears.

   If you see a message that **Secure Keys are not restored on this server**, shown in Figure 6.28, this means you should restore the encryption key exported from the RMS.

   After resolving any prerequisite problems, click **Verify Prerequisites Again**. If verification is successful, click **Next**.

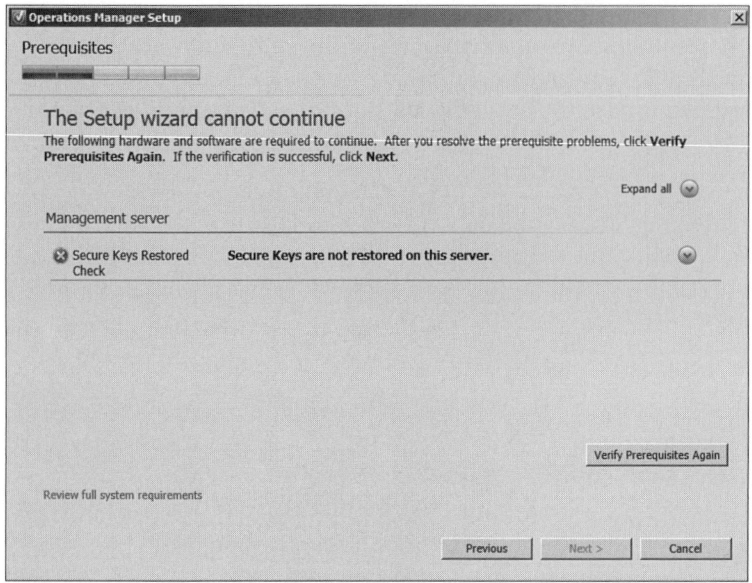

FIGURE 6.28 This warning means you have not restored the encryption key.

5. If you did not install the optional data warehouse feature in OpsMgr 2007 R2, a new data warehouse database is created at this time, since all OpsMgr 2012 management groups must have data warehouse databases.

   Type the *<ComputerName>**<instance>* of the SQL Server to be used for the data warehouse database. Modify the port if needed from the default 1433. Once Setup validates the SQL Server for the data warehouse database, the Database name section of the page becomes modifiable.

   For a new installation, leave the default database name of **OperationsManagerDW**. Modify the data file and log file folders if different from the SQL defaults as determined by Setup. Click **Next**.

6. At the Configure Operations Manager accounts page, specify the credentials for the System Center Configuration service and the System Center Data Access service (the OM_SDK account used in this book).

   If installing a new data warehouse database, you need to specify the Data Reader and Data Writer accounts (OM_DRA and OM_DWWA in this book) as shown in Figure 6.29. The System Center Data Access service account must be a member of the Operations Manager Administrators role. Click **Next**.

7. At the Ready to Upgrade page, review your selections for the features you are upgrading, and click **Upgrade**.

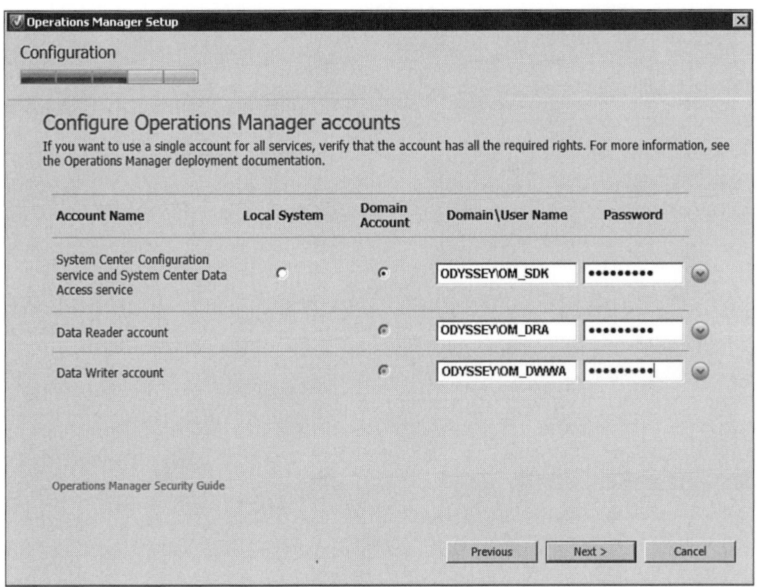

FIGURE 6.29 Upgrading the operations database and adding the data warehouse database.

8. Upgrade is complete when all green check marks appear in the left column as seen in Figure 6.30. You now have a new RMSE. Any component that failed to install is marked with a red "X." Consider ticking the option to **Launch Microsoft Update when the wizard closes**. Click **Close** to complete the wizard.

- You will also want to **Exit** the OpsMgr installer that is still open, unless you wish to review the other online links such as Product Documentation, or if you need to upgrade the ACS collector, which can be performed immediately as a next step if the new RMSE is also an ACS collector.

- To upgrade the management group from a secondary management server using the command line, open an elevated command prompt, navigate to the folder containing the OpsMgr software media distribution, and run the command in either Listing 6.10 or Listing 6.11, depending on whether you have a pre-existing data warehouse database.

LISTING 6.10 Command line upgrade: Management group from secondary management server with pre-existing data warehouse database

```
setup.exe /silent /upgrademanagementgroup
/AcceptEndUserLicenseAgreement
/DASAccountUser:<domain\UserName>
/DASAccountPassword:<password>
```

LISTING 6.11 Command line upgrade: Management group from secondary management server when no data warehouse is present

```
setup.exe /silent /upgrademanagementgroup
/AcceptEndUserLicenseAgreement
/DWSqlServerInstance:<ComputerName\instance>
/DWDatabaseName:<DWDatabaseName>
/DatareaderUser:<domain\UserName>
/DatareaderPassword:<password>
/DataWriterUser:<domain\UserName>
/DataWriterPassword:<password>
/DASAccountUser:<domain\UserName>
/DASAccountPassword:<password>
```

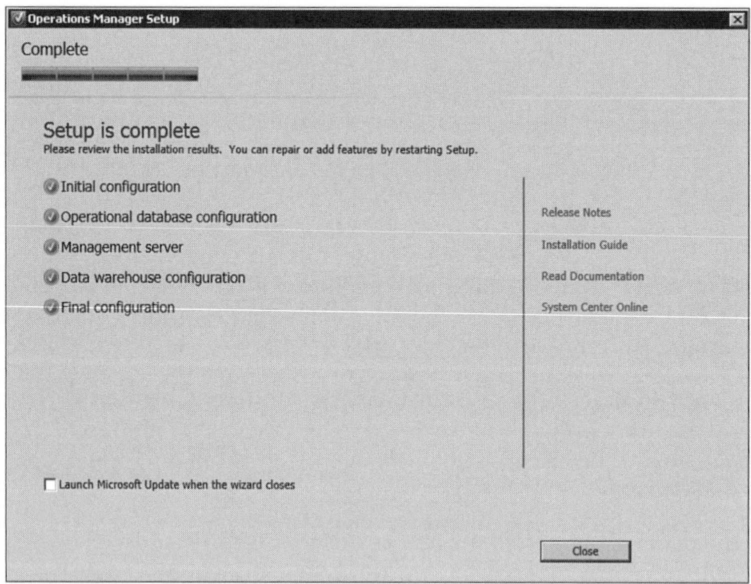

FIGURE 6.30 Successful upgrade from a secondary management server.

9. After completing the management group upgrade from the secondary management server, resume the checklist in the "Upgrading the Distributed Management Group" section at step 18. Additionally, perform the steps in the next section to edit the report server configuration file.

Additional Procedure Following Upgrade from Secondary Management Server

After upgrading your management group from the secondary management server, manually edit the rsreportserver.config configuration file for the reporting server. If you attempt to upgrade reporting without making this change, the Upgrade Wizard will report a critical prerequisite issue, because Operations Manager cannot connect to the reporting server. (If you upgraded your management group from the RMS, you do *not* have to update the configuration file manually for the reporting server.) Follow these steps if necessary to modify the reporting server configuration file:

1. On the computer hosting the reporting server you plan to upgrade, open the rsreportserver.config file using Notepad. The path is typically *%ProgramFiles%*\Microsoft SQL Server\MSRS10.MSSQLServer\Reporting Services\ReportServer, where MSSQLServer is the name of the SQL Server instance.
2. From the Edit menu, click **Find**. Search for <ServerName>. Note the <ServerName> element appears in two places in the configuration file, in the Security Extension and in the Authentication Extension.
3. Replace the name of the management server from the old RMS name with the name of an upgraded management server.
4. Search for <ServerName> again, and update the server name.
5. Save and close the configuration file.

TIP: THE RETIRED RMS OR RMS CLUSTER NODES NEED A NEW OS

The act of "seizing" the RMSE role by upgrading the management group from a secondary management server truly orphans the old RMS. You will not be able to start the System Center services to uninstall OpsMgr 2007 R2 components properly, so use of any System Center components on former RMS computers is inhibited. If you will be reusing the physical or VM computers previously running the RMS or RMS cluster, plan to reload the operating system(s).

Performing a Multi-Homed Upgrade

An early consensus in the Microsoft TechNet OpsMgr forums is that many administrators are electing the multi-homed upgrade path to System Center 2012 Operations Manager. Regardless of the current state or upgradability of your OpsMgr 2007 R2 server components, there are many business and technical reasons to require or prefer to use this side-by-side upgrade approach. In this scenario, you will deploy a fresh OpsMgr 2012 management group, dual-home all agent-managed computers, and then retire the old OpsMgr 2007 R2 management group. The main operational effect of this method is that your OpsMgr database will begin again in a default and empty state, without management packs imported or agents deployed—at square one.

Here are the most common reasons for proceeding with a multi-homed upgrade rather than an in-place upgrade of the OpsMgr 2007 R2 database:

- Current OpsMgr 2007 R2 configuration and/or performance have deficiencies and could use a *do-over*. Starting over with fresh management packs and overrides, while applying lessons learned running previous releases of OpsMgr, is expected to create a more useful, stable, and responsive OpsMgr experience.

- Current OpsMgr 2007 R2 operational database is *too large* to upgrade in place. Since you need to expand the database to have at least 50% free space before an in-place upgrade of the database, this can result in an operational database that is too large. Operational databases over 100GB should be avoided.
- Current OpsMgr 2007 R2 management group is running on *mostly non-supported configurations* such as 32-bit Windows, releases of Windows before Server 2008 R2, and installations of SQL 2005 that for whatever reason cannot be upgraded. In this scenario, upgrading in place is more work than starting over with a new, parallel OpsMgr 2012 management group on all-supported platforms, using the multi-homed upgrade path.
- Upgrade timing for Operations Manager coincides with *hardware refresh* cycle, and all-new computers to run System Center components are being deployed as part of the refresh. If the computer refresh involves relocation to a new data center, you may want your OpsMgr servers physically in your most densely populated data center.
- Your organization is making the strategic decision to leverage multiple System Center 2012 components, or all of System Center 2012, in a *private cloud scenario*. This involves OpsMgr integration with components like System Center Virtual Machine Manager (VMM) and Data Protection Manager (DPM). You probably would want to deploy OpsMgr 2012 in an optimized manner in the private cloud, and this precludes an in-place upgrade of an existing OpsMgr 2007 R2 management group.
- You may attempt an in-place upgrade of the management group and have a *fatal database upgrade*. After restoring the management server(s) and databases from backup, rather than risk repeated failure, you elect the multi-homed upgrade method. There may be other advantages to the multi-homed method, such as fewer service interruptions and more time for validation and testing.

Deploy OpsMgr 2012 Management Group

This is the "easy" part—just follow the initial installation instructions in Chapter 5 to deploy your server components. Recall that an OpsMgr 2012 agent can also report to OpsMgr 2007 R2 gateways and management servers. This means that every OpsMgr 2007 R2 agent in your organization can be upgraded and dual-homed—communicating with both your current OpsMgr 2007 R2 management group and a new OpsMgr 2012 management group simultaneously. Of course, the OpsMgr 2012 management group and the OpsMgr 2007 R2 management group cannot share the same management group name; you need a new, unique management group name for your OpsMgr 2012 management group.

There are no constraints on the design of your OpsMgr 2012 management group when upgrading from an OpsMgr 2007 R2 management group using the multi-homed method.

However, note that only agent-managed computers can be multi-homed. Gateway servers and management servers cannot be multi-homed. Computers running any OpsMgr 2007 R2 server components cannot participate in the OpsMgr 2012 management group. Your upgrade path using the multi-homed method is about focusing on your agents, ignoring the OpsMgr 2007 R2 server computers as far as the scope and architecture of your System Center 2012 Operations Manager management group.

Another consideration is the selection of SQL Server to run the OpsMgr databases. You may have a choice to install OpsMgr 2012 to the same SQL database servers or server clusters used by OpsMgr 2007 R2, with the plan being for the OpsMgr 2007 R2 databases to be dropped after the upgrade project is complete. If you intend to share your OpsMgr 2012 SQL servers with the current OpsMgr 2007 R2 management group during the migration, capacity demands on the involved systems will double, potentially producing poor performance in both management groups. Make sure whatever SQL platform(s) you select can handle the load when all agents are multi-homed.

TIP: THE UPGRADE HELPER MANAGEMENT PACK IS FOR THE 2007 R2 SIDE

Install and use the Upgrade Helper management pack in the OpsMgr 2007 R2 management group you are upgrading. Keep track of your progress in upgrading agents to OpsMgr 2012 using the views in the OpsMgr 2007 R2 console. There is no reason to install the management pack in the new OpsMgr 2012 management group. Once all the computers listed in the Step 3a - Upgrade Windows Agents view are in a Healthy (green) state, you know you are clear to retire the OpsMgr 2007 R2 management group, and you won't have to worry about deleting the Upgrade Helper management pack.

Selecting management packs to import to the new OpsMgr 2012 management group is very important. You can try to match the management packs and override management packs in the OpsMgr 2007 R2 management group exactly with the new OpsMgr management group, and can certainly export custom management packs from the old management group and import them to the new, either in sealed or unsealed format. However, the authors recommend you avoid wholesale export and import of management packs, particularly unsealed ones, between management groups. A new management group is an opportunity to clean house; populate it with current, sealed management packs and new unsealed override management packs that achieve the organization's business goals for monitoring.

Multi-Home All Agents

A useful feature of the OpsMgr agent is its capability to report to several OpsMgr management groups at one time, also known as *multi-homing*. The OpsMgr 2012 agent can report to both OpsMgr 2012 management groups and OpsMgr 2007 R2 (CU4 or higher) management groups. This feature is leveraged in the multi-home upgrade method to establish a parallel monitoring infrastructure whereby every agent-managed computer runs the OpsMgr 2012 agent, while reporting to both management groups.

Your task is to discover each OpsMgr 2007 R2 agent-managed computer from the OpsMgr 2012 management group, and push an agent to all computers capable of automatic agent installation. This is easy and the agent is immediately both upgraded and multi-homed. Those OpsMgr 2007 R2 agents manually installed rather than automatically push-installed require a little more work; they must first be upgraded, then reconfigured to become dual-homed.

Upgrading and Dual-homing Automatically (Push) Installed Agents

With a multi-homed upgrade, you are deploying a complete, parallel management group infrastructure that does not duplicate roles with OpsMgr 2007 R2 servers. Agents reporting to OpsMgr 2007 R2 management servers will report to new, different OpsMgr 2012 management servers. Agents reporting to OpsMgr 2007 R2 gateways in remote network segments or untrusted domains will report to new, different OpsMgr 2012 gateway servers. In some scenarios, agents may report to a management server in one management group and a gateway server in the other.

In all scenarios, the first task is to deploy the OpsMgr 2012 management server and gateway servers to which the agents will report. Be sure to first update OpsMgr 2012 server components to the latest releases by visiting Microsoft Update and installing all System Center cumulative update rollups. Once those servers are deployed, updated, and ready to go into production, run the Discovery Wizard; appropriate management servers and gateway servers will push agents to discovered computers. Chapter 5 discusses discovery and push of agents. Run the Discovery Wizard to add OpsMgr 2012 agent-managed computers (these may already be running the OpsMgr 2007 R2 agent) just as if you were deploying OpsMgr 2012 agents for the first time.

It is best you not deploy OpsMgr 2012 agents to computers running OpsMgr 2007 R2 server components; this includes management servers, Web consoles and reporting servers. Although some OpsMgr 2007 R2 server components or consoles can coexist with the OpsMgr 2012 agent, the authors recommend isolating the existing OpsMgr 2007 R2 server components from the OpsMgr 2012 upgrade path until the OpsMgr 2007 R2 management group is uninstalled, then redeploying OpsMgr 2012 components to those computers previously running OpsMgr 2007 R2 components as needed.

You must deploy a second OpsMgr gateway server on each remote network segment connected by a gateway to achieve side-by-side monitoring of all agents. In the case of gateway servers located on remote network segments with only several computers, you may not have another physical computer or virtual machine resource to run Windows Server 2008 R2 or Windows Server 2012 (to host the new OpsMgr 2012 or OpsMgr 2012 SP 1 gateway) while the OpsMgr 2007 R2 gateway is running on that network segment. Consider these options:

- Almost any computer running the Windows Server 2008 R2 OS is suitable for the gateway component in a small network managing a few other agents. The same applies for Windows Server 2012 in the case of OpsMgr 2012 SP 1. Simply add the

OpsMgr 2012 or OpsMgr 2012 SP 1 gateway component to any server running Windows Server 2008 R2 or Windows Server 2012 such as a Read Only Domain Controller (RODC) or file server. The added load of the gateway is not much for a small remote network.

- Consider accepting a loss of monitoring of agents downstream from the gateway during the time it takes to redeploy an OpsMgr 2012 gateway on the same computer that hosted the OpsMgr 2007 R2 gateway (due to the downtime while installing the new OS).
- A complex option would be manually upgrading each agent, then manually dual-homing each agent and pointing the agents to an offsite OpsMgr 2012 gateway during the transition. This could be a gateway published from another site on a wide area network (WAN) or over the Internet.

Upgrading and Dual-homing Manually Installed Agents

Each agent-managed computer with a manually installed OpsMgr 2007 R2 agent must be upgraded manually by running the appropriate setup program with either the Setup Wizard or the command line. Chapter 5 discusses the steps to upgrade an agent manually. As long as the OpsMgr 2007 R2 management server or gateway server the agent is reporting to is running CU4 or later, upgrading the agent is transparent to the OpsMgr 2007 R2 management group.

After upgrading an OpsMgr 2007 R2 agent in place to OpsMgr 2012, the agent is still single-homed to the original OpsMgr 2007 R2 management group. You can't remotely dual-home the agent because manually installed agents cannot be modified remotely. Follow these steps to multi-home an OpsMgr 2012 agent manually:

1. On the agent-managed computer, open Control Panel, then open the **Operations Manager Agent** applet.
2. Click the **Add** button. Enter the OpsMgr management 2012 group name and management server or gateway server and click **OK**.
3. Notice information for both old and new management groups appears in the list of management groups as seen in Figure 6.31, and click **OK** again.
4. Within several minutes of adding the OpsMgr 2012 management group to the agent, the computer object for the agent should appear in the Operations console in the **Administration -> Device Management -> Pending Management** view. Right-click manually dual-homed agents waiting to be approved, and select **Approve**. If there are a large number of agents to approve, consider the scripted solution in the "Make All Agents Single-Homed to OpsMgr 2012" section.

6

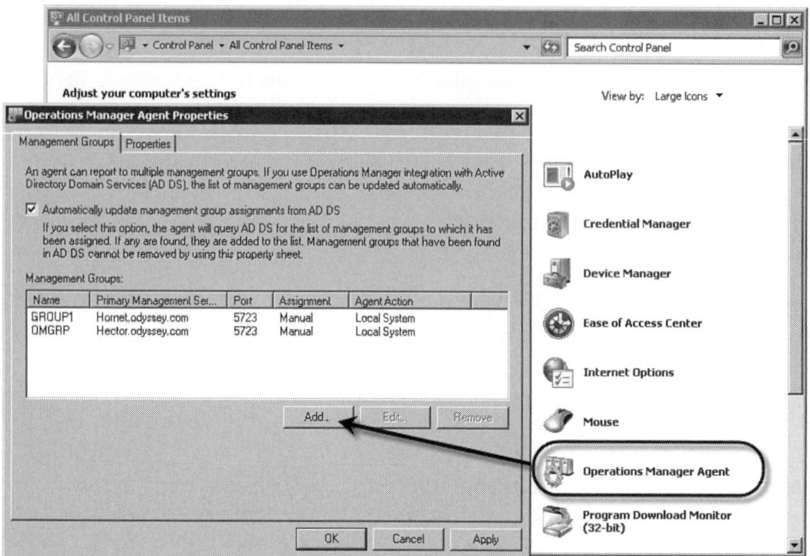

FIGURE 6.31 Manually dual-homing a manually upgraded agent.

Retire the OpsMgr 2007 R2 Management Group

Once all agents are dual-homed and reporting to the OpsMgr 2012 management group a coexistence period begins, during which you can monitor a computer from either management group. If you installed the Upgrade Helper management pack in the OpsMgr 2007 R2 management group, all computers showing green status at the Step 3a - Upgrade Windows Agents view folder is your overall "green light" to consider the agent upgrade and dual-home task complete. Now you can turn your attention to preparing the OpsMgr 2012 management group for production monitoring of your network(s).

Initially, the OpsMgr 2007 R2 management group remains your production OpsMgr instance because the OpsMgr 2012 management group does not have all required management packs imported and appropriate custom overrides created. Follow the recommendations in Chapter 7, "Configuring and Using System Center 2012 Operations Manager," to deploy management packs in a phased and deliberate approach. In particular, deploy several sealed management packs at a time and watch the effects on the management group in terms of alerting. As you discover alerts that need overrides applied, author overrides and save them in unsealed override management packs. Once monitoring is stable and effective, add another small batch of management packs until all critical business applications have end-to-end monitoring in place.

Custom management packs from the OpsMgr 2007 R2 management group that you may have authored for line of business applications can be imported (if sealed) into the OpsMgr 2012 management group as needed. Custom distributed applications (DAs) in the OpsMgr 2007 R2 management group will likely need to be authored again using the

Operations console once all required objects for the DA are discovered by OpsMgr 2012. Notification channels and subscriptions must be created, and you may have external connectors to other systems to install on the OpsMgr 2012 side.

Avoid running in multi-homed mode indefinitely as it generates twice the network traffic and agent load. Once you are satisfied you are getting the monitoring you need from the OpsMgr 2012 management group, shift production monitoring to OpsMgr 2012 and perform two main steps to retire the OpsMgr 2007 R2 management group:

- Uninstall the agents (make them no longer multi-homed to the OpsMgr 2007 R2 management group)
- Uninstall the server components

These are discussed in the following sections.

TIP: CONSIDER KEEPING RETIRED RMS FOR HISTORICAL DATA ACCESS

If you have capacity to keep the retired OpsMgr database(s) running for some months, you may consider leaving the orphaned RMS alone. You can run the retired RMS with the Operations console installed to gain access to historical data from the retired databases until such time that the OpsMgr 2012 management group meets reporting service level agreements (SLAs).

Make All Agents Single-Homed to OpsMgr 2012

An additional task is to uninstall the legacy OpsMgr 2007 R2 management group from your agent population. Unfortunately, you cannot use the OpsMgr 2007 R2 management group to remove references to itself from each agent-managed computer once the agents are upgraded to OpsMgr 2012. While running the agent install task will appear to work from the OpsMgr 2007 side, the OpsMgr 2012 agent does not respond to the instructions and the task silently fails.

The multi-homed upgrade leaves the agents dual-homed; constantly attempting to contact the old management group even after your OpsMgr 2007 R2 servers are retired. You must reconfigure all multi-homed agents to remove configuration information about the OpsMgr 2007 R2 management group being retired. This means single-homing the agents to only the OpsMgr 2012 management group. There are two ways to accomplish the agent single-homing task:

- If you have a small number of computers, access the OpsMgr control panel item as shown in Figure 6.31, but instead of adding an additional management group as previously described in the "Upgrading and Dual-homing Manually Installed Agents" section, select the OpsMgr 2007 R2 management group in the Management Groups list and click the **Remove** button.
- For a larger number of computers, a scripted solution is indicated. The OpsMgr software development kit (SDK) includes an agent configuration object documented at

http://msdn.microsoft.com/en-us/library/hh329017.aspx. Running the following small VBScript locally will remove an OpsMgr management group named GROUP1:

```
Option Explicit

Dim objMSConfig
Set objMSConfig = CreateObject("AgentConfigManager.MgmtSvcCfg")

Call objMSConfig.RemoveManagementGroup ("GROUP1")
```

Uninstall the OpsMgr 2007 R2 Servers

After all automatically and manually upgraded OpsMgr 2012 agents are no longer multi-homed to the old OpsMgr 2007 R2 management group, uninstall the OpsMgr 2007 R2 server components as appropriate. The OpsMgr 2007 R2 operational and data warehouse databases are not automatically deleted by any management server uninstallation. You can manually delete the old databases or preserve them for backup or historical purposes.

If all OpsMgr 2007 R2 servers are scheduled for retirement and there is no historical need to preserve any OpsMgr 2007 R2 databases, you can immediately repurpose these computers without an orderly uninstall of OpsMgr components. If you will be reusing the computers that were running OpsMgr 2007 R2 server components without installing new operating systems, the OpsMgr 2007 R2 server components should be uninstalled in the following order:

1. Gateway servers.
2. Report server and Web consoles.
3. Management servers other than the RMS.
4. RMS.

Case Studies

To help illustrate the many varied, valid paths to upgrade to OpsMgr 2012, the next sections describe three scenarios. For each scenario, business objectives are identified, with technical steps presented to meet the objectives. Your biggest decision is whether to upgrade the management group or multi-home the agents to a new management group. All multi-home scenarios, regardless of network size, follow the same high-level steps as those discussed in the "Large Enterprise: Multi-Home Strategy" section. Conversely, all database upgrade scenarios follow some combination of the "Small Network: In-place OS, SQL Upgrades" and the "Medium Enterprise: Preserve Database" scenarios that follow.

Small Network: In-place OS, SQL Upgrades

The objective of this scenario is to take as little time as possible and roll out the upgrade, preserving the existing operational database and management server. For the in-place upgrade, the RMS is running Windows Server 2008 R2 SP 1, and the SQL versions are SQL

Server 2008 SP 1 or R2. Figure 6.32 shows a typical small to medium topology for OpsMgr 2007 when managing up to several hundred computers.

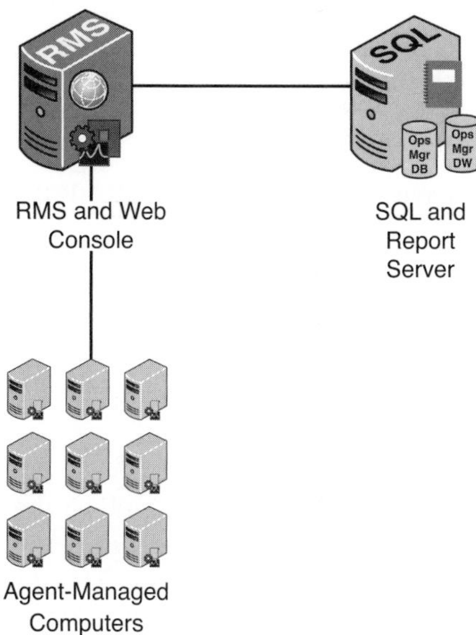

FIGURE 6.32 Small network with single management server.

This management group has the reporting server component installed on the database server and the Web console installed on the RMS. In-place upgrade of the reporting server component can be problematic. The authors recommend "sacrificing" the OpsMgr 2007 R2 data warehouse database in a small network upgrade scenario, with the goal of successfully upgrading the management group operational database on the first attempt. A fresh OpsMgr 2012 data warehouse database is created during the upgrade, and new historical reports will begin from the day of the upgrade.

Print or save to file copies of OpsMgr historical reports from the data warehouse database to which you need long term reference. To avoid unnecessary errors during the upgrade process by reducing complexity, the OpsMgr 2007 R2 agent and reporting server components are uninstalled from the SQL Server prior to upgrading the RMS and database. In addition, the Web console is uninstalled from the RMS. Here are the high-level steps to upgrade this small network management group:

1. Uninstall the agent and reporting server components from the SQL Server. The Reporting pane in the Operations console should disappear.
2. Run the ResetSRS.exe support tool to restore default settings to SSRS.
3. Delete the retired OpsMgr 2007 R2 data warehouse database (OperationsManagerDW) from the SQL Server using SQL Management Studio or other SQL administration tool.

4. Uninstall the Web console from the RMS.
5. Upgrade the management group from the RMS and create a new data warehouse database.
6. Install OpsMgr 2012 reporting on the SQL Server and push an OpsMgr 2012 agent to the SQL Server.
7. Install the OpsMgr 2012 Web console on the management server.
8. Push-upgrade the agents from the Operations console, **Administration** -> **Pending Management**.
9. Check on updates available to installed management packs at **Administration** -> **Management Packs**.

Medium Enterprise: Preserve Database

The purpose of this scenario is to continue using the existing OpsMgr management group configuration including management packs, agent performance history, and all the settings that constitute the management group—even though doing so may require some complex upgrade steps. This scenario fits the organization that is satisfied with its OpsMgr 2007 R2 configuration and does not want to re-create notifications, make new override managements packs, and discover agents again—tasks necessary when starting with a clean OpsMgr database.

For networks with OpsMgr 2007 R2 large operational databases (over 30GB), it could be impractical to perform a management group upgrade if the database must be expanded further to achieve the 50% minimum free space required for the upgrade. In this situation, you might be forced to use the multi-homed upgrade method to start over with a compact operational database.

TIP: MITIGATING RISKS IN DATABASE UPGRADE SCENARIOS

The "Upgrading the Distributed Management Group" section highlighted the importance of having backups of the operational and data warehouse databases, as well as the complete computer and system state backup of the RMS.

- This is never truer than with the large-scale upgrade, database upgrade scenario. A considerable amount of work can go into delivering an upgrade path that supports continued use of the management group database. Failure to upgrade the database, without a full RMS and database restore capability, means starting over with a new management group.
- In high-value situations, consider restoring the databases and RMS in a sandbox (isolated) lab environment. To remove all OpsMgr 2007 R2 objects from the management group, delete all the agents, gateways, and management servers, leaving the RMS the only computer in the sandbox lab copy of the management group. Then, attempt an actual database upgrade to the lab copy of the management group. Identify possibly fatal database upgrade errors before committing to a costly in-place upgrade path.

Figure 6.33 diagrams a typical large enterprise deployment of OpsMgr 2007 R2 that could be managing a thousand computers. Here are some design requirements that emerge from a study of this topology:

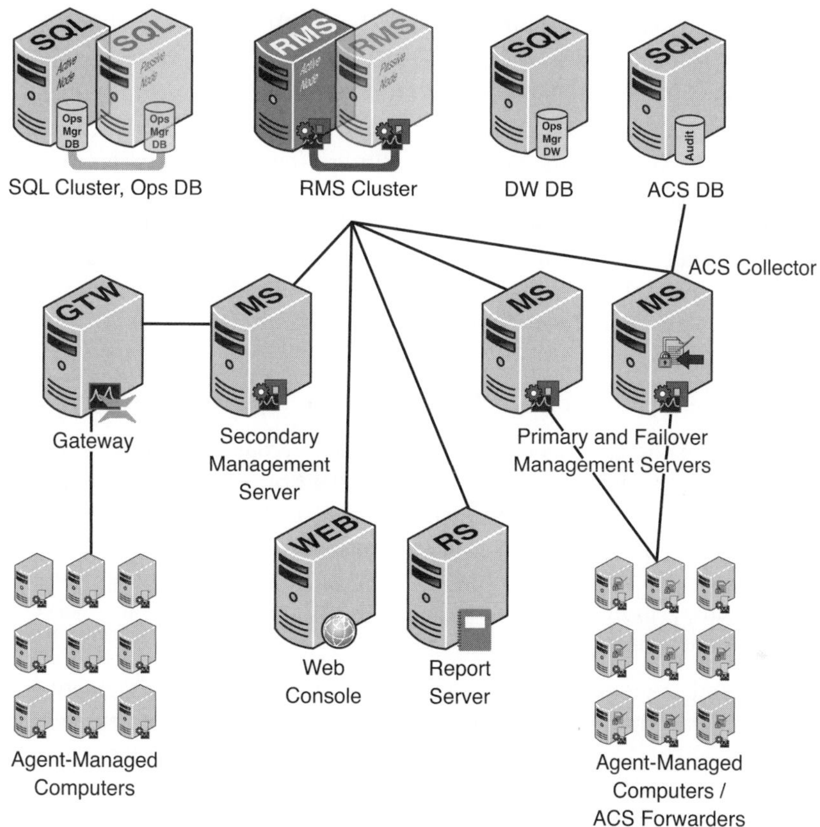

FIGURE 6.33 Distributed OpsMgr 2007 management group with clustered RMS.

- The existence of the clustered RMS means the management group must be upgraded from a secondary management server.
- The RMS will be retired, yet the reporting server and Web console still point to the RMS, so those components will be uninstalled before the upgrade. While you could uninstall and reinstall the Web console and reporting server (pointing them to management servers other than the RMS), it is simpler to just install them before upgrading.
- Assuming there is no change in the number or location of agent-managed computers, the same topology is used regarding the number of management servers (taking into account no clustered RMS).

- The gateway server must be running Windows Server 2008 R2 SP 1 to be upgraded in place—or a second computer running Windows Server 2008 R2 SP 1 (or Windows Server 2012 for OpsMgr 2012 SP 1) is required in the same remote site to install a new gateway.
- The data warehouse database is currently a non-clustered SQL Server. To achieve high availability with OpsMgr 2012, it is a good idea to cluster this database as well as continue to cluster the operational database.

A new feature in OpsMgr 2012 is enabling high availability for the Data Access Service (DAS). This allows consoles, Web consoles, and report servers not to depend on a particular management server for access to the database. While you can implement this feature using Windows network load balancing, the authors suggest a hardware or virtual appliance load balancer. In this example management group, the four OpsMgr 2012 management servers will be load-balanced and addressed by a single private DNS alias such as scom.odyssey.com.

Here are suggested high-level steps to upgrade this large network management group:

1. Upgrade the gateway. If the gateway cannot be upgraded because it is running a 32-bit OS, install a second gateway (running OpsMgr 2012 on Windows Server 2008 R2) on the remote network, and move all agent-managed computers from the 32-bit OpsMgr 2007 R2 gateway to the OpsMgr 2012 gateway. The reason to consider the gateway for upgrade first is that if the gateway is running a 32-bit operating system, the downstream agents will not have management availability if the gateway server is upgraded later in the process.
2. Upgrade all management servers except the RMS. 32-bit OpsMgr R2 management servers cannot be upgraded. Install new OpsMgr 2012 secondary management servers on Windows Server 2008 R2 SP 1 computers (or OpsMgr 2012 SP 1 on Windows Server 2012 computers) and move agents off any 32-bit management server, and then uninstall all 32-bit management servers from the management group.
3. Upgrade the ACS collector component on the upgraded management server that is the ACS collector.
4. Uninstall the agent and the reporting server components from the report server. Run the ResetSRS.exe support tool to restore default settings to SSRS.
5. Uninstall the agent and Web console from the Web console server.
6. Push-upgrade the agents from the **Administration -> Pending Management** node of the Operations console. Upgrade agents downstream from the gateway, then agents downstream from the management servers. Manually upgrade all manually installed agents (if any).
7. Upgrade the management group from the upgraded secondary management server that will become the RMS emulator in the OpsMgr 2012 management group.
8. Repurpose the former RMS cluster nodes as part of a new SQL Server failover cluster to host the OpsMgr 2012 data warehouse database. Move the data warehouse

database to a clustered SQL instance. To move the data warehouse database, see Chapter 12, "Backup and Recovery." Modify your procedure to use your clustered database server and instance name where the checklist in that chapter refers to the SQL Server-based computer.

9. Configure the hardware load balancer for a highly available DAS. Establish a DNS alias that resolves to the virtual IP (VIP) publishing the farm of management servers.
10. Install OpsMgr 2012 reporting on the reporting server using the DNS name of the highly available DAS. Push an OpsMgr 2012 agent to the reporting server.
11. Install the OpsMgr 2012 Web console on the Web console server using the DNS name of the highly available DAS. Push an OpsMgr 2012 agent to this server.
12. Check on updates available to installed management packs at **Administration -> Management Packs**.

Figure 6.34 shows the management group after the upgrade to OpsMgr 2012. The main changes are the lack of an RMS and the addition of the highly available DAS.

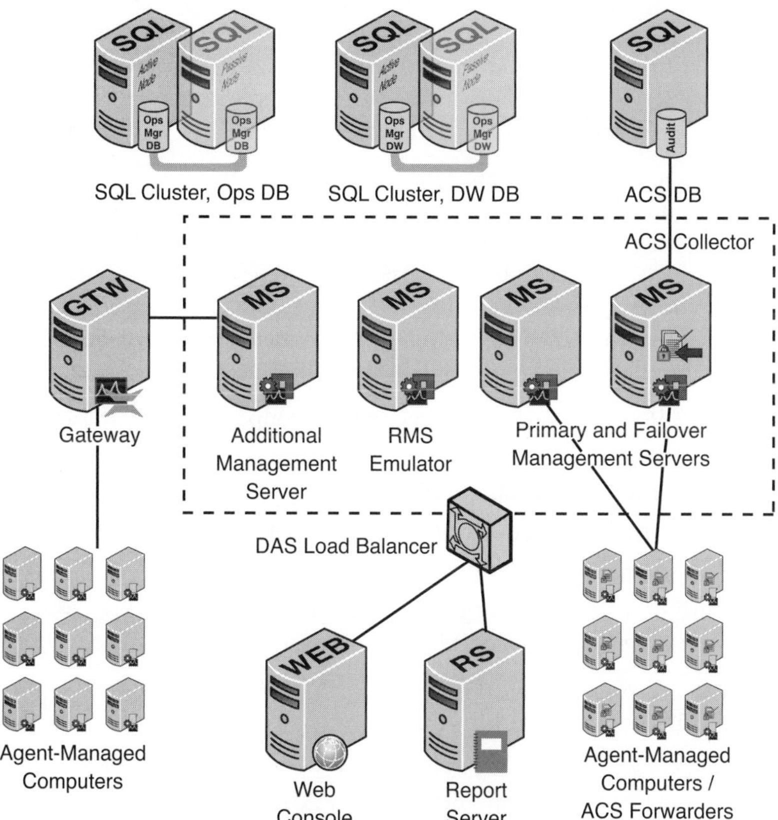

FIGURE 6.34 Distributed management group after upgrade.

Large Enterprise: Multi-Home Strategy

The final case study presented is the multi-home upgrade path. Here a large enterprise is both upgrading to OpsMgr 2012 and migrating to a new management group platform, perhaps in a new data center or private cloud. The principles demonstrated in this case study apply to OpsMgr 2007 R2 to OpsMgr 2012 upgrades of all sizes and topologies that follow the multi-home path. The business objectives are twofold:

- Moving the management group from the current site to a new one
- Starting over with best practice architecture, an optimized set of management packs and new override management packs

This solution has a higher operational expense, as it requires hardware resources to duplicate all management group components—across both management groups the agents are reporting to—during the migration project.

A challenge here is reusing company knowledge in the OpsMgr 2007 R2 implementation, in particular overrides to thresholds, monitors, and rules, as well as any custom management packs that are sealed or can be sealed and then imported into OpsMgr 2012. Unsealed management packs in OpsMgr 2007 R2 that reference only groups and classes in sealed management packs—that have the same or later version sealed management pack available in OpsMgr 2012—can be imported directly into OpsMgr 2012. However, any management pack, sealed or unsealed, that references specific objects in the OpsMgr 2007 R2 management group will fail to import into OpsMgr 2012.

Figure 6.35 represents the concept of multi-home strategy. Notice at the bottom of the diagram, there is by definition only one population of agent-managed computers (in two categories): some managed by management servers and others by a gateway. The top of the diagram shows two management groups duplicated component for component (respecting the architecture differences of the two OpsMgr versions). Each agent has a connection to both management groups. The OpsMgr 2007 R2 management group must be running CU4 or later in order to dual-home the OpsMgr 2012 agents.

Here are suggested high-level steps to upgrade a management group using the multi-home path:

1. Install the new OpsMgr 2012 management group in an optimal topology on the new platform. Do not import any management packs after initial installation other than the core Windows OS management packs.
2. Identify all sealed third-party and custom management packs in the OpsMgr 2007 R2 management group to be reused in OpsMgr 2012.
3. Evaluate the management packs installed in OpsMgr 2007 R2, particularly to identify those with little value that you do not plan to reuse.
4. Using the list of management packs identified in steps 2 and 3, stage all existing management packs you will be importing into OpsMgr 2012 to a central file location (except for the System Center and Windows OS management packs, which will already be installed).

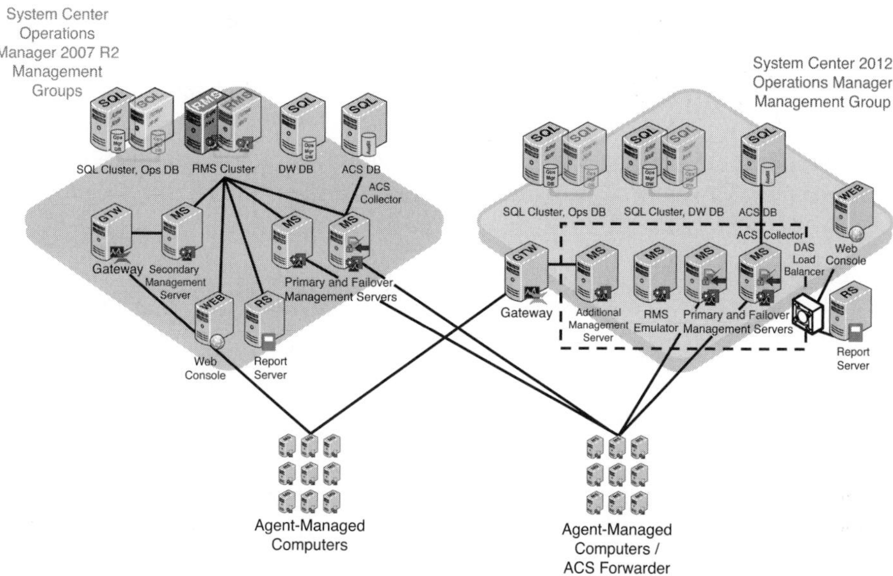

FIGURE 6.35 Multi-home upgrade for large, distributed enterprise.

5. Study the overrides in your OpsMgr 2007 R2 environment in the Administration console at Authoring -> Management Pack Objects -> Overrides.

6. Create empty override management packs in OpsMgr 2012 for each application you are planning to create overrides for, based on your review of effective overrides in OpsMgr 2007 R2.

7. Discover and push OpsMgr 2012 agents to a small, representative pool of OpsMgr 2007 R2 agent-managed computers, dual-homing them to the old and new management groups. This will be the pilot computer group when importing management packs into OpsMgr 2012.

8. Import management packs one application at a time into the OpsMgr 2012 management group. Consider checking for updated versions of each management pack as they are imported, and updating to the latest versions.

9. Create overrides in the appropriate override management pack for an application, verify alerts and monitors are configured as desired, and then proceed to the next application.

10. Install connectors and create notification channels, alert subscriptions, and scheduled reports, if any, as required for your environment. Test each feature for proper function and to confirm there are no unanticipated effects.

11. Confirm healthy management group function with all expected management packs loaded and while monitoring the pilot group of dual-homed computers. Create user roles appropriate for your OpsMgr operators, advanced operators, report operators, and authors.

12. When confident the OpsMgr 2012 management group is ready for production, discover computers running OpsMgr 2007 R2 agent, and push-install OpsMgr 2012 agents, not more than 200 at once.

13. Continue to deploy OpsMgr 2012 agents until all OpsMgr 2007 R2 agents are upgraded and dual-homed. Transition your operators to use the new Operations console for monitoring.

14. When confident OpsMgr 2012 is properly monitoring your environment, transfer primary production to OpsMgr 2012 and proceed to retire OpsMgr 2007 R2.

15. Single-home all agents, so they no longer try to communicate with the OpsMgr 2007 R2 management group. Follow one or both methods described in the "Make All Agents Single-Homed to OpsMgr 2012" section to remove the old management group from the agents.

16. When all agents are single-homed to the OpsMgr 2012 management group, you can repurpose the OpsMgr 2007 R2 management group servers.

Summary

This chapter discussed the steps involved in upgrading or migrating to System Center 2012 Operations Manager from Operations Manager 2007 R2. The next chapter discusses how to configure and use Operations Manager 2012 after your installation or upgrade.

PART III

Moving Toward Application-Centered Management

IN THIS PART

CHAPTER 7

Configuring and Using System Center 2012 Operations Manager

IN THIS CHAPTER

- Introducing the Operations Console
- Configuring the Operations Console
- Using the Operations Console
- Fast Track

This chapter discusses basic configuration and administration of System Center 2012 Operations Manager (OpsMgr), beginning with an introduction to the Operations console. You will learn about the Operations console functions and components, and how to install the console on remote machines. The chapter introduces and steps through the Operations console, discussing what work is accomplished within the various panes, and how to customize the console to your organization's requirements.

Introducing the Operations Console

This chapter assumes you have previously installed the PowerShell shell and the core server-side features of OpsMgr on one or more servers. Here are the core features to which this chapter will refer:

- OpsMgr operational database and data warehouse
- Management servers including the root management server emulator (RMSE)
- Reporting component
- (A minimum of one) Operations console
- Web console server

If you are familiar with any version of Operations Manager, you most likely will approach this chapter to become acclimated to the new System Center-based release of Microsoft's server-monitoring software and its user interfaces. The authors suggest you read Chapter 2,

"What's New in System Center 2012 Operations Manager," as an introduction. Chapter 2 discusses the history of OpsMgr and describes the differences between System Center 2012 Operations Manager and Operations Manager 2007 R2. If you are entirely new to Microsoft management products, focus on this chapter instead to begin familiarizing yourself with the product.

- If the core OpsMgr features are not installed, you might want to first read Chapter 5, "Installing System Center 2012 Operations Manager," to step through a fresh install, or Chapter 6, "Upgrading to System Center 2012 Operations Manager," if migrating from Operations Manager 2007.
- If the core OpsMgr features are installed, a first step to validate OpsMgr is installed successfully is by opening the Operations console and verifying it connects to the database server.

Connecting to the Operations Console

Let's "kick the tires" to be sure there is a stable foundation before bringing this management group into a monitoring environment. Start by verifying that all instances of the console are closed; then open a new instance of the Operations console. Even better, the authors recommend installing the Operations console on an administrator workstation, and performing all testing and production work using consoles not installed on management servers.

NOTE: WHERE TO RUN THE OPERATIONS CONSOLE

The authors do not recommend running the Operations console on a management server (MS) or using a Remote Desktop Protocol (RDP) session to the MS during testing. It is not a good practice to run the Operations console on a management server itself; you want to dedicate all MS resources for the critical OpsMgr services it hosts.

In addition, using the Operations console from a computer other than the management server tests several important communication channels between the features in the management group. You get a more complete checkup of OpsMgr's health using a separate Operations console installed on a workstation or uninvolved server. For validation purposes, the computer running the console should be a member of the domain and on the same network segment as the management server and OpsMgr reporting feature.

Connecting to the Console

Upon completing a successful installation, the default action is to open the Operations console for the first time on that computer. Here are some points to keep in mind:

- The first time you open the Operations console on a computer that is not an OpsMgr management server, you may see a Connect to Server dialog box, and you must enter the name of the OpsMgr management group and a management server for that management group. The console connects to a management server and attempts to authenticate the user logged on at the computer where the console is running.

- If the management server is not in the same Active Directory domain as the computer running the console, the Enter Credentials dialog box appears, as shown in Figure 7.1. Add user accounts or groups to roles prior to using the Operations console's Administration workspace or equivalent PowerShell commands.

FIGURE 7.1 Enter domain credentials authorized to access the Operations console.

Connecting to the Management Server

The console's Connect to Server applet remembers the identity of the management server you first connected to, and will not prompt again for the name of a management group. By default, the console connects to the management server it last connected to. To change the focus of the Operations console to another management group, select **Tools -> Connect** from the console's main menu bar. This invokes the Connect to Server applet, where you can enter the information for another OpsMgr management group. Connecting to another management group adds an entry to the Registered Servers list remembered by the Connect to Server applet, which changes the default connection to the last management group selected.

Connecting in Untrusted Domains

The Enter Credentials dialog box does not remember domain user logon information, and it only displays the local computer and those domains it is a member of or trusts as choices in the Domain drop-down selection list. The console prompts for user credentials authorized to access the Operations console in the domain where the OpsMgr management server is located. When accessing OpsMgr management groups in domains that do not trust the domain where the Operations console is located, you must manually supply appropriate user credentials and domain names on each use of the console.

Console Limitations

Theoretically, there is no upper limit on how many Operations consoles you can install in a single management group. Install the console wherever it makes work more convenient and efficient for the operations staff. However, each open console creates several network connections and causes the management server to open a connection to the operational database on behalf of the console. This means consoles are not inconsequential in terms of their impact on the network and the OpsMgr management group.

Microsoft suggests that you not plan for more than 50 simultaneous Operations console sessions in a single management group. The authors recommend you close any console sessions not in active use.

Running the Console Without Trusted Authentication

There is a potential issue when invoking the Operations console in a user context without trusted authentication between the core components of the management group and the user running the console. This issue occurs when PowerShell launches against an object in the Operations console (such as, by right-clicking the object and selecting **Open -> Operations Manager Shell**). Although the user provides credentials when starting the Operations console, those credentials are not passed to PowerShell when invoked from the console.

As an example, consider an organization with two different domains without trust relationships: Odyssey and Eclipse. If a computer is in the Eclipse domain and Operations Manager is installed in Odyssey, the user can log in to the Operations console using his Odyssey credentials. However, when the user launches a PowerShell script from the console, it fails to connect to the management server. To avoid this situation, use a computer joined to the domain where Operations Manager resides or avoid launching PowerShell from the Operations console.

Console Configuration Data

The Operations console stores configuration data locally and in the Operations database. Customizations to the My Workspace portion of the console are stored in the database, and follow the user from console to console, similar to a Windows roaming profile. This feature lets a user take advantage of the time spent creating favorite views and saved searches across all consoles in a management group. Most other console settings are locally stored in the registry key `HKEY_CURRENT_USER\SOFTWARE\Microsoft\Microsoft Operations Manager\3.0\` and will apply only to the user on that computer.

Other console settings saved in the current logged on user's registry key (only affecting the console for that user on that computer) include

- Connection history with the names of management groups the console has connected to
- Show or Hide Views selections
- Whether the console is in a window or full screen, and if in a window, the size and position of the window

The Monitoring overview always is the default location when the console opens, regardless of where the console was when closed.

Whatever child monitoring views were expanded during the last console use is also remembered. Therefore, although the console will always open to the root of the navigation hierarchy, if you have a carefully selected set of view folders that you keep open, the console saves you time by remembering those settings. The console also remembers the performance counters you previously selected in particular performance views—another major timesaver!

Confirming Management Group Health

You can install the Operations console on various systems in your environment. The authors recommend installing the console on all management servers, your OpsMgr administrators' desktops, and a terminal services or Citrix farm.

The Operations console provides a single user interface for Operations Manager. Installing and using these consoles on desktop systems running Windows client operating systems removes some of the load from the management server. Desktop access to the consoles also simplifies day-to-day administration. The authors do not recommend running the Operations console on the management servers themselves, as it is best to dedicate the management server resources to providing the Operations Manager services. However, installing the Operations console on each management server makes it available when debugging connectivity issues to your OpsMgr environment. The console binaries are also required to provide the PowerShell add-ons and to enable resource kit and third-party tools to run correctly.

After installing the core features of OpsMgr, your next step is to confirm its health. This is most easily accomplished by opening the Operations console and verifying that it connects and is able to provide information for the health of the OpsMgr servers. To open the console, select **Start** -> **All Programs** -> **Microsoft System Center 2012** -> **Operations Manager** -> **Operations Console** (or just type **operations console** in the search field). Figure 7.2 shows the initial view of the Operations console.

If you can open the Operations console successfully, this indicates the core features (including the console, operational database, and at least one of your management servers) are functional.

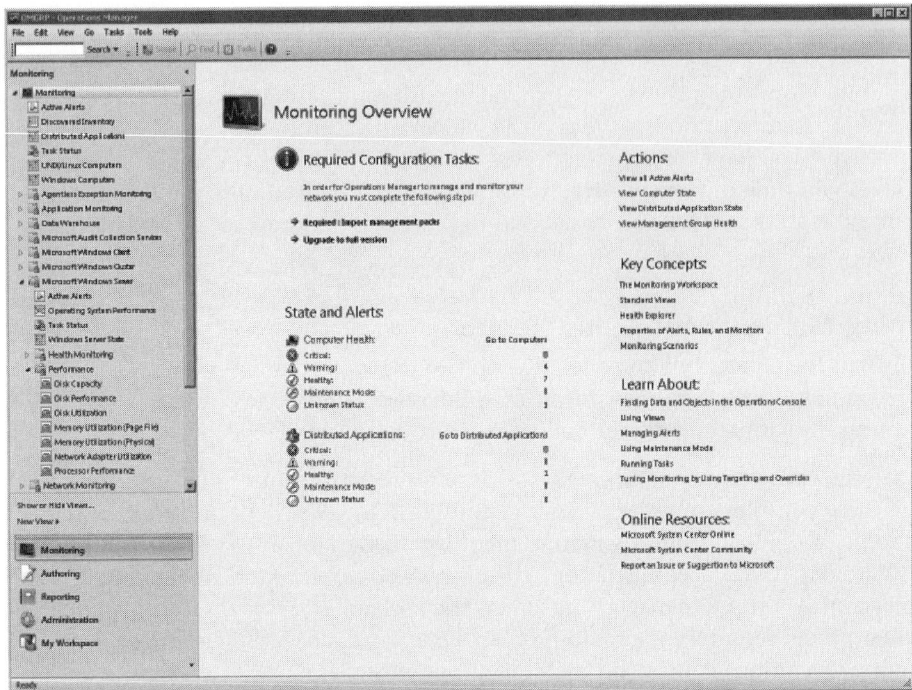

FIGURE 7.2 Introducing the Operations console.

A Quick Tour of the Operations Console

If you are new to Operations Manager or System Center, examine Figures 7.2 and 7.3. Figure 7.3 is an example of the Operations console's appearance when highlighting a server in the Monitoring pane. If this appears similar to Microsoft Outlook, it is because Microsoft designed the OpsMgr and other System Center consoles based on the Outlook user interface, making them more intuitive to navigate.

Operations Manager UI Tips

You can determine a considerable amount of information with this user interface (UI) very quickly. Here are some tips:

- The bottom left corner of the screen, known internally within Microsoft as the *WunderBar*, consists of links to the various workspaces of the Operations console, including Monitoring, Authoring, Reporting, Administration, and My Workspace. These are the major sections of the Operations console, discussed in the "Configuring the Operations Console" section of this chapter.

- Directly above the WunderBar is the folder hierarchy for the Monitoring pane, which includes a series of default views (such as the Active Alerts view) and folders for different management packs that in turn may also provide folders or views.

  The view you choose determines what appears in the center section of the screen. For example, Figure 7.3 is displaying the health of Windows Computers. Below the view displaying computer health, the Detail view shows detail for the object selected in the center pane. On the right side of the screen is the Tasks pane, showing available actions based on the highlighted object. To compare this to Outlook, this view would be very similar to what would be presented if you opened Outlook to the Inbox, highlighted an email with the preview pane turned on below and with Xobni (a third-party extension to Outlook) on the right side giving information about the person who wrote the email.

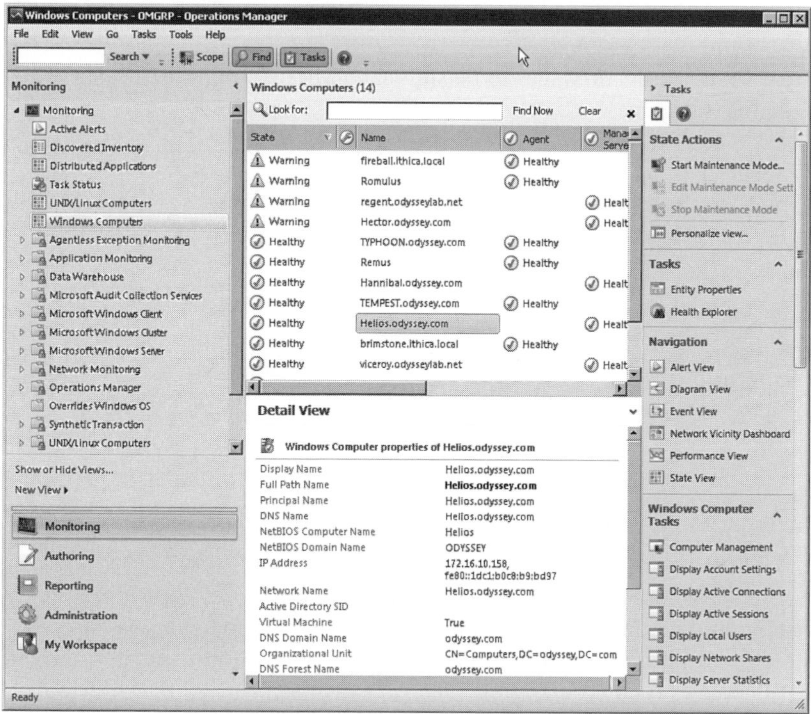

FIGURE 7.3 Touring the Operations console.

TIP: KEYBOARD NAVIGATING VIA THE WUNDERBAR

You can use Control key combinations to open different parts of the console. Highlighting an item on the WunderBar and pressing Ctrl+(1-5) opens the corresponding section pane from the WunderBar. As an example, Ctrl+1 opens the Monitoring pane, Ctrl+2 opens the Authoring pane, Ctrl+3 opens the Reporting pane, Ctrl+4 opens Administration, and Ctrl+5 opens My Workspace. This also works in Outlook but does not appear to work over RDP sessions.

- The bar at the top of the screen shows **Windows Computers - OMGRP - Operations Manager**. This indicates the management group to which you are connected is OMGRP and you are currently in the Windows Computers view. Below that is the familiar structure that provides the different tabs available (File, Edit, and so on) and a search function.

Unlike some other System Center 2012 components, this version of the Operations console does not incorporate the Outlook-styled ribbon.

- A quick look at the Operations console also indicates whether the reporting feature was successfully installed (it appears as shown in Figure 7.2, with **Reporting** in the WunderBar).

Designing the System Center user interfaces to be similar to Microsoft Outlook makes the System Center suite more intuitive.

Global Views

Below the root of the Monitoring hierarchy on the left side of the console are several view folders and the six default global views visible in Figure 7.3:

- Active Alerts
- Discovered Inventory
- Distributed Applications
- Task Status
- UNIX/Linux Computers
- Windows Computers

Global views are those views located immediately under the root of the Monitoring hierarchy. You can create new, custom global views under the Monitoring hierarchy root, as well as new view folders and hierarchies of folders. From the Navigation pane, if you open **View -> Show or Hide Views** (shown in Figure 7.4) you can specify whether the default folders are displayed or hidden.

While child views can be hidden in the Monitoring pane, global views are not listed in this figure and cannot be hidden. To avoid cluttering your Monitoring pane, the authors recommend you avoid creating additional global views unless all users of the Operations console will use them.

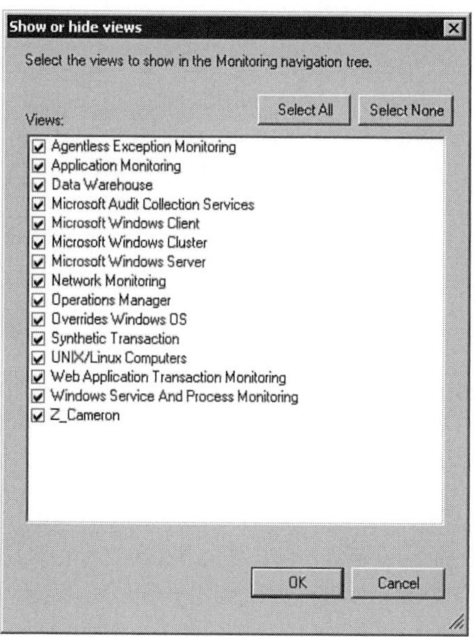

FIGURE 7.4 Configuring the default views in the Monitoring pane.

Configuring the Operations Console

Now that you have had a quick tour of the Operations console, let's go into more depth on the five navigation panes, including what they are used for and how to use them:

- **Monitoring:** Displays different types of views that enable you to analyze monitoring needs.
- **Authoring:** Lets you create additional monitoring objects to customize or supplement the default monitoring settings provided with management packs.
- **Administration:** Enables editing Operations Manager settings that affect the management group. In addition, it allows you to view and configure individual management servers and managed objects.
- **Reporting:** Displays reports included in installed management packs and enables editing customized reports.
- **My Workspace:** Enables creating and storing console customizations for later reuse.

The following sections discuss each of these panes in detail.

Using the Monitoring Pane

The Monitoring pane is the primary area where both Operations Manager administrators and operators will work on a daily basis. This pane is designed to provide what you need to quickly find and analyze the current state of the environment you are monitoring. The Monitoring pane's goal, when no problems exist, is to validate the continuing successful function of the OpsMgr instrumentation. When there is an issue with an object you are managing, the Monitoring pane's purpose is to clearly present a statement of the problem (and even propose taking suggested repair actions), or make it as easy and quick as possible to locate the root cause and achieve resolution.

The Monitoring pane is built of a series of different views. These views are included in management packs, and you can create custom views as well.

Folders

Views are stored in management packs, which in turn can contain folders. Folders in sealed management packs display with a small lock on the bottom right corner of the folder. Folders stored in non-sealed management packs are shown with the same icon but without the lock. Folders are used to create a structure to store other views in the Monitoring pane. Folders with the same name as the management pack are created automatically whenever a management pack is created.

TIP: DECLUTTERING THE MONITORING PANE

While the Monitoring pane tends to start out quite pristine, over time many folders may be added to make navigation of this pane more complicated. For information on how to remove clutter from the Monitoring pane, see the suggestions at http://blogs.catapultsystems.com/cfuller/archive/2011/05/11/quicktricks-decluttering-the-monitoring-pane-view.aspx.

You can also create custom folders and views with security applied to them, providing a more custom user experience where the user only sees those folders and views that are relevant.

Alert Views

The Alert view provides alert information from the OpsMgr operational database. You can create custom alert views that display data from a specific target or group. Properties of alert views can be created based on your requirements for the view; Table 7.1 includes conditions and examples where these would be useful.

TABLE 7.1 Alert view properties and common usage

Condition	Common Usage
of a specific severity	Severities can be Information, Warning, and Critical. This is useful when creating views that are only displaying alerts for Operations groups that may not be required to monitor Warning or Informational alerts.
of a specific priority	Priorities are High, Medium, and Low. This is often combined with specific severity settings for Operations groups.
created by specific sources	Useful when creating custom monitors and rules to show only alerts from those specific sources.
with specific resolution state	Used frequently to show those alerts not closed or with a New resolution state.
with a specific name	Often used when creating custom alerts to match based upon a naming convention.
with specific text in the description	Frequently used to match keywords listed in the description field.
created in specific time period	Useful to find alerts which have occurred in the last several hours or within a specific timeframe.
assigned to a specific owner	This is useful when creating your own views either per group or per user to see only the alerts currently owned by you or your group.
raised by an instance with a specific name	Useful when identifying an alert or rule and where it came from, based upon a wildcard search.
last modified by a specific user	Helpful when creating a view to determine what alerts a user has recently modified.
that was modified in specific time period	Helpful when tracking down a list of alerts that occurred in the last several hours or in a specific timeframe.
had its resolution state changed in a specific time period	Useful to find alerts that had state changes in the last several hours or within a specific timeframe.
that was resolved in a specific time period	This is useful when identifying alerts closed in the last day or within a specific timeframe.
resolved by a specific user	Useful when determining what alerts a specific user has resolved.
with a specific ticket ID	Helpful when tracking down a specific ticket associated with an alert.

Condition	Common Usage
was added to the database in a specific time period	This is useful when attempting to identify issues that occurred when adding data to the database.
from a specific site	Provides a way to identify alerts from a specific site based upon a wildcard.
with specific text in Custom Field1..10	Any of the 10 custom fields can provide criteria for this view based upon a wildcard.

Various fields can be displayed on the Alert view. These include Severity, Icon, Path, Source, Maintenance Mode, Name, Resolution State, Created, Age, Type, Owner, Priority, Latency, Description, Connector, Forwarding Status, Class, Time in State, Custom Field (1..10), Resolved By, Time Resolved, Last State Change, Last Modified, Last Modified By, Management Group, Site, Repeat Count, and Ticket ID.

Columns can be sorted by any of the columns you define (ascending or descending) and grouped by up to three different items in either ascending or descending order. A good example of using the properties in Operations Manager is the top-level view called Active Alerts. This is a built-in alert view with a criteria defined that all alerts are displayed other than those with a resolution state of 255 (closed), sorted by Created and grouped by Severity.

Event Views

The Event view displays event information stored in the operational database. Custom event views can be created that will display data from a specific target or group. Properties of event views can be created based on your requirements for the view; Table 7.2 includes conditions and examples where these would be useful.

TABLE 7.2 Event view properties and common usage

Condition	Common Usage
generated by specific rules	This is useful when creating custom rules to limit the view to a subset of rules that you want to display.
with a specific event number	This assists with limiting the view to show only specific event numbers. It is often combined with limiting to a specific source or severity level.
from a specific source	This assists with limiting the view to show only events that come from a specific source. It is often combined with limiting to a specific event number or severity level.
generated in a specific time period	Useful to find events that have occurred in the last several hours or within a specific timeframe.

Condition	Common Usage
raised by an instance with a specific name	Useful when identifying an event and where it came from based upon a wildcard search.
with specific severity level	Severity levels include Success, Information, Warning, Error, Audit Success, Audit Failure.
	This assists with limiting the view to show only events that come from a specific source. It is often combined with limiting to a specific event number or severity level. An example of these would be to display only error event 1000 from a specific source.
from a specific user	Most of the time this field appears as N/A, but values may also be NT AUTHORITY\SYSTEM.
logged by a specific computer	Used to restrict a view to a specific computer (or set of computers) that logged the event.

Various fields can be displayed on the Event view. These include Level, Date and Time, Source, Name, User, Event Number, Log Name, Logging Computer, and Rule Name.

Columns can be sorted by any of the columns that you define (ascending or descending), and grouped by up to three different items in ascending or descending order. A good example of using these properties in Operations Manager is the Agent Events view in the Operations Manager -> Agent Details folder. This is a built-in event view showing data related to the Health Service based on specific rules that indicate agent health. This view is sorted by Date and Time.

State Views

The State view provides state information from the operational database. Custom state views can be created that will display data from a specific target or a specific group. Properties can be created based upon your requirements for the view, and Table 7.3 includes the conditions and examples of where these would be useful.

TABLE 7.3 State view properties and common usage

Condition	Common Usage
with a specific health state	Useful when creating a view of only servers in a warning or critical state.
is in Maintenance Mode	Provides a quick way to identify those objects in maintenance mode.
with specific Display Name	Limits the view to show only objects that match a wildcard.

Condition	Common Usage
Additional conditions are available depending upon the target chosen for the state view.	As an example, additional conditions for the Health Service include with specific Authentication Name, with specific Maximum Queue Size, with specific Maximum Size of All Transferred Files, Request Compression is true, Create Listener is True, with specific Port, Is Root Health Emulator is true, Is Management Server is true, Is Agent is true, Is Gateway is true, Is Manually Installed is true, with specific Installed By, with specific Version, with specific Action Account Identity, Send Heartbeats to Management Servers is true, with specific Heartbeat Interval (seconds), Managed Through Active Directory is true, Proxying Enabled is True, with specific Patch List, with specific Agent communication Protocol, Agent initiates connection to parent agent is true, and with specific Authentication service URI. Here are additional conditions for Windows Computer: with specific Principal Name, with specific DNS Name, with specific NetBIOS Computer Name, with specific NetBIOS Domain Name, with specific IP Address, with specific Network Name, with Specific Active Directory SID, Virtual Machine is true, with specific DNS Domain Name, with specific Organizational Unit, with specific DNS Forest Name, with specific Active Directory Site, with specific Logical Processors, with specific Physical Processors, with specific Host Server Name, with specific Virtual Machine Name, and with specific Offset In Minutes from Greenwich Time.

The display fields for a state view will vary depending upon the object chosen. Fields available for Windows Computer include: State, Maintenance Mode, Name, Path, Display Name, Principal Name, DNS Name, NetBIOS Computer Name, NetBIOS Domain Name, IP Address, Network Name, Active Directory SID, Virtual Machine, DNS Domain Name, Organizational Unit, DNS Forest Name, Active Directory Site, Logical Processors, Physical Processors, Host Server Name, Virtual Machine Name, Offset in Minutes from Greenwich Time, and much more.

Columns can be sorted by any of the columns you define (ascending or descending) and grouped by up to three different items in ascending or descending order. A good example of using these properties is the top-level view named Windows Computers. This is a built-in state view that has a target of Windows Computer and displays all state information, sorted by the state of the Windows Computer.

Performance Views

The Performance view provides performance information stored in the operational database. Custom performance views can be created that will display data from a specific target or a specific group. Properties can be created based upon your requirements for the view. Table 7.4 includes conditions and examples where these conditions would be useful.

TABLE 7.4 Performance view properties and common usage

Condition	Common Usage
collected by specific rules	This condition allows you to create a custom view that shows only the performance information for objects collected by specific rules. This is useful when you have created custom rules that gather data. Rules are chosen from a drop-down list of all available rules sorted by the rule name.
with a specific object name	This condition allows you to restrict the view to show only objects that match the wildcard string specified for the object name. As an example for the processor utilization counter, the object name is Processor.
with a specific counter name	This condition allows you to restrict the view to show only objects that match the wildcard string you specify for the counter name. As an example for the processor utilization counter, the object name is % Processor Time.
with a specific instance name	This condition allows you to restrict the view to show only objects that match the wildcard string you specify for the instance name. As an example for the processor utilization counter, the object name is _Total.

You can customize performance views in several ways:

- **Date and Time:** Period of time to display data in days, hours, or minutes up to the data retention period for the Operational database (7 days by default).
- **Chart Type:** Line (default) or spline (rounded) chart that can have 3D mode enabled and point labels enabled.
- **X Axis:** Show X Axis (default is checked), Major gridlines, Interlaced strips (displays every other value in a different vertical color you specify).
- **Y Axis:** Show Y Axis (default is checked), Major gridlines (default is checked), Interlaced strips (displays every other value in a different horizontal color you specify).

The Preview section at the bottom of the Display Properties dialog provides a view of what the performance view will look like based on the settings you have chosen to customize your performance view. A good example of using the Properties view is the Operations System Performance view in the Microsoft Windows Server folder. This view is included in the Windows Server management packs and displays performance counters related to key performance indicators (KPIs) for Windows servers including processor and memory. This view was created by only showing data related to the `Windows Server Operating System` class.

When using the Performance view, you can choose what items are displayed within the view by using the Look for section; this can restrict what's shown in the chart by All Items, Items in the Chart, Items not in the Chart, or Items by Text Search. Looking for items by text search allows you to quickly provide a subset of the performance counters as shown in Figure 7.5, where the Operating System Performance view has been configured to only show items that include % processor.

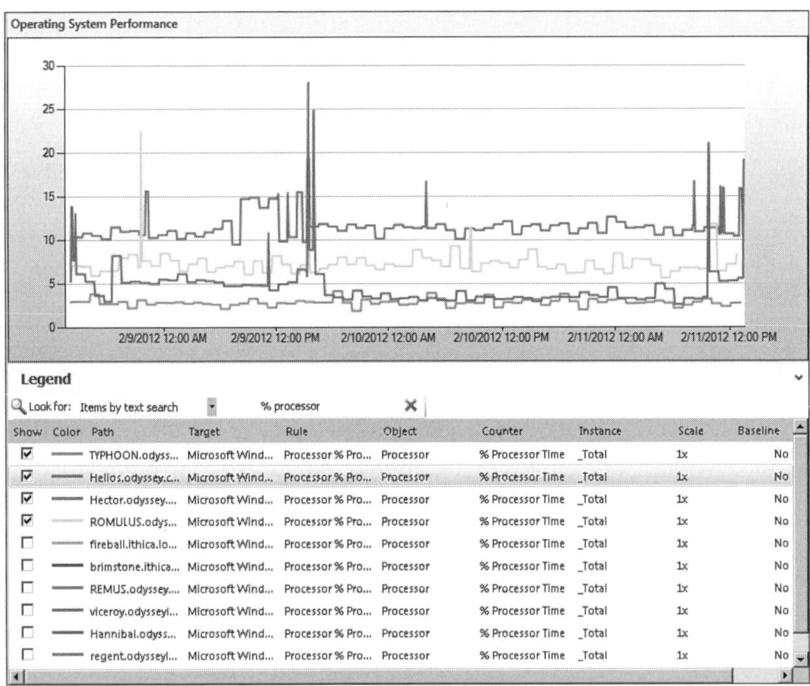

FIGURE 7.5 Using the Performance view.

This view lets you further restrict what data is displayed by using the Scope option, available above the Performance view to display only data for a specific group of servers. As an example, the Operating System Performance view could be restricted to display only servers that match a specific naming convention or that belong to a specific site using a custom group that you can create in Operations Manager.

You can easily locate which rule is gathering the performance data by right-clicking the performance counter and choosing the option to **Show or edit rule properties**. You can also change the behavior of the rule through overrides, or change the color and scale of the performance counter in the Performance view.

Diagram Views

The Diagram view provides a graphical representation for those objects you choose. These views are commonly used to display distributed applications. When creating a diagram view, you can use an existing template or create your own. The templates available when creating a new diagram view vary depending upon the object chosen. As an example, if you choose the Active Directory Topology Root object, options are available to select an existing template including AD Sites, AD Forests and Domains, Topology, and Connection Objects. If you choose to create your own template there are a variety of options available to customize this view, including

- **Diagram Properties:** The number of levels to show (default is 2), and whether the layout direction is North South (default, which expands downward when the lowest level objects are opened), South North (expanding upward when the highest level objects are opened), East West (expanding from the right to the left when the lowest objects are opened), and West East (expanding from the left to the right when the lowest objects are opened).
- **Object Properties:** Configures the object containment style for either non-box (default) or box and the maximum number of nodes per row in the box node.
- **Line Properties:** Specifies the containment line color (defaults to black), the style (defaults to solid but other options include Dot, Dash, DashDot, and DashDotDot), and the width (defaults to 1). The line properties are also configurable for the non-containment line color (defaults to blue, style defaults to DashDotDot).
- **Virtual Groups:** Virtual groups provide a way to display data in diagram views not restricted to display a maximum of eight children; if the view goes beyond that number the children are grouped under healthy, warning, and critical state. The virtual groups option allows a distributed application to either not group virtually (default) or to group virtually based upon the maximum number of children, virtual group threshold, or minimum virtual group children. Figure 7.6 shows an example of how a diagram view appears using virtual grouping compared with the same view shown using no virtual grouping (on the bottom of the figure).

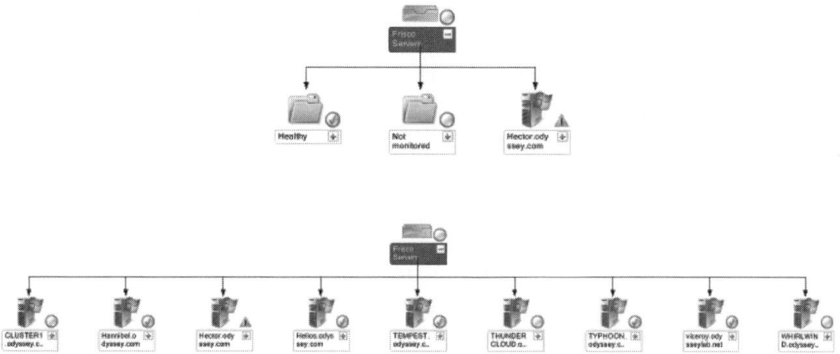

FIGURE 7.6 Computer group view in OpsMgr 2012 with and without virtual grouping.

A good example of a diagram view is the Operations Manager AD Forests and Domains view, included in the Microsoft Windows Active Directory management pack in the Topology Views folder. This diagram provides a view that defaults to opening up the first two levels of the diagram, and can be expanded to show additional levels of information as shown in Figure 7.7.

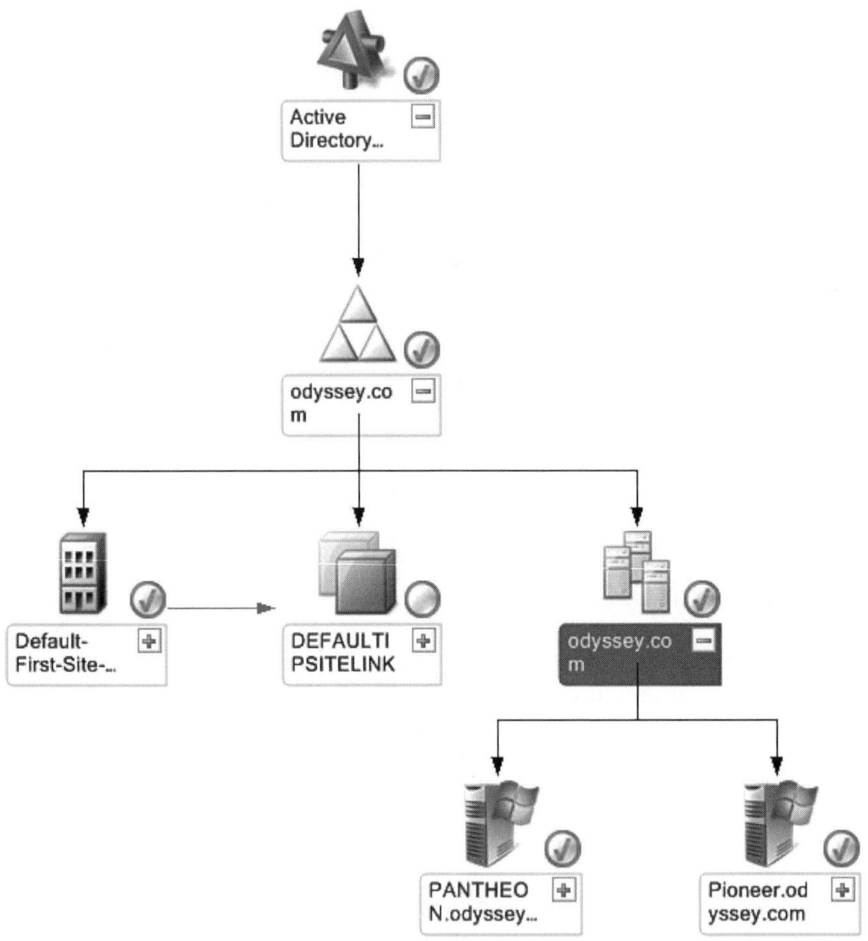

FIGURE 7.7 AD Forests and Domains Diagram view.

The Diagram view provides a way to intuitively determine where problems are in the object being displayed with options on the top toolbar to let you show the problem path, filter by health, or filter by layers. You can save your diagram view to a jpg file or VDX file you can use with Visio integration to provide state-enabled Visio diagrams that can be made available outside the Operations console.

One of the changes since OpsMgr 2007 R2 is the addition of a popup message that provides a notification when opening a diagram view with a large number of objects. The popup states **The requested view will contain at least 50 objects and may require substantial time to render. Do you wish to continue?** The default value for this is 50, which may be a low setting for organizations with large distributed applications and appropriately scaled OpsMgr hardware. This value is configurable in the Registry by creating a `DWORD` called `MaxNodesThreshold` in `HKEY_CURRENT_USER\Software\Microsoft\Microsoft Operations Manager\3.0\Console\DiagramViewParameters`.

TIP: GETTING MORE SCREEN REAL ESTATE IN THE OPERATIONS CONSOLE

In OpsMgr 2007, you could close the Tasks pane and move over the Monitoring pane for additional space to work with those items that take a considerable amount of screen real estate, such as an alerts view. You could also right-click a view and open it in a new page. Each of those options is still available, but now there are arrows at the top of the pane that shrink the various panes to the side of the screen. This provides a way to maximize screen real estate and still be able to quickly navigate or execute tasks in Operations Manager. Figure 7.8 shows an example of how you can move the Navigation pane and Tasks pane to the side. Clicking on either of these panes causes the pane to re-expand until you click on it again.

Notice in Figure 7.8 the user interface calls the minimized pane on the right side the Task pane. When expanded, it shows as the Tasks pane.

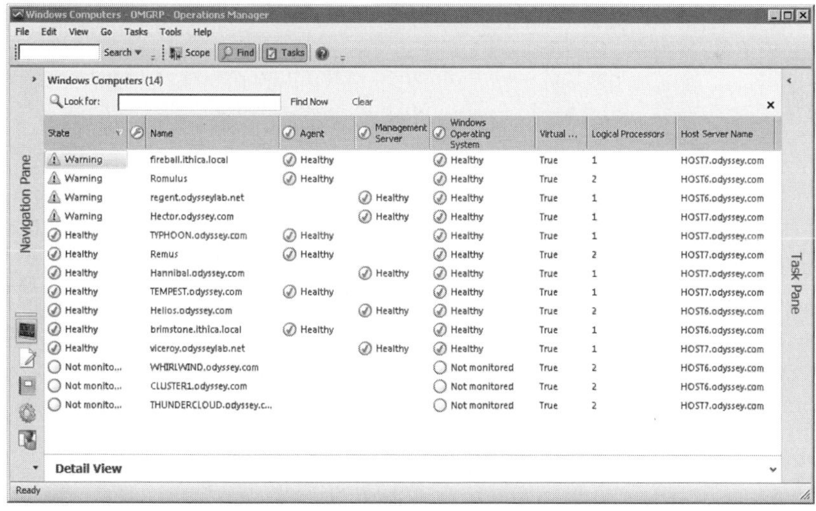

FIGURE 7.8 Shrinking the Navigation pane and Tasks pane.

Task Status Views

The Task Status view provides information on tasks that have run within Operations Manager. Custom task status views can be created that will display data from a specific target or group. You can create properties of task status views based upon your requirements for that view. Table 7.5 includes conditions and examples where these would be useful.

TABLE 7.5 Task status view properties and common usage

Condition	Common Usage
created by specific tasks	Display status for only specific tasks you want visible, such as tasks that stop a service. All available tasks are listed to choose for this condition.
submitted by specific persons	Display only tasks submitted by specific users (based upon a wildcard value you specify) to determine tasks that were executed by Operators or OpsMgr administrators
running as specific account	Useful to determine when tasks were run with elevated privileges, based upon a wildcard value you specify.
with specific status	Display tasks that were scheduled, started, succeeded, or failed. Find tasks that failed to execute successfully.
with specific output text	Useful with custom tasks to match specific output you expect from your script, based upon a wildcard value you specify.
scheduled to run in a specific time period	Show what tasks are scheduled to run in the time period you specify, based on a specific time range or in a period of time (such as the last two hours).
that started running in a specific time period	Show what tasks are started to run in the time period you specify based on a specific time range or in a period of time (such as the last two hours).
were last modified in a specific time period	Show what tasks were modified in the time period you specify, based on a specific time range or in a period of time (such as the last two hours).

The display fields available include Status, Task Name, Schedule Time, Submitted By, Run As, Run Location, Task Target Class, Category, and Task Description.

Columns can be sorted by any one of the columns you define (ascending or descending), and grouped by up to three different items in ascending or descending order. A good example of using the properties from Table 7.5 in Operations Manager is the top-level view called Task Status. This is a built-in view that shows the status of tasks in Operations Manager.

Web Page Views

The Web Page view provides a way to integrate a web page into the Operations console. The configuration for this view involves identifying the name of the view, its description, and the URL the view will display in the console. The Web Page view is extremely helpful as it can integrate various web pages into the Operations console. Here are examples of how you can use this:

- **SharePoint Document library:** Adding a top level Web Page view to the document library lets you quickly integrate documentation for your Operations Manager environment, such as standard naming conventions for management packs and overrides, detailed information on management packs in the environment, and alert escalation procedures.
- **Network Operations Center (NOC) Dashboard view:** Various dashboard solutions exist that can display Operations Manager data; generally, these are web accessible. The Web Page view provides an easy way to add these types of views into the Operations console.
- **Reports:** You can access reports in Operations Manager via the Web Page view, allowing quick access to a specific report directly through the Monitoring pane rather than navigating through the Reporting pane. To find the unique URL for the report, follow these steps:
    1. In the Reporting pane of the console, configure how you would like the report to be displayed in the Web Page view.
    2. After configuring the report, use **File** -> **Publish**.
    3. Using the Operations console, navigate to **Administration** -> **Settings** -> **Reporting** to identify the URL for the reporting site.

TIP: CHANGING THE REPORT URL FOR THE WEB PAGE VIEW

The reporting URL uses a value of "%2f" to represent the "/" character, the "%20" to represent a space " ", and the "%3a" to represent the ":" character. The Web Page view will not accept these characters, so to get the view to display the web page you must substitute the references to "%2f" to have "/" in their place, "%20" to have " " in their place, and "%3a" to have ":" in their place.

- **Websites:** You can use Web Page views to integrate additional external websites that could be useful when working in Operations Manager such as www.systemcentercentral.com, www.myitforum.com, the OpsMgr forums, or even your favorite search engine.

The Web Page view is an extremely useful method for integrating URL based information quickly into the Operations console.

Dashboard Views

Microsoft has redesigned the Dashboard view in System Center 2012 Operations Manager. This view is designed to create customizable dashboard solutions for OpsMgr natively in the Operations console through integration of widgets. Widgets are a combination of a user interface control (such as a grid or a chart) and a data provider defining what data is retrieved. As an example, you could create a grid with three cells in it and add a different widget to each cell. This allows you to generate a view quickly displaying the alerts, state, and performance information for specified objects. By combining these two concepts, you can generate dashboard solutions you can customize to your environment's requirements. For more information on dashboards, see Chapter 11, "Dashboards, Trending, and Forecasting."

Pivoting

An important concept to understand when working in the Monitoring pane of the Operations console is that each of the objects displayed is an entity that has properties associated with it. As an example, if you highlight a SQL database, the Tasks pane shows State Actions, Tasks, Navigation, SQL Database Tasks, and Report Tasks. The items displayed are context specific to the highlighted item. If you highlight a server, you see server-specific tasks and not the SQL Database Tasks as when you highlight a SQL database. Think of a SQL database as a box with various sides to it. If you look at it from the top view, it shows the health of the SQL database, if you rotate it to the side, it shows you the performance information for the database, and if you rotate it to another side, it shows the alerts you have received for that database. The database is still the same entity, but what you see varies depending on what side of the box you are looking at, which is determined by the view of the database you have chosen in the Operations console.

What pivoting means in this instance is you can take an entity from any view it is in, navigate to another view, and it retains the context it had in the previous view. As an example, if you right-click a database and open its Performance view, you see only the performance counters associated with that database (such as database free space). You can also right-click a database and open it in the Alerts view or the Diagram view. Understanding that you can pivot from one view of what you are seeing (such as performance) to another view of the same entity (such as alerts) can be extremely helpful in understanding how to effectively navigate the console.

Maintenance Mode

There are times when systems or specific objects in OpsMgr may need to undergo maintenance and you do not want OpsMgr to generate alerts letting you know what is occurring. Maintenance mode in OpsMgr provides this capability. To activate maintenance mode, highlight an object (or multiple objects) and choose **Maintenance Mode** by right-clicking or using the Tasks pane.

Options available for maintenance mode include

- **Start Maintenance Mode:** Used if the object is not in maintenance mode
- **Edit Maintenance Mode:** Used if the object is already in maintenance mode
- **Stop Maintenance Mode:** Used when the object is already in maintenance mode

When an object is placed in maintenance mode, you can choose to put only the selected object or selected objects and all their contained objects (default) into maintenance mode. Maintenance can either be planned or unplanned (default).

- For planned maintenance, these categories are predefined and available: Other (Planned), Hardware: Maintenance (Planned), Hardware: Installation (Planned),

Operating System: Reconfiguration (Planned), Application: Maintenance (Planned), Application: Installation (Planned), and Security Issue.

- The predefined options available for unplanned maintenance include Other (Unplanned), Hardware: Maintenance (Unplanned), Hardware: Installation (Unplanned), Operating System: Reconfiguration (Unplanned), Application: Maintenance (Unplanned), Application: Unresponsive, Application: Unstable, Loss of network connectivity (Unplanned).

A comment field is available to provide details as to why this object (or objects) is being placed in maintenance mode. The authors recommend providing comments when objects are put in maintenance mode to decrease confusion later as to why an object was put into maintenance mode.

Maintenance mode duration is specified with a default of 30 minutes (5 minimum) or you can specify an end date and time to remove the system from maintenance mode.

TIP: SCHEDULING MAINTENANCE MODE

The Operations console does not have an interface to schedule maintenance mode. However, the Operations Manager 2007 R2 Resource Kit (http://www.microsoft.com/download/en/details.aspx?displaylang=en&id=26139) includes a Scheduled Maintenance Mode utility enabling you to schedule and manage maintenance mode. Hopefully, this utility will be updated to function correctly in OpsMgr 2012 and be re-released in a resource kit for System Center 2012 Operations Manager. Many organizations use Tim McFadden's GUI-based remote maintenance scheduler, available for download at http://www.scom2k7.com/scom-remote-maintenance-mode-scheduler-20/.

Once an object is in maintenance mode it appears with an icon that looks like a wrench, indicating the object is in maintenance mode. During the period the object is in maintenance mode, no alerts are generated for that object. To view the maintenance mode state for an object in a State view, add the Maintenance Mode column to the display list.

MAINTENANCE MODE CHANGES IN SYSTEM CENTER 2012 OPERATIONS MANAGER

System Center Operations Manager 2012 does not block management servers from going into maintenance mode, but Microsoft does not recommend or support placing a management server into maintenance mode. Maintenance mode for management servers causes the agent assignment to force the agents to fail over to another management server to avoid data loss. If you have a single management server and place it into maintenance mode, it will not come out of maintenance mode, because there is no other management server available to perform the workflow!

Health Explorer

The Diagram view provides you with a view of the hierarchy for the object you are viewing in Operations Manager. Another way to view this hierarchy is through the Health

Explorer. Health Explorer is opened by using the Tasks pane or right-clicking an object and selecting **Health Explorer**.

If you worked with OpsMgr 2007, you may notice a change in the Health Explorer as it now defaults to showing only unhealthy child monitors. This default view populates much quicker as there are fewer objects to display, as shown in Figure 7.9. You can remove the filtering by clicking on the **Filter Monitors** object on the top bar of the Health Explorer. The web version of the Health Explorer displays all health states unfiltered, as in OpsMgr 2007.

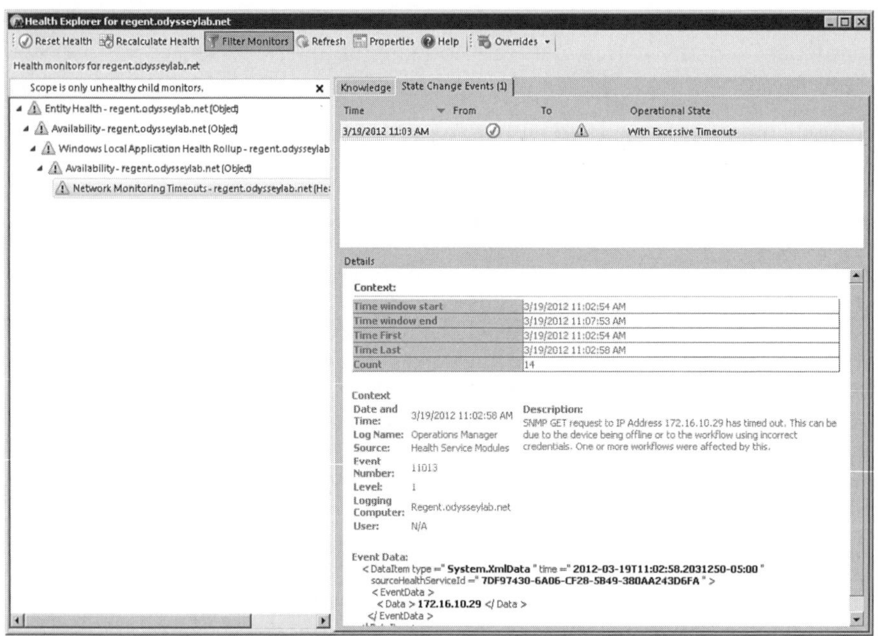

FIGURE 7.9 Health Explorer in System Center 2012 Operations Manager.

Health Explorer can provide insights into when a monitor changes health and be used to provide additional information into what caused a health state to change. As an example, a built-in diagnostic occurs when a CPU goes from healthy to critical. When this occurs, OpsMgr begins the List Top CPU Consuming Processes diagnostic, which gathers information at the time the processor changed from a healthy to a critical state. This information can be useful in debugging why a server is experiencing a performance bottleneck.

Using Health Explorer, you can reset the health state of an entity or recalculate the health of an entity. This is useful when a monitor is reporting as unhealthy, but you have reason to believe the health state may be incorrect. Here's how reset and recalculate differ:

- ▶ Resetting the health forces the monitor back to a health state.
- ▶ Recalculating health forces the monitor to reassess what it believes is the current health state.

CAUTION: RECALC DOESN'T WORK FOR MOST MONITORS

Recalculating health does not work for over 95% of all monitors in Operations Manager 2012. This is because the on demand recalculation requires both the initially defined datasource and the monitortype datasource to have a probe action to support on demand recalculation functionality.

From this view in OpsMgr, similar to others, you can pivot to other views. As an example, you can view alerts or the properties of the monitor. Within the properties of the monitor, you can create overrides or perform other changes to the monitor that determines the health state of the entity displayed in the Health Explorer.

Distributed Applications View

An important global view, introduced earlier in the "Global Views" section, is the Operations Manager Management Group distributed application. The Distributed Application (DA) view includes all DAs that exist for the management group, including the built-in Operations Manager Management Group DA, DAs for other Microsoft management packs such as the Active Directory topology, and custom designed DAs you can create in the Authoring pane for your line of business (LOB) applications.

Figure 7.10 shows navigating to the Distributed Applications state view, and then right-clicking the Operations Manager Management Group distributed application, and expanding the context-sensitive menu choices available for selection. The cursor is over the selection to invoke the Health Explorer for Operations Manager Management Group.

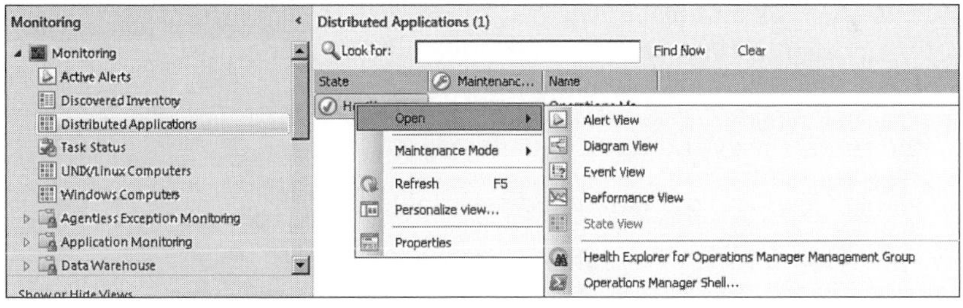

FIGURE 7.10 Right-clicking the distributed application object presents menu choices.

This distributed application object represents the health of the management group and is a convenient and centralized vehicle for overseeing the end-to-end monitoring capabilities of OpsMgr. The best tools in OpsMgr for reviewing distributed application health are the Diagram view and Health Explorer.

Discovered Inventory View

Another useful global view, introduced in the "Global Views" section, is the Discovered Inventory view. This view defaults to the Computer object, but you can use it to identify what objects exist for any target type by changing the target type on the Tasks pane, shown in Figure 7.11.

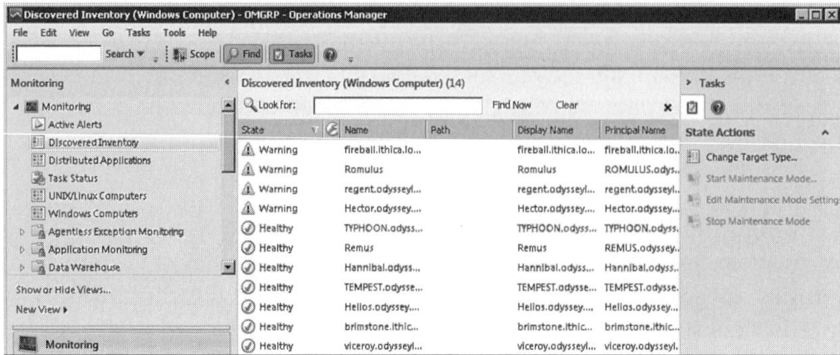

FIGURE 7.11 Changing the target type in the Discovered Inventory view.

This view is extremely helpful when attempting to identify objects and whether they are discovered. Marnix Wolf gives a nice example of how this view is useful at http://thoughtsonopsmgr.blogspot.com/2010/04/where-are-my-counters-for-windows.html, where he discusses his debugging process for monitoring performance of physical disks in Operations Manager. The article uses the discovered inventory view and changes the target to Windows Server 2008 Physical Disk to determine the discovered objects.

Customizing the Monitoring Pane

You can start using the Operations console to monitor your environment with the default views in their default configurations. However, you can get considerably more value from OpsMgr by customizing the look and feel of the console to match the business and technological aspects of your organization. The most effective use of the Monitoring space is a combination of configuration decisions involving these features:

- Personalizing the global views and other default views
- Creating new global views and views in child view folders
- Creating new child view folders or hierarchies of view folders
- Creating new tasks, specific for your environment, that automate actions related to the object(s) selected in console views

In a team-managed setting, it is important participants collaborate on and have input into modifications that affect everyone. In addition, it is critical to communicate what features have been customized or added; as people cannot use new features that they do not know about! The next sections walk though some real-world examples of using these techniques to make the Operations console more useful.

Personalizing the Active Alerts Global View

Let's begin with personalizing the properties of the Active Alerts global view. This view does not include two very useful fields for reviewing active alerts—the Last Modified field and the Repeat Count field. These fields are helpful when identifying recurring alerts and when alerts last reported a modification. One option for changing this view is to use

Personalize view from the Actions pane on the right side of the console. You can also access the Personalize view dialog from a context-sensitive menu by right-clicking the header (or any row) of the Results pane or selecting **View -> Personalize view** from the ribbon bar. Figure 7.12 shows personalizing this global view by adding the **Last Modified** and **Repeat Count** fields.

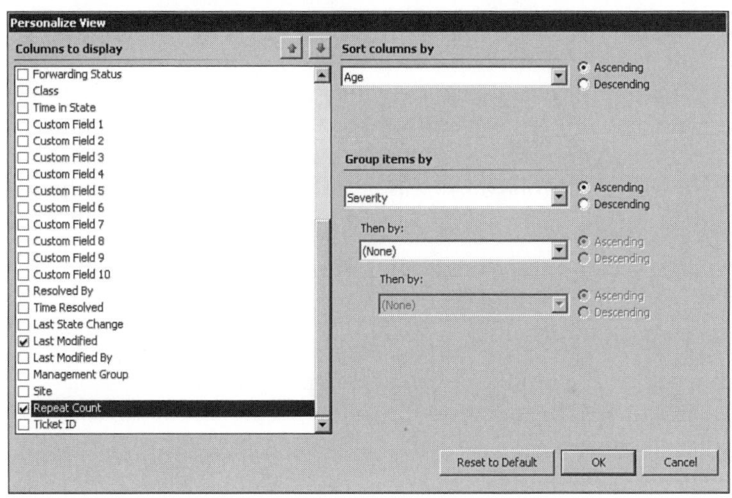

FIGURE 7.12 Personalizing the Active Alerts global view.

Personalizing the Monitoring Pane by Creating New Folders and Views

You can personalize the Monitoring pane by creating additional folders and views. When you add a management pack to your management group, a folder with the name of the management pack is automatically added to the Monitoring pane. These folders may "clutter" the Monitoring pane; they can be removed for management packs that only store overrides. See the "Decluttering the Monitoring Pane" Tip for details.

Creating additional views is a tool for scoping the Operations and Web consoles so users only see what is relevant to them when they open a console. As an example, it may be useful for a group of users responsible for a line of business application to have views created that show state, performance, alerts, and dashboards that only display their line of business application. You can define user roles in the Administration pane and restrict them to seeing only specific views in the console.

Add views in the Monitoring pane by right-clicking and choosing to create a new folder or view. The views available for creation were previously discussed in the "Using the Monitoring Pane" section. When a view is created, the content of the view can be restricted by configuring which group or object will be displayed within the view. By creating custom views in the Monitoring pane, you can personalize Operations Manager to display only those specific folders and views that can provide a more user-specific experience.

Personalizing the Monitoring Pane by Creating New Tasks

The tasks that are displayed in the Tasks pane in Operations Manager 2012 vary depending on the object that is highlighted in the console, such that if a SQL Server-related alert is highlighted, tasks associated with SQL Server are displayed in the Tasks pane.

Custom tasks can be created in the Authoring pane and will appear based upon the object that is highlighted. As an example, the ReSearch This management pack was written so that any highlighted alerts will show the tasks that are available within the management pack (ReSearch This - Internal, ReSearch This - Bing, ReSearch This - Google, and ReSearch This - Community). Other community-created management packs perform actions such as calling Green Machine to reset health state, executing Windows administration tasks, forwarding alerts via email, running tools from the PsTools Suite (available at http://technet.microsoft.com/en-us/sysinternals/bb896649.aspx), and more. To download these and other examples, go to http://tinyurl.com/SCCMPs.

To personalize the OpsMgr 2012 Monitoring pane further, you can create tasks specific to your environment and store them in your own custom management packs. See the "Management Pack Objects" section for details on creating tasks in Operations Manager.

This chapter has focused heavily on the Monitoring pane in OpsMgr as most OpsMgr administrators spend the majority of their time working in this section of the console. However, there are four other major areas of the Operations console; these are discussed next, beginning with the Authoring pane.

Using the Authoring Pane

The Authoring pane is the portion of the Operations console where you can add and customize monitoring. Common tasks performed in the Authoring pane include creating additional monitors, attributes, groups, and rules to customize or supplement the default monitoring settings in existing management packs. You can also create new management packs and distributed applications based on templates. In addition, this space is used to create and modify OpsMgr groups.

The Authoring pane includes several major sections including Management Pack Templates, Distributed Applications, Groups, and Management Pack Objects.

Management Pack Templates

Management pack templates and the Add Monitoring Wizard are used to create and target custom object types, enabling you to extend the management capabilities of System Center 2012 Operations Manager. To create a new management pack from a template, right-click the Management Pack Template node and select **Add monitoring wizard**. Alternatively, you click the **Add monitoring wizard** shortcut in the lower portion of the Navigation pane. When creating new management packs it is important you have thought through a plan for creating them and establish a strict naming standard for your management packs. Chapter 13, "Administering Management Packs," discusses management packs and topics such as this in more detail.

OpsMgr provides templates for similar object types to make it easier to create custom objects with the Add Monitoring Wizard. There currently are nine default templates (this has increased from the four available in OpsMgr 2007 when it first released):

- **.NET Application Performance Monitoring:** This template was added as part of the new .NET Application Performance Monitoring (APM) capability discussed in Chapter 15, "Monitoring .NET Applications." This template allows you to monitor ASP.NET and Windows Communication Foundation (WCF) applications hosted in IIS 7. The template is expanded in System Center 2012 Service Pack (SP) 1 to add support for applications hosted in IIS 8.0 and Windows Server 2012, Windows services built using .NET, monitoring WCF and ASP.NET MVC3 and MVC4 applications, and .NET 4.5.
- **OLE DB Data Source:** Generates synthetic transactions that monitor database availability. Use this template to run a query from a specified watcher node, connecting via a connection string. The template validates that the query executed in the specified amount of time. It does not provide the ability to perform actions or change the state of a monitor based upon the returned data (such as execute this query and if the results are more than 200, set a monitor to red, if less than 200 set the monitor to green).
- **Process Monitoring:** Generates synthetic transactions that monitor whether processes are running on the targeted group you specify. Alerts can be raised if an incorrect number of processes are running, the process runs longer than the duration you specify, or the CPU or memory exceeds thresholds specified when creating the process monitor.
- **TCP Port:** Generates synthetic transactions that monitor availability of a specified target and port. This template is extremely useful for checking the up/down status of a device that can only be validated by connecting to a specific port such as a black-box device, or providing up/down status for agents outside of the forest when a certificate infrastructure is unavailable. The template also provides response time, useful for providing up/down monitoring for devices connected across WAN links.
- **UNIX/Linux Log File Monitoring:** This template monitors UNIX/Linux log files for a specific log entry. For more information on UNIX/Linux monitoring, see Chapter 20, "Interoperability and Cross Platform."
- **UNIX/Linux Process Monitoring:** This template monitors processes on UNIX/Linux systems.
- **Web Application Availability Monitoring:** This template was added in Operations Manager 2012 to monitor availability of websites. You can add individual websites or paste in a large number of URLs from a comma-separated values (CSV) file. One of the benefits of this template over the Web Application Transaction Monitoring template is you can specify either agents or a resource pool as a watcher node. See Chapter 17, "Using Synthetic Transactions," for information on this template.

- **Web Application Transaction Monitoring:** Known in OpsMgr 2007 as the Web Application Template, this template provides monitoring for web applications, which can be recorded using the web application recorder. These synthetic transactions are executed from watcher nodes you specify.
- **Windows Service:** Generates monitors and rules that verify availability of a Windows service. The template is configured by specifying a service name and targeted group and whether the services should only be monitored if the service is set to automatic (default). Alerts can be raised if the CPU or memory exceeds thresholds specified when you create the monitor.

Distributed Applications

A distributed application service monitors the health of a distributed application that you define to OpsMgr. It creates the monitors, rules, views, and reports necessary to monitor the distributed application and its individual components. When creating a distributed application in System Center 2012 Operations Manager, first create the service that defines the distributed application monitoring object at a high level. Next, use the Distributed Application Designer to define the individual components that are part of the distributed application you want to monitor.

To create a new distributed application service and invoke the Distributed Application Designer, right-click the Distributed Applications node and select **Create a new distributed application**. You can also click the **New distributed application** shortcut in the lower portion of the Navigation pane. Here are the default templates available in OpsMgr 2012 (additional distributed application templates may be included in management packs):

- **.NET 3-Tier Application:** Used for a standard .NET 3-tier application that would contain presentation, business, and data tiers.
- **Line of Business Web Application:** Used for applications containing websites and databases.
- **Messaging:** Use this template for messaging services such as Microsoft Exchange, which includes the various components common to a messaging service.
- **Blank (Advanced):** Choose this template when starting from scratch to create your own custom distributed application.

This section of the chapter is to familiarize you with where to author distributed applications and the default templates included in OpsMgr. Chapter 18, "Distributed Applications," discusses the Distributed Application Designer in detail.

Groups

System Center 2012 Operations Manager groups can delegate authority, scope access to specific areas of the Operations console, and override default settings of management packs. To create a new group, right-click the Groups node and select **Create a New Group**, or click the **New group** shortcut in the lower portion of the Navigation pane. This invokes the Create New Group Wizard, which walks you through five steps:

1. **General Properties:** Assign a name and description, and select an unsealed management pack in which to save the new group. You can also create a new management pack for this purpose if desired.

   This is the only mandatory page of the wizard; the remaining four steps are optional. However, if you do not enter anything on one or more of the remaining steps, no objects will be members of the group.

2. **Explicit Group Membership:** Here you can choose specific objects to be members of the group. Selecting Add/Remove Objects opens an Object Selection page, where you can locate and select any existing object in the management group.

3. **Dynamic Members:** This is where you normally enter information into the wizard. As a best practice, your groups should automatically populate with objects of the type you are interested in, rather than depend on manual population of the group using the explicit group membership step. A Create/Edit Rule button opens a Query Builder where you select the desired object class and build a formula. Discovered objects with attributes matching the formula's criteria automatically become members of the group.

TIPS ABOUT GROUPS IN OPSMGR

Here are some tips about OpsMgr groups:

- You can use both explicit and dynamic memberships in the same group. Cameron Fuller discusses this at http://blogs.catapultsystems.com/cfuller/archive/2012/01/07/a-quick-question-about-groups-in-opsmgr-scom.aspx.
- System Center Central provides examples of how to create dynamic groups in OpsMgr, see http://www.systemcentercentral.com/BlogDetails/tabid/143/IndexID/89416/Default.aspx.
- To see what members are in a group in OpsMgr, highlight the group, right-click, and choose **View Group Members**.
- To determine the management pack a group is stored in, create an override on the group and use the Discovered Inventory view. Now export the MP and go through XML or use PowerShell (for more information, see http://www.systemcentercentral.com/BlogDetails/tabid/143/IndexID/69116/Default.aspx or http://blogs.technet.com/b/jonathanalmquist/archive/2009/06/30/in-which-management-pack-is-this-group-stored.aspx).

4. **Subgroups:** Here you can choose subgroups to add to the group. An Add/Remove Subgroups button opens an Object Selection page, where you can select any existing groups in the management group to include as subgroups.

5. **Excluded Members:** This is the opposite of step 2, the Explicit Group Membership screen. Just as in that step, selecting Add/Remove Objects opens an Object Selection page where you can locate and select any existing object in the management group.

Selected objects will not be members of the group, even if included by one of the other methods, such as dynamic or subgroup membership.

TIP: HOW TO MANAGE SYSTEM CENTER OPERATIONS MANAGER USING GROUPS

For additional information on groups and using them in OpsMgr, see the whitepaper at http://go.veeam.com/manage-scom-using-groups-wp.html.

Management Pack Objects

The Management Packs Objects node, found in the Authoring pane of the Operations console, is used to create objects that define how monitoring will be performed in your management group. You can view existing attributes, monitors, object discoveries, overrides, rules, service level tracking, tasks, and views by clicking the appropriate leaf object under the Management Pack Objects node. You can also create new attributes, monitors, rules, and tasks from each corresponding leaf object. Here is a description of each leaf object and its purpose:

- **Attributes:** Displays a list of attributes for each object type in your management group. Attributes are properties of classes. They can be populated by discoveries, which can be discovered based upon the Windows registry, Windows Management Instrumentation (WMI) queries, scripts, and more. You can also create new attributes for use by discovery rules and dynamic group membership criteria. After creating an attribute, you can create a group whose members are only objects with the commonality described in your attribute.

TIP: ATTRIBUTES VERSUS PROPERTIES

There is no difference between an attribute and a property—they are the same thing. Attributes are discovered properties of a class or type, which is made up of discovered instances or objects.

As an example, to monitor a set of servers with a common registry value, you would create an attribute based on that value. To find the servers with that registry value, create a group with a dynamic inclusion rule for only those servers with the newly created attribute, and target the group to only the server object type. Operations Manager will check the registry of each server to see whether that registry value exists; if it exists, the server is added as a member of the group.

Figure 7.13 shows the final page of the Create Attribute Wizard, where a custom attribute is created that checks for the existence of a registry key on Windows Server 2008 computers. This particular case checks whether Windows Update is configured for automatic updating (defined in the `HKLM\SOFTWARE\Policies\Microsoft\Windows\WindowsUpdate` key). You could use this attribute to define a group of Windows Server 2008 computers participating in automatic updates.

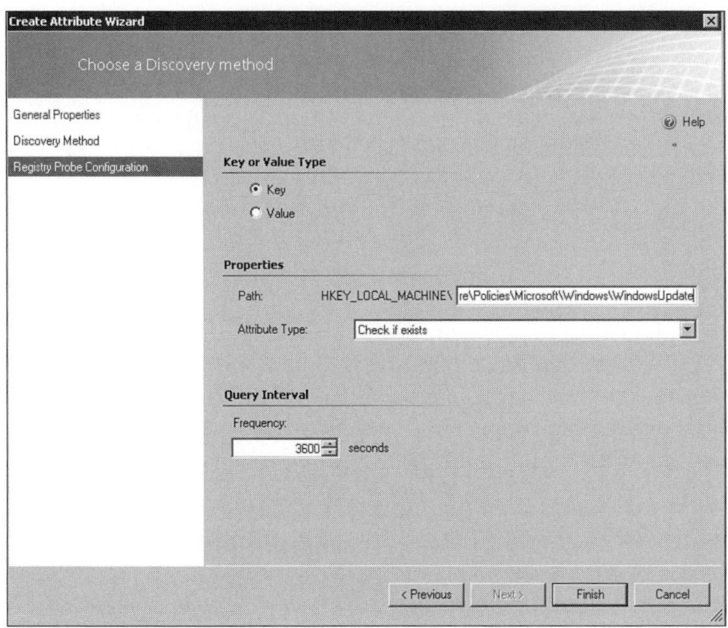

FIGURE 7.13 Creating a new attribute that checks for the existence of a Registry key.

TIP: AUTOMATICALLY GROUPING SERVERS IN OPSMGR BASED ON TIER

For additional information on how to gather a custom attribute such as the tier of a server (as an example, a development system may be a Tier 5 and a production critical system would then be a Tier 1 server), see the blog post at http://blogs.catapultsystems.com/cfuller/archive/2009/01/16/automatically-grouping-servers-in-opsmgr-and-configmgr.aspx.

- **Monitors:** Displays a list of monitors sorted by object type. Monitors continually assess the condition of specified objects. Based on this assessment, a monitor can also generate alerts and change the health state of an object.

  You can use monitors in Operations Manager to assess various conditions that can occur in monitored objects. For example, a monitor can assess the values of a performance counter, the existence of an event, the occurrence of data in a log file, the status of a Windows service, or the occurrence of a Simple Network Management Protocol (SNMP) trap. The result of this assessment determines the health state of a target and generated alerts. The three types of monitors for these assessments are unit monitors, dependency rollup monitors, and aggregate rollup monitors. Chapter 3 explains these in detail, and Chapter 14, "Monitoring with System Center 2012 Operations Manager," discusses how to create and use these monitors.

TIP: AVOID CREATING UNNECESSARY ATTRIBUTES

The Operations console does not let you delete attributes after they are created, so do not create attributes unless you know you will use them. (To remove an attribute, you must export the management pack, delete the attribute in the XML file, and reimport the management pack.) You can disable attributes by disabling the corresponding discovery rule in the Object Discoveries node.

If you create an attribute by mistake, it does not affect your management group; just don't associate the bogus attribute with other, valid management pack objects.

- **Object Discoveries:** Displays a list of discovery objects currently in use in your management group. A discovery dynamically finds the objects on your network you want to monitor. You can right-click any object discovery listed in the Results pane to view its properties or override it. You would override an object discovery if it would find objects you do not wish to monitor.

  You cannot create object discoveries from the Authoring pane. Because management pack developers do not know the specific objects in your network environment, they define only the type of objects their management pack monitors. However, the developers also include discovery objects, so once the management pack is imported, the object discoveries find the specific objects on your network that are of the types monitored by the management pack.

- **Overrides:** Provides a list of all overrides, sorted by the override target. This view lets you review the overrides that exist in the management group, filter the list based on target, or find specific overrides based upon keywords. Figure 7.14 shows an example of searching all overrides for all targets for the keyword **queue**. Using consistent naming conventions for management packs (such as prepending the override management pack name with the name of your organization) makes it easier to locate environment-specific overrides.

- **Rules:** Displays a list of rules sorted by object type. Rules collect data, such as event information, generated by managed objects. Use rules instead of monitors to generate alerts when the data collected from managed objects does not indicate the health state of the managed objects.

  An example of a rule's functionality is the collection of a specific event from the Application Event log of Windows-based computers. The collected event is stored in the operational and/or data warehouse databases of the management group, where you can analyze it in views and reports.

  Rules can also be overridden or disabled. Select the rule in the Results pane, right-click it, and select **Overrides -> Override the Rule** (or **Overrides -> Disable the Rule**). An overrides summary for a particular rule is also available to select when you right-click a rule.

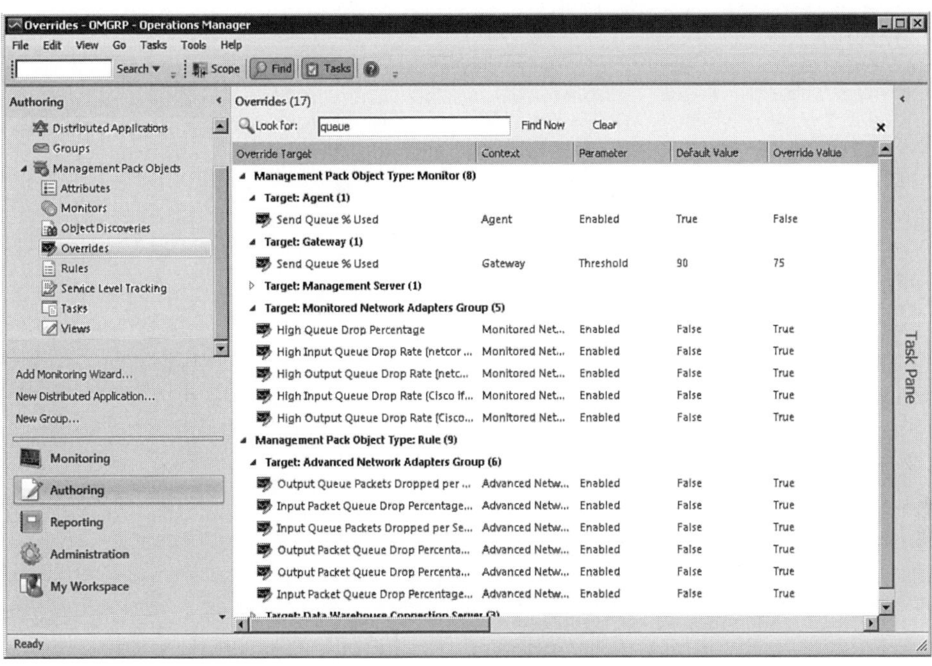

FIGURE 7.14 Finding overrides in the Authoring pane.

- **Service Level Tracking (SLT):** Operations Manager 2007 R2 added the ability to define service levels, enabling you to compare the availability and performance of the monitored applications.

  There are no service level objectives (SLOs) defined by default in OpsMgr. To define an SLO, right-click **Service Level Tracking** and choose **Create**. On the General tab, specify the name of the SLT object you are creating and provide a description. The example in Figure 7.15 creates an SLO for the Operations Manager Management Group. On the Objects to Track page of the wizard, choose a task from the targeted classes and a management pack to store it in (the Default management pack is not recommended).

  The threshold definition for availability is created using a Monitor State SLO. The threshold definition for performance is created with a Collection Rule SLO. The example in Figure 7.16 creates a monitor state SLO to monitor the availability of the Operations Manager Management Group setting a service level objective goal of 99% (the default), which only counts Critical status as being counted towards the downtime.

  After creating these thresholds, the Service Level Tracking Summary Report (available in the Reporting space in the Microsoft Service Level Report Library) will compare SLO thresholds with monitored data from the OpsMgr data warehouse database. You can also expose this service level through the Dashboard view using the Service Level Dashboard layout.

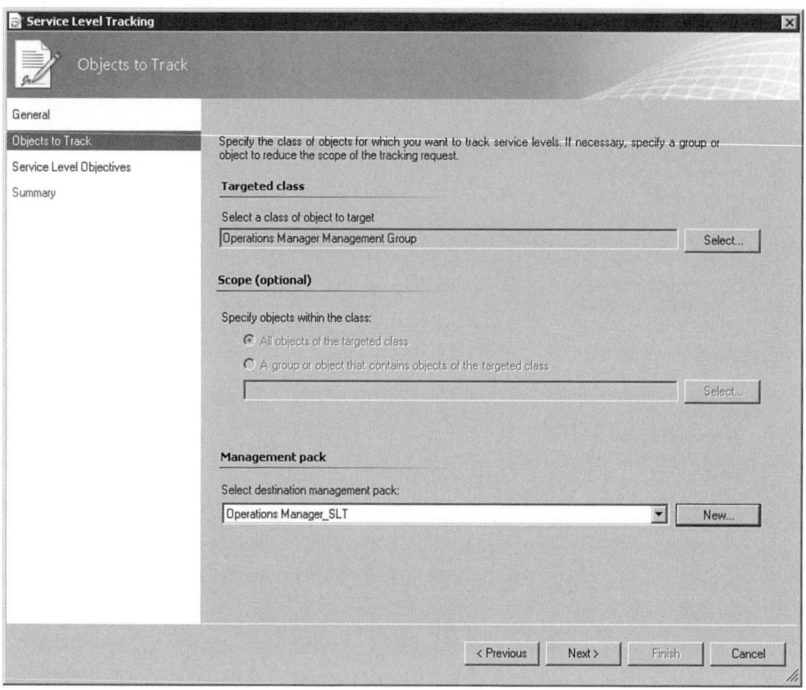

FIGURE 7.15 Objects to Track tab for Service Level Tracking.

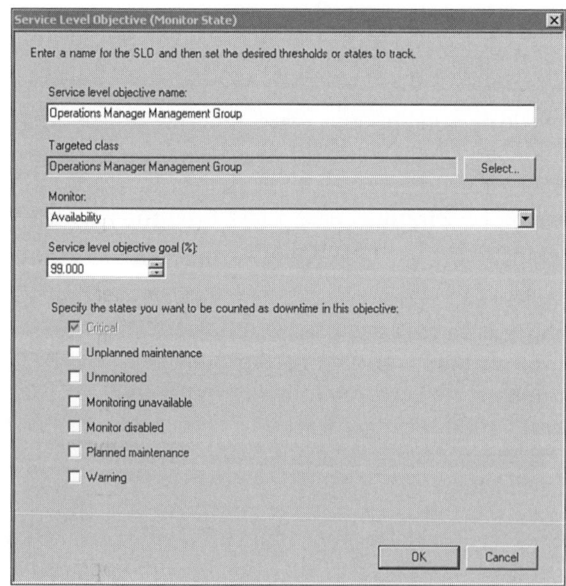

FIGURE 7.16 Service Level Objective Monitor State.

For additional reading on using Service Level Tracking functionality in Operations Manager, see

- **Developing SLTs with and without maintenance:** http://blogs.catapultsystems.com/cfuller/archive/2011/09/07/opsmgr-dashboard-integration-developing-slt%E2%80%99s-which-show-availability-with-and-without-maintenance-windows.aspx
- **Targeting in SLT explained:** http://thoughtsonopsmgr.blogspot.com/2010/01/opsmgr-r2-and-service-level-tracking.html

- **Tasks:** Lists the tasks available within your management group, grouped by object type. Tasks are predefined actions that run against a monitored object. You can view, modify, or delete tasks in the Authoring pane of the console. When creating a task, you can choose to create an agent task or a console task. Agent tasks can run remotely on an agent or a management server, while console tasks can run only on the local computer. In System Center 2012 Operations Manager, a batch file or script can run as a task remotely or locally; however, if an alert or event generates the task, the task must run locally.

  You can create new tasks by running the Create a new task action. Table 7.6 lists the task types you can create.

- **Views:** Displays a list of available views in the management group. Views display a particular aspect of monitoring settings. When you select a view, a query is sent to the operational database. The results of the query are displayed in the Results pane in the Monitoring space.

TABLE 7.6 Tasks that can be created

Type	Task	Description
Agent Tasks	Command line	Runs a batch file or starts an application on an agent or management server computer.
	Run a UNIX/Linux Shell Command	Runs a shell command on the targeted UNIX/Linux Computer.
	Run a script	Runs a script on the agent or management server.
Console Tasks	Alert command line	Runs a task targeted to an alert to run a command line application or batch file.
	Command line	Runs a command line application or batch file.
	Event command line	Runs a task targeted to an event to run a command line application or batch file.

You cannot create views from the Authoring space. You can only examine the properties of views in the Authoring space. Views are created in the Monitoring space; the list of views in the Authoring space is a convenient summary.

About the Reporting Pane

Reporting in OpsMgr 2012 refers to the process of storing, retrieving, and presenting historical data stored in the data warehouse database. Here are three ways you can access data from OpsMgr reporting:

- Targeting from the Monitoring pane
- Reports in the Reporting pane
- Scheduled reports

All three categories of reports yield the same reporting products; what differs is the method in which the report criterion is assembled. The Reporting space in the Operations console can save reports you author, save your favorite reports, and schedule reports. The next sections discuss the different report types.

Targeting from the Monitoring Pane

The most common way to use OpsMgr Reporting is the targeted report method. With this method, you access the report from the Monitoring space selecting the object for which you want report data, and clicking one of the reports displayed in the Actions pane on the right side of the Monitoring space to launch the Report view.

By targeting the object, the object of interest prepopulates the object list in the report parameters. Figure 7.17 shows a report on the processor of the Hector computer for the last seven days. It also shows a performance report, generated by selecting to view the parameters of the report (**View -> Parameters** from the Report view).

This is known as a *targeted report* because you invoke the Reporting view in the context of the Monitoring view with a particular computer selected. It only takes several mouse clicks to generate the report, and you do not need to know details about the report's construction or underlying data, such as the fact that processor performance history is part of the `Windows Operating System` object class.

TIP: FINDING OBJECTS AND GROUPS FOR A REPORT BEFORE RUNNING THE REPORT

How do you know what to use as the "object" or "group" for a report? When you open a report, you must change parameters to specify the start date and the targeted groups or objects. Before you even run the report, review the text at the bottom (the report details section). It specifies which objects provide what information.

A quick way to determine the parameters you can use is to run reports from the State views. As an example, in the **Monitoring -> Windows Computer** section, click a server. The **Actions** pane shows a list of available reports for the object. Running the report from here passes the parameters to the report. You can highlight multiple systems at the same time; the necessary parameters are passed to the report (as occurred for the results shown in Figure 7.18).

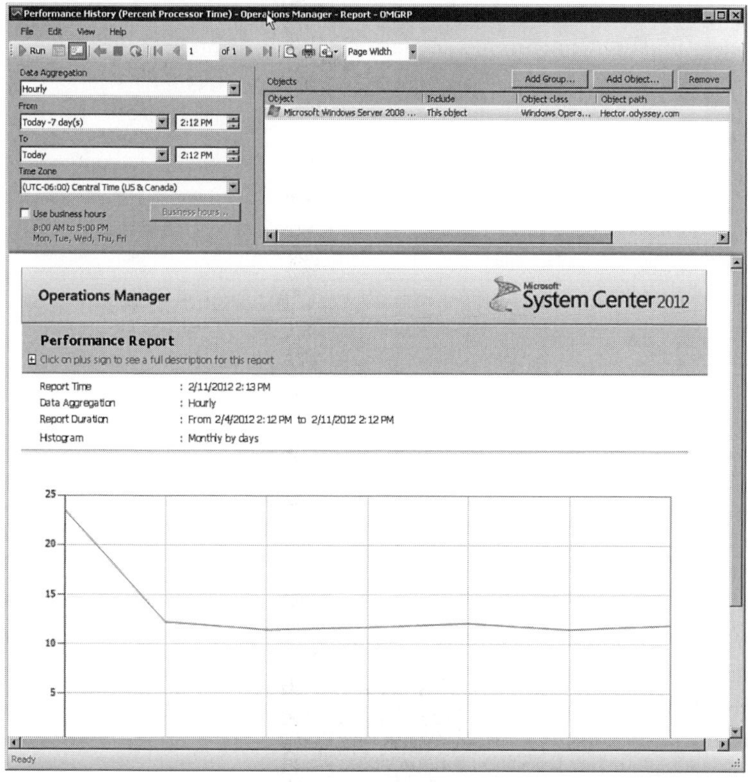

FIGURE 7.17 Percent Processor Time report for one server.

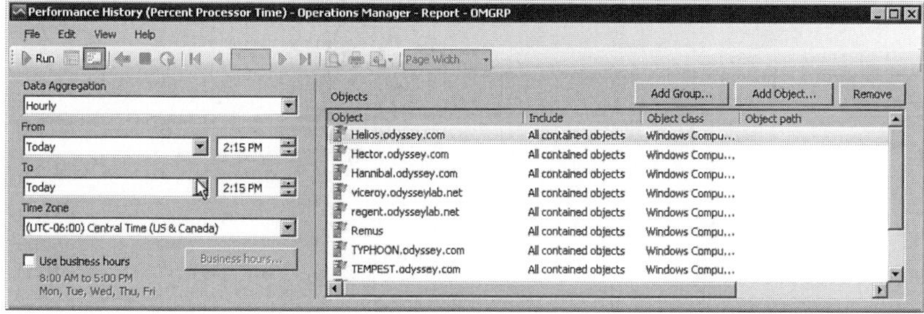

FIGURE 7.18 Performance History report for Percent Processor Time.

Reports in the Reporting Pane

You can also run reports directly from the Reporting pane. Historically this was significantly more complicated, as you needed to identify the available objects that actually had data available for the report to populate correctly. Operations Manager 2007 R2 added the

Filter Options functionality. This function simplifies the process to identify the appropriate objects to run a report in the Reporting pane. Figure 7.19 shows an example of a report where Filter Options are available, after hitting **Search**, only objects that actually have data for the report are displayed.

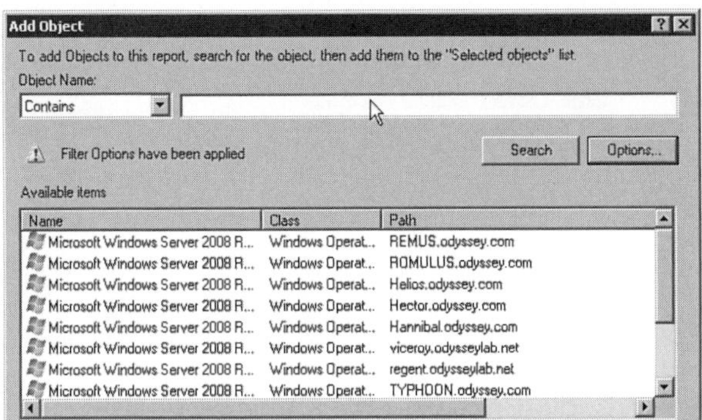

FIGURE 7.19 Processor utilization report with filter options.

New reports include the Performance by System and Performance by Utilization reports, providing answers to some commonly asked questions such as *How do you create a simple free disk space report?* These types of reports use the Filter Options functionality, or you can run the report for a specified group of servers. Figure 7.20 shows an example of the Performance by Utilization report, showing both the processor average percent utilization and the logical disk average percent space used counters, run directly from the Reporting pane after choosing the group of servers to display.

Performance By Utilization

Report Time:	2/11/2012 2:19 PM
Report Duration:	From 2/4/2012 2:19 PM to 2/11/2012 2:19 PM
Data Aggregation:	Hourly
Group:	Windows Server 2008 R2 Computer Group
Utilization:	Most
Show:	10
Management Groups:	OMGRP

Processor: Average Percent Utilization

Computer	%
REMUS.odyssey.com	20.11
Hector.odyssey.com	11.96
ROMULUS.odyssey.com	7.88
Helios.odyssey.com	5.47
Hannibal.odyssey.com	5.39
TEMPEST.odyssey.com	4.62
fireball.ithica.local	4.05
regent.odysseylab.net	3.84
brimstone.ithica.local	3.65
TYPHOON.odyssey.com	2.94

Logical Disk: Average Percent Space Used

Computer	Drive	%
fireball.ithica.local	C:	18.28
REMUS.odyssey.com	C:	13.73
ROMULUS.odyssey.com	C:	13.52
TEMPEST.odyssey.com	C:	13.13
Helios.odyssey.com	C:	11.52
Hector.odyssey.com	C:	10.47
Hannibal.odyssey.com	C:	10.3
regent.odysseylab.net	C:	9.63
TYPHOON.odyssey.com	C:	9.34
viceroy.odysseylab.net	C:	9.3

FIGURE 7.20 Performance by Utilization report.

If you find a report you like, click **File** and save it to your Favorites, making it easier to locate later (these will be available under **Reporting -> Favorite Reports**).

Scheduled Reports

Create scheduled reports by selecting **File -> Schedule** after running a report. A three-step wizard allows you to specify a delivery method, schedule, and parameter(s) for your report to automatically run and save to a file share of your selection. You can select the same file formats for scheduled reports as when exporting a targeted or generic report. A list of scheduled reports in your management group appears at the Scheduled Reports node in the Reporting workspace.

If email does not display as a delivery method option for your reports, run the Reporting Services Configuration tool on your SQL Server Reporting Services server. Specify the sender address and SMTP server in the email settings. Now reload the report; the option for email as a delivery method should be available.

TIP: SYSTEM CENTER REPORTING TIPS

For additional tips on using reporting in Operations Manager, see Cameron Fuller's Windows IT Pro article on 10 OpsMgr 2007 Reporting Tips, available at http://www.windowsitpro.com/article/microsoft-system-center-operations-manager-2007/10-system-center-operations-manager-reporting-tips-140603.

Administration Pane

The Administration space lets you edit high-level OpsMgr settings that affect the security and configuration of the entire management group. You can also view and configure individual management servers and managed objects. This space is displayed only when the user running the console is a member of the OpsMgr Administrators security group. The Administration space presents controls for various major OpsMgr functions that are highly sensitive to the integrity of the management group. Ten nodes appear in the Administration space; the next sections drill down into each of these nodes.

Connected Management Groups

A connected management group provides the capability for the Operations console user interface in one management group to query data from another management group. Use this node to add the connection information for a connected management group, which is the management group name, fully qualified domain name (FQDN) of a management server, and the credentials to use to connect to the other management group. The default credentials are those of the System Center Data Access account of the local management group.

Device Management

There are five leaf objects in the Device Management node, allowing you to perform post-installation configuration of specific management servers, agent-managed computers, agentless managed computers, and network devices:

- **Agent-Managed:** Shows all computers with installed agents. Agents are grouped under the management server to which the agent reports. Actions are provided to repair or uninstall an agent. You can also pivot to the Event, Alert, Performance, Diagram, or State views for an agent-managed computer by right-clicking the computer name and selecting **Open**. Select the properties of an agent-managed computer to override global heartbeat failure and security settings.

TIP: CONFIGURING AGENT PROXYING

Because this configuration change is extremely common and often must be performed on a large number of systems, there are a number of ways to configure agent proxying without changing systems one at a time in the Operations console. Here are several to consider:

- J.C. Hornbeck's article on enabling agent proxy for a class in System Center Operations Manager 2007 is available at http://blogs.technet.com/b/operations-mgr/archive/2009/09/29/enabling-agent-proxy-for-a-class-in-system-center-operations-manager-2007.aspx.
- Kevin Holman's article on how to set agent proxy enabled for all agents is at http://blogs.technet.com/b/kevinholman/archive/2010/11/09/how-to-set-agent-proxy-enabled-for-all-agents.aspx.
- Clive Eastwood's ProxyCFG tool is available at http://blogs.technet.com/cliveeastwood/archive/2007/08/30/operations-manager-2007-agent-proxy-command-line-tool-proxycfg.aspx.

You must enable agent proxy for systems running management packs such as the Active Directory MP, Exchange MP, SQL MP, and others. To make this change, right-click the agent in the Agent-Managed view and select **Properties**. On the Security tab, check the box that says **Allow this agent to act as a proxy and discover managed objects on other computers**.

REAL WORLD: AGENT PROXY AND SECURITY

Based on the number of servers requiring the proxy setting, many organizations consider enabling proxy for all servers in the environment. Before making that type of decision, be aware of the security ramifications. Enabling proxy allows a server to submit discovery data on instances that are higher in the hierarchy than the server itself is. This theoretically increases your attack surface, as it is possible a malicious source that gains control over a machine could inject false discovery data providing invalid information to your management group. While the authors have not heard of such a case occurring, it is important to be aware of the implications of this setting in OpsMgr.

- **Agentless Managed:** Shows all agentless managed computers, displayed under the proxy agent that monitors them remotely. You can change the proxy agent for a particular agentless managed computer and delete an agentless managed computer from the management group.
- **Management Servers:** Displays all management and gateway servers installed in your management group. Select the properties of a server to override global management server defaults such as the heartbeat failure and manual agent install settings. The RMSE for the management group is identified by a **Yes** in the RMS Emulator column. The Configure Client Monitoring action is available to begin collecting error information from managed computers. Chapter 19, "Client Monitoring," includes detailed procedures for configuring client monitoring.
- **Pending Management:** Here you can approve or reject manual agent installations awaiting approval to join the management group. The default setting in a management group automatically rejects manually installed agents, so unless you modified that setting from the **Administration** -> **Settings** -> **Server** -> **Security** menu, no computers will appear in the Pending Management node.
- **UNIX/Linux Computers:** Shows all UNIX/Linux computers with installed agents. For more information on this topic, see Chapter 8, "Installing and Configuring Agents," and Chapter 20.

Management Packs

The Management Packs node of the Administration pane lists the management packs currently installed in the management group. During installation, nearly 90 management packs are imported into OpsMgr 2012, providing a minimal amount of monitoring (the number imported varies based on the service pack level you are installing). Here are the actions you can perform through the Management Packs node:

- **View the properties of a management pack:** Management pack properties can be viewed by right-clicking a management pack and choosing **Properties** or choosing the **Properties** action from the Tasks pane. MP properties include the ID, Name, Version, Description, Knowledge, and list those management packs depending on this management pack or any management packs this management pack depends on.
- **Export Management Packs:** The Export Management Pack task exports unsealed MPs. However, you cannot export sealed management packs through the Operations console; the PowerShell cmdlet `Export-SCOMManagementPack` can perform this action.
- **Delete a Management Pack:** Delete management packs by right-clicking a management pack and choosing the **Delete** option or the **Delete** action from the Tasks pane. You must first delete any management packs that depend on the MP you want to delete.

- **Create a Management Pack:** Create management packs by right-clicking on the Management Packs node and choosing **Create Management Pack** or the **Create Management Pack** option from the Tasks pane. Management pack creation creates an unsealed management pack with the name, version, description, and knowledge provided when you create the MP. This option is commonly used when creating management packs to store overrides for customization and tuning in OpsMgr.

TIP: MANAGMENT PACK NAMING STANDARDS

Developing and using a management pack naming standard can save countless hours and problems when trying to find custom rules, monitors, or determining the appropriate place to store an override. From the authors' perspective, you should to have a standard, document it, and store it somewhere easy to locate (such as in SharePoint with a web page view pointing to the document library). Pete Zerger from System Center Central has a good discussion on how to choose appropriate naming conventions, available at http://www.systemcentercentral.com/tabid/145/indexId/73805/Default.aspx.

- **Download Management Packs:** You can download management packs from the console by right-clicking the **Management Packs** node and choosing **Download Management Packs** or choosing the **Download Management Packs** option from the Tasks pane. This option connects to the Management Pack Catalog service to allow downloads of any Microsoft management pack in the catalog.

  The Download Management Packs feature was added with OpsMgr 2007 R2. It provides a means for these actions:

  - View all management packs in the catalog
  - View updates available for installed management packs
  - View all management packs released within last 3 months, or all management packs released within last 6 months

  The download option does not install management packs; it just downloads them to a location you specify. This option is useful when you want to pre-download the management packs you need, and provides a bulk download for management packs currently available in the catalog.

- **Import Management Packs:** To download and install management packs, right-click the Management Packs node and choose **Import Management Packs** or choose the **Import Management Packs** option from the Tasks pane. This option connects to the Management Pack Catalog service to allow you to download and import any Microsoft management packs in the catalog. This feature provides the same ability to filter the view of available management packs as discussed in the preceeding bullet. This is useful when adding management packs to OpsMgr, or identifying management packs that have been upgraded compared to what is currently installed in the management group. You could also use this function to add management packs downloaded using the Download Management Packs option.

TIP: DOWNLOADING MANAGEMENT PACK GUIDES FROM THE OPERATIONS CONSOLE

To download management pack guides while working with the Operations console import or download options, click in the information section of the Download Wizard (circled in Figure 7.21 where the download link is available for the Configuration Manager 2007 R2 MP) and it will link to the web page containing the management pack guide. This tip is from Marty List, who blogged it at http://blogs.catapultsystems.com/mlist/archive/2011/03/17/the-elusive-documentation-link-in-operations-manager-2007-r2.aspx.

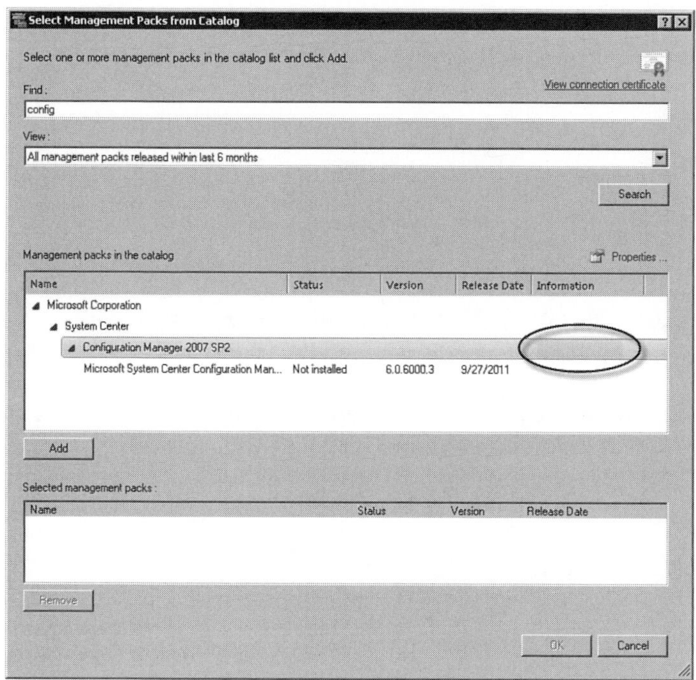

FIGURE 7.21 Download management pack guides.

There are times it is not recommended or viable to use the console to download or import your management packs from the online catalog. When these situations occur, you can download management packs using the System Center Marketplace (http://systemcenter.pinpoint.microsoft.com/en-US/home). Here are some examples:

- **Non-Microsoft management packs:** The Operations console management pack download and import options only provide downloads for Microsoft management packs, not any by third parties available in the System Center Marketplace.
- **Inability to connect to the catalog:** Depending upon the web restrictions in your environment, the console may not be able to connect to the Internet to download management packs (including some locations where administrators with locally

installed consoles cannot connect to the catalog). In these situations, you could download management packs in a remote network and transfer them to the OpsMgr environment.

- **Recently released management packs:** Occasionally the online catalog used by OpsMgr is not current and the System Center Marketplace has the download available.

The Operations Manager community has also stepped up to provide free community based management packs. Community management packs written for OpsMgr 2007 and Operations Manager 2012 include the following:

- **System Center Central MP Catalog:** http://www.systemcentercentral.com/tabid/63/tag/Pack_Catalog+MP_Catalog/Default.aspx.
- **xSNMP Management Packs:** http://xsnmp.codeplex.com/.

  These are open source management packs that were written for OpsMgr 2007 and do not work in OpsMgr 2012. The only exception is in an upgrade scenario where existing devices discovered prior to the upgrade can continue to be monitored in OpsMgr 2012. In System Center 2012 Operations Manager, the `Microsoft.SystemCenter.NetworkDevice` class is deprecated and should no longer be used. SNMP based workflows will need to be updated to use the new class `System.NetworkManagement.Node`. For additional information, see http://blogs.catapultsystems.com/cfuller/archive/2012/06/21/does-it-work-in-om12-xsnmp-management-packs-scom-sysctr.aspx.

Network Management

The Network Management node of the Administration pane provides the ability to discover and manage network devices through Operations Manager. Here you can perform the following actions:

- **Discovery Rules:** Create new discovery rules for network devices, delete the rule, make changes to the rule, or resubmit the discovery.
- **Network Devices:** Shows all network devices managed by Operations Manager. Options are available to see the properties of the network device, rediscover the device, change the proxy agent the device is communicating with, or delete the device from Operations Manager's management.
- **Network Devices Pending Management:** Lists network devices currently in a pending management state. Options are available to submit a rediscovery, delete the pending device, or change the discovery rule properties.

For details on this new functionality, see Chapter 16, "Network Monitoring." The chapter focuses on the network monitoring functionality now available in Operations Manager 2012.

Notifications

The Notifications node of the Administration pane provides administration for notification functionality in OpsMgr, including the three major components:

- **Channels:** Notification channels provide the answer to how to send notifications. Notification channels provide the methods used to provide alerts to subscribers through the subscriptions defined in the OpsMgr management group. There are four different channels available in OpsMgr:
    - **E-Mail (SMTP):** Email notification is typically the primary channel used for notification. You can configure each channel for up to three SMTP servers that can be communicated with on the port number you specify, retry intervals, and using Anonymous or Windows Integrated authentication. Each channel also contains the formatting for the message including the E-mail subject, message, importance (normal, high, and low), and encoding (Unicode UTF-8 by default).

TIP: PROVIDING MULPTIPLE SMTP SERVERS IN OPSMGR CHANNELS

OpsMgr supports up to three SMTP servers per channel to provide additional failover in situations where communication does not occur successfully to the primary SMTP server. The authors recommend using all these channels to provide failover even if the servers are highly available Exchange servers (such as an Exchange cluster). For details and why it is relevant in Exchange back pressure situations, see http://blogs.catapultsystems.com/cfuller/archive/2012/01/09/exchange-back-pressure-amp-opsmgr-notification-channels.aspx.

- **Instant Message (IM):** Instant Messaging notification can be used to send IMs for alerts. Required configuration is the name of the IM server, the return address, protocol (TCP or TLS), authentication method (NTML or Kerberos), and IM port (5060 by default). The format of the IM message can also be customized and encoding can be specified (Unicode UTF-8 is the default).
- **Text Message (SMS):** Text message channels can be created; configuration required includes the name of the channel, description, text message, and encoding (Default or Unicode).
- **Command:** The command channel notification provides a method to deliver alerts that cannot be delivered through the built-in methods (E-mail, IM, and Text Message). The command channel can run scripts by specifying the full path to the command file, command line parameters, and the startup folder for the command line. Command channel notification is like the Swiss army knife of notifications, as you can do pretty much anything with it as it is running a script. As an example, you can use the command channel to create a ticket as discussed at http://scug.be/blogs/dieter/archive/2011/05/11/scom-setup-command-notification-channel-subscriber.aspx.

Using multiple concurrent command notifications can result in failure of the alert to notify correctly. The default value in OpsMgr provides up to five simultaneous command processes. You can increase this value (although increasing the value can increase the load on the management servers providing the notification functionality) by creating the registry key `HKLM\Software\Microsoft\Microsoft Operations Manager\3.0\Modules\Global\AsyncProcessLimit` (`DWORD`). To change this value from 5 to 10, the value would be 0x0000000a. For further information, see Clive Eastwood's blog at http://blogs.technet.com/b/cliveeastwood/archive/2008/04/16/some-more-command-notification-tricks-and-tips.aspx. This registry key exists in the same location as it did in Operations Manager 2007 and has a default value of 5, a minimum value of 1, and a maximum value of 100.

TIP: CUSTOMIZING THE MESSAGE FORMAT AND RETURN ADDRESS

A common complaint heard after OpsMgr deployments is determining what alerts were sent and to whom. To avoid this issue, create a unique email channel on a per-subscription basis and specify a different return address for each channel (for example, the SQL alerts return address could be SQLAlerts@odyssey.com). Add your OpsMgr administrators to each subscription and create Outlook rules to classify the alerts based upon the return address so your SQL alerts would route to a specific folder. This provides a quick way to identify what alerts were sent, to whom, and the subscription they came from.

The message format available in notifications is customizable on a per-channel basis depending upon your requirements. Kevin Holman has gathered a list of the parameters you can use at http://blogs.technet.com/b/kevinholman/archive/2007/12/12/adding-custom-information-to-alert-descriptions-and-notifications.aspx.

- **Subscribers:** Subscribers are to whom notifications are sent. They are defined based on using a subscriber name, schedule (always send notifications or notify only during specified times), and the address to send the subscription. The subscriber specifies a channel type and delivery address for the subscription. While you can create subscribers for individual email addresses, the recommended approach is to use mail-enabled security groups to avoid the maintenance involved for individual subscriptions. Using mail-enabled security groups simplifies maintenance by using Active Directory to maintain the list of who receives subscriptions.
- **Subscriptions:** Subscriptions describe those items the subscriber is notified of, and the schedule for those notifications. You can create subscriptions directly in the Administration pane or right-click an alert in the Monitoring pane and choose **Notification Subscription** -> **Create**. Subscriptions are extremely flexible as they can be as simple as sending all alerts or be configured in a variety of ways, listed in Table 7.7.

TABLE 7.7 Subscription conditions

Condition	Common Usage
raised by any instance in a specified group	Custom groups are often used to scope the console and can be used so only those individuals interested in alerts receive the alert, based on group membership.
raised by any instance of a specific class	Classes can be used to provide subscriptions that only include the classes you specify. As an example, a subscription could be generated for Exchange administrators, which only includes the Exchange classes.
created by specific rules or monitors (e.g., sources)	Useful when identifying an alert or rule and where it came from, based on the available rules and monitors (which can be filtered to only show a specific management pack).
raised by an instance with a specific name	Used to restrict a subscription to include only specific objects in the subscription.
of a specific severity	Severities include Information, Warning, and Critical. This allows you to create subscriptions that are only sent if the severity is at least critical, as an example.
of a specific priority	Priorities are High, Medium, and Low. This is often combined with specific severity settings to subscribe to only critical high alerts, as an example.
with specific resolution state	Used frequently to include alerts that are not closed or have a New resolution state.
with a specific name	Often used when creating a subscription to include custom alerts to match based on a naming convention.
with specific text in the description	Frequently used to match keywords listed in the description field.
created in specific time period	Useful to include only alerts occurring in the last several hours or within a specific timeframe.
assigned to a specific owner	This is useful to include only the alerts owned by you or your group.
last modified by a specific user	Include only a specific user based on wildcard search. Useful when alerting based on tickets modified by specific individuals.
that was modified in a specific time period	Useful to include alerts that have had state changes in the last several hours or within a specific timeframe.
had its resolution state changed in a specific time period	This is useful for including alerts closed in the last day or within a specific timeframe.

Condition	Common Usage
that was resolved in a specific time period	Include only alerts resolved during a specific period of time such as a night shift or day shift specific alert subscription.
resolved by specific user	Include only a specific user based on wildcard search. Useful when alerting based on tickets completed by specific individuals.
with a specific ticket ID	Include alerts that match a wildcard search based upon the ticket ID.
was added to the database in a specific time period	Include alerts added to the database during a specific period of time.
from a specific site	Include alerts in the subscription from a specific site based upon a wildcard.
with specific text in Custom Field1..10	Any of the 10 custom fields can be provided criteria for this view based upon a wildcard.

When defining subscriptions, understand you cannot exclude a specific alert from notification. Whatever alerts match the criteria defined for the subscription are included as part of the subscription. As an example, if you create a subscription to email all new alerts that are critical and high priority, it will include all these alerts. To avoid subscribing to a specific alert, reconfigure the alert not to match the conditions of the subscription. One approach to accomplish this is changing the alert being generated as critical and high priority via an override to either warning severity or medium priority. Making this change alters the alert so it does not match the criteria defined for the subscription.

By combining channels (how), subscribers (who), and subscriptions (what), OpsMgr provides an extremely flexible and powerful solution for alert notification.

Product Connectors

The Product Connectors node of the Administration pane provides the ability to discover and manage product connectors through Operations Manager. This node includes the internal connectors, which exist as part of the default installation of OpsMgr:

- Network Monitoring Internal Connector
- SMASH Discovery Internal Connector
- Operations Manager Internal Connector

If you have installed connectors, use this node to administer the connectors.

Resource Pools

Resource pools were introduced in System Center 2012 Operations Manager to provide additional scalability and redundancy for management group operations and for specific monitoring workflows. There are three resource pools out of the box:

- **AD Assignment Resource Pool:** This pool is defined for automatic membership and provides the AD integration assignment functionality.
- **All Management Servers Resource Pool:** This pool is defined for automatic membership and performs functions such as group calculation, availability, database grooming, and health aggregation.
- **Notifications Resource Pool:** This pool is defined for automatic membership and provides the alert notification workflow.

This node provides the ability to create and delete resource pools, view the properties of a resource pool, or view the membership of a resource pool. For more information on resource pools, see Chapter 9, "Complex Configurations."

Run As Configuration

The Run As Configuration section of the Administration pane lists the accounts and profiles used by Operations Manager. These three leaf objects in the Device Management node allow you to configure accounts, profiles, and UNIX/Linux accounts:

- **Accounts:** Accounts are defined in this node and associated with profiles. This area allows creating, deleting, and changing Run As accounts. Run As account types include
  - **Windows:** Standard Windows credentials such as domain\user or name@FullyQualifiedDomainName
  - **Community String:** SMMP version 1 or 2 community string for network monitoring
  - **Basic Authentication:** Standard basic Web authentication
  - **Simple Authentication:** Generic user name and password combination
  - **Digest Authentication:** Standard digest Web authentication
  - **Binary Authentication:** User-defined authentication
  - **Action account:** Windows credential that can only be assigned to the Action account profile
  - **SNMPv3 account:** SMMP version 3 community string for network monitoring

  Credentials can be distributed either via two levels of security: Less secure (send the credentials to all managed computers), or More secure (manually select computers to distribute the credentials to).
- **Profiles:** Run As profiles allow monitors, rules, and tasks to run as an account with sufficient privileges. As an example, a SQL Server instance may need a different account to provide sufficient access to the databases than the default agent action account. This node provides the ability to create and delete Run As profiles, and to add Run As accounts to a profile.

- **UNIX/Linux Accounts:** Accounts defined in this node are used for UNIX/Linux monitoring. Chapter 20 provides additional information on UNIX/Linux monitoring.

Security

The Security node of the Administration pane is used to define members of various user roles in OpsMgr. There are eight user roles in Operations Manager:

- **Administrator:** Full administrator of all of OpsMgr and cannot be restricted in its scope. This role contains BUILTIN\Administrators by default.
- **Advanced Operator:** This role has limited change abilities in OpsMgr and can be scoped to specific groups, views, and tasks. The role does not initially contain any members.
- **Application Monitoring Operator:** This role provides access to the Application Diagnostics web console and cannot be scoped. This role does not contain any members by default.
- **Author:** Role designed to be able to create, edit, and delete defined tasks, rules, monitors, and views within the scope. This role does not contain any members by default.
- **Operator:** Role for editing and deleting alerts, running tasks, and accessing views based upon how the account is scoped. This role does not contain any members by default.
- **Read-Only Operator:** Role that can view alerts and access views based upon how the account is scoped. This role does not contain any members by default.
- **Report Operator:** This role can view reports in Operations Manager. This role does not contain any members by default.
- **Report Security Administrator:** This role enables integration of SQL Reporting Services security with the Operations Manager roles. This role initially includes the Data Reader and Data Writer accounts.

For additional information on security in System Center 2012 Operations Manager, see Chapter 10, "Security and Compliance."

Settings

Eight management group settings are exposed at this node, organized under the Agent, General, and Server headings. These are global settings because they control the behavior of the entire management group.

- **Agent:** The only setting here to modify is the global heartbeat interval. Agents generate heartbeats at specific intervals to ensure they are functioning properly. The default heartbeat interval is 60 seconds.

- **General:** You will find five settings under this heading:
  - **Alerts:** Here you can add new alert resolution states and modify the auto-resolution intervals. You can create up to 254 custom resolution states; you will want to expand on the two built-in states (Closed and New). The authors suggest at least adding the new resolution states of Acknowledged and Assigned to help manage alerts. The default auto-resolve settings are used to resolve active alerts in the New state after 30 days and active alerts when the alert source is healthy after seven days.

TIP: NEW ALERT RESOLUTION STATES IN OPSMGR 2012 SERVICE PACK

With the release of Service Pack 1 for Operations Manager 2012, several resolution states have been added, which include: Acknowledged (249), Assigned to Engineering (248), Awaiting Evidence (247), Resolved (254), and Scheduled (250).

  - **Database Grooming:** The OpsMgr grooming process removes unnecessary data from the database in order to maintain performance. The default setting is to purge all resolved alerts and all event and performance data after seven days. Performance signature is the only exception to this rule as it is configured to purge after two business cycles.

TIP: PERFORMANCE SIGNATURE DATA GROOMING

While the user interface says two days is the default performance signature retention period, the actual retention period is two business cycles and these are groomed once per week.

  - **Privacy:** Provides the procedures to configure what Customer Experience Improvement Program (CEIP) information, error reports, and solution responses are transmitted and received from Microsoft. The authors recommend enabling at least the CEIP and operational data reporting options; these do not affect the operation of the management group or its users, and they provide anonymous data to Microsoft that helps improve the quality of the OpsMgr product.
  - **Reporting:** This setting lets you modify the Uniform Resource Locator (URL) path to the reporting server. The default is http://<*ReportingServername*>:80/ReportServer. Only modify this setting if you change the identity of the reporting server in your management group or the composition of the URL, such as enabling SSL.
  - **Web Addresses:** If you installed the OpsMgr Web console in your management group, you can add the URL to the Web console here. Whatever URL is entered will appear in notifications as a link for the recipient to follow to the

Web console for more information about the alert that caused the notification. A default installation of the Web console would indicate a URL setting of http://<*WebConsoleServer*>/OperationsManager.

- **Server:** The two settings here are Heartbeat and Security. The security setting is described in the "Device Management" section of this chapter; it determines how manually installed agents are handled. These agents can be automatically rejected or accepted, or placed in the Pending Management node to be approved by an administrator. The heartbeat setting is the number of consecutive missed heartbeats from an agent before OpsMgr initiates a loss of heartbeat alert; the default is 3. Therefore, the default settings of OpsMgr will fire an alert on a down agent after approximately three minutes, which is the server missed heartbeat setting multiplied by the agent heartbeat interval.

My Workspace

My Workspace is a private place for you to create and store console customizations for later reuse. Many console settings, related to the configuration of the console, reside in the user area of the registry of the computer running the Operations console. This means customizations are only available on that computer running the console you customized. Microsoft has also provided a way to leverage the shared OpsMgr operational database to permit console operators to save some settings in the My Workspace area. Views saved in My Workspace follow the operator from console to console, and are also available when using the Web console.

There are three practical uses of My Workspace:

- **Create shortcuts to views in the Monitoring pane:** You can have quick access to any view in the Monitoring pane by creating a shortcut to it in your Favorite Views folder. Right-click any view in the Monitoring pane and select **Add to my workspace**. Give the shortcut a name and select the Favorite Views folder to save the shortcut in (or create a new folder). The shortcut view reflects changes to the source view, and vice versa. Note that deleting the shortcut does not delete the source view.
- **Create My Views:** These are unique views, not links to existing views. To create a My View, right-click the **Favorite Views** folder in My Workspace (or a favorite views child folder you created), and select **New**. Then you can create any view, such as an alert view or a dashboard view, just as if you were creating it in the Monitoring space. Views created here are only visible to you, so you can create all the views you want without affecting any other users in your management group. As an example, one of the first views the authors will commonly create is an All Alerts view that displays all alerts regardless of their state. This view provides a quick way to see what alerts are in the database including those in a closed state.
- **Access saved searches:** Search functions are available from all console views, accessed via the menu bar of the Operations console, and you can save complex

search criteria in My Workspace. A toolbar-style Search button is located in the menu bar, or you can select **Tools -> Search** from the menu bar. The button is not context-sensitive; it always calls up the same blank search dialog to enter search terms in. Perhaps more useful is the Advanced Search function, selectable from the bottom of the Search toolbar menu or from **Tools -> Advanced Search**. The Advanced Search dialog includes an option to save your search criteria for reuse later. Figure 7.22 shows the Advanced Search dialog with the Save parameters to My Favorites link highlighted.

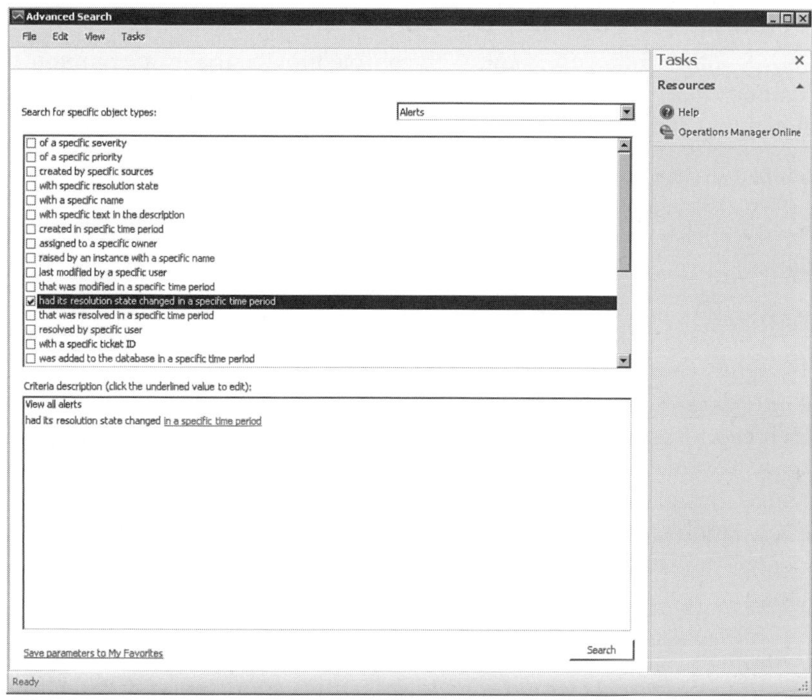

FIGURE 7.22 The option to save search criteria is available on the Advanced Search dialog.

Although the euphemistic term "fishing expedition" means an investigation with little chance of success, Microsoft urges OpsMgr administrators to teach console operators "how to fish." A good fisherman makes an educated guess about where he may find the fish, and he drops a baited hook at the appropriate spot and depth. The My Workspace area is the tackle box for your operators, where each professional can store his or her assemblage of preferred tools (views and searches) for quick access every time he or she needs to "go fishing."

TIP: ABOUT THE WEB CONSOLE

The Web console provides very similar functionality to what is available in the full Operations console, and should provide a usable alternative to the Operations console in many situations. The Web console does not provide the authoring, administration, or reporting panes available in the Operations console; it only includes the Monitoring and My Workspace views. See Chapter 4, "Planning an Operations Manager Deployment," for more details on the differences between the full Operations console and the web-based version.

Using Operations Manager: Beyond the Consoles

While the Operations Manager full console and Web console provide the most common ways to access Operations Manager, there are times that this approach may not meet your organization's requirements. The next sections discuss the following four situations:

- Custom developed interfaces
- SharePoint
- Mobile solutions
- Service Manager

Custom Developed Interfaces

Some organizations prefer to design their own interface to Operations Manager rather than using the prebuilt consoles. This often occurs when there is a requirement for extremely strict change control. A common approach is developing a web portal that interfaces with the Operations Manager software development kit (SDK) to provide a custom user experience. An example of this would be a simple portal allowing the user to deploy an Operations Manager agent to servers within their portion of the environment.

SharePoint

You can use SharePoint to provide access to Operations Manager information through a variety of methods including the addition of widgets to display dashboard data. SharePoint can also be used to display web pages such as the OpsMgr Web console or specific reports within your environment.

Mobile Solutions

Another common request for Operations Manager is to provide access to OpsMgr information via a mobile device such as an iPhone, iPad, Android, or Windows smartphone. For these situations, third-party solutions are available that include

- **Jalasoft Xian Wings:** Xian Wings provides a mobile platform for Operations Manager that supports the iPhone, iPad, Windows Phone 7, Windows Mobile, Android, and Blackberry devices, displaying information from OpsMgr that includes alerts and performance data and allows you to interact using existing OpsMgr tasks from a mobile device. (Windows Phone 8 will be supported but was not fully tested at time of writing this chapter.) More information about this product is available at http://www.jalasoft.com/xian/wings.

- **Squared Up Operations:** Squared Up provides a different way to represent data for Operations Manager that includes dashboards and alert workflows that you can run on an iPad. Information about this product is available at http://www.squaredup.com.

Service Manager

Another option for working with Operations Manager without the consoles is to use tickets generated in the Service Manager component based on Operations Manager alerts. If tickets are auto-created for alerts in Service Manager, you can work on these and resolve them in Service Manager, and then close them using the Service Manager connector. Using the existing Service Manager connectors for Operations Manager can significantly decrease reliance on the Operations console for many users.

Using the Operations Console

After you successfully install the core management group components, two major configuration activities must take place before Operations Manager can start working for you. These actions are to import management packs and to discover objects to manage. The next sections walk you through these activities after confirming the basic health of the management group.

Adding Management Packs

The installation process automatically imports a number of management pack libraries. These libraries provide a foundation of object types on which other management packs depend, and contain basic settings used by OpsMgr for the minimum functionality to manage the OpsMgr application itself, such as the management pack for System Center 2012 Operations Manager.

Source files for currently installed management packs are located on each management server at *%ProgramFiles%*\System Center 2012\Operations Manager\Server\Health Service State\Management Packs. Do not import from this folder when performing future management pack import operations, as these management packs are already part of your OpsMgr environment.

In addition to the management packs included with the OpsMgr installation, you should import other management packs into your OpsMgr management group to monitor those applications used by your organization. It is a best practice to import only the management packs required to meet your monitoring and management goals. Specifically, it is a poor practice to import every management pack you find. Each imported management pack incrementally increases the overhead load of the management group. Too many unused or unnecessary management packs can clutter the Operations console to the point that you miss indications of issues with the applications you do need to monitor.

As discussed in the "Management Packs" section, you can add management packs through the Administration pane or by downloading them from the System Center Marketplace. You can also import management packs into OpsMgr using the `Import-SCOMManagementPack` PowerShell cmdlet.

Deploying Agents

You can deploy OpsMgr agents in a variety of ways, including the Operations console in the Administration pane under the Device Management section using the Discovery Wizard. Additional information on agents and their deployment processes is discussed in Chapter 8.

Fast Track

The majority of the Operations Manager 2012 console works very similarly to the Operations Manager 2007 console. The following are key concepts to remember when using the System Center 2012 Operations console compared to the OpsMgr 2007 console:

- The Diagram view now has a popup that provides notification if more than 50 items are displayed on the diagram.
- Dashboard views are added to provide integrated dashboard functionality in OpsMgr 2012. See Chapter 11 for details.
- The Web Application Monitoring template provides a quick way to add large numbers of URLs for monitoring in OpsMgr, with agents or resource pools serving as watcher nodes.
- The Operations console has changed to provide the ability to minimize the various panes on the screen easily (Navigation, Tasks, and Alert Details as an example).
- The Health Explorer now has a default scoping to show only non-healthy monitors when opened.
- OpsMgr 2007 R2 added the Overrides and Service Level Tracking pieces of the Authoring pane.
- Maintenance Mode for management servers has changes in functionality (see the Tip labeled "Maintenance Mode Changes in System Center 2012 Operations Manager").
- Application Monitoring Operator is added as a user role.
- Network management functionality has been changed due to the new integrated network monitoring (see Chapter 16 for details).

Summary

This chapter introduced the Operations console. It discussed connecting to the console, confirming your management group's health and provided a quick tour of the Operations console. The majority of this chapter was dedicated to an in-depth discussion on the Operations console by navigating through each of the five navigation panes (spaces), working downward through the console through each setting in the user interface. All components were reviewed, including information on what each does and how to use it. The chapter also included a discussion on using Operations Manager outside of the console and specific uses of the Operations console. The next chapter discusses installing and configuring agents in System Center 2012 Operations Manager.

CHAPTER 8

Installing and Configuring Agents

IN THIS CHAPTER

- Understanding Core Concepts
- Discovering and Deploying Agents
- Managing Agents
- Troubleshooting Tips
- Fast Track

This chapter focuses on agents and their use in System Center 2012 Operations Manager (OpsMgr). There is much more to agents in OpsMgr 2012 than installation and configuration. This chapter starts with understanding core concepts, such as how the discovery and approval processes work. It explains the differences between agent-managed systems, agentless monitored systems, unknown states, and network devices. The focus then moves to different methods available for deploying and configuring the OpsMgr agent; these methods include using Active Directory Integration, System Center Configuration Manager, the Operations Manager Deployment Wizard, and manual installation. This chapter also includes the features, limitations, and procedures associated with agentless monitoring in OpsMgr.

The chapter also discusses the various configurations available when using other management software such as Operations Manager 2007, or if you have multiple OpsMgr 2012 management groups. The last part of this chapter discusses managing agents and the relationship between Agentless Exception Monitoring (AEM) and agents, and presents some troubleshooting tips associated with agents in System Center 2012 Operations Manager.

Understanding Core Concepts

The discovery process identifies systems to which you can install agents or systems you can configure for agentless monitoring. This discovery process queries Active Directory Directory Services for computer information matching the requirements you define for discovery.

How Discovery Works

Microsoft's Operations Manager team provides an excellent graphical representation of how the discovery process works; available at http://blogs.technet.com/b/momteam/archive/2007/12/10/how-does-computer-discovery-work-in-opsmgr-2007.aspx. Figure 8.1 is based on that graphic, and the specific steps for discovery follow.

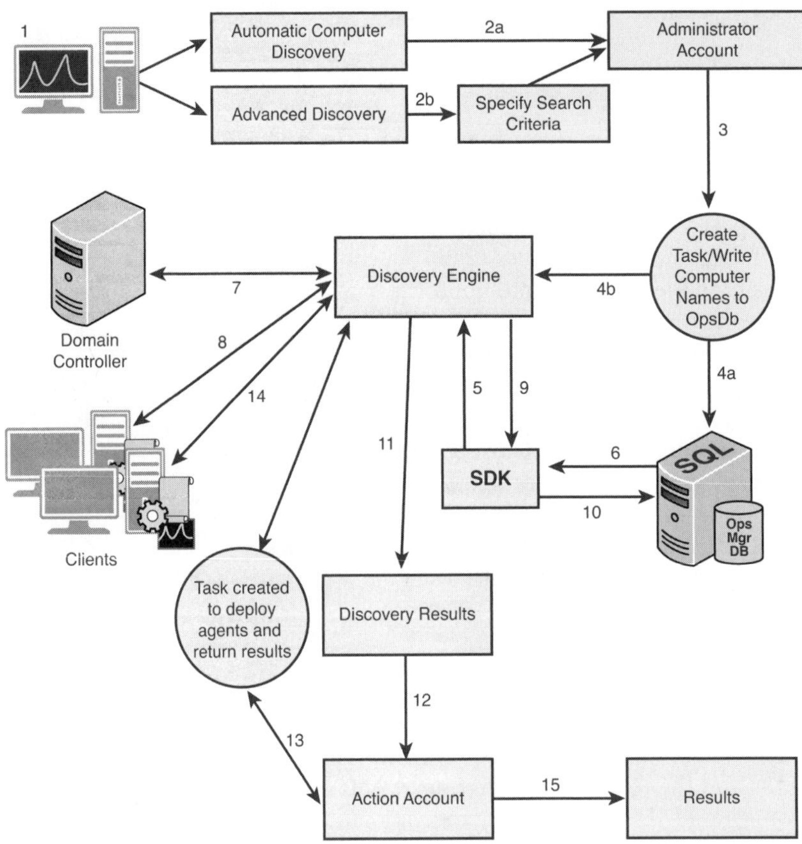

FIGURE 8.1 Agent discovery process.

To follow the steps in Figure 8.1, here is the process for computer discovery:

1. The Discovery Wizard process is initiated from the Operations console.
2. Discovery can be automatic or advanced:
    - The automatic computer discovery option scans the entire domain that the OpsMgr management server is a member of for all Windows-based computers. This option is generally only used in a small environment or a lab environment.

   - When you select the advanced computer discovery option, search criteria options are available to provide the computer and device type, specify the management server, and verify whether discovered computers can be contacted.

   Additional options are to either scan Active Directory or browse for computer names.

3. The OpsMgr admin specifies if the management server action account or another account with administrator-level privileges will be used. The specified account is used for discovery with Active Directory and to push the agent to the system that will be monitored.
4. Two tasks are created:
   - A task is created to write computer names to the operational database.
   - A task is submitted to the discovery engine.
5. The discovery process reads credentials from the database using the Data Access Service (DAS).

TIP: IS THIS THE DAS OR THE SDK?

The Data Access Service (DAS) and SDK are the same service. There is also a software development kit (SDK), used when an API such as .NET or PowerShell communicates with Operations Manager. The DAS handles interfacing with the OpsMgr databases. The OpsMgr 2007 SDK service was renamed to DAS with OpsMgr 2007 R2, but many OpsMgr administrators continue to use the terms interchangeably. The full name of the DAS is the System Center Data Access Service.

6. The current list of computers is read from the operational database.
7. The discovery engine contacts a domain controller for resources, including Active Directory computer account information.
8. If the option to verify discovered computers was selected (the advanced computer discovery option in step 2), each client is contacted through ports 135, 137, 139, 445, and 5723.
9. The discovery engine passes results of the computer discovery to the DAS.
10. The computer discovery results are written from the DAS to the operational database.
11. The discovery engine checks for the management mode and reports the discovery results.
12. The action account uses either Local System or the specified domain account to create tasks to deploy the agents.
13. The tasks are created to deploy the agents and return the results.

14. The discovery engine deploys agents and returns the results.
15. Results are gathered from deploying the agents and displayed on the Operations console.

The Discovery Wizard has capabilities for automatic discovery of all Windows-based computers, and can scan computers in a specific organizational unit (OU). To discover machines residing in nontrusted domains and workgroups, provide the computer name in the format *<domain>**<ComputerName>* or *<workgroup>**<ComputerName>*.

TIP: FAILED DISCOVERY WITH SAME COMPUTER NAME

During an OpsMgr deployment, it was determined that if the same computer name exists in multiple domains, discovery will fail on the second system if OpsMgr is already monitoring the first system. As the fully qualified domain name is the unique identifier for an agent, this situation should only occur in environments where a disjointed DNS exists with a single DNS domain that represents multiple different Active Directory domains.

Scheduling Discovery

Microsoft Operations Manager (MOM) 2005 included a built-in capability to schedule computer discovery. This functionality was replaced in OpsMgr 2007 with Active Directory Integration (discussed in the "Active Directory Integration" section later in the chapter), which applies the OpsMgr settings to systems with the agent deployed. Active Directory Integration still applies in OpsMgr 2012.

For those environments not implementing Active Directory Integration, you can use PowerShell with a scheduled task to schedule computer discovery; Pete Zerger provides a two-part blog post with an example of how to identify those computers in Active Directory that do not have the Operations Manager agent (see part 1 at http://www.systemcentercentral.com/BlogDetails/tabid/143/IndexID/94221/Default.aspx). After identifying these computers, you can automate agent installation with PowerShell (discussed in part 2, at http://www.systemcentercentral.com/BlogDetails/tabid/143/IndexID/94248/Default.aspx). You can schedule these scripts to run on a recurring basis using the Windows task scheduler. The scripts are included with the material accompanying this book; for additional information see Appendix E, "Available Online."

Approval Process

OpsMgr's default configuration rejects manually installed agents. Change this configuration in the Administration node of the Operations console by following these steps:

1. Navigate to **Administration** -> **Settings** -> **Security**. Right-click **Security** and select **Properties**.
2. The General tab shows the default configuration is **Reject new manual agent installations.** If your environment will use manual agent installation, check the option that says **Review new manual agent installations in pending management view**, shown in Figure 8.2.

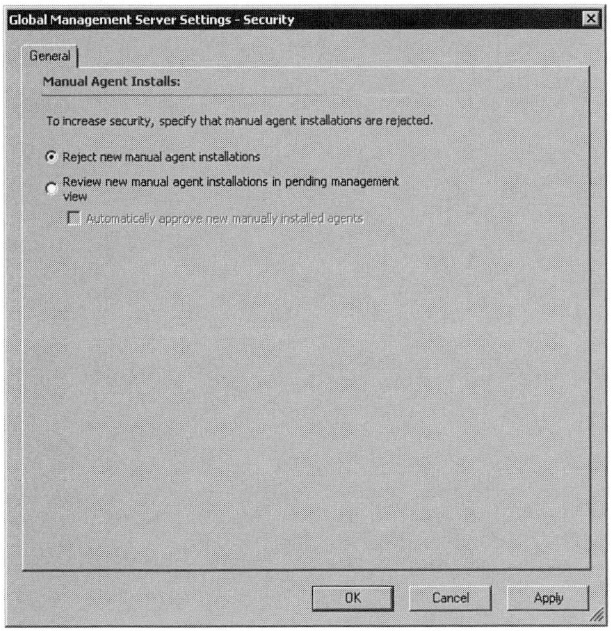

FIGURE 8.2 Configuring manual agent installs.

3. If you choose the option to review new manual agent installations, a check box is available that reads **Automatically approve new manually installed agents**. If you select this option, new manual agents are automatically approved.

   If you do not choose this second option, manually installed agents display in the Operations console, under **Administration** -> **Device Management** -> **Pending Management**, where you can approve or reject their installation.

Agent-Managed Systems

The Agent Managed node of the Administration pane shows those Windows agents that Operations Manager is monitoring. An agent-managed system runs a software component called the OpsMgr agent, which runs as a local service on each computer on which it is installed. The agent monitors the computer using management pack objects that apply to that agent. The management server updates these objects as changes are applied to the management packs used by that management group. Agents will request configuration information if they do not have configuration information or do not receive configuration information on a timely basis. (Agents are notified of configuration updates through a dirty state notification that is sent from their management server.) Typically, OpsMgr configurations use agent-managed systems.

A question often asked about the OpsMgr agent is *How large a footprint does it have?* Microsoft approaches this by adding functionality where Operations Manager itself tracks the overhead OpsMgr is adding to the system. Figure 8.3 shows agent performance information including agent processor utilization. Using these performance counters, you can determine the overhead added by OpsMgr. During testing by the authors, the OpsMgr processor impact to servers typically was less than 2%; you can display this level of granularity on the chart by personalizing the view and setting the maximum value to a smaller value such as 5.

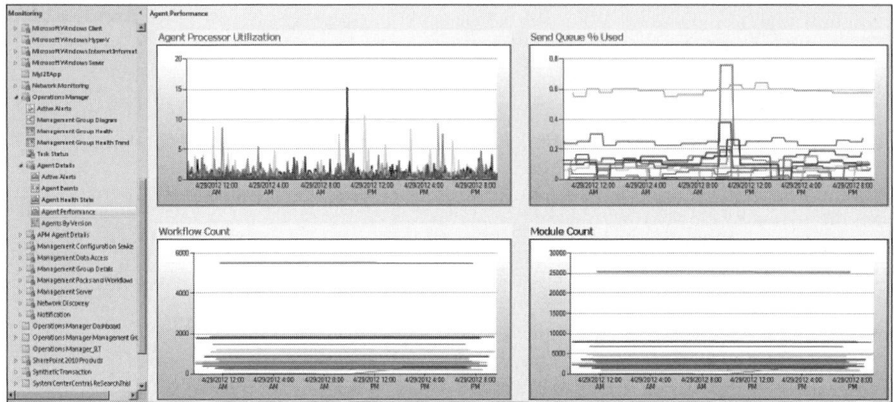

FIGURE 8.3 Agent processor utilization.

Agent processor utilization is gathered by the Collect Agent Processor Utilization rule, which works as follows (this information is in the product knowledge for the rule):

```
This rule calculates the total CPU utilization of the Operations Manager agent and
its related processes and then submits that as performance data under object "Health
Service" and counter "agent processor utilization."
This rule's underlying script works by locating and sampling the CPU utilization for
the Operations Manager agent process (HealthService.exe), its child monitoring host
process (MonitoringHost.exe), and the child processes of those monitoring host
processes (cscript.exe, PowerShell.exe, etc.). The script runs the calculation three
times and writes the average of the three consecutive samples to the operations
database and data warehouse.
```

TIP: UPDATED AGENT PROCESSOR UTILIZATION SCRIPT

The OpsMgr 2012 System Center management pack includes a new version of the agent processor utilization script that more accurately calculates CPU utilization from the agent. This script removes the CPU overestimation seen in the previous version, which caused the non-relevant alerts occurring in the older version of the script.

Microsoft has also added the Agent processor utilization monitor, which alerts if the agent utilization exceeds a threshold of 25% over a set of six consecutive samples. The monitor returns to a healthy state if the threshold is no longer exceeded for three consecutive samples.

Table 8.1 lists a comparison of resources required and time required for the OpsMgr 2012 agent installation versus an agentless monitored configuration.

TABLE 8.1 OpsMgr 2012 agent and agentless monitored resource requirements during deployment

Resource or Statistic	Agent Monitored	Agentless Monitored
Processor	1% average increase	1% average increase
Disk usage	150 average increase in pages per second	No statistically significant increase in pages per second
Disk space	348MB of data in *%ProgramFiles%*\System Center Operations Manager	No statistically significant increase in disk usage
Network	4.5MB of data sent/received during installation	< 1MB of data sent/received during the installation
Memory	31-48MB less memory available (addition of the Health Service host and Monitoring Host processes)	14MB less memory available
Deployment time	2.5 minutes to get to Not Monitored state, 6.5 minutes to Monitored state	2.5 minutes to Monitored state

Table 8.2 shows a comparison of resources required for the OpsMgr 2012 agent installation versus an agentless monitored configuration after the agents as monitored.

TABLE 8.2 OpsMgr 2012 agent and agentless monitored resource requirements after deployment

Key Performance Indicator	Agent Monitored	Agentless Monitored
Processor	1% average increase	1% average increase
Disk usage	9 page average increase in pages per second	No statistically significant increase in pages per second
Disk space	351MB of data in *%ProgramFiles%*\System Center Operations Manager	Less than 10MB of disk space decrease seen on the system
Network	No statistically significant increase in network usage	< 1MB of data sent/received during the installation
Memory	19-32MB less memory available (addition of the Health Service host and Monitoring Host processes)	< 1MB less memory available

8

With the hardware currently available in most server environments, the statistical impacts of both agent monitored and agentless monitoring by Operations Manager are minimal. The next section provides additional details on agentless managed systems.

Agentless Managed Systems

An agentless managed system does not run the OpsMgr agent. The agent component on a management server (or OpsMgr agent) collects data from the agentless managed computer through remote calls to that system.

NOTE: AGENTLESS SYSTEMS AND PROXY AGENTS

Agentless managed systems can be managed either by OpsMgr management servers or by other agents. The system that monitors the agent is known as a *proxy agent*. Proxy agents can be configured when managing a new system or changing the proxy agent on an existing agentless monitored system.

OpsMgr 2012 supports up to 10 agentless managed systems reporting to a single management server, and 60 in a management group. Agentless monitoring is commonly used in six different situations:

- **Clustered servers:** If your environment has Windows clusters where Operations Manager is monitoring the nodes with proxy enabled on the nodes of the cluster, the cluster appears as agentless monitored in OpsMgr. This type of monitoring is built in for clusters; the OpsMgr administrator does not need to configure agentless monitoring.
- **Validated systems:** These are systems where specific testing processes must occur for any changes to the configuration, including deploying agents. (A *validated system* is one that has a strict process to validate the functionality of the system anytime software is installed on it.) In these cases, the Information Technology (IT) group responsible for server management wants to avoid even the appearance of affecting an application server, thus avoiding potential liability. If you are in this situation, you can use the agentless management mode to manage servers that might otherwise be unmanaged.
- **Unsupported Windows operating systems:** Legacy systems such as NT 4.0 or Windows 2000 that do not support an installed agent are common reasons for using an agentless configuration.
- **Minimally monitored systems:** For some systems, the goal is to provide only up/down information and minimal additional information—to avoid digging deeply into what is occurring on the system. An example of this is a lab server running Internet Information Services (IIS) and SQL Server. The server may be important enough to know up/down information but not to provide alerts for issues with IIS or SQL. For these systems, agentless monitoring may be a good solution.

- **Service Manager:** The RTM version of System Center 2012 Service Manager does not support installation of an Operations Manager 2012 agent. Monitoring Service Manager requires using agentless monitored systems. With the release of System Center 2012 Service Pack (SP) 1, a Service Manager server can now have an agent installed that reports to Operations Manager in a multi-homed configuration.

REAL WORLD: ISSUES WITH SAME NAME SYSTEM BOTH AGENT AND AGENTLESS MONITORED

During initial lab testing with Operations Manager, there was a situation where the same system ended up being both agentless and agent monitored. The condition caused problems resulting in a "greyed out" management server; this was resolved by deleting both the agentless monitored and the agent monitored system from the console and then re-adding the system as agent monitored.

Agentless managed computers have a more limited set of features than agent-based managed computers. Similar to agent-based managed computers, agentless managed computers include the following capabilities:

- State monitoring
- Heartbeat
- Service discovery
- Performance collection
- Script execution
- Event collection

However, there are some significant limitations to agentless managed systems. The primary limitation is management packs that do not support agentless monitoring. This list includes these commonly used management packs:

- Active Directory (domain controllers)
- Clusters
- Exchange
- IIS
- SharePoint

Agentless monitoring also increases the resource load on the agent proxy that is monitoring the system.

Systems in an Unknown State

Unknown systems are unmanaged systems, either identified for potential management in the future (these systems are discovered but are not managed) or that have had the agent removed from them. OpsMgr does not collect information from unmanaged systems. Computers in an unknown state display in the right-side pane in the Operations console at the root of the Monitoring node.

Network Devices

Network device management is enhanced in OpsMgr 2012 and is moved from the Device Management node to the Network Management node of the Administration pane, shown in Figure 8.4.

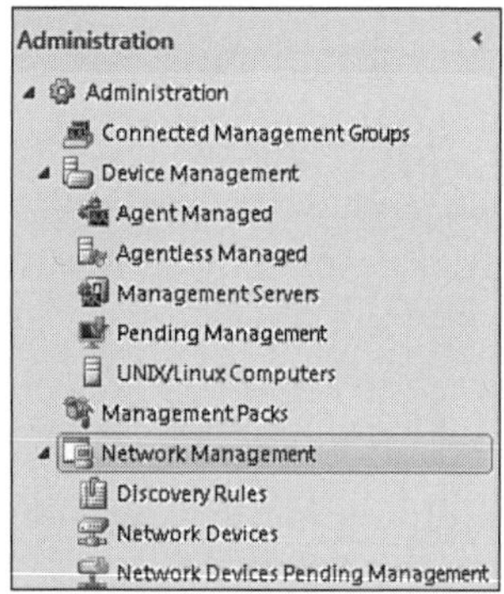

FIGURE 8.4 Network device management.

Chapter 16, "Network Monitoring," provides information on the network monitoring functionality available within Operations Manager 2012.

UNIX/Linux Systems

Microsoft added support for UNIX and Linux monitoring with Operations Manager 2007 Release 2 (R2) and enhanced it in Operations Manager 2012. System Center 2012 Operations Manager performs monitoring for UNIX/Linux systems through deploying a locally installed agent. Administration of these agents occurs in the Operations console under Administration -> Device Management -> UNIX/Linux Computers.

Discovering and Deploying Agents

A number of approaches are available for deploying agents. System Center 2012 Operations Manager continues to provide the capability available in previous versions to perform push installations from the Operations console. While the ability to deploy agents from the console is quite beneficial, it uses a proprietary approach. OpsMgr 2012 is a monitoring product; push installations to deploy the OpsMgr agent are relying on

OpsMgr itself for the software deployment, which was not the core focus that Operations Manager was designed to perform.

Along with the functionality included in the product for deploying agents (which works extremely well for most environments), you can install the agent in a variety of ways:

- Active Directory Integration (provides agent configuration information, but does not actually install the agent)
- Group policy
- Configuration Manager (ConfigMgr)
- Imaged systems
- Operations Manager Discovery Wizard
- Manual installation
- Installation using PowerShell

For small and midsized organizations, the authors recommend deployment with the Operations console using the Discovery Wizard. Larger organizations may want to evaluate Active Directory Integration coupled with other deployment methods such as Configuration Manager, group policy, and PowerShell. These techniques are discussed in the "Active Directory Integration," "Group Policy Deployment," "Configuration Manager Agent Deployment," and "PowerShell-Based Agent Installation" sections.

If you plan to push out a large number of agents over small or congested network links, the best practice recommendation is to deploy those agents outside business hours to minimize any impacts to the network environment.

Agent Supported Platforms

Operations Manager includes agents for both Windows platforms and UNIX/Linux systems, as discussed in the next sections.

Windows Agents Supported Platforms

You can deploy OpsMgr 2012 agents to the following Windows operating systems; see http://technet.microsoft.com/en-us/library/hh205990.aspx for additional information:

- Windows Server 2003 SP 2
- Windows Server 2008 SP 2
- Windows Server 2008 R2
- Windows Server 2008 R2 SP 1
- Windows XP Professional x64 Edition SP 2
- Windows XP Professional SP 3
- Windows Vista SP 2
- Windows 7

Operations Manager 2012 SP 1 adds support for the following Windows operating systems; http://technet.microsoft.com/en-us/library/jj656654.aspx provides additional information:

- Windows Server 2012
- For embedded systems, including POSReady, Windows XP Embedded Standard, Windows XP Embedded Enterprise, Windows XP Embedded POSReady, Windows 7 Professional for Embedded Systems, and Windows 7 Ultimate for Embedded Systems

TIP: AGENT SUPPORT ON WINDOWS 8

While the official support documentation for OpsMgr 2012 SP 1 (http:/technet.microsoft.com/en-us/library/jj656654) does not list Windows 8 as of January 2013, a blog post from the team (http://blogs.technet.com/b/momteam/archive/2012/09/05/windows-server-2012-system-center-operations-manager-support.aspx) states that Windows 8 will be supported for the OpsMgr agent in Service Pack 1. The assumption of the authors is that the official support documentation will be updated to include Windows 8 at a later date.

Windows Servers

While servers constitute the majority of Windows operating systems typically monitored by Operations Manager, OpsMgr can also monitor client operating systems. Operating system monitoring is provided by the Windows Server Operating System Monitoring management pack, available for download from the System Center Marketplace site at http://systemcenter.pinpoint.microsoft.com/.

Windows Clients

Although you can use OpsMgr to monitor client operating systems, most organizations typically only monitor servers (this is often a licensing-based decision). An exception might be a batch-processing system that runs business-critical functions not yet migrated to a server platform. For example, many manufacturing companies use workstation-class computers to monitor machines that produce their products.

The Windows Client management pack currently monitors Windows XP, Windows Vista, and Windows 7 systems. (Final word on whether there will be an update to monitor Windows 8 systems is pending from Microsoft.) This pack provides the ability to monitor the availability, configuration, and performance of Windows client operating systems. Download this management pack from the System Center Marketplace site at http://systemcenter.pinpoint.microsoft.com/.

Microsoft does not support Microsoft Windows NT 4.0 or Windows 2000 in an agent-managed configuration (or support any other operating systems that do not match the configurations listed in the "Windows Agents Supported Platforms" section). If you need to manage unsupported systems such as these, consider either agentless management or review third-party supplemental software for System Center 2012 Operations Manager.

TIP: EXTENDING DESKTOP MONITORING

At the Microsoft Management Summit (MMS) 2012, Infront Consulting Group demonstrated its Business Critical Desktop Monitoring management pack; this augments existing Operations Manager client monitoring by providing

- Monitoring for desktop and application health.
- Identification for currently logged on users and systems pending reboot.
- Associating users with their desktop for easier identification.
- Tasks for remediation include the ability to reboot a workstation, enable remote desktop, set current user as registered owner, and explore the remote C:\ drive.

Additional information on this pack and others available from Infront Consulting Group is available at http://www.infrontconsulting.com/software.php.

UNIX/Linux Agents Supported Platforms

You can deploy OpsMgr 2012 agents to the following UNIX/Linux operating systems; see http://technet.microsoft.com/en-us/library/jj656654.aspx#BKMK_RBF_UnixAgent for additional information including SP 1 support:

- HP-UX 11i v2 and v3 (PA-RISC and IA64)
- Oracle Solaris 9 (SPARC) and Solaris 10 and 11 (SPARC and x86)
- Red Hat Enterprise Linux 4, 5, and 6 (x86/x64)
- Novell SUSE Linux Enterprise Server 9 (x86), 10 SP 1 (x86/x64), and 11 (x86/x64)
- IBM AIX 5.3, AIX 6.1 (POWER), and AIX 7.1 (POWER)
- System Center 2012 Service Pack 1 adds support for CentOS 5 (x86/x64), CentOS 6 (x86/x64), Debian 5 (x86/x64), Debian 6 (x86/x64), and Ubuntu 12.04 (x86/x64)

TIP: THE "UNIVERSAL LINUX" MONITORING PACKS

Support for the new UNIX operating systems added with SP 1 is implemented using the "Universal Linux" monitoring packs. Here are the MP files required to add monitoring for these operating systems:

- Microsoft.Linux.Universal.Library.mp
- Microsoft.Linux.Universal.Monitoring.mp
- Microsoft.Linux.UniversalD.1.mpb (to support Debian and Ubuntu Linux agents)
- Microsoft.Linux.UniversalR.1.mpb (to support CentOS Linux agents)

Agent Requirements

Agent deployment in Operations Manager has a common set of requirements, with specific requirements for Windows or UNIX/Linux systems. These include

- **Name Resolution:** The Operations Manager management server must be able to resolve the name of the OpsMgr agent and vice versa. To validate name resolution is working correctly, ping the fully qualified name of the agent from the management server, and the management server from the agent.

- **Accounts/Profiles:** An account must exist with access to the system to install the agent. On Windows, the account requires local administrator rights. On UNIX/Linux systems, the account either needs to have privileged access or the rights to use `sudo` or `su` elevation.

TIP: UNIX/LINUX SYSTEM NOT MONITORED

When a UNIX system shows as not monitored, this is usually because a Run As account is not assigned. As there is no local system account on UNIX, you must create a UNIX/Linux account and assign it to the UNIX/Linux Action Account RunAs profile.

- **Communication:** Once an agent is installed, it must be able to communicate with the management server or pool (in the case of a UNIX/Linux system) it is assigned to. This means traffic must be able to route between the two servers, and the port the agent communicates with needs to be open for communication and reachable by the agent. To validate communication is working correctly, telnet from the agent to the server or from the server to the agent on the appropriate communication port. (This is port 5723 from the agent to the management server for Windows, 1270 from the management server to the agent for UNIX/Linux.)

Management Pack Requirements for Operating System Monitoring

Microsoft includes the management packs required to monitor Windows agents with the management group installation. You must add the specific Windows and UNIX/Linux operating system management packs before OpsMgr can monitor operating system information. The various operating system monitoring management packs are available for download from the System Center Marketplace site at http://systemcenter.pinpoint.microsoft.com/ or in the Operations console by right-clicking **Management Packs** in the Administration pane and choosing to import management packs. Use either of these approaches to add the appropriate management packs to Operations Manager.

TIP: MANAGEMENT PACKS ADDED DURING INSTALLATION

To see those management packs added in your environment during the OpsMgr installation, navigate to **Administration** -> **Management Packs** and sort by the Date Imported field. The oldest set of dates listed represents those management packs added to OpsMgr during the installation process.

Windows Management Pack Requirements

You can monitor Windows OpsMgr agents themselves even if the appropriate operating system management pack is not installed. As an example, an OpsMgr agent can be deployed and monitoring on a Windows 2008 system without adding the Windows 2008 management pack, but only the agent is monitored; the operating system shows as in a not monitored state. What this means is the heartbeat of the system is monitored, but no operating system-specific information is gathered (such as performance data for the OS, monitoring for disk space, or monitoring for Windows services). When the Windows 2008 operating system management pack is added, the operating system moves from a not monitored to monitored state after the operating system is discovered and monitoring is deployed to the system.

UNIX/Linux Management Pack Requirements

UNIX/Linux agents cannot have the Operations Manager agent installed until the appropriate UNIX/Linux OS management pack is imported. While the core UNIX/Linux libraries are imported when you install System Center 2012 Operations Manager, you must add the complete management packs for each OS version before attempting to monitor UNIX/Linux agents. These management packs are available on the installation media in the \ManagementPacks folder or you can download them from the System Center Marketplace.

The list of currently available management packs for UNIX/Linux includes individual downloads for the different versions of AIX, HP, Linux, and Solaris. Separate management packs are also available for ACS functionality on these operating systems.

TIP: VERIFY YOUR MANAGEMENT PACKS VERSIONS ARE CURRENT

During a recent OpsMgr agent deployment, agents failed to deploy with a message that "The task cannot be executed against the object(s) because the target of the task does not match any of the classes of the object."

In this environment, older (test) versions of the UNIX/Linux monitoring packs (version 6.1.7000.269) had been installed for the cross platform monitoring management packs. After upgrading these management packs to the versions available on the OpsMgr RTM media (version 7.3.2026.0), the agents deployed without experiencing this issue.

Using the Discovery Wizard

In most organizations, the Discovery Wizard is the primary method for deploying Operations Manager agents. The Discovery Wizard is available in the Administration space of the Operations console, and can be used to deploy monitoring to Windows computers, UNIX/Linux computers, and network devices. It provides an intuitive interface to add managed devices, and those devices deployed from the Discovery Wizard gain the benefit of being manageable by OpsMgr so the agent can be repaired, uninstalled, or upgraded during an update rollup (UR) deployment.

Discovery Wizard for Windows Agents

To discover Windows agents, run the Discovery Wizard and choose the default option for Windows computers. The Discovery Wizard can easily scan an entire Active Directory domain for Windows-based systems, limit its scan to specific OU structures, browse for computers, or even deploy to specific systems you enter (or copy and paste) into the wizard. Here are some things to consider when using the Discovery Wizard to deploy agents:

- Agents deployed using the Discovery Wizard do not pull their information from Active Directory, even if Active Directory Integration is in place.
- Agents deployed through the Discovery Wizard are defined to report to a specific management server. Should the management server fail, they fail over to another management server.
- The Discovery Wizard first discovers the system(s); after discovery, you can choose those specific systems to receive the OpsMgr agent. You can see deployment successes and failures displayed within both the Deployment Wizard results and the Tasks section of the console (Monitoring -> Tasks). The best practice recommendation by the authors is to use the Discovery Wizard to discover and deploy agents in all but the largest of OpsMgr environments.

Using the wizard is the easiest method to deploy OpsMgr agents. To launch the Discovery Wizard to discover Windows systems, follow these steps:

1. Open the **Operations console** and navigate to **Administration**. Right-click **Administration** and choose **Discovery Wizard** (right-clicking any item listed in the left pane provides this option).
2. On the Discovery Type page, choose **Windows computers** from the options available (Windows computers, UNIX/Linux computers, and Network devices).
3. The next page, shown in Figure 8.5, asks you to select either automatic or advanced discovery. Automatic computer discovery scans for all Windows-based computers within the domain where the management server (MS) is a member. Automatic discovery is useful in smaller organizations and very effective when selecting large numbers of systems to which to deploy the OpsMgr agent. For most agent deployments, the preferred option is to take the default of Advanced discovery. The following describes the advanced discovery process:
    - If you are deploying agents only to servers, take the default option of **Servers and Clients** from the Computer and Device Classes dropdown list (available options include Servers and Clients, Servers Only, Clients Only, and Network Devices).

TIP: AVOID USING THE SERVERS ONLY OPTION IN THE DISCOVERY WIZARD

It is a best practice to not use the Servers Only option during a discovery as the filter requires contacting each machine for verification. This process slows down the discovery and can lead to discovery failures from timeouts. The Servers Only option is most useful when doing an extremely filtered LDAP query for specific machines versus a large-scale discovery.

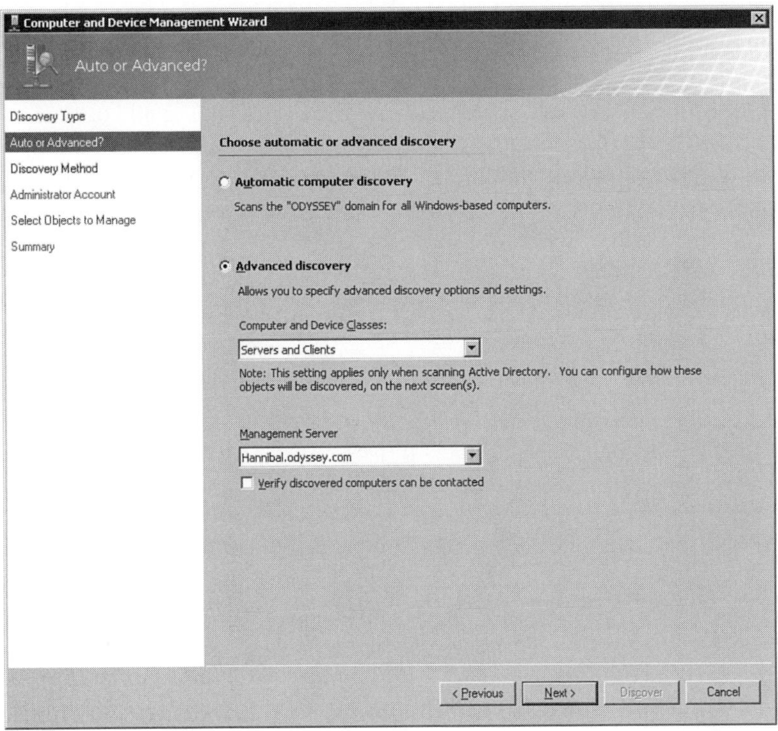

FIGURE 8.5 Choosing Automatic or Advanced discovery.

- If you will be deploying agents onto workstations, take the default configuration (**Servers and Clients**). Check the option **Verify discovered computers can be contacted**. This often increases the success rates of the deployment because only systems that can be communicated with over the network are listed for selection.
- If you select the **Servers Only** option, the option Verify discovered computers can be contacted is grayed out and checked.

The discovery can return approximately 4,000 computers if the verify option is selected, and approximately 10,000 computers if not selected.

Finally, select the management server the agent will communicate with from the drop-down list. Continue by clicking **Next**.

4. The Discovery Method page provides two options.
   - Scan Active Directory to discover computers
   - Browse for, or type-in computer names

The scan option searches Active Directory based on the criteria you specify. Click **Configure** to choose this option, which opens a Find Computers window you can use to create a custom LDAP query. Examples of this would include searching for all computers (by adding "*" to the Computer name field) or selecting all computers starting with SRV. Additional options for the LDAP query include Description, Managed By, Name, Operating System, Operating System Version, and Phonetic Display Name as shown in Figure 8.6.

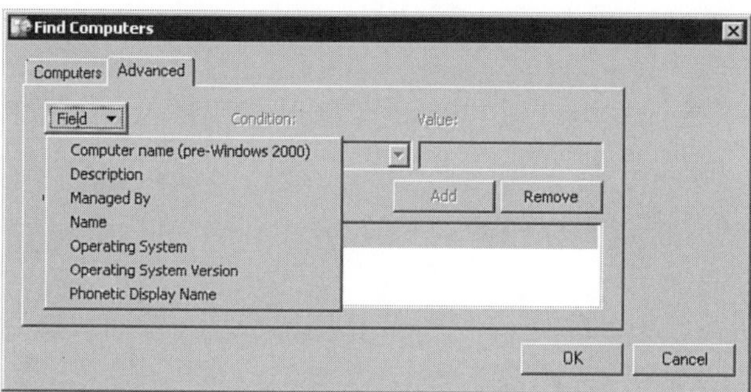

FIGURE 8.6 LDAP Query Fields.

The Browse for or type-in computer names option includes an additional option: **Browse Active Directory for computer information**. Selecting the Browse option opens a dialog where you can select computers by searching for computer names (or descriptions) as well as restrict your search to a specific organizational unit. Figure 8.7 shows a browse of Active Directory in the Computers OU for names starting with the letters HA. The selected systems are then transferred to the Browse for or type-in computer names text box. Here are some points to keep in mind:

- The type-in option is used to receive the results from clicking Browse, or can provide a location to cut and paste server names into the discovery.
- The cut-and-paste approach is useful when you have previously documented the systems that will be part of your proof of concept (POC) or pilot groups, because you can cut and paste them into this field for agent deployment. This is also useful when performing a multi-homed migration from OpsMgr 2007 to OpsMgr 2012 as you can export groups of agent names from OpsMgr 2007 and paste them here. You can enter computer names here separated by a semicolon, comma, or newline. This field works with NetBIOS or fully qualified domain names.

Enter the systems you want to configure with the scan, browse, or type-in method and click **Next** to continue.

5. The Administrator Account page allows you to choose the default account or specify another user account when installing the OpsMgr agent. The default is **Use Selected Management Server Action Account** (also referred to as the MSAA); this is the recommended option as long as the account has at least local administrative rights

to the systems to which you are deploying the agent (Domain Admin user accounts are members of the local Administrators group by default). If your MSAA account is not a domain administrator or at least a local administrator on the workstation, you can provide credentials for this discovery process. Refer to Chapter 10, "Security and Compliance," for best practice approaches on this account. Click **Discover** to continue.

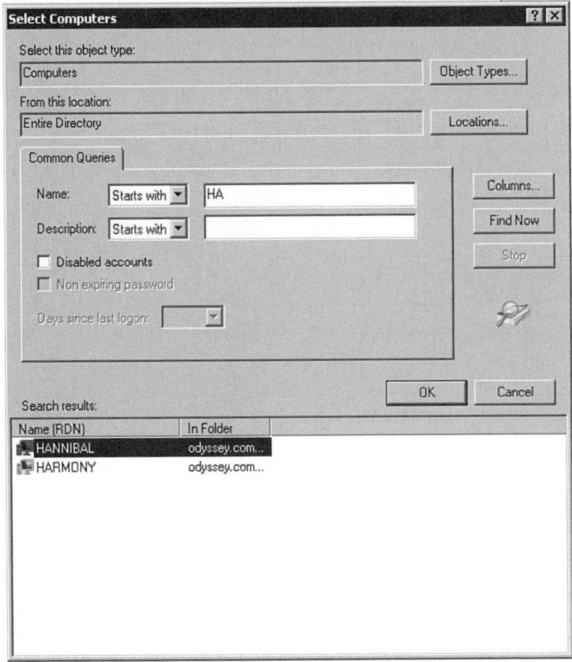

FIGURE 8.7 Browsing Active Directory with the Discovery Wizard.

NOTE: DISCOVERY WIZARD STUCK ON "DISCOVERY IS IN PROGRESS"

There are three common causes of having the Discovery Wizard become non-responsive according to an article by System Center MVP Marnix Wolf:

- SQL Broker Service is not running; see http://support.microsoft.com/kb/941409 for further information.
- SPNs are not set correctly.
- Health Service Store on the MS is corrupted.

Marnix's blog article on this topic is available at http://thoughtsonopsmgr.blogspot.com/2010/08/discovery-wizard-is-running-for-ever.html. Additional discussions on troubleshooting discovery in Operations Manager are available at http://go.microsoft.com/.

6. The next page, displayed in Figure 8.8, lists the systems available for agent installation (systems that already have the OpsMgr agent are not displayed). Select the appropriate server(s), validate the Management Mode is **Agent**, and click **Next** to continue.

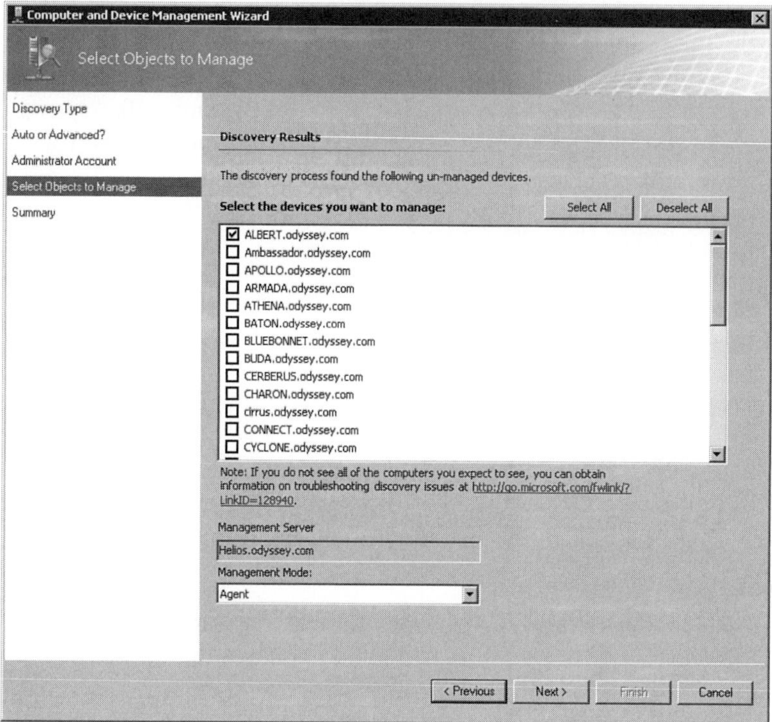

FIGURE 8.8 Select Objects to Manage page.

You can also use this dialog to install agentless systems, but the focus in this section is on agent-based installations.

7. Take the defaults on the Summary page for the agent installation folder (*%ProgramFiles%*\System Center Operations Manager\Agent) and for the agent action account to use the credentials of the Local System account. Chapter 10 provides additional information on the agent action account.

8. Click **Finish** to begin installing the OpsMgr agents.

9. The status of each agent deployment displays on the Agent Management Task Status page. The status starts at Queued, changes to Started, and moves to either Success or Failure. Should the agent deployment fail, click the targeted computer; the task output box provides details on why it failed. Click **Close** when this deployment is complete (deployments continue when the Agent Management Task Status page is closed).

TIP: TRUST REQUIREMENTS TO DEPLOY AGENTS

Agent authentication in OpsMgr requires Kerberos or certificate-based authorization to provide mutual authentication. Use certificate-based authorization for gateway configurations where agents are in untrusted domains or workgroups. Within a forest, transitive two-way trusts are automatically created that support Kerberos. There are four other types of trusts in Windows: External, Realm, Forest, and Shortcut. Shortcut trusts improve logon time and should not apply in this scenario. Realm trusts pertain to non-Windows environments, so they should not apply when deploying agents.

Forest trusts support Kerberos, but Realm trusts do not. This means that agents in domains connected to the management server's domain via an External trust will not deploy successfully unless deployed using a gateway server configuration.

Discovery Wizard for UNIX/Linux Agents

The Discovery Wizard provides an integrated method for adding UNIX/Linux systems to OpsMgr 2012 for monitoring. Prior to running this wizard, there are several prerequisites. The next sections discuss prerequisites and the discovery process.

Prerequisites for UNIX/Linux Agents

For UNIX/Linux agents to be discovered correctly, here are several required steps before running the Discovery Wizard:

- Import management packs required for UNIX/Linux monitoring, discussed in the "UNIX/Linux Management Pack Requirements" section.
- Create a resource pool for monitoring UNIX/Linux servers, performed at Administration -> Resource Pools. Create a new resource pool and add the appropriate management servers to that resource pool.
- Configure the cross platform certificates (export/import) *for each management server in the pool*. Information on this process is available at http://technet.microsoft.com/en-us/library/hh287152.aspx. Details on certificates, troubleshooting agent deployment, and other topics related to UNIX/Linux servers are discussed in Chapter 20, "Interoperability and Cross Platform."
- Create and Configure Run As accounts for UNIX/Linux systems; see http://technet.microsoft.com/en-us/library/hh212926.aspx for additional information.

Discovery Process for UNIX/Linux Agents

Using the wizard is the easiest way for deploying OpsMgr agents to UNIX/Linux systems as well as Windows systems. Before running the wizard, import the appropriate UNIX/Linux management packs, create a resource pool to monitor the agents, create configuration certificates, define the Run As accounts, and identify the IP address(es) of the systems. After completing these tasks, you can discover UNIX/Linux agents with OpsMgr.

Follow these steps to launch the Discovery Wizard:

1. Navigate to the **Administration** node in the Operations console. Right-click **Administration** and choose the **Discovery Wizard** (right-clicking any item listed in the left pane provides this option).
2. On the Discovery Type page, choose **UNIX/Linux computers** from the options available (Windows computers, UNIX/Linux computers, and Network devices).
3. On the Discovery Criteria page, select the resource pool you previously defined for your UNIX/Linux agents (see the "Prerequisites for UNIX/Linux Agents" section) and click **Add** to define the discovery criteria for the UNIX/Linux agents.
4. In the Discovery Criteria subpage, configure the discovery scope, discovery type, and credentials for the discovery (see Figure 8.9).

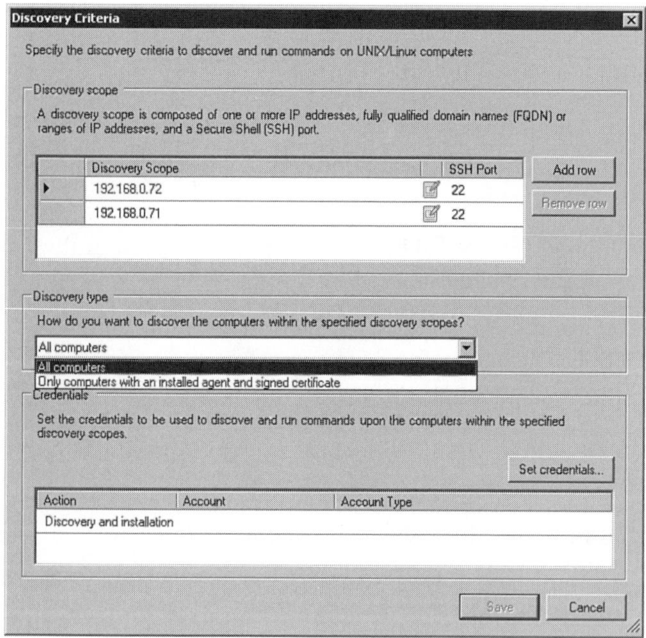

FIGURE 8.9 UNIX and Linux Discovery criteria.

- **Discovery Scope:** Contains names or IP addresses of the UNIX/Linux systems to be monitored with Operations Manager and the SSH port OpsMgr will use to communicate with each system.
- **Discovery Type:** Defines whether all computers (the default) can be discovered or only computers that already have an installed agent and signed certificate (most useful when adding manually installed UNIX/Linux systems).
- **Credentials:** Significant changes have occurred in how OpsMgr 2012 handles credentials when compared with OpsMgr 2007 R2. Credentials can be defined

to use SSH (the default) or a user name and password. For a given user name and password, the user does not need privileged access. If the user defined does not have privileged access, it can be configured to use either `sudo` or `su` elevation. The `sudo` and `su` elevation options use the default credentials to establish the connection, and then the user permissions are elevated to perform the agent installation. Figure 8.10 shows an example where discovery criteria has been defined for one system using the OpsUser account to connect to the system, using `su` elevation to perform the installation as root.

TIP: PRIVILEGED AND UNPRIVILEGED ACCOUNTS IN OPSMGR 2012

A commonly asked question is *What are the actual differences between a UNIX/Linux privileged and unprivileged account in OpsMgr 2012?*

- A *privileged account* needs to have root-level access to the system including access to security logs and Read, Write, and Execute permissions within the directories where the OpsMgr agent was installed.
- An *unprivileged account* is a normal user account without root access or special permissions, but you can use the account for monitoring system processes and performance data.

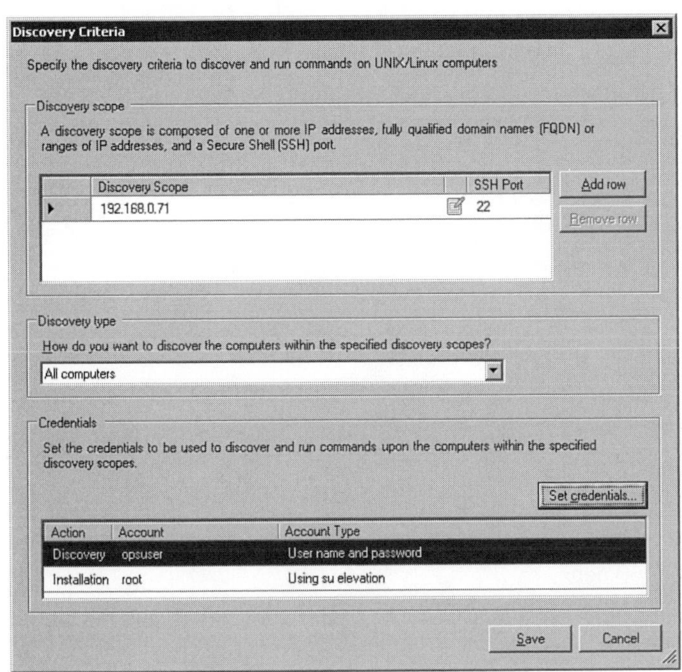

FIGURE 8.10 UNIX and Linux Discovery criteria using `su`.

5. At the Computer Selection page, select the systems that were discovered and make those systems manageable. Figure 8.11 shows an example of the Trident SUSE Linux

Enterprise Server as a system that already has the agent installed and is ready to be managed by OpsMgr 2012.

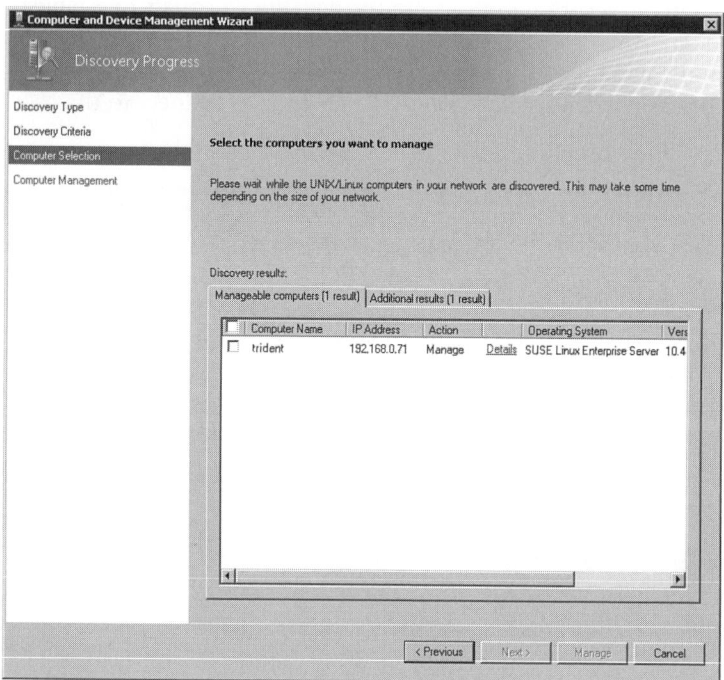

FIGURE 8.11 UNIX and Linux computer selection.

6. The Computer Management page summarizes the discovery and installation process showing systems that succeeded or failed during this process. For details on UNIX/Linux agent deployment troubleshooting, see Chapter 20.

TIP: ADDITIONAL CROSS PLATFORM DISCOVERY WIZARD INFORMATION

There are some excellent additional resources available online for UNIX/Linux agent information. Here are some of the authors' favorites:

- The wiki for UNIX/Linux agent deployment at http://social.technet.microsoft.com/wiki/contents/articles/4966.aspx
- Kevin Holman's blog article on deploying UNIX/Linux agents using OpsMgr 2012 at http://blogs.technet.com/b/kevinholman/archive/2012/03/18/deploying-unix-linux-agents-using-opsmgr-2012.aspx.

Manual Agent Installation

In general, manual agent installation should be the method of last resort for deploying OpsMgr agents. Manually installed agents cannot be remotely managed or upgraded through the Operations console. Only those agents remotely manageable can have their primary management server changed, be agent repaired or agent uninstalled from the console. The inability to upgrade these agents also adds complexity when attempting to apply update rollups.

TIP: UPGRADING MANUALLY INSTALLED AGENTS

Once an agent is installed manually, any update rollups must be manually applied. Cameron Fuller provides a method to update manually installed agents through the Operations console, available at http://blogs.catapultsystems.com/cfuller/archive/2012/04/27/how-to-upgrade-clients-to-cu5-which-were-manually-installed-in-opsmgr-scom-sysctr.aspx. This builds upon Kevin Holman's article at http://blogs.technet.com/b/kevinholman/archive/2010/02/20/how-to-get-your-agents-back-to-remotely-manageable-in-opsmgr-2007-r2.aspx.

These approaches will not work if an agent was installed manually due to network restrictions, as these restrictions would continue to block the network traffic required to perform actions such as an agent upgrade. Although written for OpsMgr 2007, the approaches discussed in these posts should still apply to OpsMgr 2012 environments.

Manual Installation for Windows Agents

A manual installation requires you log in to the system to which you will be installing the agent, make configuration changes to OpsMgr, and approve the agent installation. Typically, you will use manual agent installations when specific servers are not installing the agent using the more automated methods. To perform a manual installation, follow these steps:

1. Change the default settings to Allow Manual installations within the Operations console, under **Administration** -> **Settings** -> **Security** -> **Pending Management** -> **Review new manual agent installations**.
2. Log on to the server where the agent requires manual installation and install the agent on the system. The recommended way to install the agent is running the Setup.exe program on the root of the installation media and choosing the **Local Agent** option. This runs the MOMAgent.msi file for the appropriate platform and turns on logging during the installation. A more direct approach is to browse the installation media within the agent folder and into the appropriate version folder (AMD64, i386, ia64) and run the MOMAgent.msi program from that folder.
3. Check the Operations console under **Administration** -> **Device Management** -> **Pending Management**. The manually installed system should now be listed. Approve the manual installation.

Parameters available for a manual installation and other deployment methods not using the Operations Manager console are shown in Table 8.3, which lists the most commonly used parameters, and Table 8.4, which lists the less frequently used parameters.

TABLE 8.3 MOMAgent.msi common parameters

Parameters	Values	Usage
USE_SETTINGS_FROM_AD	0, 1	0=Set properties on the command line. 1=Use AD Integration.
MANAGEMENT_GROUP	Name of management group	Specifies the management group that will manage the agent.
MANAGEMENT_SERVER_DNS	Name of primary management server	Fully qualified domain name (FQDN) for the management server or gateway.
ACTIONS_USE_COMPUTER_ACCOUNT	0, 1	0 indicates a specified user, 1 is the Local System account (recommended).
USE_MANUALLY_SPECIFIED_ SETTINGS		If USE_SETTINGS_FROM_AD = 1 this must be 0.

TABLE 8.4 MOMAgent.msi less common parameters

Parameters	Values	Usage
MANAGEMENT_SERVER_AD_NAME	AD name of primary management server	Specify this parameter if the computer DNS and Active Directory name do not match.
SECURE_PORT	5723	Health service port number.
ENABLE_ERROR_REPORTING	0, 1	1 to enable, 0 to disable (0 by default).
QUEUE_ERROR_REPORTS	0, 1	1 to queue error report, 0 to send reports immediately (0 by default).
INSTALLDIR	Path for agent installation	This parameter can change the default path to match a specific folder.
ACTIONSUSER	Username	Only required if you specify ACTIONS_USE_COMPUTER_ ACCOUNT as 0.
ACTIONSDOMAIN	Domain name	Only required if you specify ACTIONS_USE_COMPUTER_ ACCOUNT as 0.
ACTIONSPASSWORD	Password	Only required if you specify ACTIONS_USE_COMPUTER_ ACCOUNT as 0.
NOAPM	0, 1	Installs OpsMgr without the .NET APM components. If you are using AVIcode 5.7, setting this to 1 leaves the AVIcode agent in place.

Examples of usage for these parameters are discussed in the "Group Policy Deployment" and "Configuration Manager Agent deployment" sections.

Manual Installation for UNIX/Linux Agents

Agents can be manually installed for UNIX/Linux systems and then discovered using the Discovery Wizard. Chapter 20 discusses the process to install a UNIX/Linux agent manually.

Active Directory Integration

System Center 2012 Operations Manager provides the ability to configure agents through Active Directory (AD). This takes place by publishing the OpsMgr agent configuration details to Active Directory. An OpsMgr agent performs an LDAP query to the authenticating domain controller at system startup, determining the management group it belongs to and the management server with which it will communicate. Note that Active Directory Integration does not actually deploy the agent.

To use Active Directory Integration in OpsMgr 2012, the domain functional level needs to be at least Windows 2000 or Windows 2003 Native mode. To check the functional level of your domain, open Active Directory Users and Computers, right-click your domain, and select **Properties**. To change the domain functional level, right-click the domain and select **Raise Domain Functional level**. You should only make this change with prior planning and within the change control windows in your environment.

TIP: WHEN TO USE ACTIVE DIRECTORY INTEGRATION

Jonathan Almquist provides an insightful blog article discussing when one should use Active Directory Integration in OpsMgr, available at http://blogs.technet.com/b/jonathanalmquist/archive/2010/06/14/ad-integration-considerations.aspx. His main point about AD Integration is that while it provides a way to facilitate including the OpsMgr agent in a server image, AD Integration is not very forgiving of mistakes made. In most cases, you can avoid AD Integration by using the command shell to assign primary and failover configuration, unless the goal is to include the OpsMgr agent in a server image.

Configuring Active Directory Integration

Active Directory Integration creates a container in the domain root of Active Directory named OperationsManager, this is used by clients to determine the management group and management server with which they will communicate. The steps involved in configuring Active Directory Integration include

1. In Active Directory, create a new global security group (the authors recommend something intuitive such as ADIntegrationGroup) that contains the computer accounts belonging to the AD Assignment Resource Pool. To view members of this resource pool, navigate to **Administration** -> **Resource Pools**, right-click **AD Assignment Resource Pool**, and choose **View Resource Pool Members** (this should contain all management servers in the management group by default). For the OMGRP management group used in this book, the group members include Hector, Helios, and Hannibal as shown in Figure 8.12.

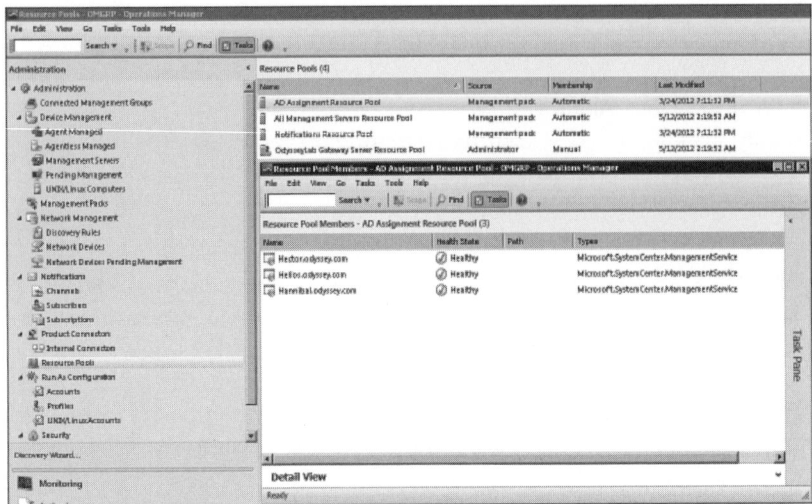

FIGURE 8.12 Resource Pool Members for the ADIntegrationGroup.

NOTE: OPSMGR AGENTS FOR WINDOWS AND SERVER POOLS

One of the common misconceptions in OpsMgr 2012 is that Active Directory Integration is no longer required and that Windows agents can now report to a pool of management servers. AD Integration is still required for agents to use Active Directory to determine the management server to communicate with, and Windows agents do not communicate with a resource pool in OpsMgr 2012.

2. To create the container OpsMgr 2012 uses to store information for AD Integration, open a command prompt and change directory to the Operations Manager\ Server folder (the default location would be *%ProgramFiles%* \System Center 2012\ Operations Manager\Server).

   Run the `MOMADAdmin.exe` program, passing it this information:

   - **Management group name:** This is OMGRP in the example for the Odyssey management group; determine the management group name by opening the Operations Manager console and looking at the name of the management group, shown on the title of the console between the two dashes in the title name. As an example, Active Alerts - OMGRP - Operations Manager.
   - **MOMAdminSecurity group name:** ADIntegrationGroup, this is the group created in step 1.
   - **RunAs account name:** Specify the account that is used for rules to run on the agent; determine this by navigating in the Operations Manager console to **Administration** -> **Run As Configuration** -> **Accounts** -> **Type of Action Account**.

- **Domain in which to create the container:** Odyssey in this example, you can find this when opening Active Directory Users and Computers.

Example: `MOMADAdmin OMGRP ADIntegrationGroup Odyssey\Administrator Odyssey`

Figure 8.13 shows the MOMADAdmin program run for the OMGRP management group in the Odyssey domain.

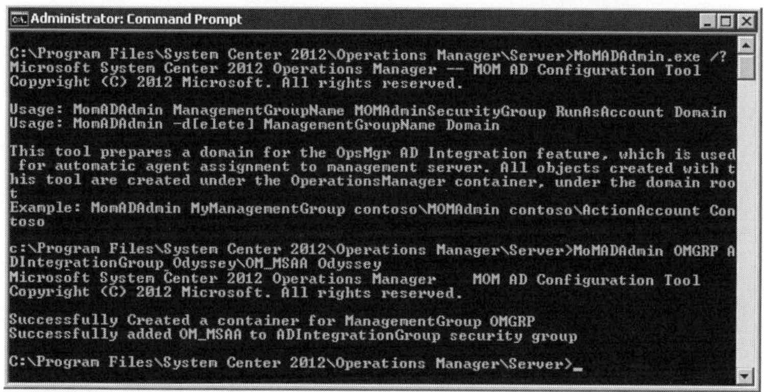

FIGURE 8.13 Running MOMADAdmin.

A successful run of MOMADAdmin indicates it successfully created the container and added the appropriate security group to the container.

3. From the Administration pane, create rules for AD Integration that indicate which servers communicate with a given management server. Configure AD Integration per management server in **Administration** -> **Device Management** -> **Management Servers** by right-clicking a server and choosing **Properties**.

   The Auto Agent Assignment tab displayed in Figure 8.14 shows an example of AD Integration where all servers report to a single management server.

   Adding an Auto Agent Assignment (the **Add** icon shown in Figure 8.14) starts the Agent Assignment and Failover Wizard, which specifies the domain and defines the inclusion, exclusion, and failover criteria:

   - **Inclusion criteria:** On the Inclusion criteria page, define those systems that will report to this management server. LDAP queries can be created based on a naming convention, or an OU or group membership. A sample LDAP query to include systems based on group membership for the Odyssey domain is `(sAMAccountType=805306369)(memberof=CN=`<*name of AD group*>`,CN=Users,DC=Odyssey,DC=com)`

   - **Exclusion criteria:** On the Exclusion page, define any systems that will not report to this management server. This works similarly to the inclusion page; here you can write an LDAP query to exclude systems from reporting to this management server.

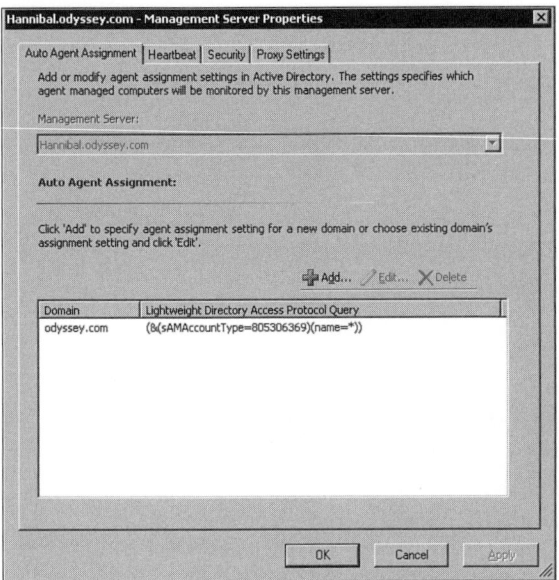

FIGURE 8.14 Configuring AD Integration.

- **Failover:** On the Failover page, either choose a random failover or specify management servers for failover. When configuring failover, consider that the failover server must be able to support the total number of agents that would report to it should the primary management server fail. As an example, if there are 2,000 servers reporting to a primary server and 2,000 servers reporting to the failover server, if the primary failed the failover server would now be expected to support 4,000 servers, which is beyond the supported number of agents per management server.

4. The group specified when running `MOMADAdmin` must be added to the Operations Manager Administrator role (**Administration** -> **Security** -> **User Roles** -> **Operations Manager Administrators**). If this step does not occur, Operations Manager raises an alert indicating that this step is required for AD Integration to function.

5. After configuring AD Integration, you must validate it is functional. There are multiple steps associated with validation, including checking AD, agent event logs, and the registry key on the agent:

NOTE: AD INTEGRATION ON A DOMAIN CONTROLLER

AD Integration will not work on a domain controller. Attempting to do so generates event number 2119 from the HealthService indicating that AD Integration has been disabled due to the health service's attempt to use AD Integration on a domain controller. The System Center Management service will also fail to start on the domain controller.

- **Active Directory:** Successful Active Directory Integration creates a container called OperationsManager (to view containers, use **View -> Advanced Features in Active Directory Users and Computers**). Within the container there should be another container matching the name of the management group (OMGRP in this example), and within the management group-named folder a HealthServiceSCP folder and a domain local security group. After defining the AD auto assignment information (step 3), a container with the name of the management server and _SCP on the end, and two domain local security groups based on the management server name (with _PrimarySG_# and _SecondarySG_#) are added to the container for the management group.

- **Agent Event Logs:** An agent must be installed without specifying management group information to use Active Directory Integration. When the System Center Management service starts, events are logged in to the Operations Manager event log, indicating AD Integration is configured and that the agent is able to identify its management server. Figure 8.15 shows an example of an agent successfully receiving management group information from Active Directory, indicated by event 20013 from the OpsMgr Connector in the Operations Manager log on the agent.

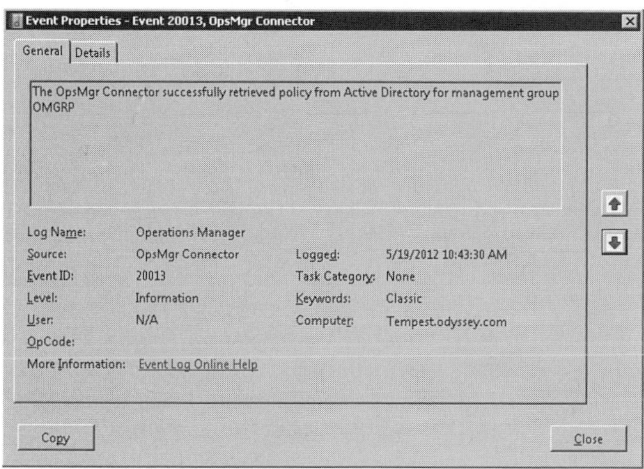

FIGURE 8.15 Agent successfully retrieving AD Integration information.

- **Registry Key:** A registry key is created on the agent indicating AD Integration is configured for the agent. This key is named `EnableADIntegration`; in OpsMgr 2012 it was moved to `HKLM\System\CurrentControlSet\Services\HealthService\Parameters\ConnectorManager`. A value of `0` indicates Active Directory Integration is turned off, and a value of `1` indicates that Active Directory Integration is turned on. This value can be changed on an agent, but do not manipulate this registry key on a management server.

TIP: HOW ACTIVE DIRECTORY INTEGRATION WORKS

Steve Rachui put together an excellent blog article explaining how AD Integration works in OpsMgr 2007. AD Integration has not changed significantly since OpsMgr 2007, so this article still applies to OpsMgr 2012 and is available at http://blogs.msdn.com/b/steverac/archive/2008/03/20/opsmgr-ad-integration-how-it-works.aspx.

Removing Active Directory Integration

To remove Active Directory Integration after it is configured, the `MOMADAdmin` utility accepts a `-d` parameter, which removes this configuration. For the configuration in the Odyssey domain, to remove Active Directory Integration, type the following (the parameters for `-d` are the management group name and the domain):

```
MOMADAdmin.exe -d OMGRP Odyssey.com
```

PowerShell-Based Agent Installation

PowerShell is another option for deploying agents in Operations Manager 2012. Here is an example of syntax used to deploy an OpsMgr 2012 agent:

```
$InstallAccount = Get-Credential

$PrimaryMgmtServer = Get-SCOMManagementServer -Name "<managementservername>"

Install-SCOMAgent -Name "<agentname>" -PrimaryManagementServer $PrimaryMgmtServer -
ActionAccount $InstallAccount
```

- The first line of this PowerShell example allows you to enter credentials into a logon dialog box that is used to deploy the agents.
- The second line sets the primary management server (be sure to use the FQDN for the management server name).
- The third line installs the agent on machine specified by the agentname (specify the FQDN for the agent name as well) using the primary management server from the second line and the action account specified in the line first line of the PowerShell script.

The script is included for your convenience with the online material accompanying this book; see Appendix E for further information.

For more details on using PowerShell for agent-based installation, see Scott Moss's article at http://om2012.wordpress.com/2011/12/07/om12-rc-deploying-agents-with-powershell.

Group Policy Deployment

Group policy can deploy software, both by software deployment and running the installation using a startup script. Group policy software deployment cannot run setup switches with an MSI package as part of a GPO; using this method requires creating a transform

(MST) file for the Operations Manager 2012 agent. As no transform files exist, this chapter focuses on how to deploy the agent using a startup script, which requires the following steps:

1. Create a file share named OpsMgrAgent on a computer (Helios in this example). Copy over the agent folder structure under the new share name, such that it contains the \amd64, \i386, and \ia64 folders. Ensure everyone in the domain has at least Read access to the share to be able to access the scripts to run the OpsMgr agent installation.

   Rename the i386 folder to x86, because this is how the Processor_Architecture environment variable is defined on the i386 platform. You can also provide this share using the Distributed File System (DFS) so the files are accessible from a locally available server in the site.

2. Create a .cmd file and save it in the newly shared folder. Name the file InstallOpsMgrAgent.cmd and include the following content (this script example is included with the material accompanying this book; for additional information see Appendix E):

   ```
   IF EXIST "%programfiles%\System Center Operations
   Manager\Agent\HealthService.exe" goto end
   Call \\helios.odyssey.com\OpsMgrAgents\%Processor_Architecture%\MOMAgent.msi
   /qn /l*v %temp%\MOMAgentinstall.log USE_SETTINGS_FROM_AD=0
   MANAGEMENT_GROUP=OMGRP MANAGEMENT_SERVER_DNS=helios.odyssey.com
   ACTIONS_USE_COMPUTER_ACCOUNT=1 USE_MANUALLY_SPECIFIED_SETTINGS=1
   ACCEPTENDUSERLICENSEAGREEMENT=1
   :end
   ```

NOTE: SECURITY AND INSTALLING THE OPSMGR AGENT

When installing the OpsMgr agent using group policy, security configuration changes may be required including disabling of User Account Control.

   The parameters used here for installation via group policy are the same as those used for manual installation on Windows and are discussed in the "Manual Installation" section.

3. Use the Group Policy Management console (GPMC; **Start** -> **Run** and then type **gpedit.msc**) to create a new GPO and browse to **Computer Configuration** -> **Windows Settings** -> **Scripts (Startup/Shutdown)**. Right-click **Startup** and then choose **Properties**.

4. At the Startup Properties page, click **Add** and browse to the file share created in step 1 to select the InstallOpsMgrAgent.cmd file. No script parameters are required, so click **OK**, and click **OK** at the startup properties page. Close the GPMC.

   Agents installed using this method are treated as manually installed agents so are rejected in the default configuration, or you can modify this configuration so they can be automatically or manually approved using the Pending Management node in the Administration pane. Refer to the "Approval Process" section earlier in the chapter for further details.

Configuration Manager Agent Deployment

You can use Configuration Manager to deploy the OpsMgr 2012 agent. The primary benefits to using ConfigMgr to deploy the OpsMgr 2012 agent include

- Strong targeting mechanisms are available through collections, including the ability to target to a group, a site, or a subnet as an example.
- Increased reporting information on agent deployments, provided with the standard software deployment reports in ConfigMgr.

Here are some negatives to using ConfigMgr to deploy the OpsMgr 2012 agent:

- You must either create the package or configure Active Directory Integration to provide this method to deploy the agent, or hard-code values into the program within ConfigMgr for a specific management group and management server.
- You need to define collections for whatever targeting will be required.
- Individual or small group agent deployments require more time than if you use the Discovery Wizard for deployment.

ConfigMgr has two primary ways to deploy software: to the user or the computer. Since the goal is to deploy an OpsMgr agent targeted at a server or a workstation, use deployment to a computer, which uses packages you create. These packages are deployed to collections of systems. Creating the package for OpsMgr is simple and only requires several steps:

1. Within the ConfigMgr console in the Software Library workspace, navigate to **Application Management -> Packages**, right-click, choose **Create Package from Definition**, and point it to MOMAgent.msi. For this example, package the amd64 version of the OpsMgr agent. Take the defaults except for the source files option, which should specify **Always obtain files from a source folder**, and point the folder to the path of the agent (as an example, d:\agent\amd64).
2. The MSI file creates a set of installation options that are not relevant for this deployment. On the Program tab for the package, delete the per-user installs and the per-system attended install because they are not required and may cause confusion.
3. Right-click the package and select **Properties**. On the General tab, change the properties on the per-system unattended command line to

```
MSIEXEC.exe /I MOMAgent.msi /qn /l*v %temp%\MOMAgentinstall.log
USE_SETTINGS_FROM_AD=0 MANAGEMENT_GROUP=OMGRP
MANAGEMENT_SERVER_DNS=helios.odyssey.com
ACTIONS_USE_COMPUTER_ACCOUNT=1 USE_MANUALLY_SPECIFIED_SETTINGS=1
```

These parameters install MOMAgent.msi in quiet mode. Specify saving the MSI log file to a log named MOMAgentinstall.log, and provide configuration information for the client; pointing it to a management server, management group, and to run the agent using Local System.

To install the OpsMgr agent for unattended installation and use AD Integration, change the per-system unattended command line to

```
MSIEXEC.exe /i MOMAgent.msi /qn /l*v MOMinstall.log
USE_MANUALLY_SPECIFIED_SETTINGS=0
```

4. Change the properties on the Requirements tab to set the maximum time allowed to **15** minutes and to specify only 64-bit platforms to run this agent on, as shown in Figure 8.16.

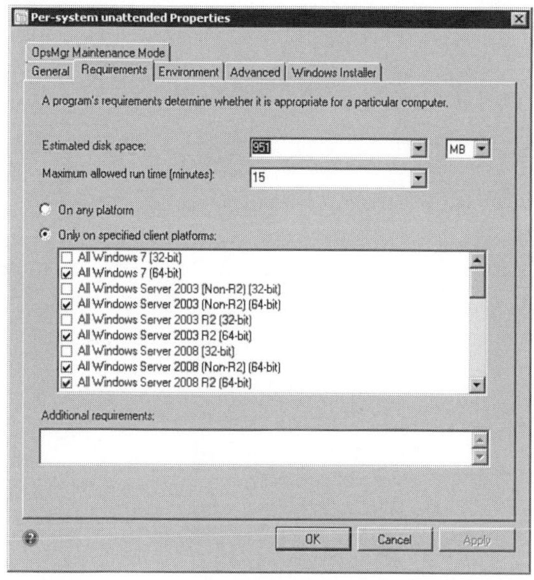

FIGURE 8.16 Per-system unattended deployment.

5. After creating the package, assign it to a distribution point in your ConfigMgr environment. ConfigMgr uses distribution points to deploy software packages.

6. Create a collection that will represent those systems to which you want to deploy the agent, and restrict the collection to the particular software platform the package supports. As an example, you could create a collection for all servers in the environment running a 64-bit platform.

7. Right-click the program and select **Deploy** -> **Program** to push the agent to a collection that requires the OpsMgr agent. This starts the Deploy Software Wizard, which is used to deploy the software to the collection. Using this wizard, choose the

software package, and set the assignment schedule for the OpsMgr agent deployment to **As soon as possible**. To check on the status of the deployment use the Deployments node in the Monitoring workspace. Figure 8.17 shows the status of the deployment of the OpsMgr agent to a single system using System Center 2012 Configuration Manager.

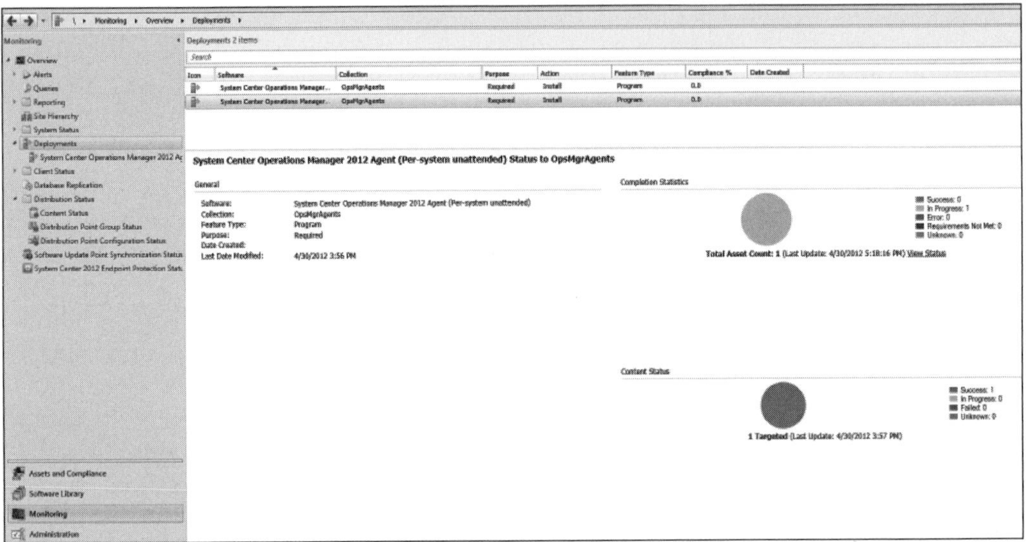

FIGURE 8.17 Deployment status in ConfigMgr.

8. If deploying agents to different platforms (such as i386 or amd64), create separate packages for each of these platforms, which means performing steps 1–7 for each platform.

Image-Based Deployment

You can use various imaging technologies to install or deploy operating systems, including Norton Ghost and System Center Configuration Manager. Imaging can deploy preconfigured operating systems that may already have applications deployed on them. Imaging provides a rapid way to install identical operating systems and software configurations on multiple systems quickly and efficiently.

Imaged systems can integrate the OpsMgr agent as part of the image. When the system starts, it looks up its configuration in Active Directory (discussed in the "Active Directory Integration" section), and the agent is able to report to the specified Operations Manager management server.

Integrating the OpsMgr agent into the image and using Active Directory Integration technologies provides a deployment method that is easy to maintain after implementation. For smaller organizations that do not frequently add systems for monitoring by OpsMgr, this approach is most likely overkill.

OpsMgr Agent Port Requirements

Microsoft documentation provides a comprehensive list of ports that are required for Operations Manager 2012, available at http://technet.microsoft.com/en-us/library/hh205990.aspx. However, the most commonly asked question focuses specifically around what ports are required to install OpsMgr agents and those that are necessary to support OpsMgr communication from the agents. Here are the ports required to install OpsMgr agents:

- Windows agent push installation, repair, or upgrade requires TCP 135, 139, 445, 5723, UDP 137, 138.

NOTE: AGENT PUSH AND FIREWALLS

The OpsMgr agent is pushed using RCP/DCOM from the management server or gateway server to the system to which the agent will be installed. For agent push installation to succeed, the Windows Firewall on the server and agent must be configured to have exceptions allowing the appropriate management or gateway server(s) to communicate with the system. If the Windows Firewall is disabled on the system, the firewall exceptions are not required. The default "Domain Profile" Windows Firewall will allow agent push without modification.

- UNIX/Linux agent push installation requires communication from the pool of management servers monitoring UNIX/Linux systems: TCP 22 (SSH), 1270 (inbound).

Once an Operations Manager agent is installed, the port requirements are decreased unless it is necessary to perform tasks on the agent, upgrade the agent, or repair the agent. The required ports to maintain communication are

- OpsMgr agent communications to management servers on TCP 5723.
- If ACS is active on the agent, the ACS forwarder port is required to the ACS collector; this is TCP 51909.
- IF AEM is active on a system, the AEM information port is required to the AEM server; this is TCP 51906.
- UNIX/Linux agent communication from the pool of management servers monitoring UNIX/Linux systems; port TCP 22 (SSH), 1270 (inbound).

Converting Agentless-Managed to Agent-Managed

To change an agentless system to agent-managed, you must first delete the agentless managed system and then deploy the agent to the system. To delete an agentless-managed system, follow these steps:

1. Navigate to **Device Management -> Agentless Managed**.
2. Right-click the agentless managed system and choose **Delete**. You then can deploy an agent to the system using one of the standard methods of deploying agents discussed previously in the "Discovering and Deploying Agents" section.

CAUTION: SITUATIONS WHERE YOU CANNOT DELETE AGENTLESS MANAGED SYSTEMS

The authors ran into a situation where it was not possible to delete an agentless managed system from the console in Operations Manager 2007, and the same workaround may still be required in OpsMgr 2012. The deletion failed and generated an error in the Operations Manager event log stating the Data Access Layer rejected the retry on a SQLError. This event occurred with each attempt to delete the record.

The error was caused because a domain controller was configured agentless managed (it could not have an agent installed because it was running Windows 2003 without Service Pack 1), and then an agent was manually installed on the machine. To resolve this issue, update the row in the BaseManagedEntity table in the OperationsManager database for the agentless system that would not delete, giving IsDeleted a value of 1. Then, delete rows from the DiscoverySourcetoTypedManagedEntity table for the system that would not delete, and approve the manual installation.

The system reappears as agentless in the Operations console, but now you can delete it and redeploy the agent. Additional information on this is available at the blog for this book (see the article "Unable to delete Agentless Systems") in the June 2007 archive at http://opsmgrunleashed.wordpress.com/2007/06/04/unable-to-delete-agentless-systems/.

Coexisting OpsMgr Agents with MOM 2005

This topic will be relevant for organizations that still have MOM 2005 either for monitoring or as part of Forefront Client Security. Due to the different agents used in MOM 2005 and OpsMgr 2012, interaction between these solutions should generally be minimal.

The MOM 2005 agent service is called "MOM," whereas the Operations Manager 2012 service is "System Center Management." The two agents run different programs under different service names, which separate them from each other when they are on the same machine. However, the agents perform similar tasks. Each agent collects information such as performance counters and events and runs scripts. There is potential for crosstalk between the two agents, where actions performed by the MOM 2005 agent create an event interpreted by OpsMgr 2012, and vice versa.

Although there are some potential challenges with coexisting MOM 2005 and OpsMgr 2007 agents, with the new OpsMgr 2012 agent these should be minor.

Multi-Homed Agents

Agents in Operations Manager 2012 can report to multiple management groups. These types of agents are *multi-homed* agents. Multi-homed agents typically are used for

- Providing horizontal support silos
- Transitioning from OpsMgr 2007 to OpsMgr 2012
- Supporting test or preproduction environments

For information on planning a multi-homed environment, see Chapter 6, "Upgrading to System Center 2012 Operations Manager."

OpsMgr 2012 supports a maximum of four management groups per Windows agent for multi-homing. Be aware there is an increase in the memory requirements of the agent when an OpsMgr 2012 agent reports to multiple management groups.

TIP: MULTI-HOMING FOR CROSS PLATFORM AGENTS

Although not officially supported, you can configure cross platform agents to communicate with multiple management groups. The process is discussed in a blog post at http://blogs.catapultsystems.com/cfuller/archive/2012/06/08/can-a-crossplat-unixlinux-agent-be-multihomed-in-opsmgr-scom-sysctr.aspx.

Deploy multi-homed agents using the Discovery Wizard for each management group, or you can manually run the OpsMgr Agent Setup Wizard on the managed computer.

TIP: USING THE CONTROL PANEL OPERATIONS MANAGER AGENT APPLET

MOMagent.msi only allows repair and removal of the Operations Manager agent. The new Operations Manager Agent control panel applet is the preferred method to configure multi-homed agents and even supports scripting APIs.

Managing Agents

A number of tasks are associated with managing either the agents or the systems you will monitor. The next sections describe validating agent functionality, Windows event log considerations, pending actions, changing agent configurations, and removing or renaming agents.

Validating Agent Functionality

Steps to validate the health of agents vary depending on whether they are Windows agents or UNIX/Linux agents. The following sections discuss recommended steps to validate that an agent is functional in OpsMgr 2012.

Validating Windows Agent Functionality

Here are recommended actions to check and verify the health of a Windows OpsMgr agent:

1. First, verify agent health in the Operations console at **Administration -> Agent Managed**. If the agent is grey, this indicates it is not communicating with OpsMgr. If the agent is not monitored, it has not reached a monitored state or it is in maintenance mode.
2. Verify agent health in the Monitoring pane under **Operations Manager -> Agent Details -> Agent Health State** view. This view provides health state information from both the agent and the Health Service Watcher.
3. Check the Computer view in the Monitoring pane to verify that the agent and operating system are monitored. Here are some reasons the OS may not be monitored:
   - The system has not been identified with an OS that can be monitored with an installed management pack.
   - The system is agentless monitored.
   - The system is experiencing issues deploying the OS-specific management pack.
4. Review the **Agent Details -> Active Alerts** view to review alerts that may be affecting the agent's health.
5. Access the Operations Manager log remotely or locally to identify critical or warning errors occurring on the system.

Validating UNIX/Linux Agent Functionality

Here are recommended steps for checking and verifying the health of a UNIX/Linux OpsMgr agent:

1. Verify agent health in the **Administration -> UNIX/Linux Computers** node. If the agent is grey, this indicates it is not communicating with OpsMgr. If the agent is not monitored, it has not reached a monitored state or is in maintenance mode.
2. Check the UNIX/Linux Computer view in the Monitoring pane to verify the agent and the operating system are monitored. Here are some reasons the OS may not be monitored:
   - The system has not been identified with an OS that can be monitored with an installed management pack.
   - The UNIX/Linux Default Action Account has not been defined for UNIX/Linux systems.
   - The system is experiencing issues deploying the OS-specific management pack.

Converting Manually Installed Agents and Applying Update Rollups

Manually installed agents (or agents deployed using any method other than pushing them from the Operations console) cannot be repaired, uninstalled, or upgraded during an update rollup deployment. To avoid these restrictions there is a work-around that changes the state of a manually installed agent to allow it to be remotely manageable.

Steps to perform this action include using a SQL query to update the agent's values for `IsManuallyInstalled` to `0`. Making this change causes this agent to be seen in OpsMgr as a remotely manageable agent. Once an agent is listed as remotely manageable, it can be repaired for you to apply the current update rollup and then flush the health cache on the agent. Here are some useful articles (written when Operations Manager updates were referred to as cumulative updates versus the current naming convention of update rollup):

- **How to upgrade clients manually installed in OpsMgr to CU5:** http://blogs.catapultsystems.com/cfuller/archive/2012/04/27/how-to-upgrade-clients-to-cu5-which-were-manually-installed-in-opsmgr-scom-sysctr.aspx
- **How to get your agents back to "remotely manageable" in OpsMgr 2007 R2:** http://blogs.technet.com/b/kevinholman/archive/2010/02/20/how-to-get-your-agents-back-to-remotely-manageable-in-opsmgr-2007-r2.aspx

Event Log Sizes and Configurations

One of Operations Manager's major data sources is the event logs of a monitored system. If the event log on a managed computer completely fills, event logging either stops or events are overwritten, depending on the configuration of the Windows event log. A full security log can even stop the computer from functioning! If the event log is not able to gather information, OpsMgr cannot provide information effectively about the status of the monitored system. Historically this was a larger issue than it is in most environments today, due to the increase in the default log file sizes for system and application logs. Here are the default sizes:

- **Windows 2000:** 512KB (half a megabyte)
- **Windows 2003:** 16,384KB (16 megabytes)
- **Windows 2008 and above:** 20,480KB (20 megabytes)

With the release of Windows 2003 and newer operating systems, the increased default log file size removes the requirement to adjust the log file sizes for most Operations Manager environments.

The exception to the default event log size rule may be applications that are extremely intensive on the application or system logs such as Microsoft Exchange (historically, this had a recommended 40MB application event log according to the Exchange Best Practices Analyzer information available at http://technet.microsoft.com/en-us/library/aa997362), or custom-built applications.

If there is a requirement to increase the log file sizes, you can do this directly through the event viewer application or by creating a group policy. For maximum recommended event log sizes per platform, see http://support.microsoft.com/kb/957662.

Pending Actions

By default, the global setting for Operations Manager 2012 does not accept manual agent installations. You can change this configuration by performing the steps discussed previously in the "Approval Process" section.

You can also configure this on a per-management server basis. Follow these steps:

1. In the Operations console, navigate to **Administration** -> **Device Management** -> **Management Servers**.
2. Right-click the management server name and select **Properties**.
3. Select the Security tab, which allows you to configure the management server to override global management server settings and allow the installation of manually installed agents.

In both configurations, a check box is available when you select the **Review new manual agent installations in pending management view** setting. This check box is labeled **Auto-approve new manually installed agents**. If it is not checked, manually installed agents are placed into a pending actions folder for approval.

Navigate to the Pending Management folder at **Administration** -> **Device Management** -> **Pending Management**. Agents failing installation are also added to this folder, where you can re-run the agent installation process.

Agent Settings

Configure agent settings in the Operations console, under **Administration** -> **Device Management** -> **Agent Managed**. Right-click an agent and choose **Properties**. The Heartbeat tab provides a method to override the global settings for the agent's heartbeat frequency (60 seconds by default).

There have been discussions in the OpsMgr newsgroups about problems when the agent heartbeat frequency is set to less than the default of 60 seconds. Additionally, if this value is increased it delays any heartbeat alerts that may occur. If your environment's requirements necessitate changing this setting, test it thoroughly prior to deploying the setting.

The Security tab has a check box labeled **Allow this agent to act as a proxy and discover managed objects on other computers**. More information on this setting is discussed in Chapter 7, "Configuring and Using System Center 2012 Operations Manager."

Agent Failover

Agent failover is often a misunderstood topic in Operations Manager. To dispel a myth here first—agent failover is built into OpsMgr even without using AD Integration. If a management server fails in OpsMgr, the agent is moved to another management server. The challenge is that within the user interface there is no way to specify a management server. To define how agents fail over you must either use AD Integration or PowerShell scripts.

AD Integration and Agent Failover

When using AD Integration in OpsMgr, define agent failover using the Agent Assignment and Failover Wizard (**Administration -> Device Management -> Management Servers**). Select a management server and right-click **Properties**. At the Auto Agent Assignment tab, click **Add** to specify agent assignment settings. The Agent Assignment and Failover Wizard provides a way to define inclusion and exclusion criteria for the management servers in the management group.

PowerShell Configuration for Agent Failover

PowerShell provides a quick way to determine the primary and failover management servers an agent is configured to use. The following commands find the primary management server for an agent:

```
Get-SCOMAgent | where { $_.ComputerName -eq "<ComputerName>"}
| Format-List PrimaryManagementServerName
```

You can also use PowerShell to configure primary and failover management servers in OpsMgr. The following PowerShell script assigns the agent to a variable, defines the primary and failover management servers as variables, and then uses the `Set-SCOMParentManagementServer` cmdlet to assign the primary and the failover server for the agent.

```
$SCOMAgent = Get-SCOMAgent -Name "<agentname>"
$PrimaryMgmtServer = Get-SCOMManagementServer -Name "<managementservername>"
$FailoverMgmtServer = Get-SCOMManagementServer -Name "<managementservername>"
Set-SCOMParentManagementServer -Agent $scomAgent -PrimaryServer $PrimaryMgmtServer
Set-SCOMParentManagementServer -Agent $scomAgent -FailoverServer $FailoverMgmtServer
```

For additional information about configuring agent failover in PowerShell or a script to bulk-set this configuration for a group of servers, see http://www.teknoglot.se/code/powershell/opsmgr-2012-agent-failover-simple-script-with-wildcards-opsmgr-powershell/.

These scripts are provided for your convenience with the online material accompanying this book; see Appendix E for information.

Agent Internals

An Operations Manager agent stores data that must be sent to the management server in a queue file. The queues prevent loss of data when a management server is not available (such as when rebooted to apply patches and other maintenance). If multiple management servers are installed in the management group, the agent fails over to another management server.

The agent queue is used as part of the normal communication between an agent and a management server, but only becomes important from a sizing perspective if the agent is unable to communicate with any available management servers.

These queues default to 15MB in size (15,360KB). For most systems, this should be sufficient to hold the OpsMgr data for several hours. There may be times, however, when the size of this queue may be insufficient, such as for servers that send a large amount of data to the management server (very intensive applications such as Active Directory or Exchange), or if there will be longer periods of time when the management server will be unavailable. You can change the size of this queue on a per-agent basis in the registry at `HKLM\SYSTEM\CurrentControlSet\Services\HealthService\Parameters\Management Groups\<Management Group Name>\MaximumQueueSizeKb`.

If the size of the queue is insufficient, alerts are raised by Operations Manager such as the alert generated by Send Queue % Used Threshold. To track history of queue utilization, use the Agent Performance view. The queue statistics were shown earlier in the top-right of Figure 8.3.

Since the release of Operations Manager 2007, this setting has not required frequent changes. While there are methods available to automate this process such as creating a task that uses PowerShell, the best approach has been to edit the registry setting directly on the system requiring the change.

Removing or Renaming Agents

The recommended method to remove agents involves using the Operations console. Perform the following steps:

1. Open the Operations console and navigate to **Administration** -> **Device Management** -> **Agent Managed**.
2. Right-click an agent and choose the **Uninstall** option. (Uninstall removes the agent from the system, versus using Delete, which only deletes the agent from the Operations console and does not actually remove the agent from the system.)
3. Selecting Uninstall launches the Uninstall Agents wizard, which prompts for credentials (the default is to use the management server action account) to uninstall the agent with.
4. Specify an account that has the permissions required (at least local Administrator) to remove the agent and then click **Uninstall**.

You can also manually uninstall the agent on the system and then delete the agent from the Operations console.

TIP: UNINSTALLING AGENTS USING POWERSHELL

The following is a PowerShell script that uninstalls agents based upon matching a naming convention. This example identifies a unique naming for the servers such as those named with "DC" indicating they are a domain controller (where odyssey.com is the name of the domain):

```
Get-SCOMAgent -DNSHostName *DC*.odyssey.com | Disable-SCOMAgentProxy
$credential = (Get-Credential)
Get-SCOMAgent -DNSHostName *DC*.odyssey.com | foreach{Uninstall-SCOMAgent -Agent
$_ -ActionAccount $credential}
```

This script is provided for your convenience with the online material accompanying this book; for more information see Appendix E. You could use this same approach to uninstall a single system by matching the system name in the first line of this PowerShell example.

Those systems monitored by Operations Manager that have their name changed must have the agent removed and reinstalled. If the renamed system does not have its agent uninstalled and reinstalled, the original system name still appears in the console, but no longer reports information back correctly to OpsMgr.

New User Interface on Windows Agents

The control panel on OpsMgr agents has a new applet called Operations Manager Agents, shown in Figure 8.18. This applet lets you add and remove management groups the agent reports to and make changes to existing management group configurations. It also provides a quick way to see the properties of the agent (computer name, product name, product version) and to change the agent action account.

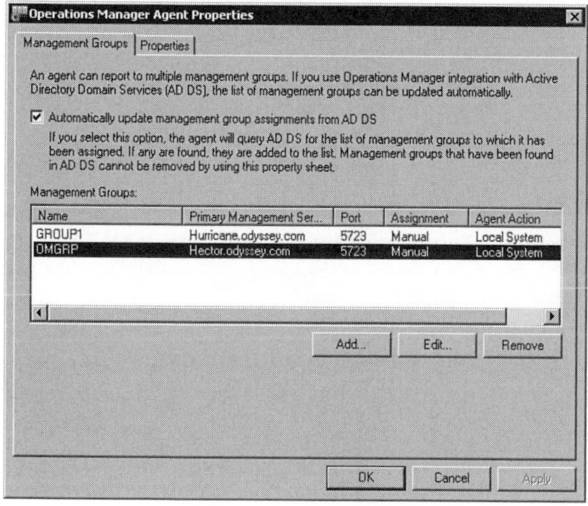

FIGURE 8.18 Operations Manager Agent control panel applet.

AEM Versus Agent-Monitored and Agentless Monitoring

An area often causing confusion is the relationship between agentless monitoring and Agentless Exception Monitoring (AEM). In short, there really isn't a relationship! The issue here is that they both are called "agentless" but do different things, which can make the terminology confusing. For simplicity, remember that agentless managed systems are systems monitored by a proxy agent that performs the actual monitoring rather than deploying an agent to the system you are monitoring, while Agentless Exception Monitoring captures aggregates and reports on application crashes (Dr. Watson errors) within your management group.

Troubleshooting Tips

There is a variety of common troubleshooting items to be aware of when debugging agents in Operations Manager 2012. Start with the "Agent Requirements" section if there are issues with agents. If those items are functional, the following sections discuss recommended troubleshooting steps for Windows and UNIX/Linux systems.

Troubleshooting Windows Agents

Here are recommended articles to review when troubleshooting deployment of Windows agents in OpsMgr:

- **Troubleshooting the Installation of the System Center Operations Manager Agent:** http://support.microsoft.com/kb/2566152
- **Console based Agent Deployment Troubleshooting table:** http://www.systemcentercentral.com/BlogDetails/tabid/143/IndexId/60047/Default.aspx

Troubleshooting UNIX/Linux Agents

Here are recommended articles to review when troubleshooting deployment of UNIX/Linux agents in OpsMgr:

- **Troubleshooting UNIX/Linux Agent Discovery in System Center 2012 - Operations Manager:** http://social.technet.microsoft.com/wiki/contents/articles/4966.aspx
- **Installing sudo on Solaris:** http://sysinfo.bascomp.org/solaris/installing-sudo-on-solaris/
- **Enable ssh root login in Solaris 10:** https://blogs.oracle.com/sunrise/entry/enable_ssh_root_login_in

Fast Track

Agents in Operations Manager 2012 work similarly to Operations Manager 2007. Here are key concepts to remember when using System Center 2012 Operations Manager compared to OpsMgr 2007:

- **Agents and pools:** Windows agents do *not* report to pools in Operations Manager 2012—they still report to Operations Manager servers. Cross platform agents do report to pools in Operations Manager 2012.
- **New Operations Manager user interface in the control panel:** See the "New User Interface on Windows Agents" section for information.
- **UNIX/Linux agent installation:** Significant changes have occurred to the discovery and installation process for UNIX/Linux agents in OpsMgr 2012. See the "Prerequisites for UNIX/Linux Agents" and "Discovery Process for UNIX/Linux Agents" sections for details.
- **PowerShell script changes:** The OpsMgr PowerShell scripts have been changed in OpsMgr 2012 to include SCOM in the command name (such as `Get-SCOMAgent`). Details on PowerShell changes in OpsMgr 2012 are available in Chapter 23, "PowerShell and Operations Manager."

Summary

This chapter discussed agents, and installing and configuring them. It also explained core concepts and provided troubleshooting tips. This chapter also discussed how to manage Operations Manager agents, including managing agent failover and agent internals. The next chapter covers complex configurations in System Center 2012 Operations Manager.

CHAPTER 9

Complex Configurations

IN THIS CHAPTER

System Center 2012 Operations Manager (OpsMgr) can provide solutions when running on a single server or can scale to multiple servers. While the software comes with a straightforward setup program, how you install OpsMgr depends on the specific needs of your organization. This chapter offers insight for deploying OpsMgr in environments that require redundancy, load balancing for the Web console, special resource pools, multi-homing, moving the root management server (RMS) emulator role to another management server, or redundant gateway servers.

Here are some things to keep in mind before installing your OpsMgr environment:

- Keep it Simple (KISS)—Don't make it complex unless necessary.
- Stay away from technical showcases.
- Build your OpsMgr environment based on facts and not assumptions.

When designing for OpsMgr, you should consider two areas: the functional area that identifies and describes the requirements, and the technical design that maps those requirements to a certain technical solution.

The functional design includes the Planning phase, which creates the set of requirements. Chapter 4, "Planning an Operations Manager Deployment," this phase. Here are some of the key areas considered during the Planning phase; the answers to which determine whether you require a complex environment:

- **Type of objects you will monitor:** In addition to Microsoft technologies, System Center 2012 Operations Manager can monitor UNIX, Linux, network devices, Java, .NET applications, virtual infrastructures, many types of hardware, and more. This means it is crucial to know when monitoring is required, versus just being nice to have.
- **Location of the objects to be monitored:** Establish whether the objects you want to monitor are in the same forest as your OpsMgr environment or an untrusted forest, where they are geographically, and the type of network connectivity between the objects and your planned management servers.

  Be aware that gateway servers are sometimes oversold and overdesigned. Here's an example: When you have trusted but geographically divided locations using slow WAN links, implementing gateway servers (traditionally used in untrusted environments) may theoretically improve the monitoring experience. However, the bandwidth savings can be overstated. Using gateways can add another challenge: Since many agents are communicating with the gateway server, it has a considerable queue that is dumped quicker (completely or partially) should there be a WAN outage.
- **How the status information is shown, and to whom:** Determine where the consoles need to reside, who will use them, who will use Web consoles, where those users reside, and whether there are existing SharePoint environments that OpsMgr could use to present its information.
- **Whether the OpsMgr environment is business critical, thus requiring redundancy for high availability:** If Operations Manager is business critical, downtime is not an option; you should consider this when designing your environment.

How you answer these questions determines your approach to building your OpsMgr environment and the level of complexity it will introduce.

Implementing High Availability

The OpsMgr 2007 RMS was a single point of failure. When the RMS was down or inaccessible, most features of the management group were unavailable. To maintain availability, you could install the RMS in a highly available cluster; however, the implementation itself was somewhat error prone, and its use introduced new challenges. For example, installing cumulative updates (CUs) had to be performed in a particular order or the clustered RMS would be rendered useless. The increased effort associated with managing a clustered RMS tended to have a negative impact on your total cost of ownership (TCO).

The architectural changes incorporated in System Center 2012 Operations Manager remove the RMS feature. With System Center 2012 Operations Manager, you can maintain availability and redundancy for your management servers by installing a minimum of two management servers in any management group, even in a lab environment. Management servers are automatically placed in the All Management Servers Resource Pool, providing overall availability of the management group. Resource pools are discussed in the "High Availability with Resource Pools" section.

NOTE: NEED FOR MULTIPLE MANAGEMENT SERVERS IN TEST ENVIRONMENTS

A test lab not running at least two management servers cannot demonstrate and test agent failover, RMS workflow failover (the first installed management server emulates the RMS for backward compatibility), or agentless workflow failover, used with UNIX/Linux/Network/URL/port monitoring.

There are many potential areas for implementing high availability in System Center 2012 Operations Manager:

- **SQL Server using Microsoft failover clustering:** Use this option when OpsMgr is business critical and the budget allows for it. When the failover cluster is configured correctly, failover occurs automatically without requiring user intervention.
- **Database high availability using log shipping:** Consider this approach when OpsMgr is business critical but budget constraints prevent database clustering. However, log shipping requires manual steps to continue operations in the event of a SQL Server failure. There are also cost-related aspects to consider, discussed in the "Using Log Shipping" section.
- **Data Access Service high availability using network load balancing (NLB):** When you open the Operations console, it connects to the System Center Data Access Service (also referred to as the SDK and DAS) of an individual management server. Should that server become unreachable, the console does not automatically fail over to another management server in that management group. Using NLB, you can create an NLB cluster of some or all management servers. When the Operations console connects to that NLB cluster and a connection to a node in the cluster fails, it is automatically redirected to another management server. The authors recommend you consider this configuration, as without the console you cannot administer nor use OpsMgr directly.
- **Web console high availability using NLB:** NLB should be used in environments where Web console availability is crucial. Using the Web console provides much of the functionality as the standard Operations console without installing additional software on a user's system. Incorporating NLB makes the Web console more useful as you can also make it highly available.
- **Audit Collection Services (ACS) high availability:** ACS (discussed in Chapter 10, "Security and Compliance") is largely unchanged in this version of OpsMgr. The approaches for creating a high available ACS infrastructure in OpsMgr 2007 remain viable.
- **Gateway server high availability:** Highly available gateway servers are appropriate when your organization requires it. For instance, when only six systems reside in a DMZ behind a gateway and those systems are critical, monitoring is also critical. In

this case, multiple gateways, configured in failover mode, are appropriate, as this removes the gateway as a single point of failure (SPOF).

- **Resource pools high availability:** Resource pools are new in this version of OpsMgr. As discussed in Chapter 2, "What's New in System Center 2012 Operations Center," resource pools are a collection of health services working together to manage instances assigned to the pool. Workflows targeted to the instances are loaded by the health service in the resource pool managing that instance. If one of the health services in the pool were to fail, the other health services in that pool pick up the work the failed member was running. Here are the three resource pools created by default in an OpsMgr management group:
    - All Management Servers Resource Pool
    - Notifications Resource Pool
    - AD Assignment Resource Pool

  You can also create your own resource pools or change the behavior of the All Management Servers Resource Pool.

Although it might be tempting to use all available options for high availability, the authors do not recommend this. Choose only those options that are required and appropriate for your corporate requirements, SLAs, and budget; remember the KISS principle introduced at the beginning of this chapter. Should something not fit the bill, something else has to give: You must either lower the requirements to meet the budget or increase your budget to meet the requirements. As this will be decided by management, involve them in an early stage and keep the communication channels open.

The next sections discuss the various high availability options.

Microsoft Failover Clustering for SQL Server

Microsoft failover clustering has come a long way since it was first introduced in Windows NT. In those days, it was quite challenging to install, configure, and maintain a Microsoft failover cluster. Adding SQL Server to the mix made clustering even more complicated.

With current versions of Windows Server Enterprise Edition and SQL Server, it has become straightforward to install, configure, and maintain a SQL failover cluster. However, failover clusters are still a special breed of server configuration and necessitate special requirements, maintenance, knowledge, and experience from the technicians managing these configurations.

TIP: EXPERIENCE IS THE BEST PREREQUISITE TO ESTABLISH SQL CLUSTERING

If you do not know the specifics or have real world experience with SQL clustering and it is a requirement for your OpsMgr environment, consider adding individuals to your team that have this experience. SQL DBAs are often good sources of knowledge and can help.

As this is an OpsMgr book, it does not discuss in detail how to install a Microsoft failover cluster for SQL Server. However, it will highlight some important steps in this process.

Failover Clustering: Things to Know

Before looking deeply into failover clustering, you should understand what it is and how it operates. You will also want to be familiar with its requirements.

A failover cluster consists of several computers called *nodes*, running Windows Server Enterprise or Datacenter Edition, and configured to be part of the failover cluster. Failover clusters use *resources* that are hardware or software components managed by the failover cluster, such as disks, an Internet Protocol (IP) address, or a network name. Each resource is owned by only one node in the failover cluster at any point in time. A *resource group* is a combination of resources that are managed as a unit, which can be moved between the nodes of the failover cluster. The *quorum* is a very important component of any failover cluster. It maintains the configuration data that is required for recovery of the failover cluster, including the details of the changes applied to the failover cluster. Finally, the process of moving resources from one node to another is *failover*, and the process to move the resources back is *failback*.

WINDOWS SERVER AND SQL EDITIONS: STANDARD OR ENTERPRISE?

A two-node failover cluster requires at a minimum the enterprise version of the Windows Server operating system and the standard edition of SQL Server.

Here are the criteria a Windows Server failover cluster must meet to be considered an officially supported solution by Microsoft Customer Support Services (CSS):

- All hardware and software components should meet the qualifications for the appropriate logo.

  For Windows Server 2008 R2, http://support.microsoft.com/kb/943984 has the official support policy for failover clusters.

- All tests in the Validation Wizard must be passed.

  This wizard is part of the failover cluster snap-in and must be run prior to installing a failover cluster.

HELPFUL RESOURCES FOR SUCCESSFULLY INSTALLING A FAILOVER CLUSTER

The Internet has many resources to assist with installing a failover cluster. You may want to look at http://technet.microsoft.com/en-us/library/cc732035(WS.10).aspx regarding information for Windows Server 2008 R2. YouTube also has some good videos about this topic, such as http://www.youtube.com/watch?v=TmyFEMXm52g.

Supported Cluster Configurations

Microsoft officially supports failover clustering for the OpsMgr operational database, data warehouse database, and audit database. Table 9.1 lists supported cluster configurations.

TABLE 9.1 Supported cluster configurations

Feature	Cluster	Notes
Operational database Data warehouse database ACS audit database	Single Active-Passive cluster. Active-Active is supported although not recommended by Microsoft.	No other OpsMgr features can be installed on the cluster nodes of the cluster.

Installing the OpsMgr Databases in a Clustered Configuration

After creating your SQL cluster, the OpsMgr database installation is essentially the same as installing a non-clustered database, as explained in Chapter 5, "Installing System Center 2012 Operations Manager." The only caveat is that installation must occur on the active node of the SQL cluster. To verify which node that is, follow these steps:

1. Start Failover Cluster Manager and connect to the cluster in question.
2. In the left part of the Failover Cluster Manager page, select the cluster and expand it.
3. Select **Services and Applications**. Right-click the SQL Server (instance name) and select **Properties**.
4. The node running the SQL Server instance is shown on the General tab of the Properties page. This is the active node. Make a note of this information, as you will use the information (shown in Figure 9.1 and Figure 9.2) while installing the operational database and the data warehouse database, respectively. (The audit database is discussed in the "ACS High Availability" section.)

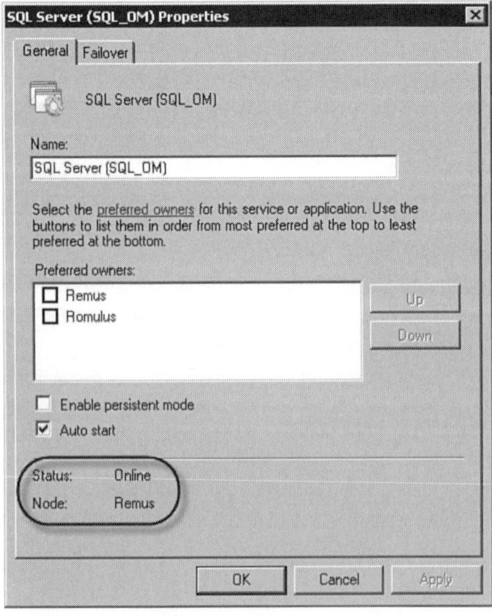

FIGURE 9.1 Verifying the active node for the operational database.

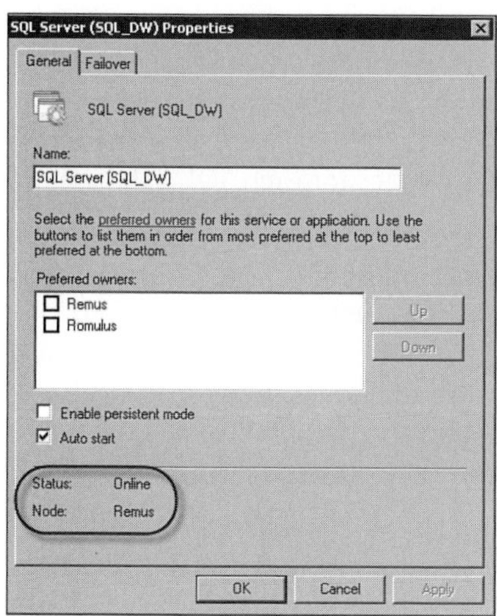

FIGURE 9.2 Verifying the active node for the data warehouse database.

SQL SERVER REPORTING SERVICES AND HIGH AVAILABLITY

Microsoft does not support making SQL Server Reporting Services (SSRS) highly available for OpsMgr, although there are some Internet resources discussing how this can be accomplished. The implementation is a load-balanced solution running two separate SSRS instances, each with its own ReportServer database, as you cannot share these databases between multiple SSRS instances.

The problem here is due to how OpsMgr reporting is implemented, which causes changes to reports to get out of sync between the different SSRS instances. When you open the Reports workspace in the Operations console, you connect to a single SSRS instance with its own SSRS database. A customized report is uploaded to only one SSRS instance, not the other load-balanced instance. Similarly, when you import management packs that contain reports, those reports are uploaded to only one SSRS instance initially. At some point, the reports are uploaded to the other instance, but it is impossible to say when that will occur. The result is these reports become out of sync.

Using Log Shipping

Log shipping is an automated backup of the database and transaction log files on the primary SQL Server, restoring these to a secondary SQL Server. The key concept here is that backup and restore of the transaction log files occurs automatically based on a specified interval. For information on SQL Server log shipping, see http://msdn.microsoft.com/en-us/library/ms187103.aspx.

While log shipping might appear to put less stress on your budget compared to using a SQL failover cluster, here are some considerations:

- **Additional disk space requirements:** By default, the OpsMgr databases are installed using the simple recovery model. Log shipping only functions when replay of the log can take place, which does not occur with the simple recovery model. This means you must change to a full recovery model for those databases, resulting in larger transaction log files, which requires more disk space for each SQL database and SQL Server system.
- **Robust secondary SQL Server systems:** Typically, the system(s) used for your OpsMgr database servers are well sized, as they run the databases crucial to your OpsMgr environment. However, each secondary SQL Server, where the transaction log files replay, requires at least the same specifications. Should the primary SQL Server go offline, the secondary SQL Server will be hosting the OpsMgr databases. Should that server not be up to the job—I/O wise—you will have a degraded or non-functional OpsMgr environment.

  Secondary SQL Server systems often run other production databases as well. This means that systems will require serious hardware to run *all* those databases when the primary database server for OpsMgr goes offline.
- **Specific collation settings for OpsMgr:** OpsMgr has specific requirements for SQL collation settings. This can be a challenge for non-English speaking countries since those countries use other collation settings by default. This often results in dedicated SQL instances for OpsMgr with special collation settings, and a secondary SQL Server must use the same collation settings as well. If this is not the case and the secondary SQL Server takes over, some management packs will not be able to upload data into your data warehouse!
- **Failover is not automatic:** With SQL clustering, failover to another node occurs automatically. This differs with log shipping, where the management servers and the OpsMgr databases themselves require manual intervention before the secondary SQL Server can be used, meaning there may be some downtime in monitoring and for end users wanting to access OpsMgr for monitoring or reporting. When the primary SQL Server again becomes available, these steps are again required before OpsMgr can use that system. In addition, reconfiguring the management servers to use another database server and databases when there is a failover is a manual process, potentially introducing mistakes that could result in a non-functional OpsMgr environment.

Enabling Log Shipping

While log shipping is not difficult to set up, realize it is only appropriate when the related logs contain information of every single transaction made to the database. This is controlled by the database recovery model setting.

The operational and data warehouse (OperationsManager and OperationsManagerDW) databases are installed using the simple recovery model. A simple recovery model results in an empty transaction log since transactions are truncated from the log once they are written to the database. Implementing log shipping requires changing to the full recovery model, meaning that all transactions are fully logged and retained until backed up. (There is also a bulk-logged recovery model. For differences between the three recovery models for SQL Server, see http://msdn.microsoft.com/en-us/library/ms189275.aspx.)

To change the recovery model of the OpsMgr databases, follow these steps:

1. Open SQL Server Management Studio and connect to the SQL Server instance hosting the OpsMgr databases, the OperationsManager database in this case.
2. In the left part of SQL Management Studio (the Object Explorer), expand the **Databases** node.
3. Select the OperationsManager database, right-click, and select **Properties**.
4. On the Database Properties page, select Options to display the options available for this database.
5. Change the **Recovery model** setting to **Full** (shown in Figure 9.3 for SQL Server 2008 R2) and click **OK** to save your changes. Repeat these steps for the OperationsManagerDW database.

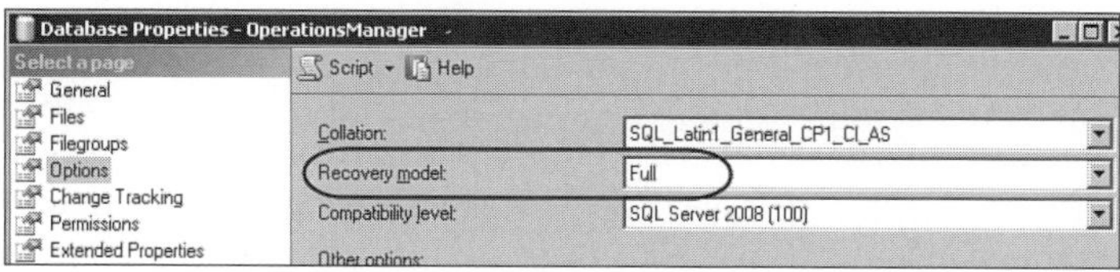

FIGURE 9.3 Changing the Recovery model to Full.

Configuring Log Shipping

With the recovery model reconfigured, it is time to configure log shipping.

TIP: ONLINE RESOURCES FOR LOG SHIPPING

For a detailed guide about configuring log shipping for OpsMgr, see http://social.technet.microsoft.com/wiki/contents/articles/11372.configure-sql-server-log-shipping-guide-for-the-system-center-operations-manager-2007-r22012-operational-database.aspx. As this is an OpsMgr book, it does not discuss configuring log shipping in detail. However, the authors will highlight some potential pitfalls.

Here are some things to consider when configuring log shipping:

- **SQL Server Agent service:** The SQL Server Agent service must run under a domain account and be a member of the SQLServerSQLAgentUser$*<ComputerName>*$*<Instance>* local group.
- **Firewall considerations:** The firewall must allow access to the primary and secondary SQL servers. Open the ports related to the SQL Server instance and those for file and printer sharing.

- **Test for disaster:** Test failover to the secondary SQL Server and document it thoroughly. Otherwise, should a real disaster occur and you are doing this the first time, there could be too much pressure and not enough experience.
- **Broker service:** The Broker service should be enabled, as well as CLR (Common Language Runtime) integration. The article at http://msdn.microsoft.com/en-us/library/ms131048.aspx discusses enabling CLR Integration.
- **Management server configuration:** Each OpsMgr management server requires modifications as described in the wiki mentioned earlier in this section for configuring log shipping for OpsMgr. Be sure you are familiar with these changes, and know where to locate the registry keys and file requiring those modifications.
- **Database modifications:** The OperationsManager database requires a modification as well, as described in the wiki mentioned earlier in this section for configuring log shipping for OpsMgr. Ensure you know the table and which record.

Network Load Balancing the Data Access Service

The Operations console is crucial for any management group; if it is not available, you cannot administer the OpsMgr environment or determine the status of the management group. The console requires the System Center Data Access Service (DAS). This was a SPOF in OpsMgr 2007, as this service ran only on the RMS. With System Center 2012 Operations Manager the service runs on any OpsMgr management server of a given management group.

However, even when one opens the Operations console in OpsMgr 2012, it connects to a particular management server from which it uses the Data Access Service. Should that management server become unreachable, the console does not automatically fail over to another management server—it simply stops functioning by freezing and throwing an error about the Data Access Service being unavailable.

You can use Network Load Balancing to make the System Center Data Access Service highly available. Using NLB lets the Operations console become robust: Should a management server become unavailable, the Operations console—connected to that particular management server—is redirected automatically to another management server, providing a highly available console.

Here are the high-level steps to set up NLB for the DAS:

1. Configure static IP addresses for all nodes participating in the NLB cluster.
2. Enable NLB for each management server participating in the NLB cluster.
3. Create the NLB cluster with its Virtual IP (VIP) address.
4. Add one or more additional hosts—running the System Center Data Access Service (this could be any OpsMgr management server)—to the NLB cluster.
5. Create a host record in DNS referring to the VIP address.

The next time the Operations console runs, it connects to the NLB cluster using the DNS name specified in step 5 and connects to a node of the NLB cluster. If that node becomes unreachable, the console is redirected automatically to another node in that NLB cluster.

TIP: RESOURCES FOR NETWORK LOAD BALANCING THE DATA ACCESS SERVICE

Microsoft TechNet is an excellent resource for information about network load balancing the DAS. You can begin with http://technet.microsoft.com/en-us/library/hh316108.aspx, which contains references to other TechNet articles about NLB. These are must-reads for anyone interested in using network load balancing for the System Center Data Access Service.

Network Load Balancing the Web Console

As the Web console is nothing but a web service, it is a perfect candidate for NLB, which would make it highly available as well.

The procedure required to network load balance the Web console is similar to that used for the System Center Data Access Service. Here are the high-level steps:

1. Configure static IP addresses for all nodes participating in the NLB cluster.
2. Enable NLB for each management server participating in the NLB cluster.
3. Create the NLB cluster with its VIP address.
4. Add one or more additional hosts—running the OpsMgr Web console—to the NLB cluster.
5. Create a host record in DNS referring to the VIP address.

ACS High Availability

There is a one to one relationship between the ACS collector and ACS database, also referred to as an *ACS pair*. This configuration makes the ACS collector a single point of failure in ACS design and setup. However, there are multiple ways to work around this. Neil Harrison of Microsoft has written a series of blog postings about ACS high availability; see http://blogs.technet.com/b/neharris/archive/2011/03/22/acs-forwarders-and-high-availability-part-1.aspx.

9

ACSCONFIG.XML: THE KEY TO COLLECTING DATA FROM ACS FORWARDERS

Central to high availability considerations is the ACSConfig.xml file. This file is present on all ACS collectors and crucial to the functionality of the ACS collector, as it contains configuration information for the collector. ACSConfig.xml is located in the %*SystemRoot*%\system32\security\AdtServer folder of each ACS collector. It contains a list of all forwarders ever known to the collector, their last contact time, and the sequence number of the last event each forwarder sent to the collector; the collector uses this information to know which events have been collected. This is important, as it prevents duplication of data in the ACS database. ACSConfig.xml is updated every 5 minutes by the AdtServer service.

Another approach is to run multiple ACS pairs and configure the ACS forwarders to use a primary and a secondary ACS collector, as shown in Figure 9.4. Notice the primary ACS collector is the last one in the override set for the ACS forwarders. Although this type of setup offers automatic failover of the ACS forwarders to the secondary ACS collector, there are some serious downsides:

- **Data duplication:** This configuration has multiple ACS collectors active at any given time, each with its own ACSConfig.xml file. When one ACS collector becomes unavailable, it automatically fails over to the secondary collector, which you can configure as shown in Figure 9.4. However, data duplication would occur since **ACSConfig.xml** on the secondary ACS collector has no previous entries for the forwarders. This means that all events are collected again by the secondary collector, and written to the audit database associated with that collector.

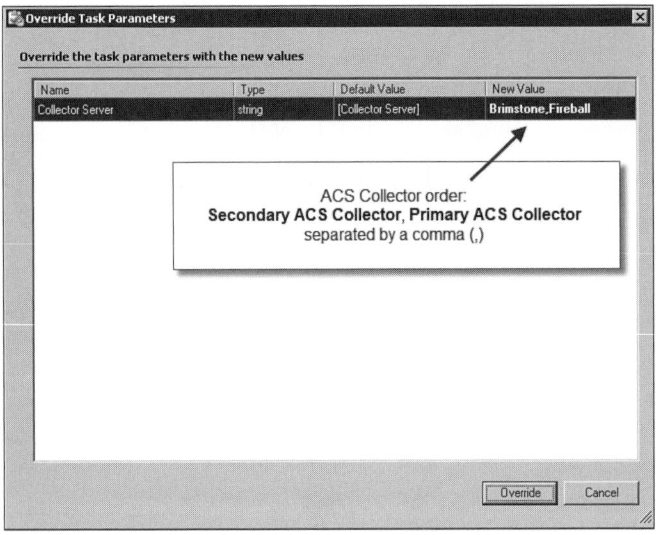

FIGURE 9.4 Assigning multiple ACS collectors to the ACS forwarders.

- **Running ACS reports across multiple databases:** As ACS data is spread among multiple audit databases, reports must query these multiple databases. This can be solved by using a third-party tool that archives the databases and uses the archive for reports. However, additional tools cost money, and add additional (complex) technologies to your ACS deployment.

Here's a third approach: Relatively unknown is that beginning with OpsMgr 2007 Service Pack (SP) 1; you can have two ACS collectors using the same audit database, as long as only one of those collectors is active at any given time.

In this case, you have two ACS collectors pointing to the same database with one collector active and the other passive at any given time. The ACS forwarders are also configured with a primary and secondary collector, as displayed in Figure 9.4.

A mechanism is in place (such as a scheduled task) that copies ACSConfig.xml every 5 minutes from the active to the passive collector. This prevents excessive data duplication in the database. While some data might be duplicated, it will be far less compared to all security events in setups with multiple ACS pairs.

The total amount of duplicated data depends on the time difference between the time when the primary ACS collector became unavailable and the last time the file ACSConfig.xml was updated by the AdtServer service of that collector.

Here are some downsides to consider with this type of setup:

- **Data duplication:** There is still some data duplication with this approach.
- **No automatic failover:** There is no automated failover, so this must be performed manually. However, you can script this and automate it using System Center 2012 Orchestrator.

To implement this type of high availability for ACS, perform the following steps:

1. Install the first ACS collector, which will become the primary collector. Make sure you use SQL Authentication and not Windows Authentication, as Windows Authentication will not work when you bring the secondary collector online.
2. When the primary ACS collector is installed and operational, stop the Operations Manager Audit Collection Service on that server.
3. Install the secondary ACS collector. Don't forget to use SQL Authentication here as well.
4. Stop the Operations Manager Audit Collection Service on the secondary ACS collector and configure it to start manually. Start this service on the primary ACS collector.
5. Create a scheduled task or an Orchestrator policy that replicates the file ACSConfig.xml every 5 minutes from the active ACS collector to the passive collector. This will minimize the amount of duplicated data in the database.
6. Enable the ACS forwarders by using the Enable Audit Collection task in the Operations console. This task requires an override configured specifying the ACS collector used by the forwarder. Here you will enter a comma-separated list of collector servers, previously displayed in Figure 9.4. Notice that the secondary server appears first in the list and the primary server appears last.

Failing Over

When the primary ACS collector becomes unavailable, start the Operations Manager Audit Collection Service on the secondary ACS collector. This starts the AdtServer service, which reads the ACSConfig.xml file and collects the security events delivered by the ACS forwarders.

You must also stop whatever process copies the ACSConfig.xml file from the "old" primary ACS collector to the new ACS collector that is now the new primary. Otherwise, the old information contained in that file will create all sorts of havoc in your ACS environment. You will also need to start the process of copying the ACSConfig.xml file from the new primary ACS collector to the new passive collector.

Failing Back

When the server hosting the primary ACS collector role is operational again, you can restore its functionality as well. The Operations Manager Audit Collection Service should not be running initially.

Copy ACSConfig.xml from the secondary ACS collector to the primary collector. Stop the Operations Manager Audit Collection Service on the secondary collector and start it on the primary collector. The ACS forwarders will now failover automatically to the primary collector. Also, remember to adjust the process that copies the ACSConfig.xml file such that the file is always copied from the active ACS collector to the passive collector.

High Availability with Resource Pools

Resource pools, introduced in Chapter 2, can also be used as a high availability solution for some OpsMgr components.

WHAT RESOURCE POOLS DO

Resource pools are a collection of health services that work together to manage instances assigned to the pool. The workflows targeted to the instances are loaded by the health service in the resource pool managing that instance. Should one of the health services in the resource pool fail, the other health services in the pool will pick up the work the failed member was running.

Modifying the Default Resource Pools Membership Behavior

As mentioned in the "High Availability" section, three resource pools are present in any OpsMgr management group by default. These resource pools are populated automatically (see the Membership column in Figure 9.5).

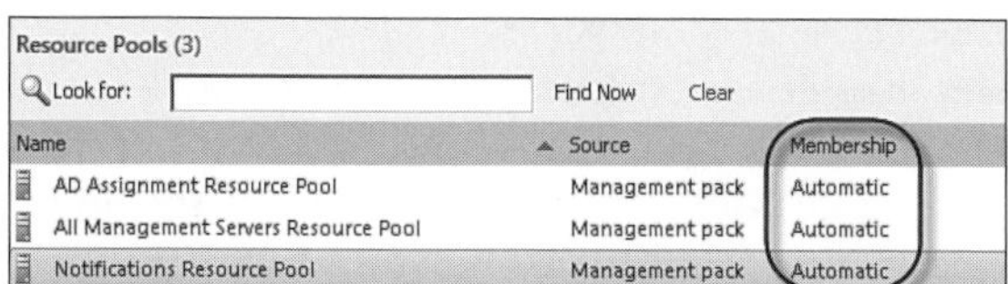

FIGURE 9.5 Automatic membership for the default resource pools.

There may be conditions where you would not want a pool to populate automatically, particularly in complex or large-scale deployments. Say you are running a management group containing many management servers. In this type of environment, you may want specific functionality for different management servers. This means that only a certain set of management servers should participate in each default resource pool. You can achieve this using a simple PowerShell command that stops the pool from populating automatically.

CAUTION: CHANGING RESOURCE POOL CONFIGURATION DISABLES ADDING MANAGEMENT SERVERS TO IT AUTOMATICALLY

Once you run the `Get-SCOMResourcePool` and `Set-SCOMResourcePool` cmdlets to change membership for the Notifications Resource Pool to Manual, new management servers are no longer added automatically to that pool. This means you must manually add any new management servers requiring membership to that particular resource pool.

The Notifications and AD Assignment resource pools can be set to manual membership through the Operations console. When you select one of these resource pools in the console, the Action panes show the option **Manual Membership**. When selected, you are asked whether you want to change the resource pool membership method from automatic to manual. Selecting **Yes** causes that resource pool to be populated manually. To reset it to automatic, you must use PowerShell.

In large-scale environments, you may want to change the resource pool membership method to manual. This gives you granular control over the resource pools, enabling you to use OpsMgr management servers for particular tasks such as monitoring a certain set of Windows servers located in certain geographical locations.

You could specify a set of dedicated OpsMgr management servers for each geographic location. Other scenarios allow for using certain management servers to monitor a large number of URLs, UNIX/Linux systems, or network devices. This lets you ensure these management servers are not used for RMS activities. The downside of this approach is additional administration is required to maintain the resource pools.

The following example changes the membership for the Notifications Resource Pool from Automatic to Manual:

1. On a management server, open the Operations Manager Shell and run this command:

```
Get-SCOMResourcePool -Name "Notifications Resource Pool" |
Set-SCOMResourcePool -EnableAutomaticMembership $FALSE
```

2. When looking in the console for the resource pools, you will see the membership for the Notifications Resource Pool now displays as Manual, as shown in Figure 9.6.

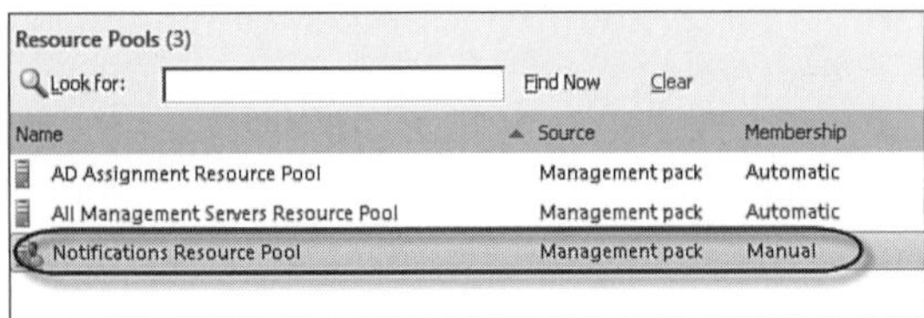

FIGURE 9.6 Notifications Resource Pool membership is changed to Manual.

3. Edit the properties of this resource pool, allowing you to add or remove management servers. This is displayed in Figure 9.7.

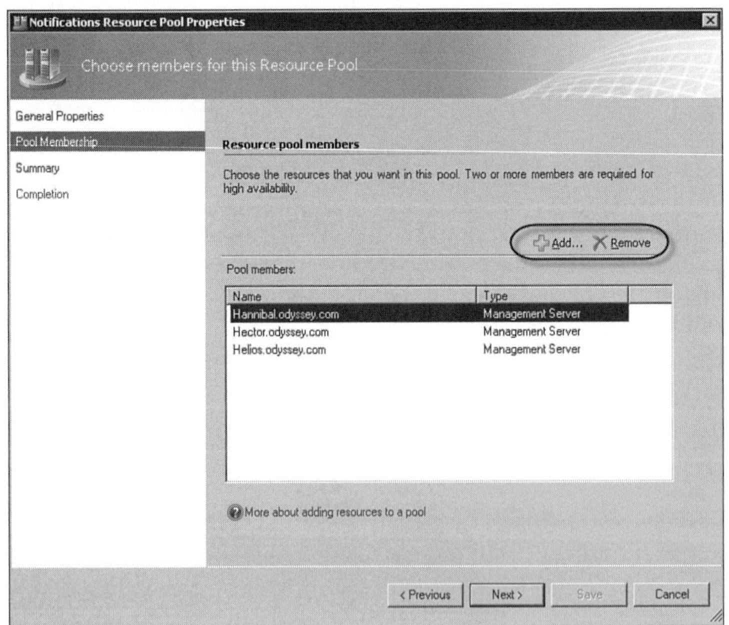

FIGURE 9.7 Editing the properties of the Notifications Resource Pool.

The authors recommend using this approach for the Notifications Resource Pool when you have attached an SMS modem to a particular management server. In this scenario, you would remove all management servers except the one to which the SMS modem is attached. Even better is to have two SMS modems, each connected to another management server, with both residing in the Notifications Resource Pool.

This is also useful when you allow Exchange relay for only specific servers or IP addresses, so not all management servers might have access to send email notifications. A minimum of two servers in this pool allows for high availability of the notifications process as well.

About Gateway Server Resource Pools and Redundancy

If you are familiar with OpsMgr 2007 gateway servers, you know this feature can be a single point of failure:

- When the gateway server becomes unavailable, the objects reporting to it cannot be monitored until the gateway server is available again.
- When the management server to which the gateway server reports to becomes unavailable, objects reporting to this gateway server are not monitored until this management server becomes available.

Anders Bengtsson of Microsoft has an excellent post on how to eliminate both SPOFs at http://contoso.se/blog/?p=831. The approach uses PowerShell cmdlets.

With resource pools available in OpsMgr 2012, you might be considering them to eliminate SPOFs for gateway servers. However, while you can add gateway servers to resource pools, it does not make them highly available. Here's why:

- When a gateway server belonging to a resource pool of gateway servers becomes unavailable, its workload is taken over by another gateway server participating in that pool. However, the agents reporting to the failed gateway server will not know to communicate with the other gateway server; you must configure agent failover using PowerShell cmdlets.
- The Gateway Server Approval Tool accepts only a gateway server name, not a resource pool name.
- Resource pools don't have "virtual health services." Although a job can be deployed to a resource pool, it is executed by a member of the pool. There is no shared health service run by all the management servers in the pool.

The behavior of gateway servers in redundancy scenarios is unchanged from OpsMgr 2007. What has changed is that gateway servers could participate in a resource pool. However, this type of approach is only valid in specific scenarios since gateway servers do not scale to the extent of management servers when used in a resource pool.

Typically, resource pool activities are network, UNIX/Linux, and URL monitoring. Gateway servers do not have the power to perform these actions on the same scale as pooled management servers. However, pooled gateway servers can come into play where there is a set of devices needing to be agentless monitored, but these devices reside in a DMZ such as a firewalled location and are not accessible from your management servers on the regular network. A resource pool of multiple gateway servers in the firewalled location will work quite well here, with the agentless workflows assigned to the resource pool containing those very same gateway servers.

As gateway resource pools do not address failures, you must use PowerShell to eliminate this SPOF. For information about configuring gateway server failover between management servers, see http://technet.microsoft.com/en-us/library/hh456445.aspx. Anders Bengtsson provides a blog posting at http://contoso.se/blog/?p=831 that also shows how to configure the agent for automatic failover.

When complete, your configuration should look similar to Figure 9.8.

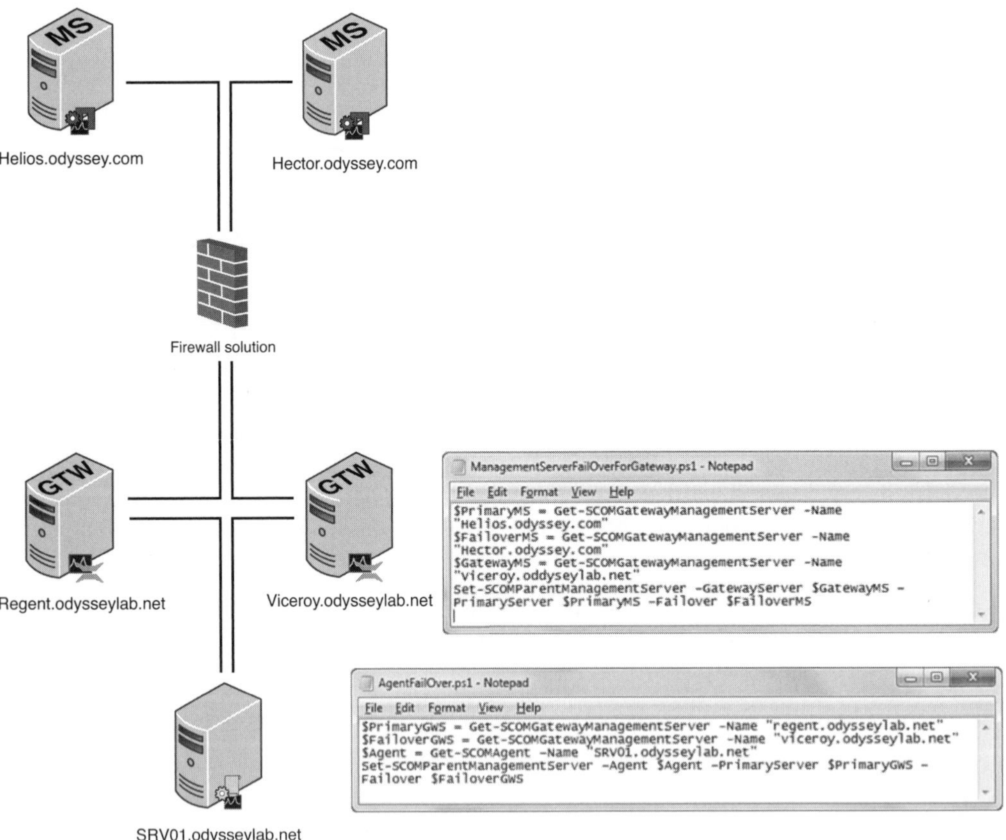

FIGURE 9.8 Robust gateway server configuration and related PowerShell scripts.

Here are the two PowerShell scripts used in Figure 9.8. For your convenience, these scripts are available with the online content for this book; see Appendix E, "Available Online," for details.

Listing 9.1 contains the PowerShell script that enables agent failover to another gateway server. Replace the NetBIOS names with NetBIOS names of your gateway servers and management server.

LISTING 9.1 AgentFailOver.ps1 PowerShell script

```
$PrimaryGWS = Get-SCOMGatewayManagementServer -Name "regent.odysseylab.net"
$FailoverGWS = Get-SCOMGatewayManagementServer -Name "viceroy.odysseylab.net"
$Agent = Get-SCOMAgent -Name "SRV01.odysseylab.net"
Set-SCOMParentManagementServer -Agent $Agent -PrimaryServer $PrimaryGWS -Failover
$FailoverGWS
```

Listing 9.2 contains the PowerShell script that enables the gateway servers to fail over to another management server. Replace the fully qualified domain names (FQDNs) with FQDNs of your gateway server and management servers.

LISTING 9.2 ManagementServerFailOverForGateway.ps1 PowerShell script

```
$PrimaryMS = Get-SCOMGatewayManagementServer -Name "Helios.odyssey.com"
$FailoverMS = Get-SCOMGatewayManagementServer -Name "Hector.odyssey.com"
$GatewayMS = Get-SCOMGatewayManagementServer -Name "Viceroy.oddyseylab.net"
Set-SCOMParentManagementServer -GatewayServer $GatewayMS -PrimaryServer $PrimaryMS
-Failover $FailoverMS
```

Creating Resource Pools

While OpsMgr 2012 lets you create your own resource pools, here are some considerations:

- Creating dedicated resource pools for UNIX/Linux, URL, and network monitoring allows you to scale out easily when having resource issues without affecting the other monitoring workflows.
- Only create a new resource pool when there is a requirement for it and an additional pool makes sense.
- Populate your new/custom resource pools wisely. For example, installing two additional management servers and placing them into three custom resource pools is counterproductive; those management servers would have to run the workloads of all three resource pools combined. A good rule of thumb is having at least one dedicated management server allocated to each resource pool you create.

If running an OpsMgr environment with more than two management servers and you want to divide the different monitoring workloads, you could create dedicated resource pools for monitoring things such as network devices or UNIX/Linux systems.

SINGLE MEMBERED RESOURCE POOLS

Although it might sound strange, you can create resource pools with only one member. While there won't be any failover in this type of resource pool, there are cases where a resource pool might be required:

- When you want to monitor a set of network devices residing behind a single gateway server, a resource pool with that single gateway server is the only valid approach—as any given monitored network device must be covered by a resource pool. In this case, you would create a single member resource pool and assign the network devices to it.
- Another scenario might be a resource pool with one management server only, allowing you to scale out in the future by adding more management servers to that pool as needed. This makes scaling out very easy.

Managing the RMS Emulator Role

OpsMgr 2012 removes the RMS feature. The RMS emulator (RMSE) role is included for backward compatibility to legacy management packs that target the Root Management Server class instance (`Microsoft.SystemCenter.RootManagementServer`). A recent management pack requiring this role is the Exchange 2010 MP, which uses the RMSE with its correlation engine.

OpsMgr 2007 assigned the RMS role to the first installed management server. With OpsMgr 2012, the RMSE role is assigned to the first management server installed in a new management group. Using a small set of PowerShell cmdlets, you can move the RMSE role to another management server, remove it, and determine which management server hosts it at any given moment. Keep in mind that when that role is removed, it can be added again using the same PowerShell cmdlet used to move that role to another management server. These actions are described in the next sections.

Confirming the RMS Emulator Role

Using the PowerShell cmdlet `Get-SCOMRMSEmulator`, you can check which management server hosts the RMSE. Figure 9.9 shows Helios is the RMSE for Odyssey.

You can also check which management server hosts the RMSE role by using the Operations console. Navigate to **Administration -> Device Management -> Management Servers**. The middle pane shows all management servers, with the RMS Emulator column showing which management server hosts the RMSE role. This is displayed in Figure 9.10.

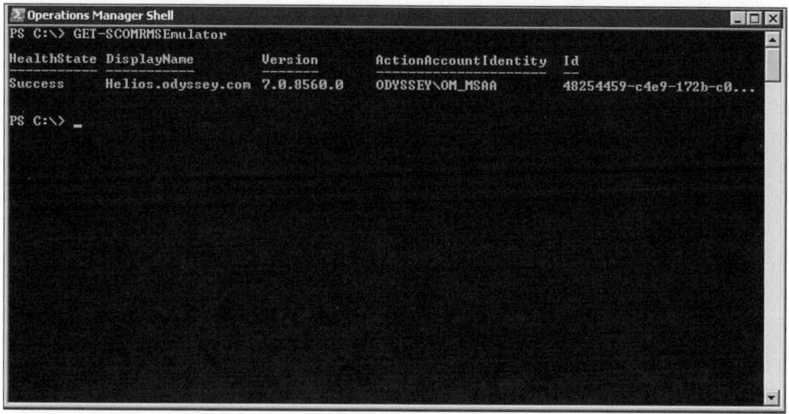

FIGURE 9.9 Confirming the RMS emulator role.

Management Servers (6)

Look for: Find Now Clear

Health State	Name	Domain	Client Monitoring Mode	Version	RMS Emulator
Warning	Helios	ODYSSEY	Disabled	7.0.8560.0	Yes
Healthy	Hannibal	ODYSSEY	Disabled	7.0.8560.0	No
Healthy	viceroy	odysseylab	Disabled	7.0.8560.0	No
Healthy	regent	odysseylab	Disabled	7.0.8560.0	No
Healthy	Hector	ODYSSEY	Disabled	7.0.8560.0	No
Healthy	lunohost1	LUNO	Disabled	7.0.8560.0	No

FIGURE 9.10 Checking where the RMSE role resides.

Moving the RMS Emulator Role

When using the PowerShell cmdlet `Set-SCOMRMSEmulator` in conjunction with `Get-SCOMRMSEmulator`, you can move the RMS emulator role to another management server.

Here is an example of the syntax:

```
Get-SCOMManagementServer -Name "Hector.odyssey.com" | Set-SCOMRMSEmulator
```

TIP: ALWAYS CHECK AND USE FQDNS WHEN MOVING RMSE ROLE

When the RMSE role is moved using the `Get-SCOMRMSEmulator` and `Set-SCOMRMSEmulator` PowerShell cmdlets, there is no confirmation of success. To confirm the action was successful, run the `Get-SCOMRMSEmulator` cmdlet again or check the Operations console as described in the "Confirming the RMS Emulator Role" section. Also, know that you must use FQDNs for the management server names when running these PowerShell cmdlets, as otherwise the cmdlets might not work.

Let's check the Operations console to confirm the move was successful. This is displayed in Figure 9.11.

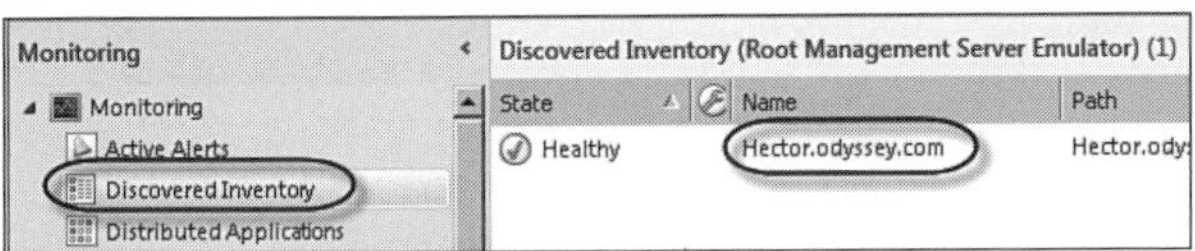

FIGURE 9.11 Checking the results of the move.

Removing the RMS Emulator Role

If you determine you no longer need the RMS emulator role, you can remove that role using the `Remove-SCOMRMSEmulator` PowerShell cmdlet. As Figure 9.12 shows, you must confirm the deletion of that role. This prevents running this PowerShell cmdlet accidentally. When you confirm the deletion, the RMS emulator role is removed.

```
Operations Manager Shell
PS C:\> Remove-SCOMRMSEmulator

Are you sure you want to perform this action?
Warning! By removing the RMS Emulator role, any workflow that targets the Root
Management Server will not load.
[Y] Yes  [A] Yes to All  [N] No  [L] No to All  [S] Suspend  [?] Help
(default is "Y"):_
```

FIGURE 9.12 Removing the RMS emulator role.

After removing the role, you can run `Get-SCOMRMSEmulator` to confirm the role is removed.

TIP: RESTORING THE RMSE ROLE AFTER IT IS REMOVED

Should you remove the RMSE role and need to restore it, you can use the same PowerShell cmdlet that moves the role to another management server to assign the role to a management server. You will want to verify afterwards that the cmdlet was successful by running `Get-SCOMRMSEmulator`.

The RMS emulator role is easily confirmed, moved, and removed. Should it turn out the removal was premature, you can easily add the role again to a management server.

WAN Links and Gateways

While gateway servers were initially used for monitoring untrusted environments, you can also use them when you have WAN links with slow or busy connections.

An OpsMgr gateway server is basically a super OpsMgr agent. Similar to any other OpsMgr agent, it compresses traffic sent to its management server. However, where a single OpsMgr agent only sends out its own traffic, a gateway server will send the information of all OpsMgr agents that report to it. This can give you increased compression rates of 4:1 or greater.

The authors strongly recommend considering a gateway server when you have to monitor a set of servers at a remote location over a slow/limited WAN link.

TIP: CERTIFICATES AND GATEWAY SERVERS

An OpsMgr gateway server requires certificates only when the OpsMgr agents residing behind that server and reporting to it reside in a non-trusted environment for the OpsMgr management group. In situations where these agents reside in the same trusted environment, no certificates are needed, as Kerberos will continue to be used.

The installation scenario for a gateway server in a trusted domain is similar to installing any other gateway server, other than not installing the certificates. Figure 9.13 shows a gateway server in a slow WAN in a trusted domain.

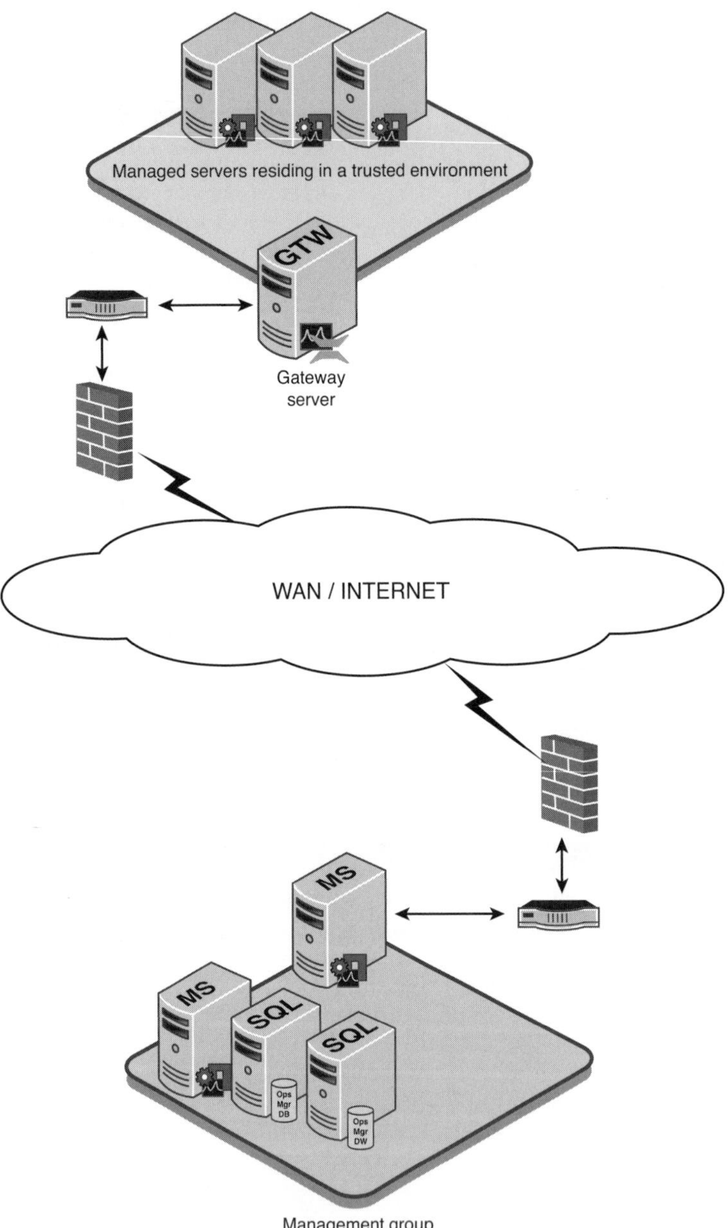

FIGURE 9.13 Gateway server deployed in slow WAN link scenario.

Multi-Homing Agents

An OpsMgr agent can report to a maximum of four different management groups in a supported configuration. Even though it might seem unusual to have a single OpsMgr agent report to more than one management group, here are several scenarios where it might be useful:

- **Migrating from OpsMgr 2007 R2 to OpsMgr 2012:** In this scenario, all managed servers run the latest OpsMgr agent. The agent reports to the OpsMgr 2007 management group and the OpsMgr 2012 management group as well, which enables the organization to migrate in a controlled manner to OpsMgr 2012 without having to upgrade the existing OpsMgr 2007 R2 management group.
- **Separating monitoring between different support groups:** Multi-homing enables you to distribute monitoring across multiple support teams, each with its own set of responsibilities and monitoring requirements. One management group can be solely used for security auditing by using ACS while another OpsMgr management group monitors the IT environment.
- **Supporting preproduction and production OpsMgr management groups:** The authors recommend a preproduction OpsMgr management group for testing purposes; say when your company develops management packs. While you would first thoroughly test management packs in an isolated lab environment, once they are ready for production, it is best not to immediately import it to your production OpsMgr management group. Instead, import these management packs into a preproduction OpsMgr management group that uses OpsMgr agents running on production systems. This lets you evaluate the impact of the management pack on the OpsMgr management group in an isolated environment.

HOW MULTI-HOMED AGENTS WORK

Multi-homed agents can report to a maximum of four different management groups. For each management group, the agent loads a set of processing rules and configuration information and processes it independently. This eliminates any possible conflict between the management groups to which the agent reports.

A multi-homed agent is deployed using the same mechanisms as discussed in Chapter 8, "Installing and Configuring Agents." Enabling an agent for multi-homing is a straightforward process: Install the agent in the first management group and then install it in the other management group(s). The process of "installing" the agent in the second management group automatically multi-homes the agent. Of course, you can do this manually as well. Figure 9.14 shows an example of multi-homed agents, reporting to two different management groups (OMGRP and OMGRP-TEST).

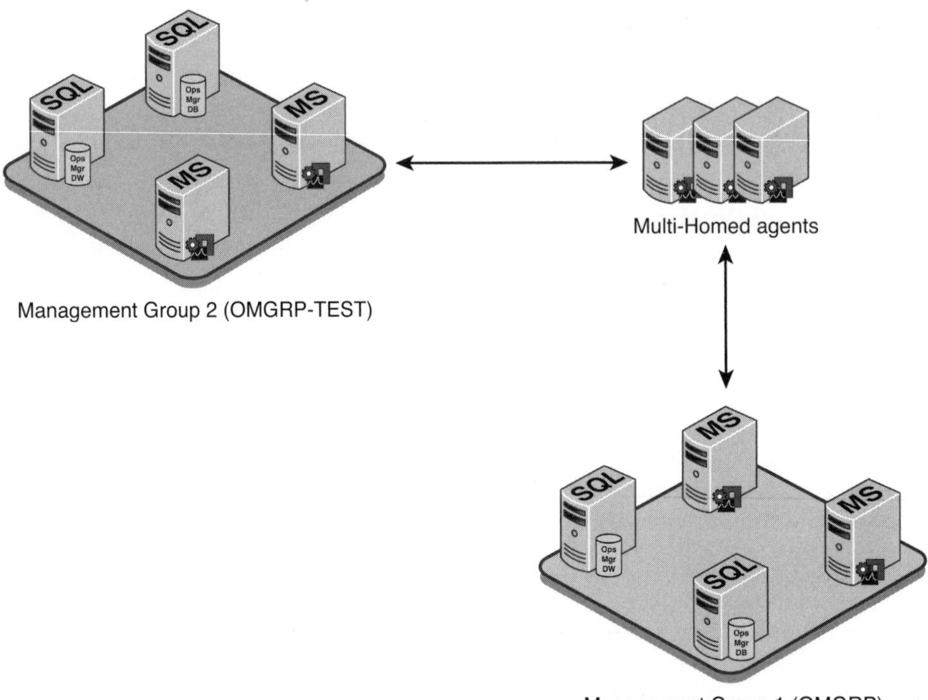

FIGURE 9.14 An example of multi-homed agents.

This example shows what is necessary to multi-home an agent manually. Note this is not recommended for production environments as it is a labor-intensive process and thus prone to error. The authors recommend automating that process using any of the techniques discussed in Chapter 8. Follow these steps:

1. Start an RDP session to the server with the agent you want to multi-home.
2. Open Control Panel and click on the **Operations Manager Agent** applet. (If this icon is not shown, select the detailed view in Control Panel.)
3. Click the **Add** button of the Operations Manager Agent Properties page, which opens the Add a Management Group dialog box displayed in Figure 9.15.

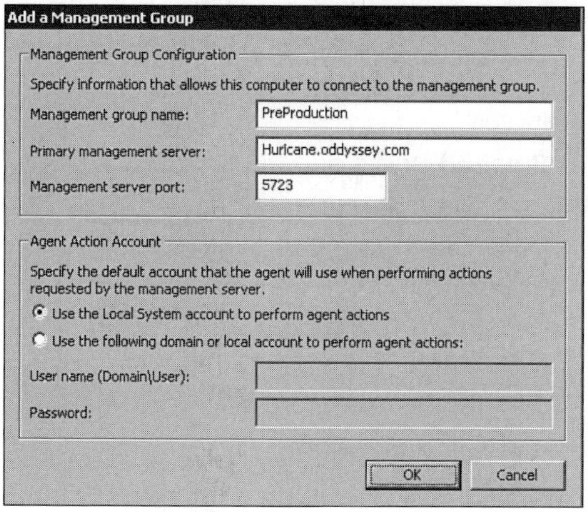

FIGURE 9.15 Add a Management Group dialog box.

4. Enter the management group name, primary management server, and management server, and click **OK** to return to the Operations Manager Agent Properties page. Click the **Apply** button in Figure 9.16 for this agent to report to two management groups.

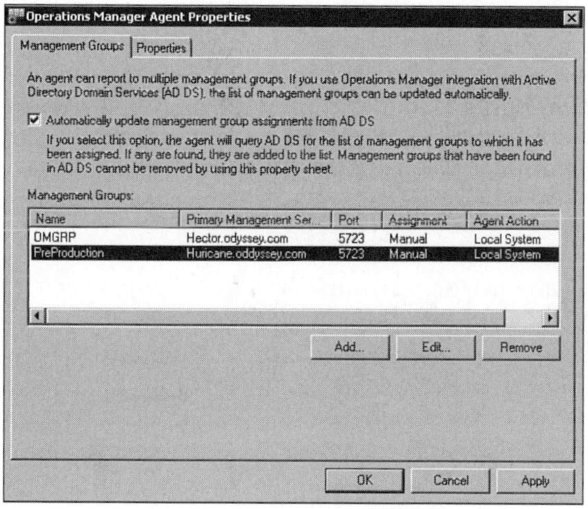

FIGURE 9.16 A multi-homed agent.

HELPFUL RESOURCES FOR MULTI-HOMING AGENTS USING SCRIPTING APIS

During agent deployment, its control panel applet is installed/registered with AgentConfigManager.dll. This DLL file contains useful .NET functions that you can reference and call using PowerShell, VBScript, and so on.

Here are some resources about how to use these .NET functions:

- **Copying and registering the script library:** http://msdn.microsoft.com/en-us/library/hh329076.aspx
- **Adding and removing a management group:** http://msdn.microsoft.com/en-us/library/hh329017.aspx
- **Displaying management group information:** http://msdn.microsoft.com/en-us/library/hh352628.aspx

The authors want to thank Kevin Holman for his posting about the agent control panel applet. The same posting also contains references about the .NET functions contained by the DLL file and using them; see http://blogs.technet.com/b/kevinholman/archive/2011/11/10/opsmgr-2012-new-feature-the-agent-control-panel-applet.aspx.

Connected Management Groups

Connected management groups have been available as a feature since OpsMgr 2007 RTM. They enable viewing and interacting with data from multiple management groups in a single Operations console, letting you respond to alerts from multiple management groups and run tasks on the monitored computers of the connected management groups.

Connected management groups are defined in a hierarchy. Microsoft uses several specific terms when referring to connected management groups:

- **Local management group:** This management group resides in the top tier of the hierarchy and is the management group that has the Operations console with the consolidated view.
- **Connected management group:** This management group contributes its data to the consolidated view of the local management group and resides in the bottom tier of the hierarchy. You can have more than one connected management group, which have a peer-to-peer relationship where each has no visibility or interaction with the other connected management groups. The visibility is only from the local management group into the connected management group.

Here are some important concepts to know about connected management groups:

- You cannot connect management groups of different builds. This also means an OpsMgr 2007 management group cannot be connected with an OpsMgr 2012 management group.
- Bidirectional communication is required between the local and connected management groups. For this, TCP ports 5723 (health service traffic) and 5724 (Operations console traffic) must be allowed.

- When the two management groups do not share the same DNS service, you must create a secondary DNS zone in the DNS service used by the local management group. This way the DNS information of the primary zone where the connected management group resides is transferred to the DNS service that the local management group queries.
- The local and connected management groups must reside in the same domain or in trusted domains. You can connect to management groups residing in untrusted domains but cannot view data from those domains until a trust is in place, since the AD account of the local management group must be added to an OpsMgr user role for the connected management group.

TIP: WORKAROUND FOR CONNECTED MANAGEMENT GROUPS IN UNTRUSTED DOMAINS

The authors have had mixed results getting connected management groups to work in untrusted domains. Be sure the account the local management group uses to connect to the connected management group also exists with the same name and password (known as shadowed or pass-through authentication) in that domain. This account must be added to an OpsMgr user role for the connected management group.

Microsoft provides documentation about OpsMgr connected management groups at http://technet.microsoft.com/en-us/library/hh230698.aspx. The authors strongly advise reading this article before connecting OpsMgr management groups.

Designing for Distributed Environments

You can deploy OpsMgr in all types of environments; small single locations with or without DMZs, spanning across multiple countries, and everything in between. Designing and building for enterprise environments or those environments spanning multiple geographical locations separated by WAN links require that you build a distributed environment.

In this type of scenario, placing all your management servers at a single location and the agents at satellite locations may not be the best approach. Often a more distributed approach is better, such as placing gateway servers at certain WAN locations and taking advantage of their compression ratio, as discussed in the "WAN Links and Gateways" section.

High-Level Steps

Here are the high-level steps that describe an approach to use when designing and building a distributed OpsMgr environment:

- Start with design. Begin with placement of your management group, including required SQL servers. Provision enough room for growth on the database servers and for additional management servers.

When a LAN segment has only four IP addresses available, it is best to use another LAN segment. When running a virtualized OpsMgr management group, ensure the hosts are not overcommitted and the storage area network (SAN) is not configured for best capacity instead of best IOPS, as that will seriously hamper I/O performance.

- Place the servers hosting the OpsMgr databases and SSRS with your management servers in the same LAN segment. This way traffic will flow quickly without routers between them, benefitting the overall performance and stability of your OpsMgr environment. This guarantees the highest bandwidth and lowest latency.
- Ensure the location where your management group resides is connected by high-speed WAN links to the other geographical locations. You will want to have the best WAN connections available for your monitoring environment. Often you will end up placing the OpsMgr management group in the corporate data center.
- For each geographical location, inventory what needs to be monitored. In addition to the total amount of servers or network devices, it is important to know the applications and services you will be monitoring. The more there is to monitor, such as business critical applications, websites, and .NET applications, the more network traffic is sent over the WAN connection to the management group.
- Some locations require Operations console access. This can be provided onsite or using a terminal server residing at the same location as the management group. The latter will improve console performance since the data does not have to be sent over the WAN connection. Only the screens, keyboard input, and mouse movements are sent across the WAN links. Chapter 4 describes this in more detail, along with some caveats.
- While often people think a minimum network speed of 64Kbps between a single agent and a management server is required, this actually is not true; this is the minimum connection Microsoft supports for an agent. Average traffic on a single agent is 500 bytes per second (~4Kb/s).
- Geographical locations connected by slow/congested WAN links might require a network upgrade. If this is not possible, consider installing a gateway server. As stated previously in the "WAN Links and Gateways" section, this gives you higher rates of compression and puts less strain on the limited WAN link. However, a gateway server will not solve a slow/congested WAN link.
- A distributed environment does not always mean distributed management of the management group. However, when one or more geographical locations have their own teams of administrators administering the OpsMgr management group, you will want to initiate delegation of control by introducing OpsMgr user roles. You may also again want to consider hosting Operations consoles with a terminal server that resides at the same location as the management group.
- A geographical location might be quite large, or have to comply with certain laws unique to that location. In this case, consider installing another dedicated management group at that location. This lets you manage that location as required by law without affecting the rest of the organization.

- Enterprise organizations may have a presence in unstable countries. In these cases, it is best to install only agents and perhaps a gateway server. Do not install an Operations console solution; offer it only through terminal services with additional security measures applied such as two-way factor authentication. Should the political situation go badly, you can pull the plug on those agents without worrying that sensitive information is out there.

Potential Pitfalls

Here are some pitfalls to consider when designing and building distributed OpsMgr environments:

- Do not mistake gateway servers for management servers. Gateway servers do not scale to anywhere near what a management server can. Consider gateway servers as agents with added gateway functionality.
- You may see statements about not using gateway servers if you have less than 10 agents. However, this introduces a considerable amount of additional administration since every managed server requires a certificate. Whether you deploy a gateway server depends on the unique requirements of each organization.
- Gateway servers introduce a SPOF. When the gateway server goes down, the agents behind it and reporting to that server cannot get their information to the OpsMgr management group. While you can eliminate this by installing a second gateway server and configuring failover, it will increase your costs.
- Refrain from installing management servers outside the LAN segment where the management group resides even when wide WAN links are in place. This will eventually hamper the overall functionality, availability, and stability of the entire management group.

  This was true with OpsMgr 2007, but is even more so in Operations Manager 2012, as the resource pools require very low latency because of heartbeat detection between management servers in any given resource pool. The management servers need to be close to or on the same segment as the databases. There are no exceptions to this design principle; when a particular geographical location is large enough for its own management server, you may want to consider providing a dedicated management group at that location.
- Keep your Operations consoles under tight scrutiny. Too many concurrent console connections can affect the overall performance of the management group. In addition, when these consoles require updates or extensions, you know exactly which consoles to update rather than having people complain that console functionality is broken. You will want to keep the installation bits required for the console installation at a location with limited access.

By keeping these pitfalls in mind along with the high-level design steps, you can design and build a well-designed distributed OpsMgr management group.

Fast Track

It may seem at first that not much has changed in terms of redundancy in System Center 2012 Operations Manager compared to Operations Manager 2007. However, when looking deeper, the changes are significant:

- The RMS no longer exists and is replaced by resource pools and the RMS emulator role. This eliminates the SPOF that existed in OpsMgr 2007.
- Sending out notifications is automatically handled by a resource pool of management servers. You can influence the membership of this pool and the way it is populated.
- Since the System Center Data Access Service runs on all management servers, it can be load balanced by using NLB, thus making the consoles highly available.

Summary

This chapter discussed some of the more complex configurations possible with OpsMgr. These include redundant SQL Servers, Web consoles, ACS configurations, gateway servers, and designing for distributed environments. The next chapter discusses security and compliance.

CHAPTER 10

Security and Compliance

IN THIS CHAPTER

- ▶ Securing Operations Manager
- ▶ Using Audit Collection Services
- ▶ Fast Track

In today's Information Technology (IT) environment, administrators must concern themselves with a number of key issues. Information is the most important asset belonging to most organizations, and system administrators will want to achieve maximum availability and optimum performance from the systems they are responsible for monitoring. This also should be accomplished in a secure manner, delegating administrative roles to reduce the risk of accidental or intentional misuse of rights. Additionally, system administrators must ensure the organization complies with internal procedures and external regulations that facilitate auditing network security. This chapter discusses these two facets of security and auditing in respect to System Center 2012 Operations Manager (OpsMgr).

Securing Operations Manager

Security is not a "one size fits all" undertaking; it should be customizable and flexible based on the needs of the organization and its applications. Securing Operations Manager includes utilizing role-based security, Run As profiles, Run As accounts, and understanding the various OpsMgr service accounts. In addition, you will want to understand how security works with the System Center Data Access Service, security across multiple domains, how the gateway server feature works when monitoring non-trusted domains, monitoring agents in workgroups, database security, monitoring an environment with firewalls, and securing communications.

About Role-Based Security

Operations Manager 2007 set the standard for System Center security with its implementation of role-based access control (RBAC), now used across System Center 2012. RBAC, which utilizes user roles, allows you to manage administrative rights efficiently so each user has only the access required for their job function. Given that an administrator with full access to your OpsMgr management group is able to perform an almost unlimited range of actions within that environment, you will want to limit this particular role to those individuals requiring that high level of access to perform their jobs. As Operations Manager can monitor many types of applications potentially administered by multiple teams, role-based security provides the ability to limit privileges users have for various aspects of OpsMgr—by task as well as scope.

The Operations console includes access to more than 150 available operations, which fall under the following categories:

- **Monitoring:** These operations include opening views, resolving alerts, executing tasks, and overriding monitors. These views help you analyze monitoring needs.
- **Authoring:** Authoring includes creating and modifying objects to customize or supplement the default monitoring settings provided by management packs.
- **Reporting:** Reporting operations consist of using and designing reports and managing report security.
- **Administration:** Administrative operations include configuring security, importing, exporting, and removing management packs, changing global settings, discovering computers and devices, configuring notification, and installing agents.

User roles determine the level of functionality a user will have and the areas of the console they can access. Roles consist of users with similar job functions that are grouped together. These groups of users are then granted the least privileged permissions in the system required to perform these job functions. Roles also limit the scope of views and tasks that are available to each user.

Here's what a very simplistic mapping of roles looks like:

```
[User] has a [Role]
```

Given that different roles often have overlapping tasks within an application, the mapping (or model) would be

```
[User] has [Role] is allowed to execute [Tasks] made up of [Operations]
```

Here's how this works:

- A *role* is a set of permissions a user must have to do a job. Well-designed roles should correspond to a job category or responsibility (for example, Operations Manager Administrators, Operations Manager Operators, or Operations Manager Authors) and be named accordingly.

- A *task* is a collection of operations, and can include other tasks. A well-designed task is inclusive enough to represent recognizable work items (for example, closing an alert, creating an override).
- An *operation* is a set of permissions that you associate with system-level or application program interface (API)-level security procedures such as reading or writing attributes. You use operations as building blocks for tasks.

When discussing roles, you will also want to understand profiles and scopes:

- **Profiles:** Operations or tasks such as resolving alerts, executing tasks, overriding monitors, creating user roles, viewing alerts, viewing events, and so on, are grouped into profiles.
- **Scopes:** A scope defines the entity groups, object types, tasks, or views to which a profile is restricted. Scopes do not apply to all profiles.

Role-based access control utilizes Microsoft's Windows Authorization Manager (AzMan) framework. This model enables an application to check whether a given user role gives an individual the right to execute a certain operation, and not worry about everything in-between. The dynamic nature of the Operations console also adjusts what is visible such that if a user does not have access to a workspace or operation, it is not viewable.

WINDOWS AUTHORIZATION MANAGER AND RBAC

AzMan provides the framework for integrating RBAC into applications. First released in Windows Server 2003, it enables administrators using those applications to provide access through assigned user roles that relate to job functions. AzMan provides an administrative tool to manage authorization policy and a runtime that allows applications to perform access checks against that policy. A key concept is that authorization policy is managed separately from an application's code. The application designer defines the set of operations considered security sensitive and then defines a set of tasks that map onto those operations. The tasks are those used by administrators and users in System Center 2012 Operations Manager and other Microsoft applications.

Information is maintained in AzMan stores that can be created in Active Directory Domain Services, Active Directory Lightweight Directory Services, SQL Server (introduced with Windows Server 2008), and eXtended Markup Language (XML) files. The OpsMgr store contains user roles and their scoping. The store for OpsMgr 2007's implementation of AzMan was an XML file named MomAuth.xml; in OpsMgr 2012, the store is maintained across multiple AzMan tables in the operational database.

Operations on the Data Access Service

The System Center Data Access Service (DAS), known as the SDK service in the initial OpsMgr 2007 release and then renamed with OpsMgr 2007 Release 2 (R2), is a Windows service running on each management server deployed in a management group. It is a

Windows Communication Foundation (WCF)-based web service that all data access in Operations Manager passes through, and represents a single point of control for security authentication and authorization checks. All database interaction goes through this service, which authenticates and authorizes users using AzMan. Think of the DAS as the gatekeeper for all access. In fact, turning on Windows auditing for this service enables you to audit actions on the database; this is applicable for any System Center component using the Data Access Service, as it is the middle-tier application server for the System Center common platform.

The DAS actually goes through another layer, called the Data Access Layer (DAL), to get to the database itself. The Data Access Layer is a set of DLLs used internally by other components of the common platform. The Data Access Service accesses the database over ADO.Net (with a default port of 1433) using the security context under which the service runs. Because user roles use the class libraries to connect to the Data Access Service, this controls not only what one can do at the console but also with PowerShell cmdlets and custom clients.

Figure 10.1 illustrates the function of the Data Access Service in System Center 2012 Operations Manager security, and Figure 10.2 shows the data flow.

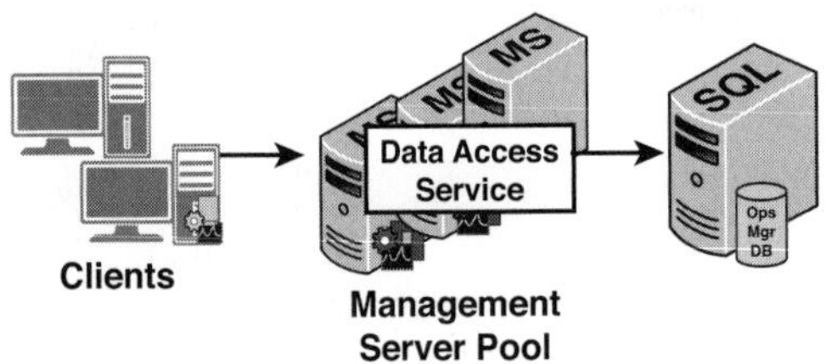

FIGURE 10.1 The Data Access Service in Operations Manager.

The DAS has a number of different operations that can be called on the API. Here are the four standard operations that are relevant to role-based security:

- **View:** Has permission to see information about an object.
- **Create:** Has permission to create an object of a certain class.
- **Edit:** Has permission to edit an object (or just some properties of an object).
- **Delete:** Has permission to delete an object from the database.

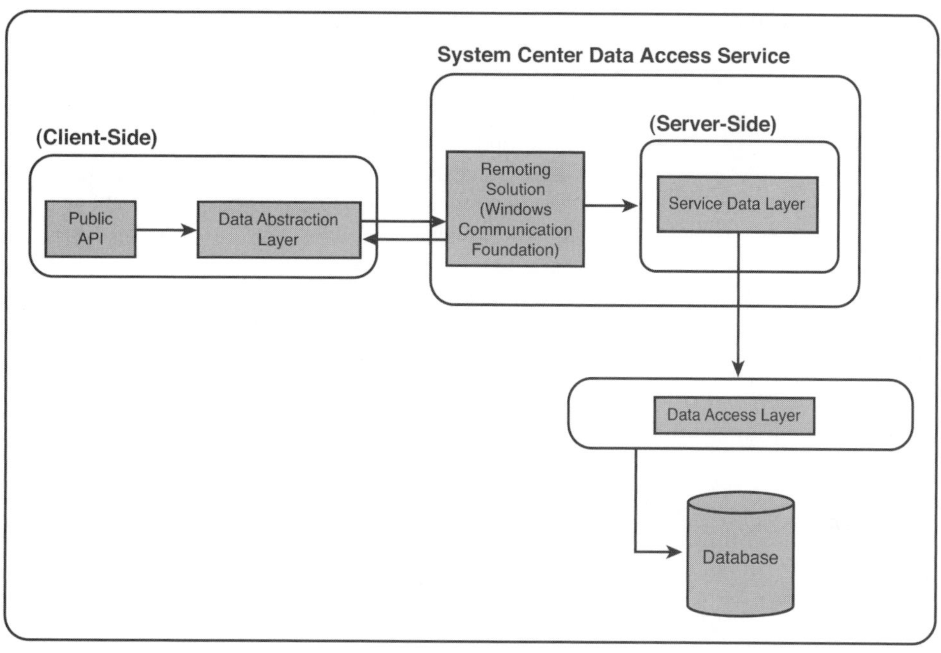

FIGURE 10.2 Data flow for the System Center Data Access Service.

User Roles and Profiles

Profiles are predefined collections of operations that can be performed on certain classes, properties, and relationships. Out of the box, each profile is associated with a user role to which you can add members. You cannot modify these preexisting user roles, but you can create new user roles based on the eight existing profiles. Out of the box, Operations Manager provides the user roles and profiles listed in Table 10.1. Information on specific operations associated with each is available at http://technet.microsoft.com/en-us/library/hh872885.

TABLE 10.1 User roles and profiles provided by System Center 2012 Operations Manager

Role Name	Profile Type	Profile Description	Role Scope
Operations Manager Administrators	Administrator	Contains privileges found in the Author, Advanced Operator, Operator, and Read-Only Operator profiles.	Globally scoped.
Operations Manager Read-Only Operators	Read-Only Operator	Ability to view alerts and access views according to configured scope.	All groups and views currently present and those imported in the future.

TABLE 10.1 Continued

Role Name	Profile Type	Profile Description	Role Scope
Operations Manager Operators	Operator	Ability to interact with alerts, run tasks, and access views according to configured scope. Includes all privileges found in the Read-Only Operator profile.	All groups, views, and tasks currently present and those imported in the future.
Operations Manager Advanced Operators	Advanced Operator	Limited change access to Operations Manager configuration; ability to override configuration of rules and monitors for specific targets or groups of targets within the configured scope. Includes all of the privileges found in the Operator profile.	All groups, views, and tasks currently present and those imported in the future.
Operations Manager Authors	Author	Grants members the ability to create, edit, and delete monitoring configuration (tasks, rules, monitors, and views) within the configured scope. You can also configure Authors to have Advanced Operator privileges scoped by group. Includes all privileges found in the Advanced Operator, Operator, and Read-Only Operator profiles.	All groups, views, and tasks currently present and those imported in the future.
Operations Manager Report Operators	Report Operator	Grants members the ability to view reports according to configured scope.	Globally scoped.
Operations Manager Report Security Administrators	Report Security Administrator	Enables integration of SQL Server Reporting Services (SSRS) security with Operations Manager.	No scope.
Operations Manager Application Monitoring Operators	Application Monitoring Operator	Grants members the ability to see the application monitoring events in Application Diagnostics and access Application Advisor.	Globally scoped.

The built-in roles do not limit scopes, meaning they have access to all groups, views, and tasks (with the exception of Report Security Administrators and Application Monitoring Operators). To narrow scope, create your own custom roles based on the Operator, Report Operator, Read-Only Operator, Author, or Advanced Operator profiles.

Creating User Roles

You can add Active Directory (AD) security groups or individual accounts to any of the predefined user roles or to a role that you create. When you create a role, you can narrow the scope of the groups, tasks, and views it can access. Should you create a user role based on the Author or Advanced Author profiles, be sure these users have access to an installation of the Operations console to perform the tasks allowed by those profiles.

NOTE: OPERATIONS MANAGER ADMINISTRATORS USER ROLE

Operations Manager 2007 required you to assign a security group to the Administrators rule during setup; by default, this was the BUILTIN\Administrators group on the root management server (RMS). With OpsMgr 2012, you no longer are asked to assign a security group during setup; it is assigned to the local Administrators group with membership modified through the Operations console or using PowerShell.

The Administrators role differs from other user roles as you can only add Active Directory security groups to this role, not individual users. In addition, when you add a group to the Operations Manager Administrators user role, you must restart the management server to which you are connected for the change to take effect.

As mentioned in the "About Role-Based Security" section, if a user does not have privileges to view a monitored object or perform an action, that object or action does not appear or is grayed out in the console. For information regarding the consoles, see Chapter 7, "Configuring and Using System Center 2012 Operations Manager."

To help you become familiar with creating a new user role, this section steps through the process of creating a new Advanced Operators user role. Advanced Operators can create overrides to rules and monitors for targets or groups of targets that are within their configured scope. To create the user role, log on as an OpsMgr Administrator and navigate to the Administration space in the Operations console. Follow these steps:

1. In the Administration pane, select **Security** and right-click **User Roles**. Select **New User role**, and then select the **Advanced Operator** profile as displayed in Figure 10.3 to initiate the Create User Role Wizard.

2. On the General page of the wizard, enter a name for the User role such as **Odyssey_Advanced_Operators** and click **Add** in the User role members section of the page.

   In the Select User or Groups dialog box, specify the AD users or groups to add to this role and click **OK** to return to the General page.

   You can also add an optional description on the General page. Figure 10.4 shows this page completed with the User role name, Descriptions, and User role members field populated. Click **Next**.

   Note that the following screens of the Create User Role Wizard will vary based on the profile type to which this user role is assigned.

3. The Group Scope page asks you to approve groups. Members of this user role can set overrides and monitor objects in approved groups. By default, the entire management group is selected. Unchecking this lets you select specific groups. In Figure 10.5, the OMGRP management group was unchecked and the All Windows Computers group selected. Click **Next** when you complete group selection.

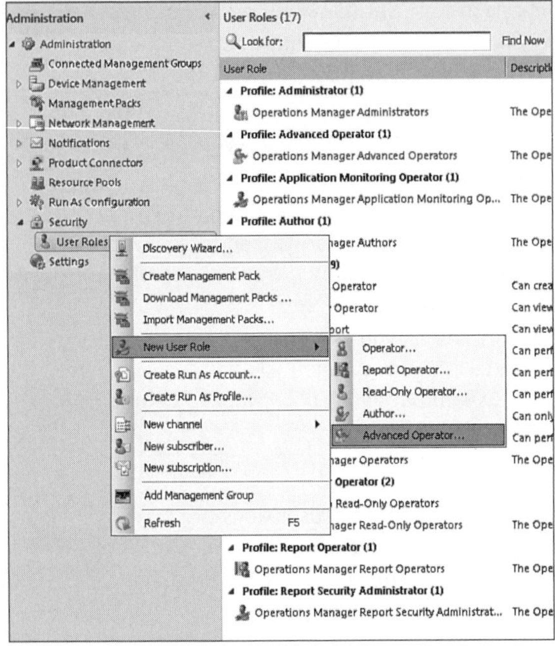

FIGURE 10.3 Starting the Create User Role Wizard.

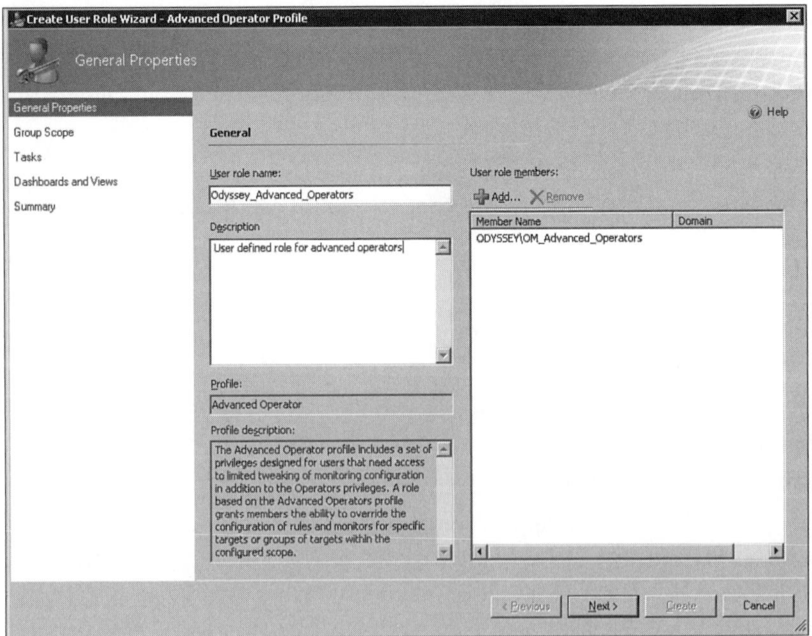

FIGURE 10.4 A completed General Properties page of the Create User Role Wizard.

4. The Tasks page asks you to Approve tasks members of this user role can execute. All tasks are automatically approved by default.

   Alternatively, you can select **Only tasks explicitly added to the 'Approved tasks' grid are approved** and press **Add** to add approved tasks to open the Select Tasks dialog, where you can check the tasks you wish to add. You can view the tasks to select either by task name or management pack order. The ability to select specific tasks gives you granularity in defining the tasks a user role is allowed to perform. For this example, the default of **All tasks are automatically approved** was used. Click **Next** when finished selecting tasks.

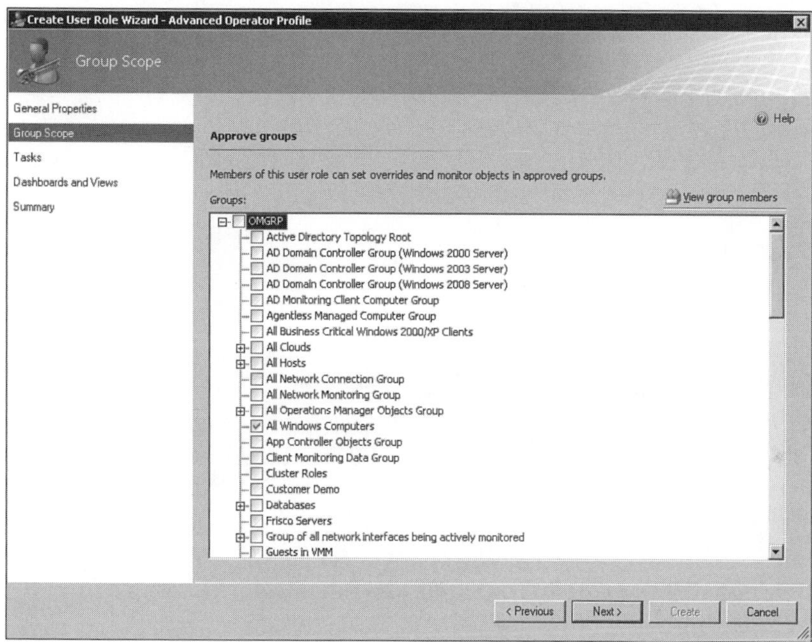

FIGURE 10.5 Selecting group scope for an Advanced Operator user role.

5. The Dashboards and Views page of the wizard lets you define the views and dashboards members of this user role can access. The default is **All dashboards and views are automatically approved**. If you select **Only the dashboards and views selected in each tab are approved**, you can select specific dashboards and views in the Monitoring Tree and Task Pane.

   Selecting any dashboard under the Monitoring Tree tab gives members of this user role access to data in the data warehouse. Be aware that should you select specific dashboards and views, members of this security role will not automatically have permissions to new views and dashboards later added to OpsMgr unless you rerun the wizard. Figure 10.6 shows the Active Alerts, Discovered Inventory, and Windows Computers view selected.

Clicking the Task Pane tab allows you to add dashboards you would like members of this user role to access and view from the Tasks pane. For this example, the Windows Server Task Pane Dashboard from the Windows Server Task Pane Dashboard MP was selected.

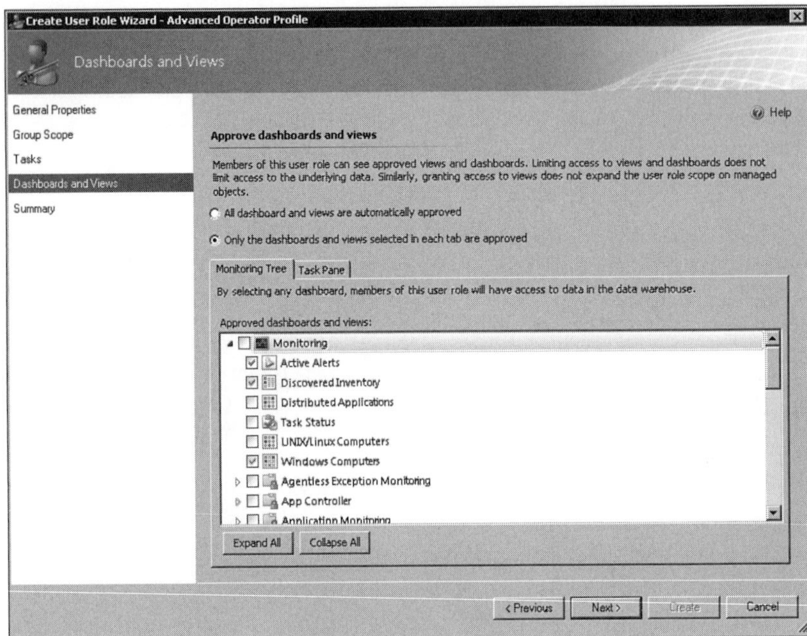

FIGURE 10.6 Selecting group scope for an Advanced Operator user role.

Click **Next** after selecting those dashboards and views that will be accessible to members of this user role.

6. The Summary page, shown in Figure 10.7, lists a summary of the properties you have assigned to this user role. Click **Create** to create the user role.

This was a fairly simple illustration of creating a user role. You could further narrow the scope of this Advanced Operators role by being more granular in setting group scope and tasks. Keep in mind that the pages of the wizard displayed and the actions you can restrict will vary based on the profile the user role is based on.

Step 3 asked that you specify groups permitted to the user role. Groups, like other OpsMgr objects, are defined in management packs. Your Operations Manager installation created a number of groups from the management packs imported during the installation process. If the existing groups do not contain those monitored objects needed for a scope, you can create a group that does. To do so, exit the Create User Role Wizard, switch to the Authoring space, and use the Create Group Wizard to create a group that better suits your needs.

Similar to Windows file system security, when a user account is a member of multiple roles, access is the combination of what is granted to all those roles.

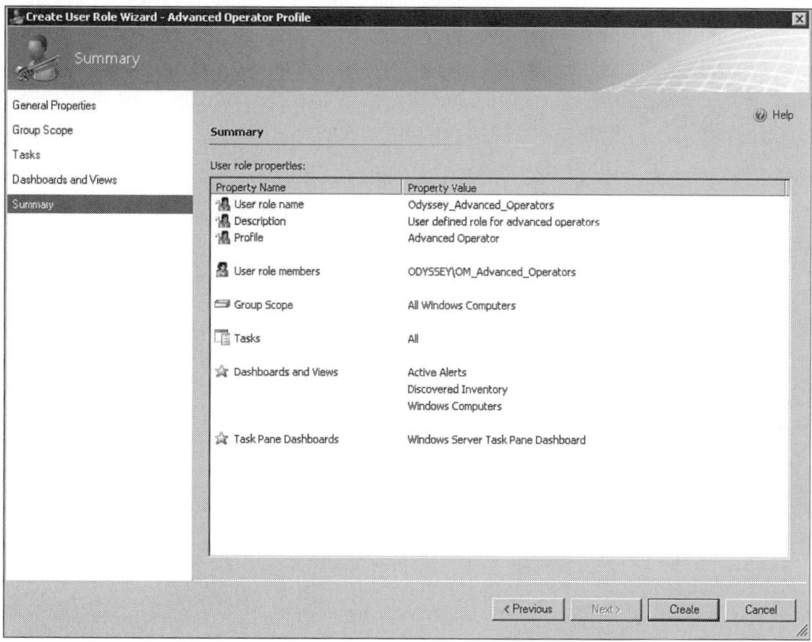

FIGURE 10.7 The Summary page of the Create User Role Wizard.

TIP: MAINTAINING USER ROLES USING POWERSHELL CMDLETS

New PowerShell cmdlets in OpsMgr 2012 let you list and configure user roles:

- `Get-SCOMUserRole` lists user roles; http://technet.microsoft.com/en-us/library/hh920219.aspx provides syntax examples.
- The `Set-SCOMUserRole` cmdlet configures an Operations Manager user role. Documentation is available at http://technet.microsoft.com/en-us/library/hh918504.aspx.

Creating a Report Operator Role

The Report Operator role grants the users belonging to that role the ability to run audit reports; however, the Operations console does not include the capability of creating this role, nor does the new PowerShell `Set-SCOMUserRole` cmdlet support creating the Report Operator role.

The good news is you can still load the OpsMgr 2007 PowerShell snap-in to use the workarounds previously developed for this. This line of code tells PowerShell to load the `Microsoft.EnterpriseManagement.OperationsManager.Client` snap-in, so the old commands will be recognized:

```
Add-PSSnapin Microsoft.EnterpriseManagement.OperationsManager.Client
```

System Center Operations Manager 2007 Unleashed (Sams, 2008) discussed using a script provided by Eugene Bykov of Microsoft to create a Report Operator role in OpsMgr 2007, modified by Neal Browne to be parameter-driven. As discussed at http://www.systemcentercentral.com/BlogDetails/tabid/143/IndexID/94404/Default.aspx, by incorporating the OpsMgr 2007 PowerShell snap-in and changing the script to be a function, you can continue to use the 2007 code rather than delving into .NET methods to create a script that would accomplish the same thing in OpsMgr 2012.

Here is the code for the `CreateReportRole` function, with updates to the 2007 script by the *OpsMgr Unleashed* team:

```
Function CreateReportRole {
param($rootMS,$roleUserName,$roleDisplayName,$roleDescription)
#Initializing the OpsMgr 2007 PowerShell provider
     add-pssnapin "Microsoft.EnterpriseManagement.OperationsManager.Client"
-ErrorVariable errSnapin;
     set-location "OperationsManagerMonitoring::" -ErrorVariable errSnapin;
     new-managementGroupConnection -ConnectionString:$rootMS -ErrorVariable
errSnapin;
     set-location $rootMS -ErrorVariable errSnapin;

#Checks to see if it failed or succeeded in loading the provider
     if ($errSnapin.count -eq 0){
    Write-host "'nOpsMgr 2007 PSSnapin initialized!'n";
     }
     else{
    Write-host "'nOpsMgr 2007 PSSnapin failed initialize!'nPlease verify you are
➥running this script on an OpsMgr management server";
    Write-Host;
     }
$mg = (-item .).ManagementGroup
$reportOperator = $mg.GetMonitoringProfiles() | where {$_.Name -eq "ReportOperator"}
$obj = new-object Microsoft.EnterpriseManagement.Monitoring.Security.
MonitoringUserRole

$obj.Name = $roleUserName
$obj.DisplayName = $roleDisplayName
$obj.Description = $roleDescription
$obj.MonitoringProfile = $reportOperator

$mg.InsertMonitoringUserRole($obj)
}

#Call function with necessary parameters to create the custom Report Operators role
```

Here is a sample command line execution:

```
CreateReportRole "helios" "ReportOperators" "Odyssey Report Operators" "Report
➥Operators for Odyssey"
```

Table 10.2 lists the parameters used by the `CreateReportRole` function.

TABLE 10.2 Parameters for the `CreateReportRole` function

Parameter	Explanation
rootMS	The fully qualified domain name (FQDN) or NetBIOS name of the RMS emulator (since there's no longer an RMS)
roleUserName	Name of the user role
roleDisplayName	Display name of the role
roleDescription	Description of the role

NOTE: AVAILABLE ONLINE

The `CreateReportRole` PowerShell function is included as value-added content on the InformIT site for this book. Appendix E, "Available Online," provides additional information.

Troubleshooting User Roles

When you create user roles and scope them to specific tasks, the associated data is stored in AzMan tables in SQL Server. You can view the contents of this store using the AzMan.msc Microsoft Management Server Console (MMC) snap-in. Follow these steps:

1. Invoke the AzMan snap-in from the Start menu (**Start** -> **Run** -> **AzMan.msc**).
2. Select the **Action** menu drop-down menu and click **Open Authorization Store**.
3. At the Open Authorization Store dialog box, select **Microsoft SQL** for the authorization store type and enter the name of the store used by your OpsMgr installation, as shown in Figure 10.8. Here is the format of the connection string, documented at http://technet.microsoft.com/en-us/library/cc770467(v=ws.10).aspx:

   ```
   mssql://Driver={SQL Server};Server={SCOMSQLSERVER\INSTANCE};/{operational
   ➥database name}/AzManStore
   ```

   For the Odyssey environment used by this book, the string is

   ```
   mssql://Driver={SQL Server};Server={thundercloud\sql_om};/OperationsManager/
   ➥AzManStore
   ```

10

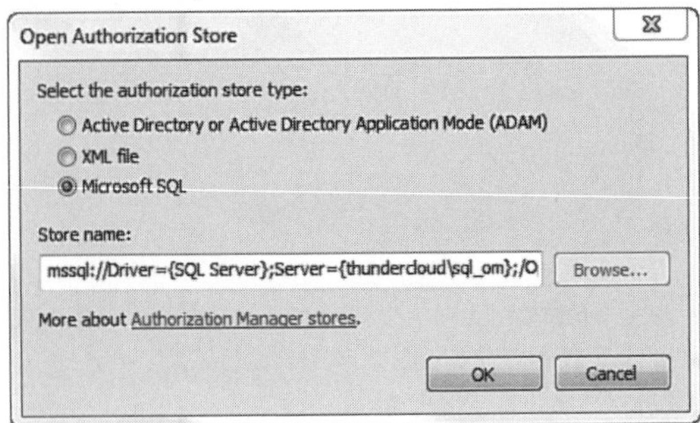

FIGURE 10.8 Opening the SQL Authorization Store for OpsMgr 2012.

4. In the MMC console, expand Microsoft System Center in the left hand pane. User-defined user roles are represented by GUIDs and located at **AzmanStore** -> **Microsoft System Center** -> *<GUID for the role you created>*.

Using this snap-in allows an administrator to browse the different rights and operations loaded into Authorization Manager, which can be useful when rights are not working as you expected. As an example, Figure 10.9 shows the mapping for the Odyssey_Advanced_Operators user role, created in the "Creating User Roles" section.

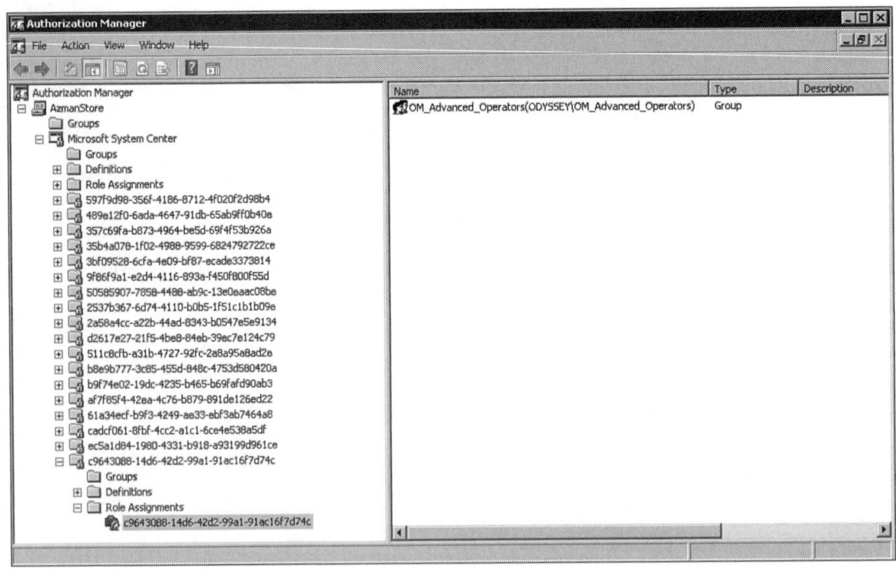

FIGURE 10.9 Using Authorization Manager to view role assignments.

CAUTION: AZMAN INFORMATION IS FOR VIEWING ONLY

While viewing the AzMan store can be interesting when troubleshooting, Microsoft does not support you making any modifications. You could enable someone to elevate to a higher level of access if modifications are made incorrectly.

Run As Profiles and Run As Accounts

Management pack components such as rules, monitors, tasks, and discoveries require credentials to run on the targeted computer. These components run using the credentials of the MSAA by default. Utilizing Run As profiles and Run As accounts enables you to change the account providing credentials.

Run As Profiles

A Run As profile allows a management pack author to associate an identity other than the default action account with a particular module, letting it run using the credentials of that entity. The account used must have the Allow Logon Locally right.

Run As profiles take a Windows local or domain user account and apply it to a specified OpsMgr profile (for information on UNIX and Linux security, see the "About Cross Platform Security" section later in the chapter). For example, the SQL Server management pack has a profile; assigning a user to this profile means it will run using the credentials of that user. A Run As account is the user account assigned to a Run As profile (discussed in more detail in the "Run As Accounts" section). Similar to the Run As accounts used by Windows, privileges are elevated only while the action targeted by the Run As profile is running.

OpsMgr 2012 automatically creates a number of Run As profiles during setup. Unless otherwise specified, the default action account is used by a Run As profile if another account is not assigned to that profile. Table 10.3 lists the Run As profiles created during initial installation.

TABLE 10.3 Run As profiles created at setup

Profile Name	Explanation
Active Directory Based Agent Assignment Account	Used by the AD-based agent assignment module to publish assignment settings to Active Directory. The management server action account (MSAA) is assigned to this by default.
APM CSM Encryption Profile	Used to store encryption key settings for collected sensitive data in client-side monitoring.
Automatic Agent Management Account	Used to automatically diagnose agent failures such as heartbeat failures and failure to receive data.
Certificate Signing Account	Windows account used to sign the certificates used to secure communication between Operations Manager and managed UNIX/Linux systems, which must be a local Administrator on the management servers. If this Run As profile is not populated, the default action account is used.

10

TABLE 10.3 Continued

Profile Name	Explanation
Client Monitoring Action Account	If specified, used to run all client monitoring modules; otherwise the default action account is used.
Connected Management Group Account	This profile is used by the Operations Manager management pack to determine the credentials used to test connectivity between connected management groups. If no credentials are provided for a given system, the default action account is used.
Data Warehouse Account	If specified, this account runs all data warehouse collection and synchronization rules. If not overridden by the Data Warehouse SQL Server Authentication Action account during OpsMgr Reporting setup, this is also used by collection and synchronization rules to connect to the data warehouse database using Windows integrated authentication.
Data Warehouse SQL Server Authentication Action Account	If specified, this logon name and password is used by collection and synchronization rules to connect to the data warehouse database using SQL authentication.
Default Action Account	This is the default Windows account under which Operations Manager processes run. The account needs sufficient privileges to gather data from providers (these are modules that gather performance counter information and events). Minimum required permissions are Allow Logon Locally, Performance Monitor Users, and being a member of the Users group. The authors recommend using Local System for this account, as Local System is a low maintenance account with local administrative rights to that operating system only.
MPUpdate Action Account	Used by the MP Notifier. This was a management pack available with Microsoft Operations Manager 2005; while still created with the management group, the account is no longer used.
Notification Account	This Windows account is used by notification rules. Its email address is used as the email and instant message From address. Ensure the credentials used for this account have sufficient rights to the Simple Mail Transfer Protocol (SMTP) server, instant messaging server, or Session Initiation Protocol (SIP) server you are using for notification.
Operational Database Account	Used to read and write information to the operational database.
Privileged Monitoring Account	Unlike other profiles, this profile defaults to Local System, but can be overridden. All tasks and workflows requiring system level access should use this profile; typically, this is discovery workflows. Do not use this profile just to guarantee access to resources, as that adds unnecessary risk to your installation.

TABLE 10.3 Continued

Profile Name	Explanation
Reporting SDK SQL Server Authentication Account	If specified, this login name and password is used by the DAS to connect to the data warehouse database using SQL Server authentication.
Reserved	This profile is reserved and should not be used.
SNMP Monitoring Account	Used for SNMP monitoring.
SNMPv3 Monitoring Account	Used for SNMPv3 monitoring.
UNIX/Linux Action Account	Used for low privilege UNIX and Linux access.
UNIX/Linux Agent Maintenance Account	Used for privileged maintenance operations for UNIX and Linux agents, and required for account agent maintenance operations.
UNIX/Linux Privileged Account	Used to access protected UNIX and Linux resources and actions that require high privileges. It is required for some rules, diagnostics, and recoveries to work.
Validate Alert Subscription Account	Used by the validate alert subscription module that validates notification subscriptions are in scope. Administrator access is required.
Windows Cluster Action Account	Used for discovery and monitoring of Windows cluster components. It defaults to the default action account unless specifically populated.
WS-Management Action Account	Used for WS-Management access.

Run As Accounts

A Run As account typically maps to an Active Directory user account, although you can also use SQL credentials, forms authorization credentials, binary credentials for certificate authorization, HTTP basic authorization, HTTP digest authorization, and SNMP community strings. This account represents an identity that can be associated with a Run As profile. The profile maps the Run As account to a specific computer. Rather than assigning additional rights to an action account, using Run As accounts and Run As profiles provides the ability to run a task, rule, or monitor using an account with the necessary rights.

There are also single use accounts—these are accounts you enter to run a single task. The Operations console allows you to use the default account or a specified account. These accounts use the same infrastructure as Run As accounts, except credentials are not retained; they are encrypted in memory and discarded after use.

USING RUN AS ACCOUNTS WITH MANAGMENT PACKS

Using a Run As account can help your organization with its monitoring requirements. Consider an example with the Odyssey company. John is working on a custom SQL management pack that includes a task to generate database statistics. He knows that the action account may not have sufficient rights to run this task. Bob, the Odyssey DBA and SQL Server administrator, has required access rights. John needs to configure the task to run with Bob's credentials.

As a management pack author, always check that you do not give the action account a higher level of privilege than is required. If something requires more than the minimum level of privilege, create a new profile; otherwise, installations will not be able to maintain reduced action account privileges.

John creates a Run As profile and associates it with the task module he is including in his management pack. When the management pack containing the database statistics task is imported into OpsMgr, the Run As profile associated with this task is included in the import and appears in the list of available Run As profiles (**Administration** -> **Run As Configuration** -> **Profiles** in the Operations console).

Odyssey's OpsMgr administrator will use the Create Run As Account Wizard to create a Run As account to run the task, configured with Bob's credentials. The Run As profile's properties are then modified to add the Run As account that the task will use. You need to specifically define the target computer on which the Run As account will run in the Run As profile.

When you configure Run As accounts, consider the rights required by the action account and choose a user account with those privileges. Using a Domain Admin account usually is not a good choice! Although a highly privileged account ensures all the management pack features will work, this introduces risks associated with using accounts that have more than those permissions required to do the job, and makes your auditors unhappy.

TIP: CHECK CREDENTIALS WHEN YOU CREATE RUN AS ACCOUNTS

The Create Run As Account Wizard does not actually verify the credentials you specify when creating the Run As account. This means that if you enter incorrect credentials, the account you create will not be able to run its assigned monitor, rule, or task successfully. Not checking credentials is by design, as the account may exist in another forest or be a local account for a member computer or one in a workgroup.

When OpsMgr tries to use that account, it will generate an alert if the account is not configured properly. As a best practice, verify the account exists and its credentials are adequate before using it as a Run As account. The authors also recommend using an account with a non-expiring password.

You can associate multiple Run As accounts with a single Run As profile. This can be useful in cases where you are using a Run As profile on different machines. As an example, there is a task that one individual has rights to run on Odyssey's Hannibal server, but someone else has rights to run on Cyclone, Odyssey's Virtual Machine Manager (VMM) server. To make this work, configure separate Run As accounts for each server, associating both individuals with a single Run As profile. This assignment is made on each computer.

As part of the installation process, several Run As accounts are identified:

- **Local System Action Account:** This is the built-in system account to be used as an action account.
- **Management Server Action Account:** This user account is the one under which all rules run on the agent by default.
- **Local System Windows Account:** Built-in system account.
- **Network Service Windows Account:** Built-in network service account.
- **Data Warehouse Action Account:** Used for the data warehouse.
- **Data Warehouse Report Deployment Account:** Used for data warehouse report deployment.

Other action accounts are specified as you add additional features. For example, the gateway action account is the user account under which all rules run by default on the agent, but does not come into play until you install a gateway server.

Required Accounts

System Center 2012 Operations Manager uses a number of service and action accounts. Here are some things to keep in mind regarding these accounts:

- If you use domain accounts and your domain group policy object (GPO) allows passwords to expire, you must either change the passwords on the service accounts according to your password expiration policy, override the settings for these accounts so the passwords will not expire, or use low maintenance system accounts. Password information entered for accounts is stored, encrypted, in the operational database.
- You may want to consider using built-in accounts where that is practical, as the operating system maintains these accounts and they are not affected by password expiration policies. In addition, the passwords to these accounts are not exposed.

When you install the first management server, it requires credentials for the MSAA and System Center Configuration Service and System Center Data Access Service account.

When you push out an agent, you can provide credentials for several accounts:

- Computer Discovery Account
- Agent Action Account
- Agent Installation Account

The default is to specify the MSAA; all other accounts default to using either Local System or the default action account (the MSAA).

Each management server and agent runs an instance of the System Center Management service, which has an associated service account. The service monitors the health of the computer and potentially the health of other computers as a proxy. The System Center Management service uses Local System; this should not be changed.

When you install the reporting feature, you must specify credentials for the Data Warehouse Write account and the Data Reader account.

Table 10.4 lists the accounts used during installation and initial setup.

TABLE 10.4 Service accounts required for OpsMgr 2012 installation

Account Name	When Used	Used For	Use for Low Maintenance	Use for High Security
Management server action account	Management server setup	Collects data from providers, runs responses, writes to operational database.	Local System	Domain account
System Center Configuration service and System Center Data Access service	Management server setup	Writes to operational database, runs services. This account is assigned to the SDK_user role in the operational database.	Local System	Domain account
SQL Server service account	OpsMgr database setup	Run database services.	Local System	Domain account
Data Reader account	Reporting server setup	Defines the account credentials SSRS uses to run queries against the Operations Manager data warehouse.	Low-privilege domain account, this must have SQL Server logon rights and management server logon rights.	Low-privilege domain account, this must have SQL Server logon rights and management server logon rights.
Data Warehouse Write account	Reporting server setup	Writes data from the management server to the data warehouse database and reads data from the operational database.	Low-privilege domain account	Low-privilege domain account

TABLE 10.4 Continued

Account Name	When Used	Used For	Use for Low Maintenance	Use for High Security
Agent action account	Discovery and push agent install, manual installations. For AD integration, this account is set to Local System, but you can modify it later.	Gathers information and runs responses on managed computers.	Local System	Low-privilege domain account
Gateway action account	Gateway server setup	Gathers operational data from providers, runs responses, and performs actions such as installing and uninstalling agents on managed computers.	Local System	Low-privilege domain or local computer account

Action Account

Every management server and agent requires an action account. This account gathers information about, and runs responses on, management and gateway servers and any computer with an installed agent. You can use the default action account (located under **Administration** -> **Run As Configuration** -> **Accounts**) or specify a different account for the action account. Unless an action is associated with a Run As profile, the credentials used to perform the action would be those defined for the action account.

Actions performed by the action account or a specific Run As account (Run As accounts are discussed in the "Run As Accounts" section) are run by the MonitoringHost.exe process. Each account has its own instance of MonitoringHost.exe, so there may be many MonitoringHost.exe processes running under many identities, at any given time.

The Monitoring Host Process

The MonitoringHost.exe process manages workflows. Here are some of the actions performed by these workflows:

- Monitoring and collecting Windows event log data
- Monitoring and collecting Windows performance counter data

- Monitoring and collecting Windows Management Instrumentation (WMI) data
- Running actions such as scripts or batches
- Monitoring and collecting application-specific log data, such as IIS logs
- Running a managed code module
- Executing tasks, performing discovery, and other useful actions

Multiple Monitoring Host Instances

It is not unusual for more than one data provider, or more than one response, to run simultaneously. OpsMgr runs each provider or response in a separate MonitoringHost instance to protect other instances of MonitoringHost.exe in the event of a failure. Workflows are merged under the same identity in the same MonitoringHost, unless a workflow has specifically requested to be isolated in the workflows definition in the management pack. Typically workflows are not isolated, as creating multiple processes incurs overhead in terms of system resources.

Management Server Action Account

The MSAA is specified during your OpsMgr installation. You can choose to use Local System or a domain or local user account.

Each management server has its own action account; you can specify the same action account or use different accounts when you have multiple management servers. The action account is granted write access to the operational and data warehouse databases. The MSAA needs at least the following privileges:

- Member of the local Users group
- Read access to the Windows event logs
- Member of the Performance Monitor Users group
- Granted the Allow Logon Locally right

TIP: BEST PRACTICES FOR THE MANAGEMENT SERVER ACTION ACCOUNT

Microsoft recommends using the same MSAA on all management servers, which should be a domain account rather than Local System, except when used in a lab or very small environment.

Using a Low-Privileged Account on the Agent

For older operating systems such as Windows XP, the agent action account must have administrative rights to the system. For other operating systems, you usually can use a low-privileged account for the action account. This is the preferred approach, as you can use Run As profiles for anything requiring a higher level of access. When using a low-privileged account, the account must have the following minimum privileges:

- Member of the local Users group
- Member of the Performance Monitor Users group
- Granted the Allow Logon Locally right

These are the lowest privileges OpsMgr supports for the action account. Other Run As accounts can have lower privileges.

When you specify a domain account for the action account, you may need to add privileges to the account for various management packs to function properly. Table 10.5 lists these privileges.

TABLE 10.5 Permissions required for the action account

Access Type	Resource
Read	Read access to the Windows event logs.
Read	Read access to the Windows performance counters.
Performance Monitor Users	The action account must be a member of the Performance Monitor Users security group.
Read	Read access to application-specific log files.
Read	If other log files or folders are monitored, the action account must have Read access to the specific log file or folder.

The actual privileges necessary for the action account and the Run As accounts vary, depending on the management packs running on the computer and how those are configured.

NOTE: CUSTOMIZING THE ACTION ACCOUNT FOR MANAGEMENT PACKS

Different management packs may have different requirements for minimum privileges for the action account, although well-written management packs will not force the action account to have higher privileges (with the possible exception of access to a particular logfile, and so on). Read the related management pack guide to understand the privileges necessary for the managed agent.

As an example, if the agent you are configuring the action account for is an Exchange server and a domain controller, you will need to combine the privileges necessary for each management pack to ensure the action account has the appropriate rights to support all the management packs that apply to it. Each management pack has its own profile; rights and privileges for each profile are added together, giving the effective rights.

Here are additional caveats to using low-privileged accounts:

- You cannot enable Agentless Exception Monitoring (AEM) on a management server with a low-privileged action account.

- If a management pack will be reading an event in the security event log, you must assign the action account the Manage Auditing and Security log privilege by using either a local or a global policy.

  Microsoft recommends using Audit Collection Services (ACS) to manage security event log data, unless that will not deliver the required functionality.

- If the operational database is installed on a separate computer from the first management server and you select the option to use a domain or local account during installation, the action account must be a domain account; a local user account on the management server will not be able to access the database and the setup process will fail.

Action Account on Older Operating Systems

For systems running Windows XP, the action account must be a member of the local Administrators security group or run as Local System. The Local System account has high privilege levels on the local system as it is a member of the Administrators security group. On a domain controller, Local System account privileges give it the equivalent to Domain Admin-level privileges on that particular system.

Newer operating systems have additional built-in accounts. The built-in Network Service account has fewer access privileges than Local System, but the Network Service account is able to interact throughout the network with the credentials of the computer account.

NOTE: ISSUES WITH USING THE LOCAL SERVICE ACCOUNT

There is a built-in account with lower privileges than Local System; this is the Local Service account. This has the same local privileges as the Network Service account and has a smaller attack surface due to its inability to communicate outside the local computer.

However, the requirement to communicate with the management server prevents use of the Local Service account, as it has no rights to communicate outside the local computer. The Network Service account has that right.

Changing Credentials for the Action Account

If the action account has a password that will expire, Operations Manager generates an alert 14 days before expiration. Change the password in Active Directory, and then update the credentials in OpsMgr. Follow these steps to change the credentials:

1. In the Administration pane of the Operations console, select **Run As Configuration -> Accounts**.
2. In the Accounts pane, under Type: Action Account, right-click the account *<domain\UserName>* you want to change, and then select **Properties**.
3. Select the Credentials tab in the Run As Account Properties dialog box (see Figure 10.10).
4. Enter the new credentials for the action account, and click **OK**.

REAL WORLD: USING LOCAL SYSTEM FOR THE DEFAULT ACTION ACCOUNT

Microsoft recommends using Local System as the default action account:

- It provides the necessary rights to monitor a local machine.
- It is secure and low maintenance.
- Many management packs require using Local System.

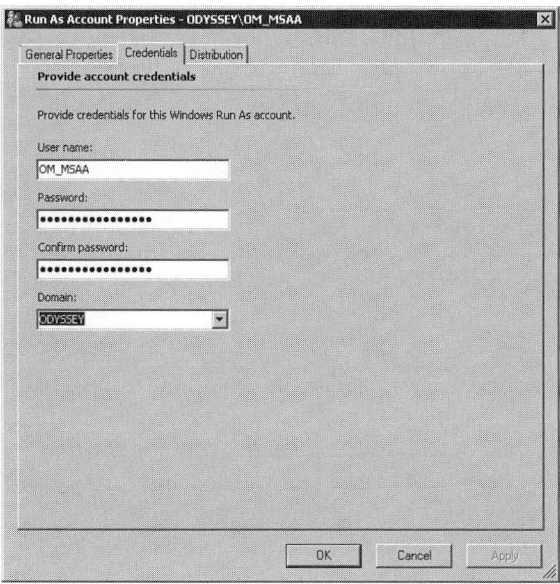

FIGURE 10.10 Run As Account Properties.

The System Center Configuration Service and System Center Data Access Service Account
Both the System Center Configuration Service and System Center Data Access Service use the System Center Configuration Service and System Center Data Access Service account to update information in the operational database. Credentials used for this account are assigned to the sdk_user role in the database. Data from managed entities written to the database may be of a security-related nature. You can run this as Local System or specify a domain user account that has local Administrator privileges; a local user account is not supported. Microsoft recommends the credentials assigned to this account are from a high-privileged account but not the same used for the MSAA.

If you install the operational database on a server other than the first management server and select Local System for this account, the computer account for the management server is assigned to the sdk_user role in the operational database.

Changing the credentials for this service is discussed at http://technet.microsoft.com/en-us/library/hh456438.aspx.

Computer Discovery Account

The account used by the Computer and Device Management Wizard for computer discovery is either the MSAA or an account with administrative privileges on the targeted computer(s). If you specify a local user account rather than a domain account to limit your security exposure, the MSAA performs discovery.

Agent Installation Account

If you use discovery-based agent deployment, you are asked to specify an account with Administrator privileges. OpsMgr uses the MSAA by default. As this account installs the agent on targeted computers, it must have local Administrator rights on all systems to which the agents are deployed. If the MSAA does not have Administrator rights, you must specify an account with those rights. Information for this account is not stored; it is encrypted before use and then discarded.

Notification Action Account

This account is not required during setup; it is used when creating and sending notifications. The account will need sufficient rights for the SMTP server, instant messaging server, or SIP server you will use for notifications.

Data Warehouse Write Account

The Data Warehouse Write account is used to insert and update information in the data warehouse database. This account writes data from the management servers to the data warehouse and reads data from the operational database. The credentials used for this account are assigned to the OpsMgrWriter role in the data warehouse database, and the dwsynch_users role in the operational database. This account must be a domain account. If you change the password for the credentials that you entered for this account, you must also make the same password changes for the following Run As accounts (see http://support.microsoft.com/kb/2681388 for details):

- Data Warehouse Action account
- Data Warehouse Configuration Synchronization Reader account

Data Reader Account

The Data Reader account runs and manages reports. The credentials used for this account are assigned to the OpsMgrReader role in the data warehouse database, and are added to the Operations Manager Report Security Administrators role. The Data Reader account becomes the identity for the Report Server application pool in IIS. This account must be a domain user account. If you change the password in AD for the Data Reader account, you must also change it in the Reporting Services Configuration Manager, the IIS Report Server Application Pool, and the Windows service account for SSRS. This is discussed in the next sections.

Changing the Execution Account Password in Reporting Service Configuration Manager

When the password is changed for the Data Reader account, you must also change the Reporting Services execution account in Reporting Services Configuration Manager. Perform the following steps:

1. On the reporting server, select **Start** -> **All Programs** -> **Microsoft SQL Server 2008 R2** -> **Configuration Tools** -> **Reporting Services Configuration Manager**.

   If prompted **Do you want to allow the following program to make changes to this computer?**, click **Yes**.

2. Click **Connect** in the Reporting Services Configuration Connection dialog box.
3. In the left pane of Reporting Services Configuration Manager, select **Execution Account**.
4. In the Execution Account pane on the right, enter the new password for the account (see Figure 10.11).
5. Select **Apply**, and then click **Exit** to close Reporting Services Configuration Manager.

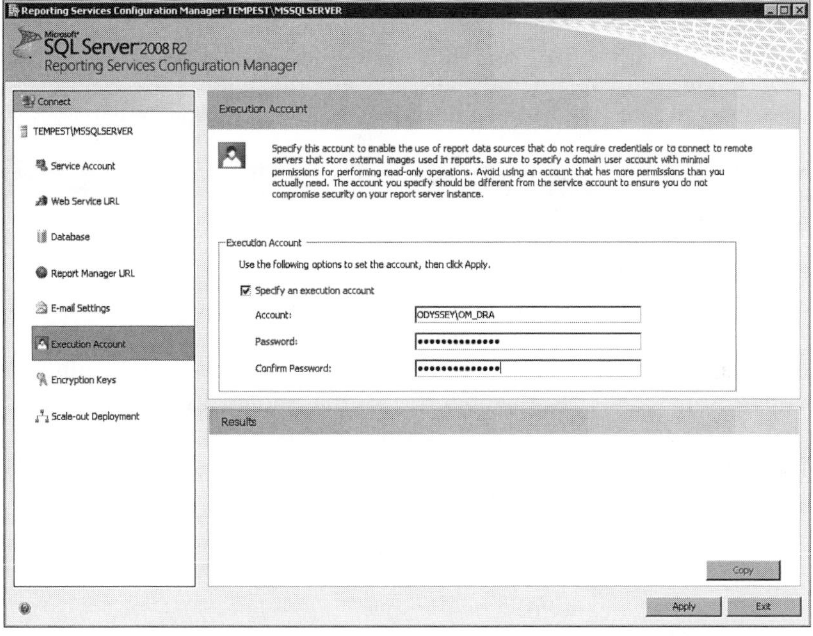

FIGURE 10.11 Changing the password for the Reporting Server execution account.

Changing the IIS Report Server Application Pool Account Password

When the password is changed for the Data Reader account, you must also change the IIS Report Server Application Pool account password. Follow these steps:

1. On the system running SSRS, click **Start** -> **Programs** -> **Administrative Tools** -> **Internet Information Services (IIS) Manager**.
2. Expand *<ComputerName>* **(local computer)** -> **Application Pools**. Right-click **ReportServer** for the instance you are using, select **Properties**, and click **Identity**.
3. In the Password box, type the new password and then click **OK**.

Changing the Windows Service Account for SSRS

When the password is changed for the Data Reader account, you will need to change the password for the service account. Perform the following steps:

1. On the system running SSRS, click **Start** -> **Administrative Tools** -> **Services**.
2. In the Services (Local) console, scroll down to SQL Server Reporting Services for that instance, right-click and select **Properties**.
3. In the Properties dialog box, click **Log On**.
4. In the Password and Confirm Password boxes, type the new password, and then click **OK**.

System Center Management Service Account

The System Center Management service account must run using the credentials of Local System. This account registers SPNs (Service Principal Names); using credentials other than Local System results in duplicate SPNs. Microsoft does not support running the System Center Management service account under any credentials other than Local System.

NOTE: ABOUT SPNS

SPNs are used by clients to uniquely identify an instance of a service. If, as in the case of Operations Manager, you install multiple instances of a service on computers throughout an AD forest, each instance must have a unique SPN.

The System Center Management service process is separated from the single and multiple uses of the MonitoringHost process. This separation means that should a script running on the computer stall or fail, it does not affect the functionality of the System Center Management service or other responses on that computer. As discussed in Chapter 3, "Looking Inside OpsMgr," there is only one System Center Management service, although it has two implementations:

- The agent System Center Management service runs on monitored computers and executes tasks, collects performance data, and so on.
- The other implementation runs on a management server or gateway server.

The service's functionality is defined by the setup, binaries, and installed management packs.

Gateway Action Account

If you install a gateway server, you must provide credentials for an action account. This actually is an MSAA for the gateway server. Gateway servers in remote domains (and workgroups) will need their own unique action account, which functions as a Run As account for that domain, and allows you to monitor other servers in that external domain such as a DMZ (demilitarized zone).

The gateway action account can run with the credentials of Local System or a domain/local account. It is a best practice to use a low-privilege account. Using a domain account enables the gateway servers to have the permissions required to install agents and perform necessary actions.

Database Security

Operations Manager uses the operational database and data warehouse database. It also uses an audit database if you implement the ACS feature. OpsMgr-specific logins are added to the Master database on the database server instance hosting that database, with corresponding users and database roles to the user databases. The next sections discuss security aspects for the OpsMgr databases.

Operations Database Security

During installation, the setup process adds SQL logins for the MSAA and the System Center Configuration Service and System Center Data Access Service account. Setup then adds these logins as OperationsManager database users and grants them Connect permission for the database. Operations Manager setup also creates several database roles in the operational database:

- configsvc_users
- dbmodule_users
- dwsynch_users
- sdk_users

The MSAA becomes a member of the dbmodule_users role, which is granted Execute permissions for the database. The System Center Configuration Service and System Center Data Access Service account becomes a member of the configsvc_users and sdk_users database roles. The configsvc_users role is granted the Execute database permission, and the sdk_users role is granted Execute and Subscribe query notifications permissions. The MSAA, the System Center Configuration Service and System Center Data Access Service account, and the four special database roles become members of the db_datareader and db_datawriter roles. These are default user roles, which come from the Model database.

Installing APM adds the apm_datareader and apm_datawriter roles to the operational database. The Data Warehouse Write account, apm_datawriter, and dwsynch_users are members of the apm_datareader role. The apm_datawriter role has the Data Warehouse Write account added to it.

Data Warehouse Database Security

OpsMgr reporting setup adds SQL logins for the Data Warehouse Write account and Data Reader account. Setup then adds these logins as database users to the data warehouse database. Setup also creates two database roles in the data warehouse database:

- OpsMgrReader
- OpsMgrWriter

The Data Reader account becomes a member of the OpsMgrReader role, and the Data Warehouse Write account becomes a member of the OpsMgrWriter role. The OpsMgrWriter is granted specific permissions to required database tables. For example, the role is granted Select and Update permissions for the AlertStage table.

ACS Database Security

ACS, described in more detail in the "Using Audit Collection Services" sections later in the chapter, is designed to be separate from OpsMgr administrators and OpsMgr security. Each ACS collector has its own database, OpsMgrAC by default. The authors recommend using SQL authentication for ACS rather than Windows security. When using SQL authentication, the system hosting the database server should have a local group that has a login to the audit database with db_datareader permissions. The local group will allow for user accounts that are not local administrators to view ACS reports, such as user accounts for auditors.

Mutual Authentication

An agent and management server use Windows (Kerberos v5) or certificate authentication to mutually authenticate before the management server will accept data from the agent.

Because OpsMgr requires mutual authentication, the agents and management server optimally belong to the same Active Directory domain. If they are in separate domains, a forest trust between the domains provides the capability for mutual authentication. After mutual authentication occurs, the data channel between the agent and management server is encrypted. These actions take place automatically. The next sections discuss communications between the management server and agent when they are not in domains with trust relationships.

ABOUT MUTUAL AUTHENTICATION

Mutual authentication means that all data sent between a management server, gateway server, and the agent is signed and encrypted by default, and these systems must authenticate each other before communications will occur. Mutual authentication uses the Kerberos v5 authentication protocol or certificates. OpsMgr does not support unencrypted communications.

Using mutual authentication with encryption and signing helps mitigate a man-in-the-middle attack, since the keys are exchanged in such a manner that a person in the middle cannot intercept communications. A man-in-the-middle attack could occur if an attacker simulates an OpsMgr agent or sever, establishing communication with the system on the other end of the conversation, with the potential to perform a harmful action on one of these systems.

OpsMgr and Non-Trusted Domains

Due to DMZs, mergers, or other business situations, companies may have domains that are in separate forests. Without a trust, agents in one domain cannot authenticate with a management server in the other domain. In this case, mutual authentication occurs with certificates. Once mutual authentication takes place, data is encrypted using a public/private key pair, as discussed in Chapter 24, "Operations Manager for the Service Provider."

As an alternative to installing certificates on each agent in a remote domain, you could use a gateway server as the communication mechanism between two domains. The gateway server serves as a proxy server, forwarding monitoring information between the two environments that otherwise could not communicate with each other using Kerberos. Using a gateway server offers these advantages:

- **Simplicity:** When monitoring an untrusted domain, only two certificates need to be installed and updated (on the gateway server and a management server).
- **Isolation:** There is no direct communication between the gateway server and the operational database server or management servers (other than the management server with the installed certificate).
- **Certificate support:** This scenario utilizes standard support for certificate authority (CA)-issued certificates or third-party certificates. Assigning a certificate to the gateway server rather than each agent in the DMZ reduces the amount of configuration effort required.

For the environment used by this book, Odyssey is the domain containing the management servers and other OpsMgr server features, and Continent is a DMZ with systems to be monitored by OpsMgr. A gateway server is installed in the Continent DMZ. Mutual authentication between OpsMgr servers in the Odyssey domain takes place using Kerberos, and mutual authentication between the gateway servers and the agents in the Continent domain uses Kerberos.

Because there is no trust between the two domains, a certificate has been installed on the gateway server and a management server to provide mutual authentication and data encryption. The advantage of using a gateway is only one certificate is needed in the second domain (Continent) and one port (5723) opened through the firewall, as shown in Figure 10.12.

Here is the process of sending data from the agent in an untrusted domain to a management server:

1. As the gateway and agent are in the same domain, Kerberos is used between the agent and the gateway server to authenticate the agent to the gateway, where a key pair exchange occurs once the channel has been authenticated.
2. The information is decrypted by the gateway, re-encrypted by the certificate, and then encrypted using the dynamically generated key pair, which is a function of the health service.
3. When the management sever assigned to the gateway receives the data, it decrypts the data.
4. Data is written to the operational database.

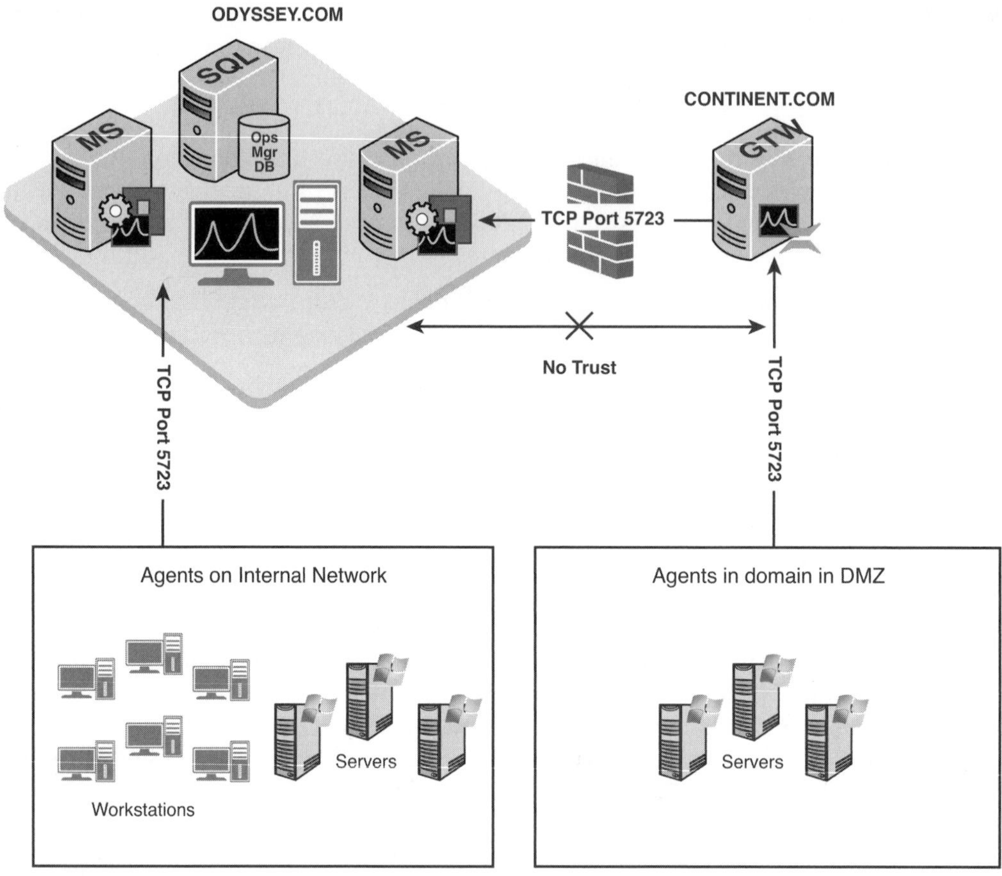

FIGURE 10.12 Using a gateway server with a DMZ and internal network.

Data sent from a management server to an agent may include user credential information such as confirmation data and tasks. When an agent is deployed, it automatically generates a public/private key pair, sending the public key to the management server. Any time the management server will send user credential information to the agent, it uses that public key for an additional layer of protection. The public/private key pair is generated automatically, at startup, when the keys expire, or by a request from the System Center Management Configuration service.

NOTE: ABOUT USING THE GATEWAY SERVER

Use a gateway server when a firewall separates agents from management servers if deploying agents and management servers in separate domains without a forest trust. You can also use a gateway server when you have a requirement to monitor agents in a workgroup, as workgroup systems will always require a certificate.

After the gateway server is deployed, agents connect directly to the gateway and the gateway connects to the management sever. Using a gateway server, you only need to open one port in the firewall—for the gateway server—rather than opening a port for each agent. This improves security.

Additionally, when deployed in an AD environment, a gateway server reduces the number of certificates because the gateway and agent in the same AD forest mutually authenticate by using the Kerberos protocol. Traffic with the management server is also reduced as the gateway server installs the agent software and collects information from the agents to send to its management server.

Gateway servers can also be placed in the same domain as the management servers to reduce wide area network (WAN) traffic in a site with minimal bandwidth as discussed in Chapter 4, "Planning an Operations Manager Deployment." In this scenario, certificates are not required.

OpsMgr and Workgroup Support

Although agents in a workgroup environment can use a gateway server, you must install certificates for communication between the agents and the gateway server to provide a secure channel. These certificates are in addition to the certificate installed on the gateway itself to communicate with the management server.

As an alternative to installing a gateway server, you can configure the agents to use certificate-based authentication directly with a management server in the domain. This could be feasible when there are a small number of agents to monitor in the workgroup. Here is the basic configuration:

- Ensure the management server has a copy of the trusted root CA in the computer certificate store, and that it was imported into the local computer certificate store. The subject name should match the FQDN of the management server with the private key.
- Run `MOMCertImport.exe` on the management server.
- Be sure the agent has a copy of the trusted root CA, and that there is a certificate with a subject name matching the NetBIOS name of the agent in the local certificate store; then run `MOMCertImport.exe`.

Instructions for configuring the certificate and running MOMCertImport are in Chapter 5, "Installing System Center 2012 Operations Manager."

TIP: WORKING WITH MANUALLY INSTALLED AGENTS

For both the untrusted domain and workgroup scenarios, agent installation and any changes to agent settings are made manually.

You will also want to deselect the **Reject new manual agent installations** option in the Operations console, under **Administration** -> **Settings** -> **Server** -> **Security**. This setting does not allow newly installed agents to establish communications with the management server. Choose the setting to **Review new manual agent installations in pending management view**, and optionally to **Automatically approve new manually installed agents**. These settings allow the agent to establish its initial communication with the management server.

Once all manually installed agents are deployed and communicating with their management server, change the setting to **Reject new manual agent installations**. This prevents unauthorized manually installed agents from trying to communicate with the management server.

Agent Proxying

OpsMgr supports agent proxying. When you will be managing an agentless managed computer, it must be assigned to a management server or agent-managed computer to provide remote (proxy) agent functionality. As discussed in Chapter 8, "Installing and Configuring Agents," computers are managed as agentless when you either cannot or do not want to install an agent on them.

Not all management packs work in agentless mode, and agentless management will not work when the agentless computer and its proxy communicate through a firewall. Proxying is the capability for an agent to relay or forward information from or about other computers or network devices to the management server. The proxy can be any agent managed-computer in the management group configured to be a proxy, including a management server.

Disabling agent proxying prevents spoofing by an attacker pretending to be an agent because the management server matches information sent from the agent to a known agent name before accepting the data. Agent proxying is disabled by default. To configure agent proxying on an agent-managed computer, follow these steps:

1. In the Operations console, navigate to **Administration** -> **Device Management** -> **Agent Managed**.
2. Right-click the agent-managed computer you want to act as a proxy agent, select **Properties**, and then select the Security tab. Check the box to **Allow this agent to act as a proxy and discover managed objects on other computers**, and click **OK**.

To configure a management server as a proxy for agentless managed computers, perform the following steps:

1. In the Operations console, navigate to **Administration** -> **Device Management** -> **Management Servers**.
2. Right-click the management server you want to act as a proxy, select **Properties**, and then select the Security tab. Check the box to **Allow this agent to act as a proxy and discover managed objects on other computers**, and click **OK**.

This procedure must be performed for each agent of management server for which you want to allow agent proxying.

A number of management packs use agent proxying. For example, the Active Directory management pack requires agent proxying to populate its topology views. The File Replication Service (FRS) management pack also requires agent proxying for monitoring replica members.

Using SSL to Connect to a Reporting Server

Many organizations are implementing secure websites using SSL technology. If you have installed SSL on your reporting server, you must configure the Operations console to use SSL. Port 443 is used for secure http (https). Perform these steps:

1. In the Operations console, navigate to **Administration** -> **Settings**. Right-click on **Reporting** and select **Properties**.
2. In the General tab, under the Report Server Settings section, click the Reporting Server URL drop-down list and select **https://**.
3. Edit the URL, replacing :80 with **:443**, and click **OK**.

Using the Health Service Lockdown Tool

On computers requiring high security such as domain controllers, you may want to deny certain identities access to rules, tasks, and monitors that could jeopardize the security of your organization. The Health service lockdown tool (`HSLockdown.exe`) includes command-line options to control and limit the identities to run rules, tasks, and monitors.

Here is the syntax for HSLockdown:

```
HsLockdown <ManagementGroupName> /<Option>
<Option>:
/L - List accounts/groups
/A - Add an allowed account or group
/D - Add a denied account or group
/R - Remove an allowed/denied account or group
```

Accounts must either be specified in NetBIOS (domain\username) or UPN (username@fqdn.com) format.

Executing Health Service Lockdown

Run HSLockdown from the command prompt. The utility is located in the *%ProgramFiles%*System Center 2012\Operations Manager\Server folder.

If you use the Add or Deny options, you must restart the System Center Management service for the changes to take effect.

Unlocking the Action Account

The System Center Management service will start, but its availability shows as Red if you used HsLockdown to lock out the action account. To resolve this, perform the following steps:

1. Log on as an administrator, select **Start** -> **Run**, type **cmd** in the Run dialog box, and click **OK**.
2. Navigate to *%ProgramFiles%*\System Center 2012\Operations Manager\Server.
3. Type `HsLockdown <ManagementGroupName> /A <action account>`, and press **Enter**.

10

About Cross Platform Security

One of the major features added with OpsMgr 2007 R2 was cross platform support on UNIX and Linux. In cross platform monitoring, the System Center Management service on the management server or gateway server runs all the monitoring intelligence. (You can also use a management server pool, reducing a potential single point of failure.) This service communicates with the monitored computer through a WSMan layer that is on both the management server and the monitored system. Installation of the WSMan layer is a prerequisite. Communication between the WSMan layers occurs over TCP port 1270, originating from the management server or gateway server. If the WSMan layer is not present on the monitored computer or it has failed, there is no communication and there will be a heartbeat failure. You can use SSH to install the WSMan layer or perform diagnostics.

UNIX/Linux has both privileged and unprivileged accounts:

- A privileged account needs to have root-level access to the system, including access to security logs and Read, Write, and Execute permissions in the directories where the OpsMgr agent was installed.
- An unprivileged account is a normal user account without root access or special permissions. You can use this type of account for monitoring system processes and performance data.

The UNIX/Linux Run As Account Wizard is used to create two types of Run As accounts:

- **Agent maintenance account:** This account establishes SSH connections to the monitored computers. This account, which must be a privileged account, performs actions such as upgrading, uninstalling, or restarting the UNIX/Linux agent.
- **Monitoring account:** Use this for ongoing monitoring. You will want to create Run As accounts both for unprivileged and privileged monitoring.

OpsMgr has three Run As profiles for UNIX/Linux, which you configure in the Operations console under **Administration** -> **Run As Configuration** -> **Profiles**, and previously introduced in the "Run As Profiles" section:

- **UNIX/Linux Privileged Account:** This profile will be associated with a privileged Run As account (root or similar), or an unprivileged account that has been configured with elevation via sudo. This is what a workflow will execute, as that requires elevated rights.
- **UNIX/Linux Agent Maintenance Account:** Use a monitoring Run As account to this profile that has privileged credentials or credentials that are elevated.
- **UNIX/Linux Action Account:** This is used by your basic monitoring workflows. Add a monitoring Run As account with unprivileged credentials to this profile.

TIP: USING SUDO ELIMINATES THE NEED FOR ROOT IN UNIX/LINUX DEPLOYMENTS

Using elevation lets an unprivileged account assume the identity of a privileged account on a UNIX/Linux system. The UNIX su (superuser) and sudo programs use the credentials the management server supplies to perform the elevation process. For privileged agent maintenance operations that use SSH (such as discovery, deployment, upgrades, uninstalls, and agent recovery), support for su, sudo elevation, and support for SSH key authentication (with or without passphrase) is provided. For privileged WS-Management operations (such as viewing secure log files), support for sudo elevation (without password) is added.

However, you must enable sudo for the user and turn off the prompt for password. This is not a security issue if intended use of Run As credentials is observed. If the UNIX administrators enter the sudo-enabled Run As account credentials, the no prompt requirement is of less consequence. For information on configuring sudo, see http://social.technet.microsoft.com/wiki/contents/articles/7375.configuring-sudo-elevation-for-unix-and-linux-monitoring-with-system-center-2012-operations-manager.aspx.

Cross platform security requirements are also discussed at http://technet.microsoft.com/en-us/library/hh212926.aspx and http://technet.microsoft.com/en-us/library/hh212886.aspx. Scott Weisler has an excellent discussion of cross platform security and discovery recommendations at http://www.systemcentercentral.com/BlogDetails/tabid/143/indexId/94460/Default.aspx and http://opsmgrunleashed.wordpress.com/2012/07/07/cross-platform-discovery-settings/. Chapter 20, "Interoperability and Cross Platform," discusses UNIX and Linux monitoring in depth.

Firewall Considerations and Communications Security

The "OpsMgr and Non-Trusted Domains" section discussed using a gateway server as a proxy to communicate with a management server across a firewall. This section discusses other considerations for a firewalled environment.

Ports

Table 10.6 shows OpsMgr 2012 component interaction across a firewall. The table lists the ports used to communicate between components, which direction to open the inbound port, and if the port number can be changed. This information can also be illustrated using Figure 10.13, previously shown in Chapter 3.

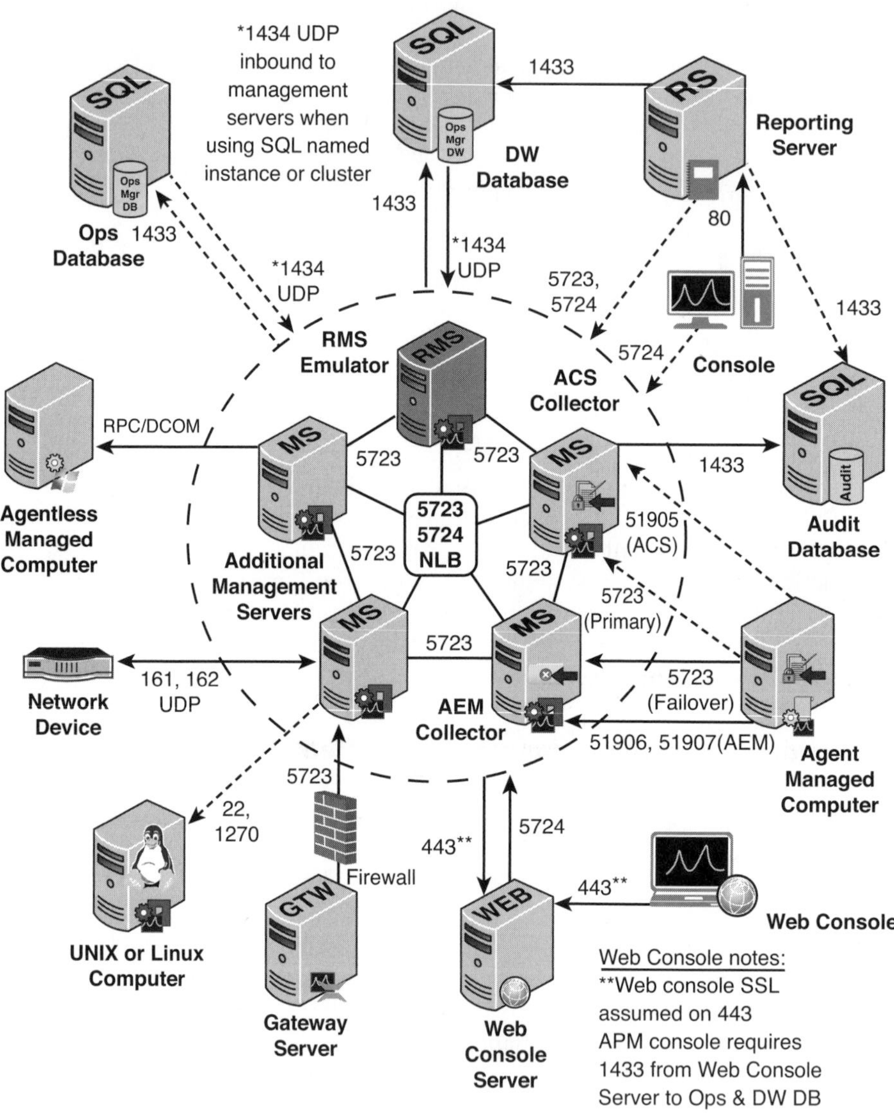

FIGURE 10.13 Communication channels between computers in a management group.

TABLE 10.6 Ports across a firewall

Component A	Port/Direction	Component B	Configurable
Management server	OLEDB (SQL) 1433 -->	Operational database	Yes (Setup). In a cluster, the second node requires a unique port number.
Management server	UDP 1434 <--	Operational database	No
Management server	5723, 5724 -->	Management server	No
Management server	OLEDB (SQL) 1433 -->	Data warehouse database	Yes (Setup). In a cluster, the second node requires a unique port number.
Reporting server	5723, 5724 -->	Management server	No
Operations console	5724 -->	Management server	No
Connector Framework source	51905 -->	Management server	No
Web console server	Selected website port	Management server	No
Web console (for Application Diagnostics)	1433 -->	Operational database	Yes (Setup)
Web console (for Application Advisor)	1433 -->	Data warehouse database	Yes (Setup)
Web console (for Application Advisor)	80 ->	SSRS	No
Web console browser	80, 443 (SSL) -->	Web console server	Yes (IIS Admin)
Agent installed by using MOMAgent.msi	5723 -->	Management server	Yes (Setup)
Agent installed by using MOMAgent.msi	5723 -->	Gateway server	Yes (Setup)
Gateway server	5723 -->	Management server	Yes (Setup)
Agent (ACS forwarder)	51909 -->	ACS collector	Yes (Registry)
AEM monitoring data from client	51906 -->	Management server AEM file share	Yes (Client Monitoring Wizard)

TABLE 10.6 Continued

Component A	Port/Direction	Component B	Configurable
CEIP data from client	51907 -->	Management server (CEIP) endpoint	Yes (Client Monitoring Wizard)
Operations console (reports)	80 -->	SSRS	No
Reporting server	OLEDB (SQL) 1433 -->	Data warehouse database	Yes
ACS collector	OLEDB (SQL) 1433 -->	ACS database	Yes
Management server	161, 162 <--> SNMP (UDP) and ICMP must be allowed bi-directionally through firewalls	Network device	Yes
Management server Gateway server	1270 -->	UNIX or Linux system	No
Management server Gateway server	22 -->	UNIX or Linux system	Yes

Determining the SQL Server Port

Table 10.6 shows a port number of 1433 for SQL connections. This assumes SQL Server is installed using a default instance. If SQL Server is installed with a named instance, it will use a dynamic port unless statically configured. To identify the port, follow these steps:

1. Run SQL Server Configuration Manager on the system hosting the SQL Server (**Start -> All Programs -> Microsoft SQL Server 2008 R2 -> Configuration Tools -> SQL Server Configuration Manager**). Select **Yes** if User Account Control asks **Do you want to run the following program to make changes to this computer?**
2. In the left-hand pane of the console, expand **SQL Server Network Configuration**.
3. Select **Protocols for** <instance name>.
4. In the right-hand pane, double-click on **TCP/IP**.
5. Select the IP Addresses tab.
6. The TCP/IP Properties page shows settings for a number of IP addresses. The port is under the IPAll section, which is at the bottom of the list. Figure 10.14 shows an example for the Odyssey operational database.

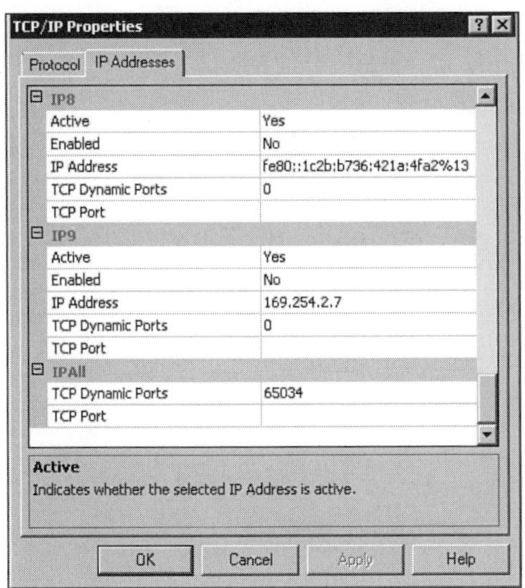

FIGURE 10.14 Determining the port used by a SQL Server database in a named instance.

Agents Across a Firewall

If you are installing agents on any computer running the Windows Firewall, it is necessary to modify the default firewall configuration. This is also true for computers utilizing the agentless managed feature of OpsMgr.

If you are certain the Windows Firewall is disabled on all prospective managed computers, you do not need to perform this action. However, the Windows Firewall is often deployed, particularly on managed desktop computers.

The authors recommend using the Group Policy Management Console (GPMC) to create and deploy an OpsMgr firewall exceptions GPO in the domain(s) where OpsMgr will manage computers. Here are the steps to create and deploy the GPO using the GPMC:

1. Right-click the Group Policy Objects node and select **New**, and create a new GPO named **OpsMgr Firewall Exceptions Policy**.
2. Right-click the new GPO and select **Edit**. The Group Policy Management Editor will open in its own window.
3. Navigate to the **Computer Configuration** -> **Policies** -> **Administrative Templates** -> **Network** -> **Network Connections** -> **Windows Firewall** -> **Domain Profile** node.
4. In the setting **Windows Firewall: Allow inbound remote administration exception**, enable the setting, then at the **Allow unsolicited incoming messages from these IP addresses** section, enter the Internet Protocol (IP) addresses and subnets of the primary and secondary management servers for the agent.

If all computers are on the same subnet, you can enter the word **localsubnet**. This setting opens TCP ports 135 and 445 to permit communication using Remote Procedure Call (RPC) and Distributed Component Object Model (DCOM).

Click **OK**.

5. In the setting **Windows Firewall: Allow inbound file and printer sharing exception**, enable the setting, then at the **Allow unsolicited incoming messages from section**, enter the IP addresses and subnets of the primary and secondary management servers for the agent in the same manner as the previous step. This opens TCP ports 139 and 445, and UDP ports 137 and 138 to permit network access to shared files.

   Click **OK**.

6. In the setting **Windows Firewall: Define inbound port exceptions**, enable the setting and click the **Show** button, and enter the port the agent uses to communicate with the management servers (the default is 5723): TCP:*<IP address of management server><subnet>*:enabled:OpsMgr Agent. An example entry would be: `5723:TCP:localsubnet:enabled:OpsMgrAgent`.

   Click **OK**, and then click **OK** again.

7. Close the Group Policy Editor and return to the GPMC. Go to the Settings tab of the new OpsMgr Firewall Exceptions Policy and select to **show all**. Verify that the settings are what you configured.

8. Navigate in the GPMC to the domain and/or organizational unit (OU) where the computers to be managed are located, then right-click and choose to **Link an Existing GPO**; then select the **OpsMgr Firewall Exceptions Policy**.

9. Allow the GPO to take effect on prospective managed computers. Automatic group policy refresh occurs within an hour on most Windows computers. To have the new GPO take effect immediately on a particular computer, either restart it or execute the command `gpupdate /force`.

CAUTION: RESTRICTION ON AGENTLESS SYSTEMS

Agentless systems are not supported on firewall systems.

Configuring Internet Proxy Settings for a Management Server

You must configure proxy settings for a management server if it will be communicating over the Internet (for example, if you configured Client Monitoring to transmit or receive data from Microsoft). Follow these steps:

1. In the Operations console, navigate to **Administration** -> **Device Management** -> **Management Servers**. Select the management server, right-click and select **Properties**, and then select the Proxy Settings tab.

2. Click on the option to **Use a proxy server for communication with Microsoft** and then select **http://** or **https://** from the drop-down list, typing the name of your proxy server in the address text box.

3. Enter the Port number and click **OK**.

Using Audit Collection Services

This portion of the chapter covers the primary activities necessary to take advantage of the ACS features in OpsMgr 2012. ACS provides a means to collect events generated by audit policies and store them in a central database. Figure 10.15 illustrates that the ACS feature on a managed computer operates independently of OpsMgr, forwarding events to a dedicated server process that has its own SQL Server database.

By deploying and using the ACS features of Operations Manager, the organization achieves a crucial capability—being able to prove it is secure in some valuable measurements of security. ACS provides evidence of how well your environment complies with specific security policies. A question that often arises, particularly from administrators that already have security solutions deployed, involves where ACS fits in a layered security approach. Table 10.7 shows how ACS compares to a conventional intrusion detection system (IDS).

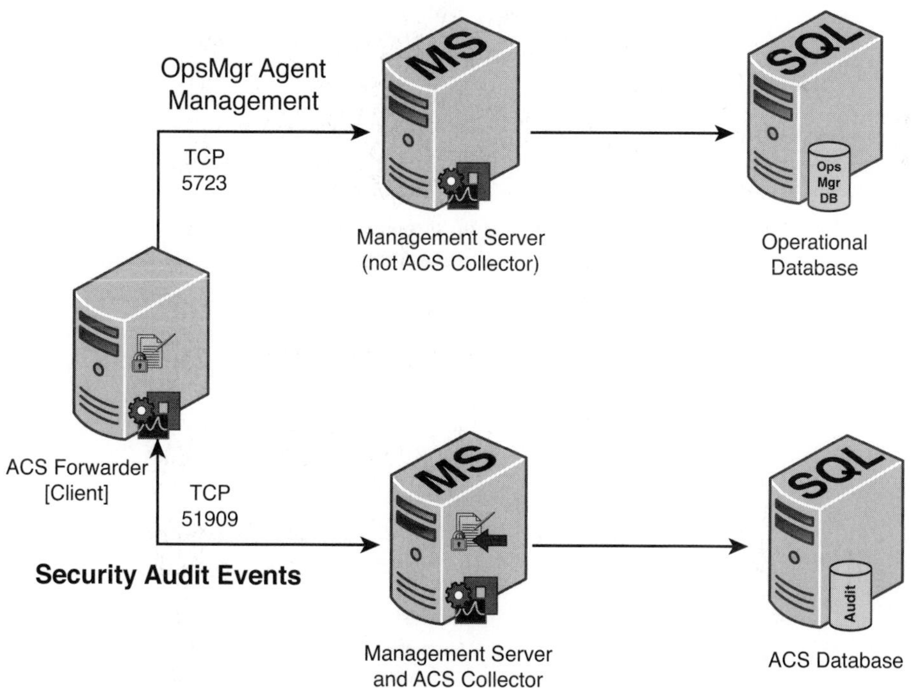

FIGURE 10.15 The ACS forwarder sends security events to the ACS collector.

TABLE 10.7 IDS compared to ACS

Consideration	Conventional IDS	ACS
Sensor	Hardware appliance or agent	ACS forwarder (managed by OpsMgr agent).
What it does	Looks for symptoms across spectrum of intrusions	Audits if specific intrusions have occurred or not.
Deliverable	Alerts of possible intrusions	Reports listing intrusions, or confirming the absence of specific intrusions.
Target environment	Multi-platform	Windows networking, some UNIX/Linux support.
Cost	Can be high	Low, ACS included with Operations Manager.
Complexity	Can be complex to set up and to use, continuous attention required	Setup of ACS is not complex and ACS reports are easy to read; however, defining domain security and auditing policies, then corresponding ACS reports can be a time consuming one-time activity.
Ongoing administration	Can be intense to evaluate alerts; dedicated/exotic consoles	No alerts, just reports; ACS agent administration integrated into the Operations console.

Consider ACS for augmenting your existing, conventional intrusion detection systems. IDS and ACS serve different purposes, and in some scenarios, ACS provides more meaningful or actionable data than an IDS. In an infrastructure where all users and sensitive data exist in a Windows Active Directory domain environment, ACS provides invaluable intelligence in auditing targeted resources, such as changes to privileged groups, and knowing of unauthorized attempts to connect to hidden file shares.

Chapter 5 covered basic steps to install ACS. This section provides additional detail on each of these activities, with references to Chapter 5 so as not to duplicate material. Here are the three high-level aspects of ACS to be covered:

- **Planning:** Development of audit policies (auditing objectives, plans, and reports), and ACS component architecture.
- **Deploying:** Installing and configuring the ACS database, collector, and reports; enabling audit forwarders.
- **Administering:** Executing your audit policy; managing ACS database and reports.

Planning for ACS

The planning activity for ACS has two main phases: Audit policy planning and ACS architecture planning. The authors do not recommend you deploy any ACS features until these two planning activities occur. You must manage the expectations of ACS report consumers such as auditors or network security staff, and match those to architecture decisions, audit policies, and reports during the planning process. Server, storage, and network bandwidth considerations must be included in planning before you activate ACS.

Audit Policy Planning

To get audit data into the ACS database, auditing must be enabled at the Windows operating system level on each ACS forwarder. This means that you first cause the security audit events to exist, and then deploy ACS to transport security audit events to the ACS collector and write them to the ACS audit database. By default Windows does not perform security auditing; you must explicitly turn this on for ACS to collect the data. You enable auditing through *security policies*. Security policy in Windows is found in three locations:

- **Local Security Policy:** Accessed via **Start -> Administrative Tools -> Local Security Policy**.

  Local security policy only exists on client computers and member servers; domain controllers do not have a local security policy. Settings in the local security policy are effective on the local computer unless overridden by domain security policy.

- **Domain Security Policy:** Accessed using the GPMC.

  Settings in domain security policy are effective on all non-domain controller computers in the domain and override settings in the local security policy. Domain security policy has no effect on domain controllers. You can override domain security policy on non-domain controllers using custom GPOs; however, it is a best practice to use a standard domain security policy across your organization as much as possible.

- **Domain Controller Security Policy:** Accessed using the GPMC.

  Settings in the domain controller security policy are effective on all domain controller computers in the domain. This is the only security policy that affects domain controllers.

Comparing the Different Windows Security Policies

Domain controller security policy and domain security policies have the same settings; the local security policy is a subset of these settings. Figure 10.16 compares Windows Server domain (and similarly domain controller) policy side-by-side with Windows Server local policy. Essentially, you can do much more with domain policy than with local policy, but recall that a local policy is always present (except on domain controllers).

Notice the Event Log folder in the domain security policy seen on the left of Figure 10.16; this is where retention periods and parameters for event logging are set. While not a security policy, event log settings are involved in ACS functionality—the security event log must not be too small. The Local Policies folder, immediately above the Event Log folder in the figure, contains the audit policy that provides key ACS settings. Table 10.8 provides details on audit policies and settings.

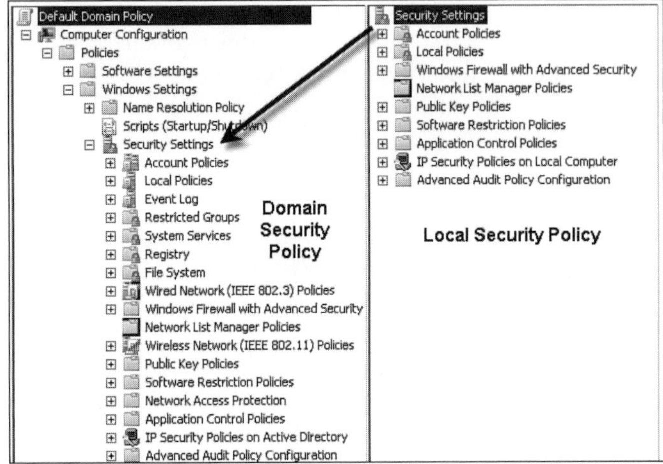

FIGURE 10.16 Domain security policy is a superset of local security policy.

Using Local Security Policy

Any ACS forwarder not a member of an Active Directory domain must use local security policy to enable auditing. You can set local security policy manually at each computer using the local security policy tool (**Start -> Programs -> Administrative Tools -> Local Security Policy**). Local polices can be manually exported from one computer and imported to another computer's local policy. If you need to restore a computer's local policy to the defaults, use the Security Configuration and Analysis MMC snap-in.

Using Domain and Domain Controller Security Policies

In a domain environment, you could enable auditing to a certain extent on some computers and in a different manner on others (except in the case of domain controllers).

- Domain controllers always enable the complete domain controller security policy, no more and no less. (The domain controller security policy should not be linked to any OUs other than the Domain Controllers OU.)
- Non-domain controller computers (clients and member servers) have the default domain security policy applied and optionally one or more other security policies applied by GPO.

The authors do not recommend creating custom GPOs with security policies unless absolutely necessary; it is best to work within the default (single) domain security policy to have consistency across the enterprise. Complexities in GPO inheritance and security settings can cause unintended results. A valid reason to deploy a custom GPO with a security policy would be to enforce auditing at a high level for a subset of servers in an OU while maintaining modest auditing for all other domain member computers.

TIP: NO DIRECT CONNECTION BETWEEN SECURITY POLICIES AND ACS

Changes to domain controller and domain security policies take effect on computers regardless of their state as ACS forwarders. Every computer in the domain will begin auditing in accordance with the domain security policy as soon as changes are applied to the GPO. Avoid inadvertently enabling overaggressive auditing; this can literally stop the network due to saturation with auditing processing and logging.

Windows Server Auditing Categories

There are nine categories of auditing available in the Local Policy -> Audit Policy section of all types of security policies (domain and local) as they appear in the GPMC, as seen in Figure 10.17. Table 10.8 lists each audit policy category, a description of its effect, and the recommended "secure" configuration settings. The selection of category and audit settings contained in Table 10.8 should be effective for collecting useful security audit data for most organizations, particularly when applied to the domain controller security policy. These policies are identical for Windows Server 2008 and Windows Server 2012.

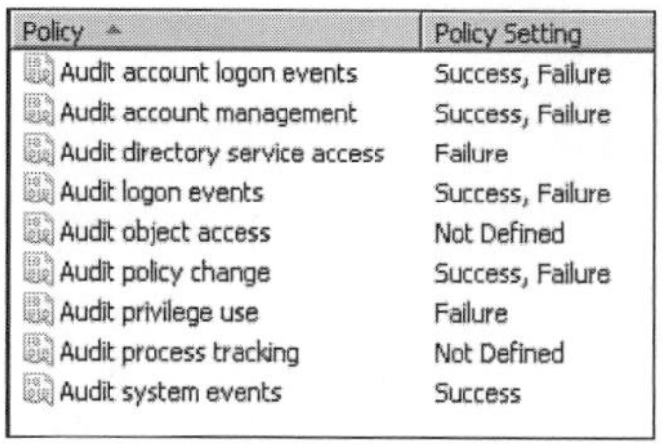

Policy	Policy Setting
Audit account logon events	Success, Failure
Audit account management	Success, Failure
Audit directory service access	Failure
Audit logon events	Success, Failure
Audit object access	Not Defined
Audit policy change	Success, Failure
Audit privilege use	Failure
Audit process tracking	Not Defined
Audit system events	Success

FIGURE 10.17 Audit policy categories as viewed in GPMC.

TABLE 10.8 Windows Server audit policies

Category	Description	Nominal Setting
Account logon events	Audits each instance of a user logging on to or logging off from another computer from which this computer validates the account.	Success, Failure
Account management	Includes when a user or group is created, changed, or deleted, renamed, disabled, enabled, or a password is set or changed.	Success, Failure

Category	Description	Nominal Setting
Directory service access	Audits the occurrence of a user accessing an Active Directory (AD) object that has its own system access control list (SACL) specified.	Failure
Logon events	Audits each occurrence of a user logging on to or logging off a computer.	Success, Failure
Object Access	Audits the occurrence of a user accessing a file, folder, registry key, printer, or other non-AD object that has a SACL specified.	None (Not defined)
Policy Change	Audits every incident of a change to user rights assignment policies, audit policies, or trust policies.	Success, failure
Privilege Use	Audits each instance of a user exercising a user right, with the exception of Bypass traverse checking, Debug programs, Create a token object, Replace process level token, Generate security audits, and Backup or restore files and directories.	Failure
Process Tracking	Audits detailed tracking information for events such as program activation, process exit, handle duplication, and indirect object access.	None
System Events	Audits when a user restarts or shuts down the computer, or when an event occurs that affects either the system security or the security log, such as clearing the security log.	Success

In addition to deploying the appropriate audit settings through domain group policy or local security policy, you should enforce minimum security log sizes for domain controllers and other computers. In a domain environment, configure the **Security Settings -> Event Log -> Maximum security log size** settings in the domain and the domain controller security policies. A recommended initial setting for domain controllers is 160MB, with 16MB for non-domain controllers. In a workgroup environment, apply these settings manually at each computer (**Event Viewer -> Security -> Properties -> Log size**). Figure 10.18 shows the event log settings in the domain controller security policy.

The security auditing for Windows is divided into domain controller and non-domain controller modes of operation, as most relevant security events occur on domain controllers. Domain user accounts receive their authentication token from a domain controller and present that token to access resources across the domain. Capturing issue of that token on the domain controller is how any audit trail begins involving domain security.

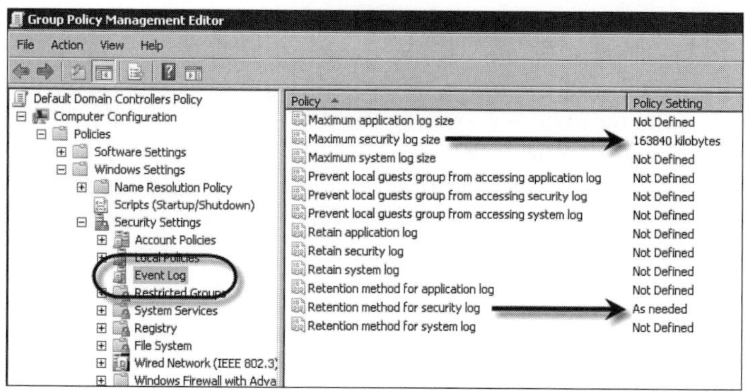

FIGURE 10.18 Event log settings to enforce on domain controllers.

ACS Architecture Planning

ACS design decisions are driven by the size of your organization, any desired administrative split between OpsMgr and ACS, and availability of the audit database. Here are five questions for you to answer when making ACS architecture decisions:

- Will you host any of your databases on clustered SQL servers?
- Will you implement a security partition between your OpsMgr environment and the audit database?
- Will you integrate the ACS reporting feature with the OpsMgr reporting feature by sharing the same SQL Service Reporting Server, or will you install ACS reporting to a dedicated SSRS instance?
- How many ACS collector/database pairs will you deploy in your management group(s)?
- Will you use SQL Standard or Enterprise edition for your ACS database server(s)?

Clustering ACS Database SQL Servers

The simplest of these architecture decisions might be whether to cluster one or more of your ACS database SQL servers. Here are some reasons to consider clustering the ACS database server:

- Cost of downtime and possible emergency system restore costs.
- Loss of ability to collect or analyze security events while replacing or performing extended maintenance on a failed SQL Server hosting the audit database.
- Liability or service level agreement (SLA) failure for possible loss of safeguarded audit data.

Because OpsMgr 2012 does not require an agent on the ACS database server, the procedures for audit database installation and configuration on a single SQL Server or multi-node SQL cluster are identical.

Creating a Security Partition

A small organization has little reason to create a security partition between ACS reporting and the OpsMgr management group. The same person or small group of individuals responsible for the security of the network is reviewing the ACS reports. The larger your organization, the more likely you have a separate security team and/or auditing and inspection team. If you need to deliver ACS reporting products to a separate team, consider deploying a security partition scheme between the production OpsMgr management group and ACS database and reporting server.

Separating the ACS database and reporting from OpsMgr accomplishes several important security and compliance-related objectives. Figure 10.19 illustrates the database and reporting features installed in a different domain and without OpsMgr agents that report to an audited domain's management group. The vertical dashed line in the center of Figure 10.19 represents the security partition. In this scenario, the ACS collector uses local SQL account security (not Active Directory security) to write to the ACS audit database in the untrusted domain. Reports are generated by SSRS or viewed directly in the SSRS report manager web interface.

An obvious security risk mitigated by a security partition is that a careless or criminal user with elevated access to an OpsMgr configuration cannot run tasks on managed computers that completely compromise organizational security. The architecture of SSRS enables extending user access to the SSRS website and administrative level access to the ACS database and report server to auditing staff without giving them access to the Operations console.

Integrating ACS with OpsMgr Reporting

If you are not deploying a security boundary between the production domain where OpsMgr runs and the ACS database and report server, there are two models for deploying ACS reports in the same domain as OpsMgr:

- Install ACS reports in a dedicated SSRS instance, as described in the previous section. However, since the SSRS computer is in your domain, there is naturally no security isolation.

  Consider installing ACS reports on a dedicated SSRS instance if the consumers of ACS data, such as a security team, would be better served with not having access to "too much data," that being all the reports already installed in the OpsMgr management group. ACS reports appear in a folder named Audit Reports. While in the SSRS website, the Audit Reports folder is the only folder in a dedicated SSRS instance, it is one of many folders in the primary OpsMgr SSRS instance.

- The default architecture, and certainly recommended for smaller organizations, is to install the ACS reports in the same SSRS instance used by OpsMgr reporting. This is convenient for OpsMgr administrators, since they do not need to leave the Operations console to run and view ACS reports. In a same SSRS instance scenario, you can still view ACS reports in SSRS, where the ACS reports will appear along with all OpsMgr reports installed from all management packs.

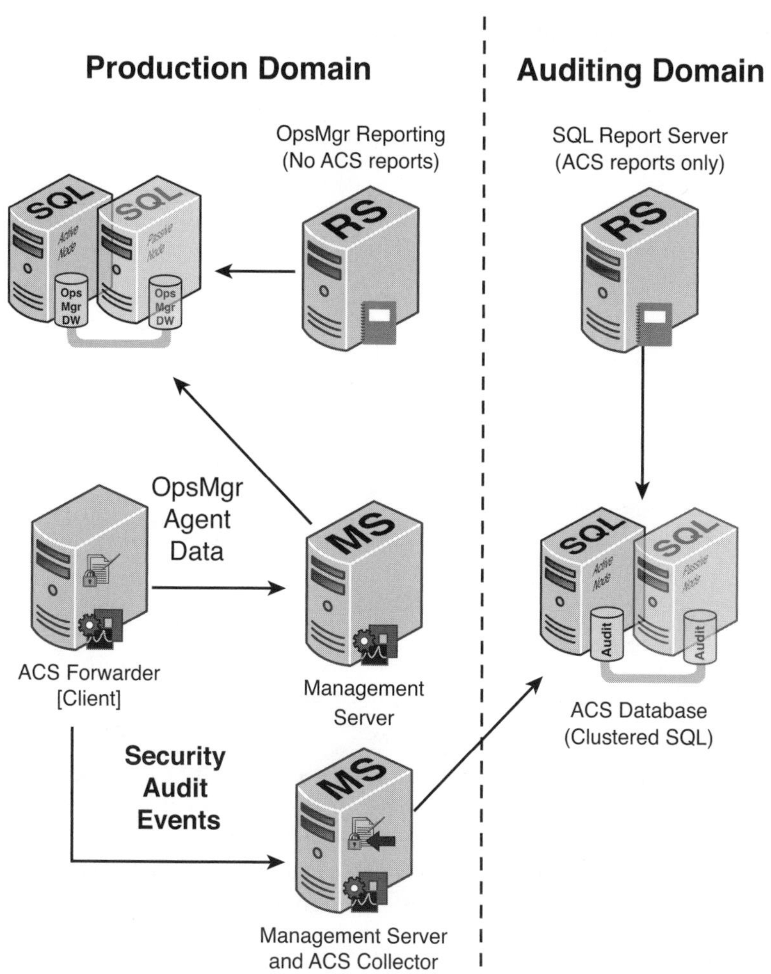

FIGURE 10.19 ACS topology for an organization with separation of audit control.

How Many ACS Collectors Are Required and Their Placement

This is a capacity decision based on how many ACS forwarders will connect at once to a particular ACS collector and other factors. The metrics vary significantly based on local network conditions, the variety and quantity of audit events, the input/output (I/O) limits of storage hardware, and the bandwidth between forwarders and collectors. A good metric to get a handle on is the number of events per hour that you expect to be written to the audit database.

Figure 10.20 shows the 48-hour ACS report Hourly Event Distribution for a group of about 30 servers that are ACS forwarders, including three domain controllers. The hourly event count averages about 110,000, spiking to about 200,000 around 3 AM each day. A moderately busy domain controller generates over 500,000 security events in a day (about 21,000 events per hour).

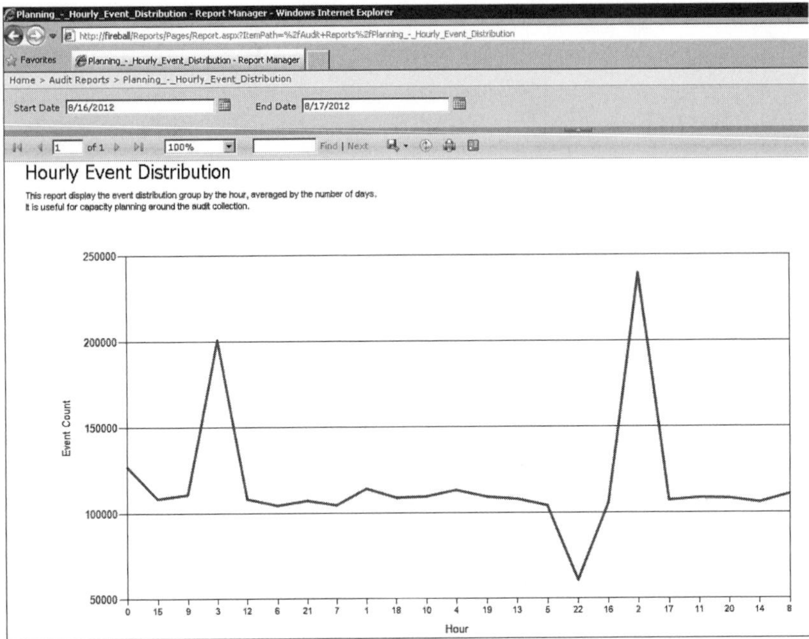

FIGURE 10.20 The quantity of events drives ACS capacity decisions.

Since ACS capacity planning is driven by the number of forwarded security events per hour, determining this number answers most ACS capacity design questions. You should strive to have only one ACS collector and database in your design; adding additional collector/database pairs only when needed for capacity. The capacity constraints that might prompt addition of more collectors could be any of the following:

- **Storage size limits on the SQL database:** The audit database needs sufficient disk space to grow to contain the desired number of days of data. The total size of the database in TB can be calculated by this formula:

  ```
  [Events per second all computers] * [0.4KB, which is the size of event] * 60
  sec *60 min * 24 hr /1024MB /1024GB /1024TB * [retention period in days]
  ```

  Pete Zerger, System Center Cloud and Data Management MVP and contributor to this book, put together an ACS database-sizing calculator. This tool, ACS DB Size Calculator.xlsx, is provided with the online material accompanying this book and is described in Appendix E. The sizing calculator uses this same formula, but allows for additional granular adjustments in security event logging options. (The calculator is from OpsMgr 2007 but is equally valid for OpsMgr 2012 ACS sizing.)

- **I/O limits on the SQL database:** The storage system for the ACS database server must keep up with high volumes of data. Here are two formulas to calculate the number of disks (spindles) required for optimum ACS capacity:

- The number of disks required to handle I/O for the transaction log can be calculated by this formula:

  ```
  [1.384, which is the average number of disk I/O per event for transaction
  log]
  * [Events per second for all computers] / [disk RPM] * 60 sec/minute =
  [number of required drives] * [2 for RAID 1]
  ```

  Note: The average number of logical disk I/O per event (for the transaction log file) has been calculated by the Operations Manager engineering team to be 1.384.

- The number of disks required to handle I/O for the database can be calculated by this formula:

  ```
  [0.138, which is the average number of disk I/O per event for database
  file] *
  [Events per second for all computers] / [drive RPM] * 60 sec/minute =
  [number of required drives] * [2 for RAID 1]
  ```

Note: The average number of logical disk I/O per event (for the database file) has been calculated by the Operations Manager engineering team to be 0.138.

- **Network bandwidth to one ACS collector:** A large number of ACS forwarders cannot share a low-bandwidth connection to a remote ACS collector. In this scenario, you may need to deploy several collectors, each in proximity to the largest forwarder populations.

  To estimate the bandwidth a particular forwarder requires to communicate with its collector, multiply the average size of a security audit event compressed for transmission (140 bytes) by the average number of security audit events in the event log of the forwarder for a given period.

- **Processing load of one ACS collector:** This is the most variable of the factors and highly sensitive to the performance characteristics of the ACS collector computer. Assuming high-performance server and storage resources are provided, a single ACS collector can support a maximum of about 150 domain controllers or 3,000 member servers simultaneously.

SQL Standard Versus Enterprise Edition

The Enterprise edition of SQL Server is recommended because of the stress of daily ACS database maintenance. If you use SQL Server Standard edition, the database must pause during daily maintenance operations when the database tables are groomed. During this period, the ACS collector queue begins to fill with requests from ACS forwarders. A full ACS collector queue causes ACS forwarders to be disconnected from the ACS collector. To ensure no audit events are lost, specify a sufficient size for the local security log on all ACS forwarders, particularly domain controllers.

SQL Server Enterprise edition can continue to service ACS forwarder requests, although at a lower performance level, during daily maintenance operations. In high value auditing scenarios, SQL Server Enterprise edition is probably mandatory to avoid the risk of lost audit data.

Deploying ACS

Chapter 5 covered the prerequisites and basic installation steps for the ACS collector and database. This chapter picks up at that point; after the ACS forwarders have been configured to report to the ACS collector, but before specific security policies are deployed. Without modifying domain or local security policy to enable auditing, there may not be much auditing activity occurring, so not many security audit events will be forwarded to the audit database.

Modify your domain controller and domain security policy to activate auditing, using the GPMC to make changes to the auditing and event log settings as shown previously in Figure 10.17 and Figure 10.18 (or importing local security policies and event log settings on non-domain computers). On a normal Windows network, these secure settings cause meaningful security audit events to be added to the database, such as proof of logon and logoff activity, and will provide evidence of network security status in the default ACS reports.

Extending auditing beyond the secure settings demonstrated in this chapter can have unintended effects, such as causing the collection of overwhelming quantities of security audit events. Many organizations will not need to enable more intensive or more specific auditing, or need to run custom reports to meet their business objectives. Extending auditing (such as for specific file system access) is covered in the upcoming "Administering ACS" section.

There are some additional ACS configuration requirements for the organization with split administration of OpsMgr and ACS, as well as for organizations with a team of auditors or inspectors without access to the Operations console that need to run ACS reports. If your organization does not have split administration or an external audit team, skip ahead to the "Administering ACS" section.

TIP: ABOUT THE ODBC DATA SOURCE

The ACS collector communicates with the ACS database server using an ODBC data source of the System DSN type. The data source is created during ACS collector setup. You can view this data source with the ODBC Data Source Administrator, launched from the Data Sources (ODBC) program in the Administrator Tools group on the Windows Start menu. Selecting the System DSN tab displays the OpsMgrAC data source. Click **Configure** to change settings of the audit database connection, such as switch from Windows to SQL authentication type, or moving the audit database associated with the collector to another SQL Server.

Optionally Create ACS Auditors Security Group

The material in this section discussing the ACS auditors group applies only to those environments with separate OpsMgr administrator and security auditing teams. In these scenarios, you must create an ACS auditors security group. ACS installation itself does not create or require any security groups. The group you create will contain the user accounts of the individuals authorized to browse to the ACS reporting SSRS website and run on-demand ACS reports.

Here are the steps to create a local security group, containing domain user accounts, and granting that local security group read-only rights to the audit database at the SQL Server security level:

1. Create a domain or local group that will contain the user accounts of the ACS auditors. In the example in this section, a local group named ACS Report Operators is created on the SSRS computer (Fireball) where the ACS reports are installed.
2. Add the domain user accounts of the auditing team to the domain or local security group created in step 1.
3. Open SQL Server Management Studio on the ACS database server and navigate to **Security -> Logins**. Right-click and select **New Login** to start the new login wizard.
4. Next to the Login name field, click **Search.**
5. On the Select Users or Group dialog box, select **Object Types** and add the **Groups** type of object. Click **OK.**
6. The From this location field should already contain the name of the ACS database server. If it does not, click **Locations** and select the ACS database computer name. Click **OK.**
7. Enter the name of your local group (for example, **ACS Report Operators**) and click **OK.** This returns you to the New login wizard. You should see the Login name populated with your ACS auditors security group.
8. In the Default database drop-down list, select **OperationsManagerAC** (the default audit database name) and click **OK.**
9. Navigate to **Databases -> OperationsManagerAC -> Security -> Users.** Right-click **Users** and select **New User.**
10. In the User name field, type a meaningful name, such as *<Company Name>* ACS Auditors. (Odyssey ACS Auditors in this example.)
11. Click the selector button to the right of the Login name field. In the Select Login dialog box, click **Browse.**
12. In the Browse for Objects dialog box, locate the SQL login for the ACS database computer's local ACS auditors security group you just created. Check the box in the left column next to the ACS auditors security group and then click **OK** twice.
13. At the Database User, General tab of the ACS auditors user, select the **db_datareader** role in the lower Database role membership list as seen in Figure 10.21 and click **OK.**

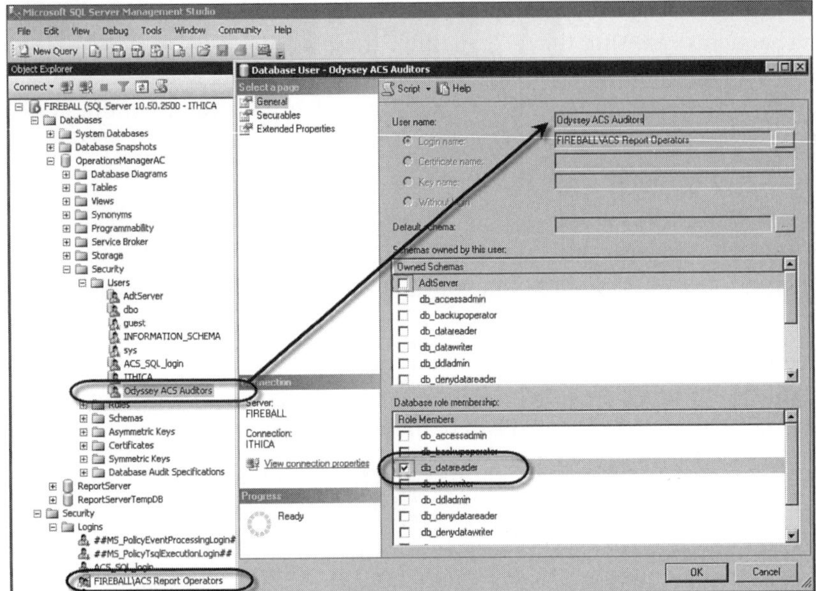

FIGURE 10.21 Creating the ACS Auditors login to the ACS database.

ACS Reporting Server Integration Scenarios

Depending on if or how you integrated your ACS reports, ACS reporting might be fully independent of OpsMgr, or the ACS reports might appear in the Reporting space of your Operations console. In all scenarios, an SSRS instance is the source of the reports and you can log in and run reports through a web browser, locally or remotely, using the SSRS Report Manager URL.

If you deploy ACS reporting on the same SSRS instance as OpsMgr reporting, the same role-based security applies to all reports. This means that ACS reporting users must be assigned to the Operations Manager Report Operator Role to access the ACS reports.

Complete integration Scenario

If users will be using the Operations console to run audit reports and you do not have a separate auditors group, there are few reasons to ever open the SSRS web instance with a browser. All the ACS reports can be run from the Reporting space in the Operations console. The only difference is the source of the data; the report data is coming from the audit database and not the data warehouse database.

Integration with Security Boundary

This scenario retains a security boundary between OpsMgr administrators and auditors, such that ACS reports cannot be run in the Operations console and can only be run in the SSRS web instance. This is an administrative separation and not the same as a security partition involving an untrusted domain or workgroup. Basically, you can use SQL Server security to control which domain accounts have rights to the audit database.

Access to reports in the Operations console occurs in the security context of the Data Reader account (DRA). If the OpsMgr DRA (or a member of a security group that the DRA is a member of) appears in the Databases -> OperationsManagerAC -> Security -> Users list with at least db_datareader permission, you can run ACS reports in the Reporting space of the Operations console. Conversely, if the DRA is not listed as a user of the database, you cannot run ACS reports in the Operations console, and trying to do so generates the following error message:

```
An error has occurred during report processing.
Cannot create a connection to data source 'datasource1'
```

The Operations console will always try to use the DRA to run reports. However, when you open the ACS reports SSRS website using a browser, you can access the audit database under credentials other than the DRA. If you grant permissions to security auditors as described previously in the "Optionally Create ACS Auditors Security Group" section, members of the ACS auditors group will be able to run ACS reports directly from a browser.

Modifying the Data Source Credentials

The default SSRS data source connection credential created by ACS installation uses Windows integrated security, and the DRA logs in using integrated security in a default configuration when running reports in the Reporting space of the Operations console. For ACS security boundary and some security partition scenarios, you must modify the data source connection credential type. Figure 10.22 highlights the default setting at the bottom (Windows integrated security) and the settings when using a security boundary. Here are the steps to modify the SSRS data source connection credential:

1. Open the SSRS Report Manager website in your browser. The URL is http://<*ReportServerName*>/Reports.
2. Click the **Audit Reports** folder to open it.
3. In the Audit Reports folder, click the **Show Details** button on the upper right side of the page.
4. Click the **Db Audit** data source object to open it.
5. Under Connect using, select **Credentials supplied by the user running the report** and check **Use as Windows credentials when connecting to the data source**. Figure 10.22 shows the DB Audit data source modified for this scenario.

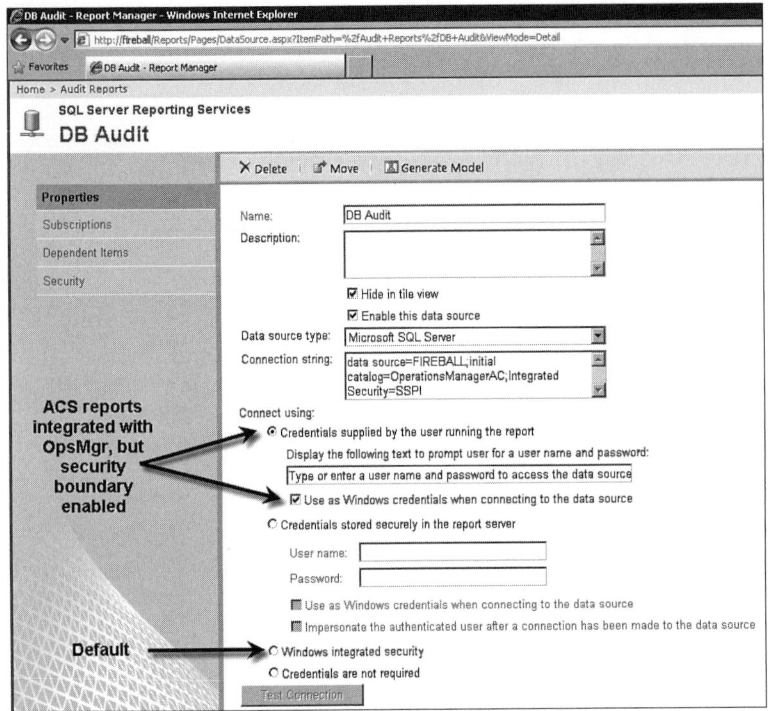

FIGURE 10.22 Default and optional settings for SSRS data source credentials.

Administering ACS

With security policy configured and ACS features deployed, your organization now enters the long-term operating phase of the auditing solution. You achieve the business goal of ACS when audit reports are reviewed in a timely and recurring fashion by responsible internal staff and/or external auditing personnel. Here are some considerations regarding implementing a sustained ACS deployment:

- **Who are the consumers of the security audit reports?** Clearly identify the individuals or teams charged with reviewing security audit reports. Unless you plan to use ACS only for forensic investigations and not proactive security policy enforcement, make sure the security stakeholders in the organization are aware of ACS and the opportunity to consume its data.
- **How will authorized viewers of audit reports physically access the reporting data?** If you extend ACS report access to auditing personnel that are not normally users of the Operations console, you may need to create a role-based security login for them, as well as train them in using the console. Alternatively, if auditing personnel will use the SSRS website to access ACS reports, there may be a SQL Report Manager training issue as well.

- **Do you need to preserve auditing data beyond the ACS database retention period?** There are two ways to persist ACS report data after the database retention period (14 days by default):
    - Export or email copies of the reports of interest and save the exported files as long as desired.
    - Perform conventional backups of the audit database.
- **Is the ACS deployment secured to prevent circumvention?** To audit individual administrator activity, each user with administrative rights must be required to use his own unique named login exclusively. A simple but proactive measure is to eliminate common or shared use of accounts, in particular the BUILTIN\Administrator (local administrator) account on non-domain controller computers.
- **Is the default 14-day ACS retention period sufficient for your organization?** If the 14-day window is satisfactory for your organization, and your audit database has sufficient storage resources, there is no need to modify the retention period. However, you might be constrained by storage space and need to reduce the retention period, or you might have plenty of storage space and you want to keep more than two weeks of data.

  To modify the retention period, you can use the AdtAdmin.exe tool with the `/setpartitions` switch, or follow these steps to modify the retention period manually:

    1. Log on to the computer running SQL Server hosting the audit database with an account that has administrative rights to that database.
    2. Open SQL Server Management Studio, and connect to the database engine.
    3. Expand the **Databases** folder, and select the **OperationsManagerAC** database.
    4. Right-click to open the context menu and select **New Query.**
    5. In the Query pane, type the following, where *<number of days to retain data + 1>* equals the number of days you want to pass before data that has aged is groomed out. For example, if you want to retain data for 10 days, enter **11**.

       ```
       USE OperationsManagerAC UPDATE dtConfig SET Value = <number of days to
       retain data + 1> WHERE Id = 11
       ```

    6. Click the **Execute** button on the toolbar. This runs the query and then opens the Messages pane, which should read (1 row(s) affected).
    7. Restart the Operations Manager Audit Collection Service on the ACS collector for this to take effect.

Running and Using ACS Reports

ACS does not behave like OpsMgr monitoring and fire an alert when there is an unauthorized access attempt. ACS is not about real-time monitoring; rather it produces reports on historical data for a given period. The time period of an ACS report can be from the present time back until the oldest date and time that daily grooming was performed on the audit database (14 days by default). ACS report ranges default to a two-day period, today and the day before; however, you can adjust the date range in the report parameters.

When thinking about using information from ACS, consider the interactive mode of using ACS reports versus the scheduled method of report delivery:

- **Audit Reports run interactively in the Operations console or a web browser:** Figure 10.23 shows the reports that appear by default in the Audit Reports folder of the Reporting space in the Operations console. Figure 10.24 shows the same view of Audit Reports in the SSRS Report Manager website. The content and format of the reports is identical in both the console and the browser.

  There are two main reasons to run ACS reports interactively (as opposed to scheduled):

  - *Proactively* using audit reports to confirm compliance with security policies.
  - *Reactively* as part of a forensic investigation. When you run the forensic reports, you search a specific computer's data, for a specific user, or for an event ID.

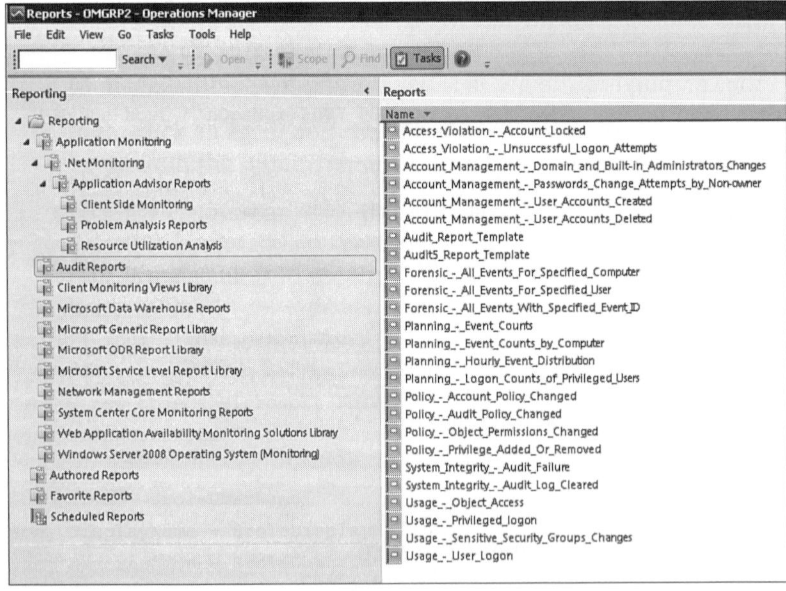

FIGURE 10.23 Audit reports integrated in the Reporting space of the Operations console.

TIP: ABOUT THE AUDIT AND AUDIT5 REPORT TEMPLATES

You may notice two cryptically named report templates in the Audit Reports folder: Audit and Audit5. These templates are used when you create a custom report. The Audit template has room for up to 22 security audit event strings, while Audit5 has room for only five strings. Shorter events index faster, and since most security audit events have five or fewer description strings anyway, select the Audit5 template for new reports unless you know the security event will contain more than five strings.

FIGURE 10.24 Audit reports viewed in a web browser using SSRS Report Manager.

- **Audit Reports scheduled to post to a file share or emailed:** For an automatic, permanent archive of "points in time" reports, schedule publishing of any audit report to a file share, such as an intranet location where audit team members can review the posted reports at their convenience. If you are implementing proactive, scheduled reviews of key audit reports, for example a weekly review, increase security by automating the generation and presentation of the reports to the auditors.

  To set up scheduled distribution of a recurring security audit report, run the report as normal, then select **File -> Schedule** in the Reporting space of the Operations console. To set up or modify subscriptions in the SSRS web interface, navigate to the Subscriptions tab of the Audit Reports folder.

  You can also email ACS reports by first enabling email on the SSRS instance. Once SSRS has an email connection defined in SQL Reporting Services Configuration

Manager, email becomes a scheduled report delivery method to select in the Operations console. Follow these steps to enable automatic emailing of ACS reports:

1. Open the Reporting Services Configuration Manager utility on the SSRS computer where ACS reports are installed.
2. Click on **E-mail Settings**.
3. Enter any desired sender address and a valid SMTP server name.
4. Click **Apply** and **Exit**.

When scheduling most security audit reports (also called creating a subscription in the SSRS Report Manager), you only need to specify the date range of the selected report. For those reports that also require the computer name parameter, there is a prompt when you schedule the report. Figure 10.25 shows the Schedule page while setting up the Account Management: Password Change Attempts by Non-owner report.

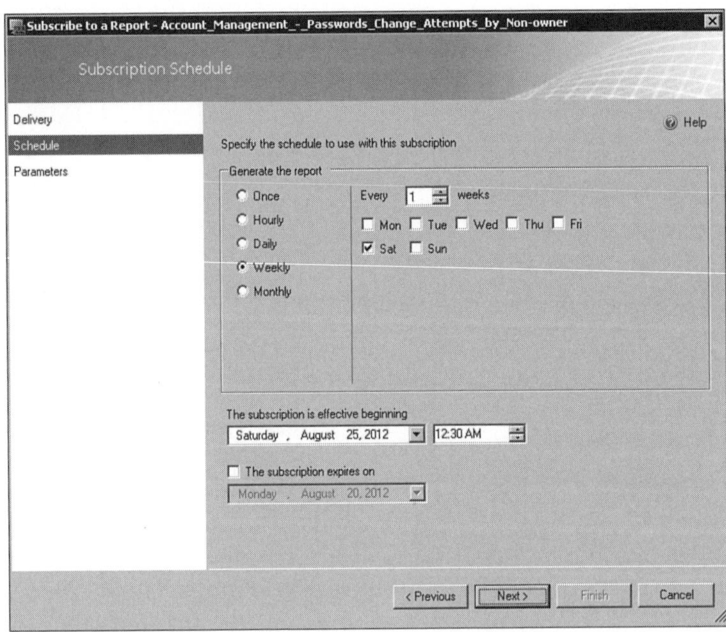

FIGURE 10.25 Setting up a weekly subscription to an audit report.

Using AdtAdmin.exe

The primary tool for administering ACS is a command-line tool, AdtAdmin.exe. The program folder for ACS is *%SystemRoot%*\System32\Security\AdtServer on the ACS collector; to run AdtAdmin.exe you need to be in an elevated command prompt in that folder. There are five categories of functions for using AdtAdmin.exe, the functions are called by various switches on the command line:

- Change the authentication method or credentials the ACS collector uses to access the ACS database. (`-GetDBAuth` and `-SetDBAuth`)
- Use as a statistical and configuration tool for connected ACS forwarders. (`-Stats`, `-ListForwarders`, `-UpdForwarder`, `-Disconnect`)
- Create Windows Management Instrumentation (WMI) queries that limit the events stored in the ACS database. (`-GetQuery`, `-SetQuery`)
- Change the retention period for ACS data in the database and modify parameters regarding daily ACS database grooming (`-GetPartitions`, `-SetPartitions`)
- Create ACS forwarder groups and assign ACS forwarders to ACS forwarder groups. (`-AddGroup`, `-DelGroup`, `-UpdGroup`, `-ListGroups`)

Creating and using ACS forwarder groups is an advanced task, only useful in very large and distributed environments where there are multiple collectors with weighted priority values, or when you need to operate against very large quantities of forwarders at once.

To see all the options, run the command `AdtAdmin -?`. The most common use of AdtAdmin.exe is to confirm the status of forwarders, and to manage WMI queries that filter out some events before writing to the ACS database. Three routine AdtAdmin.exe commands are demonstrated in Figure 10.26:

- The first command, `AdtAdmin -ListForwarders`, returns a list of forwarders that have ever connected to the collector.

```
Administrator: Command Prompt
C:\Windows\System32\Security\AdtServer>adtadmin -ListForwarders
Value,SID,Name
-1,S-1-5-21-1981609044-488691173-2582516280-2611,ODYSSEY\HANNIBAL$
-1,S-1-5-21-1981609044-488691173-2582516280-2192,ODYSSEY\HECTOR$
-1,S-1-5-21-1981609044-488691173-2582516280-2191,ODYSSEY\HELIOS$
-1,S-1-5-21-1981609044-488691173-2582516280-1638,ODYSSEY\HOST1$
-1,S-1-5-21-1981609044-488691173-2582516280-2193,ODYSSEY\TEMPEST$
-1,S-1-5-21-1981609044-488691173-2582516280-2612,ODYSSEY\TYPHOON$
-1,S-1-5-21-1981609044-488691173-2582516280-1630,ODYSSEY\HOST5$
-1,S-1-5-21-1981609044-488691173-2582516280-1631,ODYSSEY\HOST4$
-1,S-1-5-21-1981609044-488691173-2582516280-2153,ODYSSEY\HOST7$
-1,S-1-5-21-1981609044-488691173-2582516280-2189,ODYSSEY\ROMULUS$
-1,S-1-5-21-1981609044-488691173-2582516280-2232,ODYSSEY\CONCERO$
-1,S-1-5-21-1981609044-488691173-2582516280-2144,ODYSSEY\HOST6$
-1,S-1-5-21-1981609044-488691173-2582516280-1639,ODYSSEY\HOST2$
-1,S-1-5-21-1981609044-488691173-2582516280-1199,ODYSSEY\HOST3$
-1,S-1-5-21-1981609044-488691173-2582516280-2190,ODYSSEY\REMUS$
C:\Windows\System32\Security\AdtServer>adtadmin -GetQuery
Current query: 'select * from AdtsEvent'

C:\Windows\System32\Security\AdtServer>adtadmin -SetQuery -query:"SELECT * FROM
AdtsEvent WHERE NOT (HeaderUser='SYSTEM' OR Headeruser='LOCAL SERVICE' OR Header
user='NETWORK SERVICE')"

C:\Windows\System32\Security\AdtServer>_
```

FIGURE 10.26 Listing forwarders and setting WMI filters with AdtAdmin.exe.

- The second command in Figure 10.26, `AdtAdmin -GetQuery`, lists any WMI filters currently in place, and the return `select * from AdtsEvent` is the default state, that is, no WMI filter in place.

10

- The third command, `AdtAdmin -SetQuery -query:"SELECT = FROM * FROM AdtsEvent WHERE NOT (HeaderUser='SYSTEM' OR HeaderUser='LOCAL SERVICE' or HeaderUser='NETWORK SERVICE')"` creates a WMI query that will discard security events when the user account is the local computer account of the ACS forwarder. This is useful in a setting where you are interested in tracking only the activity of actual user accounts, and not machine accounts.

If you try to set WMI filters as shown in the third command in Figure 10.26 and receive an access denied error message, it may be necessary to modify the security on a registry key as shown in Figure 10.27. The registry key is `HKLM\System\CurrentControlSet\services\AdtServer\Parameters`. The Network Service account needs to have the Set Value, Allow permission granted to the Parameters key.

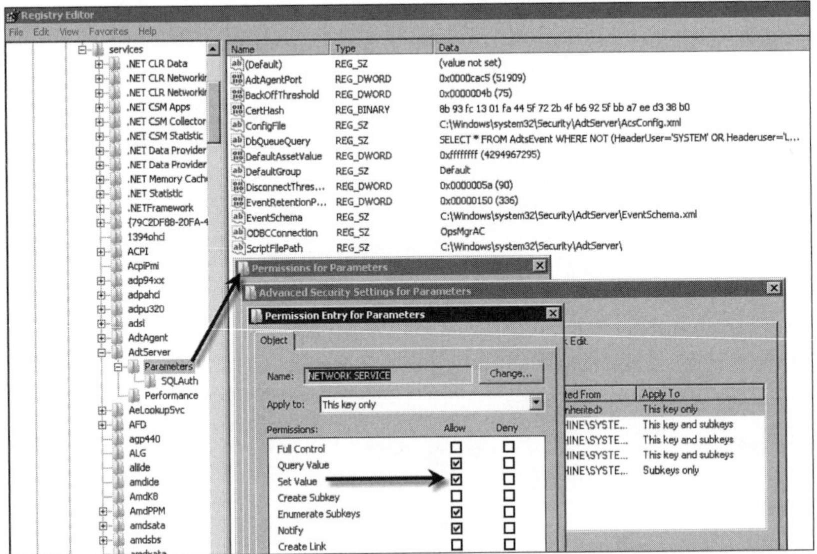

FIGURE 10.27 Allow Network Service to set values in the Parameters registry key.

TIP: REDIRECT ADTADMIN -STATS TO A CSV FILE AND OPEN IN EXCEL

The `-stats` switch for the AdtAdmin.exe tool dumps all statistics about ACS database records. Redirect the output of the `AdtAdmin -stats` command to a text file (append `"> <filename>.csv"` to the AdtAdmin.exe command line), and open it in Microsoft Excel as a comma-separated value (CSV) file. Viewed as a spreadsheet, each forwarder is listed in a row, with 17 columns of detailed data for each ACS forwarder. A value to watch is the Average time to collector(in ms) column, which is a measure of latency between when events occur on forwarders and when the collector writes them to the database. This value should be 2,000 milliseconds or less under normal conditions.

Managing ACS Collector Performance

Audit collection at scale is a high-capacity service; thousands of client forwarders may be connected at a given moment to a single collector, and busy domain controller forwarders will be sending millions of events to the audit database. You may encounter performance issues regarding the ACS collector in large and demanding environments. These issues will appear as a delay in writing security audit records to the database, or ceasing to collect events from forwarders. The capacity of a given ACS collector is finite, and the administrator of the ACS collector (the OpsMgr administrator) should keep an eye on collector performance. Three registry keys at `HKLM\System\CurrentControlSet\services\AdtServer\Parameters` can be tuned to help performance (see the keys in the upper portion of Figure 10.27). These keys work in conjunction with one another:

- **BackoffThreshold:** Default is 75%. New forwarder clients not connected above this threshold.
- **MaximumQueueLength:** Default is 262,144 events. (This registry value must be created manually.)
- **DisconnectThreshold:** Default is 90%. Active forwarders are disconnected until below this threshold.

The queue referred to in the `MaximumQueueLength` value is a memory-based queue on the ACS collector. This is a bottleneck you can throttle by increasing the maximum queue length and/or modifying the backoff and disconnect thresholds. A default collector queue, allowing 262,144 events of 512 bytes each, means about 134MB of memory is available for the queue.

During normal operation, the collector writes events to an in-memory queue, then from the queue processes writes to the database. If the collector cannot write to the database fast enough, the queue builds. When the queue reaches the `BackoffThreshold`, new forwarders cannot connect to the collector, and when the `DisconnectThreshold` is reached, the collector randomly begins to disconnect forwarders to reduce the processing load.

Your primary tools to identify and prosecute ACS capacity issues are the Audit Collection Services views in the Operations console, and the Windows Performance Monitor on the ACS collector server.

ACS Monitoring Views in the Operations Console

The left of Figure 10.28 shows the views provided in the Operations console by default. The Forwarder -> State View is very useful for detecting OpsMgr agents that do not have their ACS forwarder feature enabled; these agents will have Warning ACS forwarder health states.

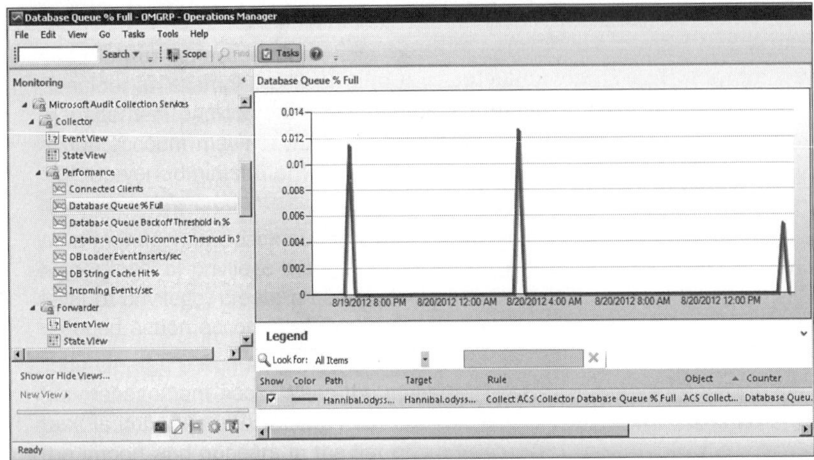

FIGURE 10.28 Monitoring ACS collector performance in the Operations console.

The chart on the right side of Figure 10.28 is a 24-hour history of the Database Queue % Full counter. A healthy ACS collector will also show similar readings—virtually no database queue situations occurring. As previously seen in Figure 10.20 (an ACS performance history report), any counters you observe in the OpsMgr performance view charts can also be captured in an OpsMgr report.

ACS Collector and Forwarder Counters in Windows Performance Monitor

To really watch the ACS collector and forwarder performance in real time, Performance Monitor (PerfMon), part of the Windows OS, is the best tool. A reason is that the OpsMgr performance charts and reports are based on 5-minute samples, while PerfMon can update its chart every second.

Figure 10.29 shows PerfMon running on the ACS collector. You can add to PerfMon any of the ACS collector counters that appear in the Operations console views, as well as the ACS forwarder statistics that you observe when running `AdtAdmin.exe -stats`. A difference is that `AdtAdmin.exe -stats` produces a snapshot of ACS activity, while PerfMon presents live and constantly updated data. Figure 10.29 is showing incoming audits per second received from each specific ACS forwarder.

TIP: DETAILED LOGGING ON ACS FORWARDERS

If you are experiencing a performance issue with a particular forwarder, you might find it useful to enable detailed logging on the forwarder temporarily. To do so, create a new DWORD value named `TraceFlags` with a decimal value of 524420 in the registry of the forwarder at `HKLM\System\CurrentControlSet\services\AdtAgent\Parameters`. After you create the registry key, restart the System Center Audit Forwarding Service (AdtAgent.exe) on the forwarder. A detailed log will be created at *%SystemRoot%*\Temp\AdtAgent.log.

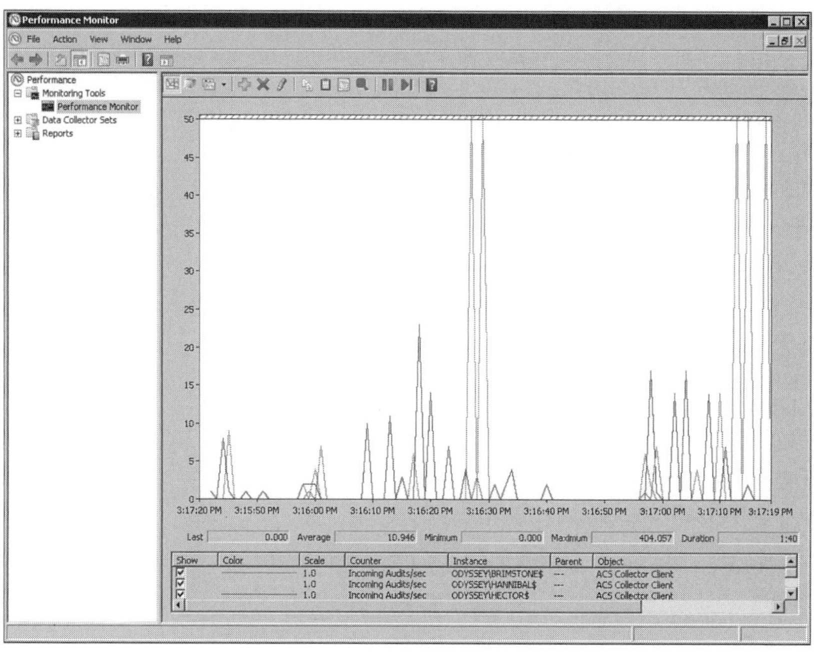

FIGURE 10.29 Monitoring ACS forwarder incoming audits in Performance Monitor.

Resolving ACS Collector Performance Issues

If you are frequently encountering the ACS database backoff and disconnect thresholds, you need to take action to provide a reliable audit collection service. You can modify the ACS collector parameters, such as increase the `MaximumQueueLength` and/or the `BackoffThreshold`. Preferred solutions are to reduce the volume of events, add resources to the collector feature, or increase performance of the SQL Server. Consider one of these approaches:

- Modify security policy to audit fewer conditions.
- Apply WMI queries at the ACS collector to filter out unnecessary events before they are written to the database.
- Reduce the population of ACS forwarders.
- Add another ACS collector/database pair and divide the forwarder population.
- Add memory or otherwise upgrade the collector.
- Upgrade the SQL Server hosting the audit database to provide faster disk writes.

10

Managing ACS Database Size

You must closely manage the audit database size on the storage system of the SQL Server hosting it. To estimate ACS database size, use the ACS database sizing calculator.xlsx workbook provided with the material accompanying this book. (See Appendix E for details.)

After installing ACS, assuming a constant number of forwarders with a constant audit event volume, the audit database will grow to reach a maximum size on the fifteenth day. Then the last day's data is dropped, reducing the database back to the most recent 14 days. The audit database will be stable in size thereafter in this "ideal world."

In the real world, of course, conditions are constantly changing. It is difficult to manage the size of the audit database precisely due to the large number of variables that can rapidly affect the quantity and type of events collected by ACS. If the SQL Server hosting the audit database is running an OpsMgr agent, the Windows Core OS management pack will monitor for low disk space on the SQL volume. If there is no OpsMgr agent on the ACS database server, make sure scheduled review of SQL disk space is provided for in your planning.

If you experience database growth beyond what the SQL Server hosting the audit database can provide, auditing will stop until more storage is provided. If no more storage is available, here are several approaches you can take:

- Collect fewer events (modify security policy).
- Discard more events at the collector (WMI query filters).
- Reduce the number of days of data you are retaining.

Default Auditing Scenario: Account Management

If you deploy the "secure" domain and domain controller security policies like those previously seen in Figure 10.17, the default set of ACS reports will provide a considerable amount of useful data about network security. This scenario detects an unauthorized change to administrative groups.

Auditing Objective

Verify that the membership of administrative groups remains the same, or contains only authorized changes.

Audit Plan

Here is a suggested audit plan:

- Audit success events in the account management category (included in Figure 10.17).
- Deploy the policy to domain controllers to detect changes in the Domain Admins and BUILTIN\Administrators groups.
- Deploy the policy to member servers to detect changes in local Administrators groups.

Audit Report: Domain and Built-in Administrators Membership Changes

The Domain and Built-in Administrators Membership Changes report, shown in Figure 10.30, lists events 632, 633, 636, and 637 (membership change events for local and global groups when the target is an administrative group). This report is a good candidate for scheduling publication to a file share or emailing to auditors for offline review. A blank or empty report indicates no changes occurred during the period.

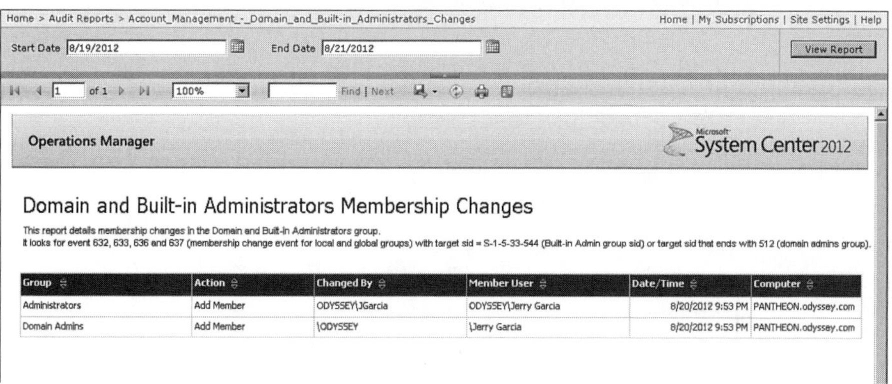

FIGURE 10.30 ACS report on changes to sensitive groups.

Advanced Auditing Scenario: Access Violation

In addition to deploying secure security policies to capture general network security audit events, you can enable advanced auditing scenarios by running targeted reports. In this scenario, you will enable object auditing, and apply audit policy to a file folder. This scenario protects high value data through visibility into unauthorized access attempts.

Auditing Objective

Detect unauthorized attempts to access confidential data in the Finance department file share.

Audit Plan

Here is a suggested audit plan:

1. Audit failure events in the object access category (included in Figure 10.17).
2. Deploy the policy to the domain controllers security policy only if the sensitive files reside on a domain controller.
3. Deploy the policy to the domain security policy to monitor sensitive files on member servers.
4. Enable auditing on the sensitive files or folders. Figure 10.31 shows the Failed, Read Attributes auditing setting being applied to the sensitive folder to be audited.

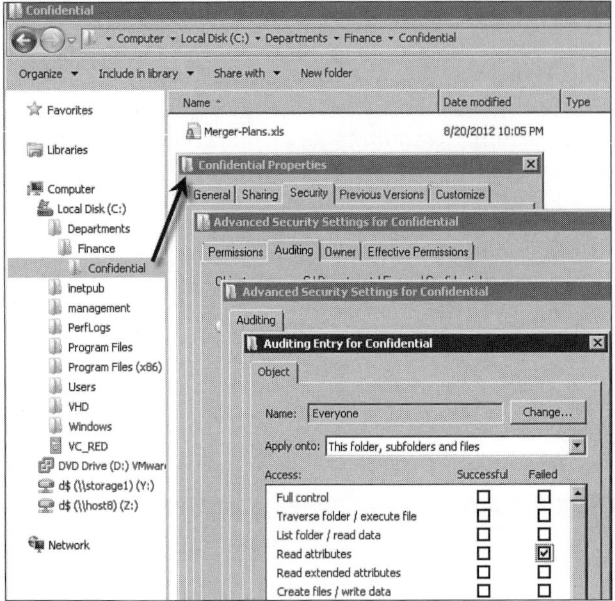

FIGURE 10.31 Enabling file and folder level auditing.

Audit Report: Object Access

The Object Access report, shown in Figure 10.32, uses events 560 (permission requested) and 567 (permission exercised) to track items with object access auditing enabled.

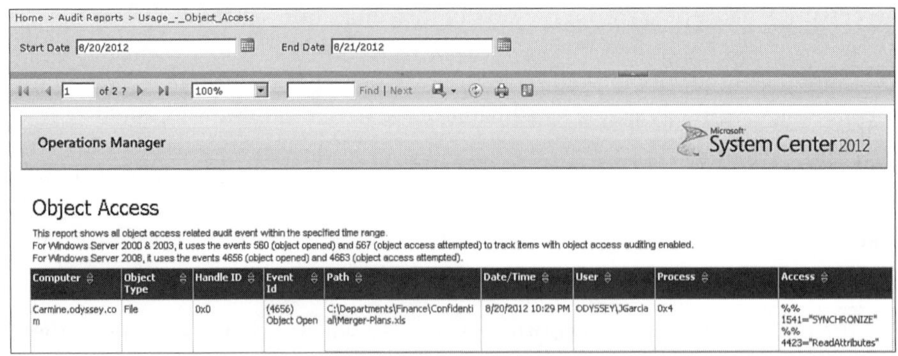

FIGURE 10.32 ACS report on object access failure.

TIP: BE SPECIFIC WHEN ENABLING OBJECT AUDITING

To reduce the volume of events generated and maximize the effectiveness of each event, only audit those actions that really interest you. For example, if you are interested in users reading a file, do not audit Full Control. Also, for best system performance, minimize the number of auditing entries for a given folder or file by using Windows groups to contain all the users and groups to be audited—then specify just that group on the Auditing tab.

Fast Track

While many of the concepts related to OpsMgr security and ACS are similar to Operations Manager 2007, here are key takeaways from this chapter:

- SDK Service was renamed to the System Center Data Access Service beginning with OpsMgr 2007 R2.
- The Authorization Manager store is now maintained in SQL Server.
- Application Monitoring Operator is a new role.
- Microsoft added support post-OpsMgr 2007 R2 for cross platform providers to write events to a local security log using a Security Event Log (SEL) write action module. Management packs for each major platform supported by cross platform have base providers with data sources for Syslog, sulog, and audit, including collection and alerting rules for key security events that should be audited.
- There are five new ACS reports: Account Locked, Account Policy Changed, Audit Policy Changed, Object Permissions Changed, and Privilege Added or Removed.
- The ACS AdtAdmin.exe tool can now change the retention period for ACS data in the database and modify parameters regarding daily ACS database grooming.

Summary

This chapter looked at a number of security-related concepts. It discussed user roles, Run As profiles and Run As accounts, and Operations Manager-related accounts. It discussed database security, mutual authentication, non-trusted domain considerations, DMZ implementations and workgroup support, agent proxying, firewall considerations, and communications security. The chapter also discussed how to use the ACS feature. Additional information on Operations Manager security is in the Operations Guide for System Center 2012 - Operations Manager at http://technet.microsoft.com/library/hh212887.aspx. The next chapter discusses dashboards for analysis, trending, and forecasting.TABLE 10.8 Continued

CHAPTER 11

Dashboards, Trending, and Forecasting

IN THIS CHAPTER

- Built-in Dashboard Functionality
- Prebuilt Dashboards
- Additional Dashboard Options
- Reports, Trending, Forecasting, and Capacity Planning
- Fast Track
- Additional Reference Links

Systems Center Operations Manager (OpsMgr) provides a framework capable of gathering a significant amount of information from a variety of sources. However, gathering this information is not the same thing as displaying it in a usable manner! Whether referring to this as surfacing data, data visualization, or simply the user experience, the concept is the same. Having the data is only half of the equation; the other half is sharing that information and making it meaningful.

This chapter focuses on techniques for sharing information gathered by Operations Manager, with a goal of providing options to identify the best method to display the specific data in which you are interested. The chapter starts with reviewing built-in dashboard functionality in OpsMgr 2012 and discusses how you can also display information through reporting and additional dashboard solutions. It also includes a discussion of trending, forecasting, and capacity planning using Operations Manager.

Built-in Dashboard Functionality

Operations Manager 2007 incorporated built-in dashboard functionality; however, it was only capable of gathering different existing views into a single view. As an example, you could create a view that displayed alerts, performance counters, and the state of a group of servers in your environment. While these views are important, they are far from the type of functionality generally expected in a dashboard.

Operations Manager 2007 R2 included a solution accelerator that provided visualization for service level objectives

(SLOs), enabling you to track the availability of a variety of items in Operations Manager such as distributed applications, network devices, or servers. Microsoft later released the Visio 2010 Add-in for OpsMgr 2007 R2. This provided a way to state enable Visio diagrams, upload them to SharePoint, and make them available via a unique URL. Microsoft has updated this functionality to work with System Center 2012 Operations Manager.

In OpsMgr 2012, dashboard functionality is added as an integrated solution. You build dashboards by defining the structure of a dashboard, choosing various templates, and adding widgets into the templates. You can also integrate these widgets into SharePoint. In addition, two additional dashboard types are prebuilt for this version of OpsMgr: the Summary and Service Level dashboards.

The System Center Virtual Machine Manager (VMM) management pack does not currently include dashboards. This chapter will focus on creating a series of VMM dashboards that provide a practical example of dashboards and how you can use them in OpsMgr 2012. To start this process, perform the following steps:

1. Create a management pack called **Virtual Machine Manager Dashboards** (or create it with a different name, but rename the folder to "Virtual Machine Manager Dashboards" so it will line up with the Virtual Machine Manager and Virtual Machine Manager Views folders, shown in Figure 11.1).

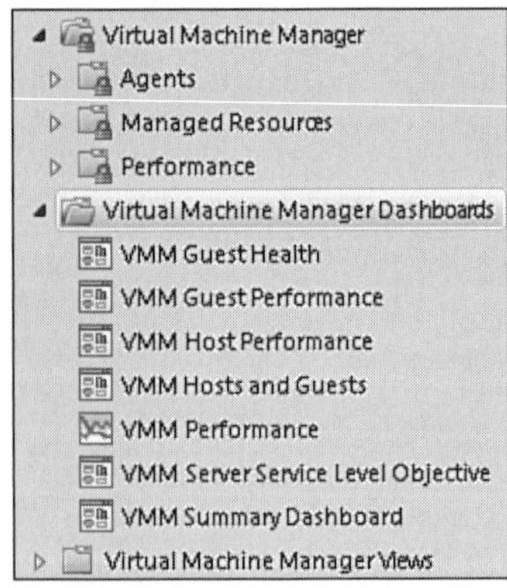

FIGURE 11.1 The Virtual Machine Manager Dashboards folder.

2. To provide a way to scope the various dashboard views created in this example, create two dynamic groups in the Authoring pane:

   - **Hosts in VMM:** This group is defined with a dynamic membership where the object is a VMHost (`Object is VMHost AND True`). This group's membership should display all hosts currently identified in VMM.

- **Guests in VMM:** This group is defined with a dynamic membership where the object is a virtual machine (`Object is Virtual Machine AND True`). This group's membership should display all guests in the environment but may need to be restricted to those guests controlled by VMM.

3. Save these groups in the management pack created for the Virtual Machine Manager dashboards.

TIP: HOW TO TELL IT IS A DASHBOARD VIEW

Dashboards use a different icon than other views in Operations Manager. Figure 11.1 shows the icons used for dashboards and performance views as a comparison, with the VMM Performance view showing the icon for a performance view and the other VMM views (such as the VMM Server Service Level Objective) showing the icon for a dashboard.

Using Templates

With the management pack created, you can choose a template to store in your new management pack. The integrated dashboard functionality for OpsMgr 2012 begins with creating a template. Follow these steps to create a new dashboard:

1. Right-click the folder in which you want to store the dashboard (Virtual Machine Manager Dashboards in this example) and choose **New -> Dashboard View** to start the New Dashboard and Widget Wizard.

2. Four options are now available:

   - **Column Layout:** The column layout divides the dashboard into a series of vertical columns you can use to add different widgets to the columns of the dashboard. As an example, you could define a two-column layout that contains one widget in each column (widget1 and widget2). You could extend this column downward by adding a third widget under widget1 and a fourth widget under widget2.

   - **Grid Layout:** The grid layout divides the dashboard into one to nine cells to which you can add widgets. Available layouts vary depending on the number of cells specified when choosing the grid layout.

   - **Service Level Dashboard:** The Service Level Dashboard provides a quick way to display service level information in a prebuilt dashboard layout.

   - **Summary Dashboard:** The Summary Dashboard offers a quick way to display summary information in a prebuilt dashboard layout that includes a Top N view, performance view, state view, and alert view. You can configure these views to display information for a specific group. This dashboard is a good starting point that you can use for the most common dashboard requirements in OpsMgr.

TIP: TEMPLATES AND WIDGETS

Additional templates or widgets are extendable functionality in Operations Manager 2012. You could also author widgets and templates, which would add to the list of available templates or widgets in this wizard.

The column layout and grid layouts can also contain a column or grid layout within the first layout chosen. As an example, you could design a two-column layout that includes a grid in the second column and a single widget in the first column. Figure 11.2 shows a grid with four cells that contain two columns on the left side.

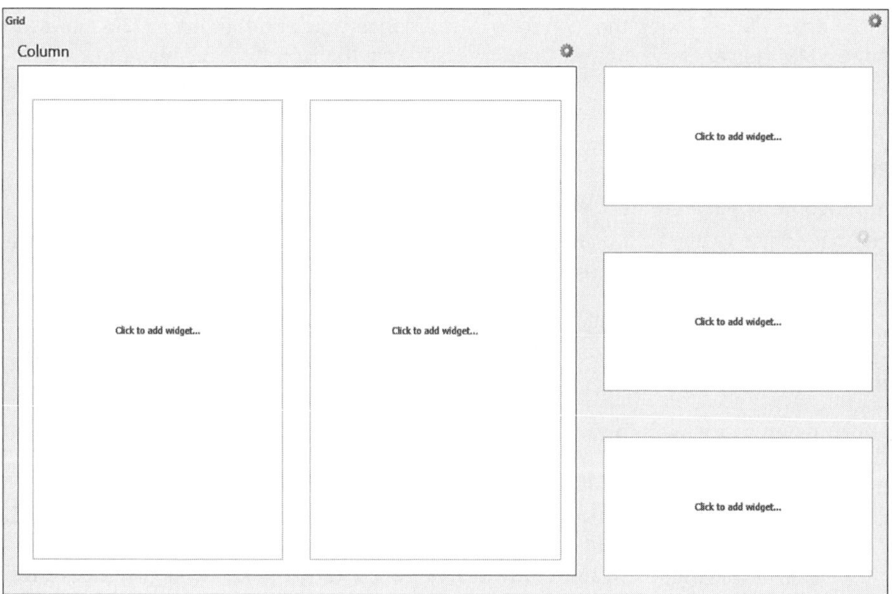

FIGURE 11.2 Grid layout containing a column layout.

The ability to nest layouts within other layouts provides a more customizable solution for meeting additional dashboard design requirements.

Using the Summary Dashboard

The Summary Dashboard provides a good starting point for the type of information that would be beneficial to show in a VMM dashboard. By choosing this option and customizing it to use the Hosts in VMM group, you can create a dashboard that displays the highest processor utilization, available memory, state, and alerts for VMM hosts for the past day (shown in the VMM Summary Dashboard displayed in Figure 11.3).

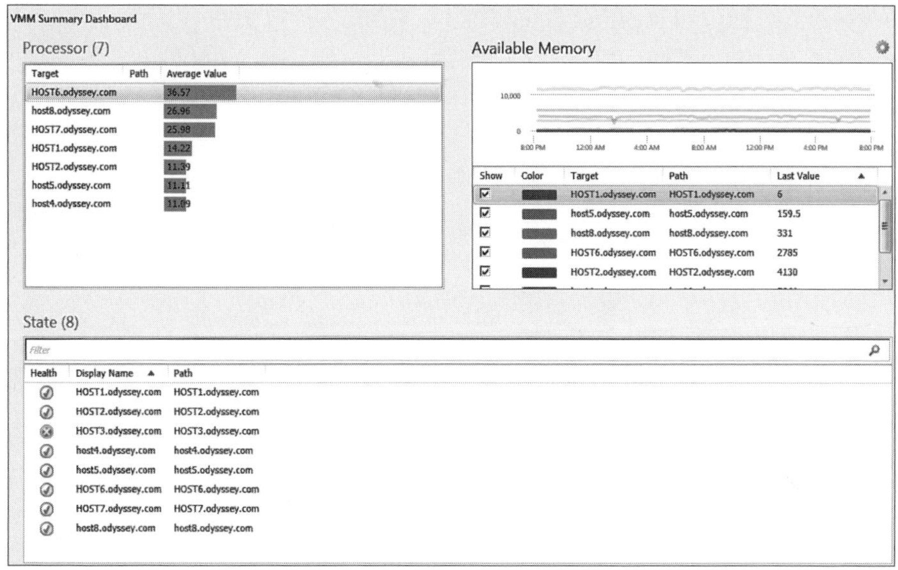

FIGURE 11.3 The VMM Summary Dashboard.

Using the Service Level Dashboard

Operations Manager 2012 includes the functionality provided with OpsMgr 2007 R2 as a solution accelerator for service level objectives, now as an integrated dashboard solution. SLOs are defined at **Authoring -> Service Level Tracking -> Management Pack Objects**.

For the VMM example, use Service Level Tracking to create a monitor state SLO for the `VMM Management Servers` class. After defining the service level objective, you can create a new dashboard that contains it by using the wizard discussed earlier in the "Using Templates" section, choosing the service level dashboard layout, and adding the SLO defined for the `VMM Management Servers` class.

Figure 11.4 shows the VMM Server Service Level Objective Dashboard, which displays the availability of VMM management servers. You can define additional service level objectives and add them to the Virtual Machine Manager Dashboards view; however, this example shows how service level information can be integrated into a series of views to display data for a specific topic (VMM availability in this case).

Up to this point in this discussion, the focus has been on using existing prebuilt layouts such as the Summary and Service Level dashboards and showing how to use them to meet common dashboard requirements. To provide more customized dashboard solutions for OpsMgr 2012, you can use the column and grid templates to add widgets that you can customize to provide dashboard solutions.

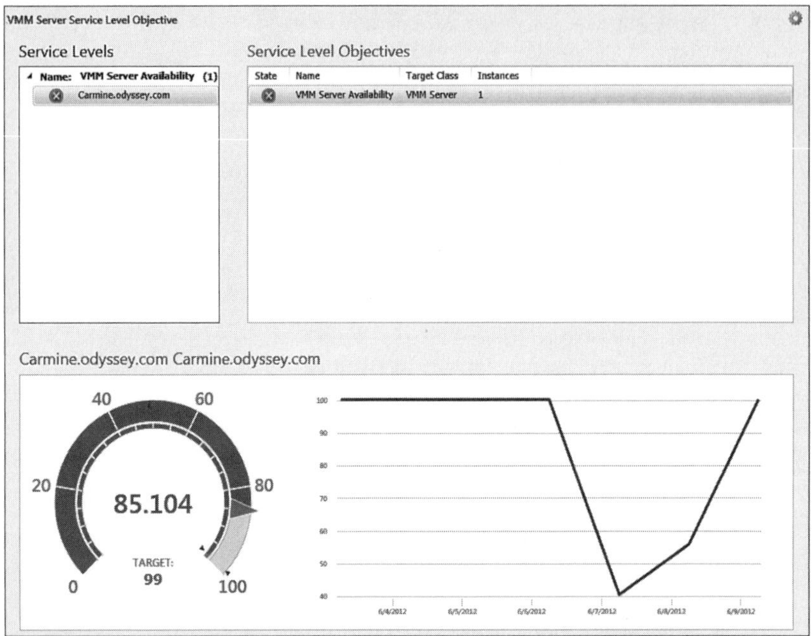

FIGURE 11.4 VMM Server Service Level Objective Dashboard.

Using Widgets

You can add widgets to the templates available in the OpsMgr 2012 console. Here are the prebuilt widgets included with this release:

- **Alert:** The Alert Widget provides a way to display alert information in a dashboard view. It can be scoped to a group or object, and you can define criteria to restrict the view to display only alerts of specific resolution states (New, Closed, and custom resolution states), severities (Critical, Warning, Informational), or priorities (High, Medium, Low). Column choices are available for all available informational fields, from the name of the alert to the custom fields for the alert. You can specify the sort order and grouping for the alert and also enable the option to display alert details inline.

TIP: ENABLING DETAILS INLINE

The Alert Widget's option to enable alert details inline works well when you are not using a Details pane to show alert details. Using this option, the details for the highlighted alert are displayed in the Alert Widget.

- **Details:** The Details Widget displays the details for the object highlighted in the Dashboard view. For example, if an alert is highlighted in the Dashboard view, then the widget shows the details of the alert, such as the description, source, path, monitor or rule, and when the alert was created. If a virtual machine is highlighted, the Details Widget displays the Display Name, Path, Health, Object Display Name, Number Of Processors, Number Of Virtual Disks, Number Of NICs, Virtual Machine Manager Server Name, Virtual Machine State, and other information for that agent.

- **Instance Details:** The Instance Details Widget is similar to the Details Widget, but the specific group or object for which it displays data in the dashboard is configured when the widget is added to the template, rather than when an object is highlighted in the Dashboard view.
- **Objects by Performance:** The Objects by Performance Widget provides performance information for the specified object or group of objects, based on the performance counter you specify, for up to 10 days. The widget shows either a specified number of top or bottom number results. See the "Objects by Performance" section for an example of how you can utilize this widget.
- **Performance:** The Performance Widget provides a way to display performance information in a dashboard. To add counters to this widget, choose a group or object and then add one or more performance counters. You can add multiple counters, such as % Processor Time, % Free Space, and PercentMemoryUsed to the same widget. The time range to display for the performance counters defaults to 24 hours, but you can raise this value up to the retention period for the data warehouse, or lower it.

TIP: PERFORMANCE DASHBOARD VIEW VERSUS PERFORMANCE VIEW

Performance views read from the OperationsManager database, where data is retained for a period of 7 days by default. The Performance Widget does not have the same limitation as a performance view in Operations Manager because the widget reads from the data warehouse database (named OperationsManagerDW by default). As a result, the widget can provide data that spans longer periods (up to the retention period of the data warehouse, which is 400 days by default).

- **State:** The State Widget lets you display state information in a dashboard. You can scope state views to include groups or objects that you choose. You can specify the class to display (such as the `Windows Computer` class). These views can restrict the State Widget to display data only in specific health states (Healthy, Warning, Critical, or Not Monitored) or to display only objects in maintenance mode. You can choose various columns from the available informational fields (the path and health of the object), and can specify the sort order and grouping for the state information displayed.

For VMM, these widgets can be used to provide dashboards for a variety of additional requirements:

- **VMM Guest Resources:** This dashboard displays the highest guest resources assigned for CPU, virtual disk, and RAM using the Objects by Performance widget in a three-column layout. This topic is discussed in the "Objects by Performance Widget" section.

- **VMM Host Performance:** This dashboard displays the host performance information for processor, disk, memory, and network using the Performance Widget in a four-cell grid layout. This topic is discussed in the "Performance Widget" section.
- **VMM Guest Health:** This dashboard displays the health state of the VMM guest systems using a three-cell grid layout using the State, Alert, and Details widgets. This is discussed in the "State, Alert, and Details Widgets" section.
- **VMM Host and Guest Dashboard:** This dashboard displays the state, alerts, and performance information for both custom groups created in this chapter. See the "Column Layout" section for additional information.

TIP: CHANGING WIDGET LOCATIONS

You can move widgets by clicking on the gear associated with a widget and choosing the **Swap with next widget** or **Swap with previous widget** options. Widgets can be swapped within a column layout or a grid layout.

Objects by Performance Widget

The Objects by Performance Widget provides an easy way to display the top values for a large number of objects. This works well when displaying the statistics for guests in VMM as there could be a large number of guests in the VMM environment. To create this dashboard, choose a three-column dashboard layout. Add three different Objects by Performance widgets, adding the CPU, memory, and disk values restricted to the Guests in VMM group you created. For this example, use the top 20 for CPU Count, Total Size of Virtual Disks, and Total RAM as shown in Figure 11.5.

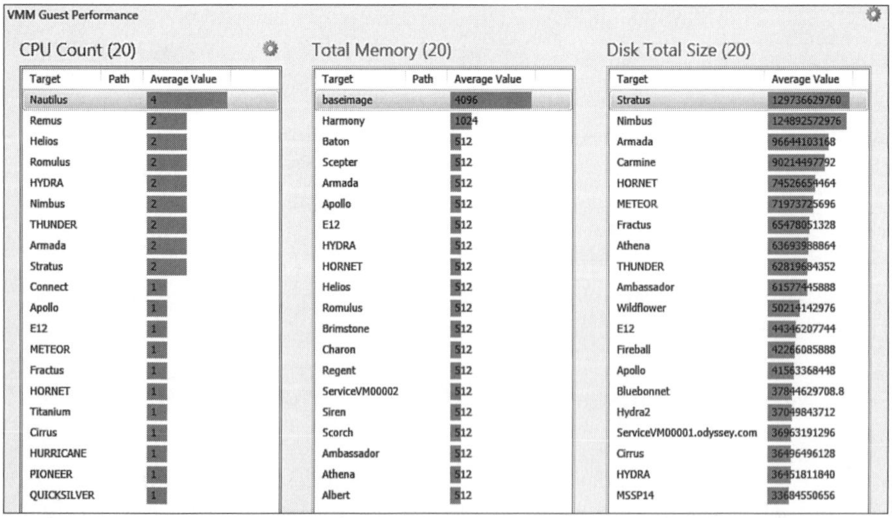

VMM Guest Performance

CPU Count (20)

Target	Path	Average Value
Nautilus		4
Remus		2
Helios		2
Romulus		2
HYDRA		2
Nimbus		2
THUNDER		2
Armada		2
Stratus		2
Connect		1
Apollo		1
E12		1
METEOR		1
Fractus		1
HORNET		1
Titanium		1
Cirrus		1
HURRICANE		1
PIONEER		1
QUICKSILVER		1

Total Memory (20)

Target	Path	Average Value
baseimage		4096
Harmony		1024
Baton		512
Scepter		512
Armada		512
Apollo		512
E12		512
HYDRA		512
HORNET		512
Helios		512
Romulus		512
Brimstone		512
Charon		512
Regent		512
ServiceVM00002		512
Siren		512
Scorch		512
Ambassador		512
Athena		512
Albert		512

Disk Total Size (20)

Target	Average Value
Stratus	129736629760
Nimbus	124892572976
Armada	96644103168
Carmine	90214497792
HORNET	74526654464
METEOR	71973725696
Fractus	65478051328
Athena	63693988864
THUNDER	62819684352
Ambassador	61577445888
Wildflower	50214142976
E12	44346207744
Fireball	42266085888
Apollo	41563368448
Bluebonnet	37844629708.8
Hydra2	37049843712
ServiceVM00001.odyssey.com	36963191296
Cirrus	36496496128
HYDRA	36451811840
MSSP14	33684550656

FIGURE 11.5 VMM Guest Resources.

Performance Widget

The Performance Widget provides a useful VMM Host Performance dashboard as the number of objects would be less than displayed in a dashboard showing guest performance.

NOTE: LIMITS OF THE PERFORMANCE WIDGET

The Performance Widget provides some capabilities that the Performance view does not have, such as the ability to sort on average values of a performance counter (see the "The Performance Widget" Tip). However, several things you cannot accomplish with the widget are possible using the Performance view. Here are some examples:

- You cannot decrease the size of the legend (and the legend cannot be removed). The result is that when using smaller views, such as the one shown in the rightmost column of Figure 11.8, the size of the chart may be less useful.
- Once the widget is configured, you cannot filter the performance counters that are displayed (such as filtering by items in the chart, not in the chart, or by text search).

Whether you use the Performance Widget in a dashboard or use the Performance view will vary, depending upon your requirements.

To create this dashboard, choose a four-cell grid layout. Add four different performance widgets, adding four key metrics around the host utilization adding the CPU, Memory, and Disk values restricted to the Hosts in VMM group. For this example, use the HyperV Logical Processor (All), Availability Mbytes (All), Logical Disk/% Free Space, and Network Interface (All). Figure 11.6 shows the results of adding these widgets.

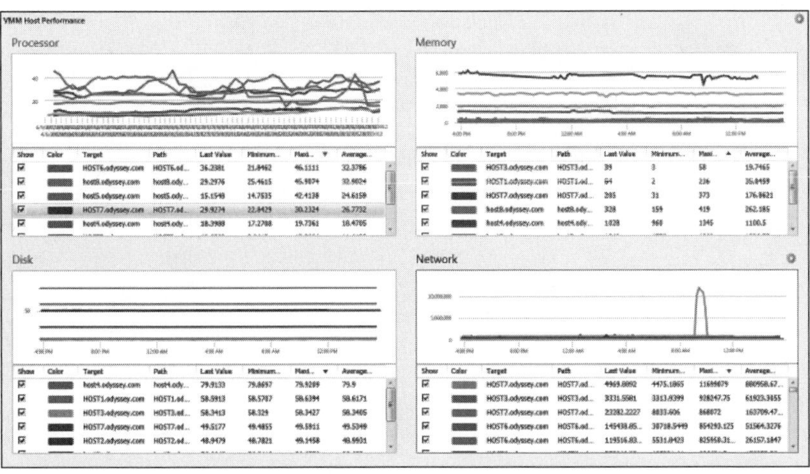

FIGURE 11.6 VMM Host Performance.

TIP: THE PERFORMANCE WIDGET

When choosing a performance counter to add to the widget, add the minimum, maximum, and average fields so the performance counters can be sorted by these values. As an example, you can add the minimum, maximum, and average values for the performance counter in the Performance Widget to make it easier to identify systems that are experiencing high processor utilization. Figure 11.6 shows multiple performance counters, which have the minimum, maximum, and average fields added for the HyperV Logical Processor, Availability Mbytes, Logical Disk/% Free Space, and Network Interface counters.

This same approach can easily be used for other performance counters, such as % Free Space, and then order these to sort by the minimum value to identify low disk space conditions.

State, Alert, and Details Widgets

The State, Alert, and Details widgets work together to provide an example of a dashboard displaying the health and alerts associated with the guest systems in VMM. To create this dashboard, use a three cell grid layout and add a state view (showing only the Guests in VMM group) to the top left cell, add an alert widget (also scoped to the Guests in VMM group) to the top right cell, and add a Details widget to the bottom cell. Figure 11.7 shows this dashboard where the Details Widget shows the last item that was highlighted in this dashboard.

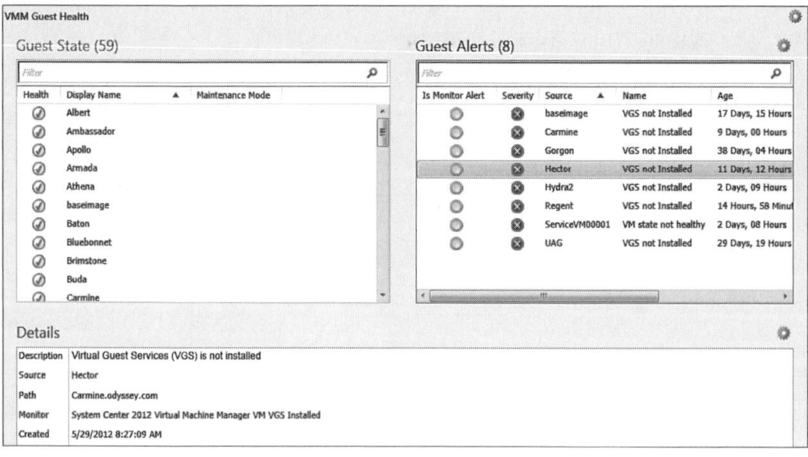

FIGURE 11.7 VMM Guest Health.

TIP: ALERT FROM RULE OR MONITOR?

The State view does not provide an easy way to identify those alerts created by a rule versus those created by a monitor. This differentiation matters because you can close alerts generated by rules, but alerts from monitors should not be closed as the health state is still impacted (for more information, see http://blogs.catapultsystems.com/cfuller/archive/2011/04/15/opsmgr-never-close-an-alert-for-a-monitor-%E2%80%93-the-exception-to-the-%E2%80%9Crule-of-the-monitor%E2%80%9D.aspx, provided as a live ink in Appendix D, "Reference URLs.") Using the Alert Widget, you can easily add the Is Monitor Alert field as shown in Figure 11.7 to categorize alerts created in a monitor.

Column Layout

The VMM dashboards example discussed in this chapter focused primarily on the grid layout and ways to use it. This section focuses on the column layout, showing where it is a more beneficial layout to utilize for custom dashboards in OpsMgr 2012.

When defining a scoped view in Operations Manager 2007 R2, a common approach was to use state, alerts, and performance views, scoping these views to a group of servers, and assigning permissions to these views for a group of users. This approach works well in a column layout where there are three columns and each column is defined to match the State, Alerts, and Performance widgets. Since this is a column layout, you can add additional cells beneath the original cells and scope them to different groups. Add additional cells to a column layout by right-clicking the gear in the top right of the column layout and adding a cell. Additional cells are added from the left to the right under the existing cells. Figure 11.8 shows an example where this column layout is used to display VMM host and guest information in a single dashboard.

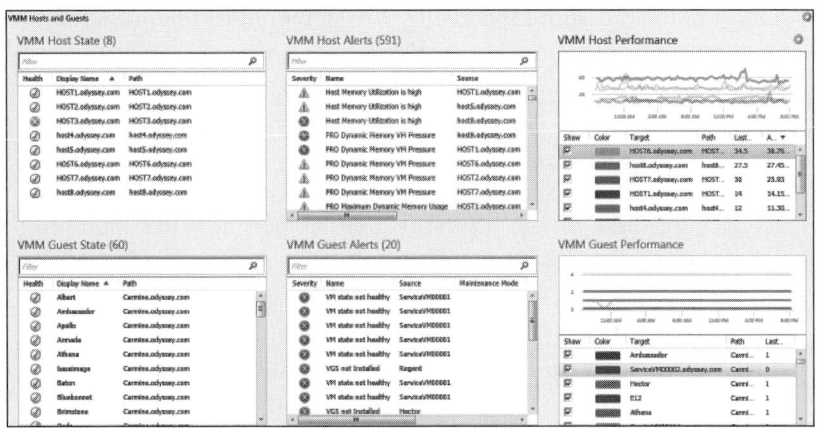

FIGURE 11.8 VMM Hosts and Guests.

The various dashboard views in this chapter provide examples of how you can use the built-in dashboard functionality in OpsMgr 2012 to generate custom dashboards to support a wide range of dashboard requirements quickly. The VMM dashboard management pack is included with the material accompanying this book; for additional information see Appendix E, "Available Online."

Using Widgets in SharePoint

Operations Manager 2012 widgets are designed to be integrated with SharePoint 2010. There are several benefits to integrating widgets into SharePoint rather than using only the Operations Manager consoles to display this information. These benefits include

- **Increased flexibility:** Using the SharePoint framework with OpsMgr widgets provides a flexible framework where you can integrate a variety of different dashboard items together in a SharePoint site.
- **Spanning System Center:** The built-in OpsMgr dashboard functionality currently displays information only from Operations Manager. Using SharePoint provides a framework where you can combine OpsMgr widgets with other technologies to create a dashboard that spans System Center and other Microsoft products.
- **Enterprise dashboard scaling:** Using a SharePoint 2010 farm, you can deploy OpsMgr dashboard components in a farm rather than individual Operations Manager Web console servers.
- **PerformancePoint:** PerformancePoint provides an extremely powerful framework to create dashboards you can easily integrate into SharePoint. More information on this topic is available in the "PerformancePoint" section.

To add OpsMgr 2012 widgets to an existing SharePoint 2010 environment requires the following:

1. **Deploying the OpsMgr web part:** Copy the install-OperationsManager-DashboardViewer.ps1 script and the Microsoft.EnterpriseManagement.SharePointIntegration.wsp file from the OpsMgr installation media (in the Setup\amd64\SharePoint folder) to the SharePoint server. Open the SharePoint 2010 Management Shell, change to the folder where you copied the files, and run the .ps1 file, passing it the appropriate path to the .wsp file and the URL for the SharePoint site (see the TechNet article later in this section for examples and details of how to run this script).
2. **Configuring the OpsMgr web part:** In SharePoint Central Administration, navigate to Site Actions, and view all site content. Create a new item on the list pointing to the URL of the existing OpsMgr Web console (http://<*servername*>/OperationsManager by default).
3. **Adding the OpsMgr web part to a SharePoint page:** Create a new page and insert the Operations Manager Dashboard Viewer web part. Edit the web part and point it to the URI for the dashboard (open the Operations Manager Web console, browse to the dashboard, and copy the dashboard URL into this field).

Microsoft provides excellent documentation on the details of this process, available at http://technet.microsoft.com/en-us/library/hh212924.aspx#bkmk_howtodeploytheoperationsmanagerwebpart. Tim McFadden also provides an excellent step-by-step on this topic, available at http://www.scom2k7.com/how-to-view-scom-2012-dashboards-in-sharepoint-2010/.

What Built-in Dashboard Functionality Does Not Do

Microsoft has gone a long way to providing a powerful and flexible framework to integrate dashboard solutions into OpsMgr 2012. However, it is reasonable to consider common dashboard requirements that would not be met by current OpsMgr 2012 dashboard functionality. (Note: These may change as new widgets and templates are written, with management pack updates, service packs, or updated releases of System Center.)

- **State enabled diagrams:** Operations Manager 2012 dashboards do not currently provide a way to create state-enabled diagrams where you can lay out components graphically and re-label them as required. Technologies available to address these types of requirements are discussed in the "Additional Dashboard Options" section.
- **Gauges and Charts:** While both the Service Level Dashboard and the Network Node Dashboards contain a gauge control and the Network Vicinity Dashboard provides a graphical layout feature, you cannot currently use these controls in other ways as individual widgets. Details on prebuilt dashboard solutions are discussed in the "Prebuilt Dashboards" section.
- **Data from outside OpsMgr:** As discussed in the "Using Widgets in SharePoint" section, the current OpsMgr widgets do not display data from a source other than Operations Manager.

This section focused on built-in dashboard functionality and its use in OpsMgr 2012. In the next section, the discussion moves to an investigation of the prebuilt dashboards that exist in OpsMgr 2012.

Prebuilt Dashboards

Using the built-in dashboard framework, Microsoft provides a series of prebuilt dashboards that are included with OpsMgr 2012. Currently, three management packs include prebuilt dashboards: Network Monitoring, Operations Manager, and Application Performance Monitoring (APM).

Network Monitoring Dashboards

The improved network monitoring functionality added in OpsMgr 2012 includes three prebuilt dashboards that use the new OpsMgr 2012 dashboard functionality:

- **Network Summary Dashboard:** This dashboard displays the network devices with the slowest response time, network devices with the highest CPU, interfaces with the highest CPU, and interfaces with the most send errors (over the past 24 hours). This dashboard is available in the Monitoring pane under the Network Monitoring folder.

- **Network Node Dashboard:** This dashboard shows the devices in the vicinity of the network device, average availability in gauges (today, yesterday, previous 7 days, and previous 30 days), instance details, average response time, processor usage, health of interfaces on the node, and active alerts generated by the node. This dashboard is available as a task when a network device is highlighted in the Operations console. Figure 11.9 shows an example of the Network Node Dashboard.
- **Network Vicinity Dashboard:** This dashboard displays the vicinity view (discussed in the Network Vicinity Dashboard) and the instance details. This dashboard is available as a task when a network device is highlighted in the Operations console.

The integrated network monitoring dashboards add solid functionality to Operations Manager 2012 and show potential approaches that may be used for additional future dashboard functionality.

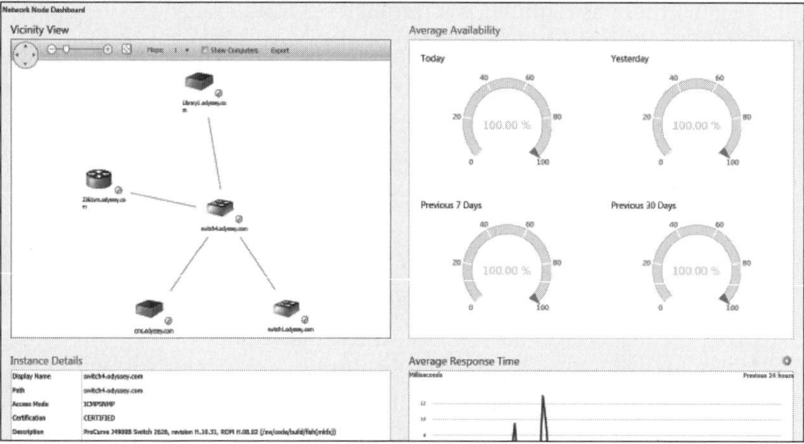

FIGURE 11.9 Network Node Dashboard.

TIP: WHERE DASHBOARDS ARE STORED IN OPSMGR 2012

Dashboard solutions in Operations Manager 2012 are stored in the following management packs:

- **Microsoft SystemCenter DataProviders Library:** This pack includes the data provider components that receive data from the operational and data warehouse databases for display in the UI controls.
- **Microsoft SystemCenter Visualization Configuration Library:** This pack includes components that enable personalization and configuration of all dashboards.
- **Microsoft SystemCenter Visualization Internal:** This pack includes internal components that the dashboard UI framework uses.

- **Microsoft SystemCenter Visualization Library:** This pack includes the majority of the UI controls that comprise the widgets. Widgets are used both in custom built dashboards and out-of-box dashboards, such as the network dashboards discussed in the "Network Monitoring" section.
- **Microsoft SystemCenter Visualization Network Library:** This pack includes the components and implementation for the majority of the network dashboards.
- **Microsoft SystemCenter Visualization Network Dashboard:** This pack includes the definition of the network dashboards and references the components in the Microsoft SystemCenter Visualization Network Library.
- **Microsoft SystemCenter Visualization ServiceLevelComponents:** This management pack includes the dial service level gauges used in the network summary dashboard.

Operations Manager Dashboards

Operations Manager's base functionality in 2012 includes four prebuilt dashboards that use the new dashboard functionality available from the Monitoring pane in the Operations Manager folder:

- **Management Group Health:** This dashboard provides the health of the management group functions and the management group infrastructure, as well as active alerts, agent configuration information, and agent version information.
- **Management Group Health Trend:** This dashboard displays the number of active alerts and the agent health state (over the past 7 days), displayed in Figure 11.10.
- **Summary Dashboard - Map:** This dashboard (and the Detailed Dashboard - List) are available when Web Application Availability Monitoring synthetic transactions have been created in the Authoring pane. These dashboards are available in the Monitoring pane under **Application Monitoring -> Web Application Availability Monitoring -> Test State** by highlighting a synthetic transaction and clicking the **Detailed Dashboard - Map** option on the task bar. The dashboard displays a map dashboard for the items that were highlighted when the task was run. A number of websites can provide locations for various cities, including http://www.timegenie.com/latitude_and_longitude/. Figure 11.11 shows an example of this dashboard for servers in a variety of locations.
- **Detailed Dashboard - List:** This dashboard displays a variety of information including the test status, total transaction time, time to first byte, content time, DNS resolution time, time to last byte, and content size for the Web Application Availability Monitoring synthetic transactions, which were highlighted when navigating to this dashboard. Figure 11.12 shows an example of this transaction monitoring www.bing.com from multiple different locations.

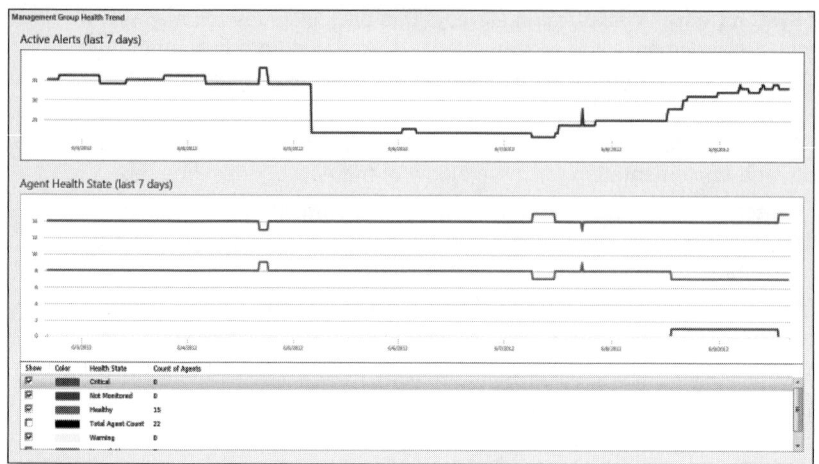

FIGURE 11.10 Management Group Health Trend.

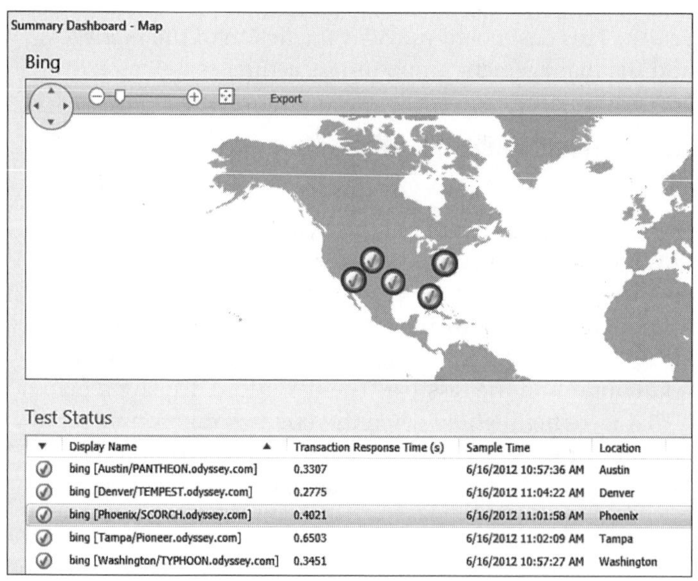

FIGURE 11.11 Summary Dashboard - Map.

NOTE: DEFINING AND REMOVING LOCATIONS IN OPSMGR

Locations are added in OpsMgr using the `New-SCOMLocation` (which requires the display name, latitude, and longitude) and `Set-SCOMLocation` PowerShell cmdlets. As an example to define the location for Austin, Texas:

```
New-SCOMLocation -DisplayName "Austin, Texas" -Latitude 32.85 -Longitude -96.85
```

To assign the location to a server, use the `Set-SCOMLocation` cmdlet:

```
$Location = Get-SCOMLocation -DisplayName "Austin, Texas"
$Agent = Get-SCOMAgent -Name "<FQDN of the server monitored by OpsMgr>"
Set-SCOMLocation -Location $Location -Agent $Agent
```

For an example of using these PowerShell cmdlets to define locations for this map, see http://blogs.catapultsystems.com/cfuller/archive/2012/06/15/creating-a-map-with-server-locations-in-opsmgr-2012-scom-sysctr.aspx or http://thoughtsonopsmgr.blogspot.com/2012/06/om12-how-to-remove-location-association.html.

The `Remove-SCOMLocation` cmdlet is used to remove the associations from the agent, management server, or pool based on the parameter specified such as

```
Remove-SCOMLocation -Agent
Remove-SCOMLocation -ManagementServer
Remove-SCOMLocation -Pool
```

To remove the location, use `Remove-SCOMlocation` as in this example:

```
Get-SCOMLocation -DisplayName "Austin, Texas" | Remove-SCOMLocation
```

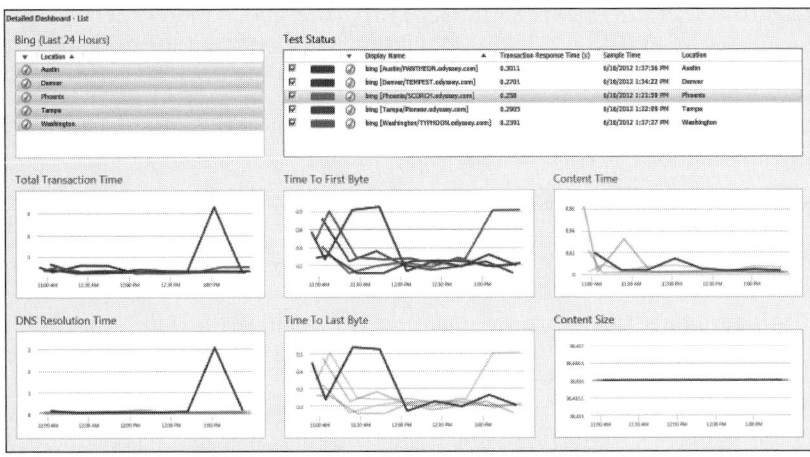

FIGURE 11.12 Summary Dashboard - List.

For further details on Web Application Availability Monitoring synthetic transactions on these dashboards, see Marnix Wolf's article at http://thoughtsonopsmgr.blogspot.com/2012/06/how-to-use-web-application-availability.html, and the OpsMgr product team's article at http://blogs.technet.com/b/momteam/archive/2012/05/31/using-the-web-application-availability-monitoring-to-monitor-web-applications-health.aspx.

APM Dashboards

The integrated application performance monitoring functionality in OpsMgr 2012 includes two prebuilt dashboards that use the new OpsMgr 2012 dashboard functionality:

- **Applications:** This dashboard shows the health of the .NET applications monitored by Operations Manager 2012 including their average response time, availability, performance, and service level agreements. The dashboard is stored in the Microsoft.SystemCenter.ApplicationMonitoring.360.Template.Dashboards management pack.
- **Web Application Status:** This dashboard displays the health of the web application availability monitors. The dashboard is stored in the Microsoft.SystemCenter.WebApplicationSolutions.Library management pack.

The authors' expectation is that over time Microsoft will supplement existing management packs (such as SQL Server, Exchange, Windows Server and others) and provide additional prebuilt dashboards for OpsMgr. As an example of this, the Operations Manager team recently released a series of dashboards for OpsMgr 2012 to display Windows Server 2008 information, available at http://blogs.technet.com/b/momteam/archive/2012/06/12/free-windows-server-2008-dashboards-for-opsmgr-2012-and-tool-to-help-create-your-own-customized-dashboards.aspx. This download provides two prebuilt dashboards for Windows Server 2008 (the Windows Server Summary Dashboard and Windows Server Task Pane Dashboard), and includes a tool called GMTTool. The GMTTool incorporates three items you cannot do from the Operations console:

- Removes management group GUIDs from dashboards so that dashboard management packs can be shared
- Gives the ability to add dashboard views to any folder in the monitoring pane
- Provides the ability to launch a custom dashboard from the Task pane

Figure 11.13 shows the Windows Server Summary dashboard where the Instance Details section displays the information for the server highlighted in the Health State of Windows Servers section.

Figure 11.14 shows the Windows Server Task pane dashboard for a specified server, showing key metrics around CPU, memory, disk, and network.

As shown by the recent addition of Windows Server dashboard functionality, Microsoft's dashboards provide a framework that can be used to show information in even more areas going forward as new management packs are written that focus on dashboards.

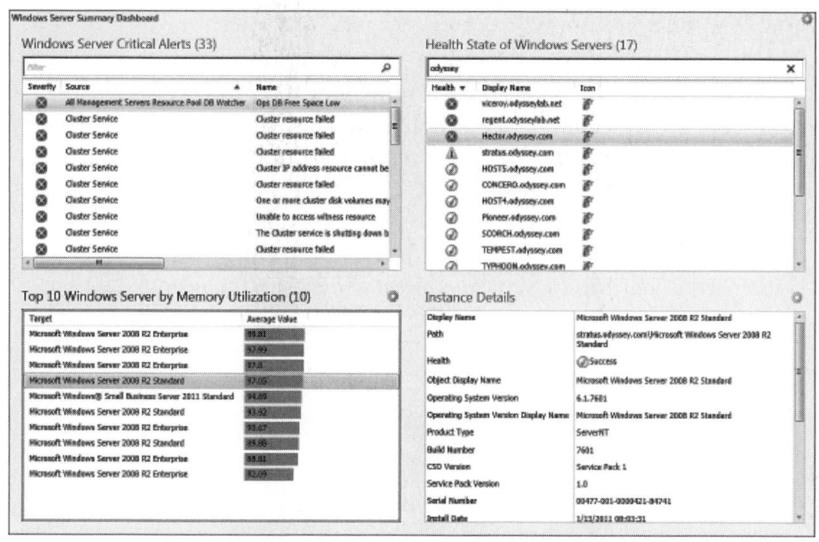

FIGURE 11.13 Windows Server Summary Dashboard.

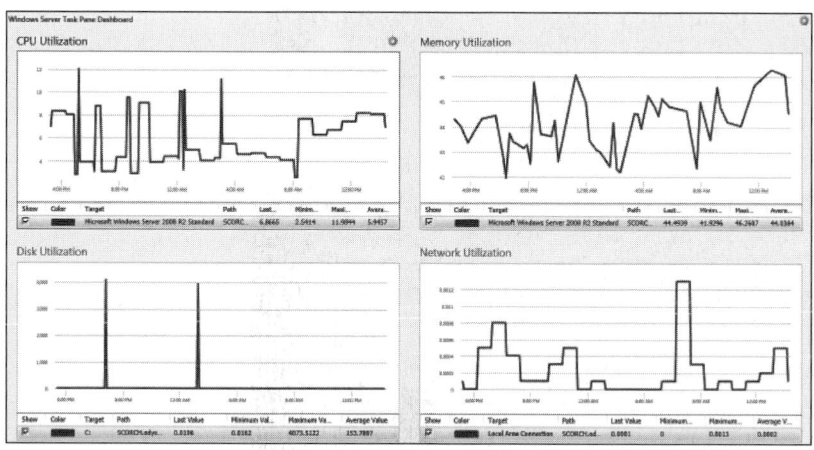

FIGURE 11.14 Windows Server Task Pane Dashboard.

Additional Dashboard Options

While OpsMgr 2012 built-in dashboard functionality provides an extremely powerful and flexible framework to create dashboards, there are items not currently viable (see the "What Built-in Dashboard Functionality Does Not Do" section for details). A number of vendors are providing a variety of options to augment dashboard solutions for OpsMgr 2012, including solution accelerators from Microsoft and third-party solutions, discussed in the following sections.

Visio Integration

As discussed in the "Built-In Dashboard Functionality" section, Microsoft created the Visio 2010 Add-in for OpsMgr 2007 R2, now updated to work with Operations Manager 2012. This solution provides a way to state-enable Visio diagrams, which you can upload to SharePoint and make available using a URL that is unique per dashboard. OpsMgr provides the ability to export a Diagram view to a .vdx file you can customize in Visio and upload to SharePoint. As an example, a network device was exported using the Diagram view option to export to a .vdx file, and then edited in Visio and uploaded to SharePoint 2010 as shown in Figure 11.15. This example shows how any entity (including a network device) can be displayed using this technology, re-labeled, and displayed in a customized manner.

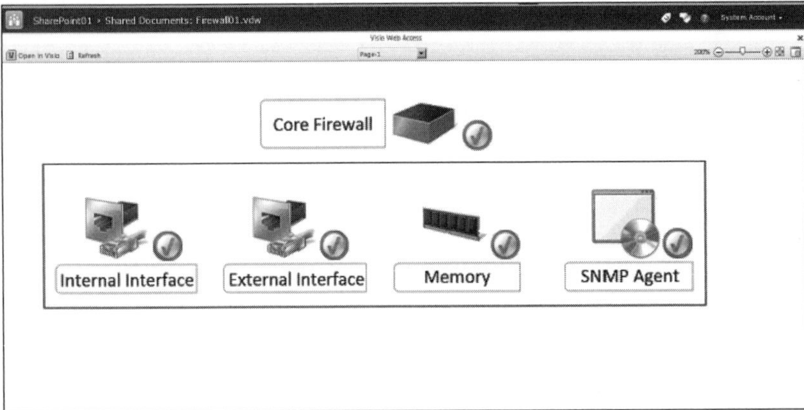

FIGURE 11.15 Visio integration and network devices.

TIP: UNIQUE URLS FROM SHAREPOINT FOR VISIO DIAGRAMS

SharePoint 2010 Enterprise edition provides a way to store .vdx files and display them as a live web diagram with a URL that is unique per .vdx file. The benefit of this unique URL is useful in multiple ways, such as creating a web page view in the Operations Manager console that points to the Visio diagram. This approach provides a quick way to generate custom dashboards that provide a more intuitive layout for a distributed application, which you can customize based on user requirements.

The strength of Visio integration versus other state-enabling diagram technologies is that it is built into Visio. The ability to export a distributed application to a Diagram view, manipulate the diagram, and upload it directly to SharePoint 2010 makes this a very useful tool. Visio integration also works extremely well with existing Visio diagrams to make them able to be state-enabled.

Savision Live Maps

Savision is a third-party vendor offering a product called Live Maps. Live Maps has provided a state-enabling dashboard solution that has been available since November 2007 (released at TechEd 2007 Barcelona). Savision provides its own authoring experience, which provides an easy to learn approach to generating dashboard solutions for Operations Manager.

The strength of Live Maps is its integration with Operations Manager. Live Map entities are treated similar to other entities in the Operations console. This means you can right-click any entity in the map and have the same options available that are throughout the rest of the Operations console (such as opening the Alert view, State view, Performance view, Diagram view, or Health Explorer), and run tasks and reports off the entities in OpsMgr. This level of integration makes Live Maps feel like a native part of Operations Manager rather than a third-party or add-on solution.

Using the VMM dashboard integration theme of this chapter, the various entities that are part of the VMM environment can be added to a diagram and displayed, as shown in Figure 11.16.

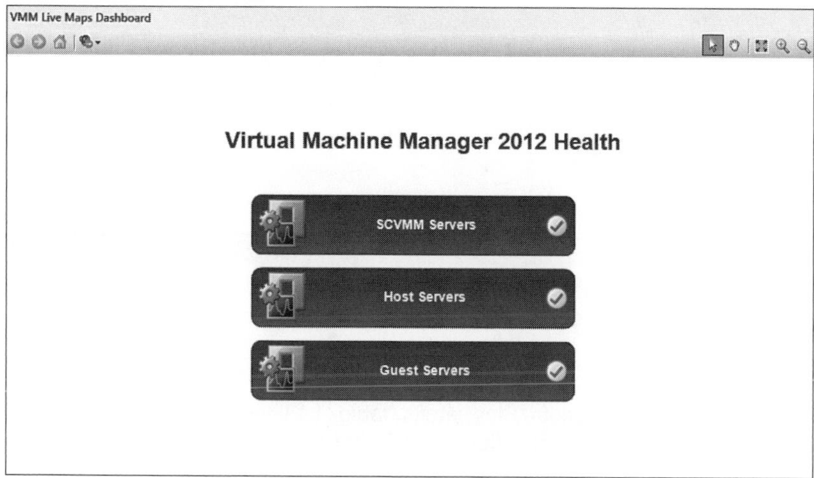

FIGURE 11.16 Savision VMM Diagram.

This top-level dashboard is linked to dynamically populating sub-dashboards that determine their membership based upon criteria defined for them. As an example, the VMM servers links to a dynamic list based upon the class of the VMM servers (`All objects of type VMM Server where the property Display Name property matches wildcard "*"`). The Hosts Servers sub-dashboard was linked to the members of the Hosts in VMM group defined in the "Built-in Dashboard Functionality" section, and the Guest Servers was linked to the members of the Guests in VMM group, defined in the same section.

Savision recently announced the release of Interactive Maps, which uses a .csv input file containing latitude and longitude information for entities in Operations Manager. This information can now provide a geographical overlay that shows where these entities exist on an Interactive map. Figure 11.17 shows an example.

FIGURE 11.17 Savision Interactive Map.

TIP: CREATING DASHBOARDS IN SAVISION LIVE MAPS

The dashboard shown in Figure 11.16 was created in less than one hour (including integration of a custom image for VMM) using the Savision Live Maps authoring console. Additional examples of Live Maps and how they can be used to display OpsMgr information are available at

- http://www.systemcentercentral.com/BlogDetails/tabid/143/IndexID/75218/Default.aspx: Taking Distributed Applications to the next level with Savision Live Maps
- http://blogs.catapultsystems.com/cfuller/archive/2010/09/14/taking-distributed-applications-to-the-next-level-with-savision-live-maps-%E2%80%93-part-2.aspx: Taking Distributed Applications to the next level with Savision Live Maps – Part 2
- http://blogs.catapultsystems.com/cfuller/archive/2011/10/11/opsmgr-2012-savision-amp-dashboards.aspx: OpsMgr 2012, Savision & Dashboards
- http://blogs.catapultsystems.com/cfuller/archive/2011/04/28/quicktricks-getting-the-url-for-a-savision-live-map.aspx: Finding the URL for a Live Map

More information on Savision and its products, including Live Maps and Vital Signs, is available at www.savision.com.

Silect Software

Silect's ConfigWise product provides another option for displaying Operations Manager (and other System Center components) information through dashboards. ConfigWise uses a Silverlight application and gathers information using SQL queries you can use to read from any database (including the Operations Manager operational database or data warehouse). Details on the ConfigWise product and using it to display Operations Manager data are available at http://blogs.catapultsystems.com/cfuller/archive/2011/10/17/opsmgr-dashboard-integration-third-party-dashboarding-solutions-silect-configwise.aspx. Additional information on Silect and its ConfigWise product is available at http://www.configwise.com/.

Bay Dynamics

Bay Dynamics' IT Analytics product provides another option to display Operations Manager (and other System Center components) information through dashboards. IT Analytics for Microsoft System Center 2012 uses cubes to display data from System Center. With the addition of cubes into System Center 2012 Service Manager, you will want to investigate this solution if there are dashboard requirements for your organization that are not covered by the built-in dashboard options.

Details on the IT Analytics product and information on how you can use it to display Operations Manager data is available at http://blogs.catapultsystems.com/cfuller/archive/2011/10/19/opsmgr-dashboard-integration-third-party-dashboarding-solutions-bay-dynamics-it-analytics-for-microsoft-system-center.aspx. Additional information on Bay Dynamics and its IT Analytics product for System Center is available at http://www.baydynamics.com/Products/ITAnalytics/SystemCenter/.

InFront Consulting System Center Dashboard

At the Microsoft Management Summit 2012, InFront Consulting demonstrated a framework designed to surface information for System Center in a Silverlight user interface. Information on this solution is not yet online, but when released should be available at InFront's website at http://www.infrontconsulting.com/.

Dundas Dashboards

Dundas dashboard technology was used as part of the Service Level Dashboard solution accelerator released for Operations Manager 2007 R2. Dundas provides a variety of dashboard components that are available to visualize data for a variety of products including System Center 2012. Additional information is available at http://www.dundas.com/dashboard/. Figure 11.18 was developed by Catapult Systems (www.catapultsystems.com) as part of its A3 + System Center solution offering using the Dundas dashboard technology to display Operations Manager data.

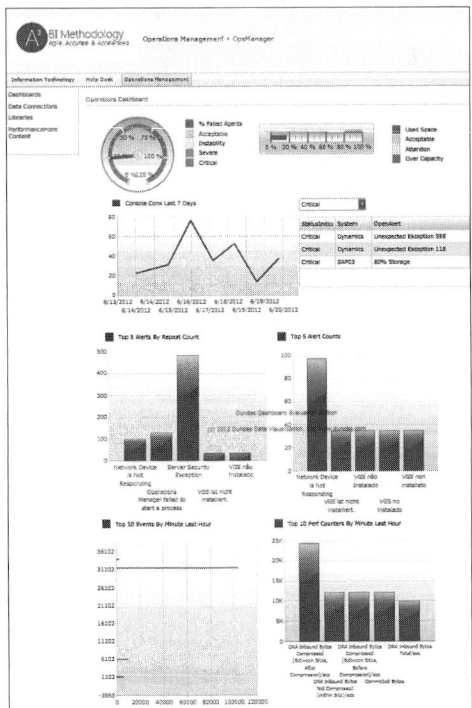

FIGURE 11.18 Displaying OpsMgr data in Dundas.

SharePoint 2007 Dashboards

As irony would have it, Configuration Manager 2007 and Service Manager 2010 each had a solution accelerator that would have been extremely beneficial for Operations Manager. Both products used modifiable SQL queries and displayed data through SharePoint using a configurable dashboard solution. While both products had dashboard solutions designed to display information in SharePoint 2007, these have not been updated to work on SharePoint 2010.

TIP: USING THE SERVICE MANAGER DASHBOARD TO DISPLAY OPERATIONS MANAGER DATA

You could adapt both of these dashboard solution accelerators to display information from the Operations Manager databases. A variation of the dashboard for Service Manager was created for use with OpsMgr 2007 R2, available for download at http://www.systemcentercentral.com/Downloads/DownloadsDetails/tabid/144/IndexID/86702/Default.aspx.

While important from a historical perspective, these dashboards most likely will not be updated to support SharePoint 2010 and so are not a recommended approach to creating dashboards going forward in OpsMgr 2012. As the SharePoint 2007 dashboards require SQL queries to gather information to display in a dashboard, identifying useful SQL queries can be helpful in developing dashboard solutions for OpsMgr.

SQL Queries

There are a number of different areas for gathering SQL queries for Operations Manager, including

- **Kevin Holman's blog:** Kevin Holman gathered a series of useful Operations Manager 2007 queries that are available at http://blogs.technet.com/b/kevinholman/archive/2007/10/18/useful-operations-manager-2007-sql-queries.aspx.
- **System Center Central:** System Center Central has a downloadable set of SQL queries to use for OpsMgr dashboards and gadgets at http://www.systemcentercentral.com/Downloads/DownloadsDetails/tabid/144/IndexID/86822/Default.aspx.

Prebuilt Gadgets

Several prebuilt gadgets are currently available that display state information for Operations Manager as part of a gadget that can be added to a Windows desktop, as part of the gadget bar.

- **OpsMgr 2007 Resource Kit:** Microsoft created a gadget for OpsMgr available for download at http://go.microsoft.com/fwlink/?LinkId=94593. Additional information on this resource kit utility was blogged by the OpsMgr Unleashed team at http://opsmgrunleashed.wordpress.com/2007/09/19/opsmgr-2007-resource-kit-the-vista-gadget-bar/. This gadget is designed to provide state information.
- **Savision Gadget:** Savision has a gadget available as part of its Live Maps product at http://www.savision.com/resources/blog/sneak-preview-live-maps-vista-gadget. This gadget is designed to provide state information.

You can also create custom gadgets, which you can use to provide both state and performance information from OpsMgr.

Custom Gadgets

PowerGadgets from SoftwareFX provides a way to generate a gadget quickly based upon an existing SQL query. Figure 11.19 shows a series of gadgets including Savision Gadget, a custom PowerGadget, and the OpsMgr 2007 Resource Kit Gadget together in a gadget bar with the Windows 7 Weather gadget.

Additional information on PowerGadgets is available at http://www.softwarefx.com/sfxSqlProducts/powergadgets/.

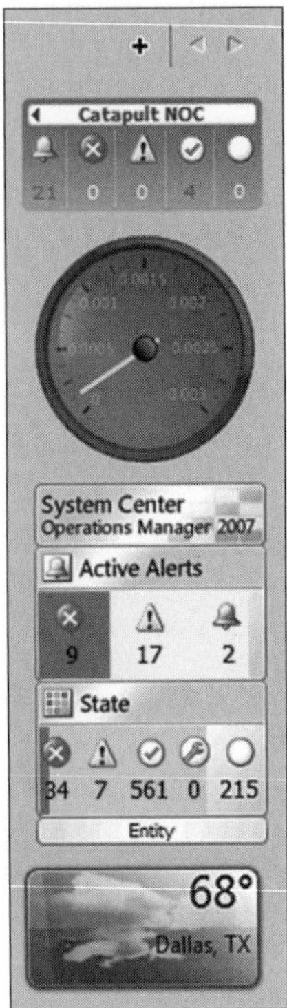

FIGURE 11.19 OpsMgr data and gadgets.

PerformancePoint

PerformancePoint Services is a performance management service within SharePoint 2010 that allows users insight into their business. Data is based on cubes served through SQL Server Analysis Services for easy drill down and scorecarding capabilities, providing users with a full business intelligence solution.

PerformancePoint can provide extremely powerful dashboard solutions, such as the one shown in Figure 11.20, developed by Catapult Systems (www.catapultsystems.com) as part of its A3 + System Center solution offering.

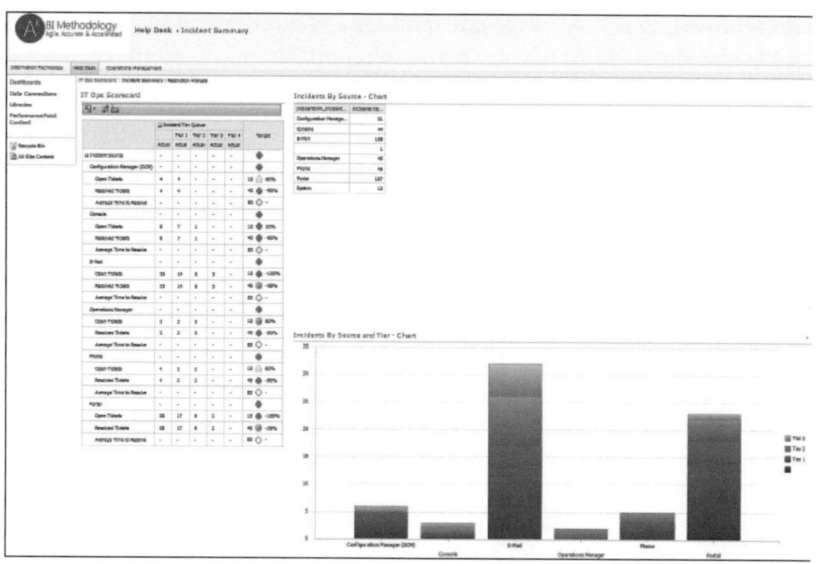

FIGURE 11.20 Displaying System Center data in PerformancePoint.

Power View

Power View is a Silverlight browser application that is a feature of SQL Server 2012 Enterprise edition. It provides a rich interactive view of data allowing users self-service capabilities.

Power View can be pointed to earlier versions of SQL Server (such as SQL 2008 R2, currently the supported database platform for Operations Manager) to provide the same type of functionality even though the application is not running on SQL Server 2012. An example of Power View is available via YouTube at http://www.youtube.com/watch?v=7k77Pzf5Dlg. Power View may provide functionality that can be used to replace the current approach towards statically designed dashboard solutions in Operations Manager and System Center.

Reports, Trending, Forecasting, and Capacity Planning

With dashboards, widgets, gadgets, and more available to display data for Operations Manager, do you still need to use reporting in Operations Manager or are reports now obsolete? Exploring this led to an interesting perspective by Satya Vel of the Operations Manager product team: "While reports are a good way to get data that is specific for a certain time period, customers such as you wanted a rich way to visualize data which you could then project and share with your organization." (See http://blogs.technet.com/b/momteam/archive/2011/11/10/how-are-opsmgr-2012-dashboards-different-from-reports.aspx.) While this quote is directed to the need for dashboards, it points out one of the strengths of reporting—providing access to specific data for a certain period of time. Taking this concept forward, here are several areas where reports are more useful than dashboards for displaying data:

- **Detailed Nature:** Dashboards are designed to provide quickly digestible information versus a report that may often be more verbose. As an example, a dashboard may show the percentage of agents in different health states, but a report may show the list of the agents in the various states.
- **Reporting Functionality:** Since Operations Manager's reporting functionality is built upon SQL Server Reporting Services (SSRS), OpsMgr gains benefits such as the ability to schedule delivery of reports via email to a file share.
- **Existing Reports:** It is difficult to justify a requirement to spend time and money developing a different way to provide data from OpsMgr when one already exists through a prebuilt report. The OpsMgr report library is extensive, and reports are added as management packs are imported into the management group. As an example, importing the Windows Server 2008 Operating System management pack adds several Windows operating system specific reports to the reporting pane in the Windows Server 2008 Operating System (Monitoring) folder.
- **Historical Trending:** While dashboards may provide a limited historical trend, more often a report will be used to answer a question such as *How did my application perform this same time last year?*
- **Forecasting:** Using the information trends in the OpsMgr database, data can be forecasted to determine an estimate for what level performance metrics may be in the future.
- **Capacity Planning:** The information available in OpsMgr's data warehouse can be utilized to assist with capacity planning.

The topics discussed in this section provide the focus areas for where reporting provides a recommended approach for data visualization in OpsMgr.

Reporting in OpsMgr

Operations Manager provides an extremely powerful and flexible reporting engine built on a data warehouse designed to gather raw data and store aggregated data for use in historical reports. OpsMgr uses SQL Server to store the data, and SSRS to provide the reporting functionality. The next sections focus on common challenges with OpsMgr reporting, with tips on how to use the OpsMgr reporting features more effectively.

Avoiding the Blank Report

Although Operations Manager's reporting structure is extremely powerful and flexible, it can be unintuitive and difficult to work with. One of the most common complaints is an inability to identify correct objects to use for a report and that running reports return blank results. The following sections focus on methods to use reports that will not result in a blank report.

Filter Options

OpsMgr 2007 R2 includes a new feature called *filter options*. This option is available in most of the new reports to reduce the objects available for a report and only display those objects with data. Filter options are active by default on the various OpsMgr reports for which they are supported. You can tell if filter options are available when you attempt to add a group or an object to a report and the report and the **Filter Options have been applied** text is displayed, as shown in Figure 11.21.

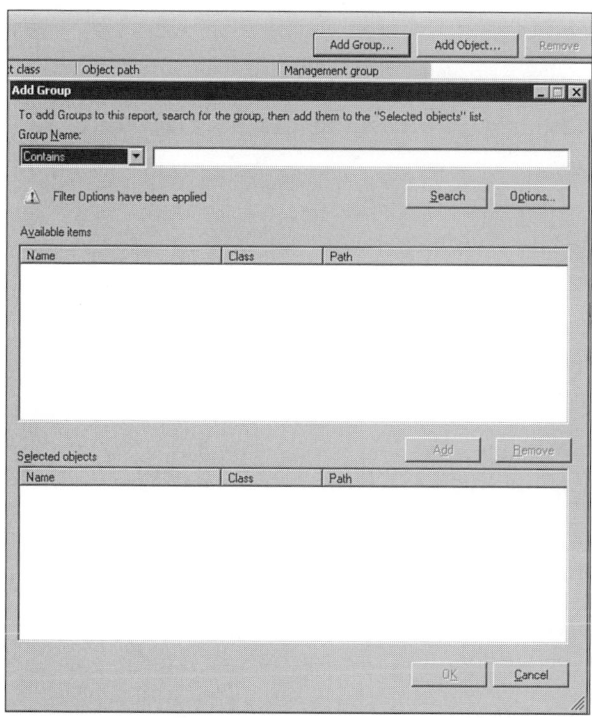

FIGURE 11.21 Filter Options have been applied.

This functionality provides a more targeted list of what objects have data and goes a long way towards removing problems where a blank report is run in OpsMgr.

TIP: INTEGRATING REPORTS INTO VIEWS

For details on reports and how they can be integrated into the Operations console using a web page view, see Chapter 7, "Configuring and Using System Center 2012 Operations Manager."

Predefined Objects

Many reports in OpsMgr 2012 have objects predefined for the report, so they do not need to be chosen when the report is run. Here are some examples of views that include reports with predefined objects:

- Application Monitoring / .Net Monitoring / Application Advisor Reports / Resource Utilization Analysis
- Client Monitoring Views Library
- Exchange Server 2010 Report Library
- Microsoft Data Warehouse
- Microsoft Generic Report Library
- Operational Data Reporting Management Pack
- SCC Health Check Reports (discussed in more detail in the "Existing Reports" section)
- SQL Server 2008 Monitoring
- System Center Core Monitoring Reports

Reports with predefined objects do not require choosing a specific object or group to report on, which simplifies the process of running the reports.

Reports with Documented Objects

For reports that do not have filter options available and do not have predefined objects, look at the report details prior to running the report to see what objects are expected to have data available for the report.

As an example, the All IIS Servers report (part of the Windows Server Internet Information Services 2003 view) provides documentation for objects that will have data for the report. As this information is not available after you run the report, you should first check the reporting details in the Reporting pane before you run a report to identify which objects will have data. This information makes it much easier to locate the appropriate object for a report and prevent running a blank report in OpsMgr.

TIP: SAVING REPORTS TO FAVORITES AND THE MY WORKSPACE VIEW

Once you have identified the appropriate objects for a report or identified a useful report, you may want to add the report to the My Workspace pane. In the Operations console, favorite reports appear in the Reporting pane under the Favorite Reports folder. If you want to access favorite reports through the Operations Manager Web console, use the My Workspace pane to provide an area where these reports are available.

Running Reports from the Operations Console Monitoring Pane

Another trick to remember when running reports is that reports do not necessarily need to be run from the Reporting pane. When an object is highlighted in a view in the Monitoring pane, those reports available for the object are listed under the Report tasks. Multiple objects can be highlighted, so that when the report is run through the Report task the appropriate objects are passed to the report so that the objects or groups do not need to be selected.

Another approach is to create a State view that lists the objects for commonly run reports. You can use this view to highlight objects and run reports instead of using the Reporting pane. Details are available at http://blogs.catapultsystems.com/cfuller/archive/2010/08/04/quicktricks-creating-really-easy-multiple-server-performance-reports-amp-how-to-create-a-report-for-multiple-objects-when-you-don%E2%80%99t-know-what-objects-to-choose.aspx.

Mitigate problems with running blank reports by knowing the correct object to pick for a report by using the filter options, running reports with predefined objects, reviewing the report details to find object documentation, and running reports from the Monitoring pane.

Reporting Functionality

Since Operations Manager 2012 uses SSRS for its backend reporting, it provides built-in functionality for reports such as scheduling and delivering reports.

You can generate reports in a variety of formats including Microsoft Excel, RPL Renderer, Microsoft Word, Adobe PDF, Tiff, MHTML, CSV, HTML 4.0, and eXtended Markup Language (XML). These reports can be stored in a folder structure to provide historical copies or the most recent execution of a report.

Emailing reports is commonly used to provide daily or weekly information focused to a specific group of users, providing performance information for their servers. For example, application owners might want to receive weekly Performance by System or Performance by Utilization reports for all servers in a web farm; Operations Manager administrators might want to receive daily reports of all agents currently down using the SCC Health Check Reports: Agents - Down Agents (OM) for a daily notification of those agents currently not reporting to OpsMgr.

The ability to schedule Operations Manager report generation and delivery is very useful. Although this functionality is built into SSRS, it is frequently overlooked in Operations Manager environments and can often provide benefits.

Existing Reports and Trending

Microsoft and third-party management pack vendors include reports in most of their management packs; you can use these reports to meet the majority of OpsMgr reporting requirements. Microsoft recently added reports to cover a common question of how to generate a report that tracks the key performance indicators (KPIs) for a group of servers. Microsoft's new reports are available in the Windows Server Operating System Reports folder, and include

- **Performance by System:** This report shows the KPIs for a system (or for several systems with each system shown on its own page of the report) over a period of time. Figure 11.22 shows an example of this report for a single server over a 14-day history. This report is useful when displaying historical KPI information for a specific server or small number of servers.

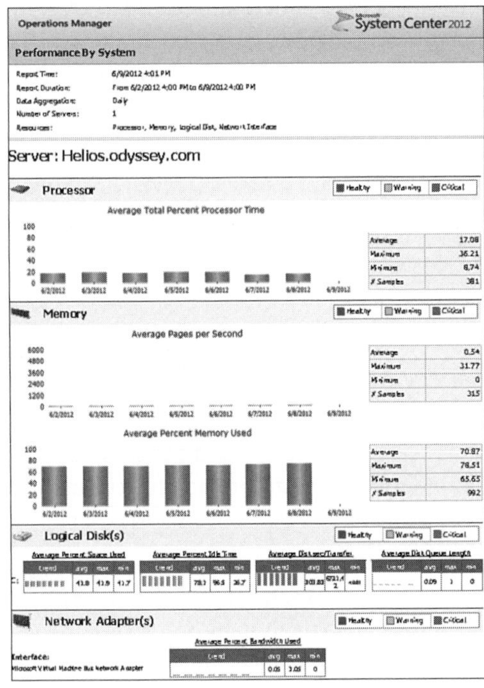

FIGURE 11.22 Performance by System report.

- **Performance by Utilization:** This report shows the top KPIs for a group of systems chosen for the report. This report does not show the historical information for the KPIs as the Performance by System report does, but is useful to see trends over a period of time to identify conditions such as high processor utilization, low disk space, average milliseconds per transfer, average disk queue length, and average percent of physical memory used. Figure 11.23 shows an example of this report for a group of servers (Operations Manager Agent Managed Computer Group).

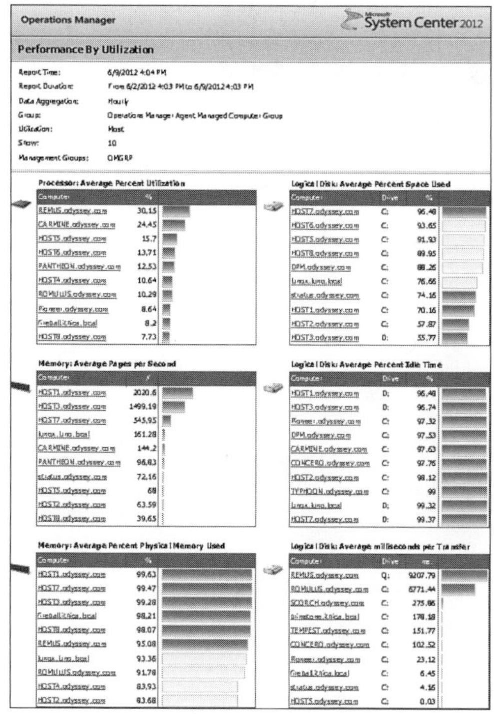

FIGURE 11.23 Performance by Utilization report.

The Operations Manager community has also stepped up to provide additional reports for Operations Manager, provided at no cost:

- **System Center Central Health Check Reports:** Released by System Center Central (http://www.systemcentercentral.com/), this report management pack provides a series of reports that help identify what is occurring in Operations Manager. These reports all function for OpsMgr 2012 with the exception of the Hotfix related reports, which would need to be updated to identify the current cumulative updates for OpsMgr 2012. These reports provide information for agents, configuration churn, events, performance, state, and general OpsMgr reports. This management pack is available free from System Center Central in the management pack catalog (http://tinyurl.com/SCC-HealthCheck).

- **Veeam Extended Generic Report Library:** Released by Veeam (http://www.veeam.com) at TechEd 2012, this reporting pack provides a series of reports that extend the report library Microsoft provides with OpsMgr. These reports include Veeam Alert Statistics Report, Veeam Performance Details Report, Veeam Generic Performance Top (Bottom) N Report, and the Veeam Performance Report. This management pack is available at no cost from Veeam and is available at http://www.veeam.com/extended-generic-report-library.html. Figure 11.24 shows an example of the Veeam Performance Details Report displaying the performance of a synthetic web transaction including the performance trend.

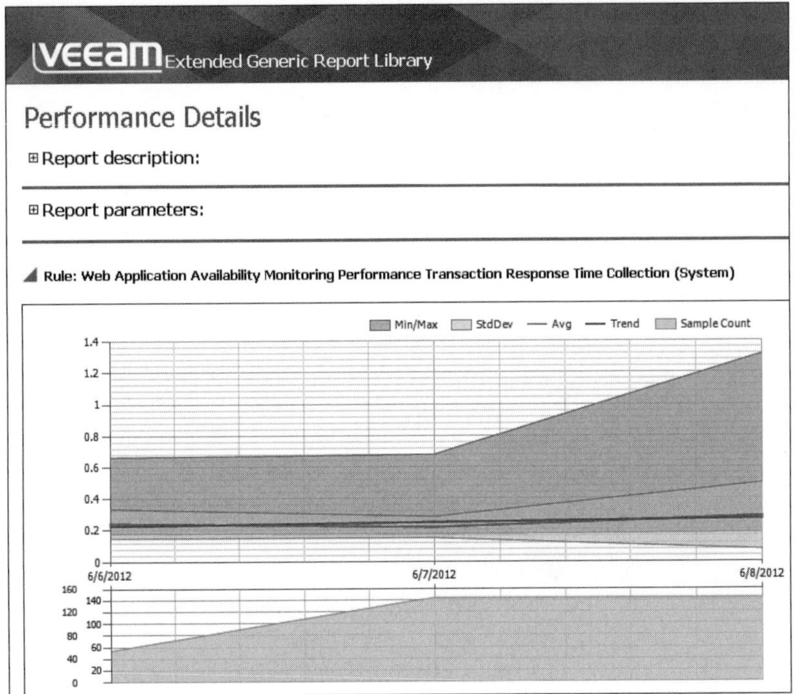

FIGURE 11.24 Veeam Performance Details report.

Reports such as those shown in Figures 11.22, 11.23, and 11.24 are examples of how you can use OpsMgr's historical information to identify performance trends. These types of reports can be used not only for KPIs on a server including disk, memory, CPU, and network, but also for any performance counter that OpsMgr gathers including custom performance counters and performance counters gathered by synthetic transactions.

Microsoft, the community, and third-party vendors provide a vast number of reports for Operations Manager 2012 that you can use to meet most report requirements. You can use the Microsoft Generic Report Library and Veeam Extended Generic Report Library to create custom reports for many situations. Should you need to create custom reports, these are discussed in Chapter 22, "Authoring Management Packs and Reports."

Forecasting and Capacity Planning with OpsMgr

While useful to see performance trends, being able to forecast performance information helps identify where likely bottlenecks will take place before they occur in OpsMgr. Examples include forecasting when a disk will run out of disk space, or when a website will need additional web servers due to increases in time to display web pages. The community has stepped in to fill in the gap in OpsMgr's current inability to provide forecasting natively using two different approaches:

- **Community MP:** Daniel Savage of Microsoft wrote a sample management pack that provides forecasting in OpsMgr 2007, available at http://blogs.technet.com/b/momteam/archive/2010/04/29/reporting-scenarios-more-samples.aspx.
- **OpsLogix Capacity Intelligent Management Pack:** OpsLogix has written a management that provides the ability to project trends and forecast capacity for OpsMgr. The updated version of the OpsLogix Capacity Intelligent Management Pack includes a widget (shown in Figure 11.25) that displays the performance counter selected well as its trend and forecasted values. This widget also displays what threshold levels are defined as warnings and critical for the performance counter. Using a feature of the widget the user can create a monitor that will generate an alert when the performance counter will exceed these thresholds. This approach allows the user to be proactively notified so that additional capacity can be ordered. Information on this management pack is available at http://www.opslogix.com/products/capacity-management-pack.

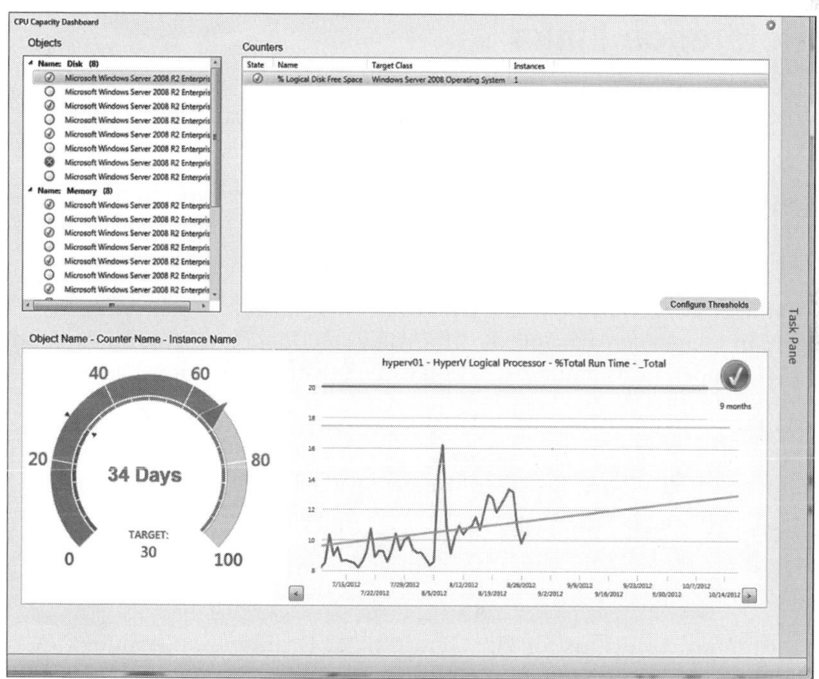

FIGURE 11.25 OpsLogix Capacity widget.

While Operations Manager does not provide out of the box forecasting and capacity planning capabilities, the OpsMgr community has stepped in to augment the OpsMgr framework to provide these solutions.

Fast Track

Here are key concepts to remember related to dashboards and reports in OpsMgr 2012:

- **Built-in dashboards:** All content in the "Built-In Dashboards" section of this chapter is new to OpsMgr 2012.
- **Prebuilt dashboards:** All content in the "Prebuilt Dashboards" section of this chapter is new to OpsMgr 2012.
- **Additional dashboard items:** This section of the chapter contains content that has been updated around solutions available for OpsMgr 2012.
- **Reports, trending, forecasting, and capacity planning:** As discussed in this section, while reporting in OpsMgr 2012 has not changed significantly since OpsMgr 2007 R2, Microsoft, third-party vendors, and the community are adding new reports regularly.

Additional Reference Links

Due to the variety of requirements that may apply to how data is displayed from Operations Manager, there are a number of good reference links that can assist on these topics. The authors recommend the following for additional reading:

- **Introducing Operations Manager 2012 Dashboards:** Blog article written by Dale Koetke of Microsoft, available at http://blogs.technet.com/b/momteam/archive/2011/09/27/introducing-operations-manager-2012-dashboards.aspx
- **Operations Manager 2012 Dashboards - The Alert Widget:** Blog article written by Microsoft's Akin Olugbade, available at http://blogs.technet.com/b/momteam/archive/2011/10/17/operations-manager-2012-dashboards-the-alert-widget.aspx
- **Operations Manager 2012 Dashboards - The Performance Widget:** Blog article written by Chris Harris of Microsoft, available at http://blogs.technet.com/b/momteam/archive/2011/10/04/widgets-performance-widget.aspx
- **Dashboards in OpsMgr 2012:** Windows IT Pro article by Cameron Fuller, available at http://www.windowsitpro.com/article/system-center/dashboards-operations-manager-2012-141491
- **Third-Party Dashboard Solutions for OpsMgr 2007 R2 Dashboards:** Windows IT Pro article by Cameron Fuller, available at http://www.windowsitpro.com/article/systems-management/operations-manager-dashboards
- **Top 10 Reporting Tricks:** Windows IT Pro article by Cameron Fuller, available at http://www.windowsitpro.com/article/microsoft-system-center-operations-manager-2007/10-system-center-operations-manager-reporting-tips-140603
- **Dashboard Integration Blog Series:** Blog series on dashboard integration by Cameron Fuller, at http://blogs.catapultsystems.com/cfuller/archive/2011/12/06/opsmgr-dashboard-integration-series-1.aspx

- **Operations Manager 2012, Savision & Dashboards:** Blog article written by Cameron Fuller, available at http://blogs.catapultsystems.com/cfuller/archive/2011/10/11/opsmgr-2012-savision-amp-dashboards.aspx
- **How Are OpsMgr 2012 Dashboards Different from Reports:** Blog article written by Satya Vel of Microsoft, available at http://blogs.technet.com/b/momteam/archive/2011/11/10/how-are-opsmgr-2012-dashboards-different-from-reports.aspx
- **Using SharePoint to View Operations Manager Data:** TechNet library content available at http://technet.microsoft.com/en-us/library/hh212924.aspx

Summary

This chapter discussed a variety of methods available to display data gathered by Operations Manager. These include the new built-in dashboard functionality with information on prebuilt dashboards included in Operations Manager 2012. This chapter also focused on additional dashboard solutions from Microsoft and third party vendors. The chapter completed with a discussion on reporting, trending, forecasting, and capacity planning. The next chapter discusses backup and recovery in Operations Manager 2012.

PART IV

Administering System Center 2012 Operations Manager

IN THIS PART

CHAPTER 12

Backup and Recovery

IN THIS CHAPTER

- Roles of Key OpsMgr Files and Databases
- Establishing a Backup Schedule
- Database Grooming and Maintenance
- Backing Up and Restoring the SQL Server Databases
- Backing Up Key Files
- Using Data Protection Manager
- Disaster Recovery Planning
- Fast Track

All production systems should have established backup and recovery procedures in place, and a System Center 2012 Operations Manager (OpsMgr) infrastructure is no exception. Unlike System Center 2012 Configuration Manager, Operations Manager does not include a backup process out of the box. This means that if one of the databases becomes damaged through corruption or a hardware failure and you are without a backup, you will have to reinstall that OpsMgr feature and recreate the database. If there is damage to the operational database, you will have to reinstall the entire management group. This creates all kinds of headaches.

Recreating a database without the ability to restore what was previously there means you lose all the information in the database. In the case of the operational database, you lose all customization and operational data collected in the database. If you lose the data warehouse database, you lose the reporting data you have accumulated. Losing the SQL Server Reporting Services (SSRS) database means you lose any customized reports. If you install Audit Control Services (ACS) and lose the audit database, you have lost your security logs and audit information.

There are also critical files you will want to secure through backup. This includes customized management packs, reports, the encryption keys utilized by SSRS, and the Internet Information Services (IIS) metabase. These types of potential data loss make it critical to create a backup and recovery plan for your OpsMgr implementation.

This chapter discusses backup and recovery strategies for Operations Manager. It also looks at a methodology for handling large report databases and requirements for disaster recovery.

Roles of Key OpsMgr Files and Databases

Backing up appropriate files and databases in a timely manner facilitates minimal data loss if there is a catastrophic failure in your OpsMgr infrastructure. An Operations Manager installation includes system databases, user databases, and significant files you will want to protect from data loss.

SQL SERVER SYSTEM AND USER DATABASES

Microsoft SQL Server system databases include databases established during the database engine installation. These databases are integral to the functionality of the database engine, and include the Master, Msdb, model, and tempdb databases. Other databases, created for application-specific purposes, are user databases.

Operations Manager-specific user databases include the operational database, data warehouse database, and audit database used by ACS. Installing the SQL Server Reporting Component (required for the OpsMgr reporting feature) creates two additional databases: the ReportServer and ReportServerTempDB databases.

Note that the Operations Manager setup process allows you to specify database names for the databases it creates. This chapter will refer to the default names.

You should include the following items in your backup strategy. This includes various system and user files and databases:

- **The operational database (named *OperationsManager* by default):** This database is installed in every management group, and is the most important user database to back up. If you lose this database due to hardware failure or corruption and do not have a database backup, you must reinstall the first management server and recreate the database, losing all management pack customizations, discovery rules, and operational data collected. This database is shared among management servers within a management group and must be backed up for every OpsMgr management group.
- **The data warehouse database (*OperationsManagerDW* by default):** This database stores aggregated data used for reporting, used by SSRS for trend analysis and performance tracking. Based on the amount of data you are collecting and the degree of aggregation, this database may be large and thus require special handling. In OpsMgr 2012, the data warehouse database is installed when you create the management group, whether or not you install the reporting feature.
- **The SSRS ReportServer database:** This database is used by SSRS. It stores the report definitions used for OpsMgr reporting and is updated when new reports are defined or definitions of existing reports are changed.

- **The ReportServerTempDB database:** The only reason to back up this database is to avoid having to recreate it if there is a hardware failure. If you have a hardware failure, you do not need to recreate the data in the database, but you do need the table structure. If you lose ReportServerTempDB, the only way to get it back is by recreating the SSRS ReportServer database.
- **The audit database (named *OperationsManagerAC* by default):** This database is associated with the Audit Collector service, which runs on the ACS collector. The database uses an agent to track cleared Security event logs and adds a new table daily for each day's security events. If you have multiple collectors, each uses its own audit database.
- **The Master database:** This is a system database, which records all information used by a SQL Server instance, such as database file locations, configuration settings, and security and login information. This database should be backed up whenever there is a change to your SQL Server configuration. If you installed the operational, data warehouse, reporting, or audit databases on separate database servers or instances, each will have a Master database that should be backed up. This is also true for a separate database server or instance using SSRS.
- **The Msdb database:** The Msdb database is also a SQL Server system database, containing scheduled tasks information for jobs, including regularly scheduled database backups. If you have installed the operational, data warehouse, reporting, or audit databases on separate database servers or instances, each will have an Msdb database that should be backed up.
- **Management packs and reports:** Management packs contain information pertaining to how Operations Manager monitors applications, services, and devices. The management packs are stored in the operational database, which you should back up as part of your standard procedure. The authors recommend separate backups of non-sealed/customized management packs, as this provides the granularity to import them directly into Operations Manager if necessary and to save a self-contained copy of any management pack customizations. Instances of importing management packs could include rolling back changes to an unsealed management pack or moving a customized management pack from a development to production environment.
- **IIS metabase:** The Web console server uses IIS. Most IIS settings are saved in its metabase, although several settings are in the registry. You could back up the server including the metabase, or redeploy the Web console server as part of your disaster recovery plan.
- **Custom files:** Custom files include the encryption key file for the reporting server. Customizations to console views are saved in the local user profile on the computer running the console. You could back up these personalizations with a physical disk backup or SystemState copy of the local operating system.

Establishing a Backup Schedule

As part of setting up backups, you should determine a regular backup schedule. Tables 12.1 and 12.2 give suggested time frames for backing up significant databases and files used by Operations Manager.

Establishing a daily backup schedule for those files that change regularly helps ensure that any data loss affects less than 24 hours of data. It also makes it possible for you to meet your service level agreements (SLAs) if you have backups of the information necessary to restore the various OpsMgr components.

TABLE 12.1 OpsMgr databases with recommended backup schedule

Database	Name	Type of Data	Recommended Backup Schedule
Operational database	OperationsManager (default)	This database contains the majority of the OpsMgr configurations, settings, and current operations data. Loss of this database would require completely reinstalling and reconfiguring the management group and result in the loss of all operational data.	Daily
Data warehouse database	OperationsManager DW (default)	This database holds all data used for reporting and can become quite large. The loss of this database would mean the loss of all historical operations and reporting data.	Daily
SQL Reporting database	ReportServer	This database holds all report definitions, as well as linked reports, cached report information, and snapshots. Loss of this database would mean having to reimport reports and recreate subscriptions, so it is of relatively minimal impact. If you install ACS, it has its own reporting subsystem and instance of the ReportServer database.	Monthly
Audit database	OperationsManager AC (default)	This database, present when using the ACS feature, tracks Security event logs being cleared by an agent. A new table is created daily for each day's events.	Daily

Database	Name	Type of Data	Recommended Backup Schedule
Master database	Master	This database is a SQL system database and records the system information for SQL Server. Back up the Master database for every SQL Server instance in your environment.	Daily or when there are changes
Msdb database	Msdb	This database is a SQL system database and holds information on all jobs scheduled through SQL Server. It is found on every SQL Server instance in your OpsMgr environment. While OpsMgr 2012 does not use this database as it schedules its maintenance internally, if you create any jobs yourself within SQL Server (backups or database maintenance for example), you should back up the Msdb database to retain that information.	Monthly or if there are changes

TABLE 12.2 Significant files with recommended backup schedule

File	Type of Data	Recommended Backup Schedule
Management packs and reports (.mp and .xml files)	Source files for management packs and reports. Enable more granular restoration than entire operational database; also used for moving management packs and reports from one management group to another.	After changes to management packs or reports. Since it can be difficult to always back up after changes, the authors recommend a daily backup.
Custom files	Encryption key files, the IIS metabase, and so on.	As needed.

Database Grooming and Maintenance

As part of maintaining the integrity of your database environment, you will want to manage data retention for your operational and data warehouse databases. Data retention also affects the size of the database and the amount of data that is backed up, which affects your backup requirements and scheduling.

Grooming the Operational Database

The OpsMgr Operations console includes the ability to modify data retention settings under **Administration** -> **Settings** -> **General** -> **Database Grooming**. The default setting for each of the data types is to remove or groom the data after seven days (see Figure 12.1). Updates to the grooming settings are applied immediately. Once the data is groomed, it is not recoverable unless it was previously backed up.

NOTE: ACTIVE ALERTS

Active alerts are never groomed. You must close an alert before it will be groomed.

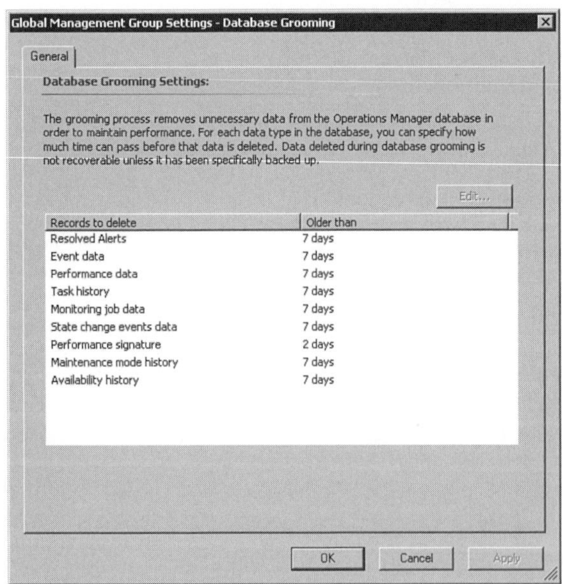

FIGURE 12.1 Operational database grooming settings.

Application performance monitoring (APM) is new with OpsMgr 2012. APM event data is groomed separately from the Database Grooming dialog in the Operations console. See the "Grooming APM Data" section for details.

Grooming the Data Warehouse Database

The Operations console does not include a graphical interface for modifying data retention settings for the data warehouse. You can groom the data warehouse settings by modifying columns in certain tables inside the OperationsManagerDW database. Data is groomed out at different intervals depending on the degree of aggregation. The data is stored by type, and data retention ranges from 10 days to 400 days by default, depending on the type of data. Defaults are listed in Table 12.3.

TABLE 12.3 Data warehouse datasets, types, and retention periods

Dataset	Aggregation Type	Retention (Days)
Alert	Raw data	400
State	Raw data	180
State	Hourly aggregations	400
State	Daily aggregations	400
Event	Raw data	100
AEM	Raw data	30
AEM	Daily aggregations	400
Perf	Raw data	10
Perf	Hourly aggregations	400
Perf	Daily aggregations	400

There is no graphical user interface to change these settings, although you can change them using SQL Server Management Studio. The next sections discuss how these settings are maintained and how they work.

Grooming Settings

Microsoft stores grooming-related settings in two areas in the MaintenanceSetting table in the data warehouse database:

- **Instance space:** Discovered objects with their properties and relationships.
- **Config space:** This is space that contains information about your management packs, the rules they contain, overrides you have created, and so on.

Tables 12.4 and 12.5 show columns of interest and their default values.

TABLE 12.4 MaintenanceSetting table instance space settings

Column	Value
LastInstanceGroomingDateTime	The last time grooming operations were performed.
InstanceOptimizationFrequencySeconds	How often optimization of the instance occurs (default: 60). This is the frequency of execution of the Standard Data Warehouse Data Set maintenance rule.
InstanceGroomingFrequencyMinutes	Frequency of the grooming process start in minutes (default: 480).
InstanceMaxAgeDays	Maximum age (since the day the instance was deleted) for the instance space objects (default: 400).
InstanceMaxRowsToGroom	Maximum number of objects to delete in one run (default: 5000).

TABLE 12.5 MaintenanceSetting table config space settings

Column	Value
LastConfigGroomingDateTime	The last time grooming operations were performed
ConfigOptimizationFrequencySeconds	How often optimization of the config space occurs (default: 60)
ConfigGroomingFrequencyMinutes	Frequency of the grooming process start in minutes (default: 60)
ManagementPackMaxAgeDays	Maximum age for the management pack (since the day the management pack was uninstalled) (default: 400)
NonSealedManagementPackMaxVersionCount	Maximum number of non-sealed management pack versions to preserve (independent of age) (default: 3)

Data Retention Settings

Settings controlling data retention are located in the StandardDatasetAggregation table. You can view the grooming settings by running this SQL query, sorted by GroomStoredProcedureName for ease of readability:

```
USE OperationsManagerDW
SELECT AggregationIntervalDurationMinutes, BuildAggregationStoredProcedureName,
GroomStoredProcedureName, MaxDataAgeDays, GroomingIntervalMinutes, MaxRowsToGroom
FROM StandardDatasetAggregation ORDER BY GroomStoredProcedureName
```

Table 12.6 displays the default settings returned by the SQL query.

The following applies to the results shown in Table 12.6:

- The first column is the interval in minutes that data is aggregated. NULL is raw data, 60 is hourly, and 1440 is daily.
- MaxDataAgeDays is the maximum number of days data is retained. Depending on the type of data and its degree of aggregation, defaults can range from 10 to 400 days.
- GroomingIntervalMinutes is the grooming process frequency. Performance, Alert, Event, and AEM data is groomed every 240 minutes (4 hours); State data is groomed every hour.
- If System Center Data Protection Manager (DPM) is installed, the SQL query will return data for DPM-grooming settings.

TABLE 12.6 Data returned from StandardDataSetAggregation table

Aggregation Interval Duration Minutes	BuildAggregation StoredProcedure Name	GroomStored ProcedureName	MaxData AgeDays	Grooming Interval Minutes	MaxRows ToGroom
NULL	NULL	DPMBackupGroom	400	240	300000
NULL	NULL	EventGroom	100	240	100000
NULL	NULL	StateGroom	180	60	50000
NULL	NULL	AlertGroom	400	240	50000
NULL	AemAggregate	AemGroom	30	240	100000
1440	AemAggregate	AemGroom	400	240	100000
NULL	PerformanceAggregate	PerformanceGroom	10	240	100000
60	PerformanceAggregate	PerformanceGroom	400	240	100000
1440	PerformanceAggregate	PerformanceGroom	400	240	100000
60	StateAggregate	StateGroom	400	60	50000
1440	StateAggregate	StateGroom	400	60	50000

To make sense of the grooming settings in this table, look at non-aggregated EventGroom data, which is the second row of information in Table 12.6. The GroomStoredProcedureName refers to the procedure EventGroom, indicating this refers to Event information. The information returned from the query shows that this data is not aggregated (`AggregationIntervalDurationMinutes=NULL`) and that it is saved for 100 days (`MaxDataAgeDays`). The `EventGroom` stored procedure is responsible for grooming data (`GroomStoredProcedureName`), and runs every 240 minutes/4 hours (`GroomingIntervalMinutes`). Each time the stored procedure runs, it will groom a maximum of 100,000 rows (`MaxRowsToGroom`).

Here is SQL code you can use to change the grooming frequency for each type of data:

```
USE OperationsManagerDW
UPDATE StandardDatasetAggregation
SET MaxDataAgeDays = <number of days to retain data>
WHERE GroomStoredProcedureName = '<procedure name>' AND
AggregationIntervalDurationMinutes = '<aggregation interval duration>'
GO
```

Alternatively, you can edit the settings in the StandardDatasetAggregation table directly. Follow these steps:

1. Select **Start** -> **Programs** -> **Microsoft SQL Server 2008 R2** -> **SQL Server Management Studio**.
2. In the Connect to Server dialog box, select **Database Engine** in the Server Type list, select the server and instance for your reporting data warehouse in the Server Name list (for example, WHIRLWIND\SQL_DW), select **Windows Authentication**, and click **Connect**.
3. In the Object Explorer pane of SQL Server Management Studio, select **Databases** -> **OperationsManagerDW** -> **Tables**.
4. Right-click dbo.Dataset and select **Open Table**.
5. Locate the dataset for which you want to change the grooming setting in the DatasetDefaultName column, and note the GUID (globally unique identifier) in the DatasetId column.
6. In the Object Explorer pane, right-click dbo.StandardDatasetAggregation and select **Open Table**.
7. In the DatasetId column, locate the dataset GUID you noted in step 5. Multiple entries of the same GUID might display.
8. Locate the aggregation type in the AggregationTypeID column by using these values:
    - **0:** Non, aggregated data
    - **10:** Subhourly
    - **20:** Hourly
    - **30:** Daily
9. After locating the dataset and its aggregation type, scroll to the MaxDataAgeDays column and edit the value there to set the grooming interval. Changes take effect immediately.

About Datasets

Data in the data warehouse is retained by data type. Each data type is stored in a separate structure, called a *dataset*. Examples of these datasets include a performance dataset for performance data, a state dataset to monitor state transactions, an event dataset for events, and so on.

Management packs may also introduce new datasets. Microsoft refers to all datasets in existence (that is, known today) as *standard datasets*. Microsoft maintains a set of tables for standard datasets that hold a description of the dataset including its data retention policies. A non-standard dataset does not have to follow these rules; data retention settings for non-standard datasets are dataset-specific.

Data retention for the standard dataset is set at the aggregation level, meaning that performance raw data (the samples themselves) is stored a certain number of days. The number of days may differ from the number of days the daily aggregates are stored for say, performance counters. These settings are stored in the StandardDatasetAggregation table, shown in Table 12.5 in the previous section.

The primary key for the StandardDatasetAggregation table is composite and consists of the database ID (from the Dataset table) and the Aggregation TypeID (from the AggregationType table). Default values vary by dataset/aggregation type. The aggregation types, defined in the AggregationType table (which consists of the `AggregationTypeID`, `AggregationType DefaultName`, and `AggregationTypeGuid` columns), are 0, 10, 20, and 30, and were defined in the "Data Retention Settings" section.

For performance reasons, data is not always groomed row-by-row. If the data inflow is high (typically the case for medium and large organizations for performance and event data), the data warehouse database uses additional tables to store data. This makes the grooming process (database row deletes) more efficient, as an entire table can be deleted rather than individual rows.

As an example, 10 million performance samples are stored in the first instance of a table. After 10 million records, OpsMgr creates a new table that holds the additional data and calculates a minimum and maximum date for the data in the first table. This information is stored separately in the StandardDatasetTableMap table. Grooming looks at this table to determine what data exists in each table and grooms accordingly.

NOTE: DWDATARP TOOL

OpsMgr 2007 Service Pack (SP) 1 included a ResKit tool named DWDATARP that allows you to view and set the data retention policies for all configured datasets. You can also edit the data directly to configure your data warehouse retention, as discussed in the "Data Retention Settings" section. At the time of writing this chapter, Microsoft has not released a resource kit for OpsMgr 2012. (Chapter 14, "Monitoring with System Center 2012 Operations Manager," discusses the resource kits and utilities that are available.)

Here is the logic used by the grooming process:

- For a certain dataset/aggregation type combination, check to see if there is only one table in the data warehouse.

- If there is just one table, delete records row-by-row using the `DELETE TOP` SQL statement and MaxRowsToGroom parameter from the StandardDatasetAggregationTable.
- If there is more than one table, find the table with the oldest maximum date for data in it. If this date is older than the retention period, drop the entire table; otherwise, do not delete any rows.

The implication of following this process is that the data warehouse may not always be "current" on grooming. When the data in a table spans a month, some records are kept one cycle or month longer than necessary. However, there are enormous performance gains in dropping an entire table rather than performing individual row deletes in SQL Server, so storing the data a little longer seems a reasonable tradeoff. Because report selection includes a time period, any additional data is not visible to the end user.

NOTE: HOW GROOMING IS ACTUALLY PERFORMED

There are separate stored procedures to groom the different types of data such as performance, state, alerts, events, AEM data, and so on. The GroomStoredProcedureName column in Table 12.6 specifies the grooming procedures used for the data warehouse.

You can use the `standarddatasetgroom` stored procedure in the data warehouse database to manually trigger grooming. The procedure uses a parameter, *datasetid*. This value, listed in the dataset table, represents the type of data on which to act. Steve Rachui has a post documenting this at http://blogs.msdn.com/steverac/archive/2007/12/13/scom-2007-operational-and-datawarehouse-grooming.aspx. (Although the post is written for OpsMgr 2007, the stored procedure has not changed.) OpsMgr calls the `standarddatasetmaintenance` stored procedure to execute `standarddatasetgroom`.

As OpsMgr aggregates most of the data in the data warehouse database, its growth on a day-to-day-basis is less than the operational database. However, since the retention period is longer, it will grow to be considerably larger.

Data Warehouse Backup Considerations

Because the data warehouse database has longer data retention periods, it can become quite large, although initially it is smaller than the operational database. Large databases often present potential backup issues. A terabyte database, for example, can take a considerable amount of time to back up and restore.

One approach is to create archived (segmented) versions of the data warehouse database, separating it by different months, quarters, or years, depending on its size and your specific reporting requirements. Segmenting gives you granularity in backups; once a database is archived, it does not need to be backed up on a regular schedule. Segmenting also makes potential restore operations quicker.

A sophisticated backup schedule that accommodates archive databases would back up the current data warehouse but retain online copies of archived versions. As you backed up each archived database when it was current, you would simply maintain those tapes in long-term storage as long as required for reporting purposes. Segmenting reporting information allows you to reduce the volume of data backed up on a daily basis while maintaining long-term availability of the data using archived databases and long-term tape storage.

Here are several caveats to this approach:

- Adjusting the grooming sections (discussed in the "Grooming the Data Warehouse Database" section) to groom only at the end of your designated archival period.
- Administrative overhead incurred in managing the backup process at the end of each retention period. The end-of-period backup process adds complexity, illustrated in Figure 12.2.
- Added complexity in tailoring reports to run against archived data as necessary.

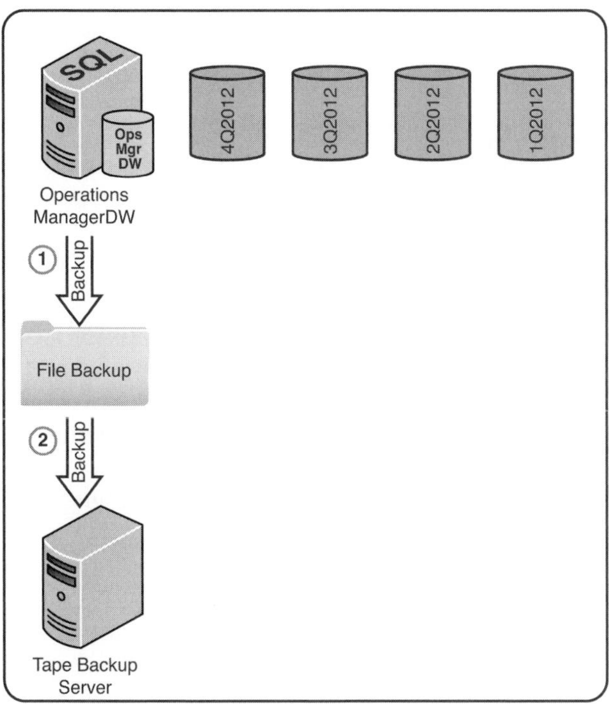

FIGURE 12.2 Backup of data warehouse with archives.

For purposes of illustration, consider an organization monitoring 3,000 servers and 1,000 network devices. For simplicity's sake, assume this company uses Microsoft SQL Server's backup capability for its database backups. The organization needs access to one year's worth of data. You can use the sizing helper, introduced in Chapter 4, "Planning an Operations Manager Deployment," to determine the amount of space required for the data warehouse. Results from the sizing helper, illustrated in Figure 12.3, estimate that with a 1-year retention period, the data warehouse will be close to 3 terabytes (TB), which is too large to easily back up directly to tape. In addition, backup to a disk file requires equivalent storage on disk for the backup file, for a total of almost 5.7TB. This is also too much storage for practical operations.

DB Size	
Number of Days for Data Retention	7
Number of Server Computers	3000
Number of Network Devices	1000
Number of APM-enabled Computers	0
Total Size (MB)	**73880.71**
Total Size (GB)	**72.15**
Total Size (GB) with 50% Buffer	**108.22**
DW Size	
Number of Days for Data Retention	365
Number of Server Computers	3000
Number of Network Devices	1000
Number of APM-enabled Computers	0
Total Size (MB)	**2984386.99**
Total Size (GB)	**2914.44**
Total Size (GB) with 10% Buffer	**3205.88**

FIGURE 12.3 Data warehouse size for an organization with 3,000 monitored servers and 1,000 monitored network devices.

However, data for a single quarter will be somewhat over 725GB. This amount is within the capability of the tape backup system. The company decides to break the data warehouse into quarterly archives and accordingly sets the data warehouse grooming sets to groom data after each quarter (120 days). This configuration has been running for over a year now with no incidents.

Figure 12.3 illustrates the backup process.

You can perform this backup process weekly, daily, or at whatever period best meets your business requirements, with the procedure remaining the same. The amount of disk storage required is based on the size of the database, which is based on the data captured by the agents. Calculating size for a 725GB database with one quarter of data, the company will require disk space to hold five databases (5 * 725GB) plus an additional 725GB for the file backup that is archived to tape. This is a total of 3,625GB (3.6TB). You can contrast this figure with the original 5.7TB storage requirement and see the savings on disk storage! In addition, only 725GB needs to be backed up at a time, rather than nearly 3TB; making the backup operation more efficient.

Procedures are a bit more complex for the end-of-quarter backup process, shown in Figure 12.4. The following steps outline the process of transitioning at the end of 1Q2013:

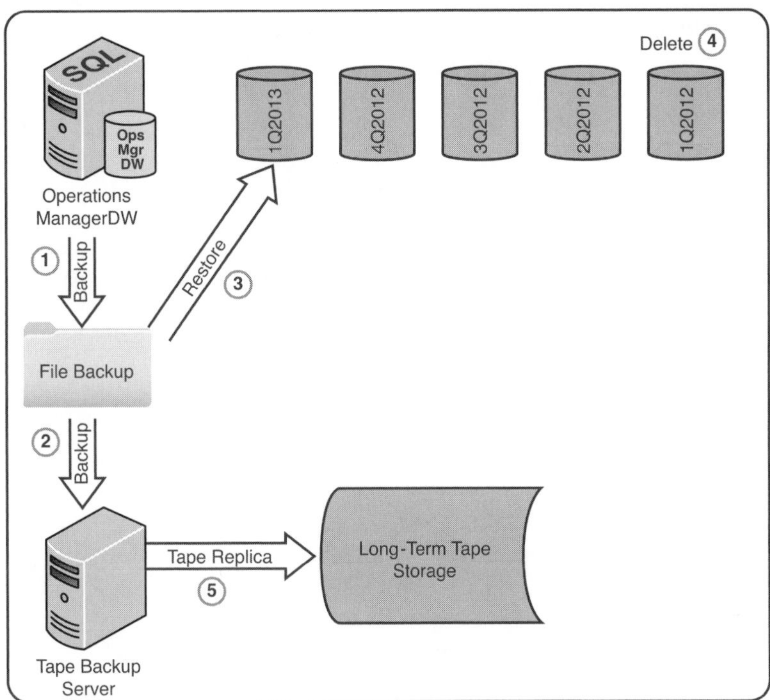

FIGURE 12.4 Quarterly backup of data warehouse with archives.

1. First, the data warehouse is backed up to a disk file. This is an online SQL Server backup, so there is no interruption in availability.
2. Next, the backup file is copied to tape. In the event of a disaster, this tape backup can easily be restored.
3. The backup file is restored to a new SQL Server database storing data for that quarter (in this example, 1Q2013).
4. The database now outside the one-year data retention requirement (1Q2012) is deleted.
5. The tape backup of the data warehouse in step 2 (1Q2013) is replicated for long-term tape storage.

You can automate these processes using scripts and jobs, or run them manually as end-of-period procedures. The overall process is flexible and can be adjusted to support monthly archives rather than quarterly. The advantage of using monthly archives is that the backups are correspondingly shorter, but the report horizon will also be shorter and only cover a single month. You could also extend this process to occur every 6 or 12 months. If it becomes necessary to query data in an archive, you could restore the archived backup as a database file and change the data source in SSRS to point to that specific database.

This process is outside any mechanisms designed or supported by Microsoft.

Grooming the Audit Database

Data is groomed from the audit database based on the data retention specified during setup, with the default being 14 days. The ACS collector calls a SQL procedure to remove a partition that is outside the data retention period. You can find this procedure on disk on the collector at *%SystemRoot%*\system32\security\AdtServer\DbDeletePartition.sql. The data retention period is specified in the dtConfigtable in the database.

To update the data retention period, run the following SQL query:

```
USE OperationsManagerAC
UPDATE dtConfig
SET Value = <number of days to retain data + 1>
WHERE Id = 6
```

To retain seven days of data, set Value to 8. Data is accumulated at approximately 7.6MB per day per workstation.

Further ACS database sizing information is available in Chapter 10, "Security and Compliance."

Grooming APM Data

If you are monitoring applications using APM, the new APM events data type will begin to take up space, and you will eventually want to groom your databases for APM events; these are stored in both the operational and data warehouse databases. You can groom APM events using several interfaces:

- The Application Diagnostics console lets you configure grooming settings for APM events in the operational database.
- In Application Advisor, you can configure grooming settings for APM events in the data warehouse.
- You can use the Data Transfer rule to override parameters related to time-based APM event grooming in the data warehouse.

These are discussed in the next sections.

Grooming the Operational Database of APM Data

Application Diagnostics is installed on the Web console server. In the Odyssey environment, this is at https://typhoon/AppDiagnostics. By opening the Application Diagnostics console, navigating to **Tools -> Options**, and selecting the Data tab, you can select how many APM events you want in the operational database and how long you want to keep them. Figure 12.5 displays data options for APM events in the operational database.

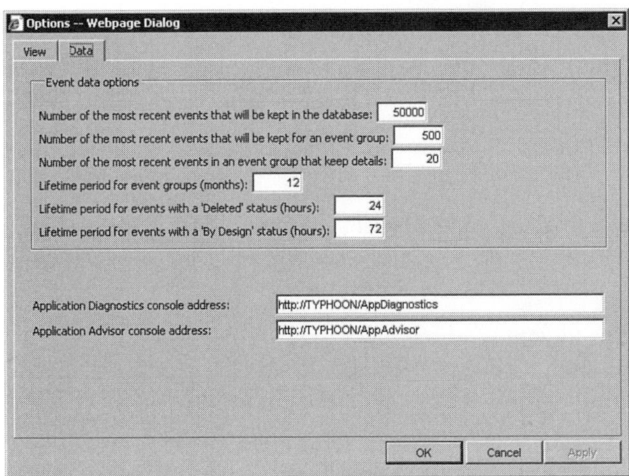

FIGURE 12.5 Using Application Diagnostics to configure APM event grooming in the operational database.

The default settings are 50,000 events with 500 per event group and 20 in an event group that keeps details. The lifetime period for event groups is 12 months. For additional information about APM, refer to Chapter 15, "Monitoring .NET Applications."

Grooming the Data Warehouse of APM Data

Use Application Advisor (http://typhoon/AppAdvisor in the Odyssey environment) to configure data warehouse grooming settings for events with a status of Deleted or By Design. Select **Tools -> Options** to bring up the Data tab, shown in Figure 12.6. The settings shown here are the defaults.

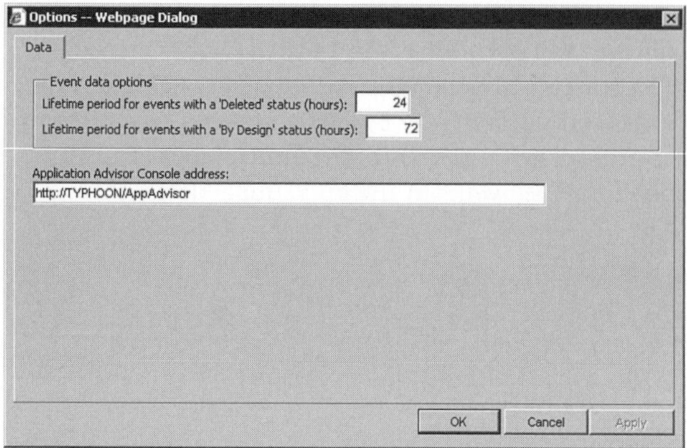

FIGURE 12.6 Using Application Advisor to configure APM event grooming in the data warehouse database.

The OpsMgr APM Data Transfer rule is targeted to the Operations Manager APM Data Transfer Service object. It includes overrides for events and counters. The setting for events applies to those events where grooming is controlled by Application Advisor and not previously marked as Deleted or By Design. If events are left in the New status, they are retained in the data warehouse for the number of days indicated by this setting. To view the override options, follow these steps:

1. Navigate in the Operations console to **Authoring** -> **Management Pack Objects** -> **Rules**.
2. Click on **Change Scope**. Enter **APM Data Transfer Service** in the Look for: box, select **View all targets**, and click **OK**.
3. In the Rules section, right click on the **Operations Manager APM Data Transfer** rule, select **Overrides** -> **Override the Rule** -> **For a specific object of class: Operations Manager APM Data Transfer Service** to display the dialog shown in Figure 12.7.
4. Make appropriate changes to the **Store Event Period** and **Store Performance Counters Interval** parameters.
   - **Store Event Period:** This determines the number of days you will keep APM events.
   - **Store Performance Counters Interval:** This parameter lets you determine how many days of performance counters to keep in the data warehouse. The setting applies to hourly performance aggregations, which can take up a considerable amount of space.

   Both parameters are set to 91 days by default. Select an existing unsealed management pack or create a new management pack to store your overrides in, and click **OK**.

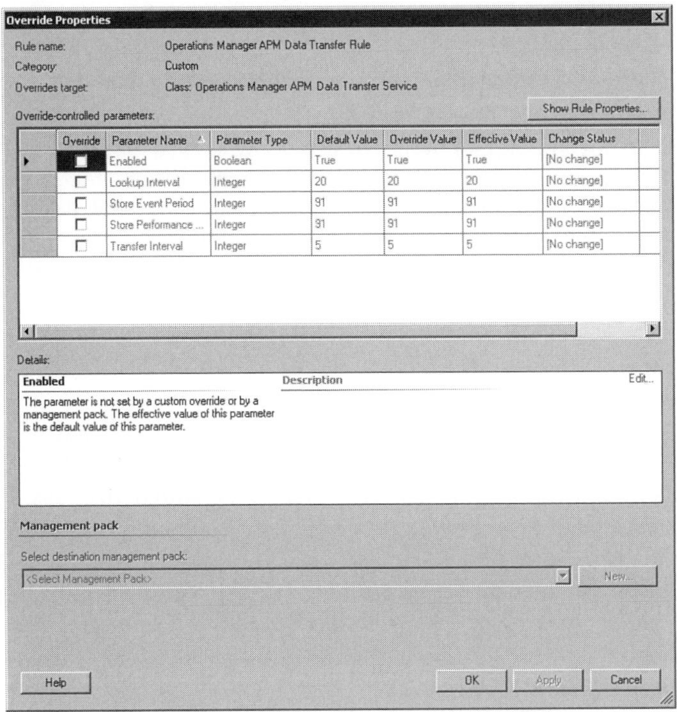

FIGURE 12.7 Using Application Advisor to configure APM event grooming in the data warehouse database.

You cannot configure daily performance aggregations, which default at 182. However, daily aggregations use considerably less disk space than hourly aggregations.

Database Maintenance

Normally DBAs do regular maintenance on SQL Server databases. With OpsMgr, Microsoft designed the databases to be self-maintaining to a degree. The next sections discuss types of maintenance you may want to consider.

SQL SERVER EDITION AFFECTS BEHAVIOR DURING MAINTENANCE WINDOW

Implementing SQL Server Standard versus SQL Server Enterprise Edition affects how the database components behave during the daily database maintenance window. This is particularly true for the audit database. The ACS collector queue stores events received from ACS forwarders prior to sending those events to the database. The number of events in the queues increases during periods of high-audit traffic, or when the database is not available to accept new events—such as during database purging. As part of daily database maintenance, those database partitions with time stamps outside the data retention schedule (four days by default) are dropped from the audit database. The two SQL Server editions behave differently during this activity:

- SQL Server Enterprise Edition continues inserting processed security events but only at 30% to 40% of the regular insertion rate.
- When using Standard Edition, security insertion halts, and events queue up on the ACS collector until database maintenance is complete.

The ACS collector is configured to queue 262,144 events by default. While this may seem a large number of events, you may quickly reach this limit if several forwarders are sending security events. You can reduce the number of events by carefully configuring the maintenance window for the daily database maintenance. Select a time frame when there is the least amount of user and application activity on the network.

Operational Database Maintenance

Microsoft built reindexing into Operations Manager for the more significant tables in the operational database; the Optimize Index rule in the System Center Internal Library management pack executes the `P_OptimizeIndexes` stored procedure daily at 2:30 AM, which cannot be modified. This means you must ensure no other SQL maintenance jobs are running at 2:30 AM.

Here are several queries you can run to view the built-in `UPDATE STATISTICS` and `DBCC DBREINDEX` jobs history:

```
select * from DomainTable dt
INNER JOIN DomainTableIndexOptimizationHistory dti
ON dt.domaintablerowID = dti.domaintableindexrowID
ORDER BY optimizationdurationseconds DESC
```

This first query indicates when the `P_OptimizeIndexes` stored procedure ran (normally every day), time to complete, and average fragmentation of the tables before and after running the stored procedure.

```
SELECT * from DomainTable dt
INNER JOIN DomainTableStatisticsUpdateHistory dti
ON dt.domaintablerowID = dti.domaintablerowID
ORDER BY UpdateDurationSeconds DESC
```

The update/optimization duration seconds column in this second query will show you how long your maintenance typically runs; this should not take long in a healthy environment.

To view the fragmentation levels of the tables in the database run

```
DBCC SHOWCONTIG WITH FAST
```

Optimally the scan density will be high (above 80%) and the logical scan fragmentation is low (below 30%). Because the built-in maintenance does not reindex all tables, some tables will be more fragmented than others. Here is a query you can run separately from the scheduled job that comes with OpsMgr against the operational database:

```
USE OperationsManager
GO
SET ANSI_NULLS ON
SET ANSI_PADDING ON
SET ANSI_WARNINGS ON
SET ARITHABORT ON
SET CONCAT_NULL_YIELDS_NULL ON
SET QUOTED_IDENTIFIER ON
SET NUMERIC_ROUNDABORT OFF
EXEC SP_MSForEachTable "Print 'Reindexing '+'?' DBCC DBREINDEX ('?')"
```

12

`DBCC REINDEX`—used in the previous query—is preferred for reducing fragmentation, but the tables that reindexed are not accessible during its execution. This is an offline operation and runs faster when there is a high level of fragmentation. If you need shared access to the database during this operation, use `DBCC INDEXDEFRAG` instead.

You can schedule this using the SQL agent, but you will want to ensure it does not conflict with the `P_OptimizeIndexes` stored procedure running at 2:30 AM each day.

NOTE: FREE SPACE REQUIREMENT FOR OPERATIONAL DATABASE

The operational database needs 50% free space at all times for growth and for re-index operations to be successful. An alert is generated when free space falls below 40%.

Autogrow is turned off for the operational database. It should not be turned on. Here's why:

- Autogrow grows the database in small increments, which can lead to fragmentation and performance issues.
- Should there be issues (such as an alert storm) that lead to requests for additional space, when autogrow is enabled the database could continue to grow until the disk is full!

Data Warehouse Database Maintenance

Similar to the operational database, the data warehouse database is fully self-maintaining. The Standard Data Warehouse Data Set maintenance rule, which is targeted to the Standard Data Set object type, is called every 60 seconds. It performs a number of tasks, including index optimization. All necessary tables are updated and reindexed as needed, and reorganized when fragmentation hits 10%. Because the maintenance runs every 60 seconds, it is not necessary to run additional jobs. This rule calls the stored procedure `dbo.StandardDatasetMaintenance`, which calls several other stored procedures, as follows:

- dbo.StandardDatasetOptimize
- dbo.StandardDatasetGroom
- dbo.StandardDatasetAggregate

The `dbo.StandardDatasetOptimize` procedure is responsible for indexing. If the average fragmentation is between 10% and 30%, the index is reorganized. If fragmentation is over 30%, the index is rebuilt.

Here is a query that reports the optimization results. It displays the optimization method applied to each table, and levels of fragmentation before and after the optimization jobs. This also is available as online content as Optimization_results.sql; see Appendix E, "Available Online," for information.

```
USE OperationsManagerDW
GO
select basetablename, optimizationstartdatetime, optimizationdurationseconds,
      beforeavgfragmentationinpercent, afteravgfragmentationinpercent,
      optimizationmethod, onlinerebuildlastperformeddatetime
from StandardDatasetOptimizationHistory sdoh
inner join StandardDatasetAggregationStorageIndex sdasi
on sdoh.StandardDatasetAggregationStorageIndexRowId =
sdasi.StandardDatasetAggregationStorageIndexRowId
inner join StandardDatasetAggregationStorage sdas
on sdasi.StandardDatasetAggregationStorageRowId =
sdas.StandardDatasetAggregationStorageRowId
ORDER BY optimizationdurationseconds DESC
```

Autogrow is turned on for the data warehouse database. The authors recommend changing this from the default (percent) to a defined number, such as 500MB for the database file and 100MB for the transaction log.

ACS Database Maintenance

ACS uses a SQL partition (table) for each day's worth of new data. This partition is closed and then indexed every night, table by table. This means that normally the only maintenance necessary for the ACS database is to perform backups.

However, it is possible the indexing can fail; this is most likely when the table is quite large. In this case, you may want to perform a reindex operation on the database or table itself for improved query and reporting performance.

TIP: WHEN IT IS APPROPRIATE TO REINDEX THE AUDIT DATABASE

Do not perform an index operation on the audit database if there is a high insert rate. Reindexing has a large impact on the database server's performance and would greatly slow down the available insert rate for ACS operations.

Running `DBCC SHOWCONTIG WITH FAST` in SQL Server Management Studio will show the level of fragmentation on the database tables.

About Recovery Mode

Operations Manager setup sets the recovery mode as simple on the OpsMgr databases, meaning transactions are not logged and restores are to the last full backup only. Due to the high transaction rate on the operational and data warehouse databases, the transaction log can become quite large should you use full recovery mode. Database recovery is also more complex when using the full recovery model, as you must restore to the last full backup and then restore each log backup.

OpsMgr does support log shipping for redundancy on the operational and data warehouse databases. If you want to implement log shipping, set the database to full recovery mode. The authors do not recommend this for the audit database, as it already has high processing requirements. If you are looking for fault tolerance, clustering is a less resource-intensive approach.

Backing Up and Restoring the SQL Server Databases

Many Information Technology (IT) organizations have a database support group responsible for their Microsoft SQL database servers and in charge of backing up and restoring SQL Server databases. Work with your database group to ensure that an appropriate backup and restore plan exists for your OpsMgr databases. If there is not a group responsible for database backups, you will need to create your own backup and restore plan. This plan includes scheduling times for backups, identifying actual database files, and defining procedures to back up and restore those files. Be sure that backups are not scheduled to occur during other Operations Manager database maintenance such as grooming. The grooming jobs perform database reads and writes. Backing up a database while grooming is occurring could cause failures in the backup job, the grooming job, or both, due to locks.

Most enterprise backup implementations, including System Center Data Protection Manager, include a separate software module that can be installed to back up a SQL Server database while it is running. The authors recommend that this type of backup agent be employed in your design to provide for online backups of the OpsMgr databases.

Alternatively, you can use SQL Server's backup feature to back up the databases to (local or remote) file or local tape, and then back up the resulting files during your normal backup process. This does not require a SQL backup agent and has the advantage of being very fast. The downside is that you need sufficient disk space to hold a backup the size of the entire database, which in the case of the data warehouse database can be quite large.

CAUTION: BACKING UP TO LOCAL DISK IS NOT SUFFICIENT

Do not just perform a SQL Server backup to local disk and think you have adequate protection. If the system running the database server crashes and your only backup is on that server, it is like having no backup at all.

Operations Manager Database Backups

This section uses SQL Server's backup feature to back up the operational database as an example of the process you can use for the other databases used by OpsMgr. SQL backups are defined using SQL Server Management Studio. (For backups using DPM, see the "Using Data Protection Manager" section later in this chapter.)

Always perform a complete backup rather than an incremental or differential backup of the operational database; by default, Operations Manager supports a simple recovery from a full backup only, not a forward recovery using the transaction log. Members of the sysadmin fixed server roles and the db_owner and db_backupoperator fixed database roles by default have permissions to back up a SQL Server database.

TIP: TYPES OF DATABASE RECOVERIES

Without diving too deep into database technology, Microsoft SQL Server supports three types of recovery: Full, bulk-logged, and simple:

- A full recovery uses the database and transaction log backups for full recoverability.
- Bulk-logged uses minimal transaction logging for bulk load types of operations—if a recovery is necessary, those transactions must be reapplied.
- Simple, used by the Operations Manager databases, recovers the database without using the transaction logs as part of the process. Using a simple recovery model, any database changes made since the previous full backup are lost. However, this model is the simplest for performing restore operations.

You can change the recovery mode if this is required for your installation. Chapter 9, "Complex Configurations," discusses the procedures to set the operational database to full recovery and configure log shipping. You could also use log shipping on the data warehouse database. You might decide to implement log shipping for a high availability environment. Additional information on recovery models is available at http://msdn.microsoft.com/en-us/library/ms189275.aspx.

The operational, data warehouse, and audit databases should be backed up daily. The following procedure defines a backup job for the operational database:

1. Open SQL Server Management Studio and navigate to **Databases -> OperationsManager**. Right-click the OperationsManager database, select **Tasks**, and then choose **Back Up** to bring up the Back up Database General page, shown in Figure 12.8.

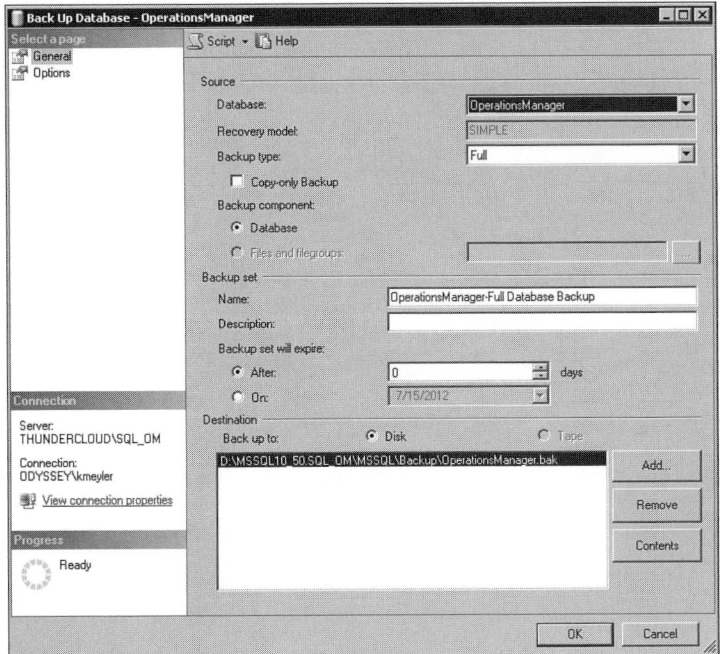

FIGURE 12.8 SQL Server Management Studio 2008 R2 database backup page.

2. The default backup type is **Full**, which is the backup type used for the OperationsManager database. This backup type backs up the entire database file, rather than just those changes since the previous backup. (Because the OpsMgr databases have a simple recovery model by default, the transaction log is truncated as each transaction completes, meaning you cannot do an incremental backup unless you change the recovery model in the database options to Full.)

   Under Destination, select the backup destination, which can be disk or tape. For this example, the OperationsManager database is backed up to **Disk**, which is the default.

3. Select **Add** under Destination. The wizard provides a default location. To enter the location and filename where the backup will be stored, click on the button with the ellipsis (...), and name the file **OperationsManager_Full_OMGRP.bak**. This example uses a folder named C:\Backups, rather than the default folder. Figure 12.9 shows the location specified for the backup file. Click **OK**.

4. SQL Server Management Studio next displays the Select Backup Destination dialog, shown in Figure 12.10. Click **OK** to confirm the destination.

5. After specifying the general requirements for the backup, select the page shown in Figure 12.11. You must decide whether you will override the backup set (file). By default, SQL Server appends the current backup to the end of the backup file if it already exists. Alternatively, you can overwrite (replace) the file.

The option to truncate the transaction log is grayed out because the database recovery type is defined as simple. If you want to truncate the log, you will have to add a step to do this manually. Simple recovery is similar to truncate log on checkpoint; meaning you do not need to truncate the log.

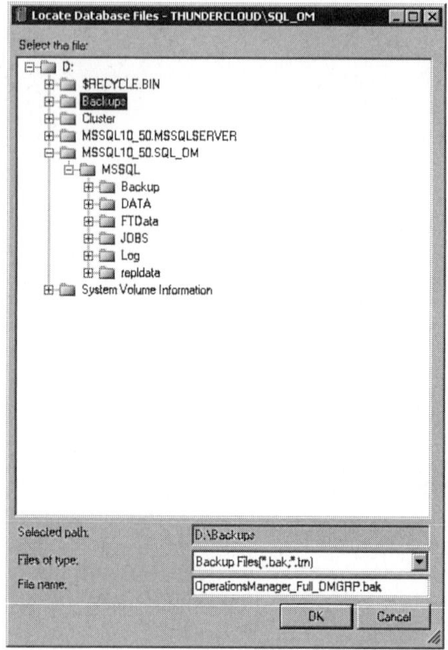

FIGURE 12.9 Specify the backup device location.

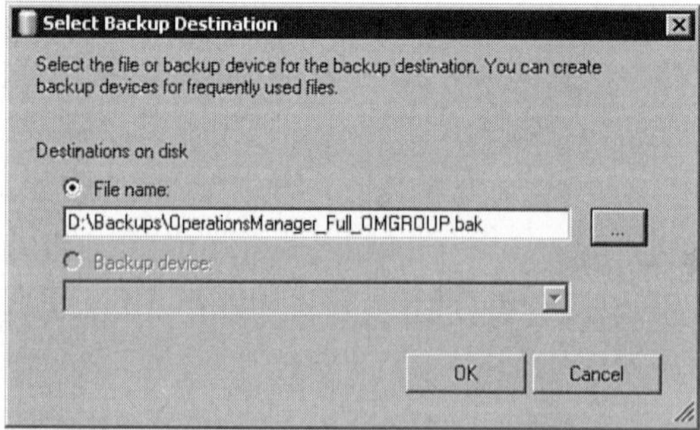

FIGURE 12.10 Select Backup Destination.

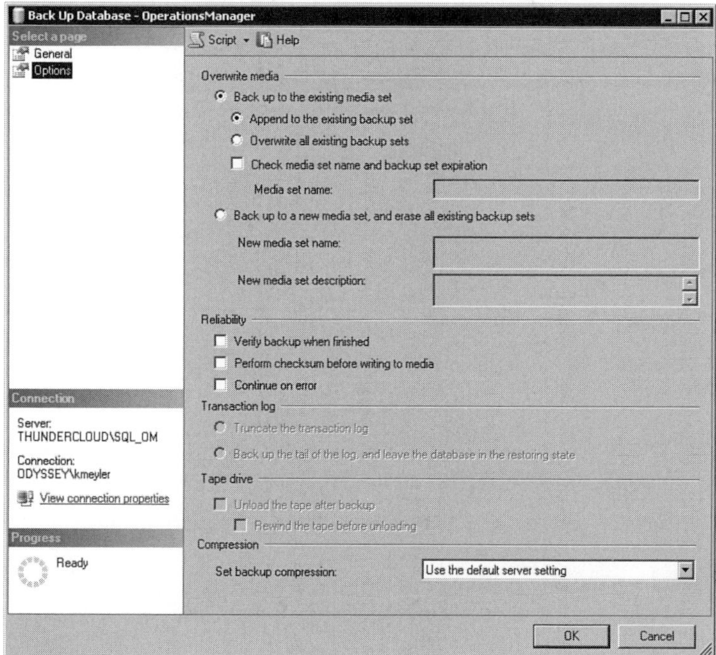

FIGURE 12.11 The backup options page.

6. Selecting the **Script** option at the top of Figure 12.11 generates Transact SQL code you can use to schedule the backup rather than having to return to SQL Management Studio each time you want to back up the database.

   Once the script is generated, the progress status shows that scripting completed successfully.

7. After generating the script, select the **Script** menu at the top of the panel to bring up the scripting options. You can select one of several options:

   - Script Action to New Query Window
   - Script Action to File
   - Script Action to Clipboard
   - Script Action to Job

   To schedule the backup as a SQL job, select the **Script Action to Job** option, displayed in Figure 12.12. SQL jobs are run by the SQL Server Agent service.

8. Define the parameters of the backup job. Selecting the Script Action to Job option opens the New Job dialog. At the General page, you can change the owner and category of the job. Figure 12.13 shows the default options.

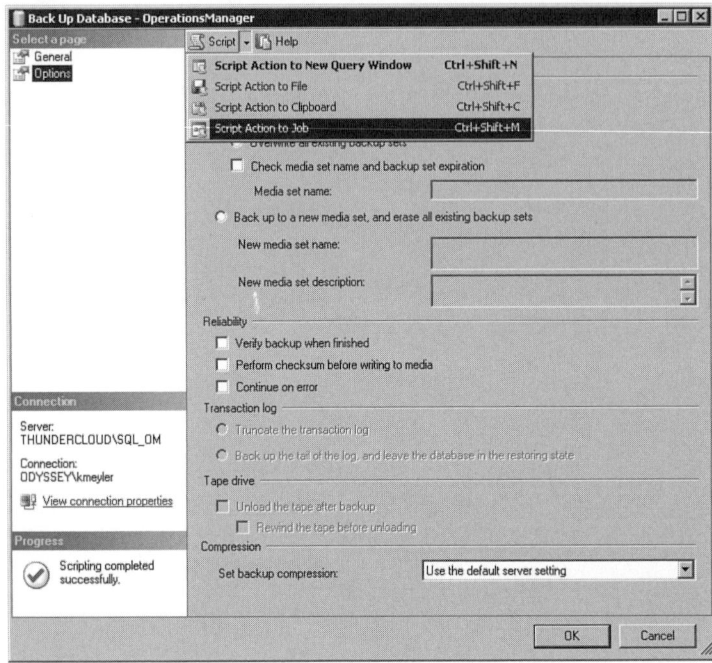

FIGURE 12.12 Create a SQL backup job.

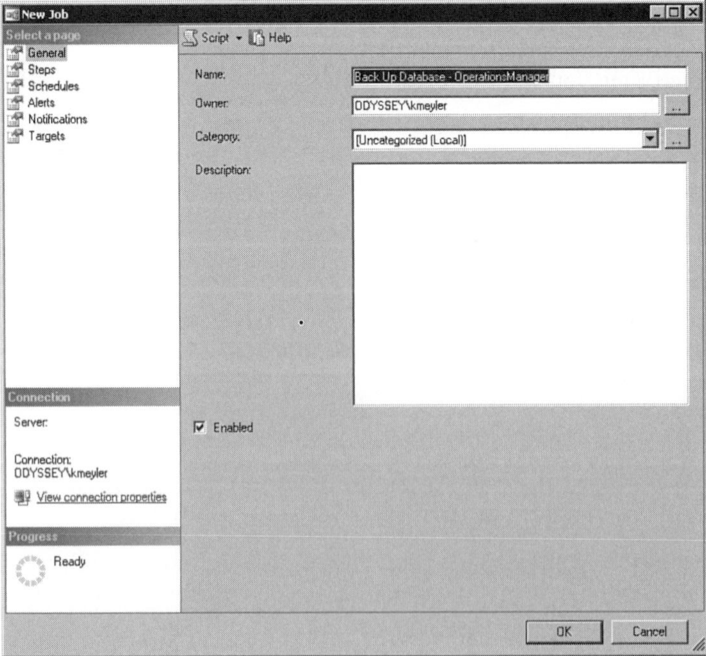

FIGURE 12.13 The New Job page.

9. Select the Schedules page and click **New** to add a new schedule.
10. You can now define the details of the schedule. Figure 12.14 shows a Schedule type of **Recurring** with a backup frequency of **Daily** and a start time of **3:00:00 AM**. After completing this page, you can also specify notifications and targets as part of the job properties. Click **OK** to save the job. The job information is saved to the Msdb database.

TIP: SCHEDULING DATABASE BACKUPS

SQL Server uses an online backup process, allowing a database backup while the database is in use. During a backup, most operations are possible such as `INSERT`, `UPDATE`, or `DELETE` statements. For general processing efficiency, the authors recommend performing backups during a period when you do not expect a high volume of updates on the database you are backing up.

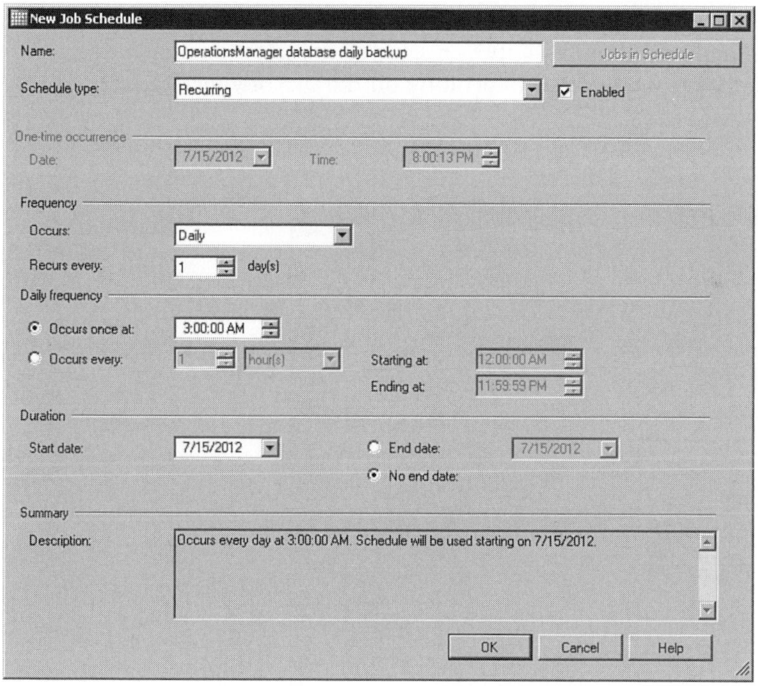

FIGURE 12.14 The new job scheduled to recur on a daily basis.

Performing Operations Manager Database Restores

If one of the Operations Manager databases becomes corrupt or a hardware issue causes you to lose a database, you will need to restore the affected database(s). This section builds on the example in the previous section that created a backup of the operational database using SQL Server Management Studio. The scenario assumes that the operational database is corrupt and cannot be repaired; therefore, the strategy is to restore from the latest backup. Follow these steps to restore the operational database:

1. Stop the System Center Data Access Service on your management servers to ensure Operations Manager will not try to write data to the database. All database access goes through this service.
2. Before performing a full restore for a SQL Server database, you must delete the existing database. Launch **SQL Server Management Studio -> Databases -> OperationsManager**. Right-click the database and select **Delete**. Uncheck the option to delete and back up and restore history information from the database; then click **OK** to delete the operational database.
3. Restore the database from the most recent backup. Right-click **Databases** and select **Restore Database**. In the Source for Restore section, select **From Database**, and select **OperationsManager** from the drop-down list. This displays the Restore Database page, shown in Figure 12.15.
4. If you have more than one backup, verify you selected the latest one for restore and click **OK** to begin the restore process. Depending on the size of your database, this may take several minutes.

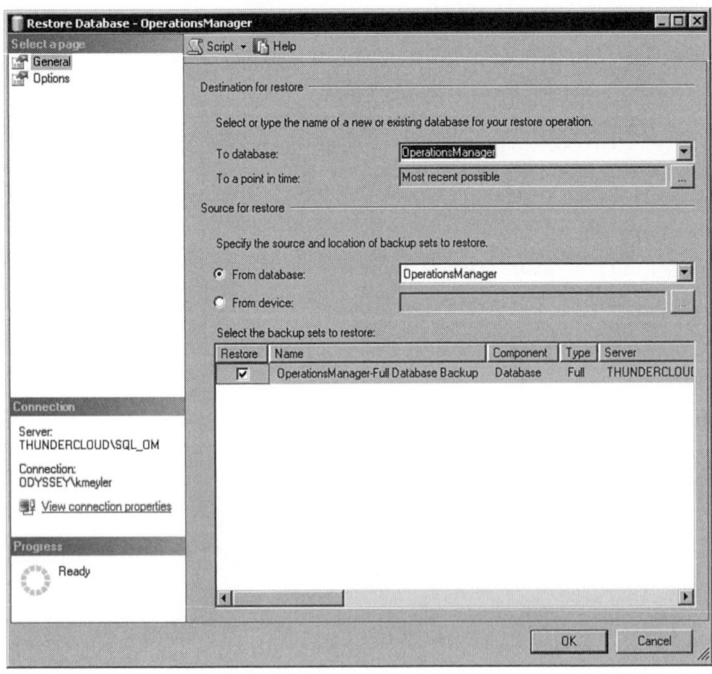

FIGURE 12.15 The Restore Database dialog.

NOTE: ROLE OF OPSMGR QUEUE FILES

OpsMgr data is stored in queue files when the database is inaccessible, minimizing the chance of loss of current data not yet written to the database.

After restoring the database, restart the System Center Data Access Service and launch the Operations console. Open the Administration node to verify it has the correct rule groups and configuration. You can also launch the Monitoring node to confirm the agents are sending heartbeats. This validates OpsMgr is operational.

CAUTION: RESTRICTIONS AND BEST PRACTICES ON DATABASE RESTORES

When restoring any of your databases, be sure the database server software installed is at the corresponding service level of your database backup. The operation is blocked if you do not have matching levels of maintenance.

In addition, you really should restore both the operational and data warehouse databases at the same time, from a backup taken at the same time. This is because many items are synchronized to both databases; therefore restoring only one of the databases creates a situation where the two will be out of sync, which can create issues with availability reports.

Moving the OpsMgr Databases to a Different Database Server

As part of a disaster recovery scenario, or perhaps if necessary for some other reason, you may have a requirement to move the OpsMgr databases to a different SQL Server database server. The next sections discuss moving the OperationsManager, OperationsManagerDW, and OperationsManagerAC databases.

TIP: VERIFYING THE MANAGEMENT GROUP IS USING THE NEW DATABASE SERVER

To be sure you are not accessing the old database server, take the appropriate (old) database offline after the move and related configuration changes are complete. Then use the Operations console to verify the health of the management group and accessibility of the new database server.

Moving the Operational Database

The operational database is installed during setup and cannot be reinstalled without reinstalling the management group. If you need to move the database to another database server, you can perform the following steps:

1. Stop the OpsMgr services (System Center Data Access Service, System Center Management, and System Center Management Configuration) on all your management servers.
2. Using SQL Server Management Studio, connect to the source database server and instance running your operational database and back up the OperationsManager database. You should also back up the Master database.

3. Connect to the destination database server and instance you will be using, navigate to **Security -> Logins**, and create logins for these OpsMgr accounts: DAS (also known as SDK), the management server action account, and the data writer account.

   Also add a login for the DAS computer account and Web console server computer account, using the format `domain\ComputerName$`.

4. Copy the OperationsManager database backup file to the destination server, and restore the database to the destination database server and instance you will be using.

5. Using SQL Server Management Studio on the destination database server, right-click the OpsMgr DAS login, then select **Properties**.

6. Select the User Mapping page and click the OperationsManager database. Ensure the following database roles are assigned to the DAS account:

   - ConfigService
   - db_accessadmin
   - db_datareader
   - db_datawriter
   - db_ddladmin
   - db_securityadmin
   - public
   - sdk_users
   - sql_dependency_subscriber

7. Click **OK**. Close SQL Server Management Studio.

8. On each management server, make the following changes:

   - Edit the registry by running `REGEDIT`.

     Browse to `HKLM\Software\Microsoft\SystemCenter\2010\Common\Database`, and update the string called `DatabaseServerName` to reflect the name of the new database server. If you are using a named instance of SQL Server, be sure to use the `ComputerName\instance` format.

     Browse to `HKLM\Software\Microsoft\Microsoft Operations Manager\3.0\Setup`, and update the `DatabaseServerName` string to the name of the new database server. Use the `ComputerName\instance` format if using a named instance of SQL Server.

     Close the registry editor after completing your changes.

   - Edit *%ProgramFiles%*\System Center 2012\Operations Manager\Server\ConfigService.config. In the `<Category>` tab for `Cmdb`, change the value for `ServerName` to the name and instance of the new SQL Server.

9. Update the operational database with the new database server name and the location of the APM tables:

   - In SQL Server Management Studio, expand **Databases -> OperationsManager -> Tables**. Right-click **dbo.MT_Microsoft$SystemCenter$ManagementGroup**, and then select **Edit Top 200 Rows**. Change the value in the **SQLServerName_6B1D1BE8_EBB4_B425_08DC_2385C5930B04** column to reflect the name of the new database server and instance. (Note: the GUID part of this column name may vary.)

   - Under **Databases -> OperationsManager -> Tables**, right-click **dbo. MT_Microsoft$SystemCenter$OpsMgrDB$AppMonitoring**, and then select **Edit Top 200 Rows**. Change the value in the **MainDatabaseServerName_5C00C79B_6B71_6EEE_4ADE_80C11F84527A** column to reflect the name and instance of the new database server and instance.

   - Close SQL Server Management Studio after completing your changes.

10. Enable the Broker service. On the new database instance, open a Query window and execute this command:

```
SELECT is_broker_enabled FROM Sys.databases WHERE name='OperationsManager'
```

    If the result is a value of 0, run these commands:

```
ALTER DATABASE OperationsManager SET SINGLE_USER WITH ROLLBACK IMMEDIATE
ALTER DATABASE OperationsManager SET ENABLE_BROKER
ALTER DATABASE OperationsManager SET MULTI_USER
```

11. Enable CLR to allow assembly execution. On the new database instance, open a Query window and execute these commands:

```
sp_configure 'show advanced options', 1
reconfigure
sp_configure 'clr enabled', 1
reconfigure
```

12. Ensure that error messages specific to the operational database are available on the new SQL Server. During Operations Manager setup, error messages specific to Operations Manager are stored in the sys.messages catalog view in the Master database. When you move the operational database to another server, these messages are not automatically moved as they are in Master. See Appendix E for the Fix_OM12DB_ErrorMsgs.SQL script to run on the new database server.

13. Reboot each management server. You may also need to start the SQL Server and SQL Agent services on the database server running the operational database.

Moving the Data Warehouse Database

Different from OpsMgr 2007, the data warehouse database is installed as part of the initial setup. Should you decide after setup to move the data warehouse to another database server, follow these steps:

1. Stop the Operations Manager Services (System Center Data Access Service, System Center Management, and System Center Management Configuration) on all management servers in your management group.
2. On the current data warehouse server and instance, use SQL Server Management Studio to back up the data warehouse database (default name: OperationsManagerDW) to a shared folder on the server. You will want to back up the Master database as well, as a precaution.
3. On the new data warehouse server, map a local drive to the folder containing the backup file. Use SQL Server Management Studio to restore the data warehouse database you backed up in step 2. Be sure to restore to the desired instance.
4. On each management server, edit the registry by opening `REGEDIT`.

   Browse to `HKLM\Software\Microsoft\Microsoft Operations Manager\3.0\Setup`, and update the `DataWarehouseDBServerName` string to the name of the new database server. Use the `ComputerName\instance` format if using a named instance of SQL Server.

   Close the registry editor when changes are complete.
5. Start the System Center Data Access Service on the management server associated with the reporting server.

   On this server, change the connection string for the data warehouse:

   - Open a web browser and go to the reporting webpage (http://<*ComputerName*>/reports_instancename).
   - Select **Details View** on the right and then select **Data Warehouse Main**.
   - Change the Connection string to contain the new data warehouse server and instance name, and then click **Apply**.
6. On the server hosting the operational database, open SQL Server Management Studio to update the operational database with the new database server name:

   Expand **Databases** -> **OperationsManager** -> **Tables**. Right-click **dbo. MT_Microsoft$SystemCenter$DataWarehouse**, and then select **Edit Top 200 Rows**. Change the value in the **MainDatabaseServerName_2C77AA48_DB0A_5D69_F8FF_20E48F3AED0F** column to reflect the name of the new SQL Server and instance.

   Again under Tables, right-click **dbo. MT_Microsoft$SystemCenter$DataWarehouse$AppMonitoring**, and then select **Edit Top 200 Rows**. Change the value in the **MainDatabaseServerName_2C77AA48_DB0A_5D69_F8FF_20E48F3AED0F** column to reflect the name of the new SQL Server and instance.

Close SQL Server Management Studio.

7. On the new data warehouse server, open SQL Server Management Studio.

   Expand **Databases** -> **OperationsManagerDW** -> **Tables**. Right-click **dbo.MemberDatabase**, and then select **Edit Top 200 Rows**. Change the value in the ServerName column to reflect the name of the new SQL Server and instance.

   Navigate to **Security** -> **Logins**, and add the data writer account, data reader account, Web console server account, and DAS account if they are not already there. Use master as the Default database (this is the default).

   For the Data Access Service (DAS) computer account, add the following user mappings if they do not already exist:

   - db_datareader
   - db_datawriter
   - OpsMgrReader
   - OpsMgrWriter
   - apm_datareader
   - apm_datawriter

   Close SQL Server Management Studio.

8. Verify the registry settings on the SSRS server are correct, and change as necessary:

   - **Server name and instance name of the data warehouse database:** `HKLM\Software\Microsoft\Microsoft Operations Manager\3.0\Reporting\DWDBInstance`
   - **Data warehouse database name:** `HKLM\Software\Microsoft\Microsoft Operations Manager\3.0\Reporting\DWDBName`
   - **Reporting Server URL:** `HKLM\Software\Microsoft\Microsoft Operations Manager\3.0\Reporting\ReportingServerUrl`

   For additional information on these settings, see Appendix C, "Registry Settings."

9. Restart the Operations Manager services on all management servers in the management group.

Moving the Audit Database

Each ACS collector writes to its own database. You can install this database on the ACS collector or elsewhere. To move the audit database to another database server, perform the following steps:

1. On the original ACS database server, stop the Audit Collection service, then use SQL Server Management Studio to back up the database (OperationsManagerAC by

default) to a shared folder on the server. It is also a good idea to back up the associated Master database.

2. Using SQL Server Management Studio, delete the OperationsManagerAC database. Be sure that the Delete backup and restore history information for databases and Close existing connections options are both checked.

3. On the new database server, use SQL Server Management Studio to restore the backup.

4. On the new database server, use SQL Server Management Studio to create a login for the ACS server. The format is *<domain\ComputerName$>*, where computername is the name of the ACS server.

5. In SQL Server Management Studio, set the correct permissions for this account in **Security** -> **Logins**. Right-click the account corresponding to the computer where the ACS service is running (*<domain\ComputerName$>* format), and select **Properties** -> **User Mapping**. Check the box in the Map column corresponding to the OperationsManagerAC database, and then select db_owner in the Database role Membership for: OperationsManagerAC box.

   Close SQL Server Management Studio.

6. On the system hosting the Audit Collection service, edit the registry key `HKLM\Software\ODBC\ODBC.INI\OpsMgrAC`. Double-click the `Server` value, and set it to the name of the new ACS database server. Close the registry editor and start the Audit Collection service on this server.

7. Verify the database move was successful by checking the audit database for entries in the most recent dtEvent-*<GUID>* table. The datetime stamp should be more recent than when you restarted the Audit Collection service.

Creating a New SSRS Database

If you have issues with the SSRS database or have to move it, the best practice is to simply reinstall SSRS. However, this loses your catalog items, including linked reports (which actually aren't reports, they are shortcuts to existing reports with predefined parameters). Marnix Wolf discusses this at http://thoughtsonopsmgr.blogspot.nl/2011/12/exporting-linked-reports-to-another.html. The Reporting Services Scripter, written by Jasper Smith, lets you transfer all SSRS catalog items from one server to another. The tool is documented and available from http://www.sqldbatips.com/showarticle.asp?ID=62. You should also extract any customized reports into RDL format and import them into the new SSRS database; see the "Backing Up Reports" section for details.

Backing Up Key Files

Databases are not the only critical components to back up to prevent loss to management group functionality. The next sections discuss procedures to back up management packs, reports, SSRS encryption keys, and the IIS metabase.

Backing Up Management Packs

It is just as important to back up modifications to management packs as it is to back up the SQL Server databases used by Operations Manager. All overrides and custom rules and monitors are saved to user-specified unsealed management packs stored in the operational database. Backing up and maintaining management packs as separate objects gives you granularity to restore a specific management pack rather than the entire database. The authors suggest creating separate management packs to store overrides for each of the various sealed management packs loaded into OpsMgr.

You can back up (export) unsealed management packs in an ad-hoc manner using the Operations console. This technique is discussed in Chapter 13, "Administering Management Packs." For purposes of regularly scheduled jobs, the authors recommend you back up your unsealed management packs in a batch mode, using PowerShell cmdlets to export the management packs. As sealed management packs are not modified, you should only need to export unsealed management packs.

NOTE: IMPLEMENTING A FULL CHANGE CONTROL PROCESS

A good change control process will include backing up management packs and storing them in a code repository solution.

Microsoft's PowerShell command-line shell is included with Operations Manager 2012. This is a customized instance of PowerShell; it is a superset of PowerShell with cmdlets specific to OpsMgr functions. Chapter 23, "PowerShell and Operations Manager," includes an in-depth look at the Operations Manager Shell.

Chapter 7, "Configuring and Using System Center 2012 Operations Manager," references the `Import-SCOMManagementPack` cmdlet as a tool to import management packs in a batch mode. This chapter will export management packs using `the Export-SCOMManagementPack` cmdlet.

Microsoft helps make the cmdlet easy to use by giving a syntax example when you type `Get-Help` for this cmdlet. The following example exports all unsealed management packs (`$_.Sealed -eq $false}`) to the Backups folder on the C:\drive:

```
$all_mps = Get-SCOMManagementPack where-object {_.Sealed -eq $false}
foreach($mp in $all_mps)
{
Export-SCOMManagementPack -ManagementPack $mp -path "C:\Backups"
}
```

To put this syntax into a script, perform the following steps:

1. Open Windows Notepad and add code to load the OpsMgr PowerShell module. Note that the script accepts a parameter for a management server name:

   ```
   param ($ServerName);
   |
   ```

```
$MS = $ServerName;

Import-Module OperationsManager
Get-SCOMManagementGroupConnection -ComputerName $MS | Set-
SCOMManagementGroupConnection
```

2. With the OpsMgr extensions loaded, you can run your script from the standard PowerShell environment, without needing to run from inside the OpsMgr Shell. This is useful when you want to run scripts in a batch mode.
3. Now, just add the code from the earlier example in this section:

```
$all_mps = Get-SCOMManagementPack | where-object {_.Sealed -eq $false}
foreach($mp in $all_mps)
{
Export-SCOMManagementPack -ManagementPack $mp -path "C:\Backups"
}
```

4. Save the text file with a .ps1 extension for it to be executable by PowerShell. Figure 12.16 shows the ExportMP.ps1 PowerShell script created to export all unsealed management packs.

```
param ($ServerName);

$MS = $ServerName

Import-Module OperationsManager
Get-SCOMManagementGroupConnection -ComputerName $MS | Set-
SCOMManagementGroupConnection

$all_mps = Get-SCOMManagementPack | where-object {_.Sealed -eq $false}

foreach($mp in $all_mps)
{
export-SCOMManagementPack -ManagementPack $mp -path "C:\Backups"
}
```

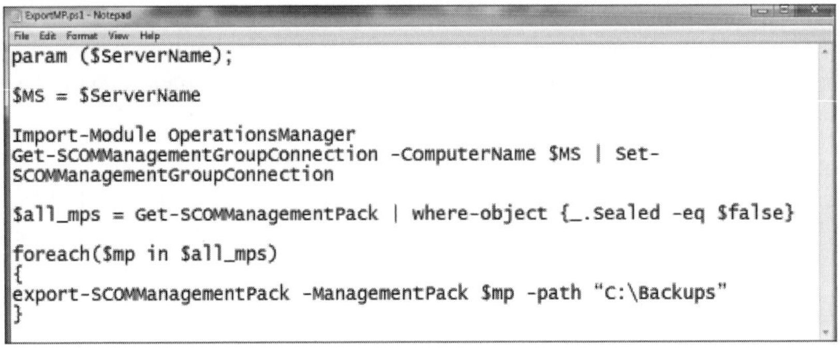

FIGURE 12.16 A PowerShell script to export all unsealed management packs.

From the PowerShell prompt, type the following, specifying the name of a management server for the `ServerName` variable:

```
Z:\ExportMP.ps1 -ServerName:<ComputerName>
```

ANOTHER APPROACH FOR EXPORTING MANAGEMENT PACKS

If you want to back up management packs associated with a particular application or service, you can use the following PowerShell script as a starting point. This example, which also uses the `Export-SCOMManagementPack` cmdlet, searches for management pack names that include the literal "AD" and then exports all management packs (sealed or unsealed) related to Active Directory:

```
param ($ServerName);
|
$MS = $ServerName
Get-SCOMManagementGroupConnection -ComputerName $MS | Set-
SCOMManagementGroupConnection

$AD_mps = get-SCOMManagementPack | where {$_.Name -match '.AD.'}
foreach($mp in $AD_mps)
{
Export-SCOMManagementPack -ManagementPack $mp -path "C:\Backups"
}
```

Backing Up Management Packs from a Batch File

You can take the script example a step further by creating a batch file that invokes a PowerShell script, which can be part of a nightly backup routine. Save the ExportMP.ps1 script to the C:\Backups folder and execute it from a batch file containing the following command:

```
%SystemRoot%\system32\WindowsPowerShell\v1.0\powershell.exe
"C:\Backups\exportMP.ps1 -ServerName:<ComputerName>"
```

Using the Operations Console to Export Management Packs

Chapter 13 discusses exporting and importing management packs. The functionality can also be used as part of your backup strategy. This chapter focuses on those steps of particular significance when backing up management packs.

The Operations console only allows you to export unsealed management packs. To use the Operations console to back up and restore management packs, follow theses steps:

1. In the Operations console, navigate to **Administration -> Management Packs**. In the Details pane, right-click a management pack to bring up the option to **Export Management Pack**, shown in Figure 12.17 (this option is grayed out for sealed management packs). This option is also available in the Tasks pane, although it is grayed out unless you are highlighting an unsealed management pack.

   This example backs up (exports) the Virtual Machine Manager Dashboards management pack, introduced in Chapter 11, “Dashboards, Trending, and Forecasting.”

2. You are prompted to browse to the folder where the exported management pack will be saved. Figure 12.18 shows the Virtual Machine Manager Dashboards management pack will be exported to the C:\Backups folder. You are not given the option to specify a filename.

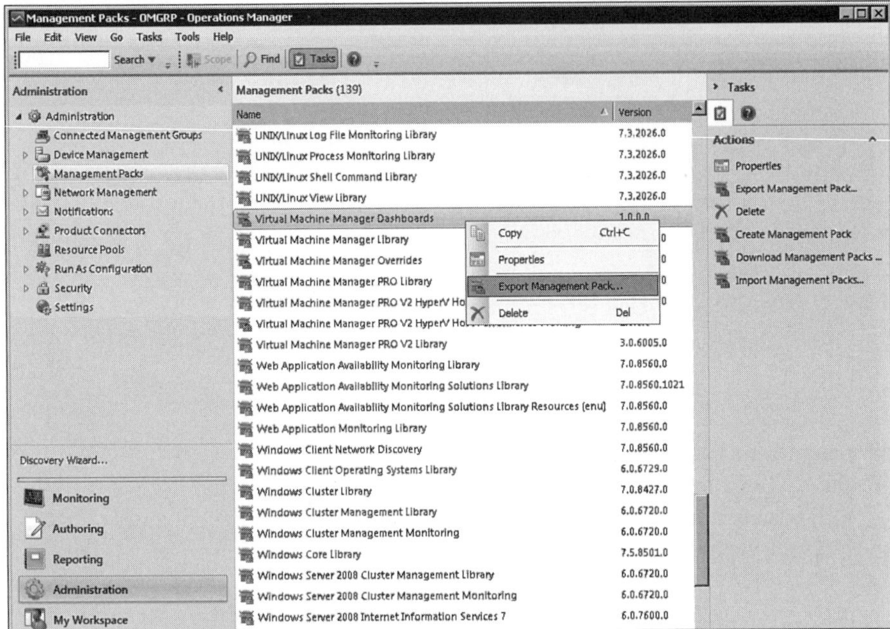

FIGURE 12.17 Specifying a management pack to export.

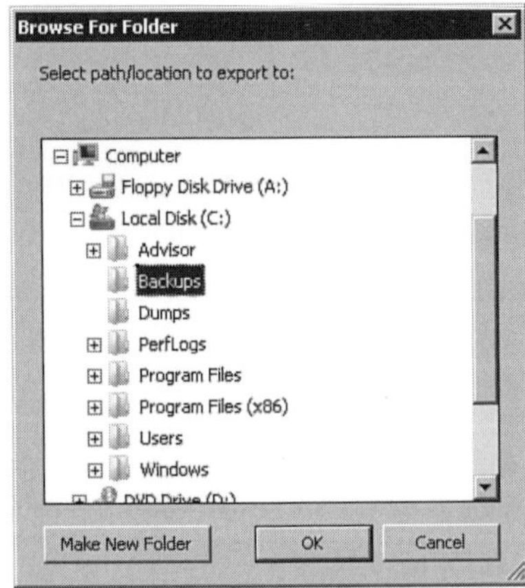

FIGURE 12.18 Specifying the folder to store the management pack.

3. If the management pack was previously exported to that folder, you are asked if you want to overwrite the previous version (see Figure 12.19). If you choose **No**, the management pack is not exported and you are not given an option to save to another filename or folder.

4. Successfully exporting the management pack using the Operations console brings up the message displayed in Figure 12.20.

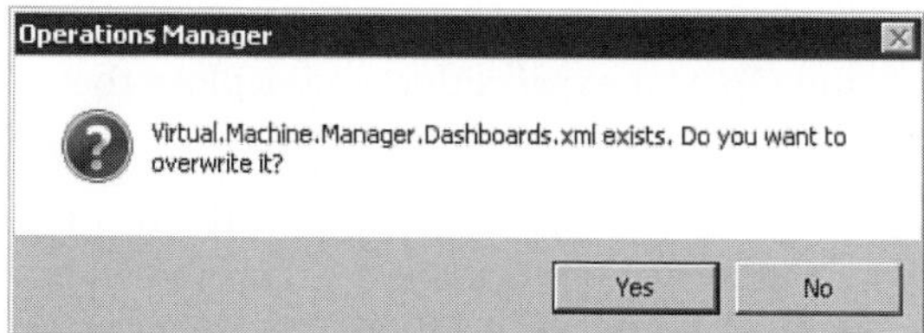

FIGURE 12.19 Prompt to replace a previously exported management pack.

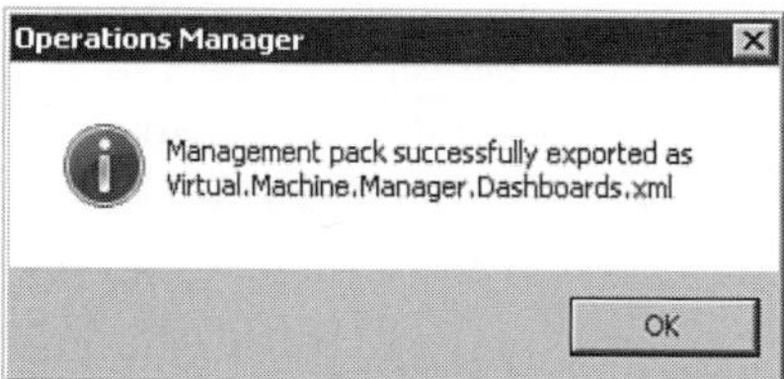

FIGURE 12.20 Management pack export complete.

Restoring the management pack using the Operations console is accomplished using the Import function discussed in Chapter 13.

Backing Up Reports

Before having a discussion about backing up reports, let's discuss how reports work. Operations Manager uses SSRS as its report engine. You can also access the OpsMgr reports from the SQL Reporting console, but that is not the recommended approach as the report names display with their GUIDS and the metadata information about the report is only displayed in the Operations console.

When you display the report hierarchy in the Operations console, you are actually seeing information from two places:

- SSRS provides the list of reports.
- The management pack provides metadata such as the report display name, knowledge about the report, and information to assist in returning data for that report.

The reports displayed in the Reporting node of the Operations console are actually those found in the SSRS root folder. This means that any report is visible, whether or not it is part of a management pack—and is one reason why you want a dedicated SSRS for Operations Manager Reporting (a second reason is that installing OpsMgr reporting changes security such that any existing reports are no longer accessible).

This model also means you can create a folder in SSRS, store a report under it, and have it appear in the OpsMgr console. This makes it easy to add reports, but because it is outside the Operations Manager management pack framework, it doesn't help when you want to deploy a new report to a new management group, deal with localization or dependencies, or easily back up any new reports you create for Operations Manager. Out of the box, reports are included with management packs, and OpsMgr expects that and deploys them to SSRS for you.

There are two steps to backing up custom reports you develop. You can export the report as a Report Definition Language (RDL) file, which saves it in eXtensible Markup Language (XML) format, and optionally package it in a management pack. To keep things simple administratively, the authors recommend you package your reports in management packs.

Backing Up OpsMgr Reports

To export your custom report as an RDL file, open it in Report Builder and choose **File -> Save as File**. This creates the RDL file, which is in XML format. To package the RDL in a management pack, edit it in a text browser and paste its content in an unsealed management pack under the **Reporting -> Report -> Definition** node in the management pack. Here's an example:

```
<Reporting>
     <Reports>
          <Report ID="Sample.Report" Accessibility="Public" Visible="true">
               <Definition>
                    [RDL XML file content here ...]
               </Definition>
          </Report>
     </Reports>
</Reporting>
```

Where

- **ID:** This is the name of your report in SSRS. It must be a unique name within the management pack.
- **Accessibility=Public:** This allows other management packs to reference this report. If the report is Public, the ID must be unique in your OpsMgr reporting environment.
- **Visible=True:** This setting makes your report visible within the catalog.

You can specify many other parameters within the node. Chapter 22, "Authoring Management Packs and Reports," provides information on writing management packs.

For purposes of backup, this chapter assumes you have saved your RDL files and included them in unsealed management pack .XML files. You should place these files in a folder with your other customized and unsealed management packs where they can be backed up.

Backing Up ACS Reports

Microsoft does not support including ACS custom reports in management packs, as by default an OpsMgr administrator does not have access to ACS reporting. Customized ACS reports should be extracted using Report Builder and stored in a separate folder. By default, Report Builder saves to your \My Documents folder; the authors suggest establishing a common location to save all customized ACS RDL files. You can use Report Builder to import RDL files back into the SSRS environment.

The ReportingConfig.exe utility, found in the installation media under the \SupportTools folder, is used to reload Microsoft-supplied ACS reports. Chapter 10 provides additional information on ACS.

Backing Up SSRS Encryption Keys

The SSRS setup process creates encryption keys that are used to secure credentials, connection information, and accounts used with server operations. If you should need to rebuild or repair your SSRS installation, you must apply the key to make the ReportServer database operational. If you cannot restore the key, database recovery will require deleting the encrypted data and re-specifying any values that require encryption.

You can use the `RSKeyMgmt.exe` utility to extract a copy of the encryption key from the ReportServer database. The utility writes the key to a file you specify and scrambles the key using a password you provide. This file should be backed up as part of your backup and recovery procedures. You should also document the password used for the file. Table 12.7 lists the parameters used by RSKeyMgmt.

TABLE 12.7 RSKeyMgmt parameters

Parameter	Value	Description
-e		Extract a key from a report server instance.
-a		Apply a key to a report server instance.
-d		Delete all encrypted content from a report server database.
-r	installation ID	Remove the key for the specified installation ID.
-f	file	Full path and filename to read/write key.
-i	instance	Server instance to which operation is applied; default is MSSQLSERVER.
-j	join	Join a remote instance of report server to the scale-out deployment of the local instance.
-l	list	Lists the report servers announced in the ReportServer database.
-m	remote computer name	Remote computer that hosts the report server instance you are joining to the report server scale-out deployment.
-n	Remote report server instance name	Required if report server is not installed on default instance of MSSQLSERVER.
-p	password	Password used to encrypt or decrypt key.
-s	reencrypt	Generates a new key and reencrypts all encrypted content.
-t	trace	Include trace information in error message.

TABLE 12.7 Continued

Parameter	Value	Description
-u	user name	User name or an administrator on the machine to join to the scale-out deployment. If not specified, current user is used.
-v	administrator password	Password of an administrator on the machine to join to the scale-out deployment.

Use the following syntax to create a backup of the encryption key:

```
RSKeyMgmt -e -fC:\Backups\rsdbkey.txt -p<password>
```

Run RSKeyMgmt locally on the computer hosting the report server. SSRS books online (http://msdn.microsoft.com/en-us/library/ms159106.aspx) discusses managing the encryption keys in the "Managing Encryption Keys" section.

Backing Up the IIS Metabase

The IIS configuration on Windows 2008 R2 and Windows 2012 servers is split between the web.config files and the applicationHost.config files. The applicationHost.config files include configuration information for the sites, applications, virtual directories, application pool definitions, and the default configuration settings for all sites on the Web server. To back up the IIS configuration, follow these steps:

1. Log on to the server hosting the OpsMgr 2012 Web console server, using an administrator account.
2. Open a command prompt using the Run As Administrator option and go to the %*windir*%\system32\inetsrv folder.
3. Type the following command to back up the configuration:

   ```
   appcmd add backup <backupname>
   ```

   If you do not specify the name of the backup, the system will name it using a date/time format.

Information on appcmd is available at http://technet.microsoft.com/en-us/library/cc772200.aspx.

AUTOMATING THE BACKUP PROCESS

To assist with backing up the files discussed in this chapter, the authors have created a simple batch file that automates the process from the command line. The backup scripts in the batch file are intended as an example and can be customized to your own environment.

The batch file (backup.bat) is available as online content for this book. You must have a functional Operations Manager environment to run the batch file. Here are the installation steps:

1. Copy the full "\backups" folder provided to each OpsMgr 2012 server, including database servers. (This content should include backup.bat and ExportMP.ps1.)
2. Customize the script to enable the installed components on the server for each OpsMgr 2012 server.
3. Schedule the backup.bat program to run according to your schedule; daily is recommended.

Using Data Protection Manager

As System Center 2012 includes a license to use all System Center components, you can use System Center 2012 Data Protection Manager to protect any computer managed by OpsMgr 2012. If you do not have an enterprise backup solution in place, consider deploying DPM right away. If you want to centralize and monitor your OpsMgr backups, DPM is the supported solution from Microsoft.

This portion of the chapter assumes you have installed a DPM server in your environment but not added OpsMgr servers to a DPM protection group. The discussion begins with installing DPM agents on untrusted computers and trusted computers, principally the SQL servers for each OpsMgr database, and servers running IIS such as the report server and Web console servers. Next, a DPM protection group is created that includes the necessary OpsMgr features. Monitoring of protection group health is covered. The discussion ends with using DPM to recover an OpsMgr management group to a point in time, and from scratch.

ABOUT ALSO BACKING UP THE VIRTUAL MACHINE

If you have a virtualized OpsMgr environment, consider "snapping" or otherwise backing up at the virtual machine (VM) level as an additional method of disaster preparedness. VM-level backups do not replace SQL application backups of the OpsMgr databases. If you perform VM-level backups, you should also perform in-guest backups of the SQL application. To protect an OpsMgr VM with DPM, deploy a DPM agent to the Hyper-V host containing the VM.

Installing DPM Agents on Untrusted Computers

Install DPM agents on untrusted computers such as the SQL database server for the audit database used by ACS. Follow these steps:

1. Run **DPMAgentInstaller_x64.exe** on any computers in untrusted domain environments. The installer file is located by default on the DPM server at *%ProgramFiles%*\Microsoft System Center 2012\DPM\DPM\ProtectionAgents\RA\4.0.1908.0\amd64.

2. On each agent computer, change directory to *%ProgramFiles%*\Microsoft Data Protection Manager\DPM\bin and run **SetDPMServer.exe** as follows (replacing *<DPM_agent>* with the name of the account you want created for DPM communication):

```
SetDPMServer -dpmServername <DPM_Server> -isNonDomainServer -userName <DPM_
agent>
```

3. Repeat steps 1 and 2 on each agent computer. Step 2 creates a local account on the agent computer (or in the domain if the agent is running on a domain controller).
4. From the Management pane of the DPM 2012 console, select **Install** in the Agents section of the ribbon.
5. Select the option to **Attach agents** to a **Computer in a workgroup or untrusted domain** and click **Next**.
6. At Select Computers, enter the computer name and username/password credential for the computer to be added, this is the account created in step 2. When the list of selected computers is complete, click **Next**.
7. At the Summary page, click the **Attach** button. The computers will appear under **Management** -> **Agents** -> **Unprotected computers with protection agent** list.

Installing DPM Agents on Trusted Computers

Install DPM agents on domain computers such as the OpsMgr database servers, report server, and Web console server. It may be necessary to disable the Domain profile of the Windows Firewall on the agent computers temporarily while pushing the DPM agent. After the agent is installed, you can enable the firewall on the Domain profile. Follow these steps:

1. In **Management** -> **Agents** in the DPM 2012 console, select **Install** in the Agents section of the ribbon.
2. Select to **Install agents**. Browse and select the computers to add from the list of domain computers. Click **Add** until all computers desired are listed and then click **Next**.
3. At the Enter credentials page, type the domain credentials DPM will use to install the agents and click **Next**.
4. Select whether to allow the computers to be restarted after installing the DPM protection agent if necessary and click **Next**. (Cluster servers are not automatically restarted in any case.)
5. At the Summary page, select **Install**. The computers will appear under the **Management** -> **Agents** -> **Unprotected computers with protection agent** list.

Creating a DPM Protection Group for OpsMgr

After you deploy DPM agents to desired computers and restart any computers that require it after DPM agent installation, create a DPM protection group. The protection group will include the SQL databases and OpsMgr management group computers running IIS. Perform the following steps:

1. From the Protection pane of the DPM 2012 console, select **New** in the Protection group section of the ribbon.
2. After the Welcome page, at Select Protection Group Type, select to create a protection group for **Servers** and click **Next**.
3. At the Select Group Members page, expand the servers in the Available members box to expose the database names. Databases in cluster servers appear under the name of the cluster, not under the failover cluster computer nodes. Select those databases previously listed in the "Roles of Key OpsMgr Files and Databases" section. For example, Figure 12.21 shows the ACS database files being selected for backup.

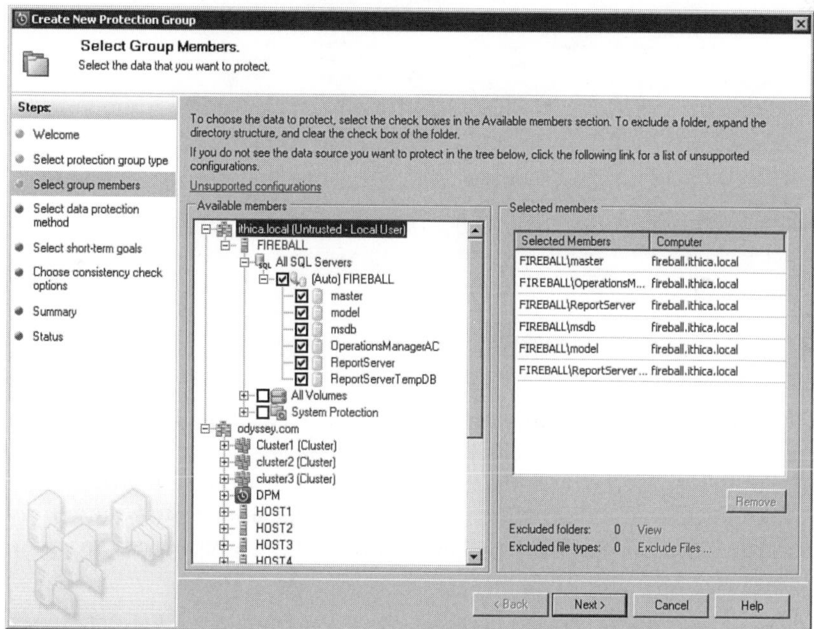

FIGURE 12.21 Including the ACS database in the DPM protection group.

4. Add the system volumes (C:\ drive) and System protection (system state backup) for OpsMgr servers running IIS. When all databases and computers desired are listed in the Selected members box, click **Next**.
5. At Select Data Protection Method, give the protection group a name, such as **OpsMgr Protection Group**, select **short term protection using disk**, and click **Next**.
6. At Specify Short Term Goals, specify desired retention range and synchronization frequency and click **Next**.

7. At the Review Disk Allocation, Replica Creation Method, and Consistency check options pages, accept the defaults or select settings appropriate for your environment.

8. At the Summary page, select **Create Group**.

Monitoring the DPM Status of the OpsMgr Protection Group

Since the one DPM protection group includes all resources needed to back up and restore the OpsMgr management group, you can monitor the health of the protection group to monitor OpsMgr backups. Figure 12.22 shows the **Jobs -> In progress** view of the Monitoring space of the DPM Administration console while creating the initial DPM replicas in the OpsMgr protection group. The DPM console is the primary means of administering DPM—DPM generates its own alerts, and if you don't have OpsMgr, you can use the DPM console to set up emailing of DPM alerts independent of OpsMgr.

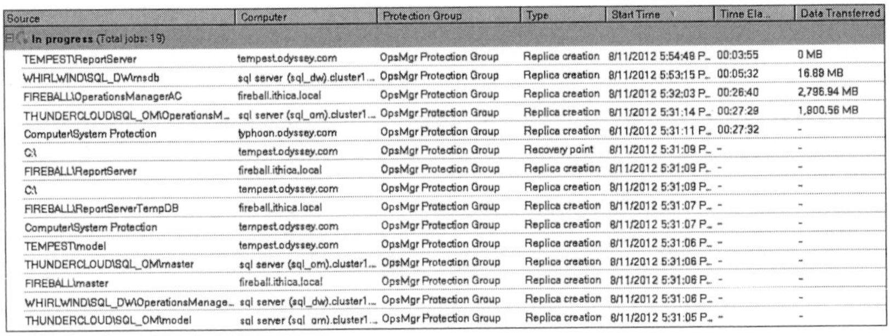

Source	Computer	Protection Group	Type	Start Time	Time Ela...	Data Transferred
In progress (Total jobs: 19)						
TEMPEST\ReportServer	tempest.odyssey.com	OpsMgr Protection Group	Replica creation	8/11/2012 5:54:48 P...	00:03:55	0 MB
WHIRLWIND\SQL_DW\msdb	sql server (sql_dw).cluster1...	OpsMgr Protection Group	Replica creation	8/11/2012 5:53:15 P...	00:05:32	16.88 MB
FIREBALL\OperationsManagerAC	fireball.ithica.local	OpsMgr Protection Group	Replica creation	8/11/2012 5:32:03 P...	00:26:40	2,796.94 MB
THUNDERCLOUD\SQL_OM\OperationsM...	sql server (sql_om).cluster1...	OpsMgr Protection Group	Replica creation	8/11/2012 5:31:14 P...	00:27:29	1,800.56 MB
Computer\System Protection	typhoon.odyssey.com	OpsMgr Protection Group	Replica creation	8/11/2012 5:31:11 P...	00:27:32	-
C:\	tempest.odyssey.com	OpsMgr Protection Group	Recovery point	8/11/2012 5:31:09 P...	-	-
FIREBALL\ReportServer	fireball.ithica.local	OpsMgr Protection Group	Replica creation	8/11/2012 5:31:09 P...	-	-
C:\	tempest.odyssey.com	OpsMgr Protection Group	Replica creation	8/11/2012 5:31:09 P...	-	-
FIREBALL\ReportServerTempDB	fireball.ithica.local	OpsMgr Protection Group	Replica creation	8/11/2012 5:31:07 P...	-	-
Computer\System Protection	tempest.odyssey.com	OpsMgr Protection Group	Replica creation	8/11/2012 5:31:07 P...	-	-
TEMPEST\model	tempest.odyssey.com	OpsMgr Protection Group	Replica creation	8/11/2012 5:31:06 P...	-	-
THUNDERCLOUD\SQL_OM\master	sql server (sql_om).cluster1...	OpsMgr Protection Group	Replica creation	8/11/2012 5:31:06 P...	-	-
FIREBALL\master	fireball.ithica.local	OpsMgr Protection Group	Replica creation	8/11/2012 5:31:06 P...	-	-
WHIRLWIND\SQL_DW\OperationsManage...	sql server (sql_dw).cluster1...	OpsMgr Protection Group	Replica creation	8/11/2012 5:31:06 P...	-	-
THUNDERCLOUD\SQL_OM\model	sql server (sql_om).cluster1...	OpsMgr Protection Group	Replica creation	8/11/2012 5:31:05 P...	-	-

FIGURE 12.22 Monitoring initial replica creation in the DPM console.

The Protection pane of the DPM console presents a state-based view of the health of each protection group. Figure 12.23 shows the healthy status of the protection group after successful creation of initial replicas. Notice the composition of the protection group includes individual computers (ACS database server and IIS servers) and clustered resources (the operational and data warehouse databases). The healthy state of a protection group in the DPM console indicates all replicas are up to date.

Since this is a book about OpsMgr, it is likely you have OpsMgr deployed in your environment. The good news is that OpsMgr 2012 is the central console for DPM 2012, and there is a full-featured OpsMgr 2012 management pack for DPM 2012. Figure 12.24, the DPM All Data sources state view, illustrates how OpsMgr centralizes the management view of all DPM workloads.

The desired mode of operation with DPM backups is that you can allocate to DPM sufficient disk-based storage resources such that you are not disturbed by endless "low disk space to create replica" type DPM alerts. Given sufficient disk space, DPM operation is a set it and forget it type of experience.

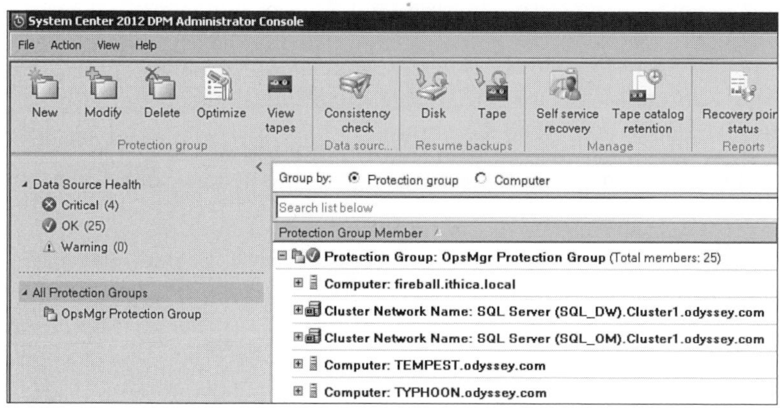

FIGURE 12.23 Monitoring protection group health in the DPM console.

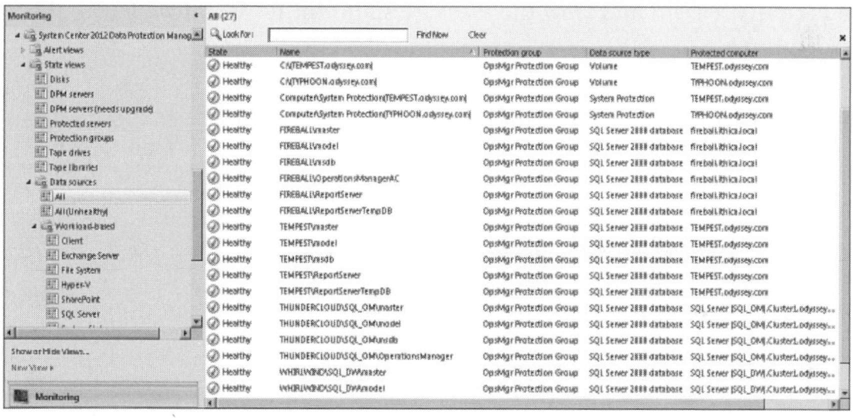

FIGURE 12.24 Monitoring all DPM protection group data sources in OpsMgr.

OpsMgr enables a management-by-exception experience for long-term DPM monitoring and support. Once the protection groups are successfully replicated, you should monitor DPM from OpsMgr. Use OpsMgr alerts of DPM failures rather than configuring email alerting on the individual DPM server.

OpsMgr Recovery Scenarios Using DPM

There are two situations where you might use DPM to recover some or all of your management group data. First is when you want to return your management group databases to a point in time, such as after discovering corruption in the database. Second is when you are recovering your OpsMgr management group "from scratch" after a disaster. Both scenarios use the same steps for DPM recovery; here are the primary differences in the scenarios:

- **Point-in-time:** You recover to existing servers, replacing the current data with the recovered data.
- **From-scratch:** You recover to empty, same-named databases on new same-named servers.

Follow these steps to restore an OpsMgr database from backup using DPM:

1. In the DPM console, navigate to **Recover -> Recoverable Data,** and browse the folder structure to locate the database to restore. Figure 12.25 shows the OperationsManagerAC database selected for restore.
2. Select the date and recovery time from the calendar. Click the **Recover** button in the toolbar.
3. After the Review Recover Selection page, on the Select Recovery Type page, select to **Recover to original instance of SQL Server (Overwrite database)** and click **Next**.
4. At the Specify Database State page, accept the default to **Leave database operational** and click **Next**.
5. At the Specify Recovery Options page, enable SAN recovery or Notification as desired, click **Next**, and at the Summary page click **Recover**.
6. Close the Recovery Wizard and view the recovery status in the Monitoring task area of the DPM console.

After successfully recovering the OpsMgr databases with DPM, you should be able to start the OpsMgr services on your management server(s), open the OpsMgr console, and resume operations as of the time of the database backup job.

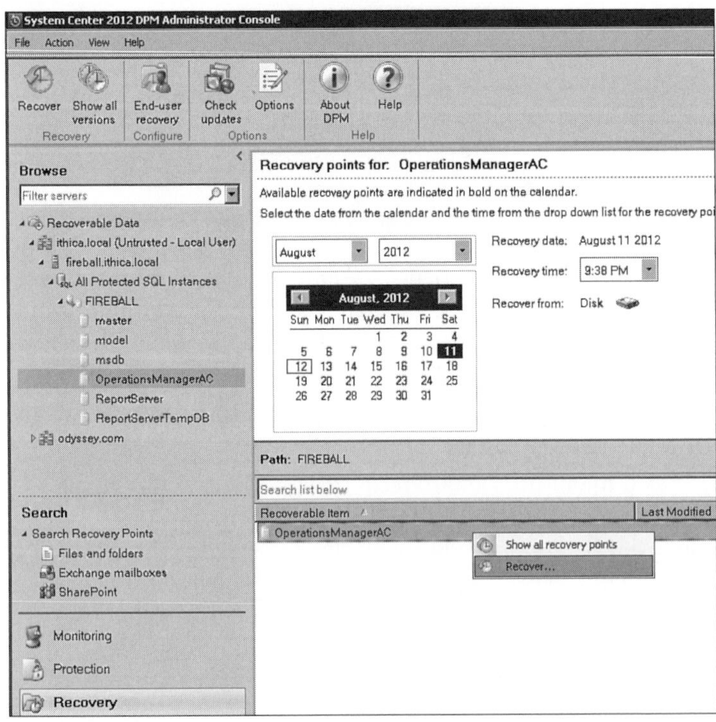

FIGURE 12.25 Recovering the ACS database from backup using the DPM console.

Disaster Recovery Planning

Although you may never need to restore Operations Manager from a catastrophic failure, you must be prepared for the possibility that this could happen. You should have a well-documented recovery plan that would work for every conceivable type of disaster that could occur, from hardware failures to a total datacenter loss. Essentially, you want to be able to get OpsMgr up and running with minimal data loss.

Your plan should assume the worst but be able to concisely and efficiently restore Operations Manager at a minimum to the last backup of your databases. You need to develop a detailed plan for the various contingencies, and practice the various scenarios in a development environment until you (and others on your staff in case you are hit by the proverbial truck) are comfortable with the process.

There at least two potentials for disaster recovery (DR), discussed in the next sections.

Recovering from a Total Loss

What would it take to recover OpsMgr assuming a "total loss"? Assume the following somewhat simplified scenario:

- The operational database is installed on the first installed management server.
- The management server is monitoring 200 agent-managed systems.
- There is only one management server in the management group.
- The Web console is installed.
- OpsMgr reporting is installed.
- ACS is not installed.

Although this is a very simple implementation of Operations Manager, it is intended to show you the steps necessary to recover OpsMgr from a complete hardware failure of the management server. Assume the server team has already built a new server using the same NetBIOS name in the same domain, installed SQL Server and SSRS, and enabled IIS, which will be used for the OpsMgr 2012 Web console. The appropriate level of service packs and security patches are applied—always be sure to be at the same level of software maintenance you had with your original system. It is time to recover Operations Manager.

At a general level, here are the steps involved:

1. Install OpsMgr 2012 from the installation media. Use the same management group name as the original install. Remember this name is case sensitive. Specify the same service accounts as used by your original installation.

This type of information should be documented as part of your disaster recovery planning. For detailed information on installing OpsMgr, see Chapter 5, "Installing System Center 2012 Operations Manager."

2. After the installation completes, immediately stop the three OpsMgr services on the management server to prevent the management server from sending data to the operational and data warehouse databases, as you will be overlaying these databases as part of your recovery process. As any data written to the databases will be lost; immediately really means immediately!
3. Install any additional hotfixes and maintenance previously installed with your original installation.
4. Delete the OperationsManager and OperationsManagerDW databases created from your OpsMgr installation in step 1.
5. Restore the latest OperationsManager and OperationsManagerDW databases created from your SQL backups.
6. Install the OpsMgr reporting and the Web console.
7. Restore the SSRS encryption keys.
8. Restore the IIS metabase.
9. Import any additional management packs and reports that were loaded to your old management server, or changed and backed up after your last database backups.
10. Start the OpsMgr services on the management server. Operations Manager will now be functional.

These steps constitute a high-level process for recovering Operations Manager. Your actual plan should contain more detail, including specific hard drive configurations, the exact installation options, SQL steps necessary to delete and restore the databases, and so forth.

Using Log Shipping

Another approach for disaster recovery is to implement log shipping. As discussed in Chapter 9, log shipping automates the process of backing up database transaction logs and storing them on a standby server. This process keeps your production and standby SQL Server systems in sync. Figure 12.26 shows a sample disaster recovery solution that includes log shipping for the operational and data warehouse databases.

In addition to deploying log shipping, you will need the SSRS encryption key and other files discussed throughout this chapter for a successful recovery.

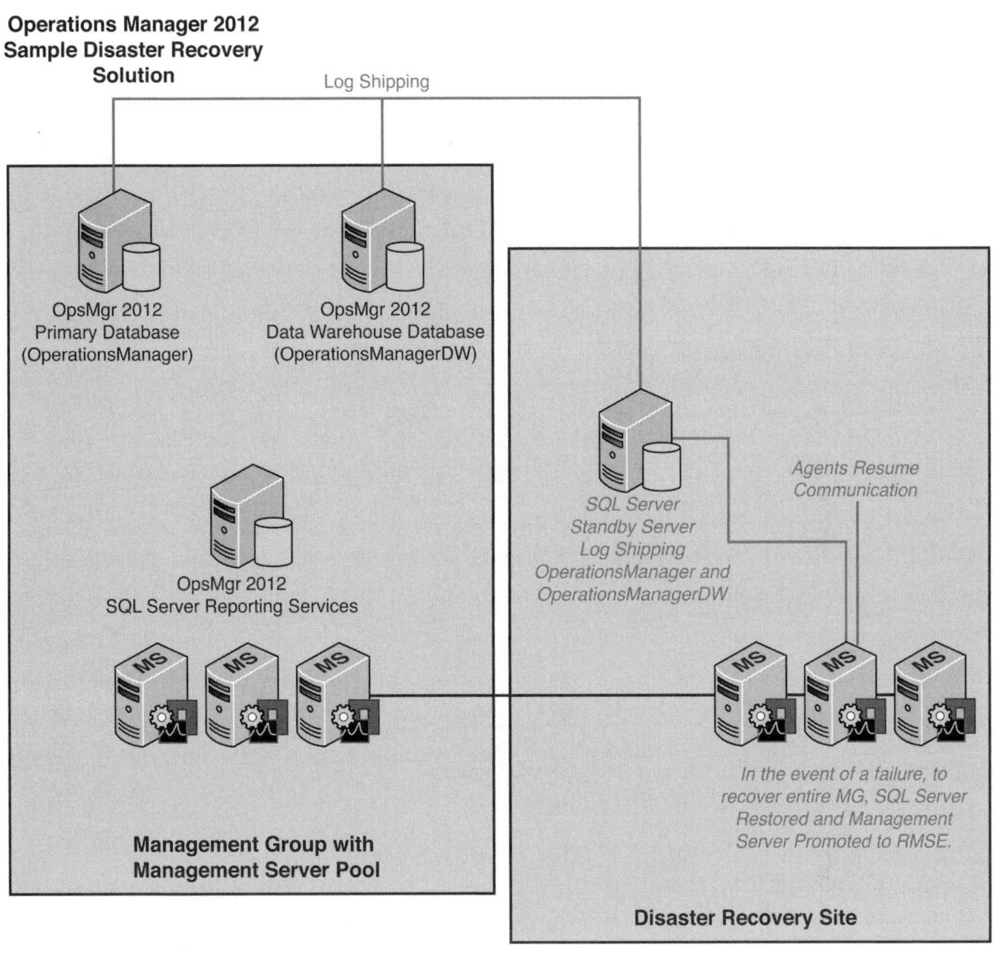

FIGURE 12.26 A sample disaster recovery solution using log shipping.

Other Approaches for Database Disaster Recovery

SQL Server 2012 includes AlwaysOn technology, which uses Windows Server Failover Clustering and enables cross-site SQL Server database disaster recovery (see http://msdn.microsoft.com/en-us/library/ff877884.aspx for an overview of AlwaysOn). Prior to System Center 2012 Service Pack 1, which includes support for SQL Server 2012, organizations wanting to utilize this functionality must rely on other solutions.

An approach suggested by the OpsMgr product team is geo-clustering, a supported configuration with OpsMgr beginning with OpsMgr 2007 R2. A geo-cluster is effectively the same as a regular two/multi-node cluster, except each node is located in a geographically remote location from each other. It utilizes SAN replication and switch trunking:

- SAN replication synchronizes data between two SANs, keeping the data on both systems current. Should one SAN fail, the other can immediately assume responsibility for the cluster connections, keeping the system online.
- Switch trunking allows a switch VLAN to stretch across two or more switches located remotely to one another; this means that for the cluster heartbeat, data can be transmitted as if the machines were plugged in to the same physical switch or hub.

Geo-clustering does requires a large hardware investment and significant bandwidth between sites in large environments.

REAL WORLD: A VIRTUAL SOLUTION FOR SQL DATABASE DISASTER RECOVERY

If you are running SQL Server on virtual machines and are using the VMware hypervisor, an approach the authors have seen for cross-site disaster recovery utilizes VMware's Site Recovery Manager. Using Site Recovery Manager and NetApp storage, this organization is able to fail over its OpsMgr databases from one data center to another. Each data center has four management servers, and the database servers at the remote site use the same NetBIOS names as the primary site. The solution was implemented as an automated process; SRM is also able to automatically assign IP addresses to the recovery VMs. When the VMs fail over they reregister on the DR subnet—rewriting the original production DNS entries.

As this organization prefers to rely on Microsoft-supported technologies for SQL Server disaster recovery, the plan is to utilize SQL Server 2012 AlwaysOn after they implement System Center 2012 SP 1.

Recovering from a Downed Management Server

Another potential scenario to discuss is if you only lose one of your OpsMgr management servers and it happens to be the RMS emulator (RMSE). In this case, you can switch the RMSE role to a functional management server, using the steps discussed in Chapter 9. Alternatively, you can recover a failed management server by running `setup.exe` with the `/recover` switch in a command prompt window. For syntax examples, see http://technet.microsoft.com/en-us/library/hh531578.aspx and http://technet.microsoft.com/en-us/library/hh531577.aspx.

A VIRTUAL PLAN FOR DISASTER RECOVERY

With many installations now using cloud and virtualized services, an additional approach for disaster recovery planning is virtualizing your disaster recovery environment. If you are using physical servers, the concept is that you would take backups of the physical drives you used when installing and configuring Operations Manager, and convert them to virtual drives.

Fast Track

While many of the concepts related to backup and recovery are similar to Operations Manager 2007, here are key takeaways when considering your backup and disaster recovery planning for System Center Operations Manager 2012:

- APM is new with Operations Manager 2012; it includes tables in the operational and data warehouse databases you will want to groom.
- Disaster recovery planning becomes simpler with the removal of the RMS feature used in OpsMgr 2007.
- SQL Server 2012, supported with System Center 2012 SP 1, includes AlwaysOn technology, which uses Windows Server Failover Clustering and enables cross-site SQL Server database disaster recovery.

Summary

This chapter discussed the need for backups, the OpsMgr features to back up regularly, and the tools available for performing backups, including System Center Data Protection Manager. It also discussed an approach for backing up the data warehouse and overall disaster recovery planning for Operations Manager. The next chapter covers administering management packs, including best practices for implementing management packs, and Microsoft resources to assist with management pack administration.

CHAPTER 13

Administering Management Packs

IN THIS CHAPTER

This chapter discusses the underlying concepts and fundamental uses of management packs (MPs). It includes the process of importing and exporting management packs, and discusses best practices for incorporating management packs into your Operations Manager (OpsMgr) environment. It also covers a number of utilities and resources developed by Microsoft to simplify management pack administration.

Any discussion of management packs invariably leads to questions about the information managed by those management packs. To that end, the chapter includes a brief discussion of some tuning and troubleshooting techniques that can help when implementing management packs.

Management Packs Defined

Management packs make it possible to collect and utilize a wide range of information from various sources. An OpsMgr management pack is an eXtensible Markup Language (XML) document that provides the structure to monitor specific hardware or software. It contains the definitions of the different components and the information needed by an administrator who must operate that application, device, or service, which will collectively be referred to as *objects*. MPs operate by discovering and monitoring these objects. After an object is discovered, it is monitored according to the health model defined in the management pack.

MPs describe what data to examine and provide analysis of that data, giving a snapshot of the monitored component's health. You will find management packs authored by Microsoft and third parties. You may decide to write rules or monitors to augment or improve the functionality of an existing MP or choose to write a management pack from scratch, particularly if you need to manage a product where Microsoft or a third party has not released a corresponding management pack. Chapter 22, "Authoring Management Packs and Reports," discusses the process of developing management packs.

One of the strengths of Operations Manager is its management packs are often produced by the same engineers who wrote the particular application or service. For instance, the Microsoft product teams produce the management packs for Microsoft products. The management packs represent the best efforts of the developers to expose relevant and useful monitoring-related information, to determine what issues require attention, and to assess the level of product knowledge required for administrators to resolve a given situation.

NOTE: MANAGEMENT PACKS IMPORTED DURING INSTALLATION

As part of the Operations Manager 2012 installation, a number of management packs are imported by default, many of which are libraries. Libraries are MPs that provide a foundation of object types (classes) and settings that other management packs depend on. The management packs you import to monitor applications, services, and devices will require (have dependencies on) one or more of these libraries.

Model-Based Management

Operations Manager employs models as its basis for monitoring applications, devices, and services. The use of models makes it possible to define the semantics of an object, discover the object, and observe the health of the object.

A model refers to a definition of the application, device, or service, and the components making up that entity. It describes the relationships between the components; and how the application, device, or service relates to other applications, devices, and services. Model-based management requires that monitored applications, devices, or services are modeled in management packs.

Operations Manager provides a core model for management packs. This core model is used to declare common types of objects (classes), and provides a starting point for management pack authors to refine the model and define particular monitoring logic. The model consists of a collection of classes, relationship types, modules, data types, and other building blocks. Monitoring capabilities are defined in an extensible way through management packs.

Management Pack Structure and Functionality

A management pack contains knowledge about an application, including the following:

- The structure of an application
- How to discover the application

- How to monitor the application
- What to do when the application breaks

The defined schema file used for OpsMgr 2012 management packs is ManagementPackSchema.xsd. XSD (XML Schema Definition) files define what elements and attributes may appear in an XML document, the relationship between the elements, and the data that may be stored in those elements.

MPs include collections of types (classes), rules, monitors, tasks, views, overrides, and reports; these components are used to determine how an object collects, handles, and responds to data related to a specific monitored application, device, or service. Operations Manager uses the object type to target rules and monitors. Here's how that works:

- Create an object type (class).
- Create the discovery for that type.
- Create a rule or monitor targeted to that type.

This is also discussed in some depth in Chapter 14, "Monitoring with System Center 2012 Operations Manager."

Not only are management packs written in XML, they can be sealed. A sealed management pack has an extension of .MP, while an unsealed MP has an extension of .XML. An unsealed management pack can reference other (sealed) MPs, but cannot be referenced by another MP.

Sealed management packs are binary and read-only, and cannot be modified. They are digitally signed by the vendor. Here are benefits of using sealed management packs:

- **Contents cannot be modified:** A sealed management pack cannot be changed. You must change the .xml file, which is then sealed again with the same certificate. The updated management pack must be backward compatible to be reinstalled in the same management group.
- **Enforces version control:** Only sealed management packs enforce version control when an updated version of the MP is installed. If you have an unsealed management pack, the new version is always installed regardless of backward compatibility.
- **Enables the management pack to be referenced by other management packs:** A management pack can only reference an element in another management pack if the management pack being referenced is sealed. This ensures modifications to a management pack do not break other management packs referencing it—because sealed MPs maintain version control, updates to the sealed MP are backward compatible.

By being read-only, the vendor knows the objects in the MP cannot be modified, as the only changes allowed by OpsMgr are to disable and override rules and monitors. Most vendor-supplied management packs for OpsMgr are sealed, and thus easier for the vendor to support.

Here are some of the more interesting features of OpsMgr management packs:

- **Dependency checks:** Dependencies on other management packs are defined within each MP. You cannot import a management pack if you have not already imported the management packs it depends on. Many management packs rely on libraries that include core definitions.

  As an example, you cannot import the SQL Server 2008 (Monitoring) management pack unless you have already imported the SQL Server Core Library MP. Conversely, you cannot delete a management pack that other MPs depend on; before deleting the SQL Server Core Library management pack, you must delete all SQL Server management packs that reference it. Figure 13.1 shows the SQL Server Core Library management pack with dependences on a number of other management packs, and depended on by other management packs.

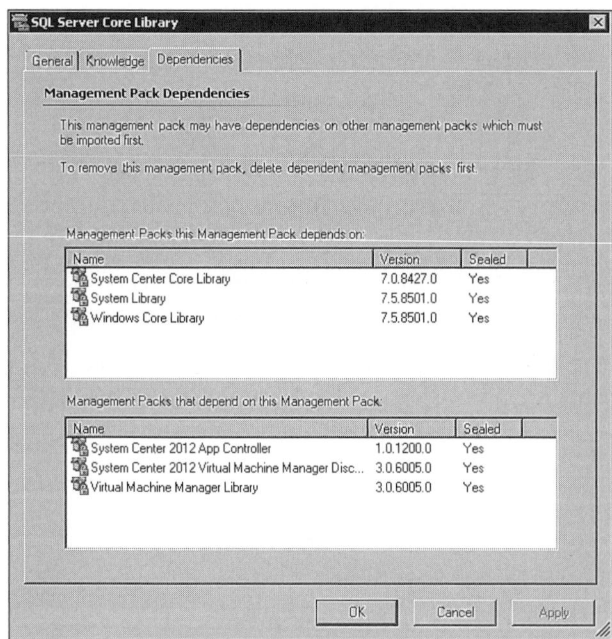

FIGURE 13.1 The SQL Server Core Library management pack both depends on other management packs and has management packs that depend on it.

NOTE: ABOUT THE SYSTEM CENTER CORE LIBRARY

The System Center Core Library MP contains type definitions for System Center.

- **Ability to upgrade to new versions of (sealed) management packs without losing overrides:** This capability is possible because overrides are saved in a separate management pack. As discussed earlier in this section, overrides cannot be saved to a sealed vendor management pack.
- **Ability to export and store overrides:** This item is related to the previous bullet. Because overrides are saved separately, you can easily export your changes for backup purposes or in preparation for importing them to another management pack.
- **Knowledge improvements:** This includes the ability to include inline views and tasks in the knowledge portion of the management pack, and the ability to use Microsoft Word to edit knowledge. Chapter 14 discusses the process of adding company knowledge.
- **Extensible monitoring:** Operations Manager allows you to plug in new types of monitoring at any time, and you can customize existing monitoring definitions to meet your needs. (The standard monitoring types are defined in system libraries imported during setup.)
- **Ability to uninstall a management pack:** Should you need to delete a management pack, just do it through the Operations console. Note the Delete capability in the Tasks pane of the Administration space in Figure 13.2.

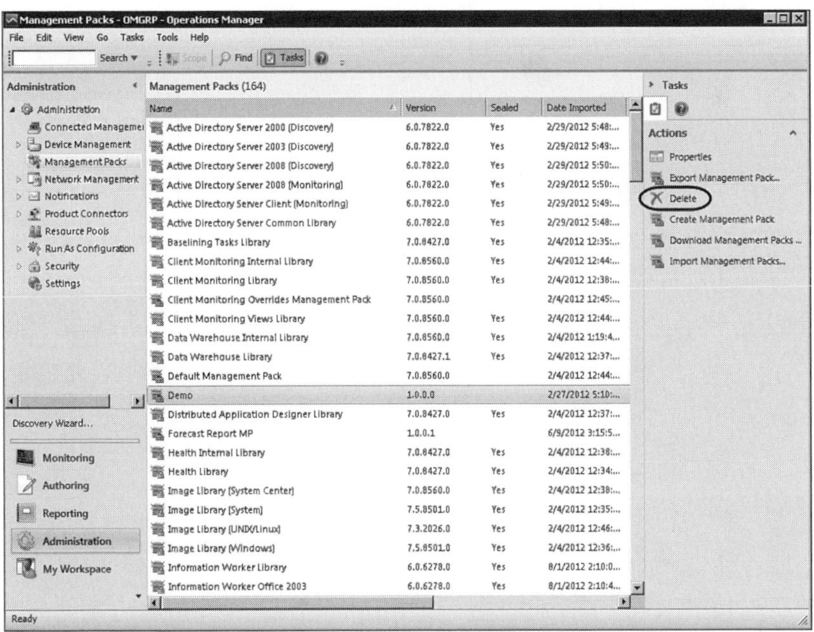

FIGURE 13.2 Delete action in the Operations console.

About Objects

Management packs focus on discovering and managing applications, components, and devices—referred to as objects. Discovered objects are monitored according to the health model defined in the management pack. An object is an instance of a class. Every class, or object type, has a health model. Health models will represent the status (health) of even the simplest managed object.

Objects can have different levels of specialization. Chapter 3, "Looking Inside OpsMgr," uses the analogy of parts of a body to describe objects and relationships. Figure 13.3, which also appeared in Chapter 3, describes object types (classes) showing increasingly specialized objects, and relationships between objects.

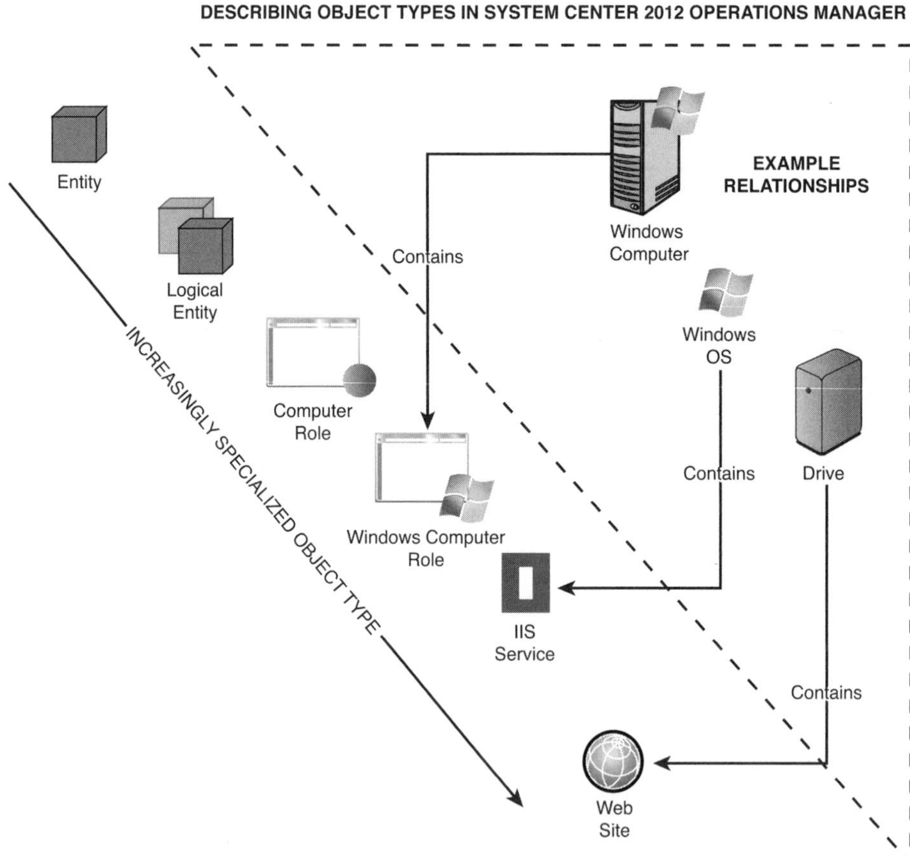

FIGURE 13.3 Operations Manager object types.

Performing Diagnostics and Recovery

Management packs may contain diagnostic and recovery actions. These actions include tasks that can run automatically or on demand. A management pack can also contain common administrative tasks, which you can launch from the Operations console or the Health Explorer.

- Console tasks can include loading management consoles or running utilities such as `ipconfig` and `ping` against a targeted computer. Figure 13.4 shows tasks loaded into OpsMgr associated with a Windows computer. These tasks are listed under the Tasks pane in the Operations console when the focus is on Windows Computers.
- Figure 13.5 is an example of running an inline task. This figure shows restarting the Orchestrator Runbook Service as a recovery task initiated from the Health Explorer.

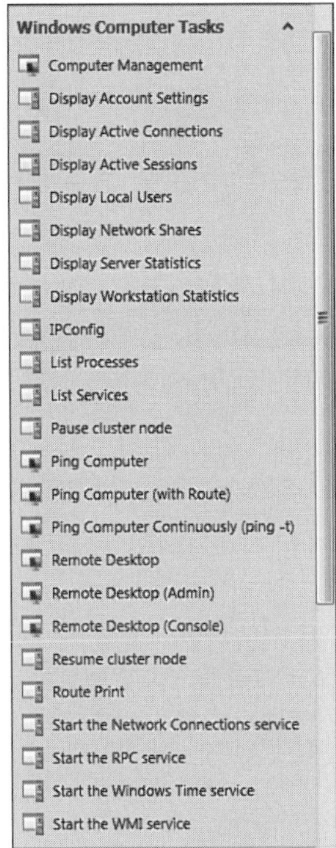

FIGURE 13.4 Tasks included with the Windows Computer object.

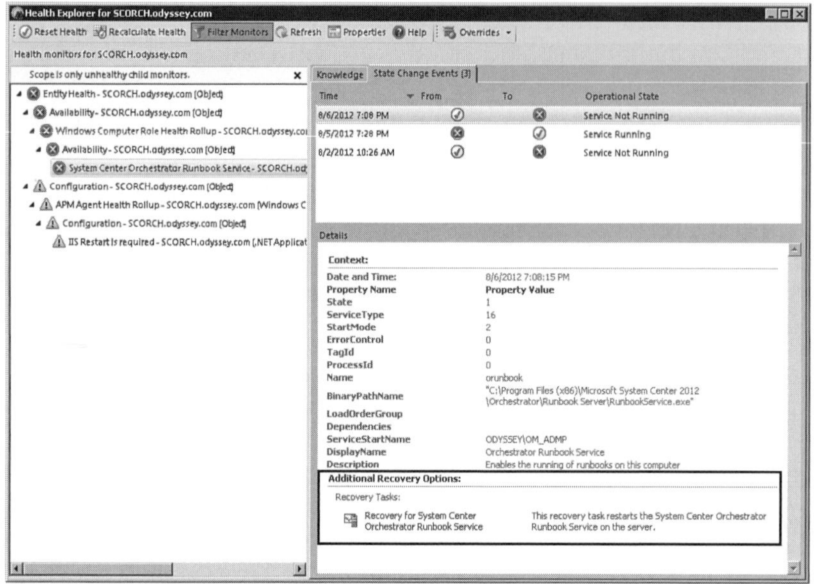

FIGURE 13.5 An inline task to run from the Health Explorer.

TIP: SCOPE SET IN HEALTH EXPLORER TO ONLY SHOW UNHEALTHY MONITORS

System Center 2012 Operations Manager changes the initial appearance of the Health Explorer to clean up the clutter so to speak, with the scope set to show unhealthy child monitors only. This can help you zero in faster on the issues at hand.

About Workflows

Monitoring is based around the concept of *workflow,* which is how information flows to support tasks. An OpsMgr agent and server will run many workflows simultaneously to discover and monitor applications, devices, and services. Some workflows are loaded by the health service on the agent or server and run continuously; others are loaded as required. A management pack may ship with one workflow or thousands. As discussed in Chapter 3, workflows are used in many ways—including collecting information and storing data in the operational and data warehouse databases, running timed scripts, creating alerts, and running tasks on demand.

Each workflow is targeted at a type of object or a class. The workflow only runs where an object of the specified type is discovered and managed by Operations Manager. A separate workflow will execute for every object of that type (class). Workflow types include rules, discoveries, tasks, monitors, diagnostics, and recoveries. The next sections discuss these different types of workflows.

How Rules Work

A *rule* uses three module types: data source, condition detection, and write action. The rule will include one or more data source modules, zero or one condition detection modules, and one or more write action modules. It is not enough to say just that a rule has a source, optionally detects a condition, then performs an action; because OpsMgr is model-based, each module is of a particular module type, with the type defining the behavior of the module.

Rules are loaded into memory when an object of the type the rule is targeting begins to be managed by the health service. The rule stays in memory, waiting for data items to be generated from the specified data source(s). Rules end with at least one write action that performs an action such as generating an alert, running a script, or collecting and storing data in the database.

A rule is a generic workflow that can do a number of things. Here are ways you can use rules:

- **Collecting and storing data in the operational database or data warehouse (collection rules):** Collection rules can be event, performance, or probe based. Event and collection rules collect data from various data providers, while probe-based rules collect data from data sources based on a probe.
- **Generating an alert (alert-generating rules):** Alert-generating rules are event based. Alerts can be based on generic comma separated value (CSV) text logs, generic text logs, Windows event logs, Simple Network Management Protocol (SNMP) traps, Syslog information, Windows Management Instrumentation (WMI) events, and more.
- **Running a timed action (timed command):** Timed commands execute a command-line task or a script based on a recurring timed interval.

Rules are primarily used to collect data to show in the console or reports and to provide stateless alerting.

About Discoveries

A *discovery* is a special type of workflow that discovers one or more objects of a particular type. It is used to discover instances of classes. A discovery can discover objects of multiple types at one time. A discovery uses a single module, which must be a data source module type.

Discovery is important because monitoring cannot occur for a class of objects without prior discovery. Discovery usually uses a probing action to discover instances of a class. Probing actions include querying WMI, querying the registry, or executing a script to discover instances of a class. Once instances of a class are discovered, these instances can be monitored.

Discoveries are actually a specialized type of rule. A discovery inserts discovery data into the operational database. This data may be object or relationship instances. Unlike rules, discoveries do not include condition detection or write action modules. All discoveries have an implicit write action that OpsMgr handles internally; the write action inserts the discovery data into the database. For performance reasons, discovery data is cached; it is only sent to the management server and database if it has changed from the previous execution of the discovery.

About Tasks

A *task* is a workflow, but it is not loaded by the health service until requested by the user (through the Operations console or an SDK call); it is typically initiated by a user using the Operations console. The user will execute the task for one or more objects. After a task executes, it is unloaded from memory until the next time it is called. The default account used to run tasks is the action account.

Tasks do not have data sources or condition detection modules.

Using Monitors

A *monitor* detects the health state of an associated managed object. A monitor uses a monitor type, which utilizes modules and defines workflows using those modules. Here are the three types of monitors:

- An *aggregate monitor* rolls up health from child monitors according to some algorithm. The current algorithms in OpsMgr for aggregate monitors are *Worst of* and *Best of.*
- A *unit monitor* monitors an object, and is discussed further in the "UnitMontiorType" section.
- A *dependency monitor* rolls up health of other objects across a containment or hosting relationship, based on an algorithm. Health cannot be rolled up across a reference relationship. Algorithms available are *Worst state of any member, Worst state of specified percentage of members in good health state,* and *Best state of any member.*

These types define the states the monitor can be in and the conditions causing each state. The monitor type can also have on demand detection defined, meaning it will recalculate state on its own, rather than waiting for the next instrumentation to appear.

Monitors are used to determine the state of a monitored object, and are the only thing that can affect the health state of an instance. Each monitor is a state machine with a set number of states. A monitor can only be in a single state at any one time.

About Diagnostics

A diagnostic is an on demand workflow and is attached to a specific monitor. Diagnostics are a specialized type of task. The workflow is either initiated immediately when a monitor enters a particular state or on demand by a user when the monitor is in a specific state. Multiple diagnostics can be attached to a monitor as required. A diagnostic should not change an application state.

How Recoveries Work

A recovery is another type of on demand workflow and is a specialized type of task attached to a specific monitor or diagnostic. The recovery workflow is automatically initiated whenever a monitor enters a particular state, a diagnostic runs, or on demand by a user request. Recoveries are typically designed to take an action to resolve the problem that caused the unfavorable health state. Multiple recoveries can be attached to a monitor.

Understanding Data Types

Looking at the concept of a data type can help you better understand module types and workflows.

OpsMgr passes data between modules. The format of that data varies depending on the module sending the data. A data source reading Windows performance counters will output a different type of data from a module reading and sending WMI data, or one that reads from an event log. Different module types expect different types of data; a threshold module type expects performance data, while a module type writing data to the operational database may expect event data. This means that OpsMgr must define and use multiple data types.

These data types are defined in management packs. Because management packs are object oriented, they follow an inheritance model—similar to class definitions. While a class hierarchy will start with a base class of `System.Entity`, a data type module starts with a data type of `System.BaseData`. All data types eventually inherit from the base data type.

When a module type is first defined, its definition includes the specification of the input and output types it will accept and provide. Each of these data types must be defined in the management pack containing the module or in a referenced management pack. These data types must also be compatible with other modules used with the workflow.

Management Pack Elements

The list in this section includes XML elements contained in a management pack; these are also known as management pack elements. Each element has an ID attribute; the ID must be unique across all elements in that management pack.

- Workflows:
    - Discovery
    - Rule
    - Task
    - Monitor
    - Diagnostic
    - Recovery
- Class Type
- Relationship Type

- Data Type
- Schema Type
- Module Types:
    - DataSource Module Type
    - ProbeAction Module Type
    - ConditionDetection Module Type
    - WriteAction Module Type
- UnitMonitor Type
- Override
- Template
- ViewType
- Image
- UIPage
- UIPageSet
- Console Task
- View
- Folder
- Report
- ReportParameterControl
- Run As Profiles

Some elements in a management pack will have child elements called *sub-elements*; these are referenced by other objects in the management pack. An example of a sub-element is a property of a class. Using the analogy from Chapter 3, a class would be an eye, and the property would be whether the eye color is brown or blue.

The "Workflows" section discussed the Rule, Discovery, Task, Monitor, Diagnostic, and Recovery elements. The next sections discuss the other elements.

ClassType

The class type defines a type of object that is discovered and optionally monitored by OpsMgr.

RelationshipType

Objects (classes) can have relationships with other objects. A relationship type defines a relationship between two class types. It optionally defines properties that can be populated during discovery.

DataType

The data type defines types of data that OpsMgr modules can use and pass between each other. The data type is a pointer to a native or management implementation. Data types are not extensible, except by Microsoft.

SchemaType

Any time you define a new monitor module, you must define the schema for that type. When the type is used, the configuration provided must validate against the schema specified. If you plan to use schema elements across multiple modules, it is easiest to define those elements once, and then reference them in the multiple modules.

Module Types

Module types define the core monitoring capabilities of OpsMgr. OpsMgr 2012 module types come in four types: data source, condition detection, probe action, and write action, displayed in Figure 13.6. Each module type performs a distinct role.

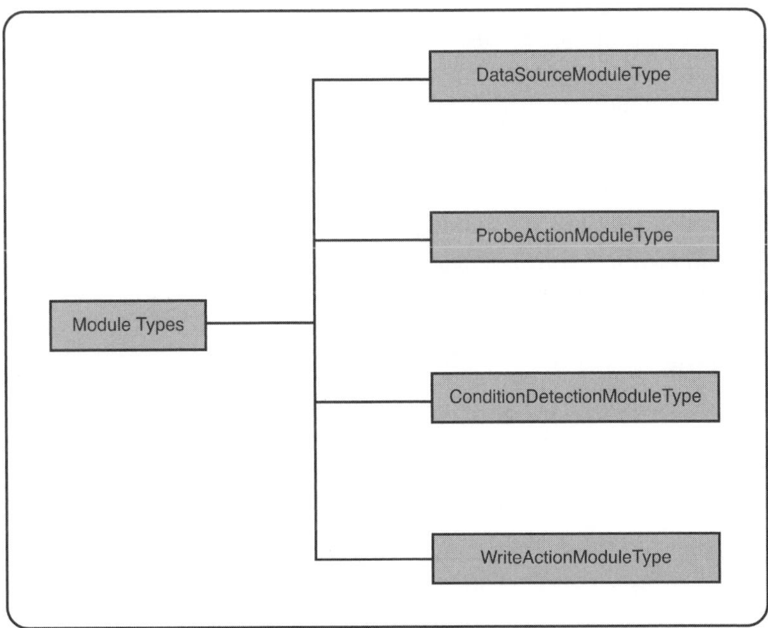

FIGURE 13.6 OpsMgr 2012 module types.

DataSourceModuleType

The data source module type requires a single output type, which must be a valid data type defined in the management pack or a referenced MP. It does not define any additional attributes.

ProbeActionModuleType

The probe action module type requires a single output type to be declared, similar to the data source module type. It also requires either a declared input type or that the trigger only flag is set.

Trigger only specifies that the input data item is only used to trigger execution of the module; the data is actually not used by the module.

ConditionDetectionModuleType

The condition detection module type has two additional attributes; these are the PassThrough and Stateful boolean attributes. These attributes are optional and default to a value of False.

WriteActionModuleType

The write action module type does not define additional attributes. It requires that a single input type is declared, and optionally an output type.

UnitMonitorType

A unit monitor watches (monitors) a particular aspect of an object. This could be an application, device, or service. A unit monitor uses instrumentation or a probing action to determine the current state of the aspect (Windows events, performance data, log file, WMI information, SNMP information, scripts, OLEDB, LDAP, and so on).

A unit monitor is defined to be of a particular unit monitor type. OpsMgr ships with more than 200 monitor types; these are predefined workflows that monitor for specific types of instrumentation.

Unit monitors always roll up health to a parent aggregate monitor; the health is ultimately rolled up to the health of an object.

Understanding Overrides

Each management pack contains default settings and thresholds set by the author or vendor of the MP, and represent that vendor's definition of a health state for its products. As an administrator, you can use overrides to adjust these default settings and customize them for your organization. Figure 13.7 illustrates how overrides fit architecturally in Operations Manager.

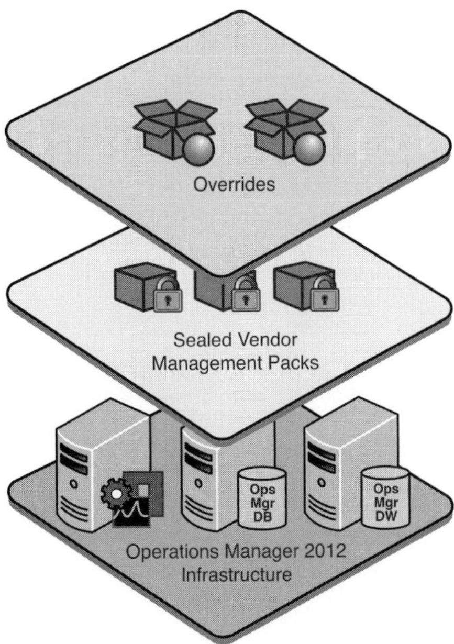

FIGURE 13.7 Structure of overrides in OpsMgr 2012.

Overrides are the only way to modify sealed management pack behavior. Overrides are stored separately from the sealed vendor management pack in a new management pack. Because most management packs are sealed, you must create an override to change the behavior of the MP.

After testing your overrides, you can export the management pack containing the overrides and import it into your production management group.

You can apply overrides to rules, monitors, discoveries, or tasks:

- Rule overrides change the frequency of a rule or a parameter such as enabled/disabled, whether to create an alert, severity, priority, and so on.
- Monitor overrides change a parameter such as a threshold.
- Discovery overrides change the frequency of the discovery. They can also enable/disable the discovery, or configure special information about what should be included or excluded in some discoveries.
- Task overrides are used to change one of the parameters the MP author allowed for override.

Overrides can be applied at several levels:

- **Type:** A *type* refers to the type of object being monitored. Examples of types would be all SQL Server databases, all Exchange mail servers, all DNS servers, and so on.
- **Group:** A *group* is a subset of a type. For example, rather than monitoring all Exchange mail servers, you may want to apply the override to only the back-end mail servers in a particular domain, or the DNS servers in a branch office.
- **Object:** An *object* would be a particular instance of a type (class). You may decide to apply an override to a particular database—perhaps the operational database, or a specific DNS server.

If overrides conflict with each other, OpsMgr applies a hierarchy. The Object override is the most granular and wins over a Group or Type override; a Group override wins over a Type override.

Override types (classes) include the following:

- Category
- Monitoring
- Rule Configuration
- Rule Property
- Monitor Configuration
- Monitor Property
- Diagnostic Configuration
- Diagnostic Property
- Recovery Configuration
- Discovery Configuration
- Discovery Property

Each of these overrides changes monitoring behavior in some manner. You can view which overrides are affecting a managed object by navigating in the Operations console to **Authoring -> Management Pack Objects -> Overrides**, selecting the specific Management Pack Object Type, and selecting a target, illustrated in Figure 13.8.

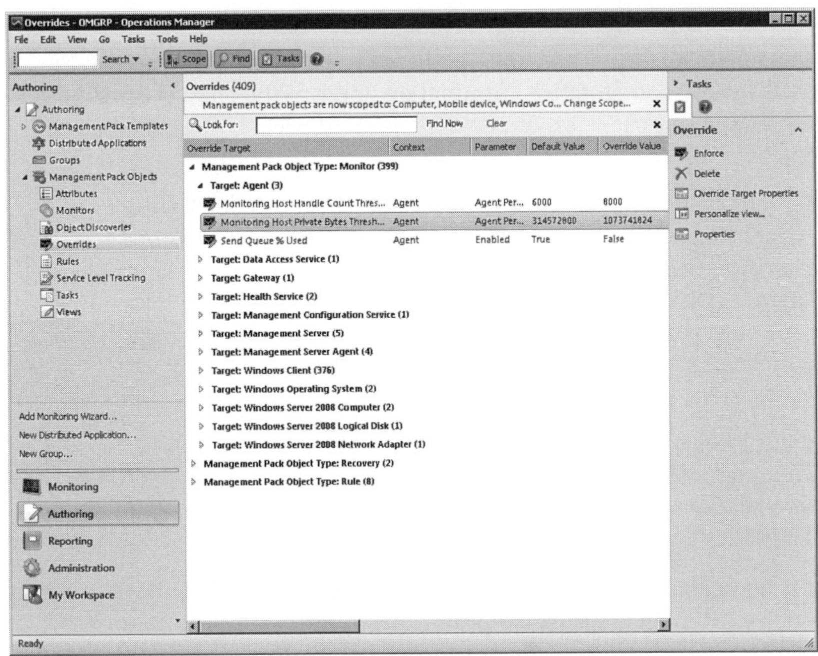

FIGURE 13.8 Viewing overrides.

REAL WORLD: STORING OVERRIDES

In Operations Manager 2007, by default, any time you created an override or other monitoring setting, those changes were saved to the Default management pack. This tended to create issues, partly because the Default MP could become quite large, and because it did not provide granularity. Saving overrides in the Default MP also made it difficult later to remove the management pack the override applied to, as there was now a dependency between the two that was not removed even when you removed the override. With OpsMgr 2012, Microsoft changed the user interface so the Default management pack no longer is the default for storing customizations to management packs.

A question often asked is *what is a best practice when it comes to storing overrides?*

- The authors suggest you create a separate MP for each workload (Exchange, SQL Server, DNS, and so on), to simplify managing overrides.
- Use a naming convention that follows the management pack holding the original settings. As an example, if you are customizing settings defined in the Windows Core Library, create an unsealed MP named "Windows Core Customizations." You can use this MP to save overrides and any other customizations, such as new monitors, that supersede the default settings of the Windows Core Library. Alternatively, you could create separate management packs for overrides only and prepend "Overrides - " to the management pack name, such as "Overrides - Exchange 2010," as Pete Zerger discusses at http://www.systemcentercentral.com/tabid/145/indexId/73805/Default.aspx. Determine your approach for naming standards and be consistent with that approach.

Management Pack Templates

A template is used in a manner similar to templates in other applications such as Microsoft Word. Users specify configuration information and run the template, with the result being a new management pack or part of a management pack, based on the information in the template.

You can use templates to create classes, rules, monitors, tasks, and so on. They are intended to fulfill common monitoring scenarios such as monitoring a Windows service, monitoring a Transmission Control Protocol (TCP) port, or monitoring an Object Linking and Embedding Database (OLE DB) connection. Rather than having to create the individual management pack objects, the configuration information is provided using a wizard; OpsMgr runs the template and creates that portion of the MP.

In the Operations console, select the Authoring space. On the left pane in the Authoring space, shown in Figure 13.9, is the Management Pack Templates section, containing management pack templates for APM monitoring, OLE DB data sources, process monitoring, TCP ports, UNIX/Linux log file and process monitoring, web application availability and transaction monitoring, and Windows services.

The Management Pack Objects section also contains several templates (wizards) for management pack objects to help you create monitors, rules, and tasks. These are discussed in Chapter 14.

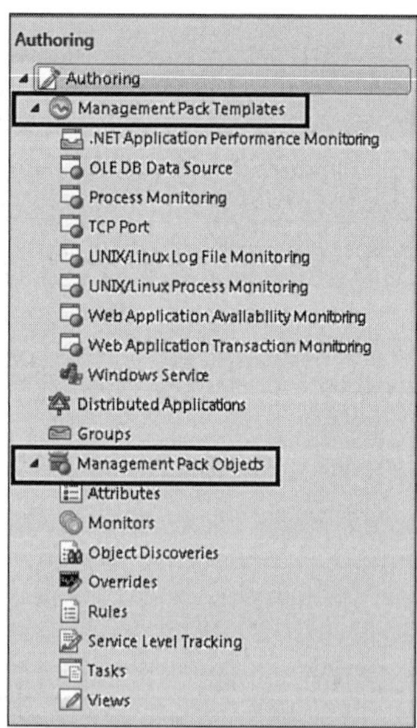

FIGURE 13.9 The Authoring node of the Operations console.

Presentation Types

Presentation types include view types, images, UI pages, and UI page sets, discussed in the following sections.

ViewType

Views are created in the Monitoring space of the Operations console. View types include alert, event, state, performance, diagram, task status, web page, and dashboard views; when you create a new view, you can choose from one of these available types.

The Default management pack is an unsealed management pack containing common elements including the views at the top level of the Monitoring space. If you create a new view or folder at this level, store those in the Default management pack. The Default MP should not be used for any other purpose, as mentioned in the Real World sidebar in the "Overrides" section; use a new management pack when creating other management pack elements.

Image

An image element contains a binary blob of data. Images are assigned to classes or other management pack objects and rendered in the console when instances of that targeted object are shown.

UIPage

A UI page references a managed code implementation of a WinForm page. The page is used to configure a module, monitor type, or template. You can share pages between different types.

UIPageSet

A UI page set defines a flow of UI pages shown when configuring a template, monitor type, or module type. This page set can define pages that show on creation, on edit, or both. The page set can define exact pieces of configuration that are passed to each page and optionally transform the configuration. The output configuration is a composite of all the output on each page.

ConsoleTask

Tasks were previously defined in the "Tasks" section. A console task is a workflow that runs on demand, initiated through the console.

View

A view is a customized subset of information available in the console. As discussed in the "ViewType" section, view types can include alert, event, state, performance, diagram, task status, web page, and dashboard views.

Folder

Folders organize information in the console. They are used for views, the rule and task wizards, the unit monitor wizard, and management pack templates.

Report

Source definitions for reports are included in OpsMgr management packs.

ReportParameterControl

You can use parameters to control which data is retrieved from a data source when a report is processed; you can also use parameters to filter the data after it has been retrieved.

Run As Profiles

A management pack can contain one or more Run As profiles. Run As profiles and Run As accounts (discussed in Chapter 10, "Security and Compliance") are used to select users with the privileges needed to run rules, tasks, and monitors.

Management pack authors can create a Run As profile and associate the profile with one or more rules, monitors, tasks, or discoveries. The named Run As profile is imported with the management pack into OpsMgr. The OpsMgr administrator then creates a named Run As account and specifies a credential and the distribution. The administrator associates the Run As account to the Run As profile and specifies the target computers the account should run on. The Run As account provides the credentials to run the rules, monitors, tasks, and discoveries associated with the Run As profile to which the Run As account belongs.

Sealing Management Packs

When a management pack is sealed, it is converted to a binary file with an .mp extension. You can install the sealed or unsealed version of a management pack to a management group, although you cannot have both installed at once.

MPSeal is used to seal management packs. This is a command-line tool located in the SupportTools folder of the OpsMgr distribution media. Sealing requires a client certificate to validate the identity of the author. The certificate should be a valid public certificate from a certificate authority such as VeriSign. If you are developing MPs within your own organization for internal use only, you can use a private certificate authority.

CAUTION: SEALING A MANAGEMENT PACK DOES NOT SECURE IT

Sealing a management pack does not hide its contents; you can export any sealed management pack from a management group using PowerShell and get full access to its XML code.

Running MPSeal creates a sealed .mp file from an unsealed .xml file. Once you seal the MP, you can install it in your management group.

Here is the syntax for MPSeal; Table 13.1 describes the command-line options:

```
MPSeal <Management Pack> [/I Include Path]* /Keyfile Key File Path
/Company Company Name [/Outdir Output Directory] [/DelaySign] {ccc} [/Copyright
Copyright text]
```

TABLE 13.1 MPSeal options

Option	Description
Management Pack File Name	The full name of the .xml file to seal. If the file is not in the current folder, include the full path to the file. If the path includes a space, enclose the path in quotes.
Include Path	The path to a folder containing .mp files referenced by the management pack you are sealing.
Key File Path	The file containing the public and private key used to seal the MP. This is the same key pair used for signing .NET assemblies and created using the Strong Name tool (sn.exe), documented at http://go.microsoft.com/fwlink/?LinkID=231266 and included with the Microsoft Windows SDK (http://go.microsoft.com/fwlink/?LinkID=231265).
Company Name	Your company name. Enclose this in quotes if it includes a space.
Output Directory	The folder to store the output file. If unspecified, the current folder is used.
DelaySign	Use this option if you will only be specifying the public key at this point. This allows you to restrict access to the private key to selected individuals. You can complete the signing with the private key just before you release the management pack.
Copyright text	Text to include for copyright information. While this option is functional, the text is not currently accessible from Operations Manager.

Here's an example that seals a management pack named Sample.Management.Pack.xml and creates a file named Sample.Management.Pack.mp in the current directory:

```
MPSeal Sample.Management.Pack.xml /I c:\mp /keyfile odyssey.snk /Company Odyssey
```

MPSeal also verifies the management pack file and reports, and reports any errors that would prevent it from installing (In OpsMgr 2007, MPVerify was used for this purpose). While a management pack may be valid according to its schema, it actually may not be valid because not all validation rules can be defined within the XML schema.

For MPSeal to perform this function, it must be able to access all management packs referenced by the management pack in the process of being sealed. These must be sealed versions of the file, have an .mp extension, and be at least the version specified by the management pack being sealed.

Use the `/I` (Include Path) option to specify a folder to search .mp files, using multiple `/I` options if the required files are in multiple folders. The standard library management pack files included with OpsMgr are located on the installation folder of the management server; you must obtain other management pack files separately.

TIP: DETERMINING THE MPS REFERENCED BY A MANAGEMENT PACK YOU ARE SEALING

If you are unsure of the management packs referenced by the management pack you are sealing, run MPSeal using any folder. A list of all required management packs is returned.

Finding Management Pack Information

Microsoft has developed management pack guides providing in-depth information and deployment details for many management packs written for Microsoft products. When you download a management pack, there usually is a second download link for the guide, although in some cases the management pack guide is included in the downloaded .msi and extracted during installation. You can also find management pack guides at http://technet.microsoft.com/en-us/library/dd347500.aspx.

The Microsoft System Center Marketplace at http://systemcenter.pinpoint.microsoft.com includes management guides as well. You can search by System Center component; Operations Manager content is at http://systemcenter.pinpoint.microsoft.com/en-US/applications/search/operations-manager-d11?q=.

Management Pack Updates

The System Center Marketplace includes the option to select management packs by release date, enabling you to look for updates within the last 30, 90, 120, or 365 days. You can also check within the Administration space of the Operations console. Navigate to the Management Packs node, right-click on **Download Management Packs**, and select **Add** on the Select Management Packs page. The View drop-down in the Select Management Packs from Catalog page includes options to display all management packs released within the last 3 or 6 months, as well as to show updates available for installed management packs. This is discussed further in the "Importing Management Packs through the Operations Console" section.

MANAGEMENT PACKS AND OLDER VERSIONS OF OPERATIONS MANAGER

The System Center Marketplace (Pinpoint) lists management packs for earlier versions of Operations Manager. OpsMgr 2007 management packs are almost 100% compatible with OpsMgr 2012, as the schema has not changed (the exception is network device management packs, as the `Microsoft.SystemCenter.NetworkDevice` class is deprecated and SNMP-based workflows must now use the new `System.NetworkManagement.Node` class). Pinpoint also lists some third-party management packs for Microsoft Operations Manager (MOM) 2005, although Microsoft no longer supports that version.

Determining Management Pack Versions

For any particular management pack, the System Center Marketplace listing includes a description of the management pack and a link to its vendor's website. The management pack description may or may not include its version. Figure 13.10 shows the listing for the SQL Server monitoring management pack.

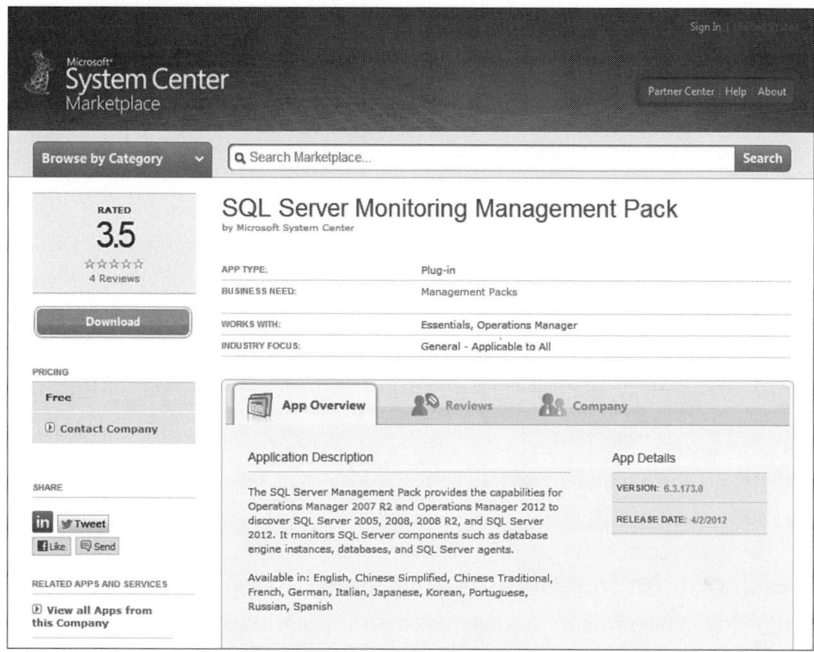

FIGURE 13.10 Management pack listing on the System Center Marketplace.

For a Microsoft management pack, clicking the Download link takes you to the download center page for that management pack. Information at the download page includes the name and size of the downloaded file and its published date and version; Figure 13.11 shows an example.

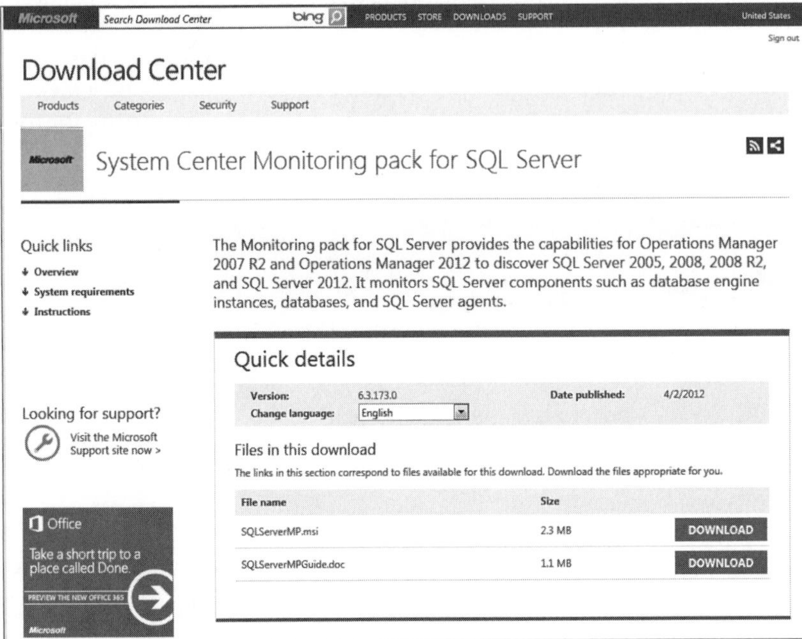

FIGURE 13.11 Quick details for a management pack at the Microsoft Download Center.

Checking the Version of an Installed Management Pack

To determine the installed version of any management pack, open the Operations console and navigate to **Administration -> Management Packs**. Select the specific management pack you are interested in and right-click to open the property sheet. The version number is in the middle of the Properties tab, as displayed in Figure 13.12.

MANAGEMENTPACK TABLE IN THE OPERATIONAL DATABASE

The operational database contains information regarding each installed management pack. You can query this information, which is maintained in the ManagementPack table. The table contains a row for each management pack installed in the management group.

To find all installed management packs, run this SQL query:

```
SELECT * FROM ManagementPack
```

Output query includes the globally unique identifier (GUID) of the management pack, name, friendly name, whether the MP is sealed, and when last modified.

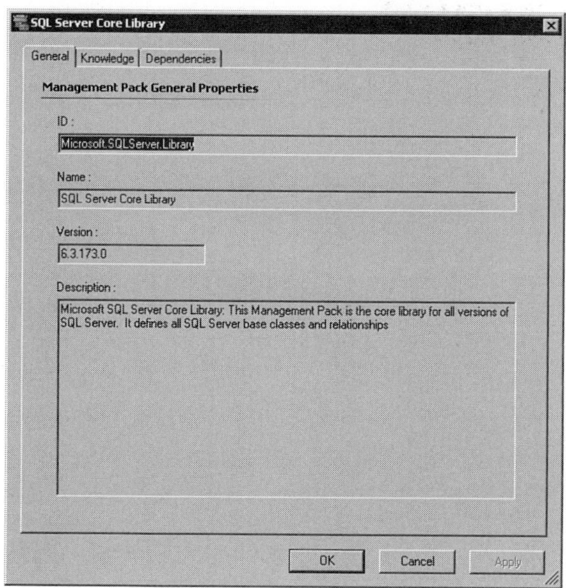

FIGURE 13.12 Checking the version of an installed management pack.

Importing Management Packs through the Operations Console

First introduced with OpsMgr 2007 Release 2 (R2), you can download MPs using the Administration node of the console, although this approach may be problematic as discussed in the Real World sidebar in this section. Follow these steps to download management packs using the console:

1. Navigate to **Administration** -> **Management Packs**. From the Tasks pane on the right, select **Download Management Packs** to start the Download Management Packs Wizard.

2. The first page of the wizard asks you to select a local folder in which to store the downloaded management packs. Click on **Browse** to browse for a folder such as C:\Management Packs, then click **Add** to add the management packs you want to download.

3. When selecting management packs, the search criteria in the View section of the Select Management Packs from Catalog page enables you to select from several search options:

    - All management packs in the catalog
    - Updates available for installed management packs
    - All management packs released within last 3 months
    - All management packs released within last 6 months

This example is searching for updates to all installed management packs. Figure 13.13 shows an update to the Windows Server Core OS management pack.

4. Click **Add** in Figure 13.13 to select management packs for download.

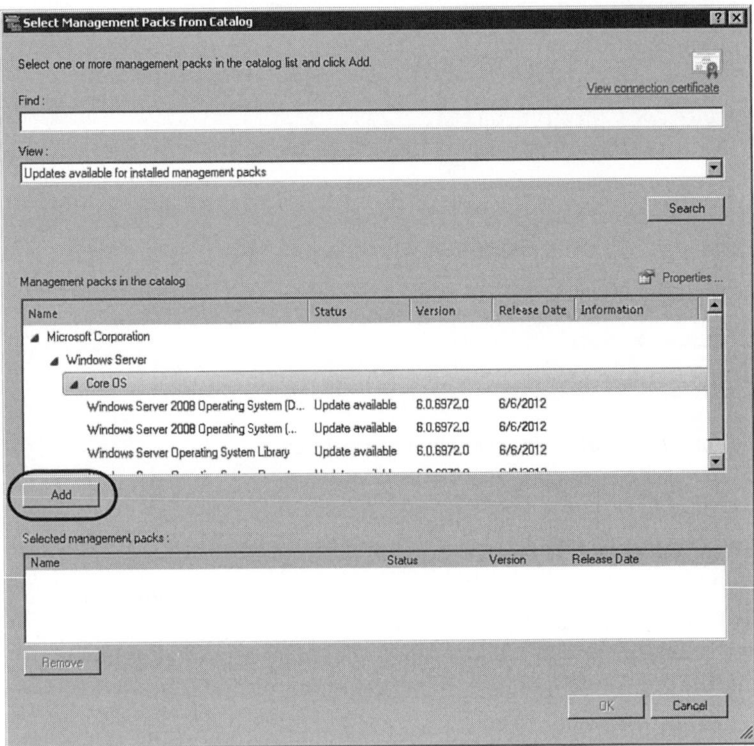

FIGURE 13.13 The list of updates to installed management packs.

5. The wizard will alert you if there are dependencies on other management packs or versions; you can download those also to resolve the issue. Once you complete your selection, select **OK** to view the download list, displayed in Figure 13.14. Select **Download** to initiate the download process.

6. Once the management packs are downloaded to the file system, they can be imported into the console using the **Import Management Packs** task in the Tasks pane, discussed in the "Importing Management Packs" section.

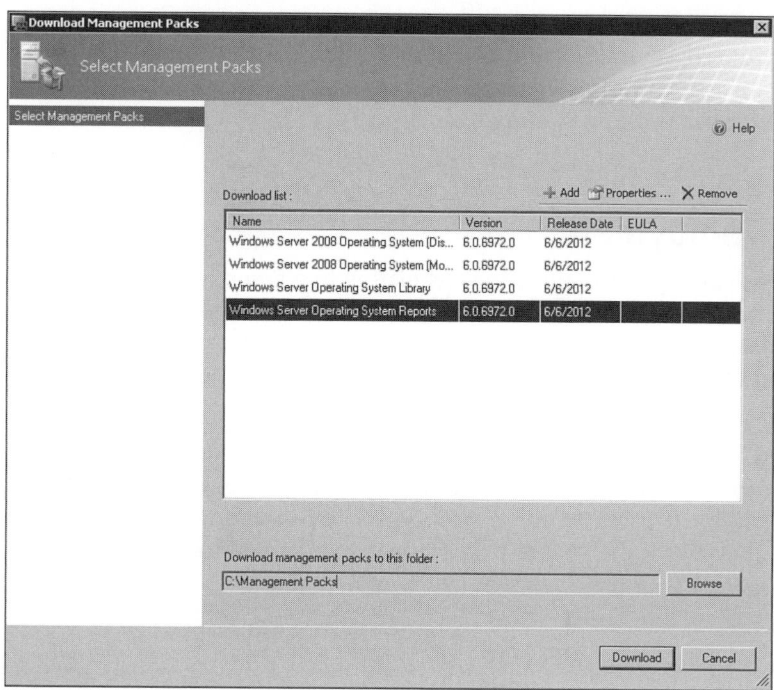

FIGURE 13.14 The list of management packs to download.

13

REAL WORLD: DOWNLOADING MANAGEMENT PACKS THROUGH THE CONSOLE NOT THE BEST APPROACH

While using the console to import management packs directly can be useful for checking for new management packs and comparing versions, it can be of limited use when actually importing management packs, and has actually created more support cases than it has helped. Here's why:

- **Unsealed management packs are not imported:** Some management packs ship with unsealed XML files that are critical to the function of the management pack.
- **Management pack guides are not downloaded:** In some cases, the guide includes steps to take that are necessary before importing a management pack.

Management Pack Bundles

With OpsMgr 2012, Microsoft includes a new packaging format for management packs, known as management pack bundles (.mpb files). Bundles use the .msi file format and were first introduced with Service Manager 2010. They enable you to include resources such as images or even assemblies in a management pack. Additional information on how bundles work is at http://blogs.technet.com/b/servicemanager/archive/2009/09/04/introducing-management-pack-bundles.aspx.

To extract files from an MP bundle, see Daniel Grandini's post at http://nocentdocent.wordpress.com/2012/02/28/opsmgr-2012-how-to-dump-management-pack-bundles/ and Stefan Stranger's discussion at http://blogs.technet.com/b/stefan_stranger/archive/2012/03/06/opsmgr-2012-how-to-dump-management-pack-bundles-small-improvement.aspx.

Planning for Deployment

Deploying management packs involves planning, evaluating in a preproduction or limited production environment, and importing and exporting management packs. Just as you evaluate a new software program before deploying it into production, you should assess management packs before importing and deploying them across your production environment.

Testing gives you an idea of how the management pack operates, what monitoring features are important for your organization, and any additional configuration that may be needed for the management pack. Testing may also reveal possible adjustments you will want to implement as overrides. After testing, tuning, and configuring a management pack, you will export it from your preproduction environment and import it into your production system.

TIP: INSTALL ONLY THE MANAGEMENT PACKS YOU NEED

The authors recommend only installing those management packs you need. Extra rules and monitors impose a cost on your system resources, including increased memory utilization of the agents targeted by the management pack and increased traffic between the managed computers and the management servers.

Determine an Order to Implement Management Packs

When planning management pack deployments, you will want to decide which ones to deploy, and in what order. Some applications have dependencies on others, so you may want to implement the related management packs as you deploy those products. As an example, say you use Exchange Server. Exchange requires Active Directory, which in turn utilizes DNS. Another consideration is how you might get the most "bang for the buck"; that is, which management packs will give you the most benefit for the least amount of cost measured in time, resources, or effort. Typically, you would examine this from a functional viewpoint. Here are several examples:

- You may decide that monitoring Active Directory is a high priority for your organization. Monitoring directory services would best be accomplished by using the Active Directory (AD), DNS, and Group Policy management packs. You might also consider implementing the Windows Server management packs as part of this, or perhaps prior to any of the other management packs.

- Alternatively, you may decide to focus first on monitoring your messaging environment. This would include using one or more of the Exchange-related management packs. As mentioned in this section, Exchange has dependencies on Active Directory, so monitoring Exchange could include monitoring AD.

The order in which you implement management packs really depends on the priorities of your organization and your goals for monitoring.

REAL WORLD: IMPLEMENTING MANAGEMENT PACKS

It is best to deploy a single management pack at a time. This practice makes it easier to deal with management pack issues as they occur. When you have more than one management pack involved, it may be difficult to determine what initially caused a problem.

Initial Tuning: Tuning by Function

Presume you have determined your strategy and order for deploying management packs and have started to import selected management packs one at a time into your preproduction environment. As part of your approach, you should refer to the management pack guide for each management pack. Management pack guides discuss particulars for installing, configuring, and tuning management packs. The management pack guides are often included in the download package with the management pack. For insight into the authors' experiences with implementing and tuning management packs, see Appendix A, "OpsMgr by Example: Configuring and Tuning Management Packs."

NOTE: IMPORTING MANAGEMENT PACKS

The process of importing management packs is described in the "Importing Management Packs" section.

You will want to perform some initial tuning, as testing and tuning in a non-production environment is always advisable prior to unleashing something new into production. Testing at this point also helps minimize the information load and unnecessary work for your production computer operators.

After evaluating a management pack's behavior, you may decide to tune one or more monitors or rules to meet your organization's needs. As an example, you may find a performance monitor generating an alert at a threshold value inappropriate for your environment. You can tune that setting by overriding the default settings for that monitor.

TIP: MANAGING ALERTS

As you implement a management pack, it will generate alerts that you will want to review and evaluate for tuning. Some rules and monitors may generate low severity alerts; depending on your environment, these may not be worth investigating or resolving, and you may consider disabling that rule or monitor.

For sealed management packs, the option to uncheck the enabled check box in the general properties sheet is grayed-out; go to the Overrides tab of the object and select the Disable button. You can choose whether to disable the action for all objects of that type, a group, a specific object or type, or all objects of another type.

Changes are saved to an unsealed management pack. Remember that you can document your actions using the Company Knowledge section of the object.

A suggested approach for tuning a management pack is to work on a server-by-server or application-by-application basis, tuning from the highest severity alerts and dependencies to the lowest. Here are several ways to approach this:

- A server-by-server approach addresses issues identified while deploying servers into Operations Manager.
- After addressing issues by server, the process should be an application-by-application/service-by-service basis, focusing on the overall health of the application or service. You can look at alerts first, and then open the Health Explorer to drill down specifically into the problem.
- Consider dependencies. If your example is to monitor DNS, AD, and Exchange, you would first implement and tune the DNS management pack because Active Directory and Exchange are dependent on DNS.
- Limit which object types display using the Scope feature, which applies a temporary filter. Select the **Scope** button on the Operations console toolbar, and the Change View Scope dialog box displays, as shown in Figure 13.15.

  This box displays a list of existing groups and distributed applications. If the list is long, you can find a specific group or application by entering a word or phrase in the Look for box, also shown in the figure. After making your selection, click **OK**; only the objects meeting your scope criteria display in the results pane. (To remove the scope, click the **X** at the top-right corner of the scoping area at the top of the results pane.)

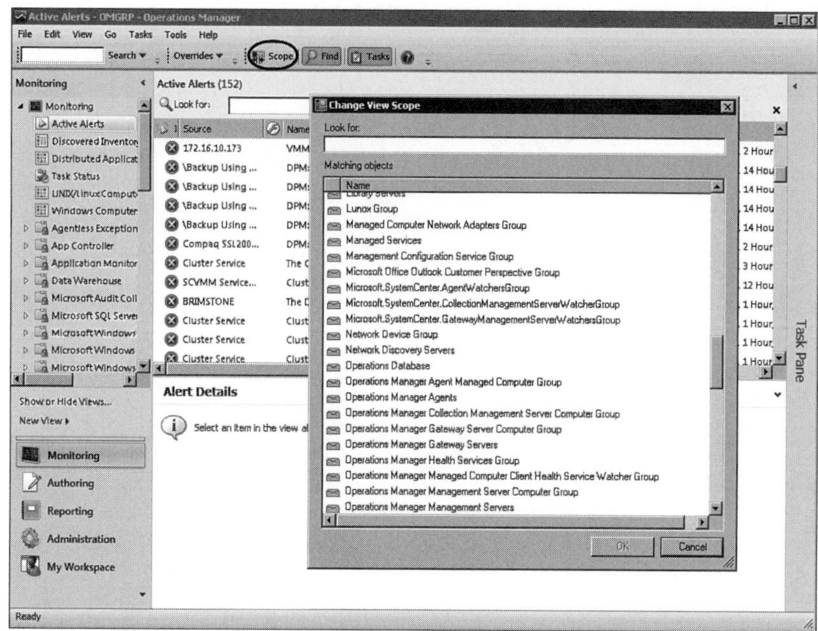

FIGURE 13.15 Changing the viewing scope.

- While the Active Alerts view provides detailed information, the State view and Health Explorer are better methods for monitoring and seeing the high-level health of your management group. As an example, you can select Windows Computers in the Monitoring space to show the servers running Windows, along with the monitored state areas with their health status (see Figure 13.16). You can then right-click any listed system to open other views or the Health Explorer for that system, also shown in Figure 13.16.

  Opening the Health Explorer for Hannibal lets you view the various monitors associated with that rollup monitor, enabling you to view associated information and check the properties for that monitor. Figure 13.17 shows the Health Explorer for Hannibal.

- You should also investigate which events are sent to the management server. In the Monitoring pane, right-click **Monitoring** and select **New -> Event View**. Give the view a name and optional description, and choose under the criteria (see Figure 13.18) if you want to limit the events returned.

  Review the console regularly to see whether events captured are unnecessary for your particular environment, as this could take up an excessive amount of storage in Operations Manager. Use the Monitoring section of the Operations console to disable or override unnecessary events. Using the Event view just created, right-click on a specific event, and select to disable or override the rule, as shown in Figure 13.19.

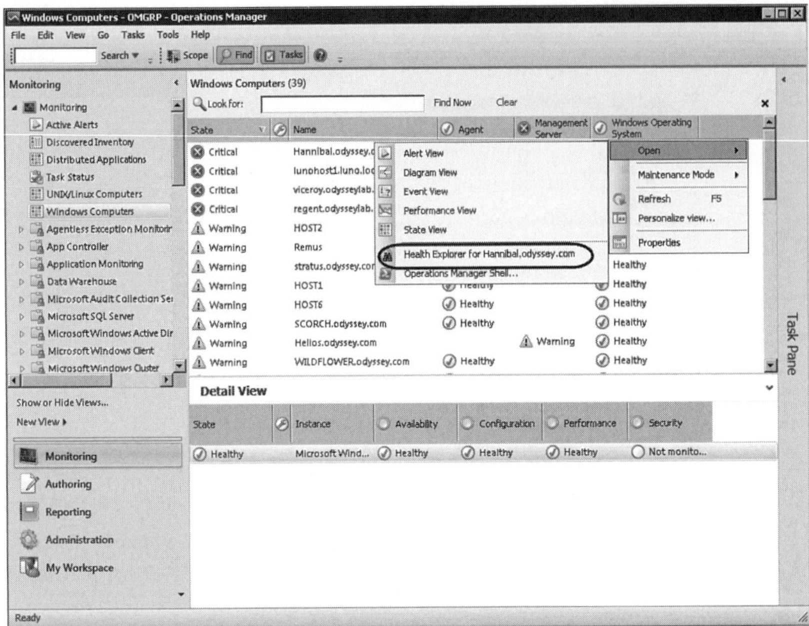

FIGURE 13.16 Viewing server health in the State view.

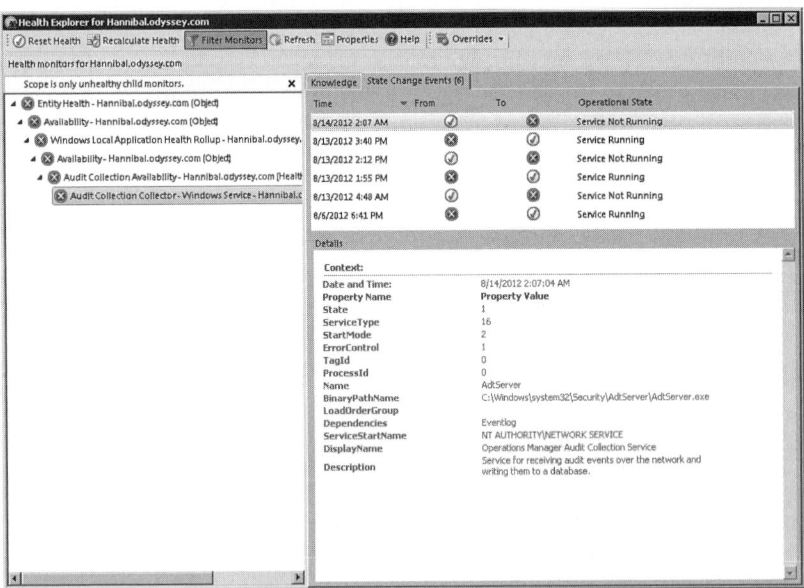

FIGURE 13.17 Viewing monitor health in the Health Explorer.

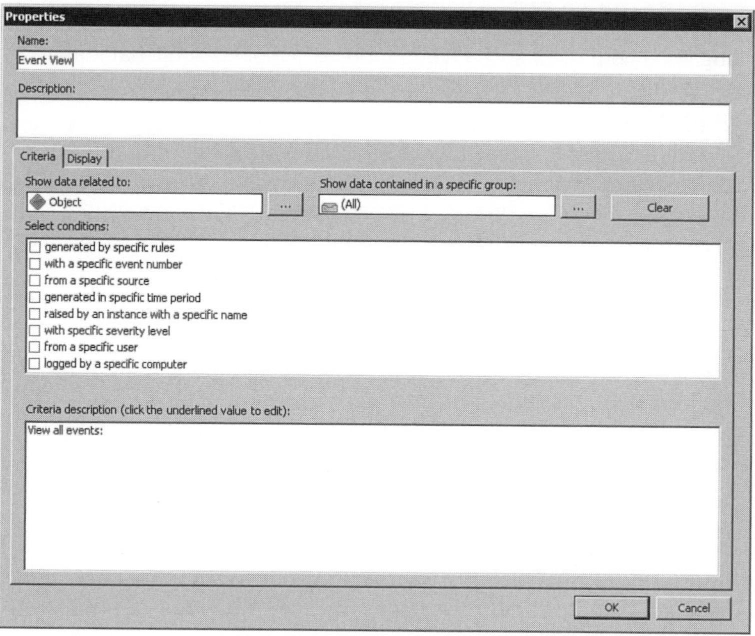

FIGURE 13.18 Creating a view for events.

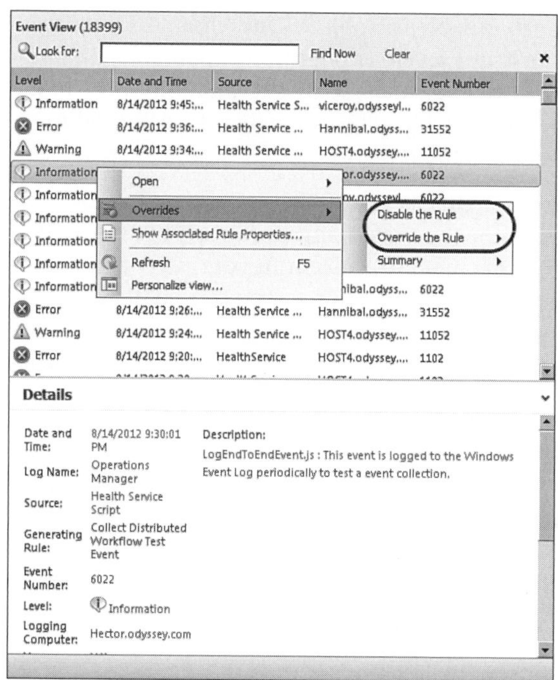

FIGURE 13.19 Disable or override a rule generating an event.

TIP: WHERE DOES ALL THAT DATA GO?

Remember that everything seen here uses space somewhere in the operational database. If the information is not relevant, you should adjust the underlying monitors, rules, or conditions so it is no longer collected.

After you have resolved alerts and events in each function and management pack, implement the next management pack on your list. After it is functional, work through the Operations console, changing the viewing scope as discussed previously in this section.

Tuning Thoughts

Here are some general guidelines for testing and tuning management packs:

- Review any new alerts reported for the server monitored with the new management pack. Operations Manager includes the Alerts and Most Common Alerts reports to help you discover your most common alerts. These reports are under **Reporting -> Microsoft Generic Report Library**. If alerts are occurring, there are several actions to consider:
    - **Resolve the issue generating the alert:** View the product knowledge base information regarding the specific error that is occurring. When a management pack is first installed, it typically uncovers a multitude of previously unknown issues in your environment. Monitor the alerts to determine potential areas of concern.
    - **Override the monitor or rule:** Go to the specific object for that management pack in the Authoring space of the Operations console; open its properties sheet, and under the Overrides tab, disable the object. Only disable a monitor or rule after concluding the issue is not severe enough to warrant an alert, and that you do not need to be made aware of the specific situation monitored for that object type or group. Some rules are initially disabled when delivered in management packs because they may not apply in all situations.
    - **Change the threshold of a monitor that is generating an alert:** This is applicable when you want to monitor the underlying condition, but the alert is generated before the condition is actually a problem in your particular environment. Consider this option if the monitor is not a good candidate for an override or disable/enable. An example of where this may occur would be free space thresholds for databases monitored by the SQL Server management pack.

      Since OpsMgr incorporates self-tuning thresholds, in some instances the software will do this for you.

TIP: WHICH RULE IS IT?

Identify the rule of interest by opening the alert in the Monitoring space and looking in the Alert Details pane in the bottom section of the Active Alerts section. The Details pane includes a hypertext link to the properties page of the rule. You can also run a PowerShell command to search on the display name of the rule (or by wildcard by surrounding the string with asterisks):

```
Get-SCOMRule -DisplayName '*<displayname>*'
```

- If a new management pack generates many alerts, you may want to disable monitors or rules in that management pack. You can turn them on gradually, making the new management pack easier to tune and troubleshoot.

How Long to Tune?

There is no simple logic about how long to tune a management pack. Evaluate and tune each management pack until you are comfortable with its functionality and behavior. This may include resolving any outstanding alerts that are not actual problem indicators or adjusting underlying rules and alerts for issues not significant in your environment. You probably will want to go through a full application production cycle for your applications in each area being examined:

- For example, if you are tuning the SQL Server management pack and have heavy month-end processing activity, go through a month-end cycle to see whether OpsMgr turns up anything unexpected.
- Gauge the effect of any new application added to your environment. Are new alerts being generated?
- Tune and test the impact of any new management pack or new version of an existing management pack.

After you complete initial tuning, you may want to continue to tune management packs after they are in production or when new applications are introduced into your server environment.

HOW MANY TEST ENVIRONMENTS ARE NECESSARY?

The Operations Manager 2012 Operations Guide speaks of a preproduction management group that is multi-homed, where agents on the production network can belong to the preproduction management group. This gives you a testing bed of real data (or at least real-life monitoring). This is a great way to test some of the capabilities of new MPs before they go into production.

However, for any new management pack not previously tested (including those written in-house!), you would want to first import it into an isolated environment. This is because there could be a rule or monitor that needs some serious tuning (or is just misconfigured), which produces a significant amount of network activity generating alerts or performance counters. If you are multi-homing the computers in your production network, you could generate more traffic on your production network segments than would be acceptable.

Here's an approach you may want to consider:

1. Maintain an isolated test environment. Import your MP(s) and do some initial testing and tuning.
2. Export out any customizations, and import those along with the sealed MP(s) into the preproduction environment. Test again, using the multi-homed agents.
3. When you have a comfort level (and a backup plan in place just in case), export the customizations from your preproduction environment. Import those along with the sealed MP(s) into production.

While this may seem onerous or hardware heavy, you only need to "get bit" once to change your mind! Also, consider using virtual machines for your test and preproduction servers to help save on hardware costs.

Troubleshooting Recap

To recap some key approaches for managing management packs:

- Introduce management packs one-by-one into your management group, to isolate changes more easily in performance and behavior.
- Only install the management packs you need. MPs increase the load on the management servers; they also increase the size of the agent on any computers targeted by the management pack.
- Work with your in-house experts for each application to understand how the rules will function in your particular organization; you may decide to disable some monitors or modify threshold limits that would trigger an alert. (Chapter 14 describes the structure of an alert.)
- Identify rules and monitors that are generating the most activity and focus on understanding what is occurring. Use Microsoft's reports you can use to start investigating your most common alerts and issues, located in the Microsoft Generic Report Library. Figure 13.20 lists the Generic Report Library reports available with OpsMgr 2012.

FIGURE 13.20 Operational Health Analysis reports in the Generic Report Library.

After identifying the system generating the messages, you need to determine what is generating those events and how to resolve unnecessary alerts—which can include disabling rules or monitors, using overrides, or utilizing consolidation rules.

TIP: DETERMINE HOW MUCH DATA YOU ARE COLLECTING

A quick way to find out how many event and performance records are in the operational database is by running these two SQL queries:

```
SELECT count(*) as COUNT from eventview
SELECT count(*) as COUNT from performancecounterview
```

- The Agent Send Queue may be full; this can be indicated by event IDs of 21006, 2024, and 2034. You can modify the size of the send queue by changing a registry value on the affected agent:

  ```
  HKLM\SYSTEM\CurrentControlSet\services\HealthService\Parameters\Management
  Groups\<ManagementGroupName>\MaximumQueueSizeKb
  ```

  <ManagementGroupName> is the name of the management group to which the agent reports. The agent queue size is 15,360KB by default. Restart the System Center Management service on the agent-managed system for the changes to take effect.

REAL WORLD: THE QUEUE IS FULL ERROR

A stopgap approach to dealing with a full queue is to increase the temporary storage settings on the affected system. The authors do not recommend this other than for debugging purposes. Increasing the queue size is only a short-term solution; if the underlying problem is not corrected, the queue eventually fills again.

Now that initial approaches for tuning your management packs have been discussed, let's look at the process to move management packs with their changes from a preproduction to production environment. Remember, the recommended approach for implementing management packs is to test them in a preproduction environment, make tuning changes as necessary, and then import your customized management packs into your production OpsMgr environment.

Exporting Management Packs

The Operations console allows you to export any unsealed management pack. Use the Export function to back up or move management packs from one system to another (such as from test to production). Perform the following steps:

1. In the Operations console, navigate to **Administration -> Management Packs.** Highlight the management pack you want to export, right-click, and select **Export Management Pack**. This example selects the Virtual Machine Manager Overrides management pack. You can also select **the Export Management Pack** option from the Tasks pane. Both options are highlighted in Figure 13.21.

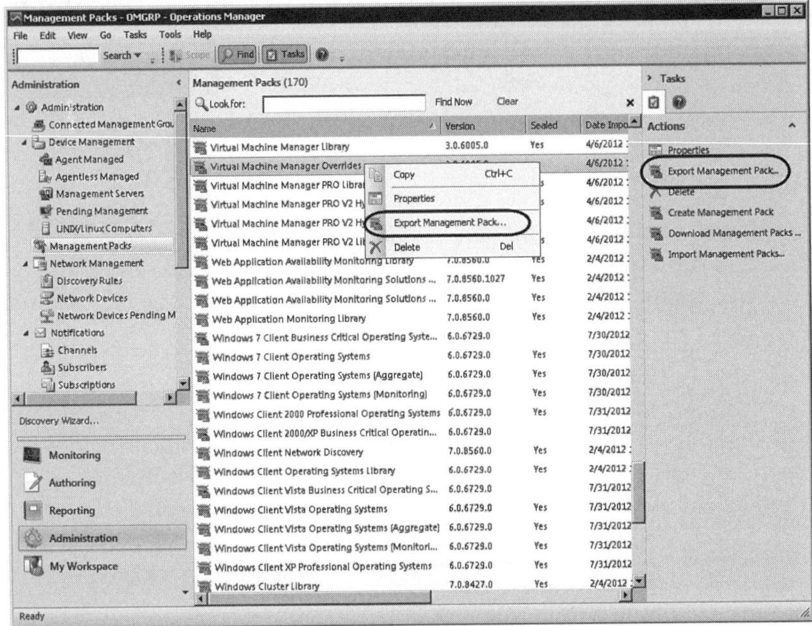

FIGURE 13.21 Select the management pack you want to export.

2. You are asked to browse to or create the folder into which to export the management pack. Select the folder, and the management pack is exported, with the success message displayed as in Figure 13.22. You do not get to specify the name of the exported file.

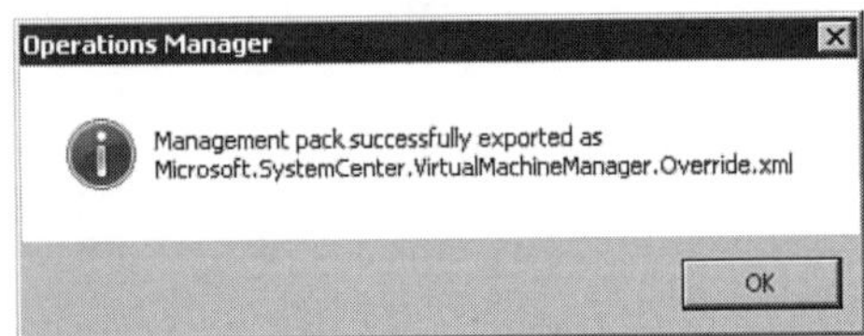

FIGURE 13.22 Successful export of unsealed management pack.

You can also export management packs in a batch mode, using PowerShell. Chapter 12 describes PowerShell export procedures.

With the management pack exported from your test environment, your next step is importing it to a production management server and integrating the management pack into the targeted management group.

VIEWING SEALED MANAGEMENT PACKS

You can find management packs in XML format in several places:

- On a monitored agent, look in the *%ProgramFiles%*\System Center Operations Manager\Agent\Health Service State\Management Packs folder. The sealed management packs are pushed down to the agent and stored in raw XML format, allowing you to look through them and glean what you can from them.
- The *%ProgramFiles%*\System Center 2012\Operations Manager\Server\Health Service State\Management Packs\ folder on a management server has management packs in XML format.

Chapter 12 also discusses approaches for exporting sealed management packs.

Importing Management Packs

The Administration space in the Operations console is used to import management packs. You can also use the `Import-SCOMManagementPack` PowerShell cmdlet, introduced in Chapter 7, "Configuring and Using System Center 2012 Operations Manager," to bulk import management packs.

REAL WORLD: GUIDELINES WHEN IMPORTING MANAGEMENT PACKS

Murphy's Law, which states that if anything could go wrong, it might, definitely can come into play when importing management packs. To minimize the impact of human error, here are some tips to keep in mind:

- Only replace an existing production management pack with one you have checked out in your test or preproduction environment.
- If you are importing a newer version of a previously imported unsealed management pack, be sure you have a backup of your production version, enabling you to return to your former management pack state by importing the backup should that become necessary.
- If you modify any of the original vendor rules or monitors, use an override to disable the original rule—you will be making your changes to a copy of the rule in an unsealed, custom management pack.

If you obtain management packs through the System Center Marketplace, extract the contents of the package into files that can be utilized by Operations Manager. Copy the executable package to a system with the Operations console installed and run the package to extract the files to the file system. Extract to the same server and folder all management packs you want to import in order to simplify the installation process later.

Packages contain one or more management packs (with an extension of .MP or .XML if management packs are unsealed), and may include documentation such as a management pack guide or readme file.

You can import management packs using the Operations console or with PowerShell, discussed in the next sections.

Using the Operations Console

To import a management pack, open the Operations console and perform the following steps:

1. Navigate to **Administration** -> **Management Packs**. Right-click and select **Import Management Packs** to start the Import Management Packs Wizard.

   You can also select the **Import Management Packs** option from the Tasks pane on the right-hand side of the console. Both options are highlighted in Figure 13.23.

2. Click **Add** in the wizard to select a management pack to import. You can add from the management pack catalog or from disk:

   - Selecting **Add from catalog** lets you query Microsoft's management pack catalog directly from the Operations console, rather than going through System Center Marketplace.

     Enter a search string in the Find: box and select whether you want to search all management packs in the catalog, updates available for installed management packs, or management packs released within the last 3 or 6 months. Click **Search** to return the catalog listing matching your criteria. From the data returned, you can select the management packs you want to add, and then click **Add** to add them to the list of management packs to import. Figure 13.24 shows SQL Server 2008 management packs selected for import. Click **OK**.

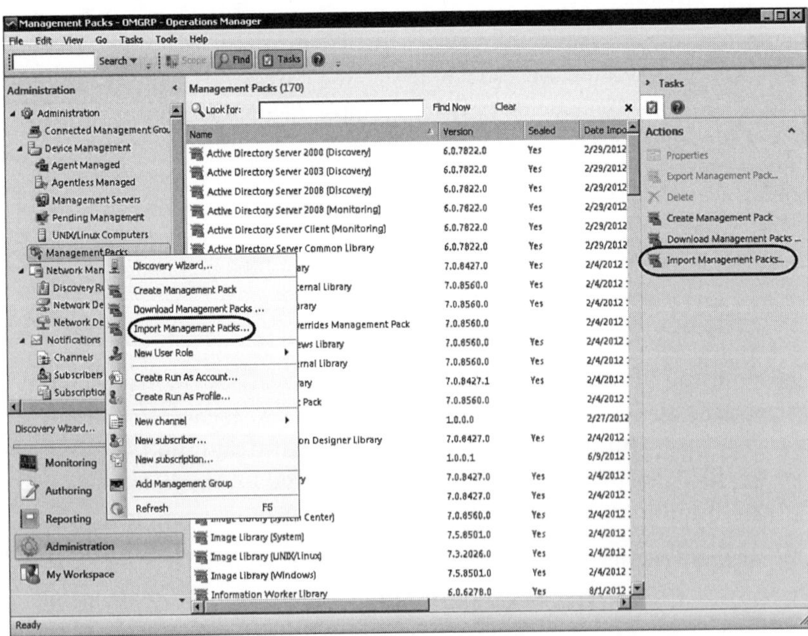

FIGURE 13.23 Begin the process to import a management pack.

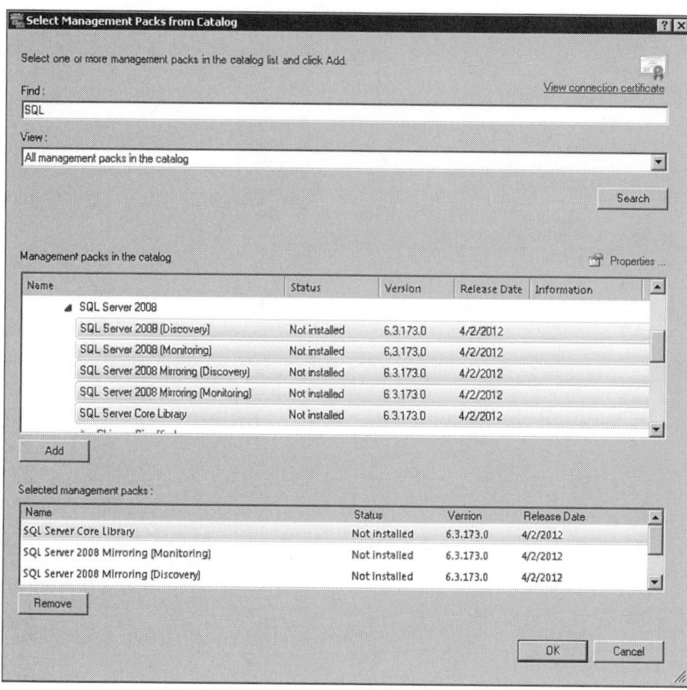

FIGURE 13.24 Selecting management packs from the catalog through the Operations console.

Figure 13.25 shows the selected management packs ready to import. Notice you can continue to add management packs to the import list by clicking **Add** again. Click **Install** to begin the installation process.

- Selecting **Add from disk** lets you import previously downloaded management packs or management packs exported from another environment such as test or preproduction.

  You will be prompted as to whether you want to search the online catalog for dependencies should you select management packs with dependencies that cannot be located locally.

  The Select Management Packs to import dialog opens, where you can navigate the file system for the management packs you wish to import. After selecting management packs of interest, click **Add** to continue to add additional management packs from the catalog or from disk. When you complete selecting management packs, click **Install** to begin the installation process.

3. If a management pack has dependencies on another management pack not already loaded to the management group or in the list to import, you will receive an error.
4. Figure 13.26 shows management packs being imported. A green check mark indicates success.
5. Click **Close** when installation is complete.

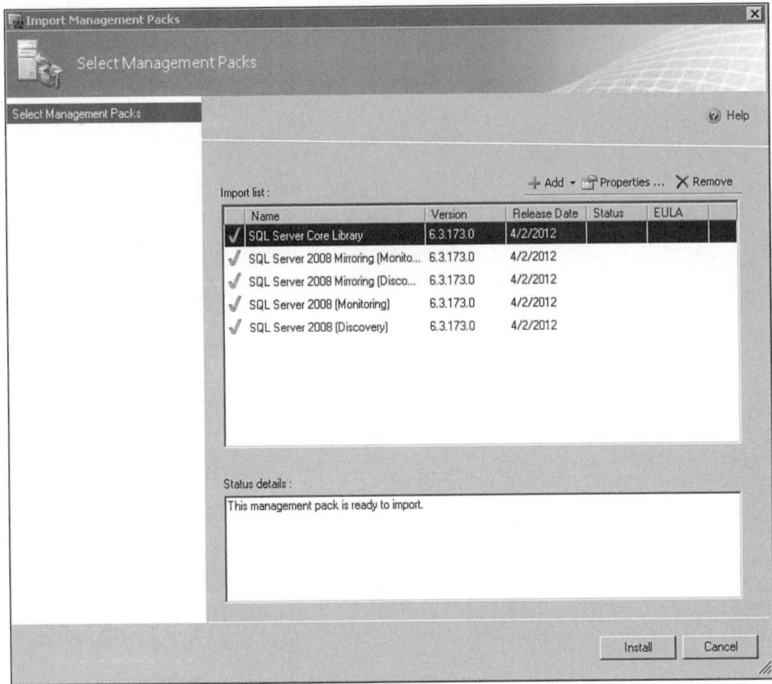

FIGURE 13.25 Management packs ready for import.

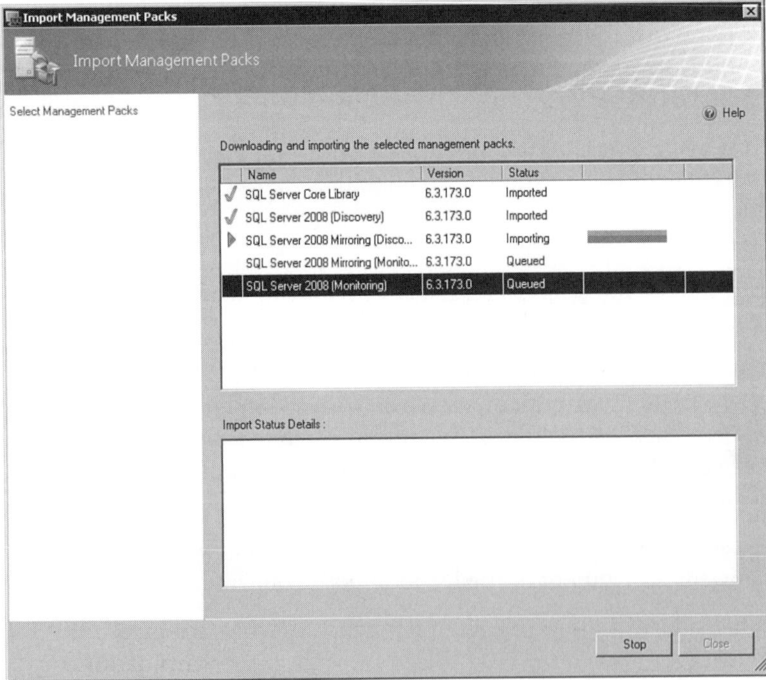

FIGURE 13.26 Management packs ready for import.

Using PowerShell Cmdlets

PowerShell gives OpsMgr administrators the capability to automate many activities using script files with cmdlets. You can create a text file with an editor such as Notepad, where each line contains an `Import-SCOMManagementPack` PowerShell cmdlet to import a management pack into your management group in batch mode. This capability allows you to schedule maintenance activities during off-hours and have a record of your steps for change control purposes.

As an example, the PowerShell syntax for importing the Windows Server Operating System Customizations management pack would be as follows:

```
Import-SCOMManagementPack
<path>Windows.Server.OperatingSystem.Customizations.xml
```


Deploying Changes

The enabled settings in your imported management packs begin monitoring as soon as they are deployed to an agent; these updates occur as needed.

TIP: INFORMATION ON AGENTS

OpsMgr agents are discussed in Chapter 8, "Installing and Configuring Agents."

Verifying the Management Pack Installation

After installing a management pack, you will see changes in several areas of the Operations console:

- At Administration -> Management Packs, the Details section in the center of the console shows the name of your new management pack.
- At Authoring -> Groups, you will see any new groups related to the management pack. Under the Management Pack Objects node, new attributes, monitors, object discoveries, overrides, rules, service level tracking, tasks, and views will be visible if these were included in the management pack.

NOTE: MORE ABOUT ATTRIBUTES

An OpsMgr attribute can check the registry or a WMI query; this is controlled by the discovery type. When creating an attribute, you must specify an object type as its target. The object type can include a number of attributes, such as a number of registry values. You could then create a group with a dynamic inclusion rule for servers with only that object type.

- The Monitoring space displays the results of monitoring. It contains folders and views defined by each imported management pack.

  On the left side under the Monitoring node, you should see a folder structure for your new management pack; it will have subfolders for any alerts, events, tasks, and other objects defined by the new management pack.

- If the Reporting feature is installed and the management pack import included reports, the Reporting space lists reports for that management pack.

Managing Management Packs

This section looks at several utilities and management packs that assist in managing management packs.

TIP: CONFIGURING FOR A FIREWALL

If your organization has a firewall, ensure the web browser settings on the server you will be using include appropriate proxy information. See Chapter 10 for additional information.

System Center Internal Library

The System Center Internal Library MP helps analyze which rules and monitors are running for a server and which rules and monitors have failed. This management pack is loaded into OpsMgr during installation and adds four tasks to the Health Services Task pane:

- Show Failed Rules and Monitors for this Health Service
- Show Running Rules and Monitors for this Health Service
- Start Online Store Maintenance
- Flush Health Service State and Cache

These tasks are displayed in the Operations console when you navigate to **Monitoring** -> **Operations Manager** -> **Agent Details** -> **Agent Health State** and select a monitored computer.

System Center Core Monitoring Agent Management

The System Center Core Monitoring Agent Management MP, loaded into OpsMgr during the installation process, extends monitoring by providing diagnostics and recoveries related to agent management. By default, all recoveries that involve automated remediation are initially disabled. If a problem or alert occurs on a monitored server, this management pack can restart, restore, or even reinstall the agent on the monitored device, depending on the diagnostic conditions of the remote agent and if the recoveries are enabled.

Before OpsMgr can automatically recover agents, you must add a Run As account to the Automatic Agent Management Account Run As profile. This Run As account must have administrator-level access on the target computers. OpsMgr uses the management server action account if you do not add a Run As account.

Viewing Management Pack Content and Overrides

Because management packs are written in XML, it can be daunting to try to view and understand the content. This is particularly the case with overrides. For OpsMgr 2007, Boris Yanushpolsky of the OpsMgr product team developed several utilities to assist with viewing management pack content. These have been updated for OpsMgr 2012 by Daniele Muscetta and can be downloaded from http://blogs.msdn.com/b/dmuscett/archive/2012/02/19/boris-s-tools-updated.aspx.

- To view management pack content, use MPViewer 2.1. MPViewer has a graphical view as well as a raw XML view. Version 2.1 includes support for .mpb files, including the ability to unseal and unpack MP bundles (this is currently limited to bundles that contain a single management pack).
- The Override Explorer can assist specifically with overrides. It provides two views, type-based and computer-based.
    - The type-based view shows types for rules, monitors, and discoveries for which overrides were created.
    - The computer-based view is basically a resultant set of overrides that apply to a computer. It also allows you to drill in and see what overrides are applied to various components such as the operating system, databases, and websites.

Listing All Management Packs Associated with a Server

You can use PowerShell to list all management packs associated with a server using the `Get-SCOMRule` cmdlet. Follow these steps to extract the list to a CSV file:

1. Open the Command Shell (**Start** -> **All Programs** -> **Microsoft System Center 2012** -> **Operations Manager** -> **Operations Manager Shell**).
2. In the command window, type the following:

```
Get-SCOMRule  | select-object @{Name="MP";Expression={ foreach-object
➥{$_.GetManagementPack().DisplayName }}},DisplayName | sort-object -property MP
➥ | export-csv "c:\rules.csv"
```

You can open the c:\rules.csv file using Excel, and it will have two columns of information: the name of the management pack and a display name.

Fast Track

While many of the concepts related to management pack administration are similar to Operations Manager 2007, here are key takeaways from this chapter:

- The Default management pack is no longer the default when creating new objects in the Operations console. It should be used only when creating common elements such as views at the top level of a workspace.

- MP bundles are now supported in OpsMgr 2012.
- Beginning with OpsMgr 2007 R2, the ability to download management packs from Microsoft's management pack catalog is integrated into the Operations console.

Summary

This chapter introduced you to management packs and tuning techniques. It discussed the process to implement management packs and best practices for deployment. The next chapter looks at how OpsMgr 2012 manages systems by using the various monitors and rule types you find in its management packs. It also discusses monitoring tips and techniques you can use.

CHAPTER 14

Monitoring with System Center 2012 Operations Manager

IN THIS CHAPTER

- The Importance of Monitoring
- About Rules
- Using Monitors
- About Alerts
- Adding Knowledge
- Locating Rules and Monitors in the Operations Console
- Using Overrides
- Creating Custom Resolution States
- Maintenance Tuning
- Maintenance Mode in OpsMgr
- Resource Kit Utilities
- Fast Track

System Center Operations Manager 2012 (OpsMgr) facilitates monitoring of servers, clients, applications, operating systems, network devices, and business services, using a combination of built-in technology and third-party additions. The monitoring architecture of Operations Manager 2012 is basically unchanged from OpsMgr 2007. Rules and monitors can generate alerts within Operations Manager. Rules and monitors, together with everything else needed for monitoring, are assembled into management packs, which are grouped by application or operating system, such as the Windows Server 2012 and Exchange 2010 management packs.

Chapter 13, "Administering Management Packs," discusses the structure of a management pack. This chapter discusses rules, monitors, and alerts (defined in Table 14.1), including the process for locating them in a complex environment. It also discusses providers; these dictate the data OpsMgr will collect. This chapter also discusses methods available to store company knowledge for Operations Manager. Using overrides enables you to change the default behavior of a management pack; this chapter explains the process to create an override and locate a previously created override. The chapter completes with a discussion of approaches to monitor and tune alerts in OpsMgr.

TABLE 14.1 Primary monitoring objects used by OpsMgr 2012

Object	Description
Rules	Rules define what you want to monitor. They define the data to collect, and describe how to process and respond to that data.
Monitors	Monitors represent the state of individual components of a system. They gather data from events, performance counters, scripts, and other sources such as Windows services. You can configure monitors to "roll up" their state; this allows for the creation of dependencies that assist in accurate mapping and monitoring of complex and distributed systems. Monitors can generate changes in state and perform diagnostic and recovery tasks based on that change.
Alerts	Alerts are raised by either rules or monitors and call attention to issues that are occurring. Although monitors and state changes are more prevalent than alerts in Operations Manager 2012, using alerts provides additional information to an issue by interfacing with the OpsMgr knowledge base. An alert generated by a monitor in OpsMgr could be automatically resolved when the monitor returns to normal, reflecting the fact that the issue no longer exists.

The Importance of Monitoring

Information Technology (IT) systems are continually evolving and adapting to changes in business requirements. The continual evolution and change of business systems often results in an increase in potential issues within IT systems. As businesses become increasingly more reliant on their IT systems, these issues are more noticeable and failures have a greater impact. Ensuring your systems are working correctly is a difficult and time-consuming task, particularly in a distributed environment.

Traditional monitoring for IT systems tends to be reactive, with problems unidentified until there is a noticeable impact. Businesses need to know what problems will occur in advance so they can be proactively resolved. With the ever-increasing automation of systems and reliance on the cloud, reactive response to issues is unacceptable in today's business and IT environments. Operations Manager 2012 provides a means to consolidate and automate system monitoring and maintenance into a single user interface where you can identify potential issues early on. This capability enables you to address and resolve a large number of issues before they affect your production systems!

OpsMgr collects data from monitored systems about the operational health state of each computer and the applications and components that make up those systems, including hard drives and databases. This data enables an accurate and up-to-date overview of your IT environment. In addition, OpsMgr is able to initiate scripts and responses based on a schedule or meeting a condition, such as a certain event appearing in a monitored system's Windows event log.

In complex environments with a large number of installed management packs, the number of rules and monitors can run into the thousands, making management cumbersome. This makes it critical to tune the alerts in OpsMgr and minimize the number of non-actionable alerts appearing in the Monitoring section of the console. While the use of monitors, first introduced in OpsMgr 2007, makes this process significantly less difficult than before, tuning is still an essential part of any OpsMgr deployment.

The process of tuning involves adjusting thresholds or disabling rules and monitors that are not required. To assist in this effort, this chapter begins with focusing on the major types of rules and monitors available in Operations Manager 2012.

About Rules

Rules exist to perform various functions. Although monitors have been available since the release of OpsMgr 2007, rules are still a key part of monitoring. Rules are used where it is not appropriate to create a monitor—and a large amount of OpsMgr monitoring continues to utilize rules.

TIP: INTERVIEWING QUESTION—THE DIFFERENCE BETWEEN A RULE AND A MONITOR

A common "weed-out" question in Operations Manager is *what is the difference between a rule and a monitor*? There are several differences but here are some primary ones to consider:

- Rules do not affect state. Monitors do impact state.
- Rules that generate alerts do not auto-close the alert when the condition causing the alert has been resolved.
- Monitors have a repeatable start and end point and can self-heal due to the expected end point. Rules have a start point but do not have an end point, so they cannot self-heal.
- Monitors do not collect performance data. Rules can collect performance data.

While there are many other differences between rules and monitors, this is a good start.

Rules exist primarily to generate alerts, collect performance data, execute timed tasks, and launch scripts. OpsMgr 2012 has three major rule types:

- Alert-generating rules
- Collection rules
- Timed commands

The next sections focus on these three different types of rules.

Alert-Generating Rules

You can use an alert-generating rule to generate an alert for a condition that does not call for a monitor (such as a backup success event, or when you do not want to impact health state but still need to monitor for the existence of a condition). A number of different providers are supported by alert-generating rules. Here is the list of alert-generating rule providers, which is similar to the list of providers available for monitors (discussed in the "Unit Monitors" section):

- **Generic CSV Text Log:** Collects log file entries from a generic text log file that uses a delimiter character to separate different fields.
- **Generic Text Log:** Collects log file entries that match a specified expression from a generic text log file that does not have a delimiter to separate different fields.
- **NT Event Log:** Collects Windows events from the various Windows event log files.
- **SNMP Trap:** Collects Simple Network Monitoring Protocol (SNMP) traps specified. Collection can occur for all traps or for specific SNMP Object Identifiers.
- **UNIX/Linux Shell:** Alerts on the filtered output from a UNIX/Linux shell command.
- **Syslog:** Collects syslog entries forwarded to the Windows computer that match a specified expression.
- **WMI Event:** Collects Windows Management Instrumentation (WMI) events that match a WMI Query Language (WQL) query.

The following procedure explains the process to create an alert rule by creating a basic Windows Event Log alert rule. The rule generates an alert if the Background Intelligent Transfer Service (BITS) service stops. Follow these steps:

1. Open the Operations console and navigate to **Authoring -> Monitoring Objects**.
2. Right-click **Rule** and select **Create New Rule** to initiate the Create Rule Wizard.
3. The wizard displays the Select a Rule Type dialog shown in Figure 14.1. From here, select **Alert Generating Rules -> Event Based -> NT Event Log (Alert)**.

   Event-based alert generating rules are not limited to alerts generated based from events occurring in Windows event logs; they can also be used for Generic CSV files, Generic Test logs, Snmp Traps, Syslog, UNIX/Linux Shell Commands, and WMI Events as shown in Figure 14.1.

   You must select a destination management pack to store the new rule you are creating. For this example, use **Sample Management Pack**. (If you need to create the management pack here, select **New** and enter the name of your new management pack.) Click **Next** to continue.

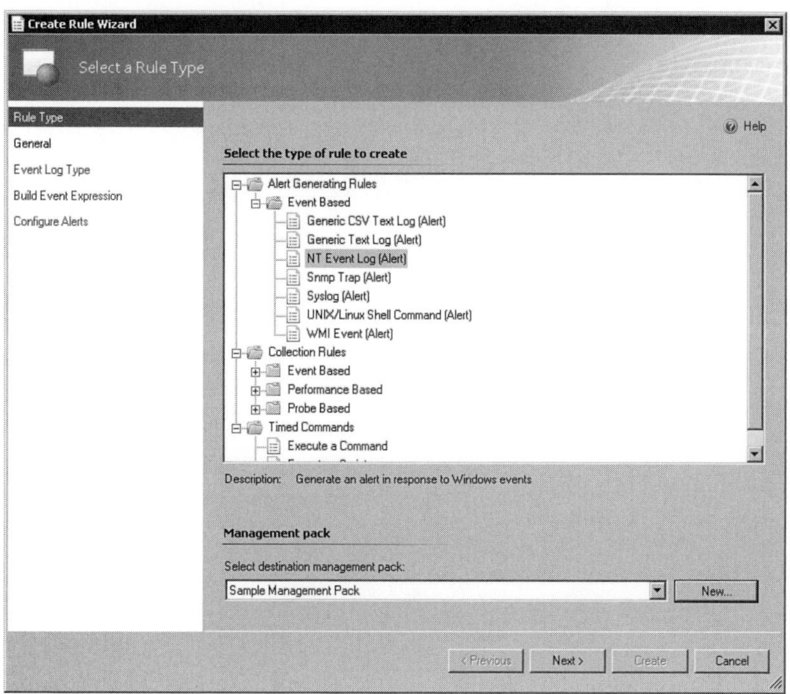

FIGURE 14.1 Alert rule selection page with the NT Event Log rule type selected.

4. In the General page of the Create Rule Wizard, name the rule and configure a target for the rule. Name this rule **Background Intelligent Transfer Service Stopped**. Target the `Windows Server Operating System` class so this rule will apply to all Windows servers. This page provides the option to enable (default) or disable the rule. When targeting to the generic classes (such as `Windows Server Operating System`) it is a best practice to disable the rule, and enable the rule for the group of servers to which the rule should apply.

   Figure 14.2 displays the completed Rule Name and Description page. Click **Next** to continue.

5. On the following page, select the Event log in which to look for the event. In this particular case, it is the System log. You can click the **...** button to browse and select the log, or you can simply type in the name of the log. Click **Next**.

6. At the next page, configure the condition to match for the alert rule. The condition is those items OpsMgr checks against to find the event when it appears in the event log. Figure 14.3 displays the event (Event ID 7036, from the source of Service Control Manager with the description `The Background Intelligent Transfer Service service entered the stopped state`) in the System event log.

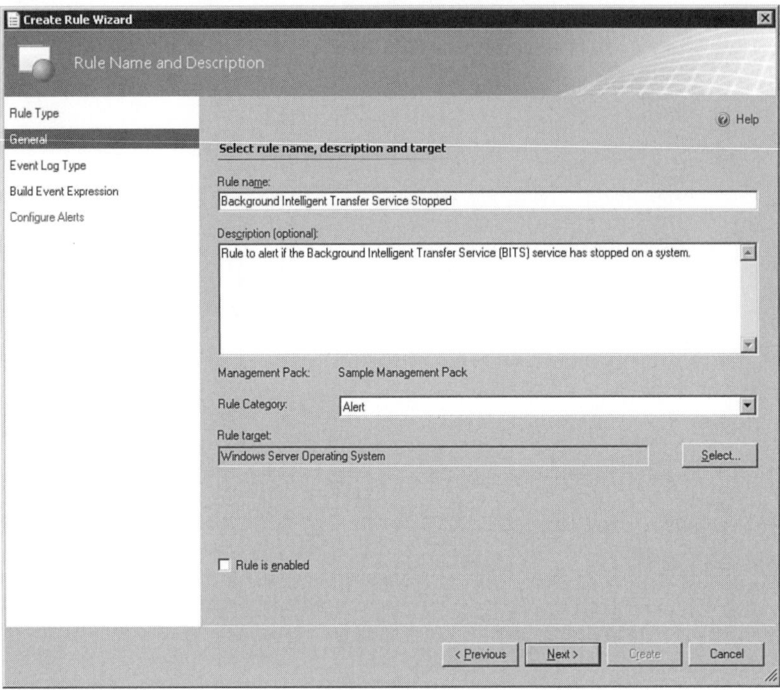

FIGURE 14.2 Defining the general properties of the rule.

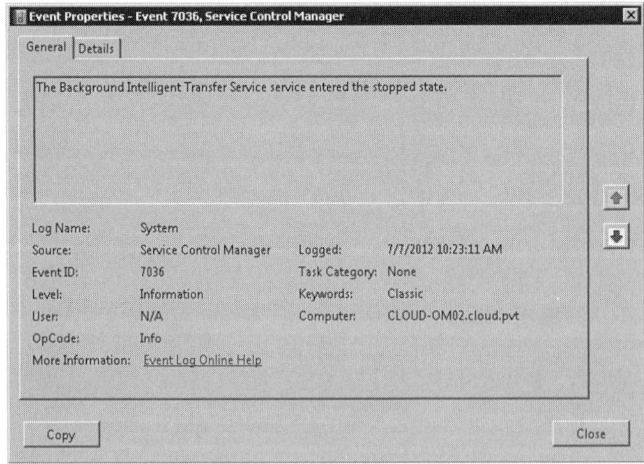

FIGURE 14.3 Background Intelligent Transfer Service event in the System event log.

7. Use the Build Event Expression page in the wizard to match the Event ID and Event Source parameters. Configure the Event ID as **Event ID Equals 7036** and the Event Source to be **Event Source Equals Service Control Manager**. This expression (known as a *filter*) is shown in Figure 14.4. Click **Next** to continue.

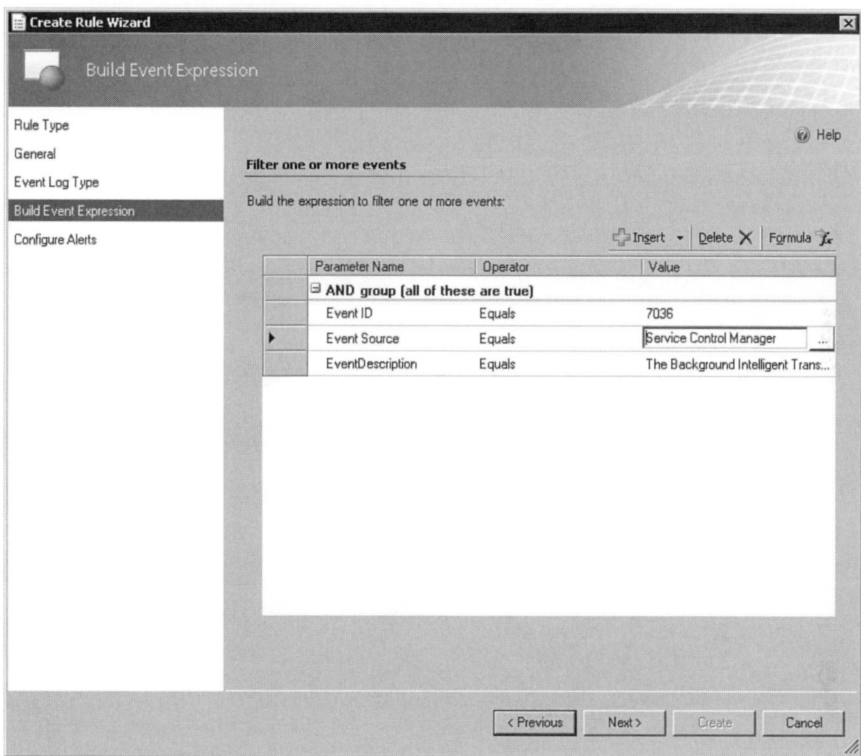

FIGURE 14.4 The Build Event Expression page completed.

8. The final page of the Create Rule Wizard configures the actual alert OpsMgr will generate. Leave the alert with the default name (Background Intelligent Transfer Service Stopped) and add the description text **This alert indicates the Background Intelligent Transfer Service has Stopped** (see Figure 14.5). Notice this rule has a Priority of **Medium** and a Severity level of **Warning** (the default is Critical; loss of this service would in most cases not be a critical situation). Click **Create** to create the new alert rule.

NOTE: CLOSING ALERTS

When you configure an alert using an alert-generating rule, the resulting alert does not close automatically, as is the case with alerts generated by monitors. You must close these alerts manually after resolving the root cause, or they will be auto-resolved after a set amount of time has passed based on your management group settings.

9. After this rule is created in a disabled state, use an override to enable this alert for the group of servers you want the alert to apply to, as shown in Figure 14.6.
10. Figure 14.7 shows an example of the alert created when the Background Intelligent Transfer Service was stopped on a system where this rule was enabled.

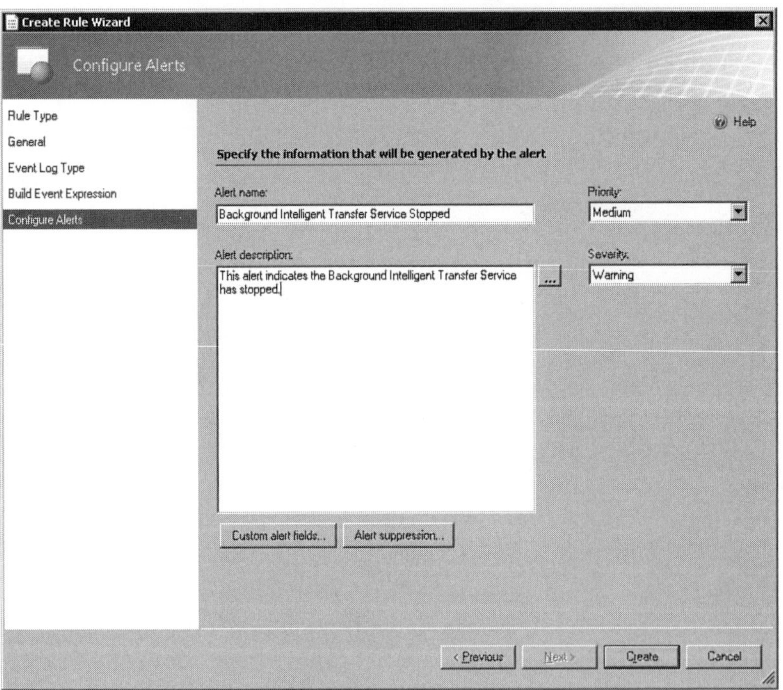

FIGURE 14.5 Configure Alerts page in the Create Rule Wizard.

FIGURE 14.6 Creating an override to enable the custom rule.

For services such as this, it may be more useful to use the Windows Service management pack template (discussed in Chapter 17, "Using Synthetic Transactions"). The template provides a simple user experience to create monitoring for a service, and generates required monitors and rules.

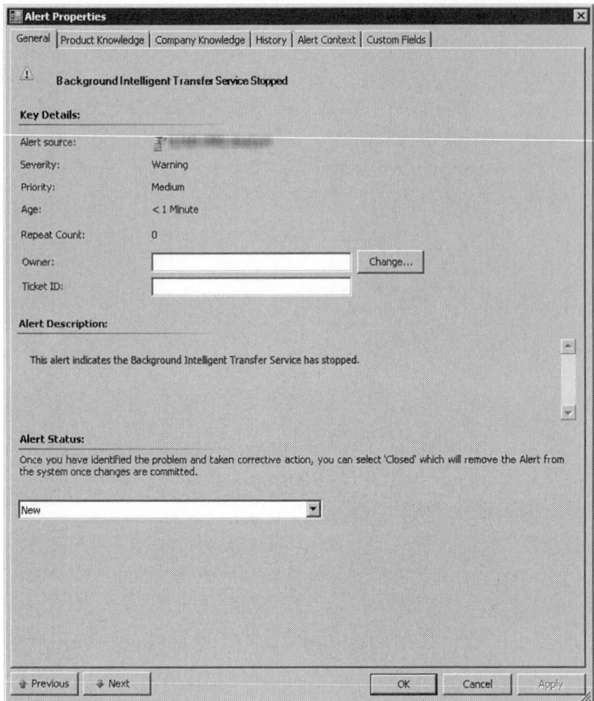

FIGURE 14.7 BITS service alert.

Collection Rules

Collecting data is an important function of rules. Whereas OpsMgr uses monitors to represent the health of a component based on an event or performance threshold, rules provide the means to collect this data for trending and reporting purposes.

You can configure collection rules to collect event or performance data and can additionally configure them to launch a script, which generates an event for collection. This is referred to as a *probe*. There are three different types of collection rules:

- Event based collection
- Performance based collection
- Probe based collection

The first of the collection rule types is used to gather event information.

Event Collection Rules

Event collection rules can collect information from a variety of sources, similar to alert-generating rules:

- **Generic CSV Text Log:** Collects log file entries from a generic text log file that uses a delimiter character to separate different fields.
- **Generic Text Log:** Collects log file entries that match a specified expression from a generic text log file that does not have a delimiter to separate different fields.
- **NT Event Log:** Collects Windows events from the various Windows event log files.
- **SNMP Event:** Collects a list of SNMP Object Identifiers.
- **SNMP Trap (Event):** Collects specified SNMP traps. Collection can occur for all traps or for specific SNMP Object Identifiers.
- **Syslog:** Collects syslog entries forwarded to the Windows computer that match a specified expression.
- **WMI Event:** Collects WMI events that match a WQL query.

Event collection rules are only required to collect the events, not to alert on the events. As shown in the example in the previous section that monitors for events for the Background Intelligent Transfer Service, OpsMgr can generate an alert based upon an event that occurs without actually collecting the event.

Event collection rules are commonly used to gather event information for custom applications. Once these events are collected, you can display them in a view in the Monitoring pane so application developers can see the events occurring within their application, across the servers where the application was installed.

Creating a Performance Collection Rule

Performance collection rules are the most commonly used collection rules. Use this rule type to collect performance data from three different sources in OpsMgr:

- **SNMP Performance:** Collects SNMP performance data. This source is used to gather performance information from devices (generally network devices) that OpsMgr can communicate with via SNMP.
- **WMI Performance:** Collects WMI performance data. This source is used when information is not available as part of the Windows performance counters. Kevin Holman provides an example in a blog posting at http://blogs.technet.com/b/kevinholman/archive/2008/07/02/collecting-and-monitoring-information-from-wmi-as-performance-data.aspx to gather the total number of processes running on a system.
- **Windows Performance:** Collects Windows performance data from performance counters available in the Performance Monitor tool. If your custom line of business applications is written to create Windows performance counters, Operations Manager can also gather these counters.

As Windows Performance collection rules are most often used, this section discusses the steps required to gather a performance counter not collected by OpsMgr by default. For this example, you will be collecting the % Processor Time counter for the IIS worker process (w3wp.exe). Perform the following steps:

1. In the Operations console, navigate to **Authoring** -> **Monitoring Objects**.
2. Right-click **Rules** and select **Create New Rule**.
3. The Create Rule Wizard displays the Select a Rule Type page. This is similar to the dialog shown in Figure 14.1, but here you are selecting **Collection Rules** -> **Performance Based** -> **Windows Performance** as the rule type. Select the **Sample Management Pack** you previously created as a target for the rule and click **Next** to continue.
4. On the Rule Name and Description page, name the rule and configure a target for it. For this example, the rule will be called **IIS worker process CPU Time**. Target the most specific existing class for this example, which is the `IIS Server Role` class. Since the rule is targeted to the most specific existing class, it can be enabled so it runs on all IIS servers (instead of creating the rule as disabled and enabling the rule for a group of systems).
5. Next, select the performance counter to collect. While you can type this manually, this is often confusing and time consuming. It is usually easier to browse and select the **Process** -> **% Processor Time** counter for the **w3wp** process (select instance from list). For this example, select the counter on **Typhoon**, as this is the server hosting the Web console in the Odyssey lab environment. Figure 14.8 shows the performance counter selected.

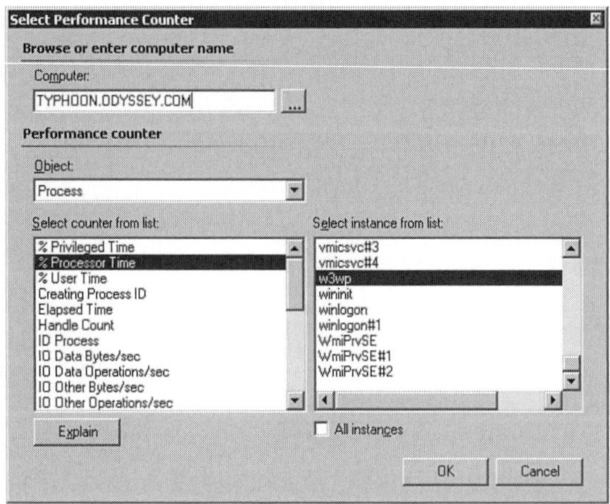

FIGURE 14.8 Selecting the performance counter for the w3wp process.

6. At the Performance Object, Counter, and Instance page (displayed in Figure 14.9), leave the collection interval at the default of 15 minutes. Click **Next** to continue to the final page of the wizard.
7. The last page of the wizard allows you to configure optimized collections. OpsMgr uses optimized collections to reduce the amount of disk space a performance counter collection uses in the data warehouse. This is explained in the "Optimized Collections" section. Click **Create** to create the performance collection rule.

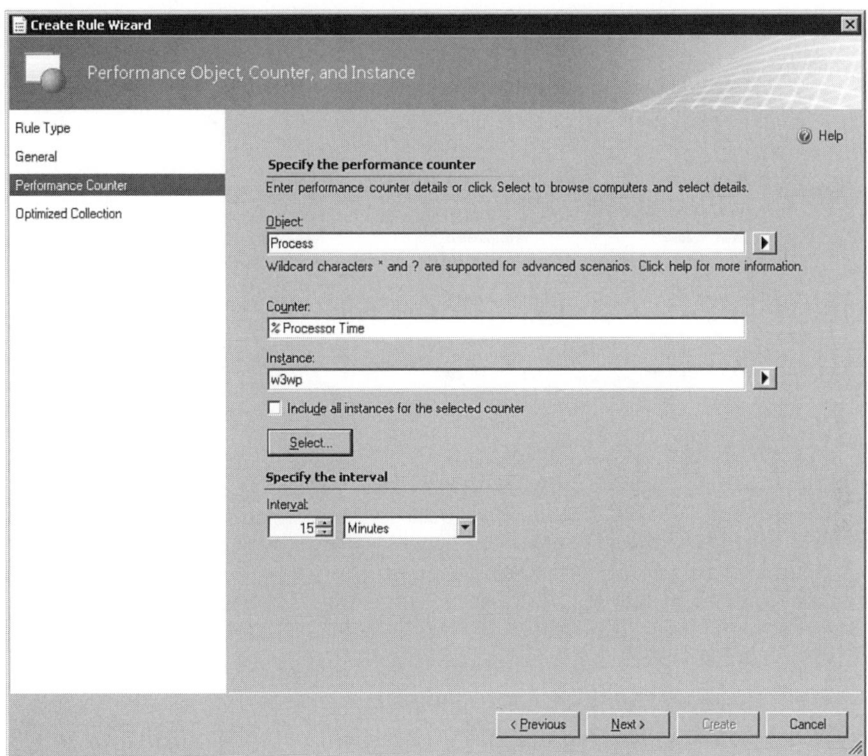

FIGURE 14.9 The counter collection page with all settings specified.

Optimized Collections

In Microsoft Operations Manager (MOM) 2005, performance data constituted a large part of the data warehouse, and it was very easy to generate huge amounts of data (inadvertently) with a small number of performance counters. Microsoft implemented optimized collections beginning in OpsMgr 2007 as one of the methods used to decrease the size of the data warehouse.

Use the Optimized Performance Collection Settings page to enable optimized collections and set the tolerance level for the performance data you are collecting. You can configure two options on this page (shown in Figure 14.10):

- **Absolute number:** This is where you specify the top value for a collection, regardless of the collection schedule. For example, if the value is set to 90% for CPU and the CPU hits 90%, a data collection takes place regardless of the collection schedule.
- **Percentage:** This is the percentage of change that must occur for a data collection to occur. For example, if the percentage were set to 10%, the performance counter would need to change by 10% (say, from 60% to 70%), for a data collection to occur.

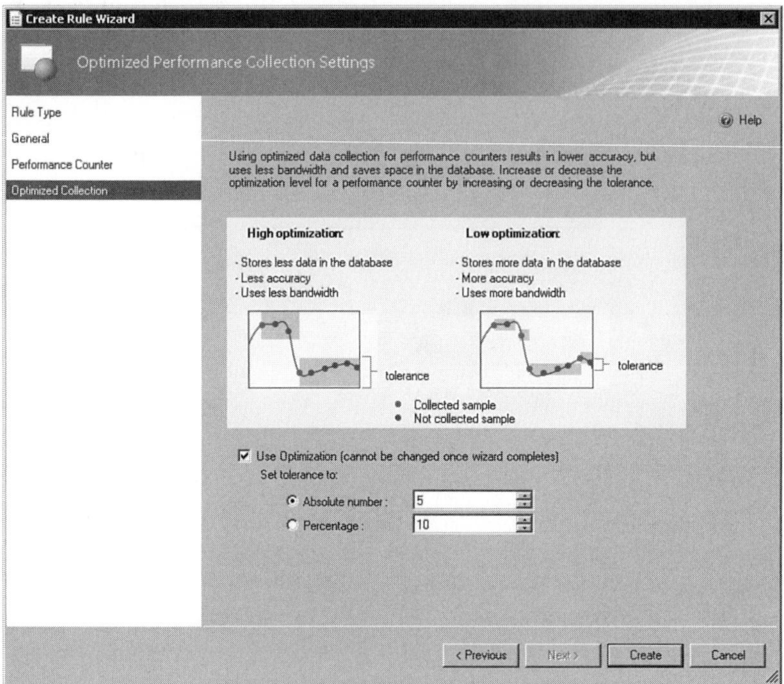

FIGURE 14.10 Optimized performance collection.

REAL WORLD: WHEN NOT TO USE OPTIMIZED DATA COLLECTION

Optimized data collection is not recommended for those performance counters where you need near real time information. As an example, say you have a custom line of business application that is extremely processor intensive running on several Windows 2008 servers. You create a Windows performance view for the application owners showing the Windows Processor utilization for those servers. Your application owners notify you they are not seeing performance counters every 5 minutes as you expected, based upon the 5 minute performance collection interval for the rule that gathers the information.

The counters are not appearing because the Processor % Processor Time 2008 rule is configured to use optimized collection, meaning when the processor reaches a level and holds to that level, it does not report the next value until there is a change. This means when the processor reaches 100% and generates an alert, it does not continue to report data as long as it is in the same absolute value range for the counter (in this case the Processor % Processor Time 2008 rule is set to an absolute value of 5). To address these types of situations, create a group for those servers requiring near-real time monitoring, create a new rule to gather their performance counters, and disable the original performance collection rule for the same group.

To summarize, optimized data collection is not recommended in an environment where you are monitoring processor utilization for a server with the OpsMgr performance views. Optimized data collection is suggested for performance collection rules that would generate a large amount of data and do not require near real time performance monitoring.

Probe-Based Rules

Probe-based rules are generally used when you want a script to generate events for a condition, but do not want those events appearing in the log files on the computer or want to pass more information to OpsMgr than is possible in a basic Windows event. These conditions are relatively uncommon and not discussed in detail in this chapter. There are three different sources available in OpsMgr 2012 for probe-based rules:

- **Script (Event):** Collects script data as events
- **Script (Performance):** Collects script data as performance data
- **UNIX/Linux Shell Command (Performance):** Collects performance data from a UNIX/Linux shell command

With this method, the script is inserted into the probe rule and the VBScript object objPropertyBag is used. This object is a container for the information that OpsMgr understands. Information on property bags and how they are used is included in Chapter 22, "Authoring Management Packs and Reports."

Timed Commands

A timed command rule is the third major rule type. Timed command rules are very simple and can launch a script or execute a command based on a schedule. Two different types of timed commands are available:

- **Execute a command:** Runs a command line on a recurring time interval
- **Execute a script:** Runs a script on a recurring time interval

This section shows you how to launch a batch file using a timed script. The batch file that will be launched is a very simple one that restarts the print spooler service. The file has the following two lines of code and should be saved as **C:\SpoolerRestart.bat**:

```
@echo off
Net stop spooler & net start spooler
```

TIP: A SCRIPTING TIP USING AN AMPERSAND

You can use the ampersand (&), as in the preceding example, to allow two commands to exist on the same line.

Perform the following steps to create a timed command rule to launch a batch file:

1. In the Operations console, navigate to **Authoring -> Monitoring Objects**.
2. Right-click **Rules** and select **Create New Rule**.
3. From the Select a Rule Type page, select **Timed Commands -> Execute a Command**. Once again, select the **Sample Management Pack** to store this rule. Click **Next**.
4. At the Rule Name and Description page, name the rule and configure a target. For this example, the name rule name is **Print Spooler Service Restart**. Target the `Windows Server Operating System` class and configure the rule as **Disabled** (it will later be enabled using an override for a group of servers).
5. Next, create the schedule for running the batch file, in this example it will run daily at midnight. Click the **Base on fixed weekly schedule** radio button and select **Add**. Check **Daily** and specify the time range as between **12:00 AM** and **12:01 AM**, as shown in Figure 14.11. This configures the script to run once a day at 12:00 AM every day of the week to start the spooler service. Click **OK**.

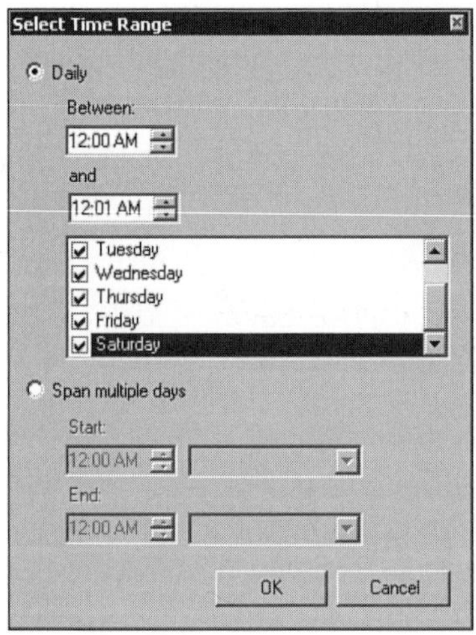

FIGURE 14.11 Specify the time range for the schedule.

6. After creating the schedule, click **Next** to continue.
7. The final page of the wizard is where you configure the actual command to execute. Configure the timed command to run the C:\SpoolerRestart.bat file created earlier in this section. There is no need to specify parameters in this example. The working directory can be set to **C:**. Click **Create** to create the timed command line. Figure 14.12 displays this completed page.

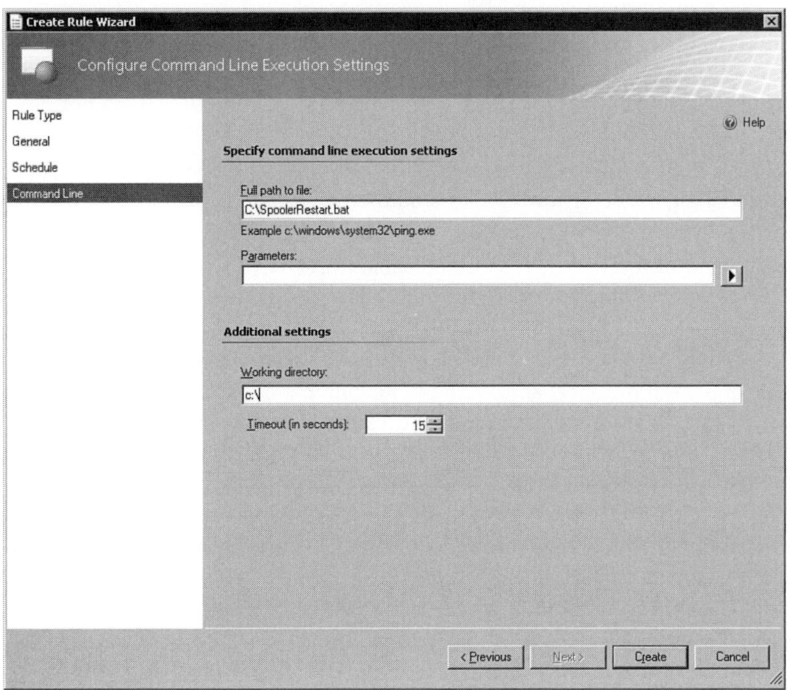

FIGURE 14.12 Select the command to execute.

14

ABOUT TARGETING RULES AND MONITORS

Brian Wren provides information about targeting at http://blogs.technet.com/ati/archive/2007/05/14/targeting-rules-and-monitors.aspx. Here are the key points of his article:

When discussing rules, you may have noticed the use of the word *target*. OpsMgr 2012 requires you specify a target to use for a particular rule or monitor. Consider the component that generates the information: OpsMgr will determine those agents holding instances of the component, deliver the rule or monitor to those agents, and execute that object for each instance.

OpsMgr 2012 also works against multiple instances of a class. Look at an example using SQL Server databases. The SQL scripts in MOM 2005 were enormous because they enumerated the entire list of databases and other SQL objects each time they executed. Now those rules are applied to the `SQL Database` class, and OpsMgr executes the rule for each database instance it discovers. For each rule or monitor, OpsMgr enumerates all instances of the target class and applies the rule/monitor to each. If there are no instances of the target class on that agent, the rule does nothing.

Groups are classes, just like any other object, although they are seldom targeted. If you apply a rule or monitor directly to a group, it executes against the group object itself and does not enumerate members of the group.

To target some groups of objects—e.g., get a particular rule or monitor to a subset of components—you have two options. Consider a subset of websites to which you want to apply a particular rule. You could target the rule at the `IIS 7 Web Site` class, but then the rule would apply to all instances of that class, and probably to sites that you did not want to include.

- Create a new class and target the rule at that class. For an IIS site, you would have to go to the Authoring console or raw XML to create a new class and discovery. That's a fairly advanced approach!
- Create a rule targeted at the whole class and disable it. Next, create a group with the sites you want and create an override for that group to enable your rule.

The easiest way to validate you are using a target that actually has instances to use is with the Discovered Inventory view in the Operations console. Check here before creating your monitor. The Tasks pane (previously known as the Actions pane) has an option called **Change target type**, which brings up the same Select a Target Type dialog box you see when selecting the target for a rule or monitor. This view lists all instances of the target class you are selecting. Use this technique to validate which agents have an instance of that class, and how many instances each has.

If no instances are listed in the view, the rule does nothing. If there are instances, you will know that this is the rule/monitor executed on the agents, and you can view the properties of the instance that will be accessible to what you are targeting at it.

Steve Rachui, a Microsoft PFE, also discusses this topic in an article available at http://technet.microsoft.com/en-us/magazine/2008.11.targeting.aspx?pr=blog.

Using Monitors

OpsMgr 2012 includes monitors in addition to rules. Monitors perform similar functions but are representative of a specific component on a managed machine. This capability makes them extremely powerful. Monitors also update in near real time (depending on the type of monitor), so they accurately represent the current state of the managed computer.

TIP: HEALTH MODELS AND OPERATIONS MANAGER

A health model describes the health of an entity. As an example, you can create a health model for a computer based upon the key performance indicators (KPIs) that apply to that entity. There are four KPIs for a server: Processor, Memory, Disk, and Network. Using these four KPIs lets you determine the overall health of a server. See http://www.windowsitpro.com/article/microsoft-system-center-operations-manager-2007/Operations-Manager-Key-Performance-Indicators-128969 for a discussion on KPIs and OpsMgr.

You can create a health model for a smaller entity such as a specific disk. The disk may be healthy depending upon the amount of free space, number of read/writes, fragmentation level, and whether the disk is physically healthy (such as a failed drive in a RAID5 array). A health model could also be created for a larger entity such as Active Directory, which contains multiple domain controllers existing in different locations.

OpsMgr has a large number of monitors that observe every aspect of a managed entity, down to the component level. You can appreciate the sheer volume of monitors when looking at the Health Monitor for a managed computer, shown in Figure 14.13. (The default view for Health Explorer shows only unhealthy child monitors; Figure 14.13 shows Health Explorer with this filter removed and all monitors displayed regardless of their current health state.)

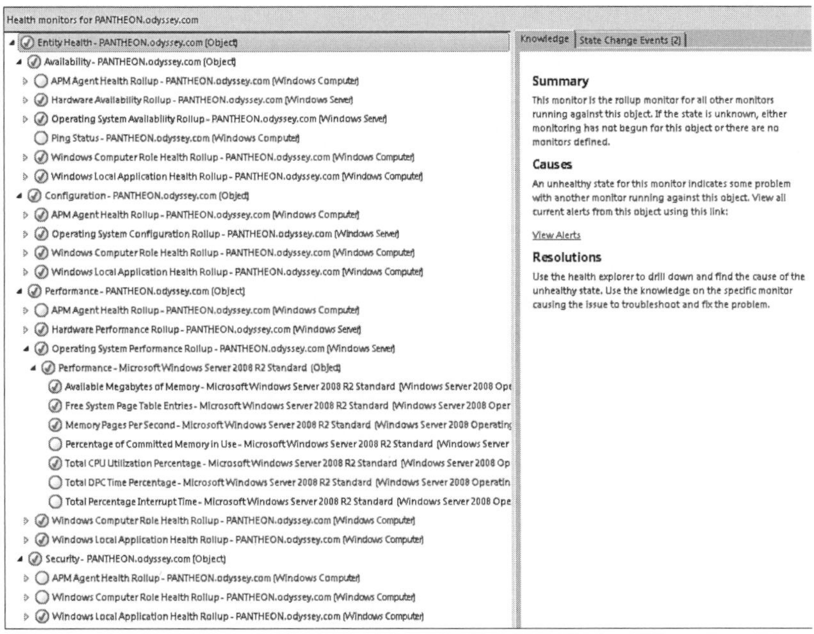

FIGURE 14.13 Health Explorer for a domain controller.

While monitors are used for monitoring, they are not responsible for collecting performance data. You must use rules for this purpose. The functionality and capabilities of rules were discussed in the "About Rules" section.

Unit Monitors

While there are three primary types of monitors in OpsMgr, this chapter focuses on unit monitors as they are the most commonly used monitor in Operations Manager. This is the lowest level of monitor and charged with actually carrying out the monitoring of a particular component or aspect of a monitored entity. Unit monitors can be rolled up using either dependency or aggregate rollup monitors.

There are many different unit monitors in Operations Manager that you can create based on your monitoring requirements. Figure 14.14 shows some of the different unit monitor types available in OpsMgr 2012.

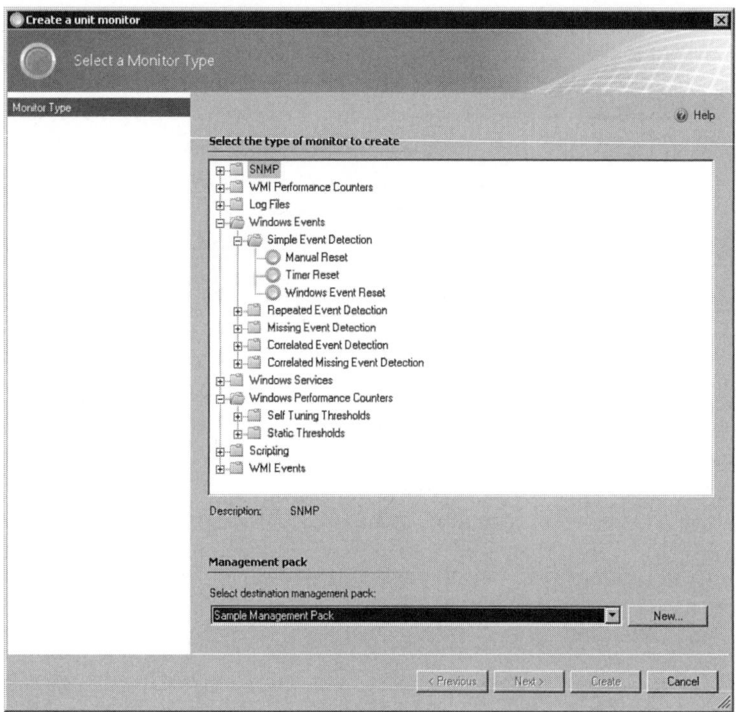

FIGURE 14.14 Types of unit monitors you can create.

Here are the eight main categories of unit monitors and their subcategories:

- **SNMP:** This includes Probe Based Detection and Trap Based Detection.
- **WMI Performance Counters:** WMI Performance counters cover both Static Thresholds (Average Threshold, Consecutive Samples over Thresholds, Delta Threshold, Simple Threshold), and Double Thresholds.
- **WMI Events:** This monitor provides either Simple Event Detection or Repeated Event Detection. Each of these monitors can be Event Reset, Manual Reset, or Timer Reset.
- **Log Files:** Log file monitoring includes Text Log (Repeated Event Detection, Simple Event Detection), and Text Log CSV (Repeated Event Detection, Simple Event Detection). Each of these monitors can be Event Reset, Manual Reset, or Timer Reset.
- **Windows Events:** Windows event monitors include Simple Event Detection, Repeated Event Detection, Missing Event Detection, Correlated Event Detection, and Correlated Missing Event Detection. Each of these monitors can be Event Reset, Manual Reset, or Timer Reset.

- **Windows Services:** This monitor provides the Basic Service Monitor functionality.
- **Windows Performance Counters:** These monitors provide Self Tuning Thresholds (2-State Above, 2-State Baselining, 2-State Below, 3-State Baselining) and Static Thresholds (Double Thresholds or Single Threshold). The Single Thresholds can be Average Threshold, Consecutive Samples over Threshold, Delta Threshold, or Simple Threshold.
- **Scripting:** This monitor provides the generic scripting functionality that is a Timed Script Three State Monitor, Timed Script Two State Monitor, UNIX/Linux Shell Command Three State Monitor, or UNIX/Linux Shell Command Two State Monitor.

SNMP Monitor

You can create a monitor to monitor an SNMP-enabled device without using the built-in network monitoring functionality in OpsMgr 2012. Here are several approaches:

- The monitor can react to an SNMP trap received by the server.
- You can configure an SNMP probe that will actively run an SNMP query based on a schedule you specify; the monitor will update depending on the results of the query.

To configure SNMP monitoring, you must first add the network devices into OpsMgr; then create SNMP trap-based or performance-based rules, depending on your requirements. When creating these rules, you use the OIDs (object identifiers) of the SNMP objects. OIDs are unique labels for SNMP counters and traps. To collect SNMP traps on the management server, you must first install the Windows SNMP trap provider (**Control Panel -> Programs and Features**).

SNMP monitoring is particularly useful for those devices or servers you wish to monitor that run non-Windows operating systems, or for monitoring hardware appliances such as firewall nodes. Chapter 16, "Network Monitoring," discusses network monitoring in detail.

WMI Event and Performance Monitors

WMI event and performance monitors behave in a manner similar to regular event and performance monitors. However, the data is not obtained using the operating system and application programming interfaces (APIs) but instead is collected with WMI. Due to the nature of these performance counters, self-tuning thresholds are not available with WMI performance monitors.

These particular monitor types are typically configured for machines monitored using the Agentless monitoring mode.

Log File Monitor

If the data you want to gather is located in a log file rather than an event log, you can configure OpsMgr to monitor for a particular line or string appearing in a log file of your designation. Multiple options are available for the log file monitor. The different log file monitor types allow you to watch for a single event or text string, or for repeated events or text strings.

Here are some points to keep in mind:

- Watching for a single event is simple. OpsMgr looks for an event that appears in an event log or a text string that appears in a log file.
- Looking for a repeated event is the same as looking for a single event, although the health state is not updated and no alerts are generated until an event has appeared a certain number of times within a certain time period.

Windows Events Monitor

One of the most basic types of monitors is the Windows Events monitor, which detects Windows events and uses these events to update its status. These monitors can vary in complexity from simple, single-event detection to a complex correlation of events; even missing events can contribute to the status of a Windows Events monitor. Since these monitors are among those most commonly used in OpsMgr, this chapter includes an example of how to create a basic Windows event monitor. Follow these steps:

1. Open the Operations console and navigate to **Authoring -> Management Pack Objects**. Select **Monitors**, as displayed in Figure 14.15.

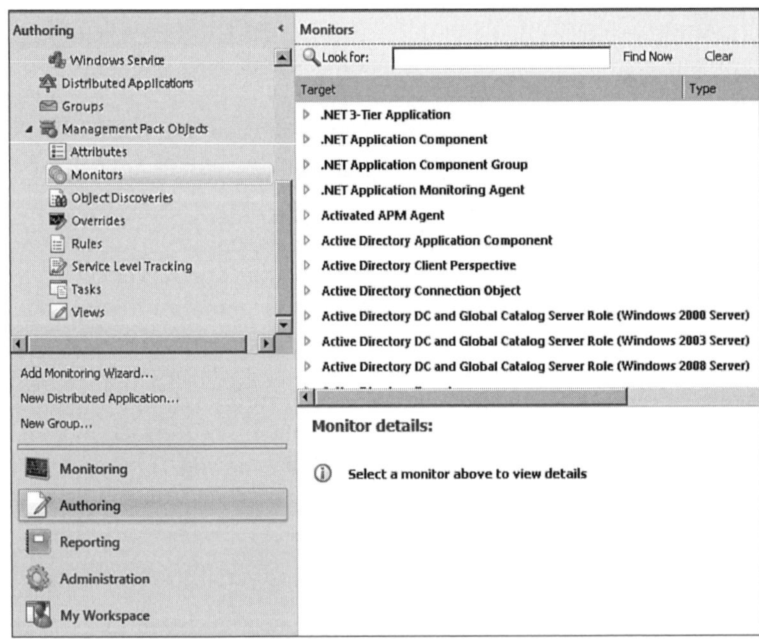

FIGURE 14.15 Monitors in the Authoring pane.

2. To create a new monitor, right-click **Monitors** in the left pane, then select **Create a monitor**. The three options available are Unit Monitor, Dependency Rollup Monitor, and Aggregate Rollup Monitor.

3. As you typically will create simple monitors, this example creates a Windows Event monitor, which is one of the many types of unit monitors. Select **Unit Monitor** to open the Select a Monitor Type page, shown in Figure 14.16.

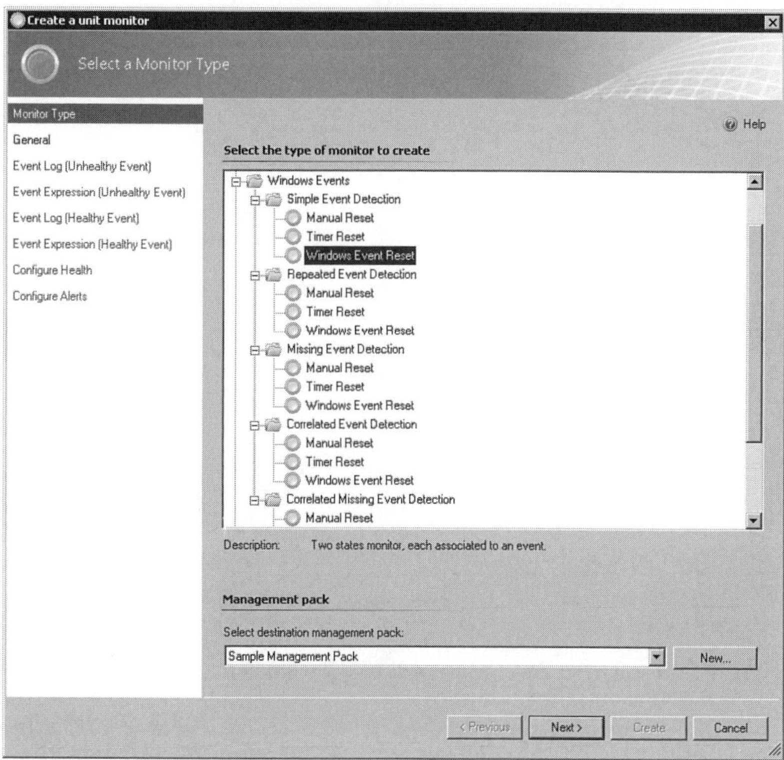

FIGURE 14.16 Selecting a Windows Event unit monitor.

4. This monitor will be configured to fail based on a Windows event and return to a normal state based on a different Windows event. From the Select a Monitor Type page, select **Windows Events -> Simple Event Detection -> Windows Event Reset.** You must also specify the management pack to which you want to add the monitor (as with other examples in this chapter, use the **Sample Management Pack**). Click **Next.**

5. Enter a name, description, monitor target, and parent monitor for the new monitor. Type a name for the monitor and a description if desired. This monitor will be called **Server Time out of Sync.**

   Set the target for the monitor to Windows Server Operating System by browsing to the object and selecting it. As shown in Figure 14.17, set the parent monitor (the monitor under which this one will reside) to **Configuration** and uncheck the **Monitor is Enabled** option (it will be enabled using an override). Click **Next.**

14

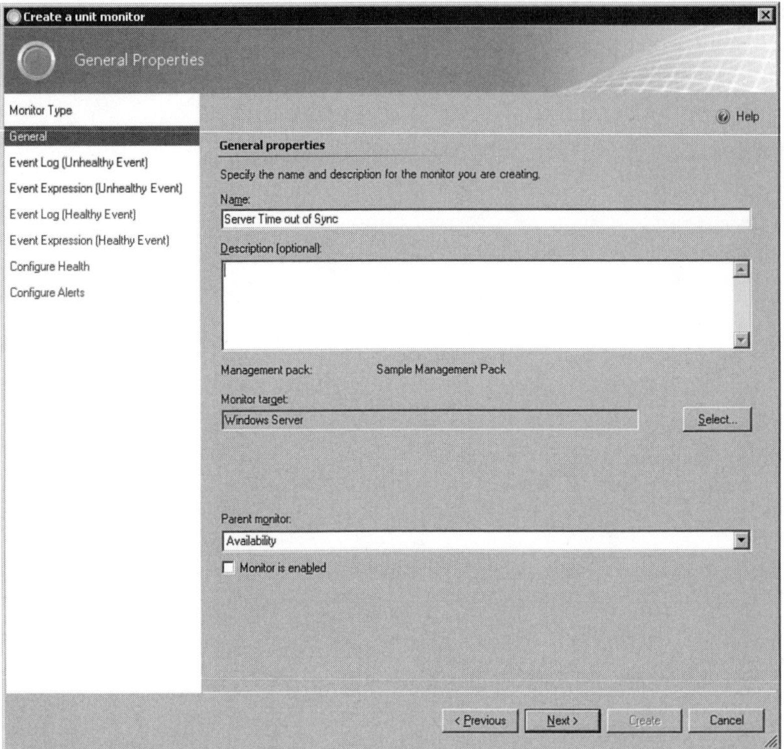

FIGURE 14.17 General properties for the Server Time out of Sync monitor.

6. The next few pages of the wizard configure Windows events that alter the state of the monitor, both healthy and unhealthy.

   On the first page, select the source of the Windows events for the event that will cause the monitor to register an unhealthy state. For this example, set the log to **System** either by typing the name or choosing ... to select the log. The System log is where the events will appear. Click **Next**.

7. On the next page, specify the formula by which OpsMgr will match the unhealthy state event. This is displayed in Figure 14.18.

   The Build Event Expression page is where you specify the parameters of the event that enables OpsMgr to accurately detect and update the state to unhealthy when the event appears in the System log. By default, the wizard adds the Event ID and Event Source parameters. You can remove these parameters as required, and you can add different or additional parameters such as Event Description and Logging Computer Used. To add a new parameter, simply click **Insert**, and then use the ... button on the newly created row to specify the parameter you want to add.

In this example, the rule will look for an event with an event ID of 50 and a source of W32Time. This event indicates time synchronization is not working.

Once you have specified the event information for the unhealthy event, repeat the processes illustrated in Figure 14.18. This will define the event that causes the monitor to return to a healthy state. Use an event from the System log with an Event ID of 37 and a source of W32Time. Event 37 indicates that time synchronization is now working correctly.

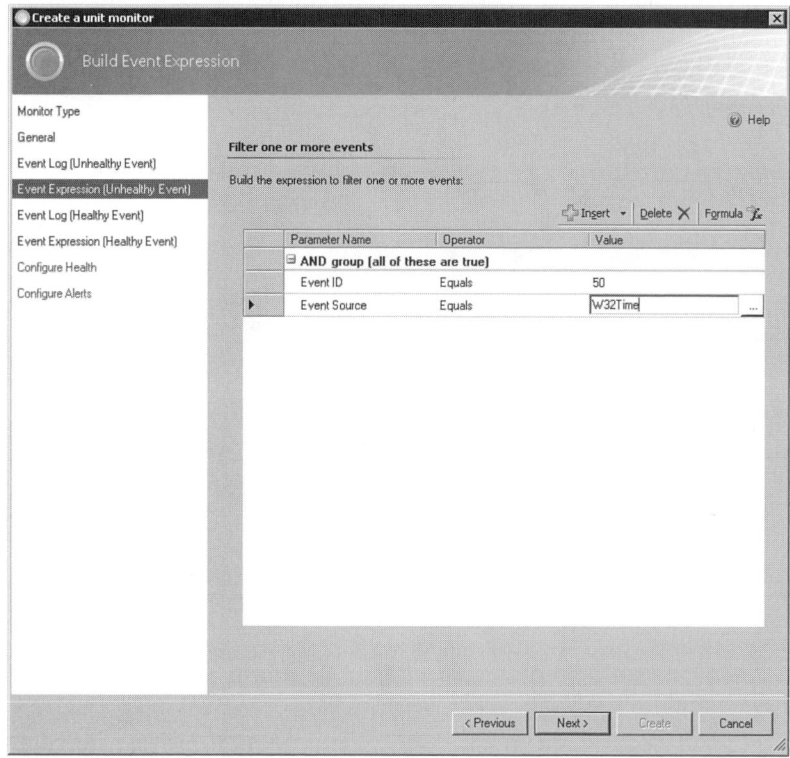

FIGURE 14.18 Server Time of Sync Monitor unhealthy state event.

8. After you complete these steps and click **Next**, the Configure Health page displays, shown in Figure 14.19.

   Here you can specify the severity of the different states of the monitor. For this example, leave both of these configurations in their default states for warning and healthy. Click **Next**.

9. In the final page of the wizard, you can specify if the monitor will generate an alert (explained in more detail in the "About Alerts" section). Choose the option to create an alert for this monitor. Once you check the **Generate alerts for this monitor** check box, a number of options appear:

- You can configure the level the monitor must be at before an alert is generated (Warning or Critical). In this case, change the setting to **Warning** as the health state was defined to be Warning or Healthy. Use the check box below this option to specify whether OpsMgr will **Automatically resolve the alert when the monitor returns to a healthy state**. You will want to do this in most cases—by enabling monitors to resolve their own alerts, you minimize the number of excess alerts residing in the console at any one time.
- Configure the details of the alert in the bottom section of the page; this defines what appears when it is generated. The information includes the name of the alert, any descriptive information, and the priority and the severity of the alert. The alert description field has similar functionality to the event expression builder used in step 7.

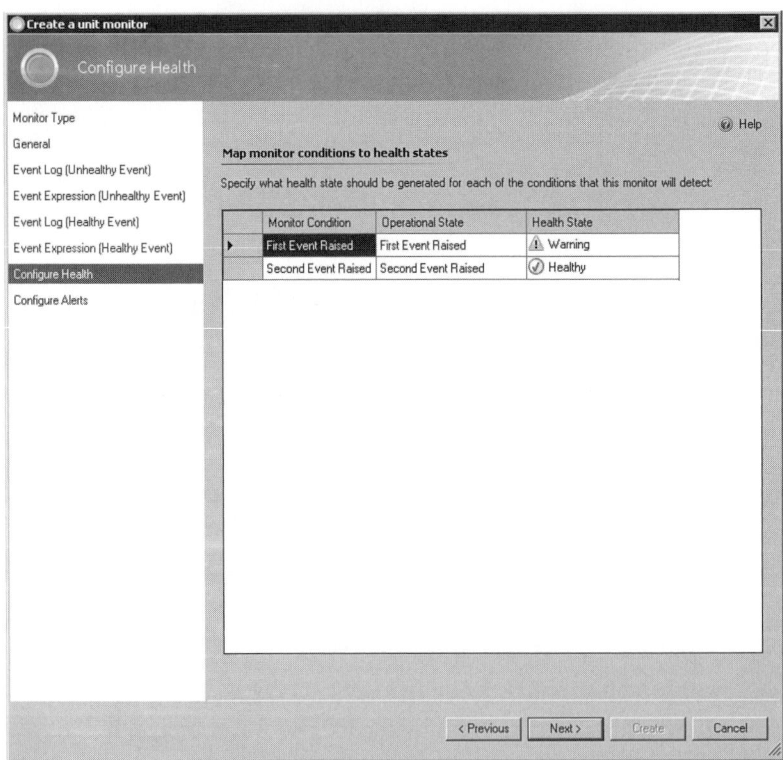

FIGURE 14.19 Configuring the health monitor for the Server Time of Sync Monitor.

10. When satisfied with the alert details and other settings in the wizard, click **Create**. Creating the monitor will take several seconds; when complete, the monitor is visible and accessible in the console.
11. To enable this monitor for a group of servers, create an override to set the Enable flag to **True**.

Windows Services Monitor

A Windows service monitor does what the name suggests. It monitors a Windows service and updates the status of the monitor based on whether the service is running or not. You can also monitor a Windows service with a management pack that creates a Windows service monitor.

Using the management pack template creates a class for the monitored service. This is useful when you want to monitor the service as an individual item and potentially add it to a distributed application (DA). Distributed applications are covered in more detail in Chapter 18, "Distributed Applications."

REAL WORLD: NOT ALL SERVICES APPEAR WHEN USING THE MONITOR WIZARD

When you use the Monitor Wizard to create a monitor for a Windows service, you can browse to see the services available for monitoring. However, you may notice that the list is shorter than the list of services in the Services MMC (Microsoft Management Console). This is because this version of OpsMgr only monitors services that are not shared. If a service is shared, it runs under svchost.exe and it is not picked up by the wizard! This is a known problem. If you are developing your own services in house, ask your developers to create separate services for their applications so you can monitor them.

As monitoring services is common in OpsMgr, the next procedure creates a Windows service monitor to monitor the Print Spooler service. Follow these steps:

1. In the Operations console, navigate to **Authoring** -> **Monitoring Objects**.
2. Right-click **Monitors** and select **Create a Monitor** -> **Unit Monitor**.
3. Select **Windows Services** -> **Basic Service Monitor**. Select **Sample Management Pack** as a target for the monitor. Click **Next** to continue.
4. On the next page, name the monitor and configure a target for it. Name this rule **Print Spooler Service Monitor** and target the `Windows Server Operating System` class, as this should apply to all Windows servers. Notice here, unlike when you created rules, you are asked to specify the parent monitor. In this case, leave the setting at the default of **Availability**. Click **Next** to continue.
5. Now, configure the service you want to monitor. In this case, it is the Print Spooler (Spooler) service. You can click the **...** button to browse for the service or type **Spooler** into the service name box. Click **Next**.
6. The next page of the wizard is the Configure Health page. This is where you define what the health of the monitor will be in relation to the state of the service. Because this is a basic service monitor, it is already correctly defined, as displayed in Figure 14.20.
7. The final page of the wizard configures the actual alert OpsMgr will generate. Check the **Generate alerts for this monitor** check box, leave the alert name as it is, and add an alert description. Also, leave the check box enabled for **Automatically resolve alert when...**. This means that once the monitor returns to a Healthy state,

any generated alerts are automatically resolved. Click **Create** to create the new service monitor.

TIP: MONITORING A PROCESS WITH OPSMGR

Sometimes you may want to know if a process (not a service) is running on a server. This scenario is common for functions such as batch processes, which often run logged in to a console as a specific user and are launched using a shortcut on the desktop. OpsMgr 2007 R2 added the ability to do this as part of the Process Monitoring management pack template. More details on this functionality are available in Chapter 17.

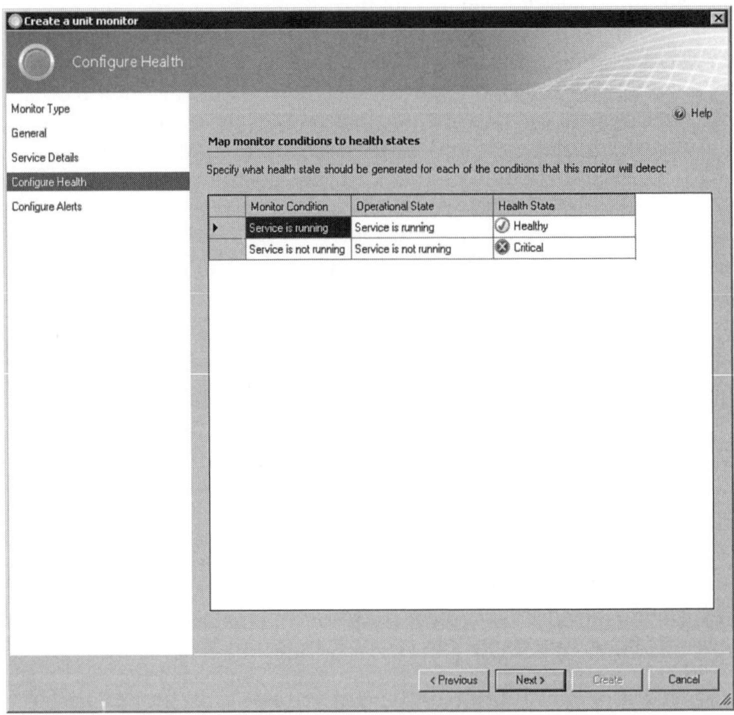

FIGURE 14.20 Health state for a service monitor.

Windows Performance Counters Monitor

The Windows Performance Counters monitor collects data from a Windows operating system or application performance counter and reacts to that data. There are two key types of Windows Performance Counters monitors, discussed in the following sections:

- ▶ Static Thresholds
- ▶ Self-Tuning Thresholds

Static Thresholds Monitor

The Static Thresholds monitor is the simplest monitor type. It is used to monitor for changes in a static threshold, such as exceeding a threshold of 90% CPU utilization. With that said, you can still create five distinct types of Static Threshold monitors for additional granularity in the monitoring process using either a single threshold or two thresholds:

- **Average Threshold:** Single threshold

  The Average Threshold monitor takes the average value of a performance counter over a certain number of samples. The state changes if the average is above the specified threshold.

  This monitor is particularly useful when you need to receive an alert when a performance counter is running near to or over a threshold for a defined period, rather than every time the performance exceeds a threshold. Figure 14.21 displays the average threshold configuration page.

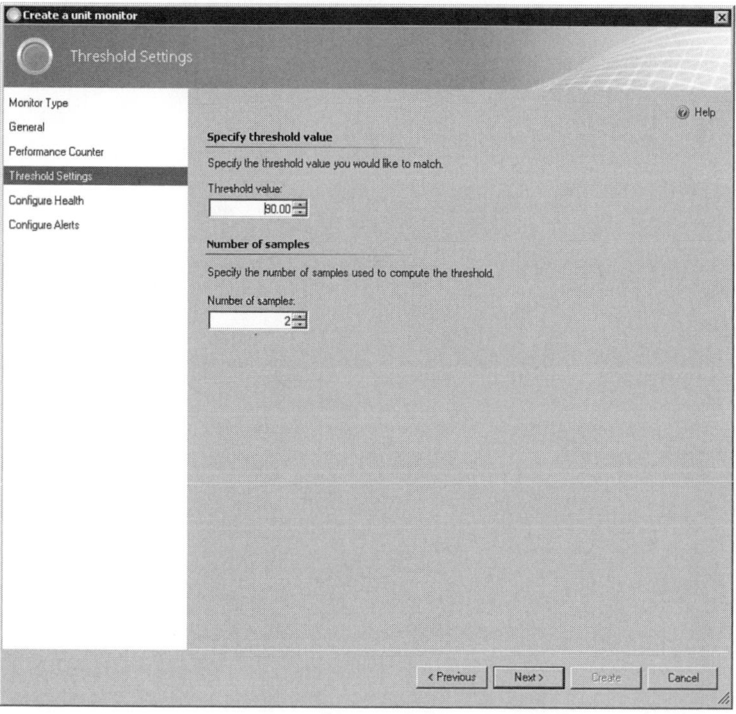

FIGURE 14.21 Threshold settings for the average threshold configuration page.

- **Consecutive Values over Threshold:** Single threshold

  Use the Consecutive Values over Threshold monitor when you need to reflect the state of a computer that consistently and repeatedly exceeds a threshold (so monitoring the average threshold is not appropriate). This capability is useful for systems that may occasionally have spikes on performance counters that do not indicate a problem, although it is an issue if a spike does not return to normal.

  Figure 14.22 shows this monitor configured. It checks for a value greater than or equal to 20 (the threshold), but collects four samples for comparison before defining it as a concern.

- **Double Threshold:** Two thresholds

  OpsMgr allows you to configure a double threshold where a single monitor checks both a high and low threshold. For example, you can configure the health state of the monitor to be affected if a performance counter falls below a "low" value or exceeds a "high" value.

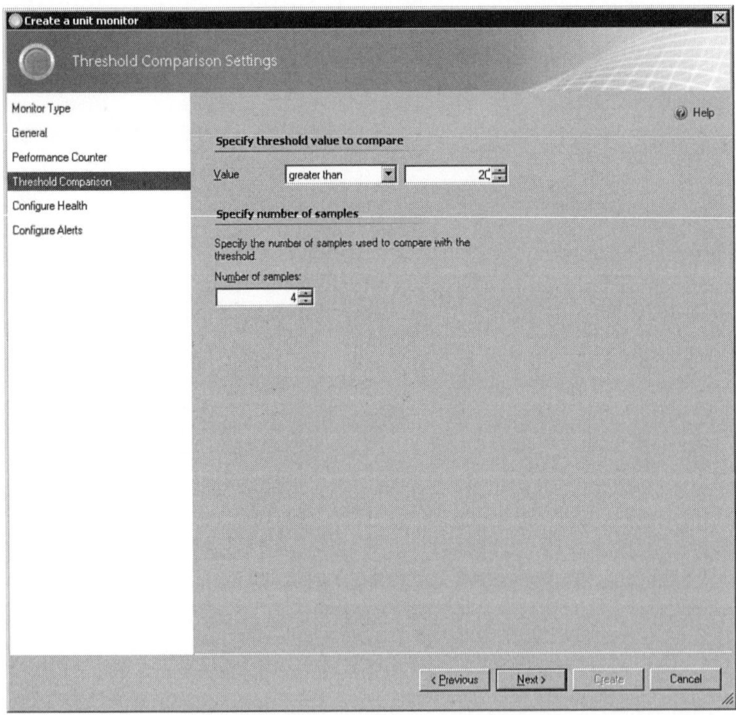

FIGURE 14.22 Threshold Comparison Settings page.

- **Delta Threshold:** Single threshold

  A Delta Threshold monitor does not measure the actual value of a performance counter but rather the change in value. For example, if you were measuring a change of 50, a performance counter change from 75 to 20 would be of interest, whereas a change from 75 to 30 would not. You can also configure the monitor to measure for a percentage drop rather than a physical value change. Figure 14.23 shows the configuration page for this monitor.

- **Simple Threshold:** Single threshold

  The Simple Threshold monitor does exactly what is says. It simply monitors a performance counter and changes the status of the monitor when the threshold is exceeded. This is the most basic and easiest to configure a Performance Threshold monitor in OpsMgr 2012. Figure 14.24 displays the Threshold Value page for configuring the Simple Threshold monitor.

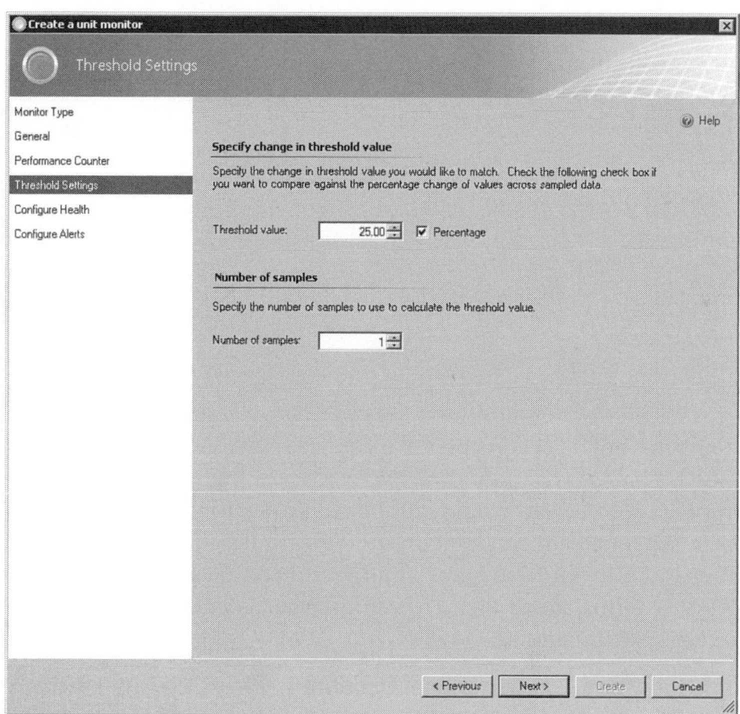

FIGURE 14.23 Delta threshold settings page.

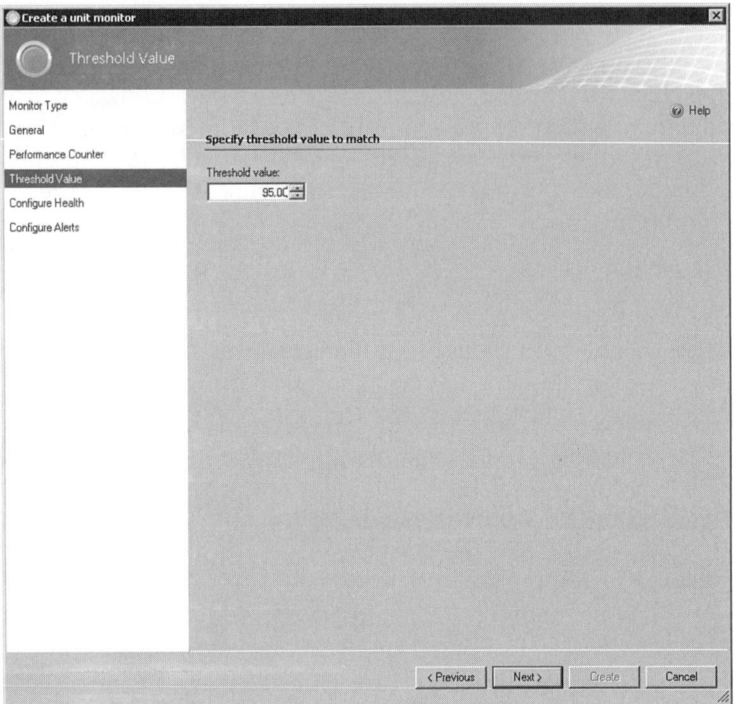

FIGURE 14.24 Simple Threshold monitor configuration page.

Self-Tuning Thresholds

Static thresholds react to performance issues only if the particular counters deviated outside a predefined value. This method of monitoring is effective, although it has its drawbacks. The main issue is that not all servers perform equally, even servers that fulfill the same role (Exchange servers being a good example). When servers perform differently, a performance value appropriate for one server may not be applicable for another system, making it necessary to create separate performance thresholds for different servers. This can be very time consuming and difficult to manage in large and complex environments. Self-tuning thresholds (STTs) were first added with Operations Manager 2007 to provide an option to address these types of situations.

Using STTs enables dynamic monitoring of performance counters, where OpsMgr adapts the thresholds as appropriate. As an example, if you monitor an Active Directory domain controller (DC) for CPU utilization using a self-tuning threshold, the threshold will "learn," noticing repeating CPU fluctuations on the server, such as extra demand placed when users log in at the same time on a Monday morning. The monitor then ignores these CPU fluctuations, and the state of the monitor only changes if the fluctuations are sufficient to move outside the baseline the monitor has learned.

A self-tuning threshold is also particularly useful to collect a baseline of a particular performance counter. When you view the associated performance graph, you can overlay the baseline, giving an overview of the trend of the counter in addition to the exact values.

Baselines

OpsMgr 2012 uses baselines to continually monitor and collect the usual running values for a performance counter. This allows it to automatically set and adjust alert thresholds to limit the amount of extraneous alerts that appear. Baselines are also available in performance graphs to show the trend of a particular performance counter. To access a baseline from a performance view graph (where available), simply generate the graph, right-click, and select **Show Baseline**. Figure 14.25 shows an example of a self-tuning threshold defined for a performance counter that gathers a baseline for the processor utilization for a series of servers over a one day baseline. The performance graph was configured to display a time range starting two days in the past and moving one day into the future so the right side of this graph shows the baseline projected into the future by one day.

The process for configuring a self-tuning threshold is similar to configuring a normal threshold. The only real difference is in configuring the logic for the self-tuning threshold to "learn." This is defined using the wizard when the threshold monitor is created, by creating an override, or editing the InnerSensitivity and OuterSensitivity values directly in the monitor. The key to tuning STTs is the inner sensitivity values, which can be changed with an override. Here are the override values for STTs:

- **Low:** 4.01
- **Low-Mid:** 3.77
- **Mid:** 3.29
- **Mid-High:** 2.81
- **High:** 2.57

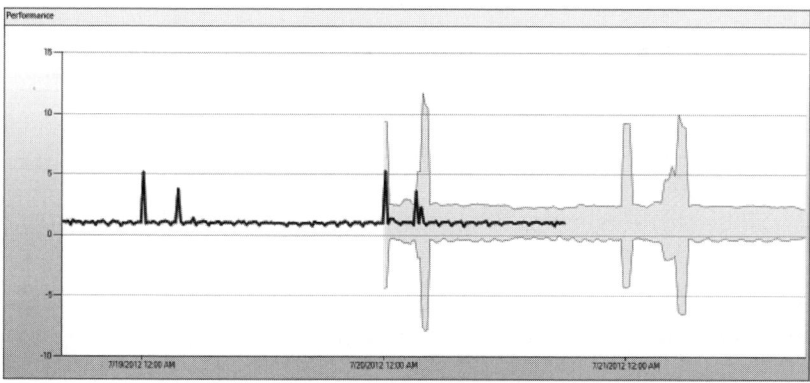

FIGURE 14.25 Performance graph with self-tuning threshold baseline.

Changing sensitivity using the wizard is straightforward. Follow these steps:

1. After selecting the performance counter you will use, the Baselining Configuration page appears, shown in Figure 14.26.

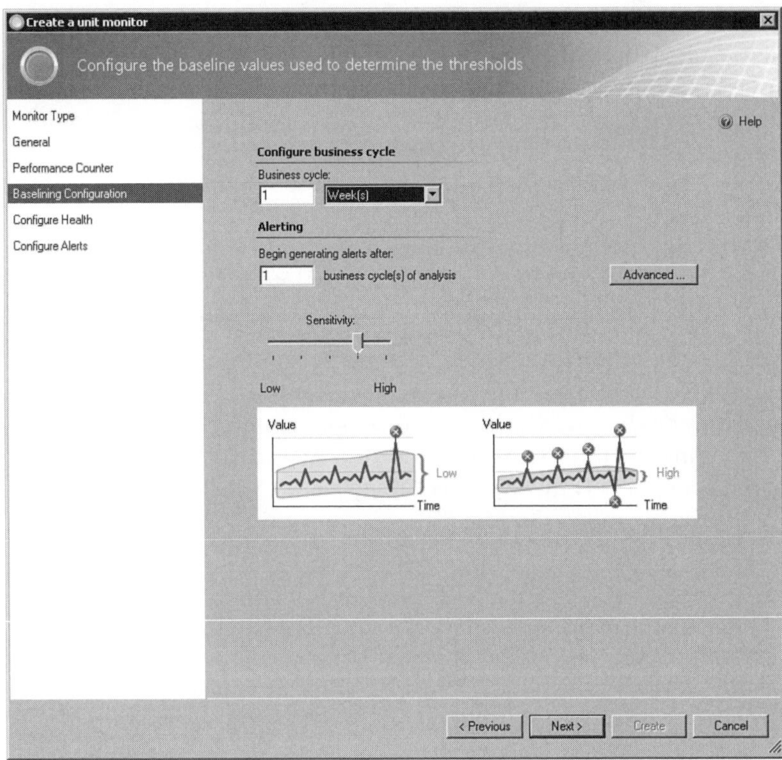

FIGURE 14.26 Self-tuning threshold Baselining Configuration page.

2. From this page, you can configure your business cycle, meaning what you consider a unit of time to monitor. A business cycle is defined in terms of days or weeks; the default is 1 week.

   The Baselining Configuration page also allows you to configure how many business cycles should pass before generating alerts. This is useful because the monitor is able to learn efficiently before it begins generating alerts for exceeded thresholds.

3. You can also specify how sensitive (or insensitive) the threshold monitor will be. Moving the sensitivity slider automatically adjusts the sensitivity, or you can configure it in more detail by clicking **Advanced**, which displays the dialog shown in Figure 14.27.

4. From the Baselining - Advanced page, you can manually configure the two settings for sensitivity: the learning rate and time sensitivity settings.

- Learning rate is the rate at which the baseline is adjusted, based on frequency of occurrences.
- Time sensitivity is the rate at which the baseline is adjusted based on a time interval.

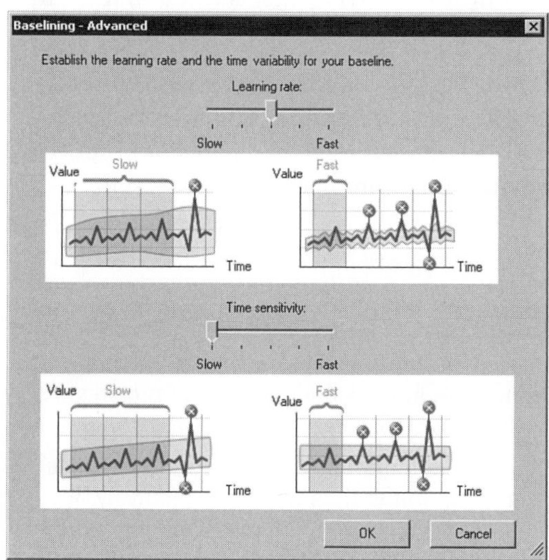

FIGURE 14.27 Baselining Advanced threshold sensitivity configuration.

There are a number of different self-tuning thresholds:

- **2-state Above:** The 2-state Above baseline is used to generate a status change and alert when the performance counter strays above the learned baseline. When it is below the baseline, the status of the monitor is normal.
- **2-state Baselining:** This monitor is very much the same as the 2-state Above threshold monitor except that the baseline information is recorded for use in performance graphs.
- **2-state Below:** The 2-state Below baseline is the opposite of the 2-state Above baseline. If the counter strays below the learned baseline, the status is updated and an alert generated.
- **3-state Baselining:** The 3-state Baselining monitor collects the baselining information. It also allows the monitor to update the health state when the performance deviates both above and below the learned baseline.

Issues with Self-Tuning Thresholds

Self-tuning thresholds have become well known in the OpsMgr community as “noisy” monitors. There are two primary reasons for this:

- There were several performance counters chosen in OpsMgr 2007 that were extremely noisy as STTs. Examples of common noisy STTs include items with consistently low values such as 0 or 1; these trigger when almost any value occurs for the performance counter, even if only for a short duration, regardless of how sensitive the monitor is tuned to be. (An increase from 0 to 1 is a huge increase in value mathematically, versus an increase from 300 to 301 which is not a significant increase.)
- There were challenges with tuning self-tuning thresholds to decrease the sensitivity of the STT. Microsoft uses a proprietary algorithm to determine how sensitivity is applied to STTs. Kevin Holman discusses STTs and how they are created and tuned correctly at http://blogs.technet.com/b/kevinholman/archive/2008/03/19/self-tuning-thresholds-love-and-hate.aspx.

REAL WORLD: SHOULD YOU USE SELF-TUNING THRESHOLDS?

Despite the benefits of self-tuning thresholds, there are drawbacks to using this technology. Currently, self-tuning thresholds are unable to take into account periods of prolonged inactivity, such as weekends and holidays. Here's an example:

OpsMgr may calculate a baseline for a server during the month of November. The baseline is automatically calculated over the period of a month, and is thus assumed relatively accurate.

However, during December many businesses close or run reduced operations over the Christmas period, which negatively affects the baseline. The monitored servers are less heavily utilized during the holiday period, and the baseline adjusts to reflect this. When everyone returns to work the server has a more typical load, and its new baseline is no longer accurate. When the server now becomes busy, it will have unnecessary alerts generated for performance counters outside the baseline, because OpsMgr still thinks the server should not have that much activity.

Currently, the only way to work around this issue is to temporarily disable the baseline rule using an override for the periods of extended inactivity, or place the machine or class object the performance counter applies to in maintenance mode. The authors do not recommend the latter method because it results in the computer or class object no longer being monitored. The other commonly used option is to replace an STT with a static threshold.

Manually Resetting or Recalculating a Monitor

The Health Explorer includes the option to Reset Health and to Recalculate Health. Figure 14.28 displays the Reset Health and Recalculate Health buttons.

TIP: MANUAL RESET MONITORS

This chapter has stated the assumption that monitors can automatically identify when they return to a healthy condition. The exception to this is a manual reset monitor. A manual reset monitor only resets state when the monitor is manually reset by a script or an OpsMgr administrator. Russ Slaten has an excellent article on manual reset monitors, available at http://blogs.msdn.com/b/rslaten/archive/2010/06/25/the-challenges-with-manual-reset-monitors.aspx.

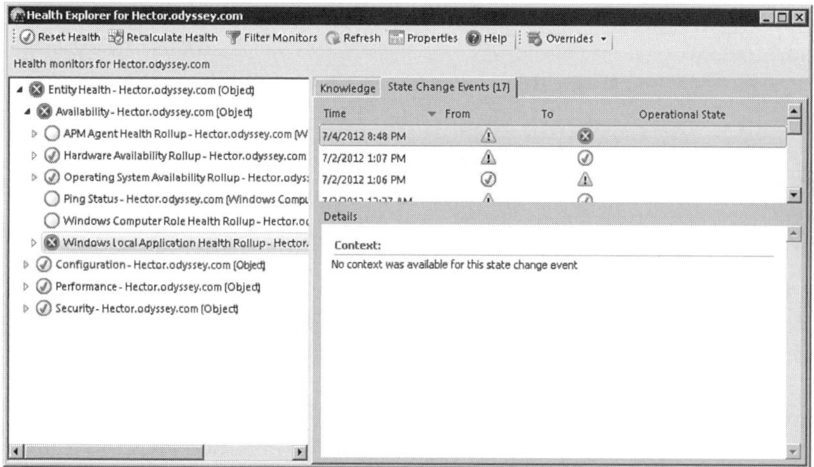

FIGURE 14.28 The Reset and Recalculate Health buttons in the Health Explorer.

The Reset and Recalculate Health buttons perform different actions:

- **Reset Health:** The ability to reset the health state is a good idea in principle, because sometimes monitors do not reset themselves when the corresponding alert closes itself. In extreme cases, it may be necessary to restart or even reinstall the agent to reset the monitor. The Reset Health button avoids this and provides a way to reset a monitor to a healthy state. To reset a monitor, open the Health Explorer for the object, find the monitor, highlight it, and choose the **Reset Health** option.
- **Recalculate Health:** The Recalculate Health button allows you to initiate a recalculation of the state of any monitor in real time, rather than having to wait for the configured schedule. However, this only works on monitors that implement On Demand Detection; the majority of monitors do not have this implemented yet. To recalculate a monitor, open the Health Explorer for the object, find the monitor, highlight it, and choose the **Recalculate Health** option.

TIP: RECALCULATING AND ON-DEMAND DETECTION IN OPSMGR

Recalculating health does not work for more than 95% of all monitors in Operations Manager 2012. This is because the on-demand recalculation requires both the initially defined datasource and the monitortype datasource to have a probe action to support on-demand recalculation functionality. To understand on-demand detection, read Boris Yanushpolsky's article on the topic at http://blogs.msdn.com/b/boris_yanushpolsky/archive/2008/06/03/on-demand-detection.aspx.

Additional reading on unit monitors is available from Steve Rachui, available at http://blogs.msdn.com/b/steverac/archive/2009/08/30/understanding-monitors-in-opsmgr-2007-part-i-unit-monitors.aspx.

Dependency Rollup and Aggregate Rollup Monitors

As discussed in the "Unit Monitors" section, OpsMgr 2012 has three different types of monitors: Unit, Dependency Rollup, and Aggregate Rollup. These are discussed in the next sections.

Dependency Rollup Monitor

The Dependency Rollup monitor is configured to roll up the health state of a particular monitor or component to the next level in the monitored computer's health state. For example, if a SQL Server database resides on a physical disk and the disk fails, a Dependency Rollup monitor included in a management pack for SQL would ensure the state of the physical disk affects the state of the database relying on it. Steve Rachui provides details on dependency rollup monitors at http://blogs.msdn.com/b/steverac/archive/2009/10/05/understanding-monitors-in-opsmgr-2007-part-iii-dependency-monitors.aspx.

Aggregate Rollup Monitor

An Aggregate Rollup monitor is designed to reflect the state of a collection of Unit monitors, Dependency Rollup monitors, or other Aggregate Rollup monitors. For example, the state of multiple SQL servers can be grouped and rolled up to a SQL Servers group. Steve Rachui writes about aggregate rollup monitors at http://blogs.msdn.com/b/steverac/archive/2009/09/06/understanding-monitors-in-opsmgr-2007-part-ii-aggregate-monitors.aspx.

Rules and monitors perform a variety of functions, but the primary function is generating alerts in the Operations console (discussed in the next section) that you can then distribute to subscribers through subscriptions.

About Alerts

As discussed in the "About Rules" and "Using Monitors" sections, both rules and monitors generate alerts. Alerts represent an overview of all active issues in the system. Alerts contain more information than monitors do, which makes them very useful for troubleshooting. In addition, alerts are not necessarily resolved when a monitor's status returns to normal. You can configure alerts to remain active, assisting in visibility and hopefully resolving the issue in question. You will find alerts in the Active Alerts view in the Monitoring space of the Operations console.

Alerts contain a number of pieces of information in the Monitoring -> Alert Details pane of the console; Figure 14.29 displays an example.

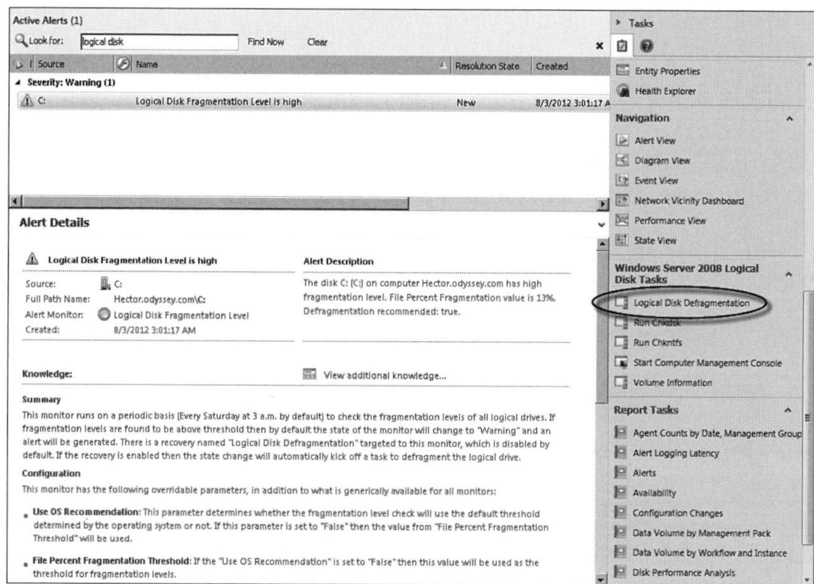

FIGURE 14.29 The Alert Details pane.

The alert details in this figure provide specific information about the alert, such as the computer that raised it, the source of the alert (the application or operating system component generating the alert), and any additional knowledge included by the vendor or that you created yourself.

A useful feature in OpsMgr is the ability to embed tasks within the Alert Details section. This allows the user discovering the alert to carry out troubleshooting steps, such as restarting a service directly from the Alert Details section in the console, which reduces administrative overhead. Figure 14.29 is an example of this capability, including an embedded task to defragment a drive identified as highly fragmented.

TIP: DASHBOARDS AND ALERTS FROM RULES AND MONITORS

The new dashboard functionality in OpsMgr 2012 provides a quick way to identify which alerts are generated by monitors or by rules. By creating a dashboard view with the Alert Widget, you can display the Is Alert Monitor field and sort alerts into those created by a monitor or rule. Additional information is available at http://blogs.catapultsystems.com/cfuller/archive/2012/01/30/quicktrick-find-alerts-from-a-monitor-or-rule-in-opsmgr-2012-scom.aspx.

Generating Alerts

Both rules and monitors generate alerts. Monitors can automatically resolve alerts when the state of the object returns to normal (rules cannot). This helps minimize the number of inactive alerts resident in the console at any one time.

OpsMgr 2012 uses a notification workflow, which is the engine that underpins all aspects of alert generation. The notification workflow manages the generation and resolution of alerts, and includes the following capabilities:

- Creating and forwarding email messages and other external notifications such as instant messaging and Short Message Service (text messaging)
- Alert aging
- The ability to customize the messaging format at the user levels

User-level formatting requires at least one notification channel to be previously configured by an OpsMgr administrator, and allows individual users to configure their own recipient object and notification subscriptions. For redundancy, use multiple Simple Mail Transport Protocol (SMTP) servers.

The authors recommend alternate methods of notification beyond email notification. It is not particularly useful to try to send emails with Exchange saying that Exchange is down!

TIP: EXCHANGE, OPSMGR, AND BACK PRESSURE

The authors recommend multiple SMTP servers even in environments where the Exchange environment is highly available. This is due to a condition called *back pressure* where Exchange will stop receiving inbound email temporarily. More information on this situation and OpsMgr is available at http://blogs.catapultsystems.com/cfuller/archive/2012/01/09/exchange-back-pressure-amp-opsmgr-notification-channels.aspx, and additional information on Exchange back pressure is at http://technet.microsoft.com/en-us/library/bb201658.aspx.

Configuring Notification

Configuring notification involves performing the following steps:

1. Establish a notification channel.

   This can be via SMTP, instant messaging, or Short Message Service (SMS).

2. Create notification recipient(s).

   Defining notification recipients includes specifying the scheduled hours during which they will receive notifications, with the address information for each channel on which the notification is available.

   Recipients are defined in the Operations console under **Administration -> Notifications -> Recipients**.

3. Create notification subscription(s).

   Each subscription defines those management groups and objects for which alert notifications are sent, the alert criteria (severity, priority, and category), email format, and resolution state criteria for filtering out unnecessary alerts. You can even specify alert aging as notification criteria. Establish subscriptions in the Operations console under **Administration -> Notifications -> Subscriptions**.

4. Create a Notification Action account (introduced in Chapter 10, "Security and Compliance").

   The email address associated with the Notification Action account is used as the email and instant message "From" address. Be sure to give this account the appropriate rights for the notification channel it will be using.

These steps are well documented in the white paper "Notification Setup Guide for Operations Manager 2007" developed by Anders Bengtsson and Pete Zerger. You can download this white paper from http://contoso.se/blog/?p=132. For your convenience, the authors include this as a live link in Appendix D, "Reference URLs."

Forwarding Alerts by Email

In *System Center Operations Manager 2007 Unleashed* (Sams, 2008), the authors developed a small management pack that creates a task you can use to forward alerts. This management pack was later improved by Ron Williams. The Forward Alerts via Email MP provides a right-click capability for forwarding the alert name and description to someone via email.

On current operating systems, this seems to work only if Outlook is installed locally on the system (which works well on an administrator's workstation but not on the management server, but remember it is not a best practice to use the Operations Manager console on a management server). The Alert Forward MP is available from System Center Central, at http://www.systemcentercentral.com/tabid/145/indexId/11518/Default.aspx.

This management pack is a useful tool for forwarding alerts to those individuals without subscriptions that need to be aware of a specific alert.

Using the Notification Workflow Engine

Once you configure notification, administrators no longer have to create alert rules to generate email alerts; they simply need to subscribe to the alert using the notification workflow engine. The next section covers notification workflow and the creation of alert subscriptions.

The Life Cycle of an Alert

Alerting is configured using the Subscription Workflow capability of Operations Manager. In addition to managing alert generation, you can configure subscriptions to alerts to ensure only the appropriate alerts are forwarded via email, and only to the correct subscribers. You can also send alerts and monitoring data to different subscribers during off-hours. Notification Workflow in OpsMgr is also used to configure which alerts are passed to connectors for forwarding to third-party systems. More information on integrating OpsMgr with other systems is in Chapter 21, "System Center Integration."

Figure 14.30 shows the structure of the notification workflow.

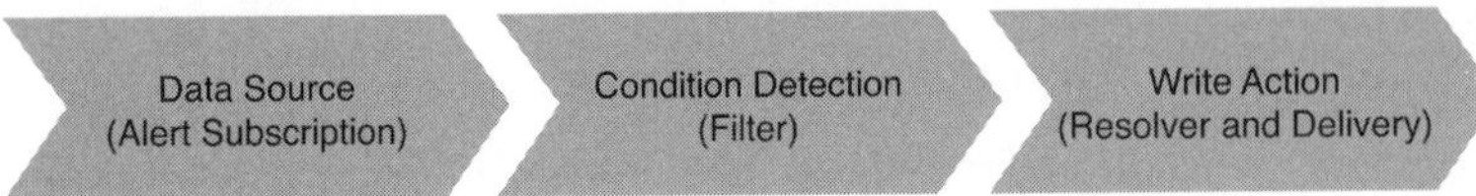

FIGURE 14.30 Notification workflow.

At a high level, here are the steps OpsMgr takes to create the workflow:

1. Create the subscriber and subscription.

   This is where you configure the subscriber to which to send the alerts. This can be an email recipient, IM recipient, SMS message recipient, or based on a command (useful for sending notifications to a third-party message system).

2. Create a subscription for generating notifications.

   Here you create the actual subscription that defines which alerts to send and to which subscriber.

3. Generate an alert.

   The alert is generated by OpsMgr.

4. The AlertSubscription Data Source module periodically polls subscriptions.

   Periodically, the OpsMgr notification workflow polls the subscriptions and enumerates the configuration to define whether the alert(s) generated since the last poll need to be forwarded to a subscriber.

5. The Resolver module processes (filters) alerts that match.

   Matching alerts are passed to the next stage of the notification workflow.

6. The Resolver module enumerates the subscriber list, addresses, and schedule for each notification.

   At this point, the alert is identified as matching the filter, but OpsMgr performs one final check to ensure the subscription is configured to receive alerts during the specified time. In other words, if an alert is found that matches the conditions defined for the subscription at 5 a.m. and the subscription is not configured to receive alerts between 1 a.m. and 6 a.m., the alert is not forwarded.

TIP: USING GROUPS WITH SUBSCRIPTIONS

The *Unleashed* authors developed a series of blog posts discussing how to use custom groups to simplify the Operations console for server owners. Here is a post providing information about how to use custom groups in subscriptions: http://opsmgrunleashed.wordpress.com/2009/08/28/how-to-use-customized-groups-to-simplify-the-opsmgr-console-for-server-owners-%E2%80%93-using-custom-groups-with-subscriptions-one-off-notifications/. Cameron Fuller expands upon this topic with a webinar and whitepaper provided by Veeam, available at http://go.veeam.com/rs/veeam/images/whitepaper_How_To_Manage_SCOM.pdf.

7. Subscription subject and body are generated for each device per subscriber.

   The subscription message is created and generated, based on the default subscription format and any additional changes to the default format configured in the rule or monitor generating the alert.

8. Delivery Action executes the delivery, with subscription content included.

   The message is delivered. OpsMgr now passes responsibility of the message to the subscription delivery software (Microsoft Exchange, for example). OpsMgr does not monitor to verify that the message arrives. If the message does not arrive, you will need to attempt to locate it in the subscription delivery device.

As OpsMgr monitors its own subscription workflow, if no alerts are generated in the Operations console to suggest there is a problem with the workflow, it assumes the message has left the OpsMgr subscription workflow and is passed to the configured subscription device.

The next sections describe the process to create a channel and a subscriber. Channels and subscribers are used together to provide part of a subscription. Subscriptions identify the criteria for the alert. This is combined with the subscriber and channel information to deliver the alert information.

Creating a Channel

There are four different types of channels you can configure in OpsMgr 2012:

- **E-mail (SMTP):** This is the primary type of channel used for notifications in Operations Manager.
- **Instant Message (IM):** The Instant Message channel is generally used for a small number of extremely targeted alerts that are of higher priority (such as a server down situation).
- **Text Message (SMS):** The Text Message channel also is generally used for a small number of extremely targeted alerts that are of higher priority (such as a server down situation).
- **Command:** The command channel is used when there is a requirement to run a script or to perform an action as a result of an alert condition.

E-Mail (SMTP) Channel

To create a channel, open the Operations console and navigate to **Administration -> Notifications**. Right-click and select **New Channel**. E-mail is the primary option chosen for most channels in Operations Manager.

For all channels, the first page of configuration defines the channel name and the description for the channel. This example creates an E-mail channel by specifying the description, settings, and format for the channel. Figure 14.31 shows an example configuration where a single SMTP server has been configured with a return address for the channel (SC2012OM@odysseylab.net) and a retry interval of 5 (default).

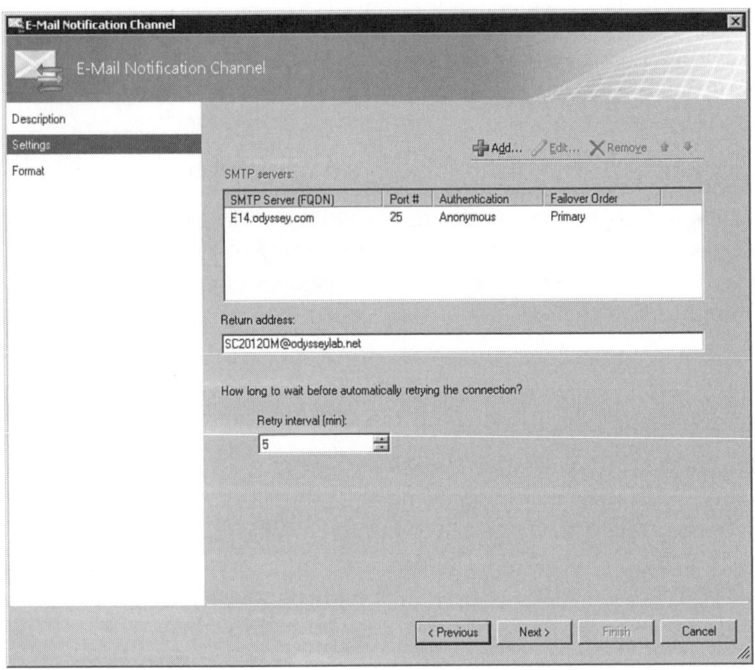

FIGURE 14.31 E-mail notification channel settings.

Figure 14.32 shows the default format E-mail channel format. You can configure the E-mail subject, E-mail message, Importance, and Encoding for this channel. You can customize each field based on your requirements for the channel, including altering the email message itself to contain the fields shown on the right side of the figure.

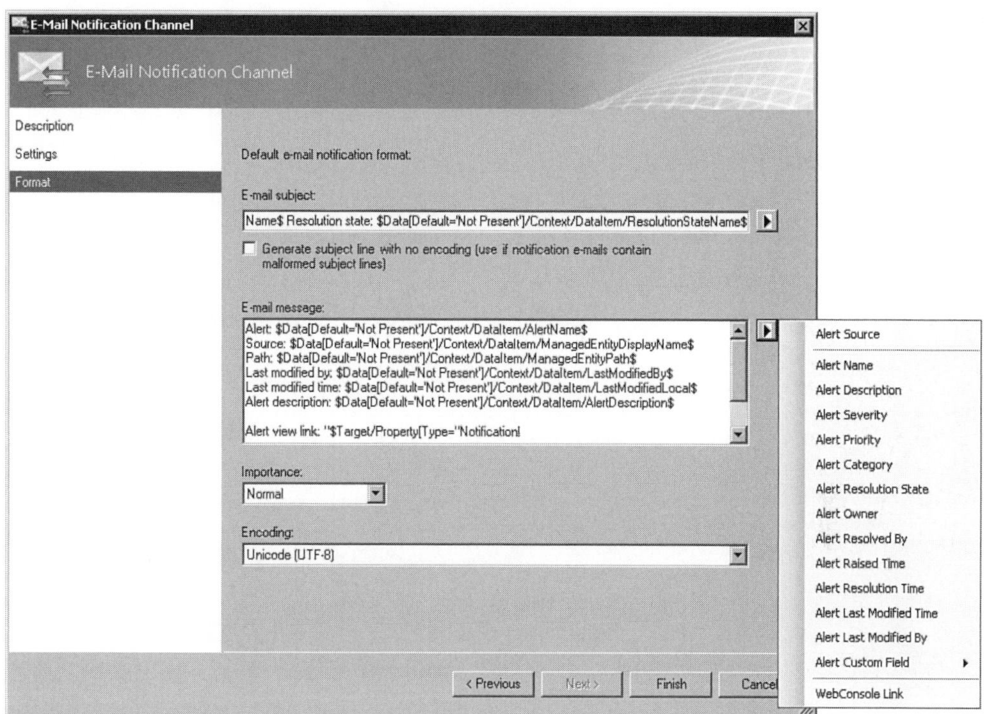

FIGURE 14.32 E-mail format channel settings.

TIP: BENEFITS OF USING MULTIPLE E-MAIL CHANNELS

Channel configuration includes the return address for the channel. By creating and using a unique channel for each subscription in Operations Manager, you can define a different return address for each subscription that users could use to categorize alerts into different folders in Outlook. For example, SQL alerts can be routed to a SQL folder and Exchange alerts to an Exchange folder. This is also beneficial to the OpsMgr administrator, as he can receive all email alerts from OpsMgr and can easily determine those alerts sent by OpsMgr and which subscription actually sent the alert.

Instant Message (IM) Channel

You can also configure instant message channels, as shown in Figure 14.33 and Figure 14.34. The settings for the IM Notification Channel include the name of the IM Server to communicate with, return address, protocol option (TCP or TLS), authentication method (NTML or Kerberos), and IM port (5060 for TCP, 5061 for TLS).

Figure 14.34 shows the IM notification channel format. You can customize the IM message and Encoding fields depending upon your requirements for the IM channel, including alterations of the IM message itself to contain the fields shown on the right side of this figure. The Operations Manager Unleashed team provides information on the steps required to enable Instant Messaging in OpsMgr 2012 at http://opsmgrunleashed.wordpress.com/2012/02/24/enabling-instant-messaging-notifications-in-system-center-2012-operations-manager/.

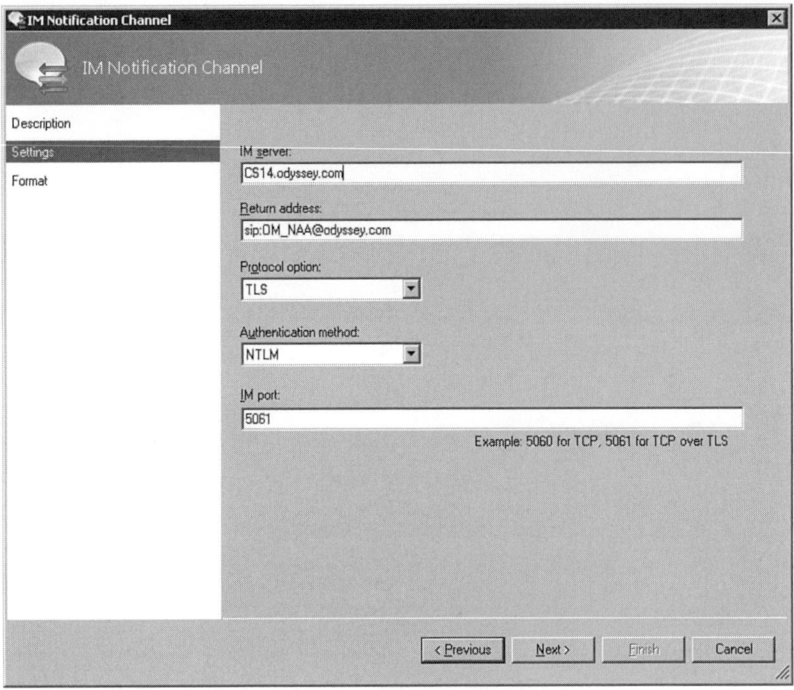

FIGURE 14.33 IM notification channel settings.

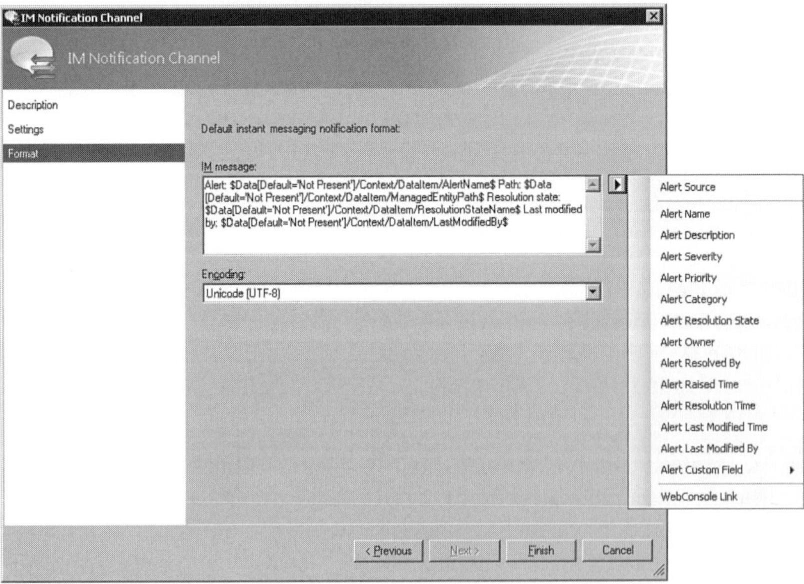

FIGURE 14.34 IM notification channel format.

Text Message (SMS) Channel

The SMS notification channel requires a modem supporting SMS Protocol Data Unit (PDU) mode. After configuring the channel name and description on the first page of the wizard, configure the text message and encoding as shown in Figure 14.35. Marnix Wolf discusses the steps to get SMS functional in OpsMgr at http://thoughtsonopsmgr.blogspot.com/2010/06/sending-out-sms-messages-with-scom.html. System Center Central also has a series of articles at http://www.systemcentercentral.com/tabid/143/IndexId/60339/Default.aspx.

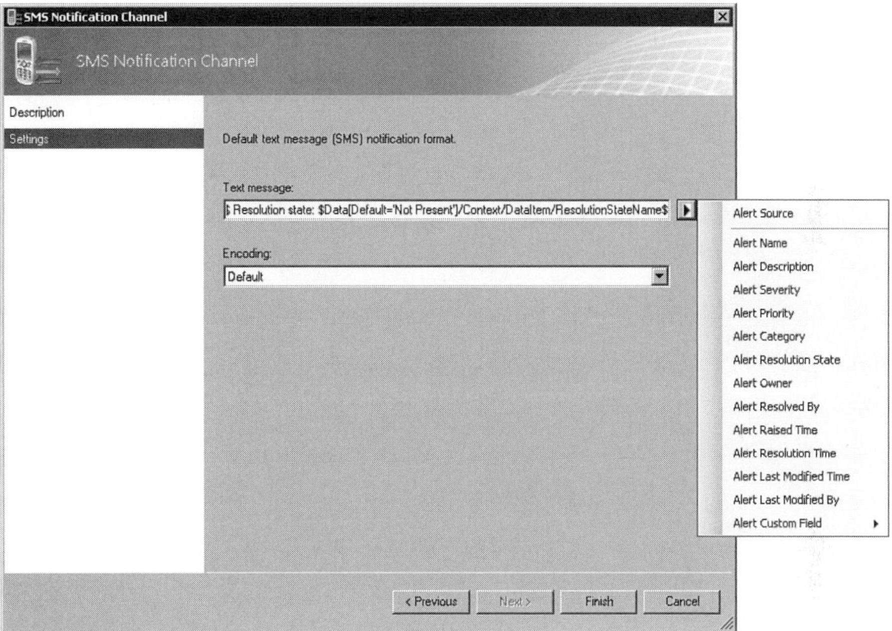

FIGURE 14.35 SMS notification channel settings.

Command Channel

The command channel is the Swiss-army knife of channels in Operations Manager. You can use this channel to run a script that can provide a variety of functions. As an example, the command channel can be used to update alert history to include the subscriptions that sent the alert. See an example of how to accomplish this at http://blogs.catapultsystems.com/cfuller/archive/2012/05/04/how-can-i-tell-if-opsmgr-scom-actually-sent-me-an-email-step-by-step-sysctr-[storing-information-on-subscriptions-sent-in-alert-history].aspx.

Creating a Subscriber

Before you can configure alerts and monitors to send data via email, you must configure a subscriber that includes an address to which to send emails. Follow these steps:

1. Navigate to **Administration** -> **Notifications**. Right-click and select **New Subscriber**. This opens the Notification Subscriber Wizard.
2. Begin by naming the new recipient. The easiest way to do this is searching Active Directory (AD). (If the user does not exist in AD, you must enter the information manually.) Click the **...** button to browse the directory. Type the user's name and click the **Check Names** button to validate your entry. Figure 14.36 shows the name after being selected from Active Directory. Click **OK**.

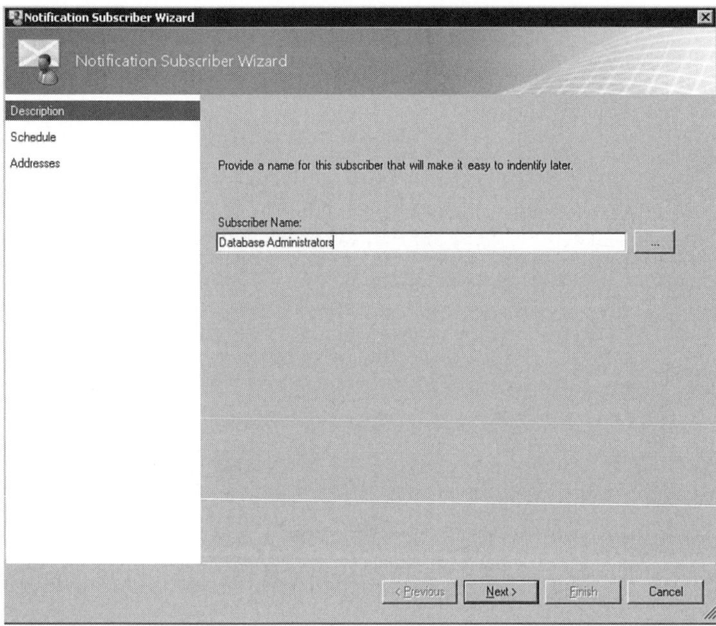

FIGURE 14.36 The description page for the Notification Subscriber Wizard.

3. The user's account name now displays in the subscriber name field. On this second page, you can also choose to configure a schedule for sending emails. For this example assume notifications will always be sent and accept the defaults on the page. You can use schedules to allow notifications during specific time ranges by a date range, weekly recurrence, selected days of the week, and based upon a specific time zone as shown in Figure 14.37. This is most frequently used when providing one form of notification during business hours and another form of notification outside business hours.
4. Choose the type of notifications to send to this address (in this example, email), then click **Add** to start the Subscriber Address Wizard.

5. Specify the name of the subscriber on the General page such as **Database Administrators** in this example.

6. Choose the channel type you want for your subscriber, such as the E-Mail (SMTP) channel example as shown in Figure 14.38. Specify the delivery address to send the subscription to such as DatabaseAdmins@odyssey.com shown in the figure. Note you can add individual email addresses as individual subscribers, or you can add distribution lists, using Microsoft Exchange to maintain the membership of the distribution list.

7. Specify the schedule for the subscriber and click **Finish** to complete the wizard. You can configure scheduling for the subscriber or for the subscription. The schedule applies to all subscribers within the subscription.

   This example illustrated how to set a business day schedule for the subscriber so alerts would only be sent during those hours. You can configure the subscription to send during any hours, and different addresses could be specified to send emails during business hours and a pager notification off-hours. The new recipient (Database Administrators) is displayed in Figure 14.39. You can add additional subscribers to this subscription.

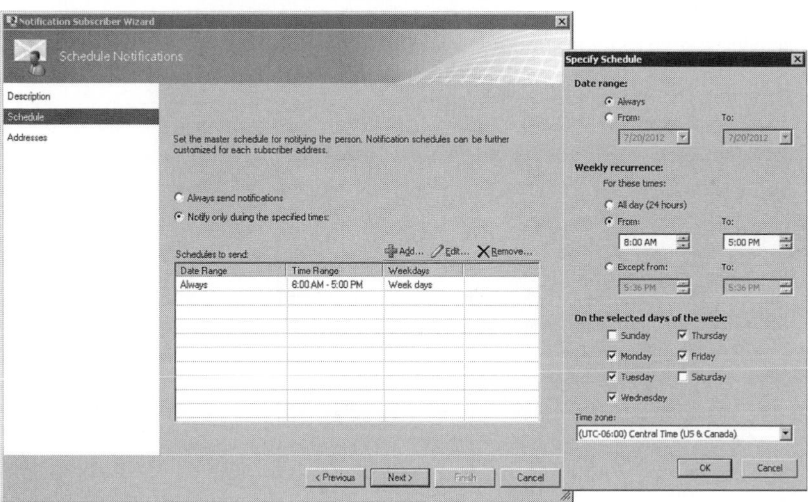

FIGURE 14.37 Configuring the notification schedule.

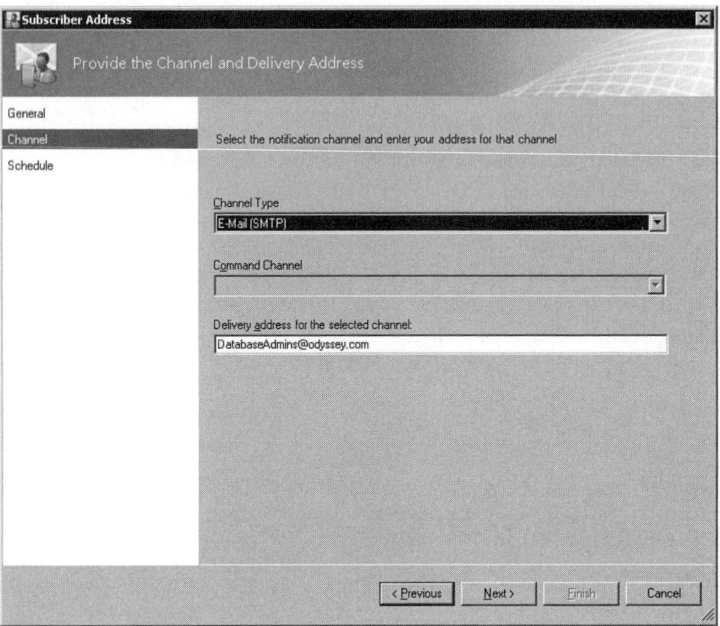

FIGURE 14.38 Specifying the channel and address for the subscriber.

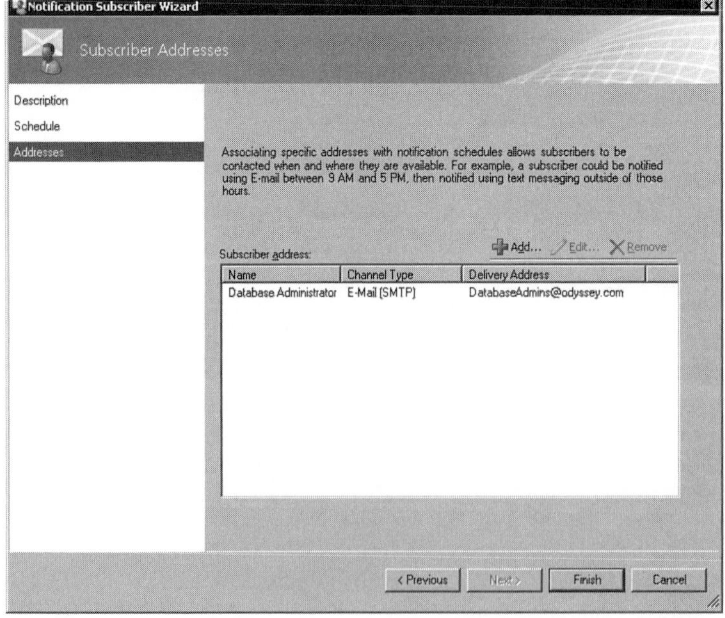

FIGURE 14.39 Configuring the notification address for the subscriber.

Creating a Subscription

After creating a subscriber, you must create a subscription for the recipient to get email alerts. Perform the following steps:

1. In the Administration space, navigate to **Notifications** -> **Subscriptions**. Right-click and select **New Notification Subscription** to display the General properties page of the Notification Subscription Wizard. This page is where you name the subscription, in this example **Alerting to Database Admins**. Click **Next**.

2. The Criteria page identifies the criteria applied to determine if a subscription will include an alert. Multiple conditions can be applied as part of the subscription criteria. Table 14.2 shows the various conditions that can be used as part of a subscription and their common usage.

TABLE 14.2 Subscription properties and common usage

Condition	Common Usage
raised by any instance in a specific group	Groups are commonly used to scope the Operations Manager console so users only see those items that are relevant. These same groups can be used in a subscription to limit the scope of what alerts are sent to those users, which they also see within the Operations console.
raised by an instance of a specific class	Classes can be used to restrict that alerts are sent via the subscription to only those that match specific classes. As an example, you could create a subscription for all SQL-related classes to send to the database administrators group.
created by specific rules or monitors (e.g., sources)	Subscriptions can be limited to specific rules or monitors. This is commonly used when creating subscriptions from the OpsMgr Monitoring pane.
raised by an instance with a specific name	Subscriptions can be limited to specific objects based upon this condition.
of a specific severity	Severities can be Information, Warning, and Critical. This is useful when sending critical alerts for Operations groups that may not be required to receive Warning or Informational alerts.
of a specific priority	Priorities are High, Medium, and Low. This is often combined with specific severity settings for Operations groups.
with specific resolution state	Used frequently to select alerts in a New resolution state.
with a specific name	Often used when creating custom alerts to match based upon a naming convention.

TABLE 14.2 Continued

Condition	Common Usage
with specific text in the description	Frequently used to match keywords listed in the description field.
created in specific time period	Useful to send alerts that have occurred in the last several hours or a specific timeframe.
assigned to a specific owner	This is useful when sending alerts owned by a specific owner or group.
last modified by a specific user	Helpful when sending alerts a user has recently modified.
that was modified in specific time period	Helpful when tracking down a list of alerts that occurred in the last several hours or in a specific timeframe.
had its resolution state changed in a specific time period	Useful to send alerts that had state changes in the last several hours or within a specific timeframe.
that was resolved in a specific time period	This is useful when sending alerts closed in the last day or within a specific timeframe.
resolved by a specific user	Useful when sending alerts a specific user has resolved.
with a specific ticket ID	Helpful when sending alerts for a specific ticket associated with an alert.
was added to the database in a specific time period	This is useful when attempting to identify issues that occurred when adding data to the database.
from a specific site	Provides a way to send alerts from a specific site based upon a wildcard.
with specific text in Custom Field 1..10	Any of the 10 custom fields can provide criteria for this view based upon a wildcard.

As an example for commonly used criteria, a subscription was created (see Figure 14.40) that sends all critical severity alerts in a New resolution state matching any of the classes included in the SQL management pack.

3. You can define new subscribers in the Notification Subscription Wizard or add existing subscribers to the subscription at this point. For this example, add the Database Administrators subscriber defined in the "Creating a Subscriber" section, as shown in Figure 14.41.

4. On the Channels portion of the Notification Subscription Wizard you can create new channels, add existing channels, and configure alert aging.

   For this example, configure the channels as shown, using a custom channel for the Database Administrators. The benefit to using a custom channel is you can customize the channel to send alerts from a different return address, letting you define Outlook rules to route those emails into a specific folder based on the return address.

5. The summary page of the Notification Subscription Wizard provides the summary of the subscription you created and a check box (checked by default) to enable the subscription. Figure 14.42 shows the channel configuration for a subscription once a channel is added.

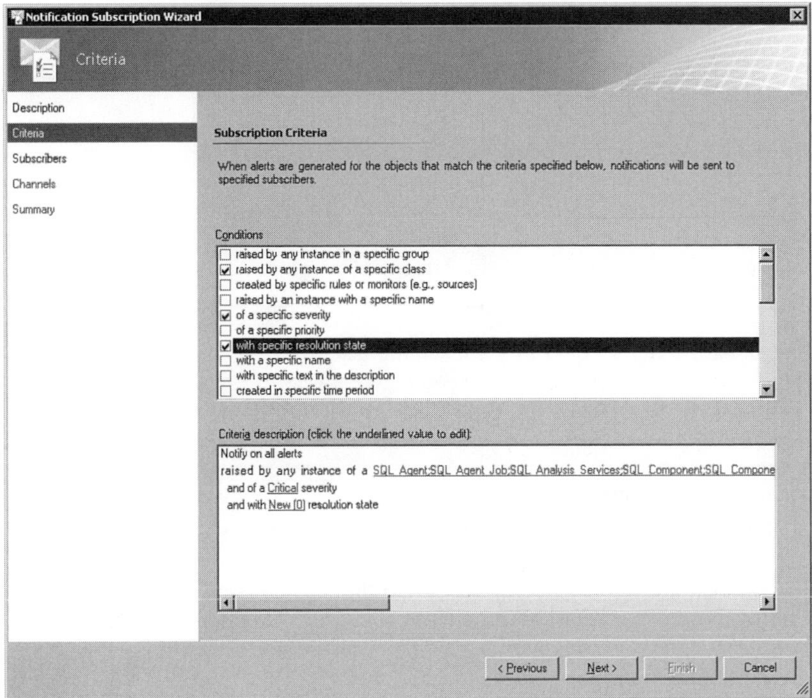

FIGURE 14.40 Configuring the Subscription Criteria in a subscription.

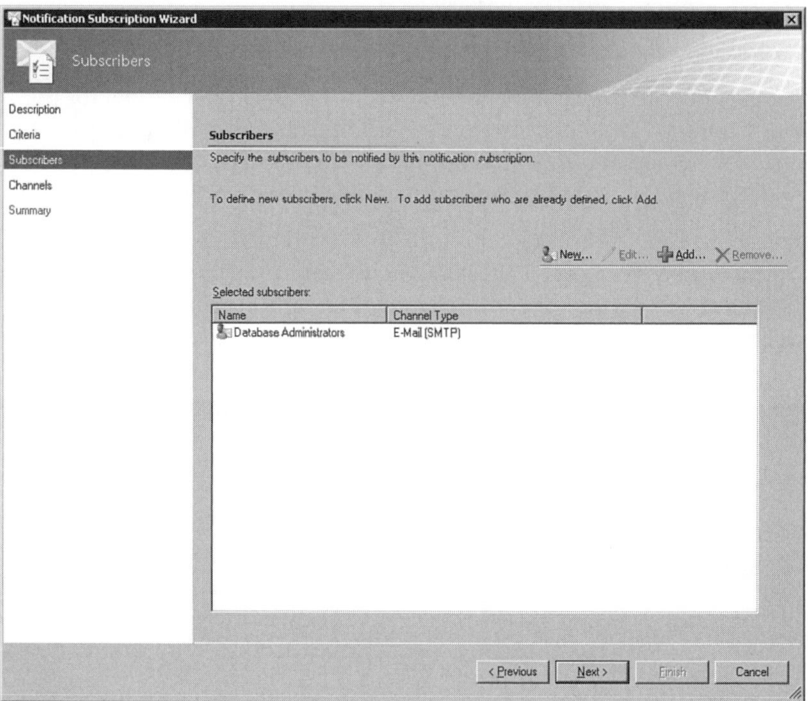

FIGURE 14.41 Configuring the Subscribers in a subscription.

TIP: WHEN TO USE ALERT AGING

Alert aging is primarily used for three situations:

- **Sending an alert for conditions that often change state within a short amount of time:** As an example, a service configured to restart automatically may alert when the service is offline, and would close quickly when the service is brought back online. By setting a 5-minute delay, alerts already resolved will no longer match the criteria of the subscription since the criteria for the subscription is set to New but the alert would now be in a Closed state.
- **Providing a repeating alert notification:** By creating multiple subscriptions to the same conditions for alerts and using alert aging, you can configure an alert that notifies immediately to one group, one hour later to a second group, and an hour after that to a third group.
- **Changing alerts by a subscription after they are found to be in a new state:** For example, alerts routed to a ticketing system have their resolution state changed to indicate they were sent to a ticketing system. By setting alert aging for subscriptions to several minutes, alerts routed to the ticketing system would not be processed by the other subscriptions (because their criteria would no longer match since the resolution state is no longer New).

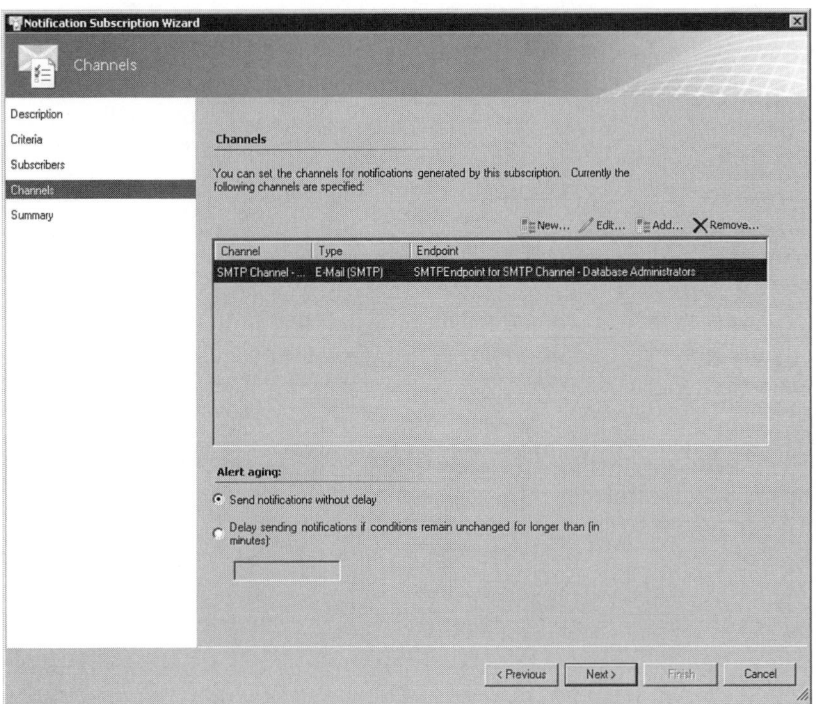

FIGURE 14.42 Configuring channels in a subscription.

TIP: CANNOT EXCLUDE FROM A SUBSCRIPTION

The OpsMgr user interface does not include functionality to define a subscription that excludes specific alerts. Here are some options to work around this restriction:

- Create a subscription targeted to the specific pieces (rules/monitors); see http://blogs.technet.com/b/kevinholman/archive/2008/10/12/creating-granular-alert-notifications-rule-by-rule-monitor-by-monitor.aspx. The problem is that with large management packs you cannot edit the subscriptions once there are a large number of rules/monitors.
- Use XML based exclusions as discussed at http://sethisageek.blogspot.com/2012/03/how-to-exclude-specific-alerts-from.html. The issue here is you cannot edit the subscription in the UI after these changes are made, so this has significant negatives.
- As a long-term approach, the best solution may be an Orchestrator workflow to exclude specific alerts from a subscription, using a table reference that includes the subscription name and the exclusion alert name.

For now, the authors suggest creating granular subscriptions that match the requirements for alerting as closely as possible.

Creating a Subscription Based on an Alert

One of the new features in Operations Manager 2007 R2 was the ability in the Monitoring pane to create a subscription from an alert. To use this feature, highlight an alert, then choose the option in the subscription section of the Tasks pane to create or modify the subscription.

The Create task starts the Notification Subscription Wizard, passing information based on the highlighted alert. This includes the name of the alert as the subscription name and the alert description as the description field. The subscription criteria are configured to notify on alerts that match the rule or monitor that generated the alert. When using this approach to alerting, the authors recommend making the description field more generic (this field often contains server specific information not relevant to all alerts), and setting the criteria to match a New resolution state.

TIP: BLOG POSTING ON SUBSCRIPTIONS

Kevin Holman provides an excellent blog posting on subscriptions in OpsMgr 2012 at http://blogs.technet.com/b/kevinholman/archive/2012/04/28/opsmgr-2012-configure-notifications.aspx.

Adding Knowledge

Despite the fact that monitors are the preferred method for monitoring servers and applications because they are "real time," alerts are still the primary source of information in OpsMgr. This is the reason many monitors are configured to generate alerts.

A typical alert contains a large amount of knowledge and information about the problem that occurred, troubleshooting tips, and often will include steps to assist in resolving the problem. When you select an alert in the Monitoring pane of the Operations console, the bottom (Alert Details) pane displays additional information about an alert as shown in Figure 14.43.

As shown in the figure, some alerts contain quite a bit of information. However, the information supplied by the management pack vendor may not be applicable for your organization, or there may be other specific information you want to include such as additional troubleshooting steps or the names and telephone numbers of the engineers managing the system in question.

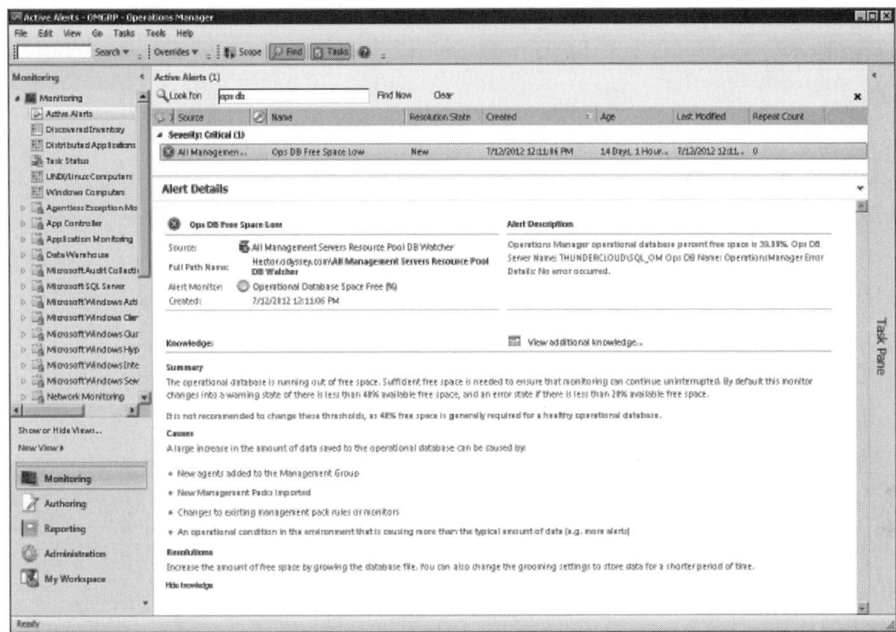

FIGURE 14.43 Viewing the Alert Details pane.

Using Company Knowledge

By incorporating company knowledge, you can add information into an alert so that when that alert appears in the console it appears with your customized information in addition to the vendor-supplied product knowledge.

The following procedure documents the steps to add company knowledge to an alert:

1. Editing company knowledge requires additional software. There are several restrictions and prerequisites to consider:

   - Due to how editing of company knowledge is built into Operations Manager, it can only be performed on a 32-bit operating system. Given the shift towards 64-bit operating systems, this is more of a restriction than it was several years ago. For environments that must use this approach to storing company knowledge, you should install a shared 32-bit Windows 7 system you can use for editing company knowledge. Note that these restrictions are only on editing company knowledge, not viewing existing company knowledge.

   - You must install the Operations Manager console on the system where you will be editing company knowledge. As a reminder, the console requires .NET Framework 4.0 (http://www.microsoft.com/en-us/download/details.aspx?id=17718) and Microsoft Report Viewer 2010 (http://www.microsoft.com/en-us/download/details.aspx?displaylang=en&id=6442) for installation. It is also best to have at least 2GB of memory on the system, although the console will install with less than that amount of memory (the authors do not recommend using less than 2GB as performance will likely be unusable).

- After you install the console, there are two additional prerequisites:

  Microsoft Word (Word 2003 with the .NET Programmability feature, or Microsoft Office Word 2007 or Office Word 2010 Professional edition)

  Visio Studio 2005 Tools for Office (http://www.microsoft.com/en-us/download/confirmation.aspx?id=24263)

- For details on company knowledge and requirements to add knowledge, see http://technet.microsoft.com/en-us/library/hh212900.aspx.

2. Open the Monitoring space in the Operations console. Select an alert and open the properties for the alert. This example uses the Ops DB Free Space Low alert, but the specific alert is not important for this process.

3. On the Alert Properties page, select the Company Knowledge tab. To add company knowledge, click the **Edit Monitor** button, which displays the Properties page for the monitor. Select the Company Knowledge tab here and you will see an **Edit** button.

4. Select the destination management pack drop-down. With the change in how the default management pack is implemented in OpsMgr 2012, the destination management pack now defaults to select a management pack. From this dialog, you can use the **New** button to create a management pack in which to store company knowledge, or choose an existing unsealed management pack from the list provided. Select the **Sample Management Pack** created earlier and then click **Edit**, which will load Microsoft Word.

REAL WORLD: ERROR OPENING WORD WHEN EDITING COMPANY KNOWLEDGE

With OpsMgr 2012 (even on a 32-bit operating system using a 32-bit version of Word later than Word 2003, the Operations console and all additional software installed), editing company knowledge fails when opening Word with this response and error message:

```
Failed to launch Microsoft Word. Please make sure Microsoft Word is installed.
Could not load file or assembly
'Microsoft.Office.Interop.Word,Version=11.0.0.0, Culture=neutral, PublicKeyTo-
ken=71e9bce111e9429c' or one of its dependencies. The system cannot find the
file specified.
```

If you are attempting to edit company knowledge using Word 2010, Satya Vel has blogged a resolution to this issue at http://blogs.technet.com/b/momteam/archive/2012/10/10/how-to-get-knowledge-editing-to-work-in-operations-manager-2012-with-office-2010.aspx. Another option is to use third party products such as SquaredUp (www.squaredup.com) that can edit company knowledge without using Microsoft Word. The authors suggest not using the built-in functionality to edit company knowledge in Operations Manager 2012 and that you store this information in SharePoint instead.

5. After Word loads, you are presented with a Word document you can edit and store company knowledge in.
6. Edit the company knowledge and click the **Save** icon in Microsoft Word. After saving the knowledge, you can close Word. The knowledge is added to the monitor. Click **OK** to save your changes.

Integration with System Center Service Manager

Using the Operations Manager Alert Connector, you can use System Center 2012 Operations Manager with System Center 2012 Service Manager to generate incidents in Service Manager. Figure 14.44 shows an example of an alert created as a Service Manager incident using this connector.

Using the integration provided by the connector, the knowledge in alerts can also be captured in Service Manager. Figure 14.44 highlights a task to search knowledge articles you could use to search an existing in-house knowledgebase.

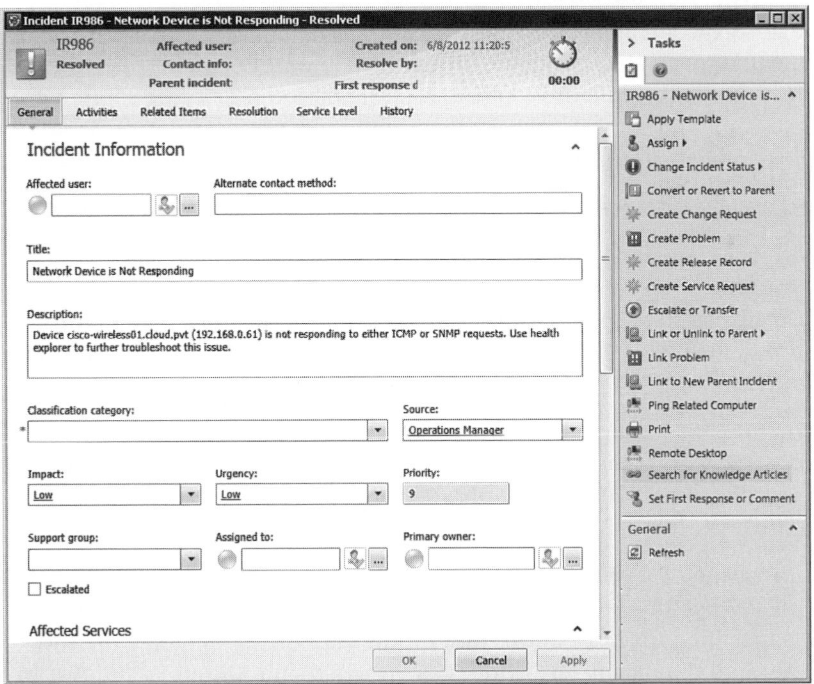

FIGURE 14.44 Service Manager incident from OpsMgr alert.

Service Manager 2012 also facilitates integration back to the Operations Manager Web console (configured under **Administration** -> **Settings** -> **Incident Settings** -> **Operations Manager Web Settings** in the Service Manager console). An incident created from an OpsMgr alert can be tied back to the OpsMgr Web console, so when the incident is opened you can open the OpsMgr Web console directly from the incident. This functionality tightens the integration between these System Center components. You can configure the connector between OpsMgr and Service Manager to keep alerts and incidents synchronized (so that incidents that are closed will close the corresponding alert), but this interaction provides a way to see the original alert in the Operations console without requiring the user to open the console or OpsMgr Web console and the navigate to the alert.

If your organization is using both System Center components, the best option for storing company knowledge may be Service Manager. For additional information on all aspects of Service Manager 2012, see the upcoming *System Center 2012 Service Manager Unleashed* (Sams, 2013).

ReSearch This: Internal and SharePoint

As discussed in the "Using Company Knowledge" section, using the company knowledge feature available in OpsMgr can be challenging unless you are running 32-bit operating systems and older versions of Microsoft Office. Another option for storing company knowledge uses SharePoint and the ReSearch This community management pack. Perform the following steps to implement this solution in Operations Manager 2012:

1. In SharePoint, create a document library, browse to the library, and copy the URL.
2. Download and install the ReSearch This management pack available from System Center Central at http://www.systemcentercentral.com/PackCatalog/PackCatalogDetails/tabid/145/IndexID/21716/Default.aspx. Version 6.5.0.6 of this management pack includes a task designed to search internal websites for alert resolution information.
3. On SharePoint, identify a sample URL by opening the SharePoint document library where the KB article will be stored and searching on the word **TEST**. Copy the URL for later use. A URL for a SharePoint site on a server named sp01 would be http://sp01/KB%20Articles/Forms/AllItems.aspx.
4. In the Authoring pane of the Operations console, navigate to **Management Pack Objects** -> **Tasks**. Scope this view to **Windows Computers** and find **research this – internal**. Change the properties of this task on the command line: Paste the URL from SharePoint into the parameters field replacing TEST with **$Name$** as shown in Figure 14.45.
5. Once this is in place and KBs are uploaded to the document library, you can highlight an alert and the ReSearch This - Internal task can be used to search the internal SharePoint site and identify relevant documents as shown in Figure 14.46. You can open these documents using any version of Microsoft Word or the Word reader.

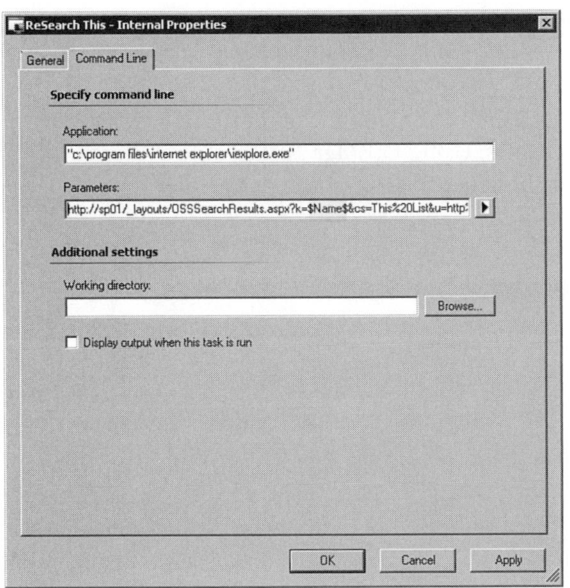

FIGURE 14.45 Searching SharePoint for company knowledge.

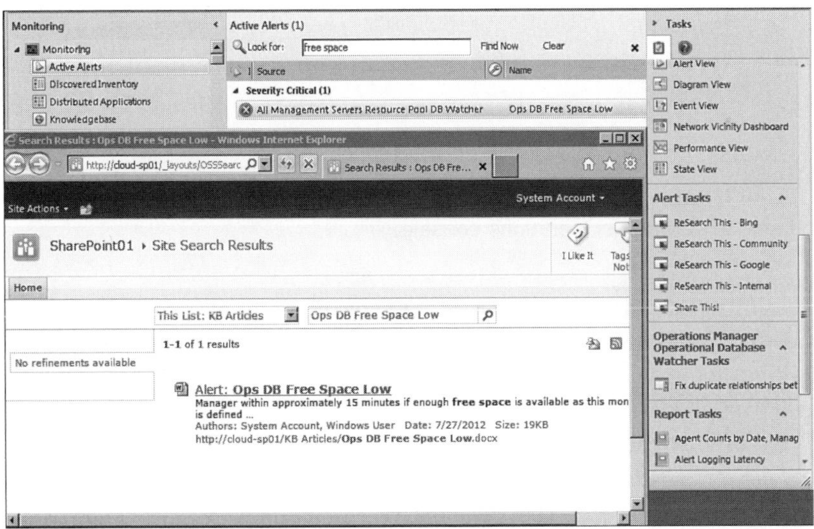

FIGURE 14.46 Results of searching SharePoint for company knowledge.

Using SharePoint as an internal knowledgebase repository and the ReSearch This management pack provide a way to share alert resolutions quickly in your organization using any Windows platform or version of Word.

Locating Rules and Monitors in the Operations Console

Operations Manager is designed for you to search throughout the user interface. Objects are indexed for efficiency when finding objects. Using OpsMgr 2012, you can search in your current view using the search bar shown at the top of the Active Alerts pane in Figure 14.47 (the Look For box).

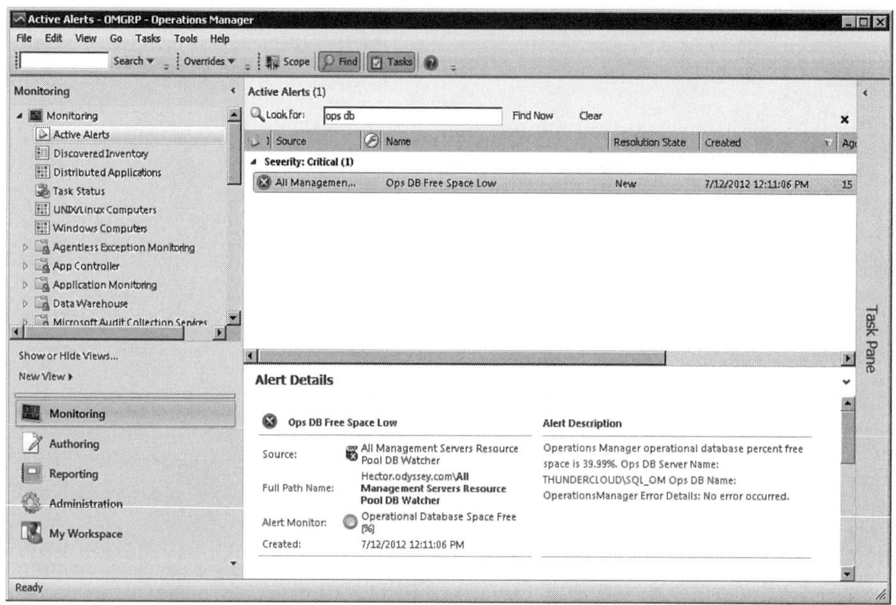

FIGURE 14.47 The search bar in the Operations console.

You can use the Search text box in the top left corner of this figure to quickly identify those object types containing the specified text. As an example, Figure 14.48 shows a search for **Ops Db**. You can also use the advanced search capability located in the Tools menu (**Tools -> Advanced Search**). This menu allows you to target your search at a particular type of object in OpsMgr, rather than searching just the view you are looking at in the console. Figure 14.49 displays the Advanced Search page.

Due to the large number of classes and objects in OpsMgr, the authors do not recommend displaying objects for all classes at one time in the Authoring section of the console. You can scope the console to a particular class or set of classes to minimize the number of items you are displaying, making searching for items easier and faster.

When navigating the Monitoring, Authoring, or My Workspace panes, you will notice at the top of the pane on the right, just underneath the section title bar, a narrow yellow strip with a Change Scope option on the far-right side. This is the scoping bar. You can use this to re-scope the console to a specific class or group of classes.

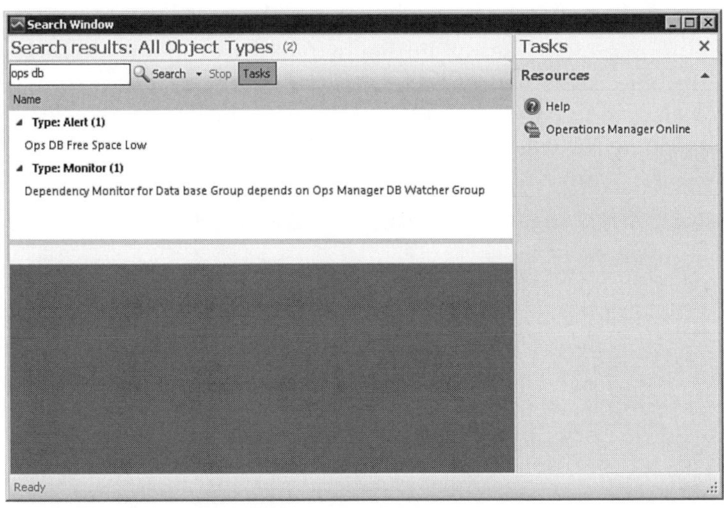

FIGURE 14.48 Searching all objects in OpsMgr.

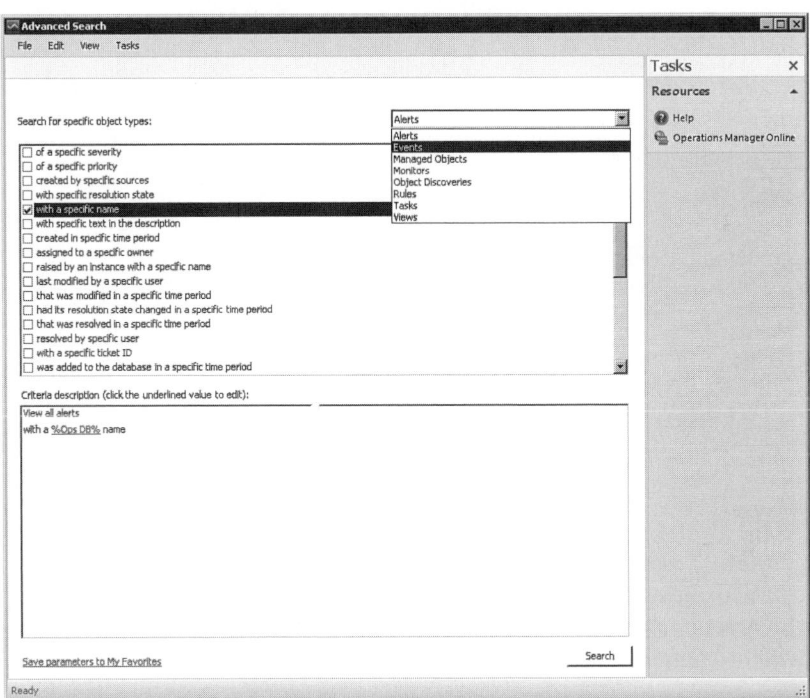

FIGURE 14.49 The Advanced Search page.

After clicking **Change Scope**, the Scope Management Pack Objects by target(s) dialog appears. From here, you can choose to view either common targets or all targets using the radio button near the top of the page. Once the scope is changed, the displayed objects are filtered based on that scope as shown in Figure 14.50.

To select the objects you wish to scope or filter by, scroll through the list of targets and select the appropriate objects, or narrow the search further by typing text in the Look For box. Once the list displays the objects you wish to select, tick the check boxes next to them, and click **OK**. The console's right pane will reload to display your selection, and the list of objects on the yellow scoping bar will include those items.

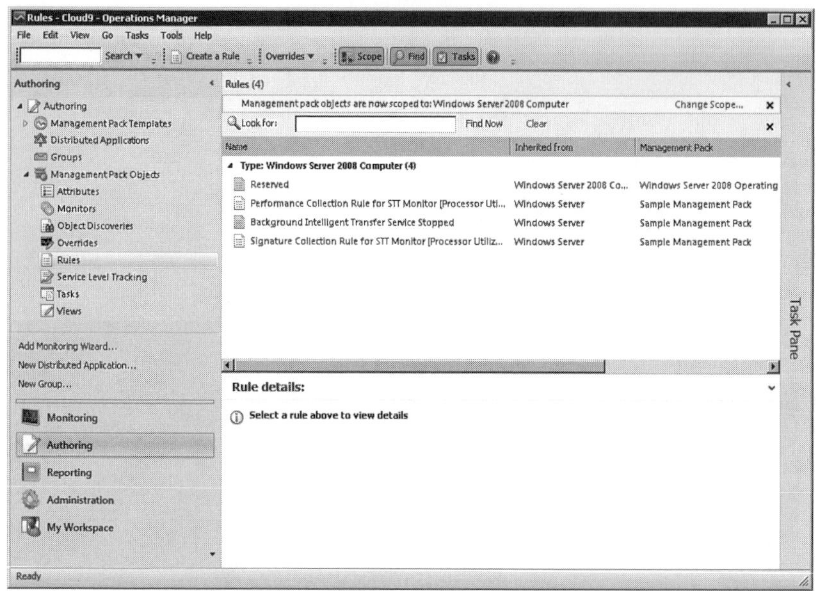

FIGURE 14.50 Selecting the scope of management pack objects you wish to view.

The scoping feature is particularly useful, not only to locate rules and monitors, but also for finding alerts and objects in the Monitoring space of the console. The ability to select scope is invaluable when there are a large number of objects and/or alerts present at any one time.

Using Overrides

Using overrides significantly reduces the need to change rules and therefore edit the rule base. You cannot edit management packs directly in OpsMgr 2012; all changes to management pack objects incorporate overrides. Overrides are the primary method to change how Operations Manager management packs function to match your environment's specific requirements.

Defining Overrides

Overrides enable you to modify settings in a rule or monitor for a particular object such as a managed computer—without actually editing the rule. As an example, you could use an override to disable a rule for a specific monitored computer without affecting the rule for all other monitored systems. Alternatively, you could specify a higher CPU threshold value for a heavily utilized server to prevent false alerts, without affecting the value used with other monitored computers.

Rule settings such as the Enabled flag (which defines whether a rule or monitor is enabled) are presented as values that can be overridden. Overrides themselves, once created, are stored in a custom management pack of your choice. The overrides are grouped together, forming a set of policies to be applied to managed computers. When rules pass to OpsMgr-monitored computers, those policies are applied before the rules arrive. Because the overrides are applied, the copy of rules on the client will differ from the rules on the management server(s). Figure 14.51 illustrates this process.

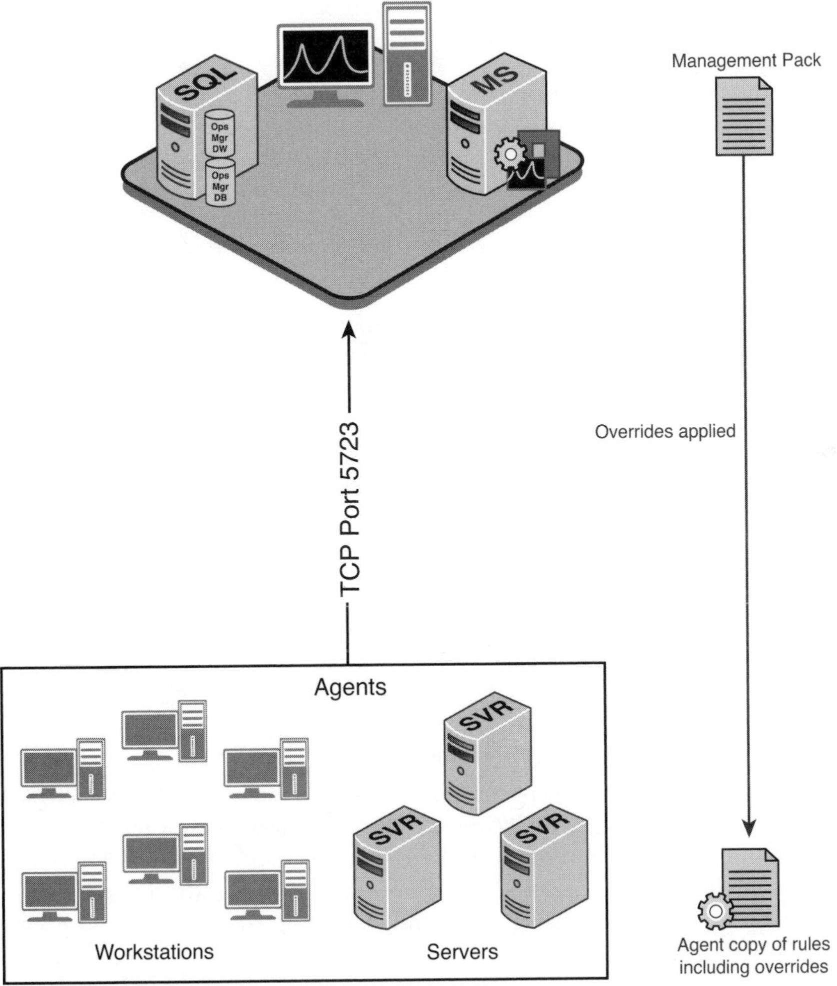

FIGURE 14.51 How overrides are applied in OpsMgr 2012.

Creating an Override

This section looks at the process for creating an override against a monitor. Here are the steps to create an override from the Authoring pane in Operations Manager. Overrides can also be created in the Monitoring or My Workspace panes.

1. Navigate in the Operations console to **Authoring -> Monitors**.
2. Using one of the search methods discussed in the "Locating Rules and Monitors in the Operations Console" section, locate the monitor you wish to override. This example will override the Available Megabytes of Memory monitor located under the `Windows Server 2008 Operating System` class. Using the scoping bar, scope the console to this class. You will find this monitor under the Performance aggregate monitor, as shown in Figure 14.52.

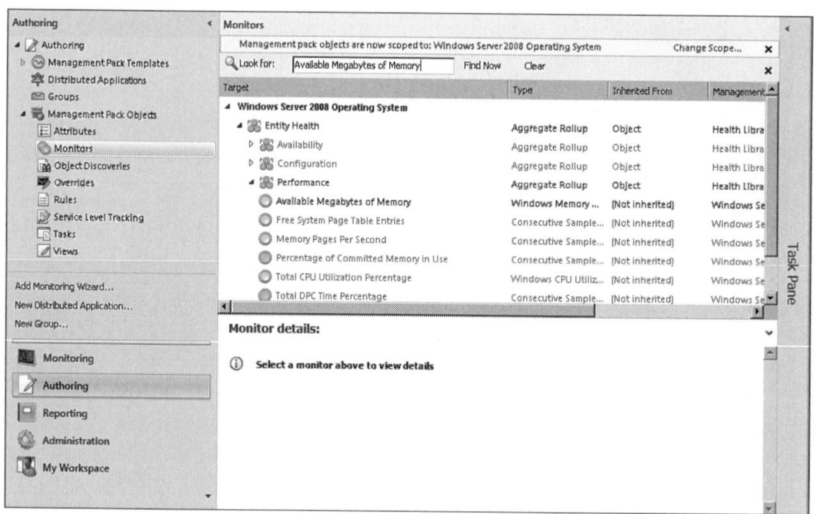

FIGURE 14.52 Locating the monitor.

3. After locating the monitor, right-click and select **Overrides**. Next, choose **Override the Monitor**.

   Notice there is also the option to Disable the Monitor, which is a simple way to disable the monitor for an object, class, or group without going through the steps listed in this section. In OpsMgr 2007 using the disable option was not recommended, as disabling stored the override in the Default management pack. This is no longer the case in Operations Manager 2012. The Disable the Monitor option creates an override that sets the Enabled flag to False and stores it in the management pack that you specify.

   Choosing **Override the Monitor** opens a submenu with the following options:

- **For all objects of class:** *<Class the monitor is attached to>*

  The For all objects of class: option creates the override and targets it at all objects encompassed by the class to which the monitor is attached. In this particular case, the override is targeted to all objects that are members of the `Windows Server 2008 Operating System` class.

  An example of this configuration would be if you needed to update a threshold value for all occurrences of a performance counter. To change the threshold value for the Total CPU Percentage Utilization monitor for all Windows Server 2008 computers, you would create an override on that monitor using the For all objects of type: option.

- **For a group...**

  The For a group... option allows you to select a group instead of a class or object.

  This is useful when you need to apply the override to a group rather than a class, such as a specific collection of computers. You can create a group, populate it with those computers, and then apply the override to that new group.

- **For a specific object of class:** *<Class the monitor is attached to>*

  The For a specific object of class: option is similar to the For all objects of type: option, other than the fact that this option gives you the opportunity to select a specific object (perhaps the processor on a specific monitored computer) to which to target the override.

  This option is useful if you want to create an override for a specific object. Take the CPU Percentage Utilization monitor used in the For all objects of a type: example. The For a specific option of type: option would be useful if you want to update the performance threshold for a single instance of the counter, on a single computer.

- **For all objects of another class.....**

  The For all objects of another type... option allows you to apply the override to all objects of a type different from that of the rule or monitor you are overriding.

  This option is only used in extremely advanced and complex scenarios and should not be used without a detailed understanding of the classes involved. This type of an override does not re-target a workflow to another class; it only allows you to target an override to another existing class.

  These options define which object or group of objects the override will target.

4. For this example, assume a single computer running Windows Server 2008 is causing excessive alerts. For this override, choose specific object of class **Windows Server 2008 Operating System**. Selecting this option presents the Select Object dialog, as shown in Figure 14.53. From this page, select the server (in this case Helios) for the computer that is experiencing heavy usage and therefore generating alerts.

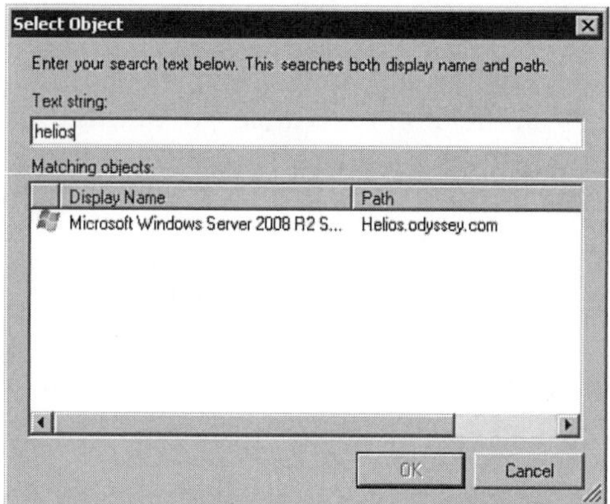

FIGURE 14.53 Select an object for override.

5. Highlight the object and click **OK** after selecting the object you wish to override. The Override Properties page displays, as shown in Figure 14.54.

6. The Override Properties page displays all the parameters you can override for the monitor. This particular monitor includes a large number of parameters you can override. Because the interest is to modify the threshold values, focus on the Available Memory Threshold (Mbytes) parameter.

   To modify this parameter, scroll down to tick the check box next to the parameter and type the new value in the Override Value column, which should highlight automatically when you put a tick in the check box. The default value is 100MB, but you can change this as necessary. For this example, change the value to 50MB. Type **50.0** into the column, select the management pack in which to store the override, and click **Apply** (see Figure 14.54).

   The next column (Effective Value) will change to reflect the change you made. Click **OK** to apply the override.

7. To verify the override, look in the Overrides Summary page. To locate this page, right-click the monitor, and choose **Overrides Summary**. You will see the override listed in the Overrides Summary page. From here, you can delete or edit any overrides as required.

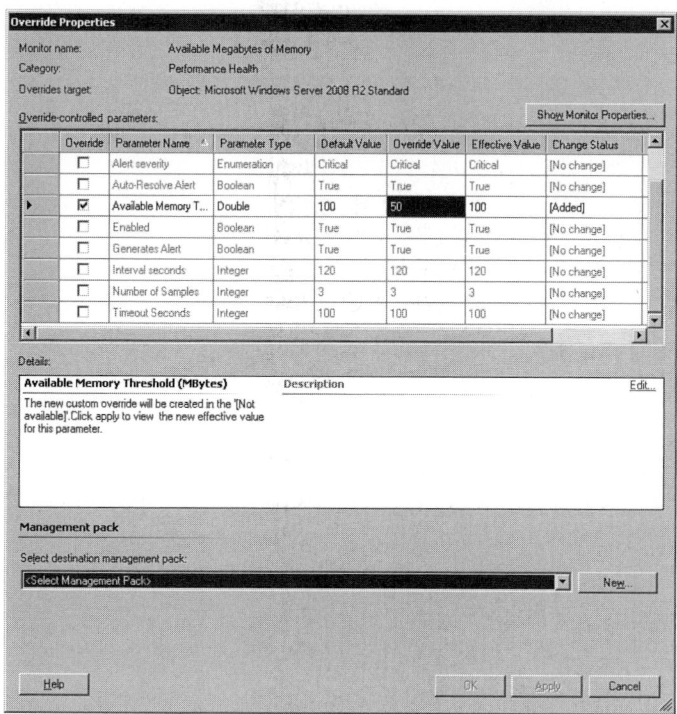

FIGURE 14.54 Changing the Available Memory Threshold parameter.

NOTE: OVERRIDING PARAMETERS

Not all parameters in monitors and rules can be overridden. If you cannot find the parameter you wish to override, it may not be possible to override that parameter. If that is the case, it may be necessary to disable the rule/monitor using an override and create a custom rule or monitor to edit the values you require.

This section looked at overrides and stepped through configuring an override to a Windows performance monitor.

Using the Authoring Pane to Locate Overrides

Operations Manager 2007 R2 added new functionality to the Authoring pane to locate overrides more easily in the console within **Authoring -> Management Pack Objects -> Overrides**. This functionality also exists in Operations Manager 2012, as shown in Figure 14.55.

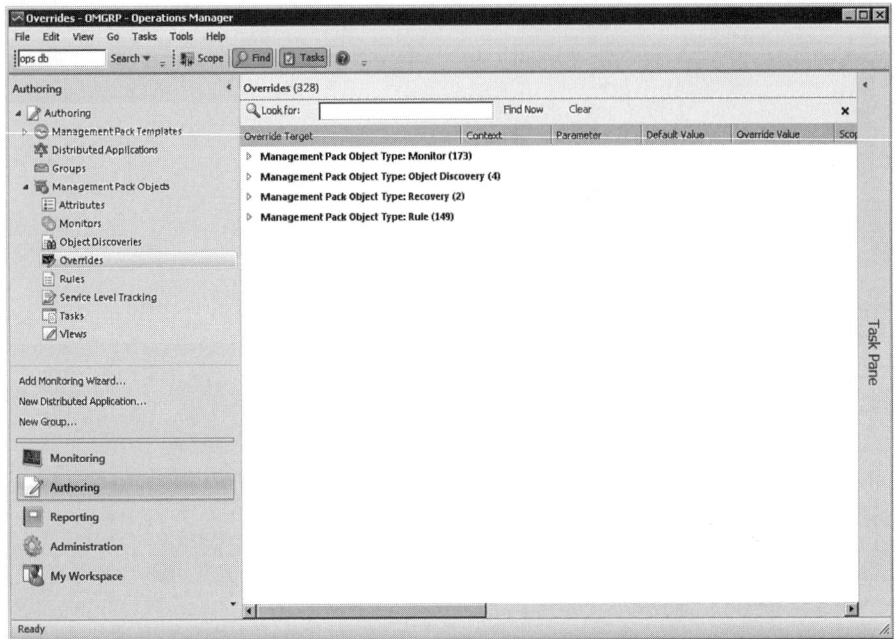

FIGURE 14.55 Overrides in the Authoring pane.

The same search functionality discussed in the "Locating Rules and Monitors in the Operations Console" section applies throughout the Authoring pane, making it much easier to locate an override created in the management group. Overrides can also be changed or removed from the Overrides section of the Operations Manager console in the Authoring node.

Using the Reporting Pane to Locate Overrides

Microsoft includes a prebuilt overrides report (shown in Figure 14.56) available in the Operations console under **Reporting -> Microsoft Generic Report Library -> Overrides**. You can configure this report to show which overrides are defined and what they are applied to, limiting it to those management packs you specify. You can also choose to include or exclude overrides from sealed management packs (overrides in sealed management packs are often created as part of the management packs Microsoft provides and can make it difficult to identify where custom overrides are located). Running this report with default settings to include all management packs and exclude sealed management packs enables you to identify custom overrides created for a particular environment. While this report still includes some of the prebuilt overrides created in non-sealed management packs, it significantly decreases the number of overrides in the report (in a lab environment the report decreased from 8 to 3 pages).

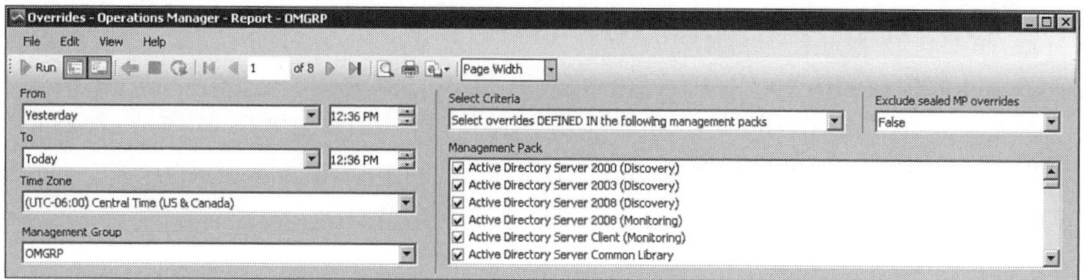

FIGURE 14.56 Overrides report example.

Using the Command Shell to Locate Overrides

Finding overrides in the Operations console is not difficult, but in large, complex implementations where there may be many hundreds and even thousands of overrides, it can become difficult and time consuming to locate them in this manner. In this case, consider using the Operations Manager Shell.

The Operations Manager Shell builds on Windows PowerShell. It contains the Operations Manager functions and cmdlets you can use to manage Operations Manager from the command line. Some features, such as configuring connected management groups, are only possible using the Shell, so you will want to familiarize yourself with it. More information on the Operations Manager Shell can be found in Chapter 23, "PowerShell and Operations Manager."

REAL WORLD: BEST PRACTICES FOR OVERRIDES

Microsoft provides recommendations and best practices when creating overrides. This guide is available at http://support.microsoft.com/kb/943239. Although written for OpsMgr 2007, most of what this guide states is still applicable with the exception that disabling alerts now does not store the override in the Default management pack.

The best practice recommendation is to create separate override management packs for each management pack.

Other best practices for overrides include

- Develop and document your standards for overrides and where they are stored. Pete Zerger writes about this at http://www.systemcentercentral.com/tabid/145/indexId/73805/Default.aspx.
- Document each override and custom management pack created based on the rule and explain why it was created. Store these in SharePoint or potentially in the Service Manager knowledgebase. Using this approach from the beginning is far easier than figuring it out on an existing environment.
- Configure overrides for groups or classes instead of specific instances whenever possible.

The next section discusses creating custom resolution states in OpsMgr 2012.

Creating Custom Resolution States

Operations Manager 2012 ships with two defined resolution states: New and Closed. You can define your own custom resolution states to provide additional granularity. Here is the process to create a custom resolution state:

1. Open the Operations console and navigate to the Administration space.
2. Select **Settings**. You will see the Settings pane on the right and open the properties of the Alerts setting.
3. Double-click **Alerts** to open the Global Management Group Settings - Alerts page displayed in Figure 14.57.
4. Click **New**.
5. The Edit Alert Resolution State page appears. Type a name for the new resolution state and select a unique ID for it. (The ID affects where it appears in the context menu. The number 1 appears at the top, whereas 255 is at the bottom.) For this example, call the resolution state **Assigned to Next Scheduled Maintenance** and give it an ID of **240**. Figure 14.58 displays this page after it is filled out.
6. Click **OK** and **OK** again to finish creating the new alert resolution state.
7. To use the new state, navigate to the Active Alerts view in the Monitoring space, right-click an alert, and select **Set Resolution State**. The Support resolution state is now available. Figure 14.59 shows the context menu where you can highlight an alert and assign it to the resolution state you created.

TIP: NEW RESOLUTIONS STATES IN OPSMGR 2012 SERVICE PACK 1

With the release of Service Pack 1 for Operations Manager 2012, several resolution states have been added, which include:

- Acknowledged (249)
- Assigned to Engineering (248)
- Awaiting Evidence (247)
- Resolved (254)
- Scheduled (250)

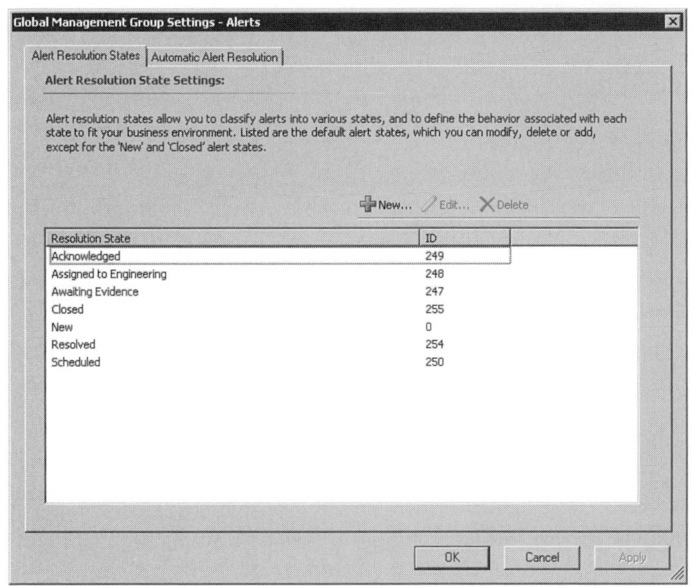

FIGURE 14.57 Alert Resolution States page.

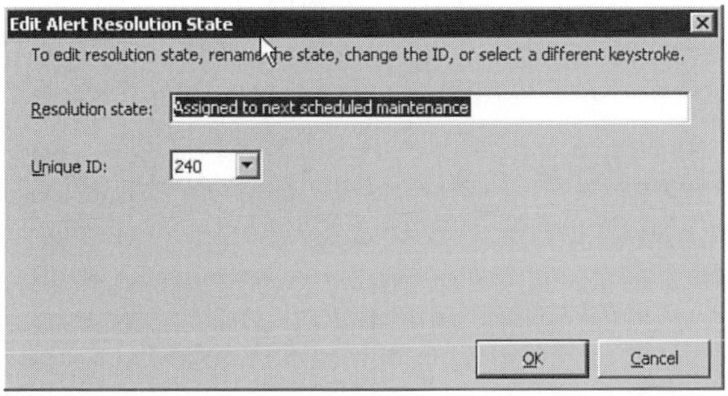

FIGURE 14.58 Edit Alert Resolution State page.

TIP: WHY YOU SHOULD CREATE CUSTOM ALERT RESOLUTIONS STATES

Custom resolution states are often used to categorize alerts that are being worked on by different groups within an organization. As an example, there is often a requirement to create a resolution state for OpsMgr Admins, Database Admins, Web Admins, and such. You can use these resolution states in subscriptions, or to create views targeted to a resolution state.

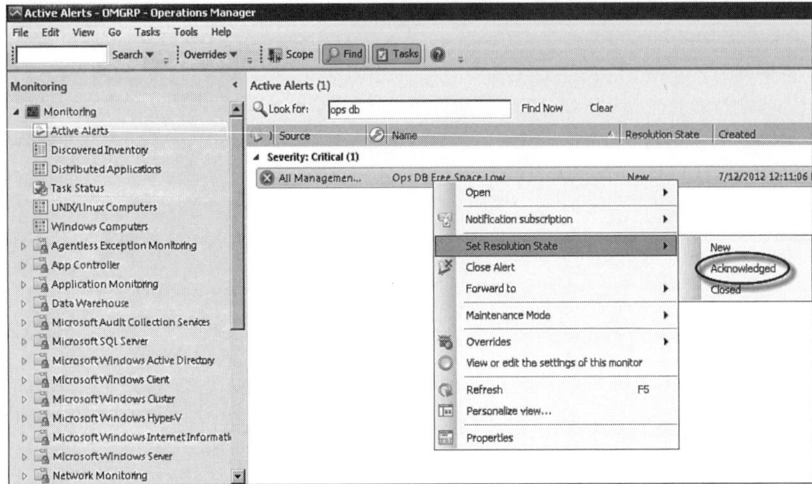

FIGURE 14.59 Using alert resolution states.

Maintenance Tuning

Tuning Operations Manager to meet your organization's specific requirements is one of the most important steps in implementing Operations Manager 2012. This section discusses concepts regarding fixing or tuning, how OpsMgr approaches alerting when compared to other products, tuning alerts "by color," and managing alerts in OpsMgr.

Whether to Tune or Fix

As an Operations Manager administrator, you will want to approach tuning for OpsMgr to fix what is found, and to only tune what is not applicable for the environment. While it is more expedient to tune OpsMgr to ignore the majority of the alerts, this destroys the benefit of the tool. OpsMgr is designed to find issues proactively when possible, so resolving issues it identifies provides a more stable and well-functioning environment. There are situations where tuning will need to occur to match your environment, but fixing should be the default response; and only tune when the issue is not a concern for your environment.

Operations Manager Versus Other Tools: A Difference in Approach

Operations Manager 2012 provides alerting that you then tune to match your environment's requirements—referred to as *tuning down*. Other tools take a different approach to alerting, where they are tuned to match your environments through adding things to alert on; this is referred to as *tuning up*.

Tuning Down

The approach of Operations Manager is to alert on conditions when they are broken and before they will break. The benefit is this approach to generating alerts means that conditions that cause problems in your environment should generate an alert when an issue occurs. The problem with this approach is a significant amount of alert volume can occur from using this approach.

Tuning Up

The flip side is to generate alerts on very few conditions and activate conditions if they are applicable in your environment. The benefit to this approach is it results in very actionable alerting. The problem with this approach is that issues might be missed, and problems that could be preventable may occur.

TIP: TUNING UP IN OPSMGR

An OpsMgr subject matter expert at the Microsoft Management Summit (MMS) 2012 discussed a different approach to tuning OpsMgr alerts where alerts are tuned by only alerting once they are in an approved state. The process used to identify this approved state can be performed by configuring relevant alerts in a lab management group that is then moved to a production management group. Additionally, smartphone web access to the Operations console enables alerts to be tuned up when identified in production. This is an interesting approach to consider when using Operations Manager.

Tuning by Color

Do you remember when you first installed Operations Manager and everything was healthy and green? Take a screenshot because it will take a lot of work to get it to stay green once the full set of management packs are in place!

The easiest way to carry out alert tuning is using the status of a managed machine to prioritize the tuning. There are three main color states in OpsMgr, which should be self-explanatory:

- Critical/Error (Red)
- Warning (Yellow)
- OK/Success (Green)

Using these colors, you can focus your tuning and alert analysis on the systems that are marked as critical (red) first, working down to warning (yellow). Unless any specific overrides must be created for a managed machine, machines that are showing as OK (green) can usually be left alone unless their status changes.

State Monitors Versus Alerts

As discussed in the "About Rules" and "Using Monitors" sections, alerts from monitors and rules are very different:

- Alerts from monitors are updated based on the current status of the system, and return to a healthy state when the failure condition is resolved.

  Although monitors can generate alerts, these alerts are typically managed by the monitor, meaning that if the state monitor condition returns to normal, not only does the status return to Healthy but any alerts raised by the monitor are automatically resolved.

  Monitor-managed alerts require little human intervention, because the monitors resolve alerts automatically once the error condition is resolved. However, these alerts still require some degree of watching, and the number of alerts will continue to increase with the number of systems you are managing.

- Alerts raised by rules behave differently than those created by monitors. These alerts will not resolve by themselves and require managing.

TIP: THE EXCEPTION TO THE RULE OF THE MONITOR

The rule of the monitor states that an alert should not be closed if a monitor generated it. The reasoning here is that the monitor is still in a non-healthy condition but there are no alerts that are active to indicate why the monitor is not healthy. The only exception to this rule is for alerts created by monitors that should have auto-closed but did not due to a technical issue. For additional information, see http://blogs.catapultsystems.com/cfuller/archive/2011/04/15/opsmgr-never-close-an-alert-for-a-monitor-%E2%80%93-the-exception-to-the-%E2%80%9Crule-of-the-monitor%E2%80%9D.aspx.

You should consider these differences in status monitors and alerts when creating custom rules and monitors, because creating a large number of alert-generating rules can affect the number of alerts appearing in the system and increase your management overhead for those alerts. Chapter 22 includes additional information on creating management pack objects.

Managing Alerts

When you are managing issues, they might fall outside your knowledge, expertise, or responsibility. In those cases, you will want to reassign the issues to a more knowledgeable party. OpsMgr allows you to manage this escalation process using the Alerts view in the Operations console. OpsMgr supports creating custom resolution states as discussed in the "Creating Custom Resolution States" section of this chapter.

Out of the box, OpsMgr 2012 RTM has two resolution states: New and Closed. (Service Pack 1 adds 5 additional resolution states, described in the "New Alert Resolution States in OpsMgr 2012 Service Pack 1" Tip.) However, you may add additional alert resolution states as necessary to assign alerts to different support groups, as discussed in the "Creating Custom Resolution States" section. After creating customized alert resolution states and using them, you may want to create custom views to view alerts from specific groups separately from the rest.

There are many different types of views, including alert views, performance views, and event views. The process for creating each type is discussed in Chapter 7, "Configuring and Using System Center 2012 Operations Manager."

For additional information on tuning in Operations Manager 2012 see Appendix A, "OpsMgr by Example: Configuring and Tuning Management Packs."

Maintenance Mode in OpsMgr

After tuning your alerts and configuring overrides, you will want to keep new false alerts to a minimum. Sometimes it is necessary to shut down or reboot computers when applying patches and performing essential maintenance; when you have planned outages, alerts and health status changes in OpsMgr are not particularly welcome.

The maintenance mode feature enables you to stop monitoring a monitored system during scheduled maintenance periods. OpsMgr 2012 lets you target maintenance mode at any object, not just a managed computer. This means, for example, that you could put a single SQL Server database into maintenance mode to take it offline while still monitoring all other databases on the server and all other components of that server such as disk and CPU. This granular level of applying maintenance mode mirrors the level of granularity found throughout OpsMgr 2012.

TIP: MAINTENANCE MODE AND CONFIGURATION MANAGER

When you use System Center 2012 Configuration Manager (ConfigMgr) to deploy software, Configuration Manager 2012 includes an option to put the system into maintenance mode for the duration of the software deployment. In OpsMgr 2007/ConfigMgr 2007, this feature did not work completely as discussed in http://blogs.msdn.com/b/steverac/archive/2008/07/18/configmgr-and-opsmgr-maintenance-mode.aspx. The option in Configuration Manager 2012 does not put the agent into maintenance mode in Operations Manager 2012 but will pause the OpsMgr agent so alerts are not generated during the software deployment.

As an example of how to apply maintenance mode to an object, the following procedure shows how to put the C: drive of the Typhoon computer in maintenance mode for 30 minutes to carry out some essential maintenance.

The easiest way to put a component into maintenance mode is to use the Diagram view of the monitored computer to locate the component. Perform these steps:

1. Navigate to **Monitoring** -> **Computers** and right-click the Typhoon computer. From the context menu, select **Open** -> **Diagram View**.
2. A diagram view similar to the one shown in Figure 14.60 appears.

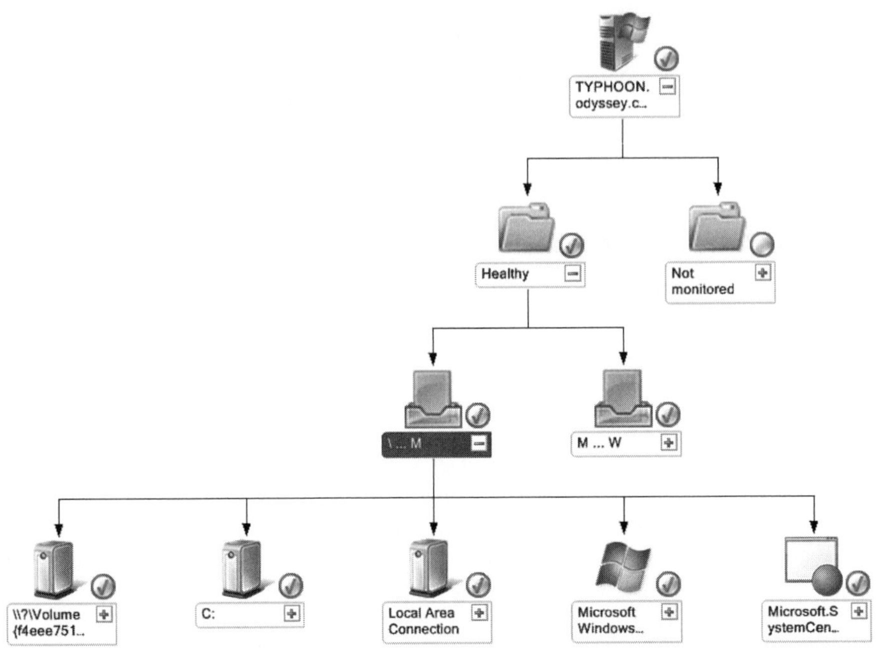

FIGURE 14.60 The OpsMgr Diagram view for Typhoon.

3. Now right-click the C: drive object (displayed at the bottom of Figure 14.60) and from the context menu, select **Maintenance Mode -> Start Maintenance Mode** to open the Maintenance Mode Settings page.

4. Check the **Planned** box on the right and the **Selected objects only** radio button. Now, select a category for planned maintenance, as displayed in Figure 14.61. Select the **Hardware: Maintenance (Planned)** category from the drop-down list. Click **OK**, and add a comment if you like. Set the number of minutes to **30** and click **OK**.

5. If you refresh the view, you will see that the object now has a small spanner icon (highlighted in Figure 14.62) to indicate it is in maintenance mode. You can edit maintenance mode and remove a managed computer or object from maintenance mode using the same context menu used in step 3.

   Of course, you can put higher-level objects in maintenance mode, including an entire managed computer.

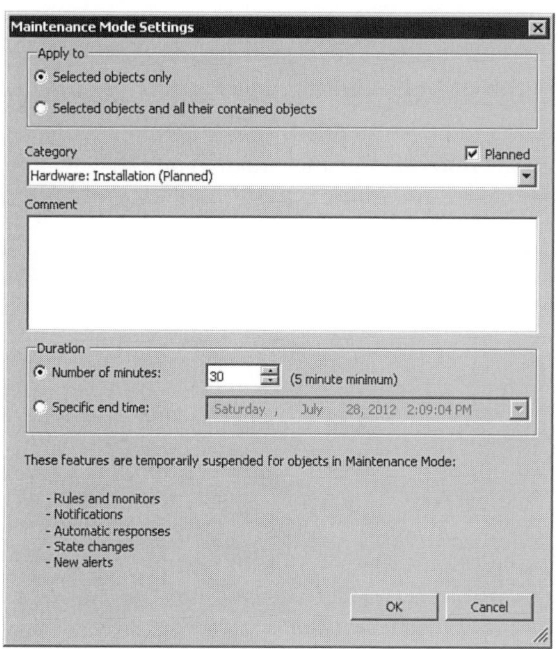

FIGURE 14.61 The Maintenance Mode Settings page.

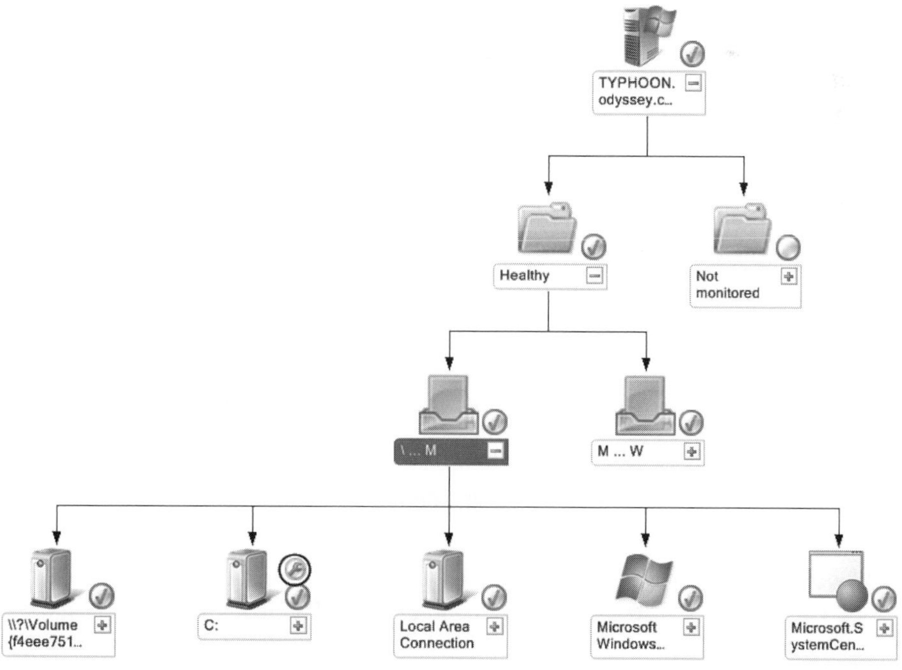

FIGURE 14.62 Looking at the Diagram view while in maintenance mode.

14

By default, maintenance mode automatically filters down to lower-level objects. As shown with the example for the C: drive on Typhoon using the Maintenance Mode Settings page, you can change this by choosing **Selected objects only**.

You can also initiate maintenance mode using the OpsMgr Shell. This is useful when you want to script the adding of monitored objects into maintenance mode. You can find additional information on using the OpsMgr Shell in Chapter 23.

TIP: MAINTENANCE MODE RESETS HEALTH STATE

One of the side effects of using maintenance mode is that all monitors are reset to a healthy state. This can be useful when there are situations where it is not feasible to manually reset the state of the various monitors involved, even when using PowerShell scripts.

Resource Kit Utilities

As of January 2013, Microsoft has not released resource kit utilities for Operations Manager 2012. However, due to the similarity of how OpsMgr 2007 R2 and OpsMgr 2012 work there is a high degree of likelihood that the utilities written for OpsMgr 2007 R2 will work on OpsMgr 2012.

The System Center Operations Manager 2007 R2 Authoring Resource Kit is available at http://www.microsoft.com/en-us/download/details.aspx?id=18222 and includes the following utilities:

- **Authoring Console:** This provides a method to develop MPs within a GUI environment but cannot be used for the new features added in OpsMgr 2012, such as dashboards or the new network monitoring functionality.
- **Management Pack Best Practice Analyzer:** This tool integrates with the Authoring console to scan management packs for best practice compliance and provides automated resolution for a variety of issues.
- **Management Pack Spell Checker:** This tool integrates with the Authoring console to check spelling in management packs to eliminate errors in display strings.
- **Management Pack Visio Generator:** Allows you to generate a class inheritance and class relationship diagram using Microsoft Office Visio.
- **Management Pack Diff:** Shows the differences between two management packs.
- **Management Pack Cookdown Analyzer:** Identifies workflows that may break cookdown and provides suggestions for how to fix the performance problems.
- **All References Add-in:** Helps find all management pack elements that reference the specific element chosen. For example, the ability to right-click a class and find all rules, monitors, overrides, as well as anything else that targets that class is provided.

- **Workflow Analyzer:** Provides the ability to analyze all types of workflows and allows the user to trace workflows running on any health service.
- **Workflow Simulator:** This tool integrates with the Authoring console and can be used to test certain types of workflows such as discoveries, rules, and monitors without a management server or management group.
- **Management Packs:** The commonly required management packs needed to open the Authoring console are provided with the Authoring Resource Kit.

The System Center Operations Manager 2007 R2 Admin Resource Kit includes the following resource kit tools (utilities and their descriptions are a subset of the text provided by Microsoft at http://blogs.technet.com/b/momteam/archive/2011/06/03/system-center-operations-manager-2007-r2-admin-reskit-released.aspx):

- **Scheduled Maintenance Mode:** Ability to schedule and manage maintenance mode in the management group.
- **Clean MOM:** Helps remove all installed R2 components.
- **MP Event Analyzer:** MP Event Analyzer tool is designed to help a user with functional and exploratory testing and debugging of event based management pack workflows like rules and monitors.

The System Center Operations Manager 2007 Tools and Utilities include the following resource kit tools (utilities and their descriptions are a subset of the text provided by Microsoft at http://technet.microsoft.com/en-us/systemcenter/bb625978.aspx):

- **Active Directory Integration Script:** Enables you to extract a list of computer names from your custom SQL Server database, based on a specified query parameter, and add them to an Active Directory security group. You can assign the members of the security group to a specific management server.
- **Sample Vista Gadget:** Enables you to view the state of a specified set of objects from a computer running Windows Vista and Windows 7.
- **Operations Manager Cleanup Tool:** A command-line utility you can use to remove all of the components of Operations Manager from a local computer when the typical method using the Programs and Features applet in the control panel has failed.
- **Action Account Tool:** A Windows PowerShell script that allows you to set the action account on multiple computers.
- **Effective Configuration Viewer:** A tool that displays the set of rules and monitors that are running on a computer, distributed application, or any other managed entity after any configured overrides have been applied.
- **Operations Manager Inventory:** A command-line utility that captures the configuration of your Operations Manager management servers and stores it in a .cab file that can be sent to Microsoft support to assist in problem analysis.

- **AEM Validation:** A command line utility that allows you to perform end-to-end validation of Agentless Exception Monitoring to verify AEM is properly configured and operational.
- **AEM Management Pack:** A management pack that enables you to identify generic errors sent by Windows Error Reporting (WER) clients to AEM-enabled management servers.

Fast Track

The majority of Operations Manager 2012 monitoring functions similarly to Operations Manager 2007. Here are key concepts to remember when monitoring an environment with System Center 2012 Operations Manager compared to OpsMgr 2007:

- **Company knowledge:** With the current restrictions in the product allowing only 32-bit operating systems to edit company knowledge, more of this functionality is moving into Service Manager or SharePoint repositories.
- **Resolution States:** With Service Pack 1 for Operations Manager 2012, several reolution states have been added:
  - Acknowledged (249)
  - Assigned to Engineering (248)
  - Awaiting Evidence (247)
  - Resolved (254)
  - Scheduled (250)
- **Overrides:** The option to disable a monitor no longer stores the override in the Default management pack. Disabling now sets the Enabled flag to False and provides you with an option to specify the management pack in which to store the override. The Authoring pane added an Overrides section in OpsMgr 2007 R2.

Summary

This chapter focused on an in-depth discussion of the various rule and monitor types in OpsMgr 2012, the life cycle of an alert, and the importance of monitoring an environment. The chapter reviewed and provided examples for many of the types of rules and monitors that are available in Operations Manager 2012. Notifications were discussed including creation of channels, subscriptions, and subscribers. It also discussed how to add custom knowledge and locate rules and monitors in the Operations console. Resolution states were discussed, including the process to create custom resolution states in OpsMgr. Tuning and overrides were discussed in detail, including how to find overrides in the Operations console. The chapter discussed the process for tuning alerts and provided information on maintenance mode and its use in OpsMgr 2012. It concluded with a discussion of the current state of resource kit tools for OpsMgr 2012.

PART V

Service-Oriented Monitoring

IN THIS PART

CHAPTER 15

Monitoring .NET Applications

IN THIS CHAPTER

- What Is APM?
- APM Architecture
- Installing APM and Configuring .NET Application Monitoring
- APM in the Operations Manager Console
- Troubleshooting Applications Using the Application Diagnostics Console
- Using the Application Advisor Console
- Understanding APM Rules
- APM Global Configuration Options
- Sensitive Data Considerations
- Advanced APM Architecture
- For AVIcode 5.7 Customers
- New with Service Pack 1

System Center Operations Manager 2012 (OpsMgr) introduces the .NET application monitoring capability to enhance monitoring by collecting application performance information, including performance violations and failure details from ASP.NET and MVC applications, Windows Communication Foundation (WCF), and Web Services hosted on Internet Information Services (IIS) 7 and 7.5 (and IIS 8 in Service Pack 1).

Prior to System Center 2012, monitoring .NET applications was available with AVIcode 5.7, which was a stand-alone product and included a management pack for Operations Manager 2007 R2. This chapter discusses how to use the application performance monitoring (APM) feature to monitor .NET applications.

SURVIVAL GUIDE FOR THE INFORMATION TECHNOLOGY (IT) PRO

.NET monitoring by necessity includes exposure to elements of code. While the authors have done their best to provide introductions to acquaint you with some of the application development (appdev) terminology and concepts, you may still find yourself in unfamiliar territory. When you find yourself struggling with an appdev concept or term, consider marking your place in this chapter and then doing some additional searching and reading online.

You may even ask an application developer to help familiarize you with the terms with which you are struggling. This is a *great* way to begin the dialogue with your appdev team. You will need to work together with your developers to get the most from .NET monitoring in OpsMgr 2012!

As background, here are some terms for the IT Pro to become familiar with:

- **ASP.NET MVC Framework:** This web application framework implements the model-view controller (MVC) pattern. Information about MVC is available at http://en.wikipedia.org/wiki/ASP.NET_MVC_Framework.
- **AJAX:** AJAX is an acronym for Asynchronous JavaScript and XML (eXtended Markup Language) and is a group of interrelated web development techniques used on the client side to create asynchronous web applications. ASP.NET AJAX is a set of extensions to ASP.NET developed by Microsoft for implementing Ajax functionality. It is released under the Microsoft Public License (MS-PL). Read more about AJAX at http://en.wikipedia.org/wiki/ASP.NET_AJAX.
- **Windows Communication Foundation (WCF):** Previously known as "Indigo," this is a runtime and a set of APIs (application programming interfaces) in the .NET Framework for building connected, service-oriented applications. You can read more about WCF at http://en.wikipedia.org/wiki/Windows_Communication_Foundation.

What Is APM?

Application performance monitoring is a discipline within systems management that focuses on monitoring and managing the performance and service availability of software applications.

APM software typically has no or very little requirements on the application that will be monitored, and does not require code changes and recompilations. It monitors application runtime behavior by watching all requests coming in and out and collecting statistical information as well as detailed reports of the failures and performance issues.

Previously, monitoring an application required writing a management pack. Operations Manager's APM feature allows IT to instrument a .NET web application using a template present in the OpsMgr Operations console, without the need to author and design the service model for the application in a management pack. This template generates the monitoring based on the selections made in the template. With AVIcode APM functionality embedded in OpsMgr, organizations can deliver in-depth monitoring of .NET web applications and services without spending weeks writing complex management packs or requesting the application developer(s) to instrument the application as it is being developed.

APM in OpsMgr 2012 supports monitoring applications running on the Microsoft .NET Framework 2.0 and later, hosted inside IIS 7 and IIS 7.5. This translates into ASP.NET, Web Services, WCF hosted inside IIS, and MVC applications. System Center 2012 Service Pack (SP) 1 adds support for discovery and monitoring of MVC applications, IIS 8, and Windows services built using Microsoft .NET 4.5.

APM Architecture

The OpsMgr 2012 installation includes most APM components by default, including

- ▶ APM classes and types, installed during management server setup
- ▶ APM dashboards and wizards templates, installed with the Operations console
- ▶ Application Diagnostic and Application Advisor Web consoles, installed with the OpsMgr Web console
- ▶ APM OLTP and DW database stores, integrated with the Operations Manager databases
- ▶ APM agent, deployed as a module within the Operations Manager agent

APM agent components include a Windows service and application monitoring core. System Center Management APM is a Windows service and is installed as disabled by default; it is enabled after you configure monitoring using the .NET Application Performance Monitoring template. This service is mainly responsible for collecting infrastructure and application processes performance counters and usually runs under a high privilege account. The application monitoring core is a set of DLLs automatically loaded inside your .NET application when you enable it for monitoring. These collect application request information including deep troubleshooting data regarding problems such as performance violations and failures. Figure 15.1 shows APM integration with Operations Manager 2012 features.

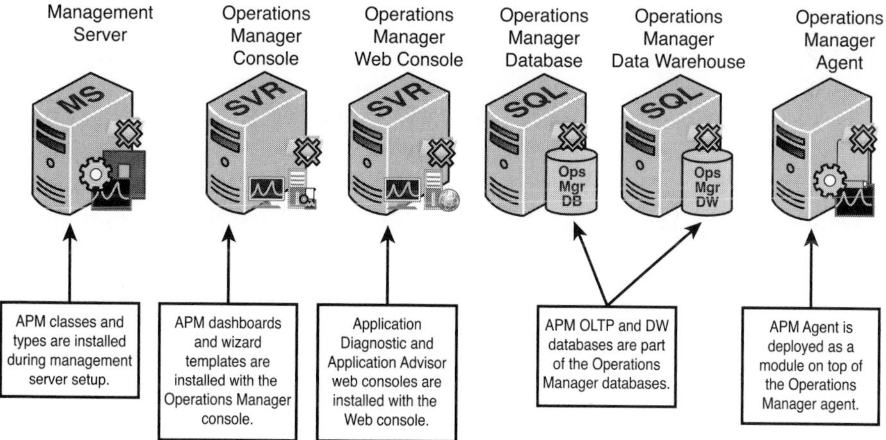

FIGURE 15.1 APM deployment architecture.

The client-side monitoring feature of APM collects performance information of browser-based applications from the end user perspective. This is implemented by automatic injection of monitoring JavaScript code into your application's response; the script then runs in the browser, collects all details, and then sends the data back to the APM agent.

To be able to collect that client-side data, APM installs an additional IIS web application, CSMCollector, on each IIS website where your applications are hosted. Figure 15.2 shows the APM client-side components and integration of the .NET modules on an APM-monitored server.

Integration of the APM agent and OpsMgr is implemented as OpsMgr rules and discovery scripts, found inside the APM management packs. Full integration into the standard architecture means that the APM agent leverages security settings, scalability, database maintenance, and so on available from Operations Manager, without requiring separate configuration.

Service: The System Center Management APM service installed with OpsMgr is started.

Data Source: Custom performance counters and a data source are registered on the monitoring service.

IIS folder: CSMCollector IIS application is created on each monitored web site when client-side monitoring is enabled.

Core Components: APM DLLs are registered on the system and loaded inside the monitored application process (w3wp.exe).

FIGURE 15.2 APM components.

Installing APM and Configuring .NET Application Monitoring

Microsoft put a lot of effort into combining the components of AVIcode in OpsMgr, including its two databases, separate agent, and configuration console. While this means the Operations Manager database will potentially be much larger than it would be without the APM feature, there are some definite upsides. Perhaps most important is that the installation of APM is straightforward, since most components are integrated within the standard OpsMgr setup. You are required to install the OpsMgr Web console, as the OpsMgr Web console feature contains the Application Diagnostic and Application Advisor consoles; these are must-have features of APM.

The only additional action required is installing the following management packs:

- Windows Server Internet Information Services 7.0 management pack
- Operations Manager Web APM IIS 7 management pack

If monitoring IIS 8 applications, install the IIS 8 applicable management packs.

OpsMgr 2012 includes a single wizard for configuring .NET application monitoring; this is the .NET Application Performance Monitoring Wizard. Use this wizard to manage the configuration options, including server-side and client-side monitoring, in one place. To configure APM, follow these steps:

1. In the Operations console, navigate to **Authoring** -> **Management Pack Templates** -> **.NET Application Performance Monitoring**. Right-click and select **Add Monitoring Wizard**, which brings up the page shown in Figure 15.3. Select **.NET Application Performance Monitoring** and click **Next** to continue.

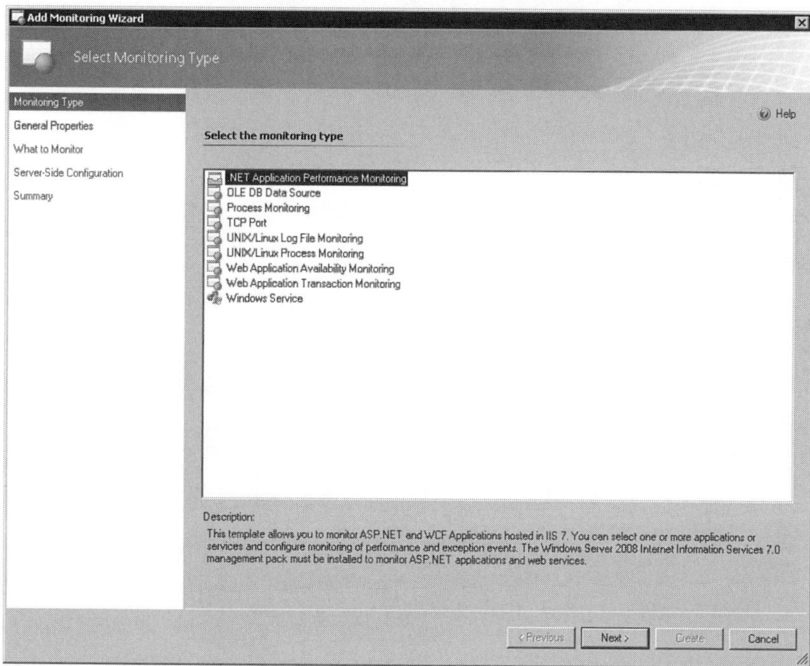

FIGURE 15.3 The Select Monitoring Type page of the Add Monitoring Wizard.

2. Figure 15.4 shows the General Properties page of the wizard, where you select a destination management pack. Notice you will receive a warning if the Operations Manager APM Web IIS 7 management pack is not imported.

   The standard part of the configuration begins with defining a friendly application name and description. This is the name used to update the configuration in the future and to find data in the OpsMgr dashboards. The name should reflect your line of business (LOB) application name or a subset of that. The authors recommend defining a name based on the application components you plan to place into that logical application.

   As the application defined here will include common default configuration settings, it makes sense to combine application components of the same type and meaning. This could be front-end components of one application, or middle-tier application components, and naming the application group accordingly.

15

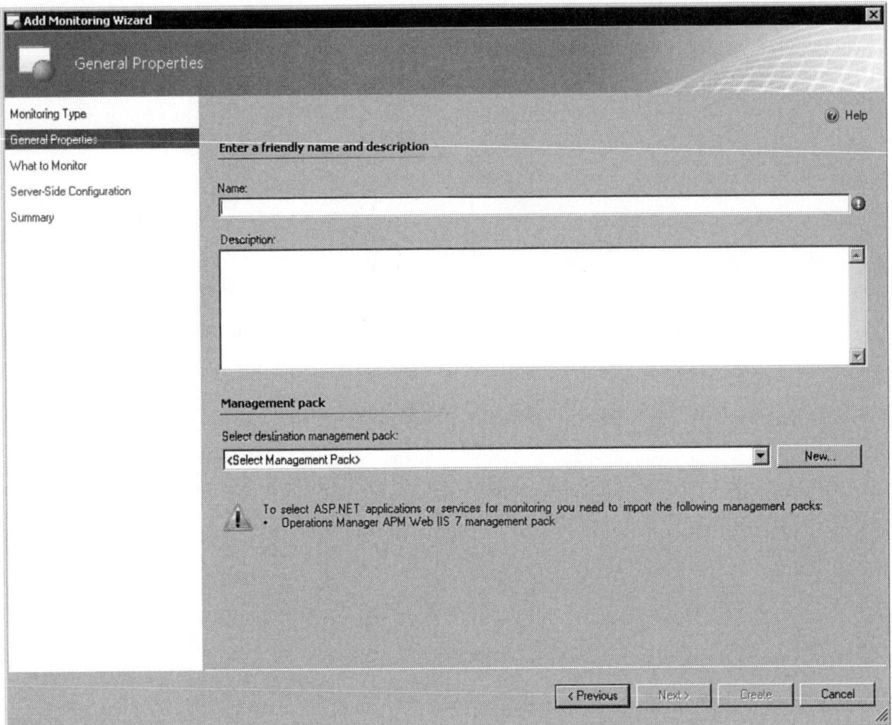

FIGURE 15.4 The General Properties page of the Add Monitoring Wizard.

A management pack stores all settings related to the application monitoring. Create a new management pack for each application to keep application settings separate, and then click **Next** to continue.

3. The next page, shown in Figure 15.5, asks you to add application components to monitor.

TIP: ABILITY TO MODIFY THE MANAGEMENT PACK

You can either select the simple configuration and select only the primary settings to start monitoring quickly, or enable advanced configuration options to set up granular monitoring settings. It is always possible to go back to the settings and change them.

Click **Add** to include application components that will be part of this application; these components are discovered by the management packs included in the installation. The OpsMgr 2012 RTM version includes support of ASP.NET web applications and web services using .NET 2.0/3.0/3.5/4.0 hosted in IIS 7.0/7.5. System Center 2012 SP 1 adds applications hosted in IIS 8.0 and Windows Server 2012, support of Windows services built using .NET and improvements for monitoring WCF and ASP.NET MVC3 and MVC4 applications, and support of .NET 4.5. Application components are displayed in Figure 15.6. Click **OK** when you complete adding components to return to the What to Monitor page.

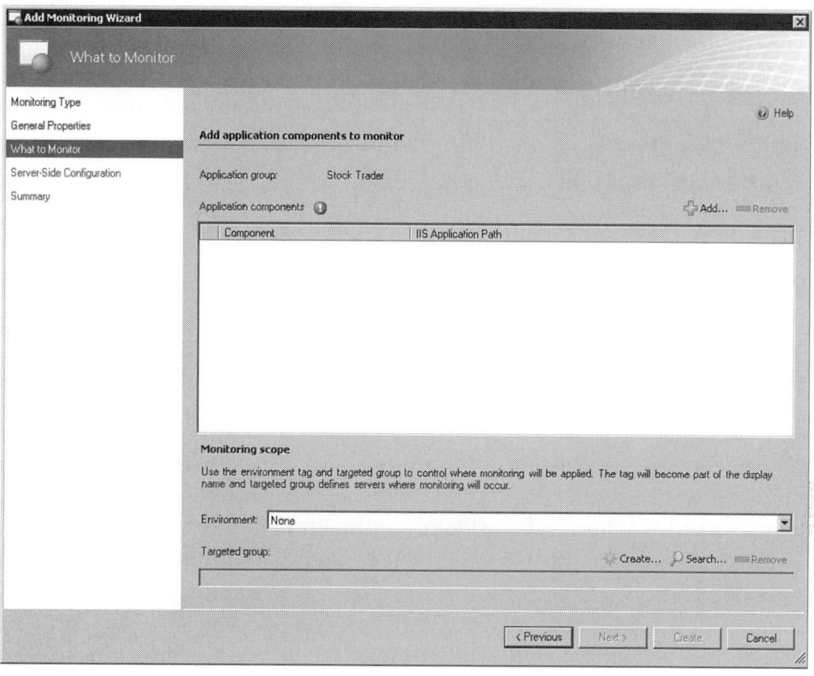

FIGURE 15.5 Configure the components to monitor.

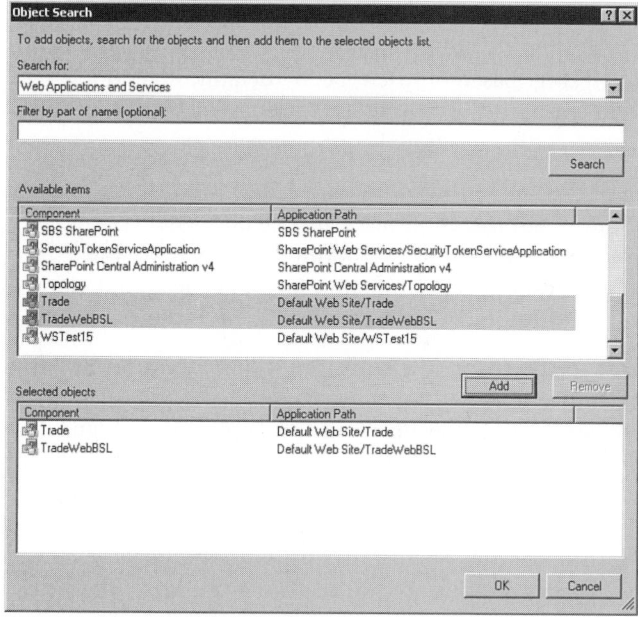

FIGURE 15.6 Select application components.

15

4. The rule that defines how application components are discovered is explained in the "Advanced APM Architecture" section. In short, default configuration includes scanning only the website and one level of subapplication folders, and searching only for files with certain extensions including .aspx, .asmx, and .svc. Based on these criteria, the application components are prefilled into the wizard grouped by the application full path on the IIS (such as Default Web Site\DinnerNow) and not based on the file system path. You can adjust the discovery mechanism by overriding the rule's properties.

   You can also tag this configuration by selecting the Environment drop-down in Figure 15.5 and assigning it to Production, Staging, Test, Development, or giving it a custom tag. This is useful when you have multiple environments hosting the same application that should be managed separately and potentially have different application monitoring settings.

   The last option on this page is to limit the monitoring to a specified group of servers by selecting a Targeted group; this is a standard OpsMgr computer group that can include static or dynamic members. Consider defining groups to separate environments from one another and limiting the number of excessive discoveries when you know where the application will be running. You might also define groups if you want to roll out application monitoring in stages; you can add new computers to the group determined by your current deployment phase.

   After completing the What to Monitor page, click **Next** to continue.

5. The next page of the wizard is the Server-Side Configuration page, shown in Figure 15.7.

   The settings for monitoring performance and exception alerts control the type of alerts that need to be fired in OpsMgr based on the type. By default, exception alerts include only security and connectivity failures and not application failures. To change these and other settings requires additional configuration.

   The alerting threshold is one of the key settings for performance monitoring and defines what is considered as normal transaction performance and what is slow. Each time a transaction is executed, the APM agent monitors its duration and compares this with the alerting threshold; a performance alert is generated if the transaction runs slower than that threshold.

   Even if the performance events alerts setting in Figure 15.7 is not checked, the alerting threshold is still important since it is used for the events collected by APM agent against the application component(s) and is available in the Application Diagnostics console. Picking a threshold is always not obvious, and you should adjust thresholds over time based on application performance. Thresholds defined for business logic components such as web services or WCF should be less than those for the front-end application components, as front-end components call business logic and run slower since they contain their own logic in addition to those calls.

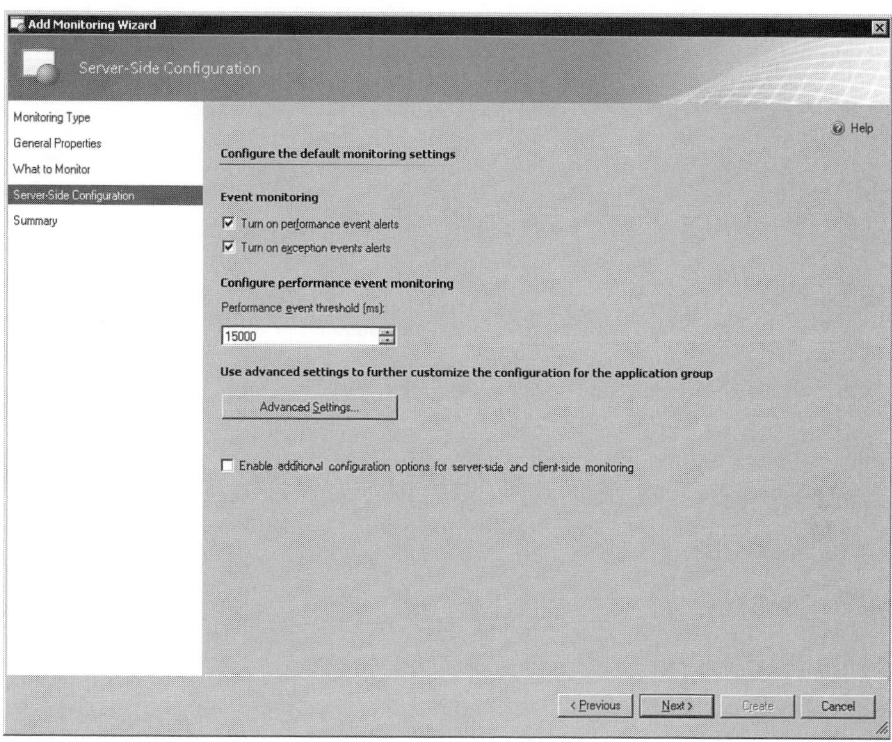

FIGURE 15.7 Server-side basic configuration.

6. After configuring these settings, you can complete the wizard, which will apply the settings to the application components, create required dashboards in OpsMgr, and alert when it is appropriate. You must recycle IIS services on the monitoring servers to start .NET performance monitoring.

Advanced Settings

Advanced settings allow fine-tuning of the .NET monitoring configuration and provide access to almost all configuration settings you might ever need. IT Pros should become familiar with several terms before proceeding in this section:

- **.NET namespace (namespace):** The .NET Framework provides a huge number of base classes, data types, algorithms, and so on. If each of these items had to be declared with a unique name, the task of naming each element would be enormous and leave few good names available to .NET developers. Instead, namespaces are used to ensure that naming conflicts do not occur within the .NET Framework or your own programs. A namespace provides a named group of classes, structures, enumerations, delegates, interfaces, and other (child) namespaces. Within a namespace, all declared items must be uniquely named. However, the same name may be duplicated in different namespaces. Observe namespace `MyAppNamespaceOne` with a class of `MessageState`:

```
namespace MyAppNamespaceOne
{
 class MessageState
 {
     public void WriteMessage()
     {
         Console.WriteLine("This is the first namespace!");
     }
 }
 }
```

The second namespace, `MyAppNamespaceTwo`, also has class `MessageState`:

```
namespace MyAppNamespaceTwo
{
class MessageState
{
    public void WriteMessage()
    {
        Console.WriteLine("This is the second namespace!");
    }
}
}
```

Although both namespaces have a class with the same name, this does not cause a naming conflict because the two classes are logically separated by the namespaces. This means the program will compile without errors.

MSDN includes many examples of .NET namespaces. Reviewing actual namespaces may help you better understand this concept. The namespaces in the OpsMgr 2012 SDK can be found at http://msdn.microsoft.com/en-us/library/hh329046.aspx.

- **.NET method (method):** A method is a segment of code that performs a specific task. For example, for mathematical functions, you could define one method to add, one to subtract, another one to divide, and another method to multiply. The idea is that when you want to add up, you just call the Add Up method.
- **.NET entry point (entry point):** Entry point is a term introduced in APM. An entry point is a method like any other method; technically any method can be named as an entry point.

  Why are entry points necessary and which methods are default entry points provided by the APM default configuration? The .NET process has multiple classes loaded, and methods are calling one to another based on the logic contained in the classes. Microsoft wanted to define a place that identifies a transaction in terms of having the unique transaction identifier and containing all other methods that belong to this transaction logic. For example, for ASP.NET pages the entry point is the ProcessRequest method, which processes requests. ProcessRequest includes the URL as one of the parameters so you can uniquely identify the transaction and calls all internal methods that are part of this transaction. APM starts monitoring the request at the entry point and finishes when the method completes processing. This automatically includes all subsequent calls for that transaction.

With this information now firmly within your grasp, you are ready to continue with APM advanced settings.

Advanced settings can be divided into two areas:

- Server-side monitoring settings and OpsMgr alerting and health monitoring settings
- Client-side monitoring settings

These settings will be your standard default monitoring configuration for all application components in this application, unless overridden in the Advanced Settings page shown in Figure 15.8. Click on **Advanced Settings** in Figure 15.7 to open this page.

Notice the second section of Figure 15.8, where you can configure the sensitivity threshold for performance monitoring. The sensitivity threshold is rarely changed from its default value (100ms). It controls the amount of data collected when transaction runs slower than the alerting threshold; this is collecting the child calls made during the transaction execution such as calls to the code, calls to SQL, I/O, web calls, and so on. This means the performance event contains only calls that were slower than the sensitivity threshold. This is one of the differences of APM versus a profiler (like Visual Studio Intellitrace), which collects performance information of every single method. The APM agent instead reduces overhead by reporting only methods slower than a sensitivity threshold, which always shows the slowest execution path and the slowest resources.

ABOUT PROFILERS

An example of a profiler or debugger is Visual Studio Intellitrace, a feature of Visual Studio. These tools, used by software developers to diagnose and debug problems during the development cycle, provide deep level visibility into the application code performance issues and failures. Profilers allow you to investigate issues easily but cannot be used to monitor applications in production. The primary difference with APM is the monitoring software is less intrusive and provides very little overhead compared to profiler or debugger tools, particularly when the application is under high load. As such, the APM agent component is sometimes referred to as a *lightweight profiler*.

Adding Namespaces and Methods

You can also set namespaces and methods by clicking the Set Namespaces and Set Methods buttons in Figure 15.8. Namespaces, classes, and methods are the items that define the application code. Methods are the single operations created by developers or provided by Microsoft or custom frameworks. Methods are combined into classes, and classes are organized into namespaces. By adding your application's namespaces, you enable better visibility into the code performance. Selecting **Set Namespaces** opens the dialog shown in Figure 15.9.

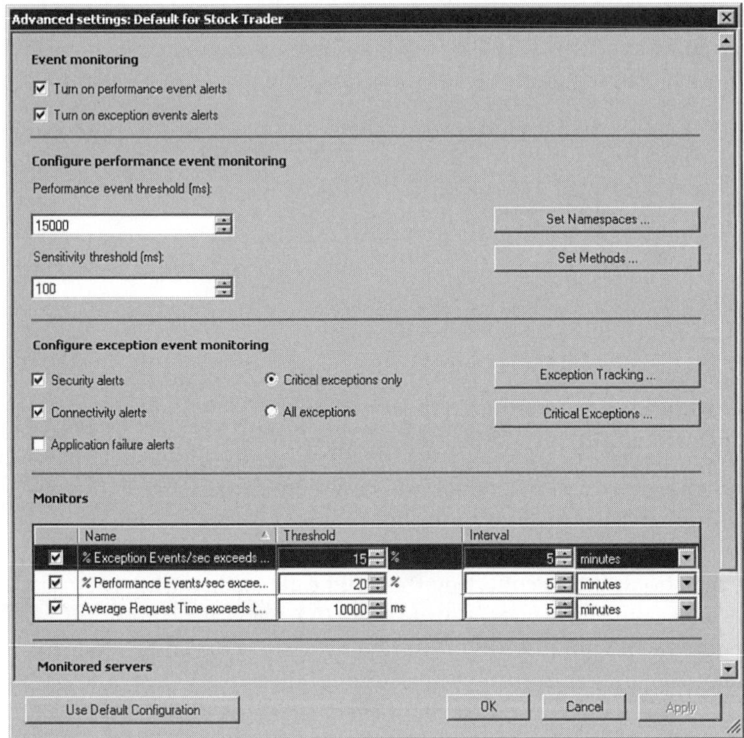

FIGURE 15.8 The Advanced Settings dialog.

In the Namespace dialog, you can define additional namespaces or classes to track for performance when the transaction is running over the alerting threshold. While the default list of namespaces is not visible in Figure 15.9, it includes a number of namespaces disabled for monitoring such as Microsoft, System, IBM, Infragistics, java, and so on. This means when you choose the predefined **All namespaces** item for performance monitoring, it only enables monitoring of the custom code other than those namespaces explicitly disabled in the default configuration or this list.

Why are some of the namespaces disabled? They are excluded for one of two reasons:

- There are too many methods in the namespace and monitoring all of them would introduce noticeable overhead on the monitored server.
- Microsoft customers will not find this information actionable since they cannot change .NET even though they would see all internals. On the other side, APM brings the most actionable data and details about the application and its code performance/failures.

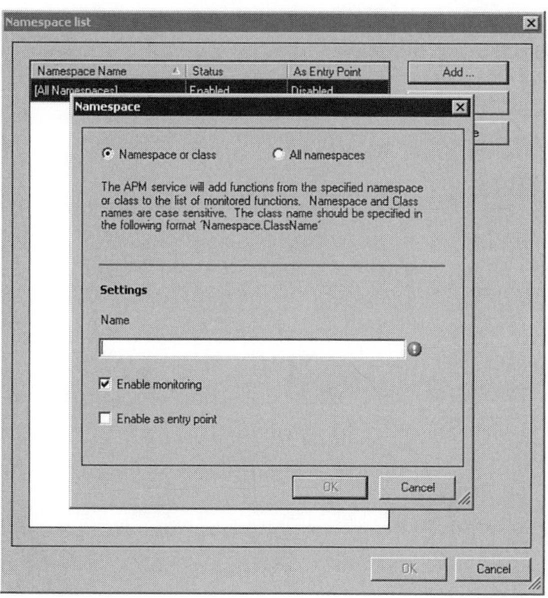

FIGURE 15.9 Adding Custom .NET namespaces for monitoring.

CAN I USE WILDCARDS WHEN SPECIFYING .NET NAMESPACES?

A question the authors frequently hear is *Can I use wildcards to specify multiple custom namespaces*? The short answer is *no*; while when specifying namespaces (shown in Figure 15.9) it may tempting to try odyssey.com.* or odyssey*, using wildcards like these will not result in additional monitoring of custom namespaces.

However, you can add multiple custom namespaces for monitoring with a single entry. When you specify any namespace, it automatically works as a "starts with" wildcard. When you add the namespace DinnerNow, this means that all of sub-namespaces and classes starting with DinnerNow. will be monitored, that is, all namespaces and classes "inner" to the one specified.

Example 1: "DinnerNow.CardSpace" will be monitored.

Example 2: "DinnerNowLogic" will not be monitored.

You can also enable namespaces to act as an entry point; this option triggers performance monitoring of the execution when the first method of this namespace is started and an entry point was not previously detected. Use this option when monitoring Windows services or other custom code components to detect proper entry points without specific configuration.

- Methods differ from namespaces. When adding a method for performance monitoring, you can enable collecting parameter values in that method. On the other hand, when adding a namespace, APM adds all methods from that namespace only for performance tracking and contains only duration without parameter values. Figure 15.10 shows the Method dialog, accessible by selecting **Set Methods** shown previously in Figure 15.8 and clicking **Add**.

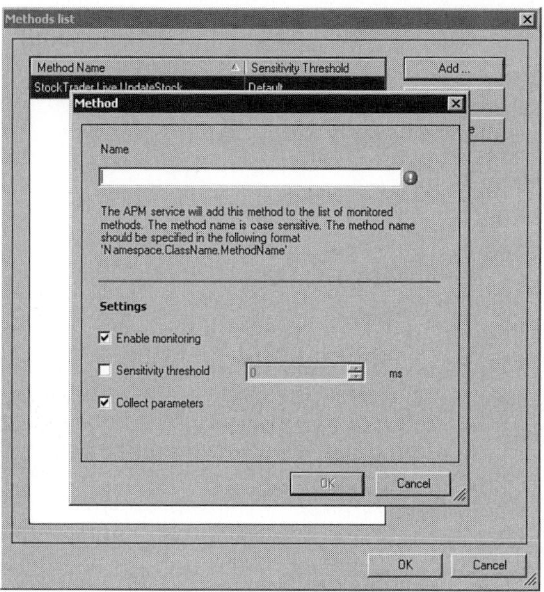

FIGURE 15.10 Configuring methods.

Do not add too many unnecessary methods to the list of methods, as this will increase overhead. The general approach for picking methods is to add only those methods where knowing the parameter values helps explain the root cause of a performance problem, which you could not troubleshoot by investigating an execution call stack.

An example would be a SQL Server call that passes a query or stored procedure name with optional parameters. Here the same method is always used to execute a query against a database, but the duration differs based on the query and the call stack is always the same since the execution is performed on the SQL Server, not the application code. As all standard methods such as SQL calls, web service calls, web calls, I/O calls, and such are included in the standard APM agent configuration; you only need to specify custom methods here.

Configuring Exception Event Monitoring

Exception event monitoring settings, also configured in Figure 15.8, are somewhat different. You can configure the type of alert you want to fire in OpsMgr based on the type of failure, which can be connectivity-related, security, or an application failure. The other settings in the figure describe what data the APM agent should collect from the application when a failure occurs.

Selecting **Critical exceptions only** or **All exceptions** (also in Figure 15.8) specifies whether the APM agent needs to collect only unhandled exceptions not caught inside the code itself. All .NET exceptions are handled somewhere, but the agent tracks where each exception is handled and this determines how it is categorized. If the exception is not handled within the code but is handled by one of the standard .NET system level handlers, the exception is unhandled and treated as critical. Typically, critical exceptions are visible to the end users as a custom error page or something similar. All exception monitoring includes collecting critical exceptions and handled exceptions. Handled exceptions are those exceptions handled somewhere in the code.

Collecting all exceptions helps to identify hidden errors in the application, but may expose exceptions that are part of the business logic rather than failures. All exception monitoring is dependent on the exception-tracking list, as the APM agent tracks handled exceptions only in the methods defined there.

TIP: WHEN SHOULD I ENABLE "ALL EXCEPTIONS?"

As mentioned in this section, collecting all exceptions can help identify hidden errors in the application, but will almost certainly result in more non-actionable alerts being raised. While it is common to enable the All exceptions option in development and QA environments where code is being tested, enabling this setting in production environments should be approached with caution. Adding more alert data to the Operations console can take focus away from critical exceptions. If undetected errors (with critical exceptions only enabled) continue to impact usability of your production applications, enabling tracking of all exceptions may help provide clues to expose the source of the problem.

Exception tracking (see Figure 15.11), accessed by selecting **Exception tracking** in Figure 15.8, may appear similar to namespaces and methods in performance monitoring settings but is configured separately from performance monitoring. However, exception-tracking settings appear similar to configuring namespaces and methods, as they may include namespaces, classes, or methods. The APM agent will collect parameter values for the methods belonging to that list when the exception is raised.

When exception monitoring is configured to collect all exceptions, only exceptions captured in the methods specified in the exception tracking list are collected. The default configuration contains key methods from Microsoft .NET Framework preconfigured for exception tracking; the list includes but is not limited to the methods for SQL operations, I/O calls, web calls, conversion and parsing logic, and so on.

Critical exceptions, shown in the Exception handler dialog in Figure 15.12, allow tuning APM agent monitoring to identify and collect critical exceptions from the non-standard exception handlers. Some applications may be designed to capture critical failures and store them in an event log, file, or a database. Those are critical failures from the application perspective but not for the APM agent since technically they are handled in the application's code. For these situations, you can add the methods used for handling exceptions to the exception handlers list, and the APM agent then would collect those as critical.

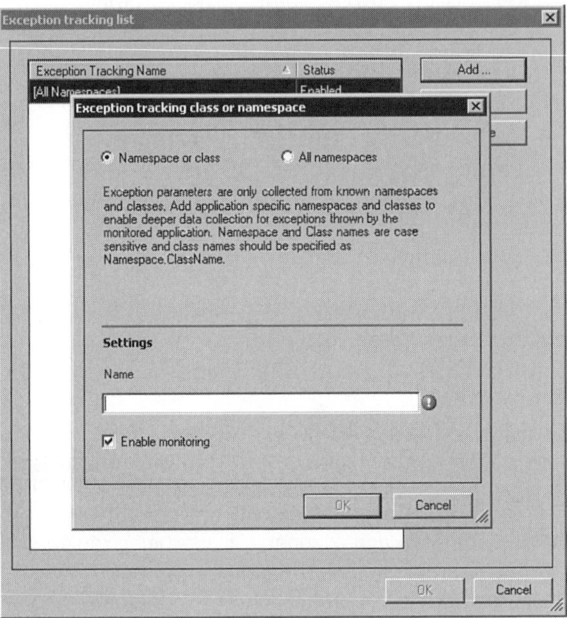

FIGURE 15.11 Exception tracking.

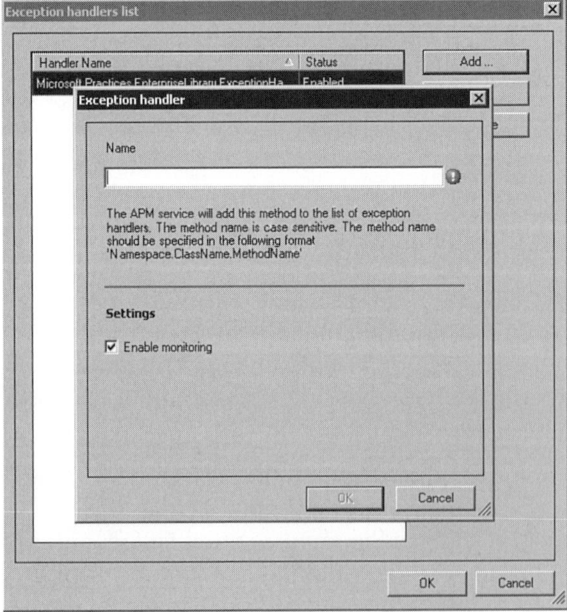

FIGURE 15.12 Configuring critical exceptions.

The last settings shown in Figure 15.8 are monitors used in OpsMgr to identify the high-level state of application components. It does not make sense to determine the state of the component based on the particular failure or performance violation, as other requests may be successful and running at that time. Therefore, the monitors use overall application component metrics calculated across all requests being processed.

There are three types of monitoring, previously displayed in Figure 15.8, that determine component state:

- **Exception events/sec exceeds threshold (% of all requests):** These are calculated based on number of exception events detected in the application according to the exception monitoring settings (all or critical as previously defined in Figure 15.8), compared to the total number of requests processed.
- **Performance events/sec exceeds threshold (% of all requests):** Performance events per second are calculated based on total number of requests running slower than alerting thresholds compared to the total number of requests. The default value is 20%.
- **Average Request Time exceeds threshold (ms):** Average request time is calculated as average duration of all requests processed by the application component independent of the thresholds or other configuration.

By default each monitor checks component state every 5 minutes by comparing average value during that period with a threshold defined in the template, and changes state in case of violation. State monitors run on each application component of a computer, so if a component is deployed to *N* servers behind a load balancer rather than each server, the APM agent checks if there is a violation on the component performance of that exact server. OpsMgr aggregates the state coming from all application component instances to the application component state and then to the application state, available on the dashboards, and discussed in the "APM Views" section.

Additional Configuration

Additional configuration, available after performing server-side configuration, enables you to define more granular monitoring settings by changing the settings individually for each application component, and enabling and configuring client-side monitoring.

Server-Side Customizations

Figure 15.13 shows the initial screen for server-side customizations.

- Customizing monitoring for individual application components adds flexibility by letting you change some or all of the monitoring settings for a component. You can customize monitoring for all the settings described including thresholds and namespaces, defining them on a component basis. Typically, you make these customizations immediately after initial APM configuration, but they can be adjusted later as you determine some settings should be tuned differently from others.

- You could also define specific transactions to monitor individually. These transactions could be web pages, web service methods, or individual functions.

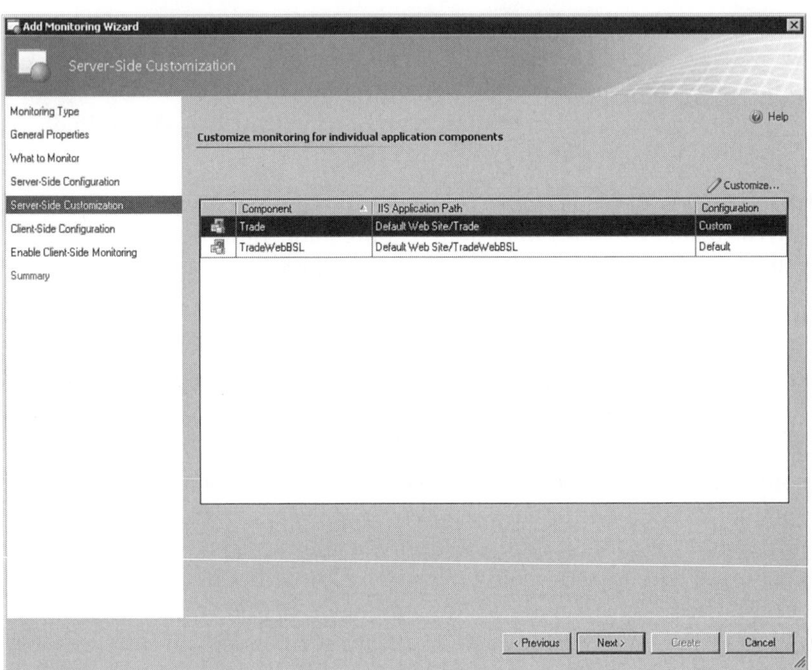

FIGURE 15.13 Server-side customizations.

Select **Customize** in Figure 15.13 to open the dialog displayed in Figure 15.14. Adding specific transactions allows monitoring the transaction's health separately from the application's overall health and collecting alerts for that specific transaction. This lets you select the most critical transactions and make them fully visible while keeping overall application monitoring at a standard level. For example, as shown in Figure 15.15, you can configure collecting connectivity and security alerts for the overall application but for several critical transactions such as the default home page, login, search, and such; configure those separately and collect all alerts including performance and application failures.

Based on the type of transaction, specify how it is identified; this could be by URL, web service method or class names, or method names for a function. Use monitors to set up different health criteria.

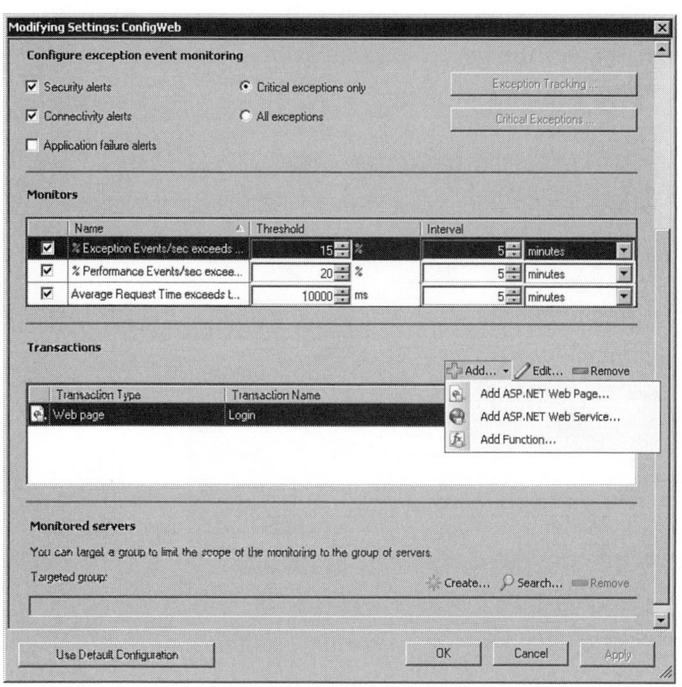

FIGURE 15.14 Customizing component configuration.

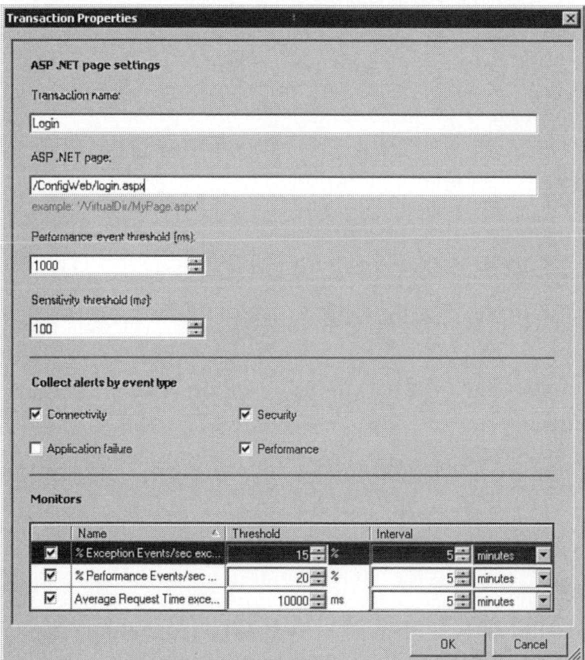

FIGURE 15.15 Adding a custom transaction.

Client-Side Customizations

After configuring server-side transactions, the next step of the wizard allows you to enable client-side monitoring configuration. Figure 15.16 shows this dialog.

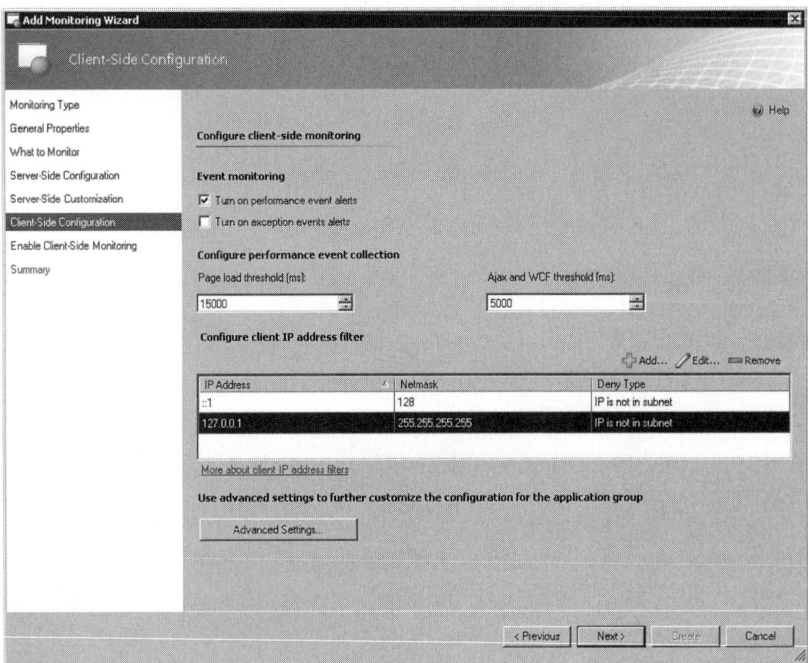

FIGURE 15.16 Client-side configuration page.

Client-side configuration options define monitoring settings to monitor client-side application components. This includes high-level settings as well as granular tuning. Tuning under Advanced Settings are client-side monitoring configurations.

Client-side monitoring (CSM) runs on the end user's browser. It collects application performance information from the end user perspective, which includes slow performance problems and failures.

- Performance events are collected when page load and rendering run slower than a threshold or an AJAX call runs slowly.
- Exception events are collected for JavaScript failures on the browser.

Similar to server-side monitoring settings, you can configure OpsMgr to generate alerts as performance or exception events.

General settings include page load and AJAX/WCF thresholds. Alerting is applied for the overall page loading time performance monitoring, and AJAX/WCF for the client-side response time based on AJAX calls made from the browser. The client IP address filter, shown in Figure 15.17, allows you to define IP addresses that are disabled for client-side monitoring. By default, these are set to disable all JavaScript injection; you should adjust them later to gradually enable client-side monitoring—first to internal testing groups and then to the application users.

TIP: GETTING HELP CONFIGURING IP FILTERS

The built-in help provides excellent guidance on how to configure the IP filters for client-side monitoring. Simply click the **More about client IP address filters** hyperlink shown in Figure 15.16 and Figure 15.17.

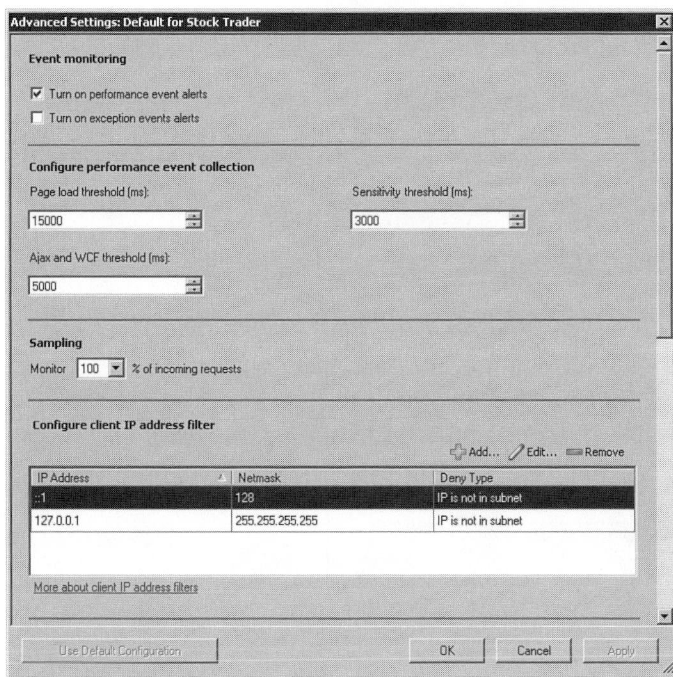

FIGURE 15.17 Configuring the IP address filter.

The advanced settings shown in Figure 15.18, which enable you to tune client-side monitoring, contain Microsoft-recommended default values. You can change the sensitivity threshold, which is responsible for collecting slow performance JavaScript per page load and AJAX response processing. Sampling allows instrumenting the percentage of page requests to decrease overhead from the injection logic and decrease the amount of monitoring traffic.

The last section of the settings introduces performance problems detail levels where you can specify additional information to collect: This includes a list of loaded images with full URLs and timing, a list of loaded scripts with full URLs, lists of CSS files and HTC files if your pages use these. Global variables and the exception stack are collected for each exception event as they occur.

From a performance perspective, each option adds a small amount of overhead for the end users, which is seen as increased time to render a page in the browser. Although the overhead is typically small, the authors recommend first monitoring with default settings, and then enable monitoring of images and scripts—enabling CSS and then HTC last since they introduce the most overhead. For exception details, try enabling call stack and then global variables, as call stack typically returns more details for reproducing JavaScript failures. Ensure your website is running HTTPS, which will secure the global variables and parameters from the call stack while transferring these from the browser back to the web server.

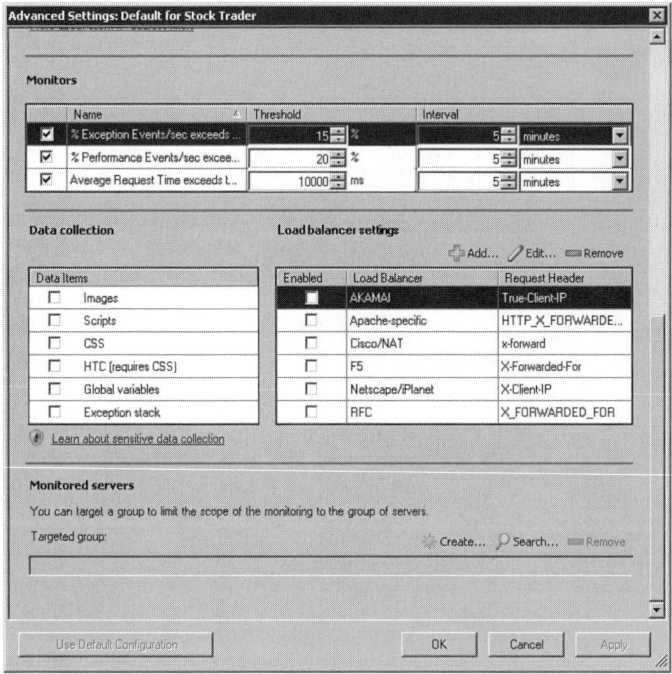

FIGURE 15.18 Additional client-side advanced settings.

The most common settings enabled are images, scripts for performance problems, and call stack for failure. Discuss what configuration is the best with an application developer familiar with the application. Figure 15.18 shows the check boxes to enable these settings.

Configuring load balancer settings is key to IP filtering working properly. The typical production deployment has a firewall with a load-balancer at the front, which redirects the request to one of the servers from the pool based on configuration. When this occurs, the incoming IP address at the server level is always the address of the load-balancer, such as an F5 server. This would make it impossible to apply IP filters, since all addresses are the same. However, most load balancers have an option to preserve the original IP address in the request header when forwarding it to the application server; typically, this option must be specifically enabled. Be sure to run this by your network engineer to include the correct header in client-side monitoring; this allows the client-side module to read the proper client IP address to filter by and report correctly.

Before enabling client-side monitoring (see Figure 15.19), you should check your web application for compatibility. It is highly recommended you run the client-side compatibility check task before configuring monitoring.

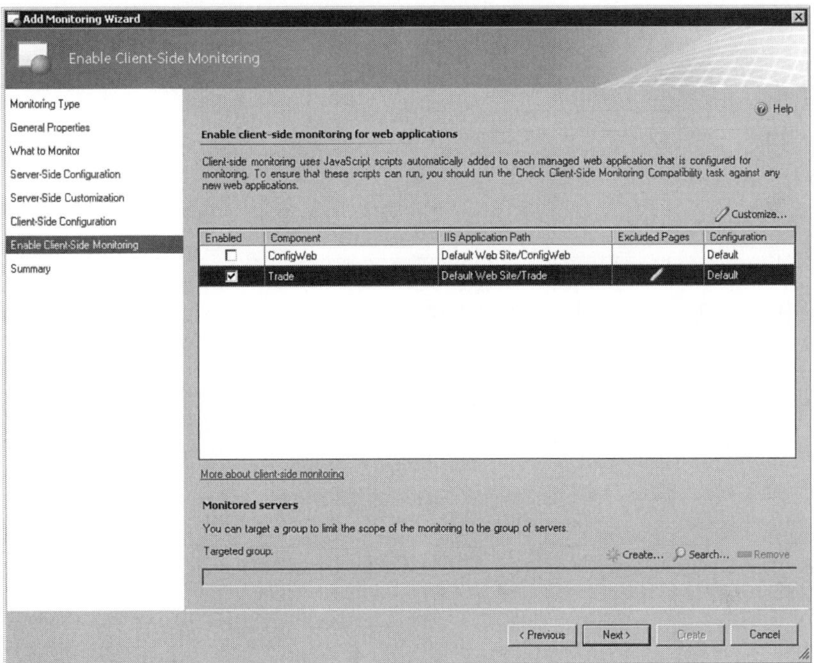

FIGURE 15.19 Enabling client-side monitoring.

This task is located under the Monitoring view. In the Operations console, navigate to **Monitoring -> Application Monitoring -> .NET Monitoring -> ASP.NET Web Application Inventory**. Select the website or application you plan to monitor for client-side performance and run the Check Client-Side Monitoring Compatibility task, and then check the task status for the details. Figure 15.20 shows output from this task.

Figure 15.21 is an example of a compatibility warning. Always review the warning and error messages with the description to isolate and fix the cause; when the issue is related to individual pages you could remediate it by excluding those pages in the configuration. Otherwise, consider following the recommendations and if necessary avoid enabling client-side monitoring, or be sure to test it first in your preproduction environment.

This particular example advises you to change the master page and add meta tags to the proper position on the page to ensure it is fully compatible with client-side monitoring. In this case, it is best to fix the problem since the master page is common for every URL; if the problem is related to a specific page or pages, you can simply exclude them from the monitoring settings when enabling client-side monitoring.

Task Output:

Application: FeedLogin

Compatibility check result: Passed

Rule ID	Rule name	Result
1	Webpage contains VBScript code	Passed
2	Webpage uses an ASP.NET Substitution control	Passed
3	Client scripting code overrides standard objects or functions	Passed
4	Webpage contains an instruction for changing the compatibility view	Passed
5	Webpage contains an instruction for changing charsets	Passed
6	Webpage contains calls to the HttpWebResponse.Flush() method	Passed
7	Webpage contains calls to the HttpWebResponse.End() method.	Passed

FIGURE 15.20 Output from the compatibility check task.

4 **Webpage contains an instruction for changing the compatibility view** **Critical incompatibility**

Knowledge base:

Description: This meta tag is expected to be the first on the page right after the <!Doctype> and <html> tags. In client-side monitoring, the tag becomes positioned after the client-side monitoring injected code, so the page rendering process might run incorrectly(might slow-down the loading or have other effects).
Critical Environments: Internet Explorer 7, Internet Explorer 8 and Internet Explorer 9.
Resolution or mitigation options:
- **General:** The affected web pages might not be compatible with client-side monitoring. To make them compatible, the application code needs to be revised.You have the option to disable client-side monitoring for the application to prevent the unexpected behavior that client-side monitoring incompatibility causes.
- **Rule-specific:** Disable client-side monitoring for the whole application. Server side monitoring can remain enabled since the issue only affects client-side monitoring.The resolution option is based on the following:

There are incompatible resources of the following file types:

a. Master page
b. Other files that contain incompatibilities with extensions that differ from those mentioned above.

Monitoring cannot be excluded only for these particular resources.

Incompatible resources (1):

Master page: **C:\stocktrader\StockTrader\StockTraderWebApplication\Trade\Site.master** - Line: 6, Character: 1.

FIGURE 15.21 Compatibility warning.

At the Summary page, review all your APM settings. The wizard will create classes, objects, views, discovery scripts, and rules for this application and save these to the specified management pack.

ADDITIONAL READING ON APM RULES, MONITORS, AND WORKFLOWS

Here is some recommended additional reading on APM rules, monitors, and workflows:

- **System Center .NET application alerts versus events:** http://blogs.technet.com/b/shawngibbs/archive/2012/04/13/system-center-net-application-alerts-vs-events.aspx
- **Custom APM rules for granular alerting:** http://blogs.technet.com/b/momteam/archive/2012/01/23/custom-apm-rules-for-granular-alerting.aspx

- **Working with alerts:** http://blogs.technet.com/b/momteam/archive/2011/08/23/application-monitoring-working-with-alerts.aspx

These links are also available in Appendix D, "Reference URLs."

IIS Restart and Recycle

IIS restart is required in the following situations:

- When you apply monitoring on the server for the first time
- When you disable monitoring for all applications on the server

After enabling or changing .NET monitoring settings, you will find an alert and warning state change introduced on the servers where the configuration has changed. Once the APM agent configuration is applied, the Health Explorer will have an IIS restart or recycle warning on the computer state (see Figure 15.22) as well as a separate alert, displayed in Figure 15.23.

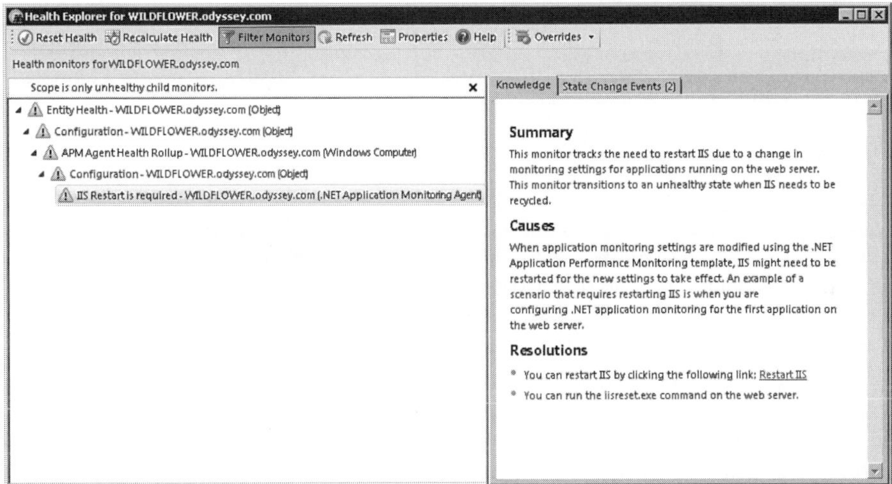

FIGURE 15.22 Warning in the Health Explorer.

While it is not necessary to restart IIS immediately, the new settings are not applied until the restart. You can wait until the next maintenance window if you cannot immediately do so. The best view showing IIS restart/recycle is required is at **Monitoring -> Operations Manager -> APM Agent Details -> IIS Restart / Recycle Required** in the Operations console.

This warning would require either IIS restart or recycling the IIS application pool; you could perform the restart from the current view using the tasks enabled there.

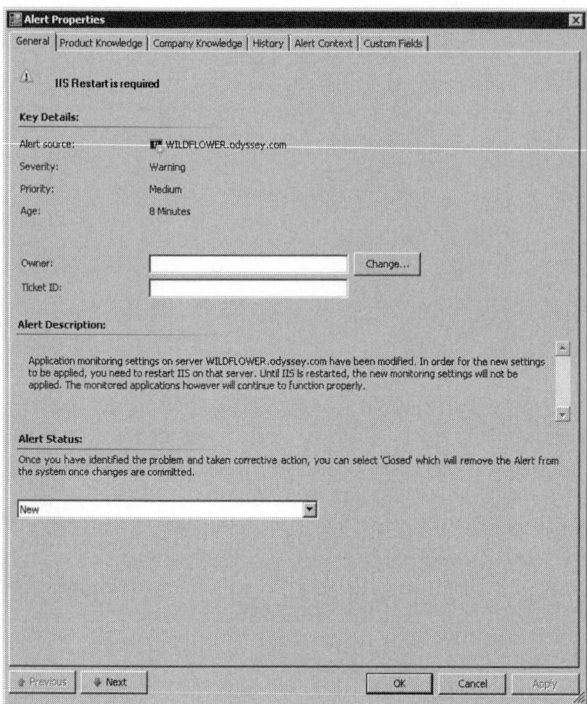

FIGURE 15.23 Alert to perform IIS restart.

NOTE: ABOUT IIS RESTART AND RECYCLE REQUIREMENTS

APM agent settings require IIS restart or recycle depending on the configuration. The APM agent never restarts or recycles IIS by itself, but it may notify the administrator if that is required to finalize the configuration. Here's how it works:

- IIS restart is required if no application components are being monitored by the APM agent and OpsMgr applies new configurations to one or multiple components on the server. Each time monitoring is started or stopped completely on the server an IIS restart is required. It is possible to apply the configuration and restart IIS later during a service window or wait until the next server reboot.
- IIS application pool recycle is required to finalize the configuration change when at least one application component is monitored on the server and there are new configuration changes to any of the namespaces, performance methods, and critical exception handlers. In addition, any change that adds new components for monitoring, removes components from monitoring, or enables or disables client-side monitoring will necessitate a restart.

  An application pool recycle is less critical than IIS restart because it doesn't completely stop the service; this starts a new instance of the worker process to handle new requests and waits until the old instance completes work on current requests and then shuts it down. Refer to the IIS 7 documentation to understand how application pool recycle works at http://technet.microsoft.com/en-us/library/cc770764(v=ws.10).aspx.

- A restart or recycle is not required when at least one application component is already monitored on the server and the new configuration changes alerting or sensitivity thresholds only. The All/Critical exceptions monitoring switch discussed in the "Advanced Settings" section, or any of the OpsMgr alerting and health monitoring settings, as well as CSM settings, can also be applied dynamically without restarts or recycles.

Configuration Conflicts

Configuration conflicts may occur in certain situations with alerts shown in the OpsMgr dashboards. Conflicts can occur per server-side monitoring configuration when multiple application components are running on the same server.

The APM agent includes some settings defined globally on the server, but not by application component. These settings are performance namespaces, exception tracking configuration, and the critical exception handlers list. Should different application components have those settings conflict with each other, they may not be resolvable; however, the conflict occurs only if those components are deployed to the same web server.

Conflicts could be critical or not critical:

- Critical conflicts may occur when same configuration item has different settings coming from two or more components; for example, one namespace is enabled for one component, and the same namespace is explicitly disabled for another component.
- Non-critical conflicts happen when one component has some settings enabled or disabled but another component does not have any of those settings specified. In this case, the second application component would "inherit" some of the settings from the first component.

OpsMgr generates a warning alert when it discovers a critical configuration conflict; the alert context identifies the affected applications. The sample alert shown in Figure 15.24 shows a critical configuration conflict that cannot be resolved automatically. Alert context details show those applications with conflicting configurations.

Identifying Thresholds and Namespaces

The next sections discuss best practices on choosing monitoring settings. The most critical settings for application monitoring are performance thresholds and namespaces, as they control when to report a problem and what data to include per each incident.

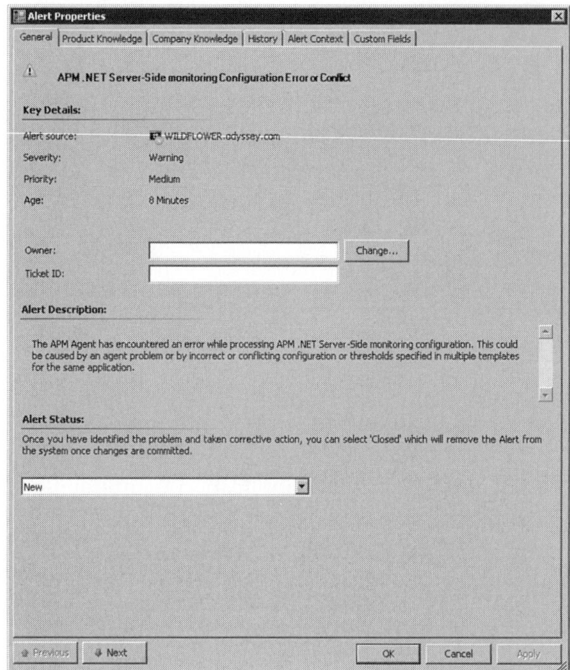

FIGURE 15.24 Example of a critical configuration conflict.

Choosing Performance Thresholds

There are several approaches to identifying a proper threshold. For example, if there is already an established service level agreement (SLA) for the application, you would want to set an alerting threshold to that SLA to monitor all violations. The default threshold is 15 seconds; determine whether that will work for your application.

- Setting the alerting threshold to zero causes APM to not collect all requests because of event throttling logic; for more information see the "Advanced APM Architecture" section of this chapter. This would be correct only for those applications with almost no load; for real production applications this means collecting details regarding the first *N* requests no matter the duration, this makes it difficult to analyze which are problems versus normal performance.
- The alternative is to keep the alerting threshold high. This would target only outliers but also has disadvantages. In this situation, the APM agent won't collect deep dive information since the events will primarily be light. For additional information about light events, see the "Advanced APM Architecture" section.

Proper thresholds are those that address performance violations as 1%–10% of the application overall load based on the response time. The most common approach to identifying threshold is to start with an initial configuration and tune it up or down over time based on application performance trend information, which you can learn from Application

Advisor reports. Usually you would pick an initial value from 5–15 seconds depending on your application's normal performance, and then tune that value up or down depending on the volume and actionability of the data presented.

Setting Namespaces

Configuring namespaces defines the amount of data collected for performance or exception problems. These settings are different for performance and exception monitoring, but the approach is similar. The default configuration does not include custom namespaces and only collects what is defined with the default agent configuration. This gives you visibility into the outgoing database, web service, I/O, and other outgoing calls but lacks visibility into the custom code.

If you select all namespaces for monitoring, APM collects complete details regarding the custom code of your application, can be tremendously useful to the development team when troubleshooting an issue. However, this may introduce more overhead. Enabling all namespaces may not bring your application to its knees, but the overhead may be noticeable in some situations.

The approach recommended by the authors is based on where the application is running:

- If in a preproduction or QA environment, it is best to enable all namespaces or several custom namespaces used in your application code. You can then run performance tests and measure the resource usage as well as response time and throughput to compare it with a baseline without monitoring being enabled.
- In a production environment, you should scope the configuration to enable additional namespaces only on a limited number of servers and observe their behavior. If there is a concern with overhead, disable some of the namespaces used in your application; utilize the development team to identify those namespaces.

What APM Collects

Data collection is enabled primarily by the configuration defined in the Template Wizard; the advanced configuration defines the amount of data collected. Two types of data are collected: statistics and events. These are discussed in the next sections.

Collecting Statistics

Statistics come from custom performance counters registered by .NET monitoring and client-side monitoring modules on each computer when you enable application monitoring. These counters are exposed and updated by monitoring modules, based on application behavior and performance. Here is the list of counters registered when you enable application monitoring for an application component(s) on the server:

- **.NET Apps:** Categories of this counter introduce overall application performance on the machine per each application component.
- **.NET Statistics:** These show overall performance per each transaction defined.

- **.NET CSM Apps:** These counters collect overall client-side performance information of the application components reported back to the CSMCollector web service on the current machine.
- **.NET CSM Statistics:** These counters aggregate performance information over the client-side transaction's performance.
- **.NET CSM Collector:** These collect internal information of client requests and tokens.

Collecting Events

Events cannot be accessed directly on the server. Events can come from a .NET monitoring module or client-side monitoring module and contain detailed problem reports to identify the root cause of a performance issue or application failure. Two types of rules collect and submit events: One creates alerts in Operations Manager; the second delivers events to the Application Diagnostics console. Figure 15.25 shows the flow of server-side events.

Client-side events have a similar flow and two types of rules as well. These events are initiated on the browser by executing the client-side monitoring JavaScript and then sent to the CSMCollector web service installed on each monitored website. This is depicted in Figure 15.26.

All application events are submitted to the Application Diagnostics and Application Advisor consoles. The rule responsible for this data transfer is the APM event collection rule; this runs on every instance of the `.NET Application Monitoring Agent` class.

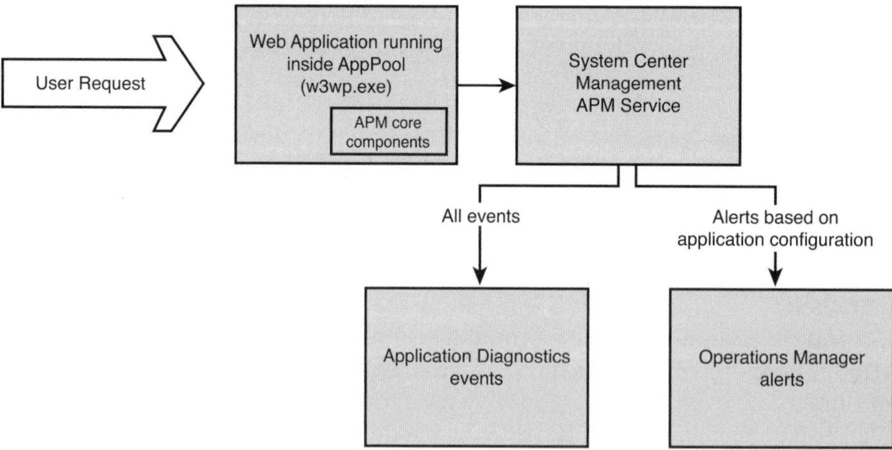

FIGURE 15.25 Server-side events flow.

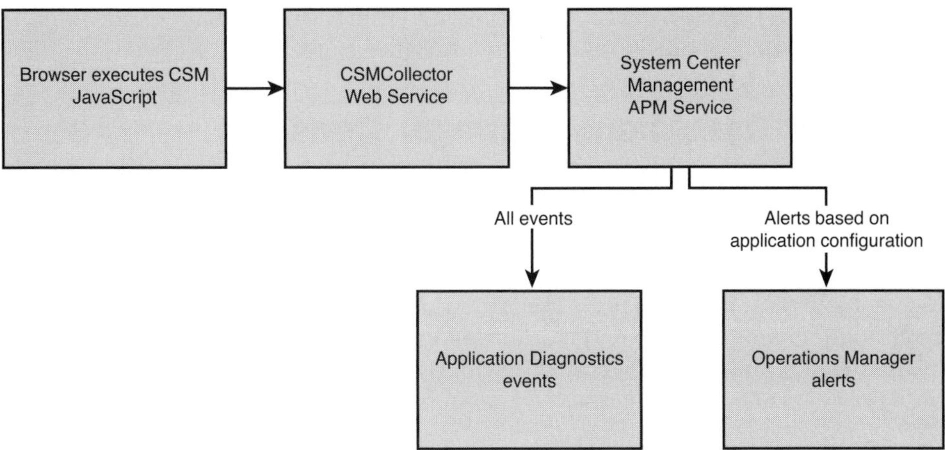

FIGURE 15.26 Client-side events flow.

A second type of rule is based on the configuration you defined using the Template Wizard and delivers only the exceptions or performance alerts you configured. These rules are enabled or disabled for the application instances created with the wizard. There are four rules for the APM events and two rules for the CSM events; these run on the instances of `APM Application` and `Client-Side Monitoring Application` base classes.

Each of these rules generates or updates an alert based on the event type and problem hash-code included in the event data to identify unique alerts for similar events and attaches a link to the event details to drill into the full event with the Application Diagnostics Web console. Here are the rules that generate alerts for APM events:

- **Generate Alert for Performance APM Event:** Generates alerts per performance violations detected in the application.
- **Generate Alert for Security APM Event:** These generate alerts per failures related to the security nature.
- **Generate Alert for Connectivity APM Events:** Generates alerts for the failures related to the connectivity nature.
- **Generate Alert for Application Failure APM Events:** These generate alerts for the failure related to the application itself but not the configuration.

There are rules to generate alerts for CSM events:

- **Generate Alert for Performance CSM Events:** These generate performance issues detected on the client browser like slow page loading and slow AJAX calls.
- **Generate Alert for Application Failure CSM Events:** Generates alert for the failures on the client browser such as JavaScript failures.

Similar sets of metrics and rules exist for all transactions that you configure inside the advanced configuration, as previously shown with Figure 15.14.

APM in the Operations Manager Console

You can leverage data collected by APM agents differently using different consoles. The APM dashboard in the Operations console is designed for operators and provides high-level information of the state, top metrics, and alerts. Compare this to the Application Diagnostics console, which provides views to perform low-level analysis and is useful for development and operations (devops), application support, debug engineers and developers. Application Advisor is based on the data coming from Application Diagnostics and has a number of reports and navigation controls with the ability to drill into the Applications Diagnostics view to identify root cause.

Using Dashboards

OpsMgr 2012 creates dashboards automatically after you configure monitoring using the .NET Application Monitoring template. Figure 15.27 shows an example.

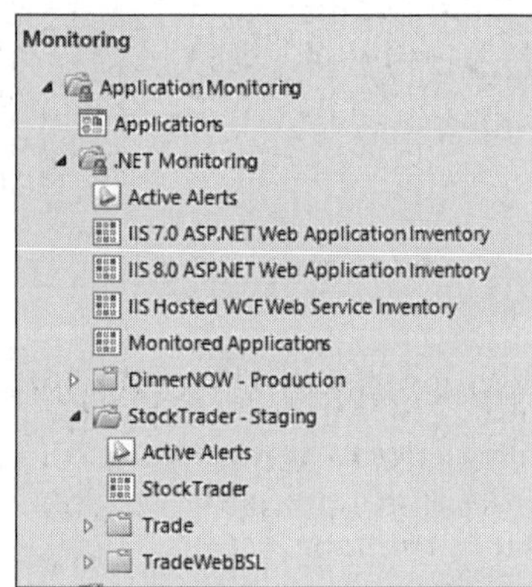

FIGURE 15.27 Operations console dashboards and views.

Top level views show aggregated information from all applications:

- **Active Alerts:** Shows active alerts from all applications.
- **ASP.NET Web Application Inventory:** Shows all .NET web applications discovered on the servers. From this view, you can run the Check Client-Side Monitoring Compatibility task to check an application's compatibility with APM client-side monitoring.
- **Monitored Applications:** Shows high-level state of the applications.

APM Views

Multiple views are created automatically for each application when you complete the configuration template:

- **Active Alerts view:** Shows the alerts from all components of current application.
- **Application State view:** Shown in Figure 15.28, named to match the .NET application component, the Application State view displays the health of all components of this enterprise application monitored by APM.

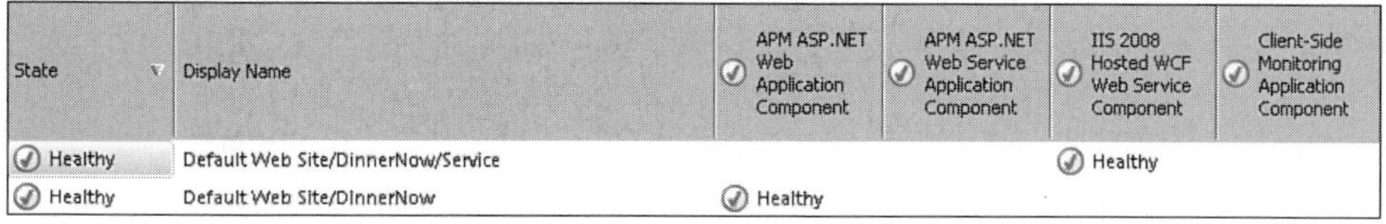

State
Display Name
APM ASP.NET Web Application Component
APM ASP.NET Web Service Application Component
IIS 2008 Hosted WCF Web Service Component
Client-Side Monitoring Application Component
Healthy
Default Web Site/DinnerNow/Service
Healthy
Healthy
Default Web Site/DinnerNow
Healthy

FIGURE 15.28 Application State view.

Each component has its own subfolder with subviews for server-side monitoring and client-side monitoring:

- **All Performance Data:** This brings all performance metrics for this component from all machines, including average response time, load, and so on.
- **Overall Component Health:** This view shows the health of each component per server where it is monitored.

Alerts and Drill-Down

Alerts represent problems found in the application. They are created based on the monitoring settings you specified in the Template Wizard and could be of different types: security, connectivity, application failure, and performance. You will find different alerts for your application if they occurred due to different problems; for example, performance alerts are organized by web page URL, and application failure alerts will be separated by action and exception class.

Each alert has standard properties such as creation date, age, repeat count, and so on. The repeat count is increased each time a new occurrence of this root cause is detected, and each alert contains a link to the problem details in the Application Diagnostics console. Figure 15.29 is an example of an APM alert.

Drilling into the alert details opens the Application Diagnostics console, which is secured and limited to those individuals allowed to access it.

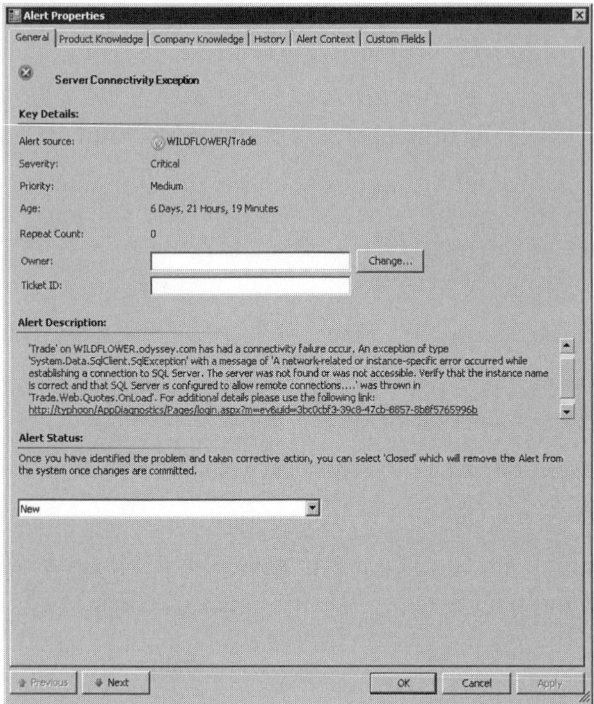

FIGURE 15.29 Sample APM alert.

Troubleshooting Applications Using the Application Diagnostics Console

The Application Diagnostics console is designed to provide reporting capabilities for devops, developers, and debug engineers to investigate the root cause of the failures or performance problems. It is a web console and requires Internet Explorer.

Using Views and Dashboards in the Diagnostics Console

The Application Diagnostics console has multiples dashboards providing views on different data. Computers and applications dashboards show more high-level data, and events dashboards give access to individual problems with the ability to filter, group by, and analyze details.

The Computers dashboard, displayed in Figure 15.30, shows currently reporting computers with installed agents. It displays data for the last hour for CPU, memory, I/O, and application load. Each category displays the total value for the machine and the monitored application, which covers processes running the application that is enabled for monitoring. For example, comparing total CPU and application CPU could identify what is consuming processor time. Load shows total number of requests processed by the applications monitored on the current computer versus the number of events, that is, failures and performance problems.

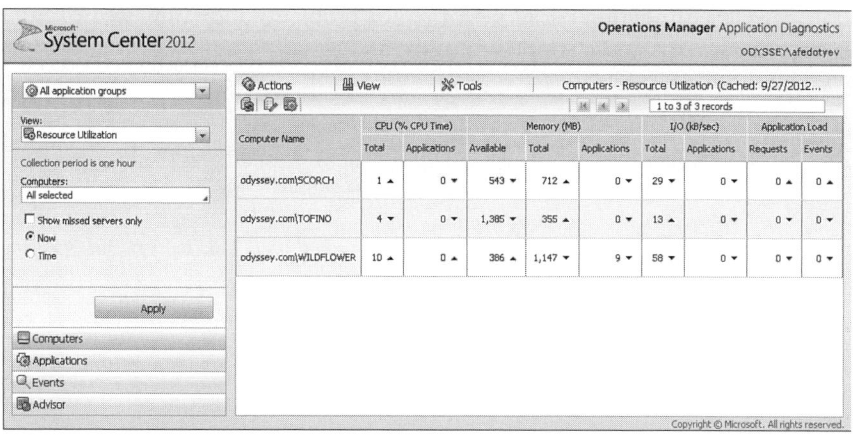

FIGURE 15.30 The Computers dashboard in the Application Diagnostics console.

Drilling down into computer details opens a new page with additional details, the ability to trend together any type of counter, a list of currently running processes that includes only the processes where the APM agent is monitored, and statistics on the load of each application on the current computer. Figure 15.31 provides an example.

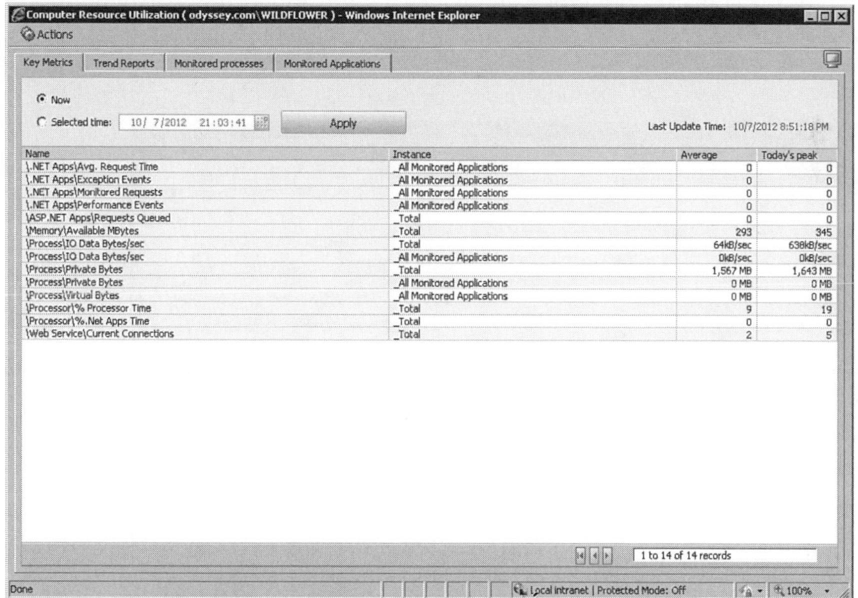

FIGURE 15.31 Computer resource utilization.

The Applications dashboard (see Figure 15.32) shows all application components that are monitored; each IIS application is grouped separately. Each application in this dashboard aggregates data from all computers and shows overall behavior. The dashboard includes load information, response time, number of performance problems and failures, and the number of server/processes this application is running on.

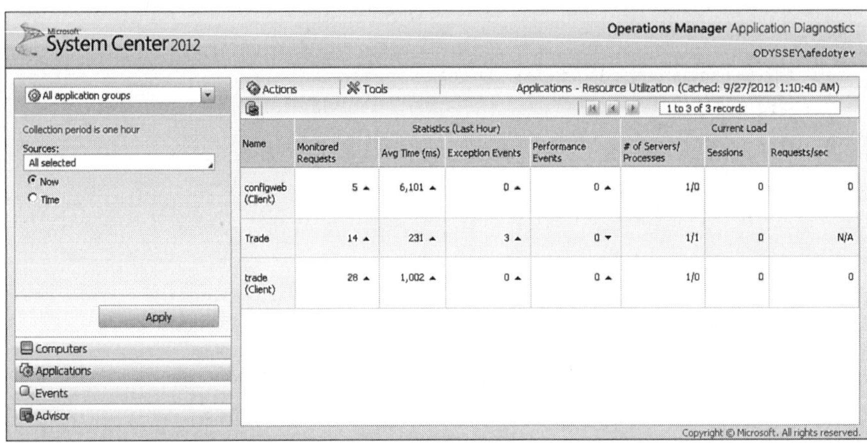

FIGURE 15.32 Applications dashboard.

Drill-down provides the ability to see problem breakdown based on the root cause, trending information of the application metrics, and reviewing the application behavior on different servers in the web farm. Figure 15.33 shows an example of application resource utilization.

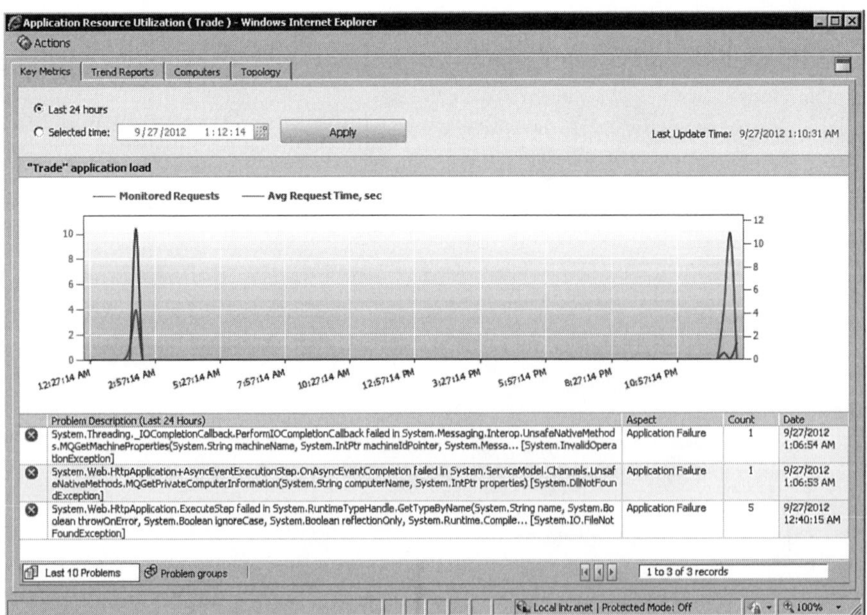

FIGURE 15.33 Application resource utilization.

The Events dashboard, shown in Figure 15.34, provides many options for navigating through the events collected from the monitored application. It includes options to view all events, or by performance or exception events. Selecting a specific view changes the filtering options to provide the best search fields. For example, the Exception Events view has the ability to search by exception class or error code. When investigating a problem, you will want to leverage all options including using the specific view for failure or performance issues, grouping by different values, filtering by dates and problem details, and so on.

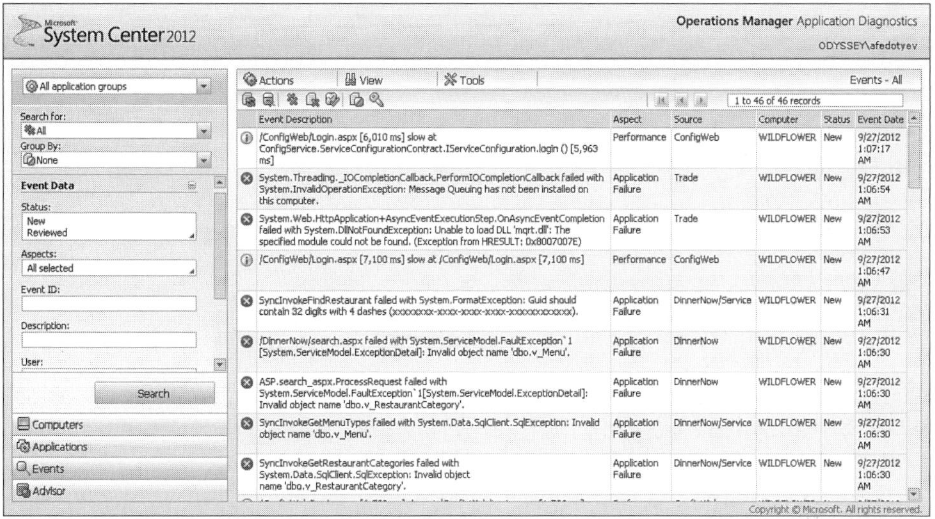

FIGURE 15.34 The Events dashboard.

The Advisor node in Figure 15.34 opens Application Advisor in a new window. Application Advisor is described in the "Using the Application Advisor Console" section.

Managing Events

The key value of APM is the results it collects, which include issues describing information from the application runtime. Data for each alert differs based on the type of alert, be it an exception from the .NET server-side or an AJAX call running slowly on the client side. Figure 15.35 shows common properties of an event.

Each type of the event has its own specific properties and shares a number of common properties that are listed at the top of each event. Common properties include

- **Computer name:** The name of the computer where the problem was collected.
- **Source:** This is the name of the application component where the problem was detected; for ASP.NET applications, it will include the IIS application name.
- **Event date:** The date and time the problem was detected.

- **Aspect:** The type of the problem; there are four possible aspects: application failure, performance, security, and connectivity.
- **User name:** Name of the user that executed the transaction that failed or ran slowly.
- **Status:** The state of the event defined by the APM rules management; it can be New, Reviewed, Deleted, and By Design.

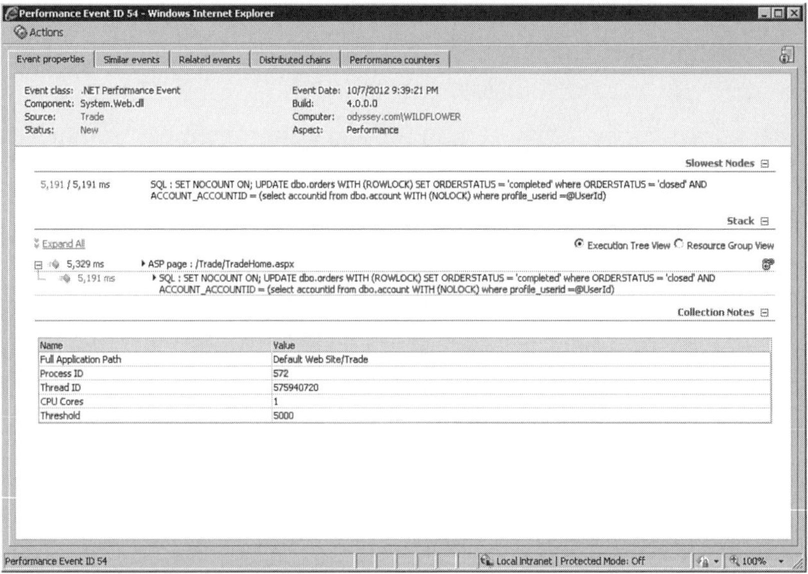

FIGURE 15.35 Event common properties.

Each event represents a specific problem. The problem is used to group events that have the identical root cause. Performance events are grouped into problems based on the unique URL; exception events belong to the same problem if they have the same call stack and exception class.

Exception Event

Exception events are based on .NET exceptions in the runtime. Exceptions include the exception itself with the call stack and parameters for the methods in the call stack. Figure 15.36 shows an exception event.

The (green) arrow icon on the left of Figure 15.36 identifies parameters; when you see that icon, you can expand the method and read the parameter values that were passed as well as the member variables the object had during execution. Additionally (see Figure 15.37) there is a cube (blue) icon near some of the methods. This means source code information was collected; it shows where in the code the exception was raised by a source file name and a line number. Source code information is collected only when PDB files were deployed to the server together with the actual DLL files. PDB files are program database files holding debugging and project state information that allows incremental linking of debug information of the application. These files are created when the application is compiled with the **Generate Debug Info** option enabled. This is located in Visual Studio at **Project** -> **Project Properties** -> **Configuration Properties** -> **Linker** -> **Debugging** -> **Generate Debug Info**.

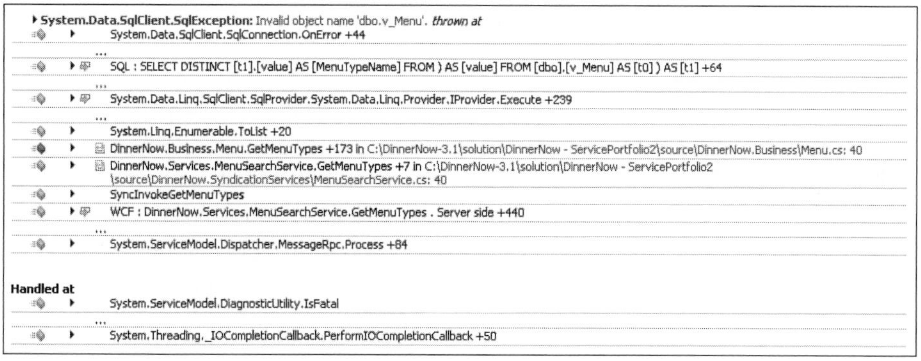

```
▸ System.Data.SqlClient.SqlException: Invalid object name 'dbo.v_Menu'. thrown at
    System.Data.SqlClient.SqlConnection.OnError +44
    ...
    SQL : SELECT DISTINCT [t1].[value] AS [MenuTypeName] FROM ) AS [value] FROM [dbo].[v_Menu] AS [t0] ) AS [t1] +64
    ...
    System.Data.Linq.SqlClient.SqlProvider.System.Data.Linq.Provider.IProvider.Execute +239
    ...
    System.Linq.Enumerable.ToList +20
    DinnerNow.Business.Menu.GetMenuTypes +173 in C:\DinnerNow-3.1\solution\DinnerNow - ServicePortfolio2\source\DinnerNow.Business\Menu.cs: 40
    DinnerNow.Services.MenuSearchService.GetMenuTypes +7 in C:\DinnerNow-3.1\solution\DinnerNow - ServicePortfolio2
    \source\DinnerNow.SyndicationServices\MenuSearchService.cs: 40
    SyncInvokeGetMenuTypes
    WCF : DinnerNow.Services.MenuSearchService.GetMenuTypes . Server side +440
    ...
    System.ServiceModel.Dispatcher.MessageRpc.Process +84

Handled at
    System.ServiceModel.DiagnosticUtility.IsFatal
    ...
    System.Threading._IOCompletionCallback.PerformIOCompletionCallback +50
```

FIGURE 15.36 Exception event.

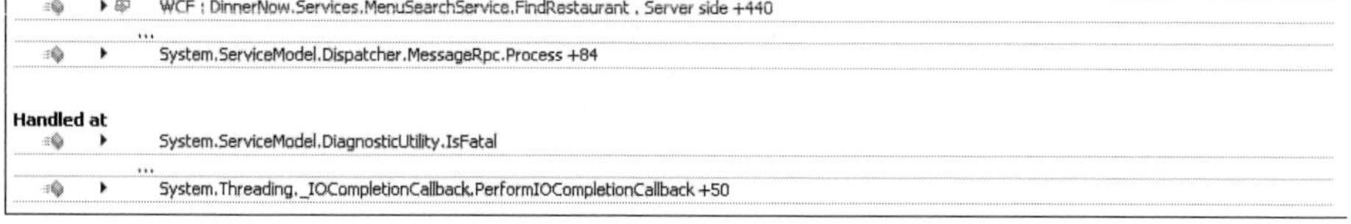

```
▸ System.FormatException: Guid should contain 32 digits with 4 dashes (xxxxxxxx-xxxx-xxxx-xxxx-xxxxxxxxxxxx). thrown at
    System.Guid..ctor +1409
    DinnerNow.Services.MenuSearchService.FindRestaurant +27 in C:\DinnerNow-3.1\solution\DinnerNow - ServicePortfolio2
    \source\DinnerNow.SyndicationServices\MenuSearchService.cs: 53
```

Parameters(4) | Member Variables(0) | Source

Name	Value	Structure
postalCode	98101	
menuType		
restaurantCategoryId		
deadline	45	

```
    SyncInvokeFindRestaurant
    WCF : DinnerNow.Services.MenuSearchService.FindRestaurant . Server side +440
    ...
    System.ServiceModel.Dispatcher.MessageRpc.Process +84

Handled at
    System.ServiceModel.DiagnosticUtility.IsFatal
    ...
    System.Threading._IOCompletionCallback.PerformIOCompletionCallback +50
```

FIGURE 15.37 Exception with parameters from custom namespaces.

Parameters are collected as specified in the configuration per the list of monitored functions, which can be a method or a class/namespace. By default, that configuration already contains a number of methods from the .NET Framework itself that are interesting from a failure perspective. During configuration, administrators can enable all user namespaces or specific methods to collect parameter values if the exception occurs in that method.

Exceptions could be critical (unhandled) and non-critical (handled). .NET does not actually have unhandled exceptions. Each exception is handled with a handler of some type;

the difference is where the exception is handled. A handler is a method in the code that catches an exception, performs some logic to store the failure details on the disk or event log, and then "hides" the failure. This allows users to see a friendly message on the web page rather than the error page. Implementing exception handlers is performed by developers and is typically defined by company coding standards. Exception monitoring settings allow you to configure collecting exceptions logged with custom handlers.

The APM configuration contains a list of exception handlers, which by default has all standard .NET Framework system level handlers. When an exception is handled in one of those handlers, it is critical, meaning that it was not handled inside the application code. Each exception event has four properties by which it will be possible to search, filter, and group:

- **Action:** The action identifies what functionality failed from the user perspective. For an ASP.NET application, the action would be a URL to the .aspx page; for a web service or WCF object, the action would be a method that was executed.
- **Failed function:** This is the method in the call stack causing the exception. It is the last method in the code that either raised an exception itself or called some system framework method that raised an exception, or a call to the external resource that caused a failure.
- **Exception class:** The type of the .NET exception that was raised, this typically identifies the high-level type of the problem. Examples are System.Data.SqlException and System.NullReferenceException.
- **Problem:** Technically the problem is identified by a hash code that is calculated based upon the full call stack including the code offsets and the exception class. The next time the exception is raised in the same place called by the same methods and the exception class is the same, it is assumed it is the same problem. This property is used for grouping and finding similar problems.

The APM agent has built-in knowledge used to determine the aspect (type) of the exception; this could be connectivity, security, or application failure:

- **Connectivity exceptions:** These are failures to complete a request caused by no connection to a dependent resource, such as a call to a database or web resource. Examples of a connectivity issue would be a failure due to no connection to SQL Server, no network to connect to remote web service, or a file that does not exist when trying to read configuration information.
- **Security exceptions:** Security issues can occur when there is no permission to insert a row into the database table, not enough permission to create a new file on the disk, or a service account is not allowed to call a remote WCF method. Security exceptions are those that failed due to no permissions to complete an operation; this could be a call to a database, accessing a file, and so on. Figure 15.38 displays a security event.

Description ⊟

Security failure in "DinnerNow.Business.Menu.GetMenuTypes()" has been detected: "Cannot open database "DinnerNow" requested by the login. The login failed. Login failed for user 'IIS APPPOOL\Classic .NET AppPool'.".

Name	Value
⊟ Target	
SQLServer/Database	dinnernow/DinnerNow
⊟ Actions	
Method	Open
⊟ Security context	
ConnectionString	Data Source=dinnernow;Initial Catalog=DinnerNow;Integrated Security=True
Thread identity	IIS APPPOOL\Classic .NET AppPool

Exception Chain ⊞

Exception Data ⊞

Stack ⊞

Modules List ⊞

Collection Notes ⊞

FIGURE 15.38 Security event.

NOTE: ADDITIONAL INFORMATION COLLECTED FOR SECURITY AND CONNECTIVITY ISSUES

For each security and connectivity issue, the APM agent tries to collect information to identify the resource for which access failed. For example, if the problem was while opening a SQL connection, this will contain the connection string, service account used to open the connection, and SQL Server and database name. This information is displayed on top of the event to make these events friendlier to the administrators; this means they could fix it quickly rather than having to read the call stack to identify the root cause of the security issue.

- **Application exceptions:** An application failure is assigned to those exceptions that failed because of the failure in the code, rather than due to security or connectivity.

Performance Event

Performance alerts are raised when the duration of the particular functionality runs slower than alerting thresholds defined in the configuration for this application. Figure 15.39 is an example of a performance event.

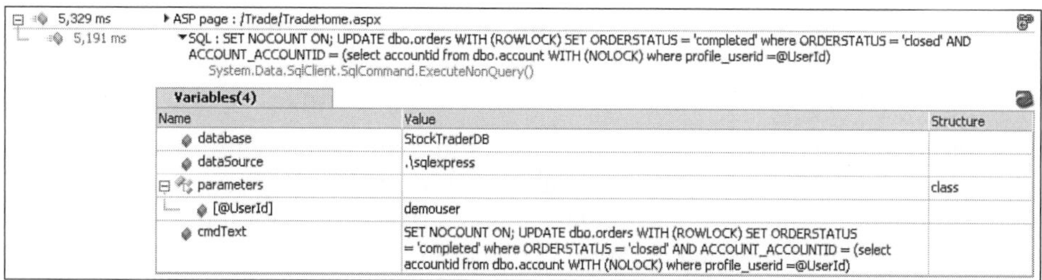

FIGURE 15.39 Performance event.

The performance event has two views: execution tree view and the resource group view. Both views show the top method with the duration on top, as shown in the tree views in Figure 15.39 and Figure 15.40. This method identifies the functionality that is slow and the duration. For example, for an ASP.NET application, the top method would be the .aspx page name and path; for a WCF object, it would be the method name that was called.

Figure 15.40 shows a performance event with custom namespaces. The execution tree view shows the calls flow with the duration information inside the tree, so users can track which method called what other methods, as well as parameter values when those were collected. Some of the methods in the execution tree view have a small triangle icon on the left and some do not; that icon is displayed when the parameters values were collected. The user can click on the method to expand it and read the values. Parameters are collected only for those methods defined as resources in the configuration. By default, configuration includes resources from .NET Framework; those cover standard methods to access the database, web calls, I/O calls, and so on. Administrators can extend the list of the resources when configuring monitoring.

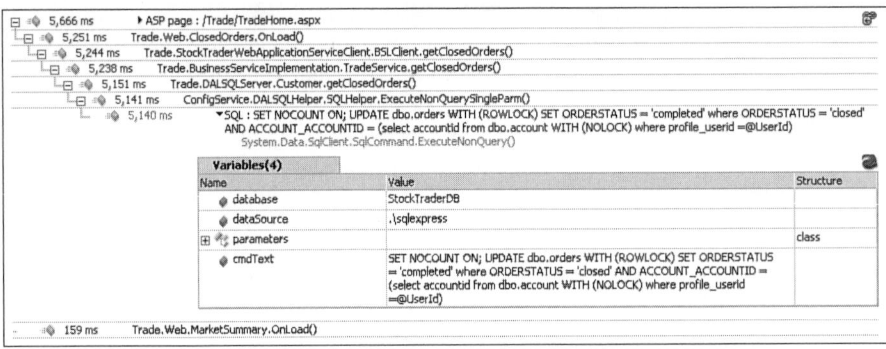

FIGURE 15.40 Performance event with custom namespaces.

Often standard resource calls are displayed with a friendly name in addition to a method name. For example, method System.Data.SqlClient.SqlCommand.ExecuteNonQuery is aliased as SQL: sp_MyProcedure, where sp_MyProcedure is an actual SQL query that was executed. This is implemented by aliases, allowing you to define friendly names for any methods; more importantly, they allow using the parameter value to become a part of the method alias. That allows you to search, filter, and group by the new aliased method description.

When the execution tree view shows the call stack information with a list of the methods and duration, you can mouse-over the time value on the left from each method and see additional information. This includes the start and end date on the local machine and self-time. Self-time is the calculated duration of the time spent in the method itself; this is equal to the difference from the duration of the method minus total duration of the direct children method calls and shows actual time spent in the method. Those methods that do not call other methods do not have self-time, since 100% of the time was spent in the method. Self-time value is used to build the heavy resource calls list; only methods with duration more than 10% of the total request duration are displayed in this list.

Occasionally users may find a performance event that contains no data, and the notes say the event is light or no data was collected due to light logic. Light events are explained in the "Advanced APM Architecture" section. Figure 15.41 shows an example.

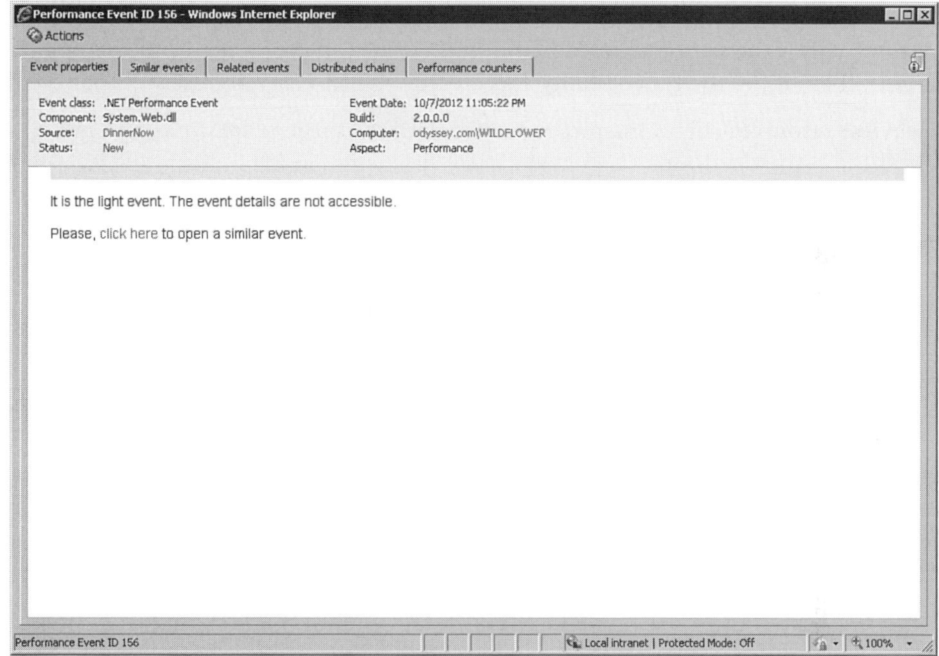

FIGURE 15.41 Performance light event.

Light logic is a technique used to optimize APM agent resource usage when collecting performance violations over the thresholds. .NET application monitoring configuration includes an alerting threshold to collect only requests running slower than the defined threshold. The APM agent does not know the duration of the request until the request execution completes; to report only violations, the agent would need to track all requests and submit details only for those running slowly. This logic would introduce overhead excessive for a production environment, thus leading to development of a light event optimization algorithm. The algorithm tracks status for each request whether it was light or not, meaning it ran faster or slower than a threshold.

The APM agent does not collect any detailed problem information for light requests. In the event the request was marked as fast (under threshold) last time and now is slow, for the first occurrence the agent reports an alert similar to Figure 15.41, and marks in memory that the request was slow this time. If the same request runs slowly the next time, the agent would collect a full problem report including execution tree view and resource information; otherwise, it will be again marked as fast.

The light logic algorithm is more complicated and has rules for switching from light to normal and back, but generally causes some events not to have details. When you see a light event, look for a similar event with the same action that is not light. This will not be exactly the same event but is the same action running slower than a threshold; you might have to analyze different performance events with the same action to identify all possible root causes to determine a resolution.

Each performance event has the following properties:

- **Action:** This is the same in most situations as the Action properties in the exception events; it identifies the functionality executed by the end user or other component.
- **Heaviest resource:** This is the method name with the greatest self-time, and introduces the biggest performance degradation.

Client-Side Event

A client-side performance alert is collected for the performance violation of the page loaded in the browser of the client itself. When the full execution cycle of the page is slower than a configured threshold, APM detects where the time was spent. Figure 15.42 shows an example.

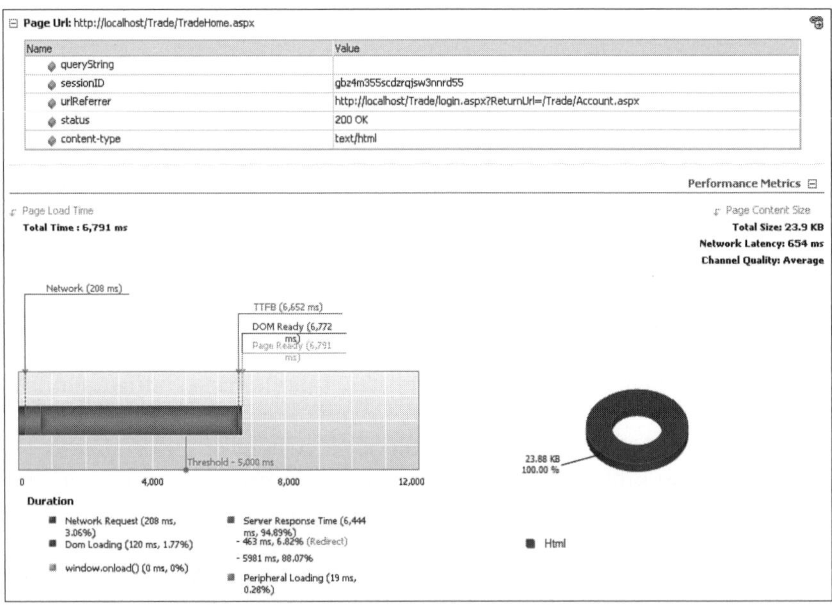

FIGURE 15.42 Client-side performance event.

This type of alert covers the following phases of the page load cycle:

- **Network time:** Network time from previous page post to the first byte of the new page excluding the server execution time

- **Server response time:** Actual server processing time
- **Document object model (DOM) loading:** The time it takes to load everything into the document object model in the browser
- **Peripheral loading:** The time to load peripherals like images
- **window.onload JavaScript execution time:** The time to run scripts attached to the page onload logic

In addition, each event includes information about downloaded content (see Figure 15.43), AJAX calls made on the page, and user and browser information. The monitoring configuration controls the information that is collected.

FIGURE 15.43 Client-side additional details.

Client-side monitoring also collects JavaScript exceptions that occurred on the page and sends those back to APM. Exception event data collection is controlled by monitoring settings and can collect JavaScript stack and global variables. Figure 15.44 shows an example.

FIGURE 15.44 Client-side exception event.

Distributed Chains

Most modern applications are developed using service oriented architecture (SOA) and have several layers that communicate with each other. In situations where the performance problem or failure is related to a call to another component using a standard .NET mechanism such as a web service, WCF, .NET Remoting or COM+, client-side and server-side calls, APM will correlate the problems information from the layers into a chain, as shown in Figure 15.45.

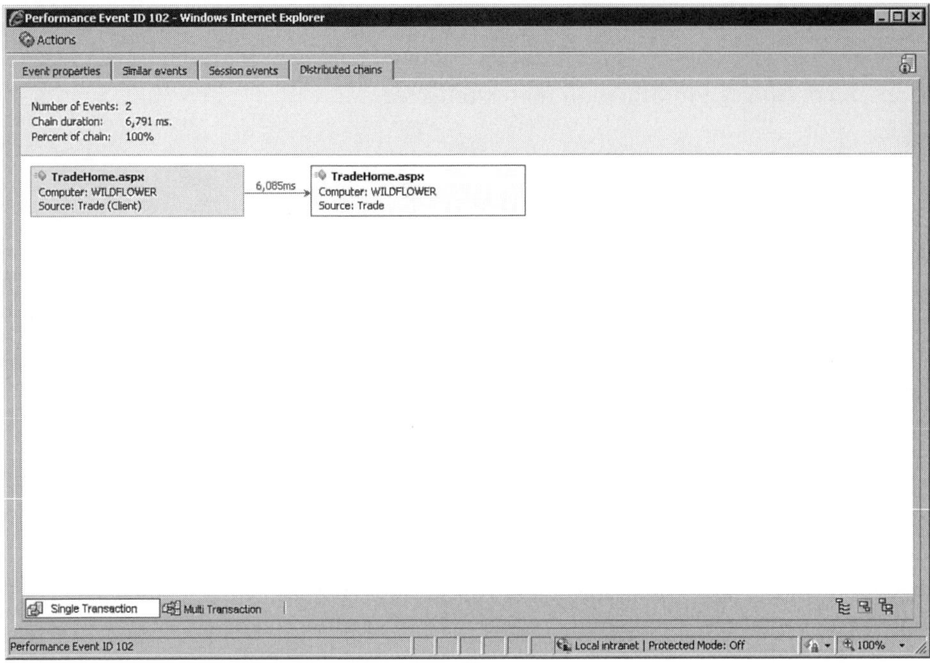

FIGURE 15.45 Distributed chains.

Distributed chains logic is based on heuristics and includes multiple parameters including date and time, service method name, duration for performance events, and exception information for failures. There are two views:

- **Single:** This is a more narrowly focused view and allows only a 1-minute window difference from the node being called (callee) and the caller and checks actual parameters values passed to the call on both sides.
- **Multi:** This wider view does not filter parameter values and allows a wide range of date and time filters that the user can define. Use this view for general analysis of the component's communication.

The chain information is not always available for the user when the performance or exception problem is caused in the callee. Here are some reasons this could occur:

- The agent is not installed on the callee server(s) (the callee server is the server hosting the component being called, and the callee is the application component being called).
- Alerting threshold for the callee application component is too high; therefore, no performance violation is collected.
- There is event throttling logic that blocked collecting this particular event (more detail in the "Advanced APM Architecture" section later in this chapter).
- The information about the callee has been removed by the database maintenance.

Tuning the configurations described in these bullets will fix most of these issues, as it includes wide agent deployment and better thresholds configuration.

Using the Application Advisor Console

Application Advisor introduces a set of multi-purpose reports for use by the operations team, managers, devops, developers, and QA teams. The value is not only in the reports but also in the user interface, as it gives you the ability to continuously drill down into subreports to investigate until you determine a root cause. The authors highly recommend clicking on every link in the report to find where it goes (this would be either a subreport or an event in the Application Diagnostics console).

Within the Application Advisor reports, your best place to start is generally the Problems Distribution Analysis and Application Status reports. The next sections discuss these reports.

Problems Distribution Analysis Report

The Problems Distribution Analysis report is designed to bring together monitored results from multiple components of your application and prioritize them based on the number of problems in each IIS application. The authors recommend running this report across long intervals to help assess the state of your .NET applications globally and to identify top problems.

Begin by defining report start and end dates, and the sources and computers you want to include. These are typically grouped into one report based on the LOB application to which they belong. Then, configure whether you want to see all problems; you can define additional thresholds to filter only the top problems. The report only analyzes data already collected; if the agent was configured to collect only performance problems running over 5 seconds you can filter them in the report by setting the value to be more than 5 seconds. Trying to show performance problems running less than 5 seconds will not return data if that was not collected. Figure 15.46 shows a sample report.

The report displayed in Figure 15.47 shows all sources selected, sorted descending by the number of problems. This can help identify where you have issues and need to concentrate your efforts on fixing those problems. Clicking on the source will navigate to the application details and highlight the top reasons for the problem.

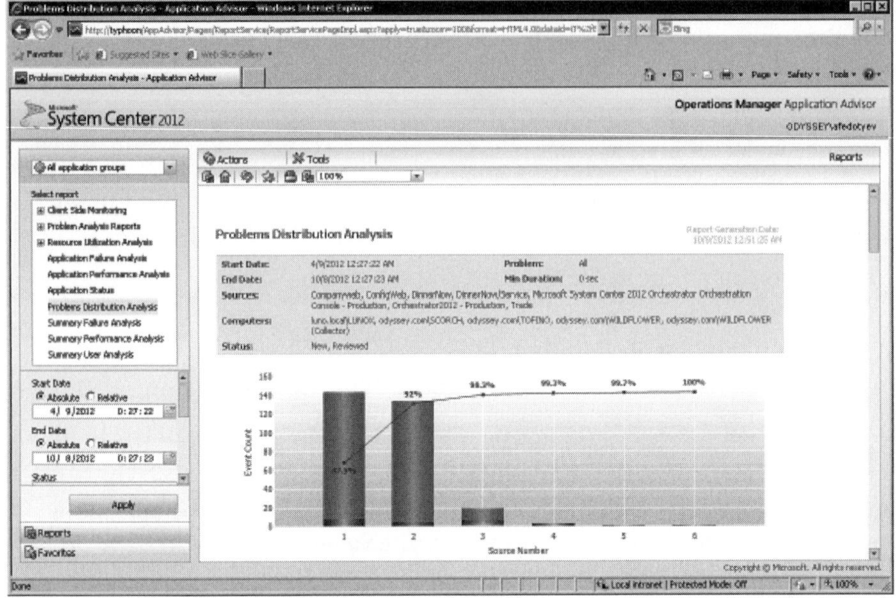

FIGURE 15.46 Problems Distribution Analysis report.

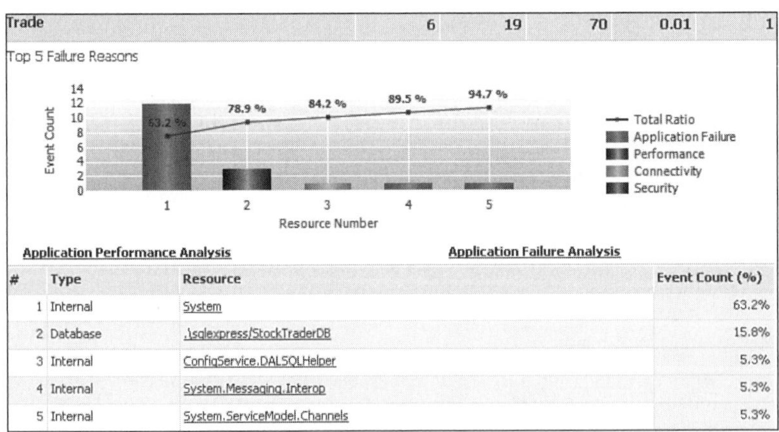

FIGURE 15.47 Source problems distribution summary.

These reasons could be database or web service related in the case of external problems. The details would show the database name or web service URL. When the problem is caused by application code issues, the reason would identify the namespace of the code of which component is failing or running slowly.

Internal execution means that there is no common reason of the problem or the monitored configuration did not enable namespaces for performance monitoring, meaning there is no data to identify which part of the code is causing performance problems.

By clicking on a link with a specific reason, Application Advisor opens a list of the individual events representing that problem, and you can select any of those, opening the Application Diagnostics interface to show the actual event.

Application Status Report

The Application Status report differs from the Problems Distribution Analysis report because it is designed to show the difference between the current application state and the historical average.

This report, shown in Figure 15.48, is limited by up to five components to be included into one report, typically selected from the same LOB application. You can also filter by computers, critical problems, or all problems, and an additional threshold filter.

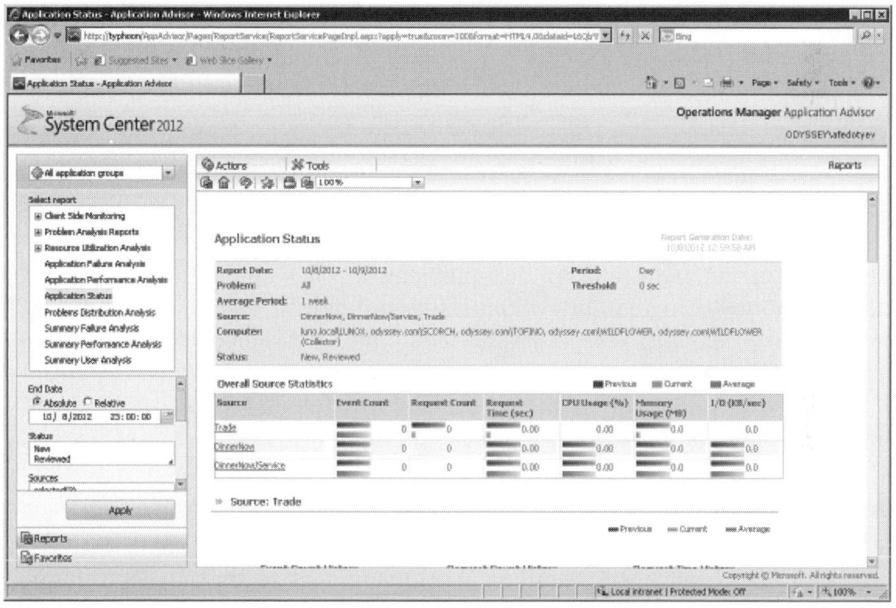

FIGURE 15.48 Application Status report.

It is important to define the end date of the report, which can be absolute or relative, the type of the report (daily, weekly, or monthly), and the time range for the historical baseline calculation.

For each application component, you can find two types of details: overall performance and problem trending. Overall performance shows resource metrics; these are CPU, memory, and I/O. Application performance metrics are also displayed; these are load, response time and rate, and problems. The chart for each metric shows the current period trend versus previous period versus historical average. As an example, when executing a weekly report with three months of historical data you will find the current week performance compared with previous week and compared with a three-month baseline.

Scrolling down, you find each component, containing the trend for each individual problem for the top 10 exception and performance problems as shown in Figure 15.49. For example, you can see that a specific problem occurred *N* times, but it is less than in previous time range (*-M*).

Event Statistics

Event Type	Problem Count		Event Count		New Problem Count
Performance	3	+3	7	+7	3
Exception	10	+10	121	+121	9

Top 10 New Problems

Performance Problems

#	Description	Event Count	Avg Dur. (sec)	Max Dur. (sec)
1	/DinnerNow/Default.aspx slow at DinnerNow.WebUX.MenuSearchService.IMenuSearchService.GetRestaurantCategories (). Client side	3	25.21	32.92
2	/DinnerNow/search.aspx slow at Opening connection to the database 'AspNetDB' on the server 'DinnerNow'	1	16.60	16.60
3	/DinnerNow/Default.aspx slow at DinnerNow.WebUX.MenuSearchService.IMenuSearchService.GetRestaurantCategories	1	17.70	17.70
	Total (Top 10) 100.0 %	5		
	All others 0.0 %	0		

FIGURE 15.49 Top source problem trends.

An additional status report shows a list of new problems for each application. Note that changing the monitoring configuration will most likely bring you "new" problems; they will be new since they were not previously collected. Running this report for the application on a periodic basis with the same monitoring configuration lets you identify critical trends and new problems. (It is always interesting to run the report after releasing a new version of the application or during/after a peak load.)

Best Practices for Scheduling Reports

Proactively leveraging the Application Advisor reports helps you to improve the quality of your applications more quickly. The authors recommend scheduling delivery of those reports to ensure the information is analyzed on a timely basis. Here are some suggestions:

- **Schedule a report after you render it to make sure it contains required data:** There are two options for scheduling a report: by the menu using a wizard, or after rendering the report using a toolbar command. This second approach is recommended since you can review the report results and verify it before actually scheduling the report. It also will reuse the report parameters and put those immediately into the wizard, so you do not need to configure it twice.
- **Use relative dates, as they are relative to the date/time when you schedule the reports to be executed:** All scheduled reports require using relative dates. It is important to remember that the date will be relative to the date when you want to send the report. For example, if you want to send a weekly report for the previous week each Monday, you should use the beginning of the previous week to the end of that week as relative dates. Figure 15.50 shows an example.

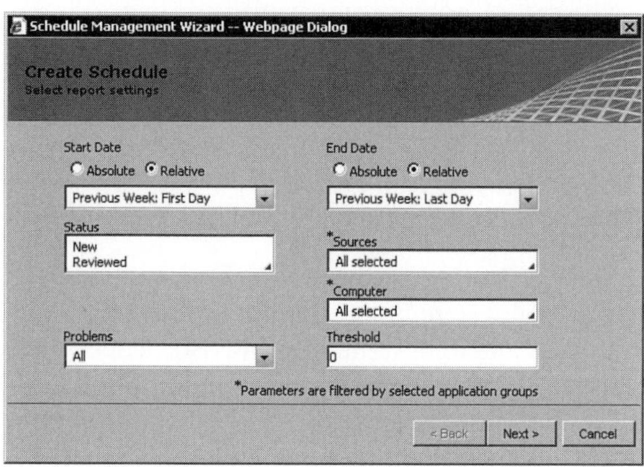

FIGURE 15.50 Scheduling an Advisor report.

- **Limit the scope of the report and assign it to the proper audience:** Group the application components (sources) into the same reports and schedule these to be delivered to the appropriate person(s). This ensures that during analysis you are not mixing data from completely different applications and that the proper individuals can act on them.

- **Name the scheduled reports accordingly—you may end up having from 10 to 50 subscriptions:** A typical recommendation would be to include the report name, application name, and period into the subscription name. For example, Problem distribution analysis – Front End – weekly.

- **Schedule reports to be rendered during different times of a day:** Reports are rendered using SQL Server Reporting Services (SSRS). Using a different time of the day for a large number of subscriptions would increase the responsiveness of SSRS and decrease database load.

- **Keep copies of exported monthly/per three-month reports to ensure you have the information even when data is purged from the data warehouse database:** The reporting database has limited capacity and keeps the data for three months by default. The authors recommend archiving exported reports so you could review those later and compare them with the current state of your applications.

USING APM REPORTS TO BRIDGE THE "DEVOPS GAP"

As described on Wikipedia (http://en.wikipedia.org/wiki/DevOps), many organizations divide Development and System Administration into different departments. While Development is usually driven by user needs for frequent delivery of new features, Operations departments focus more on availability, stability of IT services, and IT cost efficiency. These two contradicting goals create a gap between Development and Operations, which slows down IT's delivery of business value.

Through proactive communication to your application developers using APM reports, you can help your developers identify code defects more quickly and effectively, minimizing the devops gap.

Understanding APM Rules

Rules are a concept introduced as part of the Application Diagnostics console and are different from OpsMgr monitoring rules. APM rules were first introduced in AVIcode 5.7. These rules only exist in the Application Diagnostics and Application Advisor scope and are not applied to OpsMgr alerts. Rules are used for managing Application Diagnostics events to filter events based on their status; they allow filtering the noise and known problems from all exception and performance events, resulting in APM reporting that is focused on actionable events.

When you enable APM monitoring for your applications, you will most likely find a wide variety of exception and performance events are collected. During analysis, you may find that some of the exceptions are not critical in your environment; other events are raised for application components that are working as designed but many events that are actionable. Rules can help to automatically filter the non-critical or irrelevant events and let you work on the important ones.

With rules in place, when APM agents detect problems and collect corresponding events, these events are evaluated against the APM rules, with problems identified as non-critical according to these rules categorized accordingly. A demonstration of how to create an APM rule is included in the "Working with Rules" section.

Here are examples of situations where you would use rules:

- You do not need to report specific types of problems because they are not an issue.
- Events do not need to be displayed in reports because they are already reported and promised to be fixed by a specific date.
- Problems are caused by external providers and cannot be resolved.

Working with Rules

Each rule has a set of conditions and an action. Conditions could be general such as the computer name or source, or specific to the nature of problems whether it is an exception or performance problem. The action could be only to change the state of the event. Here is the list of allowed states; these cannot be modified:

- **New:** This is the default state of each event and has a standard lifetime as defined in Application Diagnostics configuration.
- **Reviewed:** This is a custom state to allow filtering acknowledged events; it has a standard lifetime.

- **Deleted:** Deleted events have 24-hour lifetime by default and are removed automatically.
- **By design:** These events have a 72-hour default lifetime.

The authors recommend starting with filtering noise by assigning those events into the deleted state; noise events are usually exceptions and not critical, such as exceptions caused by 404 (not found) calls. Next, proceed to mark events as by design to let you concentrate on real issues. By design events have a longer lifetime; this gives you time to review them and confirm you are not removing anything that is important. Now you can start assigning the reviewed state to events. This state is often used to mark some problems as acknowledged, so you could filter those in the Application Diagnostics console and Advisor reports.

Avoid making rules that cover many events; these should be configured to be quite narrow in terms of filtering. Here are the conditions usually used to filter exception events:

- Exception class
- Full call stack
- Description
- Failed function
- Action

These conditions are usually used for filtering performance events:

- Action
- Event duration
- Slow call
- Slow call duration

To create a rule, use the Rules Management Wizard; you can open this from the Application Diagnostics using the Tools menu, or from any event window using the Actions menu.

Figure 15.51 illustrates an exception filter, and Figure 15.52 shows a performance filter.

You then define actions and the status you want to assign by this rule along with other rule properties, as shown in Figure 15.53.

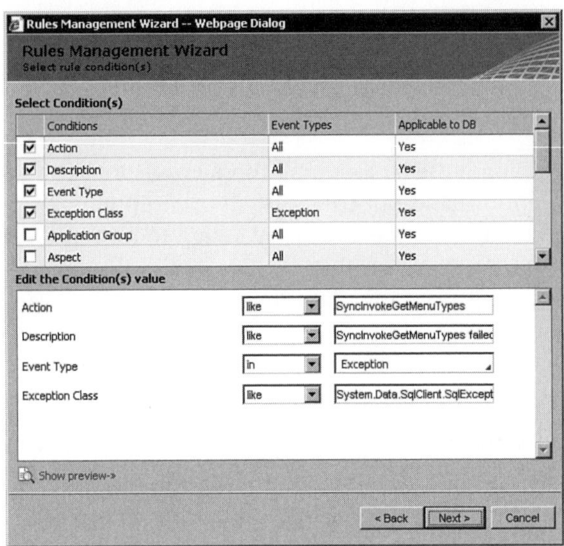

FIGURE 15.51 Exception filter in the Rules Management Wizard.

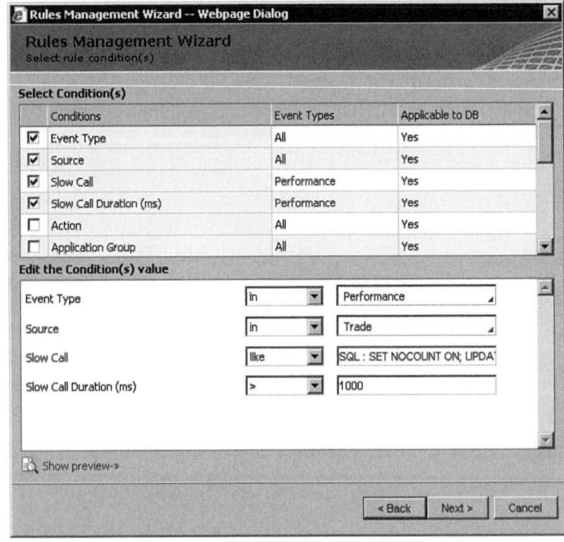

FIGURE 15.52 Performance filter.

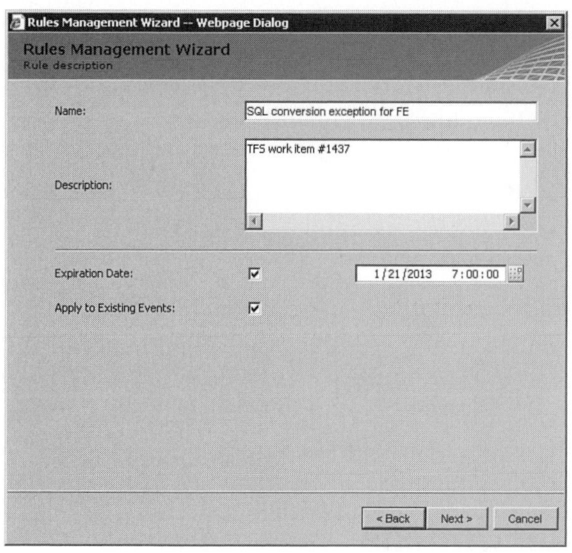

FIGURE 15.53 Rule configuration.

Best Practices for Using Rules

Here are some best practices developed during client implementations:

- **Configure new rules from existing events:** While you create a rule using the wizard in the Application Diagnostics console, the authors recommend you use an existing event and create the rule from the event view. Doing this automatically fills every condition value based on the current event.
- **Include general filters such as source, computer(s), and event type:** Be sure to limit the scope of the rule by specific source(s), computer(s), or event type. This improves performance when evaluating rules and ensures rules do not execute status change for non-desired events.
- **Use preview:** Always use preview after configuring the conditions. Preview is evaluated using all events in the database and gives a good sense of those events included into the filter.
- **Rules naming:** Naming rules properly is important to keep them manageable. Naming conventions should include the type of rule (deleted, by design, or reviewed) and short description of the rule conditions such as application component name, exception class, and so on. For example, if you were creating a rule filtering a known issue related to the AddItem() method in the shopping cart of the DinnerNow web application, you might name it DinnerNow ShoppingCart AddItem() Known Issue.

- **Use meaningful rule descriptions:** Meaningful descriptions help you and others. Descriptions should be detailed and explain the type of problem covered by this rule. Also include additional information; the Team Foundation Server (TFS) work item number for example if corresponding problems are tracked there.
- **Expiration date:** Set expiration date for by design and reviewed rules. This helps you not miss a problem when it is not resolved by a new version of your application. When a rule expires, it stops changing the state and new events will show up in the reports to indicate that the problem still exists.
- **Filter out reviewed events in Advisor and Diagnostics consoles:** By default, the Application Diagnostics and Application Advisor consoles do not enable events with reviewed status. Enable and review those events periodically to ensure no important data is lost, should some data start matching one of the rules after there are changes to the application.

APM Global Configuration Options

Several configuration options could be useful and help with understanding the APM functionality. While these settings are not officially called "Global Configuration Options," the settings referenced here are related to settings that control console behaviors and data retention settings for the APM deployment as a whole. These are discussed in the next sections.

Application Diagnostics Configuration

The Application Diagnostics configuration includes several useful items for configuring global behaviors of the Application Diagnostics console. While the default settings are generally fine for most organizations, some are situationally useful, such as when you move the APM consoles to a new server or when you need to configure APM to retain more event data longer than the defaults.

- Figure 15.54 shows the Data tab of the Options page (**Tools -> Options**). This lets you configure data retention time for events in the operational database and to specify the URLs of the two consoles:
  - **Number of the most recent events that will be kept in the database:** Total number of events from all applications to retain; default is 50,000.
  - **Number of the most recent events that will be kept for an event group:** Maximum number of events to be stored with the same problem, such as the same exception occurring with the same call stack or same the page violating the alerting threshold; default is 500.
  - **Number of the most recent events in an event group that keep details:** The execution call stack with parameter values is stored only in the most recent events collected for a recurring problem; default is 20 events.

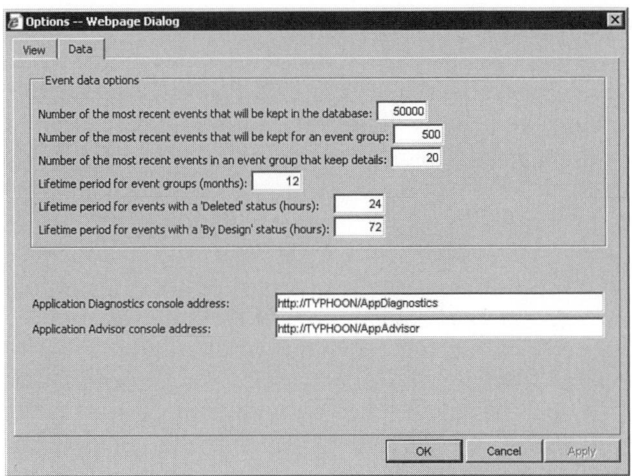

FIGURE 15.54 The Data options tab.

- **Lifetime period for event groups (months):** When to delete information about a problem and its events if there were no new events; 12 months is the default.
- **Lifetime period for events with a 'Deleted' status (hours):** When to permanently remove events marked as 'Deleted' from the database; default 24 hours.
- **Lifetime period for events with a 'By Design' status (hours):** When to permanently remove events marked as 'By Design'; default 72 hours.
- **Application Diagnostics console address:** Base URL used when events are exported.
- **Application Advisor console address:** Base URL used when clicking on the Reports link.

- The View tab, shown in Figure 15.55, lets you specify the amount of data viewed on a page and cache options. Caching can improve UI performance.
- The Tools menu also has an option to define application groups, which could be useful when there are too many application components (sources). This is the Application Groups Management Wizard, the first page of which is shown in Figure 15.56.

An application group is a flexible combination of sources and computers that allows you to define the high-level scope of Application Diagnostics and Application Advisor views to improve navigation. The authors recommend creating application groups in a similar manner to the applications defined in the Operations console when you defined monitoring of your .NET applications.

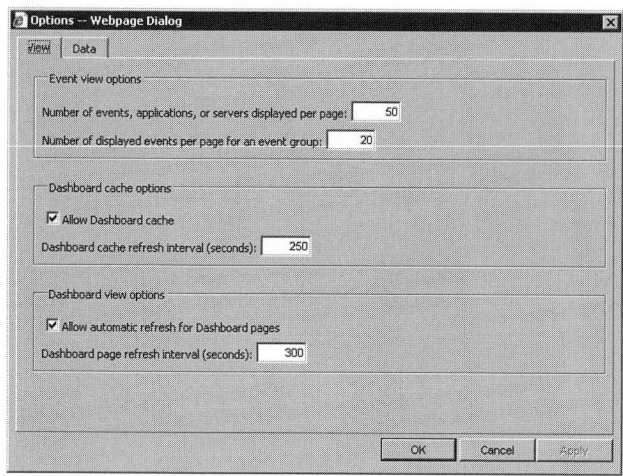

FIGURE 15.55 Configuring view options.

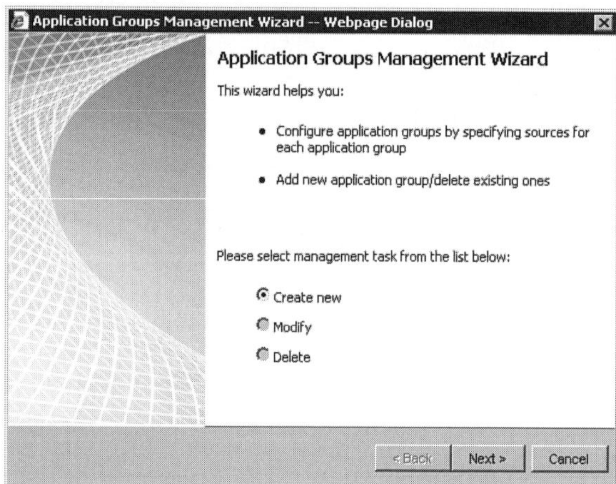

FIGURE 15.56 Application Groups Management Wizard dialog.

Configuring Application Advisor

Configuring Application Advisor is relatively simple. The Advisor options page (select **Tools -> Options** in the Application Advisor console) is shown in Figure 15.57.

- Event data options control how long to store events in the operational database. Although these events do not contain problem details such as call stack and parameters and only have high level information, these events still can be reported on if selected. The default settings in Figure 15.57 show that it doesn't make sense to build a report for deleted events older than one day, as those events are no longer available.

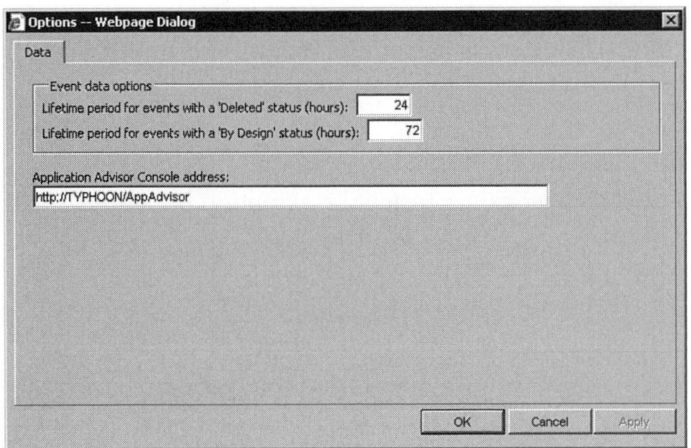

FIGURE 15.57 Advisor options.

- The Application Advisor console address is used to support smart links from exported or scheduled reports back to the Application Advisor or Application Diagnostics consoles to drill down into the problem details.

Sensitive Data Considerations

Since the APM components might collect parameters values from the monitored application, this may also expose sensitive data, usually called personal identifiable information (PII). Typical PII data could be a user name, social security number, password, income details, date of birth, and so on.

This will depend on the application itself; whether it actually receives user input of PII data, stores or operates with PII data, and whether data collected by APM could make that sensitive information visible. However, it is important that you are prepared to remove this information. There are three approaches on how to secure the data and each of them secures data on a different level. These are discussed in the following sections.

Role-Based Access Approach

Role-based access allows limiting data access to ensure you have everything secured. However, before restricting data access you need to understand who has access to it.

Since data center monitoring is usually secure by nature and only a limited set of people have access to monitoring results, this might be sufficient to secure sensitive data in APM. However, if you open up access to monitoring data to a broad audience within your organization, you can also leverage role based-access control (RBAC) in OpsMgr to limit access to the Application Diagnostics and Application Advisor Web consoles, as these can expose the parameter values submitted by end users and customers, and may contain personal and sensitive data. The Operations console does not expose the call stack parameters values, as alerts only include general information.

Establish permissions for Application Monitoring Operators by adding them to the members of the Operations Manager Application Monitoring Operator role under **Administration** -> **Security** -> **User Roles** in the Operations console.

Configuring Data Collection and Using Sensitive Rules

Sensitive data could be collected as parameter values inside the exception or performance events in the Application Diagnostics console; the rest of the information would only include URLs of the pages and the computer name and possibly methods in the call stack. However, inside the parameters you can see actual values that the end user passed to the system.

You generally can control the data collection via the monitoring configuration templates when you define the namespaces, classes, and methods for exception and performance monitoring; to limit data collection you could revisit those settings and adjust them to collect less data. Sometimes it is enough to disable a specific namespace, class, or method from monitoring.

If sensitive data is inside the standard system level methods but not in the custom code, you may not be able to limit data collection there. In this case, you should consider using sensitive rules.

Sensitive rules are part of the APM functionality; they are implemented as low-level RegEx expressions that can specify the information you want to exclude from the data the APM module collects from your application. These rules are executed on each monitored server after the APM module collects the exception or performance event and before it is sent to the management server; thus, PII data is never saved to disk.

Each rule could be a value or field type or both. The authors recommend not using both to reduce confusion and the complexity of the regular expression. A field type sensitive rule should be used when you need to exclude the whole value completely based on the parameters/field name. Value type rules could mask part of the value, such as masking a password inside the connection string. Sensitive rules for both "password" and "pwd" values and fields are included into the standard configuration and masked by default.

The example in Figure 15.58 shows the default data collected when custom namespaces are enabled for exception monitoring. In this case the password value was masked, but SSN was collected both as a value of a long string passed to a "Register" method as well as a parameter passed to a "CreateUser".

The code here collects every value except the SSN for troubleshooting should a problem occur.

```
<Hidden>
<Expression>(SSN=?)[^;]*</Expression>
<CompareExpression>(SSN=?)[^;]*</CompareExpression>
<Replacement>$1*****</Replacement>
<Type>value</Type>
</Hidden>
```

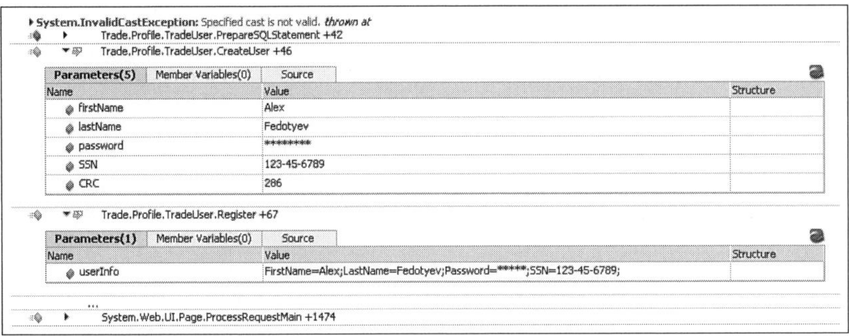

FIGURE 15.58 Sensitive data.

This hidden rule filters the SSN part from the long string value. Each rule filter has a format of

- **<Expression>:** Used to identify whether the value contains sensitive data
- **<CompareExpression>:** Identifies where in the string the value exists
- **<Replacement>:** Tells what to do with the sensitive piece of information
- **<Type>:** Is value, field, or both

The next example removes SSN value from the CreateUser method. A sensitive rule to filter out values is simpler, as it does not require a compare expression because it masks the entire parameter value.

```
<Hidden>
<Expression>SSN</Expression>
<CompareExpression/>
<Replacement/>
<Type>field</Type>
</Hidden>
```

After applying these rules, SSN values are filtered with both methods with the rest of the values still collected. This is displayed in Figure 15.59.

Sensitive rules are part of the core APM functionality. There is no UI to apply these; you must leverage overrides. Figure 15.60 shows an example:

- **Rule type:** .NET Application Monitoring Agent
- **Rule:** Apply APM Agent configuration
- **Override:** Sensitive data rules
- **Value:** Hidden rules in XML format stored as one line, <Hidden>...</Hidden><Hidden>...</Hidden>

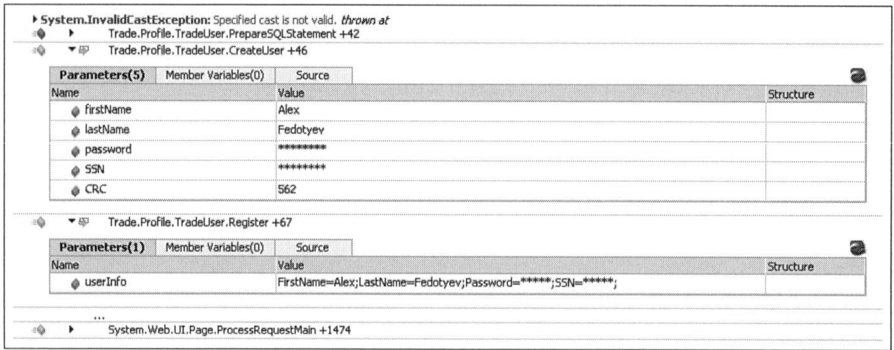

FIGURE 15.59 Filtered sensitive data.

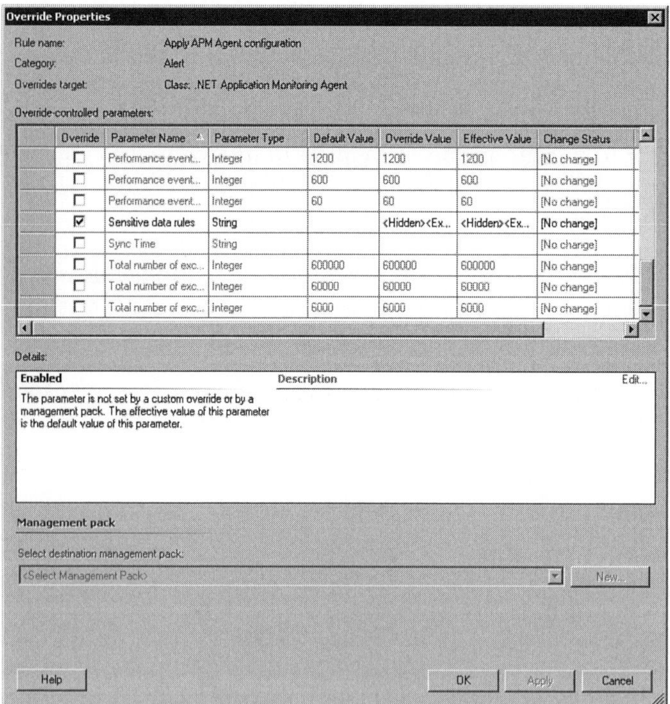

FIGURE 15.60 Configuring sensitive rules as an override.

Advanced APM Architecture

This section of the chapter contains a number of advanced topics that you may not need to use while implementing APM, although some of them might become useful and improve overall understanding of APM functionality.

Light Events

Performance events are collected based on the violation of a threshold defined in the configuration. How this process works at the APM agent level is not fully addressed in the product documentation and deserves further explanation. The agent tries to collect information about the slow methods in the execution stack for slow events, but it is unknown whether the request is slow or fast until it completes. Alternatively, tracking performance for all methods for all requests is an expensive proposition.

Light and regular events are internal logic allowing APM to determine how much information to collect about an event to avoid overhead while still collecting sufficient detail about performance problems. APM collects less information for light events compared to regular events; here's how this works:

- The APM agent keeps additional status information for each request that identifies if the previous execution was above or below the alerting threshold. When the request completes normally and below the sensitivity threshold, the agent does not collect information about the call stack and parameters for the next request. The event is considered light.
- If the next occurrence of the request is above (slower than) the sensitivity threshold, no details are included because the APM agent considered this a fast event before the breach occurred. On the first failure, the event is considered light, and the agent sends an event without details and just overall duration. However, since the sensitivity threshold was breached, the event is now marked as regular (or "heavy" as some might think of it).
- If the next occurrence of the same request is also slow, full information is collected about the call stack and parameters passed to methods and functions. You can find those events in the Application Diagnostics console quite often. If the next event is heavy, the agent collects the execution stack. Dropping the flag back to light occurs on an internal threshold monitored by the agent that clears the heavy state after 50 events below the threshold or after 24 hours by default.

How does the APM agent decide which events are light and which are heavy at the outset? Actually, all entry points are initially flagged heavy. When your application steps through a particular entry point for the first time, here is what occurs:

- If the entry point breaks the threshold, the full stack trace is collected, parameters and all. The entry point remains heavy and the APM agent collects all the stack trace data until you restart the application or the entry point transitions back to light per the 50/24 threshold algorithm mentioned in the previous bullet.
- If the entry point does not break the threshold for the first time, no event is collected and the entry point is immediately considered light and remains light until it breaks the threshold. The first time it breaks the threshold, the light event is collected and the entry point reverts to heavy status. It remains heavy and the APM agent collects the full stack trace until you restart the application or the entry point transitions back to light per the 50/24 threshold algorithm.

Finding these light events (events without full call stack detail) in the Application Diagnostics console when researching a problem can be frustrating. Fortunately, it is possible to create a rule that would automatically mark light events as deleted, ensuring you can easily filter down to only those events will full details of the call stack, including parameters using the same Rules Management Wizard demonstrated in the "Working with Rules" section earlier in this chapter. Figure 15.61 illustrates the menu item to select to mark light events as deleted.

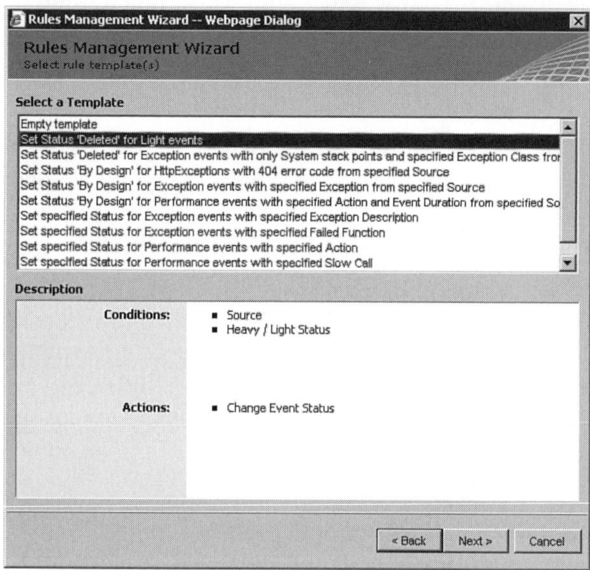

FIGURE 15.61 Rule to delete light events.

Event Throttling

Data collection is expensive logic and can cause overhead. Therefore, there are certain limitations on the APM agent on how often to collect performance, exception, and client-side events.

Event throttling introduces multiple limits of when to stop collecting events on different levels. These settings are in the PMonitor.default.config file; see the "Low-Level Agent Configuration" section for additional information.

- **Performance events per domain per minute:** 60
- **Performance events per domain per hour:** 6,000
- **Performance events per domain per day:** 1,200
- **Performance event groups per minute:** 3
- **Performance event groups per hour:** 30
- **Performance event groups per day:** 60

The performance events per domain settings limit the total number of events from the same application component; performance event groups settings limit the number of performance events collected for the same problem (the same URL or same web service method). When the limit is reached, the agent stops collecting additional performance events, so it will collect the first *N* events per minute, hour, or day:

- **Exception events per domain per minute:** 15
- **Exception events per domain per hour:** 60
- **Exception events per domain per day:** 300
- **Exception event groups per minute:** 3
- **Exception event groups per hour:** 15
- **Exception event groups per day:** 30

Exception event limits work in a manner similar to performance event limits, but here the same problem would mean exactly the same exception class and call stack. Exception throttling settings are more aggressive as this logic is more expensive from a performance perspective:

- **Total number of exception collected per minute:** 6,000
- **Total number of exception collected per hour:** 60,000
- **Total number of exception collected per day:** 600,000

The total number of exception settings are the top limits of exception events being collected and implemented to ensure the overhead is minimal. All counters for exception and performance events drop to zero when the monitored processes restart.

Generally, you do not have to change the event throttling settings, but there could be specific occasions where you need to collect more details to identify the problem; in this case, you could use overrides to update the settings. Figure 15.62 illustrates applying an override. Here are the settings:

- **Rule type:** .NET Application Monitoring Agent
- **Rule:** Apply APM Agent configuration
- **Override:** Corresponding throttling setting(s)

Aliasing Rules

Aliasing is a rarely used configuration but still an important part of the APM functionality. You can create an alias for any method to change how the information is displayed and stored, which can improve understanding and analysis through friendly labeling and more logical grouping in reports.

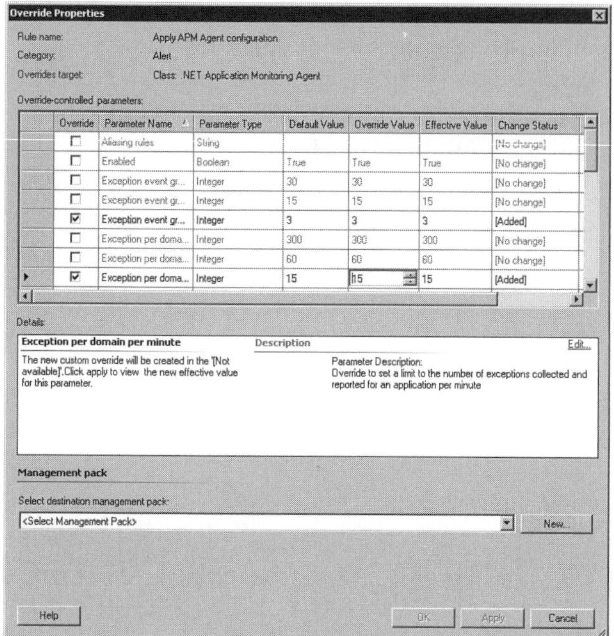

FIGURE 15.62 Changing event throttling settings via an override.

Several default aliasing rules are provided out of the box. Perhaps the best example to explain this concept is the aliasing rules for SQL calls made from .NET applications. Developers know there are several methods to execute SQL queries against the database. For example, one of these methods is the ExecuteNonQuery method of the `SqlCommand` class. From the execution perspective, this and several other methods are always used to run a query, but the response time and results depend on the actual query. Therefore, APM has an alias to use the query name for naming, grouping, and reporting slow operations or failures that occur due to specific SQL calls. The result is SQL related issues could now be readily grouped by the problematic SQL query instead of the more esoteric method name. Figure 15.63 shows an example for the results of the SQL calls aliasing; this is implemented out of the box with APM.

5,157 ms SQL : SET NOCOUNT ON; UPDATE dbo.orders WITH (ROWLOCK) SET ORDERSTATUS = 'completed' where ORDERSTATUS = 'closed' AND ACCOUNT_ACCOUNTID = (select accountid from dbo.account WITH (NOLOCK) where profile_userid =@UserId)
System.Data.SqlClient.SqlCommand.ExecuteNonQuery()

Variables(4)

Name	Value	Structure
database	StockTraderDB	
dataSource	.\sqlexpress	
parameters		class
cmdText	SET NOCOUNT ON; UPDATE dbo.orders WITH (ROWLOCK) SET ORDERSTATUS = 'completed' where ORDERSTATUS = 'closed' AND ACCOUNT_ACCOUNTID = (select accountid from dbo.account WITH (NOLOCK) where profile_userid =@UserId)	

FIGURE 15.63 SQL calls alias.

After the alias is applied, it is still possible to see the actual .NET method—System.Data.SqlClient.SqlCommand.ExecuteNonQuery. However, the actual query will be used for all filtering, grouping, search, and analysis in the Application Diagnostics console and Application Advisor reports.

You may need to configure an alias when you configure transactions using custom functions or performance methods to collect parameter value for a specific resource method. An example would be if an application uses a custom API to access an external resource that may run slowly or even fail based on the parameter passed, which makes it a good candidate for creating an alias. Here's an example:

```
<function match="functionName">
<name>System.Data.SqlClient.ExecuteNonQuery()</name>
<aliases><aliasGroup>
<alias>SQL : {0}</alias>
<param name="cmdText" />
</aliasGroup></aliases>
</function>
```

Here an alias is defined for a specific method; it defines and aliases itself and the parameter(s) to use as part of the alias in an order numbered starting with zero. This example uses a "cmdText" parameter.

Useful Overrides

Several overrides can help in tuning APM for specific scenarios.

- When there are a large number of .NET web applications running on an IIS server, it could be difficult to enable all of them for monitoring in OpsMgr, which may potentially result in raising a large number of less important, non-actionable alerts in the Operations console. However, you may still want APM to collect information about performance or exception problems for presentation in the Application Diagnostics console.
- There could be a situation where your service delivery obligations do not require IT operations to raise alert on failures in all applications, but APM data collection is still required from a quality/continuous improvement perspective.

For these situations, you could enable monitoring all web applications to report only to Application Diagnostics and Application Advisor, but not to Operations Manager.

All web applications monitoring settings are available in the Discovery of APM agent properties object discovery, which is available on the `.NET Application Monitoring Agent` class:

- **Enable monitoring all web applications:** Enables monitoring all web applications on the server.
- **Performance threshold:** Default alerting threshold to monitor all web applications.

- **Sensitivity threshold:** Default sensitivity threshold.
- **Enable all critical exceptions:** Enables monitoring of all exceptions.
- **Enable event throttling:** This setting could disable event throttling completely; it is not recommended to disable it in production.

The .NET Application Performance Monitoring template presents a list of web applications and services for users to choose those applications to monitor. If there are applications not listed in the template, you can customize the rule responsible for discovering IIS web applications and services by applying required overrides:

TIP: FINDING THE RULE THAT DISCOVERS IIS WEB APPLICATIONS AND SERVICES

It may be difficult to locate the rule that discovers IIS web applications and services. To find this rule, limit the scope by selecting only the **IIS 7 Web Server** target, then you will see it displayed in the rules list.

- **Class:** IIS 7 Web Server
- **Rule:** IIS 7.0 Web Application Discovery
- Overrides:
  - **Additional file name extensions for ASP.NET Web Application discovery:** Provide a list of file name extensions, semicolon separated, to use to identify an application as an ASP.NET web application. The default behavior is to check for .aspx files in the root application folder. A common approach is to extend this to aspx;asax, but only if you are missing applications.
  - **Additional file name extensions for ASP.NET Web Service discovery:** Provide a list of file name extensions, semicolon separated, to use to identify an application as an ASP.NET web service. The default behavior is to look for .asmx files in the virtual directory.
  - **Discover all directories as ASP.NET Web Application:** Set to True to discover an application that was not previously discovered as an ASP.NET web application or ASP.NET web service. This flag configures the IIS discovery workflow to discover the unknown applications as ASP.NET web applications so that you can monitor them with the .NET Application Performance Monitoring template.
  - **Discover empty directories as ASP.NET Web Application:** Set to True to treat applications with an empty root virtual directory as an ASP.NET web application.
  - **Discover empty directories as ASP.NET Web Service:** Set to True to treat applications with an empty root virtual directory as an ASP.NET web service.

APM discovers WCF applications deployed to IIS based on the existence of files with the .svc extension by default. Should your WCF application be missing in the list of available application components, you can tune that discovery:

- **Class:** .NET Application Monitoring Agent
- **Discovery:** IIS 2008 WCF Web Service Discovery Rule
- Overrides
  - **WCF Web Service Discovery DataSource Additional Extensions Override:** List of file extensions that would present a WCF service, for example "foo;bar"
  - **WCF Web Service Discovery DataSource Empty Directory discovery Override:** Enable discovery of empty IIS folders as WCF components

Low-Level Agent Configuration

Some people like to know all the details of how everything works behind the curtain. Low-level configuration is one of these areas and explains some of the default behaviors, although the authors do not recommend changing them. The default configuration contains all the standard settings such as namespaces, methods, classes, aliases, and so on.

Agent configuration is stored inside the standard management pack in a number of resource files. The OpsMgr agent performs the following steps each time the APM configuration is changed for one or more applications monitored on the server:

1. The agent gets the default configuration from the resource files.
2. The agent identifies all configuration changes intended to be applied to the current server's applications from the user management packs.
3. The agent applies these changes on top of the default configuration file and then pushes the complete configuration to the APM agent components.

This flow protects the configuration from the occasional corruption and enables having consistent configuration at any given moment.

The easiest way to locate that configuration is to access the monitored server inside the OpsMgr agent temp resources folder, by default at *%ProgramFiles%*\System Center Operations Manager\Agent\Health Service State\Resources\. You could also obtain it from the agent folder when it is merged with the application configuration, by default *%ProgramFiles%*\System Center Operations Manager\Agent\APMDOTNETAgent\V7.x.xxxx.x\Configuration\.

Here are the configuration files containing the most interesting details:

- **PMonitor.config:** This defines on a high level which application to monitor, the namespaces to collect and not collect for performance and exceptions, and high-level settings to enable or disable event throttling or to enable monitoring of all web applications.

In this file, you can find a default list of disabled namespaces like "Microsoft," "System," "Infragistics," and so on. You also can find the list of default methods used to identify calls to the databases, web services, or other resources.

- **PMonitor.default.config:** This file has detailed descriptions of how to collect data. It contains instructions to collect not more than 10 members of a class, not more than 10 items in the array, and not go deeper than three levels when collecting subclasses.

  It also includes how to collect data defined either as prebuilt instrumentation classes that are part of the APM agent components, or defined in a declarative way and specify which members of the classes to collect.

  The end of this file includes the event throttling settings and limits applied per minute, per hour, and per day.
- **CSM.action.config:** This file is where the client-side monitoring configuration includes details from the high-level configuration down to specific instructions on how to inject the JavaScript and which data to collect.
- **AgentHandlers.config:** This contains definitions of all aliases and sensitive rules.

For AVIcode 5.7 Customers

For AVIcode 5.7 customers, Microsoft does not have an automated upgrade story as AVIcode stored most or the entire configuration inside the agent configuration files, while OpsMgr 2012 has the configuration fully centralized and stored inside the management packs. However, the configuration is mostly identical or has direct mapping between the 5.7 and 2012 versions, therefore migration should not be particularly painful.

Side by side installation is limited to have only one .NET monitoring agent, either the 5.7 or 2012 version. This allows you to keep AVIcode 5.7 monitoring enabled as is but to start leveraging Operations Manager 2012 to monitor other components without .NET monitoring, and then migrate over time.

New with Service Pack 1

System Center 2012 Service Pack 1 introduces several important improvements for the APM feature:

- Support for IIS 8 and Windows Server 2012
- Monitoring Windows Services built using .NET Framework (this extends the APM templates)
- Automatic discovery of ASP.NET MVC3 and MVC4 applications
- New transaction types for MVC pages and WCF methods

- Azure SDK support by collecting resource information Azure storage, SQL, queues, tables, and blobs
- Improved devops scenarios including exporting events in Intellitrace format and Team Foundation Server integration
- Advanced configuration for monitoring web applications running on Microsoft SharePoint

These changes are implemented via an updated APM template, which you can use for configuring monitoring of Windows server components in addition to Windows .NET applications. In the Object Search window on the What to Monitor page of the APM Add Monitoring Wizard, you will now see an option to scope the object search to Windows services.

Monitoring Windows services built using .NET usually requires additional configuration by defining additional entry points. The only exception is when the Windows service hosts a WCF component; here no extra configuration is required because WCF entry points are already part of the default configuration.

Detecting entry points requires interaction with your development team; ideally, they should be able to supply the operations team with the proper entry points for the tasks the Windows service performs. The authors recommend identifying business tasks that Windows services perform and configuring entry points that start those tasks. For example, it is not wise to propose long running methods to be entry points, it is better to include methods called by timers or message processing or something similar. This enables monitoring of performance and failures occurring during each job or message processing but not the overall service state.

The System Center Management Pack for Microsoft Visual Studio Team Foundation Server 2010 Work Item Synchronization is a new add-on that allows deep integration between APM and Team Foundation Server. This is a new component introduced in System Center 2012 SP 1. It brings full integration between operations and development and allows forwarding alerts from Operations Manager to the Microsoft Team Foundation Server and back.

When you install and configure this management pack, it extends the TFS schema by registering a new work item type of Operational Issue. The operations team can then forward any APM alert to development by changing its resolution state to "Assigned to Engineering," a new resolution state introduced with SP 1. The integration service creates a new work item inside TFS, populates it with the details collected by the APM agent, and enables bidirectional synchronization between OpsMgr and TFS. This feature completes the application monitoring scenario and enables full workflow between operations and development teams.

Summary

This chapter discussed the features available in .NET Application Performance Monitoring in OpsMgr 2012 and best practices for configuring server-side and client-side APM monitoring. How to use APM reporting to bridge the "devops gap" was also discussed. The chapter also included guidance on how to optimize APM reporting using APM rules. Minimizing unnecessary OpsMgr alerts without losing useful APM event data was also explained. The next chapter discusses the expanded network monitoring capabilities of OpsMgr 2012.

CHAPTER 16

Network Monitoring

IN THIS CHAPTER

System Center 2012 Operations Manager (OpsMgr) provides extended capabilities for network monitoring. Unlike its predecessor, Operations Manager 2007, which only offers simple "up" or "down" functionality, OpsMgr 2012 provides more advanced monitoring of your network devices. With OpsMgr 2012, you can get detailed port, interface, and peripheral monitoring of your network devices, as well as virtual local area networks (vLANs) and hot standby router protocol (HSRP) groups. OpsMgr 2012 now includes monitoring of all types of devices, including firewalls and load balancers. Its new network monitoring capabilities provide the long-awaited pieces required for effective end-to-end monitoring.

This increased visibility into your network infrastructure can help you identify those failures in critical services caused by network related issues. You can drastically reduce the time spent investigating application outages using the new port stitching feature, which displays the health of the network devices connected to servers hosting those applications. For example, if an alert is raised about a particular application being unavailable, you can select that application in the Operations console and launch the Network Vicinity Dashboard task to quickly find whether the outage is due to network related issues.

Features and Capabilities

Here are network monitoring features now available in OpsMgr:

- ▶ Ability to discover network dependencies of target computers and devices

- Discovery, monitoring, and reporting supported for extended monitoring out of the box
- More than 2,000 network devices supported out of the box
- Protocols supported include
  - **Simple Network Management Protocol (SNMP) v1, v2c, and v3:** Port monitoring is available for devices that have implemented the interface Management Information Base (MIB) (RFC 2863) and MIB-II (RFC 1213) standards.

    OpsMgr 2012 can discover and monitor network devices that use SNMP v1, v2c, and v3. For a complete list of supported devices, see http://www.microsoft.com/en-us/download/details.aspx?displaylang=en&id=26831; Microsoft will update this document as new devices are added to OpsMgr 2012.
  - **IPv4 and IPv6:** Discovery is only supported using IPv4. However, it is possible to monitor IPv6 devices if these devices were discovered recursively with an IPv4 device.
- Improved SNMP stack that is more scalable and performs better than in OpsMgr 2007 R2

The next sections discuss supported device types and those capabilities available out of the box.

Supported Device Types

Depending on the device vendor and type of device, OpsMgr 2012 provides varied levels of detailed processor or memory monitoring. The "Out of the Box Monitoring" section further discusses the level of monitoring for different types of devices. Here are the types of network devices you can discover and monitor in OpsMgr 2012:

- Routers
- Switches
- Hubs
- Bridges
- Firewalls
- Load balancers
- Hosts (Any computer connected to the network with an Internet Protocol [IP] address and available only via Internet Control Message Protocol or ICMP)

Out of the Box Monitoring

There are differences in the default workflows that run on network devices, which are discussed in the next sections.

Standard Monitoring

A device will receive standard monitoring in OpsMgr if the object identifier (OID) is unknown to the discovery process. While the device may be discoverable, it will have limited monitoring out of the box; this is limited to availability (up/down status). It is possible a device that currently receives only standard monitoring may have advanced monitoring features available in the future. You can check the supported devices document at http://www.microsoft.com/en-us/download/details.aspx?displaylang=en&id=26831 for updates.

Two monitors will run against those devices that receive standard monitoring out of the box:

- **ICMP Ping:** This monitor pings devices using ICMP Echo request to determine whether the device is up.
- **SNMP Ping:** This monitor pings devices using SNMP requests to determine whether the device is up.

Extended (Advanced) Monitoring

A device will receive extended monitoring in OpsMgr if the OID is known and simulation workflows were successfully tested using standard and vendor MIBs. In addition to the ICMP Ping and SNMP Ping monitors that are included with standard monitoring, extended monitoring includes additional performance monitoring and collection rules. Here is a list of workflows that run out of the box on these devices:

- **Internal Network Management Node Discovery Data Collector:** This rule collects data related to discovery of network devices.
- **ICMP Response Time:** This rule collects response time to ICMP requests.
- **Trap received (warm start):** This rule collects events from SNMP warm start trap.
- **Trap received (cold start):** This rule collects events from SNMP cold start trap.

Many devices also have these additional workflows delivered out of the box, depending on vendor and device model:

- Connection Health (determined by analyzing the entire connection including both ends)
- vLAN Health (determined by the health state of all switches comprising the vLAN)
- HSRP Group Health (determined by the health state of individual HSRP end points)
- Port and Interface Health (Up/down status, both operational and administrative)

- Inbound and Outbound Traffic Volume:
    - Aborts
    - Broadcasts
    - Carrier sense
    - Collisions
    - CRC rates
    - Discards
    - Errors
    - FCS errors
    - Frames
    - Giants
    - Runts
    - Ignored
- MAC Transmit
- Receive Error
- Queue Rates
- % Utilization
- Drop and Broadcast Rates
- Processor % Utilization (available only for select devices)
- Memory
- High Utilization
- High Buffer Utilization
- Excessive Fragmentation
- Buffer Allocation Failures (only for select devices)
- In-Depth Memory Counters (Cisco devices only)
- Available Memory

Network Monitoring Considerations

There are a number of areas to consider before implementing network monitoring in OpsMgr. Knowledge of the points discussed in the next sections will help you understand some of the basic requirements and develop a solid plan to implement network monitoring successfully. These include firewall requirements, required management packs, understanding capacity limitations, and resource pool considerations.

Firewall Requirements

All firewalls between the management servers in the resource pool and the network devices need to allow SNMP (UDP) and ICMP bi-directionally, and ports 161 and 162 must be open bi-directionally. This includes Windows Firewall on each management server. If your network devices use a non-standard port, you must open bi-directional UDP traffic on these ports as well.

Required Management Packs

Here are the management packs required to implement network discovery and monitoring. They are automatically installed during setup of the first management server, so you do not need to install them separately:

- Microsoft.Windows.Server.NetworkDiscovery
- Microsoft.Windows.Client.NetworkDiscovery

The network adapter on the agent-managed computer must be discovered if you want to map connections between network devices and agent-managed computers. This requires installing the Windows Server Operating System and the Windows Client Operating System management packs for those versions of Windows where you want to discover network topology and dependencies. The process of discovering and mapping connections between network devices and computers is discussed in the "About Port Stitching" section.

Capacity Limitations

Although there are no hard capacity limits in OpsMgr, Microsoft has established capacity guidelines for all types of devices to be monitored in a single management group. Depending on factors such as hardware configuration and monitoring intervals, your management group may fall short of these limitations, or possibly exceed them.

Here are the general guidelines when planning capacity for network device monitoring.

- **Network devices managed by a resource pool with three or more management servers:** 1,000
- **Network devices managed by two resource pools (three management servers per resource pool):** 2,000

These limitations suggest monitoring no more than 1,000 network devices in a single resource pool, and up to 2,000 network devices per management group.

For additional information regarding capacity planning, Microsoft provides a sizing helper tool at http://www.microsoft.com/en-us/download/details.aspx?id=29270.

Resource Pool Considerations

Each management server (or gateway server) is limited to a single network device discovery rule. However, any management server can perform the discovery, as a single resource pool can monitor devices that were discovered by more than one network discovery server. This can help should you have multiple different discovery rule settings to configure and only two management servers in your network monitoring resource pool; you are not required to run discoveries from the assigned resource pool.

About SNMP

An SNMP-managed network consists of three key components. Here is the correlation of these components in OpsMgr network monitoring:

- **Managed device:** The network device to be discovered and monitored
- **Agent:** The software module residing on the managed device that understands the device's management information
- **Network management system (NMS):** Consider this as the OpsMgr 2012 network monitoring resource pool

An SNMP-managed device has two levels of access—read-only and read-write:

- In OpsMgr 2012, read-only access is sufficient to discover and monitor the device.
- Read-write access is required only if settings on the device need to be updated; typically this will not be done with OpsMgr, but with your actual NMS.

There are three versions of SNMP available for use in OpsMgr 2012 out of the box: v1, v2c, and v3. The next sections discuss the differences in using each of these versions, SNMP network communication basics, and the structure of MIBs and OIDs.

SNMP Versions

SNMP v1 is the first implementation of the SNMP protocol, which was developed in the late 1980s and became popular for its use in managing various types of network devices. However, SNMP v1 lacks security features, as the only authentication mechanism required to establish a session is a community string sent over the network in plain text. This allows anyone connected to the network to view this community string "password" and potentially use it for nefarious purposes. Figure 16.1 shows the SNMP v1 message format, also used by SNMP v2c.

The version number shown in the figure is "0" for SNMP v1 and "1" for SNMP v2c. Differences between SNMP v1 and v2c are primarily internal; OpsMgr 2012 has no additional considerations between the versions other than compatibility with the version selected in your network device discovery rules. One of the most significant changes in SNMP v2c, as indicated in Figure 16.1, is the introduction of the `GetBulkRequest` operation, which allows the NMS to request more data be returned in a single message rather than having to perform `GetNextRequest` operations until the full message is received. This is an expansion of the message body, or Protocol Data Unit (PDU).

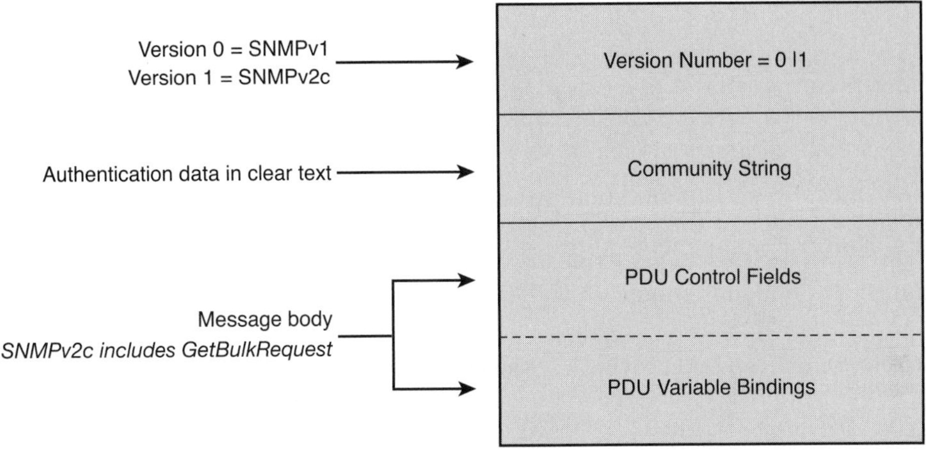

FIGURE 16.1 SNMP v1 and v2c message format.

A more practical example of viewing message format of SNMP v1 is to run a network trace from a management server that is a member of your network monitoring resource pool, and then filter on the SNMP protocol. Figure 16.2 shows what an SNMP v1 packet looks like in a Netmon trace.

```
Frame Details
 Frame: Number = 17008, Captured Frame Length = 139, MediaType = ETHERNET
+Ethernet: Etype = Internet IP (IPv4),DestinationAddress:[00-15-5D-0A-87-05],SourceAddress:[00
+Ipv4: Src = 172.16.10.154, Dest = 172.16.10.158, Next Protocol = UDP, Packet ID = 6734, Total
+Udp: SrcPort = 56299, DstPort = SNMP(161), Length = 105
-Snmp: Version1, Community = public, Get request, RequestID = 27651
  +MessageHeader:
  +Version: 0 <-------------------- Version 0 = SNMP v1
  +Community: public <------------- Community String = public
  +PDUType: Get request <---------- PDU Control Fields
  +PDU: <-------------------------- PDU Variable Bindings (message body)
```

FIGURE 16.2 SNMP v1 Netmon trace.

SMNP v3 introduces an enhanced security model with additional authentication and privacy mechanisms. Although there are other changes to the protocol stack that look much different from previous versions of SNMP, the addition of cryptographic security is the most significant change as it pertains to network monitoring in OpsMgr.

SNMP v3 provides three significant security features:

- **Authentication:** A user name and authentication key are required, which verify messages are from a valid source.

- **Encryption:** Ensures privacy by preventing unauthorized sources from reading SNMP messages.
- **Message integrity:** Ensures that an SNMP packet has not been tampered with while in transit.

These three security features are provided in SNMP v3 due to its implementation of a user-based security model, or USM. The following set of security levels in the USM are what make these security features possible in SNMP v3:

- **noAuthNoPriv:** Communication without authentication and privacy.
- **authNoPriv:** Communication with authentication and no privacy.
- **authPriv:** Communication with authentication and privacy.

The authentication feature is provided by the HMAC-MD5-96 or HMAC-SHA-96 protocol. The encryption, or privacy, feature for a standard SNMP v3 implementation is provided by the CBC-DES protocol. However, OpsMgr also implements the AES protocol for encryption. For message integrity, the USM prescribes that if authentication is used, the complete message is checked for integrity in the authentication module.

The main differences you will notice in a network trace between SNMP v2 and v3 are the community and PDU fields are unreadable.

You can find additional information about USM on the Internet Engineering Task Force website at http://tools.ietf.org/html/rfc3414.

Communications Basics

SNMP sends operation requests and responses, which consist of the PDU and header elements relevant to the SMNP version used. In OpsMgr, a network device sends data to the management server in two cases:

- When it responds to a request from a management server
- When a trap event occurs

Here are the most common types of SNMP operations used in OpsMgr:

- **Get:** Request message sent by the management server, requesting a single MIB entry on the network device.
- **GetNext:** Similar to the `Get` operation, this operation traverses the entire MIB hierarchy and returns the next OID that followed the information previously sent. This is typically used when requesting information without a particular OID instance.
- **GetBulk:** Similar to other `Get` operations, but requests the agent to send data in units as large as possible. This reduces the number of messages transmitted between the agent and management server when requesting large amounts of data. `GetBulk` was introduced in SNMP v2c.

- **GetResponse:** Network device response to a `Get`, `GetNext`, or `GetBulk` request.
- **Trap:** Message sent from the network device to the management server when an interesting event occurs.

Figure 16.3 shows an operation message originating from a management server targeted at a network device, and Figure 16.4 shows the network device responding to that request.

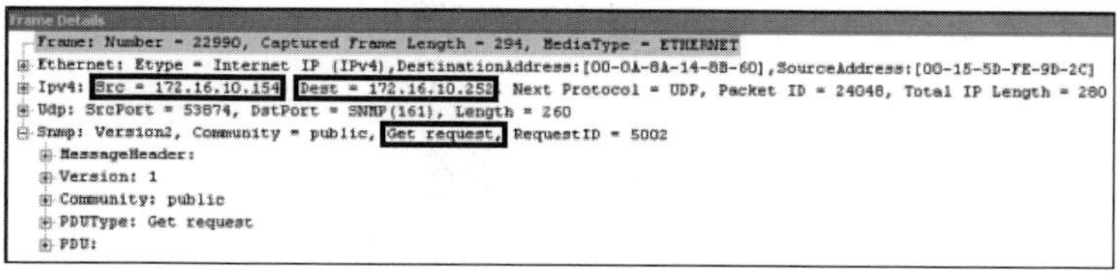

FIGURE 16.3 SNMP v2 get operation.

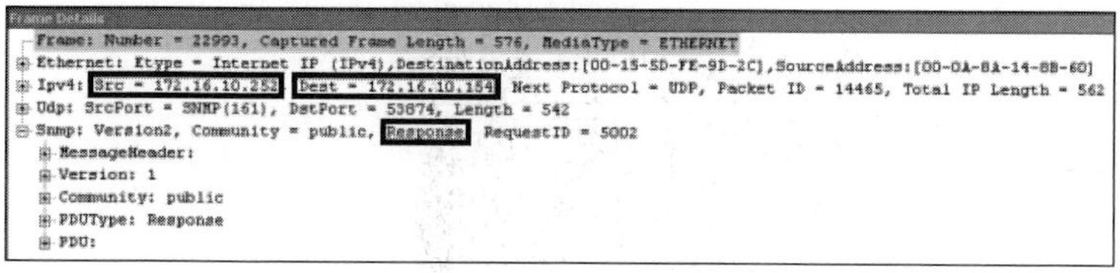

FIGURE 16.4 SNMP v2 response operation.

MIBs and OIDs

When a management server sends a type of `Get` operation to a network device, the device responds with a `GetResponse` message, returning the requested value(s) from the MIB to the management server. The MIB is a virtual database that defines objects hosted on the network device. The MIB is a hierarchical database, and the defined objects are referenced through an OID.

You can view the MIB hierarchy as a tree, where each branch is assigned by a different organization. Top-level OIDs belong to standards organizations, like IANA, IETF, and US Department of Defense. Lower-level OIDs are allocated to associated organizations, as well as private organizations such as IBM, Cisco, and Microsoft. Similar to IPv4 addresses, organizations may obtain a base OID and address objects on their particular device(s) by appending a string of numbers.

Figure 16.5 shows the hierarchical structure of an OID, indicating that Cisco may assign an OID string rooted at 1.3.6.1.4.1.9, and Figure 16.6 illustrates a network trace of an SNMP Response to a management server requesting information from a Cisco device. Notice the root OID of the Cisco namespace.

You can view a list of current, registered private enterprise OIDs on the IANA website at http://www.iana.org/assignments/enterprise-numbers.

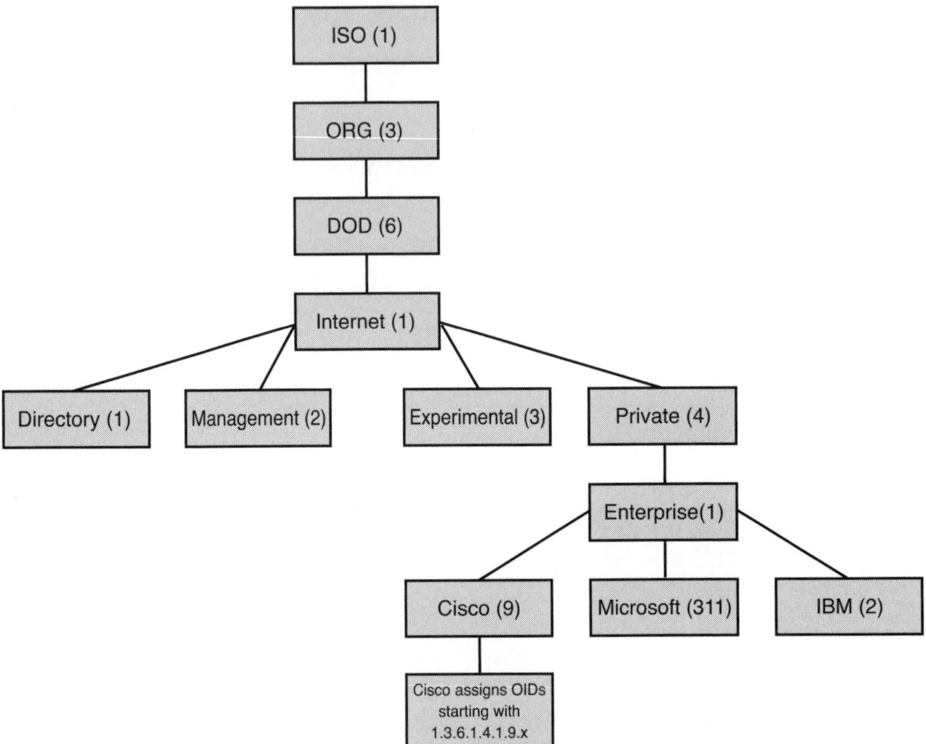

FIGURE 16.5 Sample OID tree.

```
Frame Details
Frame: Number = 22993, Captured Frame Length = 576, MediaType = ETHERNET
+ Ethernet: Etype = Internet IP (IPv4),DestinationAddress:[00-15-5D-FE-9D-2C],SourceAddress:[00-0A-8A-14-8B-60]
+ Ipv4: Src = 172.16.10.252, Dest = 172.16.10.154, Next Protocol = UDP, Packet ID = 14465, Total IP Length = 562
+ Udp: SrcPort = SNMP(161), DstPort = 53874, Length = 542
- Snmp: Version2, Community = public, Response, RequestID = 5002
   + MessageHeader:
   + Version: 1
   + Community: public
   + PDUType: Response
   - PDU:
      + RequestID: 5002
      + ErrorStatus: noError (0)
      + ErrorIndex: 0
      - VariableList:
         + VariableBindListHeader:
         - VariableBind:
            + VariableBindHeader:
            + ObjectName: UnknownOidExtension (1.3.6.1.2.1.1.1.0)
            + StringValue: Cisco IOS Software, C2600 Software (C2600-ADVSECURITYK9-M), Version 12.4(15)T8, RELEASE SOFTWARE (fc3)
         - VariableBind:
            + VariableBindHeader:
            + ObjectName: UnknownOidExtension (1.3.6.1.4.1.9.9.48.1.1.1.6.2)
            + endOfMibView: Null Value
```

FIGURE 16.6 Response with Cisco OID.

Using Run As Accounts

OpsMgr network monitoring utilizes Run As accounts slightly differently from a typical agent-managed computer. On a Windows agent-managed computer, the OpsMgr agent is installed, and there is an instance of a health service running for each management group with which the agent is configured to communicate. In this case, a Run As account is configured for those discovery and monitoring workflows requiring elevated privileges to resources on the Windows system.

In this scenario, the Run As account is the credential to be used and is associated with a Run As profile. The Run As profile is assigned to the workflow in the management pack, as shown in the following eXtended Markup Language (XML) after the `RunAs` element.

```
<DataSourceModuleType ID="SampleDataSource" Accessibility="Internal"
RunAs="SampleDataSource.RunAsProfile">
```

If a Run As profile is associated to a workflow, indicating it requires elevated privileges to access a resource, the Run As account is used during runtime of that particular workflow.

OpsMgr agents are not installed on the device in network monitoring. Instead, SNMP is used, where `Get` requests are sent to the device and responses are returned to the management server or gateway server in the resource pool.

There are two types of access permissions in SNMP: read-only and read-write. Since OpsMgr only reads the MIB on the device for monitoring purposes, all network monitoring workflows targeted at the device require only one Run As account, which is actually used by the management server(s) in the network monitoring resource pool to request information from the network device. There are no considerations for assigning more than one Run As account to the management server, so associating Run As accounts to Run As profiles is not necessary for network monitoring.

About SNMP v1 and v2c

Network monitoring in OpsMgr requires one of two types of Run As accounts:

- Community String
- SNMPv3 Account

Figure 16.7 shows these selections in the Create a Run As Account Wizard.

The community string Run As account type is always used for SNMP v1 and v2c devices, in which the only required input in the configuration is the plain text community string. You will need to configure as many Run As accounts as you have SNMP communities in your environment that you want to monitor.

Using SNMP v3

The enhanced security features available in SNMP v3 require additional configuration of the Run As account. For SNMP v3 devices, you will need to use the SNMPv3 Account shown in Figure 16.7.

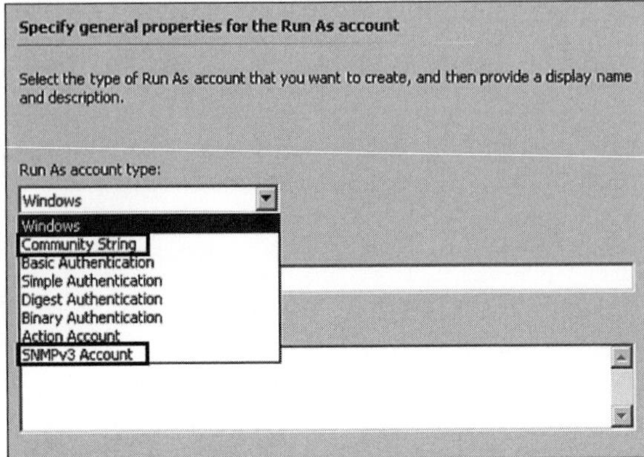

FIGURE 16.7 Network monitoring Run As accounts.

Here are the configuration parameters of the SNMPv3 Account type, including how these parameters correlate to the three security levels in the USM discussed in the "SNMP Versions" section earlier in the chapter:

- **User name:** Required

  If only user name is configured, noAuthNoPriv security level is used.
- **Context:** Optional
- **Authentication protocol:** Optional. May use MD5 or SHA.
  - If configured, then authNoPriv security level is used.
  - If authentication protocol is used, an authentication key is required.
- **Privacy protocol:** Optional. May use AES or DES.
  - If configured, then authPriv security level is used.
  - If privacy protocol is used, a privacy key is required.
  - You may not use a privacy protocol without first selecting an authentication protocol.
  - Check your device configuration to know which setting to select in the Discovery Wizard.

Creating a discovery rule and assigning a Run As account is discussed in the "Creating a Discovery Rule" section later in the chapter.

Discovering Network Devices

Network device discovery is performed by manually created discovery rules. When you create a discovery rule, you designate a management server or gateway server that runs the rule on the specified schedule. As each management server or gateway server can run only one discovery rule, you should plan how to make this work best for your environment.

The next sections discuss the differences between discovery methods and the internals of the network discovery process. You will also see how to create a new network discovery rule and how to perform some common tasks, such as removing and restoring a device.

Types of Discovery Methods

There are two types of network discovery methods: explicit and recursive. Here are the characteristics of each method:

- **Explicit discovery:** An explicit discovery rule attempts to discover only those devices that you explicitly specify in the wizard by IP address or fully qualified domain name (FQDN).
- **Recursive discovery:** A recursive discovery rule attempts to discover those devices you explicitly specify in the wizard by IP address. It also attempts to discover other network devices connected to the devices specified in the discovery rule. IP addresses of these neighboring devices are gathered through the seed device's Address Routing Protocol (ARP) table, its IP address table, or topology MIB.

TIP: RECURSIVE DISCOVERY CONSIDERATIONS

Recursive discovery could take a long time in large environments. Discovering all network devices may not be necessary in all implementations and might cause unnecessary load on the management server(s). Sometimes it is best to consult with your network team and add only the devices necessary to create the network topology connecting the systems you are monitoring with OpsMgr.

Microsoft recommends using recursive discovery only in smaller environments and that explicit discovery is used in large environments.

If you use recursive discovery, you can elect to discover all other network devices the seed device knows about, or only network devices connected to the device in a specified IP address range. You can also filter recursive discovery by using such properties as the device type, name, and OID.

NOTE: GUIDANCE ON FILTERING

Filtering can be an area of confusion. The best place to get guidance is in the Discovery Wizard, which includes a link for information on device filters.

Stages of Discovery

Three stages occur when a management server processes a discovery rule: probing, processing, and post-processing. These stages are discussed in the next sections.

Probing Stage

During the probing stage, OpsMgr attempts to contact the device using the protocol(s) specified in the discovery rule. This stage verifies whether a device is reachable. You can configure the discovery rule to use the following protocols:

- **ICMP only:** Contacts the device using ICMP only. If this is selected, OpsMgr monitors only availability of the device; advance monitoring features are not available.
- **ICMP and SNMP:** Contacts the device using both protocols.
- **SNMP only:** Contacts the device using SNMP only.

Figure 16.8 shows a network trace of the probing stage, where both ICMP and SNMP protocols are used. As you can see, only four packets are involved in this stage.

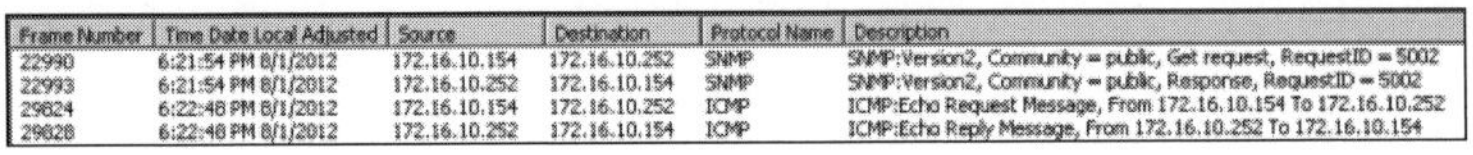

Frame Number	Time Date Local Adjusted	Source	Destination	Protocol Name	Description
22990	6:21:54 PM 8/1/2012	172.16.10.154	172.16.10.252	SNMP	SNMP:Version2, Community = public, Get request, RequestID = 5002
22993	6:21:54 PM 8/1/2012	172.16.10.252	172.16.10.154	SNMP	SNMP:Version2, Community = public, Response, RequestID = 5002
29824	6:22:48 PM 8/1/2012	172.16.10.154	172.16.10.252	ICMP	ICMP:Echo Request Message, From 172.16.10.154 To 172.16.10.252
29828	6:22:48 PM 8/1/2012	172.16.10.252	172.16.10.154	ICMP	ICMP:Echo Reply Message, From 172.16.10.252 To 172.16.10.154

FIGURE 16.8 Probing with ICMP and SNMP.

If ICMP and SNMP are used as the access mode, OpsMgr first pings the device using ICMP. If the device does not respond to the `Echo` request, probing ends without proceeding to the SNMP `Get` request and the device is not discovered.

By default, the probing stage uses SNMP v2c first. If the device does not respond within the configured retry attempts, the management server attempts again using SNMP v1. You can configure the number of retries in the advanced settings of the discovery rule.

Processing Stage

Once probing determines the device is reachable, OpsMgr attempts to match the `sysObjectId` returned in the `GetResponse` message from the probing stage to a device defined in an oid2type_*.config file hosted on the management server. If OpsMgr finds a match, the device receives advanced monitoring features. Otherwise, only availability monitoring will run on the device.

NOTE: CONFIG AND PROBE FILES

The config and probe files are located on the management server under *%ProgramFiles%*\System Center 2012\Operations Manager\Server\NetworkMonitoring\conf\discovery, by default. Probes have an .import extension. If OpsMgr matches the device to an oid2type file, it will probe the device for additional information such as device vendor, type of device, model, ports and interfaces, memory, processors, VLAN membership, HSRP groups, and neighboring devices.

When recursive discovery is configured, the IP addresses of neighboring devices are added to the discovery queue. If the IP address is not filtered out by any include or exclude filter configured on the discovery rule, the discovery process begins the probing stage for these devices. This continues until all network devices are discovered.

Post-Processing Stage

The final stage consolidates the information collected by the additional probing that occurred in the previous stage and inserts this discovery data into the operational database. Part of the post-processing stage includes mapping device ports to the servers in which they are connected. This is known as *port stitching*. Port stitching creates the topology, or network vicinity view, and is discussed in the next section.

About Port Stitching

As discussed in the previous section, port stitching maps device ports to the servers and network devices to which they are connected.

NOTE: SUPPORTED DEVICES FOR PORT STITCHING

Port stitching occurs only for supported network devices and Windows computers, and requires those Windows server or client operating system management pack(s) for which you want to create a topology of connected devices.

For port stitching to occur, the `Windows Computer` object and at least one `Computer Network Adapter` object hosted on that computer must be discovered. The `Computer Network Adapter` object is discovered by the Windows Server Network Discovery and Windows Client Network Discovery management packs, respectively.

You can view events related to port stitching in the Operations console by navigating to **Monitoring -> Operations Manager -> Network Discovery -> Network Discovery Progress Events** and searching for **12024** events. Figure 16.9 illustrates port stitching occurred for 46 computers during the last interval. Also, note the System.NetworkManagement.CollectDiscoveryData collection rule is collecting these events.

16

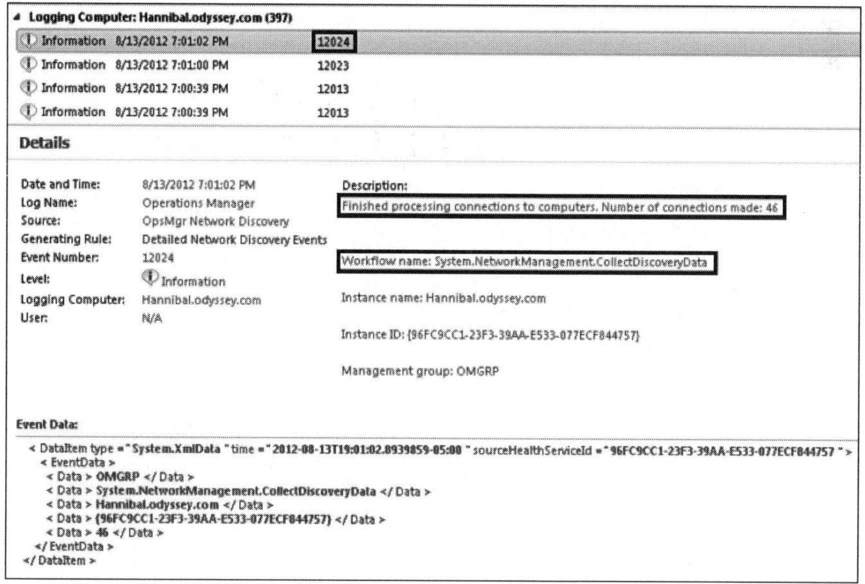

FIGURE 16.9 Successful port stitching event.

Creating a Discovery Rule

Before you can start monitoring network devices in OpsMgr, you must first discover the device(s) by creating a discovery rule. This is accomplished using the Discovery Wizard in the Operations console. Network discovery rules run at a defined interval, or may be run manually as needed. The two methods of discovery are explicit or recursive, previously discussed in the "Types of Discovery Methods" section.

NOTE: RECURSIVE DISCOVERY SUPPORT FOR IPV6

OpsMgr can identify connected devices in a recursive discovery that use an IPv6 address, although the initial device that is discovered must use an IPv4 address.

A discovery rule can perform only explicit or recursive discovery; it cannot perform a combination of these discovery methods. If you know all the network devices that you want to discover, it may be best to use explicit discovery. Recursive discovery can discover devices that you have no interest in monitoring, which can increase the monitoring workload on your management servers and potentially create a performance bottleneck in your management group.

A discovery rule can discover any combination of SNMP v1, v2, and v3 devices. There is a significant difference between how SNMP v3 devices are discovered: SNMP v3 devices must always be explicitly included in the discovery rule, whether the rule uses an explicit or recursive method of discovery.

Another key difference applies to recursive discovery. If you specify SNMP v1 or v2 devices in a recursive discovery, those SNMP v1 and v2 devices connected to the device can be discovered. However, SNMP v3 devices will not be discovered recursively, nor will recursive discovery occur beyond an SNMP v3 device that is explicitly added to a recursive discovery rule.

TIP: EXCLUSIONS FROM DISCOVERY RESULTS

Windows computers running SNMP are filtered out of discovery results in certain cases:

- The device type is "Host" and the vendor is "Microsoft".
- The sysDescription field contains "Microsoft".
- The sysOid starts with .1.3.6.1.4.1.311.1.1.3.1.
- The sysOid contains 1.3.6.1.4.1.199.1.1.3.11.

When configuring the discovery rule, specify whether OpsMgr will use ICMP, SNMP, or both to communicate with the network device. When the discovery rule runs, the specified discovery management server attempts to contact the network device(s) included in the rule. The authors suggest specifying both ICMP and SNMP in the discovery configuration for advanced monitoring of your network devices. If you specify ICMP only, monitoring of discovered devices will be limited to availability.

NOTE: DEVICES MUST BE REACHABLE VIA ICMP

If ICMP and SNMP are used as the access mode, OpsMgr first pings the device using ICMP. If the device does not respond to the `Echo` request, probing ends without proceeding to the SNMP `Get` request and the device is not discovered.

A number of settings are available to configure for a network device discovery rule; these range from basic discovery configuration to more advanced settings. You can view a full list of configuration settings at http://technet.microsoft.com/en-us/library/hh230715. At a minimum, the following information is necessary to create a network device discovery rule:

- The IP address or FQDN of each device you want to include in an explicit discovery, or as seed devices in your recursive discovery.
- The version of SNMP each device uses (SNMP v1, v2, or v3). Remember SNMP v3 devices must always be explicitly added to your discovery rule, whether it is explicit or recursive.
- The SNMP community string of each SNMP v1 or v2 device you want to discover.
- The user name for each SNMP v3 device you want to discover. Optionally, if you require authentication and privacy, the authentication protocol, authentication key, privacy protocol, and privacy key are also needed. Check your device configuration to know which setting to select in the Discovery Wizard.
- The name of the network monitoring resource pool that will monitor the devices discovered.

16

TIP: INCLUDING ONLY SPECIFIC IP ADDRESS RANGES

If using recursive discovery and you only want to discover network devices that fall within a specified IP address range, you can specify that IP address range in your discovery rule. This may be a desired configuration when specifying a resource pool consisting of gateway servers in a different geographic location.

Before creating a network device discover rule, ensure your firewalls are configured properly as discussed previously in the "Firewall Requirements" section.

Network Device Discovery Walk-Through

To create a network device discovery rule, open the Operations console and perform the following steps:

1. Navigate to **Administration** -> **Network Management** -> **Discovery Rules**. Right-click in the Discovery Rules pane and select **Discover Network Devices**. You may also right-click any node in the Administration tree, select **Discovery Wizard**, select **Network devices**, and click **Next**. Each method opens the first page of the Discovery Wizard.

NOTE: USER ROLE REQUIREMENT

You must be a member of the Operations Manager Administrators user role to create discovery rules.

2. On the General Properties page, enter a logical name for your new discovery rule. You must also select a management server that will perform the discovery. Note that the server performing the discovery will not be the server that monitors those devices. Next, select a resource pool that will do the actual monitoring of the devices. Figure 16.10 illustrates these options.

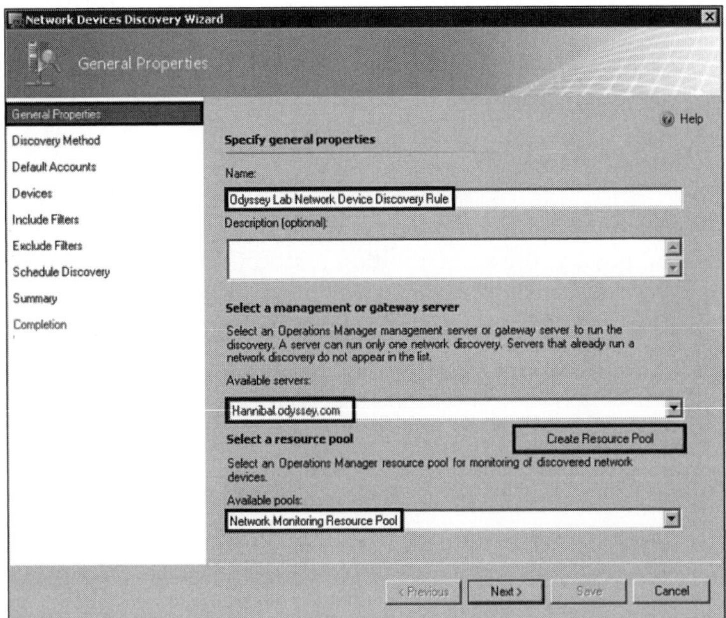

FIGURE 16.10 Discovery rule general properties.

If you have not yet configured a resource pool to monitor the network devices that will be discovered by your new rule, you may elect to create one now by clicking **Create Resource Pool**. This opens a new wizard that guides you through the resource pool creation process. The information required for this wizard is the resource pool name and selected management server(s) that will be included in the resource pool membership. Careful planning of discovery servers and resource pools may be required in more complex and geographically dispersed environments; however, you can modify discovery rules at any time.

3. Click **Next** to select the discovery method: explicit or recursive. In this example, recursive discovery is used.

4. On the following page, Default Accounts, configure the Run As account(s) to use. You must select all Run As accounts that may be used to communicate with any device in your discovery rule. This may be one or many, depending on your environment.

NOTE: TRAP EVENTS FROM UNSUCCESSFUL LOGINS

The discovering management server attempts to use each Run As account selected in the Default Accounts configuration until it reaches a successful login. If configuring multiple Run As accounts, be aware that this may result in network devices generating trap events about failed login attempts at each discovery interval.

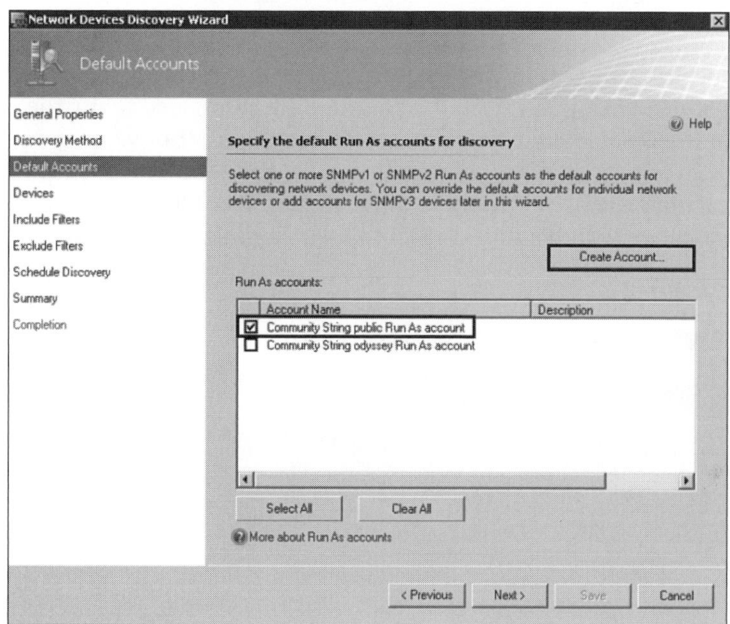

FIGURE 16.11 Discovery rule default accounts.

Figure 16.11 illustrates the Default Accounts page, where only the **Community String public Run As account** is selected, since all the devices in this example discovery rule use the same SNMP v1 and v2 community string.

If you have not yet created a Run As account, you may do so now by clicking **Create Account**. This launches a separate wizard, guiding you through the new Run As account process. The Run As account wizard, when launched from this page, only allows you to configure community string accounts.

NOTE: DEFAULT ACCOUNTS IN THE NETWORK DEVICES DISCOVERY WIZARD

You will notice that only SNMP v1 and v2 are configured at this stage in the wizard; you can only add community string accounts here. SNMP v3 discovery settings are entered later in the wizard. If you are creating a recursive discovery rule, you must select at least one community string Run As account on this page. These are the accounts that will be used to recursively discover connected network devices.

5. After selecting the default account(s) to use, you are presented with a Devices page. This page is equivalent to an explicit discovery, in that you will enter specific configuration for devices you want to discover. This page must have at least one device configured. If you are configuring a recursive discovery, the device(s) entered here are considered "seed" devices. Recursive discovery starts at the seed device and then attempts to discover connected devices included in the discovery rule until all devices are discovered.

   You may either add devices by selecting **Add** in the wizard or by importing a text file containing a list of IP addresses. By default, all devices are configured to use the accounts specified on the Default Accounts page, and to use SNMP v1 or v2, port 161, and ICMP/SNMP access mode. If you import a text file, the device(s) added are automatically configured to use these default settings. Figure 16.12 illustrates the Devices page, where a device with IP address 192.168.1.1 was added by importing a text file.

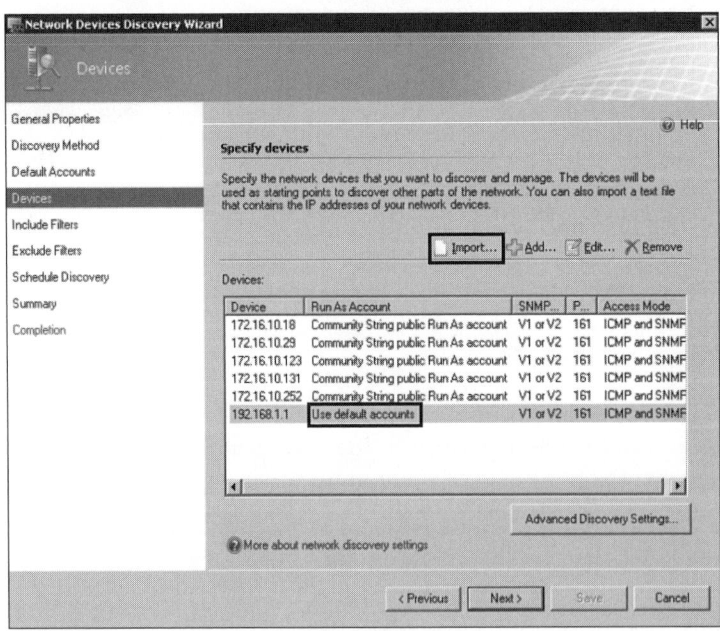

FIGURE 16.12 Discovery rule devices.

If you choose to add a device manually, the Add a Device configuration page appears. Several options are available here, most notably the option to add an SNMP v1 or v2 device, or an SNMP v3 device. Figure 16.13 illustrates adding an SNMP v1 or v2 device, whereas Figure 16.14 shows the difference in adding an SNMP v3 device.

CAUTION: MONITORING A DEVICE IN MORE THAN ONE RESOURCE POOL

Use caution when adding devices to your discovery rule, whether explicitly or recursively. If a device is monitored by more than one resource pool, the device cannot be deleted later.

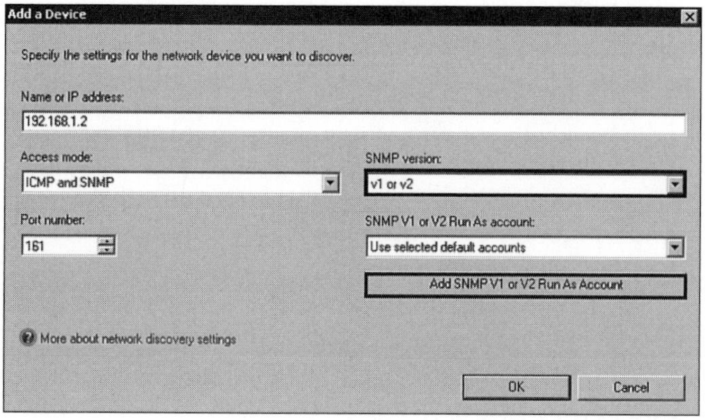

FIGURE 16.13 Add SNMP v1 or v2 device.

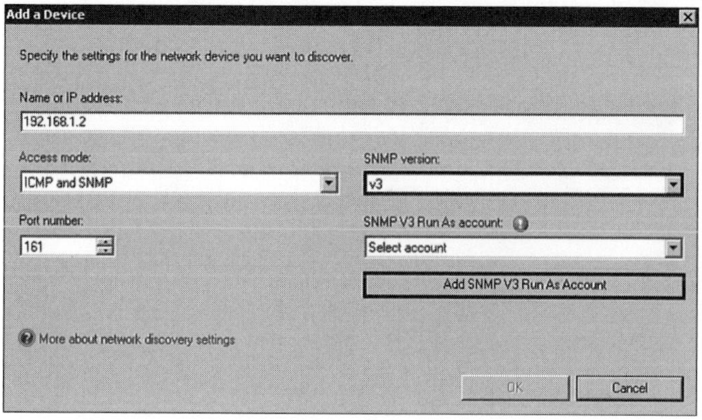

FIGURE 16.14 Add SNMP v3 device.

- If SNMP v1 or v2 is selected, you will have the option to select an SNMP v1 or v2 Run As account or create one now.
- Alternatively, if SNMP v3 is selected, you will have the option to select an SNMP v3 Run As account or create one at this time.

This example demonstrates adding SNMP v1 or v2 devices. On the Add a Device page, specify the IP address of the device and select the access mode, port number,

SNMP version, and Run As account. Click **Next** on the Devices page after all seed devices are configured in your recursive discovery.

TIP: ADDING SNMP V3 DEVICES

Configuring SNMP v3 devices for discovery is only available at this stage in the discovery configuration process, whether you choose explicit discovery or recursive discovery. Also, note that recursive discovery does not occur for devices connected to SNMP v3 devices, and SNMP v3 devices always require explicit configuration in either discovery method. Adding an SNMP v3 device is discussed further in the "Adding an SNMP v3 Device" section later in the chapter.

6. The next page in the wizard, Include Filters, allows you to discover only devices within a specified IP address range. This can be useful in cases where your network monitoring resource pool is located in a particular geographic area, and you only want devices in this location to be monitored by this resource pool. You may add as many IP address ranges as necessary to the filter.

NOTE: USING WILDCARD MATCHING IN FILTERS

Filters can be configured with basic IP addresses ranges, such as 192.168.1.1-192.168.1.100, or can be more complex by using wildcard matching patterns. An example of a valid wildcard pattern that includes the same IP address range is 192.168.1.<1-100>. Read more about wildcard patterns at http://technet.microsoft.com/en-us/library/hh230715. You can also learn more about filters by selecting the **More about device filters** link in the wizard, shown in Figure 16.15.

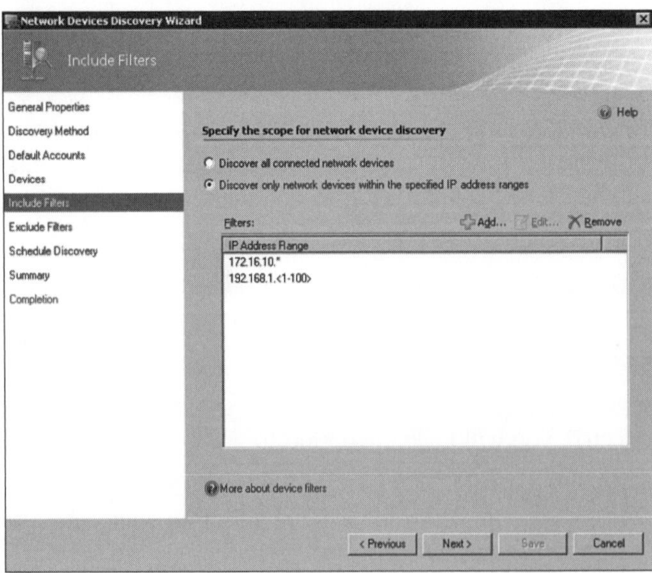

FIGURE 16.15 Sample include filter.

Figure 16.15 illustrates filters to include IP address 172.16.10.1-172.16.10.255 and 192.168.1.1-192.168.1.100.

In addition to including specific IP address ranges in your filter, you may also specify which types of devices to discover; such as bridge, firewall, router, or switch. You also have the option to discover only those devices that match OID attributes. For example, if you want to discover only Cisco devices, you would filter on OID 1.3.6.1.4.1.9.*.

Click **Next** after completing the Include Filters page.

7. The next page in the wizard, Exclude Filters, allows you to enter a range of IP addresses you want to exclude from your discovery rule. Unlike the Include Filters page, the only option available is an IP address range. Click **Next** after completing the Exclude Filters page.
8. The last step in configuring your discovery rule is setting the schedule.
   - By default, the discovery rule will run every Saturday at 2:00 am. The rule will be run once per day at the configured schedule, and can be scheduled to run any day at any time.
   - You may choose not to run the discovery rule on a schedule by selecting **Run the discovery rule manually**. If your environment is relatively static and new devices are not frequently added, electing to run the rule manually may be suitable and can reduce unnecessary discovery workloads. If devices are added or changes are made to the network, you can simply run the discovery rule manually by right-clicking and selecting **Run**.
9. After configuring the schedule, click **Next** to proceed to the Summary page. Review your discovery rule configuration and click **Create** to finish.
10. After the discovery rule is saved, you may be prompted to distribute the Run As account(s) to the selected discovery server and network monitoring resource pool, as indicated in Figure 16.16.

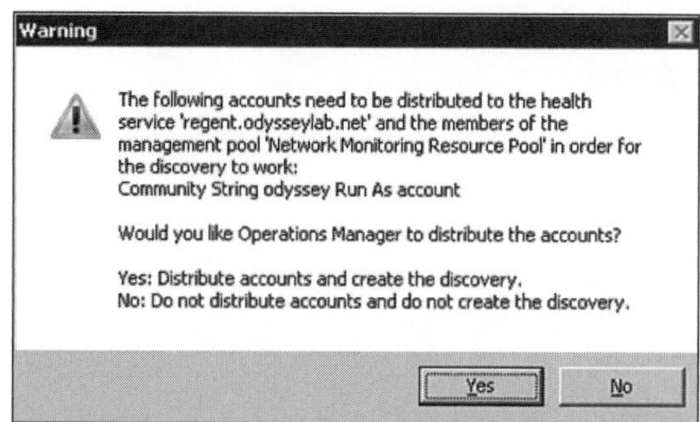

FIGURE 16.16 Distribute credentials.

16

Choose **Yes** to have OpsMgr automatically configure this for you. If you select **No**, the discovery rule is not created. After saving, you are presented with a Completion page, at which time you may elect to run the discovery rule after the wizard closes.

Adding an SNMP v3 Device

As mentioned in the "Network Device Discovery Walk-Through" section, SNMP v3 devices are explicitly added to a discovery rule, whether it uses the explicit or recursive method. This section discusses how to add an SNMP v3 device to your discovery rule.

NOTE: RUN AS ACCOUNTS FOR SNMP V3 DEVICES

Unlike SNMP v1 and v2 Run As accounts, where you can use a single community string Run As account across multiple devices, each SNMP v3 device requires a unique Run As account. If you have multiple SNMP v3 devices to include in your discovery rule, you may want to configure your Run As accounts beforehand to streamline the discovery rule creation process. Read more about SNMP v3 Run As accounts at http://technet.microsoft.com/en-us/library/hh212920.aspx.

SNMP v3 devices are added on the Devices page of the Network Devices Discovery Wizard. You may elect to import a text file containing a list of SNMP v3 IP addresses, or add each device manually. Settings for each device must be configured using either method. If you create the SNMP v3 Run As account before launching the discovery wizard, you could simply select the Run As account in the drop-down box as illustrated in Figure 16.17.

If the Run As account did not previously exist, you can create one now. Follow these steps:

1. Select **Add SNMP V3 Run As Account** to launch the **Create Run As Account Wizard**.
2. On the General Properties page, name your new Run As account and optionally enter a description. Since each SNMP v3 device requires a unique Run As account, it may be helpful to include the device name in the name of the Run As account or its description.

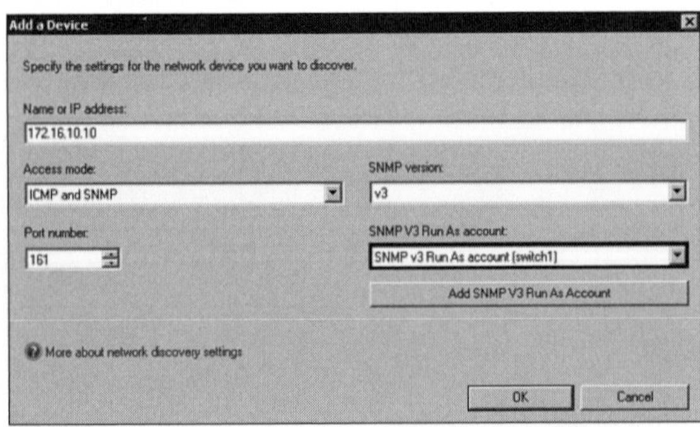

FIGURE 16.17 Adding an SNMP v3 device.

3. After naming the Run As account, click **Next** to enter the credentials that will be used to access the device. Figure 16.18 illustrates the details you can enter on this page.

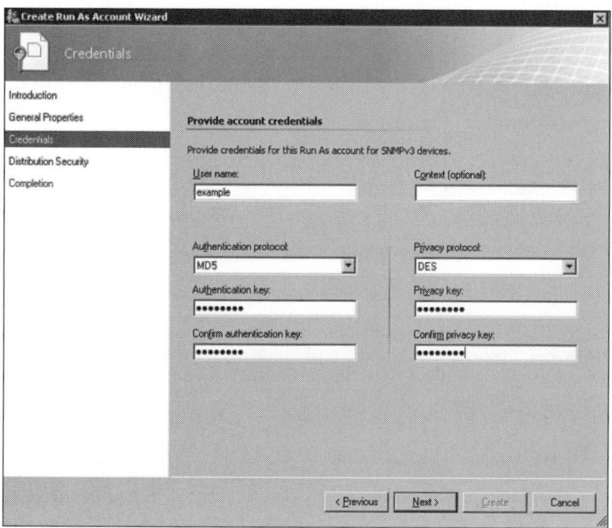

FIGURE 16.18 SNMP v3 Run As account details.

Only the user name is required for the SNMP v3 Run As account; however, providing just the user name almost defeats the purpose of using SNMP v3. Typically, you would use an authentication protocol, and optionally a privacy protocol. The only required configuration is the user name. These protocols were discussed earlier in the "Using SNMP v3" section.

4. After entering all the details for your SNMP v3 device, click **Create** to return to the Add A Device page. After making your selections on the Add A Device page, click **OK** to add the device and return to the Devices page of the Network Devices Discovery Wizard.

Deleting a Network Device

After OpsMgr has discovered and is monitoring a network device, you might want to stop monitoring the device for some reason. To suspend monitoring of a network device temporarily, you can place it into maintenance mode. If there is no need to monitor the device any longer, you can choose to remove the device from OpsMgr entirely.

To remove a device, follow these steps:

1. In the Operations console, navigate to **Administration** -> **Network Management** -> **Network Devices**.

2. Right-click the device you want to remove and select **Delete**.

If the device is the starting point for recursive discovery (seed device), you must remove the device from the discovery rule or delete the discovery rule. If you attempt to delete a seed device in a recursive discovery rule, you will receive a dialog similar to that displayed in Figure 16.19.

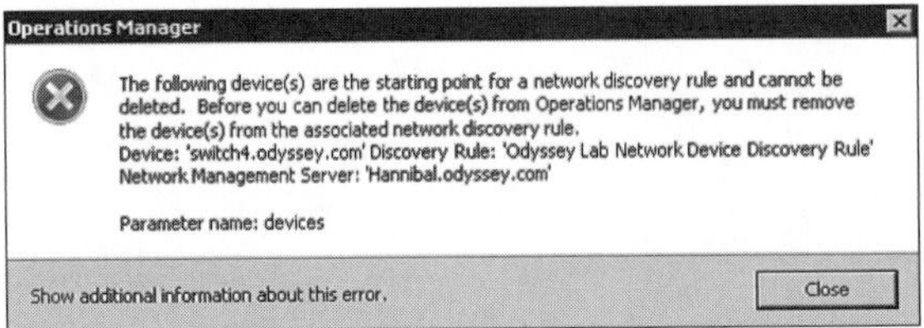

FIGURE 16.19 Delete seed device dialog.

NOTE: RECURSIVELY DISCOVERED DEVICES

If you delete a device that was recursively discovered, OpsMgr adds the device to the exclude filter list of the discovery rule.

Perform the following steps to remove a seed device:

1. In the Operations console, navigate to Administration -> **Network Management** -> **Discovery Rules** and open the discovery rule indicated in the dialog in Figure 16.19.
2. Click on the Devices page, select the device that you want to remove from OpsMgr, and click **Remove** as illustrated in Figure 16.20.

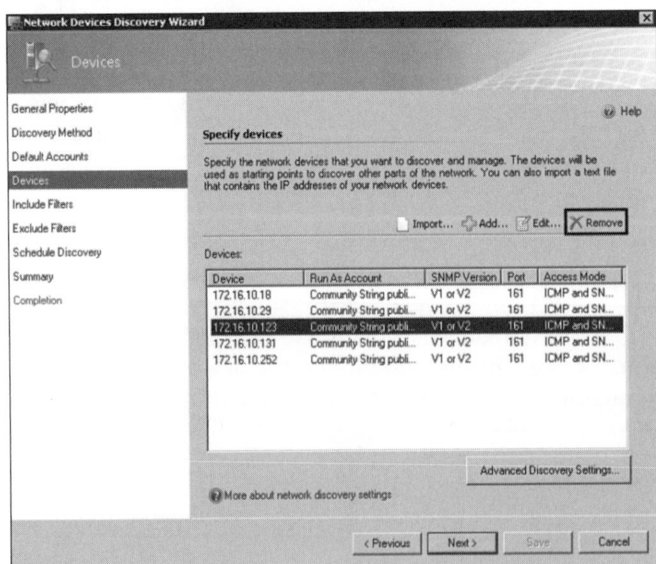

FIGURE 16.20 Delete seed device in recursive discovery.

3. Select the Summary page and click **Save**. The device will be removed from OpsMgr at the next discovery interval, or you can run the discovery manually to expedite this change.

Restoring a Network Device

There may be cases where you need to restore a device that was previously removed from OpsMgr. There are two ways to restore a device, depending on how the device was initially discovered.

If the device was originally discovered as a seed device in a recursive discovery or by an explicit discovery, proceed to step 5 in the "Network Device Discovery Walk-Through" section.

If the device was originally discovered recursively, follow these steps:

1. In the Operations console, navigate to **Administration** -> **Network Management** -> **Discovery Rules** and open the discovery rule that initially discovered the device.
2. Click on the Exclude Filters page, select the device you want to restore, and click **Remove**.
3. Click on the Summary page and click **Save**. The device will be restored at the next discovery interval, or you can run the discovery manually to expedite this change. Note that it may take some time for the device to be rediscovered, depending on the size of your environment and how far down in the recursive discovery this device is located.

Monitoring Network Devices

Many new and enhanced monitoring features are available in OpsMgr 2012. In addition to a much wider range of supported devices, OpsMgr now delivers more advanced monitoring out of the box. The next sections discuss what is available out of box and how to retrieve detailed information about monitoring workflows. Not all devices, ports, and interfaces are discovered and monitored the same.

By default, out of the box monitoring occurs only on device ports discovered as connected to another discovered device or Windows agent-managed computer in the same management group. This is to avoid unnecessary monitoring workflows running against ports that are not active on the network or connected to devices or computers in the management group.

Port and interface monitoring is only available for those devices implementing the interface MIB (RFC 2863) and MIB-II (RFC 1213) standards; and peripheral monitoring, including processor and memory, is only available on a subset of devices. For a list of supported devices that include this extended peripheral monitoring, refer to http://www.microsoft.com/en-us/download/details.aspx?displaylang=en&id=26831.

NOTE: THE LIST OF NETWORK DEVICES WITH EXTENDED MONITORING CAPABILITY IN OPERATONS MANAGER

The page at http://www.microsoft.com/en-us/download/details.aspx?displayang-en&id=26831 links to a spreadsheet containing a list of devices with extended monitoring capability in Operations Manager 2012. However, as of January 2013, this spreadsheet was last updated July 25, 2011, prior to the beta release of System Center 2012 Operations Manager. What has occurred is Microsoft first looked at network monitoring in OpsMgr 2012 as the capability to monitor generic devices or certified devices having extended monitoring capabilities, but then moved towards standard and advanced (extended) monitoring. The intent is to provide the same monitoring capabilities for all devices implementing MIB (RFC 2863) and MIB-II (RFC 1213) standards, rather than certifying one device at a time.

Key performance and availability monitoring is covered through standardized port/interface monitoring functionalities. Advanced or extended monitoring simply means it may include device processor/memory monitoring—which is really just contextual data. Since it is most important to provide standardized part/interface monitoring, updating the spreadsheet has been of low priority.

Network Monitoring Groups and Usage

Several groups in OpsMgr contain device peripherals, ports, and interfaces in which advanced monitoring will be enabled. For advanced monitoring to occur on a device, these objects must be a member of at least one of these groups. Here is information about each group and its usage in OpsMgr:

- **Managed Computer Network Adapters Group:** This group contains ports and interfaces of network devices to which managed Windows computers are connected. Ports and interfaces are automatically added to this group during the post-processing stage of discovery, specifically, when port stitching occurs.
- **Critical Network Adapters Group:** This group is manually populated and will contain network ports and interfaces of type Network Adapter (Network Base) that need to be monitored. For example, if you have a mission critical server that is not agent-managed in the same management group as the discovered network device, but want to monitor the device's interface that is connected to this computer, you can explicitly add that interface to this group to enable monitoring. This will extend network monitoring workflows to the mission critical computer that is not managed by OpsMgr.
- **Advanced Network Adapters Group:** Similar to the Critical Network Adapters Group, this group is manually populated and contains network ports and interfaces of type Network Adapter (Network Base). The difference is a port or interface that is a member of this group will receive advance monitoring, such as processor and memory performance monitoring.

  Typically, it is not necessary to add an interface to both the Critical Network Adapters Group and this group; members of the Advanced Network Adapters Group receive the same monitoring in addition to enabling advanced monitoring workflows that are otherwise disabled out of the box.

- **Relay Network Adapters Group:** This group contains network ports and interfaces of network devices that are directly connected to each other, such as routers and switches. Interfaces are automatically added to this group during the discovery process.
- **Group of All Network Devices Actively Being Monitored:** This is the top-level group for all the above network adapters groups; those groups are nested within this group. All ports and interfaces in the nested groups are visible in network monitoring operational views.

NOTE: DEVICES THAT ARE UNREACHABLE

If a network device is disconnected or the network monitoring resource pool cannot reach it for some reason, an alert is generated indicating the device is offline. However, unlike a typical agent-managed computer, monitoring data is not queued, so performance, availability, and event data is not collected while the device is unreachable.

Retrieving Built-In Monitoring Workflows

As of OpsMgr 2012 Update Release 3, there are over 400 monitoring workflows delivered in the Network Management - Core Monitoring and Network Management Library management packs, of which almost 250 workflows are enabled by default. You can view the current monitoring workflows by running the following SQL queries against your operational database.

NOTE: AVAILABLE ONLINE

For your convenience, the SQL queries in this section are available with the online content for this book. See Appendix E, "Available Online," for further information.

To view out of the box rules, run the query in Listing 16.1 against the operational database.

LISTING 16.1 Rules included in network monitoring management packs

```
SELECT vMP.DisplayName,
    vRule.DisplayName,
    vRule.Enabled,
    vRule.Category,
    vRule.Description
FROM RuleView AS vRule INNER JOIN
    ManagementPackView AS vMP ON vRule.ManagementPackId = vMP.Id
WHERE vMP.DisplayName IN (
    'Network Management - Core Monitoring',
    'Network Management Library')
ORDER BY vMP.DisplayName, vRule.DisplayName
```

To view out of the box monitors, run the query in Listing 16.2 against the operational database:

LISTING 16.2 Monitors included in network monitoring management packs

```
SELECT vMP.DisplayName,
    vMonitor.DisplayName,
    vMonitor.Enabled,
    vMonitor.Category,
    vMonitor.Description
FROM MonitorView AS vMonitor INNER JOIN
    ManagementPackView AS vMP ON vMonitor.ManagementPackId = vMP.Id
WHERE vMP.DisplayName IN (
    'Network Management - Core Monitoring',
    'Network Management Library')
ORDER BY vMP.DisplayName, vMonitor.DisplayName
```

These queries return management pack name, workflow name, whether enabled by default, and a description of the workflow. You can further filter these queries to return what workflows are enabled or disabled by default by adding an additional `WHERE` clause. For example, to return a list of rules that are enabled by default, you can run the following query in Listing 16.3.

LISTING 16.3 Network monitoring management packs rules enabled by default

```
SELECT vMP.DisplayName,
    vRule.DisplayName,
    vRule.Enabled,
    vRule.Category,
    vRule.Description
FROM RuleView AS vRule INNER JOIN
    ManagementPackView AS vMP ON vRule.ManagementPackId = vMP.Id
WHERE vMP.DisplayName IN (
    'Network Management - Core Monitoring',
    'Network Management Library') AND
    (vRule.Enabled <> 0)
ORDER BY vMP.DisplayName, vRule.DisplayName
```

Notice the last `WHERE` clause:

```
(vRule.Enabled <> 0)
```

Alternatively, you can return all rules that are disabled by default, by changing the `WHERE` clause to

```
(vRule.Enabled = 0)
```

You can do the same for the monitors query by replacing `vRule` with `vMonitor`.

Listing 16.4 is an example that returns rules targeting Cisco devices:

LISTING 16.4 Return rules that target a specific type of device

```
SELECT vMP.DisplayName,
    vRule.DisplayName,
    vRule.Enabled,
    vRule.Category,
    vRule.Description,
    vMTV.Name
FROM RuleView AS vRule INNER JOIN
    ManagementPackView AS vMP ON vRule.ManagementPackId = vMP.Id INNER JOIN
    ManagedTypeView AS vMTV ON vRule.TargetMonitoringClassId = vmtv.Id
WHERE vMP.DisplayName IN (
    'Network Management - Core Monitoring',
    'Network Management Library')
    (vMTV.Name LIKE '%cisco%')
ORDER BY vMP.DisplayName, vRule.DisplayName
```

Notice the last `WHERE` clause:

```
(vMTV.Name LIKE '%cisco%')
```

Alternatively, you can return all rules that target another device by changing the `WHERE` clause:

```
(vMTV.Name LIKE '%juniper%')
```

You can also use the Operations Manager Shell, with the Get-SCOMRule and Get-SCOMMonitor cmdlets, to retrieve the same information. Here is an example to create a csv file of all monitors targeting Cisco devices.

```
Get-SCOMMonitor -Target (Get-SCOMClass -DisplayName *cisco*) | select
DisplayName, Description, Enabled | Export-Csv out.csv
```

Open c:\out.csv with Excel to display an expanded, formatted list of monitors. You can use this same query to retrieve rules targeting Cisco devices by replacing `Get-SCOMMonitor` with `Get-SCOMRule`. To return similar information for other device types, replace the `-DisplayName` parameter with the device vendor for which you want to export the information.

Another option to retrieve management pack details quickly is using MPViewer, available for download at http://blogs.msdn.com/b/dmuscett/archive/2012/02/19/boris-s-tools-updated.aspx. This tool has been updated to work with the new OpsMgr 2012 management pack schema and network monitoring management packs, and can offer additional insight such as performance counter names and monitoring intervals. This information can be helpful in tuning network monitoring management packs to meet business needs before installing into production.

Sharing this type of information with your network engineering team and management staff will help them understand what is being monitored and collected, which should empower you to make informed and proactive decisions to maintain a healthy environment.

Viewing Operational Data

OpsMgr 2012 introduces the dashboards feature (discussed in Chapter 11, "Dashboards, Trending, and Forecasting"), which enables you to access data quickly to more efficiently troubleshoot operational issues. These operational dashboards are included out of the box in Microsoft-authored management packs and many vendor management packs, and can be easily created on-demand in the Operations console to include monitoring data collected by any management pack. Dashboards can include any combination of alert, health, state, or performance information of your network devices. The next sections discuss identifying network device health through the Health Explorer and using the built-in dashboards and reports.

Using the Network Device Health Explorer

The most valuable view in OpsMgr to ascertain the state of systems quickly is the state view. In the case of network monitoring, network administrators should check on a daily basis the Network Devices state view located under Monitoring -> Network Monitoring.

Figure 16.21 illustrates the Network Device state view, sorted by state with the top instance reporting an unhealthy state. To view the state of all monitored instances on that device, launch the Health Explorer by double-clicking the State column of any network device. You can also launch the Health Explorer by right-clicking the object and selecting **Open -> Health Explorer**.

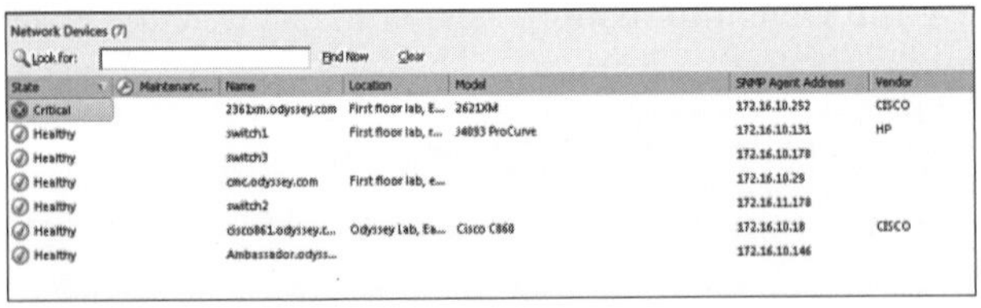

FIGURE 16.21 Network Devices state view.

By default, the Health Explorer expands to show all unhealthy instances, as shown in Figure 16.22.

Figure 16.22 indicates free memory and processor utilization has exceeded monitor thresholds. Clicking the Knowledge tab of the unhealthy monitor(s) provides more information about the issue, and the State Change Events tab gives details about when this monitor changed state. The State Change Events tab also includes information about the sampled data that generated the state change event.

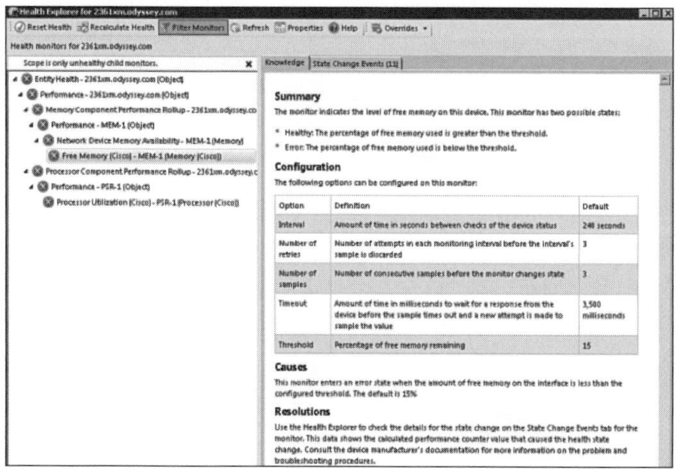

FIGURE 16.22 Viewing a network device in the Health Explorer.

The next sections highlight the dashboard features built into the network monitoring management packs.

Network Vicinity Dashboard

Network monitoring in OpsMgr 2012 includes the Network Vicinity Dashboard. This dashboard displays network topology health in relation to the instance experiencing a problem, given it is hosted by a `Windows Computer` object. Earlier versions of OpsMgr fell short of this type of network health information, which could cause systems administrators some grief when troubleshooting application latencies or server outages. These problems are sometimes caused by degraded network health or network device outages. The Network Vicinity Dashboard provides key information to help administrators more effectively resolve these types of network related issues.

Figure 16.23 illustrates the Network Vicinity Dashboard after selecting a database instance from the Microsoft SQL Server Database state view. Since SQL Server databases are ultimately hosted by a Windows Computer, the Network Vicinity Dashboard can draw a topology health map related to the computer hosting the database.

This example shows a problem with the SQL Server database. Launching the Network Vicinity Dashboard confirms it is not a network related issue, as three hops from the Windows Computer hosting the unhealthy database (stratus.odyssey.com) to the switch connected to the computer hosting the client application (cmc.odyssey.com) is green, indicating a healthy network connection.

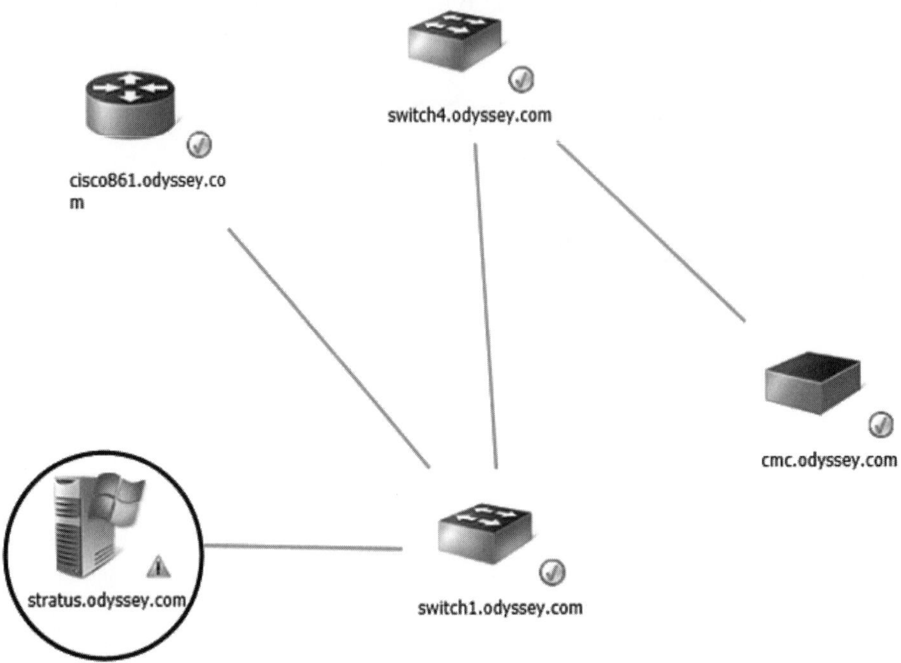

FIGURE 16.23 Network Vicinity Dashboard.

Network Node Dashboard

The Network Node Dashboard provides information such as

- ▶ Vicinity of the network device selected and the devices it is connected to
- ▶ Device availability as far back as 30 days
- ▶ Key device performance metrics
- ▶ Health of monitored interfaces on the device
- ▶ Any active alerts that were generated from any monitored component on the device

This dashboard is useful if you want to know current state of a particular device, as well as historical performance and availability statistics.

Access the Network Node Dashboard by selecting an instance in any of the state views under the **Monitoring** -> **Network Monitoring** folder and selecting **Network Node Dashboard** in the Tasks pane.

Network Summary Dashboard

The Network Summary Dashboard provides sorted lists of the most unhealthy network devices and monitored network device components in your environment. This is particularly useful if you want to view a snapshot of current unhealthy interfaces and connections in the network. You can also view network interface health details from this view; select an interface in the Interfaces with Highest Utilization pane, then select Network Interface Dashboard in the Tasks pane. The Network Interface Dashboard is discussed in the next section.

Launch this view by selecting **Network Summary Dashboard** under the **Monitoring -> Network Monitoring** folder. Figure 16.24 displays an example of this dashboard.

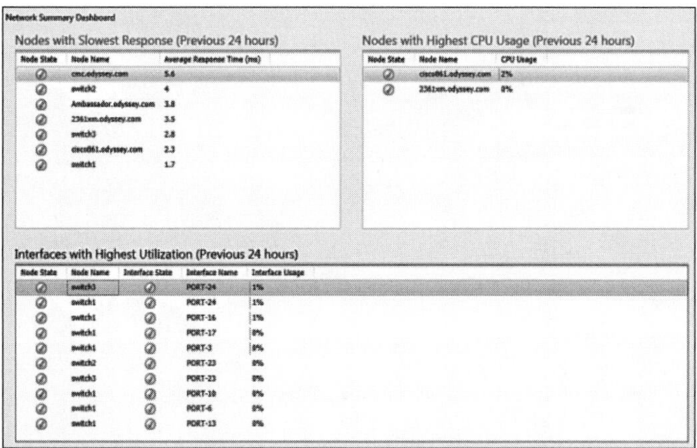

FIGURE 16.24 Network Summary Dashboard.

Network Interface Dashboard

The Network Interface Dashboard provides network traffic details about the interface, including bits and packets sent and received, a network utilization gauge, as well as discovered interface details. Figure 16.25 illustrates the Network Interface Dashboard.

This dashboard can be accessed in several ways. One method was described in the "Network Summary Dashboard" section. Another method is to select an interface in the Health of Interfaces on the Node pane in the Network Node Dashboard, and then select Network Interface Dashboard in the Tasks pane.

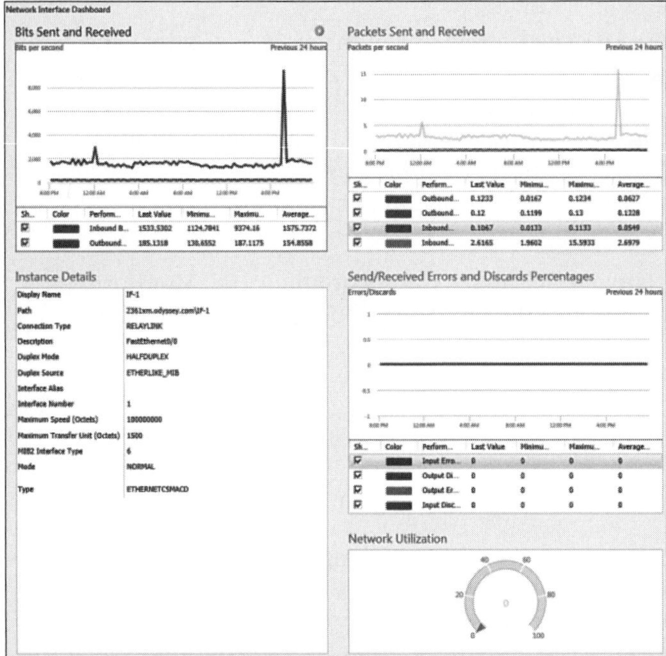

FIGURE 16.25 Network Interface Dashboard.

Viewing Historical Data

A library of reports come bundled in the network monitoring management packs. OpsMgr 2012 delivers five reports out of the box, including

- Interface Error Packet Analysis
- Interface Packet Analysis
- Interface Traffic Volume
- Memory Utilization
- Processor Utilization

In addition to the out of the box network monitoring reports, you can generate detailed reports using the Microsoft Generic Report Library. The next sections discuss the Interface Traffic Volume Report included in the network monitoring management pack and the Availability Report included in the Microsoft Generic Report Library.

Interface Traffic Volume

The Interface Traffic Volume Report can provide valuable trending information related to an interface on a network device or a series of interfaces across multiple network devices. Access this report by navigating to **Reporting -> Network Management Reports**, and double-clicking **Interface Traffic Volume**. This example demonstrates how to view traffic volume trends for a particular interface over the past 180 days.

After launching the report, you must provide some basic criteria. The only required parameters are date range and objects (interfaces) to include. Typically, you probably want to see data from a number of days back to the current date. In this case, click the **From** drop-down box and select **Advanced**. Click on the **no offset** dropdown and select **minus**. Provide a value for the number of days you want the report to display; in this example, **180 day(s)**, then press the green checkmark to save your selection.

Next, click **Add Object** and search for an interface in which you are interested. Enter an interface name; for example, **IF-1**, and click **Search**.

NOTE: SEARCHING AND FILTERING OBJECTS

The report discussed in this section is already scoped to include only network interface objects. However, the search string works only on the name property. If you have hundreds of interfaces named IF-1, the list returned will be quite long, and you will need to sort the list further by clicking the **path** column and searching for the IP address or MAC address of the device you want to add.

You may choose other criteria for this report as needed, but this is the only required criteria. You can also add multiple interfaces, which will result in multiple series in the report. When you have finished specifying criteria (by highlighting each and clicking **Add**, then **OK**), click **Run** to generate the report. Figure 16.26 illustrates interface traffic trends for the past 180 days.

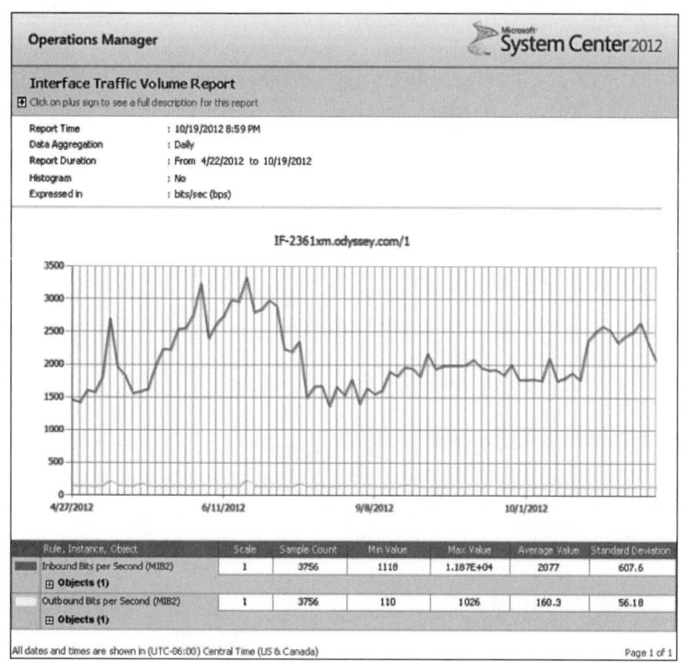

Rule, Instance, Object	Scale	Sample Count	Min Value	Max Value	Average Value	Standard Deviation
Inbound Bits per Second (MIB2)	1	3756	1118	1.187E+04	2077	607.6
Objects (1)						
Outbound Bits per Second (MIB2)	1	3756	110	1026	160.3	56.18
Objects (1)						

FIGURE 16.26 Interface Traffic Volume Report.

Availability Report

If you are interested in viewing availability history past 30 days for a specific device, you must generate a report. Use the built-in Availability Report in the Microsoft Generic Report Library; navigate to **Reporting -> Microsoft Generic Report Library** and double-click **Availability**.

Criteria required for this report are similar to the Interface Traffic Volume report discussed in the previous section, with the exception of Down Time criteria. This example uses the default Down Time criteria: Unplanned Maintenance.

The authors recommend changing the default aggregation to daily if you plan to generate historical reports spanning date ranges more than 30 days. The example in this section uses **daily** as the data aggregation. For the date range criteria, click the **From** drop-down box and select **Advanced**. Click on **no offset** and select **minus**. Provide a value for the number of days you want the report to display; in this example, **180 day(s)**; and click the green checkmark to save your selection.

To complete the report, you need to add objects. In this example, a network device is added to the report. Follow these steps:

1. Click on **Add Object**, click **Options**, and then click **Add**.
2. For your search criteria, enter **network device** and click **Search**. Click on **Network Device** in the list of available items. Click **Add** and **OK**.
3. With the filter applied, click **Search** on the Add object page to return a list of network devices. Select the network device you want to add to the Availability report and click **Add**.
4. Click **OK** to return to the main report parameters window, and then click **Run**.

Figure 16.27 illustrates availability of a particular network device over the past 180 days.

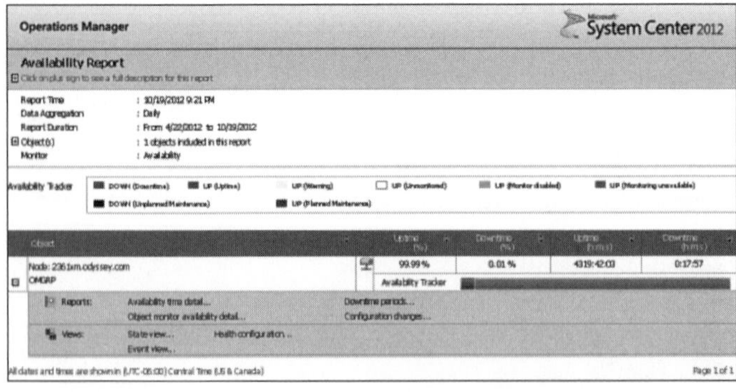

FIGURE 16.27 Network Device Availability Report.

The combination of the built-in network monitoring reports and generic reports provided by the Microsoft core libraries gives you the ability to understand availability and performance trends of your network devices.

Real World Scenarios

Similar to monitoring any service or application, you may run into issues while discovering and monitoring network devices. Several methods and tools are available for troubleshooting workflows in OpsMgr 2012. The following sections discuss some of the more common scenarios for troubleshooting issues with network monitoring as well as some considerations if you are migrating your network monitoring solution from OpsMgr 2007 R2.

Troubleshooting Network Discovery and Monitoring

In environments with complex network topologies, discovering network devices may require careful planning for everything to work as expected. Most problems with monitoring are in discovering the device; however, most troubleshooting steps related to monitoring issues are identical.

These next sections discuss some of the more common problems with network discovery and monitoring, and some options to help you solve them.

Network Discovery Views

OpsMgr 2012 has some built-in views that are a good starting point for troubleshooting discovery problems. These views are located under **Monitoring** -> **Operations Manager** -> **Network Discovery**. The data represented in these views are collected from the discovering management server(s) event log and performance counters. Here is a list of views to check if there are discovery issues, and how to interpret them:

- **Network Device Discovery Durations:** Check this view if you suspect discovery is taking too long. Typically, a discovery rule should not take longer than several minutes in an environment with less than 50 devices, and not longer than an hour in larger environments with more than 100-200 devices. If discovery duration is taking longer than expected or is unacceptable for a particular discovery rule, consider spreading the discovery load across more than one management server by creating another rule and filtering the devices accordingly. Remember not to discover the same device by more than one rule, and do not manage the same device in more than one resource pool.
- **Network Discovery Events:** This view contains summary data collected by the Network Discovery Events rule. Event ID 12008 is of particular interest, as it summarizes the entire discovery process. One element of this event is the Devices in pending list. This value will increment for each device that failed to be discovered for some reason, and these devices are added to **Administration** -> **Network Management** -> **Network Devices Pending Management**. Navigating to this view will offer more information as to why discovery failed for the device. After resolving the issue, you can submit rediscovery of the device here as well.

- **Network Device Progress Events:** This view contains detailed discovery progress events collected by the Detailed Network Discovery Events rule. The view includes the events that are contained in the Network Discovery Events view as well as several other event IDs related to the discovery process. Monitoring this view during an active discovery will yield detailed information about discovery attempts and progress for each device included in the discovery rule.
- **Network Discovery Server:** This is a state view of the management servers that have a network discovery rule defined. By opening the Health Explorer for any network discovery server that is not in a healthy state and selecting the **State Change Events** tab, you can see whether there are consistent issues with a particular rule. You should investigate any network discovery server that is persistently in an unhealthy state, as there may be some firewall rules blocking communication to some devices or issues with the management server itself.

Peripherals Not Discovered for Advanced Monitoring

One of the main reasons peripherals are not discovered is the device is not reachable via SNMP for some reason. If you are not sure a device is reachable via SNMP by the network discovery server, you can check this using various tools. One option is to use SNMPUtil.exe, which is included in the Windows 2000 Resource Kit and available for download with the online content included with this book.

With SNMPUtil.exe saved to the c:\Tools on your network discovery server, run the following command:

```
c:\Tools\snmputil.exe getnext <IP Address or FQDN> <community string> .1.3
```

Figure 16.28 indicates the device is reachable, whereas Figure 16.29 indicates the device is not reachable from the network discovery server.

FIGURE 16.28 Device is reachable via SNMP.

```
c:\tools>Snmputil.exe getnext 172.16.10.163 public .1.3
error on SnmpMgrRequest 40
```

FIGURE 16.29 Device not reachable via SNMP.

If the network discovery server can reach the device via SNMP, check whether the device should receive advanced monitoring. Peripherals are not discovered for devices that only receive standard monitoring. Here is one way to check the type of monitoring that will run on your device:

1. Log on to the network discovery server and open a command prompt.
2. Navigate to *%ProgramFiles%*\System Center 2012\Operations Manager\Server\NetworkMonitoring\conf\discovery.
3. Execute the following command, replacing the example OID with your device's OID:

   ```
   Findstr /I /S /C:1.3.6.1.4.1.9.1.469 /M *.*
   ```

   If an oid2type file is returned, advanced monitoring will run against your device.

You can also refer to Microsoft's documentation on network devices with extended monitoring capability, available for download at http://www.microsoft.com/en-us/download/details.aspx?displaylang=en&id=26831.

Additionally, check whether the device has instances in the Managed Computer Network Adapters Group or Relay Network Adapters Group.

Event Log Tracing

If a device is not being discovered as expected, you can employ native event trace logging (ETL) on the network discovery server that is having issues discovering devices. Perform the following steps to capture a verbose ETL trace of a network discovery rule:

1. Logon to the management server that runs the network discovery rule in question.
2. Open a command prompt and navigate to *%ProgramFiles%*\System Center 2012\Operations Manager\Server\Tools.
3. Type `StopTracing.cmd` and press **Enter**. Keep the command prompt open to this location for later steps.
4. Open the Operations console and navigate to **Administration** -> **Network Management** -> **Discovery Rules**. Right-click the discovery rule in question and select **Run**.
5. Quickly switch back to the command prompt, type `StartTracing.cmd VER`, ensuring VER is capitalized, and press **Enter**. Keep the command prompt open to this location for later steps.
6. Monitor the Network Device Progress Events view until the issue has been reproduced or discovery has completed. Quickly switch back to the command prompt.
7. Type `StopTracing.cmd` and press **Enter**.
8. Open Windows Explorer, navigate to *%windir%*\Logs\OpsMgrTrace, and delete all files contained in this folder except TracingGuidsNASM.etl. This step helps expedite processing when formatting the trace files, as you only want to process the network monitoring trace modules in this scenario.

9. Switch back to the command prompt, type `FormatTracing.cmd`, and press **Enter**.

10. Windows Explorer opens to the folder of the formatted ETL file upon completion. Open the TracingGuidsNASM.txt file and search for any errors or failures that occurred during the discovery. Usually you can search for **warning**, or the IP Address or FQDN of the device that is failing to discover to get more information around the issue.

Additional Considerations

Consider the following situations while planning your network monitoring solution with OpsMgr 2012. These should also be checked if discovery or monitoring is failing:

- **Device is not reachable via ICMP:** If using ICMP as part of your discovery mode, the discovery will stop if the network discovery server cannot reach the device via ICMP.
- **Using FQDN for your seed device:** Verify you can ping the device FQDN. If the name cannot resolve, ensure there is a DNS entry for the device or use the IP Address of the device in your discovery.
- **Non-standard SNMP ports:** If non-standard ports are used on devices in a recursive discovery, ensure a connected seed device is using the non-standard port; otherwise discovery will fail for those devices included in a recursive discovery.
- **Device uses IPv6:** OpsMgr 2012 cannot discover devices specified in an explicit discovery, or seed devices defined in a recursive discovery. Devices using IPv6 can only be recursively discovered.
- **Network discovery server uses IPv6 only:** OpsMgr 2012 does not currently support discovering network devices from a server using IPv6.
- **IP address not in Address Resolution Protocol (ARP) cache:** Recursive discovery uses information stored in the seed (or previously discovered) device's ARP cache. If a device expected to be recursively discovered does not have an IP address in a connected and previously discovered device's ARP cache, recursive discovery may not succeed.

OpsMgr 2007 R2 Migration Considerations

OpsMgr 2012 incorporates a change to the base class for network devices that is incompatible with any custom OpsMgr 2007 R2 network monitoring management packs. This requires additional planning when migrating your custom network monitoring management packs from OpsMgr 2007 R2, whether it be an in-place upgrade of your existing OpsMgr 2007 R2 management group or a migration to a new OpsMgr 2012 management group. In either scenario, you must rewrite your existing network monitoring management packs if you want to discover and monitor new devices. In a management group upgrade scenario, your custom management packs are backward compatible and monitoring remains intact for previously discovered devices.

Microsoft has deprecated the `Microsoft.SystemCenter.NetworkDevice` network devices class in OpsMgr 2012. Any custom workflows using this base class will need to be updated to the new OpsMgr 2012 base class, `System.NetworkManagement.Node`, which can be referenced in the new System.NetworkManagement.Library management pack. However, in upgrade scenarios where the management pack was not updated with the new class, you can view previously discovered inventory in the Operations console under **Monitoring -> Discovered Inventory** and changing target type to **Legacy SNMP Network Device**.

Here are the major reasons why this base class was changed:

- **Support for SNMP v3:** Community string has been changed from a property in the old class to a Run As account type in the new class. This enables an administrator to specify or update the Run As account in a discovery rule to an SNMP v1 or v2 community string or an SNMP v3 type with advanced security features.
- **Multi-instance support for ports and interfaces:** OpsMgr 2007 R2 uses an IP address of the device as a key property, which will not work in OpsMgr 2012 for advanced monitoring of ports and interfaces. To support multiple instances for each port or interface, the new class uses the MAC address of the SNMP management interface as the key property. This enables multi-instance support, which translates to advanced monitoring of ports and interfaces.

NOTE: HISTORICAL DATA AFTER UPDATING TO NEW BASE CLASS

After updating your custom network monitoring management pack with the new base class and importing into OpsMgr 2012, any historical data collected from those devices will be disjoined in your reports. This is because the rediscovered instances will actually be considered new instances in OpsMgr. Remember to select the correct legacy instance if you require reports ranging from before the updated management pack was imported.

The network monitoring SNMP stack is also rewritten in OpsMgr 2012. There are advantages to using the new modules, but it is not a requirement to update your workflows to utilize the new modules for your management pack to work. These modules are backward compatible; discovery and monitoring of new devices continues to work.

The following list highlights some advantages to updating your workflows to the new modules:

- **Discovery Module**
  - Supports non-standard ports
  - Supports SNMP v3
- **Condition Detection Module:** Variable Bindings (SnmpVarBind) can be specified by OID, rather than an indexed value.
- **Data Source Module:** Implements a condition detection with a performance mapper for simplified performance collection workflows.

Here is a list of new modules in the Network Management Library management pack you can leverage to streamline your network monitoring authoring experience:

- SnmpProbe
- SnmpDataSource
- SnmpEventDataSource
- SnmpPerformanceDataSource
- SnmpTrapProvider
- SnmpTrapEventProvider
- SnmpProbe.2SingleEvent2StateMonitorType
- SnmpProbe.SingleEventManualReset2StateMonitorType
- SnmpProbe.SingleEventTimer2StateMonitorType
- SnmpTrapProvider.2SingleEvent2StateMonitorType
- SnmpTrapProvider.SingleEventManualReset2StateMonitorType
- SnmpTrapProvider.SingleEventTimer2StateMonitorType

Here is a list of new monitor types in the Network Management Library management pack:

- HealthStateSNMPMonitorType
- ThresholdMonitor

These changes in OpsMgr 2012 make it possible to deliver advanced network monitoring of your network devices. They also enable organizations to identify network related issues more effectively, and lend themselves to a more efficient management pack authoring experience.

Fast Track

For those of you who are OpsMgr 2007 administrators, here are the key differences and advantages of moving to OpsMgr 2012 for your network monitoring solution:

- **Support for SNMP v3:** Changes to the network device base class enable the use of Run As account types, which is key to supporting the different type of Run As account necessary to support SNMP v3 devices.
- **Extended monitoring:** Discovery of ports, interfaces, and peripherals allows for a more detailed monitoring experience.

- **Port stitching:** Troubleshooting service or application outages that are related to the network layer can be easily and quickly assessed by launching the Network Vicinity Dashboard by clicking on any instances hosted by a Windows Computer object.
- **Supported devices:** Many devices have extended monitoring supported out of the box.

Summary

This chapter discussed the new features available for network monitoring in OpsMgr 2012, including support of SNMP v3 devices, port stitching to enable visibility of network related outages associated to service or application health, and differences between standard and extended monitoring features. It also included information about the SNMP protocol by describing MIBs and OIDs, and discussed how the SNMP protocol communicates over the network. Finally, the chapter discussed details of the stages of discovery, as well as how to troubleshoot discovery and monitoring issues.

CHAPTER 17

Using Synthetic Transactions

IN THIS CHAPTER

System Center Operations Manager (OpsMgr) 2012 can monitor Windows events, services, and performance thresholds, in addition to providing availability monitoring for servers, components, and distributed applications, capabilities that were covered in Chapter 14, "Monitoring with System Center 2012 Operations Manager." This detailed level of monitoring enables OpsMgr to facilitate alerting and reporting the availability status and health of servers and applications. However, just because an application has not generated errors does not necessarily mean it is working properly. The application could be running slowly or simply not responding to user requests, but without errors, one may have an artificial level of comfort regarding the application's health. Often, these types of problems are undetected until someone accesses the application and compares their experience against the results that are expected.

This chapter introduces synthetic transactions, which you can use to simulate that user experience. It looks at the different types of synthetic transactions provided in Operations Manager 2012 and the process for creating synthetic transactions.

Introducing Synthetic Transactions

Synthetic transactions, provided with OpsMgr 2012, allow you to configure and simulate a connection into an application. You run these actions in real time, against monitored objects. You can use synthetic transactions to measure the performance of a monitored object and to see how the object reacts when (synthetic) stress is placed on it. You create synthetic transactions by recording a website or by manually creating requests. Using synthetic transactions means that in addition to monitoring an application or server to ensure that it is online and working correctly, you can simulate a connection or log in to an application to validate it is actually responding to user requests. This additional aspect of monitoring helps to proactively identify potential issues with an application, typically long before an issue is identified using traditional methods such as Windows events or seeing services fail.

Synthetic transactions are particularly useful in monitoring high availability (HA) architectures, where a single or multiple components can be taken offline without the overall service being significantly affected. When monitoring HA configurations, you can use synthetic transactions to augment the service level agreement (SLA) and availability data gathered from OpsMgr for the components by actually monitoring to ensure the system is responding as expected, regardless of the status of individual components.

As an example, consider a large web farm where multiple servers can fail before users are affected; OpsMgr may show the failure of servers, and this will affect the SLA data for the farm. In reality, the servers being down do not adversely affect the farm. Configuring a synthetic transaction to monitor the websites hosted by the farm is a way to validate the availability of the farm and the websites it hosts as a whole, rather than as individual servers. If a server is offline, SLA information for this server will show a failure, but the synthetic transaction SLA that is testing the website still shows as healthy, providing more accurate availability information.

Synthetic transactions can monitor response times as well as monitoring to ensure something is online. This means you are not limited to validating that an application or website is responding; you can also track and alert against response time. This capability allows you to monitor the end user experience, as you are able to trend the response time of an application from an agent-managed end user system.

You can also configure synthetic transactions to monitor specific components of an application (especially web applications); this allows you to pinpoint problems to a specific subcomponent. As an example, you can configure a web application synthetic transaction to monitor the login process to a web-based system and the process for creating a record in the system, separately from one another. This means that should the login succeed but creating the record fail, you can identify this and take appropriate troubleshooting steps based on the subcomponent generating the errors.

Synthetic transactions utilize the OpsMgr class-based architecture; you are able to target and use these transactions just like a server object or role. When you create a distributed application, you can add the synthetic transaction as an object in that distributed application. From a monitoring and reporting perspective, this capability allows the synthetic transaction to affect the status of the distributed application, with any failure of the transaction then reflected in availability reporting. (Chapter 18, "Distributed Applications," discusses distributed applications in greater depth.)

Management Pack Templates

Before focusing specifically on the synthetic transactions that are part of Operations Manager, it is useful to be aware of the different management pack templates available in Operations Manager 2012. A management pack template refers to the object in the Operations console used to create the necessary rules, monitors, and so on. OpsMgr 2012 includes a number of management pack templates. Here are the management pack templates that do not perform synthetic transactions; those performing synthetic transactions are discussed next in the "Predicting Behavior by Simulation" section:

- **.NET Application Performance Monitoring:** This template was added as part of the integration of application program monitoring (APM) functionality into OpsMgr 2012's built-in management packs. This template does not perform synthetic transactions; it provides functionality for monitoring ASP.NET and Windows Communication Foundation (WCF) applications, including performance and exception events. The template is designed to work hand in hand with synthetic transactions to detect exceptions or performance issues from a server side and a client perspective.
- **Windows Azure Application:** This template is included with the Windows Azure Management Pack. The template is used to provide monitoring from Windows Azure applications using the Windows Azure APIs to allow Operations Manager to remotely discover and collect information for Azure applications. For more information on this template and the management pack, see Appendix A, "OpsMgr by Example: Configuring and Tuning Management Packs."
- **Power Consumption:** This template is added as part of the Power Management Pack. This template is used to define a collection of PDUs and computers running Windows Server 2008 R2 or 2012 that receive power from the PDU. For more information on this template, see http://technet.microsoft.com/en-us/library/ee808918.aspx.
- **Process Monitoring:** Process monitoring was added in Operations Manager 2007 R2 and is part of OpsMgr 2012's built-in functionality. This template monitors processes and alerts based on whether a process is running and if the process exceeds performance counters for memory or CPU utilization.
- **UNIX/Linux Log File Monitoring:** UNIX/Linux monitoring was added in Operations Manager 2007 R2 and is part of OpsMgr 2012's built-in functionality. This template monitors UNIX/Linux log files for specific entries. For more information on UNIX/Linux monitoring, see Chapter 20, "Interoperability and Cross Platform."
- **UNIX/Linux Process Monitoring:** This template monitors processes on UNIX/Linux systems.
- **UNIX/Linux Service:** This template monitors UNIX/Linux services. This template was later replaced by the UNIX/Linux process monitoring template, but this template is still available in Operations Manager.

17

- **Windows Service:** The Windows Service template generates monitors and rules that verify availability of a Windows service. The template is configured by specifying a service name and targeted group and whether the services should only be monitored if the service is set to automatic (default). Alerts can be raised if the CPU or memory exceeds thresholds specified when creating the monitor.

Predicting Behavior by Simulation

The most reliable way to ensure an application or server is working is to log in to it, perform a typical process, and observe the results. If the results are what were expected, chances are the application or server is working correctly. If not, those results often indicate where the problem is located, or at least provide a starting point for troubleshooting the problem. OpsMgr's capability to simulate a transaction and mimic the user experience makes it quite valuable.

The term *synthetic transaction* generally refers to any transaction that simulates user activity. OpsMgr provides the ability to monitor a number of different applications synthetically out of the box, and the capability is included in several of the key management packs available for download at Microsoft's System Center Marketplace (http://systemcenter.pinpoint.microsoft.com/). OpsMgr includes a number of management pack templates to create synthetic transactions, and the authors anticipate additional templates will continue to be added as Microsoft releases new management packs. The current templates that perform synthetic transactions include

- **Exchange 2007 Client Access Server Monitoring:** This template was added as part of the Exchange 2007 management pack and performs synthetic transactions by synthetically testing the client access servers in Exchange 2007.
- **Exchange 2007 Intra-Organization Mail Flow Monitoring:** This template with the Exchange 2007 management pack performs synthetic transactions by sending test email messages between Exchange 2007 servers you specify.
- **OLE DB Data Source:** This generates synthetic transactions that monitor database availability. Use this template to run a query from a specified watcher node, connecting via a connection string. The template validates the query executed in the specified amount of time. It does not provide the ability to perform actions or change the state of a monitor based upon the returned data (such as execute this query and if the results are more than 200 set a monitor to red, if less than 200 set the monitor to green). Details on this synthetic transaction are discussed in the "Using OLE DB to Monitor Databases" section.
- **TCP Port:** Generates synthetic transactions that monitor availability of a specified target and port. This template is extremely useful for checking the up/down status of devices that can only be validated by connecting to a specific port such as a black-box device, or providing up/down status for agents outside of the forest when a certificate infrastructure is unavailable. The template also reports on response time, useful for providing up/down monitoring for devices connected across WAN links.

Information on this synthetic transaction is found in the "Monitoring Network Devices Through Port Activity" section.

- **Web Application Availability Monitoring:** This template was added in Operations Manager 2012 to monitor availability of websites. You can add individual websites or you paste in a large number of URLs from a comma-separated values (CSV) file. One of the benefits of this template over the Web Application Transaction Monitoring template is you can specify either agents or a resource pool as a watcher node. Details on this synthetic transaction are discussed in the "Creating a Web Application Availability Synthetic Transaction" section.
- **Web Application Transaction Monitoring:** Known in OpsMgr 2007 as the Web Application template, this template provides monitoring for web applications, which you can record using the web application recorder. These synthetic transactions are executed from watcher nodes that you specify. Information on this synthetic transaction is found in the "Creating a Web Application Synthetic Transaction" section.

You could also create a custom script (such as VBScript or PowerShell) to perform synthetic monitoring of a particular application and launch the script using a rule or monitor. This is useful when monitoring proprietary applications that you may not be able to monitor using those management pack templates available out of the box. An example of this would be creating a script to send a SOAP message to a SOAP-enabled application and validating the response. You could configure this workflow to generate an alert as required.

The management pack templates are a set of wizards that walk you through the steps to create all the necessary rules, monitors, classes, and so on, to carry out a simulated connection to the monitored object. Using the templates makes configuring these synthetic transactions very simple and straightforward, without manually needing to create large numbers of rules or monitors to achieve the same results.

The following sections discuss the processes to create the different synthetic transactions using the management pack template wizards.

Watcher Nodes

When simulating connections to an application, you want to do more than ensure the connection is accurate and reflective of what users would do. You will want to initiate the connection from different locations, as this also simulates the user experience. You should initiate the connection from a server close to what you are connecting to, in addition to initiating the connection from a computer in the same location(s) as the users that are making the connections. You can then compare the results from each location to see whether the user experience is the same.

The agents performing synthetic transactions are known as *watcher nodes*. These watcher nodes actually perform the actions of a synthetic transaction, such as connecting to a website or querying the specified database. Placing these watcher nodes where the users are located is particularly important when those servers hosting the applications are located in geographically remote locations from the users, which often is the case with Information Technology (IT) systems.

Configure the watcher nodes (the client computers designated to run these transactions) as part of creating a synthetic transaction. Watcher nodes allow you to specify the computer(s) that will launch the simulation. The only prerequisite is that the computer you want to run the simulation from has an installed OpsMgr agent. The computer could be running a Windows server or client operating system and can be located anywhere, provided it can communicate with the OpsMgr environment and the application it is configured to "watch."

The information collected from one or more watcher nodes can assist in locating the source of a problem. As an example, say you have configured two watcher nodes, with one on the same network segment as the server you are connecting to and one located elsewhere on the client network. If your (remote) client network watcher fails to connect and your (local) client network watcher successfully connects, this would indicate a network problem because the application is still responding, yet the client network is not able to connect. This scenario is illustrated in Figure 17.1.

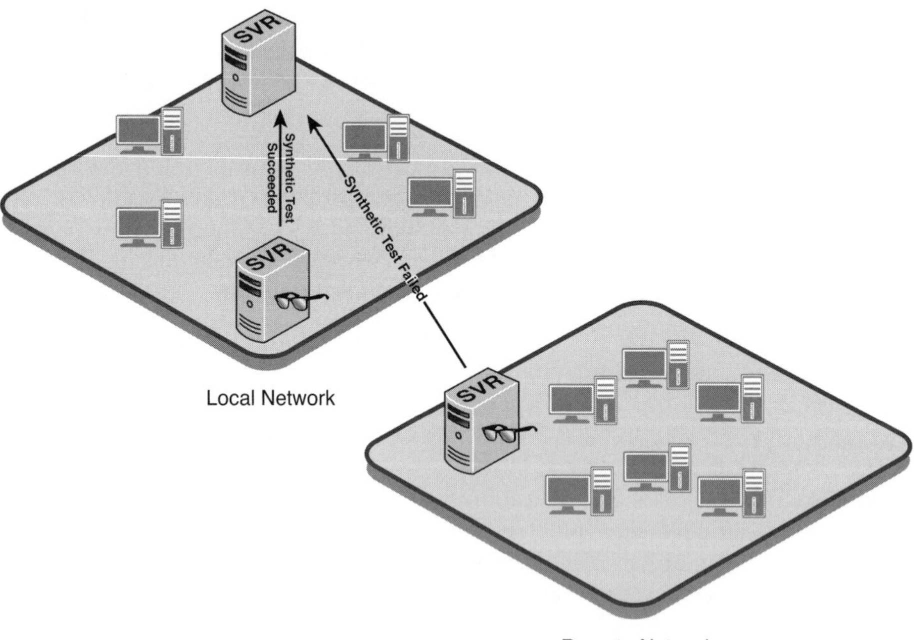

FIGURE 17.1 Remote watcher node failed.

As Figure 17.1 shows, using watcher nodes properly can help to not only detect when an application is failing, but can also be used to assist in locating the source of other problems—such as network connectivity problems when the application itself is responding correctly.

An additional way to use synthetic transactions is by using Operations Manager to assist with monitoring those network device types not supported with the out of the box network monitoring functionality in OpsMgr 2012. You can use these transactions to highlight potential network problems, and to simulate connections to network devices. You can connect to network devices using the TCP port monitor monitoring template discussed in the "Monitoring Network Devices Through Port Activity" section. You can monitor other issues external to the application with any type of synthetic transaction, as physical connectivity is always required from the client to the server, regardless of the connection type.

Using OpsMgr 2012's capability to monitor network devices means the location of network-related problems can also be determined and resolved. For additional information on network device monitoring in OpsMgr, see Chapter 16, "Network Monitoring."

TIP: WATCHER NODES AND RESOURCE POOLS

OpsMgr 2012 supports using a resource pool for Web Application Availability Monitoring (discussed in the "Creating a Web Application Availability Synthetic Transaction" section). To provide a highly available watcher node, create a resource pool with multiple management servers in a location and use the resource pool as the watcher location. Creating a resource pool with management servers in the same location removes network connectivity from consideration while providing redundancy for the web application availability monitoring. Other synthetic transactions types such as Web Application Transaction Monitoring and TCP Port Monitoring cannot use resource pools as watcher nodes.

Monitoring Web Applications

It is assumed that any company will have a website, and that the Internet is a core requirement for most companies to function. Companies use websites to display and share information within their company as well as externally. The use of Internet and web technologies brings with it a requirement to monitor these technologies, ensuring they are working correctly and within required parameters. Out of the box, OpsMgr monitors not only the core technologies behind the Internet, that being the Internet Information Services (IIS) application and services and Apache Tomcat, but also allows you to configure synthetic transactions to simulate a connection to a website. Using synthetic transactions offers an additional level of monitoring by alerting you to errors in the web application and simulating user access to the site. These transactions let you validate that the site loads correctly, displays as expected, and loads within an acceptable amount of time.

The level of monitoring provided by the Web Application Monitor in OpsMgr goes beyond loading a page and validating that the page loads correctly and does not produce any errors. The monitor also allows you to configure navigating through different pages within the website and provides the ability to input information into the web pages. For instance, you may browse a site, navigate to the search page, input search terms, and use the results to validate the website is working correctly. This capability is particularly useful for identifying issues that affect the website but are not linked directly to the site itself.

As an example, consider a website with a backend database that contains data you can search against. Although the page may display correctly, an error may be generated if the database is offline when running a search. Using the Web Application Transaction Monitoring template allows you to detect this condition.

You can also utilize the Web Application Transaction Monitoring template to collect performance data from the website, including DNS response time and total response time. The level of performance data you can collect is very impressive; Figure 17.2 shows an example of the counters you can collect using an application created with the template using the new dashboard functionality in OpsMgr 2012. The health state for web application transaction monitors is available under Monitoring -> Web Application Transaction Monitoring -> Web Application State view. From this view, you can pivot to the performance view to see the performance counters associated with the web application transaction.

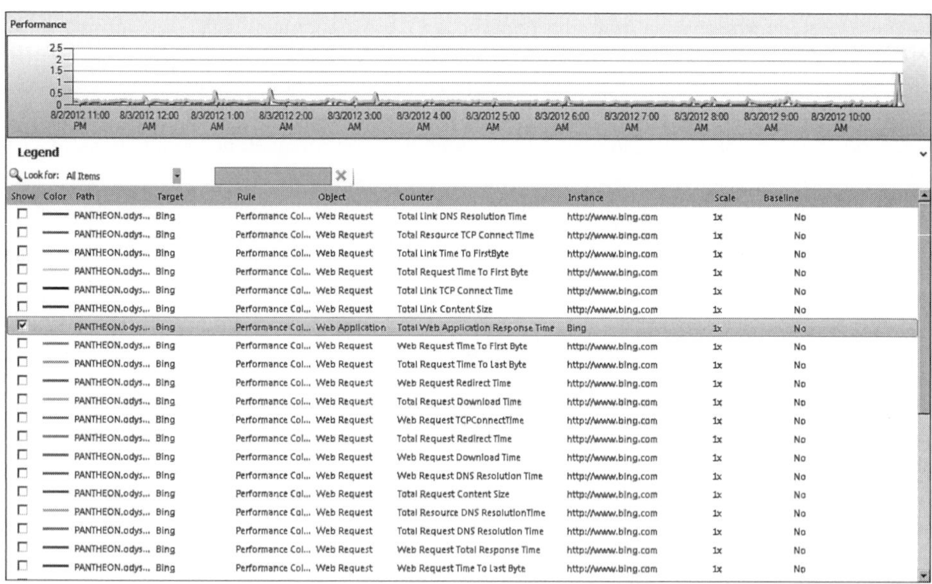

FIGURE 17.2 Website performance counters.

As Figure 17.2 illustrates, a large number of counters can be collected. After collecting the information, you can display it in a performance graph in the Monitoring space in the Operations console, or perhaps generate a report to show the trend in website performance over time.

Creating a Web Application Synthetic Transaction

This section looks at the process to monitor a web application using the Web Application Transaction Monitoring template. Configuring a web application synthetic transaction is quite straightforward; a wizard allows you to configure basic monitoring, and OpsMgr includes a Web Application Designer that allows you to configure advanced settings such as login information for the website. The designer also makes it easy to configure the website for monitoring, providing a web recorder you can use to record the synthetic transaction you will create using Internet Explorer.

Follow these steps to create a web application synthetic transaction:

1. Launch the Operations console and navigate to the Authoring space.
2. Right-click the **Management Pack Templates** subtree and select **Add Monitoring Wizard**, as shown in Figure 17.3.

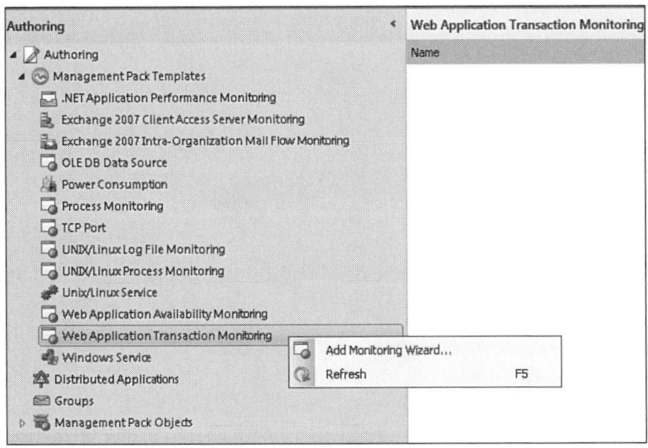

FIGURE 17.3 The Add Monitoring Wizard.

3. The wizard displays the dialog shown in Figure 17.4. From this page, select **Web Application Transaction Monitoring** as the monitoring type, and then click **Next**.
4. On the following page, input the name and a description for the synthetic transaction, and select the management pack in which to create the transaction rules. For this example call the transaction **Bing** and select the Sample management pack used elsewhere in this book or another one you have already created. Click **Next** to continue.
5. The next page is the Enter and Test Web Address page. Enter the basic URL you wish to monitor. For this example enter **www.bing.com** (although, as you will see later in this process, the information you enter here is irrelevant as you can change it using the Web Application Editor in the "Configuring Advanced Monitoring for a Website" section). After entering the URL, click the **Test** button to validate you can contact that URL. Figure 17.5 displays this completed page. Click **Next**.

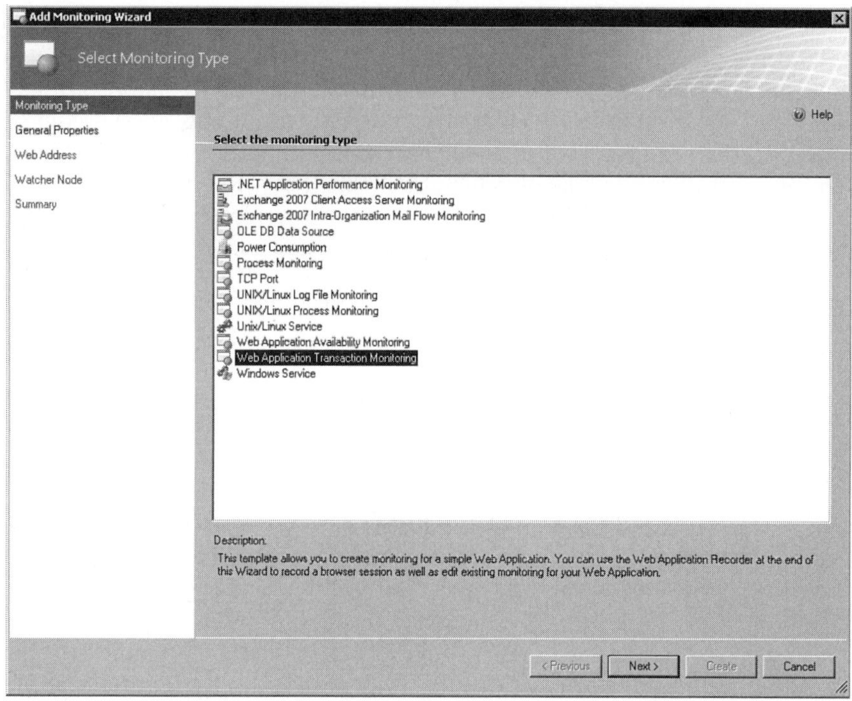

FIGURE 17.4 Select Web Application Transaction Monitoring as the monitoring type.

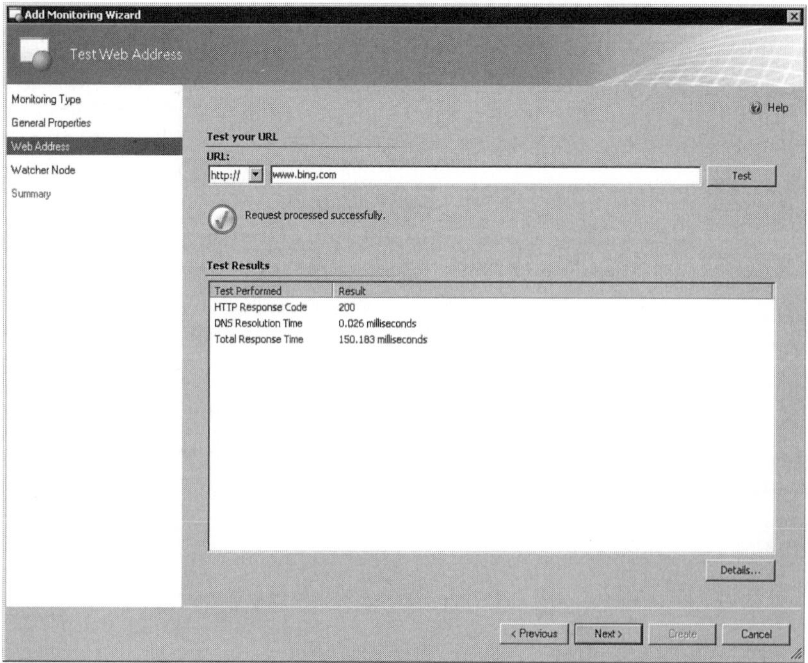

FIGURE 17.5 Test Web Address page in the Add Monitoring Wizard.

6. The next page configures the watcher nodes, where you will identify and configure the computer initiating the test. The page lists all machines running OpsMgr Windows agents, management servers, and gateways; tick the check boxes to carry out the test on the machines you choose. For this example, run the test from **PANTHEON.odyssey.com** and configure the test to run with the default setting of **2** minutes. Figure 17.6 shows the completed Choose Watcher Nodes page. Click **Next** to continue.

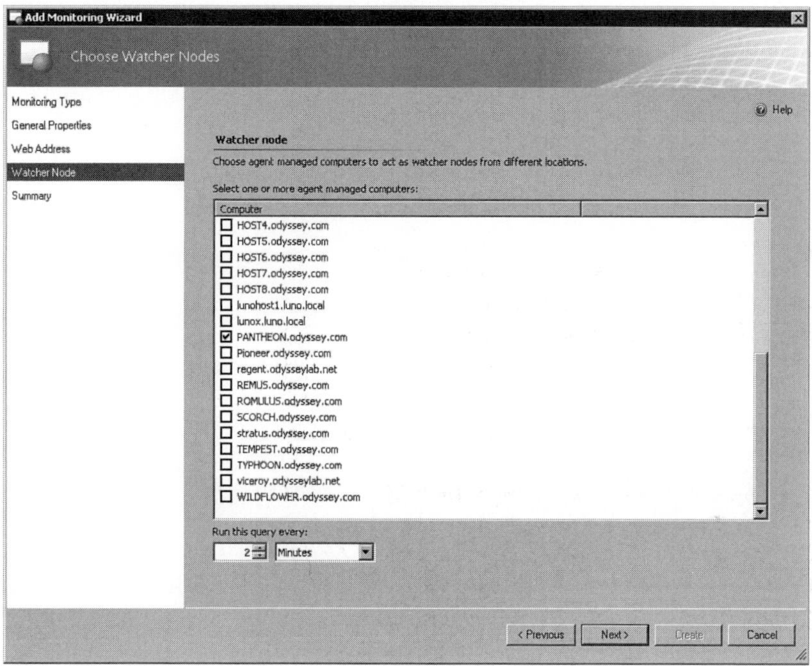

FIGURE 17.6 The Choose Watcher Nodes page in the Add Monitoring Wizard.

7. The final page displays a summary of the information you have specified throughout the wizard. The page also allows you to **Configure Advanced Monitoring or Record a browser session**. If you do not check this option, the wizard completes and the web application synthetic transaction is saved to the previously specified management pack.

   For this example, the next step is to configure more advanced monitoring of the website, so check the **Configure Advanced Monitoring or Record a browser session** check box at the bottom of the page.

The next section covers the steps for advanced website monitoring.

Configuring Advanced Monitoring for a Website

After using the Add Monitoring Wizard, you can configure advanced monitoring of a website or web application. Follow these steps:

1. When you click **Create** in the Add Monitoring Wizard with the **Configure Advanced Monitoring** option checked, the wizard closes and the Web Application Editor opens, as shown in Figure 17.7.

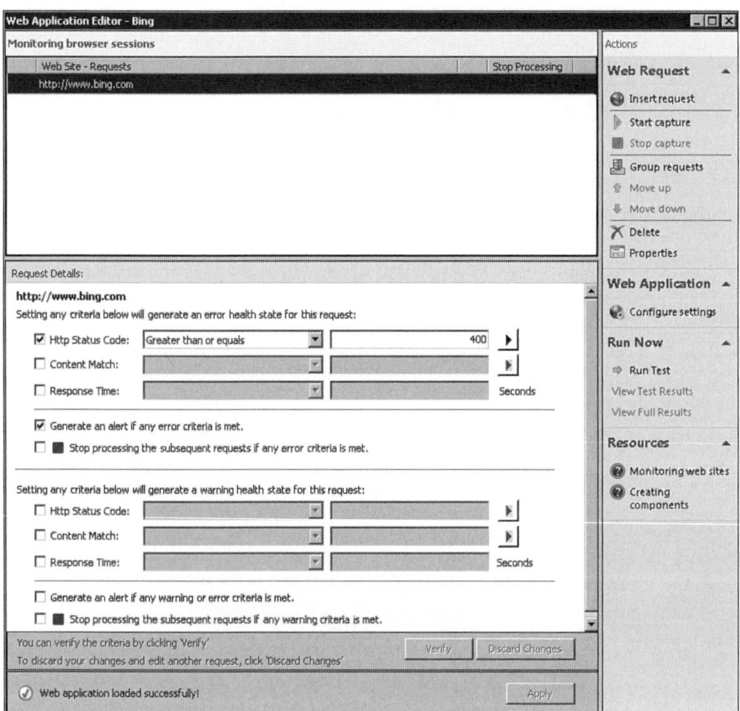

FIGURE 17.7 The Web Application Editor.

2. Using the Web Application Editor, the next step is to record a web session and look at the additional options available when creating a web application synthetic transaction. Begin by deleting any web addresses present in the editor in preparation for recording a web session. Select the website configured in the wizard in the previous section and click the **Delete** option on the right-hand side in the Actions pane under the Web Request section. Click **OK** when prompted.

3. Click the **Start Capture** button. This opens an Internet Explorer browser window with a Web Recorder pane on the left-hand side, displayed in Figure 17.8.

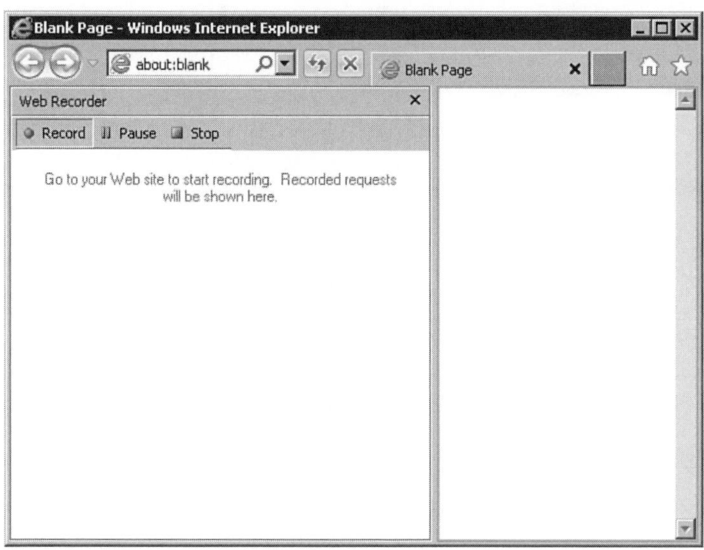

FIGURE 17.8 Starting a website capture session.

TIP: USING THE WEB RECORDER

When using the web recorder, the authors recommend performing the recording from an administrator's workstation rather than a management server. There are several configurations that need to be addressed to configure the recorder to work properly, including

- **Using the recorder with 64-bit systems:** Michael Kamp discusses the registry setting changes required to make Internet Explorer launch the 64-bit version at http://social.technet.microsoft.com/wiki/contents/articles/1307.scom-howto-use-the-webrecorder-on-windows-64bit.aspx.
- **UAC challenges, 3rd party browser extensions, IE enhanced security:** Kevin Holman discusses these topics at http://blogs.technet.com/b/kevinholman/archive/2009/06/19/web-application-recorder-r2-the-recorder-bar-missing-in-ie.aspx.
- **Recorder bar missing:** Kevin Holman discusses this topic at http://blogs.technet.com/b/kevinholman/archive/2008/11/15/recording-a-web-application-browser-session-driving-you-crazy.aspx.

Once the web recorder is working, it does a good job of recording websites that are browsed to (both http and https sites), which makes this a very useful feature to have when creating synthetic web transactions.

4. With the editor cleared, record a web session while browsing a number of pages on Bing, entering a search term, browsing to a website, and browsing to an https (SSL) site. This process demonstrates OpsMgr's capability to simulate various browser steps and record them as shown in Figure 17.9. For this example, browse to Bing (www.bing.com) and perform a search. From the search results browse to a resulting wiki page and from there open an https site.

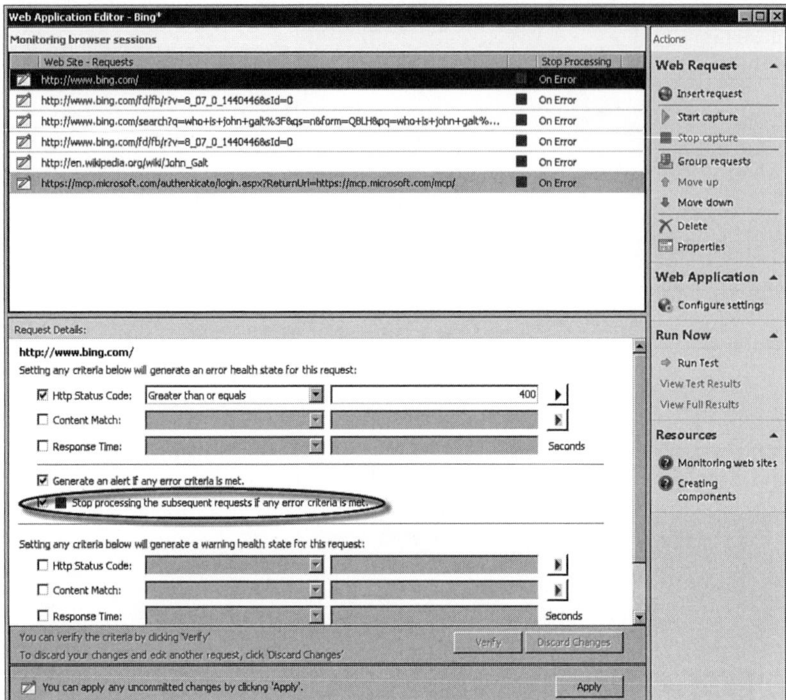

FIGURE 17.9 Recorded pages including browsing SSL sites.

5. After you complete recording the web session, click the **Stop** button in the Web Recorder pane. This closes Internet Explorer, bringing you back to the editor with the web addresses displayed in the console.

6. The next step is to configure the performance counters for this web application monitor. Click the **Configure Settings** link, which opens the Web Application Properties page, and open the Performance Counter tab shown in Figure 17.10.

7. From this tab, you can configure a number of options that affect the entire web application, including performance counters to collect, and any logon information required to access the website (logon information is specified using Run As accounts, explained in Chapter 10, "Security and Compliance"). You can also add or remove watcher nodes from this page.

   Using the Performance Criteria tab, you can also configure additional alerts to generate when the total response time for the entire website takes longer than an amount of time you specify.

8. For this example, four additional performance counters will be added that are not collected by default. On the Performance Counter tab, check the check box next to the following counters:

- Total: DNS Resolution Time
- Total: Time To First Byte
- Total: Time To Last Byte
- Total: Total Response Time

9. Click **OK** to save the options and close the options page.

   This example configured performance counters for an entire web application. Note that a large number of the options configured globally are also available to each individual website. You can also configure extra options such as custom conditions for generating alerts. Figure 17.10 shows the options configured.

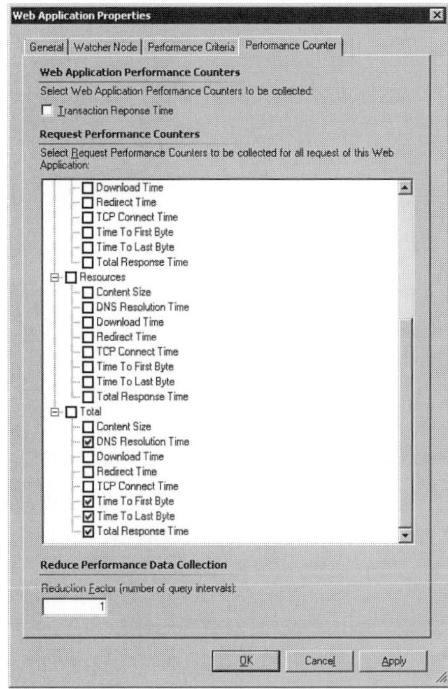

FIGURE 17.10 Performance Counter tab for configuring Web Application Properties.

10. The last configuration required will limit the number of alerts generated in the event of a failure. Although this option is not required, the authors recommend using this functionality to prevent an alert storm. To prevent the transactions continuing to process when the previous transaction fails (and limit the number of alerts generated), select all web addresses in the editor, and select the **Stop processing the subsequent requests if any error criteria is met** check box, circled in Figure 17.9.

TIP: ADDITIONAL OPTIONS FOR INDIVIDUAL ADDRESSES

When you select individual web addresses from the Web Application Editor, you can select Properties to configure additional options that are not available when configuring the options globally.

Properties for individual web addresses include custom HTTP header information and additional monitoring settings; you can also configure additional performance counters to collect for individual web addresses. This chapter does not document these individual settings in any detail as they are beyond the scope of the example that is discussed.

11. After selecting the **Stop processing the subsequent requests if any error criteria is met** option, verify the settings you have applied. Click the **Verify** button, also displayed in Figure 17.9. This button is grayed out in Figure 17.9 but becomes available after changes are made to the synthetic transaction.
12. Finally, click the **Apply** button to save the settings. This creates all of the monitoring components automatically (this button is grayed out until you verify your criteria). You can then close the editor.

Configuring Advanced Monitoring for a Secure Website

You may want to monitor websites that require authentication. In this case, you can configure authentication options from the Web Application Editor using the following process:

1. Open the editor by navigating to the Authoring Pane and the Web Application subtree. From there, left-click the web application created in the "Creating a Web Application Synthetic Transaction" section. From the Actions pane, select **Edit web application settings** (or just double-click the web application transaction monitor you wish to edit). This reopens the Web Application Editor.
2. Click the **Configure settings** link on the right side of the page, which opens the Web Application Properties page.
3. Using the Authentication drop-down (in the middle of the page), select the Authentication Method for the website from the list shown in Figure 17.11.

TIP: SETTING THE AUTHENTICATION METHOD

The authentication method should match the type used by IIS for that website. If you are using another Internet technology such as Apache, you will want to match the authentication type with that application. For reference, with IIS, the NTLM (NT LAN Manager) authentication type is the same as Integrated Authentication.

4. After selecting the authentication method, you must specify a user account. This account needs to be created as a Run As account before you can use it. More information on creating Run As accounts is in Chapter 10.

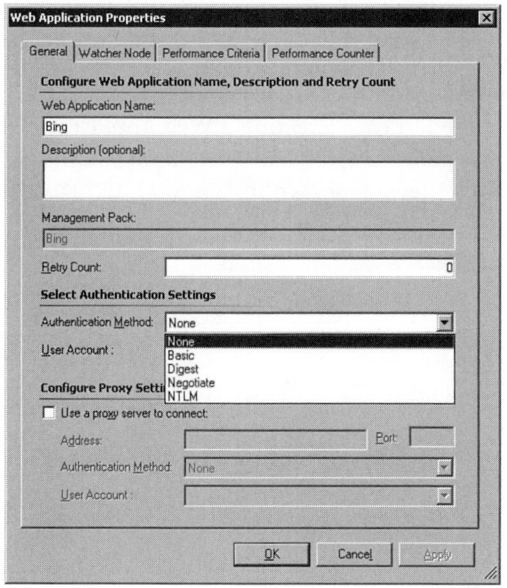

FIGURE 17.11 General tab for configuring Web Application Properties.

NOTE: TESTING THE CONNECTION

When you configure a website that requires authentication, you will not be able to test the connection from the Web Application Editor. If you attempt to test the settings, you are presented with this pop-up warning:

```
Running a test of this web application may fail. While running the test,
credentials that have been configured for this web application will not be used.
If the site you are testing does not explicitly require authentication, the test
may still succeed.
```

To test sites that are using authentication, use the monitor state and alerts generated in the Operations console.

Viewing the Website Performance Data

Now that there is a web application to monitor Bing, the performance counters specified for collection can be reviewed.

TIP: LEAVE TIME BEFORE VIEWING PERFORMANCE DATA

It can take some time to collect the performance data. The amount of time depends on the frequency of the specific test; the authors' recommendation is to wait at least an hour before viewing the data. This allows enough data to be collected to generate a report or performance view with sufficient performance data.

To view the performance counters, perform the following steps:

1. In the Operations console, navigate to **Monitoring** -> **Web Application Transaction Monitoring**, and right-click the **Web Application State** view. The right-hand pane will show the web application monitor created in the "Creating a Web Application Synthetic Transaction" section. Pivot to the performance view by right-clicking the object, then selecting **Open** -> **Performance View**, as shown in Figure 17.12.

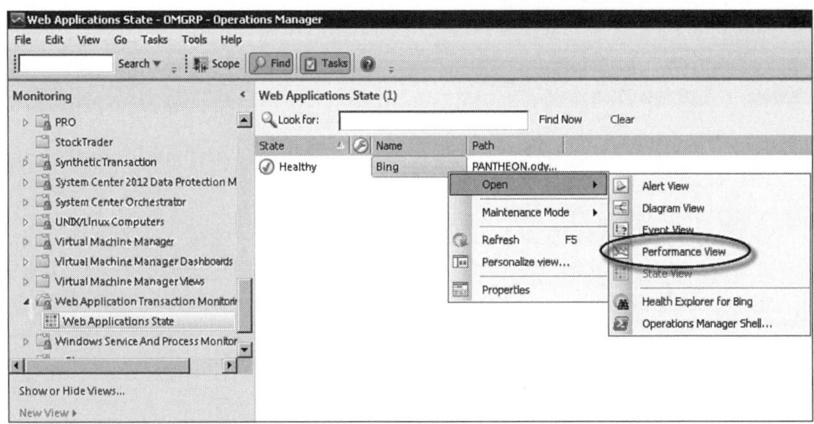

FIGURE 17.12 Opening the Performance View submenu.

2. You now see the performance view for the web application and can notice the available performance counters are the ones selected in the "Configuring Advanced Monitoring for a Website" section. To demonstrate the performance graph, select the four counters added to the web application in Figure 17.10, with the results displayed on the left side of Figure 17.13. You can also display these performance counters by creating a dashboard view and adding the performance widget (shown on the right side of Figure 17.13) or the objects by performance widget.

TIP: CREATING A DASHBOARD WITH PERFORMANCE VIEW DATA

Use the performance view to identify the path, object, counter, and instance required when adding the performance widget. Creating this view ahead of time makes it easier to determine what the appropriate information is when you are configuring the performance widget.

This section discussed the web application synthetic transaction and documented the procedures to create a web application synthetic transaction using the Web Application Transaction Monitoring template. It also discussed the Web Application Designer and the process for recording web sessions to enable advanced monitoring of websites and web applications. Finally, it covered the process for creating synthetic transactions to connect to sites that require authentication. In addition, the section highlighted the large amount of performance information you can collect with the web application synthetic transaction, and the steps to display the data using the performance view in the Operations console.

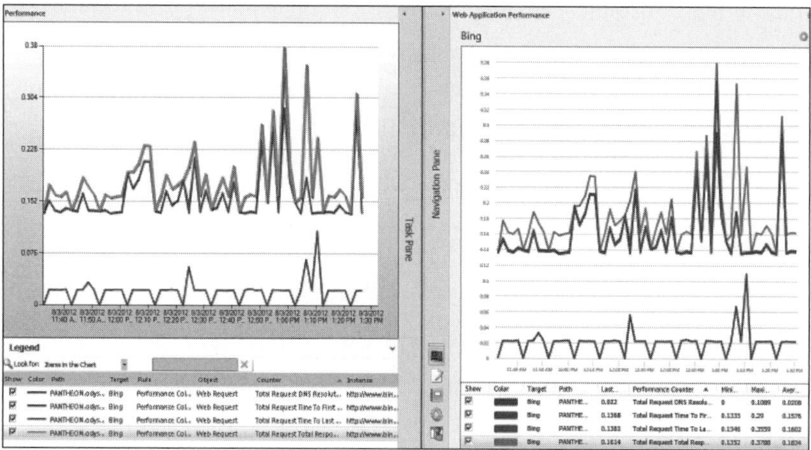

FIGURE 17.13 Viewing web application performance results.

Creating a Web Application Availability Synthetic Transaction

In addition to the Web Application Transaction Monitoring template, OpsMgr 2012 adds a Web Application Availability Monitoring template. This section focuses on the Web Application Transaction Monitoring template and its functionality compared to the Web Application Availability Monitoring template. Here are the major differences between these two templates:

- **Web Application Availability Monitoring:** You can add individual websites or paste in a large number of URLs from a CSV file. Additionally, you can specify either agents or a resource pool as a watcher node. This template does not include some of the advanced capabilities available in the Web Application Transaction Monitoring template such as recording a series of web pages.

NOTE: WEB APPLICATION AVAILABILITY MONITORING CHANGES IN SERVICE PACK 1

Web application availability monitoring in OpsMgr 2012 RTM provides the ability to execute synthetic tests from dispersed locations as long as those are Operations Manager agents within your OpsMgr environment. With the addition of the Global Service Monitoring (GSM) functionality in System Center 2012 Service Pack (SP) 1, web applications availability monitoring can perform synthetic tests for your websites from Microsoft Azure cloud locations around the world.

You can display the results in a dashboard map such as the summary dashboard map shown in Chapter 11, "Dashboards, Trending, and Forecasting." Availability monitoring is best used to provide insights into how well a website is performing across a set of testing locations that are geographically dispersed. This is the best choice when determining if a website is available.

- **Web Application Transaction Monitoring:** You can record web transactions and perform advanced configurations with the Web Application Availability Monitoring template (examples are in the "Creating a Web Application Synthetic Transaction" section). Transaction monitoring is best used to test internal website functionality and validate the website is functioning as expected. This is the best monitoring option when opening the website is insufficient as a test.

To create a web application availability monitor, perform the following steps:

1. Launch the Operations console and navigate to the Authoring space.
2. Right-click the **Management Pack Templates** subtree and select the **Add Monitoring Wizard** (shown previously in Figure 17.3).
3. The wizard displays the dialog shown previously in Figure 17.4. From this page, select **Web Application Availability Monitoring** as the monitoring type, and click **Next**.
4. On the following page, input the name and a description for the synthetic transaction, and select the management pack in which to create the transaction rules. For this example call the transaction **Bing** and select the Sample management pack used elsewhere in this book or another one you have created. Click **Next** to continue.
5. The next page is used to add URLs to monitor with this synthetic transaction. You can add bulk URLs by importing a CSV file in the format of Name, URL (include http:// or https:// as part of the URL). For this example, add a single URL named **Bing** with a URL value of **http://www.bing.com** as shown in Figure 17.14. Click **Next**.
6. The next page configures which resource pools or agents will function as watcher nodes for this synthetic transaction. Figure 17.15 shows an example where a resource pool and agents can both be configured as watcher nodes, and shows how systems locations are displayed if they have been defined in PowerShell (see Chapter 11 for details on this concept). Add the appropriate agents or resource pools and click **Next** to continue.

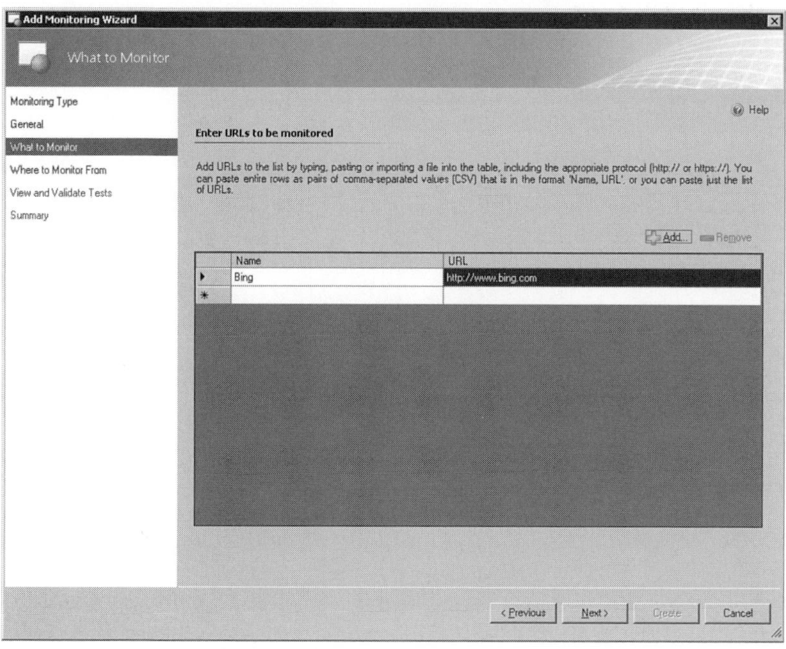

FIGURE 17.14 URLs to monitor in a web application availability synthetic transaction.

7. The next page provides an option to run a test or change the configuration for the tests. The default configuration is to run each of the tests identified (6 in the example shown in Figure 17.16) on a frequency of every 10 minutes.

8. The Run Test button shown in Figure 17.16 executes the synthetic transaction from the agent or resource pool that was highlighted. Results of the test are shown and can show data including the HTTP response and the raw data from the synthetic transaction.

9. The Web Application Availability Monitoring Change Configuration shown on the bottom of Figure 17.16 opens the Test Frequency/Performance Data Collection Interval page. A subset of the options available on this page is shown in Figure 17.17. The page provides a significant number of configurations you can customize for this synthetic transaction, listed in Table 17.1.

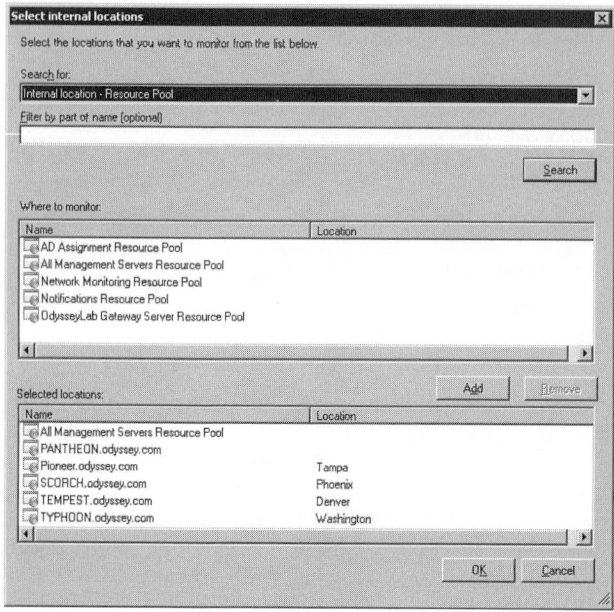

FIGURE 17.15 Configuring systems to monitor a web application availability synthetic transaction.

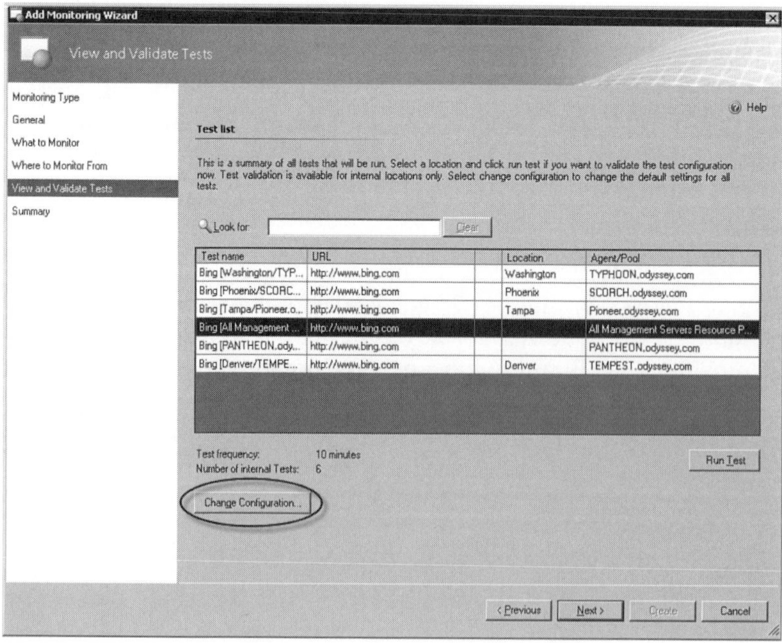

FIGURE 17.16 Configuring tests for a web application availability synthetic transaction.

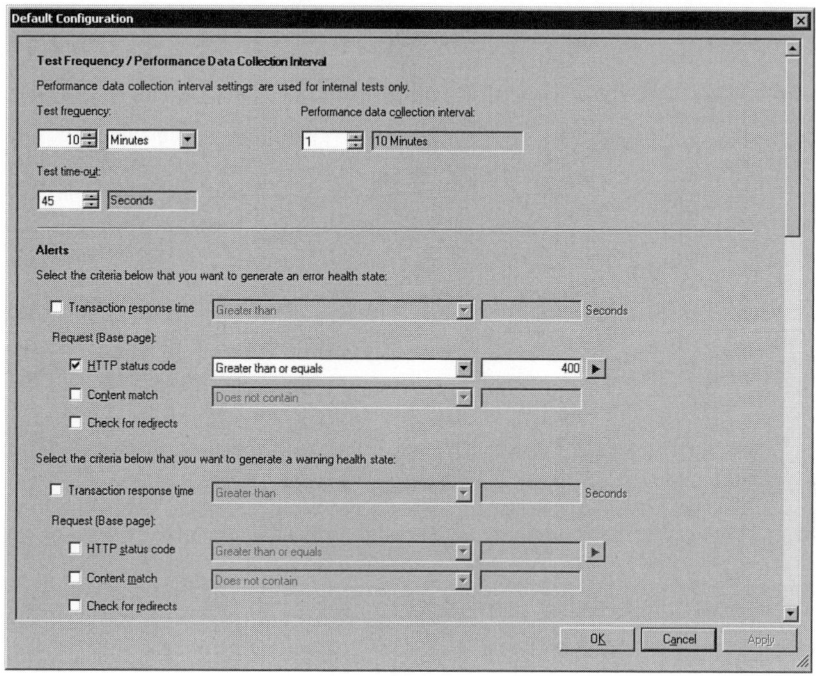

FIGURE 17.17 Testing a web application availability synthetic transaction.

TABLE 17.1 Web application availability monitoring configuration options

Configuration Type	Default Value	Notes
Test Frequency	10 minutes	Cannot be less than one minute. This option can be set in seconds, minutes, hours, or days.
Performance data collection interval	10 minutes	Cannot be less than one minute. This option matches the test frequency option for seconds, minutes, hours, or days.
Test Timeout	45 seconds	Acceptable values are from 1 second to 480 seconds.
Alerts: Transaction response time (error)	Disabled	Alert on conditions where the transaction matches the criteria defined (equals, does not equal, greater than, less than, greater than or equals, less than or equals) in seconds.
Alerts: Request (Base page) HTTP status code (error)	Enabled	Default is enabled for HTTP status codes that are greater than or equal to 400.

TABLE 17.1 Continued

Configuration Type	Default Value	Notes
Alerts: Request (Base page) Content match (error)	Disabled	Can be set to equals, does not equal, greater than, less than, greater than or equals, less than or equals, contains, matches wildcard, matches regular expression, does not contain, does not match wildcard, does not match regular expression and a text field value specified.
Alerts: Request (Base Page) Check for redirects (error)	Disabled	
Alerts: Transaction response time (warning)	Disabled	Same as the Alerts Transaction response time (error) but for the warning state.
Alerts: Request (Base page) HTTP status code (warning)	Disabled	Same as the Alerts Transaction response time (error) but for the warning state.
Alerts: Request (Base page) Content match (warning)	Disabled	Same as the Alerts Request (Base page) Content match (error) but for the warning state.
Alerts: Request (Base Page) Check for redirects (warning)	Disabled	Same as the Alerts Request (Base Page) Check for redirects (error) but for the warning state.
Alerts: Select the number of consecutive times a criteria should fail before an alert is generated	1	Acceptable values are from 1-20.
Alerts: Generate alerts from each test	Enabled	
Alerts: Generate a single summary alert	Disabled	
Performance Collection: Transaction response time	Enabled	
Performance Collection: Response time	Disabled	
Performance Collection: TCP connect time	Disabled	
Performance Collection: Time to first byte	Enabled	
Performance Collection: Time to last byte	Enabled	
Performance Collection: DNS resolution time	Enabled	
Performance Collection: Content size	Enabled	
Performance Collection: Content time	Enabled	

Configuration Type	Default Value	Notes
Performance Collection: Download time	Disabled	
General Configuration: Evaluate resource health	Disabled	
General Configuration: Allows redirects	Enabled	
General Configuration: HTTP version	Defaults to HTTP/1.1	Options also include HTTP/1.0.
General Configuration: HTTP method	GET	Other options include HEAD and POST.
HTTP Headers	Accept value */*, Accept-Language en-us, Accept-Encoding GZIP	
Proxy Server	Disabled	Can enable and provide an address and port number for the proxy.

10. The final page displays a summary of the information you have specified throughout the wizard. Click **Create** to finish this wizard and create the synthetic transaction.

NOTE: INTRODUCING GLOBAL SERVICE MONITORING IN SYSTEM CENTER 2012 (OPSMGR) SERVICE PACK 1

The Web Application Availability Monitoring template provides the foundation used to provide global service monitoring (GSM) with System Center 2012 SP 1. Hints of this direction for the product were available even before SP 1 released, as shown in Figure 17.15 from the RTM version. In this figure, the agents and resource pools are listed as "Internal," implying there would be an "External" option at a later time. GSM delivers the external view for web monitoring by providing an outside-in perspective on your synthetic web transactions. GSM allows you to use an Azure-based service to monitor your websites from geo-distributed locations around the world. For more information on GSM, see the Operations Manager team blog entry at http://blogs.technet.com/b/momteam/archive/2012/06/19/global-service-monitor-for-system-center-2012-observing-application-availability-from-an-outside-in-perspective.aspx.

The Web Application Availability Monitoring template extends Operations Manager 2012's capability to synthetically test websites and brings new functionality into the mix especially with the addition of GSM as part of Service Pack 1.

TIP: WHEN TO USE WEB APPLICATION AVAILABILITY VERSUS WEB APPLICATION TRANSACTION—IT'S ABOUT SCALABILITY

The greatest benefit of web application availability monitoring versus web application transaction monitoring is scalability. Scalability is gained from using resource pools to provide automatic workflow load balancing, and by achieving high availability without alert duplication. Additionally, the specialized design of the generated XML is far more efficient than the XML with web application transaction monitoring. The OpsMgr URL monitoring statistics and testing are based on web application availability monitoring, not web application transaction monitoring, which does not scale as well. If you are using a large number of URLs, the authors highly recommend using web application availability monitoring as a replacement for web application transaction monitoring. Web application availability is also the recommended replacement for the Bulk URL Editor in OpsMgr 2007 R2.

Using OLE DB to Monitor Databases

Operations Manager can monitor SQL Server databases, including availability, performance, and size monitoring. This is in addition to its capability for monitoring the SQL Server platform that hosts the databases. However, what about verifying the database is responding, or monitoring the databases that underpin your business critical application and are not hosted by SQL Server? This is where OLE DB synthetic transactions come in. The OLE DB (Object Linking and Embedding Database) management pack template allows you to create a synthetic connection to any database that supports OLE DB.

OLE DB is an application programming interface (API) designed by Microsoft for accessing different types of data stores in a uniform manner. It is implemented using the Component Object Model (COM) and was designed as a replacement for ODBC (Open Database Connectivity). OLE DB enables supporting connections to a much wider range of non-relational databases than possible with ODBC, such as object databases and spreadsheets that do not necessarily implement SQL technology or Microsoft SQL Server. This support for non-Microsoft SQL Server databases using OLE DB makes the management pack template in OpsMgr much more powerful, enabling it to monitor databases accurately hosted in other non-Microsoft SQL enterprise database systems such as Oracle.

Creating an OLE DB Synthetic Transaction

Here are the steps for creating an OLE DB synthetic transaction:

1. Open the Operations console and navigate to the Authoring space.
2. Right-click the **Management Pack Templates** subtree and select **Add Monitoring Wizard**.
3. The page previously shown in Figure 17.4 is displayed. From here, select **OLE DB Data Source** and click **Next**.
4. On the next page, input the name and a description for the synthetic transaction and select the management pack in which you want to create the transaction rules. For this example, the transaction name will be **Operations Manager Database**

Monitor, and select the Sample management pack used elsewhere in this book or another management pack you have created. Click **Next** to continue.

5. On the Connection String page, click on **Build**.
6. Select the appropriate Provider in the drop-down list. Because the OperationsManager database is a Microsoft SQL database data source, select **Microsoft OLE DB Provider for SQL Server**.
7. Enter the database server's name in the IP address or device name box and the database name in the Database box. For this example enter the name of the Operations Manager database server and instance (**ThunderCloud\sql_om**) and the name of the Operations Manager database, **OperationsManager**. Figure 17.18 shows an example where a query has been defined that selects the count from the basemanagedentity table.
8. On the Connection page, click **Test**.

   This test is performed from the management server and does not necessarily validate the OLE DB data source is reachable from the watcher node selected in the subsequent step. After a moment, you should see a green check mark icon and the notice Request processed successfully, as shown in the bottom half of Figure 17.18.

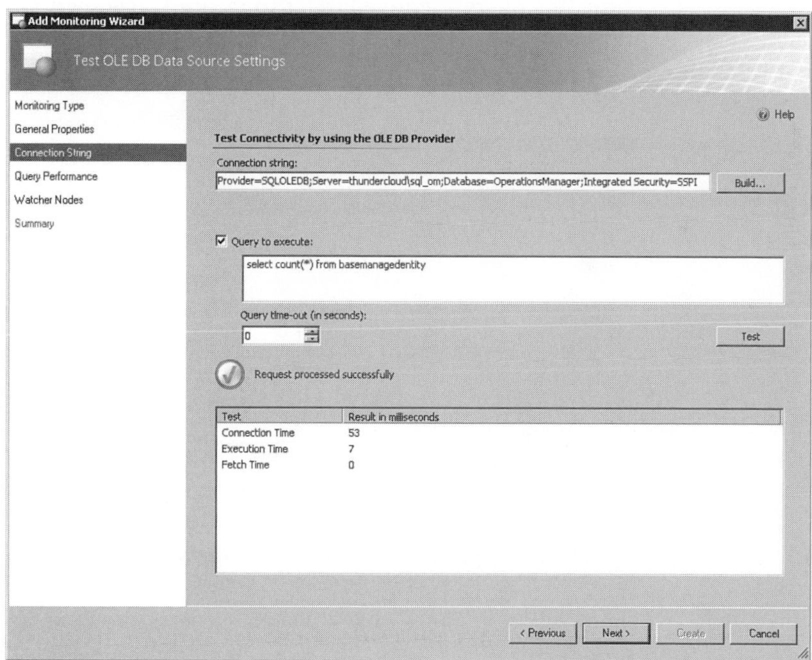

FIGURE 17.18 Entering and testing the OLE DB Data Source Settings.

REAL WORLD LIMITS OF OLE DB SYNTHETIC TRANSACTIONS

The OLE DB synthetic transaction does not output the results of the query. As an example, if you need to create an alert where there is more than *X* number of items in a table, this synthetic transaction cannot perform that action. If you need to display the output in an alert, the best approach is to create a monitor and use the Oledb.Probe write action (a standard OpsMgr write action) to generate the data for the monitor. Chapter 22, "Authoring Management Packs and Reports," includes additional information on creating management packs using XML.

More information on write actions and other components of the OpsMgr workflow is available at the AuthorMPs site at http://blogs.technet.com/b/authormps/ and Brian Wren's TechNet blog site at http://blogs.technet.com/b/mpauthor/. The OpsMgr community provides additional examples of how to query SQL and use the results in OpsMgr, including how to perform checks for a SQL full or differential backup and how to monitor the default management pack:

- http://blogs.technet.com/b/stefan_stranger/archive/2009/02/02/opsmgr-sql-full-or-differential-backup-check.aspx
- http://blogs.technet.com/b/jonathanalmquist/archive/2008/11/12/monitor-default-management-pack.aspx

---

9. The query performance page provides the ability to set error and warning thresholds based upon the connection time. If a query is entered (refer to Figure 17.18), performance thresholds can be configured for query time and fetch time. These can also be set to different values for error and warning thresholds (see Figure 17.19).

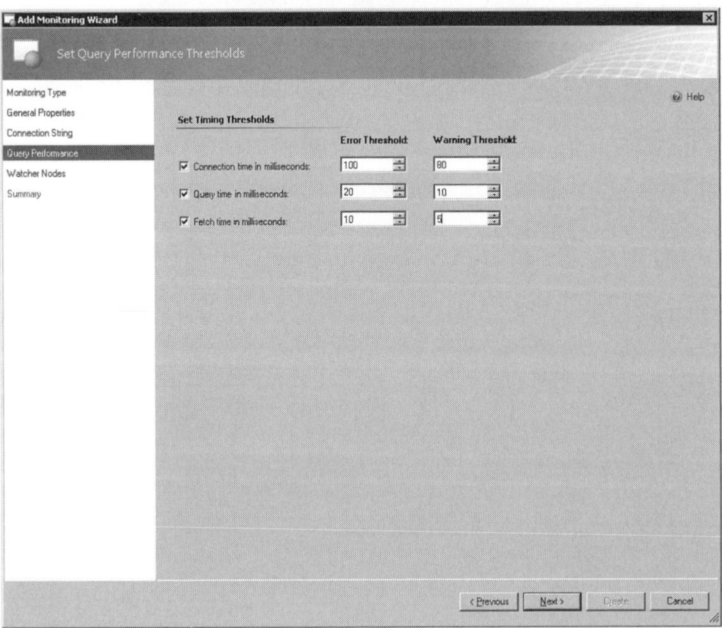

FIGURE 17.19 Configuring the Query Performance settings.

To determine appropriate threshold values, monitor the performance counters for a period of time. Figure 17.20 shows an example of how these counters can be displayed to determine what a normal value is and what thresholds should be set for error and warning thresholds. On the query performance page take the defaults, and click **Next**.

10. On the Choose Watcher Nodes page, select one or more managed computers to act as watcher nodes, ideally from several different locations.

    It is generally best to select at least two watcher nodes for each OLE DB data source. This way, when you are alerted to a problem accessing the data source, you can more easily rule out individual watcher node failure. Each instance of a watcher node monitoring an OLE DB data source creates a new object in the OLE DB Data Source State view, which becomes usable by the distributed transaction (DA).

    The default interval to run the OLE DB data source query is every two minutes. Adjust the query interval as appropriate and click **Next**.

11. On the summary page, click **Create** and wait several moments. You should then be able to locate the new OLE DB data source monitor(s) in the **Monitoring -> Synthetic Transaction -> OLE DB Data Source State** view folder. There will be one monitor for each watcher node.

You can view or modify the characteristics of the OLE DB Data Source you created at any time. Perform this task using the Authoring -> Management Pack Templates -> OLE DB Data Source node. Select the data source and click **Properties**. You can rename the data source, modify the data source connection string, and change the watcher node assignments.

By default, the OLE DB management pack template allows you to configure a synthetic transaction to connect to a database and verify the database is online. Although this level of monitoring is adequate for a large number of environments, there may be instances where an additional level of monitoring is required.

The OLEDB module defined within the System Library management pack supports an additional level of monitoring. This module allows you to configure custom queries to run against the monitored database, meaning not only can you verify that the database is online, but you can also verify that the database is responding to queries. Additionally, you can output the results of the query, allowing validation of data in the database. As an example, you can configure a SELECT statement to run against the database and then have the results of the query appear in an alert to validate the data that is returned. This capability is discussed in the next section.

TIP: OLE DB QUERIES

For an example of how to read SQL tables in OpsMgr, check out the sample management pack available on System Center Central written by Mike Eisenstein available at http://www.systemcentercentral.com/PackCatalog/PackCatalogDetails/tabid/145/IndexID/19773/Default.aspx. Additionally, Kevin Holman provides an example of monitoring a non-Microsoft database at http://blogs.technet.com/b/kevinholman/archive/2012/03/19/opsmgr-how-to-monitor-non-microsoft-sql-databases-in-scom-an-example-using-postgre-sql.aspx, and Maarten Damen provides an example of how to monitor an Oracle database with an OleDB watcher at http://www.maartendamen.com/2010/09/monitor-an-oracle-database-with-a-scom-oledb-watcher/.

Viewing the OLE DB Transaction Performance Data

After creating the OLE DB data source monitor and allowing sufficient time to pass to enable data to populate the reports, you can review the performance data related to the OLE DB data source monitor. Follow these steps:

1. Navigate to the Monitoring space and expand the Synthetic Transaction folder in the navigation tree to open the OLE DB Data Source State view. Notice the OLE DB data source monitor displayed on the right-hand side. To pivot to the performance view, right-click the object and select **Open -> Performance View**.

2. See the performance view for the OLE DB data source. The available performance counters are Connection Time, Execution Time, and Fetch Time. Select one or both of these counters and view the graph. Figure 17.20 shows the graph from the Odyssey environment. If additional watcher nodes are configured, these appear as separate counters, so you can compare the open time and connection time from different watcher nodes.

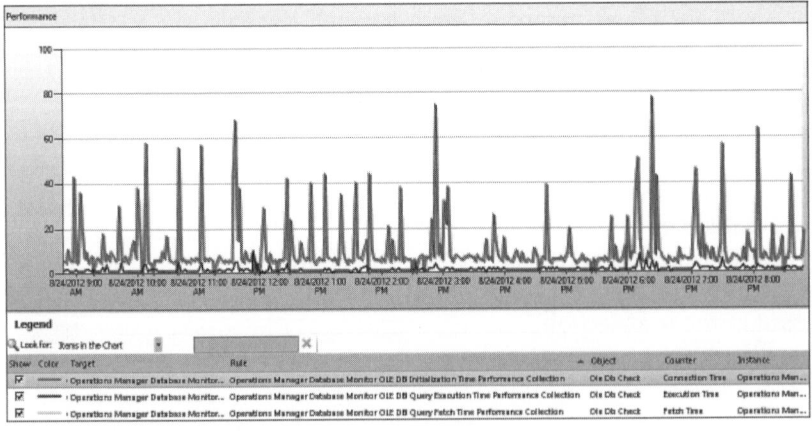

FIGURE 17.20 OLE DB connection results.

TIP: USING THE PERFORMANCE VIEW TO DETERMINE THRESHOLDS

The performance view shown in Figure 17.20 can be used to identity what normal values are for the OLE DB synthetic transaction. Once these have been identified, the query performance settings (shown previously in Figure 17.19) can be updated to reflect these values. Based upon the response times in Figure 17.20, connection time was set to an error state at 100ms or higher and a warning state at 80ms or higher. Resolution time was set based on execution time to set to an error state at 20 or higher and a warning state at 10 or higher. Fetch time was set to be to an error state at 10ms or higher and a warning state at 5 or higher.

This section looked at the process for creating a synthetic transaction to monitor a database using an OLE DB connection. The example configured monitoring for the OperationsManager database hosted by SQL Server; however, you can monitor any database that supports OLE DB as long as the OLE DB driver is installed where required. As an example, if monitoring Oracle databases, you must install the Oracle client to use either the Microsoft or Oracle OLE DB driver. The section also showed the performance data you could generate using the OLE DB data source synthetic transaction.

REAL WORLD: MONITORING ORACLE WITH THE OPSLOGIX MANAGEMENT PACK

The Oracle Intelligent management pack by OpsLogix provides a template allowing users to create rules and monitors specifically aimed at Oracle environments. An example for using such a template would be to monitor a custom Oracle enterprise application. When a specific value in an Oracle database provides an indication about the health of a particular Oracle enterprise application, the Oracle Two-State Monitor template can be used to create a new monitor for that particular application. This template is used to specify the SQL or PL/SQL statement, the value at which the monitor is considered healthy or unhealthy, and the interval at which the monitor is run. Figure 17.21 shows an example of this template and how it can be used to query Oracle and define the state of a monitor based upon the results of the query. The top left shows the query that is executed, the top right shows the threshold defined for the query, and the bottom half shows the different management pack templates available and the resulting two-state monitor created in the top half of the graphic.

Additional information on OpsLogix and their management packs is available at the website at http://www.opslogix.com/products.

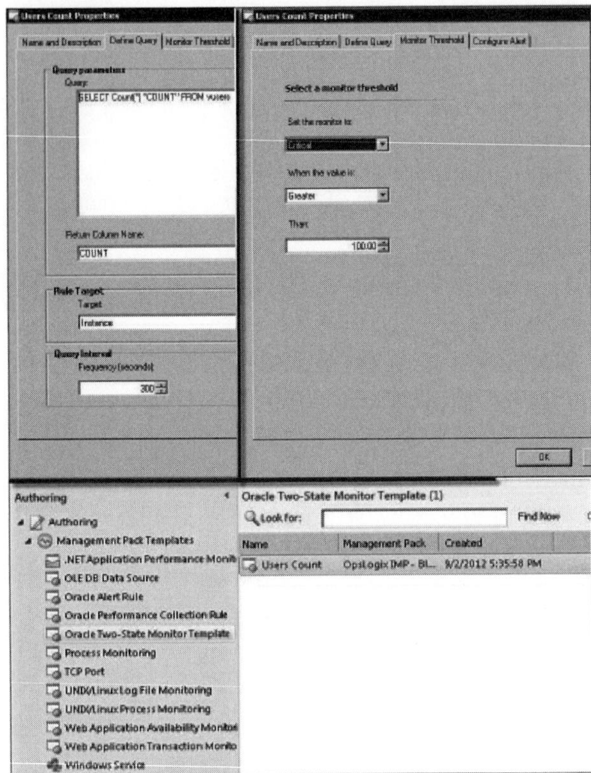

FIGURE 17.21 Querying Oracle with the OpsLogix management pack.

Monitoring Network Devices Through Port Activity

Although Operations Manager makes it straightforward to monitor applications, the level of monitoring you ultimately achieve depends on how well the application integrates with the operating system. Here are some factors that play into this:

- Whether the application logs events to the Windows event logs
- If the application runs using Windows services
- Whether there are Windows performance counters associated with the application

Even if an application is well integrated with the operating system, it still may be necessary to validate the application is actually responding. This is where the TCP Port synthetic transaction comes in.

A large number of applications use a particular TCP port to send data. Some examples include port 25, used by email applications, and port 5723, used by the OpsMgr agent. The level of integration between the application and the operating system will affect the amount and type of monitoring data that may be collected. For applications that are not integrated, TCP port monitoring may be the only way to verify whether an application is online and responding.

It is important to note that just because an application's TCP port is responding does not necessarily indicate that the application is working correctly. Monitoring a TCP port does help build a picture of application availability and response, but preferably is not the only method used to test an application. This is particularly true for non-Microsoft applications that run on the Windows platform, such as Oracle and Siebel, for example.

The TCP Port template allows you to create the necessary monitoring objects to test connectivity to a specified TCP port. The template also collects the performance and response information of that port, allowing you to analyze the response time of the TCP port.

In addition to monitoring applications using the TCP port synthetic transaction, you can also monitor hardware devices such as Simple Mail Transfer Protocol (SMTP) relay hardware devices that respond on port 25, as an example.

Creating a TCP Port Monitor

This section looks at the process for creating a TCP port monitor. The example creates two different TCP port monitors that will be used to monitor network devices:

- The first TCP port monitor will monitor the primary network link with two watcher nodes.
- The second TCP port monitor will monitor the backup network link with two watcher nodes.

Follow these steps to create the monitors:

1. Launch the Operations console and navigate to the Authoring space.
2. Right-click the **Management Pack Templates** subtree and select **Add Monitoring Wizard**, as shown earlier in Figure 17.3.
3. The different monitoring types available are displayed. From this page, select **TCP Port** and click **Next**.
4. On the General Properties page, input the name and a description for the synthetic transaction and select the management pack to which you will save the transaction rules. For this example, name the TCP Port Monitor **Denver Router (primary)** and select the **Sample management pack** to store this in. Click **Next** to continue.
5. On the target and port page, enter the TCP name or IP address of the primary network device and the port number with which to communicate. For this example, communication is occurring with the **Denver-Router1** on port **80**.

In your own environment, you would input any server or network device's IP address or DNS name, and the appropriate port to monitor. Click the **Test** button to validate the port. Figure 17.22 shows the completed page. Click **Next** to continue.

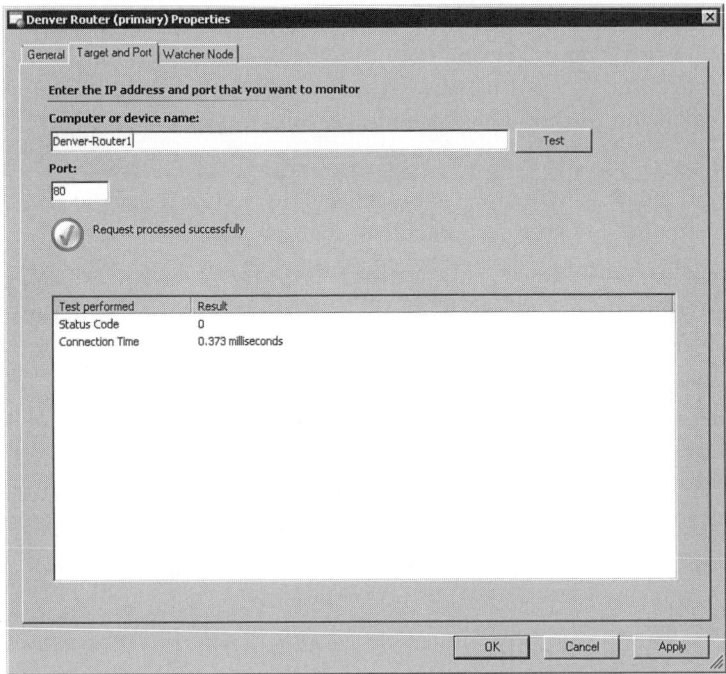

FIGURE 17.22 Entering and testing settings for the TCP port.

6. The next page is the Choose Watcher Nodes page, where the computer initiating the test is selected and configured. The page lists all computers running OpsMgr agents, and you can tick the check boxes to carry out the test on the computers you choose. In this example, run the test from the PANTHEON.ODYSSEY.COM and PIONEER.ODYSSEY.COM machines. Configure the test to run every **5** minutes instead of the default setting of 2 minutes. You can refer to Figure 17.6 for an example of the Watcher Node page. Click **Next**, and continue to the final page of the Add Monitoring Wizard.

7. The final page of the wizard summarizes the information you have input throughout the wizard. Click **Create** to complete creating the TCP Port synthetic transaction.

8. Create the second TCP port monitor for the **Denver Router (backup)** communicating with **Denver-Router2** on port **80** using the same watcher nodes used on the primary router TCP port monitor.

Viewing the TCP Port Performance Data

Similar to the other synthetic transactions discussed in this chapter, the TCP Port monitor synthetic transaction collects performance data. View this information using the process described here:

1. Navigate to the **Monitoring -> Synthetic Transaction -> TCP Port Checks State** view. Displayed on the right-hand side is the TCP port monitors configured in the "Creating a TCP Port Monitor" section. Right-click an object, then select **Open Performance View**.
2. The Performance view opens, with the only performance counter available being the Connection Time counter for the TCP port being monitored. As the example discussed in the "Creating a TCP Port Monitor" section configured additional watcher nodes, these nodes appear as separate counters, allowing you to compare the connection time from different watcher nodes.

This chapter has discussed the basics of monitoring LOB applications using TCP ports, documented the process for creating a TCP port monitor and monitoring network devices using multiple watcher nodes. Although this example focused on a network port, it is very useful to use the TCP port monitor to test ports for applications as well. Examples for where TCP port monitors are valuable include Operations Manager that communicates on port 5723, email that communicates on port 25, or Remote Desktop Protocol (RDP), which communicates on port 3389.

Using Synthetic Transactions in Application Monitoring

After creating your synthetic transactions, you will want to utilize the monitoring provided by these transactions to the maximum. You will also want to create and configure DAs using the designer tool. (For information on the Distributed Application Designer, see Chapter 18).

One very nice feature of OpsMgr is its ability to take the synthetic transaction objects you created and use them in your own distributed applications. This capability enables the results of the simulations to affect the status of the application, and thus affect your availability reports. The synthetic transaction functionality allows the status and availability of the applications to not only be based on Windows events, service status, and performance thresholds, but also on whether the application is actually responding as you expect. By measuring response time, synthetic transactions can assist you in meeting your SLAs.

The additional depth of monitoring utilized with DAs means the monitoring information obtained from a DA you configure can be very accurate when comprised of a combination of service information, Windows events, performance data, and simulated connections into the application.

When you create synthetic transactions, Operations Manager adds that transaction to the `Perspective` class. This allows these transactions to be easily located and added to DAs as required. This class will be used in this section to augment the existing monitoring for Operations Manager.

As Chapter 18 discusses how to use the Distributed Application Designer, this chapter does not focus on how to use that tool but shows how synthetic transactions can be used to augment a distributed application. Several synthetic transactions are used to augment existing monitoring provided for Operations Manager:

- **OLE DB:** The OperationsManager OLE DB synthetic transaction created in the "Using OLE DB to Monitor Databases" section is used to show how synthetic tests on the database can be used to monitor the functionality of the OperationsManager, OperationsManagerAC, and OperationsManagerDW databases.
- **Web Availability:** The websites that OpsMgr utilizes can be easily monitored using the web availability synthetic transactions. These synthetic transactions will monitor the reporting, Web console, Application Advisor, and Application Diagnostics websites.
- **TCP Port:** The TCP Port synthetic transactions are used to monitor port 5723 on the OpsMgr management servers and gateway servers.

Creating the OLE DB Synthetic Transactions for OpsMgr

You can use the steps used to monitor the OperationsManager database (discussed in the "Using OLE DB to Monitor Databases" section) to provide monitoring for each of the three major databases in Operations Manager:

- **OperationsManager:** The default name for the operational database is OperationsManager, and a sample query that can be run against this is `select count(*) from basemanagedentity`.
- **OperationsManagerDW:** The default name for the Operations Manager data warehouse is OperationsManagerDW, and a sample query that can be run against this is `select count(*) from Alert.vAlert`.
- **OperationsManagerAC:** The default name for the audit database is OperationsManagerAC, and a sample query you can run against this is `select count(*) from dbo.dtMachine`.

Creating the Web Availability Synthetic Transactions for OpsMgr

The steps used to monitor the various Operations Manager websites were discussed in the "Creating a Web Application Availability Synthetic Transaction" section, so the focus of this section is on how the process used in that section can be used to perform synthetic transactions on the following Operations Manager websites:

- **OpsMgr Web console:** The Operations Manager Web URL can be quickly determined by opening the Administration pane in the OpsMgr console under Settings -> Web Addresses.
- **Reporting:** The Operations Manager Reporting URL can be determined by opening the Administration pane in the OpsMgr console under Settings -> Reporting.
- **Application Advisor:** The URL for Application Advisor can be identified by opening the properties of the Application Advisor option on the Start menu (under Microsoft System Center 2012 -> Operations Manager).
- **Application Diagnostics:** The URL for Application Diagnostics can be identified by opening the properties of the Application Diagnostics option on the Start menu (under Microsoft System Center 2012 -> Operations Manager).

You can add each of these URLs to a single web availability synthetic transaction, which will test their availability as shown in Figure 17.23.

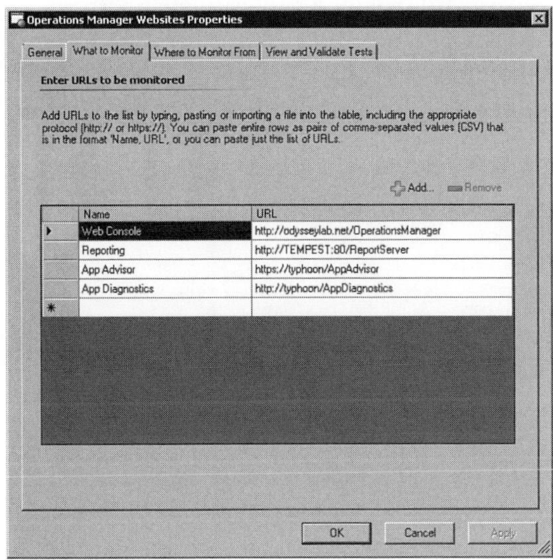

FIGURE 17.23 Web Availability testing for OpsMgr websites.

Creating TCP Port Synthetic Transactions for OpsMgr

OpsMgr management servers and gateway servers communicate on port 5723, so inbound connectivity to this port is a requirement for Operations Manager. You can use the TCP Port synthetic transactions to monitor port 5723 on the OpsMgr management servers and gateway servers. Create a TCP Port synthetic transaction for each of the management servers and gateways as shown in Figure 17.24, based on the concepts discussed in the "Creating a TCP Port Monitor" section.

17

Authoring
Authoring
Management Pack Templates
.NET Application Performance Monitorin
JEE Application Availability Monitoring
JEE Application Performance Monitoring
OLE DB Data Source
Process Monitoring
TCP Port

TCP Port (5)
Look for:

Name	Management Pack
Viceroy - 5723	Sample Management Pack
Hannibal - 5723	Sample Management Pack
Hector - 5723	Sample Management Pack
Helios - 5723	Sample Management Pack
Regent - 5723	Sample Management Pack

FIGURE 17.24 TCP port monitors for management servers and gateways.

Using Synthetic Transactions in a Distributed Application

In the model-based approach to monitoring used by Operations Manager, a variety of items can be fit into the model and combined together to form a larger object. As an example, a server's health model is built around the health of the key performance indicators such as the processor, memory, disk, and network. Other items such as applications, services, processes, and synthetic transactions are objects as well. As an analogy, think of each of these different objects as Lego™ blocks. A distributed application gathers the appropriate Lego blocks together to build something. Figure 17.25 shows how the various synthetic transactions designed to augment monitoring of Operations Manager itself can be added to a distributed application, including the dependencies where the OpsMgr URLs are dependent upon the OpsMgr databases.

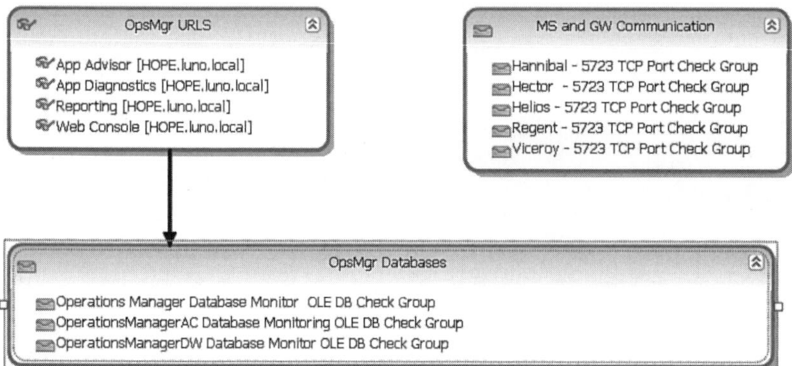

FIGURE 17.25 Operations Manager synthetic transactions in the Distributed Application Designer.

Figure 17.26 displays the same distributed application created in the Distributed Application Designer in Figure 17.25, but shows it from the Distributed Applications view in the Monitoring pane. This view provides a way to identify quickly where problems are occurring with the components of the distributed application.

This section focused on how synthetic transactions can be integrated with distributed applications to augment monitoring functionality. Synthetic transactions are a key building block (or Lego™ if you prefer) that can be used to provide a more accurate picture of how an application is actually functioning.

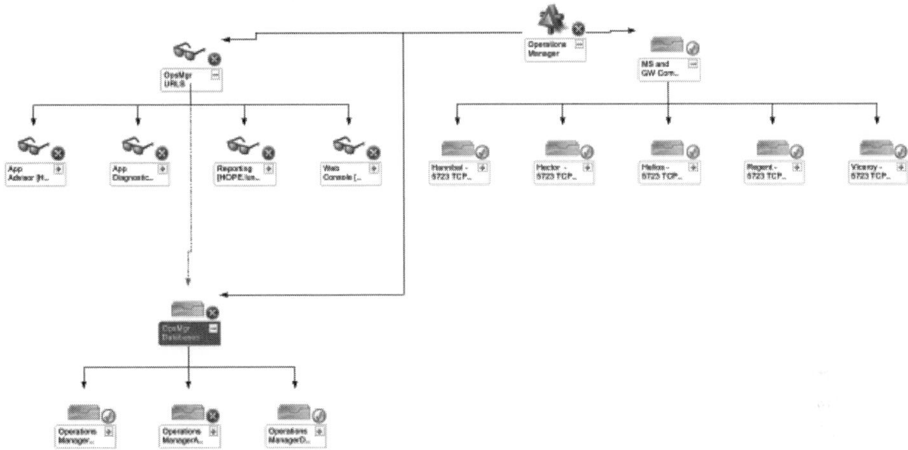

FIGURE 17.26 Operations Manager synthetic transactions in the Monitoring pane.

Fast Track

There are several key areas to focus on related to synthetic transactions and changes from previous versions of Operations Manager. These include

- **Web Application Availability:** The Web Availability Synthetic transaction was added in OpsMgr 2012 and is discussed in the "Creating a Web Application Availability Synthetic Transaction" section. The addition of GSM in System Center 2012 Service Pack 1 greatly extends this template to provide web availability testing from Microsoft's Azure cloud locations. Web application availability monitoring also provides significant enhancements to scalability by providing the ability to monitor a website from a pool of management servers or gateway servers.

- **Dashboards:** You can display performance information gathered by synthetic transactions in dashboards such as the one shown previously in Figure 17.13.

- **Web Recorder:** With changes in operating system versions, various configurations need to occur for items such as using the web recorder (see the "Using the Web Recorder" Tip for details).

- **Oracle Monitoring:** Third-party vendor solutions greatly increase the capability to perform OLE DB type synthetic transactions in OpsMgr 2012. See the "Real World: Monitoring Oracle with the OpsLogix Management Pack" sidebar for more information.

- **Synthetic Transactions in Distributed Applications:** You can use synthetic transactions to provide additional functionality for distributed applications. The "Using Synthetic Transactions in a Distributed Application" section shows how synthetic transactions, including the new Web Availability monitor, can be used in a distributed application.

Summary

This chapter discussed the various management pack templates available for Operations Manager 2012 and focused on the various synthetic transactions offered by OpsMgr out of the box. Watcher nodes were explained and both synthetic web monitors (Transaction and Availability) were discussed in depth. The chapter also discussed the OLE DB synthetic transaction, including the processes to create these types of synthetic transactions and configure advanced options. The functionality of TCP Port monitors was displayed, with an example of how to use these to monitor network devices. Finally, the chapter discussed the ability to add synthetic transactions to distributed applications created using the Distributed Application Designer.

The next chapter discusses managing a distributed environment. It covers the built-in distributed applications provided by OpsMgr and discusses using the distributed application features of OpsMgr to create your own custom management solutions.

CHAPTER 18

Distributed Applications

IN THIS CHAPTER

Beginning with the 2007 release, System Center Operations Manager (OpsMgr) has focused on end-to-end (E2E) service management. OpsMgr achieves end-to-end service management primarily with the distributed application feature, the subject of this chapter. OpsMgr also includes E2E service management in other areas, such as

- Synthetic transactions (covered in Chapter 17, "Using Synthetic Transactions"); and
- Client monitoring and Agentless Exception Monitoring (see Chapter 19, "Client Monitoring").

This chapter discusses and defines distributed applications in the systems management arena, and provides detailed coverage of built-in distributed applications in the management packs included with OpsMgr. It also explores how you can leverage the distributed application features of OpsMgr to create custom management solutions that are a perfect fit for your organization's business goals.

Distributed Applications Overview

Understanding what distributed applications are is particularly appropriate for this discussion. As Microsoft basically reinvented the term for Operations Manager, this chapter should include some definitions. The term *distributed application* originated in the software development community; OpsMgr 2007 migrated it to the systems management community with added meaning. The following sections briefly explain the programming origins of the term and then show how OpsMgr stretches that concept out to the next dimension.

The Background of Distributed Applications

Distributed applications became possible with the development of client/server computing. The capability for a single application to process and store data on both a central server and a client desktop led to the two-tiered distributed application. The earliest two-tiered distributed application, still enormously popular, is the database client, where the client application on the user desktop interacts directly with the database application on the network server.

However, for the larger enterprise, there emerged almost immediately a market for *middleware,* also known as business object applications or business logic. Middleware acts as the data-processing intermediary between the client and the backend service. Implementing middleware created the classic three-tier distributed application, often used as a model for intranet-based enterprise applications. A distributed application has three logical tiers—data, business logic, and the user interface:

- The data tier is a database such as Microsoft SQL Server.
- The business logic tier handles accessing the data and distributing it to the clients; it is the brain of the three-tier application.
- The user-interface tier (or presentation tier) often consists of both a web browser-based application and/or a traditional Windows application.

Figure 18.1 illustrates the classic three-tiered distributed application familiar to software developers.

Stratifying and segmenting a complex distributed application into defined tiers essentially creates software containers. Developing standardized software containers to host application components helps shorten development life cycles for large applications. This approach allows optimizing subordinate functions within the tiers, yet keeps the focus of the development effort on the overall distributed application.

Using distributed applications speeds the development cycle. You will often see release cycles of six months or less for major enhancements, and three months or less for minor feature additions. The application development industry has thus experienced great success by adopting the distributed application model. Using this model has markedly increased the agility of organizations, facilitating rapid rollout of major features to enterprise applications in response to changing demands and opportunities.

Using distributed applications does lead to an emerging paradigm: Because programmer-facing component models that simplify development have enjoyed such success, complexity is shifting to the operations side of managing these applications! The professional development community got its act together when it comes to rapid response to changing business goals; the widespread adoption of the distributed application development methodology has had a greatly beneficial effect on the opportunities, professionalism, and increased business value of the software development community.

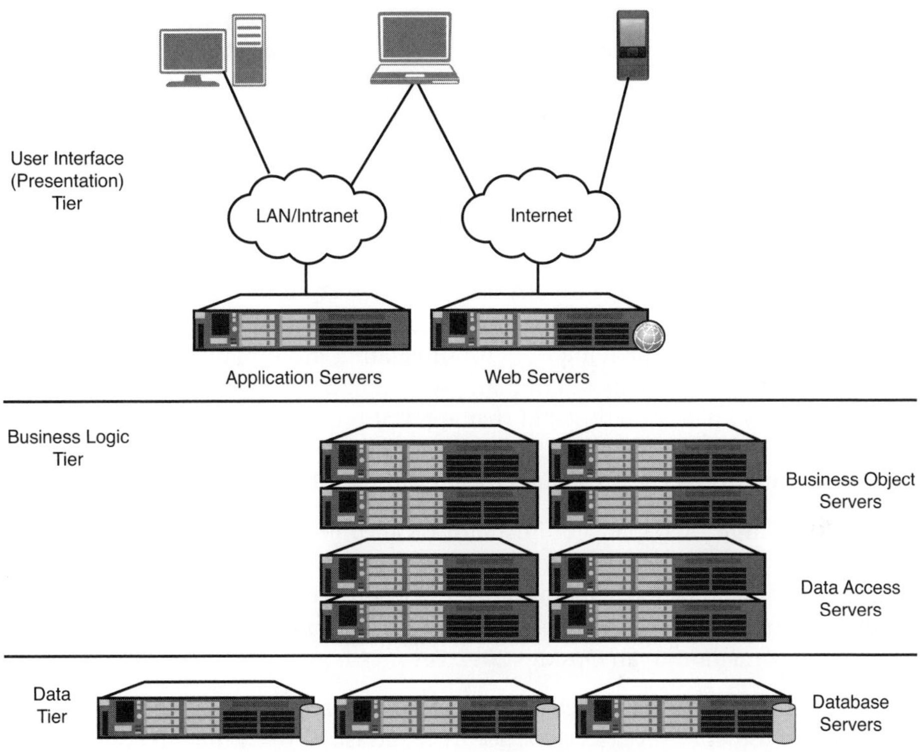

FIGURE 18.1 The classic three-tiered distributed application model used by developers.

The systems management community is now under similar scrutiny to seek efficiencies and apply holistic methodologies to its areas of responsibility. In particular, there is a clear systems management responsibility to keep up with the rapid pace of release updates to business-critical enterprise applications. Although the development side of the house may have a streamlined and efficient change management solution, the systems management team maintains responsibility for monitoring application performance and availability in production—with a high and increasing rate of application change.

As an application transitions from development to production (the release management stage), gaps in management control can occur unless the management system is prepared at that time to begin delivering service delivery metrics on the application. For prepackaged applications, one hopes that the software vendor releases an OpsMgr management pack supporting whatever new features are in the application. However, for custom enterprise distributed applications, the burden for designing a monitoring solution falls on the Information Technology (IT) staff in that organization.

IT must identify whether distributed application problems stem from a failed host, application process, network component, or other infrastructure failure. Even with a perfect monitoring infrastructure in place, it is beyond most humans' capability to synthesize the raw state of hundreds or thousands of component monitors and determine the root cause of distributed application failures. The system administrator needs a holistic way of viewing and managing the complex distributed application, processes that are also capable of rapid revision to keep in step with application change releases.

The Role of the OpsMgr Distributed Application

A holistic approach to managing complex systems offers better results than trying to manage many subsystems independently. (Aristotle's observation that *The whole is more than the sum of its parts* rings true as an early proof statement of this concept.) An OpsMgr distributed application (DA) is the framework for integrating meaningful metrics of the usability of a complex system composed of many subordinate components, such as the software containers (and hardware hosts) of that application. Using OpsMgr, a new paradigm emerges—systems management professionals are being provided with a tool that can be used to encapsulate the problem-solving processes in their heads.

Take a real world example: A system administrator is called in the middle of the night—a critical ecommerce application is down. What starts going through his mind? What does he check first, what should be looked at, what is the decision tree? You can capture those diagnostic decision trees, apply your collective event integration and synthesis knowledge, and transfer that information to an OpsMgr 2012 DA.

The OpsMgr DA represents your best bet to define what you really need to monitor for delivering your business-critical services. See the contrast between these problem-resolution techniques:

- Without a holistic means to view the health of the ecommerce application, the administrator must regularly review the status of disk arrays, network devices, firewalls, server processes, and many other components.
- Sometimes the administrator can spot an obvious failure point. However, it is just as likely that a cascading series of less-obvious failures has occurred in one or more distributed application components. This can lead to a time-consuming troubleshooting chase involving a lot of people!

Using a previously created OpsMgr DA that clearly defines the components involved in delivering the ecommerce application, a quick look at the health monitor for the application can reveal the source of the outage. The effective design of the OpsMgr DA has already done the troubleshooting work; targeted recovery operations can begin immediately to get the ecommerce application running.

How far can you take this concept? An ambitious but achievable goal of an advanced network management system is to enable a synthesis function in the monitoring engine, a step along the road toward artificial intelligence (AI) in backend support systems. If the management software can synthesize large amounts of highly diverse time-disparate data, it can do some front-line thinking and employ techniques that determine how application environments can configure and heal themselves when there are problems.

It has been postulated that increased operational complexity has reached a point where it is no longer feasible for humans to manage those applications required for running an enterprise. OpsMgr DAs are an early tool to facilitate self-managing applications—a paradigm known as *autonomic computing*, the ultimate expression of zero-touch and lights-out network management principles.

Learning how to leverage the DA feature in OpsMgr not only equips you to deal with the middle-of-the-night phone calls, it is a foundation for a new approach that foreshadows eliminating those late night calls.

Predefined Distributed Applications

Distributed applications run on many different physical tiers and often scale out over the Internet or disparate and different networks. In the Microsoft world, several applications have predefined services for monitoring. This chapter focuses on two of the most commonly encountered distributed applications in OpsMgr 2012:

- **Operations Manager Management Group:** Installed by default with Operations Manager
- **Active Directory Topology Root:** Installed by the Active Directory management pack

Figure 18.2 circles these two services at the Distributed Applications node in the Operations console in the Authoring pane on the top half of the figure, and the Monitoring pane on the bottom half. The next sections describe how you can use many of these services.

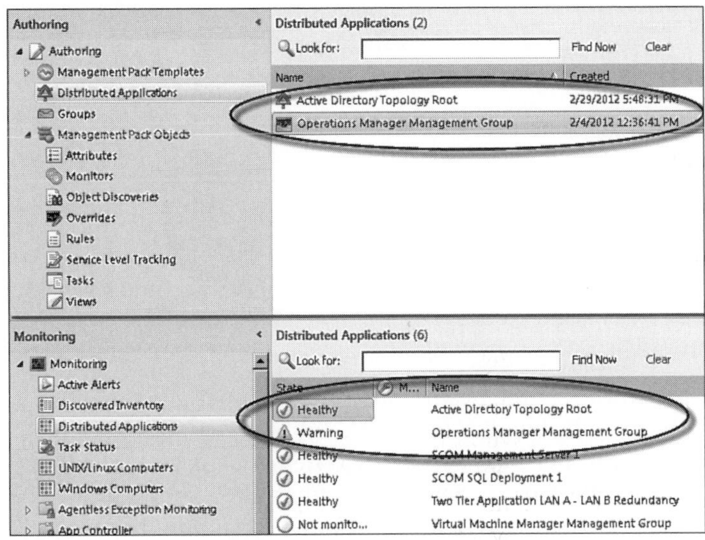

FIGURE 18.2 Commonly used Microsoft-provided distributed applications.

Operations Manager Management Group

The action of installing an OpsMgr 2012 management group automatically creates the Operations Manager Management Group DA as part of the management packs that are added when Operations Manager is installed. As a result, this distributed application is found in every Operations Manager 2012 management group. Even before you import any management packs, this service is visible in the Distributed Applications view. Microsoft created the Operations Manager Management Group DA to provide easy accessibility to the data relevant to the functioning of Operations Manager.

Using the Health Explorer

As you review the health of your management group, a great technique is to flip (or pivot) through the different views available by right-clicking the Operations Manager Management Group DA, starting with the Health Explorer. The "master view" for any DA is the Health Explorer; this is what you will open first after that middle-of-the-night phone call.

Figure 18.3 shows the Health Explorer for the Operations Manager Management Group DA, focused on a low free space alert in the Operations database. (With Operations Manager 2012, Health Explorer by default displays only those monitors in a warning or critical state as shown in this figure.)

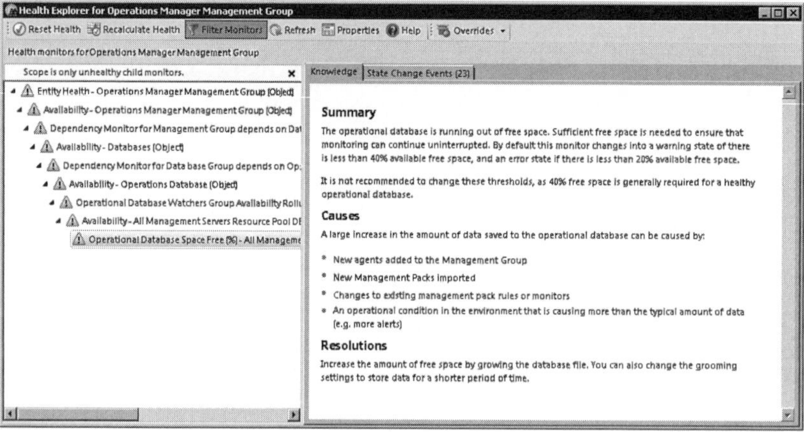

FIGURE 18.3 Operations Manager Management Group Health Explorer exposes and organizes monitors.

Figure 18.4 shows some of the branches of the health model, highlighted to point out the many different functions that can be bundled into a DA. In the lower portion of the view, notice gateway server health is watched as part of the Gateway Management Server Group Availability Health Rollup. Higher in the view, observe that three aspects of the Data Access service are watched: database connectivity, port availability, and the Windows service. These features highlight the broad scope of monitoring that a DA can perform.

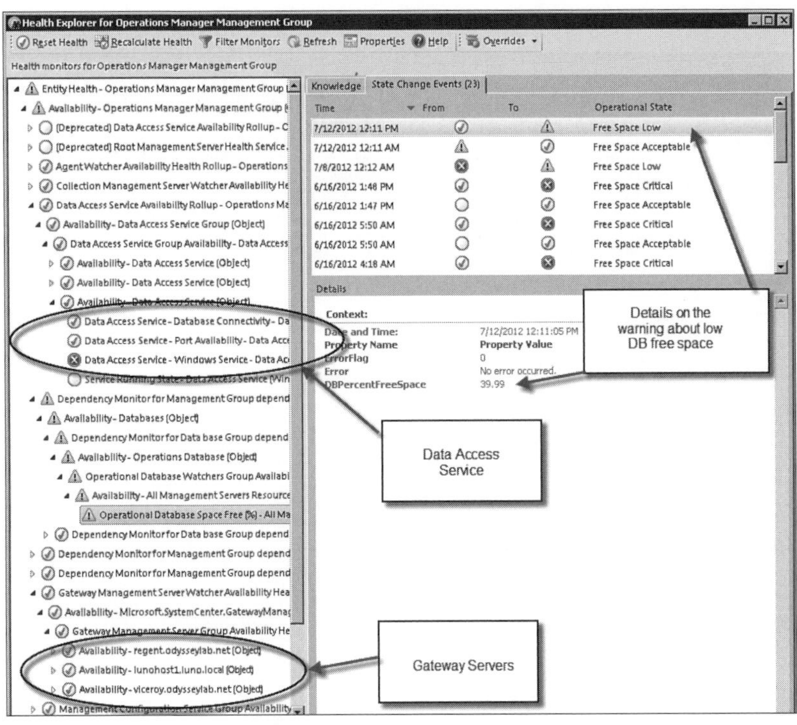

FIGURE 18.4 Management group Health Explorer Gateways and Data Access service.

Alerts and Performance Views

Figure 18.5 shows the Active Alerts view for the Operations Manager management group. This view is customized to include the Last Modified time and the Repeat Count of the alert, as this helps to triage the alerts listed.

The view is a convenient feature since it segregates those alerts dealing only with the health of the OpsMgr management group. Similarly, a performance view is available in the Operations console at **Monitoring -> Operations Manager -> Management Group Details -> Performance Data** that contains just the performance counters Microsoft believes relevant to assessing the health of the management group. Figure 18.6 shows the performance view of the Operations Manager management group.

Figure 18.6 shows the Send Queue % Used performance counter selected of a sample agent population to verify there are no unexpected connectivity issues between agents and management servers. If any send queue exceeds what is normally a near-to-zero quantity, it indicates a problem with agent communication. Microsoft provides a variety of preselected counters from both agents and management server components to add to the performance view.

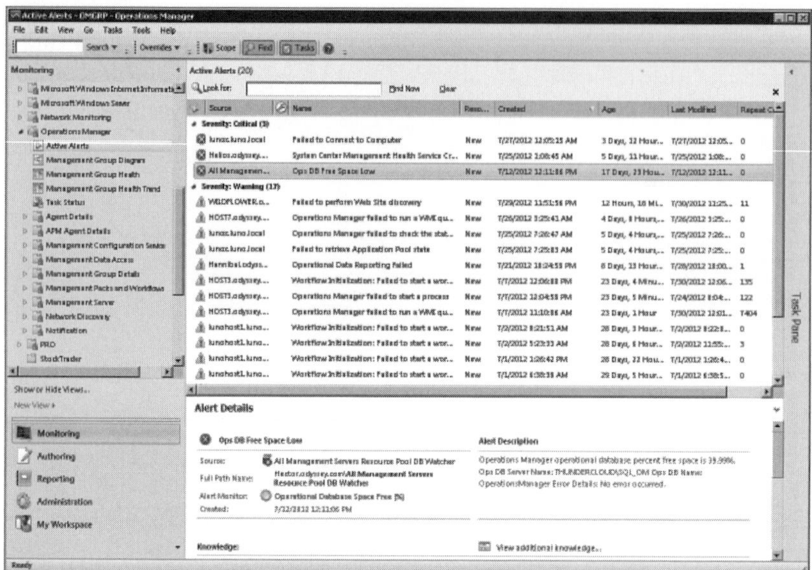

FIGURE 18.5 Examining just the alerts that are relevant to management group health.

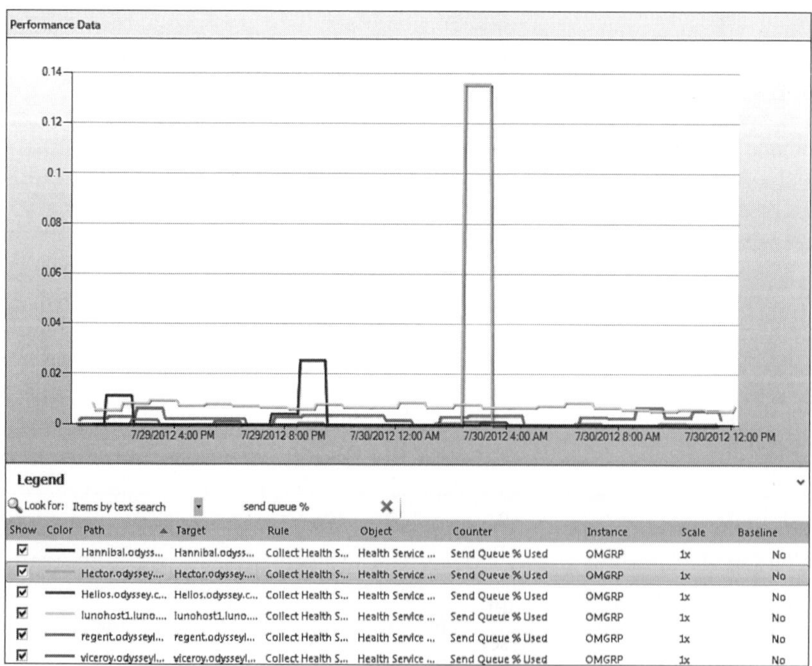

FIGURE 18.6 Performance data view for the Operations Manager management group.

The Diagram View

The most advanced view available for a DA is the diagram view. This view allows you to discover containment and dependency relationships between application components that you cannot observe in the other views. Figure 18.7 shows the diagram view of the Operations Manager Management Group DA.

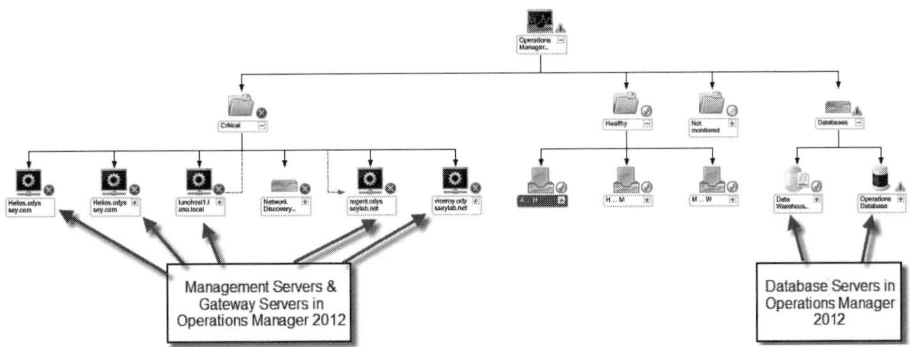

FIGURE 18.7 The diagram view of the Operations Manager Management Group DA.

> **TIP: MESSAGE WHEN OPENING DISTRIBUTED APPLICATIONS**
>
> Operations Manager 2012 includes a message that appears when opening most distributed applications: **The requested view will contain at least *X* objects and may require substantial time to render. Do you wish to continue?** The default value for this in Operations Manager is 50 objects, which means this message appears when opening most DAs in Operations Manager.
>
> To adjust the default threshold that triggers this message, change the value at `HKCU\Software\Microsoft\Microsoft Operations Manager\3.0\Console\DiagramViewParameters`, adding the DWORD `MaxNodesThreshold`. The default is 50 if the key is unspecified. For additional information, see http://blogs.catapultsystems.com/cfuller/archive/2012/03/08/opsmgr-2012-[scom]-diagram-view-requested-view-will-contain-at-least-x-objects-and-may-require-substantial-time-to-render.aspx.

Notice the left side of the diagram view in Figure 18.7 points to the management servers and gateways within the Operations Manager management group. The right side of the DA shows the database servers within the management group. That is just one small section of the DA diagram view that the authors selected to expand—when using the diagram view, you can expose just those portions of the application you want.

Comparing the DA Diagram View and the Health Explorer

In some ways, the diagram view of a DA presents the same information as the Health Explorer. For example, in the diagram view shown in Figure 18.8, the components shown for the gateway servers, which are in a green state, correspond to the availability monitors circled in the bottom portion of the Health Explorer shown in Figure 18.4.

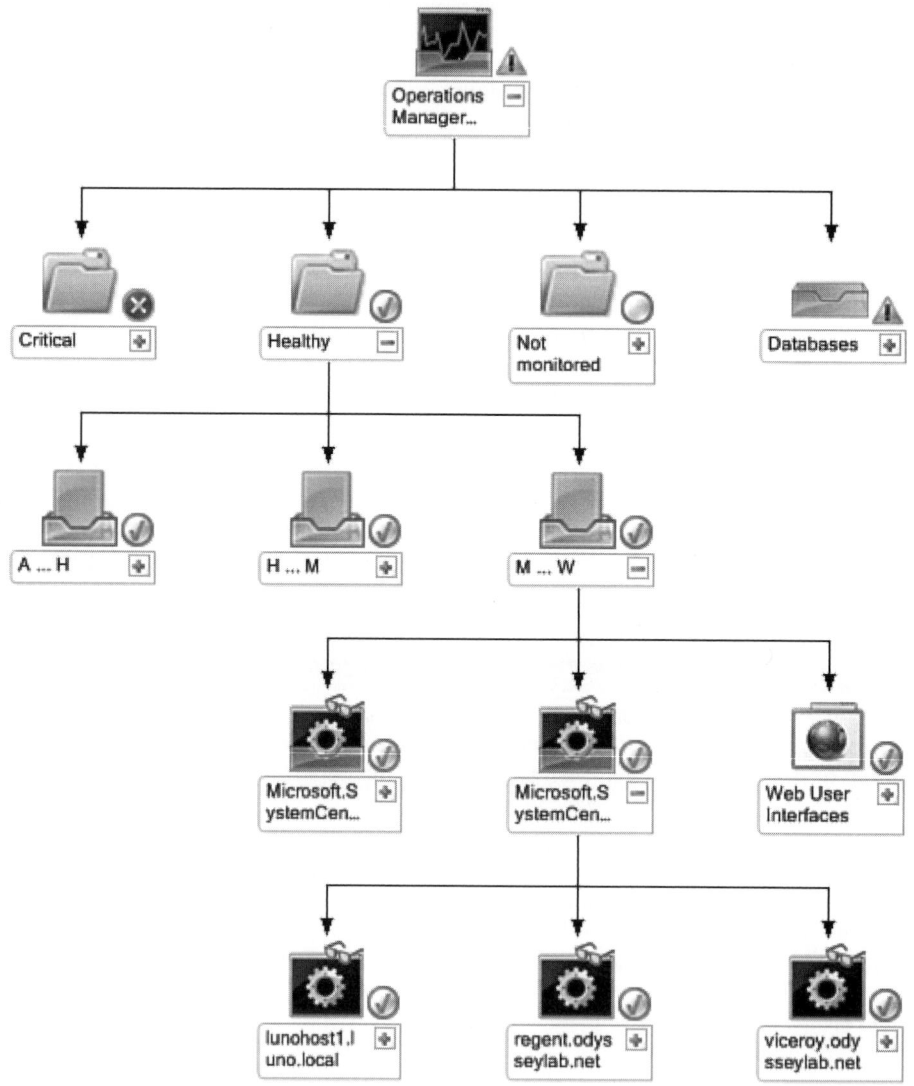

FIGURE 18.8 Gateway watcher health.

The primary difference in presentation between the Health Explorer and the diagram views is you can interact with objects in the diagram view by clicking and dragging them to rearrange the objects in the view. This causes the solid (containment) and dotted (non-containment) lines to move with the object. This capability lets you spot relationships between components that you might not otherwise detect. The "Creating a Distributed Application Health Model" section drills down into the advanced features of the diagram view.

A take-away from reviewing the Operations Manager Management Group DA is that a well-authored DA can save you a considerable amount of time when it comes to assessing the health state of the application. By identifying those classes of objects that are involved in delivering the application (and their relationships) and collecting sets of targeted views that focus on the service delivery of the application, knowledge is encapsulated, preserved, and made portable.

Active Directory Topology Root

Microsoft's Active Directory (AD) Service, so integrated with Windows networking, itself is an archetypal distributed application. Active Directory components can be on a single physical server for a small business, or distributed across hundreds of domain controllers for a global enterprise. In its simplest, small business implementation, all that matters is the local authentication experience for the user and their workstation, whereas larger enterprises will want to monitor Active Directory processes such as inter-site replication. Microsoft provides management packs to monitor both the client experience and the server-side components of Active Directory.

The left-hand side of Figure 18.9 exposes the majority of the Monitoring view folder tree added to the console when importing Active Directory management packs.

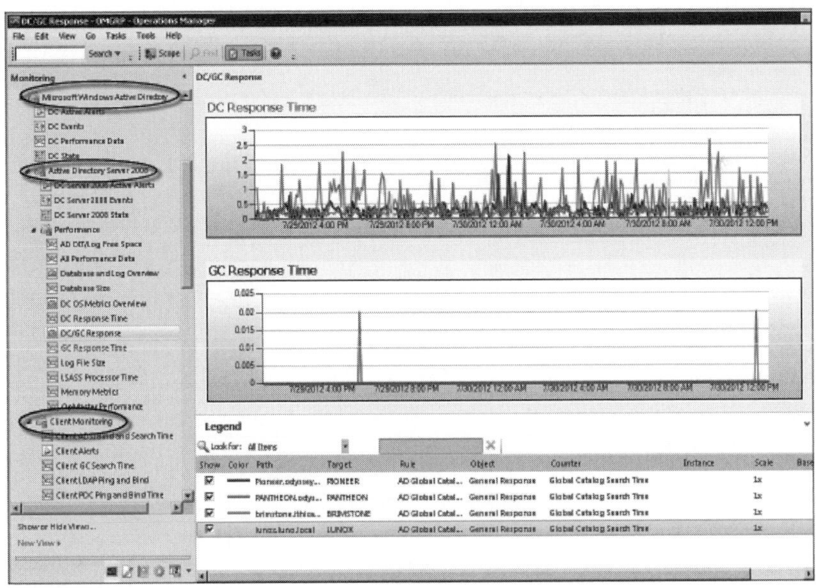

FIGURE 18.9 Active Directory management pack views.

Figure 18.9 shows the folders for the server, client, and performance monitoring aspects of the AD management packs circled (there is also a set of folders for replication monitoring and topology views that is not displayed). The Results pane displays a dashboard view with metrics showing domain controller (DC) and global catalog (GC) response time.

The Navigation pane on the left shows there are a number of very specific dashboard and performance views covering each aspect of AD health.

Using Monitors to View AD Health

What procedure should you follow to assess the overall health of AD? It's not actually necessary to open every AD view node in the Monitoring space, as Microsoft has included the Active Directory Topology Root DA with the AD management packs. By examining the Health Explorer of the Active Directory Topology Root DA, you know you are looking at a meaningful and accurate representation of your overall AD health. To illustrate the power of this DA, Figure 18.10 shows the principal monitors that constitute the health model for the Active Directory Topology Root DA.

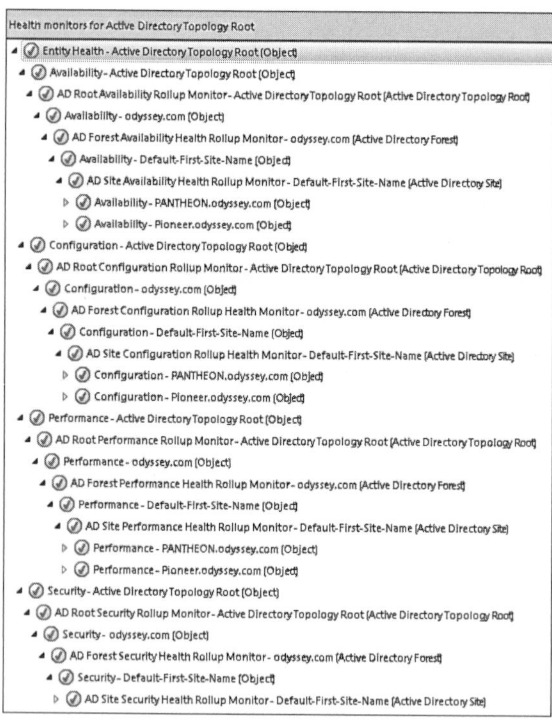

FIGURE 18.10 Principal health monitors of the Active Directory Topology Root DA.

The monitors listed in Figure 18.10 exist for each domain controller in each AD site, from the AD Database Free Space Monitor to the AD Processor Overload Monitor. Regardless of how distributed or compact your AD deployment is, Operations Manager examines all those listed health factors. Consolidating these many different types of monitors relating to AD performance and availability into a single view is an example of how OpsMgr helps you perform synthesis and integration to solve problems.

TIP: INSTALL AN AGENT ON YOUR DOMAIN CONTROLLERS FIRST

If you import the Active Directory management packs before installing OpsMgr agents on your domain controllers, the DCs appear as Not Monitored in the Computers global view in the Operations console. This occurs because the Active Directory Topology Root DA discovers the DCs in the management group's domain and makes them objects in the management group. However, without OpsMgr agents, the DCs, now identified as objects, show up as unmonitored. To prevent this from occurring, install an OpsMgr agent on your DCs before importing the Active Directory management packs.

The Active Directory Topology Root DA includes many other monitors besides the principal ones listed in Figure 18.10. For example, physical dependencies of Active Directory are also included in the health model of the DA. Figure 18.11 shows the Health Explorer of the Active Directory Topology Root DA; the upper portion highlights the Logical Disk Availability and Free Space monitors of a domain controller.

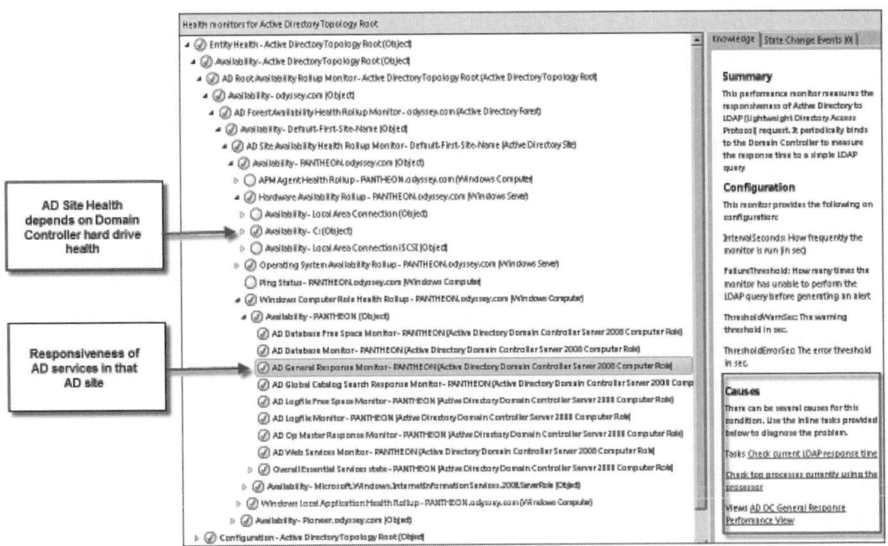

FIGURE 18.11 The Distributed Application includes hardware and service dependencies.

The lower portion of Figure 18.11 shows the selected monitor highlighted (the AD General Response Monitor), with the in-line tasks available in the lower-right corner. Using these in-line tasks when investigating a problem with general AD responsiveness provides one-click access to the following features:

- **Check current LDAP response time:** Verify the actual Lightweight Directory Access Protocol (LDAP) responsiveness at this moment.
- **Check top processes currently using the processor:** If response is slow, a process may be monopolizing the processor.
- **AD DC General Response Performance View:** Quickly look at the trending of LDAP responsiveness over the last few hours or days.

In-line Tasks

In-line tasks are another location for capturing knowledge in the DA model. The intent is that once you use the Health Explorer to zero in on the cause of a problem, the tools for your troubleshooting decision tree are there where you need them. Tactical placement of in-line tasks can help accelerate your systems management workflow.

Other Diagram Views

A very useful diagram view is available when working with the Active Directory Topology Root DA under **Monitoring -> Microsoft Windows Active Directory -> Topology Views -> Topology** and shown in Figure 18.12. This figure includes annotated arrows to point out each main feature of the diagram; the lower left shows the Logical Drive monitor highlighted in Figure 18.11 circled.

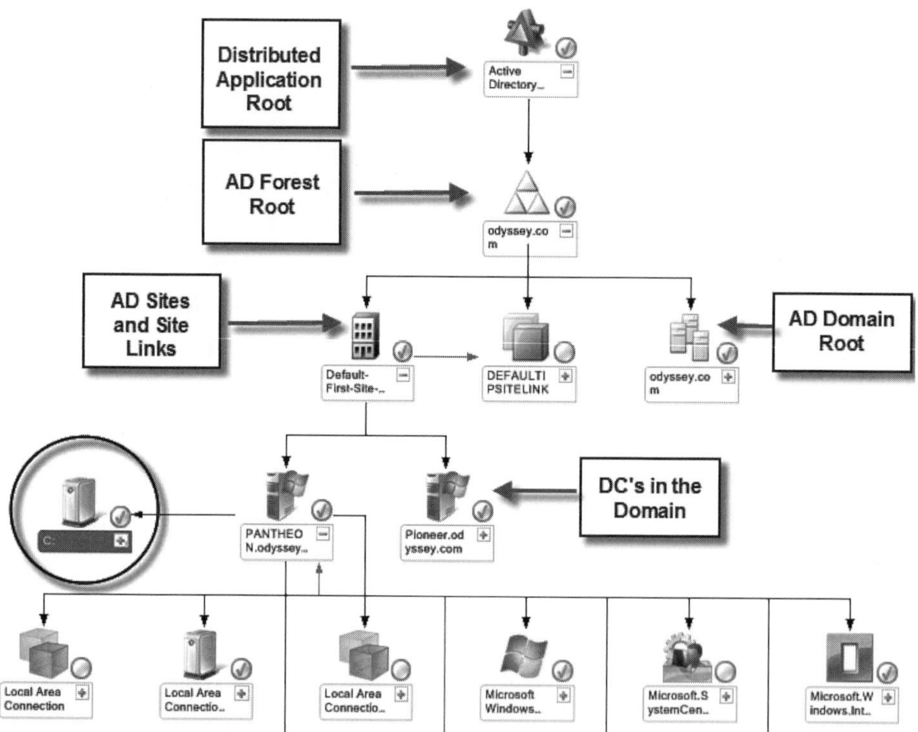

FIGURE 18.12 The Distributed Application diagram illustrates your AD topology.

The **Monitoring -> Microsoft Windows Active Directory -> Topology Views** folder includes dedicated diagram views installed by the AD management packs; these are the AD Forests and Domains, AD Sites, Connection Objects, and Topology views. Each view focuses on a particular aspect of AD health. The diagram view of the Active Directory Topology Root DA shown in Figure 18.12 is a superset view that includes all information visible in the dedicated diagram views.

Enterprise Health Monitoring

Microsoft gave Operations Manager administrators a jump-start in making use of the Distributed Application feature by including several DA templates in the Microsoft Information Worker management pack. Chapter 19 includes more depth on the Enterprise Health Monitoring view, shown in Figure 18.13.

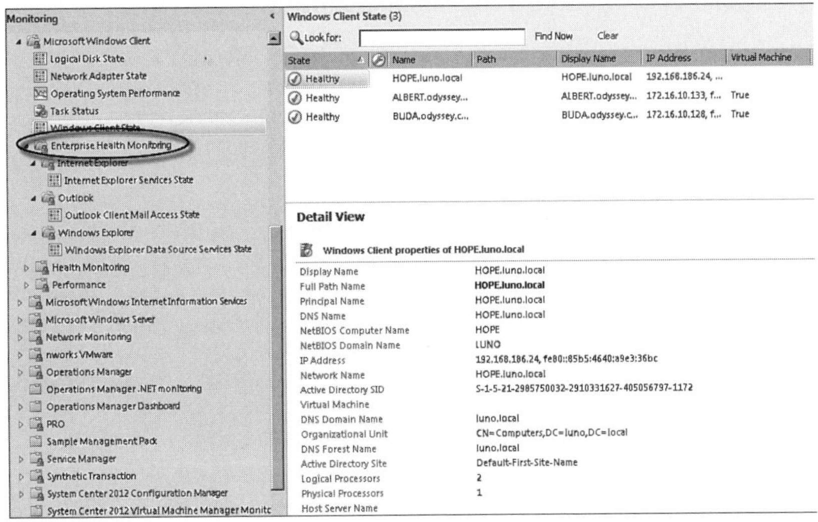

FIGURE 18.13 Enterprise Health Monitoring views.

Figure 18.13 shows the Enterprise Health Monitoring folder (circled); observe that it contains three view folders:

- Internet Explorer
- Outlook
- Windows Explorer

The Outlook Client Mail Access State view generates an alert when 10% or more client computers running Microsoft Outlook cannot contact their Exchange server(s). The Outlook Client Mail Access State view automatically populates as the management pack discovers client computers running Outlook. (As of January 2013, Microsoft has not announced plans to provide a newer version of this management pack that identifies Outlook 2010 or 2013. Objects discovered by the Information Worker management pack are listed at http://technet.microsoft.com/en-us/library/dd351478.aspx.)

The other two enterprise health monitoring views, Internet Explorer Services and Windows Explorer Data Source Services, are not populated until you create DAs based on specific predefined templates. Importing the Microsoft Information Worker management pack adds two DA templates to the Distributed Application Designer—you can choose one of these templates when you create a DA.

Here are the views added to the Monitoring -> Microsoft Windows Client -> Enterprise Health Monitoring folder and the scenarios they support:

- **View:** Internet Explorer -> Internet Explorer Services State

  Scenario: Internet Explorer Clients utilize Proxy Services and Network Services, and depend on a physical network.

- **View:** Windows Explorer -> Windows Explorer Data Source Services State

  Scenario: Data Source Clients utilize Directory Services and Network Services, and depend on a physical network.

The monitoring views are empty until you create custom monitoring services (using the Distributed Application Designer) based on the predefined templates. The names of the templates correspond to the two views. The next sections step through each of these different DAs and discuss effective means to employ these enterprise health monitoring features of OpsMgr.

Internet Explorer Service Template

Also known as the Client Web Access feature of the Microsoft Information Worker management pack, use the Internet Explorer Service template to create a DA to let you know when web browser clients cannot access critical web application resources. The websites and web-based applications you monitor can be internal to your network or on the Internet. If your organization depends on information workers accessing a web-based application for a critical business function, consider using the Internet Explorer Service template to author a DA modeling that web access. Monitoring the DA will provide visibility into the ability of client computers to use the critical web-based application.

Creating the Web Application

The first step to enable the Client Web Access (Internet Explorer Service) DA is creating one or more web applications using the Add Monitoring Wizard in the Authoring space. You then use the Distributed Application Designer, specifying the Windows Internet Explorer Service template, to add the web application as an object to monitor. The scenario demonstrates the Internet Explorer Service DA for employees accessing a business-critical website. The goal of the DA is to detect problems accessing that website.

Define the website you will monitor by creating a web application in the Authoring space. After you create the web application, you can view its health under **Monitoring -> Web Application Transaction Monitoring -> Web Applications State**. More importantly, this makes the web application selectable in the Object Picker later in the Distributed Application Designer. Follow these steps to define the critical website:

1. In the Authoring space, navigate to the Management Packs node and run the Add Monitoring Wizard.

2. Select **Web Application Transaction Monitoring** as the monitoring type and click **Next**.

3. On the Web Application Name and Description page, enter a name and description for the critical website. The name will appear as a component of the DA, so name it something that makes the most sense in that context. For this example, choose **Critical Website Access** for the name. Select (or create) a custom management pack to save your changes and click **Next**.

4. Enter and test the URL you will be monitoring. This test is performed from the management server you are currently connected to and does not necessarily validate the URL is reachable from the watcher node you select in the next step. The results of the test are displayed along with a Details button.

   The tabs in Figure 18.14 show how you can expose the actual Hyper Text Markup Language (HTML) returned from the monitored web server. You can later use details from the HTML reply to validate proper response from the critical website.

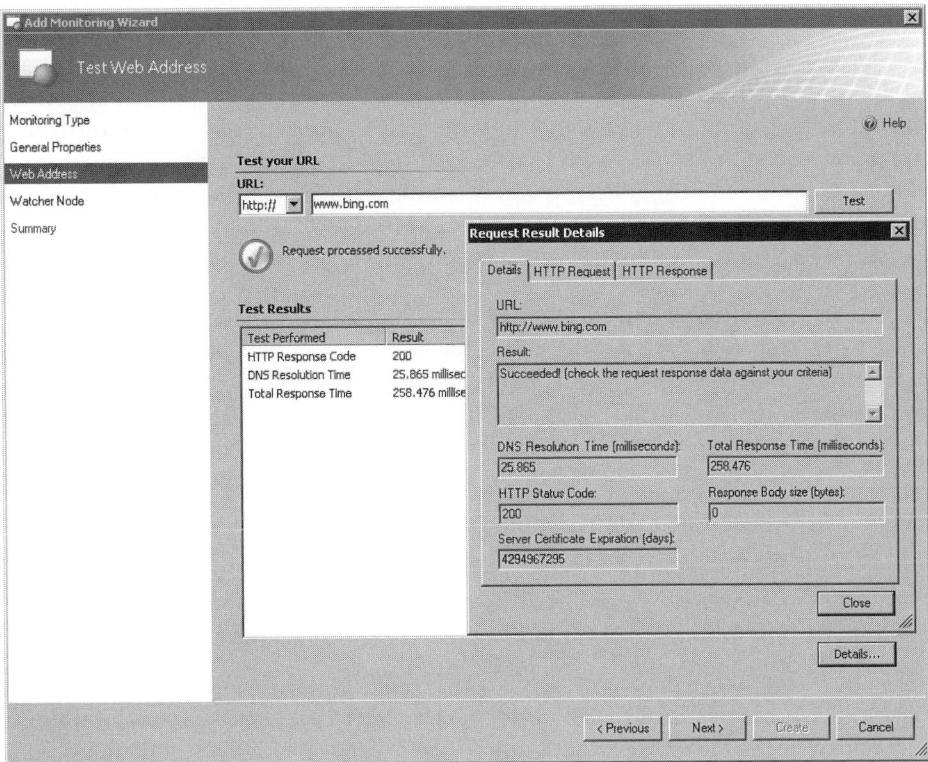

FIGURE 18.14 Viewing the detailed results of the web address test.

5. On the Choose Watcher Nodes page, select one or more managed computers to act as watcher nodes, preferably from multiple and different locations. The authors recommend monitoring an external web server through different outbound Internet

service providers (ISPs). You should also consider monitoring an internal web server from watcher nodes at each branch office or outlying building.

Select at least two watcher nodes for each web address. This way when you are alerted to a problem accessing the critical website, you can more easily rule out individual watcher node failure. Each instance of a watcher node monitoring a URL creates a new object in the Web Applications State view, which becomes usable by the DA.

By default, the web query runs every 2 minutes. This might be too short an interval if you have a larger number of watcher nodes or a complex set of web application tests. Adjust the query interval as appropriate and click **Next**.

6. Click **Create** and wait several moments. You should then be able to locate the new web application monitors in the **Monitoring** -> **Web Application Transaction Monitoring** -> **Web Applications State** view folder. Each watcher node will have a separate monitor.

You can return at any time to view or modify the characteristics of the application you created. Perform this task using the Web Application Editor, launched from the **Authoring** -> **Management Pack Templates** -> **Web Application** node. There are a number of advanced features of the web application accessible through the Web Application Editor. You can modify and fine-tune the web application to fit many business needs. For more information on web application monitoring, see Chapter 17.

Creating the Windows Internet Explorer Service DA

After configuring your web applications, the watcher nodes should appear in a healthy state at **Monitoring** -> **Web Application Transaction Monitoring** -> **Web Applications**; you can now create the Critical Website Access DA, in which the watcher nodes will participate. Follow these steps:

1. Navigate to and select **Authoring** -> **Distributed Applications**. Right-click and choose **Create a new distributed application**.
2. Enter a name and description for the DA. This name will appear in the Monitoring -> Distributed Applications global view, so use a name that communicates its purpose. For this example, select the same name **Critical Website Access** used when defining the web application.
3. Choose the **Windows Internet Explorer Service** template. (This template is available as part of the Microsoft Information Worker management pack; you must install this management pack to be able to see the template.)
4. Select a custom management pack to save the DA; this should be the same management pack to which you saved the web application.

After opening the Distributed Application Designer and choosing to use the Internet Explorer Service template, you have a logical view of four components (with relationships), as follows:

- Windows Internet Explorer Clients, which depend on Proxy Services, Network Services, and a physical network
- Windows Internet Explorer Proxy Services, which depend on a physical network
- Windows Internet Explorer Network Services, which depend on a physical network
- A physical network

This arrangement suggests that client computers depend on several components (such as proxy services and network services) to access the critical website in addition to the interconnecting physical network. Defining your DA with these components and relationships helps identify root causes when there are problems accessing the critical website. Components in the DA are containers holding one or more managed objects.

To adapt the template to your environment, determine what network services you want to associate with this DA; specifically, those services the web browser client depends on when accessing the critical website. In this example, for computer dependencies use the Domain Name Server (DNS) services on one server, and the Windows Proxy Automatic Detection (WPAD) services, hosted by Internet Information Services (IIS) on another server.

The next step is identifying the network devices, such as routers or switches, that the web browser client, DNS, and WPAD servers depend on to provide outbound access to the critical website. A failure in DNS, WPAD services, or the interconnecting network devices can result with the web browser client unable to access the critical website. The DA will rapidly disclose the failure origin if related to DNS, WPAD services, or the network devices.

It is a best practice to rename the components created by the Internet Explorer Service template so they make sense to operators in your environment. Here is how to rename the DA components in this example (right-click each in turn, and select **Properties**):

- Windows Internet Explorer Clients to **Client computer watcher node**
- Windows Internet Explorer Proxy Services to **DNS Services**
- Windows Internet Explorer Network Services to **WPAD Services**
- Physical network to **Edge Switches**

The next part of creating the DA is to add the components. The following steps populate the DA components with managed objects (clockwise from the top component, seen in Figure 18.15):

1. On the left side of the Distributed Application Designer, under Objects, double-click the **Perspective** object type tile.
2. Click the **Object** tile at the top of the object list to sort the perspectives by object name.
3. Locate and select both Critical Website Access watcher nodes; these are the ones created as web applications.

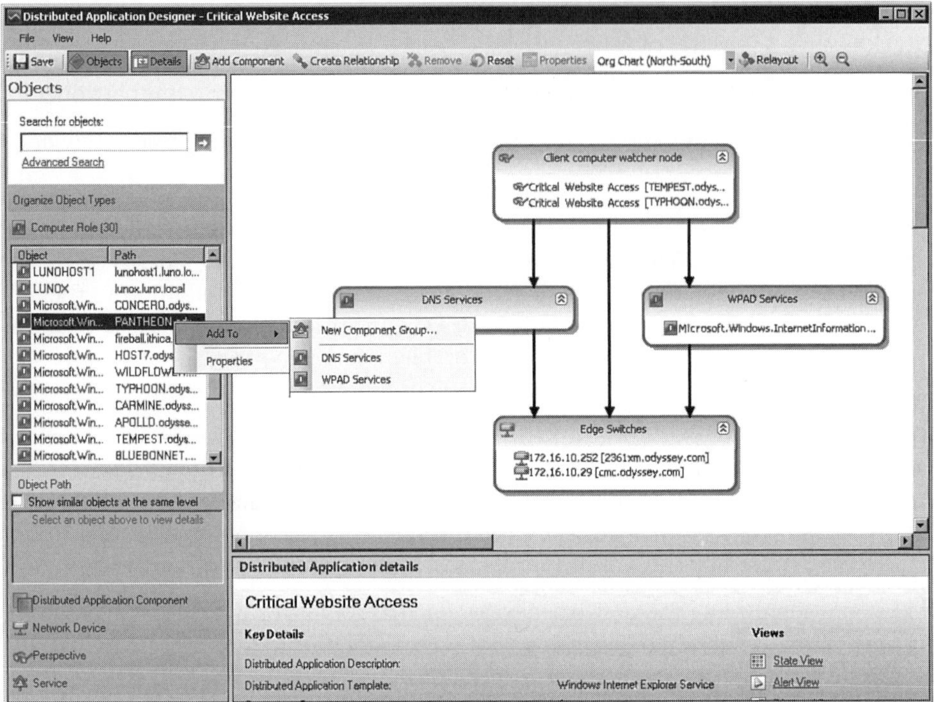

FIGURE 18.15 Creating a DA based on the Internet Explorer Service template.

4. Right-click and then select **Add To -> Client computer watcher node**. The Client computer watcher node component now contains two Critical Website Access watcher nodes.
5. Double-click the **Computer Role** object type tile.
6. Click the **Path** tile at the top of the object list to sort the computer roles by object path.
7. Locate the server name hosting the WPAD services in the path column; then select the **Microsoft.Windows.InternetInformationServices.2008.Server.Role** object for that server name.
8. Right-click and then select **Add To -> WPAD Services**. The WPAD Services component now contains the IIS Services of the WPAD server.
9. Double-click the **Network Devices** object type tile.
10. Click the **Object** tile at the top of the object list to sort the network devices by object name (IP address).
11. Locate and select one or more network devices. Select two network devices that are the edge switches the client and server computers depend on for outbound access.
12. Right-click and then select **Add To -> Edge Switches**. The Edge Switches component now contains the network devices.
13. Double-click the **Computer Role** object type tile.

14. Click the **Object** tile at the top of the object list to sort the computer roles by object name.
15. Locate the server name hosting the DNS services in the Object column. Move the cursor slowly over the server names (hover) to view a floating tip describing each object. Do so until you locate the DNS services object and select it.
16. Right-click and then select **Add To -> DNS Services**. Observe the DNS Services component now contains the DNS service object of the selected server. Figure 18.15 illustrates this step.
17. Click the **Save** icon (or select **File -> Save**).
18. Exit the Distributed Application Designer (**File -> Close** or click the X icon).

After several minutes, you can view the health status of the new DA in the **Monitoring -> Distributed Applications** view and the **Monitoring -> Microsoft Windows Client -> Enterprise Health Monitoring -> Internet Explorer Services State** view. Access to the DA object itself remains at the **Authoring -> Distributed Applications** node. You can return to that node at any time to modify the components, objects, relationships, and other settings in the DA. From that location, you can also launch the diagram view for the DA, as shown in Figure 18.16.

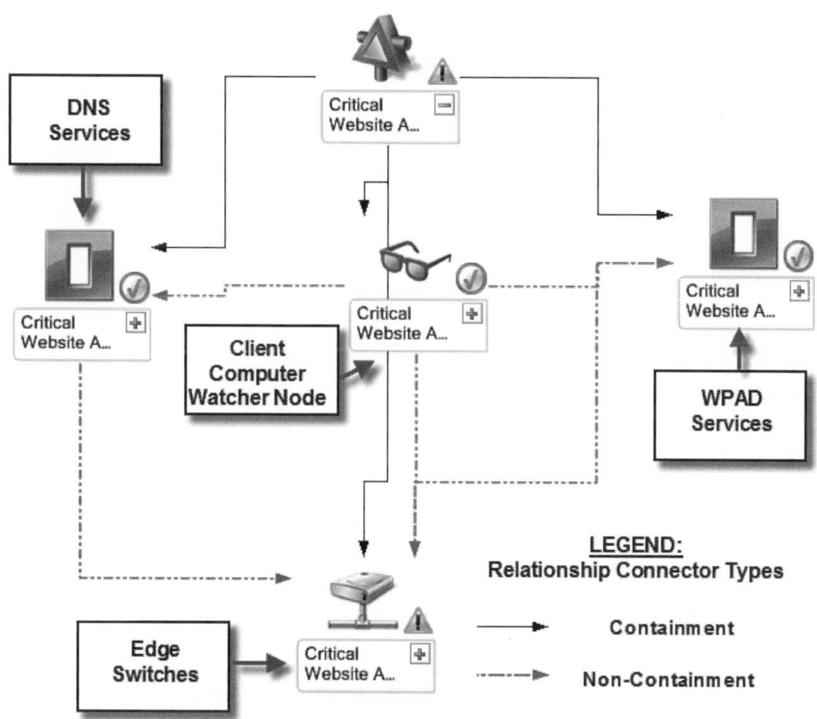

FIGURE 18.16 The diagram view of a DA based on the Internet Explorer Service template.

18

In the diagram view of the Critical Web Access DA displayed in Figure 18.16, the icons were manually moved to appear in the same topology as in the Distributed Application Designer. Text boxes were added to label which components of the DA correspond to what they were first labeled as when the DA was authored. Additionally a legend for the containment versus non-containment connector types was added in the lower right of the figure. Solid (black) relationship connector lines identify containment, while dotted (blue) lines identify non-containment dependency.

This view discloses that the Client Computer Watcher Node is dependent on (but not contained by) the DHCP Services and the WPAD Services. Likewise, the Client Computer Watcher Node, DHCP Services, and WPAD Services are all dependent on the Edge Switches, even though they are not objects contained within the Edge Switches.

TIP: VISIO INTEGRATION AND SAVISION LIVE MAPS

The inability to rename objects in a distributed application or permanently change the layout of a DA is a common reason why Visio Integration or Savision Live Maps are used in place of a DA. These technologies allow a DA to be displayed via a web page that can be customized to meet the organization's business requirements.

- For an example of this approach for Savision Live Maps, see http://blogs.catapultsystems.com/cfuller/archive/2010/09/14/taking-distributed-applications-to-the-next-level-with-savision-live-maps-%E2%80%93-part-2.aspx.
- You can find an example of using Visio integration with the Visio Add-in for Operations Manager (official name) at http://blogs.catapultsystems.com/cfuller/archive/2011/08/16/opsmgr-dashboard-integration-creating-a-visio-integrated-diagram-from-a-distributed-application.aspx.

Several infrastructure components were used in this DA to help quickly evaluate problems detected in client computers accessing a business-critical website. The next section uses the Windows Explorer Data Source Service template to create a similar DA, this time where the client accesses an important data source rather than a business-critical website.

Windows Explorer Data Source Service Template

Also known as the Client Data Source Access feature of the Microsoft Information Worker management pack, use the Windows Explorer Data Source Service template to create a DA that lets you know when data source clients are unable to access important data source providers. While this is an older management pack, it provides excellent templates that can be used to demonstrate functionality useful to include within a distributed application. The data source providers you monitor can be any of the 20 types supported by the OLE DB data source. These include Microsoft Jet sources (such as Microsoft Access legacy applications), and Open Database Connectivity (ODBC) to database sources like Microsoft SQL Server and Oracle.

If your organization requires information workers to access a data source for a critical business function, consider using the Windows Explorer Data Source Service template to author a DA that models that data source access. Monitoring the DA provides visibility into the ability of client computers to use the data source.

Creating the OLE DB Data Source

To enable the Client Data Source Access (Windows Explorer Data Source Service) DA, begin by creating one or more OLE DB data sources with the Add Monitoring Wizard in the Authoring space of the Operations console. You then use the Distributed Application Designer, specifying the Windows Explorer Data Source Service template, and add the OLE DB data source as an object to monitor.

The scenario in this section demonstrates the Windows Explorer Data Source Service DA accessing the Audit Collection Services (ACS) database. The goal is to detect problems with network access to that database's SQL data source. This demonstration of the DA using the ACS database is applicable to any two-tier (client/server) distributed application.

Define the data source you will monitor by creating an OLE DB data source in the authoring space. After you create the data source, the health of that application will be viewable in the **Monitoring -> Synthetic Transaction -> OLE DB Data Source State** view. The data source will also be selectable in the Object Picker later in the Distributed Application Designer.

Follow these steps to define the OLE DB data source:

1. Navigate to **Authoring -> Management Packs** and start the **Add Monitoring** Wizard.
2. Select **OLE DB Data Source** as the monitoring type and click **Next**.
3. On the OLE DB Data Source Name and Description page, enter a name and description of the data source. The name entered appears as a component of the DA, so name it something that makes the most sense in that context. For this example, name it **ACS Database SQL Connectivity**. Select (or create) a custom management pack to save your changes and click **Next**.
4. Click **Build** on the Connection String page.
5. Select the appropriate Provider in the drop-down list. Because the ACS database is a Microsoft SQL database data source, select **Microsoft OLE DB Provider for SQL Server**.
6. Enter the database server's name in the IP address or device name box and the database name in the Database box. For this example, enter the name of the ACS database server (**STRATUS**) and the name of the audit database, **OperationsManagerAC**. The top half of Figure 18.17 shows this configuration. Click **OK** to leave the Build Connection String.
7. Click the **Test** button on the Connection screen.

   The test is performed from the management server and does not necessarily validate the data source is reachable from the watcher node you will select in step 9. After a moment, you should see a green check mark icon and the notice **Request processed successfully**, as shown in the bottom half of Figure 18.17.
8. On the query performance page take the defaults and click **Next**.

18

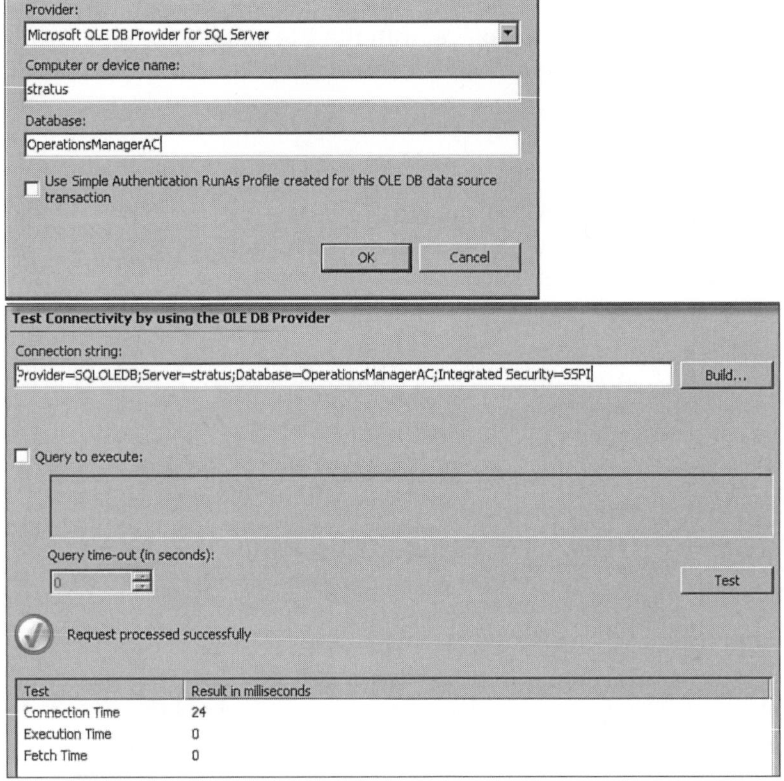

FIGURE 18.17 Successful test of OLE DB connection to the SQL database data source.

9. On the Choose Watcher Nodes page, select one or more managed computers to act as watcher nodes, ideally from several different locations. Because the ACS database can only be accessed inside the private network, it would be appropriate to select watcher nodes physically in separate physical portions of the network, such as different floors or wings.

   Select at least two watcher nodes for each OLE DB data source. This way, when you are alerted to a problem accessing the data source, you can more easily rule out individual watcher node failure. Each instance of a watcher node monitoring an OLE DB data source creates a new object in the OLE DB Data Source State view, which becomes usable by the DA.

   The default interval to run the OLE DB data source query is every 2 minutes. Adjust the query interval as appropriate and click **Next**.

10. Click **Create** and wait several moments. You should then be able to locate the new OLE DB data source monitor(s) in the **Monitoring** -> **Synthetic Transaction** -> **OLE DB Data Source State** view folder. There will be one monitor for each watcher node.

You can return at any time to view or modify the characteristics of the OLE DB data source you created. Perform this task using the **Authoring** -> **Management Pack Templates** -> **OLE DB Data Source** node. Select the data source and click **Properties**. You can rename the data source, modify the data source connection string, and change the watcher node assignments.

Creating the Windows Explorer Data Source Service DA

With the OLE DB data sources configured and watcher nodes appearing in a healthy state at the **Monitoring** -> **Synthetic Transaction** -> **OLE DB Data Source State** view folder, you can use these objects to create the ACS Database Connectivity DA. Perform the following steps:

1. Navigate to and select the **Authoring** -> **Distributed Applications node**. Right-click and choose **Create a new distributed application**.
2. Enter a name and description for the DA. The name you enter here is seen in the Monitoring -> Distributed Applications global view, so use a name that communicates its purpose. For this example, select the name **ACS Database Connectivity**, similar to how the OLE DB data source was named **ACS Database SQL Connectivity** in the "Creating the OLE DB Data Source" section.
3. Choose the **Windows Explorer Data Source Service** template.
4. Select a custom management pack to save the DA; this should be the same management pack to which you saved the web application.

After opening the Distributed Application Designer and choosing to use the Windows Explorer Data Source Service template, you have a logical view of four components and some dependencies, as follows:

- Windows Explorer Data Source Clients, depending on Directory Services, Network Services, and a physical network
- Windows Explorer Data Source Directory Services, depending on a physical network
- Windows Explorer Data Source Network Services, depending on a physical network
- A physical network

This configuration suggests client computers depend on several components, such as directory services and network services, as well as the interconnecting physical network, to access the important data source. To adapt the template to your environment, decide what network services you want to associate with this DA, specifically, those services the data source client depends on using to access the data source.

For this example, use the Active Directory Domain Controller Server 2008 Computer Role for the directory services component and the MSSQLSERVER SQL DB Engine on the ACS database server as client computer dependencies. Add the router the watcher nodes use to reach the ACS database server to the physical network component. This DA will rapidly disclose the failure origin if it is related to Active Directory, the SQL Server database service itself, or the router.

Using the Object Picker in the Distributed Application Designer, proceed to populate the components suggested by the template (following the plan of how they will be utilized), with the objects appropriate for those tasks.

The next task is to rename the DA components (which have long names that include the string Windows Explorer Data Source) with shorter, meaningful names. Here are the reassignments to make:

- Windows Explorer Data Source Clients to **ACS Database Watcher Nodes**
- Windows Explorer Data Source Directory Services to **Domain Controller**
- Windows Explorer Data Source Network Services to **ACS SQL Server**
- Physical network to **ACS DB Router**

Figure 18.18 shows what the DA looks like at this stage in its creation.

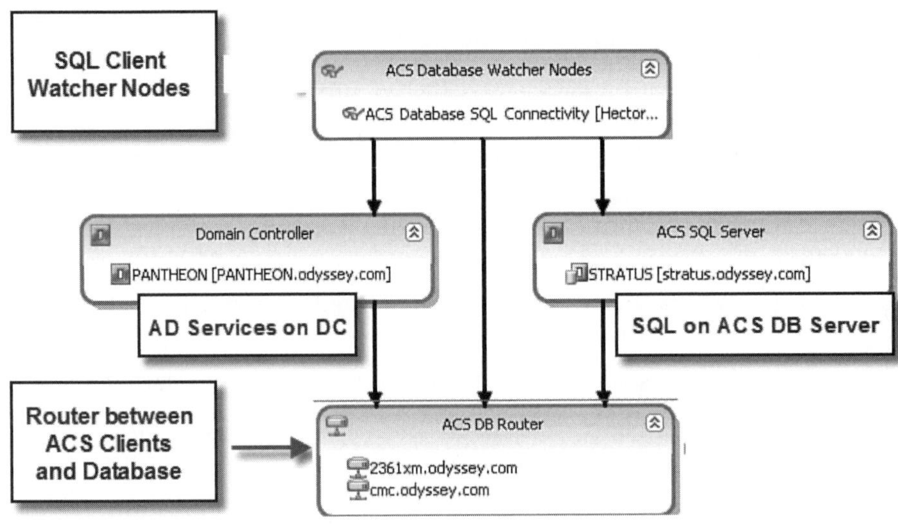

FIGURE 18.18 Initial view of the DA after assigning objects to components.

Customizing the Data Source Service DA

With the Data Source Service DA created, you can customize it with additional information about the environment it will be managing. This includes adding additional components to your custom DA and increasing the fidelity of the health model as desired. In this case, add the network switch layer to the health model. Here are the steps to add a network switch to the DA to promote failure point recognition:

1. In the Distributed Application Designer, click the **Add Component** toolbar icon.
2. Name the component with a meaningful group name and select the **Objects of the following type(s)** radio button. For this example use the name **Network Switches (Server Room)**, because this component is going to contain Network Device objects for the network switches that Active Directory and SQL Server use to connect through in the server room.
3. Select the **Device -> All Network Devices** class type. Click **OK**.
4. In the Objects area on the left, double-click **All Network Devices** to expose the list of network devices in the management group. Select the switches used by the servers.
5. Add the switches to the Network Switches (Server Room) component by either clicking or dragging, or by right-clicking and selecting **Add to -> Network Switches (Server Room)**.
6. Click the **Create Relationship** toolbar icon.
7. Click first on the **Domain Controller** component, and then click on the **Network Switches (Server Room)** component. This creates a component relationship named literally, Domain Controller uses Network Switches (Server Room). You can see that component relationship name in the Details pane when you select the relationship in the Distributed Application Designer.
8. Repeat step 7 for the ACS SQL Server component, then for the ACS DB Router component. Each of these components uses the Network Switches (Server Room) component.
9. Disengage the **Create Relationship** tool (click the toolbar icon again).
10. Click the **Relayout** toolbar icon.
11. Select the connecting (relationship) line between the domain controller and the ACS DB Router and click the **Remove** toolbar icon. Also, remove the connection between the ACS SQL Server and the ACS DB Router.
12. Click the **Relayout** toolbar icon. Figure 18.19 illustrates the DA topology after this step.

    The value of this topology is it will be easier to detect a problem if the network switches in the server room are involved. Likewise, you can rule out failure of a server room switch more quickly when troubleshooting problems in data source connectivity.
13. Click the **Save** icon (or **File -> Save**).
14. Exit the Distributed Application Designer (**File -> Close** or click the **X** icon).

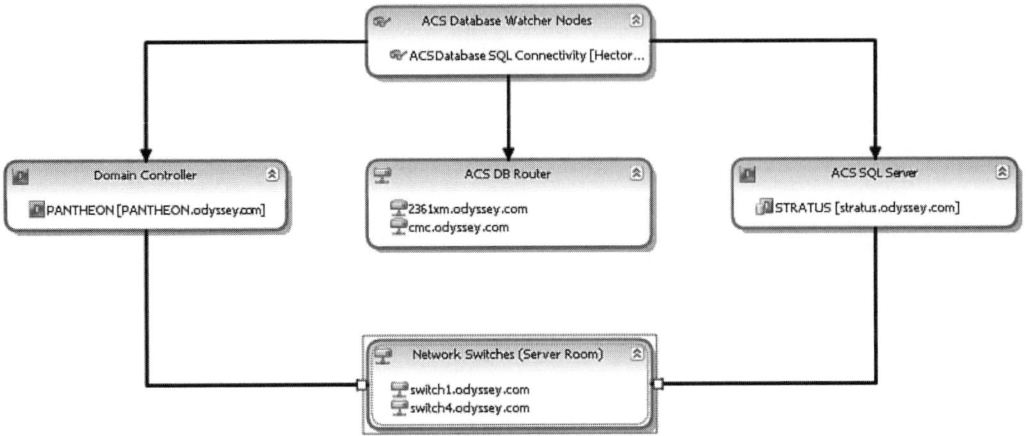

FIGURE 18.19 After adding network switches in the server room as a component.

After several minutes, you can view the health status of the new DA under **Monitoring** -> **Distributed Applications** and **Monitoring** -> **Microsoft Windows Client** -> **Enterprise Health Monitoring** -> **Windows Explorer Data Source Services**.

The last part of this section focuses on enterprise health monitoring by demonstrating the power of the Operations console and OpsMgr distributed applications, showing how you can enhance ACS monitoring to deliver a section of the console focused on these pieces of ACS.

To start this process, create a new folder called **ACS Database Connectivity**; this will contain different views of the DA. After creating a performance, alert, and state view for the DA, create a dashboard view showing the corresponding performance, alert, and state widgets. Figure 18.20 shows the completed dashboard view. For more information on dashboards in Operations Manager, see Chapter 11, "Dashboards, Trending, and Forecasting."

The dashboard view of a DA lets you synthesize data across all component groups and objects. For example, ACS database connectivity issues may correspond to performance issues with domain controllers in the same time frame. The side-by-side presentation of the dashboard view greatly facilitates the ability to compare the alert times with the performance events. Creating the DA assembles the meaningful dashboard elements used for gathering information.

Creating a Distributed Application Health Model

This section looks at monitoring custom applications. A primary purpose of the Distributed Application Designer is to help you create health models for custom applications. A DA is really just a health model—a hierarchical representation of the health of an object, where the object is the subject of the DA.

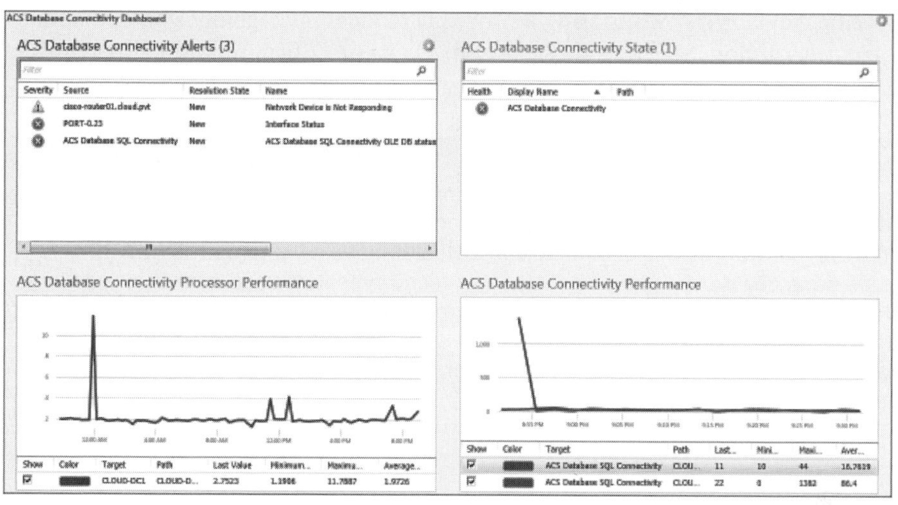

FIGURE 18.20 Using a dashboard to show multiple perspectives on the DA components.

The most fundamental way to create a health model is by authoring a management pack with the OpsMgr software development kit (SDK). However, in addition to using the SDK to author the health model for an object, you can also use the Distributed Application Designer to create a health model. The Distributed Application Designer is almost like a "layman's SDK," allowing you to transfer knowledge about how the health of an IT service should be assessed, from your mind to the DA.

REAL WORLD: DISTRIBUTED APPLICATIONS TO PROVIDE ACTIONABLE ALERTING

A major benefit of a DA is it can assist in creating more actionable alerting. For example, suppose your organization has a web-based application with several servers as part of the web tier. Out of the box, Operations Manager sends alerts when any of these web servers or the website is offline. However, in your particular environment it may only be actionable to alert if more than 50% of the web servers are offline. By adding these servers to a DA, you can configure the alerting to either not occur for the loss of a single web server or alert at a lower priority and/or severity. This means you can create alerts based on conditions affecting the overall health of an application rather than the health of an individual component of an application. For more information, see Cameron Fuller's blog posting at http://blogs.catapultsystems.com/cfuller/archive/2010/09/13/using-distributed-applications-to-generate-actionable-alerting.aspx.

To create a custom DA, you must model the end-to-end service you will be monitoring. This means you need to identify all the components that make up the service and determine the relationships between components. E2E service modeling, when done properly, is the process of instrumenting and monitoring every application layer and component, such that the appropriate level of visibility and information is provided at the right time. Remember, a potent characteristic of DAs is that they do not monitor everything; they monitor specific, key objects. Monitoring key objects reduces management burden and speeds problem resolution. Selecting those key objects is the critical task in E2E service modeling.

REAL WORLD: USING THE SDK VERSUS A DA

If your organization is critically dependent on a complex custom application, sometimes known as a Line of Business (LOB) application, consider creating a health model programmatically using the SDK as a long-term solution. Health models authored with the SDK can include advanced monitoring, diagnostic, and recovery features you cannot include in a DA. However, it is relatively easy and quick to create and deploy a DA using the graphical Distributed Application Designer, compared to authoring a management pack in eXtensible Markup Language (XML) with the SDK. You might also deploy a DA as a first step toward authoring a custom health model in the SDK, gathering initial performance data and piloting component relationships.

The tool for graphically building E2E service models is the Distributed Application Designer. This chapter has already discussed using the Distributed Application Designer. It has also shown how to use the Windows Explorer Data Source Service and the Windows Internet Explorer Service DA templates to create and customize DAs that monitor connectivity to a SQL database and access to a critical website. Here are several other templates available in the Distributed Application Designer:

- **.NET 3 Tier Application:** This is part of the default management packs included with Operations Manager and is discussed in Chapter 15, "Monitoring .NET Applications."
- **Line of Business Web Application:** This template is part of the default management packs included with Operations Manager.
- **Messaging:** This template is part of the default management packs included with Operations Manager.
- **Office SharePoint Portal Server Farm:** This template is added with the SharePoint Portal Server 2003 management pack. While not a commonly used management pack at this time, it is still relevant for organizations that have not upgraded to a newer version of SharePoint.
- **RD Session Host Farm:** This is added with the Remote Desktop Services management pack.
- **Windows Azure Application:** This template is added with the Windows Azure management pack. For more information on this template, see Appendix A, "OpsMgr by Example: Configuring and Tuning Management Packs."
- **Terminal Services Farm:** This template is added with the Microsoft Windows Terminal Services management packs.
- **Windows Explorer Data Source Service:** This template is discussed in the "Windows Explorer Data Source Service Template" section.

- **Windows Internet Explorer Service:** This is discussed in the "Internet Explorer Service Template" section.
- **Windows SharePoint Services Farm:** This template is added with the Microsoft Windows SharePoint Services management pack.
- **Blank:** This template is part of the default management packs included with Operations Manager.

TIP: FINDING MANAGEMENT PACKS THAT INCLUDE DISTRIBUTED APPLICATION TEMPLATES

There is no easy way to know which management packs include distributed application templates. This tip discusses a method used when authoring this book to identify all distributed application templates currently available.

Do not perform this process in a production environment; it should only be used in a lab environment to identify those management packs that include templates. Before attempting to import these management packs, validate there is plenty of free space in your operational database.

To identify those management packs with templates, download all the management packs from the MP catalog using the Administration -> Management Packs node in the Operations console. Right-click **Management Packs**, then select **Download Management Packs**. Search on all management packs in the catalog and add them to the download list. Once the management packs are downloaded, remove any language packs not required (in an English speaking environment, this includes CHS.mp, RUS.mp, CHT.mp, DEU.mp, ESN.mp, FRA.mp, ITA.mp, JPN.mp, KOR.mp, and PTB.mp) and import the remaining management packs. This will bring the management pack file count to less than 300.

Import all remaining management packs into OpsMgr. If there are errors listed on the management packs, resolve them or remove the MPs. (The process to add these management packs to a lab environment may take a while and stress test both your Operations Manager server and your database server—a lunch or dinner break is recommended at this point!)

As a last step, remove any additional language packs not required for this environment if any were missed. Here is a PowerShell script you can use to remove them; assuming only English management packs are required:

```
Get-SCOMManagementPack | where{$_.defaultlanguagecode -notlike "ENU"} | Remove-
SCOMManagementPack
```

This PowerShell example is a subset from http://www.systemcentercentral.com/BlogDetails/tabid/143/IndexID/93897/Default.aspx. In the Odyssey environment, adding these management packs brought the management pack count loaded in Operations Manager up from 145 to 360.

(Another option is to use the list of templates provided in this section rather than having to go through the process yourself! The list is current as of early August 2012 and created using the process discussed here.)

The "Windows Explorer Data Source Service Template" and "Internet Explorer Service Template" sections discussed the Windows Explorer Data Source Service and Windows Internet Explorer Service DA templates. These two templates are integrated with the Microsoft Information Worker management pack; both feature watcher node perspective components. Because they are part of a complete management pack solution, those two templates include enhanced predefined views and alerting features.

The other five templates exist to help speed up the deployment of DAs, so the following sections will look at the characteristics of each. The idea is that you start by selecting a template that most closely matches the DA you want to monitor.

TIP: GETTING A QUICK START WITH SERVICE MODELING

Selecting a template that matches the DA you want to monitor gives you a head start in your service modeling task. After creating the DA, add views in the Monitoring space and create custom reports as desired.

Line of Business Web Application Template

Figure 18.21 shows the Create a Distributed Application dialog, with the template selected to create a Line of Business Web Application.

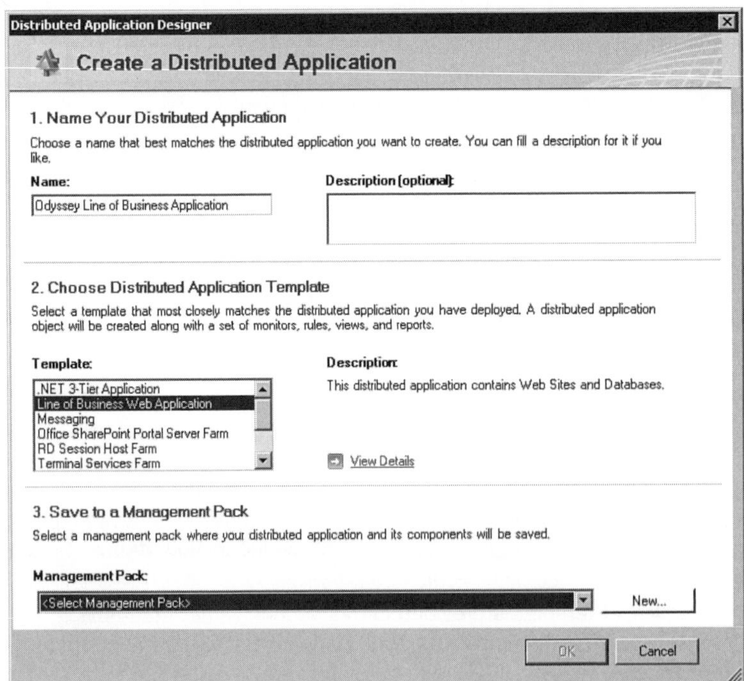

FIGURE 18.21 Creating a distributed application based on the LOB template.

A Line of Business application is generally a large application on which businesses bet their company. These applications automate large processes such as financials, customer support, marketing, sales, and commerce. Most large organizations have one or more LOB applications, which may be purchased or leased from a single LOB application vendor, or may be a patchwork assemblage of applications from various vendors that together constitute the LOB application.

Many modern LOB applications utilize a web browser as a user interface, and almost all include one or more backend databases. The components of the Line of Business Web Application DA template represent these common features of LOB applications. After creating the LOB DA as shown in Figure 18.21, the Distributed Application Designer opens with a very simple view: a Web Sites component that uses a databases component. Figure 18.22 is the initial view of the LOB DA (with the Objects pane hidden).

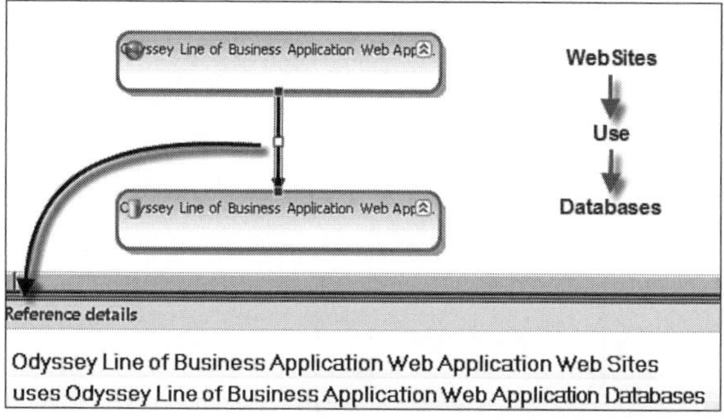

FIGURE 18.22 The core of an LOB application is websites using databases.

The default custom LOB DA has two components with a single relationship; the Line of Business Web Application template predefines those components as Web Sites and Databases.

Figure 18.22 shows the connector selected between the Web Sites component and the Databases component. This causes the header of the Details pane to change to read Reference details and the contents of the pane to spell out the relationship between the components the connection references, that being the Web Application Web Sites uses Web Application Databases. The diagram view of the DA represents the connector as a non-containment relationship.

TIP: SAVE CUSTOM DAS TO UNIQUE MANAGEMENT PACKS

Consider a policy of saving your custom DAs in dedicated management packs. This makes it easier to create custom views in the Monitoring space that target information about the DA. It also makes the DA a portable solution by causing its configuration to be stored in the unique XML file of the custom management pack. In addition, remember to save your DA as the first action you take in the Distributed Application Designer (click the **Save** icon on the left side of the toolbar). The dynamic view shortcuts in the Object Details area only become available after you first save the DA.

Before you monitor a service, you must add objects to components. Every entity in your Operations Manager management group is an object to which you can add a component in a DA. If you previously discovered the entity using a different management pack, it will be a selectable object to add to a DA component.

To utilize the function of Line of Business Web Application template, add one or more websites that use (depend on) one or more databases. Once you add a monitored object of the `Web Sites` class (a website) to the Web Sites component, that component begins to report the rolled-up health status of the objects. To add objects to the Web Sites component, you must locate suitable objects in the `Web Sites` object class. You will find those objects of interest in the Object Picker.

Working with the Object Picker

The Object Picker is the navigation and multi-purpose panel on the left side of the Distributed Application Designer. Use it to expose the objects available to select from the Organize Object Types portion of the Object Picker. Figure 18.23 is a composite illustration of the same instance of the Object Picker, showing the object picker, database objects, and website objects.

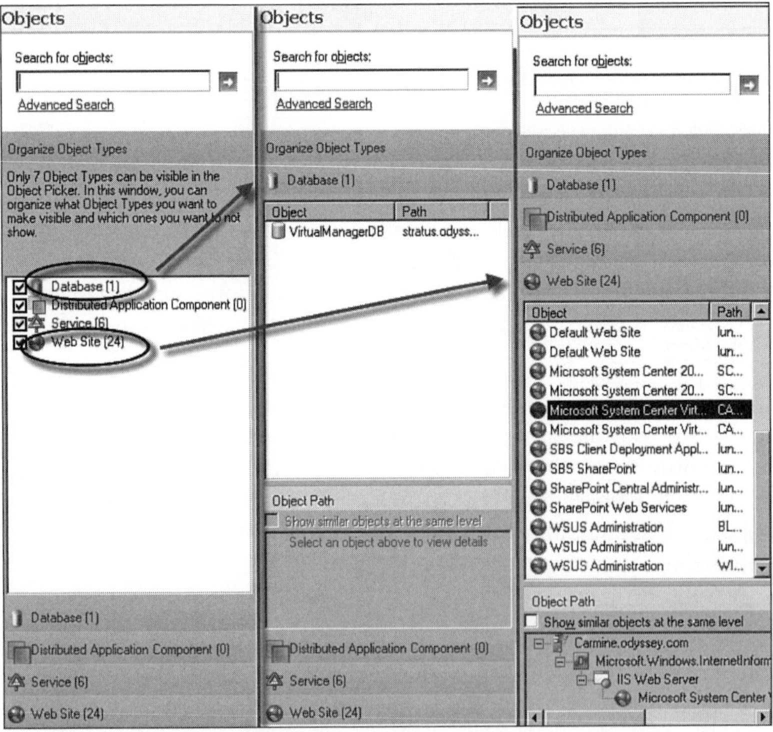

FIGURE 18.23 The Object Picker organizer (left), and object type views (center, right).

The Object Picker includes a top-level organizer window that lists all the object classes available to select objects to add as components in the DA. Seen in the left side of Figure 18.23, the new DA opens with this organizer window active. Here is a description of the purpose and usage of the organizer window:

- All eligible classes (that being those classes with components of the type that can be added to components in the DA) appear in the organizer window list.
- Only up to seven object types (classes) can be visible in the Object Picker; that is, available to select.
- It is possible more classes will be associated with the components in the DA than these seven, in this case there will be too many to be visible for selection in the Object Picker.
- Use the check marks in the organizer window to select the seven classes you currently are working with; you can change these selections on the fly as you use the Object Picker.

Object types with a check mark in the organizer window also appear as navigation tiles to select in the lower portion of the Object Picker. Here are the object types, visible in the lower-left corner of Figure 18.23:

- Database
- Distributed Application Component
- Service
- Web Site

The Distributed Application Component and Service object types are always available in the organizer. The Database and Web Site object types are available because the components in the DA based on the LOB template are associated with the `Database` and `Web Sites` object classes.

Clicking the Database navigation tile exposes the objects in the `Database` class. These are all the instances of databases on managed computers in your management group. See the center portion of Figure 18.23, with the Database object type selected in the Object Picker. In the center of this window is a scrolling list of monitored databases, with columns for the database name and the computer that hosts the database.

Hovering over the object names exposes the third dimension of the Object Picker, the object type tip, which confirms the object class. In the top center portion of Figure 18.23, hovering over the VirtualManagerDB object causes the tip **SQL Database** to appear for several seconds. The VirtualManagerDB was added to the Database component of this DA; this database is associated with the Microsoft System Center Virtual Machine Manager (VMM) application, the subject of the LOB DA. The VMM self-service website depends on the SQL database of the VMM service; this application compactly demonstrates the model of the LOB DA template.

The Web Site object type is selected in the Object Picker on the right side of Figure 18.23. When selected, all websites of all monitored computers in the management group are exposed. If you hover over the Microsoft System Center Virtual Machine Manager 2012 Self-Service Portal object in the center-right portion of this figure, the tip **IIS 7 website** appears. Selecting the object populates the Object Path panel in the bottom of the Object Picker, which exposes the Service Modeling Language of the object. The tip and the Object Path are there to assist with selecting the correct and desired object. Add that website to the Web Site component of this DA.

TIP: MONITORING SPECIFIC OBJECTS

The action of adding a specific website demonstrates a powerful concept of the DA. Operations Manager is not monitoring the IIS services on the web server; it is watching the particular website of interest. Likewise, OpsMgr is not watching the SQL services on the system running SQL Server; rather, it is monitoring the database the website depends on. In conventional server-based monitoring, if anything were amiss on the web or database servers, the state rollup would show as unhealthy. In the E2E model, some unrelated problem can exist on either server—but as long as the components in the DA remain healthy, administrators responsible for the DA are not unnecessarily alerted to those unrelated infrastructure issues. In addition, SLAs written against the health of the DA are not penalized outages that do not affect the health state of the distributed application.

Customizing the LOB DA

The DA is now ready to run in a valid minimum configuration. One website in the Web Site component depends on one database in the Databases component. You can add additional VMM websites and databases to the same two components now or in the future. You can also add other components and relationships to increase the fidelity of the health model. One recommended customization is to rename the components to **Odyssey VMM Web Sites** and **Odyssey VMM Databases**, and to name the custom DA to **Odyssey VMM**. (Rename the DA by selecting **File -> Properties**.)

The initial design of the Odyssey VMM DA is complete. Figure 18.24 shows the finished DA in the Distributed Application Designer.

In the center of Figure 18.24, see the Odyssey VMM Web Sites component (above), using the Odyssey VMM Databases component (below) in the main window of the Distributed Application Designer. This screenshot also shows the diagram view, which was launched using the shortcut in the lower-right corner of the Detail pane (circled). The Distributed Application Dynamic Diagram view opens in a new window.

The Distributed Application Dynamic view feature of the Distributed Application Designer lets you preview the appearance of your DA in the state, alert, and diagram views. These handy shortcuts let you see those views before creating associated view folders. Notice in the diagram view of the Odyssey VMM DA, the relationship **Web Sites uses Databases** is reflected in the non-containment arrow (light blue and dotted) pointing from the Odyssey VMM Web Sites icon to the Odyssey VMM Databases icon.

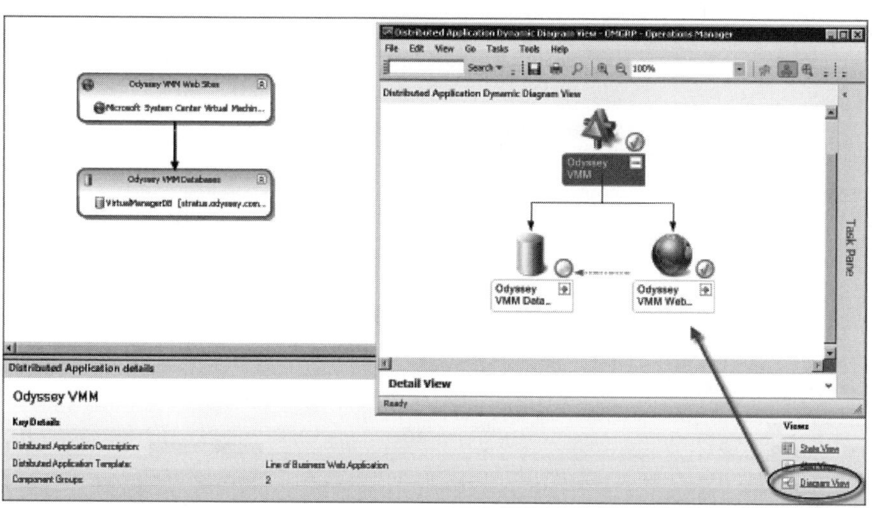

FIGURE 18.24 The Dynamic Diagram view lets you preview monitoring views.

After closing the Distributed Application Designer, a final task in deploying this LOB DA is to create views in the Monitoring space. When the Odyssey VMM management pack was created, it created an empty view folder in the Monitoring space. (This occurs with all custom-created management packs, not only those associated with the Distributed Application Designer.) To make it easy to create monitoring views focused on the DA, you can make the DA the target of custom views created in the view folder. In the Monitoring space, create an Odyssey VMM performance view and an Odyssey VMM state view in the Odyssey VMM view folder. Follow these steps to add an alert view:

1. In the Monitoring space, locate the view folder with the name of the DA. If you renamed the DA in the Distributed Application Designer, you will see the view folder with the original DA name. Right-click and select **Rename** to make the folder name match the new name of the DA.
2. Right-click this folder and select **New -> Alert View**.
3. Enter the name and description of the folder. This name will appear in the Navigation pane of the Monitoring space. For this example, use the Name **Odyssey VMM Alert View** to match the naming scheme for this view folder.
4. Next to the Show data related to Entity item, click the **...** button.
5. Locate the name of the DA in the list of targets, or type the DA name in the Look for field. If you cannot locate the DA, verify you selected the **View all targets** radio button. Figure 18.25 illustrates this step.
6. Select the name of the DA and click **OK** twice.

You could create additional custom views of the DA or a custom dashboard to display more information for your new DA. You could also enable particular notification features for alerts from the DA, such as email or instant message notification, and remember you can target the generic OpsMgr Alerts and Availability reports against the DA.

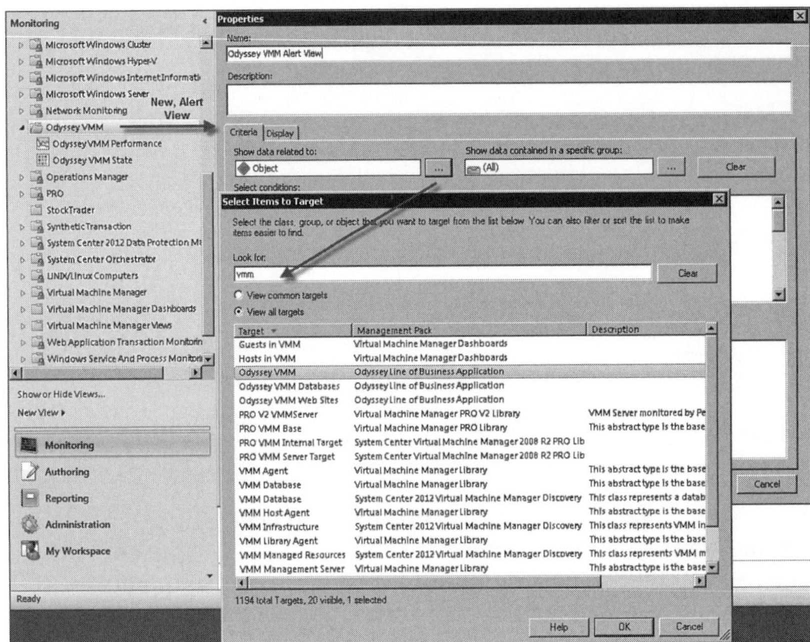

FIGURE 18.25 Creating a custom alert view for a distributed application.

Messaging Template

Regardless of whether you imported the Exchange management packs, or even if you don't use Microsoft Exchange, Microsoft includes a template you can use to create a DA that represents an enterprise messaging system.

If your organization uses Exchange, the Exchange Service DA included in the Exchange management pack may meet your requirements. However, the Exchange Service DA is part of the sealed Exchange management packs and cannot be edited, meaning you cannot define new components and relationships in this DA. A custom DA based on the Messaging template can be edited as needed. If your organization does not use Exchange, you could create a custom DA based on the Messaging template that exactly models those messaging services and components you have.

Figure 18.26 shows a completed custom DA based on the Messaging template to demonstrate how you can augment the monitoring of your Exchange organization. Table 18.1 lists the components of the Messaging template, as well as the object type each component accepts, and suggests the objects to include in your custom DA.

The Odyssey Enterprise Messaging DA, displayed in Figure 18.26, has eight object types listed in the organizer section of the Object Picker. Seven of the eight have check marks next to them, indicating that those object types are visible for selection. Trying to check an eighth object type generates the message **You will have to unselect a selected Object Type first in order to select a new one and make it visible.** You can have only seven visible object types on the Object Picker!

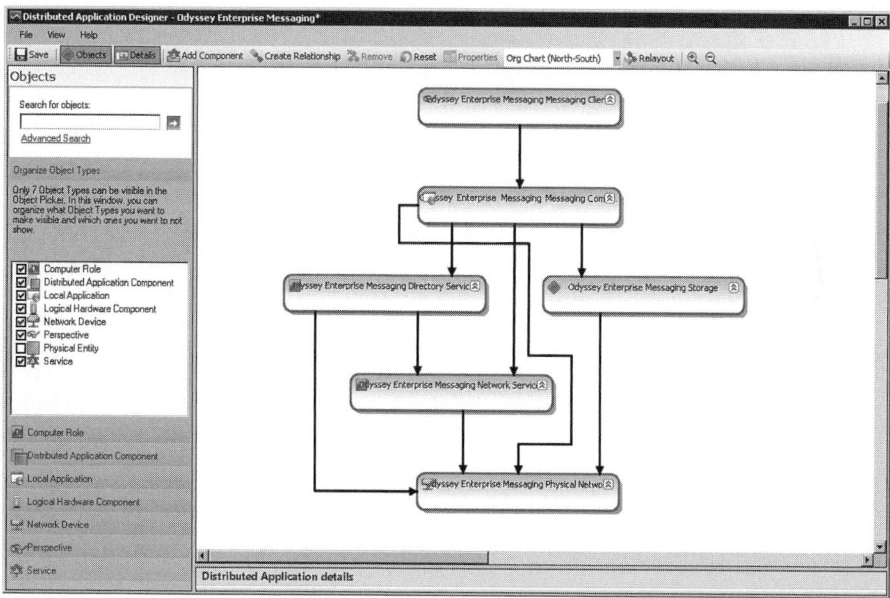

FIGURE 18.26 A custom enterprise messaging DA based on the Messaging template.

TABLE 18.1 Components included in the Messaging DA template

Component	Object Type	Suggested Uses
Messaging Client	Perspective	Create TCP Port or web application synthetic transactions to model your client messaging application; assign watcher nodes
Messaging Components	Local Application	Server applications core to messaging functions
Messaging Storage	Logical Hardware Component	Physical location(s) of the messaging database(s)
Messaging Directory Services	Computer Role	Active Directory Domain Controller(s)
Messaging Network Services	Computer Role	Other network services such as IIS or DHCP
Messaging Physical Network	All Network Devices	Routers, switches used by the components in the DA

Terminal Services Farm Template

Many organizations support groups of identical servers, known as *farms*, which work together to provide load balancing and failover for client connections. A web farm is a common scenario, where multiple web servers are load balanced either by round robin or Network Load Balancing (NLB) techniques. Another very common farm application is terminal services, using either the native Windows Terminal Services or a Citrix farm. Farm applications are by definition also distributed applications, with the same service extended across multiple computers.

While the OpsMgr software distribution media includes Microsoft Windows Terminal Services management packs available for import, the preferred approach is to download the latest version of the management packs from the System Center Marketplace (http://systemcenter.pinpoint.microsoft.com/). Importing these management packs creates views, adds reports, and adds a Terminal Services Farm DA template. The views and reports present an aggregate listing of all terminal servers and related services that exist in the management group—they do not include any diagram views or topology generation features as do the Active Directory and Exchange management packs.

Microsoft provides a template for specifying the architecture and dependencies of a Terminal Services Farm. Creating a DA based on the Terminal Services Farm template gives you a topology-based tool to monitor and troubleshoot your farm. You can create a DA for each terminal services or Citrix farm in your organization. Table 18.2 lists the components in the Terminal Services Farm DA template.

TABLE 18.2 Terminal Services Farm template

Component	Object Type	Suggested Uses
Terminal Server	Terminal Server Role	All terminal servers in the farm
Terminal Services Session Directory	Terminal Services Session Directory Role	The server specified as the session directory server in the farm configuration
Terminal Services Licensing Server	Terminal Services Licensing Server Role	The Terminal Services Licensing Server for your domain
Windows Domain Controller	Windows Domain Controller	Active Directory Domain Controller(s) used by the farm members, session directory, and licensing servers
Network Devices	All Network Devices	Routers, switches used by the involved servers

Figure 18.27 illustrates a new custom DA named Odyssey Terminal Services farm as it is being created. This example shows the Terminal Server Session Directory object (top left) and a network device object (bottom center). Domain controllers are added by selecting the DC object in the Object Picker, and then dragging and dropping it on the DC component.

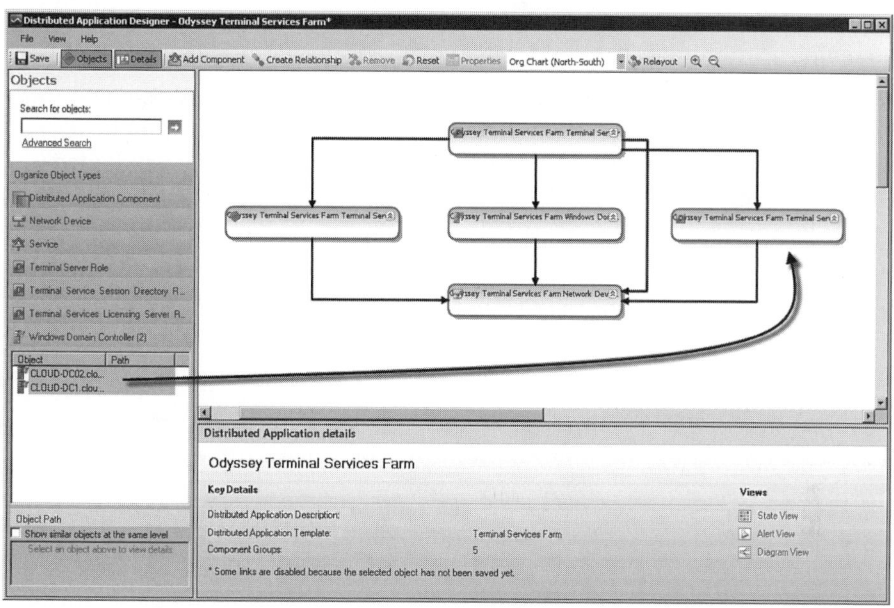

FIGURE 18.27 Adding a domain controller to the Terminal Services Farm DA.

The Terminal Server Session Directory component is a feature allowing users to reconnect automatically to disconnected sessions in a load balanced Terminal Services farm. The session directory keeps a list of sessions, indexed by user and server name. A Terminal Services farm will not function correctly if there are problems with the Terminal Server Session Directory. Likewise, the farm will fail if connectivity to the Terminal Server Licensing server is lost or the licensing service fails.

DAs based on the Terminal Services Farm template can help you track the vital services specific to the Terminal Services application. If you support more than one farm, having multiple DAs is particularly helpful to segregate views of the terminal servers and session directory server (for a particular farm) from the licensing server and those domain controllers that may be shared by multiple farms.

.NET 3 Tier Application

OpsMgr 2012 added the .NET 3 Tier Application to provide a distributed application template that includes the new .NET monitoring functionality discussed in Chapter 15. One of the interesting things to consider when using Operations Manager 2012 is the depth of monitoring that is available and extends to other System Center 2012 components. As an example, when using the .NET Application Performance Monitoring management pack template, OpsMgr identifies .NET components in App Controller, Configuration Manager, Orchestrator, and Virtual Machine Manager that OpsMgr 2012 can monitor using application performance monitoring (APM) components.

The next example uses the Orchestrator management pack created in Chapter 17 in the .NET 3 Tier Application distributed application template to highlight how .NET monitoring is integrated into DAs. Here are the steps to create a DA using the .NET 3 Tier Application template:

1. In the Authoring space, create a new distributed application. For this example name the application **Orchestrator** and save it in the **Orchestrator Monitoring** management pack. This management pack will include the .NET monitoring distributed application for System Center 2012 Orchestrator.

2. Add the components from the Objects pane for each of the four different sections of the DA (Orchestrator Client Perspective, Orchestrator Presentation Tier, Orchestrator Business Tier, and Orchestrator Data Tier). Figure 18.28 shows the Orchestrator Presentation Tier, Business Tier, and Data Tier added to the DA.

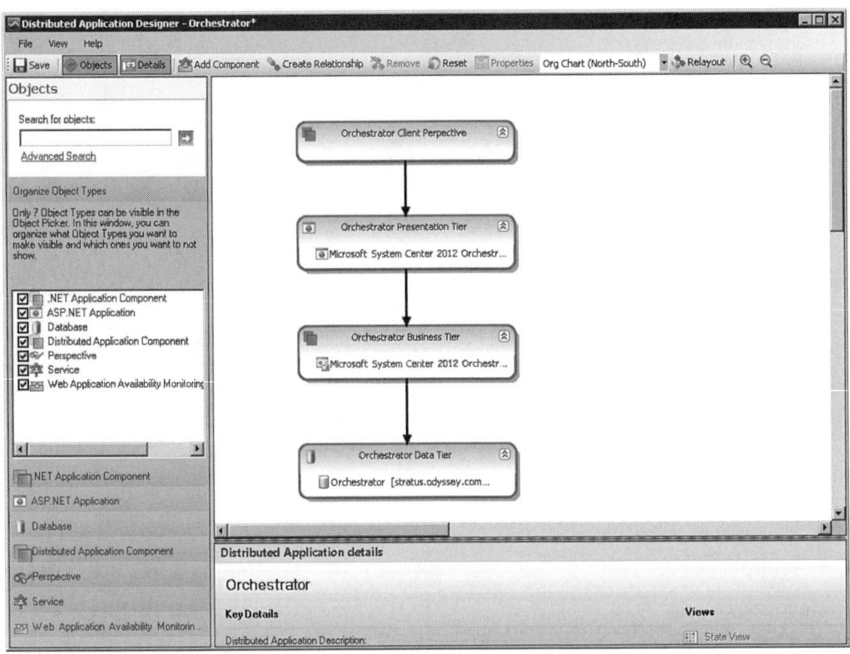

FIGURE 18.28 .NET 3 Tier Application template.

Prebuilt distributed application templates simplify the process of creating a distributed application by targeting the Distributed Application Designer to the relevant components. This provides a framework that uses these components and provides a predefined set of relationships for the DA. The Orchestrator example shows how quickly you can integrate in-depth monitoring within System Center; you can use this same functionality for in-house applications.

Blank Template

Building a new custom DA based on the Blank template in the Distributed Application Designer is about as "unleashed" as you can be in the Operations console. You have available as your palette every object discovered in your management group. The only constraint with the Blank template is you can only add objects to components matching the type (or class) for which the component was created. However, because you can also create a custom component for every class in the management group, the possibilities are infinite.

REAL WORLD: DYNAMIC DISTRIBUTED APPLICATIONS

For distributed applications to be even more useful, they should be designed so they can dynamically adjust to changes in their membership. Here's an example: An organization running a web farm with four servers adds two web servers to the farm. The DA should be able to dynamically update its membership and include the new web servers.

Implement this functionality in Operations Manager 2012 using a group with dynamic membership based upon a registry key on the system and embed this group into the design for the DA. This enables the DA to adapt as group membership changes. For further discussion on this topic, see http://blogs.catapultsystems.com/cfuller/archive/2011/11/28/opsmgr-dashboard-integration-server-health-creating-a-health-state-for-a-group-of-servers-in-a-dashboard.aspx.

When you begin creating a DA based on the Blank template, the Object Picker only contains the Distributed Application and Service object types. OpsMgr efficiently allows custom DA and DA component reuse across all DAs. The following example focuses on how to build out monitoring a network topology in OpsMgr 2012. Chapter 11 introduces the Summary Dashboard - Map, showing how to label objects with longitude and latitude information and display them on a dashboard. This dashboard map only displays geo-locations for Web Application Availability Monitoring; while extremely useful for the web application availability items, it does not provide what is required to show a full network topology view.

To create this network dashboard, here are the technologies that will be combined to provide a network topology view for OpsMgr 2012:

- **Network Monitoring:** The built-in network monitoring functionality of OpsMgr 2012 provides the health state of one of the routers in this example. For more detail on the network monitoring functionality available in OpsMgr 2012, see Chapter 16, "Network Monitoring."
- **TCP Port Monitoring:** TCP port monitoring is a synthetic transaction available out of the box in OpsMgr 2012. TCP port monitoring is useful for monitoring network devices (such as those not supported by the out-of-the-box network monitoring functionality in OpsMgr 2012).
- **Ping Monitoring:** OpsLogix has a free ping management pack that provides ping level monitoring for network devices (such as those not supported by the out-of-the-box network monitoring functionality in OpsMgr 2012). For additional information, see http://www.opslogix.com/download.

- **Visio Integration or Savision Live Maps:** You can design a map displaying the various OpsMgr entities using either of these technologies. Chapter 11 provides additional information. This chapter uses Visio integration. For an example of this type of map creation for network devices with Savision Live Maps, see *System Center Operations Manager 2007 R2 Unleashed* (Sams, 2010).

Often the built-in network monitoring functionality combined with Visio integration or Savision Live Maps is sufficient for this type of network diagram. However; for this example, the goal is to show the various technologies available and how each can be used in the dashboard and how you can gain functionality using a DA.

Monitoring Redundant WAN Links

Assume you have a geographically distributed environment using redundant WAN links to provide connectivity between locations and want to monitor these links with OpsMgr. Specifically, you want to know if a remote location is up or down, and be alerted when specific links go offline.

TCP port monitors by themselves can provide rudimentary network monitoring (up/down and response time). However, this gets more complex when you have redundant links and want alerting should you lose the link to the remote location and a critical alert occurs, or if you lose all connectivity to the remote location. This situation is one where distributed applications can be extremely useful.

Using the Distributed Application Designer to Create the Redundant WAN Link

To provide redundancy if a single watcher node fails, configure two different watcher nodes for each network link you are monitoring using a TCP port monitor that monitors the IP address of the router or switch on port 22. Create a TCP port monitor for both the primary and the backup router connections to the remote site. Use the Distributed Application Designer and a blank template to model this network configuration, as displayed in Figure 18.29. Follow these steps:

1. In the Authoring space, create a new distributed application. For this example name the application **Denver Network Link** and save it in the **Network Monitoring** management pack. This management pack will include the TCP port monitors monitoring the connections to network devices over primary and backup network links to Denver.

2. Unique naming conventions make it easier to identify components to add to a distributed application when using a blank template. For the example, searching on Denver gives the various component names containing "Denver," including the primary and backup network links.

3. Highlight the first two TCP port monitors as shown in Figure 18.29, right-click, and select **Add to New Component Group**. Add a new component group called **Denver Router (backup)** and leave the Denver Router (backup) checked for the type of objects it could contain (shown in Figure 18.30).

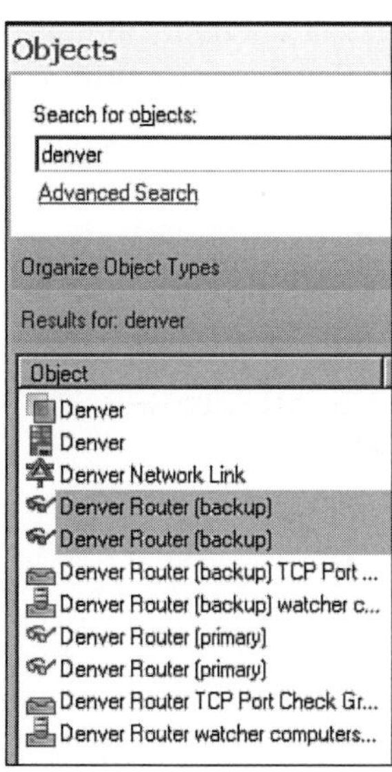

FIGURE 18.29 Searching for Denver in the Distributed Application Designer.

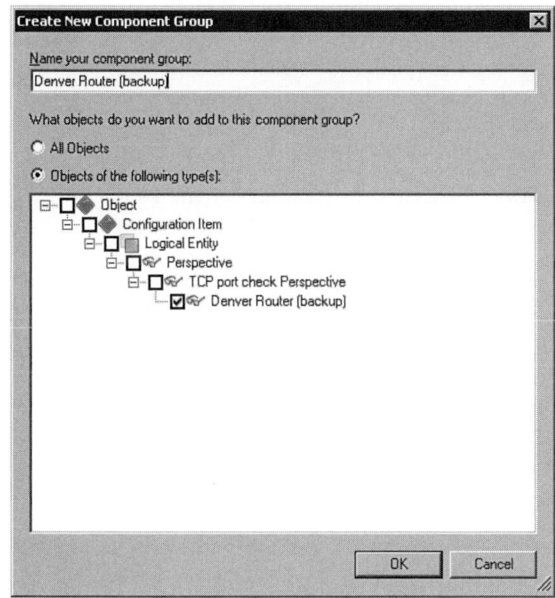

FIGURE 18.30 Component group objects.

4. Perform the same step to create the Denver Router (primary) component group with the Denver Router (primary) objects.

5. Configure the two links to provide a warning alert if both watcher nodes report an error. By highlighting one of the containers, you can use the **Configure Health Rollup - Availability** option (circled in Figure 18.31) to alter how health is rolled up.

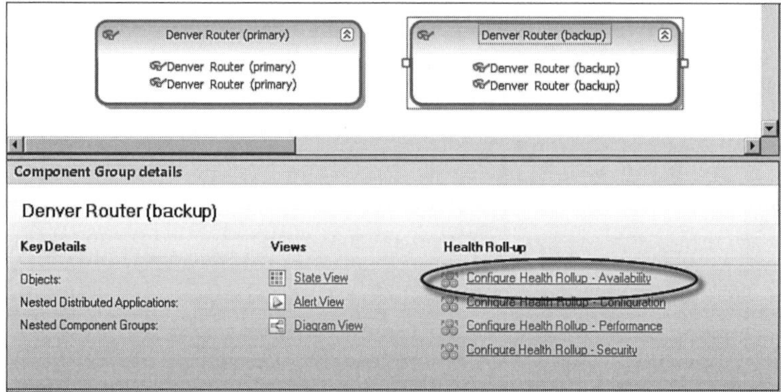

FIGURE 18.31 Denver Network link DA.

6. Use the Rollup Algorithm of Best Health State so that if a single watcher node experiences an issue, this would not be enough to indicate the network link is down. Figure 18.32 shows this configuration. Configure this for both the Denver Router (primary) and Denver Router (backup) links.

7. Save the distributed application so the relationships are applied.

8. Next, open the Monitoring pane and open the Health Explorer for the Denver Network Link. Within Health Explorer, highlight the **Availability - Denver Network Link** and change the health rollup to use **Best health state** (this is the same setting shown at the bottom of Figure 18.32). This configures the DA so it will only change state if both the network link components in the DA are in a critical state (i.e., when both the primary and backup links are critical).

9. Now, bring the Visio add-in tool into this equation. OpsMgr can provide a view of the health of a distributed application and a diagram view of the distributed application, but it lacks a user interface with the capability to represent the network topology graphically.

   Visio integration can provide a high-level overview of the state of the entire network by displaying the health of various objects (including DAs in a Visio diagram). Figure 18.33 shows an example of how you can insert objects into a Visio diagram from OpsMgr, in this case based on the `Network Device` class.

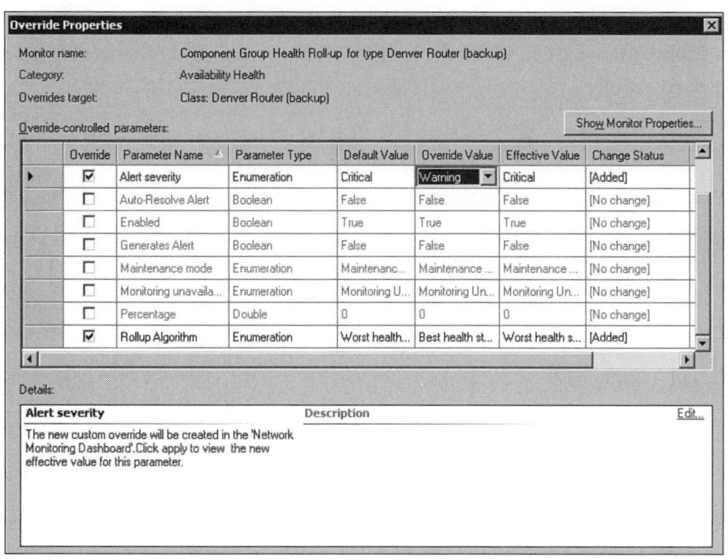

FIGURE 18.32 Configuring alerting and health state for the links.

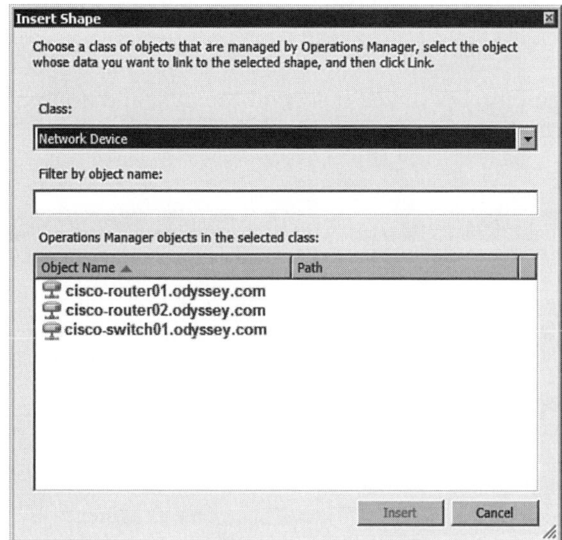

FIGURE 18.33 Inserting shapes from OpsMgr into Visio.

10. Figure 18.34 shows the network link between locations using Visio integration. This map displays the status of the network devices at each location. (Austin, Phoenix, and Washington are network devices monitored by OpsMgr, Denver is the DA designed in this section, and Tampa is a DA built using the OpsLogix Ping management pack.) The map also shows how you can add built-in network devices, distributed applications, and synthetic transactions into a web-accessible Visio diagram.

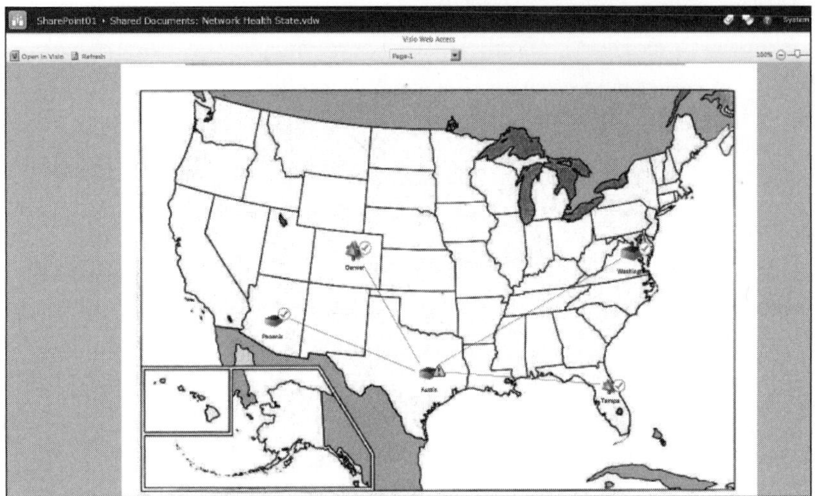

FIGURE 18.34 Visio integration using DA components and more.

11. With Visio integration, you can highlight any linked object on the map and double-click the icon to open the OpsMgr Web console for the selected object.

TIP: IDENTIFYING IP ADDRESSES FOR REMOTE NETWORK DEVICES

There are multiple ways to determine IP addresses for remote network devices:

- The recommended approach is to ask your network team for a list of IP addresses and ports you can use to validate a connection is online between your locations. If there is no port available for communication, you can use a ping monitor, previously mentioned in the "Blank Template" section.
- If your network team does not provide the necessary information, you could perform a traceroute to a server in the remote location. From that traceroute, test the IP address listed prior to the server's IP address. Using telnet, test this IP address to port 22 to determine if it is a networking device. If not, move back one IP address on the traceroute until you locate the appropriate network device. This only works when the location you are attempting to reach does not have multiple networks and network traffic for the device is not restricted to port 22.

The TCP Port monitor is only one of several options to monitor network links. Other alternatives include third-party management packs and SNMP monitoring.

Fast Track

Distributed applications and the Distributed Application Designer have not changed significantly since the release of OpsMgr 2007. The following are key concepts to remember about DAs in OpsMgr 2012 if you are already familiar with DAs in OpsMgr 2007:

- **Distributed Application Design Templates:** The "Creating a Distributed Application Health Model" section lists Distributed Application templates that are available with OpsMgr 2012.
- **.NET 3 Tier Application:** This template was added as part of the APM integration in OpsMgr 2012 and is discussed in the ".NET 3 Tier Application" section.

Summary

Congratulations, you made it through the whole chapter without monitoring a single server! The focus of this chapter was on the dispersed set of components that deliver a service to users and customers, achieving end-to-end monitoring in many applications. The chapter began by discussing the roots of the distributed application in the programming world and explained what a distributed application means in OpsMgr. It then took a close look at predefined DAs for OpsMgr and Active Directory. The chapter also discussed client perspective and watcher nodes in enterprise health monitoring scenarios. The last part of this chapter covered building DAs such as a .NET Line of Business application and a Terminal Services farm. In Chapter 19, the focus is on how to use OpsMgr to provide more insights into your client systems in addition to server systems.

CHAPTER 19
Client Monitoring

IN THIS CHAPTER

Clients are how System Center 2012 Operations Manager (OpsMgr) refers to non-server computers, sometimes referred to as workstations. Clients run Windows operating systems and may or may not have an OpsMgr agent installed. You can use OpsMgr to improve your users' experience with client computers.

With the new System Center 2012 license model, if your organization is using System Center 2012 Configuration Manager (ConfigMgr) for client management, you may be licensed to use OpsMgr on clients as well. As there is really no feature overlap between ConfigMgr and OpsMgr, you might find that adding client management to your OpsMgr implementation has a number of benefits.

Client Monitoring Features

OpsMgr includes three independent solutions designed specifically to improve the client experience. You can use any or all of these OpsMgr features on your network:

- ▶ **Agentless Exception Monitoring (AEM):** Collecting and reporting application errors and system crashes, without the OpsMgr agent installed.
- ▶ **Customer Experience Improvement Program (CEIP):** Centrally compiling and forwarding information about Microsoft product usage; requires AEM to be installed.
- ▶ **Client Operating System Management Packs:** Tailored monitoring of agent-managed client computers, optional enhanced monitoring of selected business-critical clients.

This chapter covers AEM and the CEIP; it also discusses the client operating system management packs. Together, these new features represent another way you can get value from System Center.

Simple disruptions, such as the time spent waiting for an application to restart after a crash, are a nuisance to a single user. However, when distractions from productivity occur frequently across many clients, this can have a dramatic effect—similar to or greater than that of a server outage. Using OpsMgr's client monitoring capabilities can help you alleviate that impact.

Early Steps to AEM: Dr. Watson

About 20 years ago, Microsoft released a simple debugger application for the Windows NT 3.0 beta named Dr. Watson (drwatson.exe), taking its name from fictional medical doctor John Watson, sidekick of Sherlock Holmes, the detective created by the author Sir Arthur Conan Doyle. The icon for Dr. Watson and Watson applications in Windows depicts a man carefully listening with a stethoscope. Like the icon representation, the point of Dr. Watson was to collect information, unobtrusively.

The initial drwatson.exe application created an on-demand snapshot of the computer state when a user application hung (became non-responsive). The 32-bit drwtsn32.exe version of Dr. Watson replaced drwatson.exe in Windows 2000. This version, labeled by Microsoft as a "program error debugger," included crash dump support for kernelmode crashes (blue screens), in addition to user-mode application crashes. Over time, Microsoft dropped the "Dr." title, and the term "Watson" came to describe the anonymous error collection process.

Early Watson versions wrote only crash state information such as stack traces to local files on the hard drive. This information was available to in-house developers or sent to Microsoft as part of a product support troubleshooting investigation. With the release of Office XP, Microsoft added the Watson debugger, which, with user permission, anonymously forwards crash information to Microsoft itself.

Figure 19.1 shows a Windows XP desktop with the original drwatson.exe on the left and its replacement drwtsn32.exe on the right. Drwatson.exe is a legacy program error debugger; Microsoft recommends using Drwtsn32.exe instead of Drwatson.exe if you are still running Windows XP.

Since 2001, Microsoft has collected, aggregated, and analyzed vast numbers of application error reports to identify problems that users experience with their Windows computers and applications. This information helps prioritize development resources for bug fixes and service packs.

Corporate Error Reporting: To AEM and MDOP DEM

In 2002, with the release of Corporate Error Reporting (CER) 1.0 as part of the Office XP Resource Kit, Microsoft began making Watson crash information available to network administrators as well as to Microsoft. Naturally, once administrators learned Microsoft was receiving this information, some wanted to see what that information was, and possibly make use of it in-house. Office XP was the only application that was Watson-aware at that time.

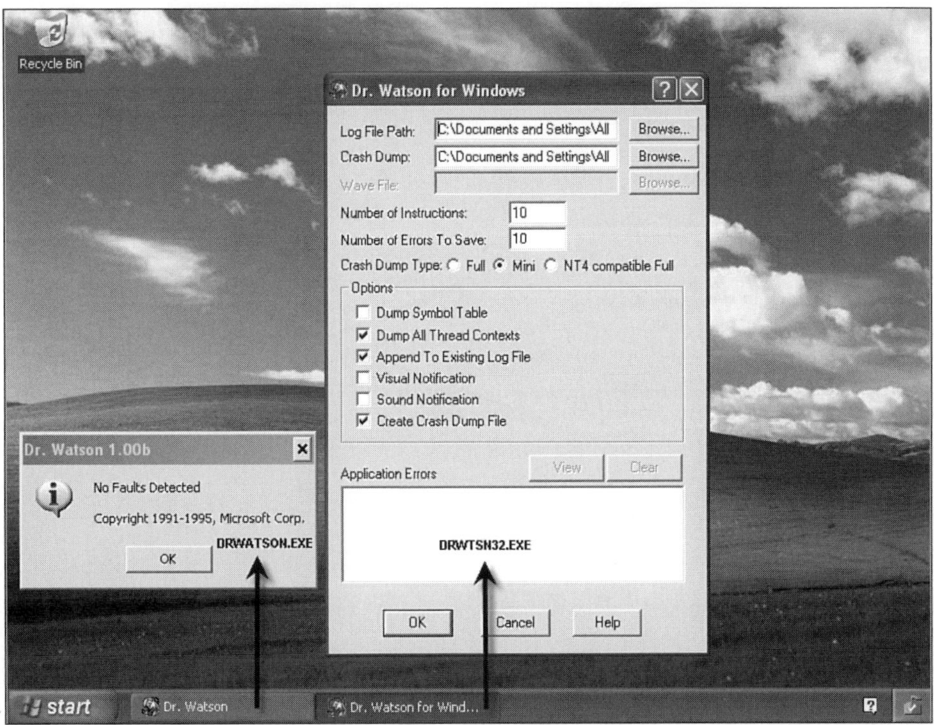

FIGURE 19.1 (Left) Legacy drwatson.exe, (Right) Updated DrWtsn32.exe on Windows XP.

In 2003, Microsoft made CER 2.0 available to Software Assurance (SA) customers through the Volume Licensing program. Installing CER creates a shared folder structure to contain error report data on the server hosting the service. The error-reporting client (Watson) accesses the root of the CER shared folder through a Universal Naming Convention (UNC) path, specified in the local computer's policy for error reporting. CER 2.0 also provides a group policy template to help administrators deploy the CER settings to workstations.

The core functionality of CER is similar in OpsMgr AEM. Microsoft renamed Watson functionality in Windows Vista to Windows Error Reporting (WER). Figure 19.2 shows the successor to Dr. Watson, the Action Center in Windows 7. Settings in the Maintenance menu of the Action Center control the behavior of WER in Windows 7.

Operations Manager 2012's AEM feature retains and extends CER 2.0's functionality. Although CER was free for those Microsoft customers with Software Assurance, the AEM feature set is no longer free, even for SA customers. Microsoft SA customers looking for a CER replacement need to either run OpsMgr 2012 (to deploy AEM along with monitoring their environment) or purchase Microsoft Desktop Optimization Pack (MDOP) for Software Assurance.

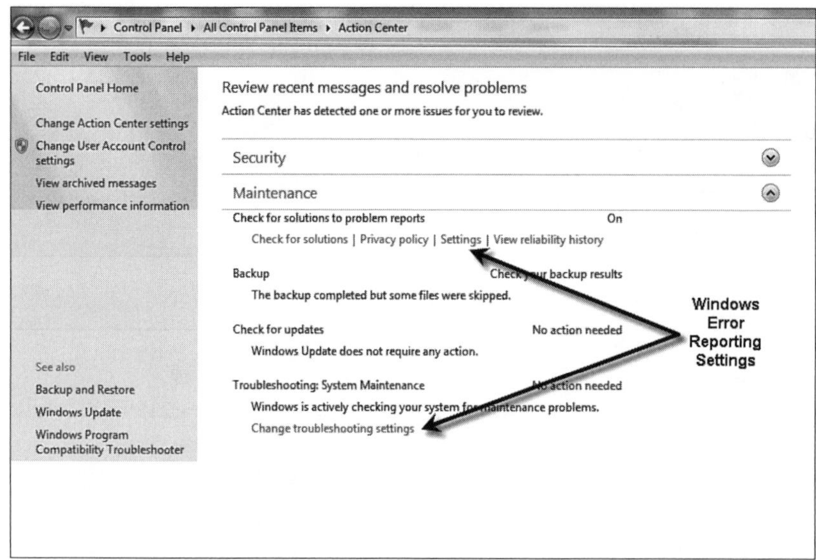

FIGURE 19.2 Error reporting settings in Windows 7: Action Center -> Maintenance.

The MDOP includes the Microsoft System Center Desktop Error Monitoring (DEM) component. DEM is a modified OpsMgr management group, with only the AEM collection and reporting features enabled. DEM (a subset of the Operations console) is essentially an updated CER console for those SA customers who do not wish to deploy the entire OpsMgr 2012 product. For more information about MDOP DEM, see http://www.microsoft.com/en-us/windows/enterprise/products-and-technologies/mdop/default.aspx.

Monitoring Client Machines

One can consider the modern desktop or portable computer as a platform service for a business or organization. The client is where the user experience occurs. Looking at the client as a platform means you are envisioning the operating system and applications on the client as a manageable service. Managing that platform holistically, rather than as many independent components, can improve the user experience as well as achieve a lower total cost of ownership (TCO) for the platform.

This manageable platform entity is constructed using the client monitoring features in OpsMgr 2012. OpsMgr assembles monitoring tools for different components involved in delivering the user experience and integrates them in the Operations console. The client monitoring features in OpsMgr 2012 allow you to measure the quality of your users' client experience.

Client Monitoring Challenges

An organization's success depends on the success of its people, and making employees more productive through communication is the primary rationale behind Information Technology (IT) investments. However, it is difficult to measure an IT organization's effectiveness in delivering the client experience to employees using traditional tools and methodologies.

Compare client support teams with server and infrastructure support teams, which often have a variety of diagnostic and reporting tools to provide metrics on their performance. For example, availability of a server farm is a valid measure of the job performance of the farm's administrator or service provider. How would you measure the quality of the user experience on your organization's desktop and notebook computers? Small gains in improving the quality and usefulness of the client experience can have immediate and noticeable impact on bottom-line productivity.

Using System Center Configuration Manager

System Center Configuration Manager focuses on initial provisioning and configuration compliance of workstations. ConfigMgr is great at deploying an operating system (OS) or application, and keeping it configured and updated as needed. However, ConfigMgr does not provide active feedback regarding the health of the OS and applications. An exception is that the Endpoint Protection feature includes an email alerting capability for endpoint protection infections and outbreaks, as shown in Figure 19.3.

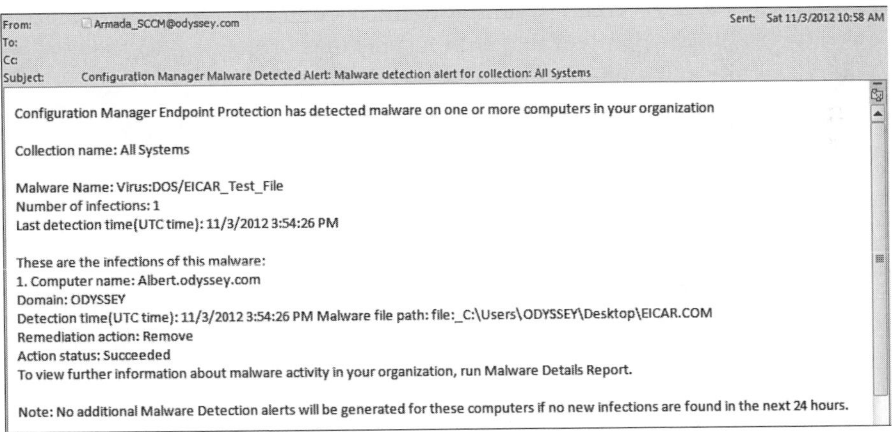

FIGURE 19.3 An emailed alert about endpoint protection status from ConfigMgr.

Using Network-Level Monitoring

Network-level monitoring of workstations, such as ping monitors, is problematic. As you expect mobile devices to be unavailable some or most of the time, a notebook computer that does not respond to a ping does not indicate a user does not have a functioning desktop! The user may be working just fine on a different network you are not pinging, or may be working offline. In actuality, a client computer that is present and alive to respond to pings tells nothing about the health or use of the OS and user experience.

End User Problems Are Costly

When an application or the operating system hangs or crashes, the typical person just reboots their computer. This is a somewhat satisfying experience for users; they remain in control of their workstation, don't need to bother anyone else, and 90% of the time, can continue work after the reboot. However, there are some steep downsides to this behavior:

- Employee productivity loss during system restart with loss of employee confidence in using the client platform.
- Possible data loss, with lost time to re-create the data lost during the crash or hang.
- IT is unaware of the event and is therefore unable to correlate issues to enterprise infrastructure changes.
- Root cause remains unknown and unrepaired, with no association determined between the problem and possible available solutions.

For users that contact the IT help desk, there are costs incurred by the help desk staff plus additional productivity loss by the employee while interfacing with the help desk. The help desk escalates issues they are unable to resolve (perhaps because they have not seen the problem before) to a desktop administrator, who often cannot devote much time to solving a "one-off" error—particularly if that error just disrupts or slows down the user, rather than completely derailing him.

Total work stoppages tend to get attention fast—a user or his supervisor quickly telephones the help desk when one or more people cannot do their job. OpsMgr gives you visibility into another dimension of the user experience—to identify intermittent work interruptions that would otherwise go unreported, or perhaps even be accepted as a cost of doing business.

Consider the incremental and recurring nature of the little productivity losses that organizations suffer. Occasional hangs and crashes of applications and client operating systems do occur with real-world users (although hopefully rarely). Real-world analysis of crash and hang information can reveal a strategically non-random distribution of errors and crashes. In fact, you can usually identify leading causes of errors, indicating where first efforts at remediation should take place.

The graph shown in Figure 19.4 highlights the distribution of the types of errors collected by Microsoft. This curve is consistent across almost all applications and components. Knowing which errors occur most often facilitates the most efficient targeting of resolution efforts. OpsMgr provides the intelligence to make the most effective decisions. Specifically, *if you can fix the top 20% of the defects, you can recover 80% of the productivity lost* to client issues. AEM develops the prioritized list of most important defects to fix.

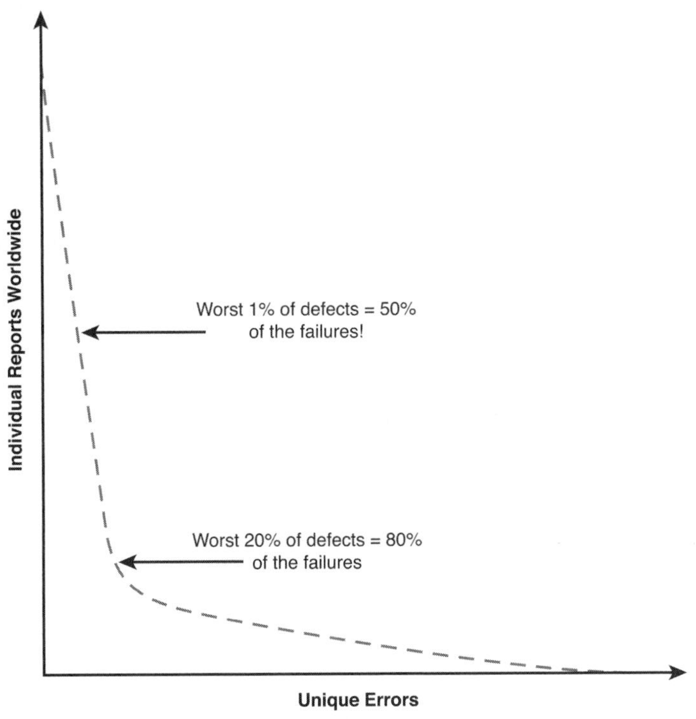

FIGURE 19.4 The shape of the error-reporting curve is what makes AEM so powerful.

Features in OpsMgr for Monitoring Clients

System Center 2012 Operations Manager combines technologies in novel ways to create a very credible client monitoring package. OpsMgr's client monitoring features effectively address the issues related to large-scale workstation populations.

There can be considerable latitude in your deployment architecture for the "right" client monitoring solution. While smaller organizations can certainly deploy an OpsMgr agent to every client computer, for larger client populations (a rule of thumb might be above about 500 client systems), you will probably get better results with a mix of agentless and agent-installed monitoring types.

The most effective deployment of client monitoring involves identifying four classes of client computers and applying a specific monitoring model to each class:

- **Agentless Exception Monitoring only:** This is the bulk of your clients, perhaps 90% or more in very large organizations. These computers have no OpsMgr agent. AEM settings, pushed by Active Directory (AD) group policy, integrate with Windows Error Reporting (Watson). AEM provides visibility for resolution knowledge for client crashes.

  Using this model, all client computers in the enterprise, including those with OpsMgr agents, have group policies enabled to use AEM.

- **Aggregated Client Monitoring:** These computers are representative of the supported client populations. A small percentage of distributed clients have an installed OpsMgr agent, leveraging the concept that a randomly selected subset of a larger population has statistical relevance to the entire population. The purpose of aggregated monitoring is to collect metrics, viewed in the Reporting space of the Operations console, that detect trends and top issues; Aggregated Client Monitoring does not raise individual alerts on clients. Alerts occur when a large number of client systems have the same problem; this is known as *aggregated alerting*.
- **Business Critical Monitoring:** This deepest level of monitoring includes individual computer alerting for key events. These will be your most important client computers—typical candidates are VIP computers, point of sale (POS) systems, kiosks, and network administration workstations. You can optionally enable alerting on loss of heartbeat for these computers.
- **Synthetic Transaction Monitoring:** These selected client computers, known as *watcher nodes*, play a key role in managing larger enterprise applications. Any client with an OpsMgr agent can host instances of synthetic transaction monitors that will perform certain client functions, measuring the success of the operation from the user perspective. Use synthetic transactions to guarantee end-to-end service delivery, such as monitoring an intranet site from a branch office.

Your tasks are to deploy AEM for the enterprise, and then identify which client computers will have OpsMgr agents installed for Aggregated, Business Critical, or Synthetic Transaction Monitoring. After installing those agents, designate selected agent-managed clients for Business Critical Monitoring and/or Synthetic Transaction Monitoring. The remainder of this chapter discusses and demonstrates the use of each of these client monitoring capabilities.

Monitoring Agentless Systems

Agentless Exception Monitoring does not use the OpsMgr agent. Implementing AEM involves just two steps: activating the AEM feature on an OpsMgr management server, and deploying a group policy object (GPO) with AD. The next sections present AEM architecture so you can understand what is happening under the hood.

AEM Architecture

To understand the architecture of AEM, consider the default behavior of the Watson and Windows Error Reporting clients without AEM, and compare this with how things work with AEM in the picture. Remember that Windows XP computers have the legacy Watson clients included with the operating system; Windows Vista and later computers have WER built-in.

These error-reporting clients, by default, request user permission after a crash or hang to transmit the information to Microsoft's back-end error reporting services. Here are the events that take place after invoking Watson/WER, illustrated in Figure 19.5:

- If the user gives permission, the Watson or WER client makes direct Internet connection using Hyper Text Transfer Protocol (HTTP) to the Microsoft back-end servers. These back-end servers have the Uniform Resource Locators (URLs) of watson.microsoft.com and sqm.microsoft.com. The Watson back-end service receives error information, and the SQM (Software Quality Metrics component of the Microsoft Customer Experience Program) back-end receives CEIP information.
- During the initial HTTP connection, a check takes place to see if Microsoft is aware of this type of error. If Microsoft has not seen the type of error before, the interface asks the user for permission to upload additional information about the error.
- The connection is changed to secure mode (HTTPS), and the crash or hang error information is uploaded, along with the additional data if it was requested and permission was granted.

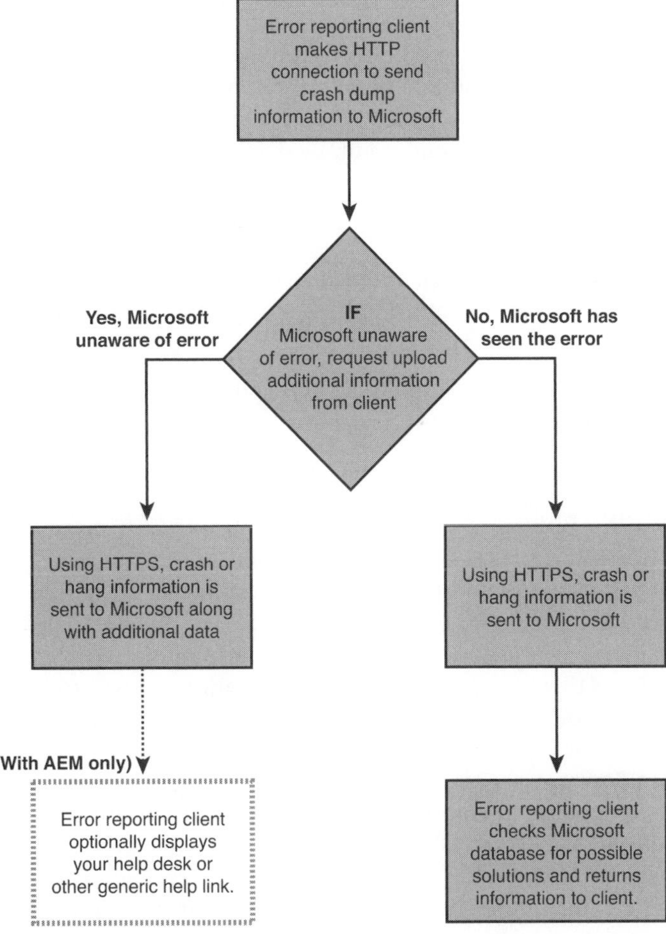

FIGURE 19.5 Error reporting client processing flow.

- The error reporting client checks a Microsoft database of possible solutions for known errors during the connection. If there is a known patch, update, or work-around for the reported error, the user gets a dialog box with a link marked **More Information**. Clicking that link opens a web page at microsoft.com on their desktop, hopefully providing helpful information. (Optionally, AEM returns a generic web link, such as a help desk link, when no possible solutions link is available.)

When you deploy AEM polices via a GPO, it configures registry keys on the client computer with values that change the behavior of Watson or WER. Error reporting clients look for these registry keys prior to sending any reports to Microsoft. If you have configured Watson or WER for AEM, the error report is redirected to the organization's AEM server. Computers configured as AEM clients no longer attempt to connect directly to Microsoft over the Internet.

Activating AEM on an OpsMgr management server creates two avenues for collecting error data. One is for legacy Watson clients (Windows XP) and the other for WER clients (Windows Vista and later). The Watson collection component is a shared folder on the AEM server accessible by all domain users and computers (but not anonymously). The WER collection component is an HTTPS listener end point, by default on port 51906.

When an error or crash occurs on a computer configured to use AEM, the report goes to the designated management server:

- The Watson client on Windows XP computers uses the Remote Procedure Call (RPC) protocol to create a folder structure, based on the error parameters, inside the expected shared folder on the management server.
- If the error or crash occurs on a Windows Vista or later computer, the WER client connects to the HTTPS listener to upload the information.

Crash and Hang Monitoring

You will want to initiate the AEM feature of OpsMgr to detect application hangs and OS crashes on computers with or without OpsMgr agents. Begin by enabling AEM on a selected management server, and then deploy the AEM GPO with Active Directory. The selected management server must have at least 2GB free disk space and cannot have an existing file share named "AEM," as this is created during AEM activation. These processes are discussed in the following sections.

Enabling AEM on a Management Server

To use AEM, you must activate one of the management servers in your environment to provide the AEM feature. Activate the server using the Operations console in the Administration pane under **Device Management -> Management Servers**. Right-click the management server and select **Configure Client Monitoring**. This starts a wizard that enables AEM on the server. Follow these steps:

1. The wizard starts with an introductory page, describing each of the steps that will occur: configuring where Customer Experience Improvement Program data is sent, where errors are sent, transmission settings, and end-user error crash behavior. Click **Next**.

2. On the CEIP Forwarding page of the wizard, configure the Customer Experience Improvement Program. You can configure how CEIP collects data in several ways:

   ▶ Continue to send data directly to Microsoft (default).

   ▶ Use the selected management server to collect and forward data to Microsoft.

   If you select the second option, you can specify whether to use the Secure Sockets Layer (SSL) protocol, whether you use Windows authentication, and the specific port number (which defaults to 51907), as shown in Figure 19.6.

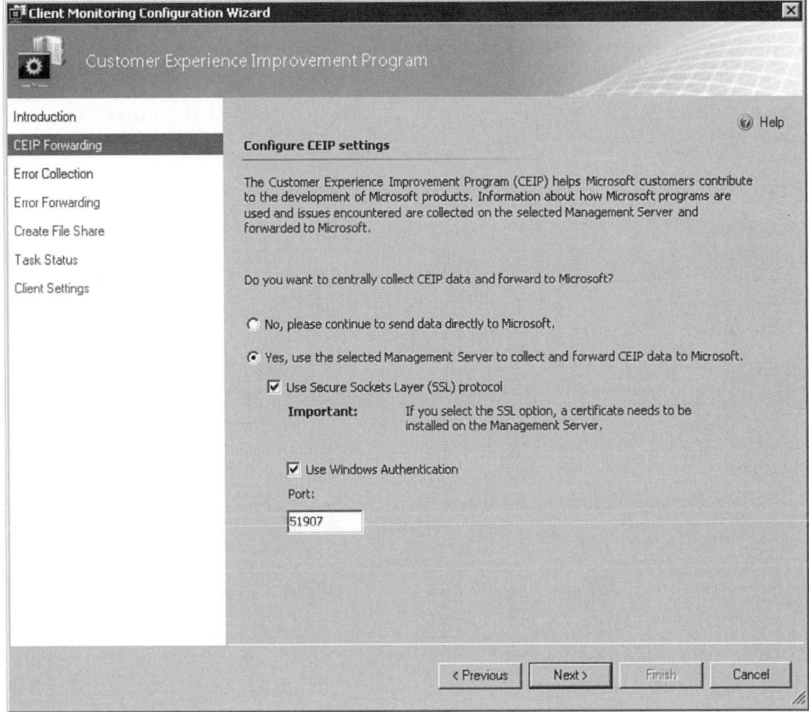

FIGURE 19.6 Customer Experience Improvement Program settings page.

3. Specify the following on the Error Collection settings page:

   ▶ The location of the file share path (which must have at least 2GB free disk space)

   ▶ Whether error reports will be gathered for Windows Vista and later computers, and if so, what port to use (defaults to 51906)

- Whether you will use SSL and Windows Authentication for Vista and later clients
- The organization name to be displayed in messages on the local client

Figure 19.7 shows this settings page configured for a local AEM file share to the folder **C:\AEM**, all Vista and later client features enabled, and the organization name specified as **Odyssey**.

4. On the Error Forwarding settings page, select to forward basic or detailed error signature information to Microsoft. Allowing detailed forwarding means that when Microsoft requests additional data about the hang or crash (because Microsoft has not seen the error before), the additional data is forwarded along with the error signature. Click **Next**.
5. At the Create File Share page, select to use the Action Account and push **Next**. The wizard will create the file share and report success, then click **Next** again.
6. The wizard completes with the Client Configuration Settings page, where you confirm the folder location to save the group policy administrative template (a file with the .ADM extension). The default is the Documents folder of the current user. Select **Finish**.

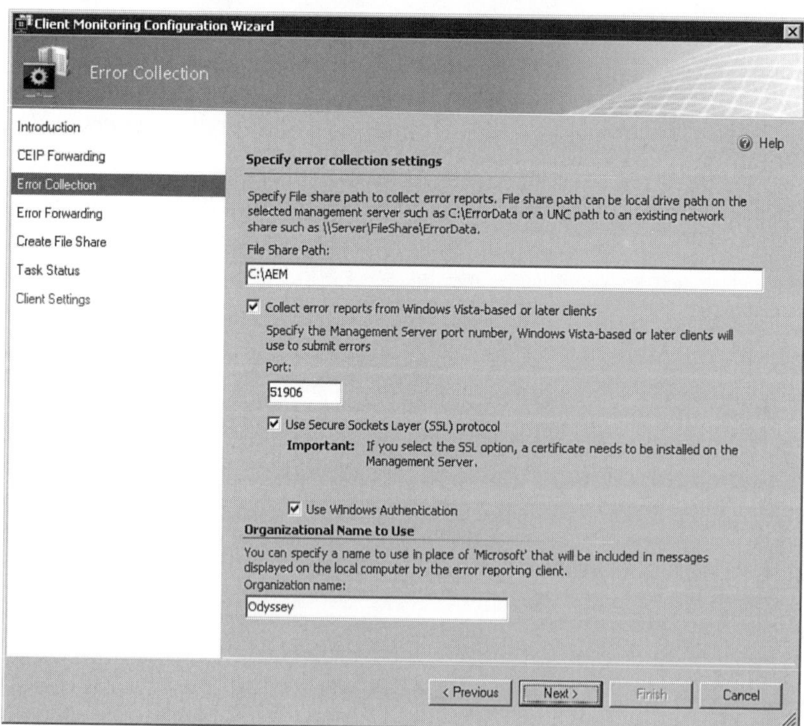

FIGURE 19.7 AEM error collection settings page.

TIP: INSTALL GPMC ON THE AEM MANAGEMENT SERVER

If your OpsMgr administrator account is also a domain administrator, save time by installing the Group Policy Management Console (GPMC) on the management server that will have AEM enabled. You will need to import, link, and edit domain group policy. To install GPMC on the management server, use the Add Features Wizard in Windows Server Manager and select the Group Policy Management feature.

Deploying the AEM Policy

Enabling AEM on a management server by running the Configure Client Monitoring wizard also saves a group policy template with the .ADM file extension. The file name will be the FQDN of the management server; for example, hannibal.odyssey.com.adm is the name of the template file for management server Hannibal. Here are the recommended steps to deploy AEM policy to your domain(s) using the GPMC:

1. Open the GPMC and navigate to the Group Policy Objects node in the domain (**Group Policy Management** -> **Forest:** *<forest>* -> **Domains** -> *<domain>* -> **Group Policy Objects**). Select the node, right-click, and choose **New**.
2. Name the policy as desired. In the example using the Odyssey domain, the name **Windows Error Reporting (Watson)** is used to distinguish this GPO.
3. Locate the new policy in the tree below the Group Policy Objects node, select the policy, right-click, and choose **Edit**.
4. The Group Policy Object Editor opens. Navigate to the **Computer Configuration** -> **Policies** -> **Administrative Templates** node, right-click and select **Add/Remove Templates**.
5. The Add/Remove Templates dialog opens; click **Add**. Browse to the location of the template file saved by the Configure Client Monitoring Wizard. For Odyssey, the path is the My Documents folder of the current user and the file name is hannibal.odyssey.com.adm. Select the file and click **Open**.
6. Observe that the Current Policy Templates list now includes the imported template, and click **Close**.
7. Returning to the Group Policy Object Editor, notice there is now a Microsoft Applications node under Computer Configuration -> Administrative Templates -> Classic Administrative Templates (ADM).
8. Expand the Microsoft **Applications** -> **System Center Operations Manager (SCOM)** node to reveal the four subordinate nodes that begin with the words **SCOM Client Monitoring**.

9. Beginning with the first node, SCOM Client Monitoring CEIP Settings, select the node on the left side of the GPMC and double-click to open each Settings item in the right side of the GPMC. With the individual Settings item open, select the **Enabled** radio button. This exposes the values for that setting that you selected when running the Configure Client Monitoring Wizard; click **OK**.

10. Walk the tree of subordinate nodes in the System Center Operations Manager (SCOM) node, selecting and enabling each feature as desired. (Repeat step 9 for each client monitoring setting you want to configure.) In all there are 11 Settings items that correspond to the questions and responses utilized by the Configure Client Monitoring Wizard.

11. Now, navigate to **Computer Configuration** -> **Administrative Templates** -> **System** -> **Internet Communications Management** -> **Internet Communications**. Double-click **Turn Off Windows Error Reporting**, select **Disabled**, and click **OK**.

12. Optionally disable the User Configuration portion of the GPO. In environments with many GPOs, user logon processing is faster when you disable the user portion of GPOs that contain no user settings. To disable the User Configuration portion of the GPO, right-click the root of the policy in the Group Policy Object Editor, and select **Properties**. Tick the **Disable User Configuration Settings** item and click **OK**.

13. Select **File** -> **Exit** (or click X) to close the Group Policy Object Editor and return to the GPMC.

14. Select where to link the new GPO. Because there is only one AEM server per management group and since you want to include all computers in the domain, you will usually link the GPO at the root of the domain.

    To enable AEM on all computers in the domain, right-click the domain object and choose **Link an Existing GPO**. Select the GPO—in the Odyssey example case, **Windows Error Reporting (Watson)**—and click **OK**.

15. The new GPO appears under the domain root with a shortcut (link) icon. Figure 19.8 illustrates the GPO linked at the domain root in the GPMC. If there are other domains in your Active Directory forest, you can expose them in the GPMC by right-clicking **Domains** and selecting **Show Domains**. Repeat the linking procedure from step 14 for each domain desired. Close the GPMC.

Verifying AEM Installation

You have now enabled centralized collection and forwarding of AEM and CEIP information in your organization. No other setup or maintenance of the AEM feature in OpsMgr is required to use this capability. Regardless of the number of client and server computers in your organization, as soon as they refresh their group policy (which can take several hours in a larger domain with multiple sites), they will start reporting crash and hang information to the management group. Domain computers also will no longer attempt to send Watson/WER or CEIP information directly to Microsoft once they apply the GPO.

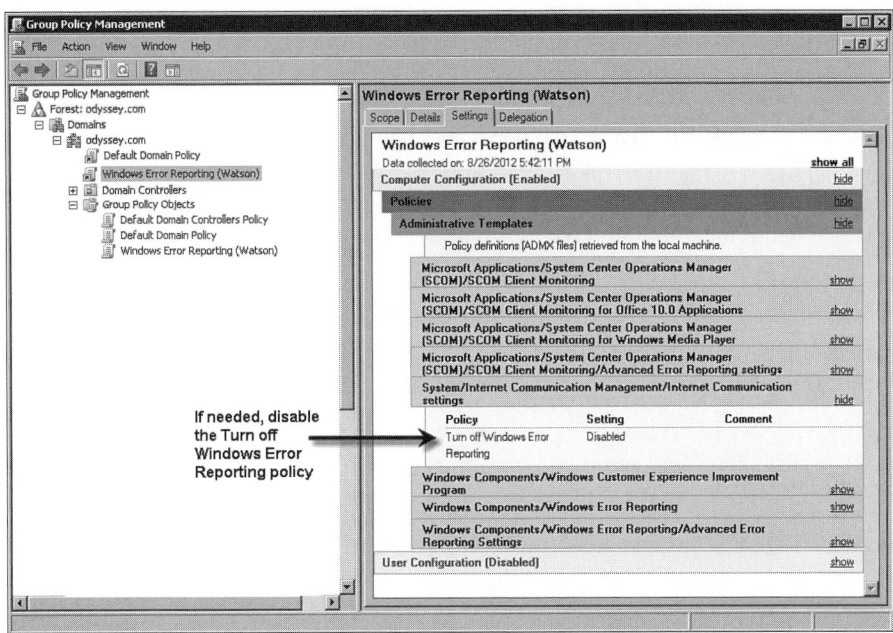

FIGURE 19.8 Displaying settings of Windows Error Reporting Group Policy object.

As the OpsMgr administrator, you may want to verify AEM is working and familiarize yourself with the console and reporting options available to view crash and hang information. If you have a known misbehaving application or invalid procedure that invokes Watson or WER, you can cause a crash or hang and observe the error reporting client in action, then see the error in the Operations console appear shortly thereafter. You can also experiment with your own crash test utilities. If you don't deliberately initiate some crashes, actual crash and hang information should appear in time in the Operations console.

WORKING WITH THE AEDEBUG REGISTRY KEY

There are several occasions where OpsMgr administrators may be interested in the software registry key that controls launching the error reporting client. On Windows XP and 2003 computers, drwtsn32.exe is the default debugger, and launching Watson is what sets AEM functionality in motion. Installing other applications with debugging features such as Microsoft Visual Studio can modify the default debugger setting, resulting in a loss of AEM reporting functionality from that computer. To restore Watson as the default debugger and thereby enable AEM, you can run this .REG script on the Windows XP or 2003 computer (this does not apply to Windows Vista, Windows Server 2008, and later systems, which use WER and not drstsn32.exe):

```
Windows Registry Editor Version 5.00
[HKEY_LOCAL_MACHINE\Software\Microsoft\WindowsNT\CurrentVersion\AeDebug]
"Auto"="1"
"Debugger"="drwtsn32.exe -p %ld e %ld"
```

A different purpose of this registry key on Windows Vista, Windows Server 2008, and later systems is to exclude processes from kicking off the debugger. This feature came from the need to exclude DWM.EXE from the "auto debug" mechanism. In the newer operating systems, DWM.exe is responsible for the display graphics; therefore, if it crashes, there is no way for DWM to display the dialog that debuggers show.

You will find an `AutoExclustionList` subkey under `AeDebug` on these systems that includes DWM.EXE. Add additional `DWORD` values to that subkey to exclude other processes you do not want to invoke WER even if they crash.

The AEM views in the Monitoring space of the Operations console are essentially windows into the shared folder structure created on the OpsMgr server. There are four folders under the root of the AEM file share, created by running the Configure Client Monitoring Wizard:

- **Cabs:** Contains subfolders based on the signature of the error report, where the last folder contains reporting data stored in a compressed archive .CAB file.
- **Counts:** Contains subfolders based on the error report, where the lowest-order folders contain counts of .CAB files collected and total reports for the error signature.
- **Status:** Holds responses from Microsoft to be relayed to the error reporting client on the next instance of a report with an existing signature.
- **PersistedCabs:** Contains .CAB files, previously sent to Microsoft, for historical reference. The AEM forwarding component on the management server clears the Cabs and Counts folders when the report to Microsoft is complete. Links in the Operations console to .CAB files in the PersistedCabs folder let the administrator browse details of past crashes.

TIP: FILE AND SHARE SECURITY ON THE AEM SERVER

The file shares created when enabling AEM on a management server have share permissions of Everyone\Full Control. Security is enforced at both the file and folder level. AEM setup creates two local computer security groups on the AEM server: AEMAgent and AEMUsers:

- The AEMAgent group membership consists of the local Administrators group with Full Control file and folder permissions.
- The AEMUsers group membership consists of all Authenticated Users—effectively all computer and user accounts in the domain—with special file and folder permissions.

These permissions allow error reports to be uploaded by client computers and processed by the management server. You should not need to modify these permissions.

Figure 19.9 illustrates the AEM shared folder structure on the OpsMgr management server. The PersistedCabs folder is expanded to expose the error report of a particular problem application. You can see the contents of the .CAB file include some text files with information about the version of Windows the computer was running and details of the application causing the crash. There is also a file with the .MDMP extension; this is a mini-dump file and accessible to application developers using Microsoft Visual Studio to assist with debugging the error condition.

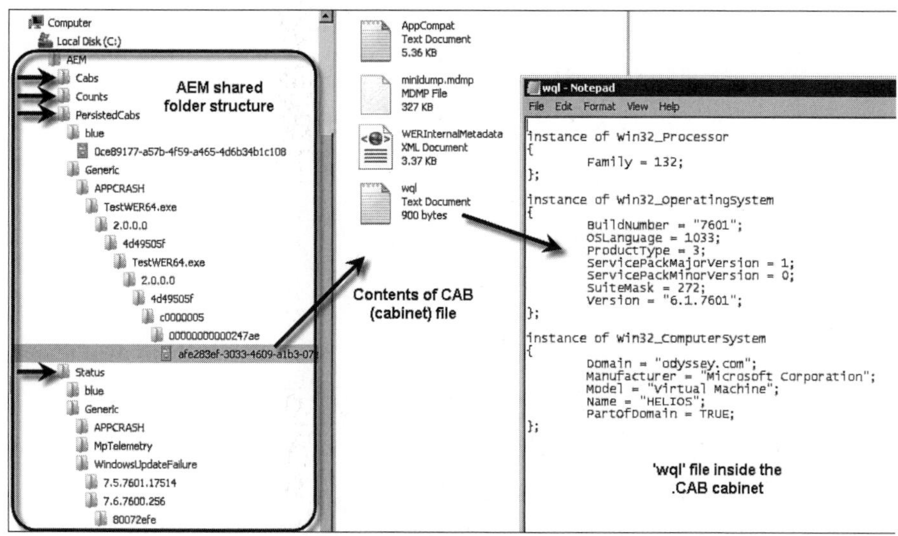

FIGURE 19.9 The AEM folder structure on the OpsMgr server stores crash histories.

AEM Console Views

The Agentless Exception Monitoring view folder contains five predefined views. When the AEM server receives crash and hang error information from client computers, it updates one or more AEM views with that information. The server processes collect reports on a timed basis—it can take up to two minutes from the moment the client transmits the error report until you see the error reflected in the console. Here is a description of each AEM view:

- **Error Events:** This is a conventional OpsMgr event view folder, containing an entry for each application error received. The other application error views list aggregated data by the application name; if you are looking for the record of a specific instance of a computer uploading an application error report, you will see it here.
- **Error Group View:** This is a dynamic view, created by reading the application names and contents of the shared folder structure where error reports are stored. The view includes an entry for each error signature reported. A single application name may appear several times if the same application reports different error signatures.

  From this view, you can select application errors and customize the error buckets, which are the settings that guide the behavior of the Watson or WER client. Bucket customization options are described in the "Customizing Error Buckets" section. Figure 19.10 shows several error groups present in a management group.

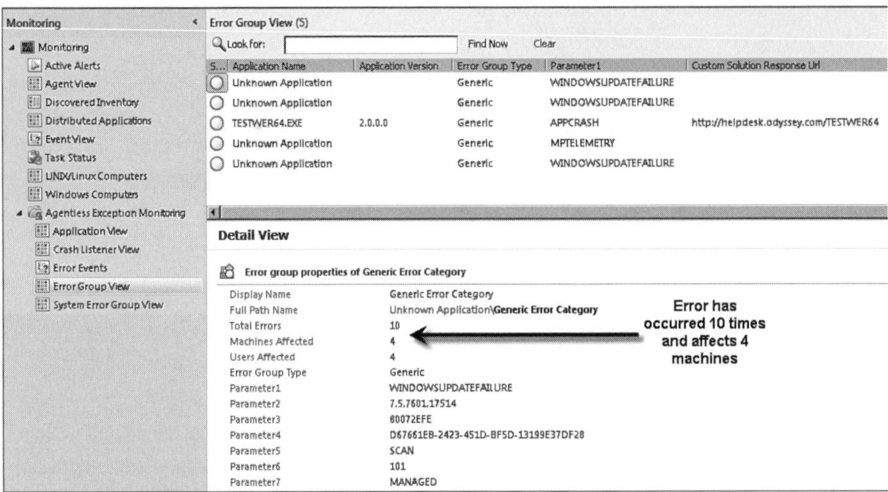

FIGURE 19.10 Each error group represents a unique error signature.

- **Application View:** This is also a dynamic view, listing application errors by application name. Each application name appears only once in this view, even if the application reports a variety of error conditions. The health monitor for an application error includes counters for computers, users, and applications; if any of these elements exceeds the threshold, that application has a Critical health state.
- **Crash Listener View:** This is a read-only view that confirms the settings of the AEM management server. The view shows only one entry, the AEM server. When you select the server, the Details pane confirms all the selections made when running the Enable Client Monitoring Wizard.

  To change one or more of these settings, disable AEM on the management server, then re-enable AEM by running the Enable Client Monitoring Wizard again with the desired new setting(s). No data is lost during the re-enable sequence, when and if you change the settings.
- **System Error Group View:** This view functions like the Error Group View, only it is for system crashes such as blue screens. The view treats each crash report as a separate object that will always have a Critical state. A link in the Details view of each crash shows the path of the .CAB file, located in the PersistedCabs folder of the AEM server corresponding to the crash report. Figure 19.11 shows the System Error Group View, with the contents of the sysdata.xml file in the linked .CAB file.

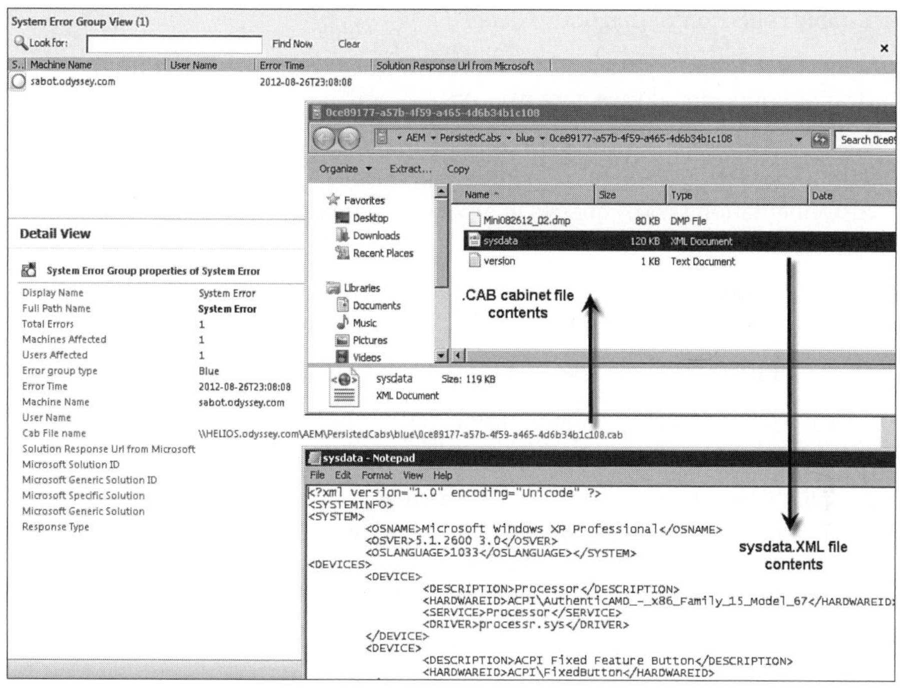

FIGURE 19.11 Viewing the contents of the .CAB file uploaded following a blue screen.

Customizing Error Buckets

In addition to identifying the top errors in your organization, AEM can collect additional, custom information and reach back to users with a custom solution link. When the AEM server receives an application error, a unique sequence of nested folders is created that match the characteristics of the error—forming an error bucket (the last folder created).

Subsequent Watson and WER clients discover an existing bucket, created by the first error report. The bucket contains an instruction text file, status.txt. The error reporting client reads status.txt in the bucket before performing the error upload. The error reporting process then executes, including any additional custom actions added to the file. Microsoft automatically modifies the status.txt file with updated information from its backend WER servers, and an administrator using the Operations console can customize it manually.

To view and modify the error bucket settings, follow these steps:

1. Navigate to the Error Group View, select the application in the Results pane, and click the **Show or Edit Error Group Properties** task in the State Actions pane on the right.

2. The Error Bucket Reponses dialog box opens. Here you can customize the actions to take the next time this error reoccurs. The options exposed by this feature include

- Disable collection of diagnostic data.
- View the diagnostic data collection options Microsoft requests for this error (this option is not always present).
- Create a custom diagnostic data collection configuration to include a memory dump, specific files from the hard disk, Windows Management Instrumentation (WMI) queries of any type, and copies of registry keys you specify.
- Select to show no error information to the user, even if Microsoft has provided a solution link for that error.
- View and test a solution link if Microsoft has provided one.
- Specify your own custom solution link, rather than none, or one Microsoft may provide.

Figure 19.12 applies most of the custom features, such as collecting the WindowsUpdate.log file, running a WMI query that returns the computer domain, manufacturer name, and other data, and collecting a registry key with the current antimalware signatures used by Windows Defender. In addition, a sample web page from an intranet help desk is specified as a Custom Solution link.

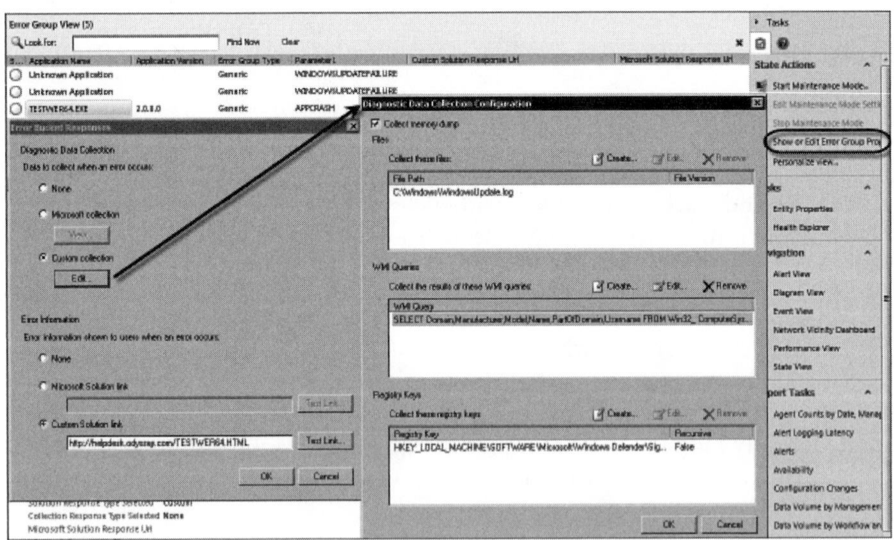

FIGURE 19.12 Specifying custom diagnostic data collection and solution link.

After applying customizations to the error bucket for an error group, you can collect custom diagnostic data and furnish users with a custom solution link each time they encounter this error. Additional options for customizing the handling and forwarding of crash and hang error information are located in the Operations console at Administration -> Settings. These options are covered in the "CEIP and the Microsoft Privacy Statement" section.

The next time a user has the error and selects to send information about it, he is directed to the custom error link on the corporate intranet—rather than the Microsoft online crash analysis link on the Internet. Figure 19.13 shows the custom in-house response on the lower left. Notice there is a pair of voting buttons and an external web hyperlink in the custom solution response.

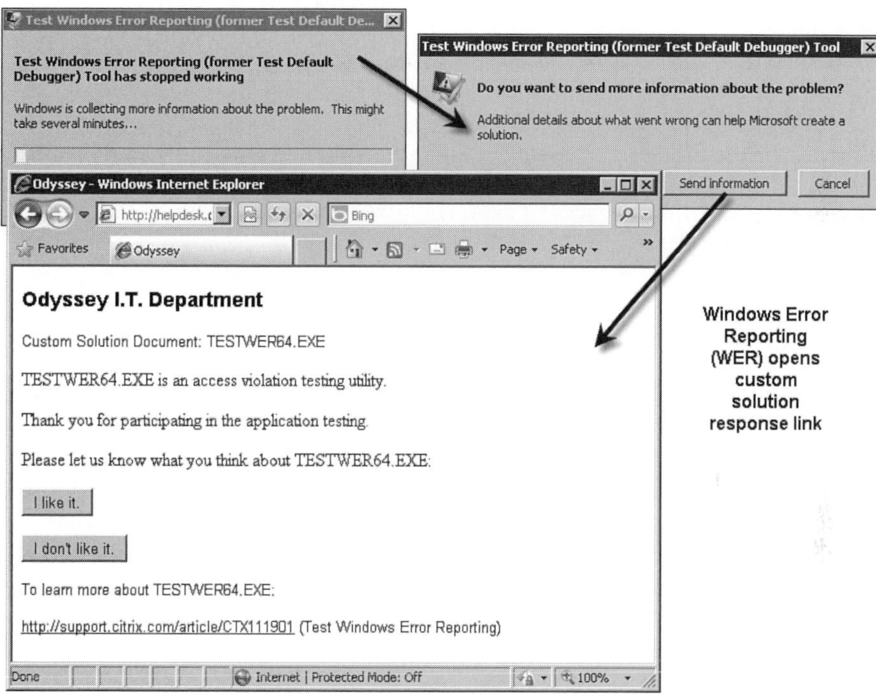

FIGURE 19.13 Custom solutions link targeted to an application's error bucket.

Incorporating Surveys

Consider employing a web-based survey technique to help solve particular errors in custom applications. You can stage a short automatic interview with the end user to gather targeted information. Here are some sample questions that might be helpful for a survey:

- ▶ What other applications (besides the one that crashed) were you running at the time of the crash?
- ▶ What steps can the IT department take to reproduce the crash that occurred?

- Will the application crash consistently if you follow the preceding steps? (Yes, Sometimes, or Never)
- Are you running any macros, COM add-ins, or templates?
- Does the crash occur for other people who log in to this computer? (Yes, No, or Unknown)

TIP: PUBLIC ACCESS TO MICROSOFT WER BACKEND DATABASE

Microsoft's Dev Center services enable software and hardware vendors to access reports to analyze and respond to problems caused by their applications. Vendors can use a Hardware/Desktop Dashboard account at no charge to view error reports.

You must register with Microsoft to participate in the Dev Center program. You can use the dashboard to view driver-specific, application-specific, or operating system-specific error reports associated with your organization, which are stored in error buckets in the Microsoft WER backend. Each error report provides details related to that bucket, and you could then request a file of the associated data. For more information about Dev Center, visit http://sysdev.microsoft.com/en-US/Hardware/signup.

Client Monitoring Reports

In addition to the five views available in the Agentless Exception Monitoring view folder in the Monitoring space, there are four client monitoring reports in the Client Monitoring Views Library in the Reporting space of the Operations console. These reports aggregate the information in the monitoring views and perform data analysis. They also provide a historical record of the performance of applications in use on the network. Since these reports are based on aggregated data, it can take up to 24 hours after you start collecting client errors before data will appear in the reports.

Along with offering further ways to gain insight from collected AEM data, the reports provide a convenient way to extend access to this valuable data across a broader audience. Because you can schedule publishing OpsMgr reports as Adobe .PDF files to network file shares or intranet sites, it is not necessary to access the Operations console or OpsMgr report server to see which applications are causing the most trouble for users. As an example, you can have weekly or monthly reports automatically generated and posted to departmental servers for viewing by application developers and desktop administrators.

USING AEM REPORTING TO TRACK SLAS

Consider the scenario where an organization wants to hold a custom application contractor accountable for the solid performance of their custom code. AEM reports provide an objective and portable means to verify whether a particular application is crashing excessively or not. A service level agreement (SLA) between the application service provider (ASP) and the organization can specify that error rates not exceed a certain threshold. The AEM reporting features can provide the metrics for compliance with such an SLA.

Top Applications Reports

The first of two application-related reports is the Top N Applications report, seen in Figure 19.14. This report displays a bar-graph chart showing the top applications reporting errors, a summary table, and a detailed table with the application name, version, crash count, and average daily crash count.

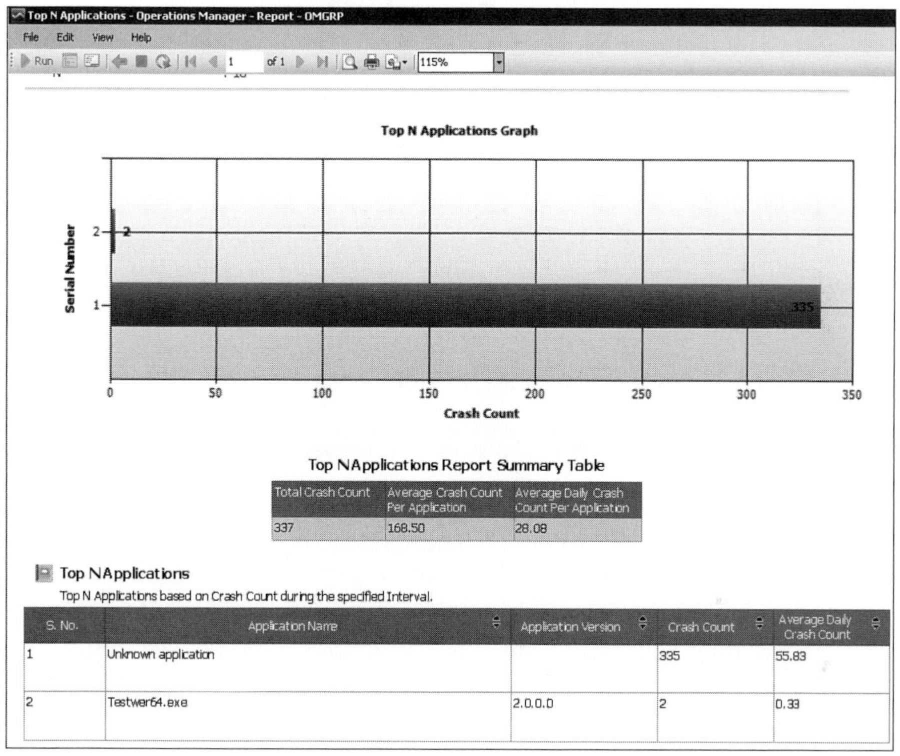

FIGURE 19.14 The Top N Applications report quickly shows which applications are causing the most problems.

The Top N Applications Report Summary table, in the center of the report, lists the average crash count per application and the average daily count per application. Knowing these average values helps you assess the statistical significance of the differences between the highest application(s) and those down the list in the detailed chart. The report defaults to including the top 25 applications. To change this report setting, modify the N value in the parameters header of the report. For example, set the N value to 5 to report on the top five applications with errors.

The other application report is the Top N Applications Growth and Resolution report. Similar to the Top N Applications report, this report defaults to N equals 25, where N is the number of top applications to include in the report. You can modify a second setting in the report parameters section, Interval Duration in Days, which defaults to 7. Because this report provides a measure of the percent of error increase over time, be careful not to specify a Previous Interval From value earlier than you have data for—this would result in an empty report. Figure 19.15 shows this report with the parameters section exposed.

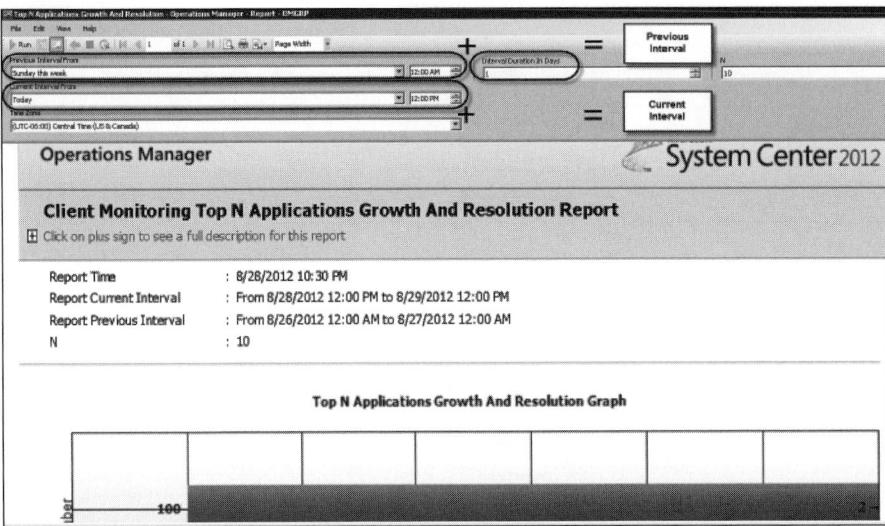

FIGURE 19.15 The Top N Applications Growth and Resolution report compares the error rates of two periods.

In the Top N Applications Growth and Resolution bar graph shown in Figure 19.15, notice the annotation (the + and = signs) in the top parameters section. A key concept to understand about the AEM growth reports is that two windows of time are compared—the current interval and the previous interval. The report construction adds the Interval Duration in Days you specify to both dates to arrive at the end dates of the two sampling periods. The length of each interval in days (the reporting window) is the same for both intervals; however, you can pick any start date for each interval, as long as the previous interval comes before the current interval chronologically.

The significance of this report is it lets you determine which applications are getting worse at a faster rate than other applications, even if the quantities of the most common errors are much higher than emerging errors. This error-trending capability is a great way to detect a problem before it affects a large number of users.

This report could help with correlating an increase in errors with a recent configuration change, such as a patch or service pack deployment. You catch the new error because of its comparatively high rate of change, even though the raw number of reports for that particular error may be less than the top applications. The report lends itself to comparing one week to the previous week, or to the same week in the previous month. Growth reports also display negative growth (applications that are falling in frequency between the previous and the current intervals).

Top N Error Groups Reports

A second pair of AEM reports focuses on error groups, rather than applications with errors. The main difference between the application error reports and the error group reports is that the application error reports list one instance of an application, summing up the errors associated with all error signatures received from that application. Compare this to the error group reports that include an entry for each error signature, regardless of what application it came from.

The error group reports display data about individual error buckets, while the application reports aggregate data from all error buckets of the same application. You can use the application-based reports to see what applications in general are causing problems, and then use the error group-based reports to identify exactly which unique errors are responsible for the most error events.

The first of two error group reports included with OpsMgr 2012 is the Top N Error Groups report. This report displays a bar-graph chart with the top reported errors, a summary table, and a detailed table with the application name, application version, error group ID, bucket type, crash count, and average daily crash count. Figure 19.16 shows the detailed table portion of this report.

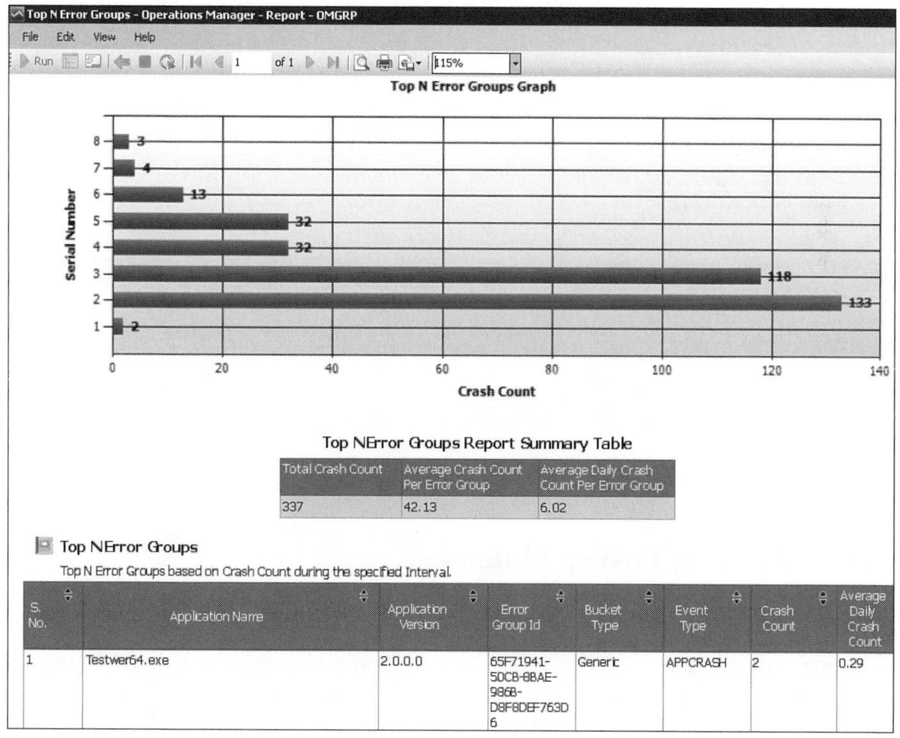

Total Crash Count	Average Crash Count Per Error Group	Average Daily Crash Count Per Error Group
337	42.13	6.02

S. No.	Application Name	Application Version	Error Group Id	Bucket Type	Event Type	Crash Count	Average Daily Crash Count
1	Testwer64.exe	2.0.0.0	65F71941-50CB-8BAE-986B-D8F8DEF763D6	Generic	APPCRASH	2	0.29

FIGURE 19.16 Spot significant crash issues in the Top N Error Groups report.

In the Top N Error Groups report displayed in Figure 19.16, notice the bucket type column. There are eight bucket types defined in the Operations Manager 2012 SDK (software development kit); these are listed in Table 19.1. The various bucket types are made available to developers to help them code WER support into their applications.

TABLE 19.1 AEM bucket types

Bucket Type	Description
AppCompat	Application-compatible bucket type
Blue	Blue screen
DW15	Watson 1.5 (legacy) error report
DW20	Watson 2.0 error report
Generic	Generic bucket type
Setup	Setup errors
Shutdown	Shutdown errors
Simple	Simple bucket type

The other error group report is the Top N Error Groups Growth and Resolution report. This report shows the top error groups based on their growth and resolution rate during the specified period. Similar to the Top N Applications Growth and Resolution report, this report compares the average daily crash count during one multi-day period (the Previous Interval), against a second multi-day period of equal length (the Current Interval). The resulting quotient, the Crash Count Percentile Increase, calls attention to error groups that are growing faster than others.

TIP: COMMUNITY RESOURCES ON OPSMGR REPORTING

For ideas on how to make OpsMgr reports more useful in customer environments, consult these community resources:

- http://contoso.se/blog/?p=537
- http://blogs.technet.com/b/jimmyharper/archive/2009/02/21/aem-views-and-tables.aspx

CEIP and the Microsoft Privacy Statement

When you run the Configure Client Monitoring Wizard to enable AEM on a management server in your management group, you can elect to participate in the Customer Experience Improvement Program. When CEIP is active on a system, it gathers information about Microsoft products used on that particular computer, processes it, and sends it to Microsoft, combining it with other CEIP data for further analysis. The transmission uses outbound TCP port 51907. The collected data is used to help Microsoft solve problems and to improve the products and features that customers use most often. Here are some examples of collected data:

- **Configuration:** Such as the number of processors, the version of Windows, and the number of network connections.
- **Performance and reliability:** Such as program responsiveness and the speed of data transmission.
- **Program use:** Such as the most frequently used features and Help and Support center usage.

Rather than having a large number of clients reporting this data individually, you can have your clients send their CEIP data to the AEM server as a central collection point for the organization. The management server hosting AEM then forwards the data to Microsoft. This feature of OpsMgr helps to minimize (or eliminate) direct access to the Internet by client workstations. In addition, some enterprise firewalls might not open port 51907 between internal networks and the Internet. Using the CEIP forwarding component of AEM means only the OpsMgr management server running AEM needs outbound port 51907 open for Internet access.

A compelling reason to use the AEM features in OpsMgr is you can control how and when your organization forwards information to Microsoft. To explore the customization options available to the OpsMgr administrator for these features, navigate to **Administration** -> **Settings** and open the Properties page of the Privacy setting as seen in Figure 19.17.

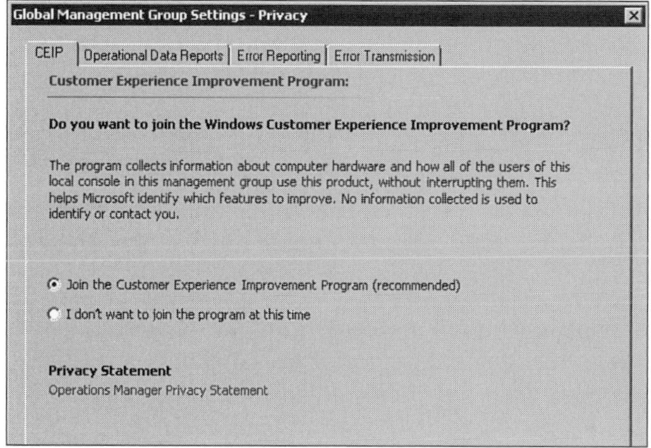

FIGURE 19.17 Privacy settings control CEIP, ODR, and WER.

There are four tabs controlling different aspects of CEIP and AEM as they relate to exchanging information over the Internet with Microsoft. The first three tabs (CEIP, Operational Data Reports, and Error Reporting) control your organization's level of participation in Microsoft's CEIP and WER programs as they relate to the function of OpsMgr itself. The fourth tab is Error Transmission and deals with handling crash and hang report forwarding for all applications in the management group, including OpsMgr. Here is a description of the functionality for each tab:

- **CEIP:** On this tab, you can select to join the CEIP program. This setting has a different function than the CEIP Forwarding screen of the Configure Client Monitoring Wizard. When you enabled AEM by running that wizard, if you chose to collect and forward CEIP data, you redirected client computer CEIP transmissions from the Internet to the management server. You were not turning CEIP on or off for any particular user or application—that is still determined by the user, unless group policy or some other mechanism is in place to force enabling of CEIP features in an application.

  The setting on this particular tab turns CEIP on or off for the Operations Manager 2012 software application in your management group. Enabling this setting facilitates CEIP data collection from the management group. Microsoft receives this data along with all the other CEIP data from other applications in your organization.

  Specifically, CEIP collects information about computer hardware that has an installed Operations console, and regarding how all Operations console users in the management group use the product. The setting for this tab is initially set when you install the OpsMgr database component for your management group—the setup process asks if you want to participate in CEIP as part of the management group setup.

- **Operational Data Reports:** This is a unique feature for Operations Manager, almost a super-CEIP. If you elect to send Operational Data Reports (ODR) to Microsoft, CEIP generates weekly reports to upload to Microsoft. ODR gathers information about OpsMgr's usage in the management group, and Microsoft collects the configuration data to understand customer environments. In addition, these reports help Microsoft determine what extra rules, monitors, or management packs can help customers lower the total cost of monitoring their networks. CEIP for OpsMgr, enabled on the first tab of the Privacy settings, only looks at use of the Operations console. ODR looks beyond console usage patterns and assesses product usage in monitoring objects.

  You must install the OpsMgr reporting feature for ODR to function. You can see the ODR reports used by this feature in the Reporting space of the Operations console. These reports are intended to be most useful to Microsoft, although you can run the reports at any time yourself and see what data Microsoft is receiving, or would receive with ODR enabled. Here are the five reports contained in the Microsoft ODR Report Library:

  - **Alerts Per Day:** This report shows the number of alerts generated per rule or monitor per day within the last week. The report has predefined settings to run with a seven-day recurring date range.

  - **Instance Space:** Shows the count of all class instances listed in the data warehouse. Figure 19.18 displays this report.

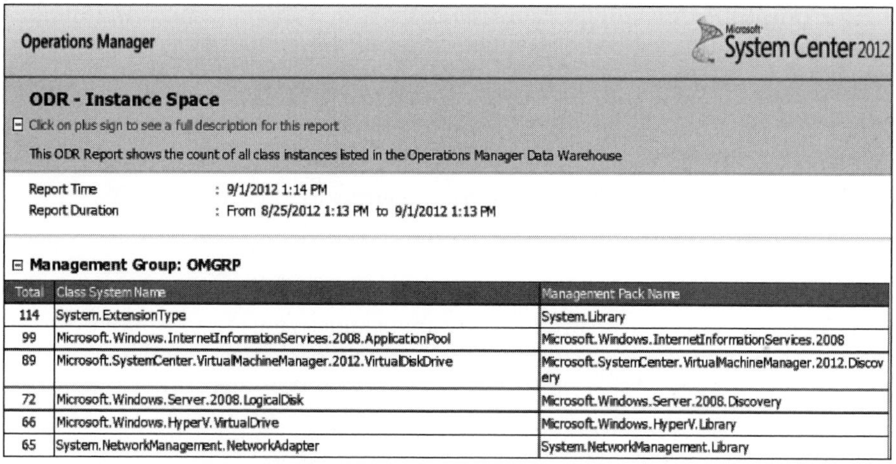

Operations Manager

Microsoft System Center 2012

ODR - Instance Space

⊟ Click on plus sign to see a full description for this report

This ODR Report shows the count of all class instances listed in the Operations Manager Data Warehouse

Report Time : 9/1/2012 1:14 PM
Report Duration : From 8/25/2012 1:13 PM to 9/1/2012 1:13 PM

⊟ **Management Group: OMGRP**

Total	Class System Name	Management Pack Name
114	System.ExtensionType	System.Library
99	Microsoft.Windows.InternetInformationServices.2008.ApplicationPool	Microsoft.Windows.InternetInformationServices.2008
89	Microsoft.SystemCenter.VirtualMachineManager.2012.VirtualDiskDrive	Microsoft.SystemCenter.VirtualMachineManager.2012.Discovery
72	Microsoft.Windows.Server.2008.LogicalDisk	Microsoft.Windows.Server.2008.Discovery
66	Microsoft.Windows.HyperV.VirtualDrive	Microsoft.Windows.HyperV.Library
65	System.NetworkManagement.NetworkAdapter	System.NetworkManagement.Library

FIGURE 19.18 The ODR - Instance Space report counts the objects in each class.

- **Management Group:** Displays workload classes (enterprise vs. standard) performed by management servers and gateway servers. This report helps Microsoft understand the infrastructure customers use to deploy OpsMgr and the amount of load on the management group.
- **Management Packs:** This very long report contains three detailed tables—the tables report on the installed management packs and their versions, the overrides applied in the management group, and the rules created through the Operations console.
- **Most Common Alerts:** Shows an overview of the top 24 most common alerts across all management packs. This is the same report you see in the Microsoft Generic Report Library, just preconfigured with a seven-day date range. Microsoft uses this information to improve management pack quality and to reduce alerting noise levels.

- **Error Reporting:** This tab allows you to control the participation of OpsMgr 2012 itself in the error reporting mechanism. You can select not to generate error reports, to prompt the user for approval before sending error reports, or to send error reports automatically without prompting the user.

  If you enable error reporting on this tab, Watson and WER clients on OpsMgr component computers initiate the error reporting process when crashes and hangs occur in the OpsMgr application process. If AEM is also enabled, those error reports are collected from the management group and forwarded to Microsoft along with all other crash and hang reports from other applications in your organization.

  The OpsMgr components using this setting are the management servers, gateway servers, and agents. Error reporting behavior for the operational database and data warehouse uses the settings specified for SQL Server, rather than those specified on this tab for the OpsMgr components.

- **Error Transmission:** The error transmission tab is the location of some important configuration settings for the management group. Figure 19.19 displays this tab, which has three sections:

    - The top section with the Filter button
    - The center section that involves uploading errors to Microsoft
    - The bottom three items controlling what links users may see after an application error occurs

  You can filter the errors sent to Microsoft by application name, user, computer, and other criteria. This lets you exempt your most sensitive users, computers, and applications from having their error reports forwarded to Microsoft. This filter capability lets the bulk of your organization contribute error information to Microsoft's backend WER servers, while reserving specific confidential information to the organization's AEM servers. Selecting **Filter** allows you to specify these exemption options:

    - Specific users (from Active Directory)
    - Specific computers (from Active Directory)
    - Specific applications
    - Specific modules
    - Specific application error types (bucket types, such as DW15 or Blue)
    - Specific event types (such as Appcrash or MPTelemetery)

  In the Diagnostic Data Collection Settings area of the Error Transmission tab shown in Figure 19.19, you can enable or disable uploading of data collection requests globally. Additionally, you can granularly enable or disable the type of data uploaded to Microsoft's backend WER services. The types of data you can control are additional files, registry information, WMI queries, and memory dumps. You can also modify the maximum number of .CAB files uploaded to Microsoft per error group (bucket). The default is 10.

  At the bottom of the Error Transmission tab is an option to specify a default solution link when no Microsoft or custom solution link is available. If you populate this field, whenever a user's Watson or WER client completes the error reporting procedure they will see an Error Reporting dialog box with a More Information link, even if neither you nor Microsoft specified a solution link for that error. If your default link points to a generic crash survey form, you can collect information from users about errors as they occur in your organization, even the first time they are reported.

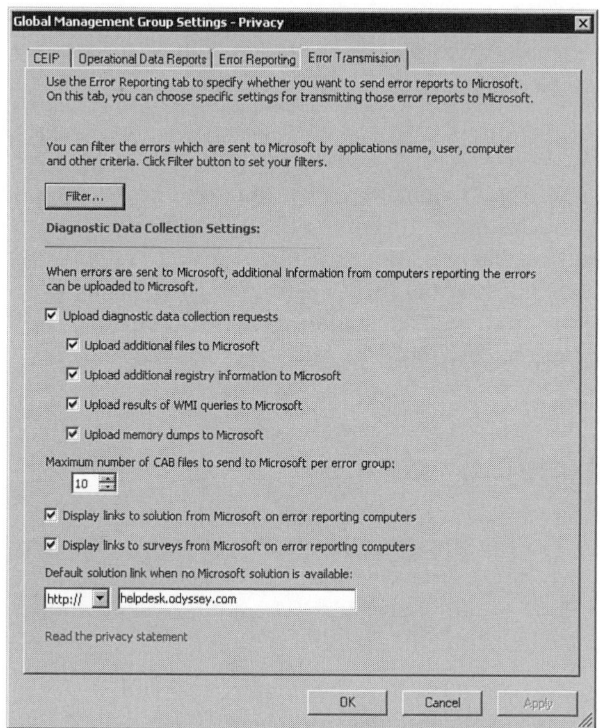

FIGURE 19.19 The Error Transmission tab in the Privacy settings.

The authors recommend Operations Manager administrators enable some or all of the Microsoft forwarding features, particularly those that apply to OpsMgr itself. Having Microsoft receive such feedback on a large scale from the real world enables more rapid and accurate improvement of the products in the Windows ecosystem. Just as Watson/WER collection shows Microsoft the top problems and allows them to target their hotfix, update, and service pack development, CEIP and ODR show Microsoft what is working in their products and those features most used. That data provides input into development of add-ons, feature packs, and new versions of software that build on the features most in demand.

If you enable all the CEIP, ODR, and Watson/WER collection and forwarding features in your AEM deployment, Microsoft will receive a considerable amount of information about your organization. There is naturally some discomfort at sharing some organizational data like server names and some user data such as file names. You can opt-out your most sensitive sources of information using the Privacy settings previously described in this section.

Error information uploaded to Microsoft is indexed by the nature of the error—that is, the target error bucket—not the identity or location of the contributing organization. The only uniquely identifiable information associated with uploading error reports to Microsoft is the source IP address. Microsoft uses the IP address to generate aggregate statistics; it is not used to identify or contact you.

As for the safety and security of the Watson/WER backend services themselves, the authors are not aware of any instances where Microsoft has been accused or suspected of misuse of error reporting data. Conversely, there are numerous occasions where error and CEIP information has resulted in improvements in Microsoft software that directly benefited all customers.

Microsoft publishes a simple three-page Privacy Statement for the Microsoft Error Reporting Service, available at http://windows.microsoft.com/en-US/Windows/microsoft-error-reporting-privacy-statement. There is also a specific Microsoft System Center Operations Manager 2012 Privacy Statement at http://technet.microsoft.com/library/hh321008.aspx. The specific OpsMgr privacy statement includes sections that address the privacy issues of each component described in this chapter, including CEIP, ODR, and WER.

Monitoring Agent-Managed Systems

Although many or most client computers in your organization may participate in AEM, some client computers should also have an OpsMgr agent installed on them. An OpsMgr agent puts a client computer in constant contact with OpsMgr and consumes management group resources. This section explores the three scenarios where it is recommended you consider deploying agents on some client computers:

- Smaller organizations, perhaps those with 50 or fewer computers, may find it simplest to deploy an agent on every client computer, particularly if their client computer hardware can leverage hardware vendor management packs imported into the management group. This also lets all the computers participate in other OpsMgr features such as Audit Collection Services (ACS).
- Midsize organizations, between 50 and 500 client computers, can make the decision on whether to have all computers with agents—or implement a mix of AEM-only and agents on clients—based on economics of the licensing and the hardware capacity of the computer(s) running the OpsMgr server and database components. A single-server OpsMgr management group can easily handle 50 client computers; however, somewhere on the road toward and above 500 computers, a single management server will begin to slow down.
- Larger organizations, such as those with more than 500 client computers, will almost certainly employ a mix of AEM-only clients and clients with agents. The large client populations let you leverage statistical techniques such as the significance of random sampling and looking for rate of change.

  The math and the economics make deploying a full monitoring agent to every client unnecessary and possibly expensive. In addition, deploying an agent to any computer incurs acquisition costs for the agent license, an incremental cost of resources consumed in the Operations Manager management group, and an ongoing cost to support the agent in terms of licensing, maintaining, and upgrading.

Organizations of any size should consider deploying OpsMgr agents on client computers in these categories and scenarios:

- **Aggregated (Collective) Client Monitoring:** This is a random, proportional sampling of client computers within each client population. The more homogeneous the client population, the smaller the sample can be and remain statistically significant. If you have a set of various desktop images for certain models of computers, try to monitor equally across each desktop model. You generally don't care if the individual computers are always on the network; these computers can be powered off, or mobile.
- **Business Critical Monitoring:** This is for VIP and high-impact workstations and application boxes such as IP telephony, kiosk, POS, supervisory control and data acquisition (SCADA) instrumentation, and network administration workstations. The authors recommend selecting at least one client computer at each branch or remote office for Business Critical Monitoring. You generally want to know if these computers go offline—you monitor them like servers for high availability.
- **Synthetic Transaction Monitoring:** Endpoint watcher nodes are defined in the health model of a distributed application as proxy agents to monitor another device, or to monitor a third-party service from a local point of presence. The authors suggest you seek ways to exploit this feature in OpsMgr. You can easily deploy multiple, smart sets of watcher nodes to measure the end-to-end service delivery of distributed enterprise applications. Watcher nodes for synthetic transaction monitoring are subject to Business Critical Monitoring as well.

A side effect of enabling AEM is it creates a Windows Computer object for every computer that ever sends a crash dump. This creates additional load as each computer is treated as a computer object in the OpsMgr database, which can cause performance issues at large scale. Very large environments should consider a dedicated management group for AEM. The guidelines at http://technet.microsoft.com/en-us/library/bb735402.aspx apply to AEM for OpsMgr 2007 and OpsMgr 2012.

TIP: COMPARING AGGREGATED TO BUSINESS CRITICAL MONITORING

Aggregated (or Collective) Client Monitoring is the default client monitoring mode for all discovered client computers after you import the client monitoring management packs. Some Aggregated Client Monitoring client computers are also selected to be subject to Business Critical Monitoring. Business Critical Monitoring and Aggregated Client Monitoring both use the OpsMgr 2012 agent to collect Aggregated Client Monitoring data; the management packs are just tuned differently. Specifically, the Business Critical management pack allows for individual alerting.

Client Monitoring Management Pack

If you are including client monitoring as a mission of your management group (in addition to monitoring servers, network devices, and distributed applications), begin by importing the client monitoring management pack. The management pack for monitoring the Windows 7, Windows Vista, Windows XP, and Windows 2000 Professional client operating systems needs to be downloaded and imported. Availability of a management pack for Windows 8 is unknown at the time of writing this chapter. On September 7, 2012, Microsoft's System Center: Operations Manager Engineering Blog at http://blogs.technet.com/b/momteam/archive/2012/09/05/windows-server-2012-system-center-operations-manager-support.aspx posted an updated comment: "We are...evaluating...and investigating building a Windows 8 client MP. Stay tuned!"

You cannot import the client management pack directly from the online catalog; download it from the Web at http://www.microsoft.com/en-us/download/details.aspx?id=15700.

Running the downloaded management pack installation file creates a folder and populates it with a number of management pack files, both sealed .MP files and unsealed .XML files. The default location is *%ProgramFiles(x86)%*\System Center Management Packs\Windows Client OS Operations Manager 2007 MP. You must manually import all management packs. The business critical management packs have dependencies even on the Windows 2000 OS management pack, so import all of them.

The unsealed business critical management packs also enable selected collective monitoring clients to be Business Critical Monitoring clients. Overrides that enable business critical monitoring for clients you select are saved in the unsealed management packs.

NOTE: ABOUT THE INFORMATION WORKER MANAGEMENT PACK

There is a legacy information worker management pack available in the online catalog. This management pack includes monitoring of Office 2003 and Office 2007 applications. Microsoft has deprecated the Microsoft Information Worker management pack, and no further management packs for Office applications will be delivered.

Import the client monitoring management packs in the conventional manner using the Operations console's Administration space. After they are imported, you will notice a single top-level view folder—Microsoft Windows Client—listed in the Monitoring space. That folder contains all the views installed by the client operating system management packs.

Aggregate Health Monitoring Management Packs

Aggregate (or Collective) Client Monitoring is Microsoft's solution for measuring the quality of users' desktop experiences without overloading the management group and IT support staff. Microsoft's design goal with the client monitoring management packs was they require zero configuration to function in a useful way and would not be noisy; that is, not create a management burden to evaluate a lot of non-critical alerts.

Aggregate Client Monitoring gathers and stores information about client computers, but does not monitor individual computers or generate alerts about specific computers. Aggregate Client Monitoring is the default configuration for the client management pack. This means that when you discover and install OpsMgr agents on client computers after importing the client monitoring management pack, those client computers are automatically and immediately subject to Aggregate Client Monitoring.

Usage scenarios for Aggregate Client Monitoring center around identifying when large numbers of client computers are experiencing the same problem (using the Monitoring views in the Operations console), and performing historical and trending analysis on collected data (using the Reporting views). Figure 19.20 displays the Microsoft Windows Client view folder in the Monitoring space.

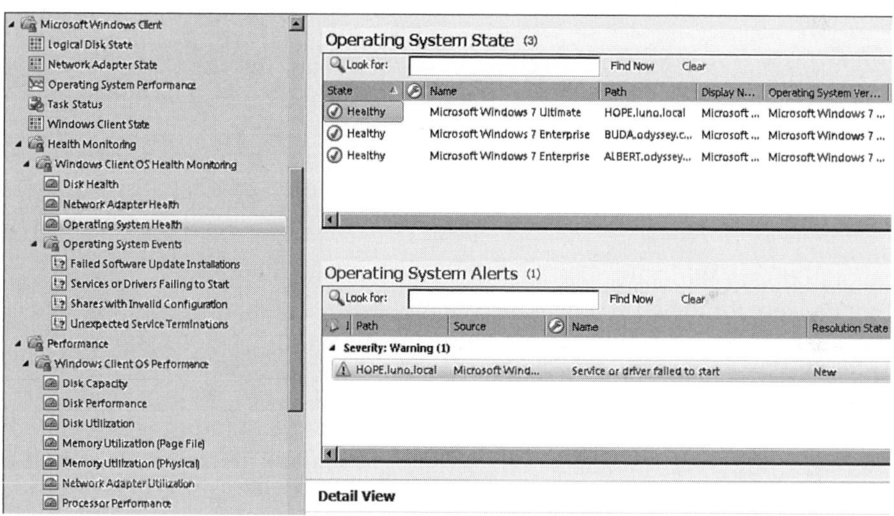

FIGURE 19.20 Views added to the OpsMgr Monitoring space by the client OS MP.

The report views added to the management group by the client monitoring management packs are probably more useful on an ongoing basis, as the Aggregate Monitoring views in the Monitoring space are most relevant when you are researching particular metrics on client performance problems. The list of client OS report folders is on the left side of Figure 19.21.

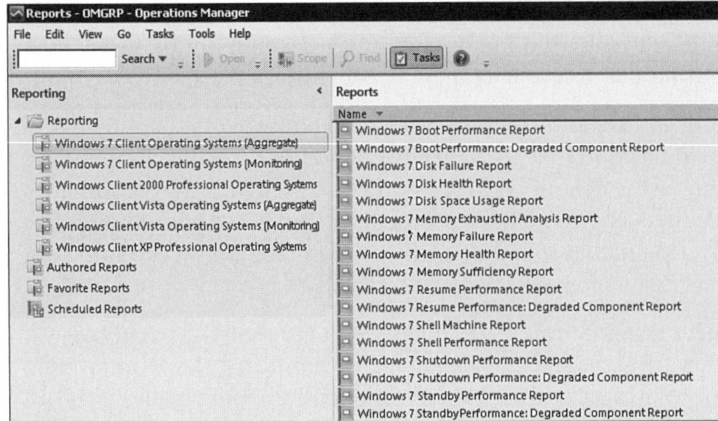

FIGURE 19.21 Windows 7 client OS aggregate monitoring reports.

TIP: AGGREGATE MONITORING ALERT THRESHOLDS

The Aggregate Collective Monitoring management pack utilizes pre-defined thresholds that are not exposed in the Operations console. Client OS thresholds are greater than 95% CPU utilization, less than 10MB available memory, or greater than 80% committed memory.

Collective monitoring of Windows 2000 and Windows XP computers provides almost identical functionality for these two operating systems. Collective monitoring of Windows Vista and Windows 7 computers, in contrast, has many more features that result from the richer diagnostics infrastructure built into Windows Vista and above. Look at the type of information that you can get from Collective Monitoring of Windows 7 clients on the right side of Figure 19.21.

Failure reports and health reports are available for slow boot performance, disk failures, memory exhaustion, resume, shutdown, and standby performance of Windows Vista and later computers. These reports are tools that really help the IT department understand issues users may be facing in more detail than “my computer is slow!”

TIP: GIVE THE VISTA AND WINDOWS 7 REPORTS SOME TIME

Initially, Client Monitoring reports for Windows Vista and later systems may contain no information. This is normal, since reports built on aggregated data require at least 24 hours of collection. Many of these reports are designed to trend data over large time-frames, such as three to six months, so there may not be much useful data for several weeks after installing the Client Monitoring management packs. Also, consider that a lack of data for reports based on failures, such as disk failure, might mean none of those failures has occurred in your organization.

Business Critical Monitoring Management Pack

Business Critical Monitoring is the most comprehensive client monitoring solution with OpsMgr. This is the only level of monitoring that can watch client computers individually and generate alerts. Adding client computers to Business Critical Monitoring requires more overhead than other types of client monitoring. You can only bring client computers into Business Critical Monitoring after discovery takes place and the clients have an agent installed on them. This means that client computers must first be made Collective Monitoring clients; then they can be promoted to Business Critical Monitoring status.

Here are the steps to perform to add client computers to Business Critical Monitoring:

1. Navigate to **Authoring -> Groups**.
2. Type **Business Critical** in the Look for box and click **Find Now**.
3. Select the appropriate group for the operating system of the client computers to add. For example, to add Windows 7 client computers, select the **All Business Critical Windows 7 Clients** group. Right-click the group and select **Properties**.
4. On the Explicit Members tab, select **Add/Remove Objects**.
5. In the Search for drop-down box, select **Windows 7 Client Computer** and select **Search**.
6. All Windows 7 computers with OpsMgr agents installed will appear in the Available items area.
7. Select one or more computers to be added to Business Critical Monitoring, and click **Add**. After confirming that the desired computers are in the Selected objects area, click **OK**, then click **OK** again.
8. Repeat steps 3 through 7 for other operating systems where you have client computers to be added to Business Critical Monitoring.

Figure 19.22 illustrates these steps to add Windows 7 client computers to the All Business Critical Windows 7 Clients group.

Populating any or all of the All Business Critical Windows Clients groups enables Business Critical Monitoring. Those groups are the target of an override that enables most of the monitors and alerts included in the client management packs, particularly those that raise individual alerts for disk health and operating system health events.

When you enable Business Critical Monitoring for one or more client computers, you can optionally enable Advanced Monitoring on selected client computer objects. Advanced Monitoring is disabled out of the box with OpsMgr; Microsoft wants to protect the performance and usability of the OpsMgr management group, at the expense of making you do a little extra work. Microsoft wanted to prevent hundreds or thousands of client computers from overwhelming a management group after they are discovered. Therefore, some monitors that are data-processing intensive are turned off, even for Business Critical Monitoring. It is up to you to identify any Advanced Monitoring features you need and enable them on a case-by-case basis.

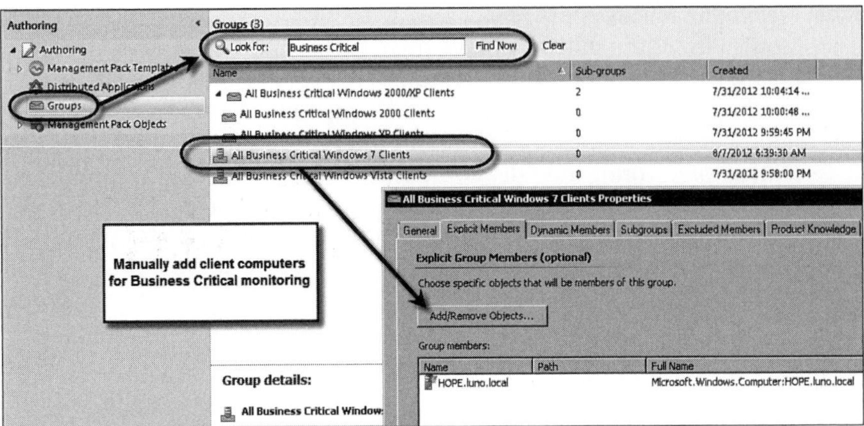

FIGURE 19.22 Manual step required to add client computers to Business Critical Monitoring.

An example of Advanced Monitoring is the Network Adapter state and performance views. Some network adapter performance information is not collected by default, even from client computers subject to Business Critical Monitoring. Examining the Network Adapter State view in the root of the Microsoft Windows Client view folder, or the Network Adapter Health dashboard view in the Windows Client OS Health Monitoring, shows all unknown status icons for each computer's network interface(s). Those monitors are in the Advanced Monitoring category. To enable Advanced Monitoring on an object of interest, such as the network interface of a VIP or mission-critical client computer, follow these steps:

1. Select the **Not monitored** status indicator in the Results pane of the monitor that you want to enable. Right-click and select **Open** -> **Health Explorer**.
2. Expand the branch of the health model that contains the monitor you want to enable. Click on the monitor to select it.
3. Click **Override** and select **Override the Monitor** -> **For a Specific Object of Type**.
4. The Select Object picker should appear; select the matching object that you want to monitor and click **OK**.
5. The Override Properties page should appear; tick the Override box in the top Enabled line and change the Override Setting from False to **True**. Save the override to a custom management pack and click **OK**.
6. Click **OK** again and close the Health Explorer. Within several minutes, the state icon for the object should change from Not Monitored to Healthy.

Although some business critical monitors fall into the Advanced Monitoring category (such as some network interface monitors), most of the monitoring views in the Operations console provide data on client computers added to Business Critical Monitoring without further configuration. This is referred to by Microsoft as Standard

Monitoring for business critical clients (requiring no additional configuration), compared to Advanced Monitoring.

All the views in the Windows Client OS Performance view folder feature Standard Monitoring and are populated for business critical client computers. Figure 19.23 shows the Processor Performance dashboard view in the Windows Client OS Performance view folder.

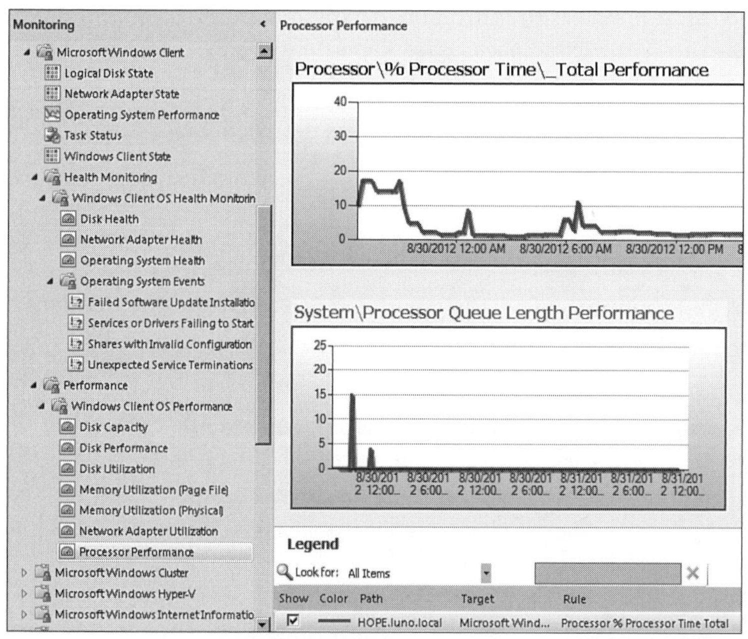

FIGURE 19.23 Standard monitoring for business critical client computers: disk, memory, network, and processor.

Notice the Windows Client OS Health Monitoring view folder about one-third down the left side of the view folders in Figure 19.23. This is where you perform operational monitoring of your client computers. There are the Disk, Network Adapter, and Operating System Health dashboard views, as well as the Operating System Events folder with four subfolders (Failed Software Update Installations, Services or Drivers Failing to Start, Shares with Invalid Configuration, and Unexpected Service Terminations).

Remember to look at the Tasks pane when you select particular business critical client monitors. Context-sensitive tasks are provided with most views, such as **Run Chkdsk** when logical disks are selected in the Results pane.

TIP: OVERRIDE NEEDED TO ALERT ON CLIENT HEARTBEAT FAILURE

By default, alerts for missed heartbeats and computer not reachable are disabled for client operating systems. To receive alerts for client operating systems, override the Health Service Heartbeat Failure and Computer Not Reachable monitors for the class Windows Client Operating System to set the Generates Alert parameter to True.

In addition to the views in the Monitoring space populated with data from business critical client computers, you can run reports to learn more details about client computer performance. Figure 19.24 shows the Disk Space Usage Report, targeted to agent-managed Windows 7 computers.

Follow these steps to produce the Disk Space Usage Report seen in Figure 19.24:

1. Navigate to the Reporting space and select the Windows 7 Client Operating Systems (Aggregate) report folder.
2. Select the Windows 7 Disk Space Usage Report and click **Open**.
3. After viewing the report, optionally save the report as a PDF, XLS, or other file type by selecting **File -> Export**.

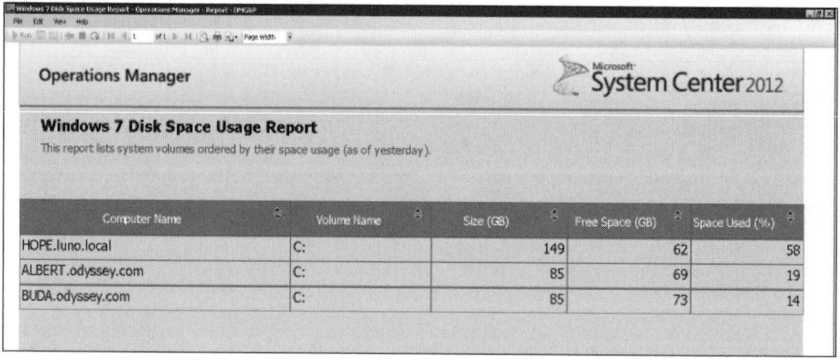

FIGURE 19.24 Disk space usage report includes all aggregate monitored clients.

Preparing for Synthetic Transaction Monitoring

Chapter 17, "Using Synthetic Transactions," and Chapter 18, "Distributed Applications," provide examples of employing client computers as watcher nodes for Synthetic Transaction Monitoring. However, this section is included to remind you to import the client management pack in order to use that feature. You cannot select client computers to be watcher nodes for your distributed applications unless you have deployed an OpsMgr agent to them.

Often, strategically located client computers are the best platform to serve as watcher nodes for end-to-end monitoring of enterprise applications. You need a monitor "at the end" to capture service delivery in the context that matters, which is usually at the user desktop. This technique is also known as *user perspective monitoring*.

The authors recommend all client computers selected as distributed application watcher nodes also are subject to Business Critical Monitoring. You need to be alerted when a watcher node for a distributed application is down or malfunctioning; otherwise, you may not be able to correlate the root cause of a distributed application failure alert to the watcher node itself being down.

Even if your organization does not intend to employ any of the client monitoring features covered in this chapter, it is still a good idea to be familiar with the client operating system management packs, and to import them into your management group if your organization supports Windows client computers. That way, your monitoring infrastructure is staged to deploy watcher nodes in support of managing end-to-end enterprise applications.

Fast Track

Very little has changed in client OS monitoring and management features between OpsMgr 2007 and 2012. Support for client operating systems newer than Windows Vista is added, as well as retaining support for legacy clients back to Windows 2000 Professional. Here is a summary of changes for client monitoring with OpsMgr:

- The new System Center 2012 license model may make it more affordable to deploy OpsMgr agents to clients. OpsMgr customers should take a fresh look at the features and benefits of client monitoring.
- Windows 7 is added as a supported client OS. There is also full business critical client OS support included for Windows Vista and above clients.
- Windows Server 2012 OS is fully supported by OpsMgr 2012 SP 1. As of January 2013, Microsoft was officially "unannounced" regarding a management pack for the Windows 8 client operating system.
- The information worker management pack and monitoring of Office applications is deprecated.
- There are two new ODR reports: Alerts per Day, and Instance Space.

Summary

This chapter began with introducing the roots of Microsoft's client monitoring initiative, Dr. Watson. After explaining the architecture of Agentless Exception Monitoring, there were examples of the value of collecting crash and hang information. The chapter discussed how to customize the AEM experience, enabling you to collect additional information from users and provide them with just-in-time solutions once errors occur. The concepts of Aggregated (or Collective) Client Monitoring and Business Critical Monitoring of client computers were introduced, and the chapter closed with a reminder of how client computers can play an important role in the end-to-end monitoring of distributed enterprise applications. The next section of the book, "Beyond Operations Manager," covers advanced topics such as cross platform monitoring, PowerShell, authoring, and cloud computing.

PART VI

Beyond Operations Manager

IN THIS PART

CHAPTER 20

Interoperability and Cross Platform

IN THIS CHAPTER

- ▶ Supported Platforms and Requirements
- ▶ Cross Platform Agent Architecture
- ▶ Cross Platform Agent DeploymentO
- ▶ Using Management Pack Templates
- ▶ Introducing Application Performance Monitoring
- ▶ Enabling Deep Monitoring of JEE Applications
- ▶ JEE Application Monitoring Templates
- ▶ Notes on UNIX Commands
- ▶ Fast Track

Cross Platform Extensions, first introduced in Operations Manager (OpsMgr) 2007 Release 2 (R2), are improved and extended in OpsMgr 2012. This enables you not only to monitor UNIX and Linux platforms using OpsMgr, but application workloads on non-Windows operating systems, such as Java enterprise applications, sometimes known as JEE. Cross platform security has been enhanced as well with the introduction of sudo functionality, which eliminates the need for root credentials. This chapter explores cross platform monitoring capabilities, configuration, and extensions in Operations Manager 2012.

Supported Platforms and Requirements

Microsoft's cross platform enhancements in OpsMgr 2012 allow you out of the box to monitor some of the more significant UNIX and Linux platforms. Table 20.1 lists the platforms and versions supported as of January 2013 (including OpsMgr 2012 Service Pack 1) and prerequisites. For additional information and updates, check http://technet.microsoft.com/en-us/library/jj656654.aspx. For those platforms not supported by the OpsMgr 2012 release, Microsoft has published the Cross Platform Providers on CodePlex (http://scx.codeplex.com/) as open source (MS-PL license). Although this does not include the entire stack, you can combine it with any Common Information Model Object Manager (CIMOM) and a WS-Management (WSMan) layer to port to the platform you want to support. You would have to write a management pack (MP) for that platform as well.

TABLE 20.1 Supported cross platform operating systems version support

Platform	Version
AIX	Version 5.3 Version 6.1 (POWER)
	Version 7.1 (Power)
CentOS*	Version 5 (x86/x64)
	Version 6 (x86/x64)
Debian Linux	Version 5 (x86/x64)
	Version 6 (x86/x64)
HP-UX	Version 11iv2 (PA-RISC/IA64)
	Version 11iv3 (PA-RISC/IA64)
Red Hat Enterprise Linux	Version 4 (x86/x64)
	Version 5 (x86/x64)
	Version 6 (x86/x64)
Solaris	Version 9 (SPARC and x86)
	Version 10 (SPARC and x86)
	Version 11 (SPARC and x86)**
SUSE Linux Enterprise Server	Version 9 (x86)
	Version 10 Service Pack (SP) 1 (x86/x64)
	Version 11 (x86/x64)
Ubuntu Linux Server*	Version 10.04 (x86/x64)
	Version 12.04 (x86/x64)

* *Only supported in OpsMgr 2012 SP 1*

** *Support added with Update Rollup 1*

Microsoft support for UNIX and Linux versions is aligned to the vendors' support rather than an N-1 strategy. New versions of operating systems are supported within 180 days of release. Old versions are supported as long as the vendor provides support for that version.

SP 1 UPDATE: SUPPORT FOR NEW LINUX SYSTEMS IN SYSTEM CENTER SERVICE PACK (SP) 1

Beginning with the release of the OpsMgr 2012 SP 1 public beta in September 2012, support is available for several new Linux operating systems:

- CentOS 5 (x86/x64)
- CentOS 6 (x86/x64)
- Debian 5 (x86/x64)
- Debian 6 (x86/x64)
- Ubuntu 12.04 (x86/x64)

Microsoft implemented monitoring support for these operating systems with the "Universal Linux" monitoring packs. Import the following MP files to enable monitoring of the new Linux operating systems:

- Microsoft.Linux.Universal.Library.mp
- Microsoft.Linux.Universal.Monitoring.mp
- Microsoft.Linux.UniversalD.1.mpb (to support Debian and Ubuntu Linux agents)
- Microsoft.Linux.UniversalR.1.mpb (to support CentOS Linux agents)

For additional information, see http://technet.microsoft.com/en-us/library/jj656654.aspx.

OS Monitoring

Monitoring of cross platform operating systems includes discovery and monitoring of core operating system (OS) subsystems, as well as management pack wizards to extend monitoring to include custom daemons (processes in Windows-speak) and log files. Detailed cross platform OS monitoring capabilities in OpsMgr 2012 include

- CPU monitoring
- Disk monitoring
- Logical disk (file system)
- Physical disk
- Log file monitoring
- Memory/swap monitoring
- Network adapter monitoring
- Process monitoring

New in 2012

In addition to the cross platform monitoring features carried forward from OpsMgr 2007 R2, there are several new features in OpsMgr 2012, including

- File system nodes monitoring
- "Three state" file system free space monitors
- All new reports
- All new MP knowledge
- Java Enterprise Edition (JEE) application performance monitoring

Cross Platform Agent Architecture

Designing a cross platform agent must have been an exercise in priorities and compromise for Microsoft. Would Microsoft go the route of highly distributed processing, offloading most of the work to the cross platform agent? Would Microsoft carry its own proprietary

Windows protocols into the non-Windows world? Would the agent source code itself be open source?

It may take years for Microsoft to gain respect in the cross platform world (a fact of which Microsoft is well aware); the second generation of cross platform extensions in the Operations Manager 2012 release is still an early step in this journey to widespread acceptance as a fully vested member of the cross platform community. In the end, the choices Microsoft made seem to have been weighted in favor of the *NIX administrator, focusing on lightweight agent architectures and open standards...all steps in the right direction.

Cross platform agent architecture, which is unchanged in OpsMgr 2012, is somewhat different from the Windows agent architecture. Figure 20.1 shows an overview of the two architectures:

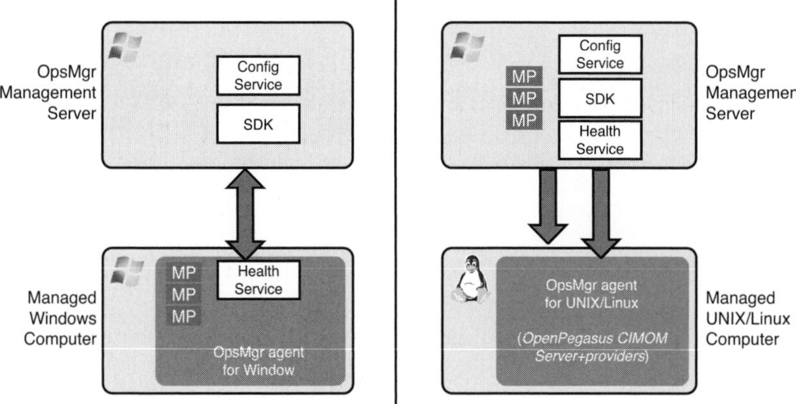

FIGURE 20.1 Windows and cross platform agent architectures.

- The Windows agent architecture is a fully distributed architecture, offloading processing to the agent that forwards collected data to a management server across a single OpsMgr channel (on port 5723).
- The cross platform agent, which leverages OpenPegasus and supports the Distributed Management Task Force (DMTF) and Common Information Model (CIM), operates much differently.

  In this architecture, the agent is a listening agent that is called by a management server to collect performance and availability data. This means the cross platform agent is a lightweight; there is less code and less processing on UNIX/Linux systems than the Windows equivalent.

Cross Platform Agent Communication

Cross platform operating systems are discovered via SSHD (the standard secure shell daemon), and monitoring data is collected by management servers using the WSMan protocol, implemented via Windows Remote Management (WinRM) on the management server. On the managed UNIX/Linux computer, the CIMOM Server is a UNIX/Linux WBEM (Web-Based Enterprise Management)-based management implementation, equivalent to Windows Management Instrumentation (WMI) on a Windows system. Figure 20.2 shows the differences between the agent architecture on the two platforms.

As with the Windows agent, a heartbeat monitor verifies agent availability. Due to the differences in agent architecture, the heartbeat monitor is a probe-based monitor initiated from the management server responsible for cross platform monitoring.

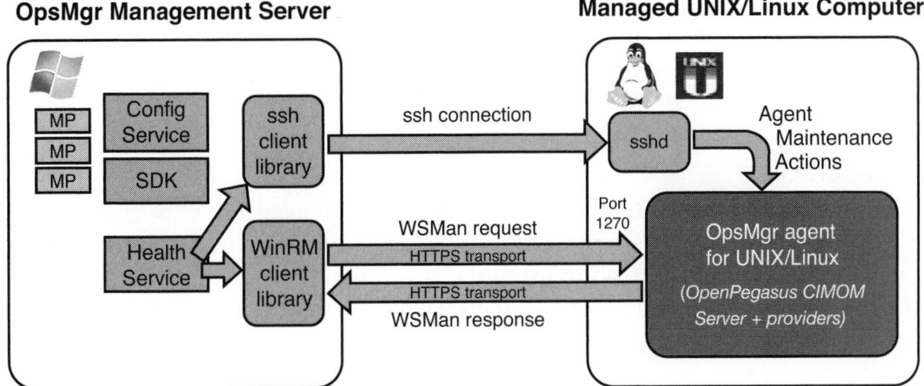

FIGURE 20.2 Detailed cross platform agent architecture.

SP 1 UPDATE: HEARTBEAT MONITORING

With Service Pack 1 for OpsMgr 2012, heartbeat monitors for Operations Manager UNIX and Linux agents now support configurable "missed heartbeats," which allows a defined number of failed heartbeats to occur before generating an alert. Failed heartbeats will cause Operations Manager to unload rules and monitors for UNIX and Linux agents until the heartbeat is restored. This makes it easy to identify those UNIX and Linux computers with failed heartbeats in the Operations console.

Performance and Scalability Implications

As with all application architectures, there are pros and cons to the lightweight agent architecture. Some of the benefits include

- Easier to maintain across nearly two dozen OS/processor architecture combinations
- Simpler for Microsoft and third parties to write management packs
- Avoids issues of MPs and modules using .NET, PowerShell, or VBScript
- Complies with Open WSMan standard
- Less overhead on UNIX/Linux computer

Here are some of the negative aspects:

- **Scalability:** Potential management server bottleneck doing the processing for hundreds of UNIX/Linux computers.
- **Communication overhead:** Frequent calls from management server to UNIX/Linux computers.
- **Potential of data loss:** Loss of communication to management server can lose data.

In short, scalability and previously high availability have been the trade-offs of this agent architecture. Perhaps the design decisions were made because Microsoft is sensitive to the probable criticisms of UNIX and Linux administrators when they learn of Microsoft monitoring of cross platform operating systems, leading them to espouse this strategy.

High Availability

Unlike its predecessor, Operations Manager 2012 delivers high availability for cross platform monitoring out-of-the-box via the new resource pool feature, which is configurable in the Operations console. In fact, administrators are prompted to configure resource pools when discovering UNIX and Linux systems. Figure 20.3 illustrates agent failover for cross platform systems. Here's how it works:

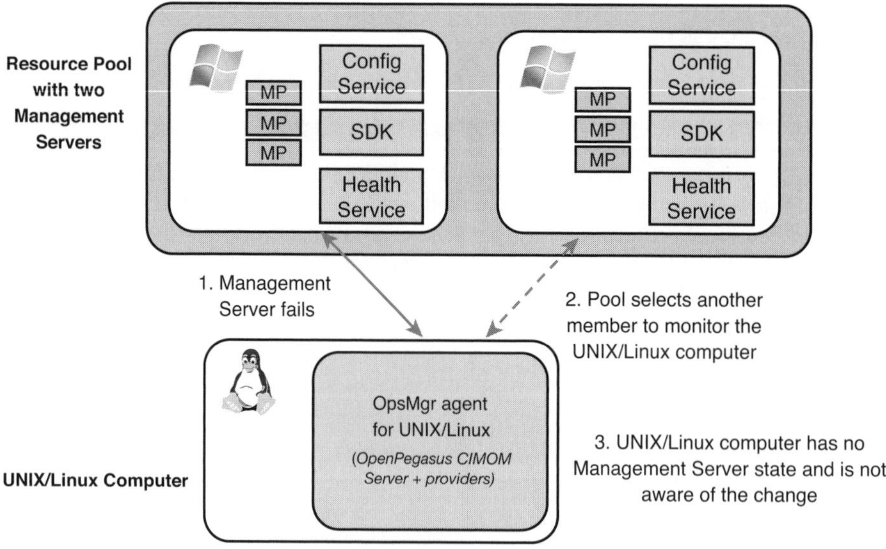

FIGURE 20.3 Cross platform agent failover.

- Administrator creates resource pool and copies certificates using `scxcertconfig.exe`.
- Administrator selects a resource pool to discover and monitor the UNIX/Linux computer.
- Resource pool selects one of its members to discover and monitor the UNIX/Linux computer.
- Management server fails.
- Pool selects another member to monitor the UNIX/Linux computer,
- UNIX/Linux computer has no management server state and is not aware of the change.

The authors recommend a strategy of configuring UNIX and Linux systems to report to a dedicated cross platform management server pool. This can be scaled out by adding additional management servers; Operations Manager will handle balancing of the agent load. As with Windows systems, you can use gateways to cross firewall boundaries; these can be pooled as well for high availability. For detailed instructions in configuring certificates across the resource pool for high availability UNIX/Linux monitoring, see http://technet.microsoft.com/en-us/library/hh287152.aspx.

UNIX/Linux Agent Architecture Details

The cross platform agent architecture is open source and Microsoft has contributed improvements to the OpenPegasus architecture. The Operations Manager Providers for Linux and UNIX project publishes the source code for the providers that make up the System Center 2012 Operations Manager agent for these operating systems. The source code is for the Microsoft-written providers that run in the OpenPegasus CIM server. The source is not for the complete agent, only for the providers. Figure 20.4 depicts the architecture.

For those platforms not supported by the OpsMgr 2012 release, Microsoft has published the providers on CodePlex (http://scx.codeplex.com). To create a complete UNIX or Linux agent, you will need OpenPegasus source code and an updated version of the DMTF CIM schema.

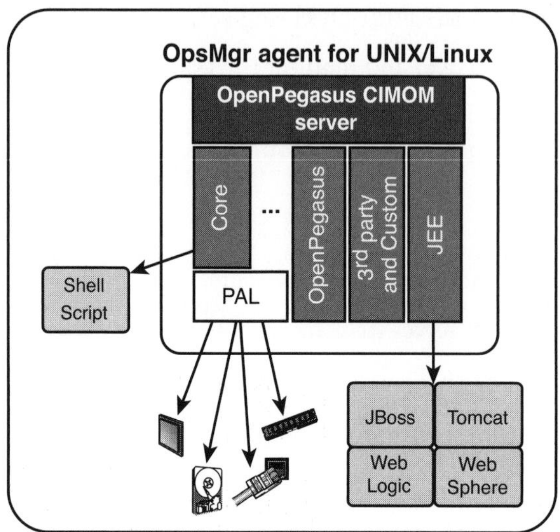

FIGURE 20.4 Additional detail on cross platform agent architecture.

OpsMgr Access to UNIX/Linux Computers

One of the most common requests voiced by UNIX and Linux administrators is minimizing the need for the root password. Cross platform monitoring in OpsMgr 2012 leverages Run As execution architecture to store privileged credentials securely and uses them only when required. Perhaps the most notable improvement to the Run As execution functionality in OpsMgr 2012 is support for "sudo" tools, meaning the root password is no longer necessary in Run As accounts. While details on the exact permissions required are sparsely documented, the authors anticipate product documentation will be updated to explain in detail when and what privileges are required to support full functionality in cross platform monitoring.

Using the new privilege architecture in Operations Manager 2012, you can specify an unprivileged account with the option to elevate to privileged status on a UNIX/Linux computer using "sudo" (or "su") as the Run As account for discovery and monitoring operations. This allows UNIX/Linux privileges to be controlled from those environments with sudo tools. It is important to note sudo must be enabled with no password required in order for privilege elevation to function as designed. Assuming knowledge of the cross platform Run As account passwords are restricted to only those who need to know (which does not have to be the OpsMgr administrator), this is a secure strategy that implements the rule of least privilege.

As a result, the "root" account or password is no longer needed in OpsMgr Run As accounts for discovery or monitoring on UNIX and Linux systems.

TERMINOLOGY: WHAT IS "SUDO" ANYWAY?

The "sudo" command on Linux and UNIX operating systems is similar to the Windows "RunAs" command; Sudo is an acronym for "Do as SuperUser."

Privilege Elevation Architecture

Figure 20.5 is an example demonstrating how the privilege elevation architecture works in Operations Manager 2012. Here is an explanation of the underlying process for cross platform privilege elevation architecture:

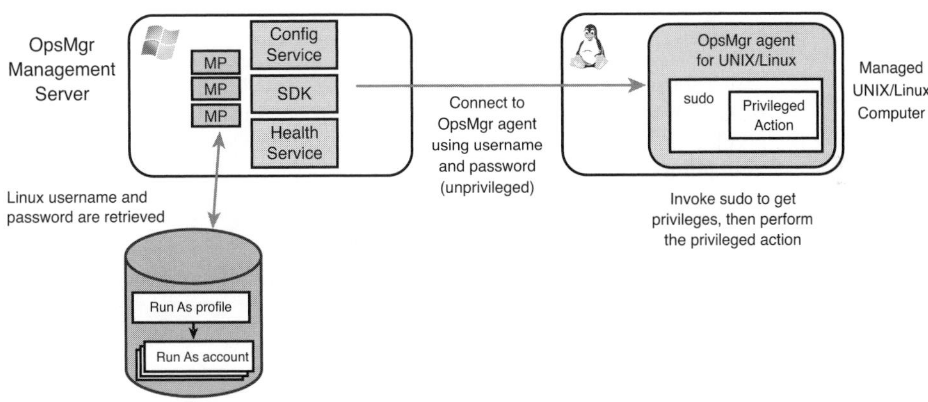

FIGURE 20.5 Cross platform privilege elevation process.

1. UNIX/Linux admin ensures sudo is set up on unprivileged account.
2. OpsMgr admin creates Run As account using info from Linux admin.
3. The management pack rule fires.
4. The UNIX/Linux username and password are retrieved by the management server.
5. Connect to OpsMgr agent using username and password (unprivileged).
6. Invoke sudo to get privileges, and then perform the privileged action.

Authentication and Data Encryption

Kerberos authentication is not possible when deploying agents to UNIX- or Linux-based computers, so certificates are used between the management server and these systems. In this scenario, the certificates are self-signed by the management server. Although you can use third-party certificates, they are not necessary.

Here are the two methods for deploying agents:

- Using the Computer and Device Management Wizard to "push" the agent to the target cross platform system
- Manually installing the agent

Manual installation is the more secure of these methods. When you use the Computer and Device Management Wizard to push agents to UNIX- or Linux-based computers, you trust that the computer to which you are deploying the agent is really the computer you think it is. Using the Computer and Device Management Wizard to deploy agents involves greater risk when you deploy to computers on the public network or in a demilitarized zone (DMZ).

Table 20.2 lists the functions the Discovery Wizard performs when you use the Computer and Device Management Wizard to deploy an agent.

TABLE 20.2 Functions performed by the Discovery Wizard

Function	Description
Discovery	The Discovery Wizard discovers the computer and tests if the certificate is valid. If the Discovery Wizard verifies the computer can be discovered and the certificate is valid, the newly discovered computer is added to the operational database.
Deployment	The Discovery Wizard copies the agent package to the UNIX- or Linux-based computer and starts the installation process.
Certificate Signing	Operations Manager retrieves the certificate from the agent, signs the certificate, deploys the certificate back to the agent, and restarts the agent.

When you manually deploy an agent, you perform the first two steps that typically are handled by the Discovery Wizard: deployment and certificate signing. You then use the Discovery Wizard to add the computer to the operational database.

Certificates are not automatically deleted when you uninstall an agent; you must manually delete the certificates that are listed in the /etc/opt/microsoft/scx/ssl folder. To regenerate the certificates at install, you must remove this folder before agent installation.

Firewall Considerations

If you have a firewall on your UNIX- or Linux-based computer, you must open port 1270 (inbound). This port number is not configurable. If you are deploying agents in a low security environment and use the Discovery Wizard to deploy and sign the certificates, you must open the SSH port. The SSH port number is configurable. By default, SSH uses inbound TCP port 22.

Cross Platform Agent Deployment

It is important to know how to prepare UNIX/Linux systems for OpsMgr agent deployment, as well as the options available when deploying the OpsMgr cross-platform agent to UNIX/Linux. Equally important is understanding how to troubleshoot error conditions should things not go as planned. These topics are discussed in the following sections.

Preparing to Discover UNIX/Linux Computers

There are several steps to perform before attempting to deploy OpsMgr agents onto UNIX or Linux systems. Most OpsMgr administrators (including the authors!) will want to start by immediately running the discovery and start installing agents. However, you will learn the hard way that this usually does not work. Check before you wreck yourself by performing the steps in the next sections before you attempt to deploy.

Name Resolution

Each of the systems you want to discover with OpsMgr must be able to resolve their Internet Protocol (IP) address to their host name. Figure 20.6 shows an example of what occurs if you attempt to discover a system via IP address and are unable to resolve the host name.

To avoid this issue, determine those UNIX/Linux systems you will be monitoring prior to performing the discovery, and if necessary add the appropriate records within the DNS Manager Microsoft Management Console (MMC) application to the DNS zone. When you create DNS records, they need to match the host name of the system. See the "Notes on UNIX Commands" section for commands to determine the host name of the UNIX/Linux system.

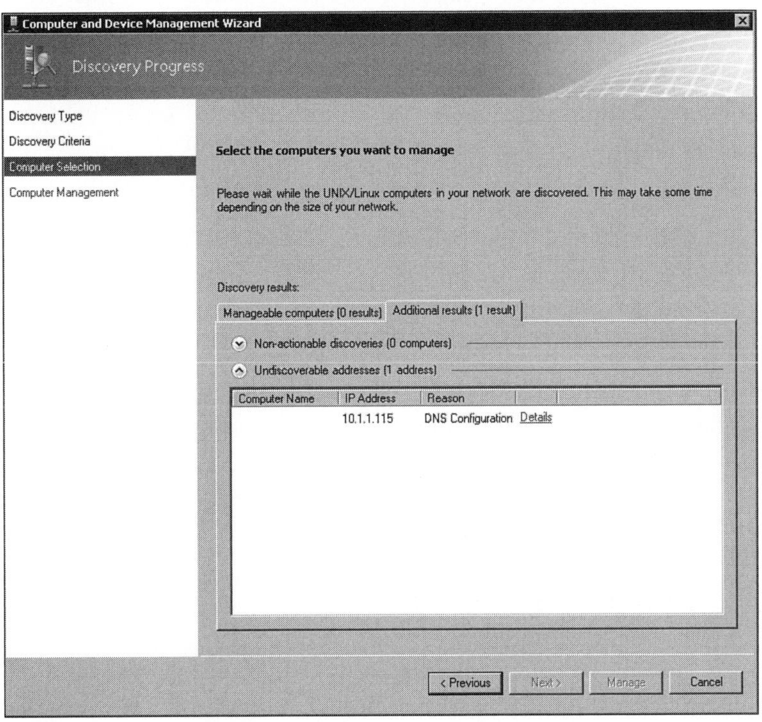

FIGURE 20.6 Discovery failure due to name resolution.

Gathering Account Information

Discovering and deploying the cross platform agent requires a username and password for those systems to which you are deploying the agent. Here are the ways you can run discovery:

- Using a superuser account (default)
- With an unprivileged user account with sudo enabled
- Supplying an SSH key

The root account typically does not have access rights to log in via Secure Shell (SSH), which is the approach OpsMgr uses to deploy the agent. The cross platform agent installation executes the scripts using the sudo command (The "Notes on UNIX Commands" section includes details on this command) as part of the installation process.

Updating WinRM

Before OpsMgr can discover any UNIX/Linux systems, WinRM must be configured to allow basic authentication.

To update WinRM, log in as an administrator to each management server in the resource pool responsible for cross platform monitoring (this requires use of Run As Administrator if using User Account Control or UAC). Here is the command to update this configuration:

```
Winrm set winrm/config/client/auth @{Basic="true"}
```

Configuring Accounts and Profiles

There are three accounts you must define as part of the cross platform functionality:

- **Linux Unprivileged Monitoring Account:** A monitoring Run As account for unprivileged monitoring
- **Linux Privileged Monitoring Account:** A monitoring Run As account for privileged monitoring
- **Linux Agent Maintenance Account:** An agent maintenance Run As account for upgrading, uninstalling, and other agent maintenance operations

Begin by configuring the UNIX/Linux Run As accounts. The process to define these Run As accounts is similar to that used for the UNIX/Linux action account, but the accounts are configured under the UNIX Privileged Accounts node in the Administration pane of the Operations console.

Using the Operations console, you will assign a user name and password to the Linux Agent Maintenance Account, Linux Privileged Monitoring Account, and Linux Unprivileged Monitoring Account. Table 20.3 further describes these accounts.

TABLE 20.3 Cross platform Run As profiles in OpsMgr 2012

Run As Profiles in UNIX/Linux MPs	Usage	Protocol
UNIX/Linux Action Account Profile	Monitoring that does not require privileges. Add a monitoring Run As account that has unprivileged credentials to this profile.	WSMan
UNIX/Linux Privileged Account Profile	Monitoring that requires privileges. Add a monitoring Run As account that has privileged credentials or credentials to be elevated to this profile.	WSMan
UNIX/Linux Agent Maintenance Account Profile	Agent maintenance operations (privileged). Add a monitoring Run As account that has privileged credentials or credentials to be elevated to this profile.	SSH

Perform the following steps to create each UNIX/Linux action account:

1. In the Operations console, navigate to **Administration** -> **Run As Configuration**. -> **UNIX/Linux Accounts**.
2. In the Tasks pane, click **Create Run As Account**.
3. On the Account Type page, choose Monitoring Account or Agent Maintenance Account.
4. On the General Properties page, provide a name and description for the account. The description is optional, but a good way to ensure other OpsMgr administrators of the account's intended purpose.
5. On the Account Credentials page, provide account credentials that can be used for the Run As account type that you selected. Select **Next** to continue.
6. Configure distribution of the Run As account:

   On the Distribution Security page, define whether these credentials will be stored in a less- or more-secure configuration, as shown in Figure 20.7:

   - **More secure:** With the more-secure approach, you select the computers that will receive the credentials.
   - **Less secure:** With the less-secure option, the credentials are sent automatically to all managed computers.

   The more-secure approach is strongly recommended, targeting the Cross Platform Resource Group for distribution.

Complete this procedure for the UNIX/Linux privileged monitoring account, the unprivileged monitoring account, and agent maintenance accounts.

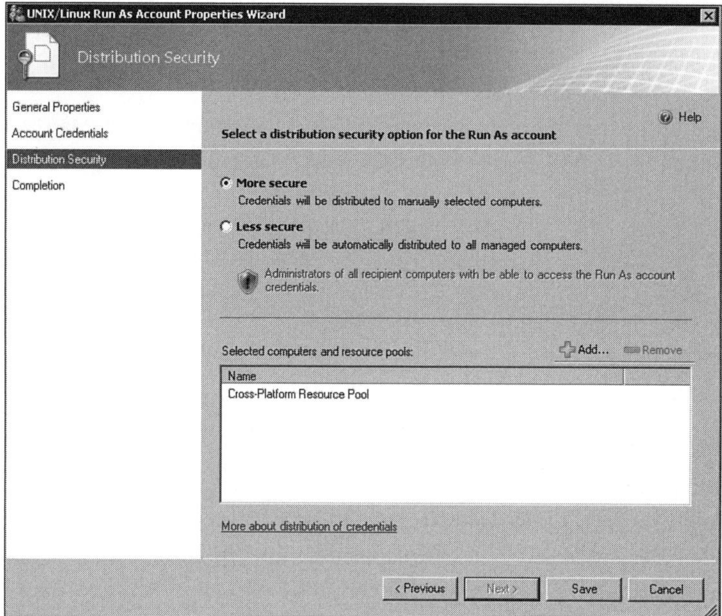

FIGURE 20.7 Cross platform Run As account distribution settings.

After creating the Run As accounts, add each Run As account to the applicable profile. There are three profiles to configure, previously mentioned in Table 20.3:

- **UNIX/Linux Action Account:** Add a monitoring Run As account to this profile that has unprivileged credentials.
- **UNIX/Linux Privileged Account:** Add a monitoring Run As account to this profile that has privileged credentials or credentials to be elevated.
- **UNIX/Linux Agent Maintenance Account:** Add a monitoring Run As account to this profile that has privileged credentials or credentials to be elevated.

To configure these profiles, perform the following steps:

1. In the Operations console, navigate to **Administration** -> **Run As Configuration** -> **Profiles**.
2. In the list of profiles, right-click and select **Properties** on one of the following profiles:
   - UNIX/Linux Action Account
   - UNIX/Linux Privileged Account
   - UNIX/Linux Agent Maintenance Account

3. In the Run As Profile Wizard, click **Next** until you get to the Run As Accounts page.
4. On the Run As Accounts page, click **Add** to add a Run As account you created. Select the class, group, or object that will be accessed using the credentials in the Run As account. Click **OK** and then click **Save**.

Repeat each of these steps for the three profiles with their matching Run As accounts.

With the UNIX/Linux Run As configuration complete, you can import the appropriate UNIX/Linux management packs and then begin discovering UNIX/Linux systems.

Importing UNIX/Linux Management Packs

Chapter 13, "Administering Management Packs," discussed the functionality available to import management packs directly from the Microsoft Management Pack Catalog rather than downloading and then installing them. This is not possible with the cross platform management packs, as they are not available in the catalog. You can find these management packs in the \MANAGEMENTPACKS subfolder of the OpsMgr 2012 installation media. You can also download the latest version of the cross platform MPs from the Microsoft website at http://www.microsoft.com/en-us/download/details.aspx?id=29696. Import the management packs for those UNIX and Linux operating systems targeted for monitoring in your environment.

You now have prepared to discover the UNIX/Linux systems. You have worked through name resolution, gathered account information from the UNIX/Linux systems, updated WinRM, configured accounts and profiles, and imported the UNIX/Linux management packs. All of this work is in preparation to discover these systems in your environment, discussed in the next section.

Discovering Systems and Deploying the Agent (Without Root)

Discovering a UNIX/Linux system is a relatively straightforward, wizard-driven process, although discovery without root is a bit more nuanced. Follow these steps to discover UNIX/Linux systems:

1. Navigate to **Administration** -> **Device Management** -> **Agent Managed** and right-click to select the Discovery Wizard. The wizard defaults to Windows computers, but select the **UNIX/Linux computers** option as displayed in Figure 20.8 and click **Next**.

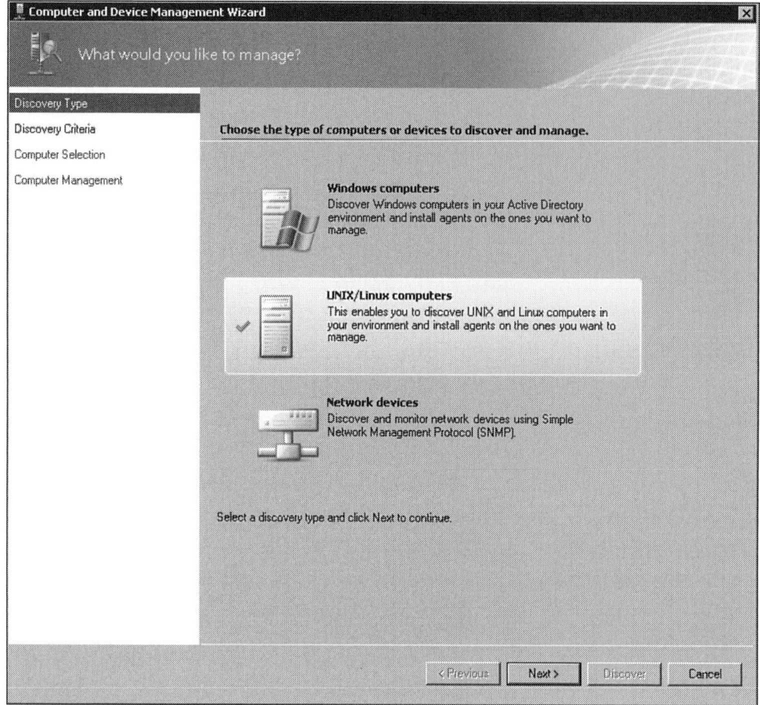

FIGURE 20.8 UNIX/Linux computers Discovery Type.

2. On the Discovery Criteria page, select the **Add** button shown in Figure 20.9. In the Discovery Criteria dialog (see Figure 20.10), enter the following information:

   - **Discovery Scope:** <*IP address* or *FQDN*> and SSH port number of the target host. To add additional hosts, click **Add row** and enter additional IP addresses and fully qualified domain names (FQDNs) as necessary, using one line per IP address or FQDN.
   - **Discovery type:** Select **All computers**.

3. Click **Set credentials** to launch the Credential Settings dialog shown in Figure 20.11.

4. To discover UNIX and Linux computers without root (using the new sudo capabilities in OpsMgr 2012), select the **User name and password** radio button and enter the following values:

   - **User name:** <*sudo_user*>
   - **Password:** <*sudo_user password*>
   - **Confirm password:** <*sudo_user password*>
   - **Does this account have privileged access?:** Select **This account does not have privileged access** from the drop-down list.

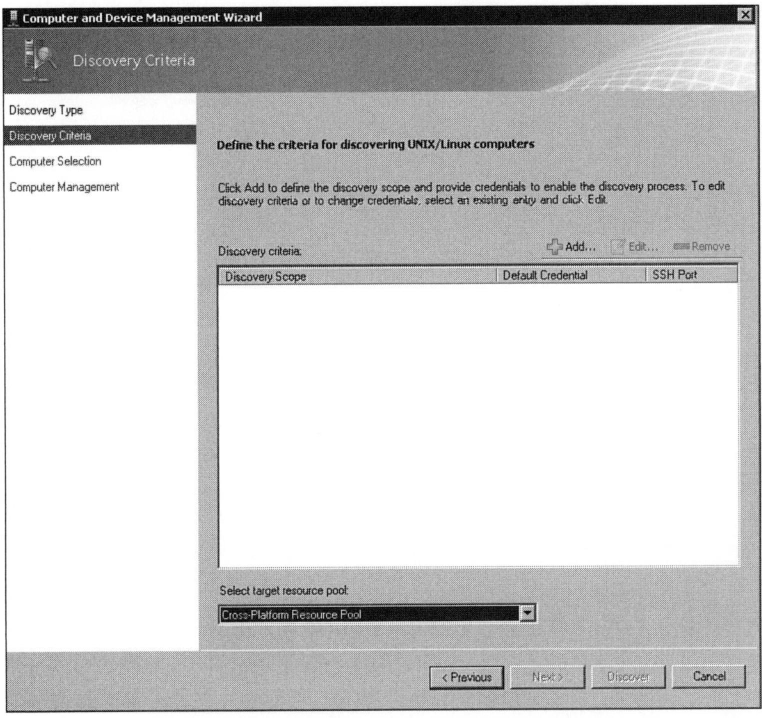

FIGURE 20.9 Cross platform privilege elevation process.

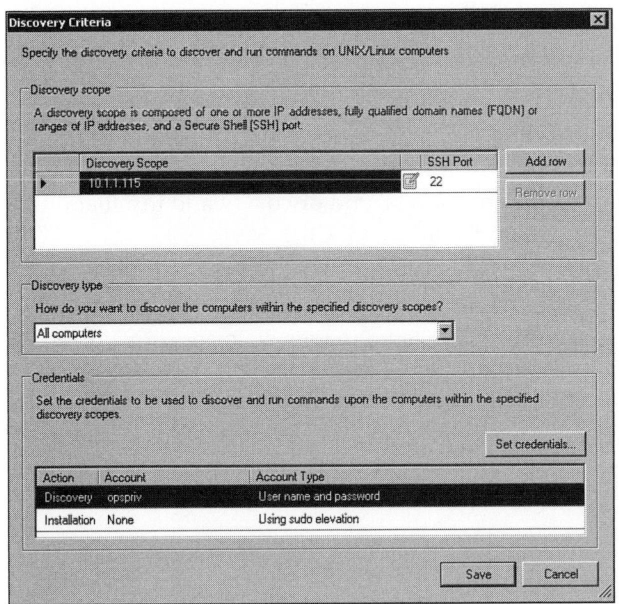

FIGURE 20.10 Cross platform discovery scope, type, and credentials.

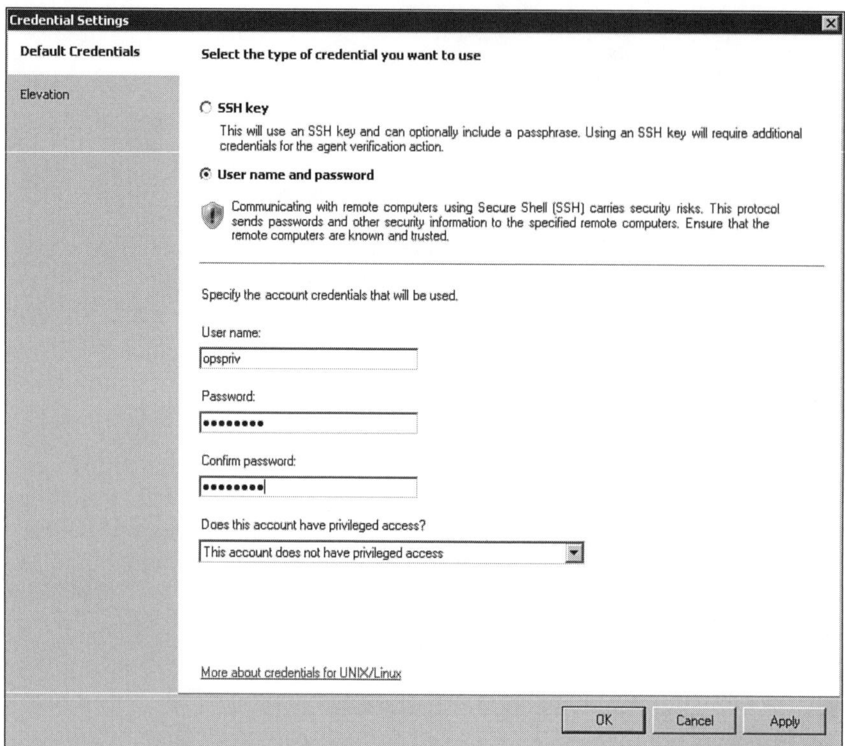

FIGURE 20.11 Specify a sudo-enabled account without privileged access.

5. Setting this option adds an extra settings tab labeled Elevation. Select this tab and verify the **Use 'sudo' elevation** option is selected, and then click **OK**. This is shown in Figure 20.12.

6. This brings you to the page shown in Figure 20.13. Click **Discover** to start the discovery process.

   Ensure the Discovery Type is set to **All computers**, and discovery and installation should proceed successfully, as shown in Figure 20.15. Click **Save**.

   The discovery process will take from several seconds to a few minutes, depending on the number of hosts in the list. When the process is complete, a list of UNIX and Linux computers is displayed in the Discovery Progress dialog as shown in Figure 20.14.

7. On the Discovery Criteria page, at the Select target resource pool drop-down, select **Cross-Platform Resource Pool** as shown in Figure 20.13, and click **Discover**.

8. Select the check box next to the computers on which you would like to install an agent and click **Next**.

9. When the process is complete, all computers to which an agent was deployed successfully will reflect a **Successful** status in the Computer Management Progress dialog, as shown in Figure 20.15.

10. Click **Done** to exit the wizard.

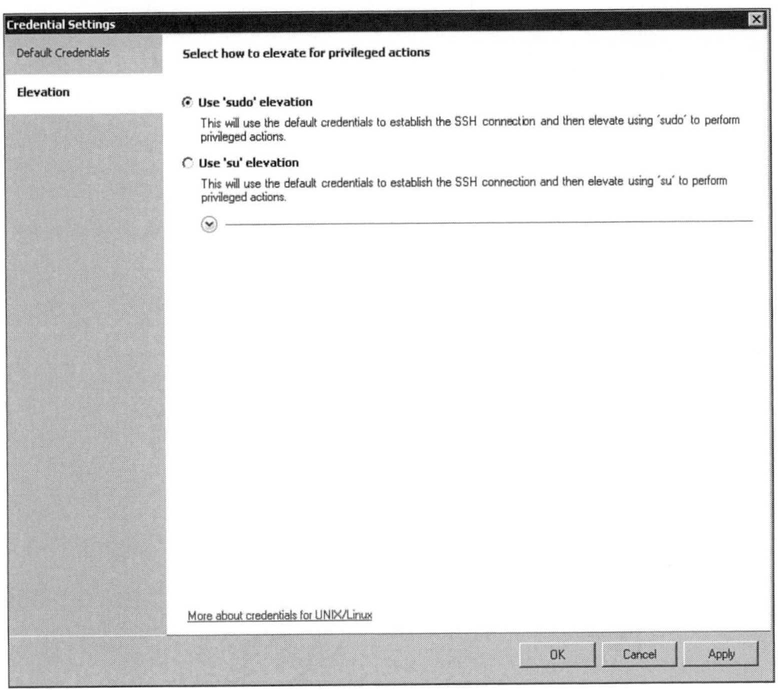

FIGURE 20.12 Verify 'sudo' elevation is selected.

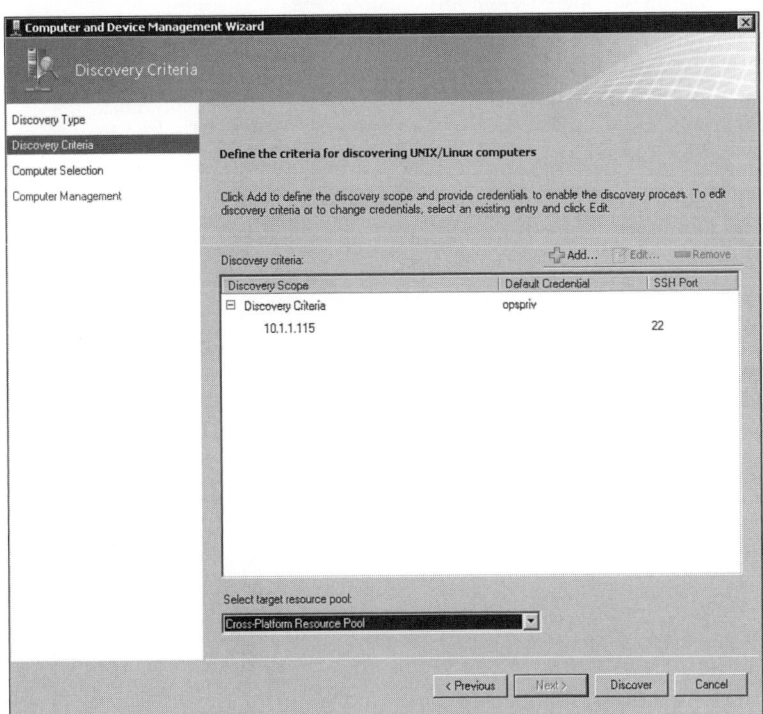

FIGURE 20.13 Discovery Criteria dialog.

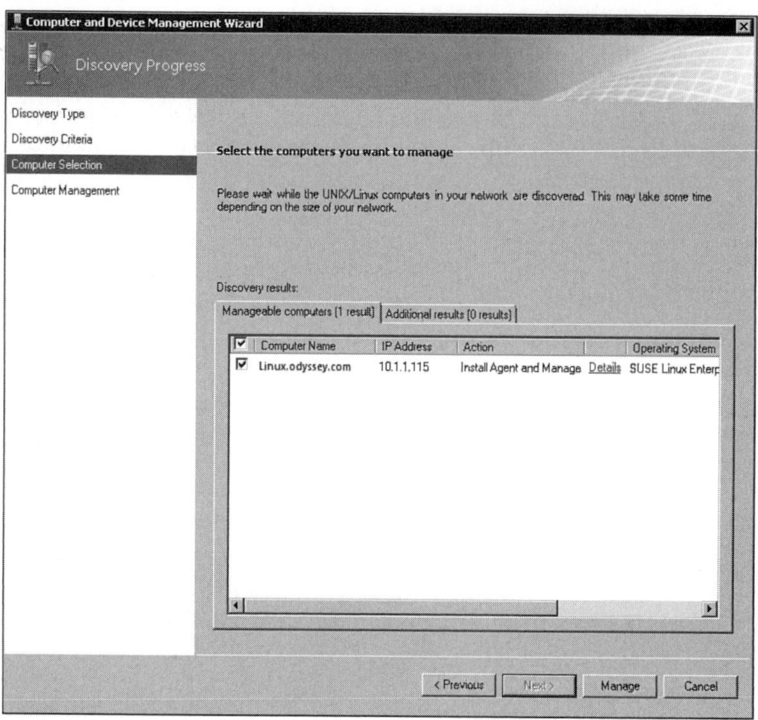

FIGURE 20.14 Discovering UNIX and Linux systems.

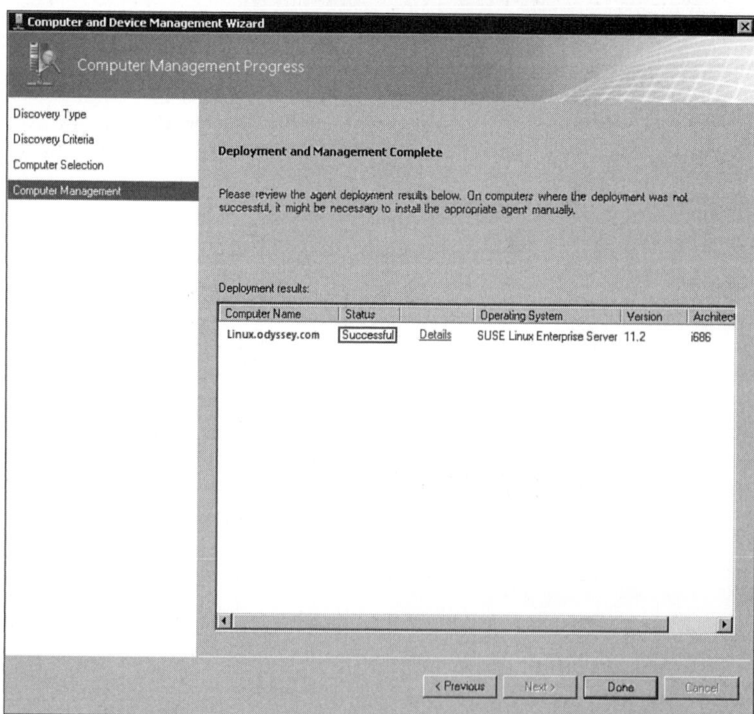

FIGURE 20.15 Cross platform agent status after successful agent deployment.

Manually Deploying the Cross Platform Agent

There are situations where you may need to deploy the cross platform agent manually. Examples include unsupported versions of UNIX/Linux or systems where an SSH connection cannot be established. This section performs a manual deployment to a SUSE 11 system named linux.odyssey.com. Follow these steps to perform the manual installation:

1. Install the FTP server on a Windows server; add the Linux agent installation files to the FTP share; then connect from the Linux system and perform an FTP `get` of the files.

   To get the files from the FTP server, log in to the Linux system, as follows:

   - **Start the ftp client: ftp**
   - **Open (ip address):** Open **192.168.0.209**
   - **Username: administrator**
   - **Password: password**
   - **Set the transfer type to binary: Binary**
   - **Get (filename): get scx-1.3.0-206.sles.11.x64.rpm**

NOTE: SECURE FILE COPY VIA SSH

You can also copy files to a UNIX or Linux system using SSH. For instructions, see http://www.garron.me/linux/scp-linux-mac-command-windows-copy-files-over-ssh.html. You could use WinSCP to copy to and from Windows to Linux. For the download location of WinSCP, see the "Notes on UNIX Commands" section.

2. Install the package using rpm (when prompted with y/n to install, choose **y**):

```
rpm -i scx-1.3.0-206.sles.11.x64.rpm
```

3. Next, verify the package installed by using the rpm command:

```
rpm -q scx
```

4. After verifying the installation, verify that the agent is running. You can use the service command, as follows:

```
service scx-cimd status
```

After manually adding this system, complete the discovery process by accessing the Operations console and discovering the system to which you manually installed the agent (see the "Discovering Systems and Deploying the Agent (Without Root)" section for details).

NOTE: COMMAND SYNTAX

The syntax of the commands you will use varies depending upon the version of UNIX/Linux to which you are deploying the agent. This particular example showed the syntax for a SUSE 11 Linux system.

Additional syntax examples for Red Hat, Solaris, HP-UX, and AIX are available at http://technet.microsoft.com/en-us/library/hh212686.aspx.

There are situations where you may need to uninstall the cross platform agent, such as when reinstalling to create a new certificate. In the following example, an issue occurred when the agent was deployed manually to a system named suse11, but the actual machine name was susesvx01.

To address this situation, remove the agent using the following syntax:

```
rpm -e scx
```

Additional details on situations where agent names do not match are available in the "Common Agent Deployment Errors" section.

Common Agent Deployment Errors

During a cross platform agent deployment, you may encounter errors needing resolution. This section includes a number of errors with the error message that occurs, and the recommended method to address the error:

- **Issue:** The certificate Common Name (CN) does not match.

  or

  Issue: The secure sockets layer (SSL) certificate contains a common name (CN) that does not match the hostname.

  Resolution: When performing a manual installation, you may have created a fully qualified name for the system that did not match the system's actual fully qualified name (as in the installation in this chapter). In this case, the certificate will not match the actual fully qualified host name. To resolve this, perform the following steps:

  1. Uninstall the cross platform agent (see the "Manually Deploying the Cross Platform Agent" section for details).
  2. Delete the certificate stored under /etc/opt/microsoft/scx/ssl named scxkey.pem.
  3. Change your DNS resolution so the name used to connect to the system will match the actual system name.
  4. Redeploy the agent manually as discussed in the "Manually Deploying the Cross Platform Agent" section.

  Another option is to reissue the certificate and restart the cross platform agent, discussed at http://technet.microsoft.com/en-us/library/dd891009.aspx.

- **Issue:** The certificate is invalid; please select the system to install a new certificate.

Resolution: Uninstall the cross platform agent, delete the certificate, and re-deploy the agent.

- **Issue:** The certificate signing operation failed.

  or

  Issue: The certificate is invalid; please select the system to issue a new certificate.

  Resolution: These can occur when there are issues connecting to the UNIX system on the SSH port. Use telnet from the management server to the SSH port to verify connectivity; if connectivity is not available, debug this issue and then re-create the certificate.

- **Issue:** Could not transfer the discovery script.

  or

  Issue: Could not create secured folder.

  Resolution: Many different connectivity issues can cause this, including IPTABLES blocking the connection, SSH not running on the client system, or (as occurred during the authors' testing) an invalid user account/password combination was specified when discovering the UNIX/Linux system.

- **Issue:** Discovery fails with error DNS Configuration.

  Resolution: Name resolution is not available for the specified IP address. Create forward and reverse records in DNS for the FQDN of the UNIX/Linux system.

- **Issue:** Agent installation failed.

  Resolution: OpsMgr was able to connect to the remote system but could not use the root or sudo-enabled credentials required to run the installation successfully. Verify the installation account password, and if this continues to fail, attempt a manual cross platform agent installation.

- **Issue:** Unable to install agent and discover computer instance into OpsMgr.

  Resolution: SSH is disabled on the UNIX/Linux system. Either enable SSH or manually install the cross platform agent.

- **Issue:** Alerts generated about "Secure Reference Override Failure."

  Resolution: The Run As profiles were not properly defined for the cross platform management packs. See the "Configuring Accounts and Profiles" section for details.

Finding Monitoring Data in the Console

OpsMgr 2012 includes many views for exploring the state, performance, and alerts related to UNIX and Linux computers. Views are organized at the top level into separate UNIX and Linux folders, shown in Figure 20.16. The subfolders present platform-specific folders for different UNIX and Linux distributions, such as AIX, Solaris, Red Hat, and SUSE, displayed in Figure 20.17.

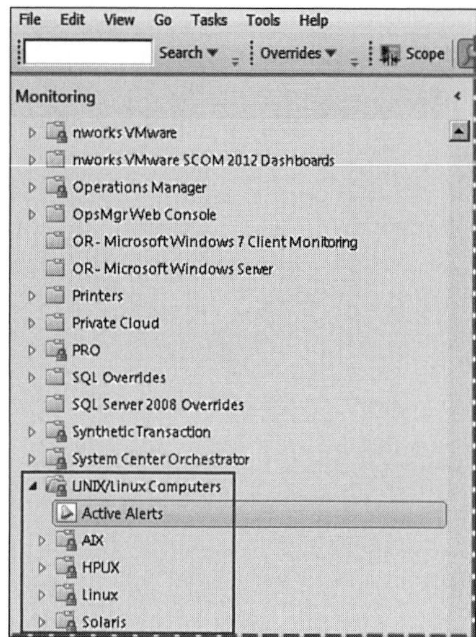

FIGURE 20.16 Top level folders for UNIX/Linux views in the Monitoring space.

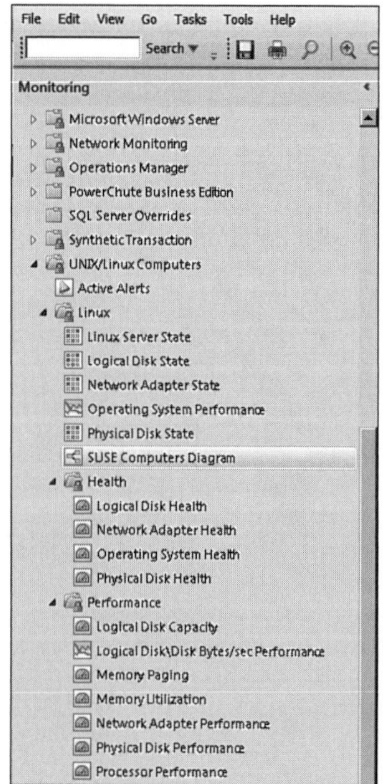

FIGURE 20.17 Linux Alert, State, Performance and Dashboard views.

Built-in diagram views provide instant visibility into ailing OS components, as shown in Figure 20.18. You can right-click any component in a diagram view to launch alert, state, and performance views, as well as the Health Explorer for the chosen component.

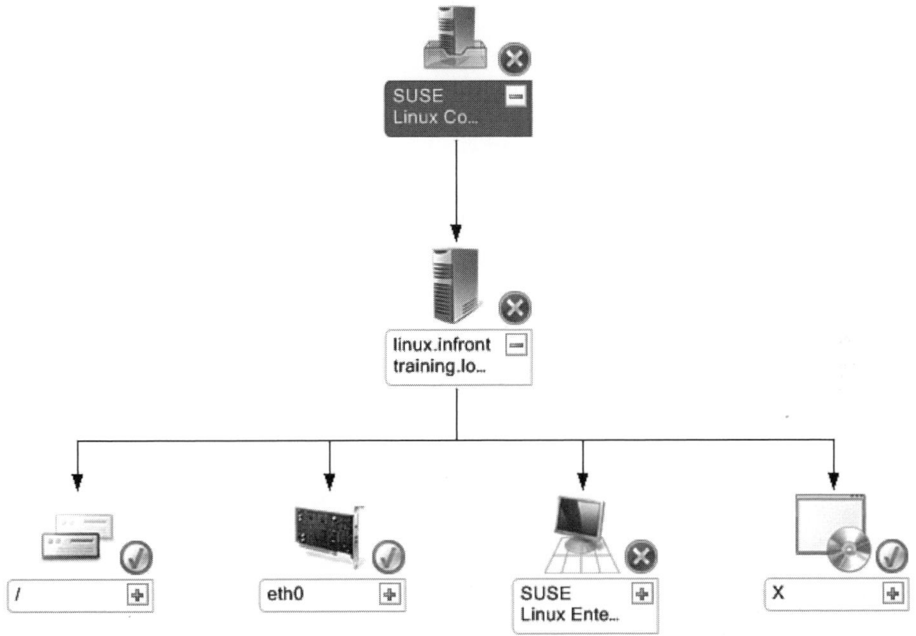

FIGURE 20.18 SUSE Linux Diagram view.

Using Management Pack Templates

In addition to the rules and monitors provided with the UNIX/Linux management packs, the OpsMgr 2012 release includes management pack templates (introduced in OpsMgr 2007 R2) specifically designed for UNIX/Linux.

- UNIX/Linux Log File Template
- UNIX/Linux Process Template
- Shell Monitor Command Monitoring Templates

These are discussed in the next sections.

UNIX/Linux Log File Template

The Log File template does exactly as its name suggests and enables you to configure monitoring a log file hosted on a UNIX/Linux system. As with other management pack templates, creating a new log file monitor is simple and wizard-based. Choosing to create a new log file monitor presents the standard rule/monitor creation dialogs where you provide the log file monitor a name and select a management pack in which to store it. Follow these steps:

1. Enter a friendly name in the textbox provided and using the drop-down, select a management pack in which to save your custom monitor, then click **Next**.

TIP: USING A DEDICATED MANAGEMENT PACK

The authors suggest using a dedicated management pack for the output of the UNIX and Linux monitoring templates.

2. This opens the dialog shown in Figure 20.19, where you will configure the log file monitor as follows:

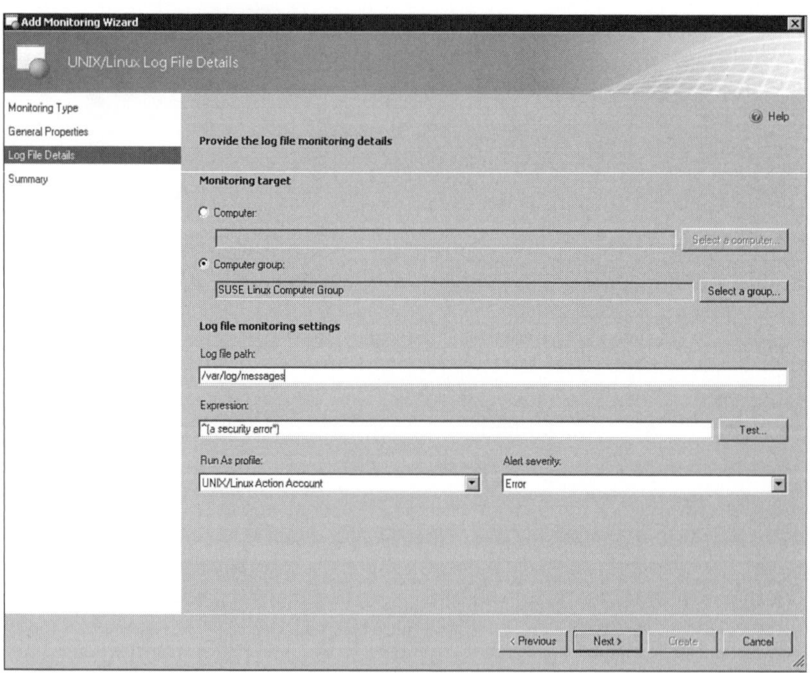

FIGURE 20.19 UNIX/Linux Log File Details dialog.

- **Monitoring target:** Select either a specific UNIX/Linux computer or computer group to target the monitor.
- **Log file monitoring settings:** Manually enter the name and location of the log file to monitor. The format of this log file path will depend on the version of UNIX/Linux you are targeting but will be similar to the /tmp/logfile format.
- **Expression:** Configure the expression (in regular expression format) to monitor for in the log file. The Expression Test section lets you test the regular expression you just created against a sample line of text you input, which replicates what is found in the log file.
- **Run As profile:** If necessary, change the Run As profile from the default configuration. This may be required if the log file being monitored requires elevated privileges to access and sudo has not been enabled on the unprivileged account.
- **Alert severity:** Configure the desired alert severity. Error is the default.

3. Click the **Test** button to test your regular expression syntax versus a line from the target log file targeted for monitoring as shown in Figure 20.20. When you have tested successfully, click **OK**.

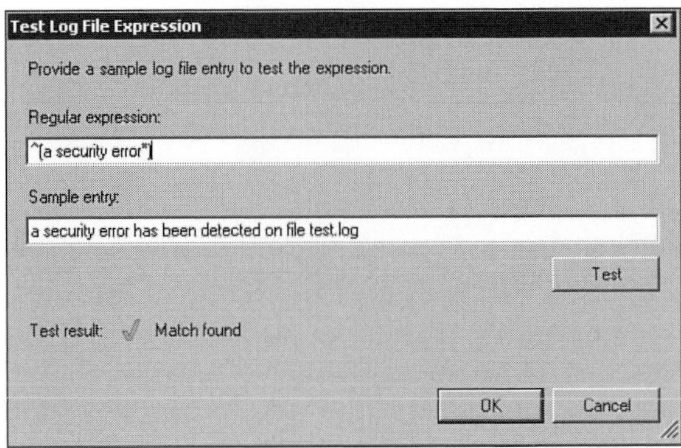

FIGURE 20.20 Test Log File Expression dialog.

4. Change the Run As profile and Alert severity defaults if necessary, then click **Next**. On the UNIX/Linux Log File Summary page, click **Create**.

UNIX/Linux Process Template

The UNIX/Linux Process template also ships as part of OpsMgr 2012. This template works similarly to the Windows Service monitoring template, enabling you to monitor the availability of a specific service (sometimes referred to as a process) running on a UNIX/Linux server. Follow these steps:

1. After choosing to create the new template and assigning it a name and destination management pack, proceed to the process details dialog shown in Figure 20.21. From this page, click **Select a process** to select a source server for the process. This server does not necessarily have to be the server you ultimately monitor but must be actively running the process.

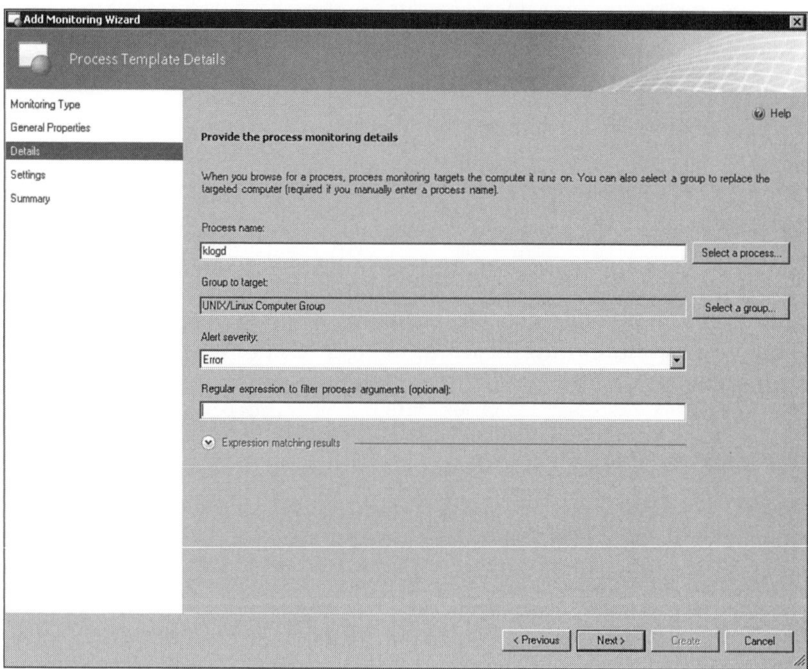

FIGURE 20.21 Process Template Details.

2. Figure 20.22 shows the server selection page. After highlighting the appropriate server and clicking **Select**, the wizard immediately begins to enumerate the processes, making it easier to select the appropriate process for monitoring, and displays the dialog shown in Figure 20.23. From this list, scroll down to select the **X** process (which represents the graphical user interface, or GUI, on the SUSE host) and click **Select**.

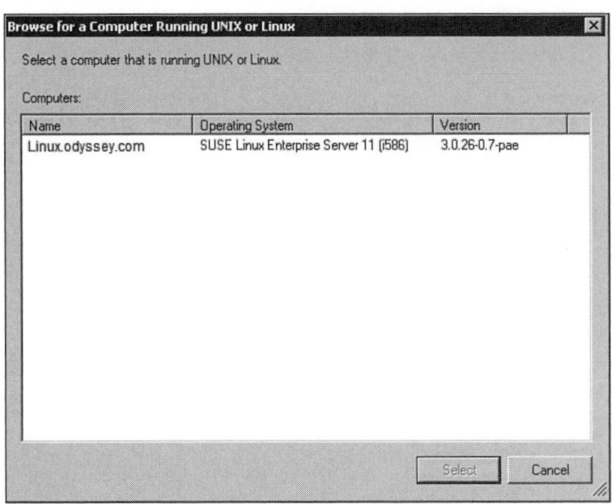

FIGURE 20.22 Server selection page.

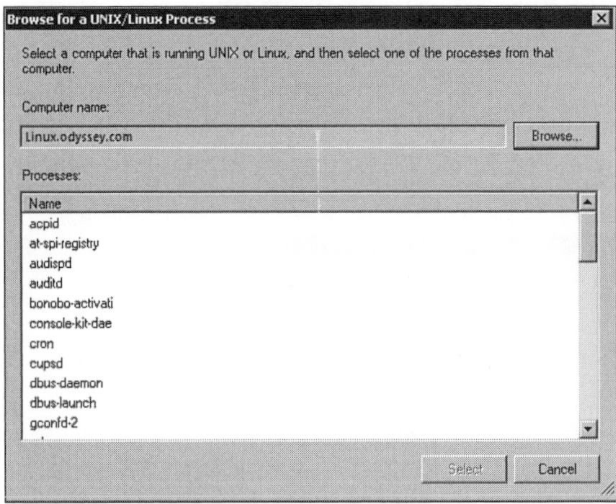

FIGURE 20.23 Select a service for monitoring.

3. Click **Next** (see Figure 20.24) to monitor the service for only the single server selected, or select the **Select a group** check box and select a computer group to target the monitor.

4. Check the **Generate an alert** check box for minimum or maximum number of service instances that should be running. To simply check that a service is running, also select the option to **Generate an alert when the minimum number of process instances is less than the specified value** and set the value to **1**, as shown in Figure 20.25.

5. To complete the wizard, click **Next** and then **Create**. Once the monitor is created, it appears in the Health Explorer under **Availability -> Application/Service Availability Rollup**. If the service stops, the monitor displays an unhealthy state.

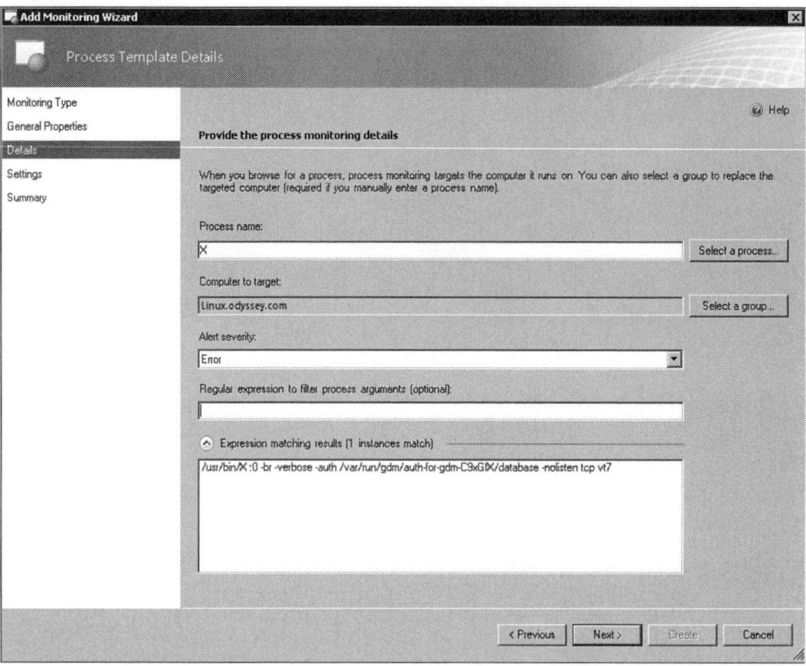

FIGURE 20.24 Process Template Details page.

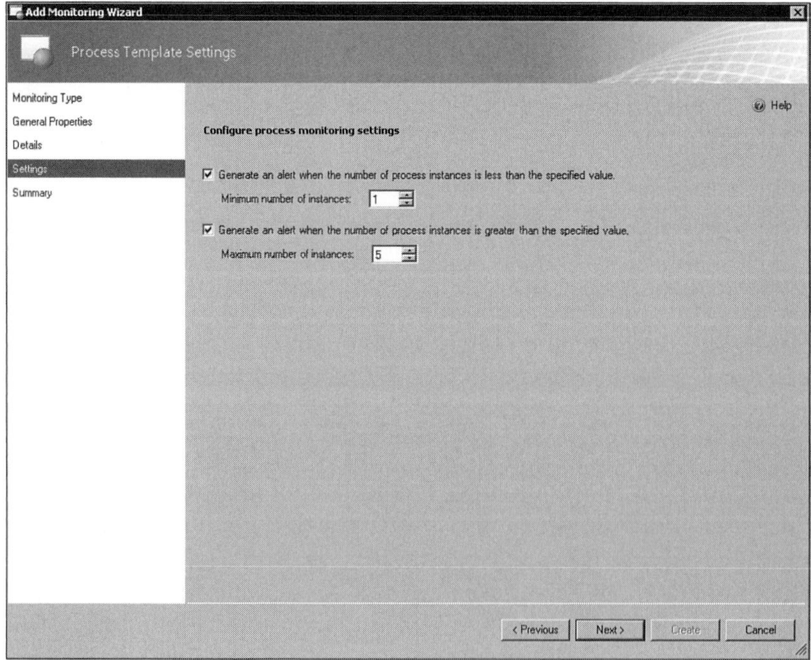

FIGURE 20.25 Process count process monitoring settings.

6. To test your configuration, you can stop the GUI for a short time to verify the configuration works as expected. It is simple to stop the GUI until the monitor transitions to an error state and generates an alert. Here's how to start and stop the GUI on SUSE 11.x:

   To stop the GUI, from a terminal session, type

   ```
   /sbin/init 3
   ```

   To restart the GUI from the command line interface, log in if prompted and type

   ```
   /sbin/init 5
   ```

Shell Command Monitoring Templates

Operations Manager 2012 includes new shell command monitoring templates. The new templates are

- Monitors
  - UNIX/Linux Shell Command Three State Monitor
  - UNIX/Linux Shell Command Two State Monitor
- Rules
  - UNIX/Linux Shell Command (Alert)
  - UNIX/Linux Shell Command (Performance)
- Tasks: Run a UNIX/Linux Shell Command

Under the cover, these templates use the ExecuteShellCommand method of the agent's script provider with the WSMan Invoke module. This method executes the command and outputs StdOut, StdErr, and ReturnCode. The command can be a path to a simple command, a command, or script existing on the managed computer, or a "one-liner" script (a shell script condensed to one line with pipes and semicolons). The templates also allow you to select whether to run with the nonprivileged action account or the privileged account (which also supports sudo elevation).

The next sections provide examples of using some of the shell monitoring templates.

Creating a UNIX/Linux Shell Command Two State Monitor (DNS Name Resolution Check)

Use the nslookup command to check name resolution health from the DNS server (specifying the local host as the server in the second argument). An example is `nslookup linux.odyssey.com 127.0.0.1`. Here is what the actual output of this command looks like:

```
lx11:/var/lib/named # nslookup linux.odyssey.com 127.0.0.1
Server: 127.0.0.1
Address: 127.0.0.1#53
Name: linux.odyssey.com
Address:192.168.1.76
```

20

```
lx11:/var/lib/named # nslookup linux.odyssey.com 127.0.0.1
Server:  127.0.0.1
Address: 127.0.0.1#53
Name:    linux.odyssey.com
Address: 192.168.1.76
```

To make this command easier to read on your monitor (and this page), you can do a bit of pipeline parsing:

```
nslookup linux.odyssey.com 127.0.0.1|egrep "^Name:.*linux.odyssey.com"|wc -l
```

This shell command returns a value of 1 if the line: `Name:  linux.odyssey.com` is found in StdOut and a value of 0 otherwise. Therefore, a value of 1 means the name resolution attempt succeeded, and a value of 0 means it failed.

Here are the steps to create a monitor using this command:

1. In the Operations console, navigate to **Authoring** -> **Management Pack Objects** and right-click **Monitors**. Select **Create a Monitor** -> **Unit Monitor**.
2. Expand **Scripting** -> **Generic**, select **UNIX/Linux Shell Command Two State Monitor**, and select a target management pack (created previously). Click **Next**, shown in Figure 20.26.

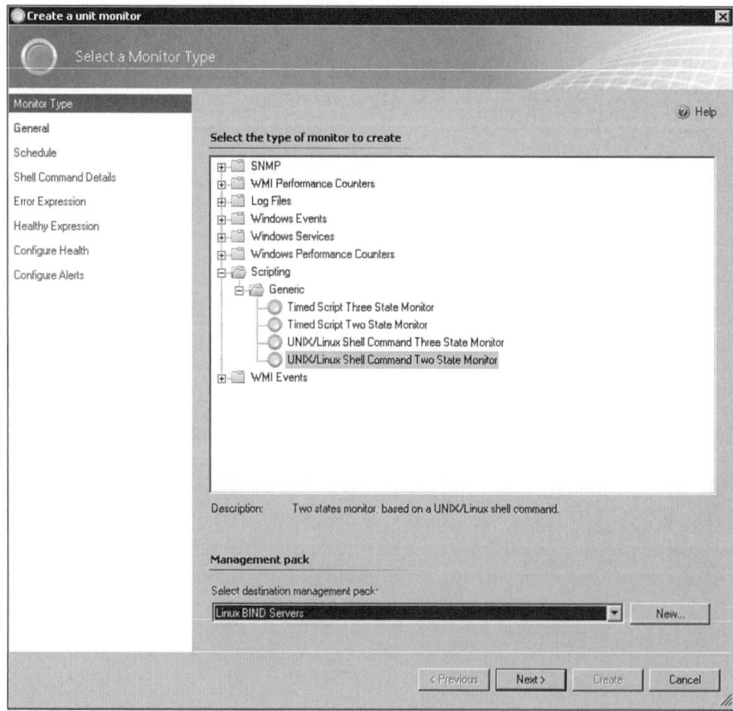

FIGURE 20.26 Select a Monitor Type dialog in the Authoring pane.

3. Input a name, description, and target (**UNIX/Linux Computer**) for the monitor. Select a Parent monitor (**Availability**) and uncheck **Monitor is enabled** as shown in Figure 20.27. Click **Next**.

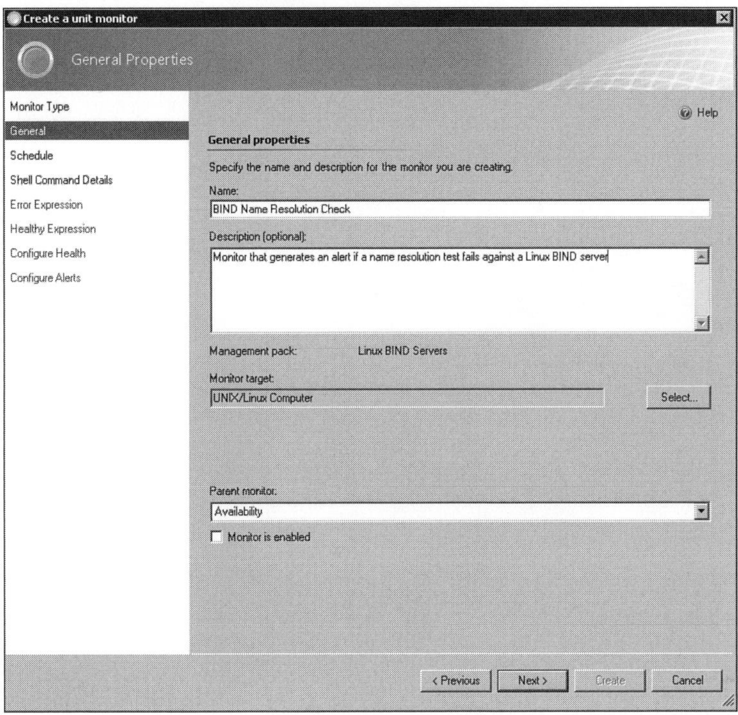

FIGURE 20.27 General Properties page of the shell command two state monitor.

4. Configure a schedule interval as shown in Figure 20.28. For performance optimization, this should be as large of a value as reasonable; 10 or 15 minutes should be sufficient for most purposes. Click **Next**.

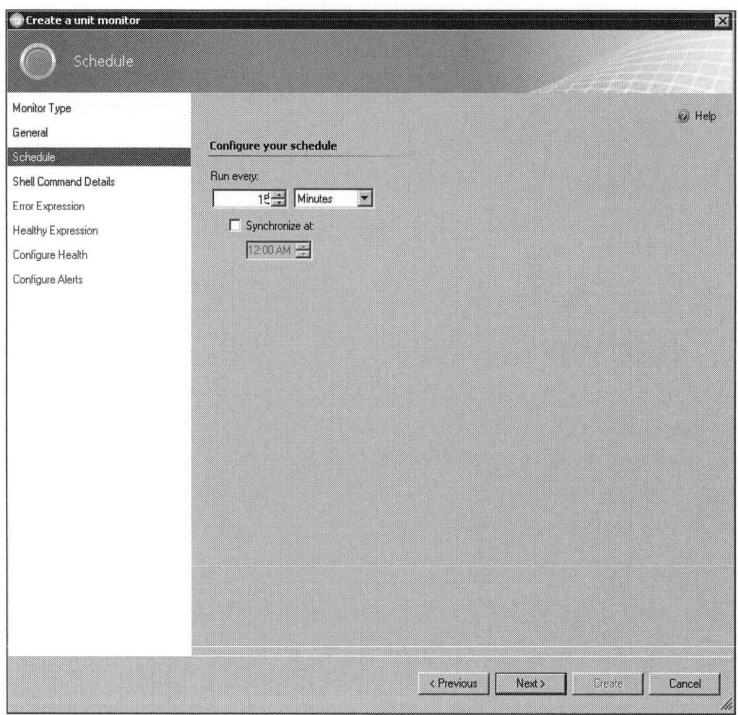

FIGURE 20.28 Schedule page for the shell command two state monitor.

5. Input the shell command (replacing linux.odyssey.com with the hostname to resolve) shown in Figure 20.29:

```
nslookup linux.odyssey.com 127.0.0.1|egrep '^Name:.*linux.odyssey.com'|wc -l
```

The **UNIX/Linux Privileged Account** Run As profile is appropriate for this command, and **120** is a sufficient value for the Timeout (seconds). Click **Next**.

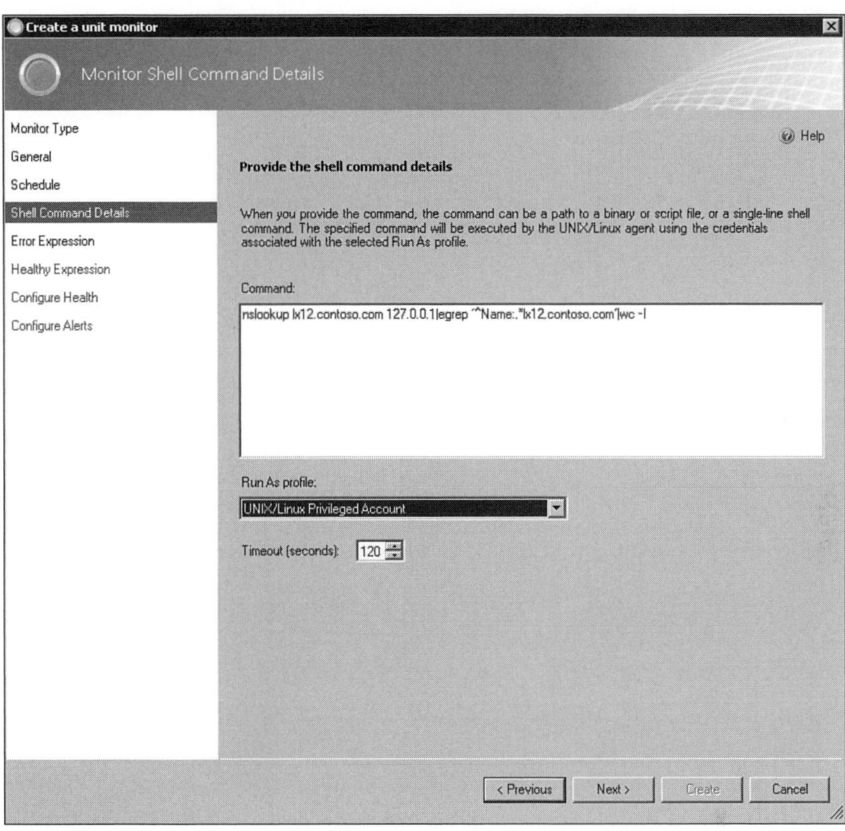

FIGURE 20.29 Command Details for the shell command two state monitor.

6. The next page of the wizard is for configuring the Monitor Error Expression. If the conditions defined in this expression are matched, the monitor goes to an error state. The Expression Filter dialog is preloaded with the following values (shown in Figure 20.30):

```
//*[local-name()="StdOut" Contains <input value>
//*[local-name()="ReturnCode"] Equals 0
```

With the shell command used in this example, the error state should be triggered when StdOut does not equal 1, so the first line can be modified to that effect. This results in an error condition triggered when StdOut does not equal 1 and the nslookup command executed successfully (ReturnCode equals 0).

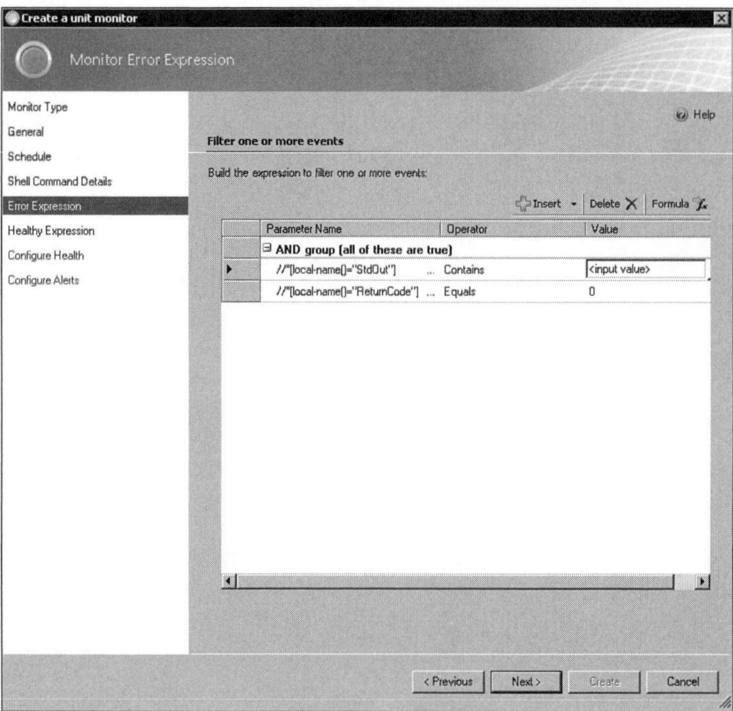

FIGURE 20.30 Shell command two state monitor - Monitor Error Expression.

7. After clicking **Next**, the Healthy Expression dialog is displayed as shown in Figure 20.31. As a StdOut value of 1 indicates a successful nslookup operation using the provided shell command, simply set the first line to: `//*[local-name()="StdOut"]` **Equals 1** and click **Next**.

8. In the Configure Health dialog, you can choose whether you want the error state to map to a Critical or Warning event by changing the Health State drop-down. This example sets the Health State to **Warning** as shown in Figure 20.32.

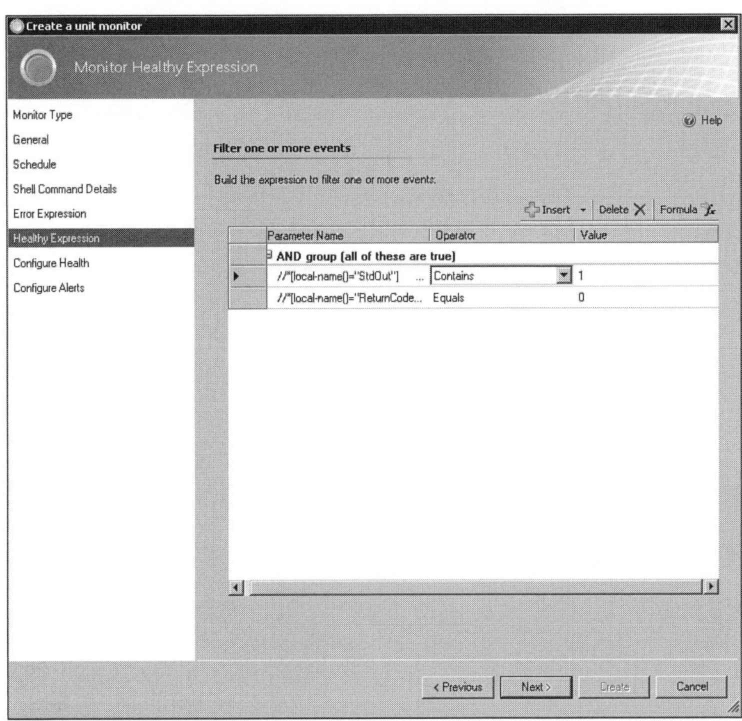

FIGURE 20.31 Shell command two state monitor - Monitor Healthy Expression.

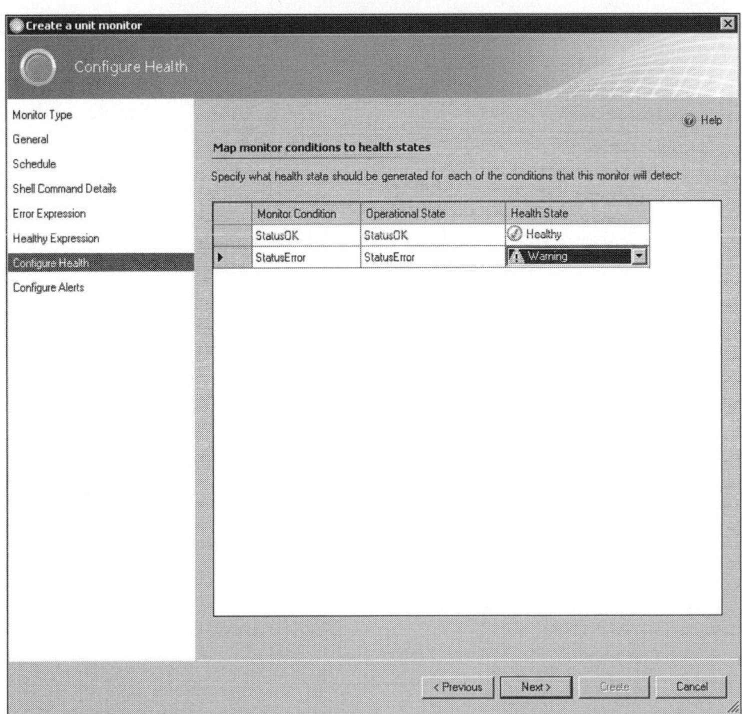

FIGURE 20.32 Configure Health page for the shell command two state monitor.

9. The next dialog is for alert configuration. Check **Generate alerts for this monitor** and select an appropriate Priority and Severity (match monitors' health) as shown in Figure 20.33. Edit the Alert name if appropriate and provide an Alert description. Standard $Target$ variables can be embedded in the Alert description by clicking [...]. Here is the syntax to include data from the shell command execution:

```
StdOut:  $Data/Context///*[local-name()="StdOut"]$
StdErr:  $Data/Context///*[local-name()="StdErr"]$
ReturnCode: $Data/Context///*[local-name()="ReturnCode"]$
```

This example uses the following description as shown in Figure 20.33:

```
The BIND DNS server: $Tar-get/Property
[Type="MicrosoftUnixLibrary7320040!Microsoft.Unix.Computer"]
/NetworkName$ failed a name resolution test. StdErr
```

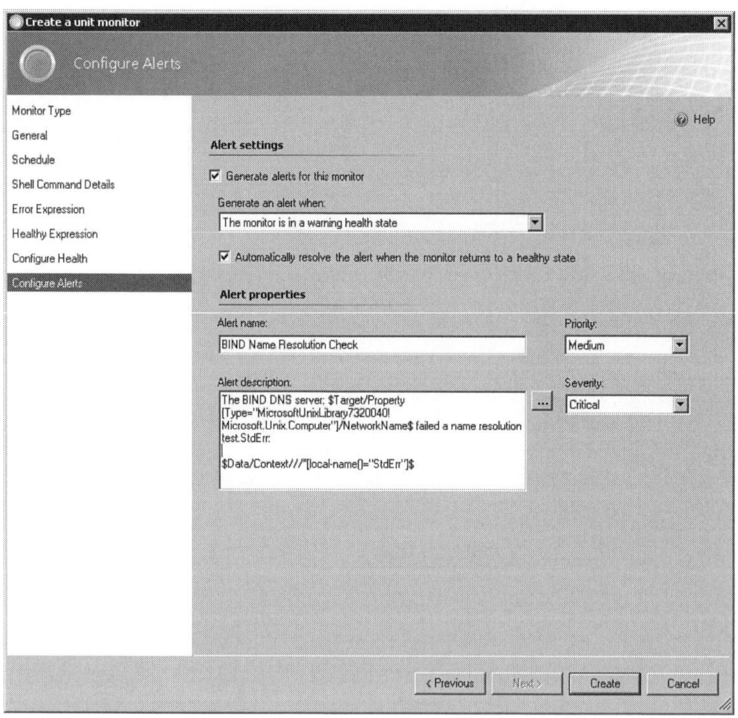

FIGURE 20.33 Configure Alerts page for the shell command two state monitor.

10. Click **Create** to complete the monitor creation.

11. As this monitor targets all UNIX and Linux computers, it was created without being enabled by default. Use an override to enable it for the group of BIND servers. Navigate to **Authoring -> Management Pack Objects**, and click on **Monitors**. In the top-right of the Monitors pane, click **Change Scope**, and check **Linux Computers** from the Scope Management Pack Objects dialog. Find the monitor just created (BIND Name Resolution Check) shown in Figure 20.34.

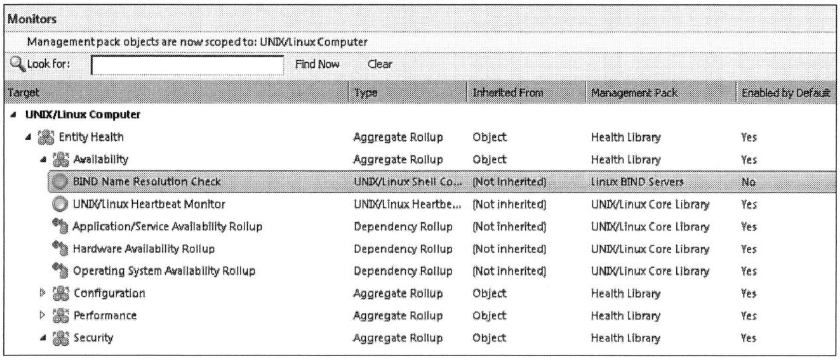

Monitors

Management pack objects are now scoped to: UNIX/Linux Computer

Look for: Find Now Clear

Target	Type	Inherited From	Management Pack	Enabled by Default
UNIX/Linux Computer				
Entity Health	Aggregate Rollup	Object	Health Library	Yes
Availability	Aggregate Rollup	Object	Health Library	Yes
BIND Name Resolution Check	UNIX/Linux Shell Co...	(Not inherited)	Linux BIND Servers	No
UNIX/Linux Heartbeat Monitor	UNIX/Linux Heartbe...	(Not inherited)	UNIX/Linux Core Library	Yes
Application/Service Availability Rollup	Dependency Rollup	(Not inherited)	UNIX/Linux Core Library	Yes
Hardware Availability Rollup	Dependency Rollup	(Not inherited)	UNIX/Linux Core Library	Yes
Operating System Availability Rollup	Dependency Rollup	(Not inherited)	UNIX/Linux Core Library	Yes
Configuration	Aggregate Rollup	Object	Health Library	Yes
Performance	Aggregate Rollup	Object	Health Library	Yes
Security	Aggregate Rollup	Object	Health Library	Yes

FIGURE 20.34 Custom BIND Name Resolution Check two state monitor.

12. Right-click the monitor, click **Overrides -> Override the Monitor -> For a Group**. Select the Linux BIND servers group created previously and click **OK**.

13. Override the **Enabled** property to equal **True** and click **OK**.

UNIX/Linux Shell Command Performance Collection Rule

This example creates a DNS name resolution time performance collection rule using the new UNIX/Linux Shell Command Performance Collection Rule in OpsMgr 2012. Perform the following steps:

1. In the Authoring pane of the console, right-click **Rules**, and select **Create a new rule**.

2. Under **Collection Rules -> Probe Based**, select **UNIX/Linux Shell Command (Performance)** and select the target management pack (previously created) as shown in Figure 20.35. Click **Next**.

3. Input the Name and Description for the rule. Select the Rule target (**UNIX/Linux Computer**) and uncheck **Rule is enabled** as shown in Figure 20.36. Click **Next**.

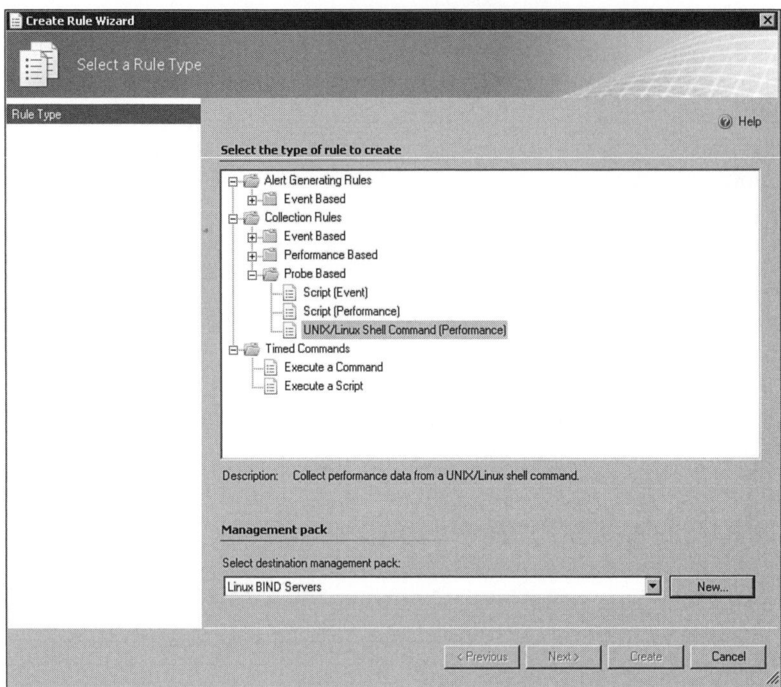

FIGURE 20.35 Select a rule type.

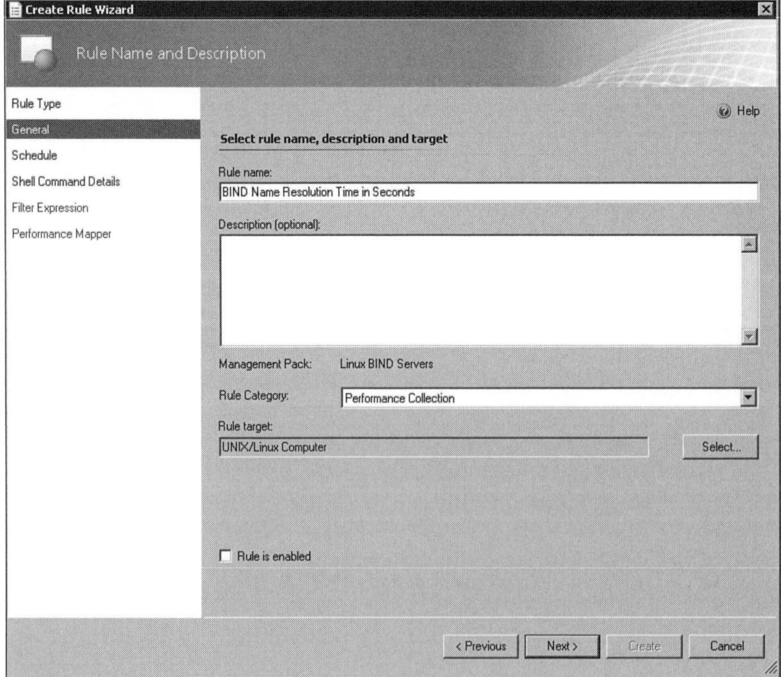

FIGURE 20.36 Add rule name and description.

4. Configure a schedule interval as shown in Figure 20.37. For performance optimization, this should be as large a value as reasonable; 10 or 15 minutes should be sufficient for most purposes. Click **Next** to continue.

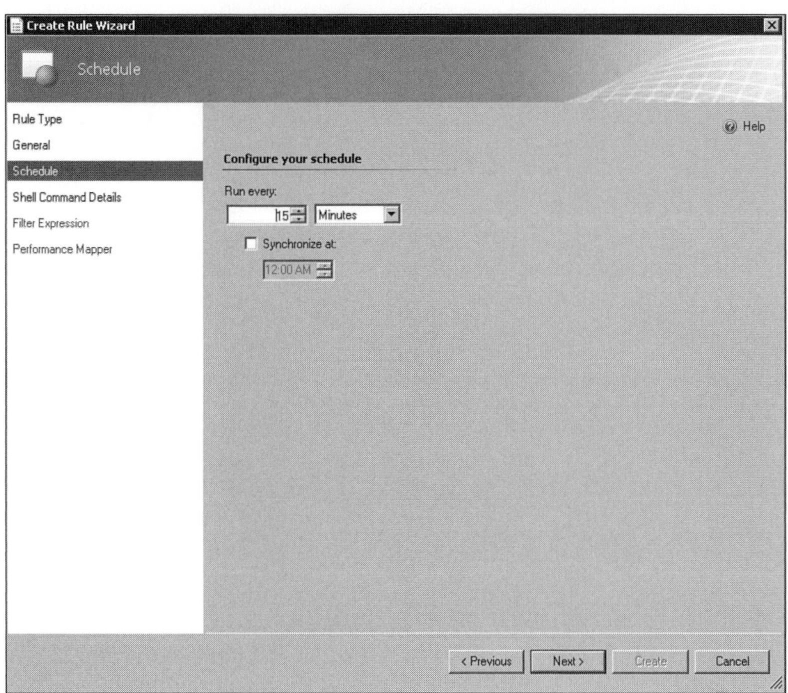

FIGURE 20.37 Schedule page for shell command performance collection.

5. On the Shell Command Details page, input the shell command `/usr/bin/time -f %e nslookup linux.odyssey.com 127.0.0.1 > /dev/null` as shown in Figure 20.38. This command will return the time in seconds (to StdErr) it takes to complete the name resolution lookup. This is a non-privileged operation, so the **UNIX/Linux Action Account** is sufficient for the Run As profile. Click **Next**.

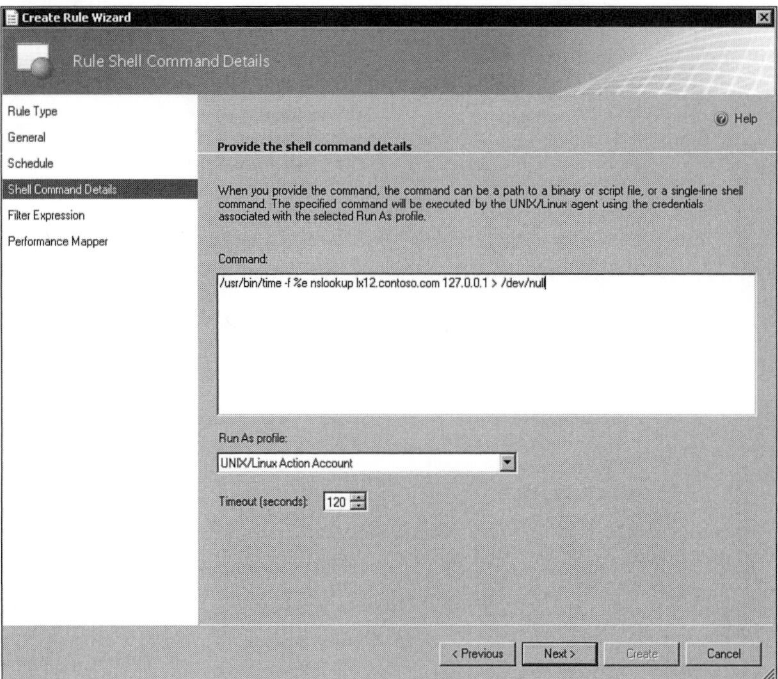

FIGURE 20.38 Command details for shell command performance collection.

6. The next page provides the opportunity to filter the output before mapping to performance data. Performance data mapping can only occur if the value is a valid double value, so the default expression syntax uses a RegExp to validate StdOut is a numeric value, and also filters that ReturnCode = 0, indicating a successful execution. While the default configuration is valid for most scenarios, the time command used in this shell command actually outputs its value to StdErr. So in this case, the first line of the filter should be modified to use a Parameter Name of `//*[local-name()="StdErr"]` as shown in Figure 20.39. Click **Next**.

7. Configure the performance mapping information as shown in Figure 20.40. Object, Counter, and Instance are arbitrary values used to identify the performance metric in performance views and reports. The default value of `$Data///*[local-name()="StdOut"]$` is the variable syntax for the returned StdOut, which is appropriate for most cases. This needs to be modified here because the time command used in this example outputs to StdErr. The StdErr variable is `$Data///*[local-name()='StdErr']$`. Click **Create**.

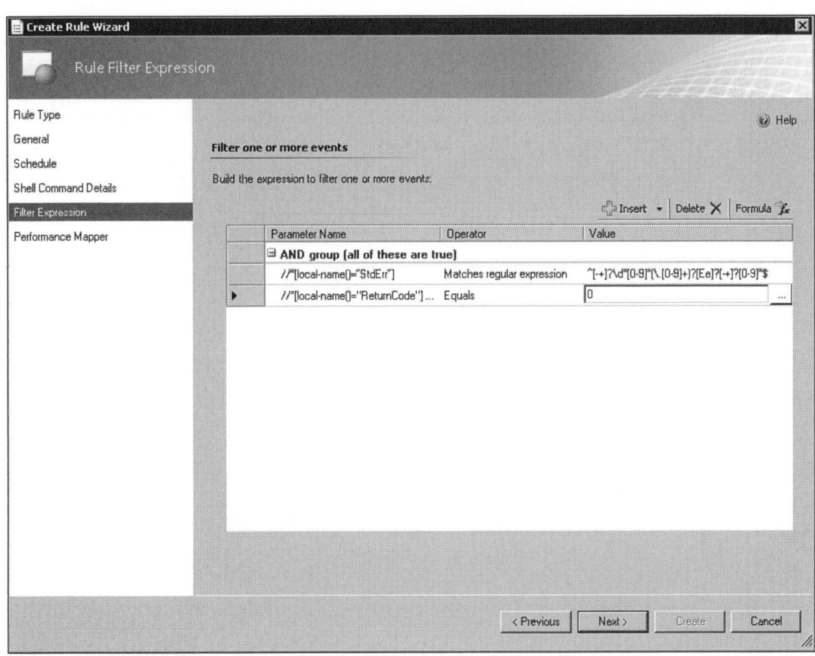

FIGURE 20.39 Rule Filter Expression for shell command performance collection.

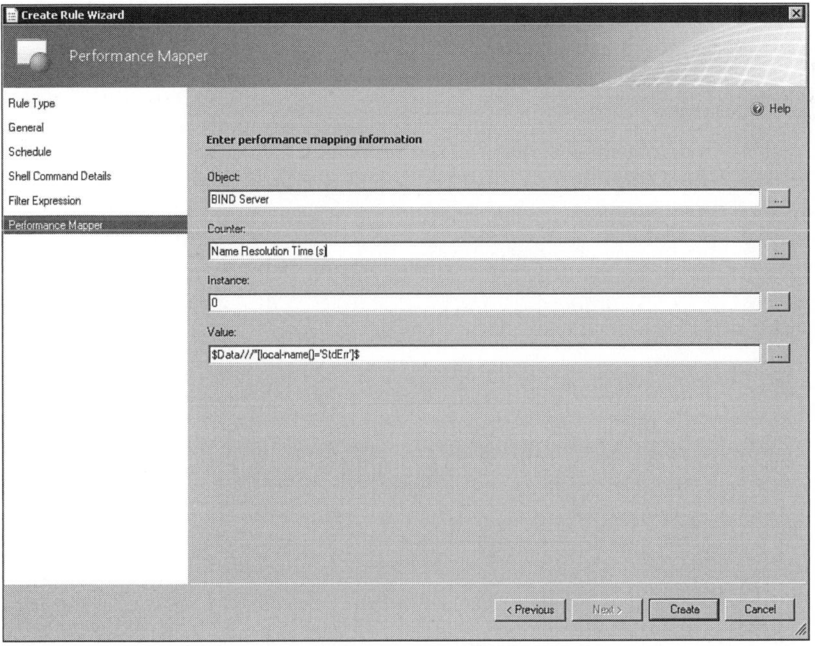

FIGURE 20.40 Performance Mapper for shell command performance collection.

8. As this rule targets all UNIX and Linux computers, it was created without being enabled by default. Use an override to enable it for the group of BIND servers. Navigate to **Authoring** -> **Management Pack Objects** -> **Rules**. In the top-right of the Rules pane, click **Change Scope**, and check **UNIX/Linux Computer** from the Scope Management Pack Objects dialog. Find the rule just created (BIND Name Resolution Test Time in Seconds) in the UNIX/Linux Shell Command Performance Collection Rule created in this procedure. The new collection rule is shown in Figure 20.41.

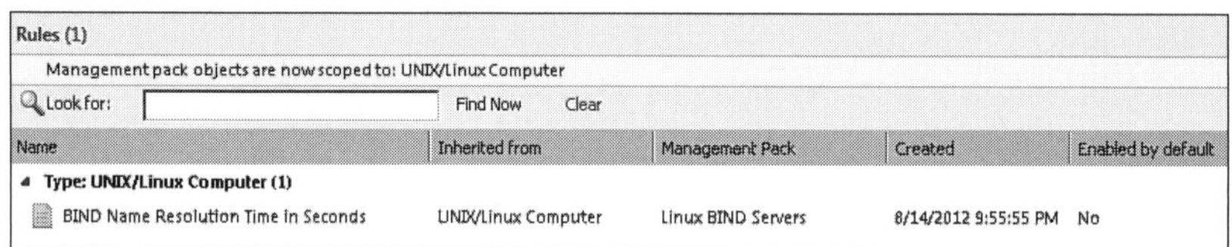

FIGURE 20.41 Custom BIND Name Resolution performance collection rule.

9. To enable the rule, right-click the rule, click **Overrides** -> **Override the Monitor** -> **For a Group**. Select a group containing the BIND servers (which must have been created previously) as shown in Figure 20.42 and click **OK**.

For detailed instructions on how to create a group in Operations Manager containing instances of the target of your rule, monitor or discovery, see Chapter 7, "Configuring and Using System Center 2012 Operations Manager."

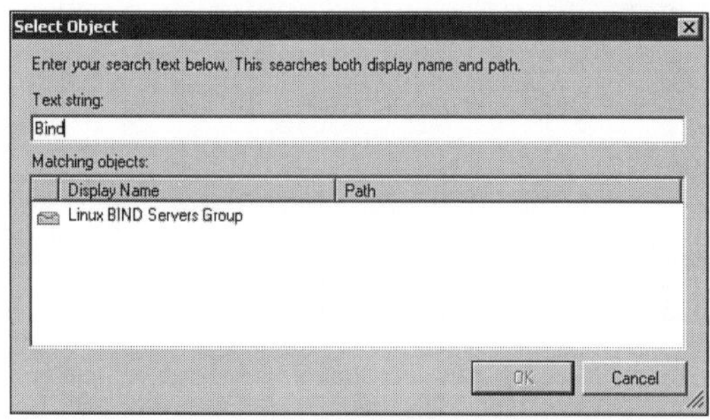

FIGURE 20.42 Select Object dialog for group selection.

10. Override the **Enabled** property to equal **True** (as shown in Figure 20.43) and click **OK**.

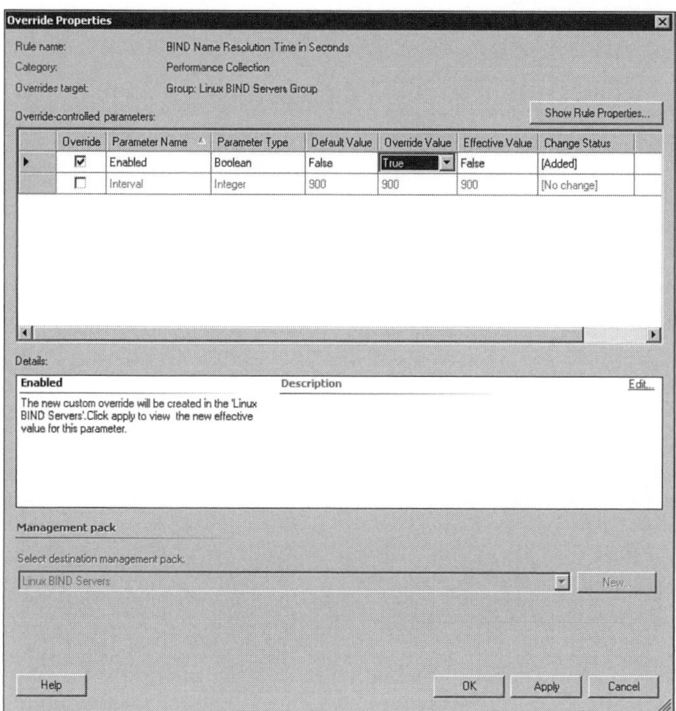

FIGURE 20.43 Custom BIND Performance collection rule override.

Creating a Run a UNIX/Linux Shell Command (BIND Restart Task)

The Run a UNIX/Linux Shell Command task wizard is the simplest of the shell command templates, and relatively easy even for those OpsMgr administrators new to UNIX/Linux shell scripting. These steps result in a task that restarts the BIND daemon on a Linux computer from the Operations console. Follow these steps:

1. Navigate to **Authoring** -> **Management Pack Objects** and right-click **Tasks**. Select **Create a New Task**.
2. Select **Run a UNIX/Linux Shell Command** from the Agent Tasks list, and select the target management pack (previously created) as shown in Figure 20.44. Click **Next**.
3. Input a name for the task (**Restart BIND Daemon**), provide a description, and select the target (**Linux Computer**) as shown in Figure 20.45. Click **Next**.
4. The command to restart the BIND daemon is `service named restart`. Type this into the shell command entry pane. Restarting a daemon is a privileged operation, so select the **UNIX/Linux Privileged Account** Run As profile as shown in Figure 20.46. The default timeout of **120** seconds should be sufficient, so click **Create**.

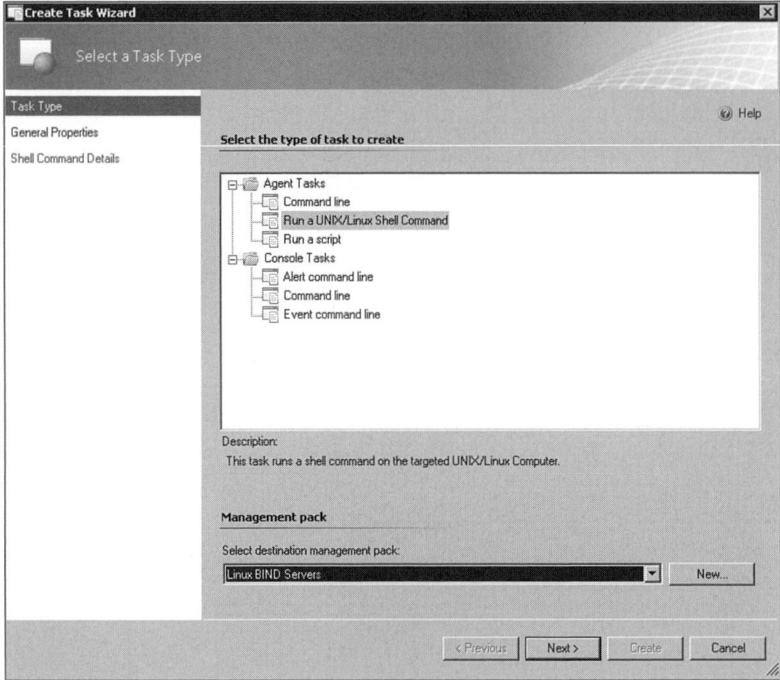

FIGURE 20.44 Create Task Wizard - Select a Task Type.

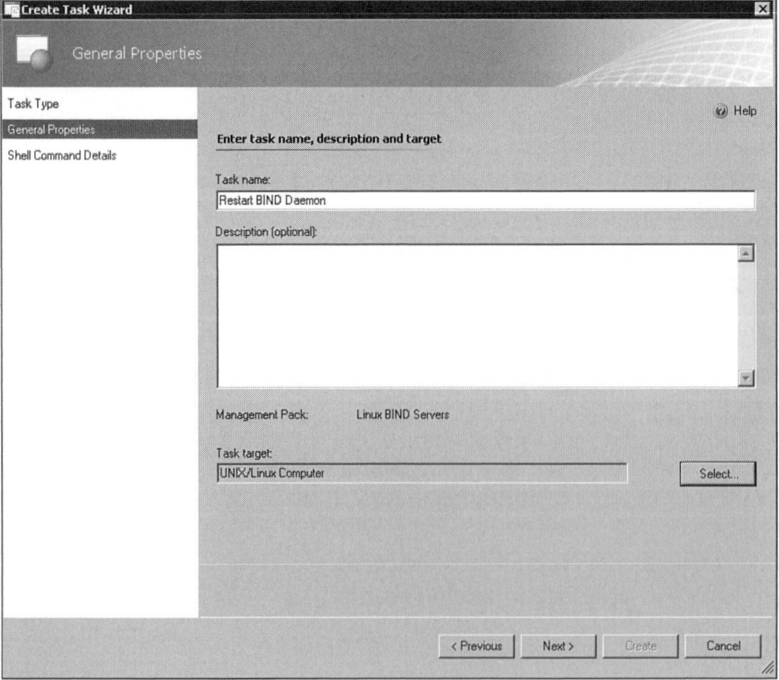

FIGURE 20.45 General Properties page of the Create Task Wizard.

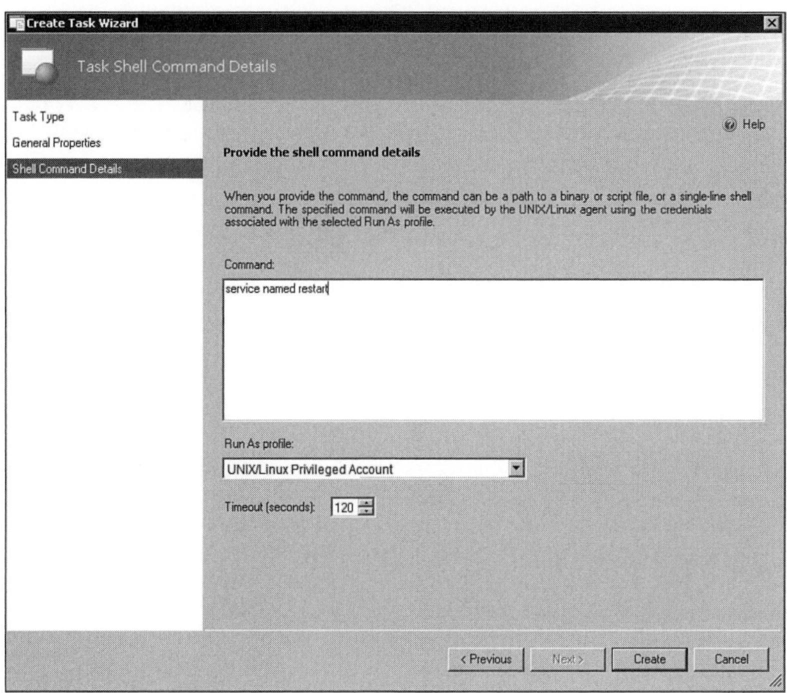

FIGURE 20.46 Command Details page of the Create Task Wizard.

When clicking on a Linux Computer instance in the Monitoring space, the Restart BIND Daemon task is listed in the right-hand task pane and can be run directly from the console.

Introducing Application Performance Monitoring

New in OpsMgr 2012 is comprehensive support for application performance monitoring (APM) for Java Enterprise Edition (JEE, formerly known as J2E) application servers. The four most common platforms are supported; Table 20.4 shows the full support matrix.

TABLE 20.4 Java application performance monitoring support matrix

	Tomcat	JBoss	WebSphere	WebLogic
Windows	X	X	X	X
RHEL	X	X	X	X
SLES	X	X	X	X
Solaris				X
AIX			X	

After importing the Java management packs applicable for your environment, the application servers are automatically discovered and standard monitoring informs you whether the application server is running and if resource utilization is within defined thresholds.

If you require deeper monitoring, Microsoft offers a Java Management Extension (JMX) application called *BeanSpy* (known during the OpsMgr 2012 beta period as the JMX Extender) that you load on the Java application server. BeanSpy is an open source technology developed by Microsoft that relies on the Java Management Extension to facilitate deep Java application monitoring. It is an HTTP-based JMX connector and servlet to install on the application server for which you want to enable deep monitoring. Information collected from the application server instances includes

- Applications deployed in the application server
- Number of garbage collections per second
- Time spent in garbage collection
- JVM memory usage and capacity
- Number of class loaded in the JVM
- Number of active threads

These additional details facilitate managing the memory allocated to the JEE application servers and ensuring resources are used efficiently.

With BeanSpy installed, the Microsoft JEE application server monitoring packs can enumerate the individual Java applications loaded in the application server. This enables you to select which applications are important to monitor. The monitored Java applications report health status, so you can determine if the application is running, as seen by the application server. Figure 20.47 shows BeanSpy and the JEE APM monitoring architecture.

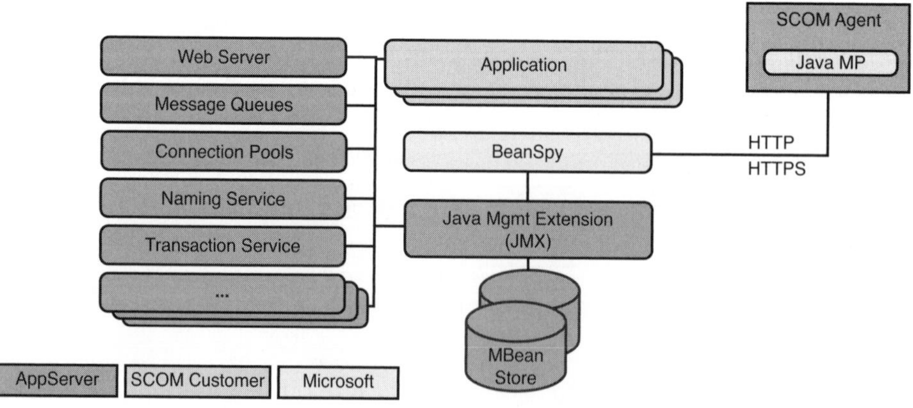

FIGURE 20.47 BeanSpy in the JEE and JMX Server Architecture (Windows).

Java applications running in a JEE application server also have a mechanism for providing application-specific management information. This mechanism is called *MBeans* and is part of the JMX standard. The application developer must choose to create custom MBeans and populate them with relevant statistics as the application runs.

MBeans provide appropriate domain-specific knowledge that can be the best way to understand an application's behavior. BeanSpy retrieves information from the MBeans, and Information Technology (IT) administrators can use a template to create Operations Manager rules that monitor and provide alerts on the values from the MBeans.

BeanSpy communicates with MBean counters (which are somewhat like performance counters in Windows but more feature-rich) to monitor individual applications running, frequency, time spent on memory garbage collection, and performance of the application server. Memory garbage collection is particularly important, as the application is unresponsive during this period.

For custom monitoring, Operations Manager 2012 offers two templates for building your own monitoring management packs; one for monitoring and one for performance; these let you monitor any simple MBean property.

JEE Configuration, Discovering, and Monitoring

Before deep JEE application monitoring can begin, you must install and configure BeanSpy on the target Java application server. This section discusses an example scenario of JEE monitoring of applications of Tomcat 7.x on Windows. Download instructions for the other Java enterprise distributions from http://www.microsoft.com/en-us/download/details.aspx?id=29270.

You can access BeanSpy through the HTTP and SSL (HTTPS) protocols, either with or without basic authentication. The following configurations are supported, listed here in the order of most to least secure:

- SSL with basic authentication (most secure)
- SSL without basic authentication[1]
- HTTP with basic authentication
- HTTP without basic authentication (least secure)[1]

If your application server is configured to use SSL, you should already have a certificate configured for your application server regardless of whether you will use OpsMgr to monitor the Java application server. However, OpsMgr requires that you specify the FQDN, instead of the host name or localhost, in the CN field of the Java application server certificate.

1. *While you will find tutorials on the Internet demonstrating JEE monitoring in OpsMgr with authentication disabled for the sake of simplicity, this is often actually not the case. You may well be faced with monitoring Java servers and applications where authentication is required.*

Security Roles Required by BeanSpy

You can find the security roles required for accessing and invoking methods in BeanSpy in the web.xml file (see Figure 20.48) located in the <*Tomcat_Install_Directory*>\webapps\BeanSpy\WEB-INF\ directory on any Java server where BeanSpy is installed. The security roles are defined in this file between the `<security-role></security-role>` tags. The roles for BeanSpy are the JEE monitoring and JEE invoke roles. You must define a user account with membership in these roles in the Java server installation and provide it to OpsMgr in Run As accounts associated with the appropriate Run As profiles.

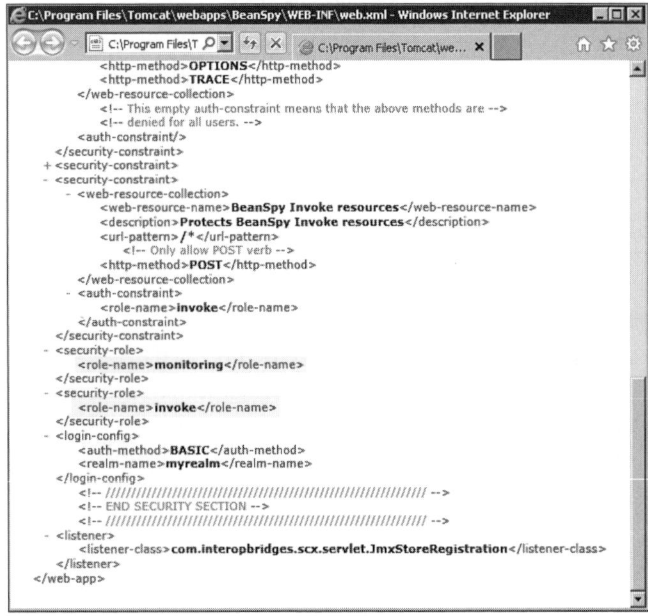

```
C:\Program Files\Tomcat\webapps\BeanSpy\WEB-INF\web.xml - Windows Internet Explorer
        <http-method>OPTIONS</http-method>
        <http-method>TRACE</http-method>
      </web-resource-collection>
        <!-- This empty auth-constraint means that the above methods are -->
        <!-- denied for all users. -->
      <auth-constraint/>
    </security-constraint>
  + <security-constraint>
  - <security-constraint>
    - <web-resource-collection>
        <web-resource-name>BeanSpy Invoke resources</web-resource-name>
        <description>Protects BeanSpy Invoke resources</description>
        <url-pattern>/*</url-pattern>
          <!-- Only allow POST verb -->
        <http-method>POST</http-method>
      </web-resource-collection>
    - <auth-constraint>
        <role-name>invoke</role-name>
      </auth-constraint>
    </security-constraint>
  - <security-role>
      <role-name>monitoring</role-name>
    </security-role>
  - <security-role>
      <role-name>invoke</role-name>
    </security-role>
  - <login-config>
      <auth-method>BASIC</auth-method>
      <realm-name>myrealm</realm-name>
    </login-config>
      <!-- ////////////////////////////////////////////////////////////// -->
      <!-- END SECURITY SECTION -->
      <!-- ////////////////////////////////////////////////////////////// -->
  - <listener>
      <listener-class>com.interopbridges.scx.servlet.JmxStoreRegistration</listener-class>
    </listener>
</web-app>
```

FIGURE 20.48 Web.xml file for BeanSpy.

Again using Tomcat as an example, users and membership in user roles are defined in the Tomcat-users.xml file, located in the <*Tomcat Install Directory*>\Conf directory on the Tomcat server. User roles are defined in the `<tomcat-users></tomcat-users>` xml tags in this file, where you will find two important types of entries:

- **<role/>**: This entry contains the name of a user role defined in a Java application (such as "Monitoring" or "Invoke"), as in the case of BeanSpy. Figure 20.49 shows several user roles listed, including tomcat, role1, manager-gui, admin, JEE monitoring, and JEE invoke.
- **<user/>**: This entry contains the name, password, and user role membership.

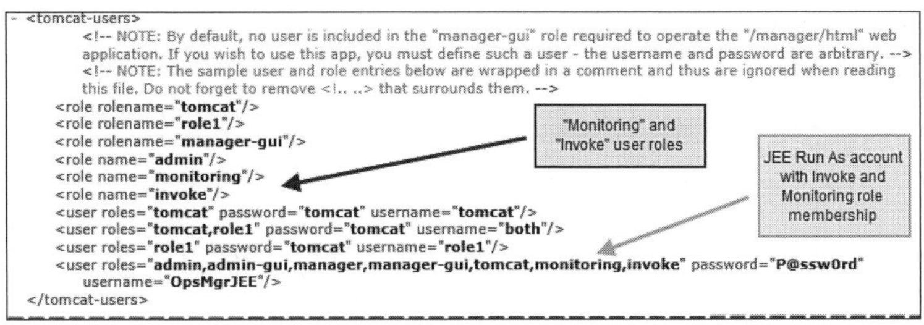

```
- <tomcat-users>
      <!-- NOTE: By default, no user is included in the "manager-gui" role required to operate the "/manager/html" web
      application. If you wish to use this app, you must define such a user - the username and password are arbitrary. -->
      <!-- NOTE: The sample user and role entries below are wrapped in a comment and thus are ignored when reading
      this file. Do not forget to remove <!.. ..> that surrounds them. -->
    <role rolename="tomcat"/>
    <role rolename="role1"/>
    <role rolename="manager-gui"/>
    <role name="admin"/>
    <role name="monitoring"/>
    <role name="invoke"/>
    <user roles="tomcat" password="tomcat" username="tomcat"/>
    <user roles="tomcat,role1" password="tomcat" username="both"/>
    <user roles="role1" password="tomcat" username="role1"/>
    <user roles="admin,admin-gui,manager,manager-gui,tomcat,monitoring,invoke" password="P@ssw0rd"
      username="OpsMgrJEE"/>
  </tomcat-users>
```


FIGURE 20.49 Tomcat-users.xml snippet with Monitoring and Invoke roles added.

Adding the User Roles in Tomcat

The JEE monitoring and JEE invoke user roles are not listed in the Tomcat-users.xml file by default; you must add these roles manually. Additionally, you should define a user entry including username, password, and role membership in Tomcat-users.xml; this is for use as the JEE monitoring and JEE invoke Run As accounts associated to the JEE monitoring and JEE invoke Run As profiles in OpsMgr 2012. Perform the following steps to create the user for the Run As account and associate to a role:

1. Save a copy of the Tomcat-users.xml file to an alternate location as a backup.
2. Type the following entries into the Tomcat-users.xml file, which are the roles defined in the web.xml file of the BeanSpy application.

```
<role name="monitoring" />
<role name="invoke" />
```

3. Next, define a new user account and grant it the appropriate role memberships by entering the following line into the Tomcat-users.xml file.

```
<user roles="monitoring,invoke" password="P@ssw0rd" user="OpsMgrJEE" />
```

REAL WORLD: AVOID MIXED CASE USER NAMES

While most JEE platforms (including Tomcat 7.x, used in this chapter's examples) support mixed case user names, OpsMgr does not seem to handle them well. A user name of OpsMgrJEE resulted in authentication failures. Switching the username to opsmgrjee (in both the tomcat-users.xml and Tomcat JEE Run As account) resolved the issue.

Configuring JEE Run As Security

Once you have configured the desired monitoring account identity and validated access to BeanSpy, the next step is to configure Run As security in OpsMgr 2012. This is discussed in the following sections.

JEE Run As Accounts

As mentioned in the "Security Roles Required by BeanSpy" section, you can use a single account for the JEE Invoke and JEE Monitoring Run As profiles. The function of these Run As accounts is defined as follows:

- **JEE Invoke:** This account is used for privileged execution of MBean method invocation.
- **JEE Monitoring:** This account is used for low privilege monitoring on JEE application servers.

The role name "Monitoring" is required by the BeanSpy servlet to query MBeans, while the name "Invoke" is required to invoke methods on MBeans. The role names must be exactly the same as in the Tomcat-users.xml file.

TIP: WHAT IS AN "MBEAN" ANYWAY?

A "Managed Bean" (or MBean for short) is a Java approach for application monitoring and management. Think of MBeans as the equivalent of Windows performance counters, exposing server and application performance metrics.

Create the JEE Run As Account

The JEE management packs include Run As profiles (shown in Figure 20.50), so you need to create a Run As account, which should be of the Basic Authentication type. For information on creating Run As accounts, see Chapter 10, "Security and Compliance." The Run As account settings for an existing account are reviewed here to ensure you understand the necessary settings:

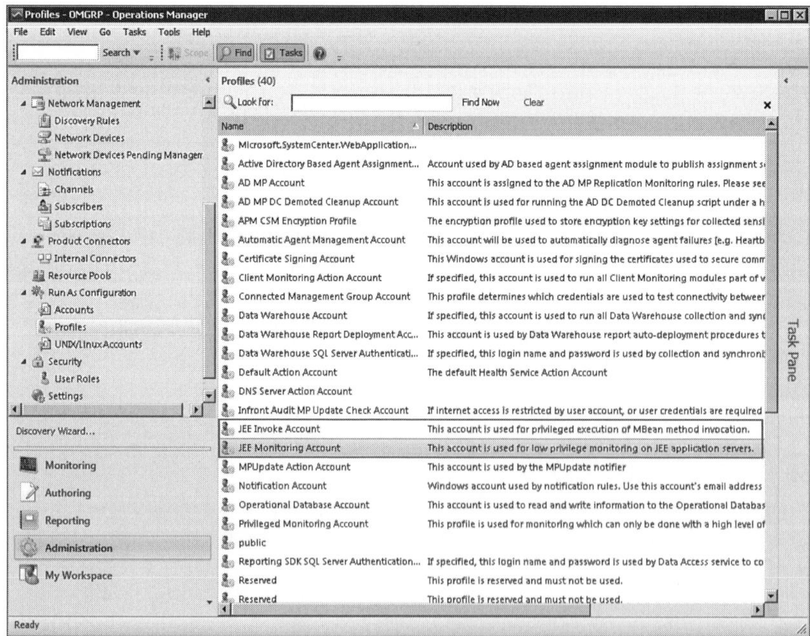

FIGURE 20.50 Tomcat JEE Run As account.

- On the General Properties tab, the Display name should have a descriptive value indicative of the account's purpose. This is just a friendly label making the account easy to identify, such as **Tomcat User** shown in Figure 20.51.

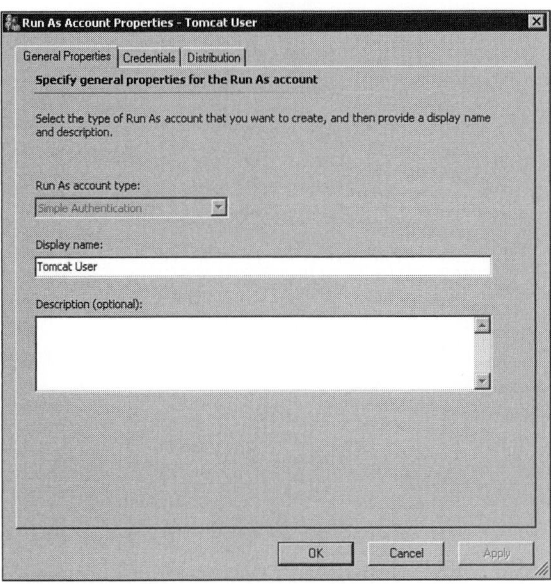

FIGURE 20.51 Tomcat JEE Run As account (General Properties).

- On the Credentials tab, use the credentials created in the "Security Roles Required by BeanSpy" section in the Tomcat-users.xml file, using **OpsMgrJEE** as the user and **P@ssw0rd** for the password, as shown in Figure 20.52.

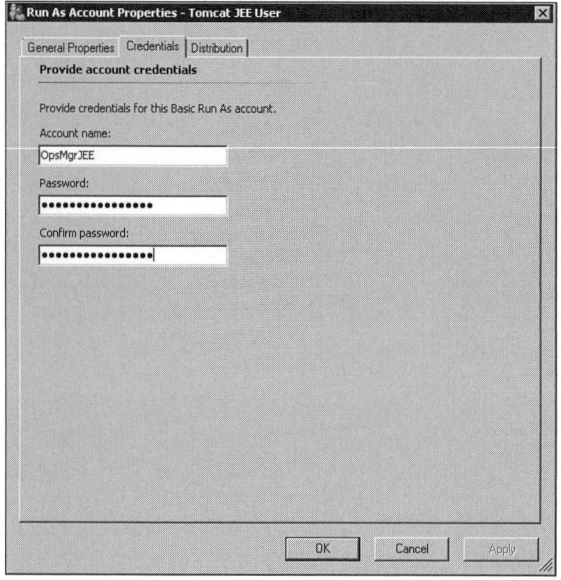

FIGURE 20.52 Tomcat JEE Run As account (Credentials).

- On the Distribution tab, select the **More Secure** option, click **Add** and configure distribution to the Cross-Platform Resource Pool, as shown in Figure 20.53. Chapter 9, "Complex Configurations," discusses creating resource pools. The completed Run As account is shown in Figure 20.54.

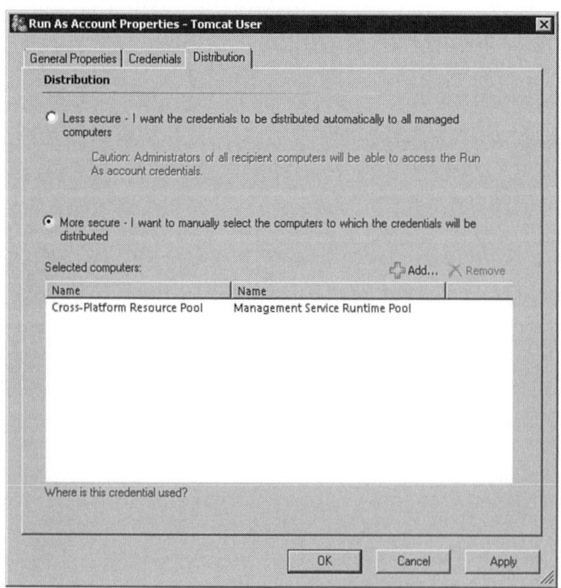

FIGURE 20.53 Tomcat JEE Run As account (Distribution).

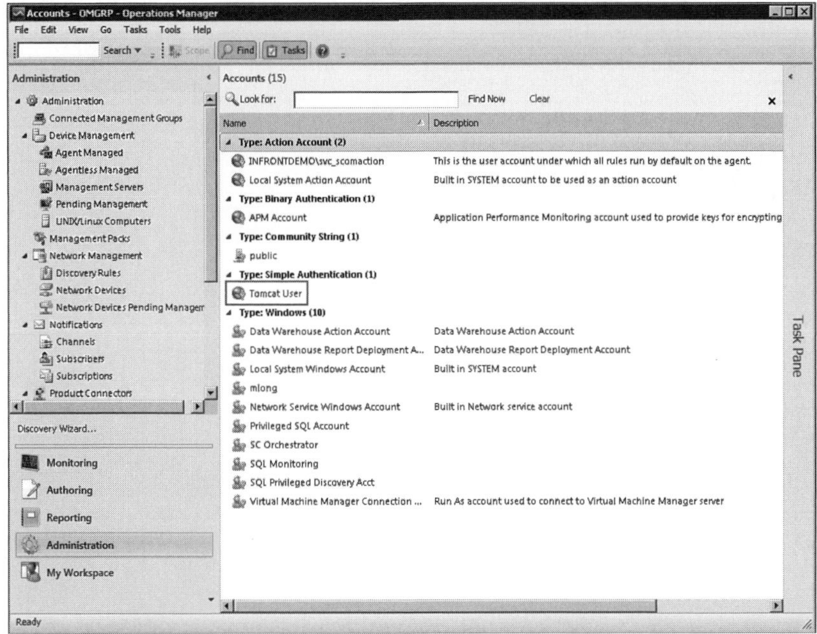

FIGURE 20.54 JEE Invoke and Monitoring Run As profiles.

Configure the JEE Run As Profiles

With the Run As account in place, you need to configure the two JEE Run As profiles, JEE Monitoring and JEE Invoke, shown in Figure 20.50.

You may want to check Run As account distribution settings in the Run As profiles, which are found in the Administration space under Run As Configuration -> Profiles, where you will find both the JEE Monitoring and JEE Invoke Run As profiles. On the Run As Accounts page in the Run As Profile Wizard, leave distribution to **All targeted objects** as shown in Figure 20.55. The distribution of the JEE run as identity is already limited to the management servers responsible for cross platform monitoring.

With the Run As profiles and accounts configured, now you can import the JEE management packs, discussed in the next section.

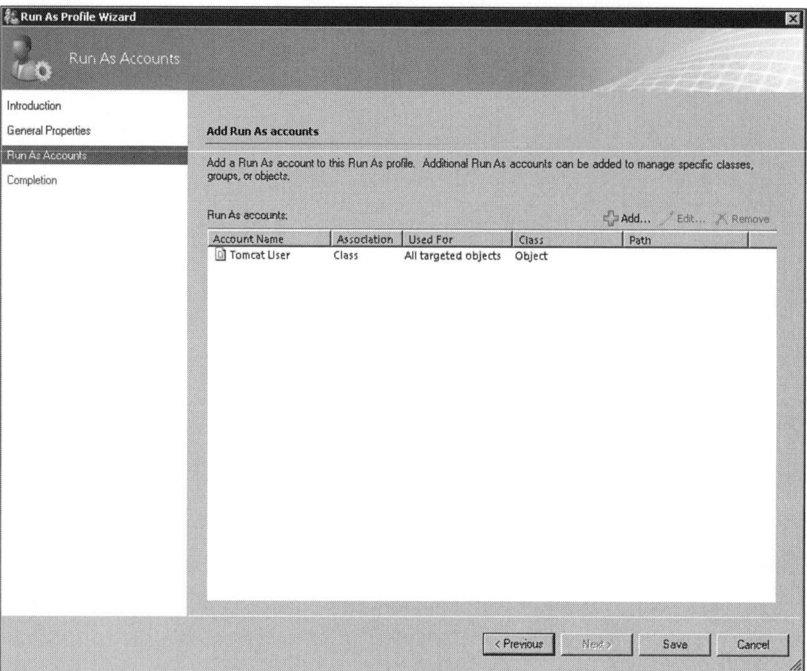

FIGURE 20.55 Run As account/profile association.

Importing JEE Management Packs

The Management Pack Import Wizard lets you connect directly to the web service on the System Center Marketplace to download management packs directly from the Microsoft website. However, as mentioned in the "Importing UNIX/Linux Management Packs" section, the JEE management packs for OpsMgr 2012 are not available in the catalog; you must download them from http://www.microsoft.com/en-us/download/details.aspx?id=29270. The management packs you download depend on those Java enterprise applications you plan to monitor. Files available for download include

- **SC2012OM_JEE_MP.msi:** All JEE management pack files
- **OpsMgr_MP_JBOSS.docx:** JBOSS management pack guide
- **OpsMgr_MP_Tomcat.docx:** Tomcat management pack guide
- **OpsMgr_MP_WebLogic.docx:** Weblogic management pack guide
- **OpsMgr_MP_WebSphere.docx:** JBOSS management pack guide
- **SC2012OM_JEE_Readme.txt:** OpsMgr 2012 Monitoring Packs for Java EE Release Notes and Quick Start Guide

After downloading the management packs, which are packaged in Windows Installer format (msi), launch the installer and extract the management packs to a local disk or shared network drive.

Import the management packs into OpsMgr using the Import Management Packs Wizard. On the Select Management Packs page, click **Add -> Add from disk** to import the management packs from the local or network folder to which you extracted the management packs. Here are the management packs you should import to support all platforms:

- Microsoft.JEE.Library.mpb
- Microsoft.JEE.Templates.Library.mpb
- Microsoft.JEE.Templates.Library.xml

Of the following management packs, import only those corresponding to the Java enterprise distributions targeted for monitoring:

- Microsoft.JEE.JBoss.4.mp
- Microsoft.JEE.JBoss.5.mp
- Microsoft.JEE.JBoss.6.mp
- Microsoft.JEE.JBoss.Library.mp
- Microsoft.JEE.Tomcat.5.mp
- Microsoft.JEE.Tomcat.6.mp
- Microsoft.JEE.Tomcat.7.mp
- Microsoft.JEE.Tomcat.Library.mp
- Microsoft.JEE.WebLogic.10gR3.mp
- Microsoft.JEE.WebLogic.11gR1.mp
- Microsoft.JEE.WebLogic.Library.mp
- Microsoft.JEE.WebSphere.6.1.mp
- Microsoft.JEE.WebSphere.7.0.mp
- Microsoft.JEE.WebSphere.Library.mp

After specifying the management packs to import, they are added to OpsMgr. The necessary management packs for monitoring Tomcat 7.x JEE applications are shown in Figure 20.56.

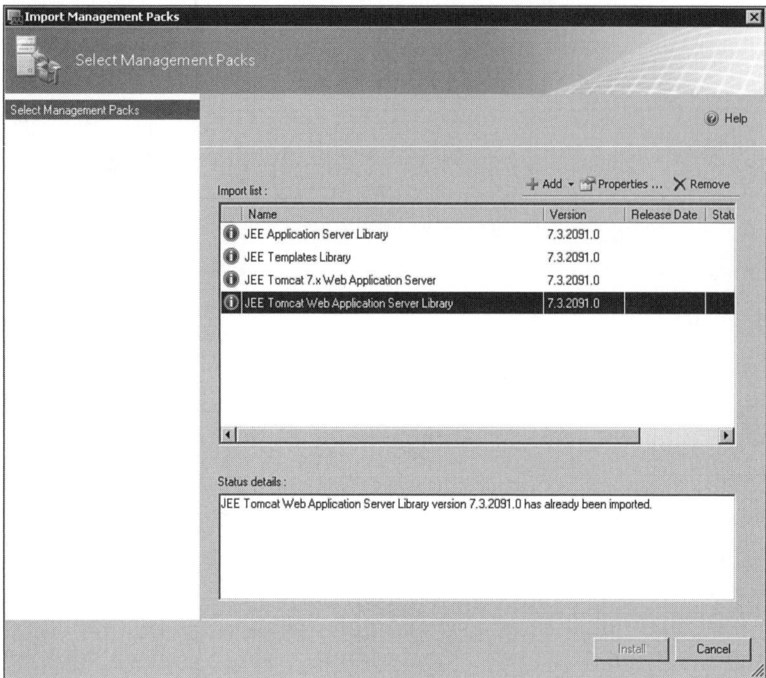

FIGURE 20.56 Importing JEE management packs for Tomcat 7.x JEE monitoring.

Deploying BeanSpy

The BeanSpy installation process is relatively easy to navigate if you have a roadmap and are familiar with potential hurdles. BeanSpy installation can be broken down into three steps:

- ▶ Locating (Deploying) the BeanSpy Files
- ▶ Installing BeanSpy
- ▶ Verifying BeanSpy is accessible

These are discussed in the next sections.

Locating (Deploying) the BeanSpy Files

To deploy BeanSpy to a UNIX or Linux computer, you must first run the following procedure that copies the files to a Windows computer, and then use a deployment method of your choosing to deploy the files to the UNIX or Linux computer. Follow these steps:

1. In the Operations console, click **Monitoring**.
2. In the Monitoring workspace, under JEE Application Servers, click the application servers for which you want to install BeanSpy.

3. In the Tasks pane, click **Copy BeanSpy files**.

   The following BeanSpy files are copied to the computer running the selected JEE Application Server, under the folder %*windir*%\temp:

   - BeanSpy.EAR
   - BeanSpy.WAR
   - BeanSpy.Http.NoAuth.EAR
   - BeanSpy.Http.NoAuth.WAR

4. Deploy BeanSpy depending on your choice of authentication and application server.

   - If you are using HTTPS with authentication, deploy BeanSpy.EAR.
   - If using HTTP without authentication, rename BeanSpy.Http.NoAuth.Ear to BeanSpy.ear and deploy.
   - If the Tomcat application server does not support EAR, deploy BeanSpy.WAR.

These files are the same for all JEE application servers; so you can run the Copy BeanSpy Files task once, retrieve the files, and deploy them to all your application servers using the deployment method of your choice.

If all of your Java apps run as Windows services, automatic discovery is not possible. This means the task used to copy the BeanSpy installation binaries (WAR and EAR files) and PowerShell discovery scripts will not be accessible. The individual files are present on each management server in a subfolder of the <*OpsMgrInstallPath*>\Server\Health Service State folder path. Since each file is located in its own subfolder in this path, it can be challenging to locate these files quickly. To expedite the process, a PowerShell script is available to retrieve these files from any management server. To obtain a copy of the script, see the article at http://www.systemcentercentral.com/BlogDetails/tabid/143/IndexID/94786/Default.aspx.

TERMINOLOGY: EAR, WAR

An Enterprise Archive (or EAR for short) is a file format used by Java EE for packaging one or more modules into a single archive so the deployment of the various modules onto an application server happens simultaneously and coherently. It also contains XML files called deployment descriptors, which describe how to deploy the modules.

A Web Application Archive (WAR for short) is a JAR file used to distribute a collection of Java Server Pages, Java Servlets, Java classes, XML files, tag libraries, static web pages (HTML and related files), and other resources that together constitute a web application.

For more information on EAR and WAR files, see these Wikipedia articles:

- http://en.wikipedia.org/wiki/EAR_(file_format)
- http://en.wikipedia.org/wiki/WAR_file_format_(Sun)

Installing BeanSpy

There are multiple methods for installing BeanSpy on a Java server. Using Tomcat on Windows as an example, the two most common methods are discussed in the following sections.

NOTE: INSTALLING BEANSPY ON DIFFERENT PLATFORMS

BeanSpy installation will vary by platform. For instructions on BeanSpy installation on Weblogic, Websphere, and JBOSS, download the corresponding management pack guide at http://www.microsoft.com/en-us/download/details.aspx?id=29270.

Automatic Deployment

The easiest way to install BeanSpy (if your Tomcat server supports it) is dropping the BeanSpy files into the \webapps directory on the Java server. By default (on Tomcat at least), when you drop a WAR file containing a sample app in this directory, it is automatically unpacked and installed. Automatic install behavior is controlled by the `UnpackWARs` setting in the \conf\server.xml file. Look for the following line and ensure `unpackWars="true"` and `autoDeploy ="true"`, as shown here:

```
<Host name="localhost" autoBase="webapps" unpackWars="true" autoDeploy="true">
```

Deployment Using Manager GUI

If your Tomcat server does not support automatic installation, you can install BeanSpy manually using the Application Manager GUI interface, http://<*Tomcat Server FQDN*>:8080/manager/index.jsp. Scroll down to the Deploy section of the Application Manager GUI shown in Figure 20.57, click **Browse**, and select the **BeanSpy.war** file. To select the file, click **Open** and then click **Deploy**.

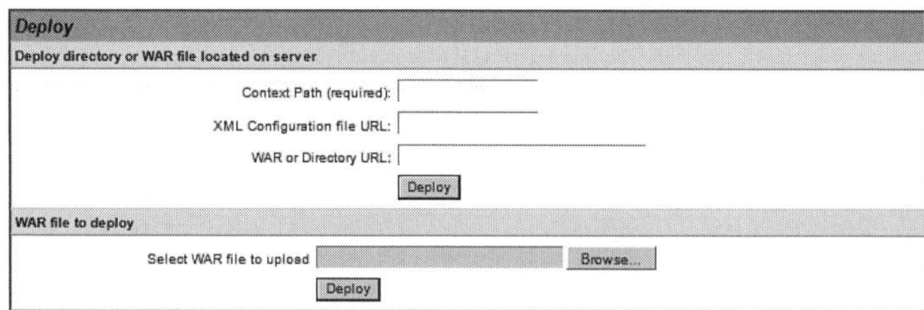

FIGURE 20.57 Deploy section of the Tomcat Web Application Manager page.

Verifying BeanSpy Is Accessible and Functional

Once BeanSpy is installed, you should verify BeanSpy is accessible with the Run As account used in the JEE Monitoring and JEE Invoke Run As profiles. On Tomcat 5.x - 7.0.x, you can verify BeanSpy by querying the Tomcat application server via a web browser using the following query. Replace *<hostname>* with the name of your Tomcat host:

```
http://<hostname>:8080/BeanSpy/MBeans?JMXQuery=Catalina:j2eeType=WebModule,name=//
localhost/BeanSpy,*
```

If authentication is enabled, you will be prompted for a username and password. When prompted, enter the username and password of the JEE Run As account you created for association with the JEE Invoke and JEE Monitoring Run As profiles.

NOTE: SYNTAX OF REQUEST VARIES BASED ON HOSTNAME AND PLATFORM

The syntax of this request not only varies by hostname, but also by JEE platform. For detailed examples of how to verify BeanSpy accessibility and functionality on other Java application server platforms, see the "Verify BeanSpy Deployment" section of the corresponding management pack guide.

Enabling Deep Monitoring of JEE Applications

If your Java applications run as Windows processes, discovery should be automatic once the appropriate JEE management packs are imported into OpsMgr and the OpsMgr agent deployed to the Windows or *NIX computer hosting the Java application server instance.

Defining Deep Monitoring

It may be easiest to describe deep availability monitoring by presenting the other application and application server monitors.

- **Application server availability:** Determines whether the process for an application server instance is running. The Health Explorer of an application server includes the availability monitor for the application server process.
- **Application availability:** This is a rollup of the application availability health to the monitored application server. In the case of Tomcat, these applications are EAR and WAR files deployed to Tomcat application servers.
- **Deep availability health:** Determines whether the application server is responding to HTTP queries.

The next sections discuss how to enable deep monitoring for JEE application servers you have targeted for monitoring.

Enabling Deep Monitoring on Automatically Discovered JEE Application Servers

To enable deep monitoring on automatically discovered JEE application servers, follow these steps:

1. Navigate to the Monitoring node in the Operations console.
2. In the Monitoring pane, select a JEE Application Server instance to which you want to enable deep monitoring.
3. In the Tasks pane, click **Enable deep monitoring using HTTP** or **Enable deep monitoring using HTTPS**.
4. In the Enable Deep Monitoring dialog, click **Run**.

After the task completes (which may take several minutes), the JEE application server instance for which you enabled deep monitoring should appear in the Deep Monitored Configurations folder in the Monitoring space.

However, if your Java applications run as Windows services, discovery will fail and manual discovery is necessary. Manual discovery requires running a PowerShell script to add the Java application servers to OpsMgr manually.

Manual Discovery and Deep Monitoring Configuration

To perform manual discovery, you must retrieve the PowerShell script files used in the manual discovery process. Here are those files:

- JEEAppServerLibrary.ps1
- NewJEEAppServer.ps1
- RemoveJEEAppServer.ps1

If you have at least one JEE application server automatically discovered by OpsMgr, you can easily get these files using a task provided in the JEE monitoring library. Go to Operations console, select an automatically discovered JEE application server instance, and run the **Copy BeanSpy and Universal discovery files** task in the Tasks pane. This copies the BeanSpy files to the *%windir%*\temp folder.

However, this task is not available if none of your Java application servers were discovered automatically. In this case, search the OpsMgr installation folder for **BeanSpy***. For example, if Operations Manager is installed under *%ProgramFiles%*\Operations Manager, BeanSpy files are located in one of the folders under *%ProgramFiles%*\System Center 2012\Operations Manager\Server\Health Service State\Resources\, and each file will be in its own folder. To make this retrieval process easier, you can get the PowerShell script referenced in the "Locating (Deploying) the BeanSpy Files" section.

To discover Java server and applications manually, perform the following steps:

1. Create a text file containing Java application server URLs, with one URL per line, as shown here, noting the port number is necessary only if the port is not 80 (HTTP) or 443 (HTTPS):

```
http://javaserver1.odyssey.com:8080
http://javaserver2.odyssey.com:8080
http://javaserver3.odyssey.com:8080
```

Save this file with the name of **MyAppServers.txt**.

2. To add JEE application servers for monitoring, run `NewJEEAppServer.ps1`. Run this script with `-help` for details of command line options. You can pipe the configuration file you created to this script, or specify a single URL on the command line. For example, to add your Tomcat 7.x Java application servers, the command line syntax would be

```
type c:\MyAppServers.txt | .\NewJEEAppServer.ps1 -JEEAppServerType Tomcat
-JEEAppServerVersion 7
```

For more information on the manual discovery process, see Christopher Crammond's article at http://blogs.technet.com/b/random_happy_dev_thoughts/archive/2012/05/21/manually-discovering-jee-application-servers-with-scom-2012.aspx.

3. After the script completes, the JEE application server instance(s) for which you enabled deep monitoring should appear in the Deep Monitored Configurations folder in the Monitoring space.

Finding Monitoring Information

After initial discovery completes, there are views in the Monitoring space that reveal the JEE applications discovered on the target server. These views can be found in Monitoring -> Application Monitoring -> Java Monitoring -> JEE Application Servers -> *<JEE distribution specific folder>*. For Tomcat, the subfolder will be Tomcat Servers, as displayed in Figure 20.58.

In the distribution specific folder (Tomcat Servers in this case), you will find state views for applications for which the default monitoring is in effect. The Deep Monitored Configurations state view presents only applications configured for deep monitoring using the JEE Application Availability Monitoring Template, discussed in the "JEE Application Availability Monitoring" section.

Several default performance views are available in the Performance subfolder, presenting performance data collected by those performance collection rules enabled by default (also shown in Figure 20.58).

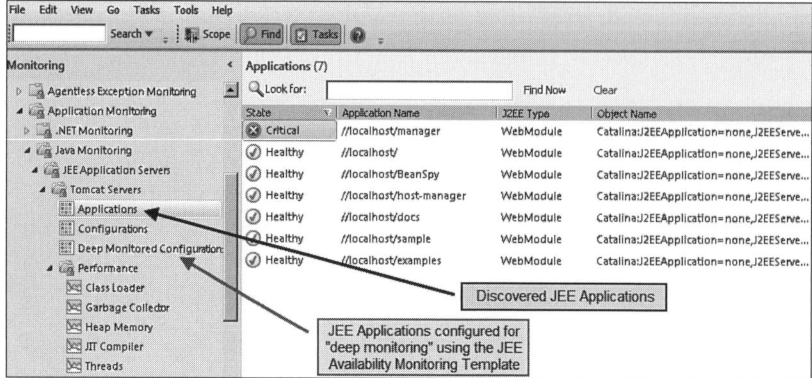

FIGURE 20.58 JEE views in the Monitoring space.

If you right-click any of the discovered applications in the Applications state view shown in Figure 20.58 and launch Health Explorer, you can view the unit monitors targeting the Application for Tomcat 7.x class, as shown in Figure 20.59.

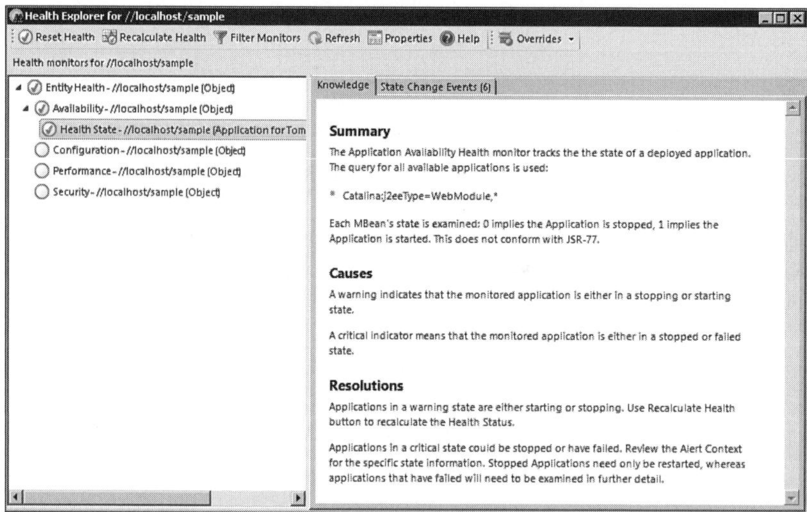

FIGURE 20.59 Default JEE unit monitors (via Health Explorer).

The only unit monitor present by default is a monitor named Health State, which checks the application availability by querying application availability with the following query:

```
Catalina:j2eeType=WebModule,*
```

The monitor examines the state of each MBean:

- 0 implies the application is stopped.
- 1 implies the application is started.

If the application is in a stopping or starting state, a warning alert is generated. If the application is in a stopped or failed state, a critical alert is raised.

Several monitors for the performance counters on each application server are disabled by default, as the thresholds for these monitors vary in each environment. Each application server has three performance monitors for each application server that you can enable, listed in Table 20.5. You may want to discuss appropriate thresholds with your JEE application administrators and developers before enabling these monitors.

TABLE 20.5 Default JEE app server performance monitors

Performance Monitor	Description	Target and Default Value
Garbage Collection Rate of a Java EE Application Server	Monitors the rate at which garbage collections are happening on the JVM associated with the Java EE Application Server.	Target: Garbage Collector 5 collections per sampling interval.
Garbage Collection Time of a Java EE Application Server	Monitors the time that the garbage collector takes to perform garbage collections on the JVM associated with the application server.	Target: Garbage Collector 5000 milliseconds per sampling interval.
Percentage VM Memory Utilized	Monitors the percentage of used heap memory compared to maximum heap memory on an application server.	Target: Monitored application server instance 90%

You may notice the default monitoring, while great for visibility, may be missing information from many of the MBeans (see the "JEE Application Performance Monitoring" section) that your application owners and developers may be interested in monitoring.

JEE Application Monitoring Templates

There are two application monitoring templates available for deep monitoring of Java enterprise applications. After importing the appropriate JEE management packs, you will see these additional monitoring templates in the Management Packs node of the Authoring space:

- JEE Application Availability Monitoring
- JEE Application Performance Monitoring

20

JEE Application Availability Monitoring

This template allows you to create a three-state availability monitor based on a JMX MBean. In this example, you will create an availability monitor for the activeSessions property of the MBean for the Tomcat Manager GUI application mentioned in the "Deployment Using Manager GUI" section. Follow these steps:

1. Browse to **Authoring -> Management Pack Templates**. Right-click and select the **Java Application Availability Monitoring** template, shown in Figure 20.60.

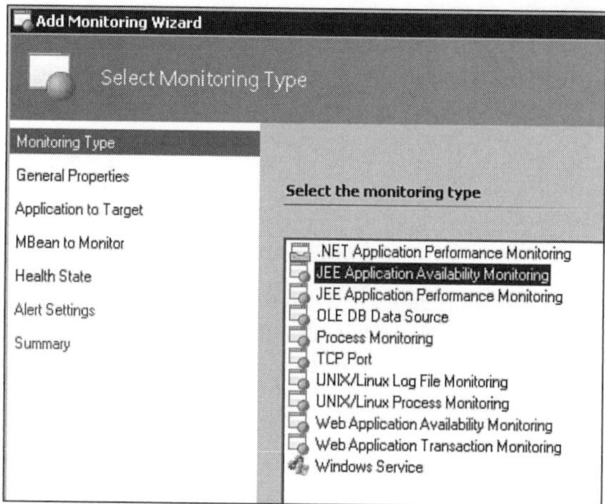

FIGURE 20.60 Select the JEE Application Availability Monitoring template.

2. Enter a friendly name for this monitor and select a management pack to store the output of this template (created earlier in the "UNIX/Linux Log File Template" section). This is shown in Figure 20.61.

3. Select //localhost/manager (see Figure 20.62) as the application to target and click **Next**.

4. Click **Browse** and choose the /Manager MBean as shown in Figure 20.63.

5. Choose the /Manager MBean and find the activeSession property. However, you may find clicking the **Run** button and browsing to the activeSessions property within the MBean a challenging task. Here is how to make this an easy process using this example as a reference:

   Type **/Manager activeSessions** in the Filter string box to filter down to the appropriate MBean before you click **Run**, as shown in Figure 20.64. This leaves you with far fewer items to choose from; in this case, only one! Once you have selected the activeSessions property for the /Manager application, click **Select**.

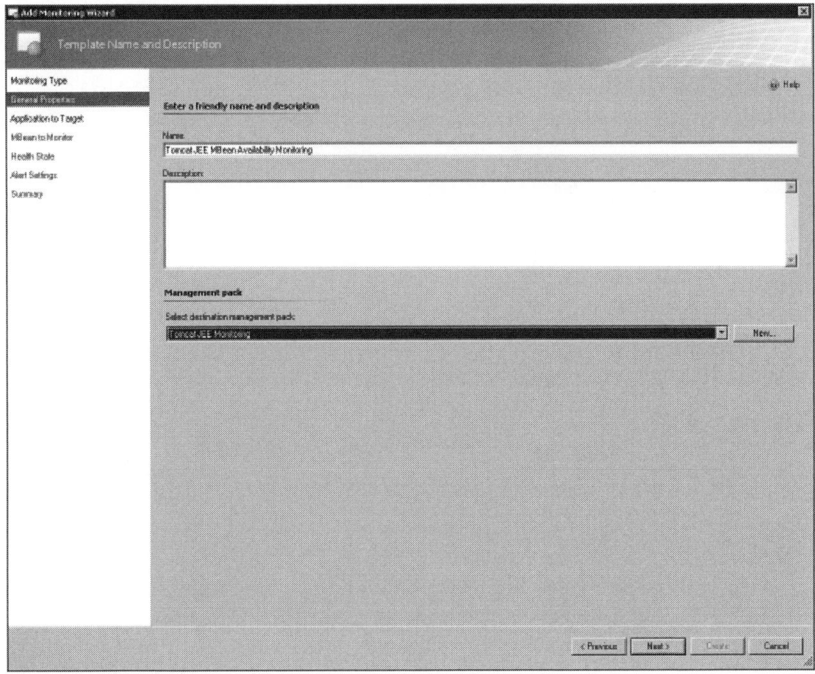

FIGURE 20.61 Template Name and Description dialog for JEE Application Availability Monitoring template.

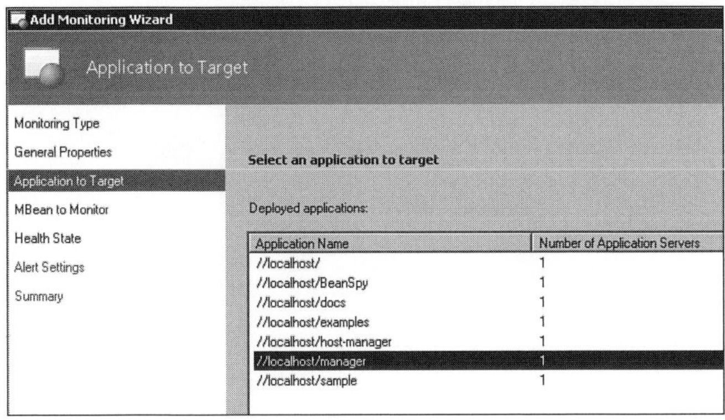

FIGURE 20.62 Choosing a target Java application.

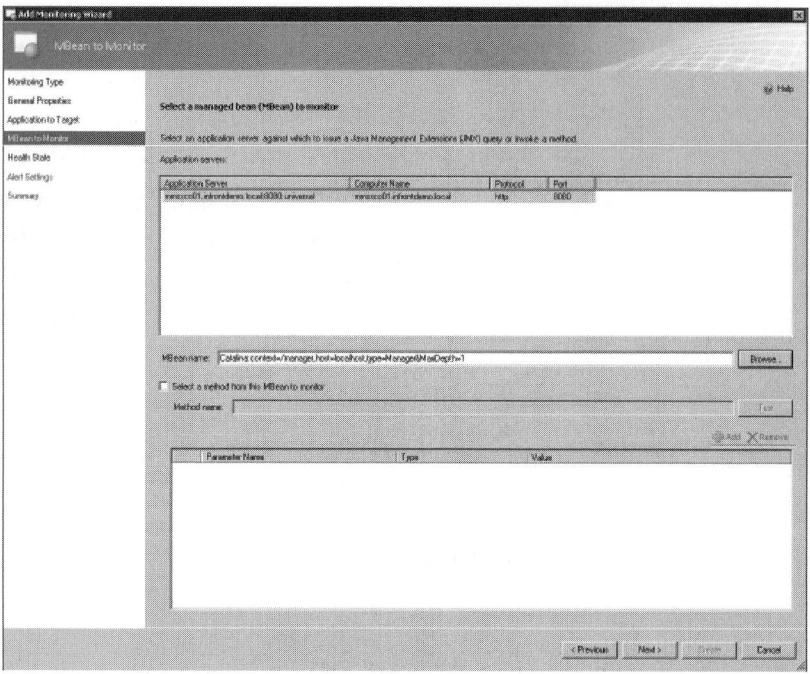

FIGURE 20.63 Choosing an MBean to monitor.

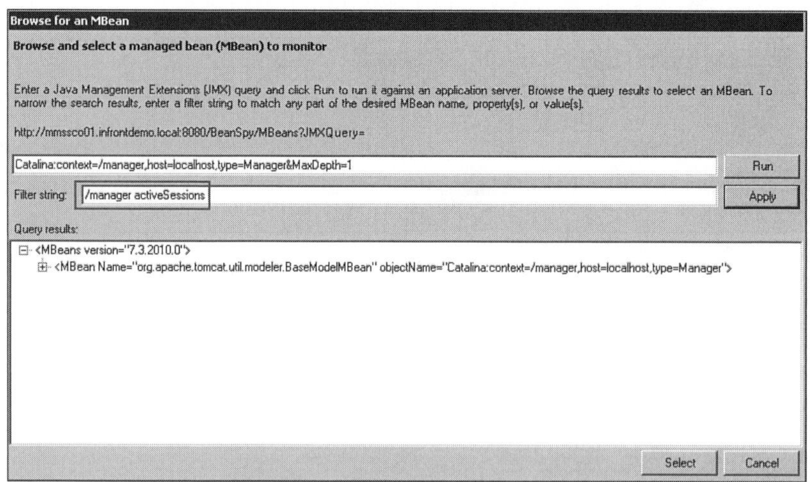

FIGURE 20.64 Browsing/searching for an MBean.

6. To configure the expressions to set the health state values, click the **Browse** button and select the activeSessions property for each health state. The activeSessions property is shown in Figure 20.65.

7. Select the activeSessions property for Healthy, Warning, and Critical states in the interface shown in Figure 20.65, using the Browse button shown in Figure 20.66 to reveal the selection dialog. Configure the following expression logic:

   - **Healthy:** Equals 0 (leave type set to Integer)
   - **Warning:** Equals 1 (leave type set to Integer)
   - **Critical:** Greater Than or Equals 2 (leave type set to Integer)

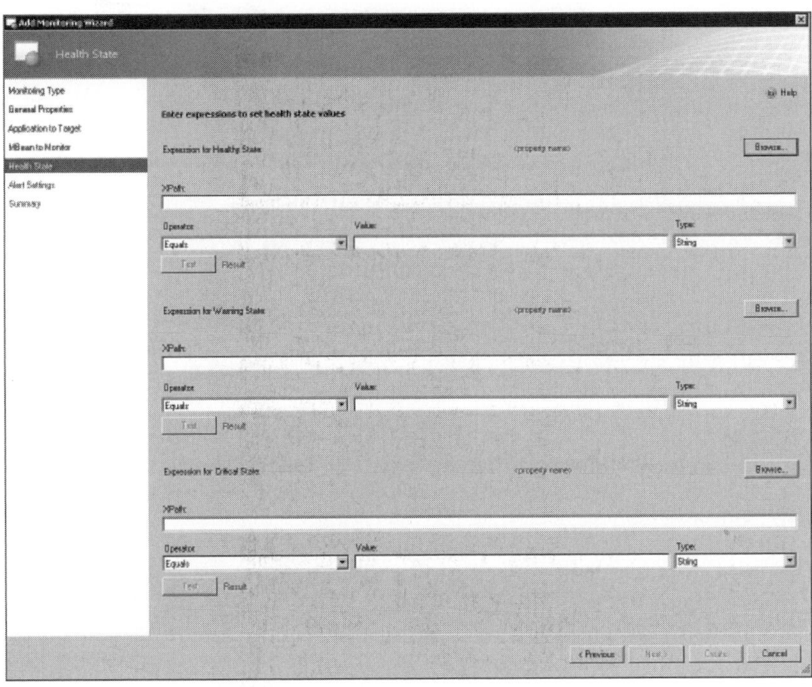

FIGURE 20.65 Configuring monitor health state.

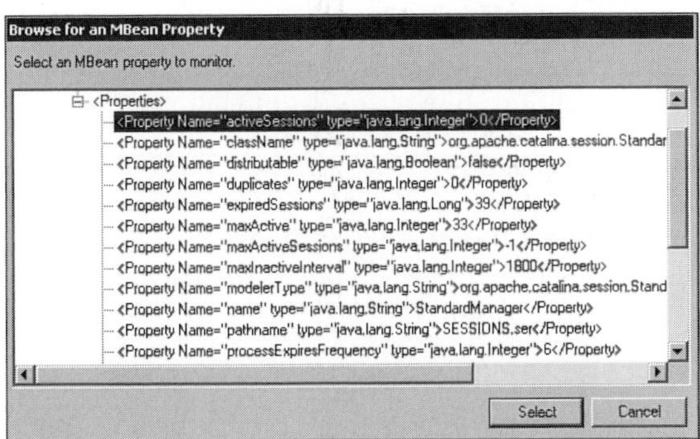

FIGURE 20.66 Browsing for MBean property "activeSessions".

20

8. The result will look as shown in Figure 20.67. Review the settings and click **Next**.

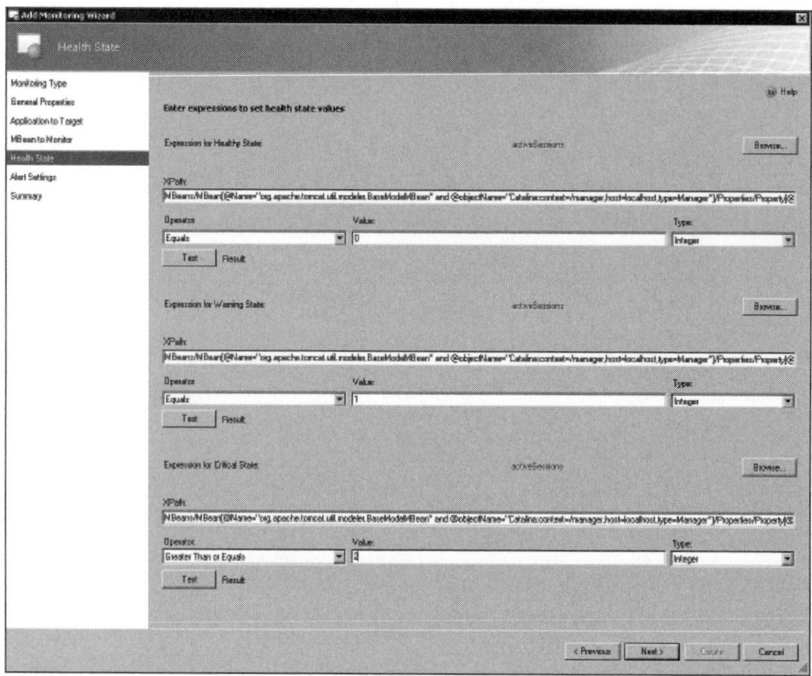

FIGURE 20.67 Fully configured monitor health state.

9. On the Alert Settings page, update the Alert name to reflect more accurately the MBean property being monitored, such as **//localhost/manager activeSessions Alert**.

10. Click **Next**, which brings up the Summary page. Review your selections and click **Create** to configure monitoring. You may need to wait 5 minutes or so before attempting to test the new monitoring.

11. To test, connect to the Tomcat Manager web application, located at http://<*ComputerName*>:8080/Manager by default. Since Healthy is defined as 0 connections, you can test this monitor simply by connecting and logging on to http://<*ComputerName*>/Manager, which will increase the activeSessions count by 1.

While it may appear this wizard simply creates a unit monitor targeting the JEE application you selected, there are several activities handled by the template in the background, including

- A new class is defined; this is a specialized class with a base class of `Microsoft.JEE.Application`, defined in the JEE Template Library MP.

- An object discovery utilizing a data source in the JEE Template Library MP.
- A new unit monitor leveraging the Microsoft.JEE.Deep.Application.ThreeState.Query.AvailabilityHealth.MonitorType monitor type defined in the JEE Template Library MP.

You can see the monitor type leveraged by this template in the Authoring space by scoping your view to **Tomcat JEE MBean Availability Monitoring extension of Microsoft.JEE.Application** and expanding the **Entity Health** -> **Availability** rollup monitor. Figure 20.68 shows the unit monitor created in this example.

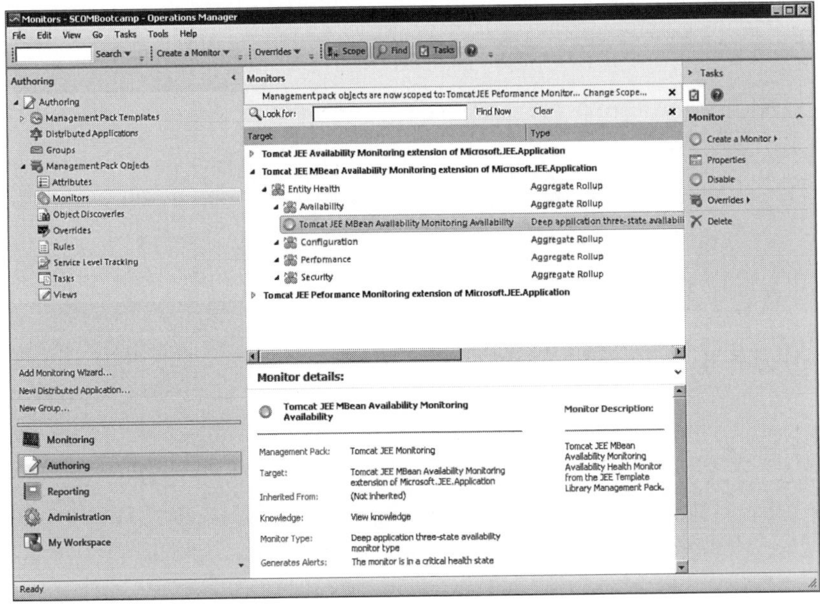

FIGURE 20.68 Unit Monitor Type Leveraged by the JEE Application Availability Monitoring template.

TIP: DEFAULT INTERVAL OF MONITOR

This monitor has a default interval of 900 seconds (15 minutes). You may want to lower this threshold before testing.

While the JEE Application Availability Monitoring template creates deeper monitoring, it does not collect additional performance data. The next section discusses JEE application performance monitoring.

JEE Application Performance Monitoring

This template allows you to create a performance collection rule based on a JMX MBean. The example in this section creates a performance collection rule for the activeSessions property of the MBean for the /Manager application. Follow these steps:

1. Browse to **Authoring -> Management Pack Templates** and select the **JEE Application Performance Monitoring** template, as shown in Figure 20.69. Click **Next.**

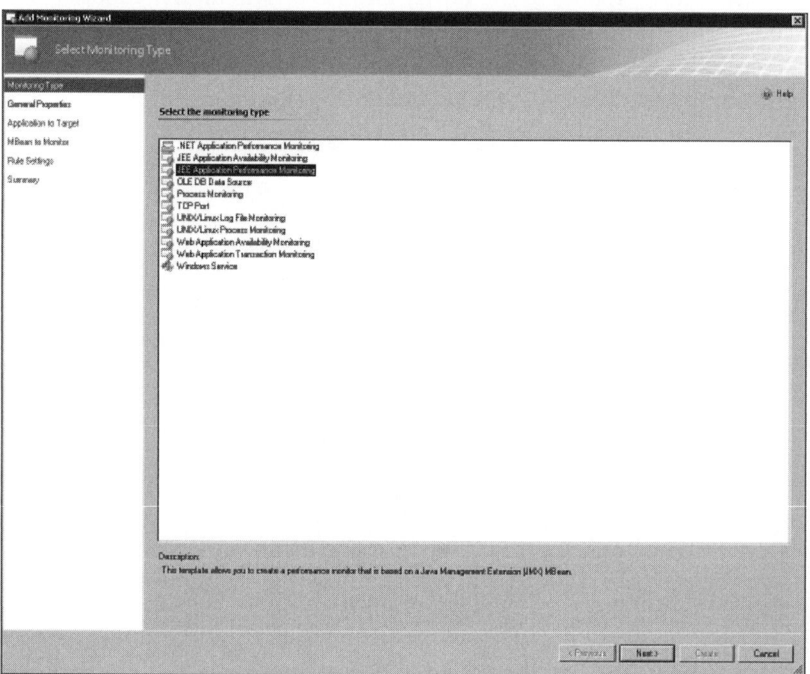

FIGURE 20.69 Select the JEE Application Availability Monitoring template.

2. Enter a friendly name and select your custom management pack (created previously to store the output of the JEE monitoring templates) as displayed in Figure 20.70 and click **Next.**
3. In the Application to Target dialog, select the **//localhost/manager** application as shown in Figure 20.71 and click **Next.**

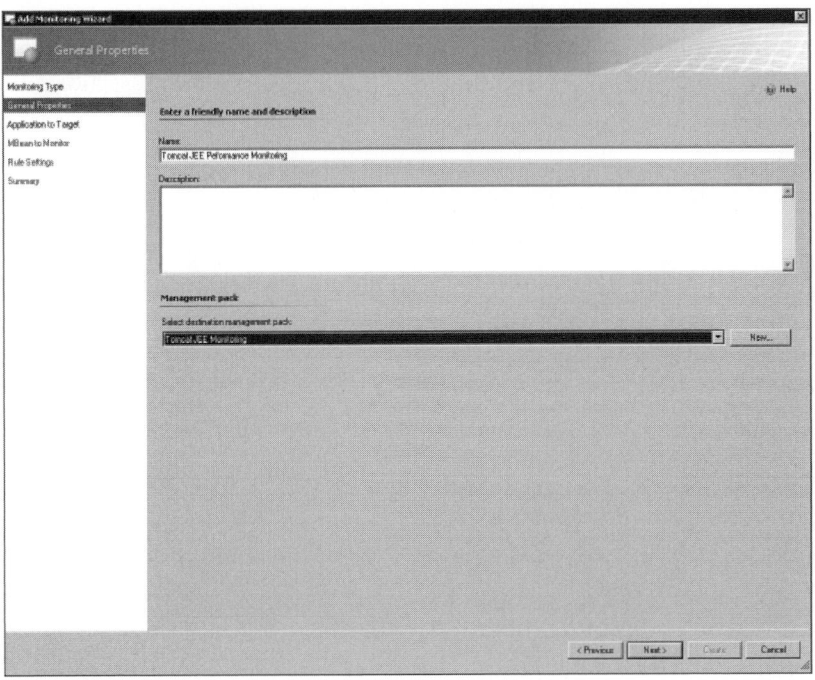

FIGURE 20.70 Template Name and Description dialog for JEE Application Performance Monitoring template in the General Properties page.

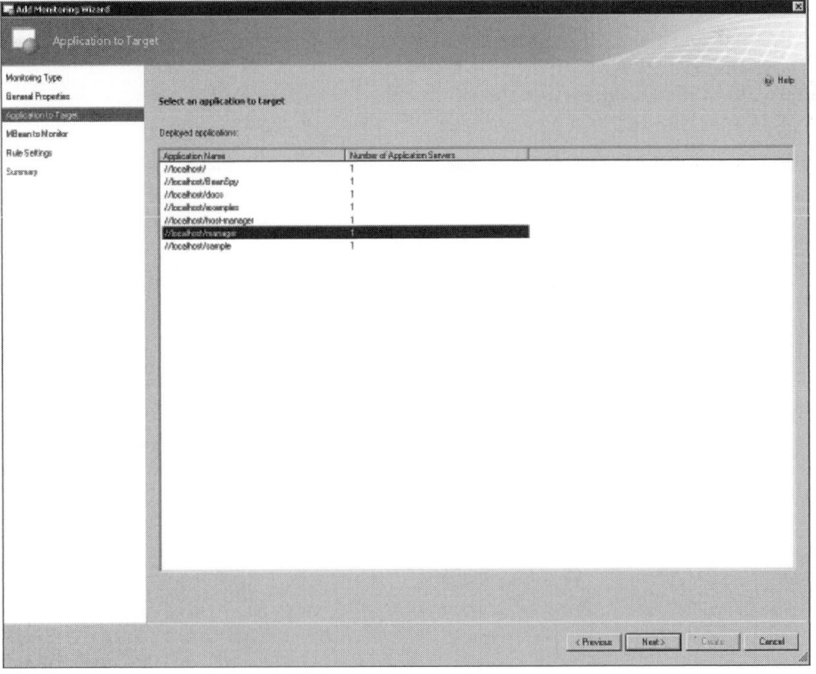

FIGURE 20.71 Choosing a target JEE application.

4. Click **Browse** and select the /Manager MBean as shown in Figure 20.72 and click **Next**. When browsing for the activeSessions property of the /Manager MBean, use the search tip suggested in the "JEE Application Availability Monitoring" section and shown in Figure 20.73.

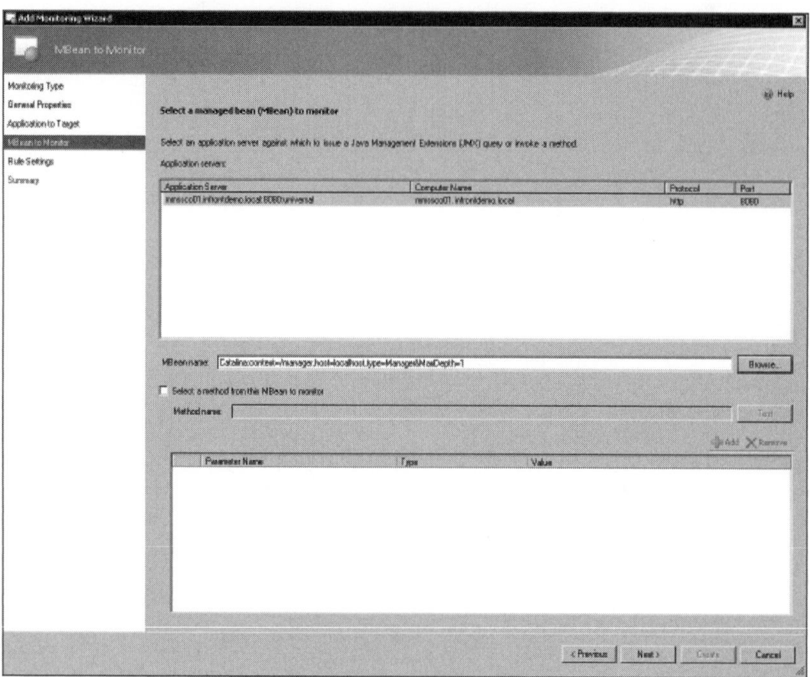

FIGURE 20.72 Select the MBean to monitor dialog.

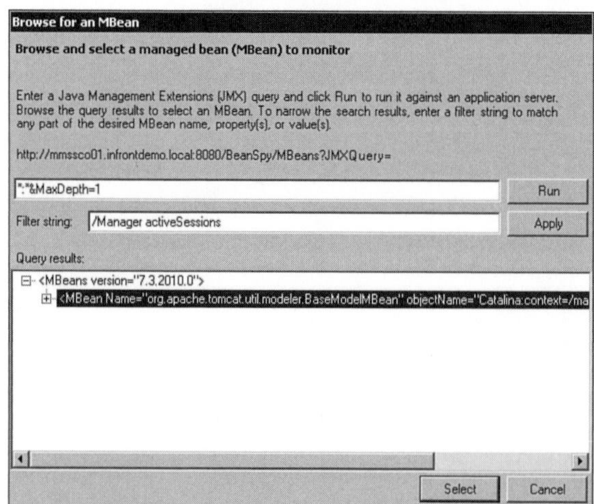

FIGURE 20.73 Browsing/searching for an MBean.

5. As you are completing the JEE wizards and browsing for MBeans, you may have noticed there are many MBean properties available for threshold monitoring and performance data, which will vary by application. Consult the product documentation for your target application. For custom Java applications that are not well-documented, consult the application developer(s) to determine which counters are relevant.

6. In the Rule Settings dialog, click **Browse**, select the activeSessions MBean property as shown in Figure 20.74, and click **Select**.

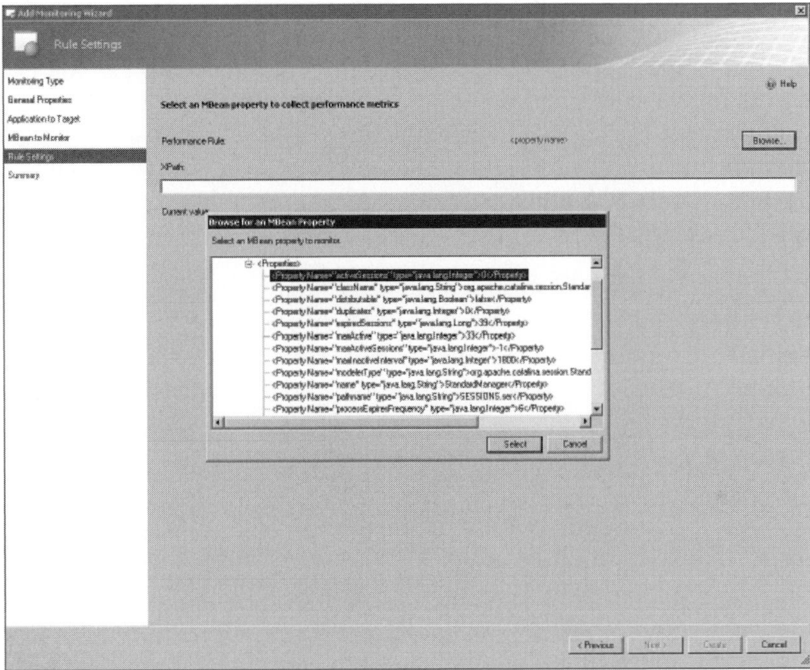

FIGURE 20.74 Rule Settings dialog for JEE Application Performance Monitoring template.

7. On the **Summary** page, click **Create**. As with the JEE application availability monitor, the default interval on this performance collection rule is 15 minutes. You may want to adjust this slightly for testing purposes.

As with the Java Application Availability Monitoring template, there is more to the JEE performance template than meets the eye. While it may appear that this wizard simply creates a performance collection rule targeting the JEE application you selected, there are several activities handled by the template in the background, including

- A new class is defined; a specialized class with a base class of Microsoft.JEE.Application, which is defined in the JEE Template Library MP.

- An object discovery utilizing a data source in the JEE Template Library MP.
- A new performance collection rule leveraging the Microsoft.JEE.MBean.Template.Query.DataSource defined in the JEE Template Library MP.

You can see the monitor type leveraged by this template in the Authoring space by scoping your view to **Tomcat JEE MBean Availability Monitoring extension of Microsoft.JEE.Application** and expanding the Entity Health -> Availability rollup monitor. The unit monitor created in this example was previously shown in Figure 20.68.

Notes on UNIX Commands

This section presents some fundamental commands you will want to remember as you deploy agents to UNIX and Linux systems, as well as additional resources for learning more about UNIX/Linux administration. This is not intended as a comprehensive list, but if you do not have access to UNIX/Linux administrators, you may find them useful during the agent deployment process. For additional information on UNIX/Linux commands, see http://en.wikipedia.org/wiki/List_of_Unix_utilities.

- Verifying UNIX/Linux connectivity

  You can use telnet to verify ssh connectivity to the UNIX/Linux system on port 22 (note the telnet client is not installed by default in Windows 2008 and above systems). Few things are more frustrating than spending hours debugging why an agent will not deploy than to find out later the management server you are deploying from is unable to reach the UNIX/Linux agent on port 22.

  If you have not stayed current with working in UNIX/Linux, a refresher course on basic commands may be useful. This section provides several commands frequently used when debugging cross platform agent deployment.

- Use ifconfig to show address information and turn on network interfaces.

  Retrieve the IP address information for the system:

  ```
  ifconfig -a
  ```

- Setting the IP address information for the system: ifconfig *<interface type> <ip address> <subnet mask> <broadcast address>*. For example:

  ```
  ifconfig hme0 192.168.0.193 netmask 255.255.255.0 broadcast 192.168.0.255
  ```

- Turning on a network interface: ifconfig *<interface name>* up. For example:

  ```
  ifconfig hme0 up
  ```

- Rebooting a system

  To reboot down a UNIX/Linux system, you need to sync twice and then init it to the correct level. Syntax:

  ```
  init 6 or shutdown -r now
  ```

- Restarting SSH

  Here is the command to restart ssh: svcadm restart (service):

```
/etc/init.d/sshd stop
/etc/init.d/sshd start
/etc/init.d/sshd restart
```

- Root command

  To execute privileged commands on UNIX/Linux systems, you will need to access the root command. Do this through su root (and then provide the password for root). Here is an example:

```
su root
```

- Specifying the DNS server

  To specify the DNS server, edit the /etc/resolv.conf file with the domain and name server information. To set the name servers to 192.168.0.230 and 192.168.0.231, here is an example for the odyssey.com domain:

```
domain odyssey.com nameserver 192.168.0.230 nameserver 192.168.0.231
```

- Creating directories

  To make a directory: mkdir (directory). For example:

```
mkdir /export/home
```

- User maintenance
  - To create a user, for example:

```
useradd teste -g users -G users,dialout,video -m -d /home/teste -p teste
```

  - To configure the account password: passwd (`UserName`). Syntax:

```
passwd Admin
```

  Then enter the password for the user specified.

  - To add a user to a group: usermod –G <*group*> <`UserName`>. This syntax adds a user (Admin) to a group named root:

```
usermod -G root Admin
```

- Remote control utilities

  Here are several must-have utilities to help remotely control the VM and perform basic file transfers (such as System Center agents) to and from the VM.

- **TightVNC:** Free remote control utility (for full screen capability), available at http://www.tightvnc.com/
- **WinSCP:** Secure copy utility, available at http://winscp.net/eng/index.php

WinSCP is really handy when correcting certificate configuration issues on *NIX systems (which occurs frequently when configuring OpsMgr cross platform agent).

- Graphical user interface

If you are a Windows person, you may want a graphical user interface (GUI). The authors like Gnome and KDE.

- To install the GNOME desktop, for example:

```
yum groupinstall "X Window System" "GNOME Desktop Environment"
```

- Install the K Desktop Environment (another UI), for example:

```
yum groupinstall "X Window System" "KDE (K Desktop Environment)"
```

To start the UI, type `startx`. You can configure the UI to load automatically, but this utilizes additional resources. To set the GUI to start automatically, set the runlevel to 5 in the /etc./inittab. People tend to run CentOS (or RHEL) at runlevel 3 or runlevel 5—both full multi-user modes. The default runlevel for the system is listed in /etc./inittab. To find out the default runlevel for a system, look for the line similar to the following near the top of /etc./inittab:

```
id:3:initdefault:
```

Fast Track

Cross platform monitoring on OpsMgr 2012 is similar to OpsMgr 2007 R2 in many ways. Here are key differences to explore if you have experience with cross platform monitoring in OpsMgr 2007 R2:

- Cross platform agent architecture is essentially the same.
- The need for root access has been eliminated with the addition of privilege elevation ("su" and "sudo").
- Resource pools provide high availability for cross platform workloads.
- Java Enterprise Edition monitoring has been added in OpsMgr 2012.
- The process and log file monitoring templates introduced in OpsMgr 2007 are still present in OpsMgr 2012. New JEE monitoring templates have been added to facilitate custom monitoring.
- OpsMgr 2012 introduces shell command rules, monitors, and tasks to make custom monitoring easier for cross platform administrators with knowledge of shell scripting.

Summary

This chapter covered the cross platform monitoring architecture in OpsMgr 2012, including both agent and server components. It demonstrated UNIX and Linux computer discovery and cross platform agent deployment. The chapter also discussed the process and log file monitoring templates, as well as the new shell command rule and monitor templates. It included in depth coverage of JEE application performance monitoring. The next chapter goes further in discussing extensibility to Operations Manager by looking at System Center integration.

CHAPTER 21

System Center 2012 Integration

IN THIS CHAPTER

- Service Manager Integration
- Virtual Machine Manager Integration
- Data Protection Manager Integration
- Configuration Manager Integration
- Orchestrator Integration
- Bringing It All Together in the Microsoft Private Cloud
- Visualization of Private Cloud Components
- Private Cloud Reporting
- Fast Track

Microsoft's rebranding of System Center 2012, with a shift from reference as a "suite of products" to a single product with "components," suggests that Operations Manager (OpsMgr) is just one component of the System Center 2012 "product." The semantics of terminology aside, the System Center components do share multiple points of integration. In fact (and as called out in Chapter 3, "Looking Inside OpsMgr"), OpsMgr shares integration points with most of the other components, including

- **System Center Service Manager:** OpsMgr integrates with Service Manager through Service Manager connectors that utilize discovery data to populate the CMDB with configuration data and OpsMgr alerts to raise incidents automatically. Additionally, Service Manager can populate its configuration management database (CMDB) with system and application data collected through Operations Manager object discoveries.
- **System Center Virtual Machine Manager:** Integration occurs through the internal connectors created with the Virtual Machine Manager (VMM) GUI to populate OpsMgr automatically with distributed application models for services deployed from VMM service templates. OpsMgr also continues to provide Performance and Resource Optimization (PRO) capabilities introduced in OpsMgr 2007 R2 and VMM 2008 R2.
- **System Center Orchestrator:** Orchestrator is the runbook automation component of System Center 2012. It includes an integration pack allowing administrators to create advanced automation sequences including OpsMgr and other System Center or monitored systems.

- **System Center Configuration Manager:** Configuration Manager provides integration to initiate OpsMgr agent maintenance mode during installation of software updates, as well as the option to create alerts when update installation fails.

While any one of these integration components may seem inconsequential, the collective integration capabilities of OpsMgr 2012 with other System Center components and third-party systems offer a very significant set of capabilities to support private and hybrid cloud scenarios in enterprise environments. This chapter discusses Operations Manager's integration with each of these components.

Service Manager Integration

System Center 2012 Service Manager provides two connectors that communicate with OpsMgr through the OpsMgr software development kit (SDK) for consuming information from OpsMgr, as well as sending updates back to Operations Manager based on the configuration of the connector.

The OpsMgr connectors for Service Manager are the System Center Operations Manager Configuration Item (CI) Connector and the System Center Operations Manager Alert Connector:

- The OpsMgr CI connector can be used to create configuration items from discovered Operations Manager objects. This will synchronize new information from Operations Manager over to Service Manager.
- The OpsMgr alert connector can be used to create a two-way synchronization between Operations Manager alerts and Service Manager incidents. You can create subscriptions that will create incidents automatically in Service Manager. When the incident is resolved in Service Manager, it is automatically closed in Operations Manager.

These connectors are highly configurable, allowing for very granular control over connector behavior based on the requirements of your environment.

System Center Operations Manager Configuration Item Connector

The System Center Operations Manager Configuration Item (CI) Connector allows automated population of the Service Manager CMDB with objects and attributes discovered in OpsMgr 2012. The nice surprise with this feature is that in addition to the default object types (classes) and properties synchronized into the CMDB, the connector can be easily customized to synchronize new objects of just about any type discovered in OpsMgr.

Configuring the CI Connector

For the System Center Operations Manager Configuration Item (CI) Connector to work as expected, you must first import a set of management packs into Service Manager. These management packs are in the Service Manager installation folder, by default in *%ProgramFiles%*\Microsoft System Center 2012\Service Manager\Operations Manager 2012 SP1 Management Packs\ and *%ProgramFiles%*\Microsoft System Center 2012\

Service Manager\Operations Manager Management Packs. The second folder contains a PowerShell script (InstallOMMPs.ps1); use this to import the management packs more quickly and easily than through the Service Manager console.

Before configuring the OpsMgr CI connector, you must first import the appropriate OpsMgr library management packs (MPs). The steps for importing management packs for OpsMgr CI connectors into Service Manager are discussed at http://technet.microsoft.com/en-us/library/hh519707.aspx.

Creating an Operations Manager CI Connector

Follow these steps to create an OpsMgr CI connector in Service Manager:

1. In the Service Manager console, click **Administration**.
2. In the **Administration** pane, expand **Administration** -> **Connectors**.
3. In the **Tasks** pane, under **Connectors**, click **Create Connector** -> **Operations Manager CI Connector**. This opens the Operations Manager CI Connector Wizard.
4. On the General page of the wizard, in the Name box, type a name for the new connector. Make sure that the **Enable** check box is selected, and then click **Next**.
5. On the Server Details page, in the Server name box, type the name of any OpsMgr management server (see Figure 21.1).
6. Use one of the following methods to enter credentials in the Credentials section of this page:
    - ▶ If you have already created a Run As account, select a Run As account for the alert connector.

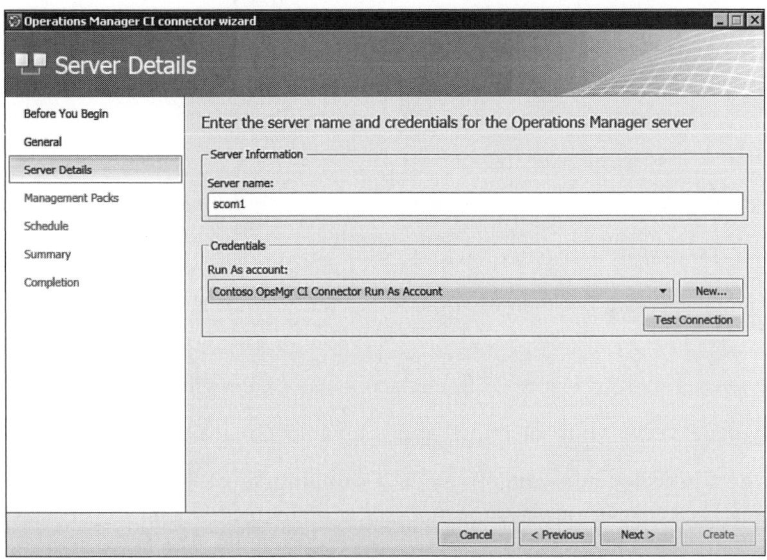

FIGURE 21.1 Server Details in the Operations Manager CI Connector Wizard.

- If you have not yet created a Run As account, click **New**. In the User name, Password, and Domain boxes that appear, type the credentials for the Run As account, and then click **OK**.

NOTE: SECURITY FOR THE CONNECTOR ROLE

To ensure full functionality of the connector, the account supplied should be a member of the Operations Manager Operators user role.

7. On the Server Details page, click **Test Connection**. If you receive the following confirmation message, click **OK**, and then click **Next**:

```
The connection to the server was successful.
```

8. On the Management Packs page, shown in Figure 21.2, click **Select all** or select the management packs that define the configuration items you want to import, and then click **Next**.

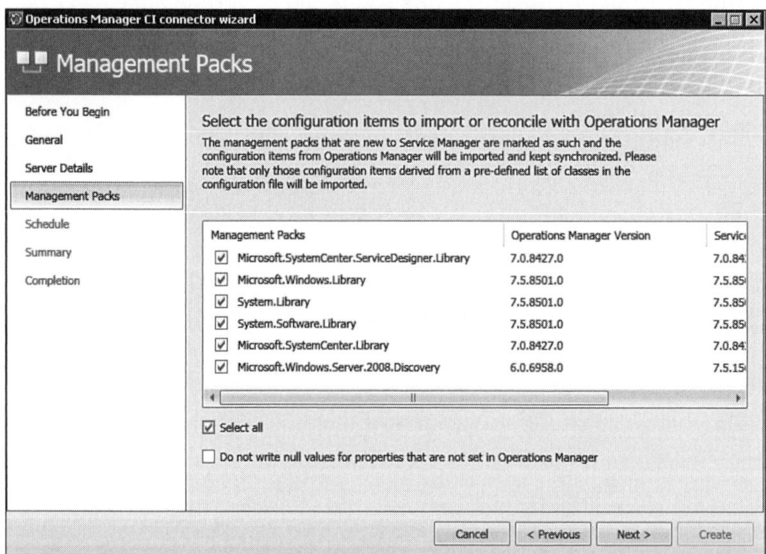

FIGURE 21.2 Selecting management packs in the Operations Manager CI Connector Wizard.

9. On the Schedule page shown in Figure 21.3, click **Next**, and then click **Create**.
10. On the Summary page, verify your selections and then click **Create** and then **Close**.
11. To synchronize the connector immediately, select **Connectors** in the Navigation pane of the console. Select your newly created OpsMgr CI connector and in the Tasks pane, click **Synchronize Now**.

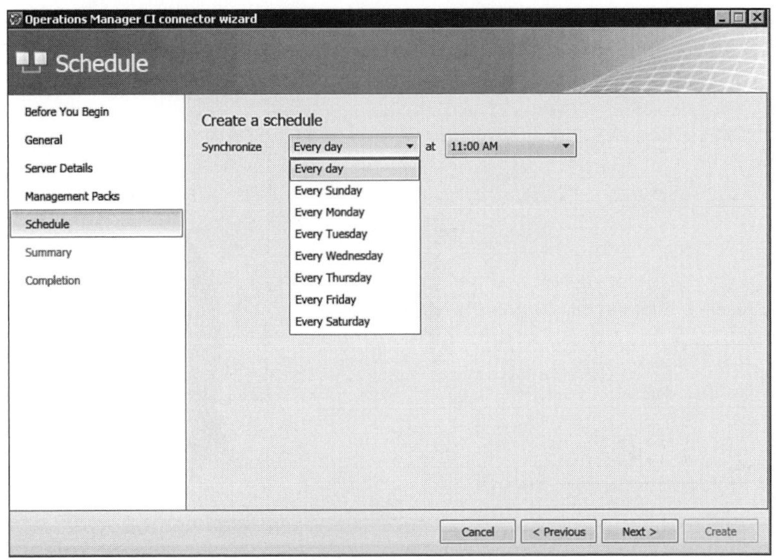

FIGURE 21.3 Creating a schedule in the Operations Manager CI Connector Wizard.

Confirming Connector Status and Viewing Results

View the columns in the **Connector** pane; the columns contain information about the start time, finish time, status, and percentage of import completion. Once the CI connector returns a status of **Finished Success**, check the new CIs or CI properties to ensure the connector updated the CMDB as expected. You want to confirm either that the objects that Operations Manager discovered are listed as configuration items in Service Manager or that existing CIs reflect new properties added via the OpsMgr CI connector.

Creating an Alert Connector

To create an Operations Manager alert connector, perform the following steps in the Service Manager console:

1. In the Service Manager console, navigate to **Administration** and expand **Connectors**.
2. In the Connectors section of the Tasks pane, click **Create Connector** -> **Operations Manager Alert Connector**. This opens the Operations Manager Alert Connector Wizard.
3. Click **Next** on the Before You Begin page of the Operations Manager Alert Connector Wizard.
4. On the General page, in the Name box, type a name for the new connector. Verify the Enable check box is selected as shown in Figure 21.4, and then click **Next**. Make a note of the connector name; you will need it in the procedure discussed in the next section.

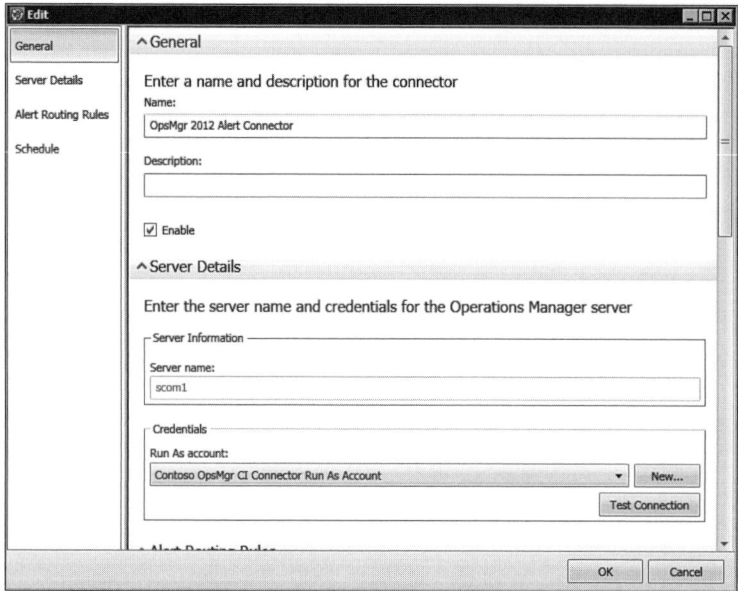

FIGURE 21.4 General settings in the Operations Manager Alert Connector Wizard.

5. On the Server Details page, in the Server name box, type the name of the server hosting an Operations Manager management server. Under Credentials, click **New**.
6. In the Run As Account dialog box, in the Display name box, type a name for this Run As account. In the Account list, select **Windows Account**.
7. In the User Name, Password, and Domain fields, type the credentials for the Run As account and click **OK**. For more information about the permissions required for this Run As account, see the "Accounts Required During Setup" section in the Planning Guide for System Center 2012 - Service Manager at http://technet.microsoft.com/en-us/library/hh495542.aspx, also available for download at http://www.microsoft.com/en-us/download/details.aspx?id=27850.
8. On the Server Details page, click **Test Connection**. If you receive the following confirmation message, click **OK**, and then click **Next**.

```
The connection to the server was successful.
```

9. On the Alert Routing Rules page, click **Add**.
10. In the Add Alert Routing Rule dialog box displayed in Figure 21.5, create a name for the rule, select the template that you want to use to process incidents created by an alert, and then select the alert criteria you want to use.

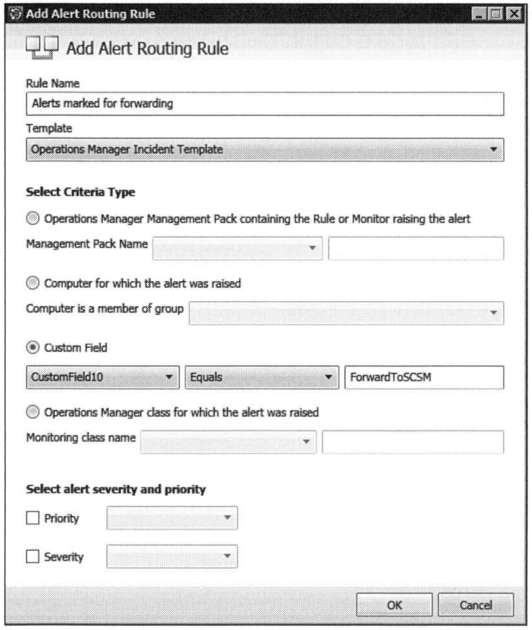

FIGURE 21.5 Add Alert Routing Rule in the Operations Manager CI Alert Connector Wizard.

REAL WORLD: USING CUSTOM FIELDS IN OPERATIONS MANAGER

The authors recommend using the custom fields in Operations Manager as a method for maximum control over which alerts are forwarded to Service Manager for creation of new incidents, as shown in Figure 21.5. You can configure automatic update of custom fields in OpsMgr alerts based on very granular criteria using PowerShell, Orchestrator runbooks, or the Operations Manager Alert Connector. It's all about controlling the volume of matching alerts flowing through the connector to raise alerts. Using the method described here ensures you have the opportunity to include volume-based throttling logic in your runbook or script when updating the custom field to trigger forwarding, minimizing the possibility that a flood of OpsMgr alerts will result in a large number of incidents being raised in Service Manager.

11. On the Schedule page, select **Close alerts in Operations Manager when incidents are resolved or closed** and/or **Resolve incidents automatically when the alerts in Operations Manager are closed**, if desired. Then click **Next**, and then click **Create**.

TIP: RECOMMENDATIONS ON ALERT CLOSURE

In testing, the authors discovered that if you select the **Close alerts in Operations Manager when incidents are resolved or closed** option on the Create a Schedule page in the OpsMgr Alert Connector Wizard, analysts could close alerts in OpsMgr that should remain open because the root cause of the alert has not been resolved.

This generally does no real harm with rule-based alerts, as rules will simply raise another alert if necessary. However, when you close an alert for a monitor, the result is a monitor that remains in an error state without an associated open alert. This becomes a blind spot, as the monitor will never raise another alert until it has transitioned back to a healthy state and then back to an error state again. To avoid this risk, you could opt to only check the box labeled **Resolve incidents automatically when the alerts in Operations Manager are closed**, as shown in Figure 21.6.

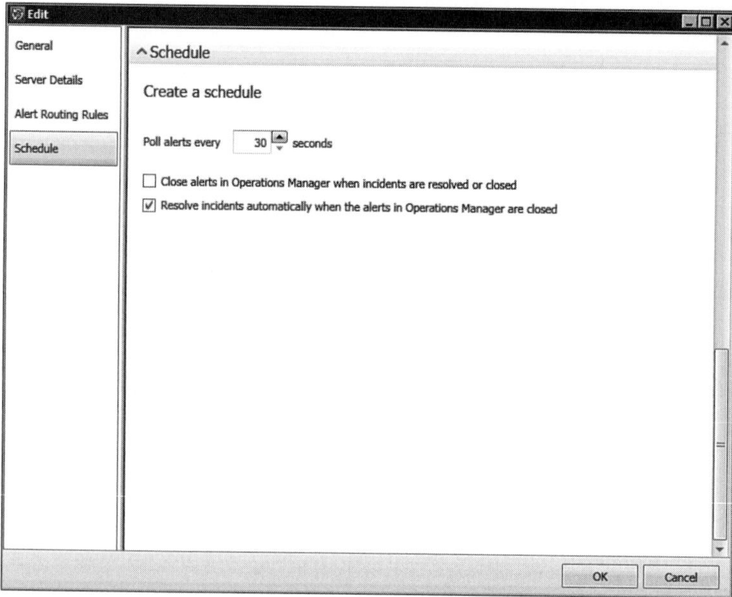

FIGURE 21.6 Create a schedule in the Operations Manager Alert Connector Wizard.

Additional Configuration in Operations Manager 2012

When you create an alert connector in Service Manager, you must add an associated alert subscription in OpsMgr. The configuration on the Operations Manager side allows you to configure additional filtering by group or class in addition to the custom field configured in the alert routing settings of the connector in Service Manager. Follow these steps:

1. Start the Operations console.
2. In the Administration pane, select **Product Connectors -> Internal Connectors.**
3. In the Connectors pane, click the name of the alert connector you specified in the "Creating an Alert Connector" section.
4. In the Actions pane, click **Properties**.
5. In the Alert Sync: *<name of connector>* dialog box, click **Add**.

6. In the Product Connector Subscription Wizard dialog box, on the General page, in the Subscription Name box, type the name for this subscription as shown in Figure 21.7, and then click **Next**.

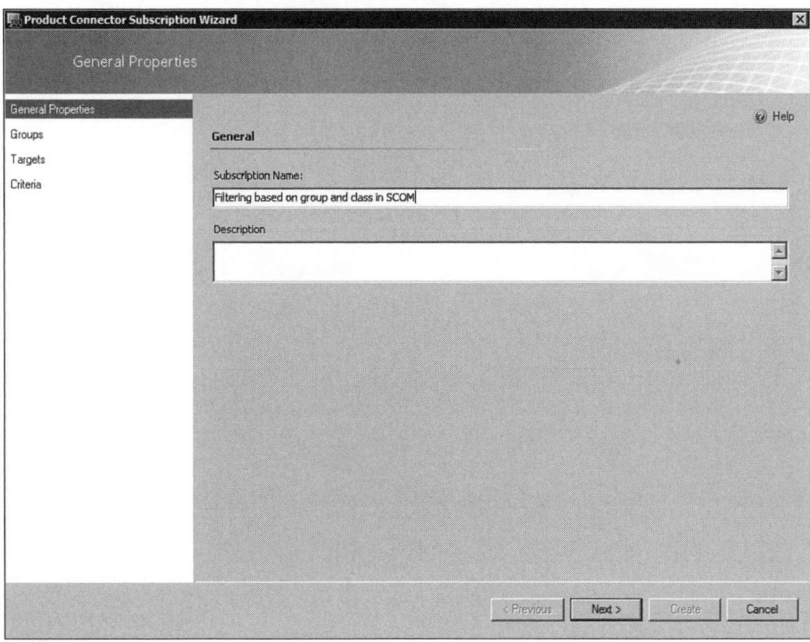

FIGURE 21.7 General Properties of the Product Connector Subscription Wizard.

7. On the Approve groups page, click **Next**.
8. On the Approve targets page, click **Next**.

TIP: MINIMIZING MANUAL CONNECTOR ADMINISTRATION

By leaving both the group and target settings at their defaults, you eliminate the need for future manual configuration when new management packs are imported, or new groups or classes are created.

9. On the Criteria page shown in Figure 21.8, select the desired criteria and click **Create**.

REAL WORLD: USE OF ALERT RESOLUTION STATE FOR SENDING TO A CONNECTOR

A strategy the authors have found effective is to use alert resolution state as the sole criteria. Using custom resolution states enables granular control over which alerts are forwarded to Service Manager with relative ease.

10. In the Alert Sync: *<name of connector>* dialog box, click **OK**.

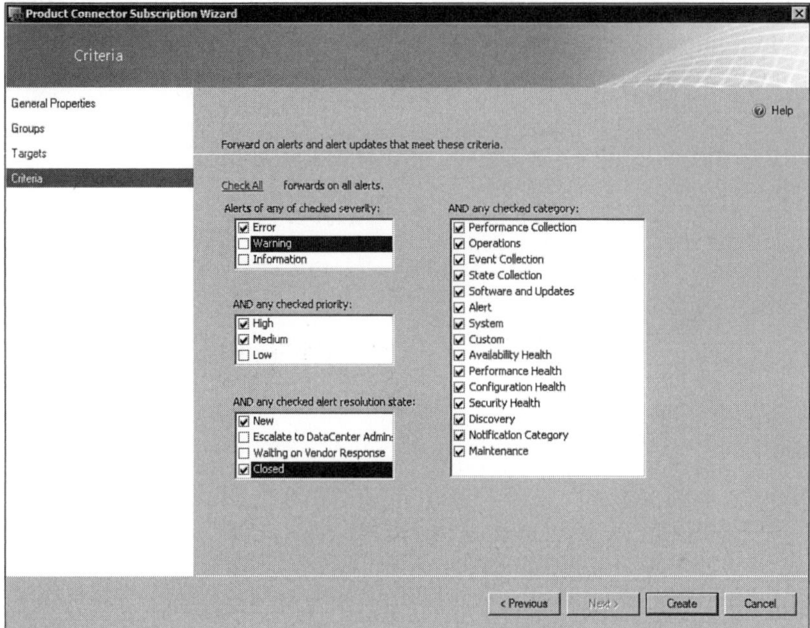

FIGURE 21.8 Criteria of the Product Connector Subscription Wizard.

Validating Creation of an Operations Manager Alert Connector

Confirm that the connector you created is displayed in the Service Manager console in the Connectors pane, and that incidents are created in Service Manager from alerts in Operations Manager. You will find all incidents created via the Operations Manager alert connector in the Work Items pane, in the All Open Operations Manager Incidents view.

Figure 21.9 shows open OpsMgr incidents in the Service Manager console.

File Language View Go Tools Tasks Help

Work Items ▸ Work Items ▸ Incident Management ▸ All Open Operations Manager Incidents

Work Items
- Work Items
  - Activity Management
  - Application Requests
  - Change Management
  - Incident Management
    - All Incidents
    - All Open Desired Configuration Ma
    - All Open E-Mail Incidents
    - All Open Incidents
    - All Open Incidents Extended
    - All Open Operations Manager Incic
    - All Open Parent Incidents

All Open Operations Manager Incidents 11

Filter

ID	Title	Assigned To	Status	Priority
IR135	Failed to Connect to Computer		Active	9
IR136	System Center Management Health...		Active	9
IR142	System Center Management Health...		Active	9
IR138	Failed to Connect to Computer		Active	9
IR141	Failed to Connect to Computer		Active	9
IR140	Health Service Heartbeat Failure		Active	9
IR143	Health Service Heartbeat Failure		Active	9
IR144	Failed to Connect to Computer		Active	9
IR137	Health Service Heartbeat Failure		Active	9
IR139	System Center Management Health...		Active	9
IR134	Health Service Heartbeat Failure		Active	9

FIGURE 21.9 All Open Operations Manager Incidents view in Service Manager console.

Double-click any alert to open, and go to the Extensions tab shown in Figure 21.10 to view extended alert properties.

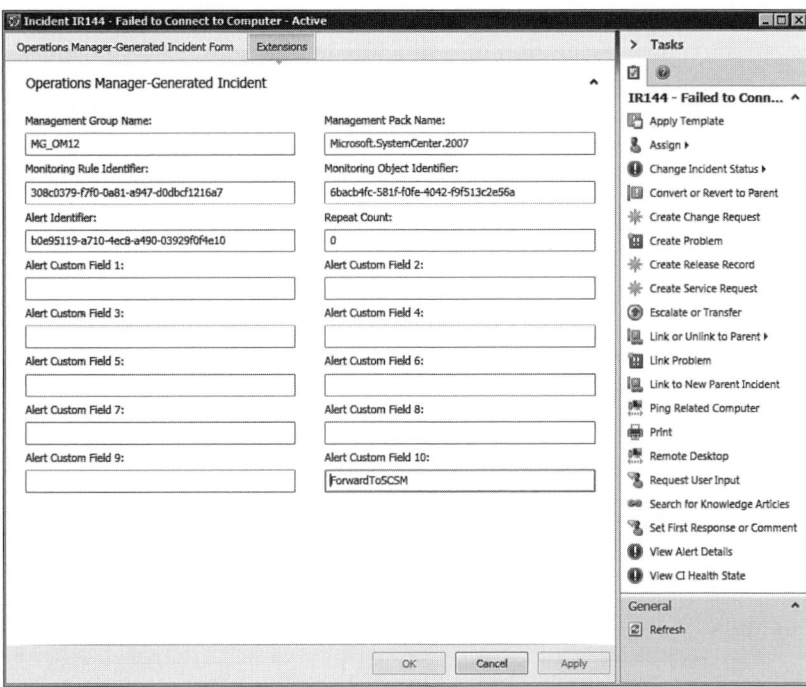

FIGURE 21.10 Extended alert properties in a Service Manager incident.

Optionally, you can close the alert in Operations Manager to verify the incident is resolved in Service Manager. If this is a monitor-generated alert, be sure to reset the monitor state to avoid the issue described in the Real World sidebar, "Recommendations on Alert Closure."

Virtual Machine Manager Integration

In a highly virtualized environment where new systems can be provisioned quickly, monitoring is a critical solution component of a comprehensive management strategy. To support this need, Microsoft has developed tight integration between OpsMgr and VMM 2012, providing deep visibility into the hypervisor and virtualization management infrastructure. The next sections discuss how to establish this integration.

Configuring OpsMgr/VMM Integration

While Dynamic Optimization and Power Optimization replace the Performance and Resource Optimization (PRO) functionality in OpsMgr for basic workload thresholds (CPU, memory, disk, and network), OpsMgr PRO still plays a large role in delivering dynamic workload management for your virtualization infrastructure by extending PRO functionality to OEM hardware, appliances, and third-party applications through PRO-enabled packs from the partner community. In addition, configuring this integration enables VMM to send information on any new services deployed from VMM (using the new service template feature in VMM 2012), where the service, virtual machines (VMs), and first class applications (WebDeploy, SQL data tier applications, and Server App-V) it contains are included in an automatically created and updated distributed application model.

While configuration of OpsMgr/VMM is not that difficult, it remains a common area of confusion. The next sections describe the configuration steps necessary to enable this functionality in your System Center 2012 deployment. Here are the high-level steps required, discussed in the following sections:

1. Install the consoles.
2. Grant permissions to OpsMgr and VMM user accounts.
3. Import the required management packs.
4. Configure System Center settings in the VMM 2012 console.
5. Validate your results.

Since you are configuring OpsMgr integration with VMM, it is assumed you have deployed an OpsMgr agent to the VMM 2012 Server, all Hyper-V hosts, and VM guests.

Installing the Consoles

Before you configure the connection, you need to install the System Center consoles to facilitate SDK access:

- Install the Operations Manager 2012 console on the VMM 2012 server.
- Install the VMM 2012 console on one of the management servers in the All Management Servers Resource Pool. You will later specify this OpsMgr management server when configuring settings in the VMM console, discussed in the "Configuring System Center Settings in VMM 2012 Console" section.

Granting Permissions to OpsMgr and VMM User Accounts

You will need an account with administrator permissions in Operations Manager 2012 and an account with administrator rights in Virtual Machine Manager 2012.

Importing the Required Management Packs

Import the Virtual Machine Manager 2012 and PRO management packs into OpsMgr 2012; these are located on your VMM 2012 server in the *%ProgramFiles%*\Microsoft System Center 2012\Virtual Machine Manager\Management Packs folder.

CAUTION: IMPORTANCE OF IMPORTING THE REQUIRED MANAGEMENT PACKS

If you do not import the VMM Manager 2012 and PRO management packs, the Operations Manager Connector setup job in VMM will fail. You must also import the IIS 2003 and 2008 management packs (and associated IIS library MP); the IIS 2003 management pack is in the references of one of the VMM packs, as shown in Figure 21.11.

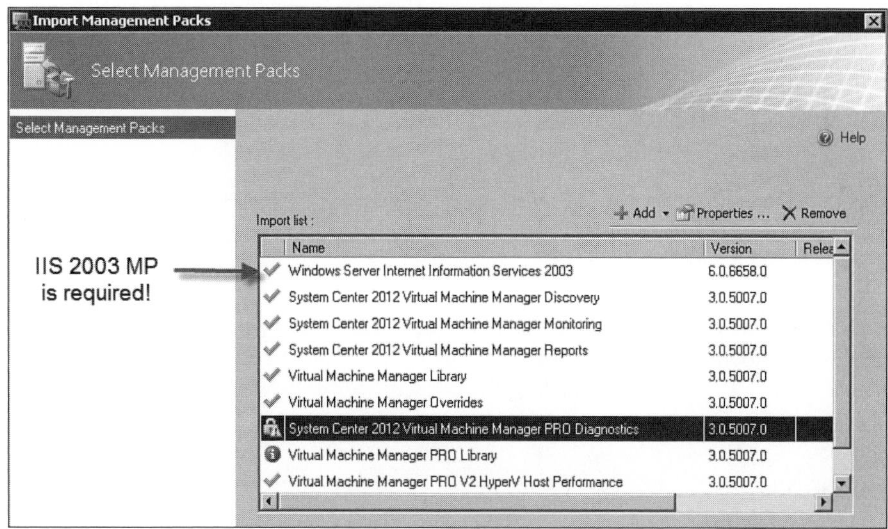

FIGURE 21.11 Import VMM and dependent management packs into OpsMgr 2012.

Configuring System Center Settings in VMM 2012 Console

To configure the System Center settings, follow these steps:

1. In the VMM 2012 console, browse to and double-click **Settings** -> **System Center Settings** -> **Operations Manager Server** to launch the wizard to configure OpsMgr integration with VMM 2012.

2. In the Connection to Operations Manager page shown in Figure 21.12, enter the fully qualified domain name (FQDN) of the OpsMgr 2012 management server where you installed the VMM console. You will need to specify an account with administrative permissions in OpsMgr. You can do this using a Run As account, which can be created in Virtual Machine Manager much as it is in OpsMgr. For instructions on creating Run As credentials, see Chapter 10, "Security and Compliance."

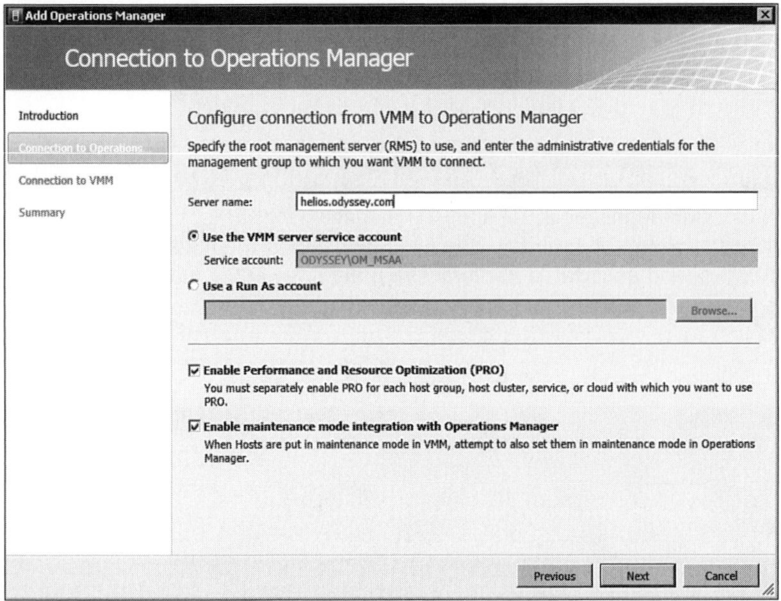

FIGURE 21.12 Add Operations Manager Wizard in the VMM 2012 console.

3. In the **Connection to VMM** dialog, enter the account with VMM administrator credentials, as shown in Figure 21.13.

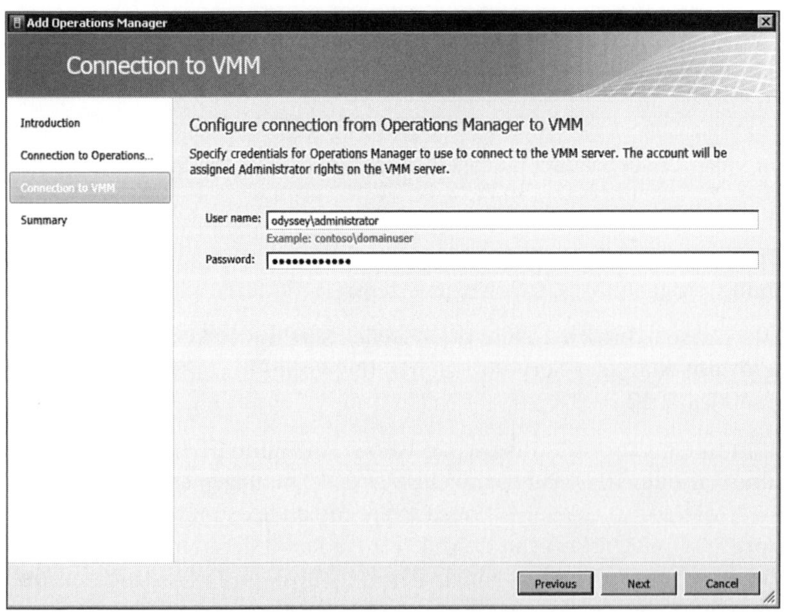

FIGURE 21.13 Specifying OpsMgr admin credentials in the Add Operations Manager Wizard.

4. Review your settings in the Summary page, shown in Figure 21.14, and then select **Finish**. This launches a job titled New Operations Manager connector.

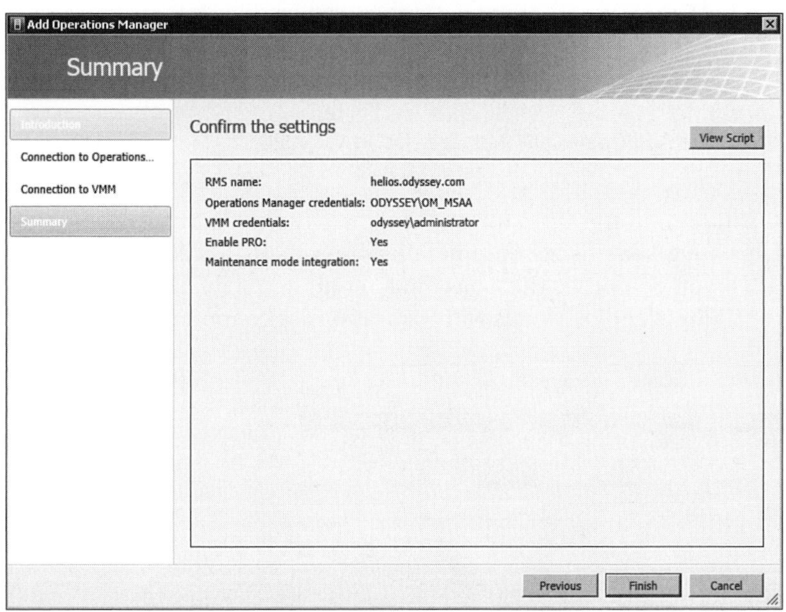

FIGURE 21.14 The Summary page of the Add Operations Manager Wizard.

Validating Your Results

You will need to validate your results first in VMM, then in OpsMgr. Once the job completes in VMM, verify a successful result. The running job is displayed in Figure 21.15.

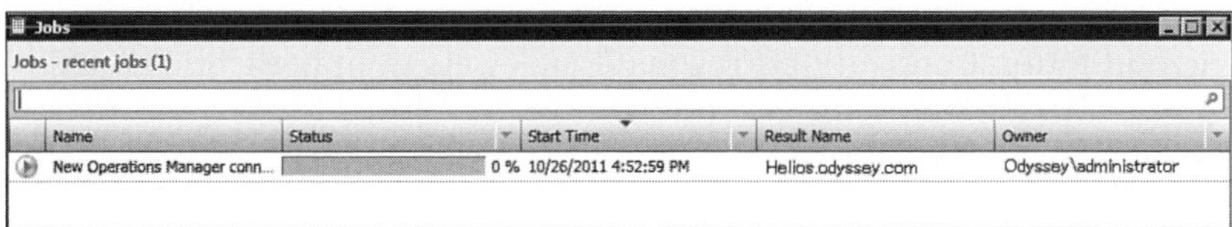

FIGURE 21.15 The Add Operations Manager connection job in the VMM console.

When the job completes, you can view the details of job results, including any problems or corrective actions that may be necessary. This is shown in Figure 21.16.

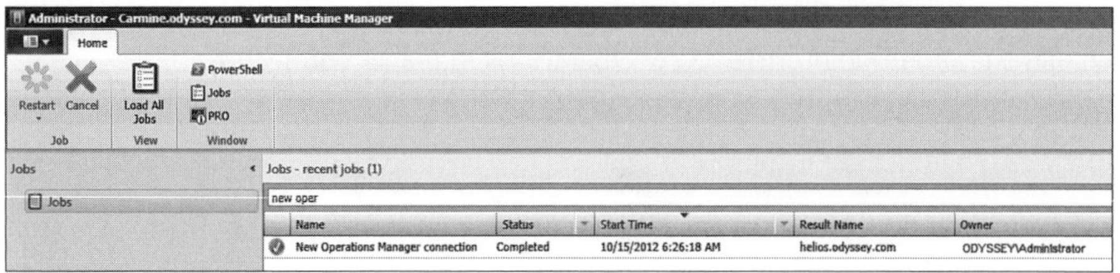

FIGURE 21.16 Results of the Add Operations Manager job in VMM 2012.

Wait several minutes, and then in the Operations console, verify the VMM Server appears in the PRO Object State with a health state of something other than "Not Monitored," as seen in Figure 21.17. If you do not see this object in a monitored state, check for Operations Manager or VMM event log events with indications of communication or permission failures.

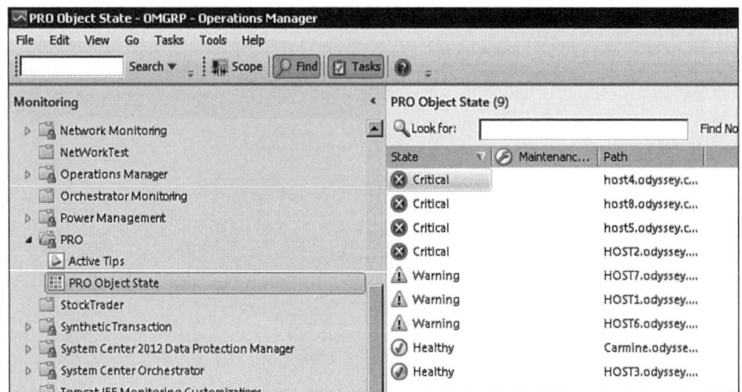

FIGURE 21.17 PRO Object State in the OpsMgr Operations console.

You should also see monitoring information for your cloud assets from the fabric up, including clouds, services, hosts, host clusters, and so on in the Virtual Machine Manager -> Agents folder displayed in Figure 21.18.

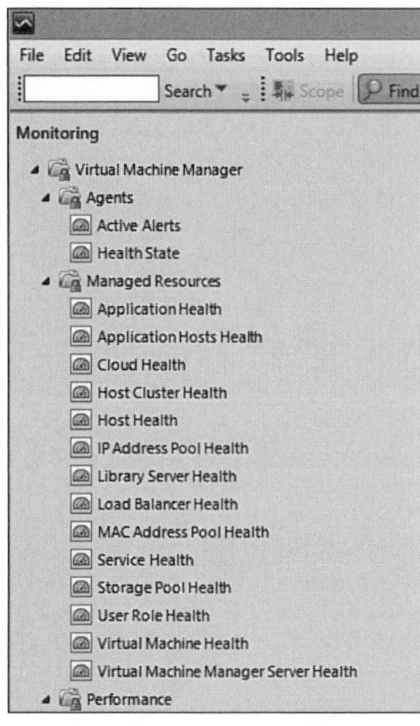

FIGURE 21.18 VMM 2012 views in the OpsMgr Operations console.

Integrated Maintenance Mode (Hyper-V Host and Host Cluster Patching)

When you patch a Hyper-V host cluster (described at http://technet.microsoft.com/en-us/library/gg675088.aspx), VMM contacts OpsMgr 2012 using an internal connector created when you configure VMM/OpsMgr integration and places the Hyper-V host in maintenance mode in Operations Manager while it is out of service and being updated. When patching is complete and the host is returned to service, VMM contacts OpsMgr to end maintenance mode for the Hyper-V host.

This requires that OpsMgr/VMM integration be configured as described in the "Configuring OpsMgr/VMM Integration" section.

Dynamically Generated Diagram Views (via Internal Connector)

When you provision a new group of VMs from a service template in VMM 2012, the resulting service instance is rendered dynamically in a distributed application model in OpsMgr 2012. This feature also requires that OpsMgr/VMM integration is configured as described in the "Configuring OpsMgr/VMM Integration" section.

SQL Server Analysis Services Integration (Forecast Reporting)

After you connect VMM and OpsMgr, you can integrate VMM with SQL Server Analysis Service (SSAS) to provide forecasting reports through OpsMgr 2012. This is required for the forecasting reports in the OpsMgr VMM 2012 management pack to be functional, and requires SSAS Analysis Management Objects (AMO) be installed on the Operations Manager reporting server. You can download AMO as part of the SQL feature pack for the SQL version you are using (SQL 2008 R2 or 2012).

Here are the forecasting reports included in the VMM 2012 MP for OpsMgr 2012:

- Host Group Forecasting*
- SAN Usage Forecasting

You must be a member of the VMM Administrator user role to configure SSAS settings in VMM. In addition, SSAS requires AMO be installed on the VMM management server. Download AMO from the Microsoft SQL Server 2008 R2 Feature Pack at http://go.microsoft.com/fwlink/?LInkID=220986, or from the SQL Server 2012 Feature Pack at http://www.microsoft.com/en-us/download/details.aspx?id=29065.

To configure VMM integration with SQL Server Analysis Services, follow these steps:

1. In the VMM console, open the Settings workspace and select **System Center Settings -> Operations Manager Server**.
2. On the Home tab, in the Properties group, click **Properties** to open the Operations Manager Settings dialog box.
3. On the SQL Server Analysis Services page, click **Enable SSAS**.
4. Enter the SSAS server, SSAS instance, and SSAS port:
    - The instance name must be the same as the SQL Server Reporting Services (SSRS) instance, which is MSSQLSERVER by default. If you used a named SQL instance during installation, provide the instance name.
    - The SSAS port is not auto-detected, so you must enter the configured listening port of your SSAS instance.
    - Verify that SSRS allows reports access using default port 80 and has HTTP access to reports.
5. Select either a Run As account or enter a user name and password, and then click **OK**. The account you specify must belong to the Operations Manager Report Security Administrator profile for full functionality.

Several hours after configuring SSAS integration in VMM 2012, the forecasting reports in the VMM 2012 Management Pack for OpsMgr 2012 should be functional.

---

* *Several separate host group forecasting reports (for CPU, memory, network, and disk I/O) have all been combined into a single Host Group Forecasting Report in the SP 1 version of the VMM 2012 Monitoring Pack that allows filtering down to the core subsystem(s) of interest, such as host CPU, memory, disk, or network.*

Data Protection Manager Integration

Data Protection Manager (DPM) 2012 administration is fully integrated into the Operations console, including

- Viewing and remediating DPM infrastructure issues in the Operations console
- Viewing and remediating DPM job failures in the Operations console

The next sections provide examples of how you can use this integration to monitor and manage backups with DPM from the OpsMgr Operations console.

Example: Recovering from DPM Backup Failure in the Operations Console

Data Protection Manager 2012 brings a considerable amount of new functionality and additional features, making it a much better fit not only in enterprise environments, but also for Microsoft private cloud scenarios. In private cloud, a high degree of automation is necessary to ensure adequate protection for self-provisioned resources, be they VM guests provisioned by application owners or Hyper-V hosts provisioned through bare-metal deployment to facilitate scale out. If there is not a data center administrator at the helm, you need to ensure resources are monitored and backed up appropriately.

DPM 2012 delivers full integration with Operations Manager 2012, allowing you to use OpsMgr tasks to launch targeted remediation actions related to DPM jobs and data sources (presented in the Operations console via views as shown in Figure 21.19) with a single click. Centralized administration and role-based delegation are delivered via the OpsMgr 2012 Operations console. OpsMgr tasks in the DPM 2012 management pack provide single-click shortcuts that lead you directly to the portion of the DPM console required to perform the necessary administrative task.

FIGURE 21.19 DPM Data sources view in the OpsMgr Operations console.

The authors tested a variety of scenarios and they all seem to work as advertised. Here are some of the areas included in testing:

- Allocation of additional space to a DPM volume that filled up.
- Automatic resolution of active alerts in OpsMgr when the condition has been corrected.
- Recovery of a SQL data source in the event of catastrophic failure (deleting the .mdf and .ldf files).
- Alert consolidation (the authors simulated failure of multiple database backup failures on a single server [due to an MSSQL service failure] and did not get an alert storm from the DPM management pack).

Centralized Management Features

The centralized management features of DPM, many of which can be driven from the OpsMgr Operations console, include

- Centralized monitoring
- Remote administration
- Remote recovery
- Role-based management
- Remote corrective actions
- Scoped troubleshooting
- Push to resume backups
- Service level agreement (SLA) based alerting (alert only when SLA violated)
- Consolidated alerts, ensuring one ticket per root cause issue
- Alert categorization (DPM infrastructure alerts are separated from backup failure alerts)
- Allowing administrators to automate/extend the base functionality using PowerShell
- Management of DPM 2010 and 2012 servers

Configuration Manager Integration

Configuration Manager (ConfigMgr) offers two points of OpsMgr integration, though the authors are not necessarily recommending that you use them. There are two small points of OpsMgr integration in the ConfigMgr console, both in the area of patch management.

If you create an automatic deployment rule (Software Library -> Automatic Deployment Rules node of the ConfigMgr console), you will find two settings on the **Alerts** tab, as shown in Figure 21.20:

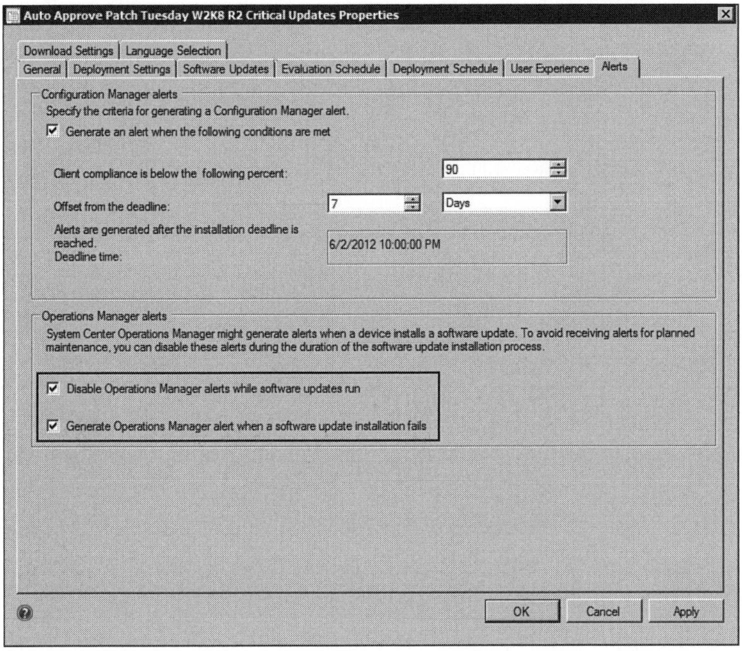

FIGURE 21.20 Operations Manager monitoring integration settings in ConfigMgr 2012.

- **Disable Operations Manager alerts while software updates run:** While seemingly self-explanatory, the **Disable Operations Manager alerts while software updates run** option triggers the ConfigMgr client to pause the OpsMgr agent during maintenance mode.

  As discussed in Chapter 14, "Monitoring with System Center 2012 Operations Manager," this does not trigger maintenance mode properly in Operations Manager, and can thus affect your OpsMgr availability reports by causing a client to reflect an unhealthy state when it is actually functioning normally. The authors do not recommend using this option; it is better to use scheduled maintenance mode scripts with OpsMgr instead, as mentioned in Chapter 23, "PowerShell and Operations Manager."

- **Generate Operations Manager alerts when a software update installation fails:** This option will raise events that generate alerts in Operations Manager; while potentially useful in alerting you when updates fail to install on systems, this could raise more alerts than you might like during patch cycles in a large environment.

The authors suggest that in most cases, using the reporting capabilities of ConfigMgr to identify failed updates would suffice, making OpsMgr alerts on the condition unimportant. At most, the authors would recommend enabling this setting only for the Critical and Security update classifications in Configuration Manager.

Orchestrator Integration

System Center 2012 Orchestrator is the runbook automation component within System Center, which allows administrators to build advanced automation sequences incorporating multiple System Center and third-party systems in a Visio-like interface. Most runbooks include little or no scripting!

RAMPING UP ON ORCHESTRATOR 2012

To appreciate the capabilities of Orchestrator integration with Operations Manager better, it pays to learn the basics of Orchestrator features, functionality, and administration. Fortunately, as this is a System Center component it is easy to get started. The authors believe just about anyone can learn the basics of Orchestrator in several hours. A number of community resources are available to help you get started, including these tutorials, available at http://www.systemcentercentral.com/BlogDetails/tabid/143/IndexID/92651/Default.aspx:

- Day 1: Runbook Concepts, Components, and Rules of the Databus
- Day 2: Advanced Features and Functionality
- Day 3: Bridging Gaps, Extending Capabilities, Best Practices

System Center Operations Manager Integration Pack

Integration packs (IPs) are prebuilt vendor-specific software packages that plug into the Orchestrator framework. They provide a number of common functions including monitoring, new event/alert/item creation, modification, and deletion. They are designed to automatically detect schema, forms, and fields from the products they connect to so that no coding is required. Additionally the IPs included in the product download are supported and updated by Microsoft.

The System Center IPs deliver more than 60 product-specific activities designed to facilitate the creation of integrated workflows incorporating multiple System Center components.

The IP for System Center Operations Manager is an add-in for Orchestrator 2012. It enables you to connect Orchestrator to a server running Microsoft System Center 2012 Operations Manager to automate actions in response to alerts raised by System Center Operations Manager. With this IP, you can also create runbooks that interact with and transfer information to the other IPs or other target systems.

For example, using the Monitor Alert activity from the Operations Manager IP, you can monitor for new alerts related to a specific error condition to trigger automatic corrective action, such as restarting a Windows service or performing an IISReset to recover a failed website. When recovery is complete, you can use the Update Alert activity to write information to the alert in Operations Manager. Figure 21.21 shows this workflow.

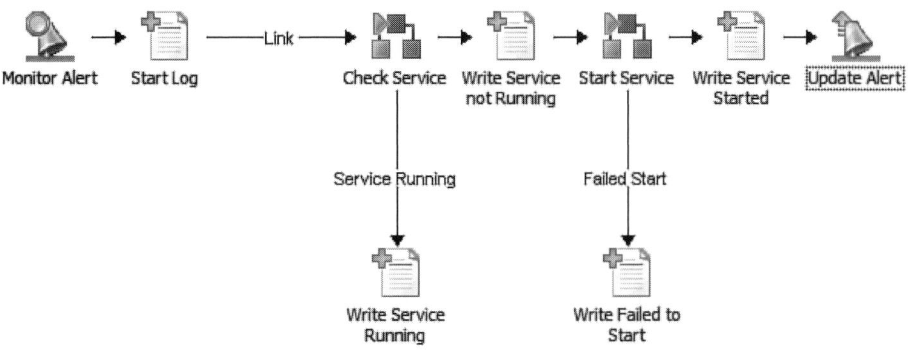

FIGURE 21.21 Service Restart Workflow incorporating activities from Operations Manager IP.

System Requirements

The IP for System Center Operations Manager requires the following software to be installed and configured before you deploy the IP:

- System Center 2012 Orchestrator
- System Center 2012 Operations Manager

You then would register and deploy the System Center Operations Manager IP in Orchestrator.

Install the System Center Operations Manager console on each computer where a runbook server or runbook designer is installed that will interact with System Center Operations Manager.

NOTE: ABOUT THE ORCHESTRATOR INTEGRATION LIBRARY MANAGEMENT PACK

The Orchestrator Integration Library Management Pack is required by the Create Alert activity. The activity installs this management pack automatically in System Center Operations Manager the first time that it runs. To uninstall this IP, remove the Orchestrator Integration Library Management Pack from System Center Operations Manager.

Activities

The System Center Operations Manager IP adds the System Center Operations Manager category to the Activities Palette in the Runbook Designer. The category contains the following activities:

- Create Alert
- Get Alert

- Get Monitor
- Monitor Alert
- Monitor State
- Start Maintenance Mode
- Stop Maintenance Mode
- Update Alert

Configuring Orchestrator Connectivity with System Center 2012 Operations Manager

Here are the required actions to configure Orchestrator connectivity with System Center Operations Manager in the Runbook Designer. Follow these steps:

1. In the Runbook Designer, from the top menu, select **Options** -> **SC 2012 Operations Manager**.
2. In the Microsoft Operations Manager 2012 dialog box, click **Add** and enter the following information, shown in Figure 21.22:
    - **Name:** Name of the Operations Manager management server
    - **Domain:** Domain of the OpsMgr 2012 management server
    - **User name:** AD account with Operations Manager administrator privileges in OpsMgr 2012
    - **Password:** Password for the AD account
3. Use the **Test Connection** button to verify connectivity.

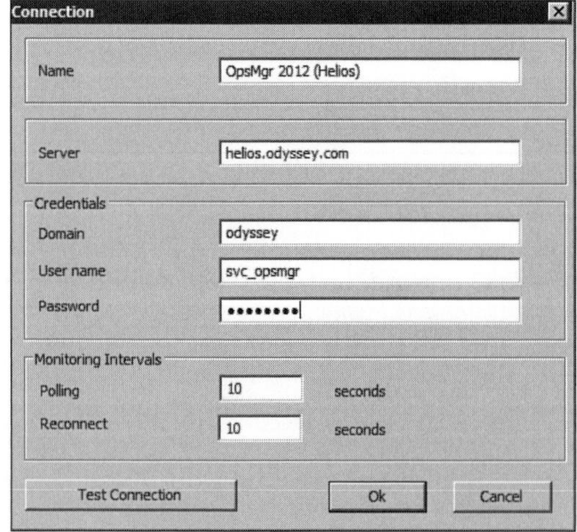

FIGURE 21.22 OpsMgr connection settings in Orchestrator Global Settings.

4. Click **OK** to create the connection.

When complete, the newly created connection in the Operations Manager 2012 dialog box should appear similar to Figure 21.23.

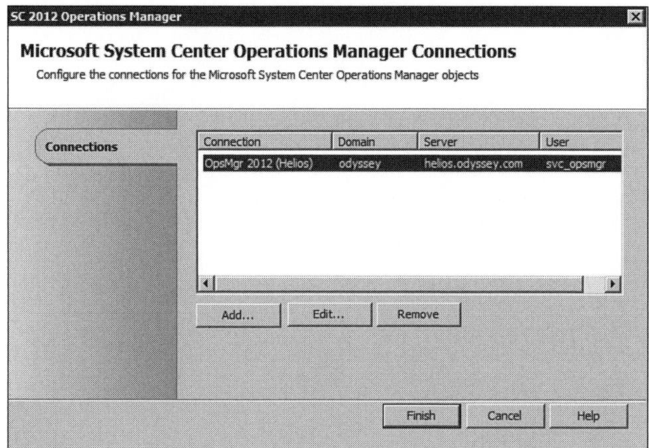

FIGURE 21.23 Click Finish to save the connection settings.

Example: Incident Remediation

This section shows a runbook in Figure 21.24 that automates recovery of a Windows service based on alert detection from a unit monitor in OpsMgr to address the intermittent Windows service failures reported by application owners. Before creating the runbook, you must establish connectivity between Orchestrator and Operations Manager 2012. This was described in the "Configuring Orchestrator Connectivity with System Center 2012 Operations Manager" section.

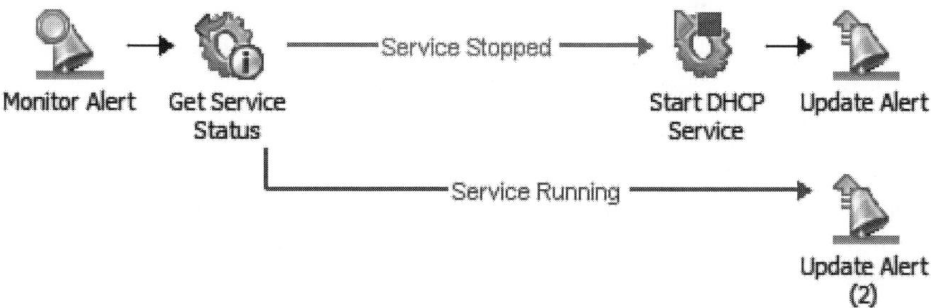

FIGURE 21.24 Sample incident remediation runbook using Operations Manager activities.

Example: Maintenance Mode for Windows or UNIX/Linux Computers

Operations Manager computer maintenance mode in Orchestrator 2012 is a common runbook request. Orchestrator includes native objects to implement computer maintenance mode on demand. Figure 21.25 shows a runbook you can use to stop or start maintenance mode, which can be easily initiated from Service Manager 2010/2012 (or other external source).

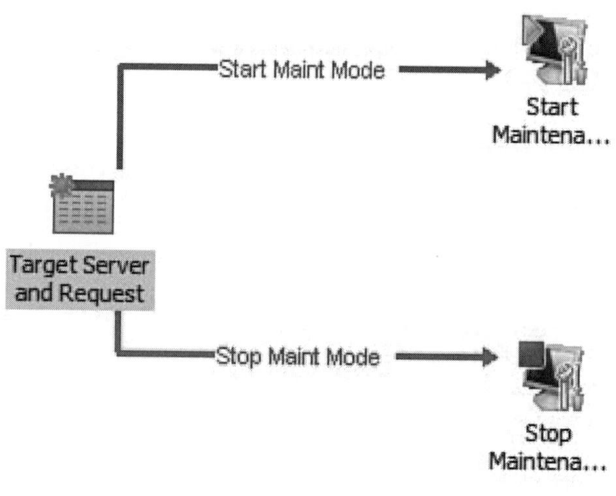

FIGURE 21.25 The integrated maintenance mode runbook.

Forwarding OpsMgr Alerts to/from Third-Party Systems

Larger organizations may have a need to forward OpsMgr alerts to third-party monitoring and management systems to allow presentation of monitoring alerts from multiple systems in a single-in-of-glass, as they tend to have more complex environments and monitoring requirements. Sometimes the request may be reversed, requiring faults in third-party management systems to be forwarded to OpsMgr as the manager of managers for enterprise monitoring.

The third-party connectors available in OpsMgr 2007 R2 (at substantial additional cost in their original incarnation) have been replaced by integration packs in Orchestrator 2012 designed to support forwarding alerts to a number of third-party monitoring systems. You simply need to purchase System Center 2012 licensing for your managed systems.

Integration packs available to facilitate alert forwarding (at the time this book was completed) include

- **HP Operations Manager:** This integration pack enables you to automate the consolidation and correlation of fault and performance events

- **HP Service Manager:** The HP Service Manager integration pack includes activities that enable you to retrieve, create, update, and monitor tickets in HP Service Manager. This integration pack does require you to configure connectivity to the remote HP Service Manager system as documented at http://technet.microsoft.com/en-us/library/hh771464.aspx.
- **IBM Tivoli Netcool/OMNIbus:** This integration pack includes activities that enable you to automate responses to alerts raised within IBM Tivoli Netcool/OMNIbus.
- **VMware vSphere:** This integration pack includes activities that enable you to automate actions in VMware vSphere.

Several additional integration packs are available for Orchestrator 2012 from System Center ISV partner Kelverion, including

- BMC Atrium v7.6
- BMC BladeLogic
- BMC Enterprise Event Manager (BEM) v7.4
- BMC Remedy ARS v7.5, 7.6
- BMC Remedy ARS v7.1
- HP Service Manager
- Service-now.com

These integration packs enable creating automation workflows to manage data forwarding and retrieval between OpsMgr and third-party systems, including

- Event forwarding to/from OpsMgr
- Automatic incident ticket creation in the target system
- Automatic update of the OpsMgr event to record the service desk ticket ID
- Monitoring of the target system for open and/or resolved events or tickets in order to update OpsMgr

The Create Alert and Update Alerts activities in the OpsMgr 2012 integration pack enable you to automate creation, update, and resolution of alerts in OpsMgr based on data retrieved from any of these third-party management systems.

As the list of integration packs shows, there is no integration pack for many third-party management systems. In these cases, you can use native activities in Orchestrator to write OpsMgr alert information to a text or xml file or even a remote database for pickup by the remote monitoring system. Technically, you could even insert information directly into the database of a third-party management system if the vendor supports direct writes to their database. Here are some native activities in Orchestrator that you could leverage in a custom automation workflow:

- **Update Database:** This activity facilitates updating existing records or creating new records in OLE DB compliant databases.
- **Run .Net Script:** This activity facilitates running scripts in Microsoft scripting and programming languages, such as PowerShell, VB.NET, and C#. PowerShell makes it very easy to write information to a variety of file formats (txt, csv, and xml) for retrieval by third-party systems.
- **Text file management activities:** There are a number of native activities that facilitate creation, update, and deletion of text files, including Append Line, Delete Line, Find Text, Read Line, Search and Replace Text, to name a few.

Ultimately, the native integration between OpsMgr and Orchestrator allows Information Technology (IT) Pros to create their own connector frameworks without the need for expensive integration solutions and services. Without the budgetary requirements of traditional third-party or custom integration solutions, more organizations will develop more mature monitoring and management processes.

Maximizing Business Value

While automation may reduce manual effort for IT, to be truly effective it should facilitate greater efficiency in the overall process. It is fine to use Orchestrator to eliminate the need to provision a virtual machine manually, but you want to ensure that speeds the overall time to deliver to the requesting party. If someone had to wait hours, days, or longer for you to get to the ticket, automating a single step of the process misses the point.

To progress runbook automation (RBA) to a truly hands-free process with proper controls (approval workflows) and governance takes more than using Orchestrator; it takes *integration.* This is why Microsoft spends so much time talking about Orchestrator in the context of System Center, but never mentions the capabilities of the component alone versus competitive products. Here's the point: Using Orchestrator in conjunction with System Center delivers an integrated capability not easily achieved with System Center Orchestrator (or any other RBA product) alone.

Bringing It All Together in the Microsoft Private Cloud

Unless you've been hiding under a rock recently, you have likely heard the phrase "cloud computing" more times than you'd care to. One of Microsoft's not-so-secret motives behind the strategic move to realign System Center as components of a single product was to position the suite as part of the Microsoft private cloud solution. Indeed, with the native integration of the suite and its capabilities to monitor and manage heterogeneous virtualization infrastructures, System Center 2012 has made Microsoft's presence felt in the private/hybrid cloud arena.

In spite of all the marketing noise, you may have questions about exactly how a private cloud differs from traditional virtualization, which has been around for well over a decade. This question and more are answered in the next sections.

What the Private Cloud Is

OpsMgr 2012 is a key component of the Microsoft private cloud solution. If you have not yet ventured into the world of the Microsoft private cloud, you may still have a fundamental question that remains to be answered: What this private cloud is actually about.

Private cloud refers to a computing model, not a location. This means that discussion of the private cloud really focuses on the computing model, not the physical location where the cloud may be running. There are a certain set of attributes and characteristics that are fundamental and core to cloud computing. This includes capabilities like the ability to offer a self-service experience so that the application or service owners can perform their own real-time deployment of virtualized services.

Cloud computing builds applications that are able to dynamically expand and contract based on business requirements. Additionally, a cloud is usage-based, meaning that you can track what's being used in terms of storage, compute, network, and charge back (or at least show back) the cost of resources consumed to service owners so the business units understand what the cost is of what they're consuming.

Core Characteristics of the Cloud

Cloud computing is the on-demand delivery of applications as standardized IT services, and inherently has four key attributes that differentiate private cloud from traditional virtualization:

- **Pooled resources:** You will often hear that cloud computing is just big virtualization, which is not the case. Cloud computing uses virtualization, but it adds significantly to virtualization. It pools those resources together and allows you to dynamically provision and scale applications.
- **Self service:** Once you pool your resources, cloud computing provides a self-service way for the business to get at those resources or more specifically by providing self-service IT infrastructure to business units and departments with an SLA. This forces service-level discussion and removes the burden to procure, provision, and manage infrastructure on a per-application, ad-hoc basis.
- **Elastic:** Scale up (or scale down) dynamically as resource needs change, enabling faster delivery of capacity.
- **Usage based:** Paying for only what you use, when you need to use it.

Benefits of the Cloud

For a private cloud solution to make business sense it must have tangible benefits above and beyond that of traditional virtualization. With the Microsoft private cloud solution, there are benefits not only to the organization, but to IT support as well, including

- **Focus:** This is about having more people able to focus on higher-level parts of the stack, managing those applications' SLAs, rolling out new applications, and not having to worry about the underlying infrastructure.

- **Agility:** This is not only about being able to deliver the applications more quickly to your users and to your customers, but also being able to respond to changes in demand. This means the next time the marketing department launches a campaign, does not tell anyone, and the company website infrastructure lacks necessary scalability for increased demand, it's very easy to scale that out quickly to meet abrupt increases in demand.
- **Economics:** Because you are running multiple workloads on the same overall infrastructure, you get better utilization across those applications. Moreover, because the cloud pools together these resources, you can buy broader sets of resources at one time, lowering the overall cost. Therefore, for agility, focus, and economics, you have great motivation to move to the cloud, and those benefits apply to both public and to private cloud computing.

Visualization of Private Cloud Components

There are several elements in OpsMgr to help visualize the health, performance, and configuration of your private cloud. Some of these features may look familiar, but Microsoft has developed new functionality to support new features in VMM 2012. The next sections discuss available views into the health and performance of Microsoft private cloud infrastructures.

Dynamically Generated Distributed Application Models

A VMM service is a group of virtual machines deployed from a specialized template, called a service template. As VMs are deployed to the service, an OpsMgr distributed application model is generated dynamically in OpsMgr (via an internal connector created when you configure OpsMgr/VMM integration, discussed in the "Configuring OpsMgr/VMM Integration" section). The model is updated when VMs are added to or deleted from the service, providing visibility into the current health state of the VMs and the service itself.

Dashboard Views

There are several dashboard views in the VMM MP for OpsMgr 2012, including

- Application Health
- Application Hosts Health
- Cloud Health
- Host Cluster Health
- Host Health
- IP Address Pool Health
- Library Server Health

- Load Balancer Health
- MAC Address Pool Health
- Service Health
- Storage Pool Health
- User Role Health
- Virtual Machine Health
- Virtual Machine Manager Server Health

Monitoring Health, Performance, and Capacity

OpsMgr with the VMM 2012 Management Pack is the best tool for monitoring not only resource performance and utilization in your Microsoft private cloud environment, but capacity as well. The next sections discuss the different ways to obtain this information.

Cloud Fabric Health and Performance

OpsMgr views presenting data on state of the cloud fabric include

- System Center 2012 Virtual Machine Manager Host Parent Partition
- CPU Utilization
- System Center 2012 Virtual Machine Manager Host CPU Utilization
- System Center 2012 Virtual Machine Manager Host Memory Utilization
- System Center 2012 Virtual Machine Manager External Switch Connection
- System Center 2012 Virtual Machine Manager Storage Pool Capacity
- System Center 2012 Virtual Machine Manager VMM Connect Virtual Center

VM Health and Performance

You can gauge the availability and performance health of the VMs in your private cloud with these views:

- System Center 2012 Virtual Machine Manager VM State
- System Center 2012 Virtual Machine Manager VM VGS Installed

Private Cloud Capacity

There are five dimensions of private cloud capacity with the Microsoft solution: CPU count, memory usage, storage utilization, VM count, and quota points. The VMM 2012 management pack for OpsMgr provides both alert-generating workflows and performance collection rules for these metrics:

- System Center 2012 Virtual Machine Manager Cloud CPUUsageCount
- System Center 2012 Virtual Machine Manager Cloud CustomQuotaUsageCount
- System Center 2012 Virtual Machine Manager Cloud MemoryUsageMB
- System Center 2012 Virtual Machine Manager Cloud StorageUsageGB
- System Center 2012 Virtual Machine Manager Cloud VMUsageCount

Private Cloud Reporting

Three common questions that come up when the topic of reporting on private cloud health, performance, and capacity include

- What is the utilization of my private cloud, right now?
- How can I trend my private cloud usage over time?
- How do I forecast future private cloud resource needs?

Usage reporting in a private cloud environment is similar to reporting in traditional virtualization infrastructure.

- You need to report on utilization in the present to identify bottlenecks to performance.
- You need to analyze utilization trends over time to understand the rate of growth in your cloud infrastructure.
- You need to project future growth to forecast future resource needs so you can budget for and procure the necessary equipment.

In a private cloud infrastructure, trending and forecasting are especially important to ensure the cloud infrastructure maintains elasticity—the ability for rapid expansion (sometimes called "cloud bursting"). Likewise, a lack of available resources and the cloud fabric can affect application availability in the event of host failure.

To address these challenges, the VMM 2012 management pack delivers reports for analyzing current capacity and resource utilization in the cloud fabric (storage, network, and compute) and VMs, as well as forecasting reports to help predict future needs. The Chargeback report provides utilization data based on the dimensions of cloud capacity. Here are the reports in the VMM management pack:

- Capacity Utilization
- Chargeback
- Host Group Disk IO Forecasting
- Host Group Disk Space Forecasting

- Host Group Forecasting
- Host Group Memory Usage Forecasting
- Host Group Network IO Forecasting
- Host Utilization
- Host Utilization Group
- Memory Utilization by Virtual Machines on Host
- CPU Utilization by Virtual Machines on Host
- Power Savings
- Resource Utilization by Virtual Machines in Host
- SAN Usage Forecasting
- Virtual Machine Allocation
- Virtualization Candidates

Health, Availability, and Performance Reporting

While there are a many views and reports included in the VMM 2012 MP, you can also report on the availability and performance of virtualization components using the generic Availability and Performance reports in OpsMgr 2012, as mentioned in Chapter 11, "Dashboards, Trending, and Forecasting."

Forecasting (What-If) Reporting

The forecasting reports analyze the historical data to create "what-if" projections of future usage to facilitate planning and budgeting for future infrastructure. This is particularly important in the private cloud environment where users perceive an environment of infinite capacity and 100% availability. Forecasting reports in the VMM 2012 management pack available in OpsMgr include

- Host Group Network IO Forecasting
- SAN Usage Forecasting

Private Cloud Usage Reporting

The integrated reporting feature in Operations Manager 2012 leverages SSRS as the reporting engine, with reporting data in the OpsMgr data warehouse.

You can find the Cloud Usage and Forecasting Reports in the Reporting space in the Operations console in the System Center 2012 Virtual Machine Manager Reports folder. You configure the report using the report parameters. At minimum, you will need to

- Choose the date range (start date earlier than NOW)
- Choose the hosts (Hyper-V, VMware, or Xen)
- Some reports may require selecting the metric (CPU, memory, disk space and IO, and network IO) you wish to include in the report

You can share reports via email or publishing to a share. SSRS supports a variety of document formats including Excel, Word, PDF, and HTML. Resource usage and utilization reports in the VMM 2012 management pack available in Operations Manager include

- Capacity Utilization
- Chargeback
- Host Group Forecasting
- Host Utilization
- Host Utilization Growth
- Power Savings
- SAN Usage Forecasting
- Virtual Machine Allocation
- Virtualization Candidates

Figure 21.26 displays the Host Utilization report.

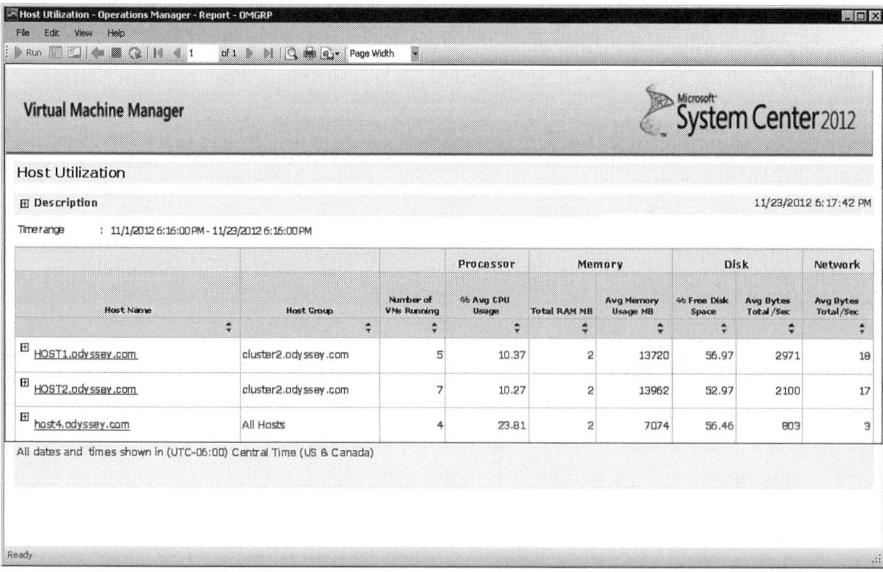

			Processor	Memory		Disk		Network
Host Name	Host Group	Number of VMs Running	% Avg CPU Usage	Total RAM MB	Avg Memory Usage MB	% Free Disk Space	Avg Bytes Total /Sec	Avg Bytes Total/Sec
HOST1.odyssey.com	cluster2.odyssey.com	5	10.37	2	13720	56.97	2971	18
HOST2.odyssey.com	cluster2.odyssey.com	7	10.27	2	13962	52.97	2100	17
host4.odyssey.com	All Hosts	4	23.81	2	7074	56.46	803	3

FIGURE 21.26 Host Utilization report.

Using Chargeback Reporting

Chargeback is a largely ignored topic that is fundamental to Microsoft private cloud operation and management that deserves some attention.

Since the Cloud Services Process Pack is not a solution that fits the bill for all (or even most) Microsoft private cloud deployments, the need arises for an alternate method of calculating resource consumption for business units across one or more clouds as defined in System Center Virtual Machine Manager 2012. This section includes several OpsMgr reports that you can leverage to answer the difficult questions around resource consumption and workload distribution in a private cloud deployment.

The most easily accessible reports actually come in System Center 2012 Operations Manager by way of the VMM management pack for Operations Manager (http://www.microsoft.com/en-us/download/details.aspx?id=29679), which contains a number of reports for tracking the logical and physical consumption of resources in your private cloud fabric (storage, network, and compute). When leveraged appropriately, this can be a good source of show back information for the business units subscribing to resources in your private cloud infrastructure. With native SharePoint integration and flexible delivery options, they can become an easily accessible source of information for stakeholders in your cloud environment who need information but are less familiar with the System Center tools.

The reports available in the VMM 2012 Management Pack for Operations Manager are shown in Figure 21.27.

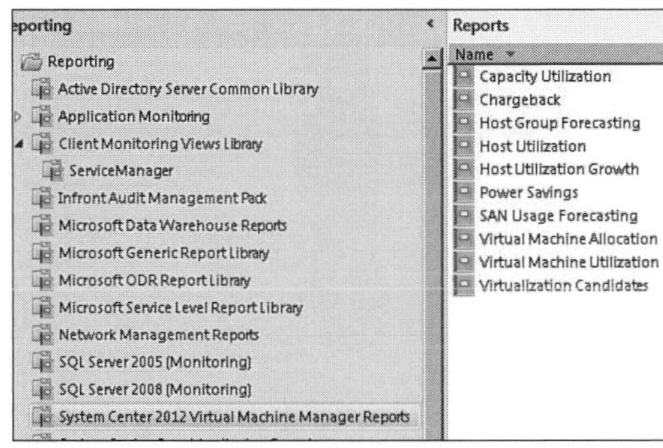

FIGURE 21.27 Available reports in the VMM 2012 management pack.

The parameter header in the Chargeback report, an example of which is shown in Figure 21.28, provides a number of fields that must be completed to provide meaningful results, including

- **Date Range:** The date picker is straightforward. The **First day of previous month** to **Last day of previous month** selection provides a rolling dataset of resource usage in the cloud.

- **Objects:** This is where you can add your virtual machines that are (or were in the past) deployed to the cloud.
- **Billing Units:** You can assign a cost to Memory, CPU, or Base Cost for VM. It is easy to make things too complicated with this setting. The authors recommend that, at least in the first iteration, you pick one of these units for your billing mechanism for chargeback in order to keep the results meaningful. You can add multiple billing units as your organization progresses in its use of chargeback.

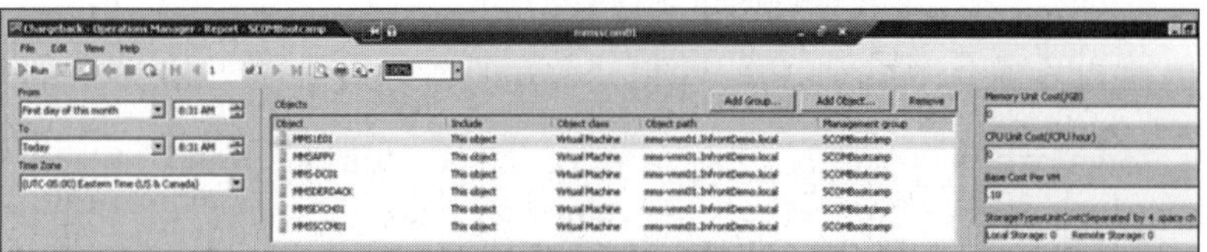

FIGURE 21.28 Smart parameter header in the Chargeback report.

The authors suggest creating a linked report to make this a dynamically populated report. Linked reports are explained in Chapter 22, "Authoring Management Packs and Reports."

The result of a sample report is shown in Figure 21.29, which logically groups infrastructure based on 1) Cloud and 2) Host Group, both of which are logical constructs defined in VMM 2012.

Virtual Machine Manager

Microsoft System Center 2012

Chargeback Report

Description

Billing period : 5/1/2012 8:31:00 AM - 5/25/2012 8:31:00 AM

Total charges : $279.25

Resources and unit costs : Memory $0.00/GB-Hour; CPU $0.00/Hour; VM $0.10/VM-Hour

Cost by resource type

Object(s) selected in report : 6 objects selected in this report

Cloud	HostGroup	Host Name	VM Name	Memory Allocated in GB-Hours	Nos.of CPU-Hours	Storage Allocated in GB-Hours	Base Cost	Total Cost
	Toronto	mms01host.infrontdemo.local	MMSSCCM01	0.00	0.00	420,757.18	25.47	**$25.47**
	Vancouver	mmshost02.infrontdemo.local	MMSAPPV	410.00	205.00	498,014.28	57.60	**$57.60**
			MMS1E01	137.63	184.50	5.34	23.39	**$23.39**
Management Cloud	Toronto	mms01host.infrontdemo.local	MMSDERDACK	1.00	1.00	619,263.90	57.60	**$57.60**
Production Cloud	Toronto	mms01host.infrontdemo.local	MMSEXCH01	1.00	2.00	879,345.54	57.60	**$57.60**
			MMS-DC01	205.50	206.00	545,966.96	57.60	**$57.60**

All dates and times shown in (UTC-05:00) Eastern Time (US & Canada)

FIGURE 21.29 Report content in the Chargeback report.

Even if you don't make this a dynamically populated report, you can save this report under My Favorites, making it a one-click report with the occasional tweak for new infrastructure to edit your cloud settings.

Fast Track

The integration between OpsMgr and other System Center components has evolved considerably in the 2012 product. The following are key differences to explore even if you are experienced with the System Center integration points of OpsMgr 2007 R2:

- OpsMgr 2012 integrates with VMM 2012 in much the same fashion as OpsMgr 2007 R2, with some additional integration to support new features in VMM and Service Manager.
- OpsMgr 2012 and ConfigMgr 2012 integration remains equivalent to that in the 2007-named releases of these components.
- OpsMgr 2012 integrates with Service Manager 2012 via two connectors: one for alerts and the other for extraction of configuration items from OpsMgr.
- Orchestrator 2012 includes an integration pack containing activities that facilitate script-free automation with Operations Manager for alert processing and automation of object or group maintenance mode.

Summary

This chapter described some of the key integration points of OpsMgr 2012 and other System Center 2012 components, as well as the role of OpsMgr in a System Center-integrated Microsoft private cloud infrastructure.

The next chapter covers management pack authoring concepts in OpsMgr 2012 in depth.

CHAPTER 22

Authoring Management Packs and Reports

IN THIS CHAPTER

A frequently asked question by new System Center Operations Manager administrators is *how does one author their own management packs*? This question is then extended to include *does that change with Operations Manager (OpsMgr) 2012?* Here's the answer: There are no real changes regarding authoring; all best practices and lessons learned are still relevant. Your existing skills can be used to build management packs in OpsMgr 2012. The real change in OpsMgr 2012 authoring is the tools available to build custom management packs.

Although Microsoft has worked to improve the authoring experience by offering two new authoring tools—one for less experienced users and one for advanced users—there is still a considerable amount to learn when authoring management packs. As a management pack author, it is crucial that you understand the basics; otherwise your management pack will almost certainly end up noisy and require tuning or rewriting.

This chapter discusses best practices for authoring and building custom management packs. It facilitates your designing a custom management pack complete with a class model, monitors, rules, and views, using the tools provided with OpsMgr 2012.

Authoring Concepts

Understanding the concepts and framework OpsMgr uses helps you write high-quality management packs and gives you a solid base to build upon. As this is often the most challenging part for those new to OpsMgr, the authors provide several examples to assist with clarifying those concepts. Chapter 3, "Looking Inside OpsMgr," explains the notion of a health model using examples of body parts; this chapter utilizes car components and discusses the process of creating a management pack to monitor a car with OpsMgr.

ABOUT THE CAR MANAGEMENT PACK

Although the car management pack used in this chapter is purely theoretical, it is not as futuristic as it may sound. Cars already have built-in computers that run an operating system (OS). When you go to a garage to service your car, the first thing the attendant does is connect it to a laptop to check its status. Some models even automatically call to schedule an appointment to replace a malfunctioning part; this is very proactive monitoring!

All that is required is a wireless connection within the car and an agent. The example used in this chapter has a connection to the management group and an agent installed in the car. A management pack author can monitor just about anything once there is a connection to a management group.

The next sections discuss management pack design and understanding related concepts.

Using Classes

Start by understanding the concept of a *class*. This is the basic component within OpsMgr, and the first component required when you begin writing a management pack. Each class is unique, is a definition of an object, and defines the properties of an object (an instance of a particular class). Here are the types of classes in OpsMgr:

- **Abstract class:** This class exists as a base class. This is used only for base classes.
- **Hosted class:** This class has a parent to child relationship. The child cannot exist without its parent or host.
- **Singleton class:** This class is single, so there can only be one instance of a (single) singleton class in your OpsMgr environment. An example of a singleton class is a group.

OpsMgr itself contains several base classes; these are defined in the system libraries created when Operations Manager is installed. These classes are abstract, meaning they only exist as a base or reference. You can use them to write and develop your own classes, which are based upon these base classes.

The entire infrastructure of OpsMgr is based on classes. All classes eventually lead up to the root class, which is the core of OpsMgr. The root class in OpsMgr may be referred to as an *object*.

NOTE: TERMINOLOGY CHANGE TO ROOT CLASS

In OpsMgr 2007 the root class was called an *entity*. This was renamed to object in OpsMgr 2012. When there are references to the root class, the word *object* is used rather than entity.

The OpsMgr 2007 health model is built from a developer's point of view, where classes and instances are commonly used and are the basis of developing an application. Many terms used throughout authoring and OpsMgr are derived from well-known developers' terms, which can make it confusing when determining the correct terminology to use. Microsoft tightened up the verbiage in OpsMgr 2012 to be clearer about what is meant when referring to classes, instances, and objects: Think of a class as a definition of an existing object, and references to an object as the same as to an instance.

Use the example in Figure 22.1 to understand the concept of classes and instances. This figure shows all the different classes and definitions and how they relate to the car example used in this chapter. The classes shown are the classes represented in a management pack. Figure 22.2 shows the results when you import a management pack and discoveries have run to discover the instances of the classes, along with the discovered class instance and its discovered properties.

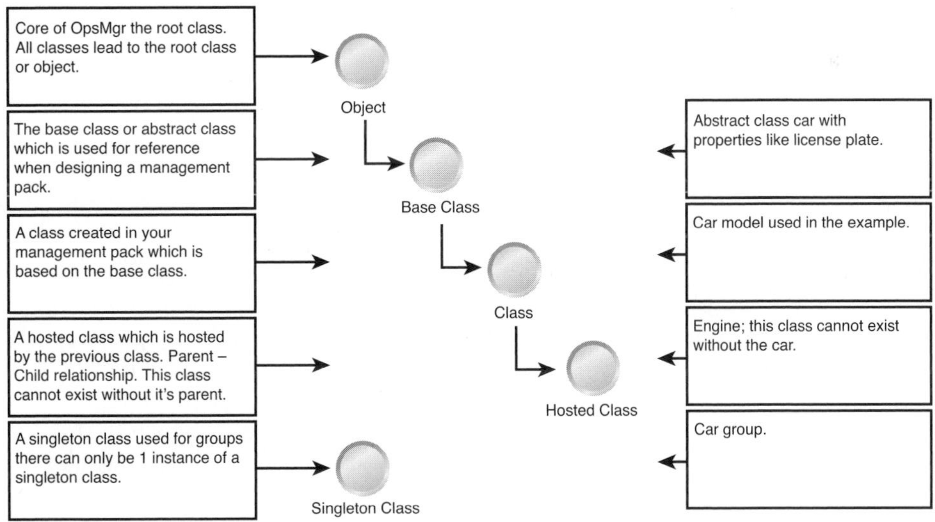

FIGURE 22.1 Classes example.

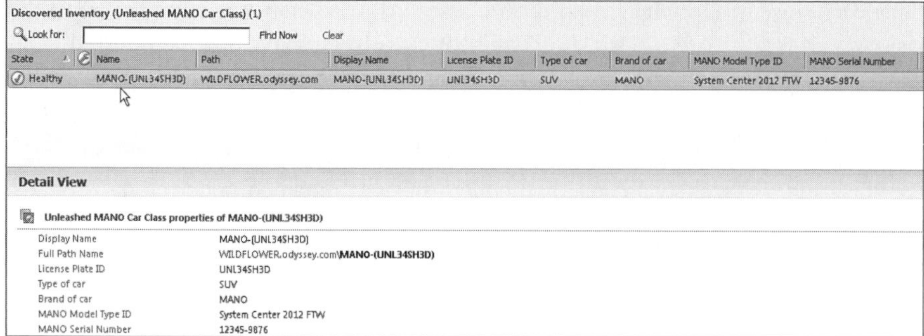

FIGURE 22.2 Discovered instance of a class.

About Relationships

How classes relate to each other depends on the relationship between those classes. Here are the three different relationships known in OpsMgr:

- **Hosting relationship:** A relationship from one to many. This is a parent-child relationship where the child cannot exist without its parent. Once the parent does not exist in OpsMgr, the hosted class is deleted, as it cannot exist without its parent.
- **Containment relationship:** This could be a one-to-many or a many-to-many relationship. The containment relationship is less restrictive than the hosting relationship.
- **Reference relationship:** An aggregate monitor for rolling up the performance health of a class.

The hosting relationship is used with a hosted class; it is defined when a class cannot exist without its parent class. A hosting relationship is actually a specialized containment relationship. The example in Figure 22.3 shows a hosting class and a hosting relationship: A gas tank cannot drive without an engine, and an engine cannot drive without a car. A hosting relationship always has one parent. In this example, one gas tank cannot have multiple engines, and an engine cannot run in multiple cars.

When using hosted classes and the hosting relationship, you must have a key property on the parent class. The key property defines the uniqueness of the parent. Figure 22.3 shows the properties of the parent class and the hosted class and the key property. If the parent class were not unique, you could not tell what class is hosting which hosted classes. Choosing the correct and unique key property for your class is crucial. Consider the following example:

Say you are using an incorrect property as the key property, such as car model. This is not unique to a specific car, as there will be numerous cars with the same model number. When you import your management pack, it discovers the cars and components. However, if you use an incorrect key property (such as car model), the unwanted result is every car discovered is not unique and therefore all hosted classes and components are discovered on every parent class. The result is each car has several engines, numerous gas tanks, and so on.

This occurs because the parent is not unique and is an incorrect key property, and every component discovered is placed in a hosting class underneath the parent. As this is not the wanted result, choose your key property carefully.

Before writing a management pack, you should understand the concept of the health model, discussed in the next section.

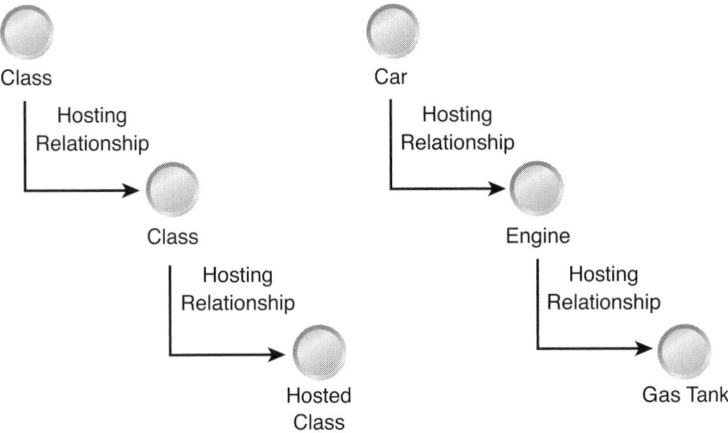

FIGURE 22.3 Hosting class and hosting relationship.

Health Model

OpsMgr is built around the health model, which is used by every class in OpsMgr and should be your starting point when writing management packs. The health model is divided into four components that make up the health of any class within OpsMgr:

- **Availability health:** A monitor for rolling up the availability health of a class.
- **Configuration health:** A monitor for rolling up the configuration health of a class.
- **Performance health:** A monitor for rolling up the performance health of a class.
- **Security health:** A monitor for rolling up the performance health of a class.

Health of an object in OpsMgr is always calculated based on these four components.

Figure 22.4 shows how health is calculated based upon the health model.

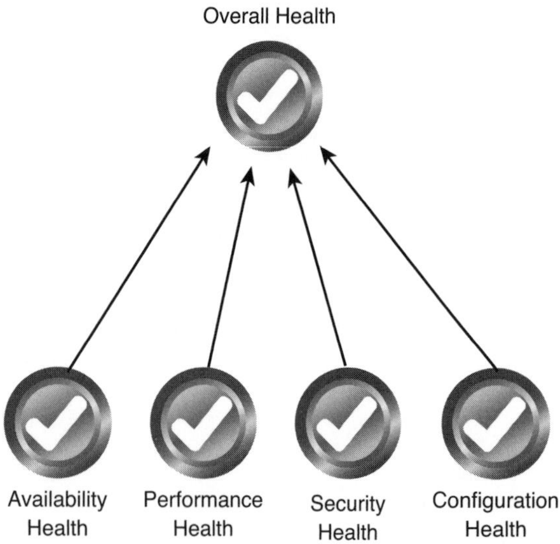

FIGURE 22.4 Health model.

Health Rollup

To make full usage of the health model in OpsMgr, you should be aware of the different types of monitors. As discussed in Chapter 14, "Monitoring with System Center 2012 Operations Manager," there are three types of monitors used in OpsMgr:

- **Aggregate monitors:** This type of monitor is used to roll up health of multiple unit or aggregate monitors for a class. Aggregate monitors are only used to roll up health; they do not monitor components by themselves.
- **Unit monitors:** Unit monitors are used to detect the state of a component. They detect the state of a particular component of a class, resulting in a healthy or unhealthy state.
- **Dependency monitors:** This type of monitor is used to roll up health between classes. It is only used to roll up the health state from one class to another class that depends on it.

Become familiar with these different monitor types and when each is used. The examples in this chapter will show how all components fit together, providing a more real world experience.

Getting Started with Authoring

Once you understand authoring concepts, the next step is gathering information about the application or device you want to monitor. This step is the most crucial in the entire process. Here's why:

Management pack authoring is similar to developing an application. Not only is the health model based on models used by developers, the process before developing a management pack is similar to that when writing an application. This means you should start by gathering monitoring requirements and designing a model before beginning to write the actual management pack.

Inexperienced management pack authors will often simply open up the authoring tools and start designing classes, discoveries, rules, monitors, and so on. Although this might work and can speed up the initial process, the result is a poorly designed management pack that could be a risk for your environment. More importantly, you have a beast of a management pack that does it all and more, but without clearly pointing out the health state of an application or service. The next section discusses approaches to streamline the design phase and avoid creating a poorly designed management pack.

Identifying Monitoring Requirements for the Application

As a management pack author, you must be more than an XML (eXtended Markup Language) "freak"; you need to identify the monitoring requirements of an application or service. This means being able to identify requirements and map them to the OpsMgr health model. Meet with your stakeholders; they have the information you require to develop the management pack. Those individuals working with the application daily at a technical and functional level are your starting point for determining design requirements. Be sure you understand their requirements and can clearly identify the components for the application.

Even when you identify those individuals responsible for the application, it could be difficult to get the information you need. This is because applications people tend to look only at the application itself, which is understandable as this is what they are responsible for and work with daily. The trick is identifying from their perspective what comprises the application—on both a functional and technical level:

- **Understanding functional requirements:** To understand the application at a functional level, work with someone familiar with its scope. He should be able to discuss bottlenecks and problems, and know exactly how the data runs through the application. Collect this information and feedback, preferably using a Visio diagram that will help you easily identify the components and dataflow. After designing the diagram, double-check your findings with the user to verify you have captured exactly how it runs.

- **Determining technical needs:** With the application identified at a functional level, talk with the technical individual(s) administering the application. He should be able to pinpoint the exact components crucial to the application. Again, make Visio diagrams of the application and follow the same process. Additionally, do not forget to talk to the Information Technology (IT) professionals responsible for the infrastructure. You might be surprised at the different way they look at the application and which components they consider crucial.

This process should give you a clear view of how the application runs and of those application components comprising the application. Combine your findings into a single Visio diagram, filtering out known components such as databases (Microsoft SQL Server, Oracle, and so on), websites (IIS, Apache), base operating systems, and such, as these should already be monitored by preexisting OpsMgr management packs. You may be able to create a distributed application without hard-core authoring by using views from existing management packs to deliver exactly what your users want. Should you discover gaps in the application that are not currently monitored, proceed with the next phase: identifying the monitoring requirements.

Identifying Monitoring Requirements for Each Component

Identifying the monitoring requirements for each component can be challenging, as not every application is designed for monitoring. This can be particularly true for in-house developed applications.

Applications typically produce a large log file with informational events. In-house developers often write everything in one executable that does everything, but without a way to separate components or determine what is occurring in that executable. This is because the application is designed and written to accomplish a particular function and nothing more. While a single executable should not be a problem, the monitoring challenge is determining which parts of the application are functional and running. The result is often a single service monitor that checks whether the service is running. Should the service fail, the developer is asked to troubleshoot the application with debugger tools. This is a time-consuming process; it would be preferable for the developer to include some checks that determine which parts of the application are running, or generate an event when the application logs critical errors. You cannot monitor a component for problems if it is not creating or logging events that you can check.

The advantage of an in-house application is you can talk with the developers directly and discuss what to build into the application to monitor it properly. Share your Visio diagrams and explain those parts of the application already monitored with existing management packs. Ask them to identify their expectations for the management pack. Give examples of services built into OpsMgr to illustrate what is achievable.

You will discover the various stakeholders have different expectations.

- A functional-oriented or service level agreement (SLA)-responsible individual is accountable for availability and not interested in Windows services, disk space, memory, CPU, and so on. This individual only wants to know if users can use the application; thus creating a high-level distributed application that only shows the components of interest is often adequate.
- Technical persons look at monitoring more proactively than do functionally oriented individuals; they will want to drill down to every component in a distributed application.

These requirements often differ from each other, necessitating additional views or dashboards. You may decide to create multiple distributed applications (DAs) in your management pack; this can be a preferred approach for reporting on availability and uptime. (Distributed applications are introduced in Chapter 18, "Distributed Applications.")

Let's return to discussing the monitoring requirements and obtaining the relevant information. For each component in your Visio diagrams, ask whether the component is significant and whether it requires monitoring. If so, what can be checked to monitor the component—services, processes, performance, or events? Avoid questions such as *What do you want to monitor?* While OpsMgr can monitor almost anything, that does not present a sophisticated overview on how to monitor the application. Put your stakeholders in the driver's seat; they are the ones who will use the management pack. Here are examples of questions you could ask:

- How does the application run?
- What does the end user expect to occur with the application?
- What services are running for the component?
- Are processes involved?
- Do you know of performance counters that could be of interest?
- How does the application perform logging? Does it log errors, or only informational events?
- Does the application currently log events in the Windows event logs?
- How can you tell the application is failing or know when it is about to fail?
- Have you experienced any significant outages for the application recently? Could these be detected, or avoided?
- How do you think the application can be monitored effectively?

The answers to these questions should provide guidance on designing the management pack and defining its components. Confirming components can easily be monitored often triggers a stakeholder's interest. Here are some considerations of which to be aware:

- You may determine that while a stakeholder can define a component and tell you it is crucial, that component cannot be monitored or discovered. This is usually caused by a misunderstanding between the technical and functional requirements of an application or an overlap between components.
- Discovering and collecting information for an application is useless when there are no monitors or you are collecting data only because it exists. Information must be usable to be valuable, or the result is a repository of all events ocurring in your environment. As this is not wanted and generally useless, you should be clear about what to collect and more importantly, why to collect it.

There is one last step before writing the management pack after you clarify and document the monitoring requirements: Verify the components in your Visio diagram are discoverable. This can be difficult for inexperienced authors. You must be able to discover the class and its relationship. You may determine you need to skip a component because it is too abstract and cannot be discovered easily. Hosted classes may also be an issue; you can only create a hosted class if the parent has a key property and you can discover the key property in your discovery. Absence of these can require redesigning your model.

When your model is finalized and complete with relationships and monitoring requirements, have your stakeholders sign-off on the design. This should give you a solid document for building your management pack and ensure its development will comply with your customers' demands.

Writing the Management Pack

With your design document accepted, you can start writing the actual management pack. This part of the chapter steps through the process of creating the entire management pack including classes, discoveries, monitors, rules, views, and reporting.

To write a management pack, you must decide which tools to use. OpsMgr 2012 has two new tools for writing management packs (in addition to the OpsMgr 2007 R2 authoring resource kit and regular XML editors); these are described and compared through the remainder of the chapter:

- **Visio MP Designer:** This tool is discussed in the beginner sections of the chapter. The Visio MP Designer is an add-on to Microsoft Visio 2010 that lets you write a management pack using Visio 2010. This tool, which is limited to a basic subset of rules and monitors, is for less experienced users.
- **Visual Studio:** Advanced sections describe creating a management pack using Visual Studio. The Visual Studio Authoring Extensions are an add-on to Visual Studio 2010 and provide numerous ways to create a management pack. This tool is for experienced authors and has a high learning curve.

Before writing the management packs used in the examples, you must first install Visio 2010 Premium Service Pack (SP) 1 and/or Visual Studio 2010; then install the extensions. Here's how:

- The System Center 2012 Visio MP Designer is available at http://www.microsoft.com/en-us/download/details.aspx?id=30170. Installation instructions are at the TechNet Wiki, http://social.technet.microsoft.com/wiki/contents/articles/6936.installing-the-visio-management-pack-designer.aspx.
- Download the System Center 2012 Visual Studio Authoring Extensions from http://www.microsoft.com/en-us/download/details.aspx?id=30169. You can find the

installation instructions at the TechNet Wiki, http://social.technet.microsoft.com/wiki/contents/articles/5236.visual-studio-authoring-extensions-for-system-center-2012-operations-manager-en-us.aspx.

Ensure you have access to a system with the Operations Manager agent installed and ready for testing. Chapter 8, "Installing and Configuring Agents," includes information on installing the OpsMgr agent.

To complete the examples in this chapter, you will need three files, available as online content with this book. See Appendix E, "Available Online," for information on using these files. The example is based on a fictional car brand called MANO, which is a new model capable of running an OpsMgr agent.

Creating Classes

The first component required for your management pack is the class model, described in the next sections, starting with the beginner level discussion intended for less experienced users.

Classes (Beginner)

The less experienced user will use the Visio MP Designer tool to create a management pack. After installing the Visio add-on, you can begin to create a new management pack, starting with the class model. Follow these steps:

1. Open Visio 2010, and select **File -> New**. Select from **Template Categories -> Software and Database -> System Center Operations Manager Core Monitoring Management Pack**. This opens the management pack template, including all shapes.
2. Select the left top shape, which is the box and hammer; the shape data box should now be visible. If not, right-click the shape and select **Data -> Shape Data** to show the shape data. Fill in the shape data as shown in Table 22.1.

TABLE 22.1 Management pack shape data

Field	Value
Management Pack Name	Unleashed MANO Car Visio Management Pack
Id	Unleashed.MANO.Car.Visio.Management.Pack
Description	Unleashed MANO Car Visio Generated MP
Version	1.0.0.0
Windows Version	All
Connector Mode	False

CAUTION: CONNECTOR MODE DEFAULT

The connector mode, listed in Table 22.1, is set to true by default, which means the tool will generate a connector management pack. Change this to false, since you want to generate a monitoring management pack.

After adding the management pack template and naming the management pack, you can add shapes manually or use preconfigured patterns, known as MP Modeling Single Server Patterns. For the Car management pack, you could use the Server Role with Component model. This example does not use a pattern; the management pack will be built from scratch. For a full pattern overview, see the TechNet wiki at http://social.technet.microsoft.com/wiki/contents/articles/6939.pattern-reference-for-visio-management-pack-designer.aspx.

3. From MP Modeling, drag and drop the server role into your drawing. Fill in the shape data as listed in Table 22.2.

TABLE 22.2 Server role shape data

Field	Value
Name	MANO Car
How To Find	HKLM Registry Key
HKLM Registry Path	Software\Unleashed Car\MANO
Affect Computer Health	False
RunOn	Always

4. After creating the MANO server role, add the server components. Drag and drop the server component on top of the Server Role component to add the connection to the server role. Fill in the shape data as listed in Table 22.3.

TABLE 22.3 Server component engine shape data

Field	Value
Name	MANO Engine
How To Find	HKLM Registry Key
HKLM Registry Path	Software\Unleashed Car\MANO\Engine
RunOn	Always
Affect Computer Health	False

5. Add the gas tank by dragging and dropping a server component on top of the engine server component. Fill in the shape data as listed in Table 22.4.

TABLE 22.4 Server component gas tank shape data

Field	Value
Name	MANO Gas Tank
How To Find	HKLM Registry Key
HKLM Registry Path	Software\Unleashed Car\MANO\GasTank
RunOn	Always
Affect Computer Health	False

You have completed the health or class model for the Unleashed Car management pack. Your Visio drawing should look similar to Figure 22.5.

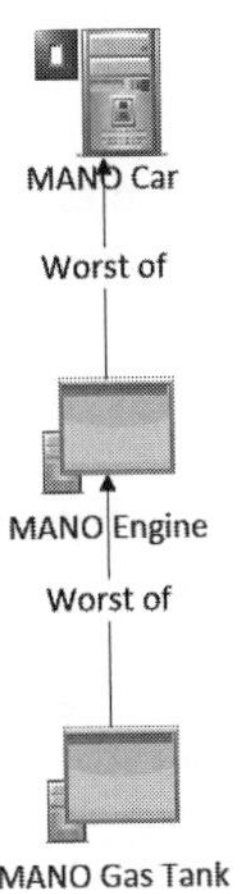

FIGURE 22.5 Visio MP Designer class model.

After creating the class model, you could generate the management pack and test it to verify all components are discovered as expected. The Visio MP Designer automatically creates the classes and discoveries as configured. It also creates an alerts view and state views for your classes. You are now ready to create monitors and rules to monitor the MANO car and finish your management pack.

Classes (Advanced)

Given the case of creating a management pack with the Visio MP Designer, why use the Visual Studio Extensions with Visual Studio to write a management pack in XML? Your decision will be based on your knowledge of management pack authoring and the management pack's requirements. There are numerous reasons to create a management pack in Visual Studio, as its capabilities are virtually infinite. Table 22.5 compares the options using the Car example.

TABLE 22.5 Creating classes in Visio versus Visual Studio

Component	Visio	Visual Studio

Base class	Limited to the same base classes:
	`Microsoft.Windows.LocalApplication`
	`Microsoft.Windows.ApplicationComponent.`
		You can to choose your base classes or create classes.
		You can write custom classes including class properties, and are not restricted to only using the local application class or application component class.

Class Displayname	Display Name of the classes will always be preconfigured and a combination of class name and computer principal name.	Display Name can be configured as desired. Use when you want to create a display name other than *<classname>* (*<principalname>*).
Class properties	Class properties are not used and there is no option to add them to your class.	Additional class properties are configurable. Use when you want to discover properties other than the display name or need to create your own class with key properties.
Class Discoveries	Discoveries possible: Registry key existence Registry value existence WMI query Server role.	All discovery methods can be used. Use when the class cannot be discovered by registry, WMI, or server role; such as script-based discoveries or to create custom discovery data sources.
Class relationships	Preconfigured relationships between components.	Define any relationship between classes. Use when you want to create relationships between classes with custom key properties.

Meeting one or more of the requirements listed in the Visio Studio column in Table 22.5 indicates you should create the management pack with Visual Studio.

This section uses Visio Studio to include base classes and their relationships, configured in a base or library management pack. The MANO car specific classes, discoveries, monitors, and rules are configured in a management pack specific to the MANO car. The first part of writing a management pack is creating a new project and adding the classes and their relationships to the project, based on your management pack design. Follow these steps:

1. In Visual Studio, select **File** -> **New** -> **Project** and select **Management Pack** -> **Operations Manager Core Monitoring Management Pack**. Name the project, select a location to save the project, and give it a friendly name, as shown in Figure 22.6.

2. Right-click **OpsMgr.Unleashed.Car.Example.Library**. Select **Add** -> **New Folder** and name the folder **Classes**. Right-click this folder and select **Add** -> **New Item**; then choose **Class**. Rename the class to **Unleashed.Vehicle.mpx** and add the class to the project.

TIP: ADD FOLDERS FOR EASY NAVIGATION

For easy navigation in your project, you could add extra folders such as classes, relationships, discoveries, rules, and monitors. These let you navigate to the components you are looking for in your management pack. You could also name your classes and relationships as the IDs in the management pack. Looking at a large MP is easier when you use folders and naming conventions.

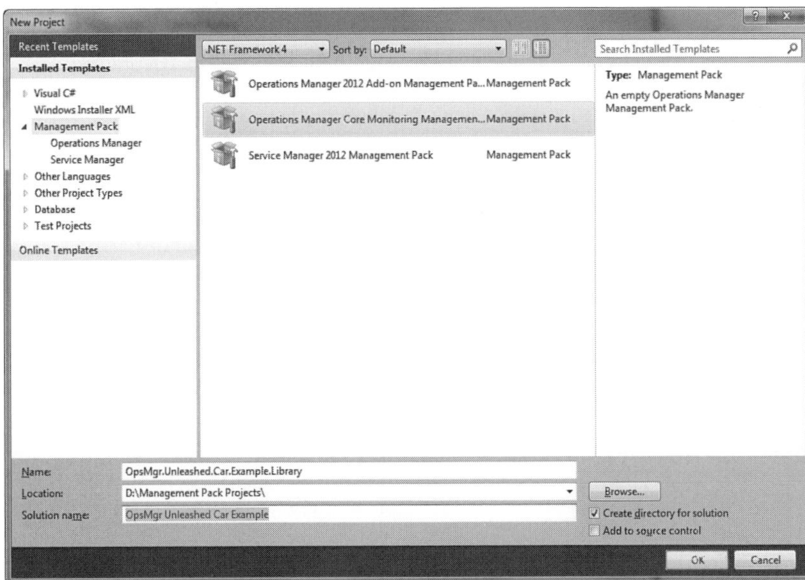

FIGURE 22.6 Creating a project.

After you create the class, the XML section opens automatically. This section contains some preconfigured settings. Edit these settings to create the class according to your needs. The Visual Studio editor has informational sections in green that explain the settings, giving you guidance on using them.

TIP: VISUAL STUDIO INTELLISENSE

A great feature of Visual Studio is Intellisense, which lets you choose from predefined settings. When you start writing XML, you can trigger Intellisense by holding the Ctrl key and pressing the space bar. With Intellisense activated, you can choose the XML components or linked classes you want to use. This makes it easier to author the XML sections.

3. Edit the XML sections with the properties in Table 22.6. To edit these sections using Intellisense, remove the existing value between "", place your cursor between the "", and use Ctrl and the space bar to trigger Intellisense as in the example shown in Figure 22.7.

TABLE 22.6 Unleashed vehicle class

Field	Value
ClassType ID	OpsMgr.Unleashed.Car.Example.Library.Unleashed.Vehicle
Base	System!System.LogicalEntity
Accessibility	Public
Abstract	true
Hosted	false
Singleton	false
DisplayString ElementID	OpsMgr.Unleashed.Car.Example.Library.Unleashed.Vehicle
DisplayString Name	Unleashed Vehicle Base Class
DisplayString Description	A base class representing vehicles

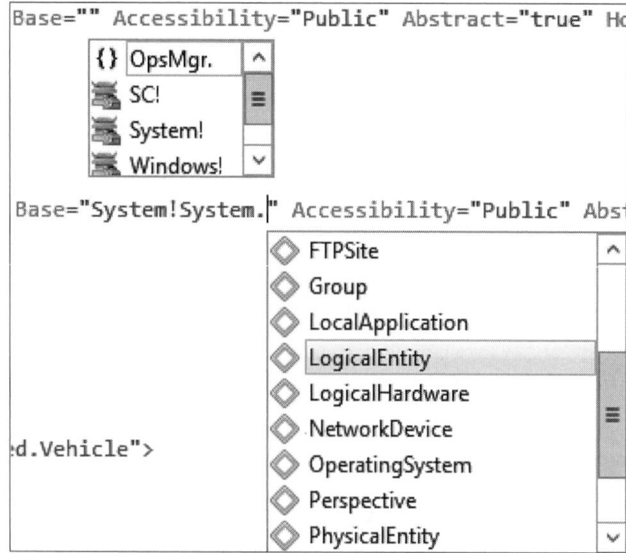

FIGURE 22.7 Intellisense in action.

TIP: COMBINING 2007 AUTHORING WITH 2012 AUTHORING

When writing a management pack in Visual Studio, you will notice Intellisense does not let you specify which values to use. For example, when you look at the registry attributes for the sample management pack, you cannot determine what PathType stands for or if it should have a value of 0 or 1. Looking up these values requires a substantial amount of effort (see the Authoring guide at http://technet.microsoft.com/en-us/library/hh457564.aspx), and writing the expressions can be difficult.

The OpsMgr 2007 R2 authoring console included wizards to help you create these settings, eliminating the need to write the expression in XML or learning 0's and 1's and their meaning. You can still use this tool; install it and follow these steps:

1. In the OpsMgr 2007 authoring console, create a bogus management pack, add a reference to the sealed management pack OpsMgr.Unleashed.Car.Example.Library.mp, and rename the management pack to the same alias as in Visual Studio, **UnleashedCarLibrary**.
2. Add a registry-based discovery to the pack, fill in all the settings required for the MANO Car class, complete the wizard, and save the discovery.
3. Now open the newly created discovery rule in the 2007 R2 Authoring console, navigate to the Configuration tab, and click **Edit** to open the configuration section of the rule in an external editor such as Notepad. Copy the contents and paste them into the data source configuration in Visual Studio, giving you the XML without writing any XML code.

This is an easier approach when designing multiple registry attributes or writing difficult expressions. Using both tools makes learning Visual Studio easier, as you can use the OpsMgr 2007 R2 Authoring console to create expressions for use in Visual Studio. Keep both tools to reference and improve your Visual Studio XML-based authoring skills.

4. Create the Unleashed.Vehicle.Car class with the properties listed in Table 22.7. Add a new class as in the previous step, but now add the class properties as well.

TABLE 22.7 Unleashed vehicle car class

Field	Value
ClassType ID	OpsMgr.Unleashed.Car.Example.Library.Unleashed.Vehicle.Car
Base	OpsMgr.Unleashed.Car.Example.Library.Unleashed.Vehicle
Accessibility	Public
Abstract	False
Hosted	True
Singleton	False
Property ID	LicenseID
Key	True
Type	String
Property ID	Type
Key	False
Type	String
Property ID	Brand

TABLE 22.7 Continued

Field	Value
Key	False
Type	String
DisplayString ElementID	OpsMgr.Unleashed.Car.Example.Library.Unleashed.Vehicle.Car
DisplayString Name	Unleashed Car Base Class
DisplayString Description	Base Class for a car. All car management packs will depend on this base class.
DisplayString ElementID	OpsMgr.Unleashed.Car.Example.Library.Unleashed.Vehicle.Car
DisplayString SubElementID	LicenseID
DisplayString Name	License Plate ID
DisplayString Description	This is the unique key property of a car.
DisplayString ElementID	OpsMgr.Unleashed.Car.Example.Library.Unleashed.Vehicle.Car
DisplayString SubElementID	Type
DisplayString Name	Type of car
DisplayString Description	Which type of car
DisplayString ElementID	OpsMgr.Unleashed.Car.Example.Library.Unleashed.Vehicle.Car
DisplayString SubElementID	Brand
DisplayString Name	Brand of car
DisplayString Description	Which brand of car

TIP: DISPLAY STRINGS IN MANAGEMENT PACKS IN SYSTEM CENTER 2012

OpsMgr 2012 and Service Manager 2012 management packs include display strings, contained in language packs. These are the display strings visible when looking at components in the console. Choose these wisely, as this is what the user sees when looking at alerts or other text. A best practice is including a description with a meaningful name so the operator understands what he is looking at.

The display settings in a management pack have a section called <LanguagePacks> with a default set to ENU (English). In addition to the default language settings, you can also change the display strings in other languages. For reference, see http://blogs.technet.com/b/servicemanager/archive/2009/07/24/localizing-management-pack-content.aspx. Although this article discusses System Center Service Manager, the language settings are identical to OpsMgr.

5. Create base classes for the Unleashed Engine, Unleashed Gas Tank components. Table 22.8 shows the names and properties for the base classes, and Table 22.9 lists the configuration for each.

TABLE 22.8 Unleashed car base classes properties

Name	Key Property	Property	Property
Unleashed.Vehicle.Car.Engine	Serial	Brand	Size
Unleashed.Vehicle.Car.Gas	Serial	Brand	Size

TABLE 22.9 Unleashed car base classes configuration

Name	Accessibility	Abstract	Hosted
Unleashed.Vehicle.Car.Engine	Public	true	true
Unleashed.Vehicle.Car.Gas	Public	true	true

After creating all classes, your management pack should look similar to Figure 22.8.

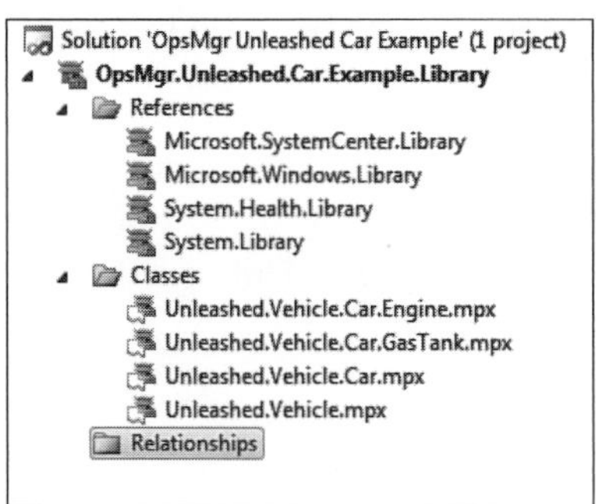

FIGURE 22.8 Base classes for the car management pack.

The management pack just created contains the base classes for a car. Although you could select existing base classes, OpsMgr does not include base classes appropriate for use in the car management pack.

After creating the classes, create the relationships between those classes. Since there are three hosted classes, create three hosting relationships. Perform the following steps:

1. Create a Relationships folder as shown in Figure 22.8. Right-click the Relationships folder in your OpsMgr.Unleashed.Car.Example.Library project and select **Add -> New Item**; then choose **Relationship**. Rename the relationship **Microsoft.Windows.Computer.Hosts.Unleashed.Vehicle.Car** and add the relationship to the project.

2. Edit the XML to include a proper ID, source class, target class, and display string as listed in Table 22.10.

TABLE 22.10 Unleashed relationships

Field	Value
RelationshipType ID	OpsMgr.Unleashed.Car.Example.Library.Microsoft.Windows.Computer.Hosts.Unleashed.Vehicle.Car
Base	System!System.Hosting
Accessibility	Public
Source	Windows!Microsoft.Windows.Computer
Target	OpsMgr.Unleashed.Car.Example.Library.Unleashed.Vehicle.Car
DisplayString ElementID	OpsMgr.Unleashed.Car.Example.Library.Microsoft.Windows.Computer.Hosts.Unleashed.Vehicle.Car
DisplayString Name	Windows Computer Hosts Unleashed Car Relationship
DisplayString Description	Hosting Relationship for Windows Computer Hosting a Car

3. Add the other two relationships based on the information shown here. Do not forget to add the display strings and follow the same procedure as in steps 1-2 for the Windows Computer Hosts Unleashed Car Relationship.

Unleashed Car Hosts Unleashed Car Engine Relationship:

- **RelationshipTypeID:** OpsMgr.Unleashed.Car.Example.Library.Unleashed.Vehicle.Car.Hosts.Unleashed.Vehicle.Car
- **Base:** System!System.Hosting
- **Source:** OpsMgr.Unleashed.Car.Example.Library.Unleashed.Vehicle.Car
- **Target:** OpsMgr.Unleashed.Car.Example.Library.Unleashed.Vehicle.Car.Engine

Unleashed Car Engine Hosts Unleashed Car GasTank:

- **RelationshipTypeID:** OpsMgr.Unleashed.Car.Example.Library.Unleashed.Vehicle.Car.Engine.Hosts.Unleashed.Vehicle.Car.GasTank
- **Base:** System!System.Hosting
- **Source:** OpsMgr.Unleashed.Car.Example.Library.Unleashed.Vehicle.Car.Engine
- **Target:** OpsMgr.Unleashed.Car.Example.Library.Unleashed.Vehicle.Car.GasTank

NOTE: ABOUT LIBRARY AND BASE MANAGEMENT PACKS

A base management pack or library is a management pack containing base components such as classes and relationships. Here's an example: The SQL Server management pack consists of multiple management packs, with one library management pack containing all basic components for SQL Server and a specific management pack for versions 2003, 2008, and 2012.

This is a best practice; when a new SQL version is released you will only have to add a specific pack and not have to re-import the base pack. Another benefit is you can remove the outdated specific pack(s) when you are no longer using the older versions of the product. Just delete the specific pack and the version specific classes are removed.

When all your classes are in one management pack, you cannot remove these without first deleting the management pack and all classes. You then would import the new management pack without the outdated classes. When you have multiple packs dependent on this pack, deleting the management pack can be a real nightmare.

The Car management pack is written according to this best practice, as the base pack contains all general settings for a CAR, and the MANO pack contains all specific settings for the MANO brand of cars.

You now have a base management pack that is ready to be sealed. Visio Studio can automatically seal your management pack after you create a key file.

REAL WORLD: ALWAYS SEAL MANAGEMENT PACKS CONTAINING CLASSES

It is a best practice to seal those management packs containing classes, as a management pack must be sealed to reuse its classes in other management packs. Failing to seal the management pack leads to issues when designing distributed applications, views, or dashboards requiring multiple classes from different management packs. When the management pack is not sealed, you must remove it (losing the discovered instances), seal the XML version, import the sealed version, and then rediscover all instances.

Before sealing the management pack, you must create a key file. Jonathan Almquist documents the process for creating a key file at http://blogs.technet.com/b/jonathanalmquist/archive/2008/08/19/seal-a-management-pack.aspx.

Creating a key file requires sn.exe, part of the .NET Framework SDK downloadable at http://www.microsoft.com/en-us/download/details.aspx?id=19988. After obtaining sn.exe, run this command to create the key file Unleashedkey.snk, which you can use to seal MPs:

```
sn.exe -k D:\MPkey\Unleashedkey.snk
```

Store this file in a safe location, as you will need it to seal your management packs. Now set up your project in Visual Studio using this key and sealing the management pack on the fly. Follow these steps:

1. Right-click the **OpsMgr.Unleashed.Car.Example.Library** project and select **Properties**. Notice you can edit the display name of the management pack by clicking **Find or Create the Management Pack Display Name and Description**. This opens an XML section where you can change the Display Name and description (visible when looking at the management pack in the Administration node of the Operations console).
2. Select the Build tab and fill in the information shown in Figure 22.9. Your project will now output an XML and sealed version of your management pack each time you build or rebuild it.

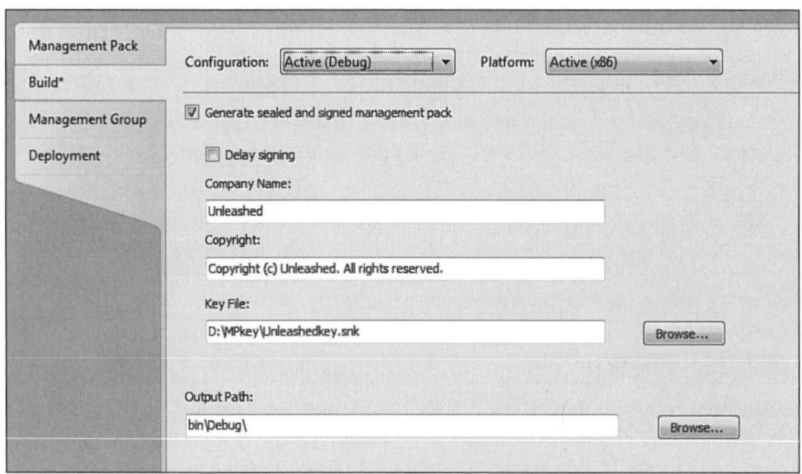

FIGURE 22.9 Sealing a management pack.

You now have everything required to create the management pack containing the base classes, which will be a core management pack required for all future car management packs. Create the management pack by right-clicking the **OpsMgr.Unleashed.Car.Example.Library** project and selecting **Build**. The project creates unsealed and sealed versions of your management pack in the location of your project, in the \bin folder under the Debug or Release folder, based on your settings in Visual Studio.

You now can create management packs for specific cars. Similar to other applications, each car has specific properties. Every brand and model will require other discoveries, rules, and monitors to discover and monitor its state.

You have two options for starting the next project: adding another project to the Unleashed car solution, or starting a new solution. The example in this chapter adds another project to the Unleashed Car solution. Follow these steps:

1. In Visual Studio, open the solution **OpsMgr Unleashed Car Example**, right-click and select **Add -> New Project**. Select **Management Pack -> Operations Manager Core Monitoring Management Pack**. Name the project **Unleashed.Car.Example.Specific.MANO.Library** and leave the location unchanged.

2. This management pack is based on the previously created library management pack containing the base classes, so you must add a reference to the base class management pack. Right-click **References** and select **Add Reference**. Select **Browse** and browse for the sealed version of the Unleashed library management pack, **D:\Management Pack Projects\OpsMgr Unleashed Car Example\OpsMgr Unleashed Car Example\bin\Debug\OpsMgr.Unleashed.Car.Example.Library.mp**.

   You now have added the library management pack as a reference and can reuse its base classes in your management pack.

3. Right-click the new referenced management pack and select **Properties**. Here you can change the alias of the reference, which makes identifying the reference easier. Change it to **UnleashedCarLibrary**.

   After renaming the reference, you can add extra folders for classes and discoveries.

4. Add the MANO specific classes to the MANO specific management pack. Add the classes as shown here. Notice you are referring to your base management pack for the base classes you created.

   Unleashed MANO Car Class:

   - **Name:** Unleashed MANO Car Class
   - **ID:** Unleashed.MANO.Car
   - **Base Class:** UnleashedCarLibrary!OpsMgr.Unleashed.Car.Example.Library.Unleashed.Vehicle.Car
   - **Accessibility:** Public
   - **Hosted:** false
   - **Property Name:** MANO Model Type ID
   - **Property ID:** ModelNumber

     Key: false

     Type: string
   - **Property Name:** MANO Serial Number
   - **Property ID:** SerialNumber

     Key: false

     Type: string

   Unleashed MANO Car Engine Class:

   - **Name:** Unleashed MANO Car Engine Class
   - **ID:** Unleashed.MANO.Car.Engine

     Base Class: UnleashedCarLibrary!OpsMgr.Unleashed.Car.Example.Library.Unleashed.Vehicle.Car.Engine

Accessibility: Public

Hosted: false

Unleashed MANO Car GasTank Class:

- **Name:** Unleashed MANO Car GasTank Class
- **ID:** Unleashed.MANO.Car. GasTank

  Base Class: UnleashedCarLibrary!OpsMgr.Unleashed.Car.Example.Library.Unleashed.Vehicle.Car.GasTank

  Accessibility: Public

  Hosted: true

The MANO car now has a class model. Before adding the management pack into your environment, you must define discovery rules for the classes. These are discussed in the next section.

Creating Discoveries

A management pack requires discovery rules to discover instances of a class. Visio MP Designer and Visual Studio create discovery rules differently, as described in the following sections.

Discoveries (Beginner)

With the Visio MP Designer, you create the discoveries when defining the shape data of the shapes in your drawing. The registry keys and values for discovering the classes in the shape data are already added; no additional actions are necessary.

Each component has several possible discoveries. Look at the shape properties of MANO car in the Visio drawing to see the row **How to Find**; this section has four types of discovery rules:

- **HKLM Registry Key:** Discovers a registry key on a Windows server agent. If the key exists, the component is discovered.
- **HKLM Registry Value:** Discovers a registry value on a Windows Server agent. It can also compare the value to a given value, using the option Compare With Registry Value.
- **Windows Server Role:** Runs a preconfigured WMI query to query the WMI class `Win32_ServerFeature`. A full list of server roles is at http://msdn.microsoft.com/en-us/library/cc280268(v=VS.85).aspx.
- **WMI Query:** Connects to WMI namespace `\\.\root\cimv2` and lets you write the query to check in WMI. The component is discovered when the query runs on the agent.

The Component Server Role targets the discovery at the class Microsoft.Windows.Server.Computer, meaning it runs on every agent on a Windows Server in your OpsMgr environment. Every server component beneath the server role queries the server role, so this only runs on agents where the role is discovered.

Because the Visio MP Designer is designed for less experienced users, by adding a shape you design the classes and discoveries. The only requirement is to have some registry and WMI knowledge, and know the server role of your server.

TIP: CHECKING SERVER ROLES USING WMI

To check the roles installed on a server, you could use WBEMTEST to query WMI. Follow these steps:

1. Select the Start button, then **Run** and type **WBEMTEST** to open the WMI Tester.
2. Select **Connect** and ensure the Name Space is **Root\Cimv2**. Click **Connect** again to connect to that namespace.
3. Click **Query** and a box will open where you can add your query. For server roles the query would be `Select * From Win32_ServerFeature`.
4. Click **Apply** and a list of all installed features by ID should display. To determine what ID stands for which feature, see http://msdn.microsoft.com/en-us/library/cc280268(v=VS.85).aspx.

You could use the same procedure to test your custom WMI queries before adding them in your discoveries.

Discoveries (Advanced)

Discoveries in Visual Studio are created separately, requiring additional effort. The primary benefit is you can reuse any existing module in OpsMgr or create your own to discover instances of a class. Table 22.11 lists several additional benefits.

TABLE 22.11 Discoveries using Visio versus Visual Studio

Component	Visio	Visual Studio
Registry based discoveries	You can query any key or value within HKEY_LOCAL_MACHINE. Keys can only be checked for existence; values can be compared to other given values.	You can query any key or value within HKEY_LOCAL_MACHINE. You can check by altering the expression for any other registry value type. You also can discover class properties, which is not possible in Visio.
WMI based discovery	You can check only in the Root\Cimv2 namespace. You can only check for existence.	You can check any namespace in WMI. You are free to discover more than one property.
Script based	None.	You can use PowerShell or VBScript to discover any class and class properties.

The examples provided in Table 22.11 are a subset and based on the capabilities in Visio. Use Visual Studio if you cannot meet your discovery requirements using Visio.

Before writing discoveries in Visual Studio, you need some background on discovery rules in general based on the Car management pack. Here are some common ways to create a discovery rule:

- **Registry discovery rule:** This rule reads the registry of the agent and searches for a particular key or keys that define if an application or component is installed.
- **WMI discovery rule:** This rule type performs a WMI query on an agent and searches for particular values to determine if an application or component is installed.
- **Script-based discovery rule:** A script-based discovery rule runs a Visual Basic script (VBScript) to discover if an application or component is installed.
- **PowerShell based discovery rule:** This rule type runs a PowerShell script to discover an installed application or component.

By becoming familiar with these methods for discovering components, you can discover any application or component running on an agent.

Discovery rules are required to discover instances of a class. The first class to discover is the `Unleashed.MANO.Car` class and its properties, which is based on the `Unleashed.Vehicle.Car` class. The base class `Unleashed.Vehicle.Car` has several properties, including a key property. Be sure your discovery discovers at least the key property of the `Unleashed.Vehicle.Car` class. Since the `Windows Server Computer` class hosts the class, you must have a key property to discover the instance of `Unleashed.MANO.Car` properly.

On the machine where you installed the example .reg files introduced in the "Writing the Management Pack" section, you can check the registry to look for a specific key that defines a MANO car. Beneath the key are the properties for the discovery rule to discover. This will be your first registry discovery rule.

TIP: ALWAYS TRY TO USE REGISTRY-BASED DISCOVERIES

Registry discoveries have the lowest performance impact; the authors recommend checking the registry first for application-specific parameters to identify your application when writing a discovery rule. To discover an application running on an agent, you generally first must target all Windows computer classes. As this makes your discovery run on every agent, it is best to keep this lightweight and use a registry-based discovery.

Even if your first discovery only discovers whether the application is present, you can create a second discovery that uses WMI or scripting to discover the other properties, targeting it at the registry-discovered application class. This lets you run the scripting or WMI discoveries, which require more resources, only on those agents running the application instead of all Windows computers. This approach is also known as *seed discovery*.

The first discovery rule in the MANO specific management pack is a registry-based discovery. Follow these steps to create the discovery:

1. Right-click your project, select **Add -> New Item**, and select **Discovery**. Name your discovery **Discoveries.**

   After adding the discovery, notice an .mptg file is added instead of an .xml file such as a class or relationship. This is a template file for you to use to write the discovery. Creating a discovery based on a template is different than adding a class; you must configure the template correctly to generate the correct XML below the template (the mptg.mpx file). When you open or double-click the .mpx file, the top has a small disclaimer that **This file has been automatically generated. Any changes made to this file may be lost the next time it is regenerated**, meaning you should make changes to the .mptg file. not the mptg.mpx file.

2. To complete the template, double-click the .mptg file to open it. Figure 22.10 shows the template with one entry. With the template open, you can double-click the entry to open the entry's property sheet as shown in Figure 22.11.

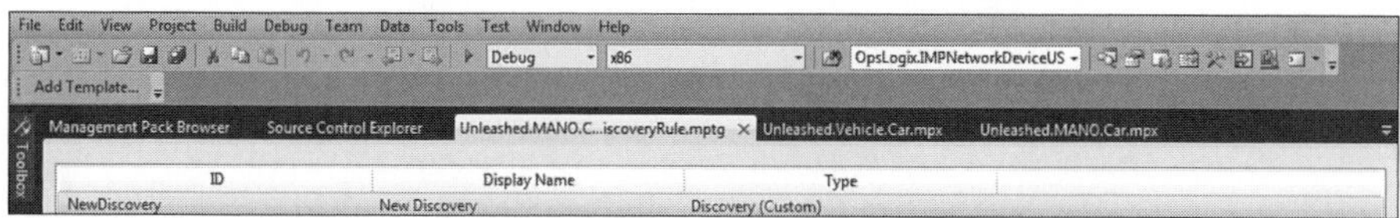

FIGURE 22.10 Discovery template.

Unleashed.MANO.Car.Discovery.Rule Discovery (Custom)

Category	**Discovery**
Comment	
Confirm Delivery	**False**
Data Source Comment	
Data Source Configuration	**(Configuration XML)**
Data Source ID	**DS**
Data Source Run As	
Data Source Type ID	**Windows!Microsoft.Windows.FilteredRegistryDiscoveryProvider**
Description	**Registry Discovery to discover MANO car class.**
Discovery Classes	**(Collection)**
Discovery Relationships	**(Collection)**
Display Name	**Unleashed MANO Car Discovery**
Enabled	**True**
ID	**Unleashed.MANO.Car.Discovery.Rule**
Priority	**Normal**
Remotable	**True**
Target	**Windows!Microsoft.Windows.Server.Computer**

FIGURE 22.11 Discovery template properties.

3. Fill in and change the properties of the discovery rule:

   - Change ID to **Unleashed.MANO.Car.DiscoveryRule** and the display name of the discovery to **Unleashed MANO Car Discovery**.

   - Click ... after **Data Source Type ID** to select the datasource **Microsoft. Windows.FilteredRegistryDiscoveryProvider**.

- Select ... after **Target** to select the **Microsoft.Windows.Server.Computer** class, against which you want to run the discovery.
- Give the discovery rule the description **Registry Discovery to discover MANO car class**.

TIP: DISCOVERY TARGET

A best practice for targeting discovery rules is to target against the `Windows Server Computer` class. If you target against `Windows Computer`, your discovery will run on every Windows system including client systems. Targeting against `Windows Server Computer` avoids running the discovery on every client.

The authors recommend being as precise as possible when targeting a discovery. For example, if you always want to discover Windows 2012 servers you should target your discovery against the `Windows 2012 Server` class instead of `Windows Server Computer`. This avoids unnecessary workload on your agents.

4. You must add the class and its properties for it to be discovered by the discovery rule. Click ... after Discovery Classes and a page opens as shown in Figure 22.12. Click **Add** to add a class, and in the Properties dialog click ... after Class to select the **Unleashed.MANO.Car** class. Click ... after Class Properties to select the properties to discover, displayed in Figure 22.13.

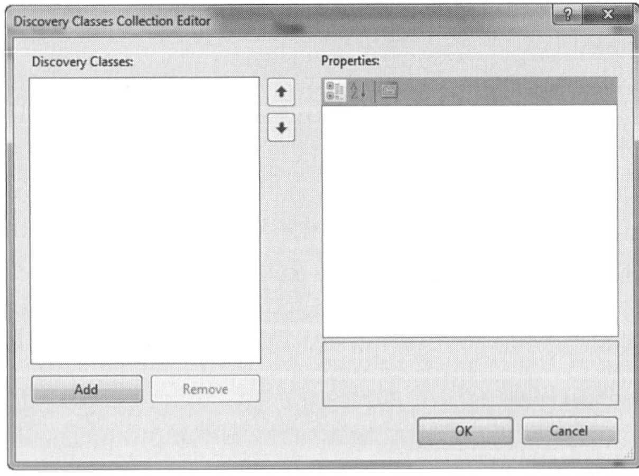

FIGURE 22.12 Discovery classes dialog in the Discovery Classes Collection Editor.

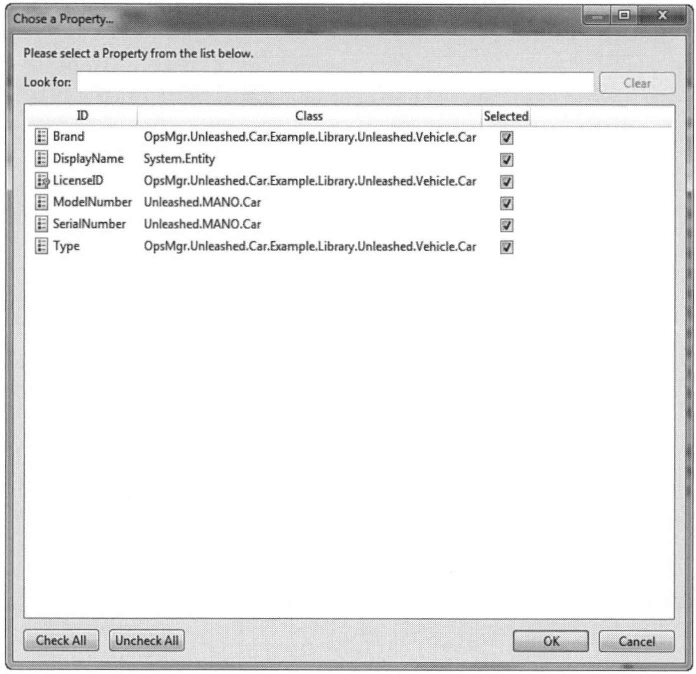

FIGURE 22.13 The Choose a Property discovery page.

5. Add the Data Source Configuration, which is the XML section of the discovery. You can use Intellisense (press Ctrl and space bar) to show the XML; it will show you where to place the different XML sections. Create the Data Source configuration using the following settings:

   - **Computer name of the computer where the discovery is running:**

     ```
     <ComputerName>$Target/Property[Type="Windows!Microsoft.Windows.
     Computer"]/PrincipalName$</ComputerName>
     ```

   - **Registry keys:** Table 22.12 lists the registry keys to be discovered. Use Intellisense to add these sections below the <ComputerName> section.

TABLE 22.12 Registry paths to discover MANO car

AttributeName	Path	PathType	Attribute Type
CarExists	Software\Unleashed Car\MANO	0	0
LicenseID	Software\Unleashed Car\MANO\LicenseID	1	1
ModelNumber	Software\Unleashed Car\MANO\ ModelNumber	1	1
SerialNumber	Software\Unleashed Car\MANO\SerialNumber	1	1
Brand	Software\Unleashed Car\MANO\Brand	1	1
Type	Software\Unleashed Car\MANO\Type	1	1

- **Interval on which the discovery should run in seconds:** `<Frequency>14400</Frequency>`
- **The ID of the class instance to be discovered by the registry discovery rule:** `<ClassId>$MPElement[Name="Unleashed.MANO.Car"]$</ClassId>`
- **Class instance properties to be discovered and their values, as follows:**

```
<InstanceSettings>
    <Settings>
      <Setting>

        <Name>$MPElement[Name="Windows!Microsoft.Windows.Computer"]/
➥PrincipalName$</Name>
        <Value>$Target/Property[Type="Windows!Microsoft.Windows.
➥Computer"]/PrincipalName$</Value>
      </Setting>
      <Setting>

        <Name>$MPElement[Name="UnleashedCarLibrary!OpsMgr.Unleashed.Car.
➥Example.Library.Unleashed.Vehicle.Car"]/Brand$</Name>
        <Value>$Data/Values/Brand$</Value>
      </Setting>
      <Setting>

        <Name>$MPElement[Name="UnleashedCarLibrary!OpsMgr.Unleashed.Car.
➥Example.Library.Unleashed.Vehicle.Car"]/Type$</Name>
        <Value>$Data/Values/Type$</Value>
      </Setting>
      <Setting>
```

```
        <Name>$MPElement[Name="UnleashedCarLibrary!OpsMgr.Unleashed.Car.
➥Example.Library.Unleashed.Vehicle.Car"]/LicenseID$</Name>
        <Value>$Data/Values/LicenseID$</Value>
      </Setting>
      <Setting>
        <Name>$MPElement[Name="Unleashed.MANO.Car"]/ModelNumber$</Name>
        <Value>$Data/Values/ModelNumber$</Value>
      </Setting>
      <Setting>
        <Name>$MPElement[Name="Unleashed.MANO.Car"]/SerialNumber$</Name>
        <Value>$Data/Values/SerialNumber$</Value>
      </Setting>
      <Setting>
        <Name>$MPElement[Name="System!System.Entity"]/DisplayName$</Name>
        <Value>$Data/Values/Brand$-($Data/Values/LicenseID$)</Value>
      </Setting>
    </Settings>
  </InstanceSettings>
```

- **Checking if the registry attribute exists:**

```
<Expression>
    <SimpleExpression>
      <ValueExpression>
        <XPathQuery Type="String">Values/CarExists</XPathQuery>
      </ValueExpression>
      <Operator>Equal</Operator>
      <ValueExpression>
        <Value Type="String">true</Value>
      </ValueExpression>
    </SimpleExpression
  </Expression>
```

With the first discovery that discovers the MANO car instance complete, you can create a discovery rule for the car engine. The registry of the server running the MANO example, displayed in Figure 22.14, indicates you can use a registry discovery for this component as well. For demonstration purposes, this section uses a script-based discovery, as discovering a component with the built-in module Microsoft.Windows.FilteredRegistryDiscoveryProvider previously introduced in this section.

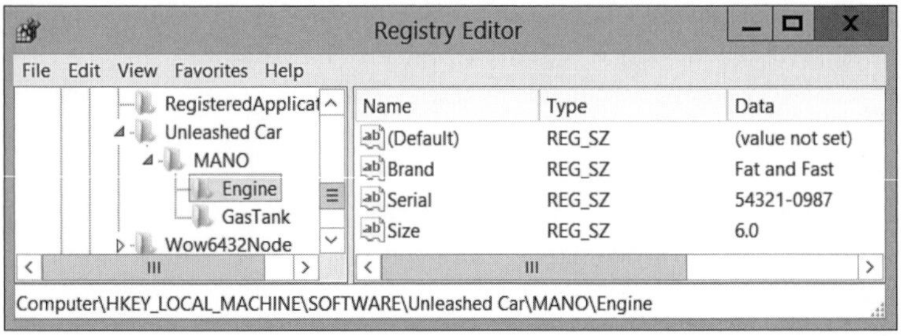
Registry Editor
File Edit View Favorites Help
RegisteredApplicat
Unleashed Car
MANO
Engine
GasTank
Wow6432Node
Name
Type
Data
(Default)
REG_SZ
(value not set)
Brand
REG_SZ
Fat and Fast
Serial
REG_SZ
54321-0987
Size
REG_SZ
6.0
Computer\HKEY_LOCAL_MACHINE\SOFTWARE\Unleashed Car\MANO\Engine

FIGURE 22.14 Registry settings.

Follow these steps to create a script-based discovery that queries the registry:

1. In Visual Studio, double-click the discovery .mptg file to open it; then right-click in the pane to select **Add Template**. When the Add Template page opens, select **Discovery(Custom)** to add a discovery rule.

2. Double-click the newly added template and fill in the settings as in Figure 22.15. Ensure you select the correct Discovery class Unleashed.MANO.Car.Engine.

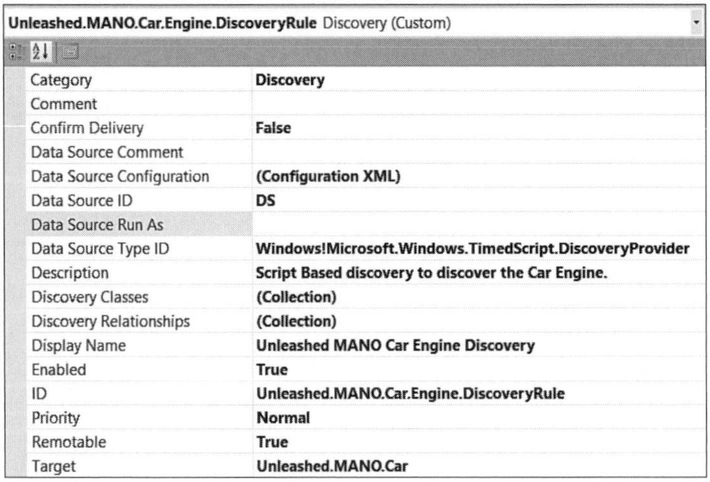
Unleashed.MANO.Car.Engine.DiscoveryRule Discovery (Custom)
Category Discovery
Comment
Confirm Delivery False
Data Source Comment
Data Source Configuration (Configuration XML)
Data Source ID DS
Data Source Run As
Data Source Type ID Windows!Microsoft.Windows.TimedScript.DiscoveryProvider
Description Script Based discovery to discover the Car Engine.
Discovery Classes (Collection)
Discovery Relationships (Collection)
Display Name Unleashed MANO Car Engine Discovery
Enabled True
ID Unleashed.MANO.Car.Engine.DiscoveryRule
Priority Normal
Remotable True
Target Unleashed.MANO.Car

FIGURE 22.15 Script-based Discovery properties page.

3. Follow the procedure discussed previously in the "Combining 2007 Authoring with 2012 Authoring" Tip for a script-based discovery. This lets you easily add the script arguments and other settings to your management pack. Copy the configuration XML into Visual Studio and add the script shown here:

```
<ScriptBody><![CDATA[
Option Explicit
SetLocale ("en-us")
Dim WSHShell,sourceId,managedEntityId,oAPI,oArgs,oInst,principalName, Serial,
Brand, Size,LicenseId
Dim oDiscoveryData
Set WSHShell = CreateObject("WScript.Shell")
Set oAPI = CreateObject("MOM.ScriptAPI")
Set oArgs = WScript.Arguments
sourceId = oArgs(0)
managedEntityId = oArgs(1)
principalName = oArgs(2)
LicenseId = oArgs(3)

On Error Resume Next
Set oDiscoveryData = oAPI.CreateDiscoveryData(0, sourceId, managedEntityId)
Serial = WSHShell.regread ("HKLM\SOFTWARE\Unleashed Car\MANO\Engine\serial")
Brand = WSHShell.regread ("HKLM\SOFTWARE\Unleashed Car\MANO\Engine\Brand")
Size = WSHShell.regread ("HKLM\SOFTWARE\Unleashed Car\MANO\Engine\Size")

Select Case Err
Case 0:

Set oInst = oDiscoveryData.CreateClassInstance("$MPElement[Name='Unleashed.
MANO.Car.Engine']$")

Call oInst.Addproperty ("$MPElement[Name='Windows!Microsoft.Windows.Computer']/
PrincipalName$", principalName)
Call oInst.Addproperty ("$MPElement[Name='UnleashedCarLibrary!OpsMgr.Unleashed.
Car.Example.Library.Unleashed.Vehicle.Car']/LicenseID$", LicenseId)
Call oInst.Addproperty ("$MPElement[Name='UnleashedCarLibrary!OpsMgr.Unleashed.
Car.Example.Library.Unleashed.Vehicle.Car.Engine']/Serial$", Serial)
Call oInst.Addproperty ("$MPElement[Name='UnleashedCarLibrary!OpsMgr.Unleashed.
Car.Example.Library.Unleashed.Vehicle.Car.Engine']/Brand$", Brand)
Call oInst.Addproperty ("$MPElement[Name='UnleashedCarLibrary!OpsMgr.Unleashed.
Car.Example.Library.Unleashed.Vehicle.Car.Engine']/Size$", Size)
Call oDiscoveryData.AddInstance(oInst)
Case Else
End Select

oAPI.Return oDiscoveryData
    ]]></ScriptBody>
```

The parts bolded in the script are OpsMgr-specific and use the MOM.ScriptAPI. Refer to http://msdn.microsoft.com/en-us/library/bb437523 for information on the different methods supported by this object.

Now that you have created the engine discovery, you can design the discovery rule for the gas tank. You can create a filtered registry discovery as with the MANO car class, or a script-based discovery. Your solution should now look like Figure 22.16; there should be two projects in the solution, OpsMgr.Unleashed.Car.Example.Library and Unleashed.Car.Example.Specific.MANO.Library. It is time to test your management pack.

To build the management packs, right-click **Solution 'OpsMgr Unleashed Car Example' (2 projects)** and select **Build Solution**. The two projects are built into management packs in the \bin folders of your projects OpsMgr.Unleashed.Car.Example.Library and Unleashed.Car.Example.Specific.MANO.Library. These are located within the OpsMgr Unleashed Example folder of your solution, as shown in Figure 22.17.

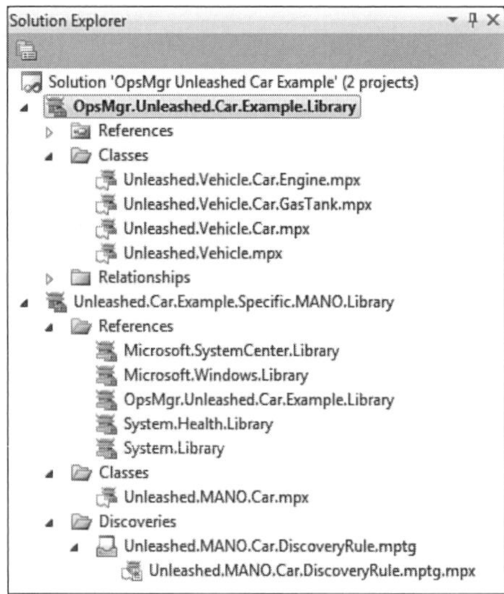

FIGURE 22.16 Unleashed car solution in the Solution Explorer.

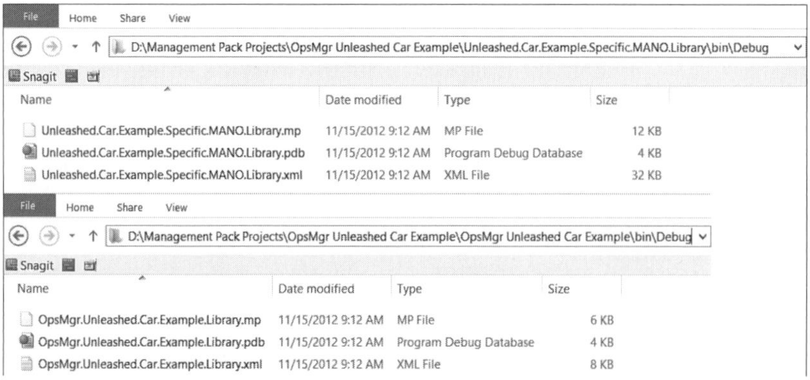

FIGURE 22.17 Management pack path.

Management Pack Results

You now have created management packs using Visio and Visual Studio. Copy the two management packs created with Visio Studio, OpsMgr.Unleashed.Car.Example.Library.mp and Unleashed.Car.Example.Specific.MANO.Library.xml, to your OpsMgr environment and import them into your management group. Do the same with the management pack created using Visio. After importing the management packs, set an override on the discovery interval of your discovery rules to a lower value to speed up the discovery while testing.

The Visio management pack already has several views; you can view the discovered instance using these views. The Visual Studio management packs do not have views; to use the discovered inventory to view the discovered instances, follow these steps:

1. Navigate to the Monitoring space and select **Discovered Inventory**, right-click in the Results section, and select **Change Target Type** to change the target to **Unleashed MANO car class**. You should now see your newly created class and its properties as displayed in Figure 22.18.

2. Compare the settings of the discovered MANO instance to the discovery rule you created to understand the discovery instance settings. Notice the display name of the instance and how it is built, based on the XML section for adding the class settings:

```
<Setting>
   <Name>$MPElement[Name="System!System.Entity"]/DisplayName$</Name>
   <Value>$Data/Values/Brand$-($Data/Values/LicenseID$)</Value>
</Setting>
```

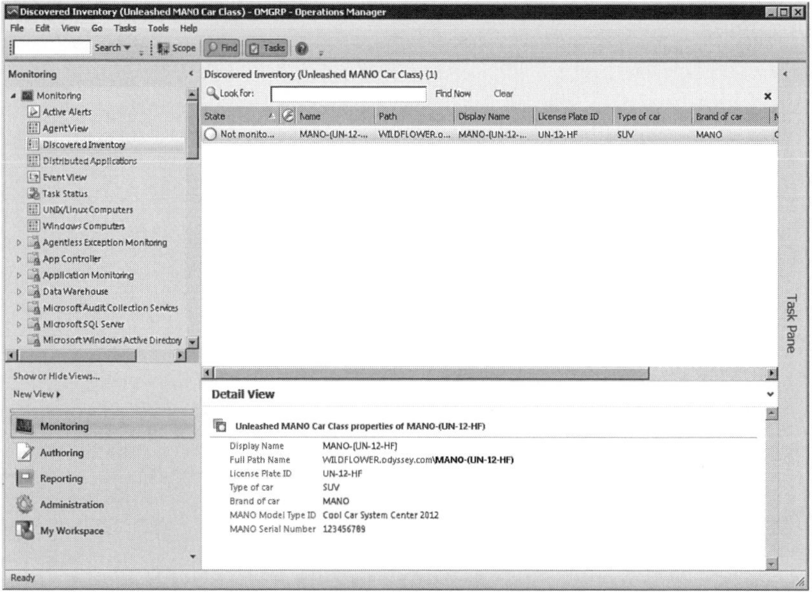

FIGURE 22.18 Discovered inventory for the MANO car.

3. Notice the combination of using plain text and OpsMgr variables. You can add both variables:

   - **$Data/Values/Brand$:** This is a variable from the discovery and is the Brand of the Car.
   - **" - (" and ")":** These parts are plain text; you could have typed in anything. The exact same text will be shown in the console.
   - **$Data/Values/LicenseID$:** This variable is from the discovery, the LicenseID of the car. The end result is a combination leading into Display Name MANO-(UN-12HF).$Data/Values/Brand$ and text " - (" $Data/Values/LicenseID$ text ")". You can change these accordingly.

4. Select the MANO Car class and right-click to select the Diagram view. Do the same with the Visio-created class by navigating to the MANO Car State view. Compare both discovered instances as shown in Figure 22.19 and Figure 22.20. Notice the difference between both discovered classes.

Figure 22.19 shows the components as created with the Visio MP Designer, which has preconfigured icons and the only detail on the classes being the displayname. Figure 22.20 shows the components as created with the Visual Studio Extensions; this has different icons you could customize if necessary and classes with detailed properties about each class.

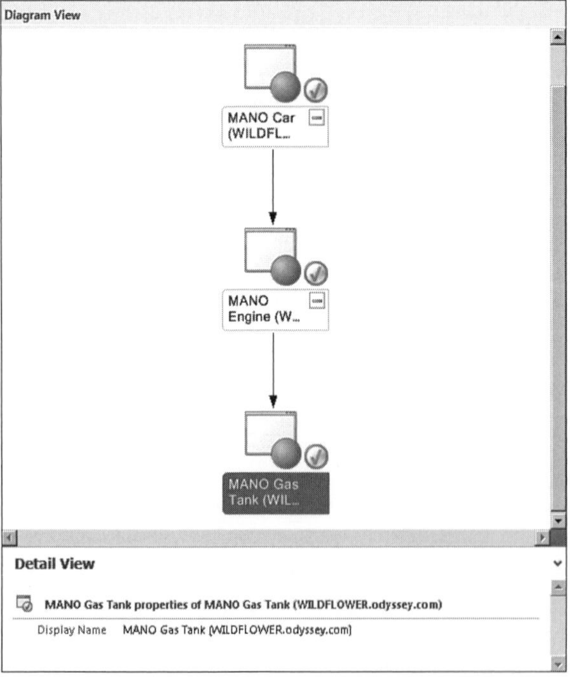

FIGURE 22.19 MANO Car Visio diagram.

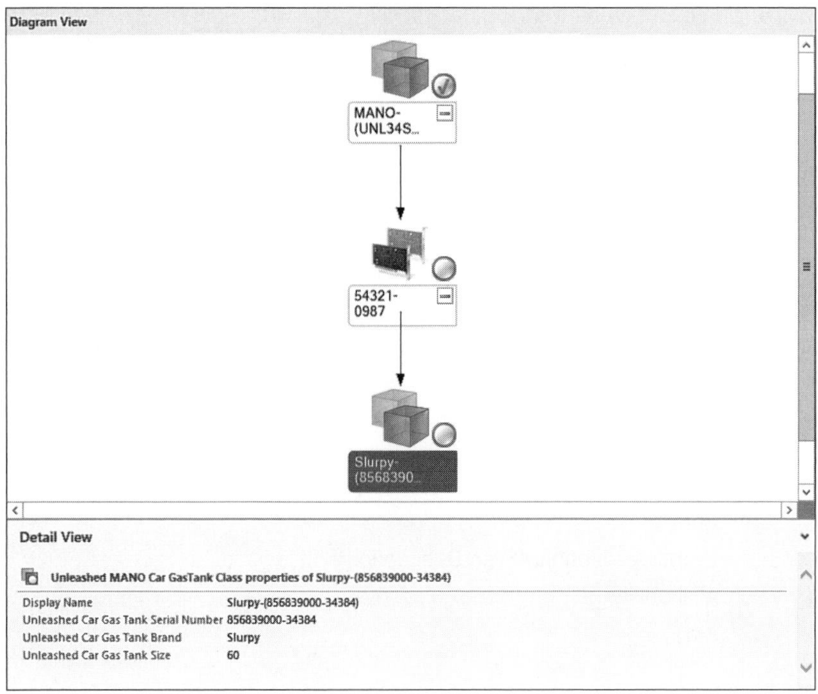

FIGURE 22.20 MANO Car Visual Studio diagram.

Creating Monitors

After creating classes and discoveries, the next step is creating monitors to monitor the health state of the discovered classes. As this is a fictional management pack, there are no actual components running on the agents that affect the health state of the MANO car. For demonstration purposes, the example will monitor for components on the system and simply rename them.

Monitors (Beginner)

With the Visio MP Designer, creating monitors is as simple as creating the other components. Select the type of monitor you want to use, and drag and drop the monitor on the component. Perform the following steps:

1. Drag and drop a Windows Event Monitor on the MANO Engine, and add the shape data shown in Table 22.13.

TABLE 22.13 MANO engine event monitor shape data

Name	Value
Name	MANO Engine
Log Name	Application
Red Event ID	999
Red Event Source	Unleashed MANO Car Engine
Monitor Behavior	Alert
Auto Reset	Green Event
Green Event ID	991
Green Event Source	Unleashed MANO Car Engine
Repeats N Times. N=	1
Advanced Alert Settings	TRUE
Alert Priority	High
Alert Severity	Critical
Alert Description	Event Description:#EventDescription#
Health Category	Availability
Run On	Always

For a complete overview on the settings and configuration references for the Visio MP Designer, see the TechNet Wiki page at http://social.technet.microsoft.com/wiki/contents/articles/6938.monitoring-and-modeling-shape-reference-for-visio-management-pack-designer.aspx.

2. Drag and drop a Windows Performance Counter Monitor on top of the MANO Gas Tank Component and fill in the shape data listed in Table 22.14.

TABLE 22.14 MANO engine event monitor shape data

Name	Value
Name	Mano Gas Tank Performance Monitor
Object	LogicalDisk
Counter	% Free Space
All Instances	False
Instance	C:
Monitor Behavior	Alert and Collect
Health Category	Performance
Comparison Type	Average
Number Of States	2 - Health & Critical

TABLE 22.14 Continued

Name	Value
Critical Threshold	50
Operator	>
Interval	300
Number Of Samples	3
Collection Interval	900
Create Performance View	TRUE
Performance View Name	Mano Gas Tank Performance View
Advanced Alert Settings	FALSE
Save Data to Data Warehouse	TRUE
Create Report	TRUE
Report Name	MANO Gas Tank Report
Run On	Always

Creating the performance monitor adds the monitor and a performance collection rule for the counter, a report filtered on the correct object, and a performance view for viewing the performance counter.

The Visio tool lets you create these by just filling in one data shape data with the correct properties. You can create any other monitor in Visio to add additional monitoring to your management pack.

The example provided with this book also contains an event monitor for the MANO Car Server role. Write this one yourself by using event source **Unleashed MANO Car**, event ID **995** Healthy, and event ID **996** Unhealthy.

Monitors (Advanced)

Creating monitors using Visual Studio offers more flexibility. You can write your own monitors or use any monitor types already existing in OpsMgr. Table 22.15 lists the different options for creating monitors using the Visio MP Designer and Visual Studio.

TABLE 22.15 Creating monitors in Visio versus Visual Studio

Monitor	Visio	Visual Studio
Windows Performance Monitor	Quickly design basic report, basic view, basic performance health monitor, and basic collection rule for only Windows performance data.	Any performance data can be monitored not just Windows performance data. Completely free to name and design your performance monitors, more advanced monitoring instead of simple threshold only.
Windows Event monitor	Monitor Windows events only on source and ID; no other options possible. No missing events monitoring.	All events can be monitored; expression filters can be used to monitor on any condition such as description contains, severity of the event. Missing events can be monitored.
Windows Service Monitor	All Windows services can be monitored. Possibility to monitor services only during business hours. Monitor CPU and Memory usage of a service.	Non-Windows services can be monitored.
Website Site monitor	Simple URL response check on response time of a website. You can also create performance collection rules and performance views.	Website monitoring can be customized in any form not only response time. Although you could create any URL monitor in Visual Studio, it is easier to use the templates in the Operations console Authoring pane.
Database Monitor	Simple Database check response time monitor. You can also create performance collection rules and performance views.	Database monitoring can be customized in any form not only response time. You can check more than just response times, as you can read contents of tables and so on. Another option is to use the OLEDB template in the Authoring pane of the Operations console.

Although creating monitors in Visio should work for most situations, Visio Studio lets you create more customized monitors with more sophisticated ways to check health state. To write monitors in Visual Studio, you must monitor the Car state and create an event log monitor. Follow these steps:

1. Open Visual Studio and create a folder named **Monitors**. Right-click the folder and select **Add -> New Item** and choose **Monitor (Unit)**. Name the file **Monitors.mptg** and click **OK**. Double-click the empty template and fill in the details as shown in Figure 22.21.

2. In the Properties pane, click **Monitor Operational States** to define the two states of the monitor: Healthy and Critical. After changing the states, click **Monitor Configuration** to add the XML. An easy way to create the monitors is using the OpsMgr 2007 R2 Authoring console to design your monitors including the expressions, and then copy the configuration to Visual Studio. Table 22.16 shows the settings for the event monitor.

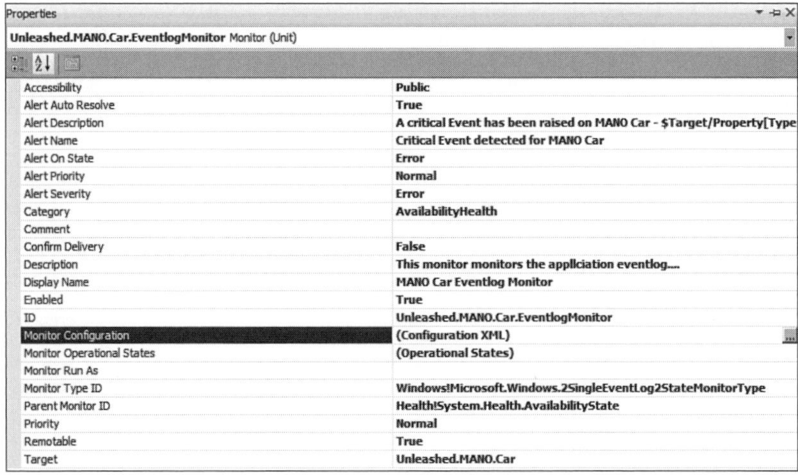

FIGURE 22.21 Two state event log monitor.

TABLE 22.16 Visual Studio events to monitor

Event State	Event Source	EventLevel	EventID
Healthy	Unleashed MANO Car	4	999
Unhealthy	Unleashed MANO Car	1	999

3. After adding the monitor configuration, you can add the alerting settings of the monitor. By default there is no alerting; only a monitor that changes the health state when an event is detected. In step 2 for creating the monitor, you added the settings for the alert (shown in Figure 22.22). All that needs to be added is the alert description.

4. Select **Alert Description** and click **...** to open the Alert Description page. Fill in the description as shown in Figure 22.22.

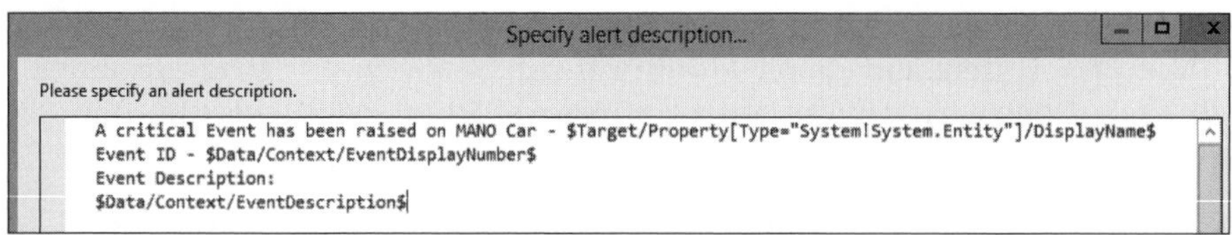

FIGURE 22.22 Alert description configuration.

5. Figure 22.22 represents the lines in the alert description. Figure 22.23 shows the result of the alert description in Figure 22.22. Compare the two to understand the configuration of the alert. Although you could write anything you want in the alert description, using the variables makes the description more specific to your alert and easier for the operator to identify the problem.

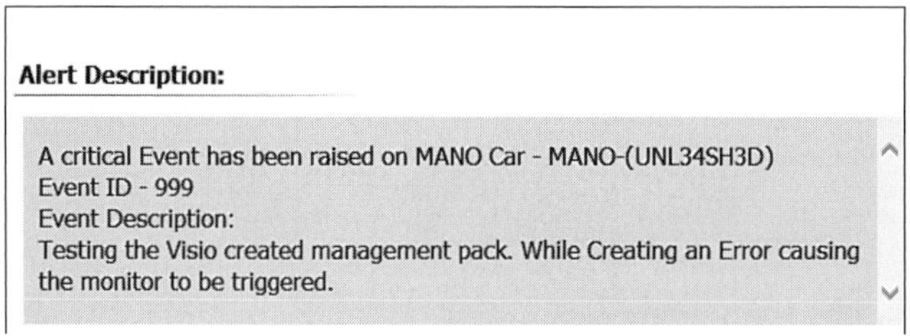

FIGURE 22.23 Alert Description - result.

6. You could add several fields of an event into an Alert Description for an event monitor similar to the one just created:

   - **EventDisplayNumber (Event ID):** $Data/Context/EventDisplayNumber$
   - **EventDescription (Description):** $Data/Context/EventDescription$
   - **Publisher Name (Event Source):** $Data/Context/PublisherName$
   - **EventCategory:** $Data/Context/EventCategory$
   - **LoggingComputer:** $Data/Context/LoggingComputer$
   - **EventLevel:** $Data/Context/EventLevel$
   - **Channel:** $Data/Context/Channel$
   - **UserName:** $Data/Context/UserName$
   - **EventNumber:** $Data/Context/EventNumber$
   - **Event Time:** $Data/Context/@time$

   Find a complete list of alert description variables in Kevin Holman's blog at http://blogs.technet.com/b/kevinholman/archive/2007/12/12/adding-custom-information-to-alert-descriptions-and-notifications.aspx.

After creating the event monitor for the Unleashed Car class, create a performance monitor to monitor the gas tank. To monitor the state of the gas tank for performance you must create a two state script monitor that queries WMI for the disk space on C:\. Writing the script monitor in Visual Studio lets you fully edit the monitor as if it was actually monitoring a gas tank! Perform the following steps:

1. In Visual Studio, double-click the **Monitors.mptg** file to open the monitor template. Right-click the Details pane and select **Add Template** to open the template. Select **Monitor (Unit)** to add a unit monitor template. Double-click the template and fill in the properties of the template as shown in Figure 22.24.

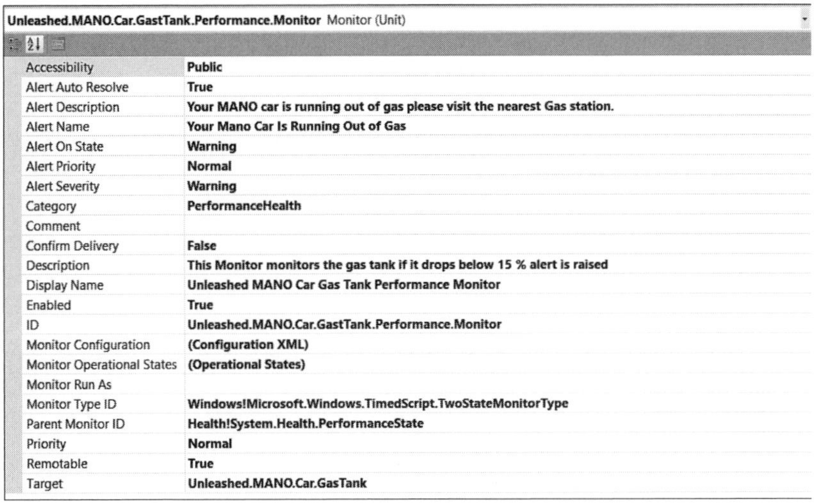

Unleashed.MANO.Car.GastTank.Performance.Monitor Monitor (Unit)

Accessibility	Public
Alert Auto Resolve	True
Alert Description	Your MANO car is running out of gas please visit the nearest Gas station.
Alert Name	Your Mano Car Is Running Out of Gas
Alert On State	Warning
Alert Priority	Normal
Alert Severity	Warning
Category	PerformanceHealth
Comment	
Confirm Delivery	False
Description	This Monitor monitors the gas tank if it drops below 15 % alert is raised
Display Name	Unleashed MANO Car Gas Tank Performance Monitor
Enabled	True
ID	Unleashed.MANO.Car.GastTank.Performance.Monitor
Monitor Configuration	(Configuration XML)
Monitor Operational States	(Operational States)
Monitor Run As	
Monitor Type ID	Windows!Microsoft.Windows.TimedScript.TwoStateMonitorType
Parent Monitor ID	Health!System.Health.PerformanceState
Priority	Normal
Remotable	True
Target	Unleashed.MANO.Car.GasTank

FIGURE 22.24 Script-based performance monitor properties.

2. After filling in the properties, change the field Monitor Operational States to warning and healthy. Now the monitor will only show a warning state and not critical.

3. Add the monitor configuration and again you can use the OpsMgr 2007 R2 Authoring console for the configuration or write the XML section using Intellisense. Table 22.17 lists the configuration requirements.

TABLE 22.17 Two-state monitor properties

Property	Value
IntervalSeconds	3600
SyncTime	00:00
ScriptName	MANOGastTank.vbs
Arguments	"15" "C:"

TABLE 22.17 Continued

Property	Value
TimeoutSeconds	300
Healthy State	Property[@Name='State'] Equal GOOD
Warning State	Property[@Name='State'] Equal BAD

4. After adding the properties, you can add this script:

```
Option Explicit
SetLocale ("en-us")
On Error Resume Next
Dim oAPI, oBag, strComputer, objWMIService, strQuery, colDisks, colDisk,
oPercentageFree, State, BAD, GOOD, oArgs, oThreshold, oDisk, oPercentageUsed
Set oAPI = CreateObject("MOM.ScriptAPI")
Set oBag = oAPI.CreateTypedPropertyBag(State)
Set oArgs = WScript.Arguments
oThreshold = oArgs(0)
oDisk = oArgs(1)
If oArgs.Count < 2 Then
Call oAPI.LogScriptEvent("MANOGasTank.vbs", 10101, 1, "MANOGastTank script was
called with fewer than two argument(s)")
WScript.Quit
End If
strComputer = "."
Set objWMIService = GetObject("winmgmts:" &
"{impersonationLevel=impersonate}!\\" & strComputer & "\root\cimv2")
strQuery = "Select * from Win32_LogicalDisk Where Name = '" & oDisk & "'"

Set colDisks = objWMIService.ExecQuery (strQuery)
For Each colDisk in colDisks
oPercentageFree = Int(100.0 * (colDisk.FreeSpace) / (colDisk.Size))
oPercentageUsed = Int(100.0 - (oPercentageFree))

Next

If oPercentageUsed < oThreshold Then
Call oBag.AddValue("State","BAD")
Call oAPI.Return(oBag)
Wscript.quit
Else
Call oBag.AddValue("State","GOOD")
Call oAPI.Return(oBag)
Wscript.quit
End If
```

The bolded parts of the script are OpsMgr-specific. As with the script-based discovery, you need to use the MOM.ScriptAPI and the methods within this API to add the script results to OpsMgr. OpsMgr scripting makes use of *property bags*, which are temporary objects in scripts to return data to OpsMgr.

Here are the three methods used with property bags:

- **CreatePropertyBag:** This method initiates the property bag in the script from MOM.ScriptAPI. It tells the script to start using property bags.
- **AddValue:** This adds a name and a value pair to a property bag. A property bag always needs to have a name and a value such as oBag.AddValue("State," "GOOD") where the name is "State" and the value is "GOOD." You add a value and a name in a property bag.
- **Return:** This returns the property bag from the script to OpsMgr. Using the description Property[@Name='State'], OpsMgr can read the value of the property bag named State that you can use further in your monitor or rule.

TIP: WORKING WITH PROPERTY BAGS

Be sure you understand how property bags work, as they are a powerful tool to change regular scripts into OpsMgr-compatible scripts. You only need several lines of code to make the script OpsMgr-aware:

Open the script API and declare it in a variable oAPI:

```
Set oAPI = CreateObject("MOM.ScriptAPI")
```

Declare to use the propertybag and put in a variable oBag:

```
Set oBag = oAPI.CreateTypedPropertyBag(State)
```

Fill the property bag:

```
Call oBag.AddValue("State","BAD")
```

Return the property bag to OpsMgr:

```
Call oAPI.Return(oBag)
```

For further reading on property bags and scripting in OpsMgr, refer to

- http://blogs.technet.com/b/momteam/archive/2009/02/13/mp-authoring-resources.aspx
- http://blogs.technet.com/b/authormps/archive/2011/02/24/property-bags-and-multi-instance-monitoring.aspx
- http://www.systemcentercentral.com/Downloads/DownloadsDetails/tabid/144/IndexID/7803/Default.aspx

After finalizing the performance monitor, the next step is including a performance collection rule in your management pack to monitor performance of the gas tank. This is discussed in the following section.

Creating Rules

Rules are primarily used for data collection or alerting only. The following sections focus on performance collection rules, as these are most commonly used.

Rules (Beginner)

The Visio MP Designer does not have an option to create rules. While you can add monitors, you cannot add rules to your management pack.

However, when you take a closer look at adding monitors, most of them have the option to Alert, Alert and Collect, or only Collect. Although it is not named as a rule, selecting Collect generates a performance or event collection rule to collect data.

When you created the MANO Gas Tank Performance monitor earlier in the "Monitors (Beginner)" section, you selected **Alert**. Now when you select **Alert and Collect**, you are creating a health monitor for monitoring performance health and a collection rule for collecting the performance data to show in a performance view. Adding the monitor in the Visio MP Designer also creates a performance collection rule.

To create collection only rules in the Visio MP Designer, ensure you set the Monitor Behavior field to **Collect**, and the designer will create a performance or event collection rule.

Rules (Advanced)

The advanced approach to creating rules has more flexibility than the Visio MP Designer. You can write your own rules to collect and manipulate the data you want before adding the collected data into OpsMgr. In the example management pack, you customize the performance data from the C:\ drive as if it was a real gas tank monitored for performance. Table 22.18 compares creating rules in Visio and Visual Studio.

TABLE 22.18 Creating rules in Visio versus Visual Studio

Collection Rule	Visio	Visual Studio
Performance Collection	Basic collection rules for only Windows performance data.	Any performance data can be collected, not just Windows performance data. You can name and design your performance collection rules and the data they collect.
Windows Event Collection	Only basic collection of Windows events.	All events can be collected including Syslog, text logs, scripted, WMI events and more. You are free to collect any data you want and store it in the OpsMgr database.

Use Visual Studio to collect data other than Windows performance data or Windows event data. You will also need to write the management pack in Visual Studio if the default settings of the collection in the Visio MP Designer are inadequate. To create the collection rule in Visual Studio, follow these steps:

1. Before writing the collection rule, you must add two management pack references. Right-click **References**, then select **Add reference**. Select **Browse** and browse for the reference folder location in the installation folder of the Visual Studio extensions. Here, select the **Microsoft.SystemCenter.DataWarehouse.Library.mp** and **System.Performance.Library.mp** management packs. You need both packs to add the performance collection rules. After adding these, you can create performance collection rules that collect data and write it to the data warehouse. Hold the Ctrl key to multi-select the packs. By default, the reference aliases are named MSDL and Perf; change the references by opening the reference properties of each reference and changing the aliases to **SCDW** and **Performance**.

TIP: RESOLVING EMPTY FIELDS IN TEMPLATES WHEN SELECTING DATASOURCE

If you run into problems when you want to add a data source or collection by selecting **...** and discover the selection is empty, or you want to add a target class but cannot locate it; you are probably missing a reference.

Be sure to have the correct management pack references in your project. Adding the referenced management pack should resolve the issue.

2. Create a folder for the rules in your project. Right-click the newly created Rules folder to add a new item **Rules (performance collection)** and name it **Rules.mptg**. Double-click Rules.mptg to begin editing the properties of the rule as shown in Figure 22.25.

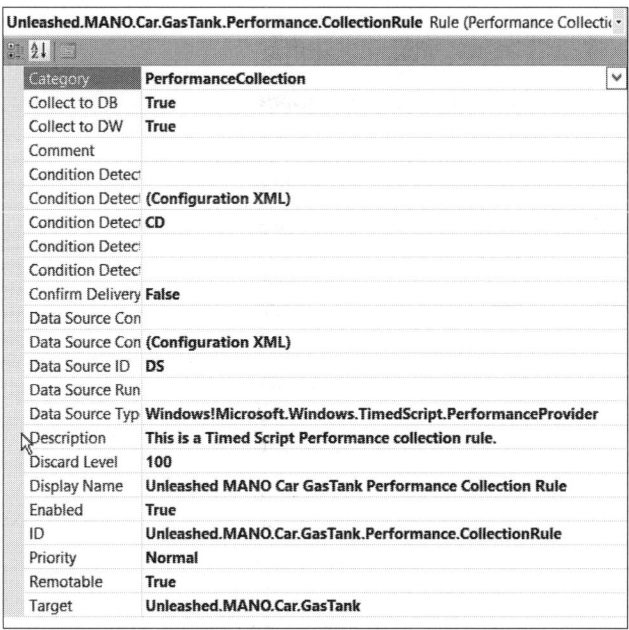

FIGURE 22.25 Performance rule configuration.

3. Add the XML section using the values and properties in Table 22.19. By using Intellisense, you should be able to add these to the data source configuration.

TABLE 22.19 Performance collection rule properties

Property	Value
IntervalSeconds	300
SyncTime	00:00
ScriptName	MANOGasTankperfCol.vbs
Arguments	"C:"
TimeoutSeconds	300
ObjectName	GasTank
CounterName	Amount of fuel in percentage
InstanceName	$Target/Property[Type="System!System.Entity"]/DisplayName$
Value	$Data/Property[@Name='PerfValue']$

After adding the XML parts, you can add the following script:

```
Option Explicit
SetLocale ("en-us")
On Error Resume Next
Dim oAPI, oBag, strComputer, objWMIService, strQuery, colDisks, colDisk,
oPercentageFree, oArgs, oDisk,PerfValue, oPercentageUsed
Set oAPI = CreateObject("MOM.ScriptAPI")
Set oBag = oAPI.CreateTypedPropertyBag()
Set oArgs = WScript.Arguments
oDisk = oArgs(0)

strComputer = "."
Set objWMIService = GetObject("winmgmts:" & "{impersonationLevel=imperson
ate}!\\" & strComputer & "\root\cimv2")
strQuery = "Select * from Win32_LogicalDisk Where Name = '" & oDisk & "'"

Set colDisks = objWMIService.ExecQuery (strQuery)
For Each colDisk in colDisks
oPercentageFree = Int(100.0 * (colDisk.FreeSpace) / (colDisk.Size))
oPercentageUsed = Int(100.0 - (oPercentageFree))
Next

Call oBag.AddValue("PerfValue",oPercentageUsed)
Call oAPI.Return(oBag)
```

With the script added to your management pack, you have created a performance collection rule to collect the amount of fuel in the gas tank. This is a great example of how you can add anything into OpsMgr using Visual Studio.

For reference, the Visual Studio projects and diagram available online as content for this book are fully functional and can be used to generate the finalized management packs.

The next section discusses creating views to view the health state of the MANO car.

Using Views

Views are important to look at an application from a user perspective. A view should give the user an overview of the health state of the application. The following sections discuss creating views in the Visio MP Designer and Visual Studio.

Views in the Visio MP Designer

Using the Visio MP Designer, when you create a server role or server component, a state view for the component is created automatically showing the state of the particular component in the Operations console. This also occurs when creating a performance monitor with the Alert and Collect or Collect settings; you can create a performance view automatically for the performance collection rule.

It is not necessary to create views when using the Visio MP Designer. Should you want additional views, you can add them directly in the console. After importing the management pack, open the Monitoring pane, navigate to the Unleashed MANO Car Visio management pack folder, and add the views. If you do not want views added in the same management pack or want to reuse the classes in other management packs, you must seal your management pack before importing it. To seal a Visio created management pack, refer to http://technet.microsoft.com/en-us/library/hh457550.

Views in Visual Studio

The approach used to create views with Visual Studio imports your sealed management packs and creates a separate views management pack. While you can create the view from scratch with Visual Studio, it is more efficient and easier to create them in the Operations console.

Keep in mind that when you use an unsealed management pack to store your views, you can only reference objects from sealed management packs, so it is important to seal your management packs when they define classes. To seal the MANO-specific management pack, follow the procedure used when sealing the base management pack in the "Classes (Advanced)" section; then import the sealed management packs.

To create a views management pack, create a new management pack and name it **Unleashed VisualStudio MANO views**. This should make a new folder visible, Unleashed VisualStudio MANO views. Underneath this folder, you can create dashboards and views for the MANO Car.

For information about creating dashboards, refer to Chapter 11, "Dashboards, Trending, and Forecasting." Chapter 7, "Configuring and Using System Center 2012 Operations Manager," discusses creating views.

Testing Your Management Packs

With your management packs created and imported into Operations Manager, you can now test their functionality:

- For the management pack created with Visual Studio, override the script arguments to choose another disk or change the threshold.
- The management pack created using the Visio MP Designer has several monitors and performance collection rules. You could set an override or change the threshold of the performance monitor to check the health state and alerting of this monitor. You can play with the settings to change severity, alerting, and resolving. You should be able to review the results in the Operations console.

To test the Windows event monitors, use the EventCreate tool, which is part of Windows. Open a command prompt on the agent running the example, and follow these steps to test the monitors:

1. For the MANO Car event monitor, run the following command to trigger an error alert and health state change:

   ```
   EVENTCREATE /SO "Unleashed MANO Car" /T ERROR /ID 996 /L APPLICATION /D
   "Testing the Visio created management pack. Creating an error, causing the
   monitor to be triggered."
   ```

   After generating an error event, watch the console to show the alert and monitor generate a critical alert. After the alert is triggered, set the monitor to healthy by running the healthy event:

   ```
   EVENTCREATE /SO "Unleashed MANO Car" /T INFORMATION /ID 995 /L APPLICATION /D
   "Testing the Visio created management pack. While Creating an Error causing
   the monitor to be triggered."
   ```

2. Follow the procedure in step 1 to test the MANO car engine error event ID 999 and healthy event ID 991.
3. Test again, changing the severity of the incidents.
   - Notice the flaws and missing options in the monitors in the Visio MP Designer. When an event ID 996 Error is created and an Information event 996 informs all is well again, the monitor cannot pick up the information since Visio can only compare on source and ID.
   - Use the same testing procedures with the Visual Studio created management pack and notice this monitor can determine the severity of the events.

   Although these are rather simple monitors, you should now have a better understanding of the differences of both packs.

4. Another major difference is how performance data is collected. The Visio MP designed rule just notifies you the C:\ drive has *x* percent of free space left, while the performance collection rule created in Visual Studio looks like a real gas tank monitor although it actually queries the same C:\ drive for free disk space performance.

The last step in creating a management pack is developing reports. Reports often are not included in a management pack because they seem overly complicated. The next section describes how to generate reports easily for custom classes or existing classes within your environment.

Creating Reports

While reporting and creating reports haven't significantly changed in OpsMgr 2012, reporting still seems very difficult for most OpsMgr users and administrators. The only change to reporting in OpsMgr 2012 is within the Visio MP Designer. Using the Visio MP Designer, you can set a simple field to TRUE to create a report in OpsMgr 2012 for the performance monitor you just created (Alert and Collect, or Collect) as displayed in Figure 22.26.

Name	MANO Gas Tank Performance Monito
Object	LogicalDisk
Counter	% Free Space
All Instances	FALSE
Instance	C:
Monitor Behavior	Alert and Collect
Health Category	Performance
Comparison Type	Average
Number Of States	2 - Healthy & Critical
Critical Threshold	50
Operator	>
Interval	300
Number of Samples	3
Collection Interval	900
Create Performance View	TRUE
Performance View Name	MANO Gas Tank Performance View
Advanced Alert Settings	FALSE
Save to Data Warehouse	TRUE
Create Report	TRUE
Report Name	MANO Gas Tank Report
Run On	Always

FIGURE 22.26 Visio MP Designer Report setting.

When you set the field to **TRUE** as shown in the figure, a report is automatically created in the management pack you created with the Visio MP Designer Tool. This is a standard report with a filter on the class and performance collection rule that are already in place.

After importing the management pack, you can run the report from the Reporting pane. Add objects by selecting **Add Object** in the upper-right corner of the report. A window opens that already has a filter in place to show only instances of the `Gas Tank` class, which is the target of the performance collection rule as shown in Figure 22.27.

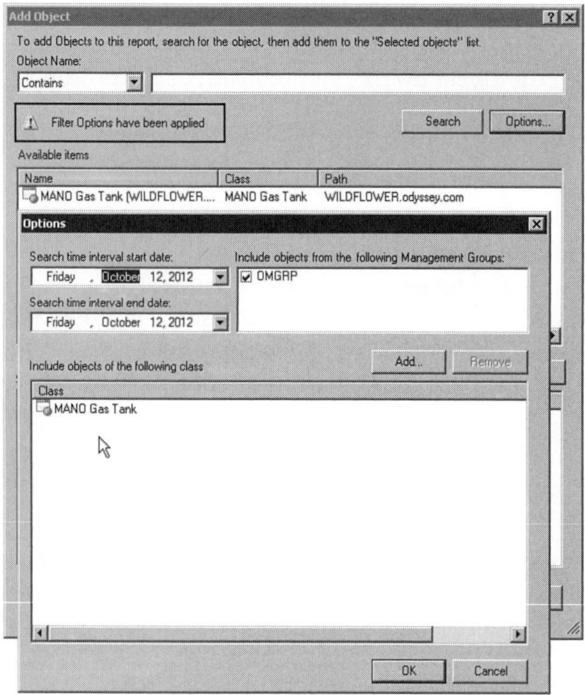

FIGURE 22.27 Report Filter placed by MP Visio Designer tool.

The Visio MP Designer delivers a quick standard report for reporting on performance collection rules created by the tool. The real benefit of this report is that it already has filters in place to report on the correct object and performance collection rule.

When you select multiple instances and run the report, you will notice the report shows only the overall graph on the combined instances. For the report to show a graph for each instance, click on the **MANO Gas Tank Performance Monitor Performance Collection Rule** link highlighted in Figure 22.28.

Rule, Instance, Object	Scale	Sample Count	Min Value	Max Value	Average Value	Standard Deviation
MANO Gas Tank Performance Monitor Performance Collection Rule	1	17	24.72	91.37	60.09	0.09943
⊞ Instances (1)						

FIGURE 22.28 Performance detail linked report.

The link takes you to the Performance Detail Report linked report, which displays additional details. If you open **Actions** and click the **Performance Detail for every object** link as shown in Figure 22.29, you generate a report that displays performance for every instance in a separate graph.

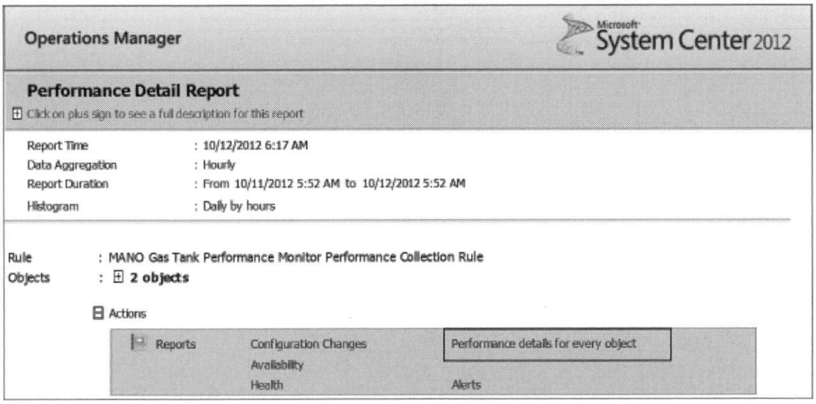

FIGURE 22.29 Performance details for every object.

You can easily create reports for newly created performance collection rules using the Visio MP Designer. Reporting on existing counters or combining counters in one report requires tools other than the Visio MP Designer; use the OpsMgr 2007 R2 reporting solutions. Here are some links discussing these tools:

- **Building reports with Report Builder by Stefan Koell:** http://www.code4ward.net/main/Blog/tabid/70/EntryId/81/How-to-use-Report-Builder-to-create-custom-reports-in-SCOM-2007.aspx
- **Building reports in SQL Server Business Intelligence Development Studio by Oskar Landman:** http://www.systemcentercentral.com/BlogDetails/tabid/143/IndexID/60805/Default.aspx
- **Building Linked reports in OpsMgr 2007 R2 by Pete Zerger:** http://www.systemcentercentral.com/BlogDetails/tabid/143/IndexID/64107/Default.aspx
- **Reporting links for creating custom reports by Stefan Stranger:** http://blogs.technet.com/b/stefan_stranger/archive/2011/01/27/opsmgr-custom-reporting-links.aspx

A big issue with custom reporting in OpsMgr is using the correct class and performance rules and targeting the reports. To target your reports correctly you must identify the target class and the performance collection rule. The explanation in this section describes how to use the standard reports in OpsMgr and how to target these reports correctly.

To create a report, you must know the class or group to target. The easiest way to determine the correct target is to open the performance view and look at the different performance rules. Select the one you are interested in, right-click the rule, and select **Show or**

edit rule properties. A Properties page opens, providing information as shown in Figure 22.30. The properties clearly state the target of the rule. View the additional properties of the rule, displayed in Figure 22.31.

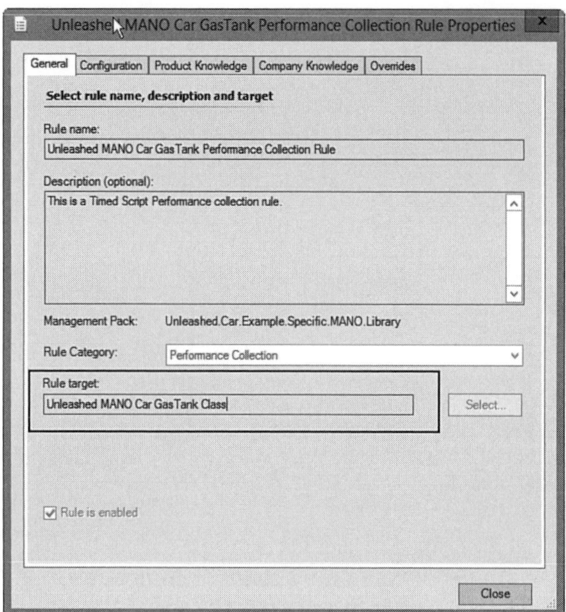

FIGURE 22.30 Performance Rule properties with target.

Rule	Object	Counter
Unleashed MANO Car GasTank Performance Collection Rule	GasTank	Amount of fuel in percentage

FIGURE 22.31 Performance rule properties.

These two figures show the Unleashed MANO Car GasTank Class target and the Unleashed MANO Car GasTank Performance Collection Rule are required for a report that includes data. With an incorrect target, you get a report without data. Now look at a performance report. Follow these steps:

1. Open the Reporting pane and navigate to **Microsoft Generic Report Library** -> **Performance**. Open the report.

2. The report opens and shows all parameters; you can change these according to your requirements. Start adding the correct objects. Click **Change** to open the Settings page.

3. Create a **New Chart** and give the chart the title **MANO Gas Tank usage**. Select **New Series** to add a series to the chart. The settings should look like Figure 22.32.

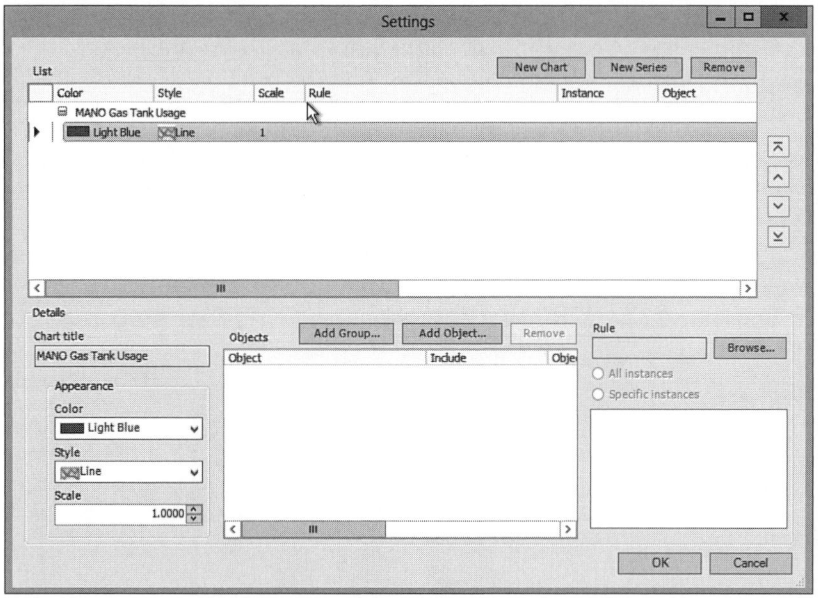

FIGURE 22.32 Performance Report settings.

4. Start adding the objects. There are two options: Add Group and Add Object. For this example, click **Add Object** and then click **Options** to add a filter.

5. On the Options page, select **Include objects of the following class**. In the Add Class dialog search for **GasTank**, add the Unleashed MANO Car Gas Tank class to the selected objects. The Options page should look like Figure 22.33.

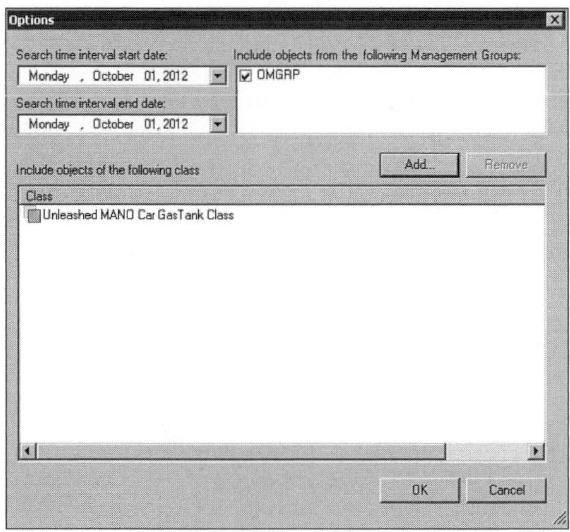

FIGURE 22.33 The Report Options filter.

6. Click **OK** to close the Options dialog. You should see a yellow exclamation mark and the text **Filter Options have been applied**. Select **Search** and a list of Unleashed MANO Car GasTank class instances should appear. Add the instance as the object, which is the target.

7. Next, add a performance rule to your graph. Click **Rule -> Browse** to browse all performance collection rules. There are several ways to search for the performance rule. The two primary search functions are by rule or by counter; as you already identified both in Figure 22.31, you can choose either. Choose **Search By Name** and fill in the search box with **Unleashed MANO Car GasTank Performance Collection Rule** as shown in Figure 22.34, and click **OK**.

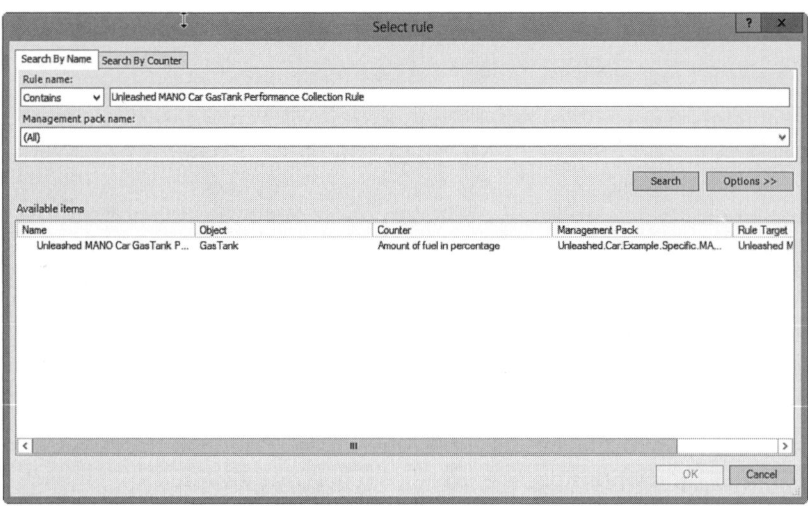

FIGURE 22.34 Select performance rule.

8. You now have selected the target and performance rule for running your report. You could also change the appearance of the graph by changing the color and style of the graph. If satisfied with the appearance, click **OK** and run the report. The result should look similar to Figure 22.35.

9. Once the report is created, you can schedule the report or save it to a management pack. To save the report to a management pack, select **File -> Save to management pack**. Name your report **MANO Gas Tank Usage Report**, and save it in a new management pack, **Unleashed Visual Studio MANO Reports**.

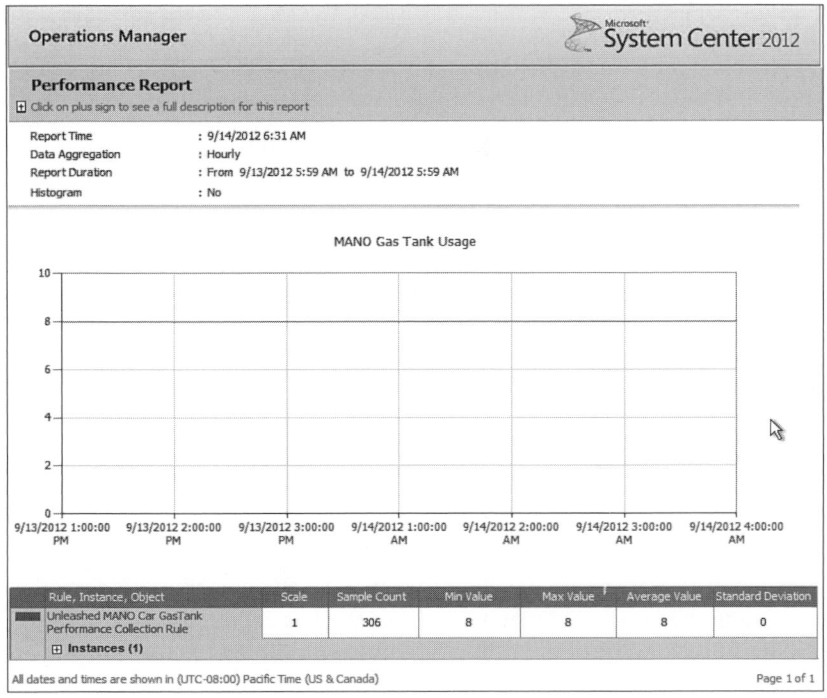

FIGURE 22.35 Performance Report result.

TIP: TARGETING IN REPORTS

The most difficult part about reporting is defining the correct target and performance rule. Use the Monitoring pane to verify you have the correct information. Navigate to the performance view containing the rule you want to report on, select the properties of the rule to determine the target class, and note the performance rule name. With the target class and rule identified, you can create any report.

Another more advanced option is writing reports based on groups. Be sure you are targeting properly. If the performance counters are targeted at the logical disk and you want to create a group, only add logical disks in this group and target your report on this group for free disk space.

The advantage to groups is they can be populated dynamically, so you only have to create a single report. If a new instance is added, the dynamic population rule automatically adds the instance to the group. The only downside is you generate the report based on the overall performance of the group and have to run a child report to get the information per instance.

This information is also is described in the article at http://www.bictt.com/blogs/bictt.php/2010/11/28/scom-reports-on-performance-counters-for-large-groups-of-servers.

Fast Track

While there are no real changes around authoring concepts in general, the real change in OpsMgr 2012 authoring is the tools available to build custom management packs.

- **Visio MP Designer:** This is an add-on to Microsoft Visio 2010 letting you write a management pack using Visio 2010. This tool is for less experienced users and is limited to a basic subset of rules and monitors.
- **Visual Studio:** The Visual Studio Authoring Extensions are an add-on to Visual Studio 2010. This tool is for experienced authors and has a high learning curve.

There are no significant changes to reporting in OpsMgr 2012. The only difference is you can now easily create reports for performance collection rules created by the Visio MP Designer tool.

Summary

This chapter discussed writing a management pack using the two new tools available with OpsMgr 2012. Using a car as an example, the chapter explained the procedures for writing a management pack, using the Visio MP Designer tool for the less experienced author and Visual Studio Extensions for advanced authors. It also showed how to combine the authoring tools currently available to create management packs for OpsMgr 2012. The chapter stepped through the development of two management packs to monitor a car to incorporate the perspective of the less experienced author and the experienced author. The next chapter discusses PowerShell in System Center 2012 Operations Manager.

CHAPTER 23

PowerShell and Operations Manager

IN THIS CHAPTER

- Windows PowerShell Cmdlet Primer
- What's New in Operations Manager 2012 PowerShell
- Working with Agents
- Managing Maintenance Mode
- Working with Alerts
- Administering Resource Pools
- Managing Licensing
- Managing the RMS Emulator
- Database Cmdlets
- Creating Overrides in Bulk
- Exploring Classes and Instances
- Managing Notification Subscriptions
- Scripting Recurring Tasks
- Fast Track

PowerShell, an object-oriented interactive command line shell integrated with the .NET Framework, has been referred to as *.NET on the command line*. As the scripting and automation language of choice for Microsoft products, PowerShell is a must-have in your administrative toolkit to be a more effective and efficient administrator. Knowing this language can save time and effort with System Center Operations Manager (OpsMgr) as well as numerous other Microsoft products.

The language has come a long way since its debut as Monad in 2005. With each version, PowerShell continues to improve in capabilities and functionality, and this release of Operations Manager includes improved PowerShell support and integration. While you will continue to leverage the Operations console on a day-to-day basis, PowerShell provides a tool for you to automate those repetitive tasks, scheduled tasks, or other bulk administrative tasks you cannot easily perform in the OpsMgr GUI.

This chapter includes a short primer on the PowerShell language and then dives into some practical examples on using PowerShell when administering your OpsMgr 2012 environment. The next several pages include some basic PowerShell information to assist those readers who may not have any experience with PowerShell. If you have experience with PowerShell, you may want to skip to the "What's New in Operations Manager 2012 PowerShell" section.

TIP: MORE INFORMATION ON POWERSHELL NAMING CONVENTIONS

The PowerShell cmdlets for OpsMgr 2012 have been renamed. For more information about the new naming standards as well as cmdlet naming collisions, see the Windows PowerShell blog at http://blogs.msdn.com/b/powershell/archive/2009/09/20/what-s-up-with-command-prefixes.aspx.

Windows PowerShell Cmdlet Primer

A *cmdlet* is a .NET program designed to interact with PowerShell. These cmdlets take the format of verb-noun with a dash between them; for example, `Get-SCOMAgent`, where Get is the verb and SCOMAgent is the noun. All PowerShell cmdlets follow this basic syntax. Here are the three common verbs used in cmdlets:

- `Get` cmdlets that fetch data
- `Set` cmdlets that set or change data
- `Format` cmdlets, which format data for output

It is important to remember that while the output to the PowerShell console may look and act like text when you copy it to the clipboard, it is just a text representation of the underlying .NET objects exposed from the code that is run.

Frequently Used and Useful Cmdlets

The next sections discuss some of the more frequently used cmdlets; familiarizing yourself with them will be useful if you are not familiar with PowerShell.

The Get-Help Cmdlet

`Get-Help` is used in combination with that cmdlet for which you need help. Here are several useful parameters:

- **–full:** This shows all the help information on a cmdlet or topic.
- **-detailed:** This shows the majority of the help file.
- **–examples:** This shows only the synopsis and the examples given in the help file.

Here is the syntax for all three parameters for you to retrieve documentation related to the `Get-SCOMAgent` cmdlet:

```
Get-Help Get-SCOMAgent -full
Get-Help Get-SCOMAgent -detailed
Get-Help Get-SCOMAgent -examples
```

For reference, the `Get-SCOMAgent` cmdlet fetches a list of agents installed and shows among other things the health state of the agents, as well as the version number of the agents. This is discussed in more detail in the "Working with Agents" section.

Using Get-Command

This cmdlet gets basic information about cmdlets and other elements of PowerShell commands, such as aliases, functions, filters, scripts, and applications, which it gets directly from the cmdlet code.

- Running `Get-Command` by itself gets all of the cmdlets, functions, and aliases in the current PowerShell session.
- Running `Get-Command` using `-Module` and specifying `OperationsManager` will retrieve all the cmdlets, functions and alias in that module.

  ```
  Get-Command -Module OperationsManager
  ```

  To make this list more readable, add some sorting to `CommandType` and `Name`. To do this, pipe the output of `Get-Command -Module OperationsManager` to the `Sort-Object` cmdlet, and specify `CommandType, Name` as the elements you wish to reorder, as shown in this example, which sorts the results alphabetically.

  ```
  Get-Command -Module OperationsManager | Sort-Object CommandType, Name
  ```


About the Get-Member Cmdlet

This cmdlet displays a list of the .NET properties and methods:

- *Properties* contain information about the object type or instance (the OpsMgr agent as an example), such as their names, whether proxying is enabled, and the Internet Protocol (IP) address they have.
- *Methods* can act on the property of the object. For example, the `Get-Process` cmdlet includes a .kill() method that can be used to kill a process for a specified process ID.

  Methods must always be called with the trailing brackets () and may require additional input, which you can find using the `Get-Help` cmdlet demonstrated in the "The Get-Help Cmdlet" section.

`Get-Member` often reveals much more information about a type or instance than you will see simply by running a cmdlet. For example, when you run the cmdlet `Get-Process`, only eight properties are returned. However, when you pass `Get-Process` to `Get-Member` via the pipeline, as shown in this example, approximately 20 methods and 70 properties are returned! Here's the syntext:

```
Get-Process | Get-Member
```

`Get-Member` is very helpful when trying to determine what information is available from the cmdlet you are working with, and indispensible when trying to write PowerShell scripts where native OpsMgr cmdlets do not provide parameters to accomplish the task at hand. Figure 23.1 shows the output from sending `Get-SCOMAgent` to `Get-Member`; it shows the properties and methods available from the `Get-SCOMAgent` cmdlet.

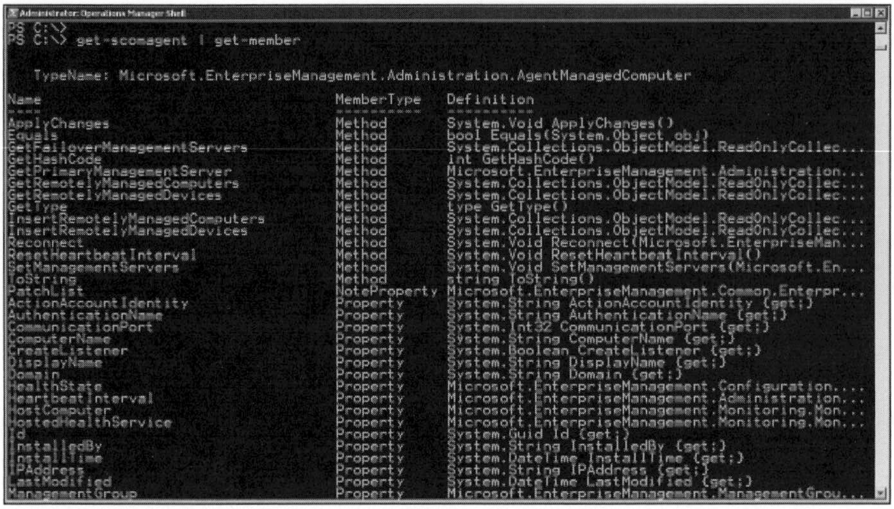

FIGURE 23.1 Properties and Methods of `Get-SCOMAgent` (via `Get-Member`).

Using Aliases

An alias within PowerShell is just another name that can be assigned to a cmdlet, function, or script. PowerShell empowers the user to assign aliases as well. To check out the built-in aliases in PowerShell, run the `Get-Alias` cmdlet.

Several examples of aliases you could use would be `FT` for the `Format-table` cmdlet or `FL` for the `Format-list` cmdlet. To see a list of specific aliases defined with OpsMgr, run the following in the OpsMgr 2012 PowerShell console:

```
Get-Alias | Where-Object {$_.Name -like "*SCOM*"}
```

Here the `Get-Alias` cmdlet fetches the alias information, which then is pipelined to the `Where-Object` cmdlet. This looks at the name of each object in the pipeline and only pulls out those objects that have the text SCOM anywhere in the name, which then is displayed in the PowerShell console.

Utilizing PowerShell Comparison Operators

To compare or filter data, use the proper comparison operators, listed in Table 23.1. Filtering data helps present exactly what you need when you need it.

TABLE 23.1 Windows PowerShell comparison operators

Operator	Description
-LT	Less Than
-LE	Less Than or Equal To
-GT	Greater Than
-GE	Greater Than or Equal To
-EQ	Equal To
-NE	Not Equal To
-LIKE	Use wild cards for pattern matching
-MATCH	A Match using regular Expressions
-CONTAINS	Used to see if a collection or group of items contains a given item

PowerShell Execution Policy

Scripting is a very powerful tool, but can be misused for malicious purposes. To protect user data and the integrity of the operating system, Windows PowerShell includes several security features, among which is the execution policy. The Windows PowerShell execution policy determines whether scripts are allowed to run and, if they can run, whether they must be digitally signed. It also determines whether configuration files can be loaded.

To see how the execution policy is applied to a specific machine, run `Get-ExecutionPolicy -list.`

For more information about the PowerShell Execution Policy, `Get-Help about_Execution_Policies` provides a comprehensive help file.

Signing PowerShell Scripts

Whether or not your environment has an existing public key infrastructure (PKI) will determine if you use self-signed scripts or signing with a certificate from a trusted certification authority.

Self-Signed Certificate

Use a self-signed certificate, using the .NET Framework 2.0 software development kit (SDK) to create the certificate, to run scripts as scheduled tasks on the OpsMgr server or administrator workstation with the Operations console loaded on it.

NOTE: CONNECTIVITY REQUIREMENTS FOR ADMINISTRATOR WORKSTATIONS WHEN RUNNING SCRIPTS

If you use an administrator workstation to run scripts, it should have similar network connectivity as a management server so your scripts will not time out or take longer than expected to run. The data will flow from the PowerShell console to the management server it needs to connect to and then to the SQL database via the System Center Data Access service, then back to the PowerShell console.

Here are two great resources that discuss using Microsoft's certificate creation tool, makecert.exe, to generate certificates to create self-signed PowerShell scripts:

- Don Jones' TechNet Magazine article "Sign Here, Please," available at http://technet.microsoft.com/en-us/magazine/2008.04.powershell.aspx
- Scott Hanselman's blog post "Signing PowerShell Scripts" at http://www.hanselman.com/blog/SigningPowerShellScripts.aspx

Existing Internal PKI

If you have an existing PKI infrastructure that can be utilized to generate a certificate, there is a great two-part series on signing PowerShell scripts with an enterprise PKI from the Microsoft Scripting Guys, http://blogs.technet.com/b/heyscriptingguy/archive/2010/06/16/hey-scripting-guy-how-can-i-sign-windows-powershell-scripts-with-an-enterprise-windows-pki-part-1-of-2.aspx and http://blogs.technet.com/b/heyscriptingguy/archive/2010/06/17/hey-scripting-guy-how-can-i-sign-windows-powershell-scripts-with-an-enterprise-windows-pki-part-2-of-2.aspx.

Certificate Authority

You could get your own code-signing certificate from a public CA (such as VeriSign or Digicert) to sign PowerShell scripts. Tom Arbuthnot, a Microsoft Lync MVP, discusses what you need to accomplish this at http://lyncdup.com/2012/03/how-to-get-a-personal-code-signing-certificate-from-a-public-ca-to-sign-powershell-scripts/.

Adding the PowerShell Integrated Scripting Environment

With the release of PowerShell version 2, Microsoft included the PowerShell Integrated Scripting Environment (ISE), a host application for Windows PowerShell. Using the Windows PowerShell ISE, you can run commands and write, test, and debug scripts in a single Windows-based graphic user interface with multiline editing, tab completion, syntax coloring, selective execution, context-sensitive help, and support for right-to-left languages. The menu items and keyboard shortcuts let you perform many of the same tasks that you would perform in the Windows PowerShell console.

In Windows 2008 Release 2 (R2), the default configuration is not to enable the Windows PowerShell Integrated Scripting Environment (this is enabled by default in Windows Server 2012). To enable the Windows PowerShell ISE on Windows Server 2008 R2, follow these steps:

1. Open Server Manager.
2. Select the **Features** option and click **Add features** to begin the Add Features Wizard.
3. Scroll down to Windows PowerShell Integrated Scripting Environment (ISE); tick the check box next to it, and then click **Next**.
4. The Confirm Installation Selections dialog box is displayed; click **Install** when ready to complete the feature installation.

5. When the installation completes the Installation Results dialog box will pop up, showing that the Windows PowerShell Integrated Scripting Environment (ISE) installed successfully.

6. Click **Close**. The PowerShell ISE is now available under **Start** -> **All Programs** -> **Accessories** -> **Windows PowerShell ISE**.

Although the PowerShell ISE is loaded on your Windows 2008 R2 computer with the OpsMgr 2012 console installed on it, this does not mean it will automatically start using the OpsMgr 2012 PowerShell modules; you must first let the ISE know about the modules (all PowerShell modules are loaded automatically on Windows Server 2012). To load the OpsMgr PowerShell module on Windows 2008 R2, open the PowerShell ISE, and in the lower interactive pane issue the following command, displayed in Figure 23.2, to import the module for Operations Manager:


```
Import-Module OperationsManager
```

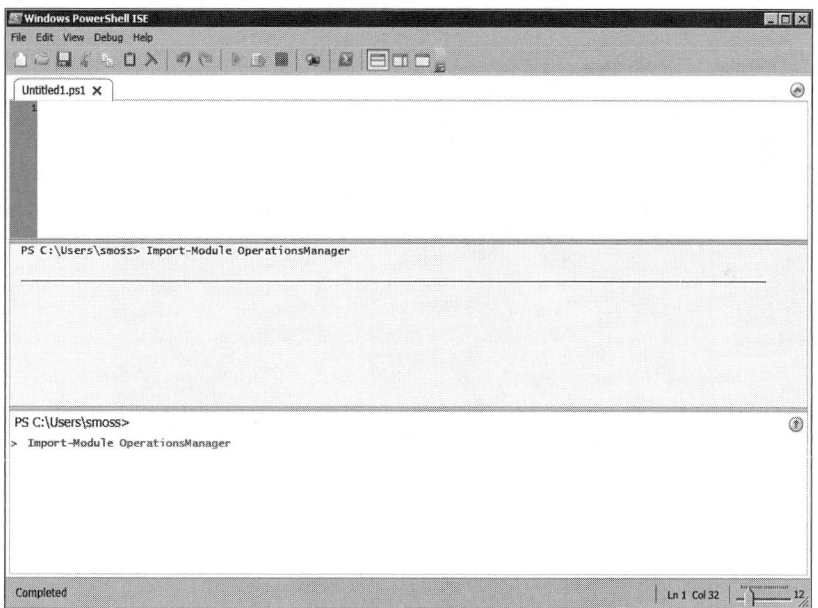

FIGURE 23.2 Using `Import-Module` to import Operations Manager cmdlets.

To verify the OperationsManager module imported properly, run this command in the PowerShell ISE lower interactive pane. This shows the cmdlets available in the OperationsManager module.

```
Get-Command -module OperationsManager
```

Once you load the OpsMgr PowerShell module in the first window, the module and its cmdlets will be known to all additional tabs opened (via the New icon or File menu item) in the same PowerShell ISE session.

Filtering, Formatting, and Grouping with PowerShell

Three formatting cmdlets format objects for output. Due to the number of options available for both `Format-List` and `Format-Table`, you would do well to check their options using `Get-Help`:

```
Get-Help Format-List -full
Get-Help Format-Table -full
Get-Help Select-Object -full
```

The `Format-List` cmdlet formats the output of a command as a list of properties, with each property displayed on a separate line. `Format-List` can display all or specific properties of an object as a list. Using these cmdlets, you can pipe objects to the cmdlet and specify those properties you want to see, automatically eliminating others. For example, the `Get-Process` cmdlet returns eight properties in its output by default, as shown in Figure 23.3.

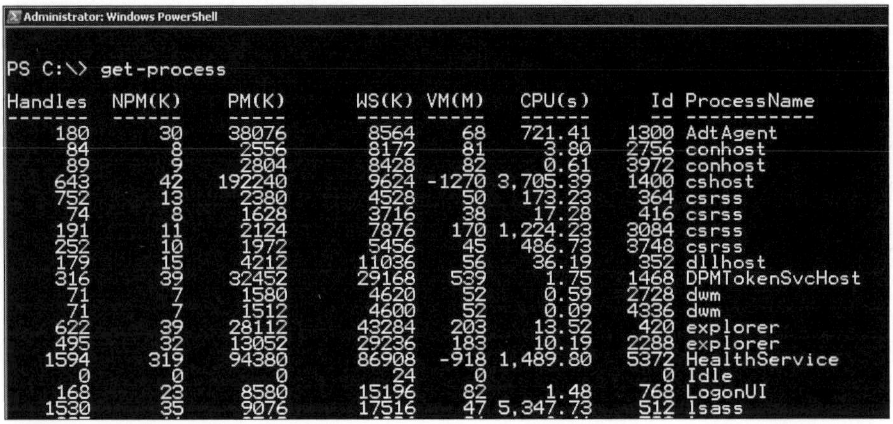

```
Administrator: Windows PowerShell

PS C:\> get-process

Handles  NPM(K)    PM(K)      WS(K) VM(M)   CPU(s)     Id ProcessName
-------  ------    -----      ----- -----   ------     -- -----------
    180      30    38076       8564    68   721.41   1300 AdtAgent
     84       8     2556       8172    81     3.80   2756 conhost
     89       9     2804       8428    82     0.61   3972 conhost
    643      42   192240       9624 -1270 3,705.39   1400 cshost
    752      13     2380       4528    50   173.23    364 csrss
     74       8     1628       3716    38    17.28    416 csrss
    191      11     2124       7876   170 1,224.23   3084 csrss
    252      10     1972       5456    45   486.73   3748 csrss
    179      15     4212      11036    56    36.19    352 dllhost
    316      39    32452      29168   539     1.75   1468 DPMTokenSvcHost
     71       7     1580       4620    52     0.59   2728 dwm
     71       7     1512       4600    52     0.09   4336 dwm
    622      39    28112      43284   203    13.52    420 explorer
    495      32    13052      29236   183    10.19   2288 explorer
   1594     319    94380      86908  -918 1,489.80   5372 HealthService
      0       0        0         24     0              0 Idle
    168      23     8580      15196    82     1.48    768 LogonUI
   1530      35     9076      17516    47 5,347.73    512 lsass
```

FIGURE 23.3 Default output of the `Get-Process` cmdlet.

Using `Select-Object`, you can narrow this list down to only the properties of interest. For example, the following single line of code (referred to as a *one-liner* in PowerShell speak) returns only the process name, process ID, and handle count:

```
Get-Process | Select-Object ProcessName, ID, Handles
```

About Sort-Object

The `Sort-Object` cmdlet works by manipulating objects for output. To sort a list of OpsMgr agents by name and output to a table requires just a couple of cmdlets in a single line of PowerShell, as shown in Figure 23.4.

The code shown in Figure 23.4, `Get-SCOMAgent | Sort-Object Name | Format-Table Name`, performs the following actions:

1. The `Get-SCOMAgent` cmdlet loads the OpsMgr agent objects into the pipeline.
2. Once in the pipeline, the objects are sent to the `Sort-Object` cmdlet, which sorts the objects by name.
3. You now have the OpsMgr agent objects in the pipeline sorted by the Name property; to display a table of just names; use the `Format-Table` cmdlet and specify what property to display, which is Name.

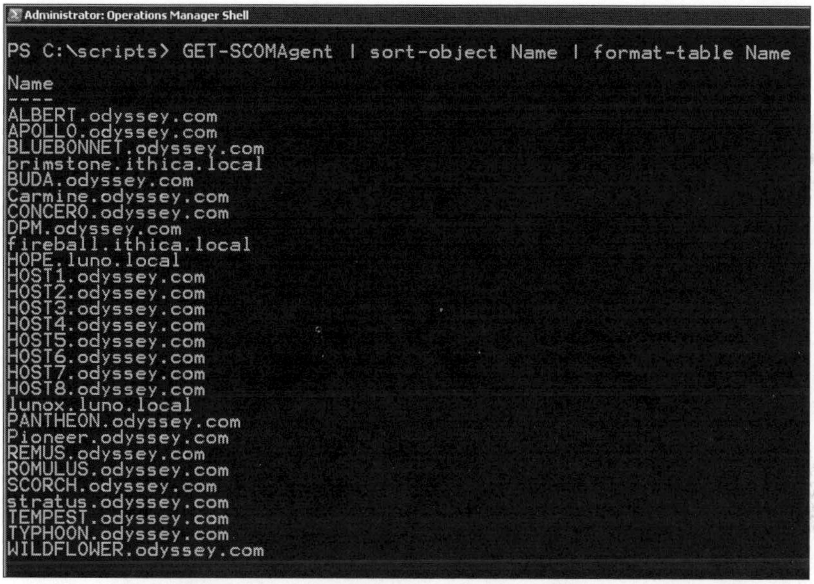

```
Administrator: Operations Manager Shell
PS C:\scripts> GET-SCOMAgent | sort-object Name | format-table Name

Name
----
ALBERT.odyssey.com
APOLLO.odyssey.com
BLUEBONNET.odyssey.com
brimstone.ithica.local
BUDA.odyssey.com
Carmine.odyssey.com
CONCERO.odyssey.com
DPM.odyssey.com
fireball.ithica.local
HOPE.luno.local
HOST1.odyssey.com
HOST2.odyssey.com
HOST3.odyssey.com
HOST4.odyssey.com
HOST5.odyssey.com
HOST6.odyssey.com
HOST7.odyssey.com
HOST8.odyssey.com
lunox.luno.local
PANTHEON.odyssey.com
Pioneer.odyssey.com
REMUS.odyssey.com
ROMULUS.odyssey.com
SCORCH.odyssey.com
stratus.odyssey.com
TEMPEST.odyssey.com
TYPHOON.odyssey.com
WILDFLOWER.odyssey.com
```

FIGURE 23.4 Using `Get-SCOMAgent` with sorting and filtering cmdlets (to format output).

TIP: MORE INFORMATION ON THE PIPELINE

A discussion about the PowerShell pipeline is beyond the scope of this chapter. For more information about the pipeline, PowerShell MVP Don Jones provides several resources:

- The article at http://technet.microsoft.com/en-us/magazine/2007.07.powershell.aspx is a nice discussion of the pipeline and about what it can do for you.
- Don created a pipeline input workbook that is a good step-by-step walkthrough of how the pipeline works, available on the morelunches.com website. See http://morelunches.com/files/powershell3/PipelineInput.pdf for information.

Using (cmdlet).count

().count is a .NET method that comes in handy when using PowerShell to answer the question *how many*? It returns the value of the count property, which tells you the number of items in a collection. Using ().count is helpful when just looking for a count of the members in a collection. For example, again using the `Get-SCOMAgent` cmdlet, you can retrieve a count of how many SCOM agent objects exist:

```
(Get-SCOMAgent).count
```

While this is useful, most environments will deploy multiple management servers, at which point distributing the Windows agent load evenly across multiple management servers becomes important. When run in an OpsMgr Shell instance, the following sample leverages the `Group-Object` cmdlet (`Group` for short) and will return the agent count by management server, as shown in Figure 23.5. This script also uses a variable named `$agent`. For information on using variables, see the "Variables in PowerShell" section.

```
$agent = Get-SCOMAgent
$agent | Group PrimaryManagementServerName -Noelement | sort Name | `
select Name, Count
```

NOTE: ABOUT THE "ONE-LINERS" IN THIS CHAPTER

Many of the "one-liners" throughout this chapter appear as multiline scripts because they are reformatted to fit on the page. The backtick symbol ` used at the end of a line of code signals PowerShell that a single sequence of code spans multiple lines. The first example of this is in the example just before this note.

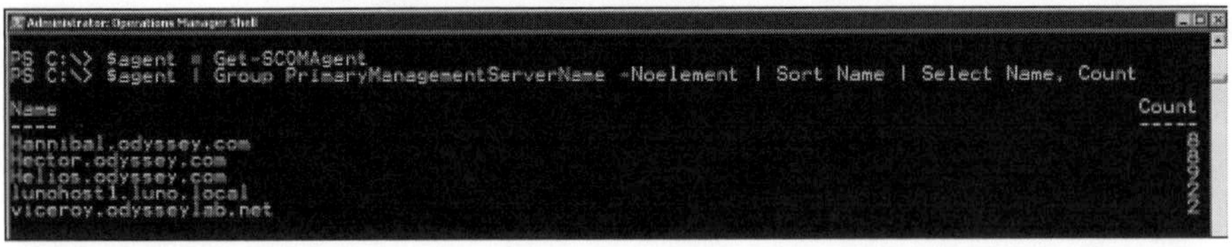

FIGURE 23.5 Agent count per management server via the OpsMgr Shell.

Notice the large amount of space between the Name and Count column in Figure 23.5. `Select-Object` (called using its alias, simply `Select`) does not format the output; it simply filters the output of the specified properties. This becomes important when exporting script output to an Excel-friendly file (covered in the "Browsing Classes" section). To format output for display on your screen, use the `Format-Table` cmdlet. `Format-Table` includes an -auto parameter that removes white space. By modifying the short PowerShell snippet to use `Format-Table` with the -auto parameter instead of `Select-Object`, the content is returned in a more concise format, as shown in Figure 23.6.

```
$agent = Get-SCOMAgent
$agent | Group PrimaryManagementServerName -Noelement | sort Name | `
Format-Table Name, Count -auto
```

```
Administrator: Operations Manager Shell
viceroy.odysseylab.net      3

PS C:\> $agent | Group PrimaryManagementServerName -Noelement | sort Name | form
at-table Name, Count -auto

Name                      Count
----                      -----
Hannibal.odyssey.com         12
Hector.odyssey.com           12
lunohost1.luno.local          2
viceroy.odysseylab.net        3

PS C:\> _
```

White space removed!

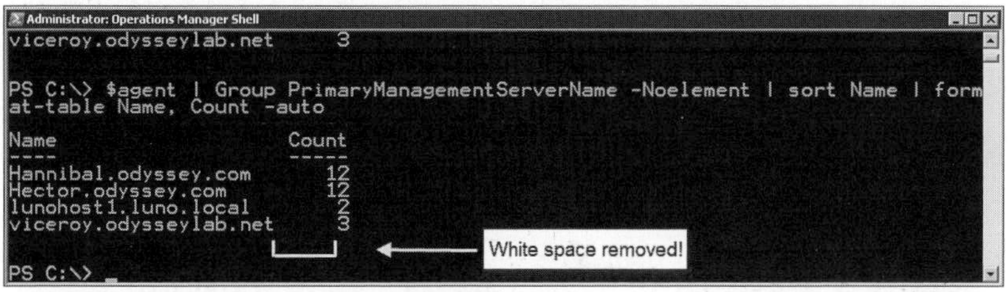

FIGURE 23.6 Agent count per management server output via `Format-Table`.

You can easily use the count method with more complex PowerShell sequences as well. Note the use of parentheses in the following example, allowing use of the count method with a more detailed one-liner including filtering courtesy of `Where-Object`; this tells PowerShell to run the code within the parentheses first, which retrieves the collection. PowerShell then returns the value of the object Count of that collection. To get a quick count of how many agents your infrastructure is monitoring whose name starts with an H, pipe the output of `Get-SCOMAgent` to `Where-Object` to filter on Name that starts with the letter H:

```
(Get-SCOMAgent | Where-Object {$_.Name -like "H*"}).count
```

Variables in PowerShell

In the example in the previous section, you may have noticed the dollar sign ($) in `$agent`. The dollar sign in PowerShell denotes a variable. Think of a variable as a container where information is stored. Two common uses of variables are to store information that will be later utilized within a script and to store information that is a result of running a script. In PowerShell, variables can contain text strings, integers, and even objects (complete with properties and methods).

For example, the following line of script saves "I Love PowerShell" to a variable called `$Text`.

```
$Text = "I Love PowerShell"
```

The next line of script echoes the contents of the `$Text` variable to screen in your PowerShell session.

```
Write-Host $Text
```

You will use variables frequently in the examples presented throughout this chapter. If you are unfamiliar with PowerShell variables, try the example in this section on your own. You can also read more about variables in the tutorial at http://www.powershellpro.com/powershell-tutorial-introduction/variables-arrays-hashes/.

What's New in Operations Manager 2012 PowerShell

There is a truckload of new cmdlets in Operations Manager 2012. With 13 aliases, 28 functions, and 125 cmdlets, PowerShell support is knocked up several notches from the OpsMgr 2007 days. For a list of these Operations Manager 2012 aliases, functions, and cmdlets, utilize the following code in the Operations Manager 2012 PowerShell console.

```
Get-Command -module OperationsManager | sort CommandType, Name | FT
```

PowerShell version 2 is supported out of the box, which means the OpsMgr PowerShell Shell is now a module and no longer a snap-in.

All cmdlets are renamed. The new cmdlet names for Operations Manager 2012 came from a PowerShell design best practice now enforced internally at Microsoft. This best practice was implemented after the OpsMgr 2007 release; this is why Operations Manager 2007 did not conform to the naming standard.

The best practice prefixes the cmdlet noun to mitigate possible naming collisions with other PowerShell cmdlets. The naming standard uses Verb-Prefix-Noun naming. The prefix is a two- to four-character name that indicates the team or product that owns the cmdlet noun. This was implemented because when a naming collision occurs, the last written cmdlet is used and could possibly break your script.

For a list of cmdlets sorted by name along with cmdlet name and definition, run the following from an OpsMgr Shell instance:

```
Get-Command -module OperationsManager | Where-Object `
{$_.CommandType -like "Cmdlet"}| Sort Name | FT Name, Definition
```

Four help topics are a great information resource if you are new to Operations Manager 2012 and PowerShell:.

- **Get-Help about_OpsMgr_whatsnew:** Discusses what is new in Operations Manager 2012 in relation to PowerShell, also discusses several of the improvements of PowerShell version 2. Connections to the management server, new cmdlets, and working with the management group object are covered. Using the deprecated Operations Manager 2007 cmdlets is the last item discussed in this help topic.

- **Get-Help about_OpsMgr_Cmdlet_Names:** Discusses the cmdlet name changes in the new version of the OpsMgr Shell. A list of the new Operations Manager 2012 cmdlets is given in this help file, also a list of Operations Manager 2007 cmdlets and the names of their Operations Manager 2012 counterparts. The final list of cmdlets is those Operations Manager 2007 cmdlets that were not ported to Operations Manager 2012.

- **Get-Help about_OpsMgr_Connections:** This help file discusses the two types of management group connections you can make from PowerShell: persistent connections and temporary connections. A discussion of management group connections and the cmdlets you can use appears in the "Management Group Connection Cmdlets" section.

- **Get-Help about_OpsMgr_RunAsAccount:**This help file goes into some of the basics of creating and associating a new Run As account using the OpsMgr 2012 PowerShell cmdlets.

TIP: HOW TO LOAD THE OPSMGR 2012 MODULE

The "Adding the PowerShell Integrated Scripting Environment" section discussed how to load the OpsMgr 2012 PowerShell module on a computer with the Operations console installed on the local machine. To utilize the OpsMgr cmdlets, run the following command in the PowerShell ISE to load the OpsMgr module:

```
Import-Module OperationsManager
```

That instance of PowerShell will have access to the last accessed Operations Manager management server. If scripting in the OpsMgr environment, this would be the first cmdlet in the script.

Before diving into examples of the OpsMgr 2012 cmdlets, let's discuss using the Operations Manager 2007 cmdlets in an Operations Manager 2012 environment.

Operations Manager 2007 Cmdlets

Microsoft installs the Operations Manager 2007 PowerShell snap-in using the Operations Manager 2012 console. If you have customized scripts that run in the Operations Manager 2007 environment and are migrating to OpsMgr 2012, you can still use your OpsMgr 2007 scripts. While Microsoft will remove this functionality in a future version, you now can load the Operations Manager 2007 snap-in in a 2012 environment, and scripts and cmdlets from Operations Manager 2007 will continue to run.

The Operations Manager 2007 snap-in is located at *%ProgramFiles%*\System Center 2012\Operations Manager\Console. (In `Get-Help about_OpsMgr_whatsnew`, the location points to a pre-RTM location of where the files are located.)

It takes only three lines of code to load the Operations Manager 2007 snap-in. As you would be using a management server to run the snap-in from, you do not need to specify a server to which the snap-in can connect. Here's how to load the OpsMgr 2007 snap-in when the Operations Manager binaries are loaded on the C: drive, also shown in Figure 23.7:

```
Add-PSSnapIn Microsoft.EnterpriseManagement.OperationsManager.Client
cd "$env:c:\Program Files\System Center 2012\Operations Manager\Console"
.\Microsoft.EnterpriseManagement.OperationsManager.ClientShell.Startup.ps1
```

```
Administrator: Operations Manager Shell
PS C:\> Add-PSSnapIn Microsoft.EnterpriseManagement.OperationsManager.Client
PS C:\> cd "$env:c:\Program Files\System Center 2012\Operations Manager\Console"
PS C:\Program Files\System Center 2012\Operations Manager\Console> .\Microsoft.EnterpriseManagement.
OperationsManager.ClientShell.Startup.ps1

    Welcome to the Operations Manager 2007 R2 Command Shell.  This command shell is
    designed to provide interactive and script based access to Operations Manager
    data and operations.  This functionality is provided by a set of Operations
    Manager commands.

    To list all commands, type: Get-Command
    To list all Operations Manager commands, type: Get-OperationsManagerCommand
    To get help for a command, type: Get-Help [command name]

Connecting to Operations Manager Management Server 'Helios.odyssey.com'.
PS Monitoring:\Helios.odyssey.com
>_
```

FIGURE 23.7 Loading the OpsMgr 2007 snap-in.

The first line loads the actual snap-in file into PowerShell, the second line changes the directory to the location where the startup script is located, and the third line runs the startup script.

Operations Manager 2012 PowerShell Connection

The Operations Manager 2012 PowerShell console is a peer to the Operations Manager 2012 console. Both connect to a management server, and the user's credentials are checked to see if the user is an authorized user of Operations Manager. The user's level of permissions in OpsMgr is determined by the user role to which the user has been assigned. As shown in Figure 23.8, the connection used by the PowerShell console to the management server is TCP port 5724. This connection is made to the management server's System Center Data Access Service (DAS).

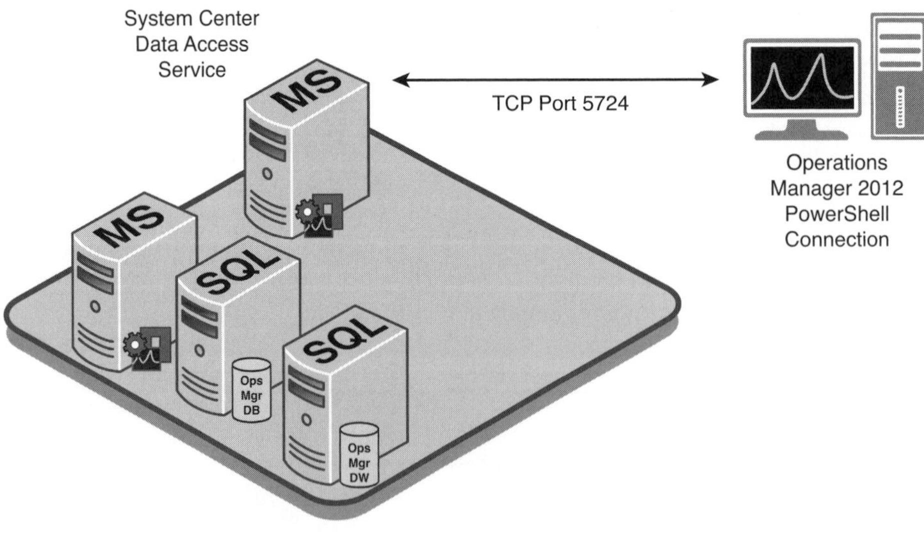

FIGURE 23.8 PowerShell connection to a management server.

Using PowerShell v2 Feature to Start a Remote Console Connection

The easiest way to access an OpsMgr PowerShell console from a machine without the Operations console installed that has PowerShell v2 loaded is to establish a connection to a remote management server using PowerShell v2, and then import the OperationsManager module using the `Import-Module` cmdlet. For more help on establishing a remote connection, see `Get-Help New-PSSession -full` from a PowerShell v2 console. Follow these steps:

1. Establish a remote session to the server with the OpsMgr module and enter the session that was created.

```
$ps = New-PSSession -ComputerName Hector.odyssey.com
Enter-PSSession $ps
```

2. Import the OperationsManager module using the `Import-Module` cmdlet.

```
Import-Module OperationsManager
```

3. Perform some OpsMgr related action.

```
Get-SCOMManagementServer
```

4. Disconnect from the remote session.

```
Exit-PSSession
```

5. Get the Session ID of the remote session.

```
Get-PSSession
```

6. Remove the remote session, which in this case was session Id 1.

```
Remove-PSSession -Id 1
```

Working with OpsMgr Management Group Connections

You often will be working with multiple management groups, such as development and production environments, when testing management packs and overrides for new management packs. The management group connection cmdlets can help you work with multiple management group connections in a single OpsMgr 2012 PowerShell console session. These cmdlets are listed in Table 23.2.

TABLE 23.2 SCOM management group connection cmdlets

Cmdlet Name	Description
Get-SCOMManagementGroupConnection	Retrieves all management group connections, including the IsActive state of these connections
New-SCOMManagementGroupConnection	Creates a new connection for the specified management group
Remove-SCOMManagementGroupConnection	Removes a management group connection
Set-SCOMManagementGroupConnection	Sets the specified connection as the active connection

To use the Operations Manager 2012 module for PowerShell, you must make a connection to an Operations Manager management group. Two types of management group connections can be made from PowerShell, persistent connections or temporary connections:

- Temporary connections are used when a management server is specified with a cmdlet, and that management server is only used in that one connection. As an example, if you are running the OpsMgr PowerShell console from ServerA in Management Group A, and need to get a list of servers from Management Group B, whose management server is on ServerB, run the following from the ServerA OpsMgr PowerShell console:

  ```
  Get-SCOMManagementServer -ComputerName ServerB.FQDN
  ```

  For the duration of the `Get-SCOMManagementServer` cmdlet that is running, there is a temporary connection established to ServerB to get a list of management servers. After the transfer of data was completed, the connection is closed.

- To make a persistent management group connection, use `New-SCOMManagementGroupConnection`. You can make multiple management group connections using this cmdlet although only one connection can be active at a time. The last connection created by the `New-SCOMManagementGroupConnection` is the active connection by default. To activate a connection, use the `Set-SCOMManagementGroupConenction` cmdlet. To verify the active connection, the `Get-SCOMManagementGroupConnection` cmdlet lists all established management group connections and notes which is active.

Working with Agents

The Operations Manager 2012 agent-related cmdlets are tailored to the operational running of agents, specifically running installs, uninstalls, repairs on the agent, and other activities related to managing an agent. There are several new cmdlets related to agents, the first that come to mind are related to the SCOM-AgentProxy cmdlets, which are discussed in the "About Enable-SCOMAgentProxy" and "Using Disable-SCOMAgentProxy" sections of this chapter.

Table 23.3 lists agent-related cmdlets, which are discussed in the following sections.

TABLE 23.3 Agent-related cmdlets

Cmdlet Name	Description
Get-SCOMAgent	Gets the agent-managed computers in a management group
Disable-SCOMAgentProxy	Disables agents from acting as a proxy
Enable-SCOMAgentProxy	Enables agents to act as a proxy
Install-SCOMAgent	Deploys one or more System Center Management agents using push install
Uninstall-SCOMAgent	Uninstalls agents from agent-managed computers
Repair-SCOMAgent	Repairs an Operations Manager agent
Set-SCOMAgentApprovalSetting	Sets the manual agent approval setting for the management group
Get-SCOMAgentApprovalSetting	Gets the manual agent approval setting for the management group

Using Get-SCOMAgent

`Get-SCOMAgent` is probably one of the more useful cmdlets for getting information about the agents in a management group. Running `Get-SCOMAgent` without any parameters dumps a general list of agent information to the display, shown in Figure 23.9.

This may not be very useful in a large environment. Let's walk through some of the items that can be obtained from this cmdlet and use the `Get-Member` cmdlet to determine the methods and properties available to the `Get-SCOMAgent` cmdlet, shown in Figure 23.10.

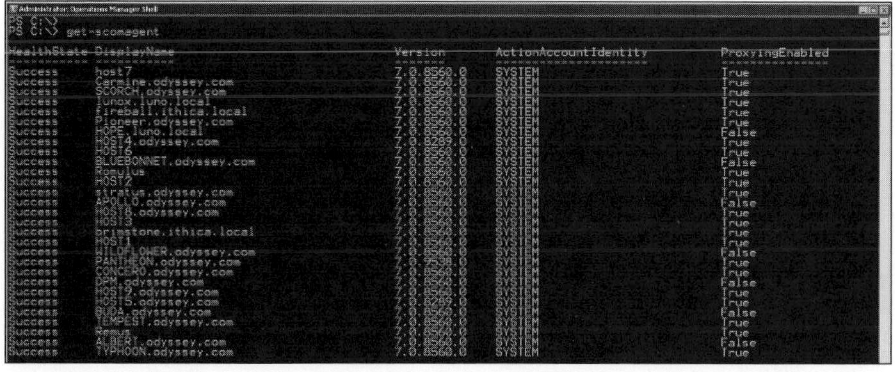

FIGURE 23.9 Output from the `Get-SCOMAgent` cmdlet.

Some of the more interesting properties an Operations Manager administrator would be interested in would be ManuallyInstalled, Name, ProxyingEnabled, and Version. There are several methods that will be of interest when determining the failover servers and that would be GetFailOverManagementServers. To get a better idea of how to utilize these properties, here are some one-liners:

- To get a list of manually installed OpsMgr agents, you will need to look at the ManuallyInstalled property, which in the listing in Figure 23.10 of `Get-Member`, shows this property specifically is Boolean. In PowerShell Boolean is treated a bit differently; it is not about a text string being set to True or False, but it is about evaluating `$True` and `$False`.

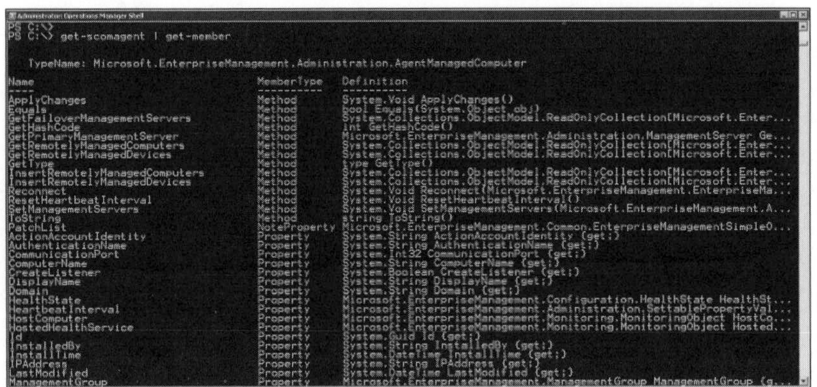

FIGURE 23.10 Using `Get-Member` with `Get_SCOMAgent` to identify properties for `Where-object`.

TIP: `$True` AND `$False`

To get the full story on Boolean values and operators see Jeffrey Snover's blog post at http://blogs.msdn.com/b/powershell/archive/2006/12/24/boolean-values-and-operators.aspx.

- The `Get-SCOMAgent` cmdlets fetch the OpsMgr agent data into the PowerShell pipeline; then the `Where-Object` acts as a filter and only keeps information about the objects that meet the criteria of `ManuallyInstalled = True`. The result of the filter action is then piped to the following `Format-Table` cmdlet, which specifies that only the `Name` object should be displayed to the output, shown in Figure 23.11.

```
Get-SCOMAgent | Where-Object {$_.ManuallyInstalled -eq $True}| FT Name
```

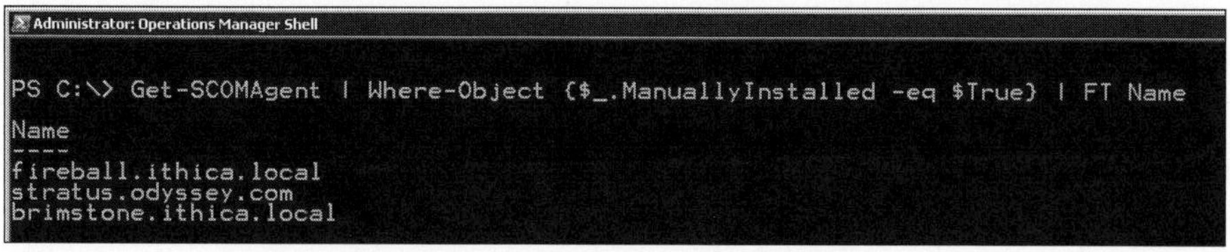

```
PS C:\> Get-SCOMAgent | Where-Object {$_.ManuallyInstalled -eq $True} | FT Name

Name
----
fireball.ithica.local
stratus.odyssey.com
brimstone.ithica.local
```

FIGURE 23.11 Retrieving a list of manually installed agents.

`Get-SCOMAgent` has several other important pieces of information that can be useful when auditing your environment to verify agents are reporting to the proper management server, as well as which management server the agent will fail over to. Referring back to the output from `Get-SCOMAgent |GM`, you will notice the property PrimaryManagementServerName; however, there is not a SecondaryManagementServerName. There is a method called GetFailoverManagementServers you can utilize to obtain this information, shown in this next line of PowerShell code:

```
Get-Agent|FT -a name,PrimaryManagementServerName,@{l="secondary";e={$_.GetFailover
ManagementServers()|foreach{$_.name}}}
```

The code snippet shown here is actually a single line of code. `Get-SCOMAgent` cmdlets retrieve agent instances, which then are pipelined to the `Sort-Object` cmdlet, which sorts the objects in the pipeline by ComputerName. The `Format-Table` cmdlet sorts the input by ComputerName, with three columns of output: ComputerName, PrimaryManagementServerName, and SecondaryManagementServers. The ComputerName and PrimaryManagementServerName values come directly from the objects in the pipeline; the SecondaryManagementServers values are retrieved via the following expression: `e{$_.GetFailoverManagementServers()|foreach{$_.name}}}`

The expression uses the GetFailoverManagementServers method, which is applied to each agent name in the pipeline.

Installing Agents with Install-SCOMAgent

Installing an OpsMgr agent via PowerShell is a great way to schedule agent discovery and deployment—a feature lacking in OpsMgr 2012. The OpsMgr administrator can set up a scheduled task that runs a PowerShell script for after-hours agent deployment. To utilize the `Install-SCOMAgent` cmdlet, there are several required pieces of information:

- The primary management server the agent(s) will report to.
- The install account credentials or Action account. This is only used if the account the OpsMgr administrator uses when logging on to the server does not have the proper admin privileges on the target box to which the agent will be deployed.

The following example uses a primary management server of Hannibal.odyssey.com with Apollo.odyssey.com as the machine to which the agent will be installed.

```
$PrimaryMgmtServer = Get-SCOMManagementServer -Name "Hannibal.odyssey.com"
Install-SCOMAgent -Name "APOLLO.odyssey.com" `
-PrimaryManagementServer $PrimaryMgmtServer -verbose
```

Using the -verbose flag gives some nice feedback when the console does not normally give feedback about the installation. This is shown in Figure 23.12.

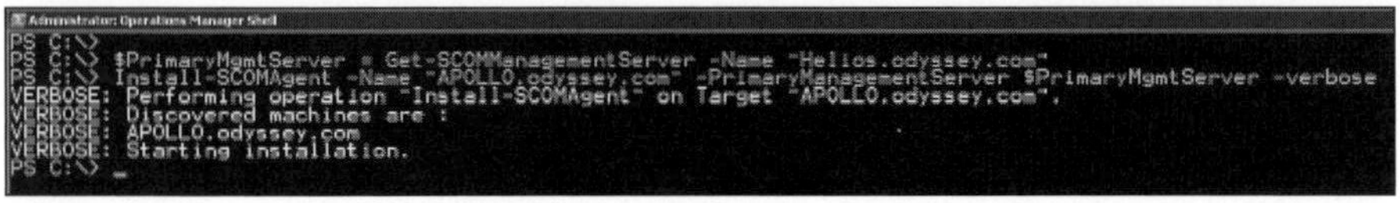

FIGURE 23.12 `Install-SCOMAgent` cmdlet with verbose flag.

An example of computer discovery and push install of the agent through PowerShell is demonstrated in greater depth in the posting on automating agent discovery and deployment with PowerShell at http://www.systemcentercentral.com/BlogDetails/tabid/143/IndexID/94248/Default.aspx.

Uninstalling Agents with Uninstall-SCOMAgent

Uninstalling an OpsMgr agent using a PowerShell script could be useful any time agent removal is required on demand or on a schedule, such as in an automated server deprovisioning in a private cloud or hosted environment. For details on setting up a scheduled task, see the TechNet Forums discussion, "How to schedule a PowerShell script through scheduled tasks," at http://social.technet.microsoft.com/Forums/en-US/exchange2010/thread/0cad57bf-1113-4622-aac3-c3278fa97d72/, which provides several good methods and resources on how to configure the task. The `Uninstall-SCOMAgent` cmdlet takes input from the `Get-SCOMAgent` cmdlet, and then the `Uninstall-SCOMAgent` is run against what is pipelined from `Get-SCOMAgent`. The one-liner shown next uninstalls the OpsMgr agent from APOLLO.odyssey.com using the -verbose flag at the end to display what additional information can be shown when there is not a status bar available, as in the user interface.

```
Get-SCOMAgent APOLLO.odyssey.com | Uninstall-SCOMAgent -verbose
```

If needed, an action account can be specified in the `Uninstall-SCOMAgent` cmdlet. The authors do not recommend using the -verbose flag in a script.

Using Repair-SCOMAgent

You can also repair an OpsMgr agent from the command line. `Repair-SCOMAgent` requires the agent object (not just the agent name) as input in order to perform the repair. The underlying repair process is the same; you are simply instantiating the repair from the PowerShell Shell. In this next example, the agent being repaired is HOST2.Odyssey.com. Figure 23.13 shows the cmdlet being executed.

```
PS C:\>
PS C:\>
PS C:\> Get-SCOMAgent -Name "HOST2" | Repair-SCOMAgent -verbose
VERBOSE: Performing operation "Repair-SCOMAgent" on Target "HOST2".
```

FIGURE 23.13 `Repair-SCOMAgent` cmdlet processing output from `Get-SCOMAgent`.

```
Get-SCOMAgent -Name "APOLLO.odyssey.com" | Repair-SCOMAgent -verbose
```


About Enable-SCOMAgentProxy

The `Enable-SCOMAgentProxy` cmdlet enables an agent to act as a proxy and discover objects not hosted on the local computer. This cmdlet is normally used in conjunction with the `Get-SCOMAgent` cmdlet, which fetches the desired agents that are then piped to the `Enable-SCOMAgentProxy` cmdlet that changes the property of ProxyingEnabled to `$True`. The next one-liner uses `Get-SCOMAgent` to fetch all OpsMgr agent information, which is then pipelined to the `Where-Object` cmdlet that will only pull out OpsMgr information that has ProxyingEnabled set to false. Those agents are then pipelined to the `Enable-SCOMAgentProxy` cmdlet that sets the ProxyingEnabled property to true. Note that `$False` and `$True` are used to represent true and false in PowerShell. Here is an example:

```
Get-SCOMAgent |Where-Object {$_.ProxyingEnabled -eq $False}| `
Enable-SCOMAgentProxy
```

To verify this one-liner has the desired effect, run the following one-liner, which returns a list of agents along with confirmation that agent proxy has been enabled.

```
Get-SCOMAgent |Where-Object {$_.ProxyingEnabled -eq $True} | `
select Name, ProxyingEnabled
```

Using Disable-SCOMAgentProxy

The `Disable-SCOMAgentProxy` cmdlet disables agents from acting as a proxy and discovering managed objects on other computers. This cmdlet is normally used in conjunction with the `Get-SCOMAgent` cmdlet, which fetches the desired agents and pipes that information to the `Disable-SCOMAgentProxy` cmdlet that changes the property of ProxyingEnabled to `$False`. The next one-liner uses `Get-SCOMAgent` to fetch all OpsMgr agent information, which is then pipelined to the `Where-Object` cmdlet that will only pull out OpsMgr agent information that has ProxyingEnabled set to `$True`. Those agents are then pipelined to the `Disable-SCOMAgentProxy` cmdlet, which sets the ProxyingEnabled property to `$False`. The authors do not recommend running this without adding filtering to change settings on only the desired subset of agents in your environment (as some agents will almost certainly require agent proxy); this example is simply intended to illustrate the possibilities of bulk administration from the OpsMgr Shell. An array of names could also be piped to `Get-SCOMAgent`.

```
Get-SCOMAgent |Where-Object {$_.ProxyingEnabled -like $True}|Disable-SCOMAgentProxy
```

To verify this one-liner had the desired effect, run the following one-liner, which returns a list of agents along with confirmation that agent proxy has been enabled.

```
Get-SCOMAgent |Where-Object {$_.ProxyingEnabled -like $False} | `
select Name, ProxyingEnabled
```

Retrieving the AgentApproval Setting

The `Get-SCOMAgentApprovalSetting` cmdlet fetches the AgentApprovalSetting for the management group to which the OpsMgr PowerShell console is currently connected. It will show either Pending, AutoApprove, or AutoReject.

```
Get-SCOMAgentApprovalSetting
```

Setting the AgentApproval Setting

The cmdlet `Set-SCOMAgentApprovalSetting` sets the AgentApprovalSetting for the management group to which the OpsMgr PowerShell console is currently connected. The three parameters are AutoApprove, AutoReject, and Pending. Here is an example to set the agent approval setting for the management group to manual:

```
Set-SCOMAgentApprovalSetting -Pending
```

To verify the changes were applied, run the following:

```
Get-SCOMAgentApprovalSetting
```

Managing Maintenance Mode

Maintenance mode is a feature of OpsMgr that enables you to suspend monitoring of an object or group of objects during scheduled hardware or software maintenance activities. You can also categorize reasons for running maintenance mode, such as software updates or hardware replacement. This is a critical feature of OpsMgr, as it enables having scheduled downtime without creating alerts, as well as not affecting service level agreements (SLAs) or reporting data for SLAs.

When an object is placed into maintenance mode, all workflows targeted against that object are suspended for the specified interval.

CAUTION: MAINTENANCE MODE ON MANAGEMENT AND GATEWAY SERVERS

OpsMgr infrastructure servers such as management and gateway servers should never be put into maintenance mode, as this will stop workflows running on the management server(s) critical to normal management group function.

There are three cmdlets associated with OpsMgr maintenance mode, which when used in various combinations can be leveraged to start, stop, or modify maintenance mode. These are discussed in the next sections.

- `Start-SCOMMaintenanceMode`
- `Get-SCOMMaintenanceMode`
- `Set-SCOMMaintenanceMode`

Starting Maintenance Mode

As you might guess, the `Start-SCOMMaintenanceMode` cmdlet can be used to initiate maintenance mode for a monitored object. The following snippet starts maintenance mode for a computer named server01.odyssey.com.

```
$Instance = Get-SCOMClassInstance -Name server01.odyssey.com
$Time = ((Get-Date).AddMinutes(10))
Start-SCOMMaintenanceMode -Instance $Instance -EndTime $Time `
-Reason "SecurityIssue" -Comment "Applying software update."
```

Modifying an Active Maintenance Mode Window

To modify an active maintenance mode window requires a combination of the `Get-SCOMMaintenanceMode` and `Set-SCOMMaintenanceMode` cmdlets. The `Get-SCOMMaintenanceMode` cmdlet is used to retrieve the active maintenance mode window and the `Set-SCOMMaintenanceMode` cmdlet to update the end time of the maintenance mode window.

```
$NewEndTime = (Get-Date).addDays(1)
Get-SCOMClassInstance -Name *.Contoso.com | Get-SCOMMaintenanceMode | `
Set-SCOMMaintenanceMode -EndTime $NewEndTime `
-Comment "Updating end time."
```

By updating the end time to the current time, you can effectively end maintenance mode for a monitored object on demand.

Working with Alerts

Alerts are an important part of any monitoring platform. Operations Manager 2012 has several different cmdlets that deal specifically with managing alerts, listed in Table 23.4.

TABLE 23.4 Alert-related cmdlets

Cmdlet Name	Description
Get-SCOMAlert	Gets the specified alerts
Set-SCOMAlert	Changes the properties of the specified alert
Resolve-SCOMAlert	Resolves an alert
Add-SCOMAlertResolutionState	Adds a custom alert resolution state
Get-SCOMAlertResolutionState	Gets the alert resolution states defined in the management group
Remove-SCOMAlertResolutionState	Removes a custom alert resolution state from the management group
Get-SCOMAlertResolutionSetting	Gets the automatic alert resolution setting for the management group
Set-SCOMAlertResolutionSetting	Sets the alert automatic resolution settings for the management group

Using Get-SCOMAlert

Before PowerShell can take action on an alert, an alert or collection of alerts must be identified. `Get-SCOMAlert` does just that; it fetches specified alerts. The `Get-SCOMAlert` cmdlet has many parameters due to the number of attributes defined in an alert. Some of the most commonly referenced properties are shown in Table 23.5; these are ResolutionState, Severity, and Priority, and are stored as numbers in the operational database.

TABLE 23.5 ResolutionState, Severity, and Priority values

ResolutionState	Severity	Priority
0 = New	0 = Informational	0 = Low
247 = Awaiting Evidence*	1 = Warning	1 = Normal
248 = Assigned to Engineering*	2 = Error	2 = High
249 = Acknowledged*		
250 = Scheduled*		
254 = Resolved*		
255 = Closed		

**Added with System Center 2012 Service Pack 1*

Examining the output from `Get-Help Get-SCOMAlert -full`, several parameters can be utilized to retrieve alerts:

- **Id:** Retrieves the alerts with the specified GUID. The Id is stored in the Id property of the object that represents an alert. To get the Id of an alert from the OpsMgr PowerShell console, type `Get-SCOMAlert | Format-Table Name, Id`.

- **Instance:** Retrieves alerts for one or more class instance objects. Enter a variable that represents the class instances, or type a command that retrieves the class instances. This parameter also accepts group objects. For information about how to get a class instance object, type `Get-Help Get-SCOMClassInstance`.
- **LastModifiedBy:** Retrieves alerts that match the specified user name for the last user that edited the alert.
- **Name:** Specifies the name of the alerts to retrieve.
- **Owner:** Retrieves alerts that match the specified owner for the alert.
- **ResolutionState:** Retrieves alerts that match a specified resolution state Id. For example, the resolution state Id for Closed is 255. You can create custom resolution states; these are maintained in the Operations console at Administration -> Settings -> Alerts on the Alert Resolution State Settings tab.
- **ResolvedBy:** Retrieves alerts that match the specified user name for the user that resolved the alert.
- **Priority:** The priority level of an alert can be 0 = Low, 1 = Normal, and 2 = High.
- **Severity:** The severity level of an alert, can be 0 = Informational, 1 = Warning, and 2 = Error.

Here are examples using the ResolutionState parameter for the `Get-SCOMAlert` cmdlet:

- **Get new alerts:** `Get-SCOMAlert -ResolutionState 0`
- **Get closed alerts:** `Get-SCOMAlert -ResolutionState 255`

Examples using the Severity parameter for the `Get-SCOMAlert` cmdlet:

- **Get severity informational alerts:** `Get-SCOMalert -severity 0`
- **Get alerts of severity warning:** `Get-SCOMalert -severity 1`
- **Get alerts of severity error:** `Get-SCOMalert -severity 2`

Examples using Priority parameter for `Get-SCOMAlert` cmdlet:

- **Get low priority alerts:** `Get-SCOMAlert -Priority 0`
- **Get normal priority alerts:** `Get-SCOMAlert -Priority 1`
- **Get high priority alerts:** `Get-SCOMAlert -Priority 2`

It is possible to combine several parameters together in one line to get some specific information, illustrated in the following examples:

- **Gets a list of new alerts with a severity of error:**

  ```
  Get-SCOMAlert -ResolutionState 0 -Severity 2
  ```

- **Gets a list of closed alerts with high priority:**

```
Get-SCOMAlert -ResolutionState 255 -Priority 2
```

- **Gets a list of new alerts with severity of error and high:**

```
Get-SCOMAlert -ResolutionState 0 -Severity 2 -Priority 2
```

Optimizing Performance When Working with the PowerShell Shell

When working with cmdlets that return large numbers of objects, syntax can make a huge difference in performance. The following one-liners perform the same task—closing all alerts with a resolution state of zero (new), but one completes the task much more efficiently than the other. The first option uses `Where-Object` (a WHERE clause) as demonstrated in the "Using Disable-SCOMAgentProxy" section.

```
Get-Alert | Where-Object {$_.ResolutionState -eq 0} | Resolve-Alert | out-null
```

This next example accomplishes the same thing as the first one, but it will run much faster in a larger environment that has more outstanding alerts:

```
Get-Alert -criteria 'ResolutionState = ''0''' | Resolve-Alert | out-null
```

The performance difference is due to that when the criteria parameter is used, the value passed is provided directly to the SQL Server database, and only the relevant data is returned. This means the data is filtered *before* it is returned to the PowerShell session, reducing the number of objects that must be passed back to the Windows PowerShell console.

Separating Alerts Generated by Rules and Monitors

Unfortunately, there is no parameter for IsMonitorAlert for the `Get-SCOMAlert` cmdlet to determine if an alert came from a monitor or rule; however, there is still a property available by that same name from OpsMgr 2007 days. To find out more about the IsMonitorAlert property, run the following in the OpsMgr Shell: `Get-SCOMAlert |GM`. The IsMonitorAlert property is of data type Boolean.

This next one-liner retrieves a list of new alerts created by a rule. To maximize performance, use the ResolutionState parameter first to get the new alerts, and then pipe that to the `Where-Object` cmdlet that will look at the IsMonitorAlert property of each alert sent to it and only show alerts matching `$False`.

```
Get-SCOMAlert -ResolutionState 0 | Where-Object {($_.IsMonitorAlert -eq $False)}
```

For those cmdlets that retrieve data from OpsMgr such as `Get-SCOMAlert` or `Get-SCOMEvent`, it is best to use the built-in criteria to scope the data that is desired. (`Get-Help Get-SCOMAlert -full` returns full details on available criteria.) In instances such as the previous example, this is not possible; there is no option to use criteria to filter out the IsMonitorAlert property of an alert.

About Set-SCOMAlert

Use the `Set-SCOMAlert` cmdlet to change or set properties of alerts. Many of the same parameters available to `Get-SCOMAlert` are available with `Set-SCOMAlert`. You can change the alert's Owner, ResolutionState, TicketID, Comment, and CustomField1 thru 10. `Set-SCOMAlert` would be helpful if you needed to make bulk changes to many alerts at one time. For example, if daily informational alerts are clogging up the Operations console; a quick fix is to schedule a task to run every hour to get all new informational (severity) alerts and set the ResolutionState to closed (255). Using `Get-SCOMAlert` gets the new informational (severity) alerts and pipes the output to `Set-SCOMAlert` with a ResolutionState of 255; to keep the console from filling up with the alerts that were just closed, pipe the output to out-null.

```
Get-SCOMAlert -ResolutionState 0 -Severity 0 | Set-SCOMAlert `
-ResolutionState 255 | out-null
```


The example here is hypothetical and not very realistic, as the more practical approach is to tune the offending management pack and tune the display to show only relevant information to the user viewing it. However, this shows the capabilities of being able to make bulk changes to specified alerts.

Setting Alert Resolution State with Resolve-SCOMAlert

The `Resolve-SCOMAlert` cmdlet does one thing; it sets the ResolutionState on an alert sent to it to closed (255). This is the same action that occurs with `Set-SCOMAlert -ResolutionState 255`. The cmdlet has many parameters similar to those available with `Set-SCOMAlert`; in essence, you could resolve alerts in bulk and modify the properties of the alert at the same time as in these examples:

- Gets a list of new informational alerts, closes them, and adds a comment to the closed alerts: `Get-SCOMAlert -ResolutionState 0 -Severity 0 | Resolve-SCOMAlert -Comment 'Chuck Norris closed these informational alerts with fists of fury and the command shell.'`
- Gets a list of new error alerts, closes the alerts, and adds a comment to the closed alerts: `Get-SCOMAlert -ResolutionState 0 -Severity 2 | Resolve-SCOMAlert -Comment 'Automated close out of alerts.'`

TIP: COLLECTION OF OPSMGR 2007 SINGLE LINE EXAMPLES IN OPSMGR 2012

For examples of OpsMgr2007 PowerShell examples migrated to OpsMgr 2012, see the collection of updated single line PowerShell scripts (one-liners) at http://www.systemcentercentral.com/BlogDetails/tabid/143/IndexID/89870/Default.aspx.

Working with Custom Alert Resolution States

The `Get-SCOMAlertResolutionState` cmdlet retrieves the alert resolution states defined in the management group to which you are connected. This would be a good way to verify the settings of an environment if you were new to it. This next example returns a full list of all alert resolution states in the current management group:

```
Get-SCOMAlertResolutionState
```

Adding Custom Alert Resolution States

The Add-SCOMAlertResolutionState cmdlet adds a custom alert resolution state to the current management group. If you are setting up a new OpsMgr environment and there is a requirement for custom alert resolution states for each IT support organization, using this cmdlet would be a quick way to create these states. All that is required is the ResolutionStateCode or number associated to the resolution state and Name of the resolution state. Other options available for this cmdlet are credentials and computer name, so you could create a temporary connection to another management group to add custom alert resolution states as well. The next example creates an OS Support resolution state with code of 15, and an Exchange Support resolution state with code of 20.

```
Add-SCOMAlertResolutionState -Name 'OS Support' -ResolutionStateCode 15
Add-SCOMAlertResolutionState -Name 'Exchange Support' -ResolutionStateCode 20
```

To verify the alert resolution state changes, run Get-SCOMAlertResolutionState.

Removing Custom Alert Resolution States

The Remove-SCOMAlertResolutionState cmdlet can remove a custom alert resolution state from a management group. First use the cmdlet Get-SCOMAlertResolutionState to fetch the custom resolution state, and then pipe the output to Remove-SCOMAlertResolutionState. The following example retrieves the alert resolution state by name and deletes it.

```
Get-SCOMAlertResolutionState -Name 'OS Support' | Remove-SCOMAlertResolutionState
```

To verify the correct alert resolution state was removed, run Get-SCOMAlertResolutionState. The next example removes the custom resolution state by using ResolutionStateCode.

```
Get-SCOMAlertResolutionState -ResolutionStateCode 20 | `
Remove-SCOMAlertResolutionState
```

To verify the correct alert resolution state was removed, run Get-SCOMAlertResolutionState.

Determining Automatic Alert Resolution Settings

The Get-SCOMAlertResolutionSetting cmdlet fetches the automatic alert resolution settings for the management group. You could use this as part of a discovery script run against a management group to verify its settings before troubleshooting the management group. In the command line, you could specify a remote server name to retrieve the alert resolution settings from a remote management group. Just running Get-SCOMAlertResolutionSetting will dump out AlertAutoResolveDays and HealthyAlertAutoResolveDays to the display.

Modifying Alert Resolution Settings

The Set-SCOMAlertResolutionSettings cmdlet is used to modify the AlertAutoResolveDays and HealthyAlertAutoResolveDays parameters in a management group. This could be used to automate changing these settings in a management group or to verify existing settings. Additional parameters such as ComputerName and Credential are also available, so these changes could also be made from a remote management group, or if alternate credentials are necessary.

To change the management group's AlertAutoResolveDays to 15 and HealthyAlertAutoResolveDays to 4, see this next example:

```
Set-SCOMAlertResolutionSetting -AlertAutoResolveDays 15 `
-HealthyAlertAutoResolveDays 4
```

To verify the changes occurred, run the `Get-SCOMAlertResolutionSetting` cmdlet again.

Administering Resource Pools

Operations Manager 2012 introduces resource pools, which are collections of management servers used to distribute work among themselves and take over work from a failed member. This eliminates the single point of failure of the Operations Manager 2007 root management server (RMS). You can use resource pools to monitor network devices and UNIX/Linux computers. For example, you could create a resource pool of management servers to monitor network elements that are located in the same data center. Table 23.6 lists the resource pool-related cmdlets.

TABLE 23.6 Resource pool related cmdlets

Cmdlet Name	Description
Get-SCOMResourcePool	Gets resource pools
New-SCOMResourcePool	Creates a resource pool
Remove-SCOMResourcePool	Removes one or more resource pools
Set-SCOMResourcePool	Changes the properties of a resource pool

Three resource pools are created by default: AD Assignment Resource Pool, All Management Servers Resource Pool, and Notifications Resource Pool. The memberships of these three groups are set to automatic, meaning any management server added to the environment takes part in these resource pools.

There will be times you need to control membership to a given resource pool, say the Notifications Resource Pool, because only one management server has the proper routing to access the email system, or only one management server has an SMS modem or pager gateway software installed. In this case, membership to the Notifications Resource Pool should not be set to automatic. While you can modify the properties of a resource pool using the Operations console, you can also use PowerShell cmdlets.

For a one-liner to change the properties of a resource pool, two cmdlets will be used: `Get-SCOMResourcePool`, which fetches a specific resource pool, and `Set-SCOMResourcePool`, which allows changes to the properties of the resource pool. To ensure the property names and the name of the resource pool are correct, run the `Get-SCOMResourcePool` cmdlet from the OpsMgr Shell and examine the output. This example uses `-Name "Notifications Resource Pool"` with the `Get-SCOMResourcePool` cmdlet. To see what you have to work with, pipe the output of `Get-SCOMResourcePool -Name "Notifications Resource Pool"` to `Get-Member` (or `GM` for short), as displayed in Figure 23.14.

```
Get-SCOMResourcePool -Name "Notifications Resource Pool" |GM
```

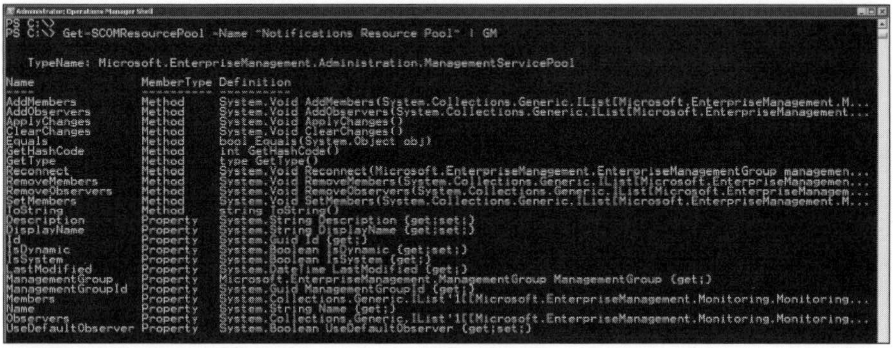

FIGURE 23.14 `Get-SCOMResourcePool` being sent to `GM`.

To learn more about what you can do with the `Set-SCOMResourcePool` cmdlet, open the help file using `Get-Help Set-SCOMResourcePool -full`. In the parameters section of the help file, there is the -EnableAutomaticMembership <Boolean>, so to change the enable automatic membership it will need to be set to `$False`. Note the following line should be a single line in the OpsMgr PowerShell console.

```
Get-SCOMResourcePool -Name "Notifications Resource Pool"|Set-SCOMResourcePool `
-EnableAutomaticMembership $False
```

Unfortunately, there is no verification or feedback of what occurred. To verify the settings were applied, run the following in the OpsMgr PowerShell console to verify the IsDynamic property is now false for the resource pool that was just changed, or check the console.

```
Get-SCOMResourcePool -DisplayName "Notifications Resource Pool" |FT Name, IsDynamic
```

To create a new resource pool, utilize the cmdlet `New-SCOMResourcePool`. For more information about this cmdlet, check the help file using `get-help New-SCOMResourcePool -full`. The following example creates a new resource pool called NetMon Tulsa, with Hannibal.odyssey.com as the management server in that resource pool. The first line gets the needed information about the management server and assigns it to the variable `$Member`; the second line creates the resource pool.

```
$Member = Get-SCOMManagementServer -Name "Hannibal.odyssey.com"
New-SCOMResourcePool -DisplayName "NetMon Tulsa" -Member $Member
```

Note because a management server is specified as a member of the resource pool, membership to this resource pool will be manual. To verify Hannibal.odyssey.com is a member of the resource pool, use `Get-SCOMResourcePool` with the -Member switch to pull a list of all resource pools to which Hannibal.odyssey.com belongs.

```
Get-SCOMResourcePool -Member (Get-SCOMManagementServer -Name "Hannibal.odyssey.com")
```

To remove this resource pool, the combination of the `Get-SCOMResourcePool` cmdlet with the `Remove-SCOMResourcePool` cmdlet is utilized with the display name NetMon*; the "*" is used because a space will not be processed properly.

```
Get-SCOMResourcePool -DisplayName NetMon* | Remove-SCOMResourcePool -verbose
```


NOTE: USE OF -VERBOSE AND -DEBUG

Most cmdlets accept standard -verbose and -debug flags. Just check the help file on -full to verify whether the specific cmdlet supports them.

Managing Licensing

Three new cmdlets included with OpsMgr 2012 deal specifically with licensing:

- `Get-SCOMAccessLicense` gets information about the current management group's licensing for System Center Operations Manager 2012. It does some slicing and dicing between management server licensing and client licensing.
- `Set-SCOMLicense` lets the OpsMgr administrators set the product license level as well as remove the evaluation expiration timeout in an evaluation installation.
- `Get-SCOMLicense` opens up an instance of WordPad and shows the Microsoft software license terms for System Center 2012.

Table 23.7 lists the license-related cmdlets, and the following sections give examples.

TABLE 23.7 License-related cmdlets

Cmdlet Name	Description
Get-SCOMAccessLicense	Gets information about licenses for System Center Operations Manager and Windows
Get-SCOMLicense	Displays the Microsoft Software License Terms for the currently active product license
Set-SCOMLicense	Sets the product license level

Retrieving License Information

The `Get-SCOMAccessLicense` cmdlet retrieves license information about the management group to which your OpsMgr PowerShell session is connected. It returns DeviceID, WorkloadRoleName, information about role type for a given computer (management server, agent-managed computer, and so on), and whether the machine is virtualized. It also returns the LogicalProcessorCount and PhysicalProcessorCount; both are important pieces of information when dealing with System Center 2012 licensing. Check out the help file for this cmdlet by running `Get-Help Get-SCOMAccessLicense -full`.

Here is an example of a one-liner report that gives a sum of both of the processor counts and physical process count for the management group to which the OpsMgr PowerShell console is currently connected:

```
Get-SCOMAccessLicense | measure-object -property `
LogicalProcessorCount,PhysicalProcessorCount -sum | `
foreach{$_.Property + " Total : " + $_.Sum}
```

Upgrading from an Evaluation Copy

If a management group was installed using an evaluation copy of Operations Manager 2012, `Set-SCOMLicense` enables an administrator to run this cmdlet with a valid product key and remove the evaluation expiration timeout. The following example is only to show proper syntax and is taken directly from the help file.

```
Set-SCOMLicense -ProductId 'C97A1C5E-6429-4F71-8B2D-3525E237BF62'
```

Managing the RMS Emulator

Three new cmdlets included with OpsMgr 2012 manage the RMS emulator role (RMSE). The first server installed in the management group holds this role by default. The role can be moved around as needed and be managed by the cmdlets listed in Table 23.8. The following sections provide examples of these cmdlets.

TABLE 23.8 Cmdlets used for managing the RMS emulator role

Cmdlet Name	Description
Get-SCOMRMSEmulator	Gets the management server hosting the RMS emulator role
Remove-SCOMRMSEmulator	Removes the RMS emulator role
Set-SCOMRMSEmulator	Moves RMS emulator role to the specified management server

Determining the RMS Emulator

The `Get-SCOMRMSEmulator` cmdlet shows the management server currently hosting the RMSE. If running locally from a management server, you can run this without options to fetch data about the management group to which the PowerShell console is connected. When running from a workstation, you can specify a management server with which to establish a connection, as well as specify alternate credentials to determine the management group's current RMSE. Figure 23.15 shows the results of running the `Get-SCOMRMSEmulator` cmdlet.

```
PS C:\>
PS C:\> Get-SCOMRMSEmulator
WARNING: column "Id" does not fit into the display and was removed.
HealthState DisplayName                    Version       ActionAccountIdentity
----------- -----------                    -------       ---------------------
Success     Hannibal.odyssey.com           7.0.8560.0    ODYSSEY\OM_MSAA
```

FIGURE 23.15 `Get-SCOMRMSEmulator` in action.

Moving the RMS Emulator Role

The `Set-SCOMRMSEmulator` cmdlet moves the RMSE to a specified management server. First retrieve the management server object (for the management server where you wish to move the role) using `Get-SCOMManagementServer` cmdlet. Then pass the output through the pipeline to `Set-SCOMRMSEmulator` to the variable, as shown in the following example, which moves the role to Hannibal.odyssey.com.

```
Get-SCOMManagementServer -Name "Hannibal.odyssey.com" | Set-SCOMRMSEmulator -verbose
```

Figure 23.16 shows the console using the cmdlets. This is not something you would do very often, but if you needed to do some work on a management server, you might decide to make a clean transition of the role before decommissioning or performing maintenance on the server hosting the RMSE role.

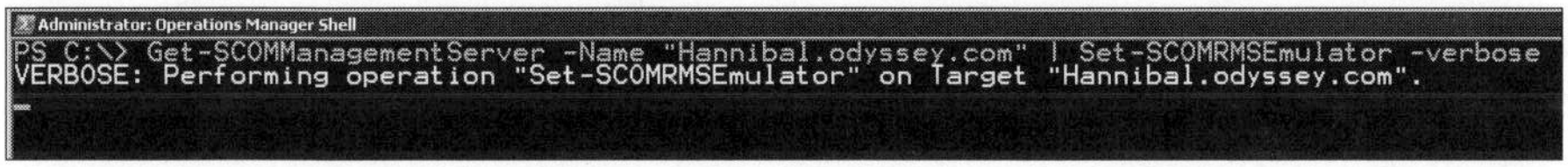

```
PS C:\> Get-SCOMManagementServer -Name "Hannibal.odyssey.com" | Set-SCOMRMSEmulator -verbose
VERBOSE: Performing operation "Set-SCOMRMSEmulator" on Target "Hannibal.odyssey.com".
```

FIGURE 23.16 Using `Set-SCOMRMSEmulator`.

Removing the RMS Emulator Role

The RMS emulator is only for backwards compatibility to legacy management packs and is in no way required for the management group to function correctly. So in theory, if you are able to confirm no workflows target the legacy `Root Management Server` class (nor would any in the future), you could remove this role. The `Remove-SCOMRMSEmulator` cmdlet removes the RMS emulator role from the management group with which the OpsMgr PowerShell console currently has a connection. Run the cmdlet with no options; it will prompt to verify this action, as shown in Figure 23.17.

```
Administrator: Operations Manager Shell
PS C:\>
PS C:\> Remove-SCOMRMSEmulator

Are you sure you want to perform this action?
Warning! By removing the RMS Emulator role, any workflow that targets the Root Management Server will not load.
[Y] Yes  [A] Yes to All  [N] No  [L] No to All  [S] Suspend  [?] Help (default is "Y"): y_
```

FIGURE 23.17 Using the `Remove-SCOMRMSEmulator` cmdlet to remove the RMS emulator role.

To verify the role was removed, rerun the `Get-SCOMRMSEmulator` cmdlet, and PowerShell should return nothing.

Database Cmdlets

Operations Manager 2012 introduced several new cmdlets to manage the operational and data warehouse databases. There are two cmdlets to manage the grooming settings for the operational database and two cmdlets to manage the data warehouse grooming settings. These are described in Table 23.9, and the following sections provide examples.

TABLE 23.9 Database-related cmdlets

Cmdlet Name	Description
Get-SCOMDatabaseGroomingSetting	Gets the database grooming settings for the management group
Set-SCOMDatabaseGroomingSetting	Sets the database grooming settings for the management group
Get-SCOMDataWarehouseSetting	Gets the data warehouse settings for the management group
Set-SCOMDataWarehouseSetting	Sets the data warehouse settings for the management group

Determining Operational Database Grooming Settings

The `Get-SCOMDatabaseGroomingSetting` cmdlet gets the database grooming settings for the management group to which the PowerShell console is currently connected, unless an alternate server and credentials are supplied. Database grooming settings are used to automatically remove unnecessary data from the OpsMgr operational database to maintain performance. Figure 23.18 shows the cmdlet and output. `Get-SCOMDatabaseGroomingSetting` can be used as part of a scheduled task to verify database grooming settings are still set to the expected values or if an update is required to return settings to their expected values.

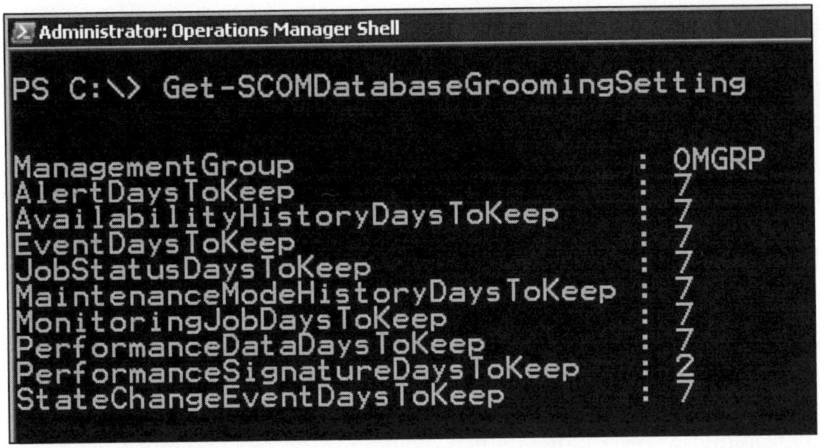

```
Administrator: Operations Manager Shell

PS C:\> Get-SCOMDatabaseGroomingSetting

ManagementGroup                      : OMGRP
AlertDaysToKeep                      : 7
AvailabilityHistoryDaysToKeep        : 7
EventDaysToKeep                      : 7
JobStatusDaysToKeep                  : 7
MaintenanceModeHistoryDaysToKeep     : 7
MonitoringJobDaysToKeep              : 7
PerformanceDataDaysToKeep            : 7
PerformanceSignatureDaysToKeep       : 2
StateChangeEventDaysToKeep           : 7
```

FIGURE 23.18 Using `Get-SCOMDatabaseGroomingSetting` to verify data retention settings in operational database.

Changing Grooming Settings for the Operational Database

Because you can easily change database grooming settings in the Operations console, it's not uncommon that administrators in larger environments might change these when troubleshooting OpsMgr management group health and performance issues. The `Set-SCOMDatabaseGroomingSetting` cmdlet sets database grooming for the operational database for the management group to which your OpsMgr PowerShell console is connected. As part of a scheduled task, you could use `Get-SCOMDatabaseGroomingSetting` to return these settings to their expected value for your environment. The cmdlet includes options to connect to a remote management group and specify alternate credentials should the account used to run the OpsMgr PowerShell console not have the rights necessary to change the database grooming settings. If you plan to make changes such as this interactively, use the -passthru parameter to show the changes made. This next example makes several changes to the grooming settings that are controlled with this cmdlet, with the output shown in Figure 23.19. The code will change these parameters using one line of code:

- -JobStatusDaysToKeep 4
- -MaintenanceModeHistoryDaysToKeep 4
- -MonitoringJobDaysToKeep 4
- -PerformanceDataDaysToKeep 4

```
Set-SCOMDatabaseGroomingSetting -AvailabilityHistoryDaysToKeep 10
-JobStatusDaysToKeep 4 -MaintenanceModeHistory DaysToKeep 4 -MonitoringJobDaysToKeep
4 -PerformanceDataDaysToKeep 4 -passthru
```

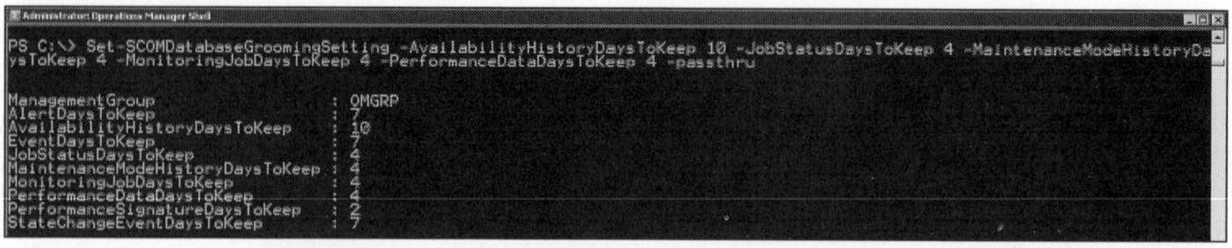

```
PS C:\> Set-SCOMDatabaseGroomingSetting -AvailabilityHistoryDaysToKeep 10 -JobStatusDaysToKeep 4 -MaintenanceModeHistoryDaysToKeep 4 -MonitoringJobDaysToKeep 4 -PerformanceDataDaysToKeep 4 -passthru

ManagementGroup                   : OMGRP
AlertDaysToKeep                   : 7
AvailabilityHistoryDaysToKeep     : 10
EventDaysToKeep                   : 7
JobStatusDaysToKeep               : 4
MaintenanceModeHistoryDaysToKeep  : 4
MonitoringJobDaysToKeep           : 4
PerformanceDataDaysToKeep         : 4
PerformanceSignatureDaysToKeep    : 2
StateChangeEventDaysToKeep        : 7
```

FIGURE 23.19 Using `Set-SCOMDatabaseGroomingSetting` to update data retention settings in the operational database.

Retrieving Data Warehouse Database Settings

The `Get-SCOMDataWarehouseSetting` cmdlet gets the data warehouse settings, which include the name of the management group, the name of the data warehouse database name, and the data warehouse server name (which includes instance name) for the management group to which the PowerShell session is currently connected. This would be helpful to use when verifying the settings for the OpsMgr data warehouse.

Updating Data Warehouse Database Settings

The `Set-SCOMDataWarehouseSetting` cmdlet sets the data warehouse settings for the management group. Some options that are available are -DatabaseName, which is the name of the data warehouse, and -ServerName, which is the data warehouse server name. If using this cmdlet from the shell, ensure you use the -passthru option to show changes after running the cmdlet.

Creating Overrides in Bulk

There are a number of potential use cases for creating overrides in bulk in OpsMgr, including

- Replicating configurations across environments,
- Disabling performance collection rules collecting counters of interest, and
- Tuning thresholds for a workflow(s) to different levels for groups of servers to meet the needs of multiple support teams.

Creating overrides (especially disable or enable overrides) is not exceedingly difficult from the OpsMgr Shell. For example, to disable rules in bulk targeting the SQL DB Engine and containing "*events/sec*" in their name, run this snippet:

```
$MP = Get-SCOMManagementPack -displayname "SQL Server 2008 Overrides" | `
where {$_.Sealed -eq $False}
$Class = Get-SCOMClass -DisplayName "SQL DB Engine"
$Rule = Get-SCOMRule -DisplayName "*Events/sec"
Disable-SCOMRule -Class $Class -Rule $Rule -ManagementPack $MP -Enforce
```

View results in the Authoring pane -> Overrides node of the Operations console, as displayed in Figure 23.20.

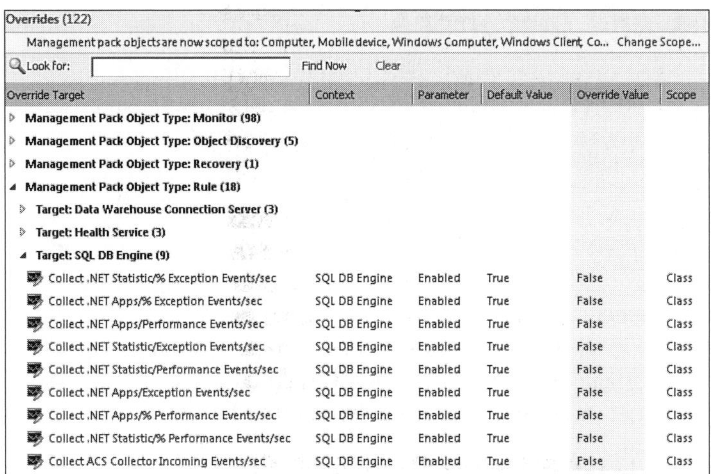

FIGURE 23.20 Viewing overrides created in PowerShell in the Operations console.

To re-enable the same rules (reversing the work performed by the previous PowerShell snippet), run the following:

```
$MP = Get-SCOMManagementPack -displayname "SQL Server 2008 Overrides" | `
where {$_.Sealed -eq $False}
$Class = Get-SCOMClass -DisplayName "SQL DB Engine"
$Rule = Get-SCOMRule -DisplayName "*Events/sec"
Enable-SCOMRule -Class $Class -Rule $Rule -ManagementPack $MP -Enforce
```

View the results in the Operations console, as displayed in Figure 23.21.

Overrides (122)

Management pack objects are now scoped to: Computer, Mobile device, Windows Computer, Windows Client, Co... Change Scope...

Look for: Find Now Clear

Override Target	Context	Parameter	Default Value	Override Value	Scope
Management Pack Object Type: Monitor (98)					
Management Pack Object Type: Object Discovery (5)					
Management Pack Object Type: Recovery (1)					
Management Pack Object Type: Rule (18)					
Target: Data Warehouse Connection Server (3)					
Target: Health Service (3)					
Target: SQL DB Engine (9)					
Collect .NET Statistic/% Exception Events/sec	SQL DB Engine	Enabled	True	True	Class
Collect .NET Apps/% Exception Events/sec	SQL DB Engine	Enabled	True	True	Class
Collect .NET Apps/Performance Events/sec	SQL DB Engine	Enabled	True	True	Class
Collect .NET Statistic/Exception Events/sec	SQL DB Engine	Enabled	True	True	Class
Collect .NET Statistic/Performance Events/sec	SQL DB Engine	Enabled	True	True	Class
Collect .NET Apps/Exception Events/sec	SQL DB Engine	Enabled	True	True	Class
Collect .NET Apps/% Performance Events/sec	SQL DB Engine	Enabled	True	True	Class
Collect .NET Statistic/% Performance Events/sec	SQL DB Engine	Enabled	True	True	Class
Collect ACS Collector Incoming Events/sec	SQL DB Engine	Enabled	True	True	Class

FIGURE 23.21 Verifying overrides created via PowerShell.

Exploring Classes and Instances

While you can use the Discovered Inventory view in the Operations console or community-developed tools such as the MP Viewer, the OpsMgr Shell enables browsing classes, relationships, and instances quickly and easily, as discussed in the following sections.

Browsing Classes

Although you can use the Discovered Inventory view or the class picker in the Authoring pane to view classes in the Operations console, it is not possible to gain insight into which classes are delivered in a specific management pack or to export class information to a consolidated format (such as csv). Fortunately, the OpsMgr Shell makes short work of such tasks, providing cmdlets for slicing and dicing classes and discovered inventory in just several lines of code. Here are some short PowerShell snippets to answer common requests:

- How to retrieve a list of all object classes present in your Operations Manager 2012 management group:

  ```
  Get-SCOMClass| format-table DisplayName, Description
  ```

- Determine the management pack in which the class is defined:

  ```
  Get-SCOMClass | format-table DisplayName, Description, ManagementPack
  ```

- Use the following to send this information to a csv file for easy reading in Excel:

  ```
  Get-SCOMClass | Select-Object DisplayName, Description | `
  Export-CSV -path c:\classes.csv
  ```

- Retrieving all the classes defined in a specific management pack is also a single line affair with the following one-liner, which retrieves all the classes in the Microsoft.SQLServer.Library management pack:

  ```
  Get-SCOMClass | where {$_.ManagementPackName `
  -like 'Microsoft.SQLServer.Library'}
  ```

Exploring Discovered Instances

Using a one-liner similar to the last one in the previous section, you can use the `Get-SCOMClass` cmdlet to retrieve a list of the discovered classes, like so:

```
Get-SCOMClassInstance| Select-Object DisplayName, Name, Description
```

You can then find the Name column in this output (not to be confused with DisplayName) to retrieve a list of discovered instances of the object class of your choice by passing output of the `Get-MonitoringClass` cmdlet for a single class to the `Get-SCOMClassInstance` cmdlet, as illustrated here for the `SQL 2008 DB` object class:

```
Get-SCOMClass -Name "Microsoft.SQLServer.2008.Database" | Get-SCOMClassInstance
```

Using the `Format-Table` cmdlet demonstrated in the "Filtering, Formatting, and Grouping with PowerShell" section, you can filter and format results in a neatly organized tabular format, to display only the database DisplayName (e.g., OperationsManager) and PathName, which represents the server and SQL instance that hosts the database.

```
Get-SCOMClass -Name "Microsoft.SQLServer.2008.Database" | Get-SCOMclassInstance | `
Format-Table DisplayName, PathName -auto
```

Exploring Relationships

The .GetRelationships() method explores the relationships between classes in Operations Manager. Given a target class, this method returns all the relationships for which the target class is either the *source* or the *target*. The simple PowerShell function below provides an easy way to enumerate relationships without the need to open multiple management packs in the MP Viewer or an XML editor.

```
function GetRelationships
 {param ($Class)

  (Get-SCOMClass | where {$_.DisplayName -eq "$Class"}).GetRelationships()|`
  fl DisplayName, Description

 }
```

To call the function, enter the function name with a class display name in quotes. Save this and the snippet above in a .ps1 file and run from an OpsMgr Shell instance.

```
GetRelationships "SQL Server 2008 DB File"
```

Figure 23.22 shows the output of the script.

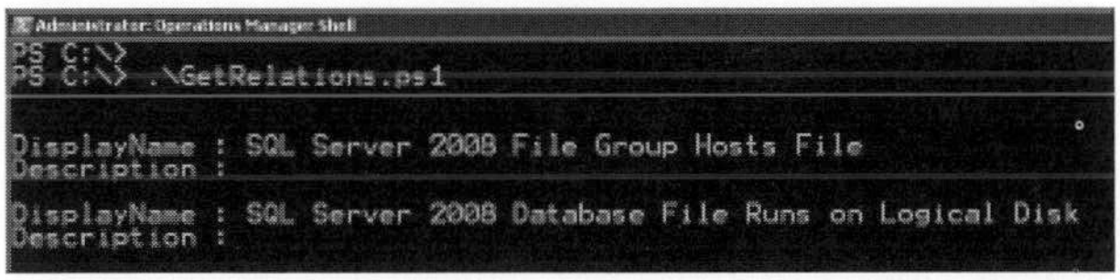

```
PS C:\>
PS C:\> .\GetRelations.ps1

DisplayName : SQL Server 2008 File Group Hosts File
Description :

DisplayName : SQL Server 2008 Database File Runs on Logical Disk
Description :
```

FIGURE 23.22 Output of the relationship enumeration function.

You can find a list of display names using the Discovered Inventory view or class picker in OpsMgr reports.

Exploring Groups

You may not be aware that each group within OpsMgr is itself a unique class. Groups in OpsMgr are a special type of class called a *singleton* class (or simply singleton), because each group in OpsMgr represents a unique class that has only once instance. That bit of trivia aside, you may find yourself wishing to enumerate members of a group for any number of reasons, such as to have application administrators (such as SQL database administrators) review to ensure OpsMgr has discovered and is monitoring all database servers and instances present in your environment.

The `Get-SCOMGroup` cmdlet makes this an easy task, facilitating enumeration of group members in a single line of PowerShell, as shown in the following example.

```
Get-SCOMGroup -DisplayName "<DisplayName of Group>" | GetSCOMClassInstance
```

Using the `Export-CSV` cmdlet demonstrated in the "Browsing Classes" section, you can send the members of the group to a spreadsheet, providing an easy format for colleagues to review to ensure all servers and instances in scope for monitoring are in fact being monitored.

```
Get-SCOMGroup -DisplayName "<DisplayName of Group>" | GetSCOMClassInstance `
| Export-CSV C:\groupmembers.csv -notypeinfo
```

Managing Notification Subscriptions

Alert notifications, introduced in Chapter 14, "Monitoring with System Center 2012 Operations Manager," consist of three core elements; the channel (how notification will be sent), subscribers (to whom notifications will be sent), and a subscription (which alert criteria will trigger notification). In the OpsMgr Shell, it is possible to work with any and all of these core elements of alert notification through the following cmdlets:

- Add-SCOMNotificationChannel
- Add-SCOMNotificationSubscriber
- Add-SCOMNotificationSubscription
- Disable-SCOMNotificationSubscription
- Enable-SCOMNotificationSubscription
- Get-SCOMNotificationChannel
- Get-SCOMNotificationSubscriber
- Get-SCOMNotificationSubscription
- Remove-SCOMNotificationChannel
- Remove-SCOMNotificationSubscriber
- Remove-SCOMNotificationSubscription

The next sections discuss several scenarios where these cmdlets can be useful.

Temporarily Disabling All Notification Subscriptions

Consider an example where you may want to temporarily disable all notification subscriptions during an extensive data center outage (planned or otherwise); this can be accomplished by retrieving all the enabled notification subscriptions with `Get-SCOMNotificationSubscription` and passing them through the pipeline to `Disable-SCOMNotificationSubscription`, as shown here.

```
Get-SCOMNotificationSubscription | where {$_.Enabled -eq $True} | `
Disable-SCOMNotificationSubscription
```


When you are ready to re-enable all notifications within OpsMgr, another one-liner reverses the effects of the previous command. You will still need to retrieve all the disabled notification subscriptions with `Get-SCOMNotificationSubscription` and then pass them to another cmdlet, `Enable-SCOMNotificationSubscription`, to re-enable all disabled subscriptions.

```
Get-SCOMNotificationSubscription | where {$_.Enabled -eq $False} | `
Enable-SCOMNotificationSubscription
```

Removing Notification Subscriptions

Removing a notification subscription is common only in the most dynamic environments. The next one-liner shows how.

```
Get-SCOMNotificationSubscription | where {$_.DisplayName `
-like "My Notification Subscription"} | Remove-SCOMNotificationSubscription
```

Should you remove a notification subscription, you may also want to remove the associated subscribers and channels using the `Remove-SCOMNotificationSubscriber` and `Remove-SCOMNotificationChannel` cmdlets. However, since subscribers and channels can be associated with multiple notification subscriptions, you will want to do a little planning first based on how you have implemented notifications in your OpsMgr environment.

Copying Subscriptions

To facilitate configuration of alert escalation scenarios using the Alert Aging feature of OpsMgr notification subscriptions, you may want to make a copy of a subscription so you can configure an alert escalation much more quickly than would be possible manually in the Operations console.

The high-level steps to copy (clone) an OpsMgr notification are

1. Retrieve the existing notification subscription.
2. Retrieve the notification channel associated with the existing notification subscription.
3. Retrieve the subscribers associated with the existing notification subscription.

4. Retrieve the notification criteria of the existing notification subscription. Criteria include the classes, groups targeted by the alerts for which you wish to send notification, as well as other alert properties, such as alert severity and priority.

The code required for copying an OpsMgr notification subscription is more verbose than can be included here in the chapter, but you will find a working example at http://www.systemcentercentral.com/tabid/143/indexid/94855/default.aspx. A copy of this script is included for your convenience in Appendix E, "Available Online;" follow the instructions in the article for customizing the script.

Scripting Recurring Tasks

The scale of your environment and the scarcity of human resources often drive the need for automation. Running one-liners in an OpsMgr Shell session is straightforward; however, if you will be running PowerShell scripts, there are several additional cmdlets you should be familiar with. These are discussed and demonstrated in the following sections.

Sample Scripts for Common Scenarios

To ensure consistency in larger OpsMgr deployments, you will want to automate many routine functions that occur on a nightly basis. What if a new OpsMgr admin deploys several hundred agents as requested but forgets to enable agent proxy on the new boxes? If there is a nightly script that enables agent proxy on all machines that do not have it turned on, this incident will not be that big a blip on the OpsMgr landscape. The same goes with automating the nightly backup of unsealed management packs and setting failover servers for agent managed machines nightly. The next sections discuss examples of using scripts.

Backing Up Unsealed Management Packs Nightly

Part of a comprehensive backup strategy for OpsMgr would include backing up unsealed management packs on a nightly basis to the file system, as discussed in Chapter 12, "Backup and Recovery." This is to ensure changes made to the OpsMgr environment, such as overrides, custom rules, and monitors, are captured and backed up. Chapter 12 includes a nice script that does just this job using the OpsMgr cmdlet `Export-SCOMManagementPack`. The following script, from Chapter 12, is available as online content as part of a suggested nightly backup procedure. See Appendix E for details.

```
param ($ServerName);
$MS = $ServerName
Import-Module OperationsManager
Get-SCOMManagementGroupConnection -ComputerName $MS | Set-
SCOMManagementGroupConnection
$all_mps = Get-SCOMManagementPack Where-Object {_.Sealed -eq $False}
foreach($mp in $all_mps)
{
```

```
Export-SCOMManagementPack -ManagementPack $mp -path "C:\Backups"
}
```

Setting Failover Management Servers to Agents

As your OpsMgr environment grows and you add hundreds (or even thousands) of OpsMgr agents on Windows servers and incorporate cross-platform and network device monitoring, you may want to configure specific failover management servers to balance the agent load.

23

This script performs the following high-level actions:

1. Retrieves the agent to be updated (host4.odyssey.com in this case).
2. Sets two variables; one for the primary management server and the second variable for the failover management server.
3. Sets the primary and failover management servers for the list of agents in the `$agent` variable.

```
#Get the agent you want to update
$AgentName = Get-SCOMAgent "host4.odyssey.com"

#Get the primary and failover management servers
$primaryMS = Get-SCOMManagementServer "helios.odyssey.com"
$failoverMS = Get-SCOMManagementServer "hector.odyssey.com"

#Set Fail-over Management Server on Agent
Set-SCOMParentManagementServer -Agent $AgentName `
-FailoverServer $FailoverMS -passthru

#Set Primary Management Server on Agent
Set-SCOMParentManagementServer -Agent $AgentName `
-PrimaryServer $PrimaryMS  -passthru
```

One behavior to be aware of when using the `Set-SCOMParentManagementServer` cmdlet is you will get a failure message if you attempt to set the primary management server to the same server as the current failover management server.

With a bit of effort, you can update agent failover settings in bulk as described in the article on updating agent failover settings from a spreadsheet with PowerShell at http://www.systemcentercentral.com/tabid/143/indexid/95393/default.aspx.

Balancing the Agent Load

While resource pools are a fantastic addition to OpsMgr 2012, one important item they do not address is balancing the agent load across management servers in the resource pool. For example, if you have two management servers and you discover and install 2,500 agents with the Discovery Wizard, all 2,500 will use the same management server as their primary. This is not a very efficient use of resources to say the least!

Fortunately, with the OpsMgr Shell, you can easily balance the agent load across multiple management servers. The sample script referenced in this section evenly distributes agents across two or more management servers. Running this script as part of a schedule task can ensure the agent load is balanced as your environment grows and evolves.

While it is relatively easy to balance agents across two management servers with PowerShell, the script logic becomes significantly more complex when you need to support 2–*N* management servers. Fortunately, that did not bother Andreas Zuckerhut, who routinely writes PowerShell-based automation solutions for OpsMgr that rate at the high end of the complexity scale. You can find a copy of this community-developed solution in the OpsMgr by Example series at http://www.systemcentercentral.com/BlogDetails/tabid/143/IndexID/96292/Default.aspx.

Group Maintenance Mode Script

Group maintenance mode scripts should be just like computer maintenance mode, short and simple. Really, maintenance mode should be an operation performed in the Operations console, but as with any other company, time and resource constraints required Microsoft to make choices and set priorities.

At the time of Operations Manager 2007 RTM, SP 1 and even R2, many people were going through a lot of unnecessary effort to put groups of objects into maintenance mode. The widely accepted methodology was

1. Retrieve the group.
2. Loop through the objects contained in the group.
3. Put object into maintenance mode.
4. Go to next object and repeat.

This was not very efficient and resulted in a script making many calls to Operations Manager 2007 (one call per agent) via the SDK.

All that was necessary in OpsMgr 2007 was to put the group object itself into maintenance mode and OpsMgr would take care of the contained objects for you! Recursion (maintenance mode for "this object and contained objects") was assumed and handled automatically by OpsMgr. However, in OpsMgr 2012, that automatic recursion (the "this object and contained objects" logic) seems to be missing in the Operations Manager Shell. You can correct this by using the .ScheduleMaintenanceMode() method in the OpsMgr 2012 SDK, which has an option to specify recursion. When you put a group in maintenance mode using ScheduleMaintenanceMode() and specify recursion, the group members are put into maintenance mode automatically. This makes for a script that is not only much shorter than versions that go the more common route (described in the numbered list in this section), but one that is also very efficient.

This sample script is actually written as a PowerShell function, making it relatively easy to pass in the required parameters for maintenance mode that you would have to enter in the Operations console for a computer.

When calling a function, the function call should be located *after* the function itself in the PowerShell file:

```
Function GroupMaintMode
#($SCOMServer, $GroupDisplayName, $DurationInMin, $Reason, $Comment)
(
[Parameter(Mandatory=$True)][string]$SCOMServer,
[Parameter(Mandatory=$True)][string]$GroupDisplayName,
[Parameter(Mandatory=$True)][Int32]$DurationInMin,
[Parameter(Mandatory=$True)][string]$Reason,
[Parameter(Mandatory=$False)][string]$Comment
){

Import-Module OperationsManager
New-SCOMManagementGroupConnection -ComputerName $SCOMServer

foreach ($Group in (Get-SCOMGroup -DisplayName $GroupDisplayName))
{
   If ($group.InMaintenanceMode -eq $False)
   {
            $group.ScheduleMaintenanceMode([datetime]::Now.touniversaltime(), `
            ([datetime]::Now).addminutes($DurationInMin).touniversaltime(),`
             "$Reason", "$Comment" , "Recursive")
   }
}
```

Save the above snippet (available online at http://www.systemcentercentral.com/BlogDetails/tabid/143/IndexID/94576/Default.aspx) to a .ps1 file and then paste the following code below the snippet, substituting your desired values for those in this sample. While the function parameters are straightforward, the function parameters are explained immediately after this snippet.

```
GroupMaintMode -SCOMServer "Helios" -GroupDisplayName "My Custom Group" `
-DurationInMin 10 -Reason "ApplicationInstallation" `
-Comment "Scheduled weekly maintenance"
```

The script is now complete. To run, call the .ps1 file from any PowerShell prompt on a computer with the OpsMgr Operations console installed. The script will import the OpsMgr PowerShell cmdlets for you.

Here is an explanation of the function parameters:

- **SCOMServer:** Mandatory parameter containing management server name (NetBIOS or FQDN)
- **GroupDisplayName:** Mandatory parameter containing display name of the target group

- **DurationInMin:** Mandatory parameter containing integer of desired duration in minutes
- **Reason:** Mandatory parameter containing reason. Acceptable values are UnplannedOther, PlannedHardwareMaintenance, UnplannedHardwareMaintenance, PlannedHardwareInstallation, UnplannedHardwareInstallation, PlannedOperatingSystemReconfiguration, UnplannedOperatingSystemReconfiguration, PlannedApplicationMaintenance, ApplicationInstallation, ApplicationUnresponsive, ApplicationUnstable, SecurityIssue, LossOfNetworkConnectivity
- **Comment:** Optional parameter with free text description of your choice

The full version of this script with additional explanation in a post by MVP Pete Zerger discussing OpsMgr 2012 group maintenance mode via PowerShell is available at http://www.systemcentercentral.com/BlogDetails/tabid/143/IndexID/94576/Default.aspx.

Some Useful One-Liners

PowerShell is a very succinct language, and it is relatively easy to do a lot of work with a relatively small amount of code when compared to some other MS scripting languages, like VBScript and JScript. This section includes a few easy-to-use one-liners that should be useful in any OpsMgr environment.

Processing Alerts in Bulk

Processing alerts in bulk may well be the most common use of the OpsMgr Shell and one you should approach with caution. Because you may find yourself trying to clean up tens of thousands of alerts in a worst-case scenario, efficient syntax is important, as explained previously in the "Optimizing Performance When Working with the Powershell Shell" section. This section includes several examples of effective use of the -criteria parameter instead of `Where-Object` to optimize performance of bulk alert processing commands.

- Resolve informational alerts created by a rule:

```
Get-SCOMAlert -criteria 'ResolutionState = ''0'' AND Severity = ''0''' | `
Where-Object {($_.IsMonitorAlert -eq $False)}| Set-SCOMAlert `
-ResolutionState 255 | out-null
```

- Resolve information alerts created by a monitor:

```
Get-SCOMAlert -criteria 'ResolutionState = ''0'' AND Severity = ''0''' | `
Where-Object {($_.IsMonitorAlert -eq $True)}| Set-SCOMAlert `
-ResolutionState 255 | out-null
```

- Get a count of warning alerts created by a rule:

```
(Get-SCOMAlert -criteria 'ResolutionState = ''0'' AND Severity = ''1''' | `
Where-Object {($_.IsMonitorAlert -eq $False)}).count
```

- Get a count of warning alerts created by a monitor:

```
(Get-SCOMAlert -criteria 'ResolutionState = ''0'' AND Severity = ''1''' | `
Where-Object {($_.IsMonitorAlert -eq $True)}).count
```

Find a longer list of one-liners for processing alerts at Pete Zerger's OpsMgr 2012 PowerShell article discussing an updated collection of one-liners at http://www.systemcentercentral.com/BlogDetails/tabid/143/IndexID/89870/Default.aspx.

Overview of Installed Patches on Agent Machines

This excellent one-liner shows the contents of the PatchList object. This is a great improvement from OpsMgr 2007 pre-SP 1 days, when an OpsMgr administrator had to keep track of individual patches via the version of files. The following one-liner shows the name of an agent and what is in the patch list.

```
Get-SCOMAgent | sort {[string] $_.PatchList} | select Name, PatchList
```

If running this in a large environment, rather than looking at the screen, dump the output to a CSV file using the `Export-CSV` cmdlet as shown here:

```
Get-SCOMAgent | sort {[string] $_.PatchList} | select Name, PatchList | `
Export-CSV -NoTypeInformation C:\output.csv
```

This information was adapted from Stefan Stranger's blog at http://blogs.technet.com/b/stefan_stranger/archive/2012/08/06/om2012-quicktip-overview-of-installed-patches-for-agents.aspx.

Agent Health State and Grey Agent Detection

System Center Cloud and Datacenter Management MVP Graham Davies sums up creating a one-liner on agent health in a blog post at http://www.systemcentersolutions.co.uk/index.php/scom/entry/agent-health-state-using-powershell. While agent health state is an important piece of information to the overall health status of an OpsMgr agent, it may not be the best indicator of an agent's true health state. If an agent is healthy when it goes offline, it still reflects its healthy state, displaying in the Operations console under Agent State as being Healthy (with a green check mark) but Grey (offline). A better measure of whether an individual agent is healthy and responsive would be checking the `HealthServiceWatcher` class's health state. Here is an example that outputs the display name of the agents with the health state of their health service watcher:

```
Get-SCOMClass -Name "Microsoft.SystemCenter.HealthServiceWatcher"|Get-
SCOMclassinstance |sort displayname|FT displayname, healthstate -auto
```

The health state value could be Success (good), Uninitialized (maintenance mode is running), or Error (the Health Service Watcher is offline).

Report on Agent Primary Management Server and Failover Management Servers

You will want to get a report monthly to check that your agents are not attempting to report to a management server previously removed from your environment. This is also a great sanity check to make sure things are set up properly.

```
Get-SCOMAgent|sort ComputerName|FT -a ComputerName,
PrimaryManagementServerName,@{l="SecondaryManagementServers";
e={$_.GetFailoverManagementServers()|foreach{$_.name}}}
```

Running OpsMgr Shell Scripts in Orchestrator

System Center 2012 Orchestrator (Orchestrator), the runbook automation component in System Center 2012, provides OpsMgr code-free integration with the other System Center components out of the box. You can read more about OpsMgr integration with Orchestrator in Chapter 21, "System Center Integration."

You will find some activities for common automation scenarios are not included by default (such as a group maintenance mode activity), requiring you, the System Center administrator, to bridge functionality gaps. Fortunately, Orchestrator is very PowerShell-friendly and includes an activity to run PowerShell scripts called Run .NET Script. However, you may not find success in your first attempt without a small bit of preparation. The following is a list of considerations and preparatory tasks to ensure your Orchestrator runbook server can successfully run OpsMgr Shell scripts:

- Enable script execution for the 32-bit PowerShell instance on the Orchestrator runbook server. While your runbook server is running 64-bit Windows Server 2008 R2 or 2012 (with System Center 2012 SP 1), Orchestrator is still a 32-bit application, and as such, always launches a 32-bit PowerShell instance.

  For details on how to set PowerShell script execution policy, see the "PowerShell Execution Policy" section.

- Install the OpsMgr Operations console on your runbook servers. Without the OpsMgr Shell present on the runbook server, OpsMgr PowerShell scripts will fail every time.

- Configure a connection to your OpsMgr management group(s) in the Global Configuration area of the Orchestrator Runbook Designer, available on the Tools -> Options menu. To ensure all scripts have adequate permissions contained within runbooks, you will need to provide an account with OpsMgr administrator privileges. For details on how to configure OpsMgr connectivity from Orchestrator, refer to Chapter 21.

You will find detailed examples of Orchestrator runbooks interacting with OpsMgr via PowerShell in *System Center 2012 Orchestrator Unleashed* (http://www.amazon.com/System-Center-2012-Orchestrator-Unleashed/dp/0672336103, Sams, 2013).

Fast Track

If you used PowerShell in OpsMgr 2007, here are key concepts to remember related to OpsMgr 2012:

- PowerShell version 2 is supported out of the box, which means the OpsMgr PowerShell Shell is now a module and no longer a snap-in.
- All cmdlets are renamed. The new cmdlet names for Operations Manager 2012 came from a PowerShell design best practice now enforced internally at Microsoft. This best practice was implemented after the OpsMgr 2007 release; this is why Operations Manager 2007 did not conform to the naming standard.
- Operations Manager 2007 cmdlets can continue to work on an OpsMgr 2012 environment, although you should test your scripts in a lab before using in a production environment.
- The best practices for use of parameters versus `Where-Object` for large datasets remain the same.
- Some of the common bulk admin tasks for which OpsMgr 2007 lacked a cmdlet are added in the OpsMgr 2012 Shell.
- Orchestrator 2012 provides a (nearly) script-free alternative for some OpsMgr PowerShell Shell scripts, providing excellent logging, error checking, and governance.

Summary

This chapter discussed Operations Manager 2012 PowerShell cmdlets. It included an introduction to PowerShell basics for those not already well-acquainted with PowerShell. A wide variety of examples was offered with the intent of presenting OpsMgr Shell capabilities for common automation and bulk administration scenarios with OpsMgr 2012. The intent of the chapter was to expose you to ideas of what you could automate, plus what can be useful in bulk administration in your day-to-day administration of OpsMgr. The next chapter discusses Operations Manager in a service provider environment.

CHAPTER 24

Operations Manager for the Service Provider

IN THIS CHAPTER

- OpsMgr and Service Delivery
- The Management Cloud
- Certificates and OpsMgr
- Multi-Tenant OpsMgr
- The Customer Network
- Introducing Server Provider Foundation
- Fast Track

Service providers, by definition, deliver a service. A managed services provider (MSP) bundles software and services into contracts called service level agreements (SLAs). Two broad categories of service can be provided by System Center 2012, in particular Operations Manager (OpsMgr). Consider these as business models, more than technical references:

- **OpsMgr as a service itself:** The service provider does not have an SLA on applications monitored by OpsMgr. Think of this as "hosted OpsMgr," an Application as a Service (AaaS). In this mode, the SLA is on OpsMgr itself, that being the availability and correct function of the OpsMgr feature of System Center. The customer pays the service provider for OpsMgr services.
- **OpsMgr as a tool to deliver a service:** The service provider has an SLA on servers, devices, and/or applications. Think of Management as a Service (MaaS) where the SLA is on availability of the business applications. The customer pays the service provider for applications and services managed using OpsMgr.

Each model deploys OpsMgr in a highly scalable, distributed model optimized for certificate-based operation using gateways and agents in remote customer networks. A difference is the hosted OpsMgr model has an SLA on OpsMgr, while the full SLA model uses OpsMgr to enable an SLA on applications and infrastructure.

This chapter discusses using OpsMgr in service provider roles and the architecture of service provider management groups and the certificate authority (CA). It explores various ways to deliver hosted and managed services with OpsMgr. The chapter concludes with an introduction to a new service provider foundation, available with System Center 2012 Service Pack (SP) 1.

TIP: SECTION ON CERTIFICATE AUTHORITY IS FOR EVERYONE

Much of this chapter covers using OpsMgr in various multi-tenant and service provider scenarios that may not apply to a single organization not performing chargeback operations to other business units. However, the "Certificates and OpsMgr" section applies to all OpsMgr administrators that will be deploying gateway servers or agents in workgroups or untrusted domains.

OpsMgr and Service Delivery

If your network or Information Technology (IT) practice is invested heavily in Microsoft technologies, you likely are already using one or more System Center components. In the System Center 2012 license model for servers, all former separate products such as OpsMgr and Configuration Manager (ConfigMgr) now are licensed together. (Chapter 4, "Planning an Operations Management Deployment," includes a discussion of how licensing works with System Center 2012.) When considering a management tool, it is logical to look at solutions utilizing software that you or your customers may already own.

The Evolution of Microsoft Management Tools

As discussed in Chapter 1, "Operations Management Basics," Microsoft's first premier management application was Microsoft Operations Manager (MOM) 2000, released in October 2001. MOM 2000 was based on a management framework acquired from NetIQ Corporation. MOM 2000 had a significant update with the MOM 2005 release in August 2004. Microsoft Operations Manager gained a well-deserved reputation as a management tool for Microsoft networks; its management packs enabled MOM to provide more relevant data about Microsoft applications than competing solutions.

The MOM 2000 and MOM 2005 Legacy

A common feature of MOM 2000 and MOM 2005, which made their application in service provider roles difficult, was a dependence on Windows Active Directory (AD) domain trusts. MOM required the domain of the MOM agents trust the domain of the MOM servers at a Windows AD (Kerberos) authentication level. This left service providers wanting to use MOM remotely to monitor multiple customers with two choices:

- Create one-way trusts and routed private network communication with each customer and use a multi-tenant MOM management group.
- Install an independent MOM management group for every customer and monitor each one remotely.

Microsoft noticed that despite the technical difficulties, a small but steady percentage of MOM licenses were being used by service providers in MSP scenarios. Management of the many AD domain trusts, DNS zones, and other infrastructure of a multi-tenant MOM model was challenging. Likewise, the high overhead and low scalability of the independent management group model limited that model's appeal.

OpsMgr 2007 Innovations

OpsMgr 2007 introduced several new technology features, such as certificate-based authentication method and the gateway server role. Certificate-based authentication overcame the AD authentication requirement, and the gateway server role removed the need for a routed private network connection to the customer network. The combination of the certificate-based authentication and gateway server role, as well as the class structure and role-based and scoped security of OpsMgr 2007, enabled a new architecture model suited to the service provider.

The OpsMgr model requires neither domain trusts nor direct network connectivity to managed networks. It supports multi-tenancy and offers a scalable remote management model. This architecture, nearly identical in the 2007 and 2012 versions, is fully described in this chapter. OpsMgr has seen some success in a service provider role for a variety of Microsoft partners and customers.

SCE and ROM Experiments

Microsoft created the System Center Essentials (SCE) 2007 product, an "all-in-one" management application, to address the needs of the small business market. SCE 2007 was the development prototype for OpsMgr 2007 and included a subset of OpsMgr features as well as software and update management features for the small business. SCE 2007 was limited to a maximum of 50 servers and 500 client computers.

Another experiment by Microsoft during this time was Remote Operations Manager (ROM) 2007; this consisted of an OpsMgr 2007 management pack imported to a service provider instance of OpsMgr and a wizard included with SCE 2007. The Enable Service Provider Mode Wizard activated an OpsMgr gateway server component on the SCE server and connected it to the service provider instance of OpsMgr over the Internet. ROM included a license for Remote Web Workplace (RWW) as a remote access solution for the service provider to the customer remote network.

ROM did not gain many subscribers, and was in fact not technically required to use OpsMgr in a service provider scenario. However, SCE 2007 gained a small but loyal following, and was part of the (ultimately ill-fated) Essential Business Server (EBS) midsized business server solution. Development continued with SCE 2010 merging Virtual Machine Manager (VMM) and OpsMgr functions in a single interface. SCE 2010 did not include an Enable Service Provider Mode Wizard or a replacement for ROM. You cannot monitor a SCE 2010 server from an OpsMgr management group.

SCE 2010 was again a prototype for future OpsMgr releases, but with a surprising outcome. After a heavy product integration development effort, Microsoft realized too much work was going into the integrated console at the expense of product functionality. A decision to continue to separate OpsMgr and VMM products played well into an eventual plan to fold all System Center-related products into one with the System Center 2012 release. While OpsMgr and VMM are tightly integrated, they remain distinct components within System Center 2012.

TIP: NO REMOTE OPERATIONS MANAGER SUPPORT IN OPSMGR 2012

Customers running SCE 2007 in Service Provider Mode do not have a direct upgrade path. Enable Service Provider Mode is non-functional in SCE 2010, and SCE 2007 customers cannot enable service provider mode to OpsMgr 2012 management groups. Service providers running Remote Operations Manager need to migrate their ROM offering to OpsMgr 2012, and their customers from SCE to OpsMgr 2012 gateways.

Intune and Service Provider Foundation

Microsoft has not yet provided an update or roadmap regarding SCE; however, SCE 2010 is probably the last release of System Center Essentials, with its functionality in the Microsoft small business roadmap migrating to the Intune product. Windows Intune is a network management service in the Windows Azure public cloud. In the first releases of Intune, a monthly subscription fee per client computer included a seat in a cloud-based management portal with an active agent running on each managed computer. Microsoft announced in September 2012 that it is changing Intune's licensing model to include per-user licensing, with rights to use Intune for up to five devices per user. With the release of Intune 4 ("Wave D") and Configuration Manager 2012 with Service Pack 1, Microsoft is taking the first step in delivering interoperability between the two products through the ConfigMgr console. Intune 4 can manage Windows Phone 8 and RT devices, with lesser capabilities for Android and IOS. See http://blogs.technet.com/b/server-cloud/archive/2012/09/10/system-center-2012-configuration-manager-sp1-beta-and-windows-intune-update-aspx for additional information.

At the time of writing this chapter, the authors are unaware of plans for an OpsMgr management pack for Windows Intune. This means OpsMgr 2012 remote monitoring of the client computer portion of remote customer networks requires OpsMgr 2012 agents, and only if a service provider SLA includes the client computers. Microsoft has a partner model for Intune, and a means for Intune customers to permit partners to access their Intune consoles by granting the service provider co-administrator permissions to their Intune subscriptions.

As described in more detail in the "Introducing Service Provider Foundation" section, a technology codenamed Service Provider Foundation (SPF) may ultimately be Microsoft's answer for the common interface between VMM and OpsMgr, as well as all Windows Server and System Center features. The common interface is not a conventional application console but is instead an oData-based web service of REST endpoints that serve up PowerShell objects.

A Microsoft vision for service providers could be that management services are delivered from public and private management clouds over the Internet to SPF endpoints in customer premise and private cloud locations. Data and instructions are executed with PowerShell and exchanged by SPF to remotely administer, monitor, and manage customer infrastructures.

The Opportunity and Challenge

The fundamental opportunity of the service provider and its customers is leveraging the economies of scale and efficiencies of mature processes to deliver better services at less cost. The provider of the service can focus on delivering the best possible experience with that service, allowing the customer to focus on his line of business rather than spending time or concern on the outsourced service.

The discipline of network management in the enterprise space can leverage economies of scale in a dramatic fashion—this is a prime mover in the economics behind the public cloud. With platform standardization and identical management approaches, vast numbers of computers can be managed and monitored through their whole life cycles with ruthless efficiency!

If a service provider could manage 10,000 computers—100 each from 100 customers—with the same efficiency as managing all 10,000 for the same organization, the cost savings compared to managing all 100 networks independently would be astronomical. Those cost savings are passed to the customer and create a profit for the service provider as well. The challenge in extending large organization-style IT efficiencies to small, midmarket, and distributed enterprises is rooted in the difficulty these markets face in adopting large-enterprise IT management techniques. For example, assembling and sharing a body of repeatable procedures to improve service, such as custom recovery tasks in OpsMgr (or even runbooks in System Center Orchestrator), can be hard to implement outside larger, more organized IT support teams.

Tools for Measuring Service

Those service providers delivering SLAs on infrastructure need eyes and ears in their managed environments to detect issues and confirm that application and service SLAs are being met. A service provider must have monitoring in place to detect problems and report these to support teams, enabling resolution of issues before serious service outages occur and thus guaranteeing the uptime of servers and applications. SLAs and tools to measure the service covered by the SLAs define the managed service provider industry.

Service Level Agreements

SLAs are legal contracts that typically focus on a customer's application needs. For example, an SLA for Exchange services might specify that employees can log into their mailboxes 99.999% of the time, equating to allowing less than 4 minutes of mailbox unavailability per month. An SLA violation occurs if the service provider fails to deliver that level of service uptime. Depending on the terms of the SLA, violations can result in the service provider paying the customer a penalty, and even lead to automatic cancellation of the contract. If one service provider cannot deliver the service properly, the customer finds another service provider.

A logical benefit of the SLA mechanism is that it aligns the business goals of the customer and the service provider. Both parties have incentive to achieve the availability metrics specified in the SLA:

- When things break, the burden is on the service provider to fix the problem, rather than the customer.
- The customer enjoys fixed costs to use the delivered service for the period of the SLA, regardless of how often the service provider has to perform preventative or corrective maintenance on the involved hardware and software platforms.

Network Management Tools

There may be some very relaxed SLAs where the service provider has no way of knowing something is broken until the customer calls. However, very few businesses (at least those that pay a network services provider!) are OK with arriving to work Monday morning to be surprised with no network service at the office. Email, web, and even telephone services could be down, so expecting managed services customers to report their own outages is generally an unsatisfying business arrangement.

Virtually every managed services provider uses one or more network management applications as tools to detect service-impacting events in the infrastructures they manage. Most commercial network monitoring tools were designed originally to monitor routers and switches and offer little more than "red light/green light" indications on device health. Deeper insight into application health requires custom automation or more sophisticated commercial tools. Service provider solutions based on Microsoft's System Center compete against products and services in three spaces:

- **Packaged MSP solutions:** In the last decade, a number of firms have emerged that offer turnkey package solutions to prospective managed service providers. These products include built-in help desk and other support utilities tailored for the small and medium business (SMB) market. Level Platforms, Kaseya, and LabTech are examples in this category, and there are no clear market favorites. Include Microsoft's own Windows Intune in this category.
- **Small and mid-market, adapted solution:** This category refers to general-purpose network monitoring applications adapted to multi-tenant and/or hosted functionality by the MSP. There is an open source option, Nagios, and industry favorites Solarwinds, What's Up, and GFI. Monitoring applications and computer resources beyond CPU, disk, network, and memory requires purchasing additional vendor modules, or dealing with numerous unsupported community add-ons. OpsMgr 2012 fits this category when used in the mid-market, including all the free knowledge in management packs without complexity or cost.
- **Large enterprise, dedicated solution:** For decades, network services SLAs have been a staple with large organizations such as airlines and credit card companies. Equally large service firms such as IBM use industrial strength monitoring frameworks such as Patrol from BMC, IBM's Tivoli, and OpenView from HP. These mature products have service provider models that generally require steep investments. OpsMgr 2012 with some adaptation is included in this category and can be employed by service providers with the most demanding enterprise SLAs.

Tools for cost-effective remote network management are difficult to architect, deploy, and support, probably a reason for slower uptake of managed services than economies might otherwise suggest. OpsMgr does not include an official service provider model or best practice blueprint, so the MSP intending to use OpsMgr in this role must make quite a few architectural and procedural decisions to reduce business risk. There are many positive indications to deploy OpsMgr in MSP roles:

- Customers may already own the System Center 2012 licenses so the service provider does not have to charge for the tool. (If customers do not own the license, Microsoft has the Service Provider License Agreement [SPLA] program to rent System Center 2012 management licenses on a monthly basis.)
- Customers or service provider may have a use case for other System Center features such as ConfigMgr or Data Protection Manager (DPM) and this brings along the OpsMgr license at no additional cost.
- Ability to leverage free OpsMgr management packs from hardware vendors and software publishers provides the best application monitoring solution in the industry. Most other management solutions charge to monitor applications and/or require a considerable amount of custom configuration.
- OpsMgr 2012 network device monitoring (via gateway servers) lets the MSP extend management to customer-premise network devices without a direct network connection.

The Management Cloud

Service providers need a network environment to deploy management tools into and from which to monitor customer networks. This is referred to as the *management cloud*. The larger the service provider's operational footprint, the more substantial the cloud must be. Above a certain scale, the service provider may need to support multiple management clouds for cloud redundancy and geographic reach.

Since OpsMgr is part of System Center 2012, deployment of OpsMgr for the service provider should occur as part of a complete Microsoft private cloud solution. Specifically, this means System Center Virtual Machine Manager virtual machine templates are used to deploy OpsMgr features as services into private clouds defined in VMM. Put another way, the hosted or managed OpsMgr service provider instance is the first tenant of a private cloud managed by the same OpsMgr instance.

Defining the Management Cloud

When you install OpsMgr and the other System Center 2012 components into the private cloud in a manner intended to host or multi-tenant the operations of other customers, you are creating a management cloud. From the management cloud, the local infrastructure hosting the cloud itself is managed, as well as all remote connected private clouds and Service Provider Foundation connections. Here are common characteristics of OpsMgr installed in a public-facing service provider management cloud:

- Owners of the monitored computers, applications, and services belong to different entities, such as customers; one customer must never be aware of another customer's presence or identity in the cloud. OpsMgr groups, classes, and scoped roles are used to segregate customers.
- There is no Windows trust relationship between the management group and the monitored computers; mutually trusted certificates validate the identity of customers to the service provider and vice versa. The service provider publishes a CA to the Internet for this purpose.
- Private or VPN network connections between the service provider's management cloud network and the customer network are not necessary. OpsMgr works perfectly using only OpsMgr gateway to OpsMgr gateway traffic over the Internet. Monitored networks may exist in many remote customer locations; any number of the remote networks may duplicate IP network numbers.
- The service provider has contracts or service level agreements with customers. In the case of internal business units that are managed like customers, these can take the form of chargeback reports at inside-sales rates.
- The service provider extends the value of OpsMgr to the customer in some fashion. Examples include using OpsMgr to monitor a hosted private cloud, publishing the OpsMgr Web console and/or establishing alert subscriptions, triaging alerts by a network operations center (NOC), and posting OpsMgr reports to a customer web portal.

Minimum Architecture Requirements

The OpsMgr service provider scenario is Internet-centric. An Internet-facing certificate authority is hosted by the service provider and issues identity certificates to all service provider management servers and gateway servers, and to all customer gateway servers. Customer computers without on-premise gateway servers can also perform certificate-based connection to service provider gateways over the Internet in the same fashion as gateways; customer agents not reporting to customer gateways are also issued certificates.

Architectural Overview of Service Provider Mode

You can begin to sketch the minimum implementation of OpsMgr in service provider mode using an Internet cloud and a pair of firewalls at each end of a communications channel. Figure 24.1 shows a customer network above and the service provider network below:

- The communications channel is a TCP port 5723 outbound connection from the customer gateway server to an Internet-based destination.
- The target is an Internet IP permitted by a firewall of the service provider, which maps that Internet IP to the private IP of an OpsMgr gateway server in a DMZ or other perimeter network.

- An SSL connection across the Internet is created between the customer and service provider gateway servers. The gateway server establishes a second SSL connection to an OpsMgr management server.
- The customer gateway server monitors other computers and devices by proxy on the remote customer network. Data travels through the gateways to the OpsMgr databases.

Once the outbound connection from the customer gateway is completed, the communication workflow becomes two-way and customer gateways and agents can receive and execute instructions delivered to them by management packs and OpsMgr Operations console tasks. This means that even if a service provider does not have direct network connectivity to the customer network, privileged instructions can still be run in customer environments by remote execution of tasks via the OpsMgr channel.

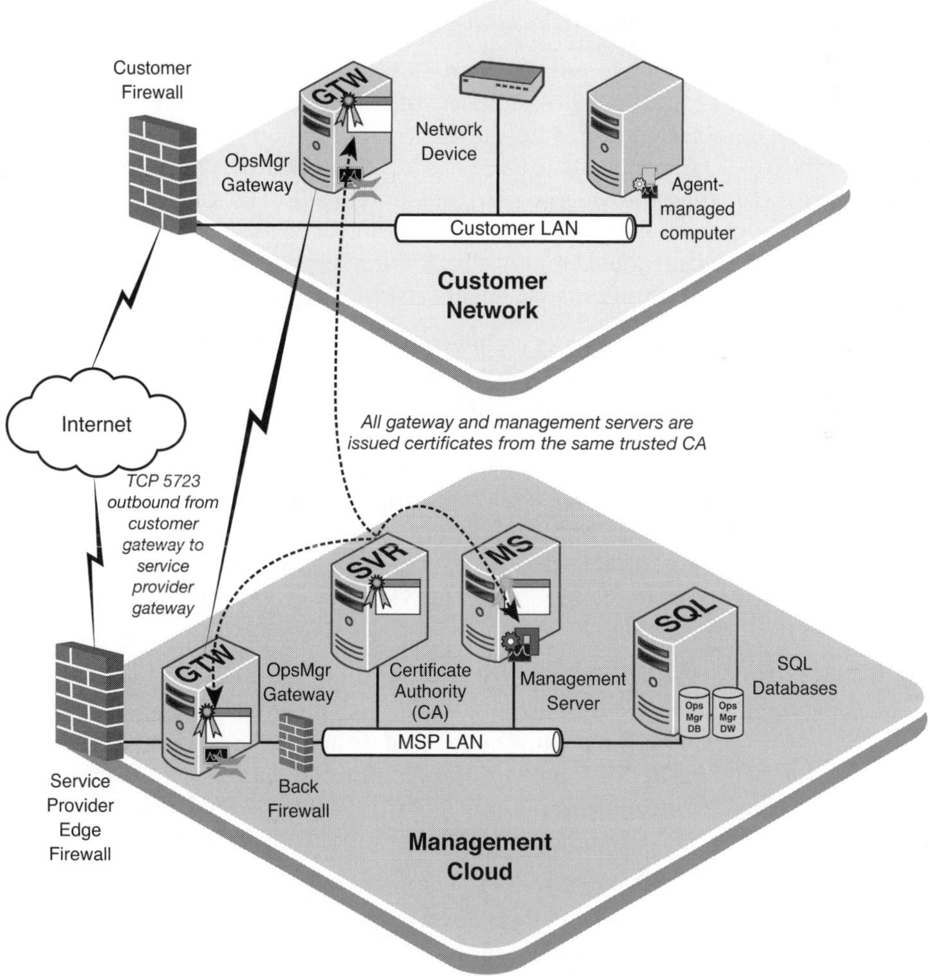

FIGURE 24.1 Overview of OpsMgr service provider mode.

Gateways and Security Considerations

It is technically possible to connect an OpsMgr gateway in a customer environment over the Internet directly to an OpsMgr management server in the service provider network. However, the authors recommend that Internet communication only occur between gateways, or between agents and gateways; there should always be a gateway server security buffer between Internet-based OpsMgr customers and the server provider's OpsMgr management servers. Here's why:

Gateway servers, which might be Internet-facing, do not have direct write access to the OpsMgr operational and data warehouse databases, while management servers do. Gateway servers also do not need AD or Kerberos to participate in the OpsMgr management group. In addition, since gateway servers only need a single outbound port (TCP 5723) opened in a back firewall scenario, an effective, single-port isolation approach is enabled that is appropriate for a screened network such as a DMZ. There is little point in putting a management server in a perimeter network since a management server needs AD, Kerberos, and SQL ports open in addition to TCP 5723.

The authors do not recommend mapping TCP port 5723 directly from the Internet to an OpsMgr management server in the service provider scenario; this would leave the management group database unprotected from a hostile process running on the management server. A gateway server is far less privileged and has less network access if compromised. A best practice is for the service provider to place one or more OpsMgr gateway servers in a perimeter network, with customer agents and gateways reporting to the service provider gateways. The service provider should employ a back firewall that permits only TCP 5723 from the gateways to their respective management servers on the internal network.

New with OpsMgr 2012, a service provider architecture consideration is the concept of gateway server pooling when monitoring network devices. While agent to gateway management remains the same as in OpsMgr 2007 where each agent reports to one primary and optionally one failover gateway server, network devices are now monitored by resource pools. You can combine up to three gateway servers into a resource pool in a large customer environment and monitor up to 1,000 network devices in the customer's remote network(s). (With more than 500 remote devices, perform load analysis before committing to higher device loads—capacity at scale can be constrained by factors such as queues and Simple Network Management Protocol [SNMP] connections.)

Scaling Models for the Service Provider

More than the traditional network administrator, the service provider must accommodate significant and constant growth in the scope and size of its monitoring operation. This business growth is usually the desired outcome of a successful managed or hosted services operation with frequent new customers and recurring new business from existing customers. The service provider should be well informed of the capacity constraints of OpsMgr in large and very large-scale scenarios.

Scale-out plans need to be developed and a valid service provider architecture determined early on. The service provider needs a monitoring infrastructure that can scale with known costs and remain on sound technical footing. Business stakeholders may be disappointed to learn that to support growth they must start over with some different, larger architecture or even some other monitoring product to scale at reasonable costs.

Service providers follow the same design guides for OpsMgr capacity as everyone else. The basic management cloud depicted in the lower portion of Figure 24.1, given one management server, one gateway server, and one database server, could monitor a maximum of 2,000 agent-managed computers. The model shown has no redundancy and thus would not be suitable for a high value SLA.

Scaling for Redundancy

The service provider must provide for redundancy first and then plan for scaling. Redundancy is very important for the service provider since availability of the monitoring tool is of paramount importance to fulfilling and confirming delivery of the SLA. For this reason, the service provider should architect for failure and maintenance of management group features. Here are ways to enable full redundancy in a high-value management group:

- **Cluster the database servers:** This allows one database node to fail or undergo maintenance and the database itself to remain highly available on the surviving cluster node(s). Failover clustering by definition locates the OpsMgr databases in higher-end shared storage, or in synchronized SQL Server 2012 AlwaysOn availability groups.
- **Add an additional management server to the All Management Servers Resource Pool and configure gateway servers with failover management servers:** This approach distributes the management group task load and allows for one management server to fail or undergo maintenance, and for connected gateways to fail over to the surviving management server.
- **Add an additional gateway server in the service provider perimeter network and configure the customer gateway servers with failover gateway servers:** This allows a service provider gateway server to fail or undergo maintenance with connected customer gateways failing over to the surviving gateway server.
- **Add an additional gateway server in the customer network and configure the customer agents with failover gateway servers:** This allows a customer gateway server to fail or undergo maintenance while connected agents fail over to the surviving gateway server.

After meeting the basic redundancy requirements, the service provider can expect near 100% availability of the monitoring infrastructure (assuming connectivity and data center power remain available). Any monitoring outage by the service provider is mission critical since customers could experience undetected outages, which provoke SLA violation on the part of the service provider and threaten the customer relationship.

It is important to remember that during failover, surviving management and gateway servers need the reserve capacity to carry the load of the agents or gateways that are failing over to them. For example, two gateways could support 4,000 agents, but not if one gateway fails. Since one gateway cannot exceed 2,000 agents, two gateways only provide redundant coverage for 2,000 agents. Load-balancing 1,000 agents on each gateway, pointing agents to the other gateway as a failover would be a good practice (an active-active deployment).

TIP: USE REDUNDANT MANAGEMENT GROUPS FOR EXTREME HIGH AVAILABILITY

To achieve extreme high availability for monitoring, consider dual-homing all agents to parallel management groups in geo-diverse management clouds. This is in addition to architecting for redundancy within the management group, and protects the service provider and customer from the risk of even a regional data center outage, although there is a high overhead to monitoring everything twice.

Scaling for Capacity

After the service provider mitigates single-component failure risks to deliver the managed service, the primary consideration shifts to capacity management. Like any OpsMgr management group, the maximum number of supported agents per management group is somewhere between 6,000 and 15,000, depending on factors such as the number of management packs and connected consoles.

As a rule of thumb, you should not exceed 1,000 agents per gateway, to allow failover to another gateway and not exceed 2,000 agents on a surviving gateway. Also, remember to reserve capacity in the management servers to which the gateway servers report. Distribute the agents-behind-gateways load among management servers and assign failover management servers to gateways, remembering no single management server should exceed 3,000 downstream agents even when one management server has failed.

In a fully scaled out service provider management group, there could be as many as 10 or more gateway servers in the management cloud and a half-dozen or more management servers. Dozens or even hundreds of customer gateways could be part of the same service provider management group. However, at a certain point, the capacity of the management group cannot be increased and the service provider is faced with a scaling decision. The next scaling increment for the service provider is the connected management group. Up to 10 or more management groups can be connected to a single top-level management group called the *local management group*. Figure 24.2 shows two connected management groups reporting to a local management group and sharing a single data warehouse database. This design could monitor the alerts of 12,000 to 30,000 computers that report to connected management groups from the local management group console.

TIP: SHARED DATA WAREHOUSE MODEL DOES NOT INCREASE DATA WAREHOUSE CAPACITY

A shared data warehouse database, even when part of a properly designed connected management group scenario, does not increase the maximum capacity of an OpsMgr data warehouse database. It does not matter how much you use OpsMgr reporting services in the management group, the limitation comes from the quantity of manageable records in a data warehouse database, which is about 15,000. Only architect for a shared data warehouse database—in the connected management group scenario—when the connected management groups will be smaller than full capacity. Specifically, the total number of managed objects in all connected management groups cannot exceed 15,000 using a shared data warehouse database.

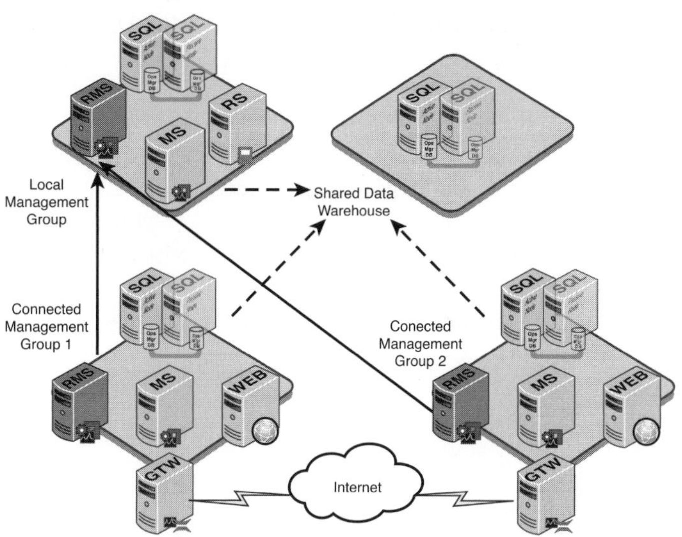

FIGURE 24.2 Connected management groups with Internet gateway scenario for maximum scaling.

If a service provider is architecting to monitor more than 6,000 computers, a multiple management group or connected management group scenario must be considered from the beginning. A multiple management group scenario not including a need for connected management groups is limited in scale only by the service provider's business processes. A maximum theoretical size for a connected management group scenario is about 10 fully populated connected management groups, or about 60,000 to 150,000 monitored computers. (There is no tier concept; you cannot "stack" downstream management groups.) Here are some considerations for this decision:

- ▶ If the service provider does not have a central point of alert escalation, for example a NOC, it may not be necessary to deploy connected management groups; for example, in a scenario of hosted OpsMgr, where customers retain responsibility for their applications and only have access to scoped OpsMgr Web consoles, emailed reports, and alert notifications.
- ▶ A service provider NOC or centralized alert processing facility will need to use a connected management group solution. This avoids the unsupportable situation of having operations staff watch separate Operations consoles for multiple management groups.
- ▶ Alerts from all connected management groups will appear in the local management group console. NOC staff or central automation act on alerts in the local management group. Tasks are also functional from the local management group to connected management groups.
- ▶ State views, customer Web consoles, and customer notification subscriptions will appear in the connected management groups. Essentially, alerts appearing in the

local management group can be investigated by shifting the focus of the Operations console to the connected management group.

TIP: ALTERNATIVE CUSTOMER CONNECTION SCENARIOS

While not covered in this book, some service providers have been successful using OpsMgr in multi-tenant models not involving gateway servers:

- You could have connected management groups in customer environments that report to a central service provider local management group instance.
- You could use OpsMgr agents at scale reporting directly to gateways over the Internet, rather than using local gateways.

Neither of these scenarios has been tested by Microsoft or is considered a fully supported environment. You should thoroughly test any service variants such as these, with all considerations carefully made before committing to a business plan.

Certificates and OpsMgr

For the service provider, publishing a certificate authority to the Internet is as critical to securely publishing gateway servers to the Internet. It is mandatory to have a solid, even permanent CA in place before proceeding with a hosted OpsMgr operation. Even though the service provider's CA is a private CA, the Certificate Revocation List (CRL) must be reachable over the Internet for the solution to work. Notice in Figure 24.1 that the management server and gateway at the service provider, as well as the gateway at the customer site, are issued certificates by the same mutually trusted CA.

The certificates are issued using fully qualified domain names (FQDNs):

- For service provider gateways, the FQDN must match DNS records or HOSTS file name records used by customer computers to locate the service provider gateway server. Since an OpsMgr authentication certificate must match the computer name, service provider gateways must have computer names that resolve to matching public FQDNs.
- Customer servers, including customer gateway computers that use Kerberos to authenticate with downstream agents and directly connected customer agents, require a certificate FQDN that matches their private Windows computer FQDN.

Each server is issued one certificate that is used for all encrypted server traffic on that server, and each server is configured to use only one certificate at a time. After manually or automatically installing an OpsMgr gateway or agent that requires certificate authentication, there is a manual step to run the MOMCertImport.exe utility to install the certificate and/or associate it with OpsMgr. The procedures for this are covered in the "The Customer Network" section.

Architecture decisions about the service provider CA involve choices between enterprise and stand-alone CAs, and root CA-only compared to root CA with subordinate CAs. The "Enterprise Versus Stand-Alone CA" and "Root and Subordinate CAs" sections discuss these decisions.

Enterprise Versus Stand-Alone CA

When installing the CA role on Windows Server, determine which of two CA modes to install. How the CA can be used will differ depending on the enterprise CA or stand-alone CA approach to OpsMgr certificates in the service provider scenario. While many service providers using OpsMgr in service provider mode have used the stand-alone model for its simplicity and repeatability, there are some useful options available in the enterprise mode as well. Table 24.1 lists considerations for these models.

TABLE 24.1 Enterprise versus stand-alone CA considerations

Enterprise	Stand-Alone
One or few instances, centralized	Repeatable, distributed
Deep Active Directory integration	Does not use Active Directory
CA used by other products	OpsMgr only CA user
CA impacts AD operations	Self-contained, no AD impact
Command line or AD GUIs	Administer with command-line

Either CA model can have important CA architecture decisions with long-lasting consequences. Using a CA for customer operations means you undertake a critical 24x7x365 support commitment to the CA infrastructure itself for a multi-year period. Once hundreds or thousands of certificates are issued from a particular CA, the value of that CA can become quite high.

Enterprise CA Model

Service providers deploying a CA to support customer operations might select the enterprise CA model when the service provider has a NOC or management cloud. The service provider's AD or a dedicated NOC AD can be extended or leveraged for management functions other than OpsMgr—such as computer certificates for System Center Configuration Manager. Changes to an enterprise CA can affect domain computers, so care is required when modifying the properties of an enterprise root or subordinate CA.

While using an enterprise CA creates a dependence on AD, it also enables some handy features that make work easier for the service provider. Here are two examples of certificate operations options available using an enterprise CA not available with a stand-alone CA:

- **Persistence and reusability of certificate templates across environments:** Certificate templates imported once to AD are available to all CAs in the enterprise. Contrast this with using stand-alone CAs, when certificate templates must be imported manually into each CA instance.

- **Using Active Directory policy to obtain certificates via the Certificates MMC:** The service provider often needs to issue certificates on behalf of customer computers. This necessitates an associated manual data entry task to issue individual certificates. While in the stand-alone model you must do this at the command line, an enterprise CA can utilize the UI of the Certificates MMC to allow operations staff to perform these tasks with less complexity.

Stand-Alone CA Model

Consider deploying a CA to support customer operations in the stand-alone CA model when the service provider wants a modular, isolated CA solution not integrated with the service provider's AD domain or any domain. This solution "drops in" to any environment and is self-contained. Changes to a stand-alone CA do not affect anyone's AD. Another benefit of the stand-alone model is you can design and replicate the entire solution in a lab or "clean" environment.

Following the stand-alone CA model requires assembling and standardizing on a set of command lines or scripts to import and operate with your service provider templates. Interaction with a stand-alone CA is similar to working with a public certificate provider. In both models, you generate certificate request files offline and then present those to the CA for processing, receiving the private keys in a response file delivered to and processed on the requesting computer(s).

Private PKI Considerations

When a user, computer, or device entity presents a certificate for authentication, it proves the entity belongs to a trusted group of users, computers, or devices. Using certificates for authentication replaces or augments traditional user name/password credentials, requiring that someone or something possess a unique certificate instead of, or in addition to, knowledge of a user name and password.

Certificates are particularly useful to confirm identity of users and systems across Windows domains using a federation concept; or when Windows networking with domain login using Kerberos is unavailable, such as with client computers in workgroups. The mutual trust for the certificate issuing authority (the CA) replaces a trust for an Active Directory forest or domain. The service provider is generally the provider of the trusted CA that makes OpsMgr work across domains.

Private Versus Public CAs

If you publish websites to the public, you probably have purchased certificates from a public certificate provider such as VeriSign, Go Daddy, or Thawte. A public cryptographic authority (that issues trusted root authority certificates) is required when you expect members of the general public or large numbers of employees, partners, or customers to trust your certificate automatically.

These SSL certificates cost $50–$350 per year or more and are a good value if you have public-facing websites, and for Outlook WebApp (OWA) and ActiveSync. Individual private certificates for user, computers, and devices from public providers range from

$10–$50 per user or more annually. This quickly becomes too expensive for all but very small organizations with very high security requirements. The successful large-scale service provider will issue many, perhaps tens of thousands of individual private certificates that could cost hundreds of thousands of dollars from a public CA. The math makes the public CA operating expenses too high to consider using a public CA in the OpsMgr service provider model.

Most client operating systems already trust the root certificates of the major industry public certificate providers. The service provider saves a lot of money using private certificates that they issue and are trusted by their customers' networks. The trick is to get the private root CA certificate of the service provider CA trusted by the client OS—this is done automatically by Active Directory group policy, but the trusted private root certificate must be manually distributed to devices and non-domain computers.

Publishing and Supporting the Private CA

The root certificate is a digital file that must be stored on, or transferred to, the storage media or memory of the device. While an administrative burden, it can also be positioned as an added security layer because members of the general public do not have the public key of the service provider's PKI solution. A properly designed root and subordinate CA infrastructure can include self-renewal features and require little administrative work for up to 20 years, the maximum recommended lifetime of a root certificate.

To use the service provider features of OpsMgr in any centralized model, you must establish a private certificate authority, or partner with a managed security service provider (MSSP) to establish and maintain one for you. Once you have a private CA properly installed and optionally published to the Internet, you can be your own certificate provider and issue the same certificates as the public providers.

The certificates you issue will be installed on all gateway servers, management servers that communicate with gateway servers and untrusted agents, and agents that use certificates rather than Kerberos trust to authenticate with management servers or gateways. The OpsMgr authentication certificate generally has a lifetime of two years. Renewing the OpsMgr certificates manually or through an automated process is a prime business challenge to the service provider using System Center on a large scale.

Root and Subordinate CAs

The advanced PKI concepts of *offline root CA* and *subordinate certificate-issuing CAs* are common to both the enterprise and stand-alone models. If your operations are large enough and/or of enough value to merit an offline root CA and subordinate CAs, you should make that determination independent of the enterprise versus stand-alone decision. The decision to go with the more complex root and subordinate CA approach is driven by the size and value of the service provider operation.

A single root CA is sufficient for small service provider scenarios. However, a service provider expecting to support more than 1,000 customer computers with individual client certificate support should consider a root and subordinate architecture. A practical consideration is that a root certificate can be issued for a 20-year validity period, while no single certificate-issuing computer can be expected to have that long a life cycle. Subordinate

CA certificates with 5–10 year validity periods allow for seamless succession of certificate-issuing computers over time—which trust the same original root certificate.

The most scalable and supportable CA solution for the large service provider involves a root CA and at least one subordinate CA. The root CA can be optionally offlined for safety and security because when the CA trust chain is deployed correctly, trust in the root certificate enables trust in all subordinate CAs issued by that root CA. The root CA truly can be offline, so normally it is powered off and/or disconnected from the network. The root CA only needs to be "rehydrated" periodically to perform the following activities:

- Issue new certificate revocation lists (annually or when a subordinate CA certificate is revoked).
- Renew existing subordinate CAs.
- Approve new subordinate CA installations.

Deploying the Certificate Authority

This section discusses the high-level steps to install an enterprise root CA and create an OpsMgr certificate template. Since the service provider will utilize the Web enrollment feature, the web server role (IIS) must be preinstalled. Also as a best practice, provision the CA computer with a second disk drive other than the system drive for placement of the CA log files, which can grow quite large. In addition, be aware you cannot change the name of a computer once the CA role is installed.

CAUTION: USE ENTERPRISE OR DATACENTER WINDOWS SERVER 2008 FOR CA

The version of Windows Server 2008 or 2008 R2 used is important to the service provider. Since only Enterprise and Datacenter editions of Windows Server 2008 and 2008 R2 include the ability to create V2 and V3 certificates with extended validity lifetimes, do not install an enterprise CA on a Windows Server 2008 or 2008 R2 Standard edition computer. (Windows Server 2012 has no restriction; all CA features are available in both Standard and Datacenter editions of Windows Server 2012.)

Perform the following steps to deploy an enterprise root CA:

1. On a Windows Server computer that is a member of a Windows domain, run the Add Roles Wizard and set up the following components of the Active Directory Certificate Service: **Certificate authorities** and **CA Web enrollment**. Online responder and network device enrollment services are not needed.
2. During CA setup, specify to install an **Enterprise** CA of the **Root CA** type. The common name of the CA is a descriptive string such as **Odyssey Service Provider Root CA**.
3. Select the longest desired validity period for the root certificate, at least 5 years.
4. Place the CA database and log on a non-system partition, such as D:\CertLog.

5. After installation, the Enterprise CA root certificate is automatically distributed via AD group policy to all domain-joined computers, and placed in the Trusted Root Certification Authorities certificate store of the local computer.

6. Export the root CA certificate to a .CER file; this file will be required later to import into the service provider and the customer gateway server computers. Run this command line on the enterprise CA computer and save the resulting file:

```
certutil -ca.cert <name of certificate file>.cer
```

Creating and Preparing the OpsMgr Certificate Template

This section adds the functionality to the Enterprise CA needed for the service provider model. Specifically, the CA will be able to issue a custom certificate type recognized by OpsMgr components such as agent, gateway, and management server. Follow these steps:

1. On the CA computer, go to Start and type **MMC**. In the MMC snap-in, select **File -> Add/Remove Snap-in -> Certificate Templates** and **Certification Authority (local computer)**. Click **OK**.

2. Select **Certificate Templates**; in the console right-click on **IPSec (Offline request)** and select **Duplicate Template** as shown in Figure 24.3.

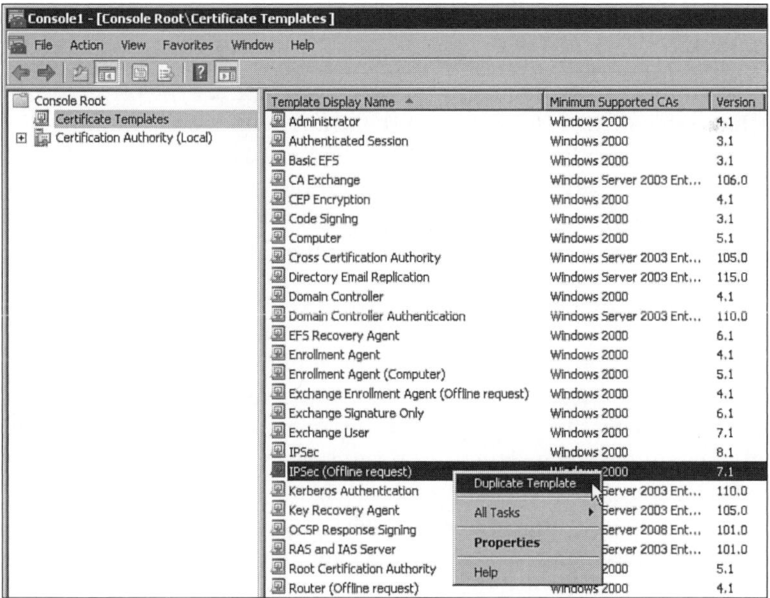

FIGURE 24.3 Duplicate the IPSec (Offline request) template for OpsMgr.

3. When prompted, select **Windows Server 2003 Enterprise**.

4. Name the certificate something descriptive like **Service Provider**.

5. On the Request Handling tab, select a key size, **1024** is appropriate for OpsMgr certificates. In addition, select **Allow the private key to be exported**.

   Also on the Request Handling tab, click the CSP button and select **Microsoft Enhanced Cryptographic Provider v1.0**, taking care not to remove the option Microsoft RSA SChannel Cryptographic Provider.

6. On the Extensions tab, edit the Applications Policies. Remove **IP security IKE intermediate** and add **Client Authentication** and **Server Authentication** policies.

7. On the Security tab, confirm that Authenticated Users have Read permissions for the new template.

   Also on the Security tab, add the computer account of the CA, and grant that account **Read** and **Enroll** permission on the certificate. (This is necessary to issue the certificate using the CA Web enrollment method.)

8. Click **OK** to create the template. The template now can be added to the CA.

9. In the MMC, go to Certification Authority. Right-click on **Certificate Templates** -> **New** -> **Certificate Template To Issue**.

10. Select the OpsMgr certificate and click **OK**. The CA can now issue OpsMgr certificates.

Publishing the Certificate Authority to the Internet

The service provider needs to publish some files to the Internet; these are the certificate revocation lists and delta certificate revocation lists of the CA. A key security feature of PKI is the CRL, which provides a positive means of locking out revoked certificates. The PKI client will always check for the CRL: to verify its own certificate and to verify that any other certificate(s) in the CA trust chain have not been revoked. Since OpsMgr service provider mode is Internet-based, the service provider needs a firewall-publishing rule permitting public access to check the private CRL.

It is important that the service provider can demonstrate to customers that an effective PKI certificate revocation scheme is operational. Less secure certificate-based authentication schemes might exist that do not include a renewal and revocation element. Customers expect the service provider to safeguard their infrastructures, including positive and immediate lockout of compromised or otherwise invalid credentials for which the service provider is responsible. A service provider using self-signed (not from a CA) and self-trusted certificates of long duration in a managed service scenario, in lieu of effective CA-based PKI with renewal and revocation plans, is less secure for its customers.

CAUTION: DON'T CIRCUMVENT CRL REVOCATION CHECKING

It is possible to design a Microsoft CA-based solution (with certificate attributes and registry changes) that disables the default behavior of computers and applications participating in PKI to perform revocation checking. This is sometimes seen in a lab environment. In the service provider scenario, it is critical for customer security that the service provider's certificate-issued CA(s) have CRLs properly published to the Internet.

When the OpsMgr agent or gateway computer in the customer environment starts up, one of the first things it does is check whether a computer certificate is ready to load for OpsMgr authentication. If there is, CRL checking on the certificate—at the operating system level—occurs before attempting application-layer authentication of the OpsMgr gateway or agent component. This enables pre-authentication CRL checking to occur.

By default, your CRL will not be accessible from the Internet. There are two areas where work must be done:

- Modifying the Certificate Distribution Point (CDP) and Authority Information Access (AIA) settings of the CA itself to stamp the public DNS location names in issued certificates, and
- Making the CDP and AIA files available over the Internet at those public DNS locations.

Figure 24.4 shows the contents of the *%windir%*\system32\certsrv\CertEnroll folder in the file system of the CA, the default publishing location for the CDP and AIA. AIA publishing to the \CertEnroll folder cannot be disabled.

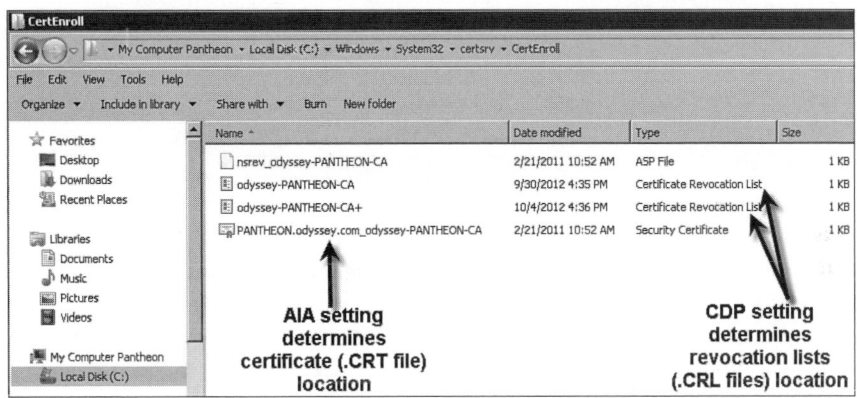

FIGURE 24.4 The CAs CertEnroll folder holds the authoritative certificate copies.

Certificate Distribution Point

In the service provider scenario, the CDP is the Internet URL where customer gateway and agent systems can expect to retrieve the CRL and delta CRL files. Adding a revoked certificate to the CRL locks out authentication processes expecting to use that certificate. The CDP URL must be on TCP port 80 HTTP and allow anonymous access. In Figure 24.4, the CRL file is odyssey-PANTHEON-CA.crl, and there is a delta CRL file, odyssey-PANTHEON-CA+.crl.

Authority Information Access

The AIA is the Internet URL where customer gateway and agent computers can expect to find the public key for the service provider's PKI, which is an authoritative copy of the server's CA or sub-CA certificate, a file with a .CRT extension. The public half of an encryption key, with for example 2048-bit security strength, is part of that certificate. The AIA URL needs to be on TCP port 80 HTTP and allow anonymous access. In Figure 24.4, the CRT file is PANTHEON.odyssey.com_odyssey-PANTHEON-CA.crt.

CDP and AIA Publishing Scenarios

As the CA Web enrollment feature is installed on the service provider scenario, by default there are also privately published web virtual directories in IIS that map to the %*windir*%\system32\certsrv\CertEnroll folder displayed in Figure 24.4. Reviewing the contents of the CertEnroll virtual directory in IIS Manager in Figure 24.5 shows how these files need to be presented to the PKI client using the standard web HTTP protocol.

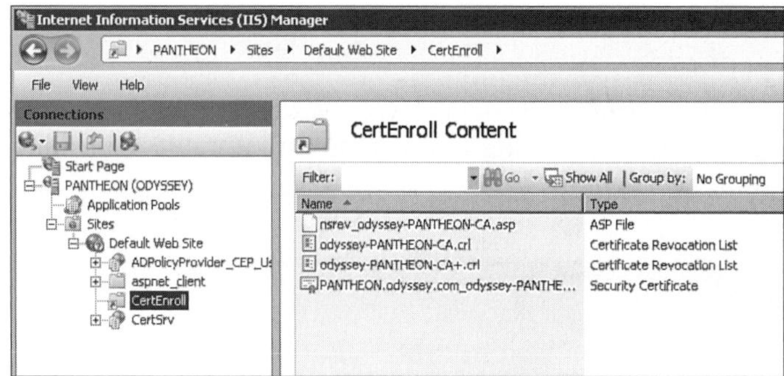

FIGURE 24.5 The CA Web enrollment feature adds IIS virtual directories.

Essentially, the PKI client reaches out over the Internet on port 80 to a URL such as http://ca.odyssey.com/CertEnroll/odyssey-PANTHEON-CA.crl, where anonymous Internet hosts can retrieve that revocation list. There are several methods available to publish the CRL to the Internet; these are described next. Each of the methods requires some customization of the AIA and CDP components of the CA or sub-CA issuing certificates in the service provider scenario.

If your service provider Active Directory name is also a public DNS name that you own and use, for example, **odyssey.com**, you have by definition a split DNS environment. If your AD name is a private name such as **odyssey.local** or a different public name such as **odyssey.net**, you have conventional DNS. If your AD is deployed in a split DNS scenario (a shared public and private DNS namespace with split public and private versions) you have the option of using the default HTTP CRL and AIA locations. The FQDN of the CA is the default HTTP location.

The goal is that accurate and publically accessible URLs are stamped into the certificate when they are issued to customer computers. You cannot change the settings in a certificate once it is issued, so whatever URLs you establish must be valid for multi-year periods and be selected for commitment to longevity from DNS hosting and Internet publishing perspectives. There are three well-known methods to publish the CRL to the Internet: the reverse proxy method, using the CA responder service, and a copy-and-publish scenario. These are discussed in the next sections.

Reverse Proxy to the Sub-CA CertEnroll IIS Virtual Directory

This is a very effective method for publishing a private CA to the Internet because it is low maintenance, always accurate, and secure through simplicity. It does require a reverse proxy solution such as that provided by Microsoft Threat Management Gateway (TMG) or a similar product. A secure reverse proxy solution caches and serves the CRL files at the Internet edge. An example secure firewall configuration for a service provider would only allow anonymous port 80 communication specifically to the /CertEnroll virtual folder with no other HTTP URL accepted.

Install the CA Online Responder Service

Large or highly distributed service providers should consider and investigate the Online Responder Service, an advanced and optional feature of Windows Server. Using Online Certificate Status Protocol (OCSP) signing certificates and online responder arrays, you can establish an effective global CRL publishing solution. For more details, consult http://technet.microsoft.com/en-us/library/cc753468.aspx.

Copy the \CertEnroll Folder Contents and Publish Separately

This is a common method because it can leverage an existing public website and co-purpose it for conveying the CRL URLs. For example, http://www.odyssey.com/ca could represent a virtual folder named "ca" that is created inside the existing public website. The contents of the \CertEnroll folder on the CA and/or sub-CA are manually (or preferably through automatic, scheduled scripting) copied to the /ca virtual folder of the public website. A downside to this method is two or more CRL copies can become unsynchronized when they depend on a manual or scripted process, making this a less preferred method.

CDP and AIA Customization

Settings for a Microsoft CA are contained in the registry of the CA computer at `HKLM\System\CurrentControlSet\services\CertSvc\Configuration`, where a key exists with the name of the CA, such as `odyssey-PANTHEON-CA`. The `CRLPublicationURLs` and the `CertPublicationURLs` multi-string values at that key determine the CDP and AIA settings stamped on certificates as they are issued.

You can modify the registry settings directly with regedit, via scripting or PowerShell, or using the Certification Authority MMC. After making changes to the registry settings, restart the CA using the Certification Authority MMC or via the command line with certutil.exe switches appropriate for your environment. To restart the CA using the MMC, select the CA root object, right-click, and select **All Tasks -> Stop Service**, then right-click and select **All Tasks -> Start Service**.

Figure 24.6 shows the MMC used to add custom CDP and AIA URLs to the CA. These settings are exposed on the Extensions tab of the Properties of the CA—flip the drop-down extensions selector between CDP and AIA management. In this example, the host name **ca.odyssey.com** is being used to publish the CRL. On the left of Figure 24.6, the CDP is customized with an HTTP URL and the options are selected to **Include in CRLs** and **Include in the CDP extension of issued certificates**. On the right, the AIA is customized as well, and **Include in the AIA extension of issued certificates** is selected.

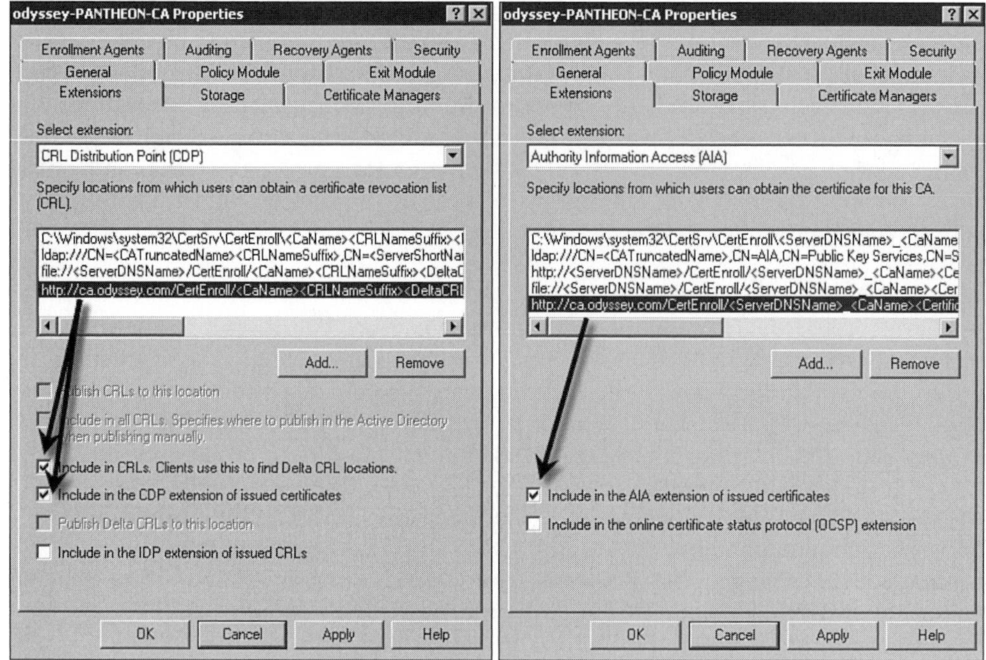

FIGURE 24.6 Customizing the CDP (left) and AIA (right) extensions of a CA.

Issuing OpsMgr Authentication Certificates

With your CA now installed and published to the Internet, the OpsMgr authentication certificate template created, and the CA CDP and AIA settings customized, you are ready to issue certificates for their intended purpose. OpsMgr certificates contain the private key, held only by the customer gateway or agent computer, which completes the PKI transaction when combined with the public key held by the CA.

There are a number of ways to interact with a Microsoft CA using various command line utilities, PowerShell, scripting, and certificate management applications such as Microsoft Forefront Identity Manager (FIM). The next sections describe three easy-to-use methods, but these are not the only solutions.

The service provider may use some or all of these methods depending on the volume of certificates to be produced at one time and whether there is private network connectivity to the customer site. Remember that only customer gateway servers, and some agents in situations where a gateway is not appropriate, need individual certificates for OpsMgr.

An MSP running a large multi-tenant mid-market instance of OpsMgr (an average load of 20 servers per customer) could consist of about 100 gateways or 2,000 managed servers. That's just several hundred, well-defined certificates to manage—one authentication certificate per customer gateway or customer agent not behind a customer gateway, and one for each OpsMgr management group gateway and management server.

If you will be issuing scores or hundreds of certificates at the same time, scripting is the best answer. If you will be managing thousands of certificates for whatever reason, scripting is the only answer! However, when just issuing several certificates at a time, as in the service provider scenario when a new customer adds one or two gateway servers, a GUI is really convenient. Fortunately, there are several choices on how to issue certificates in a service provider model.

Active Directory Enrollment Policy

From a domain member computer in the service provider's domain, you can issue certificates for any use using the Certificates MMC and Active Directory Enrollment Policy, including customer OpsMgr gateway servers and agent computers. Because the IPSEC (Offline request) certificate template was copied to use as the starting model for the Service Provider certificate, the certificate is configured to allow the details of the certificate to be manually provided rather than automatically by AD. The output of this process is a certificate file with private key with a .PFX extension that is ready to use with OpsMgr.

Follow these steps to issue an OpsMgr authentication certificate using Active Directory Enrollment Policy and the Certificates MMC:

1. On the CA computer, go to Start and type **MMC**. In the MMC snap-in, select **File** -> **Add/Remove Snap-in** -> select **Certificates** -> Add **Computer Account** -> **for Local Computer**. Click **Finish** and then **OK**.
2. Expand the Certificates\Personal\Certificates store. Right-click as shown in Task #1 in Figure 24.7 and select **All Tasks** -> **Request new certificate**. Click **Next**.
3. You should see the Select Certificate Enrollment Policy screen appear with the **Active Directory Enrollment Policy** selected. Click **Next**.
4. At the Request Certificates page of the Certificate Enrollment Wizard, click on the **More information is required to enroll for this certificate** link as shown in Task #2 in Figure 24.7.
5. In the Subject name: Type: drop-down list, select **Common name**. In the Value: field, type the fully qualified domain name of the computer the certificate is being issued for, **OpsMgrGW.customer.com** in this example. Click **Add** and the FQDN appears in the right side of the Certificate Properties as shown in Figure 24.8. Click **OK** and then **Enroll**.

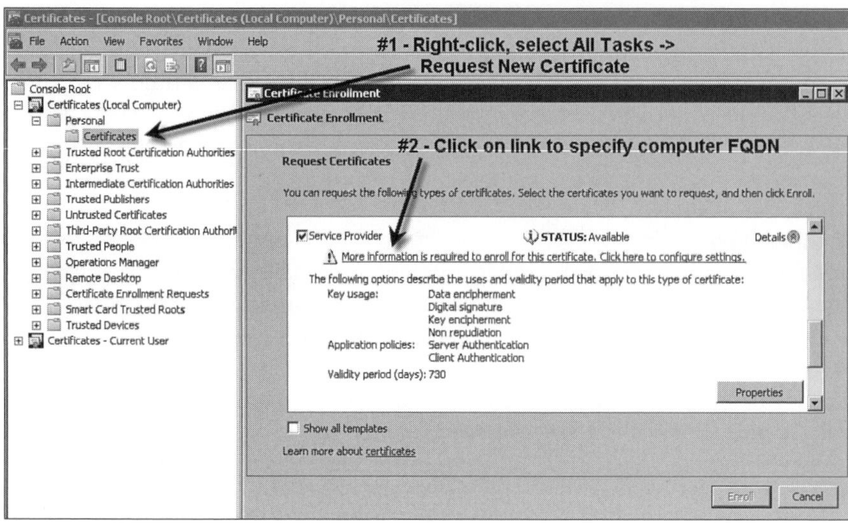

FIGURE 24.7 Requesting an OpsMgr authentication certificate using AD and MMC.

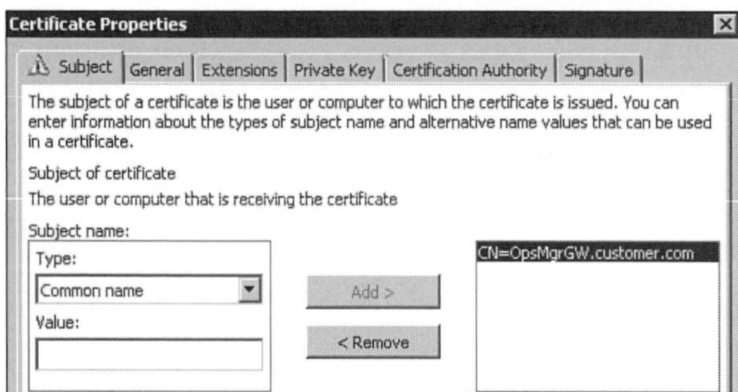

FIGURE 24.8 Type the private FQDN of the computer as value for the Common name.

TIP: DETERMINING THE CORRECT NAME FOR THE OPSMGR CERTIFICATE

To verify what to use for the Common name value in the OpsMgr authentication certificate request, confirm the private DNS FQDN of the computer. Run `ipconfig /all` and add the Host Name and Primary DNS Suffix fields together to validate the FQDN to which the certificate needs to be issued.

6. The certificate is issued by Active Directory using the credentials of the logged on user with the certificate request processed and installed in the Computer certificates store. The certificate is ready to be exported to a .PFX file and transported to the customer.

   - Export the .PFX file from the Certificates MMC by right-clicking the certificate and selecting **All Tasks** -> **Export**, and then click **Next**.

- Select **Yes**, export the private key, and then click **Next**.
- Select to **Export all extended properties** and click **Next**.
- Assign and confirm a password for the .PFX file and click **Next**.
- Select a folder and file name for the certificate, such as OpsMgrGW.customer.com.PFX, basing the certificate name on the computer name for which it is issued. Click **Next** and **Finish**.

7. After confirming a timely and successful transport of the file to the customer environment, delete the certificate from the certificate store of the service provider's domain computer where it was issued. This is a housekeeping issue and has customer privacy considerations.

A common scenario is to save the .PFX file to the desktop, save that inside a compressed .ZIP file, email the file, and delete the .PFX and .ZIP from the desktop. Open your web mail client inside the customer environment, open that same message, and save the .ZIP file to the customer gateway or agent computer. You can then extract and use the .PFX file directly with OpsMgr on the customer computer. Delete the email used for the transport for housekeeping and privacy considerations.

Web Enrollment

A second means to obtain OpsMgr authentication certificates with a GUI, in addition to Active Directory domain policy, is the Web enrollment feature of the Microsoft CA installed along with the CA role. You can use this self-service web portal to install Windows Server 2003 Enterprise CA format certificates on the computer running the web browser. (If the service provider template is based on Windows Server 2008 CA format, the certificate does not appear in the web enrollment site.) The web enrollment method is available both with stand-alone and enterprise CAs.

Unlike the \CertEnroll virtual folder seen in IIS on the CA that requires anonymous public access for the CRL, the \CertSrv virtual folder is secured by Windows authentication (Kerberos and NTLM). To obtain a certificate using this method from the desktop of a Windows server, you must disable Internet Explorer Enhanced Security Configuration (IE ESC) for the administrator while performing the work. This is because an ActiveX control is downloaded to the web browser that does the work to request the certificate, receives the response, and installs it on the computer. With IE ESC enabled, the ActiveX control cannot download.

The Microsoft CA Web enrollment feature is not a hardened website appropriate for unrestricted public Internet access. The web enrollment site should be published internally or otherwise protected from direct Internet exposure. The service provider can use the website without concerns locally, over a VPN, or a private network. If the actual CA issuing website is published over the Internet for installing certificates in the customer environment, consider using a firewall that restricts traffic to the CA to only the public IP of that customer during the certificate-issuing activity.

Follow these steps to issue an OpsMgr authentication certificate using web enrollment:

1. Open Internet Explorer on the computer where the certificate will be installed. This can be any computer, not just the computer to which the certificate is being issued, as you can export and import the resulting certificate to the actual destination computer separately.

2. Browse with the HTTPS protocol to the CA's /CertSrv virtual folder. Certificate request and issue functions will not work using HTTP (TCP port 80). For example, browse to **https://pantheon.odyssey.com/CertSrv** to request a certificate.

3. You will be prompted for Windows credentials to access the website. When you see the Microsoft Active Directory Certificate Services portal, click the **Request a certificate** link.

4. Click the **advanced certificate request** link, and then click the **Create and submit a request to this CA** link. You may see a Web Access Confirmation dialog about this website attempting to perform a digital certificate operation on your behalf; click **Yes**.

5. On the Advanced Certificate Request page, in the Certificate Template drop-down list, select the service provider template. Type the FQDN of the customer computer in the Name field. All other fields are optional. Figure 24.9 shows the web enrollment site at this step (for a computer named OpsMgrGW.customer.com).

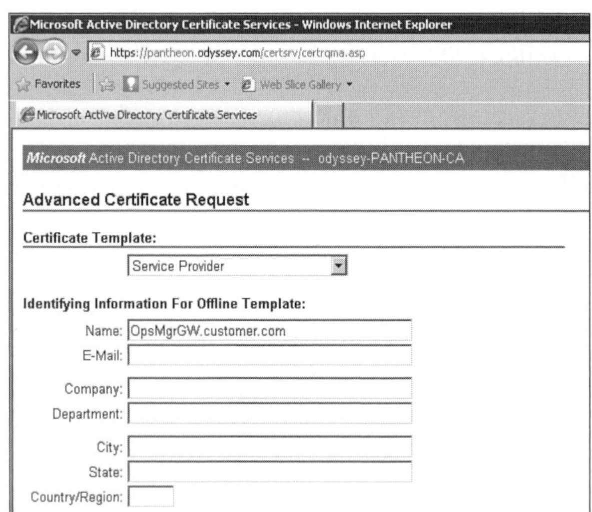

FIGURE 24.9 The private FQDN of the computer is the Name field; other fields are optional.

6. Optionally type a Friendly Name to help identify the certificate later and click the **Submit** button at the bottom of the Advanced Certificate Request page.

7. After a moment, you should see Certificate Issued; proceed to click on the **Install this certificate** link.

8. You should see the message **Your new certificate has been successfully installed**; you can either close IE or click the Home link in the upper-right corner if you want to issue another certificate.

   Something to be aware of is which local certificate store the certificate was saved to by IE. Most likely, it is the Current User Personal certificate store rather than the Local Computer Personal store. OpsMgr certificates are not useful in the User store and must be exported to a .PFX file.

9. Export the .PFX file from the Certificates MMC by right-clicking the certificate and selecting **All Tasks** -> **Export** -> **Next**.

10. Select **Yes**, export the private key, and then click **Next**.

11. Select to **Export all extended properties** and click **Next**.

12. Assign and confirm a password for the .PFX file and click **Next**.

13. Select a folder and file name for the certificate, such as OpsMgrGW.customer.com.PFX, basing the certificate name on the computer name for which it is issued. Click **Next** and **Finish**.

14. After confirming a successful export, delete the certificate in the Current User Personal certificate store. The exported .PFX file is ready to use with OpsMgr on the computer in whose name the certificate was issued.

Command Line and Request File

A third means to obtain OpsMgr authentication certificates does not require a GUI and works with a stand-alone as well as an enterprise CA. This method does not produce any .PFX files and delivers the private key directly to the requesting computer in the form of a response to the request.

Follow these steps to issue an OpsMgr authentication certificate using the command line and a request file:

1. Create a file named RequestPolicy.INF on the computer that will be requesting the certificate.

   Here are the contents of the RequestPolicy.INF file. You need to change the Subject line to match the FQDN of the computer doing the requesting (**OpsMgrGW.customer.com** in this example), and you may need to modify the certificate template name to match the name of your service provider certificate template (**ServiceProvider** in this example).

```
[Version]
Signature="$Windows NT$"

[NewRequest]
Subject = "CN=OpsMgrGW.customer.com"
Exportable = TRUE
KeyLength = 2048
```

```
KeySpec = 1
KeyUsage = 0xA0
MachineKeySet = True
ProviderName = "Microsoft RSA SChannel Cryptographic Provider"
RequestType = PKCS10

[RequestAttributes]
certificateTemplate = "ServiceProvider"
```

2. Open an elevated command prompt on the computer and change directory to where the RequestPolicy.INF file was saved. Run this command:

   ```
   CertReq.exe -new RequestPolicy.inf CertificateRequest.req
   ```

3. The resulting certificate request file **CertificateRequest.REQ** is a text file containing a 2048-bit key that also lends itself to copy-and-paste using the clipboard in a remote desktop scenario, as well as conventional file copy or emailing of attachments.

4. Transport the request file to the CA computer; open an elevated command prompt to the folder where the CertificateRequest.REQ file was saved, and run this command:

   ```
   certreq -submit -config "PANTHEON\odyssey-PANTHEON-CA" "CertificateRequest.req"
   CertificateResponse.cer
   ```

   Replace PANTHEON with the CA computer name and odyssey-PANTHEON-CA with the CA name.

5. Transport the CertificateResponse.CER file back to the requesting computer. Open an elevated command prompt on the computer and change directory to where the CertificateResponse.CER file was saved. Run this command:

   ```
   certReq.exe -accept -config "PANTHEON\odyssey-PANTHEON-CA" CertificateResponse.
   cer
   ```

   Replace PANTHEON with the CA computer name and odyssey-PANTHEON-CA with the CA name.

The OpsMgr authentication certificate now resides in the Local Computer Personal Certificates store. If you will be installing an OpsMgr gateway or agent computer manually, you can run the MomCertImport.exe utility interactively and select the OpsMgr authentication certificate directly from the certificate store. If you plan to install OpsMgr features programmatically, you may need to export the certificate to a .PFX file. Follow the same procedures as steps 9 to 14 of the "Web Enrollment" section to export a certificate copy with private key.

Multi-Tenant OpsMgr

Operations Manager was not designed to run a single management group across multiple customer environments. It expects one owner—the same owner of the management group that is the owner of the computers and applications that are monitored. Multi-tenancy exists when a service provider deploys agents or gateways to two or more customers from the same OpsMgr instance, and offers SLAs to each customer covering either OpsMgr or the monitored computers and applications.

Service Provider Business Requirements

Since there is no official Microsoft-published way to implement multi-tenancy in OpsMgr (since the Remote Operations Manager product was retired), the service provider must architect and support one or more custom business and technical models to deliver this service. Here are the business requirements of a multi-tenant OpsMgr solution:

- **System Center license:** Each monitored computer or device must be a licensed System Center 2012 endpoint. Either the customer can bring his OpsMgr management licenses, or the service provider can provide the license through monthly SPLA payments, charging the cost back to the customer. Additional licenses are not needed for the service provider's management servers or SQL Server Standard edition servers.
- **Customer isolation:** One customer must never be aware of the identities or other information about any other customer. It is acceptable for customers to know they are in a multi-tenant environment—that is a basic feature of a cloud-delivered service—but customers have a right to expect total isolation of their data to themselves and the service provider only.
- **Customer value:** Since it is not possible to extend customer access in any manner to the full Operations console in multi-tenant mode, there must be some other vehicle to deliver the value of OpsMgr. The OpsMgr Web console, alert subscriptions, and scheduled reports are the only "out of box" pieces ready to present data directly to the customer, and those features alone are often not attractive enough for a managed service. A service provider portal, other automation created by the service provider, or service provider NOC that performs remediation on some or all alerts for the customer are examples of how multi-tenant OpsMgr is made commercially viable.

Techniques to Achieve Customer Isolation

Users of public cloud email systems such as Microsoft's Hotmail/Outlook.com, Google gmail, and Yahoo mail expect to be unaffected by the other millions of mailboxes hosted in those clouds. Customers of a service provider offering multi-tenant OpsMgr should have an equivalent experience; they should be unaware of and not adversely impacted by the dozens or hundreds of other customers that might be part of the managed services operation. The concept of isolating one customer from another applies from two perspectives:

- **Service provider convenience:** A managed services operation will likely involve adding new customers, adding and removing computers and devices from management; sometimes equipment retires and customers even leave. The service provider must have a way to identify which managed objects belong to what customer, so customer objects can be managed or even deleted cleanly and efficiently. Consider creating an override to an OpsMgr rule that applies to all Windows computers of just one customer—this should be easy to do.

  Groups and classes in OpsMgr create group entities against which you can take actions. For example, an OpsMgr class or group that consists of computer objects allows you to apply a single override setting to all instances of the class or members of the group. Using a group-based and/or class-based system to collectively address all of a customer's monitored objects is pretty much required in the service provider model.

- **Customer segregation:** Information about one customer should never be inadvertently disclosed to a different customer. There is particular risk when extending customers access to the Web console, creating notification subscriptions for customers, and when running OpsMgr reports for customers. It is impossible to extend a scoped full Operations console to customers in a multi-tenant environment, such as via a Remote Desktop solution, because access to underlying data remains available—customers could see each other.

  Active Directory security and OpsMgr's role-based security allow for granular control over access to the Web console. For example, a customer guest account in the service provider's AD can be a member of an AD security group of which members are permitted some read-only operator views in the OpsMgr Web console.

Creating Groups for Customers

The simplest way to segregate customers is to use OpsMgr groups. Specifically, a nested structure in the Operations console in the Authoring space -> Groups view is created such that an All Customers top-level group contains a group for each customer. Each customer group in turn contains the site groups for that customer. An OpsMgr object of the `site` class is created when you install an OpsMgr gateway server. This class has a containment relationship to the computer and device objects managed by the gateway server in the customer location.

The reason you need to create a parent container for each customer is you could manage objects associated with the customer that do not descend from the computer or device classes, such as a synthetic transaction or a distributed application. Alternatively, the service provider may monitor directly computers with OpsMgr agents that are not behind a gateway. In these cases, the additional managed objects and groups associated with the customer are added to the parent group. Figure 24.10 shows a customer named **Luno** with this group structure.

The group arrangement supporting customers in general and customer Luno specifically is shown in Figure 24.10 and achieved by performing the following steps:

1. Manually create a customer groups management pack to store the custom group assignments.

2. Create a new top-level Group named **All Customers**; save this group to the customer groups management pack.

3. Install a gateway server at a new customer site; this creates a new object of the site class.

4. Create a new group with the name of the customer and a label such as "Customer Luno (all objects)." The management pack to which you save the name of this group depends on your management group design. Do not create a management pack for the customer and name it after the customer. Use either a codename or number for the name of customer-specific management packs, or use different management pack architecture that does not require customer-specific management packs.

5. Manually add the gateway server/site object associated with the customer as a subgroup to the customer's "all objects" group.

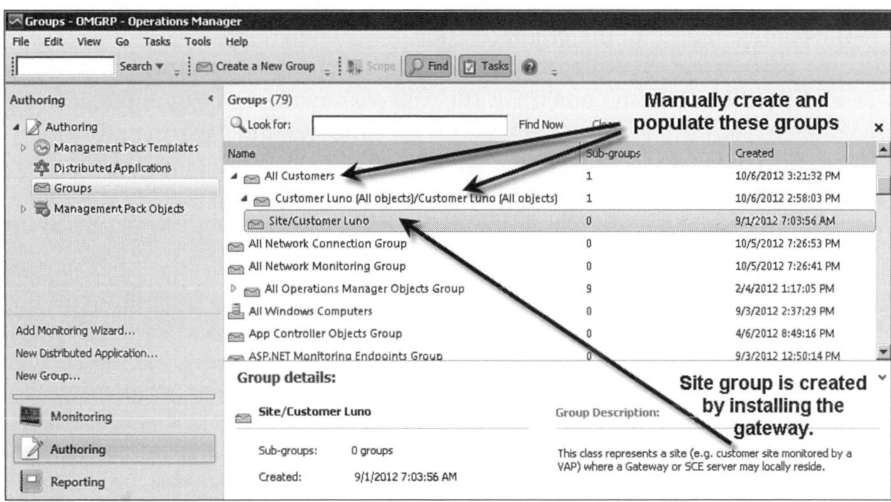

FIGURE 24.10 Add a customer's sites to an "all objects" parent group for that customer.

Moving forward with this model, computers and devices managed by the gateway are automatically added to the site and included in parent groups. The service provider can scope console views, user roles, and reports to a particular customer's "all objects" group and effectively multi-tenant those OpsMgr features. This model works for a highly trusted, centralized service provider managing up to about 2,000 computers from a single management group, or about 100 mid-market customers (with an average of about 20 managed servers each).

Here are some downsides to this group-based approach:

- Overrides to a class are delivered to all instances of the class, even if the instance is not a member of a targeted group. This means what you do in one customer environment can cause another customer's environment to load (then ignore) the uninvolved change, because you are managing all of them in the same context. This process of OpsMgr performing configuration-related work for no benefit is referred to as *churn*.

  For example, if you target an override to a class to which the customer has an instance (even in a disabled status), all customers' agents will detect the change. Customer identities (including customer site names and server names) in management pack overrides are managed with GUIDs and account credentials are encrypted, so customer privacy is maintained. What occurs is some avoidable churn being created in the entire system (the entire management group) when changes are made to a subset of the system.

- Along with increasing the overall churn of the management group, basic network utilization issues can occur at large scale when using a group-based approach to override management. With more than several thousand agents, the service provider must be careful when managing the footprint of overrides.

- Due to the manual nature of the group creation and population, it is easier to overlook adding new managed objects to the customer group. This situation could result in failing to monitor customer objects in the expected manner. For example, if a report is targeted to the "all objects" group of the customer and there are direct-reporting agents for that customer—that were not manually or dynamically added to the group—they would not be included in the report even though the customer expects them to be included.

CAUTION: DON'T INCLUDE CUSTOMER NAMES IN MANAGEMENT PACK NAMES

There is a possibility that any management pack in the management group could by design or accident be downloaded, even temporarily, to any given customer environment. While names inside the downloaded eXtended Markup Language (XML) will be masked by GUIDs, what you type as the name of the management pack will appear in the event log of every managed computer. To preserve customer privacy, come up with another way to organize and name management packs. Keep private words and customer names out of management pack names.

Creating Classes for Customers

An alternative approach to segregating customers in the OpsMgr service provider model is using a custom class to represent each customer, targeting custom rules and monitors specifically to affected customers' classes. This model is more complex than the "Creating Groups for Customers" method previously described in the section with that name. The class-based approach solves these issues for the service provider:

- Permits the service provider to achieve the highest possible scale, which is to scale beyond about 2,000 computers for the management group, due to more efficient operations.
- Better isolation of customer environments regarding application discovery overrides, which can be targeted to customer classes.
- Eliminates the need to create new discoveries for each customer application by staging a customer-specific discovery that looks for certain registry keys.

OpsMgr community contributors Rob Korving and Marc Klaver have authored and shared a class-based solution for targeting rules and customers at http://jama00.wordpress.com/category/grouping-and-scoping/. They conclude that the agent itself determines if a rule is enabled or disabled, not a management server. Therefore, some churn for overrides that target monitors in common classes like `Windows Computer` is unavoidable.

Rob and Marc suggest another solution that offers a way around this situation for common overrides at http://jama00.wordpress.com/2012/06/12/configure-custom-service-monitoring-an-alternative-method/. This method uses an alternative way for setting common configurations and overrides. The key to this solution is to rewrite or create monitors that have frequent overrides. Here's how it works:

- A script reads a registry key for a threshold value to use. An example of a threshold monitor is a custom disk free space script that uses a default value (both % and a numeric value), but when an override is present in the registry it uses that value instead.
- The registry override in turn can be set with an OpsMgr task with normal operator rights.
- The change is immediate and without configuration impact on the rest of the OpsMgr management group.

What you are doing is disabling a built-in sealed monitor that has frequent overrides and replacing it with a custom monitor that uses a script to first check a registry key for its values. If the registry key exists and is populated, the custom monitor uses that value and never looks further. Using this model, you don't create an OpsMgr override; you change the local registry to change the threshold. (This can be done manually or remotely via an OpsMgr task.)

Defining Customer Deliverables

The business and technical challenge for the service provider is to define SLAs and package service catalogs that make it obvious (to the customer!) that the service provider is adding value on the customer's behalf. When you have designed a valuable managed services offering, an accurate description of the service along with knowledge of the monthly management fee should be sufficient and compelling enough to close the deal.

Recall the default scenario for OpsMgr is that an organization deploys System Center on-premise, exclusively to manage the single enterprise. In this default model, the customer has full access to every Operations console and PowerShell function. Additional management packs can be imported and new custom management packs authored at will. This model also requires employees skilled in System Center, an outsourced Microsoft partner, or consultants to manage and maintain a conventional on-premise OpsMgr environment.

To contrast this model with the service provider employing OpsMgr in a multi-tenant model, the biggest difference is the customer cannot have access to all Operations console functions; at most, they have access to the Web console. In addition, customer use of OpsMgr PowerShell is not feasible, and the customer is unable to author custom management packs for their unique business application or update and add management packs as vendors release new editions.

The service provider needs to make up to customers for not having direct Operations console access through deliverables. The next sections cover five approaches to extend the value of multi-tenant OpsMgr:

- A NOC
- OpsMgr Web console
- OpsMgr alert subscriptions
- Scheduled OpsMgr report delivery
- Custom portal, notification, or self-service solution

Network Operations Center

Most service providers that have created an OpsMgr-based managed service offering featuring server and application SLAs include a NOC in their design. For most managed services customers, the business driver that outsourced the work in the first place was to allow their staff to be free to focus on the business rather than managing the IT network. That includes the complexities of setup and maintenance of System Center as well as prosecution and resolution of whatever alerts and unhealthy state changes may occur.

The function of an OpsMgr-based service provider NOC functions exactly like the on-premise NOC a large enterprise with 24x7 global operations might run for itself. Industry parallels include control centers at utility companies and intelligence fusion centers in the military. The NOC watches everything and fixes things as they break, hopefully discovering potential issues using OpsMgr management packs well before service outages occur.

In these full service scenarios, the service provider may be able to deliver high value from System Center without providing the customer any deliverables directly from OpsMgr. The business partner that fully outsources their IT to a trusted managed services provider will not have in-house IT staff to interpret and use the OpsMgr Web console, alert subscriptions, or scheduled reports. It is precisely this management layer that is outsourced in the full SLA model. A NOC at ClearPointe (www.clearpointe.com) appears in the photograph shown in Figure 24.11. ClearPointe is a Microsoft partner that has operated multi-tenant OpsMgr NOCs for some years, as has KPN Commercial Business Market/Getronics (www.getronics.com).

Customer interaction with the NOC will vary depending on the offerings of the service provider as well as the service provider's relationship with each customer. Simple emails between the customer and NOC staff, including customers opening their own tickets in an incident management system, are common methods of customer interaction with the NOC. The fact that the customer can telephone the NOC 24x7, speak to a Level 1 analyst and communicate a managed services instruction verbally is sometimes another key reason a full SLA model is selected by the customer.

FIGURE 24.11 A NOC at ClearPointe, a provider of full SLA services using OpsMgr.

OpsMgr Web Console

Microsoft has invested a considerable amount of development in the all-new Silverlight-based Web console for OpsMgr 2012. The OpsMgr 2007 Web console had many limitations, a principal one being that you could not access the Health Explorer control to examine the state of monitors. Beginning with OpsMgr 2007 R2, Microsoft added an AJAX-based applet to the Web console to open Health Explorer. Adding features and functionality to the OpsMgr Web console has continued with OpsMgr 2012. Figure 24.12 shows the OpsMgr 2012 Web console with a Health Explorer link opening a web-based version in a new browser window.

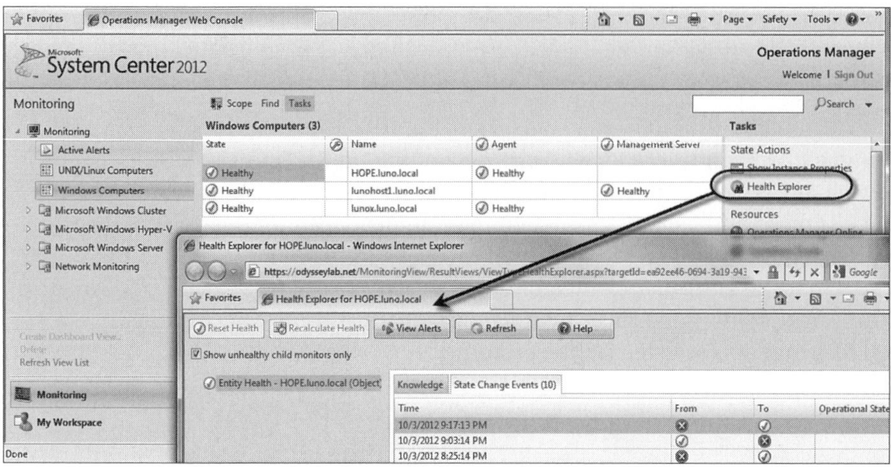

FIGURE 24.12 The OpsMgr 2012 Web console launching a web-based Health Explorer.

A common question is whether the OpsMgr Web console is an acceptable full-time substitute for the full Operations console in an operator context. The Web console is not a substitute for large-scale operations due to some limitations in the Web console compared to the full Operations console GUI. However, the Web console is an excellent tool to use in scoped OpsMgr roles with limited views, such as the customers of a service provider.

Using the Web console, a service provider can extend several OpsMgr functionalities in a multi-tenant scenario to those customers desiring it. Using read-only operator or operator roles defined in OpsMgr security and guest accounts in AD security, customer employees can log in to the service provider's Web console and only see data about their organization's infrastructure. OpsMgr Web console server farms can be load-balanced (LB) with conventional LB technology. Enabling domain guest account access to the Web console servers enables using low-privilege AD guest accounts for customers.

The Web console view in Figure 24.12 was arrived at by following these steps:

1. Create an Active Directory group to contain user accounts of customer employees, such as Customer Luno Read-Only Operator Group.

2. Create individual user accounts for each customer employee that is authorized access and add those accounts to the customer employee group. To avoid taxing the management group, issue just one or a very small number of guest accounts per customer.

3. In the Operations console, at **Administration** -> **Security** -> **User Roles**, right-click and select **New User Role** -> **Read Only Operator**. Click **Next**.

4. Assign a user role name that includes the name of the customer. Click **Add.**

5. Select the AD group, click **OK**, and then click **Next**. (Figure 24.13 shows the AD group added to the read-only operator role for customer Luno.)

6. On the Group Scope tab, deselect the root management group entity; then select only the "all objects" group for that customer.

7. On the Dashboards and Views tab, deselect the default to allow access to all views; then manually select just those views appropriate for the customer's SLA and requirements. Click **OK**.

8. Provide the customer with the URL to reach the Web console over HTTPS (SSL) as well as their user credentials. Logging in to the Web console with the AD user account (a member of the group added to the read-only operator user role) renders the tailored Web console experience previously seen in Figure 24.12.

CAUTION: DON'T BE LIBERAL WITH WEB CONSOLE ACCESS

Each instance of the Web console reduces the maximum scale potential of the OpsMgr management group. While there are no hard numbers, the service provider should take care that even with a web farm of several Web console servers, never more than 100 Web console sessions are live. Not every customer should get a Web console, and each customer should only get one instance.

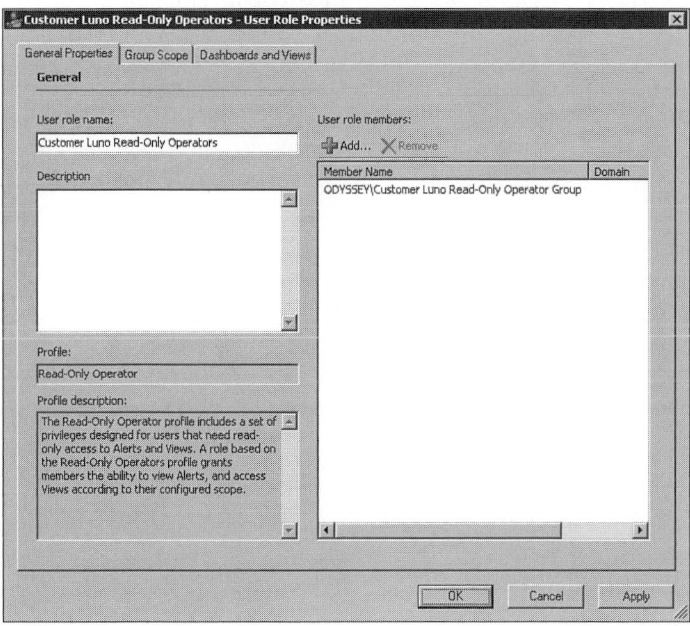

FIGURE 24.13 Adding the AD group with customer accounts to the OpsMgr role.

OpsMgr Alert Subscriptions

Another built-in feature of OpsMgr that is nearly "customer ready" is the notification and alert subscription piece. Creating an alert subscription that sends all alerts and alert status changes about a customer object to a customer email distribution list is straightforward, although effectively employing this OpsMgr feature for direct customer notification requires some thought. (The same technique for email alerts can be applied with SMS text message alerting, another OpsMgr notification technology.) Here are some considerations about using alert subscriptions to deliver OpsMgr alerts to customers:

- It is not effective to deliver all (100%) alerts as email notifications; the quantity of emails can become unmanageable.
- You can target subscriptions to alerts at either the customer's site class instance, which includes all Windows computers and network devices in that site, or the "all objects" customer group, which includes all managed objects for the customer.
- Direct alert notifications by email are best kept to a minimum of high-value, actionable events, such as direct notification of subject matter experts (SMEs) when rare but predictable events occur that only SMEs can remedy.

Figure 24.14 shows an OpsMgr alert email subscription message as viewed in Outlook. This is what a customer would receive using the default OpsMgr email notification feature. Notice the link to the service provider's Web console. The URL for the Web console is configured in the Operations console at Administration -> Settings -> Web addresses. The return address for alerts is set at Administration -> Notifications -> Channels.

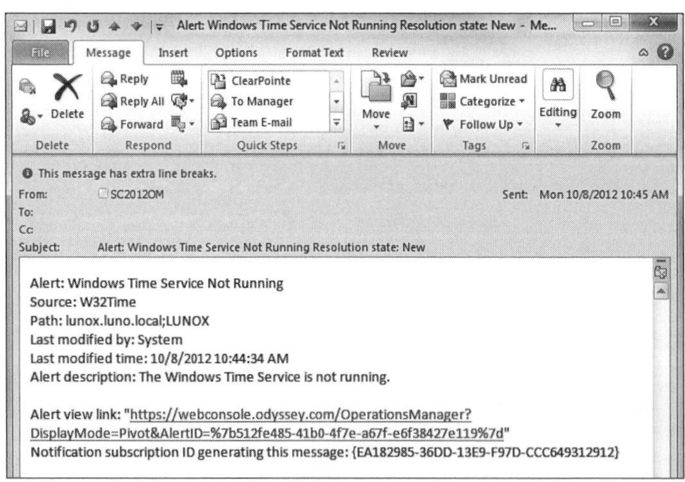

FIGURE 24.14 An OpsMgr alert notification email viewed in Outlook Inbox.

To use email to deliver alert subscriptions, you first create a notification channel, then a notification subscriber, and then the subscription. The emailed alert notification in Figure 24.14 was arrived at by following these steps:

1. In the Operations console, at **Administration** -> **Notification** -> **Channels**, right-click and select **New channel** -> **E-Mail (SMTP)**.
2. Name the channel and click **Next**. At the E-Mail Notification Channel page, click **Add**.
3. Type the name of an internal SMTP email server that will permit Internet relay of OpsMgr alert notification emails; then click **OK**.
4. In the Return address field, type the desired SMTP reply-to label and click **Next**.
5. Modify the default email notification format as desired and click **Finish**.
6. At **Administration** -> **Notification** -> **Subscribers**, right-click and select **New subscriber**.
7. For the Subscriber Name, browse in AD and select the customer group containing user accounts of customer employees, such as Customer Luno Read-Only Operator Group. Click **Next**.
8. Select to **Always send notifications** and click **Next**.
9. On the Subscriber Addresses page, click **Add**. Type a name that will help identify the address, such as Customer Luno Email Notification Subscriber. Click **Next**.
10. Select **E-Mail (SMTP)** from the Channel Type drop-down list; then type the customer email address, such as CustomerLunoContacts@luno.com, and then click **Next**.
11. At the Schedule Notifications screen, select the default to **Always send notifications**. Click **Finish**.
12. At **Administration** -> **Notification** -> **Subscription**, right-click and select **New subscription**.
13. On the Create Notification Subscription page, type a name that will help identify the subscription, such as Customer Luno New Critical Alerts Subscription. Click **Next**.
14. On the Criteria page, select one or more conditions on which to notify. In this example, all new, critical alerts from customer site Luno will be included. Figure 24.15 shows appropriate subscription criteria conditions selected. Click **Next**.

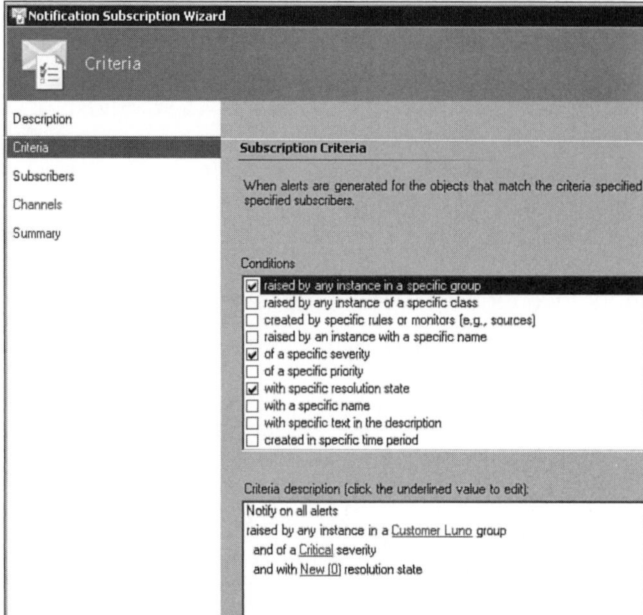

FIGURE 24.15 Selecting the criteria for a customer-based email notification subscription.

15. On the Subscribers page, click **Add**, and then **Search**. Select the subscriber created for this subscription, such as Customer Luno Read-Only Operator Group. Click **Add**, click **OK**, and then click **Next**.

16. On the Channels page, click **Add** and then click **Search**. Select the **E-Mail SMTP** channel and click **Add**; then click **OK**. Click **Next** and then click **Finish**.

17. The next occurrence of a new, critical alert on any object in the customer group will cause an email notification to be sent to the selected recipient(s).

Scheduled Report Delivery

In addition to the Web console and email notifications, a third category of customer deliverable can be achieved using OpsMgr reporting. The scheduled reports feature of OpsMgr is well suited to the service provider environment. Here are some considerations about this method of communication:

- A primary means of delivering reports is by scheduled emails created by SQL Server Reporting Service (SSRS) with reports attached as .PDF files. This is a preferred solution from the service provider perspective because the service provider does not need to retain reports on the customer's behalf.

- An alternative way to deliver reports is by posting scheduled reports as .PDF files on an intranet file share or download links in a customer-facing portal or secure-file-transfer site. In this solution, the service provider needs an archiving scheme for customer reports.

- A least preferred way is to stage reports as Favorite Reports for customers in the Web console, which function as ad-hoc on-demand reports. While this feature is very convenient and should be considered for VIP report situations, it gives customers an unpredictable ability to generate load on the service provider's OpsMgr SSRS instance.

Figure 24.16 shows a typical OpsMgr 30-day availability report targeted to a customer's site. The report will automatically contain an availability bar graph for each downstream computer and health service. OpsMgr reports can be exported to XML, CSV, PDF, MHTML, Excel, TIFF, and Word file formats. A small number of key, meaningful reports are typically of high value to customers.

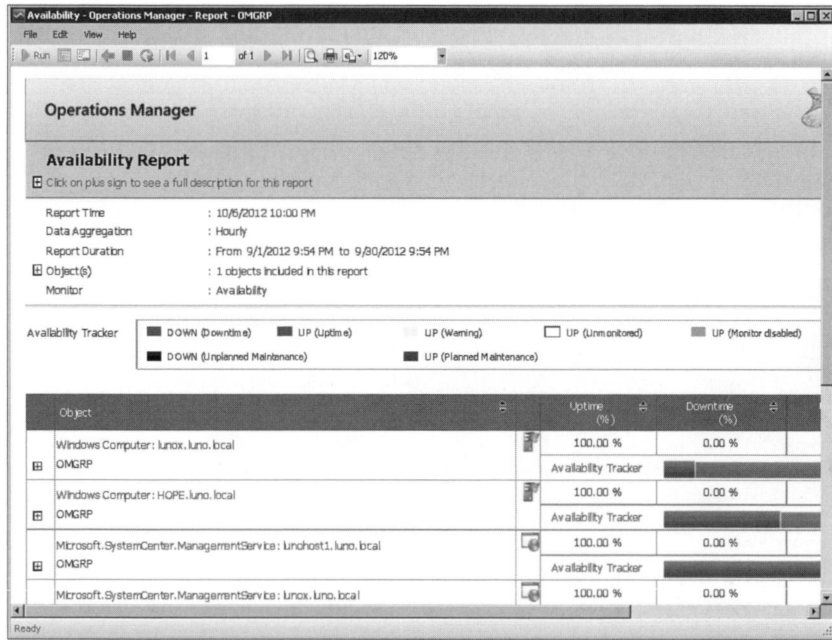

FIGURE 24.16 Availability report for a customer site includes all customer computers.

To use email to deliver report subscriptions, you must first define email settings in the SSRS instance of your management group. The report seen in Figure 24.16 was arrived at, and could be generated and emailed by a scheduled task, by following these steps:

1. Run the SQL Server Reporting Services Configuration Manager tool from the Start menu of your SSRS computer. **Connect** to the local instance, which is the server name of the OpsMgr management group's reporting server.

2. On the E-mail Settings tab, specify a Sender Address to appear as the reply-to on messages, and an SMTP Server name that can deliver email to the customer. Click **Apply**, and then click **Exit**.

3. In the Operations console, navigate to the Reporting space. In the Tasks pane, click **Schedule**.
4. For Delivery Settings, type a Description that includes the customer name such as Customer Luno Monthly Availability Report, specify the **E-Mail** delivery method, the Render Format (PDF is default), the SMTP headers such as To: and Cc: and then click **Next**.
5. On the Schedule Subscription page, select **Monthly**, select every month, and select **On the following calendar day**; then type the number **1**. Click **Next**.
6. On the report parameters page, click **Add Group** in the Object area. In the Contains field, type some text to help locate the customer site, such as the customer's name, in this example Customer Luno. Click **Search**.
7. Among the returned objects should be one of the site class for that customer. Select that item, select **Add**, and then click **OK**.
8. Select the From and To periods of the report to be the First day of the previous month to the Last day of the previous month. These selections are made in the drop-down box for each value. Figure 24.17 shows the Customer Luno site targeted for this monthly availability report. Click **Finish**.

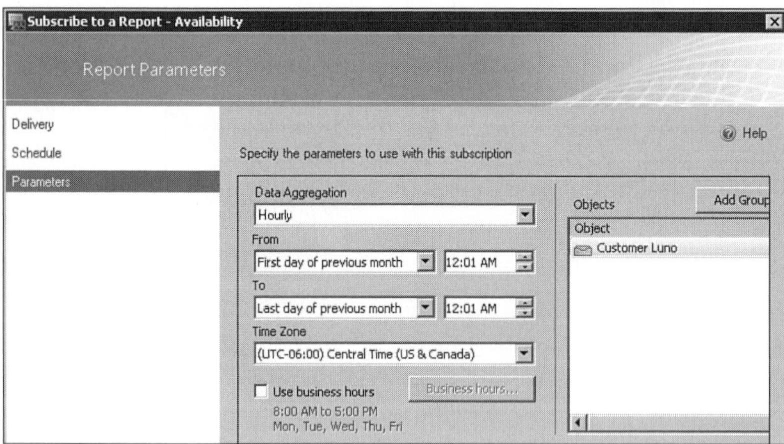

FIGURE 24.17 Setup of a recurring monthly customer availability report.

After creating the scheduled report, it appears listed in the Operations console at Reporting -> Scheduled Reports. You can edit all the settings of a scheduled report by selecting the report name in the Scheduled Reports list and then clicking the **Edit Schedule** task. Clicking **Open** with a scheduled report selected will test-run the report but not actually email it.

Custom Portal, Notification, or Self-Service Solution

Service providers frequently have a primary customer-facing portal for opening service requests; this provides feedback and other customer relationship activity. OpsMgr Web console, notification, and report features may interact with a service provider portal in many ways. For example, a service provider can run scheduled reports for customers and, rather than emailing them, post links to them on a service provider portal for review by the customer using a web browser.

Using PowerShell makes it possible to interact virtually without limit with OpsMgr, read and set data, and populate graphs, charts, and other controls that exist totally outside OpsMgr. It is possible to construct very attractive customer-facing solutions that source data from OpsMgr; these are evolved beyond the OpsMgr Web console, simple notification, and report delivery. An example would be System Center Service Manager employed as a customer-facing self-service portal, with OpsMgr alerts presented to the customer as incident tickets.

An advanced OpsMgr alert notification solution that extends the built-in features of OpsMgr subscriptions is Derdack Enterprise Alert (http://www.derdack.com). Derdack's product guarantees the delivery of critical OpsMgr alerts via voice, SMS, IM, email, and smartphone push. This software helps to deliver alarms to the right people in 24x7 scenarios. Service providers can extend their OpsMgr instance with a product such as Enterprise Alert to notify service provider and/or customer SMEs of most critical events.

An expectation of self-service provisioning is the norm in cloud computing when it comes to infrastructure as a service. Microsoft partner Nubigenus (http://www.nubigenus.com) is exploring ways to deliver self-service remediation by extending OpsMgr with adaptive and interactive dialogs. A combination of the themes of advanced notification in the Derdack product and the self-service direction in which Nubigenus is moving paints a picture of what is possible in terms of service provider automation within the OpsMgr ecosystem.

The Customer Network

The customer network requires some preparation for it to connect to the management cloud. These requirements are generally not difficult to meet. There must be a server to run the gateway, which must be a Windows Server 2008 R2 computer (or Windows Server 2012 with System Center 2012 SP 1). This is frequently a virtual machine (VM) added to the customer environment for this purpose, or a less loaded customer server selected for that role. With fewer than 100 managed agents, the effect on the server is minimal; for 200 agents or more you should reserve a dedicated gateway computer with no other roles.

There are two primary architecture considerations when bringing a customer into management:

- Placement of the gateway server(s)
- Whether any agents will not be behind gateways

A goal should be that each customer has one gateway and as few as 1 and as many as 500–1,000 agents behind it. The customer or service provider may elect to establish more than one gateway due to redundancy and latency issues in global networks. Individual agents not behind gateways are appropriate for remote customer network segments with a small number of agents that do not have network connectivity to the gateway.

Connectivity and Remote Access

Microsoft's OpsMgr solution for service providers is light on connectivity requirements for full functionality:

- Customer gateways (or agents) need only outbound TCP 80/443 and 5723 to connect to service provider gateways over the Internet.
- TCP ports 80 and 443 are required for CA/PKI functionality.
- 5723 is the native OpsMgr agent and gateway protocol TCP port.

Installing the OpsMgr agent or gateway server automatically opens outbound local Windows Firewall ports needed by OpsMgr.

Each customer typically will have one gateway located in his most connected data center. In this scenario, only the gateway server needs an Internet connection on outbound TCP ports 80, 443, and 5723. Service providers may include other connectivity options in their offerings such as a private network or VPN connection to the customer site, or another remote helpdesk solution that requires additional connectivity.

Installing the Gateway and Pushing Agents

The gateway server needs to trust the root CA of the service provider. Importing the trust certificate is a prerequisite to installing a gateway. The gateway is the only role needing either the trusted root CA or the individual certificate; all the hundreds of other computers downstream discovered and managed by the gateway will use Kerberos and AD for authentication and are unaffected by the service provider CA. Since the gateway will push agents, a gateway service account in the customer domain must be prepared with administrative and logon as a service rights (OM_GWAA in this book).

To install a customer gateway, follow the same procedure described in Chapter 5, "Installing System Center 2012 Operations Manager." Pay attention to the `/site` switch of the gateway approval tool; this determines the label for the customer site in the Operations console. Changing this after running the tool requires deleting the gateway. Remember to create the gateway with the gateway approval tool *before* installing the gateway software at the customer.

The following command line creates a gateway lunohost1.luno.local that reports to service provider gateway regent.odyssey.com; the name of the site will be Customer Luno:

```
Microsoft.Enterprise.GatewayApprovalTool.exe /ManagementServer=regent.odyssey.com
/GatewayName=lunohost1.luno.local /Site="Customer Luno"
```

After installing the gateway, navigate in the Operations console to **Administration** -> **Device Management** -> **Management Servers**, select and right-click the new gateway, and select **Properties.** On the Security tab, tick the option to **Allow this server to act as a proxy and discover managed objects on other computers**. Click **OK**.

Discovering a customer agent downstream from a customer gateway follows exactly the same procedure described in Chapter 5. Specify the customer gateway as the management server to perform the discoveries for that customer's computers.

Manually Installing Direct-Reporting Agents

The agent computer needs to trust the root CA of the service provider. Importing the trust certificate is a prerequisite for installing an agent manually and pointing the agent directly to the service provider gateway. If a service provider expects many individual agents, you should reserve gateways at the NOC for agent-to-gateway traffic, while the primary service provider gateways are used for gateway-to-gateway traffic.

Installing a customer direct-reporting agent follows exactly the same procedure described in Chapter 5 for a manually installed agent with certificate authentication. The agent will appear in the Operations console of the service provider as a manually installed agent waiting to be approved. If the service provider is using OpsMgr groups to manage customers, remember to add the individual agents to an "all objects" group for the customer that includes their gateways, as described in the "Creating Groups for Customers" section.

Discovering Network Devices

New with OpsMgr 2012 is an advanced network device discovery and monitoring capability. This is an attractive offering because the service provider can monitor network devices in remote customer locations without a VPN or private network connection. Network devices can be monitored in a highly available manner with pools of three OpsMgr gateways, which can monitor as many as 500–1,000 network devices.

Unlike OpsMgr agent traffic, which is agent -> gateway, network device polling is gateway -> device, so the service provider should ensure a customer OpsMgr gateway server is reachable via the customer's private network. Here are some service provider considerations regarding network devices:

- **Not useful for very large scale network monitoring:** Microsoft recommends monitoring a maximum of 2,000 network devices through six gateways per management group. Network device monitoring is also resource intensive for the management group.
- **Primary benefit is network location awareness:** When using this feature in the service provider scenario, the highest value is to monitor the switches and load balancers used for interserver communication in the data center. You can also monitor the routers that connect data centers and branches—this is most useful when routers are contiguous with one another, meaning a traceroute does not have a hop between monitored routers. This allows OpsMgr to "connect" them at the interface level.

The service provider should extend network device monitoring judiciously to customers and introduce the feature gradually to the management group. For network device monitoring projects of large scale—such as total device populations above the low thousands—consider connected or separate management groups that are dedicated to network device monitoring.

In the service provider scenario it is common to have a connected third-party network monitoring product such as Solarwinds provide a large-scale network device monitoring capability. A combination of OpsMgr network device monitoring for core switches and routers and Solarwinds with an OpsMgr connector for large edge router and branch switch populations is a supportable blended offering scenario.

Enabling Deliverables

Once monitoring commences, the customer site class and groups are populated with discovered objects, and the service provider is ready to enable any specific deliverables such as Web console access, notification subscriptions, or scheduled reports. These deliverables cannot be created until the object discoveries occur.

After discoveries complete, OpsMgr creates instances of discovered classes and assigns a unique GUID for every object in the OpsMgr database. Other service provider instrumentation or System Center components can now read the OpsMgr database or interact with it through the software development kit (SDK), OpsMgr connectors, and PowerShell. Discovered objects are acted on via their GUIDs.

If there are no direct OpsMgr deliverables to the customer, the service provider can now assume responsibility for consuming or conveying the value of OpsMgr in fulfillment of the SLA. While OpsMgr is not a turnkey solution for the service provider, it is very good at managing infrastructure. The challenge for the service provider is leveraging the powerful knowledge in OpsMgr across customers.

If the service provider can achieve an economy of scale with System Center in a multi-tenant fashion, the rewards can be a highly available infrastructure for customers and predictable management overhead for the service provider. The built-in deliverables from OpsMgr can form the base of a service provider offering, or extend it.

Introducing Service Provider Foundation

Service Provider Foundation is a new and important feature being released with Microsoft System Center 2012 SP 1. SPF is a web-based API for accessing the management capabilities of System Center. Design goals of SPF support developers (a consistent programming experience) and IT professionals (new capabilities and compatibility with existing management systems investments). This model is Microsoft's future direction for managing multi-tenant environments.

How SPF Helps Service Providers

Microsoft introduced SPF as the API for System Center to leverage the depth of management capabilities in System Center and Windows Server. Rather than attempt to write a single UI that does everything (like SCE 2010), Microsoft is not going to try to produce a single console experience. Rather, the company has created a programmatically standardized way for server technologies on premise and in private and public clouds to communicate with one another at the management layer.

SPF meets service provider needs to use an existing customer-facing portal, a set of web APIs to enable hosted new Internet as a Service (IaaS) portals, multi-tenancy, no dependence on individual installations of System Center components, and a means to offer value-add services such as monitoring and backup.

Some service providers report spending large amounts of time managing customer networks and IP addresses. As an example of how SPF reduces this burden, by exposing SPF management of VM networks on Windows Server 2012, service providers can essentially delegate this commodity task directly to self-service users, which in turn allows the service providers to focus more on new services that differentiate them from their competition.

Brief Overview of SPF Internals

There are three main pieces of the SPF service:

- **Resource model:** Definition of objects, or resources, which can be managed, like a VM
- **Action mapping:** Pointers to the implementation for actions that can be taken on the resources, such as create, start, or stop
- **Task execution:** Implementation like PowerShell or System Center Orchestrator runbooks

SPF is built as a RESTful web service running under IIS on Windows Server. It implements the Odata protocol for operating on collections of objects, where the URL/path directs access to the right objects and Odata query syntax controls the filtering by attribute (essentially "SELECT/UPDATE path/object WHERE filter" in SQL terms). Using Internet Explorer to do a sample GET action on the clouds associated with a particular VMM server looks like this:

http://*<SPFserver>*:8090/SC2012/VMM/Microsoft.Management.oData.svc/
Clouds?$filter=VMMServer eq '*<VMM server name>*'

Exposing System Center capabilities through a RESTful web service is consistent with other tools (such as the RESTful web service for System Center Orchestrator) and modern styles for portal code (such as Windows Azure Services for Windows Server). By producing a RESTful API for System Center and thus strengthening System Center's family of automation and integration features, Microsoft adds value with new and complementary management capabilities. Figure 24.18 shows the IIS website created by SPF, with PowerShell scripts within the virtual directory.

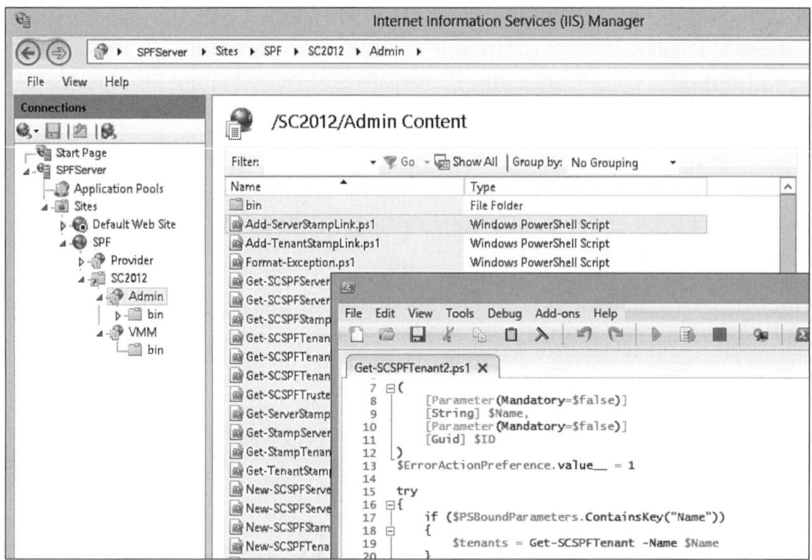

FIGURE 24.18 Service Provider Foundation: A web service calling PowerShell.

Formalizing the notion of "tenant" (or "customer" in this chapter) is central to the broader mission of making System Center a powerful tool for managing multi-tenant environments. Microsoft has selected the tenant ID in SPF as the primary customer index. The tenant name is stored in the SPF database and is used as a property on objects managed through SPF. Security for SPF is implemented such that user requests are validated against role metadata stored in the SPF database. Once it is verified that a requestor has access to the scope and specific objects in the request, SPF uses credentials for the underlying service SPF application pool to perform management tasks on behalf of the requestor.

In the case of SPF and System Center, the term *stamp* applies to a unit of scope in the management footprint. Each stamp consists of a VMM instance, with one or more companion OpsMgr servers. System Center App Controller can manage applications through SPF, supporting a scenario where a tenant who uses App Controller in a private data center can use the same tool to manage applications running on allocated assets of their tenancy in some hosted environment.

SPF setup is merged with the setup for Orchestrator, and the affinity between these System Center components is expected to grow over time. Orchestrator is a key piece of the extensibility story for SPF, particularly the automation and integration similarity between SPF and Orchestrator. Automation of repeatable customer service actions is the key to service provider business efficiency.

What SPF means to service providers using any release of OpsMgr is that complex, multi-functional consoles are recognized as a barrier to new business functionalities. A new paradigm is that the elusive single pane of glass will be achieved in a management cloud portal framework that delivers just the right amount of management information to just the right people and devices.

Fast Track

There is little change in the basic technical functionality of OpsMgr 2012 in a service provider model from OpsMgr 2007 R2. This is good news for service providers already using OpsMgr 2007 R2 for remote customer support. Here are some changes to consider from the OpsMgr 2007 era to OpsMgr 2012:

- The new System Center 2012 license model is simplified and covers the service provider infrastructure with the customer management license.
- There is no support for SCE 2007 or SCE 2010. Any legacy SCE 2007 customers (Remote Operations Manager) must be migrated to an OpsMgr gateway, and OpsMgr 2012 cannot manage SCE 2010 environments.
- New network device support creates value-add scenarios to monitor infrastructure like routers and switches.
- A greatly improved OpsMgr 2012 Web console creates a customer deliverable for the service provider.
- New with SP 1, SPF creates a framework to execute PowerShell commands including Orchestrator runbooks via a web service; this model is expected to form the basis of a new management paradigm.

Summary

This chapter presented a history of Microsoft remote management technologies and discussed the pros and cons of using OpsMgr in a service provider model. It introduced the concept of a management cloud and explained the difference between hosted OpsMgr and an OpsMgr-based SLA. The chapter also discussed how to deploy a CA to support OpsMgr in service provider mode, along with several methods to segregate customers in a multi-tenant service provider management group.

Suggestions included OpsMgr deliverables and high-level steps to bring a customer network into management. Using SPF with System Center 2012 SP 1 enables transitioning to command-line oriented remote management.

PART VII
Appendixes

IN THIS PART

APPENDIX A

OpsMgr By Example: Configuring and Tuning Management Packs

IN THIS CHAPTER

- Office SharePoint 2010
- Lync Server 2010
- Dell Management Pack
- Network Monitoring
- System Center 2012 Configuration Manager
- System Center 2012 Orchestrator
- Windows Azure Applications
- Windows Server Operating System

This appendix includes a number of "OpsMgr by example" articles that focus on configuration and tuning tips when implementing System Center 2012 Operations Manager (OpsMgr) management packs. The intent is to provide a 5000-foot/meter perspective as well as show the details for a particular type of tuning performed in a sample deployment. You could consider this as a "been there, done that, got the t-shirt" approach to implementing these management packs (see Figure A.1).

For new "by example" information and updates to existing articles, be sure to check http://opsmgrunleashed.wordpress.com/ and the OpsMgr by Example series at http://www.systemcentercentral.com/tabid/150/tag/Blog+ByExample/Default.aspx. The authors anticipate continuing to post to this series online. For this book, the "by example" series has been reformatted to provide a quick and consistent approach to implementing management packs using the following structure:

- What is this management pack? (Explained in the start of the section dedicated to the management pack)
- Where can you get the management pack?
- Where can you get the documentation for the management pack?
- What are the key installation steps?
- What are the key configuration steps?
- What are common alerts for tuning?
- What are good reference links for this management pack?

(If you have made it this far in the book, you deserve at least one Easter egg. A Jedi OpsMgr reference would have worked as well but the picture here was just too good to pass up.)

FIGURE A.1 I am "the Kevin Holman."

The goal of this appendix and the online postings is not to replace the existing management pack guides, but to provide a high-level directional overview of how to use the management pack and key points of which you should be aware. As many of the existing "by example" postings do not require updates for OpsMgr 2012, they are not included here; please refer to the sites referenced in this section to find the original articles. With no further delay (remember the goal is quick and consistent), let's delve into the management packs!

Office SharePoint 2010

The Office SharePoint 2010 management pack provides monitoring for Microsoft SharePoint 2010. SharePoint provides significant functional benefits to OpsMgr, including Visio state-enabled diagrams, the ability to display OpsMgr dashboard widgets in SharePoint, using SharePoint as a process and knowledgebase repository, and of course the monitoring OpsMgr can provide for SharePoint 2010 (for additional information, see Cameron Fuller's blog article at http://blogs.catapultsystems.com/cfuller/archive/2012/08/16/the-top-5-benefits-of-combining-operations-manager-and-sharepoint-[scom-sysctr-sharepoint].aspx).

SharePoint 2010 Management Pack Download

The SharePoint management pack includes three management packs:

- Microsoft SharePoint 2010 Products Monitoring Management Pack
- Microsoft SharePoint Foundation 2010 Monitoring Management Pack

- Microsoft FAST Search Server 2010 for SharePoint Monitoring Management Pack

Download and install the management packs for SharePoint 2010 in one of two ways:

- Through the Operations console, select **Administration -> Management Packs**, right-click on **Management packs** and select **Download management packs**.
- Search for the Office SharePoint 2010 management pack(s) from the Microsoft System Center Marketplace, located at http://systemcenter.pinpoint.microsoft.com. This is the preferred option for the SharePoint management pack.

NOTE: THE SHAREPOINT CONFIGURATION TASK AND OPSMGR 2012

The original version of the SharePoint management pack contained a task (Configure SharePoint Management) to perform configuration of the management pack, but the task did not work in OpsMgr 2012. At the time of writing this appendix, Microsoft has added a functional version of this task to the newest version of the management pack (14.0.4745.1000), available for download from the System Center Marketplace. The authors recommend downloading the newest version of the management pack, but if that is not possible you can use the previous version (14.0.4744.1000) by downloading an additional management pack available at http://www.systemcentercentral.com/Default.aspx?tabid=145&IndexId=94510; this includes a task updated to run correctly in an OpsMgr 2012 environment.

SharePoint 2010 Management Pack Documentation

The management pack guide for SharePoint 2010 is available for download at http://www.microsoft.com/en-us/download/details.aspx?id=4419.

Key Installation Steps for the SharePoint 2010 Management Pack

To install the SharePoint 2010 management pack, follow these steps:

1. Deploy the OpsMgr agent to all SharePoint web servers or SQL servers that host the SharePoint databases.
2. Download the management pack guide and have it available for reference.
3. Download and install the management packs for SharePoint 2010 as discussed in the "SharePoint 2010 Management Pack Download" section.
4. Import the relevant Office SharePoint Server 2010 management pack or packs for your environment.
5. It is not necessary to create a SharePoint_Overrides management pack manually as the configuration task automatically creates override management packs (these management packs are named Microsoft SharePoint 2010 Overrides and Microsoft.SharePoint.Foundation.2010.Overrides). You can rename these override management packs as necessary to match existing override standards for your organization.

Key Configuration Steps for the SharePoint 2010 Management Pack

After importing the SharePoint management packs, information does not initially appear in the various SharePoint 2010 views in the Monitoring pane of the Operations console. For this management pack to function, there are six steps that need to occur after the OpsMgr agents are deployed and the SharePoint management packs are added. Follow these steps:

1. Turn on proxy for all SharePoint web servers.

   This is set in the Administration pane. Navigate to Administration -> Agent Managed -> Properties of the server -> Proxy settings.

2. Create a Run As account.

   Create a Run As account that will be used for SharePoint monitoring. Here are the specific account permissions required:

   - Local admin on all SharePoint 2010 Front End and Application servers
   - Local admin on all SQL boxes that host SharePoint 2010 Databases
   - dbo for the actual SharePoint databases *or* Sys Admin SQL Role on the SQL instance (which may provide additional rights to the account but is easier to implement than configuring dbo on each database)
   - Full farm admin rights within SharePoint 2010
   - For simplicity, create a name that is easy to remember and to reference later such as "spmpa"

   If your organization has multiple farms in different environments, you may need to create multiple Run As accounts. The Run As account must be defined in the Administration pane of the Operations console as a Windows type account with credentials distributed to the SharePoint servers.

3. Find the SharePointMP.config file.

   This file will not exist if you download the SharePoint 2010 management pack from the Operations Manager console. You must download it from the System Center Marketplace (see the links in the "Key Installation Steps for the SharePoint 2010 Management Pack" section) or you will not have the required configuration file and will not see anything being monitored.

   Move the file to the *%ProgramFiles%*\System Center Management Packs folder on the management server that will run the task to configure SharePoint if it is not there already.

4. Update the SharePointMP.config file.

   Update the SharePointMP.config file with the Run As information—adding the account and information about servers in the farm:

- Association Account="SharePointService" (the Run As account discussed in step 2 with rights to the farms).
- Machine Name="spoint" (or some string that is in all your SharePoint server names). The Machine Name list needs to include both the SharePoint web servers and the SQL server(s) that SharePoint has databases on.

TIP: HOW TO FIND THE SHAREPOINT SERVERS IN AN ENVIRONMENT

As part of the configuration for the SharePoint 2010 management pack, a SharePointMP.config file must be edited to include the various SharePoint servers in your environment, including the databases used by SharePoint. Should there be a significant number of these files and you do not have an existing list, here a procedure the authors have used to identify the applicable servers:

1. Use a Windows Service monitor to monitor the SharePoint 2010 Timer service. Export the list to Excel.
2. Open the SQL view and look for SPS or SharePoint databases. Export the list to Excel.
3. Group the results into farms based on feedback from your SharePoint team.

This may not result in a complete match to what SharePoint servers exist, but it gives you a solid start from which to work!

Here is sample file content:

```
</Annotation>
<Association Account="spmpa" Type="Agent">
   <Machine Name="OdysseyWeb1" />
   <Machine Name="OdysseySQL1" />
</Association>
<Annotation Element="WorkflowCycle">
```

The following is example file content for a multiple farm configuration (subset of text provided by JC Hornbeck at http://blogs.technet.com/b/operationsmgr/archive/2011/03/10/tips-on-using-the-sharepoint-2010-management-pack-for-opsmgr-2007.aspx):

```
</Annotation>
<Association Account="Odyssey - SharePoint Farm administrator 1" Type="Agent">
<Machine Name="OdysseyWeb1" />
<Machine Name="OdysseyWeb2" />
<Machine Name="OdysseyWeb3" />
<Machine Name="OdysseyWeb4" />
<Machine Name="OdysseySQL1" />
<Machine Name="OdysseySQL2" />
</Association>
<Association Account="Odyssey - SharePoint Farm Administrator 2" Type="Agent">
<Machine Name="OdysseyWeb5" />
<Machine Name="OdysseyWeb6" />
```

```
<Machine Name="OdysseySQL3" />
</Association>
<Association Account="Odyssey - SharePoint 2010 Farm Administrator 3" Type="Agent">
<Machine Name="OdysseyWeb7" />
<Machine Name="OdysseyWeb8" />
<Machine Name="OdysseySQL4" />
</Association>
```

NOTE: ASSOCIATION ACCOUNT NEEDS TO MATCH RUN AS ACCOUNT

The association account needs to match the name defined for the Run As account in OpsMgr—exactly. In this example, the account name created was called "spmpa."

5. Run the task to configure SharePoint.

   Run the **Configure SharePoint Management Pack** command in the Tasks pane of the SharePoint folder in Operations Manager. This task is available in the Operations console under SharePoint 2010 Products -> Administration. When running this task, be sure to specify credentials with access rights sufficient to perform the action (the Run As account that was created). If an account with insufficient permissions is used, the task will fail to execute.

TIP: CONFIGURING THE SHAREPOINT 2010 MANAGEMENT PACK IN A DMZ

The SharePoint management pack task configures overrides for discoveries (stored in Microsoft.SharePoint.Foundation.2010.override.xml), and enables and configures the sync time for the management pack. If you cannot use the Configure SharePoint Management Pack task, try this approach:

1. Override the Discovery For SharePoint Foundation Installed Machine for the Windows computer running SharePoint 2010.
2. Create your Run As account, which has the needed rights according to the management pack documentation.
3. Add the Run As account to the SharePoint Discovery/Monitoring Account profile, targeted at the computer for which the override was made in step 1.

You can tweak the frequency and SyncTime in the overrides to speed things up, but probably need to wait 24 hours before everything is discovered.

If the task executes successfully, the Diagram View should be the first view with content listed. The view will show Microsoft SharePoint 2010 first as unmonitored and then as green (healthy). In addition, after running this task, there initially is no content in the Unidentified Machines view.

TIP: REBOOT THE MANAGEMENT SERVERS AFTER IMPORTING THE MANAGEMENT PACK

You may need to reboot the management servers after importing the management pack and the updated task for OpsMgr 2012 for the task to operate correctly. This was stated in the "Frequently Asked Questions and Known Issues" section of the SharePoint management pack guide.

6. Wait 24 hours.

   There are several discoveries that need to occur for the SharePoint 2010 management pack views to populate properly. It will take some time for the data to appear once this is done (some documentation suggests 30 minutes; the authors recommend 24 hours).

Common Alert Tuning for the SharePoint 2010 Management Pack

This section covers alerts encountered and resolved when tuning the various SharePoint management packs, listed in alphabetical order by alert name.

The large majority of alerts in the SharePoint 2010 management pack are generated due to SharePoint Health Analyzer (SPHA) rules, which identify a variety of SharePoint related configuration items. Table A.1 shows the list of SPHA errors identified in a recent SharePoint deployment.

TABLE A.1 SharePoint Health Analyzer common errors

SPHA Rule
Accounts used by application pools or service identities are in the local machine Administrators group.
Application pools recycle when memory limits are exceeded.
Built-in accounts are used as application pool or service identities.
Databases require upgrade or not supported.
Drives are at risk of running out of free space.
Drives are running out of free space.
InfoPath Forms Services forms cannot be filled out in a Web browser because no State Service connection is configured.
Missing server side dependencies.
People search relevance is not optimized when the Active Directory has errors in the manager reporting structure.
The paging file size should exceed the amount of physical RAM in the system.
The server farm account should not be used for other services.
The Unattended Service Account Application ID is not specified or has an invalid value.
Verify each User Profile Service Application has a My Site Host configured.
Verify each User Profile Service Application has an associated Search Service Connection.

TABLE A.1 Continued

SPHA Rule
Web Analytics: Verifies that when the Web Analytics is installed and running, usage logging is enabled in the farm.
Web Analytics: Verify that there is a data processing service started when there is a web service started.
Web Applications using Claims authentication require an update.

The SPHA rules in the SharePoint management pack are handled differently than other OpsMgr alerts. The alerts indicate there is an error related to availability, configuration, or security as shown in the following list. To find the actual error, open the Monitoring pane and navigate to **SharePoint 2010 Products -> SPHA Rules**.

- SharePoint: SPHA Availability Rule Monitor Detects Failure
- SharePoint: SPHA Configuration Rule Monitor Detects Failure
- SharePoint: SPHA Security Rule Monitor Detects Failure

Here are some common issues identified by this management pack:

- **SPHA Issue identified:** Drives are running out of free space.

  Issue: This rule checks disk space as a proportion of the RAM on the computer. When disk space is less than twice the RAM on the computer, the health rule triggers an error. If disk space is less than five times the RAM on the computer, the health rule triggers a warning. This means that server computers with high amounts of RAM are more likely to experience a failure of this rule. A 16GB server would require at least 32GB disk size for the C: drive to avoid the critical error, and 80GB disk size to avoid the warning state. For a thin provisioned environment, this could be given 80GB. Microsoft wants this space to use for the page file.

  Resolution: The resolution is to free disk space on the server if possible. However, with a requirement to have five times the amount of RAM on the computer this will likely not be viable at least in virtualized environments. This rule can be disabled on the SharePoint server itself as discussed in an article available at http://blah.winsmarts.com/2009-11-SP2010_Development_VM_-and-ndash;_Drives_are_running_out_of_free_space.aspx.

- Here is an alert that was tuned due to interaction with another management pack in OpsMgr:
  - **Alert:** IIS 7 Application Pool is unavailable
  - **Management Pack Name:** Windows Server 2008 Internet Information Services 7
  - **Management Pack Version:** 6.0.7600.0

- **Rule or Monitor:** Monitor
- **Rule or Monitor Name:** Application Pool availability
- **Rule or Monitor Notes:** This monitor checks its state every 60 seconds.

Issue: There were alerts raised by the IIS management pack indicating application pools for the SharePoint environment were in a stopped state. Per the URL at http://www.harbar.net/archive/2009/12/04/more-on-sharepoint-2010-application-pools.aspx, this is a normal configuration for this application pool with SharePoint.

Resolution: Created a dynamic group for the SharePoint Web Services root and stored it in the overrides management pack for the Windows Server 2008 Internet Information Services 7 management pack. (For an example of this for the Default Application Pool, see http://blogs.catapultsystems.com/cfuller/archive/2010/11/18/tuning-the-iis-management-packs-to-ignore-default-items.aspx). Validated the group membership by viewing the group members. This group included all application pools that contained the name "SharePoint Web Services Root." Created an override to set Enabled to False for this monitor for this group of objects.

Reference Links for the SharePoint 2010 Management Pack

Here are reference links for additional information on the SharePoint 2010 management pack:

- **Configuring the SharePoint 2010 Management Pack:** http://www.systemcentercentral.com/BlogDetails/tabid/143/IndexID/82994/Default.aspx
- **Configuring the SharePoint 2010 Management Pack for System Center Operations Manager:** http://blogs.technet.com/b/momteam/archive/2012/04/16/kb-configuring-the-sharepoint-2010-management-pack-for-system-center-operations-manager.aspx
- **How to get the sharepointMP.config file:** http://www.itwalkthru.com/2010/11/configuring-sharepoint-2010-farm.html
- **Sample sharepointMP.config file contents:** http://blogs.technet.com/b/operationsmgr/archive/2011/03/10/tips-on-using-the-sharepoint-2010-management-pack-for-opsmgr-2007.aspx
- **Discussion on the SharePoint 2010 management pack:** http://www.systemcentercentral.com/Forums/tabid/60/categoryid/4/indexid/81068/Default.aspx
- **SharePoint management pack task:** http://social.technet.microsoft.com/Forums/en-US/operationsmanagermgmtpacks/thread/0a7106ee-699d-4a6b-8da2-8cced3253003
- **SharePoint and multiple farm configurations:** http://blogs.technet.com/b/mgoedtel/archive/2012/01/07/sharepoint-2010-multi-farm-monitoring.aspx
- **Tuning the SharePoint management pack:** http://blogs.catapultsystems.com/jcowan/archive/2012/08/31/

sharepoint-2010-mp-for-opsmgr-test-and-production-multiple-db-instance-tuning-for-configuration-databases.aspx

- **Installing the SharePoint management pack in OpsMgr 2012:** http://blogs.catapultsystems.com/jcowan/archive/2012/07/10/how-to-importing-the-sharepoint-2010-mp-for-scom-2012.aspx
- **SharePoint management pack task:** http://social.technet.microsoft.com/Forums/en-US/operationsmanagermgmtpacks/thread/cea62b67-f0bc-4ae5-8b32-346698988db4

The authors owe a huge thank you to Marco Shaw, Jonathan Cowan, Simon Skinner, and Pete Zerger for their contributions to this topic!

Lync Server 2010

The Lync Server 2010 management pack provides end-to-end monitoring for Lync, including centralized discovery for all Lync Server 2010 roles and the ability to monitor Lync through synthetic transactions.

Lync Server 2010 Management Pack Download

The Lync Server 2010 management pack consists of two management packs that provide monitoring for Lync Server:

- Microsoft Lync Server 2010 Management Pack
- Microsoft Lync Server 2010 Group Chat Management Pack

Download and install the management pack(s) for Lync 2010 in one of two ways:

- In the Operations console, navigate to **Administration** -> **Management Packs**. Right-click and select **Download management packs**.
- Search for the Lync management pack(s) from the Microsoft System Center Marketplace at http://systemcenter.pinpoint.microsoft.com.

Lync Server 2010 Management Pack Documentation

The management pack guide for Lync Server 2010 is available for download at http://www.microsoft.com/en-us/download/details.aspx?id=12375. Download the management pack guide for Lync 2010 Group Chat at http://www.microsoft.com/en-us/download/details.aspx?id=8848.

Key Installation Steps for the Lync Server 2010 Management Pack

To install the Lync Server 2010 management pack, follow these steps:

1. Deploy the OpsMgr agent to all Lync servers including edge servers, which will likely be part of a workgroup configuration.
2. Download the management pack guide and have it available for reference.
3. Download and install the management pack for Lync Server 2010 as discussed in the "Lync Server 2010 Management Pack Download" section.
4. Import the relevant Lync Server 2010 management pack or packs for your environment.
5. Create a Lync_Overrides management pack to contain any overrides required for the management pack.

Key Configuration Steps for the Lync Server 2010 Management Pack

After importing the Lync management packs, several steps must occur to configure the Lync management pack. Follow these steps:

1. Turn on proxy for all Lync servers.

   This is set under Administration -> Agent Managed -> Properties of the server -> Proxy settings.

2. Configure Run As account(s).

   The profile Microsoft Lync Server 2010 Profile is defined as Network Service and cannot be changed to a different account. Only the Network Service account provides sufficient access to the Lync Server 2010 Central Management database.

3. Configure Edge server monitoring.

   Discovery of edge servers is disabled by default. To enable edge server monitoring, change the value of the DiscoverEdgeServerRole property of LS Central Topology Discovery object to **True** as shown in Figure A.2. By default, this discovery occurs every four hours (14,400 seconds) but can be changed by decreasing this value with an override and changed back to 14400 after the discovery occurs successfully.

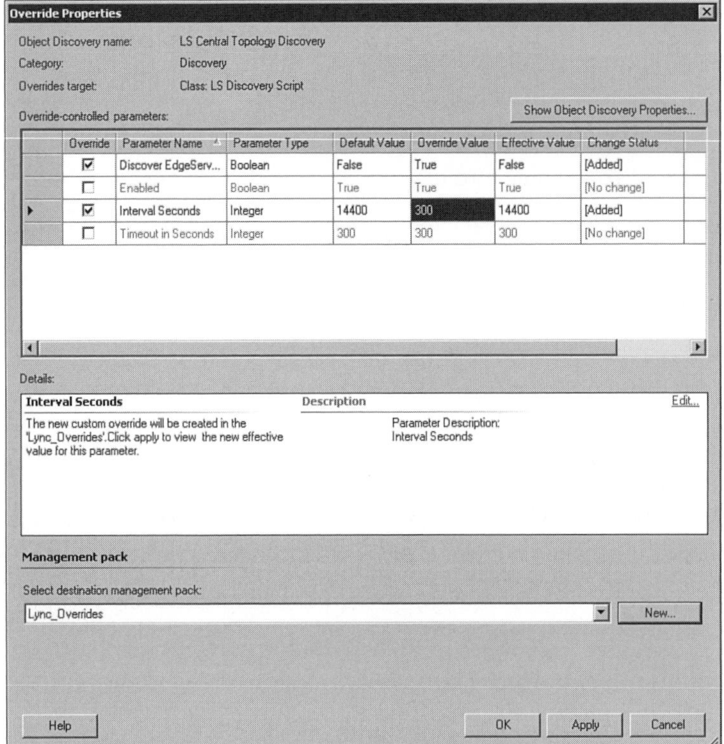

FIGURE A.2 Configuring edge server discovery.

Common Alert Tuning for the Lync Server 2010 Management Pack

This section discusses alerts encountered and resolved when tuning the various Lync management packs. Here are some common issues identified by this management pack:

- **Alert**: The following discovered partners are sending frequent invalid SIP requests to the Access Edge Server.
  - **Management Pack Name:** Microsoft Lync Server 2010 Management Pack
  - **Management Pack Version:** 4.0.7577.0
  - **Rule or Monitor:** Monitor
  - **Rule or Monitor Name:** Possible attack by Discovered Partners: traffic restricted
  - **Rule or Monitor Notes:** The alert description contains the list of partners for which this issue is occurring.
- **Issue**: This alert is indicating different organizations that want to be federated with your organization but are currently not federated.

- **Resolution**: There is an option to remove the errors manually, discussed at http://ocsguy.com/2011/04/20/a-few-words-on-federation/. Alternatively, you could create an override to disable this alert if your organization does not care to federate with the organizations listed in the alert description.

Reference Links for the Lync Server 2010 Management Pack

Here are reference links for additional information on the Lync Server 2010 management pack:

- **Deploying Synthetic Transactions for Lync:** http://www.vnext.be/2011/03/06/scom-opsmgr-lync-2010-management-pack-deploying-synthetic-transactions-sts/.
- **Clifs Notes: Lync 2010 Monitoring with OpsMgr and Lync:** http://blogs.catapultsystems.com/jcowan/archive/2012/09/26/clifs-notes-lync-2010-monitoring-with-opsmgr-and-lync.aspx.
- **Microsoft Lync Server 2010 Unleashed:** http://www.amazon.com/Microsoft-Lync-Server-2010-Unleashed/dp/0672330342/, this contains a discussion on the installation and configuration of the Lync management pack.

Dell Management Pack

Dell has updated its management pack to provide new functionality for Operations Manager. Version 5.0.1 provides agent-free out-of-band monitoring for System Center 2012 Operations Manager leveraging the Dell PowerEdge 12th generation embedded server management feature, iDRAC7 with Lifecycle Controller. The new management pack also provides agent-based monitoring with OpenManage Server Administrator (OMSA) for 9-12G PowerEdge servers.

Dell Management Pack Download

The Dell management pack contains several management packs that provide monitoring for Dell Servers. The management packs are downloaded via a single self-extracting executable named Dell_Server_Management_Pack_Suite_x86_x64.exe.

Download and install the management pack(s) for Dell by searching for the Dell management pack(s) from the Microsoft System Center Marketplace at http://systemcenter.pinpoint.microsoft.com. You can also download this management pack directly from http://www.dell.com/support/drivers/us/en/555/DriverDetails?DriverId=1YHD8.

Dell Management Pack Documentation

The management pack download includes both an installation guide and a readme file.

Key Installation Steps for the Dell Management Pack

To install the Dell management pack, follow these steps:

1. Deploy the OpsMgr agent to all Dell servers.
2. Download the self-extracting executable for the Dell server management suite and open the installation guide.
3. Running the self-extracting executable extracts a total of 22 management pack files stored in a top level folder and five subfolders (see Figure A.3) to the path of your choice (by default *%ProgramFiles%*\Dell Management Packs\Server Mgmt Suite\5.0.1). It also automatically imports three of the management packs into OpsMgr, registers DLLs with the operating system, and if you have Active Directory permissions, it creates Active Directory groups, all without prompting you. If you do not have Active Directory permissions to create groups, it notifies you that it failed after trying. These are important reasons to read the installation guide.

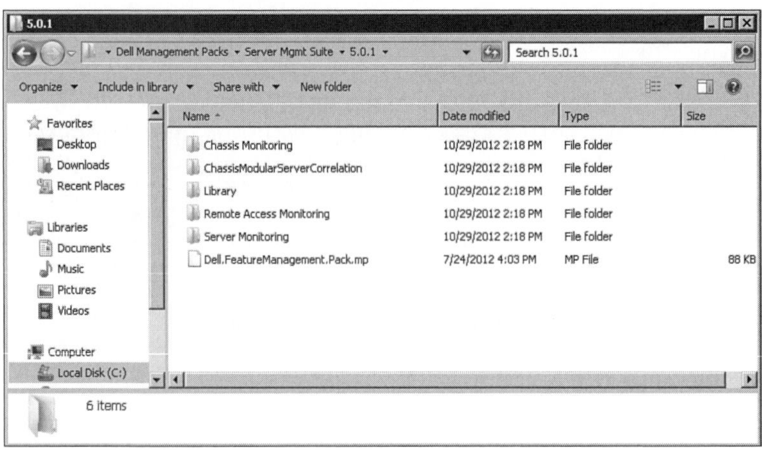

FIGURE A.3 The Dell management packs.

Dell recommends you do not directly import the Dell management packs, instead use the Dell Monitoring Feature Tasks option circled within the Monitoring pane shown in Figure A.4.

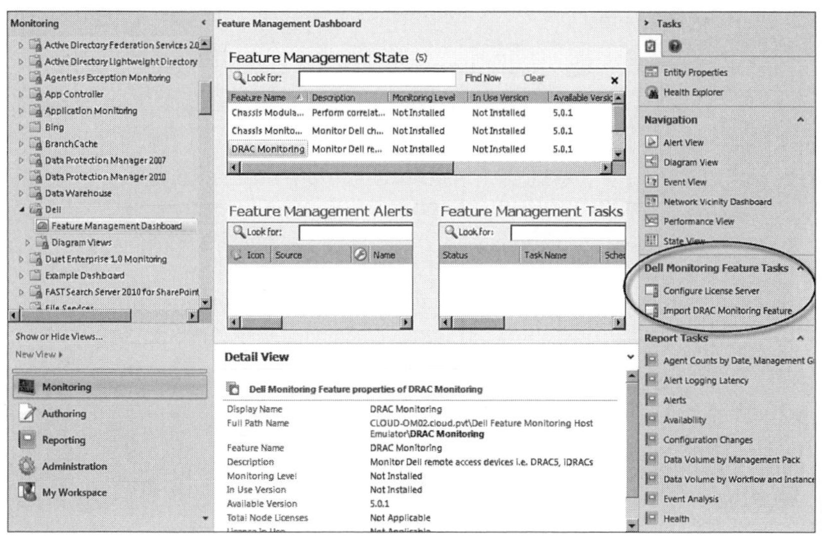

FIGURE A.4 Dell Monitoring Feature Tasks.

NOTE: DELL CONNECTION LICENSE MANAGER GROUPS IN ACTIVE DIRECTORY

Here are the groups created in the Windows Server Active Directory during installation of Dell Server Management Pack Suite or Dell Connections License Manager:

- Dell Connections License Administrators
- Dell Connections License Operators
- Dell Connections License Users

If these domain groups are not created automatically during installation, create them manually.

After creating the required domain groups, add your management server machine account as part of the Dell Connections License Users group, and add the current user account to the Dell Connections License Administrators group.

4. Create a Dell_Overrides management pack to contain any overrides required for the management pack.
5. To use the Dell tasks that are included with the management pack, the items listed in Table A.2 are required.

TABLE A.2 Dell software and purposes

Software	Purpose
DRAC Tools *or* OpenManage Server Administrator (Server Administrator)	To discover Chassis Slot Summary and Server Modules for CMC and DRAC/MC Chassis.
Dell OpenManage Power Center	Install Dell OpenManage Power Center on the management server. For more information, see Dell OpenManage Power Center Installation Guide at support.dell.com/manuals.
BMC Management Utility	To run the Remote Power Control tasks or the LED Identification Control tasks on Dell-managed systems.
Dell License Manager	To deploy licenses and collect reports from the management server. To launch Dell License Manager console, install Dell License Manager on the management server. For more information, see Dell License Manager User's Guide at support.dell.com/manuals.

Key Configuration Steps for the Dell Management Pack

After importing the Dell management packs, here are steps that need to occur to configure the management pack:

1. Turn on proxy for all Dell servers.

   This is set under Administration -> Agent Managed -> Properties of the server -> Proxy settings.

2. Configure Run As account(s).

   If you will be using the Dell Chassis Management (CMC) or Dell Remote Access Controller/Modular Chassis functionality within the management pack, Run As accounts will need to be configured for these functions.

Reference Links for the Dell Management Pack

Here are reference links for additional information on the Dell management pack:

- **Installing version 5.0.1 of the Dell management pack:** http://nocentdocent.wordpress.com/2012/09/05/making-dell-management-packs-lighter-for-your-management-servers/, and http://blogs.catapultsystems.com/jcowan/archive/2012/10/02/opsmgr-2012-dell-server-management-pack-suite-v5-0-1-installation.aspx

- **Marnix Wolf's insights on the Dell management pack:** http://thoughtsonopsmgr.blogspot.com/2012/11/dell-mp-suite-version-501-part-i-lets.html, http://thoughtsonopsmgr.blogspot.nl/2012/11/dell-mp-suite-version-501-part-i-lets.html, http://thoughtsonopsmgr.blogspot.nl/2012/11/dell-mp-suite-version-501-part-ii-know.html, http://thoughtsonopsmgr.blogspot.nl/2012/11/dell-mp-suite-version-501-part-iii.html, and http://thoughtsonopsmgr.blogspot.com/2012/12/dell-mp-suite-version-501-part-iv.html.

- **Dell Management pack wiki including videos:** http://en.community.dell.com/techcenter/systems-management/w/wiki/4118.dell-server-management-pack-suite.aspx

Network Monitoring

Operations Manager 2012 extends network monitoring capabilities with detailed port, interface, and peripheral monitoring of your network devices, as well as virtual local area networks (vLANs) and hot standby router protocol (HSRP) groups. This is discussed extensively in Chapter 16, "Network Monitoring." The information in this appendix summarizes information about the network monitoring management packs used with this new functionality.

Network Monitoring Packs Download

Two management packs are required to implement network discovery and monitoring. They are automatically installed during setup of the first management server, so you do not need to install them separately:

- Microsoft.Windows.Server.NetworkDiscovery
- Microsoft.Windows.Client.NetworkDiscovery

Network Monitoring Packs Documentation

In addition to the information provided in Chapter 16, see http://technet.microsoft.com/en-us/library/hh212935.aspx.

System Center 2012 Configuration Manager

The System Center Monitoring Pack for System Center 2012 - Configuration provides monitoring for the health of Microsoft System Center 2012 Configuration Manager (ConfigMgr). The pack provides monitoring for health, data replication between Configuration Manager sites, and monitors availability of servers and services.

ConfigMgr 2012 Management Pack Download

The ConfigMgr 2012 management pack consists of three management packs that provide monitoring for Configuration Manager 2012:

- Microsoft System Center 2012 Configuration Manager Discovery
- Microsoft System Center 2012 Configuration Manager Library
- Microsoft System Center 2012 Configuration Manager Monitoring

Download and install the management pack(s) for ConfigMgr 2012 in one of two ways:

- Through the OpsMgr Operations console, navigate to **Administration** -> **Management Packs**. Right-click and choose **Download management packs**.
- Search for the Configuration Manager monitoring pack from the Microsoft System Center Marketplace at http://systemcenter.pinpoint.microsoft.com.

Configuration Manager 2012 Management Pack Documentation

The management pack guide for Configuration Manager 2012 is available for download at http://www.microsoft.com/en-us/download/details.aspx?id=29267. This link includes two documents: ConfigMgr_MPGuide_Appendix.docx and OpsMgr_MP_ConfigMgr.docx.

Key Installation Steps for the Configuration Manager 2012 Management Pack

To install the Configuration Manager management pack, follow these steps:

1. Deploy the OpsMgr agent to all ConfigMgr servers.
2. Download the management pack guide and have it available for reference.
3. Download and install the management pack for Configuration Manager as discussed in the "ConfigMgr 2012 Management Pack Download" section.
4. Import the ConfigMgr 2012 management pack into your environment.
5. Create a ConfigMgr_Overrides management pack to contain any overrides required for the management pack.

Key Configuration Steps for the ConfigMgr 2012 Management Pack

After importing the ConfigMgr management pack there are several steps that need to occur to configure the management pack:

1. Turn on proxy for all ConfigMgr servers.

   This is set under Administration -> Agent Managed -> Properties of the server -> Proxy settings.

2. Wait for objects to be discovered.

   Discoveries are set to run every 4 hours or daily. There are three options to decrease this timeframe:

   - Use maintenance mode.
   - Restart the System Center Management Service on the Configuration Manager servers where the site roles are installed.
   - Run the tasks included in the ConfigMgr management pack (Hierarchy Discovery Task and Site Services Discovery Task) that start the discovery processes.

NOTE: THE CONFIGURATION MANAGER 2012 MANAGEMENT PACK AND SYSTEM PRIVILEGES

As documented in the OpsMgr_MP_ConfigMgr.docx file, the Configuration Manager 2012 management pack does not support low privilege account monitoring. This management pack requires Local System account privileges to run.

Common Alert Tuning for the ConfigMgr 2012 Management Pack

This section discusses alerts encountered and resolved when tuning the ConfigMgr management packs. In the case of the Configuration Manager pack, there actually is very little to tune. Here is information on the most common alert the authors have seen when tuning this management pack:

- **Alert:** SQL Server Port on Firewall Not Open
  - **Management Pack Name:** Microsoft System Center 2012 Configuration Manager Monitoring
  - **Management Pack Version:** 5.0.7705.0
  - **Rule or Monitor:** Monitor
  - **Rule or Monitor Name:** SQL Server Firewall Port Monitor
  - **Rule or Monitor Notes:** This monitor checks the value of a registry key on the ConfigMgr server at `HKLM\SOFTWARE\Microsoft\SMS\Operations Management\Components\ SMS_HIERARCHY_MANAGER\ 8D5E5CC1-CCF5-4c66-BC8A-527C9066161B\ Severity`. The value of this registry key is checked every 6 minutes.
- **Issue:** In an environment where the Windows Firewall is disabled, this alert will occur even though it is not relevant since the firewall is not enabled. The SMS_Hierarchy_Manager is in a healthy state. Validate that ConfigMgr is functional and able to communicate with the SQL Server containing the ConfigMgr site database.
- **Resolution:** As this issue is not currently occurring, delete the hman.log file that is the source of the alert, restart the SMS Executive service on the ConfigMgr server, and monitor for recreation of the log file and alert resolution.

System Center 2012 Orchestrator

The management pack (a.k.a. "monitoring pack") for System Center 2012 Orchestrator implements discovery and health monitoring of Orchestrator roles and components. Since Orchestrator, like OpsMgr, is highly connected to other System Center 2012 components, the authors recommend installing Orchestrator and its management pack into your management environment early.

System Center 2012 Orchestrator Monitoring Pack Download

The System Center 2012 Orchestrator monitoring pack consists of two management packs that provide monitoring for Orchestrator:

- Microsoft System Center 2012 Orchestrator Library
- Microsoft System Center 2012 Orchestrator

Download and install the management packs for Orchestrator in one of two ways:

- Through the Operations console, navigate to **Administration -> Management Packs.** Right-click and choose **Download management packs**.
- Search for the Orchestrator monitoring pack from the Microsoft System Center Marketplace at http://systemcenter.pinpoint.microsoft.com.

System Center 2012 Orchestrator Monitoring Pack Documentation

The management pack guide for Orchestrator and monitoring pack download are located at http://www.microsoft.com/en-us/download/details.aspx?id=29269.

System Center 2012 Orchestrator Monitoring Pack Prerequisites

There are several simple requirements to check for before installing the Orchestrator management pack:

- The Windows Server 2008 Internet Information Services 7 and the Windows Server Internet Information Services Library management packs must be imported prior to importing the Orchestrator monitoring pack.
- Windows PowerShell is required on Orchestrator management servers and runbook servers.

Key Installation Steps for the System Center 2012 Orchestrator Monitoring Pack

To install the Orchestrator management pack, follow these steps:

1. Deploy the OpsMgr agent to all Orchestrator management servers and runbook servers.
2. Download the monitoring pack guide and have it available for reference.
3. Download and install the monitoring pack for Orchestrator as discussed in the "System Center 2012 Orchestrator Monitoring Pack Download" section.
4. Create an Orchestrator_Overrides management pack to contain any overrides required for the management pack.
5. No further configuration of the Orchestrator monitoring pack is required for full functionality.

Using the System Center 2012 Orchestrator Monitoring Pack

After importing the Orchestrator monitoring pack, your Orchestrator management servers and runbook servers are automatically discovered. Here are the features of the Orchestrator monitoring pack:

- Discovered objects are the Orchestrator management servers, runbook servers, runbook targets, the Orchestrator web service, and the Orchestrator Web console.
- Three collection rules gather performance data about runbook execution as seen in Figure A.5, a view of the System Center Orchestrator monitoring pack view folder.
- Six rules fire alerts for issues like database connection failure and policy module fault.
- Four monitors watch the Orchestrator management and runbook services. Each monitor has a manual recovery task to start the monitored service.

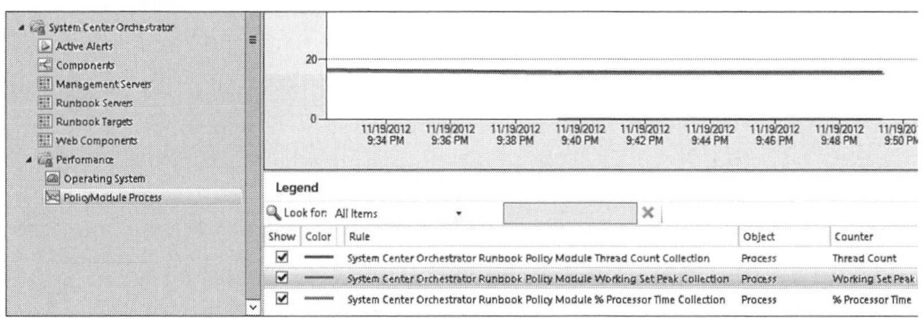

FIGURE A.5 An Orchestrator Runbook Policy Module performance chart.

Windows Azure Applications

The management pack, or "monitoring pack," for Windows Azure Applications enables you to monitor the availability and performance of applications running on Windows Azure. The monitoring pack uses various Windows Azure APIs to remotely discover and collect instrumentation information about a specified Windows Azure application.

The management pack for Windows Azure Applications provides no functionality on import. For each Windows Azure application that you want to monitor, you must configure discovery using the Windows Azure Application monitoring template. The July, 2011 version of the management pack, current at the time of writing this appendix, discovers Azure Platform as a Service (PaaS) features, specifically Windows Azure Web, Worker, and VM roles. Newer VMs of the Infrastructure as a Service (IaaS) type, which are still in "trial" period as of December 2012, are not discovered.

Windows Azure Applications Monitoring Pack Download

The Windows Azure Applications monitoring pack consists of a single management pack, Microsoft System Center Azure, which provides monitoring for applications in your Windows Azure subscription. This management pack is not available from the online catalog, you must download the management pack and the management pack guide from http://www.microsoft.com/en-us/download/details.aspx?id=11324.

Installing and Importing the Windows Azure Applications Monitoring Pack

After downloading the management pack, follow these steps to install and import the Windows Azure Applications monitoring pack:

1. Run the Monitoring Pack for Windows Azure Applications.msi, by default the installation file will be installed to *%ProgramFiles(86)%*\System Center Management Packs\Monitoring Pack For Windows Azure Applications.
2. In the Operations console, navigate to **Administration** -> **Management Packs**. Right-click and choose **Import management packs**. Browse to the installed management pack location and select the **Microsoft.SystemCenter.Azure.mp** management pack for import.

Windows Azure Applications Monitoring Pack Prerequisites

There are no prerequisites for the most basic functionality of the management pack, which is simple availability of Windows Azure role instances. For all performance monitoring, it is necessary to configure your Azure application as follows:

- The Windows Azure role must be published with full trust level. For more information about Windows Azure trust levels, see the Windows Azure Partial Trust Policy Reference (http://go.microsoft.com/fwlink/?LinkId=191346).
- Windows Azure Diagnostics must be enabled. For more information about Windows Azure Diagnostics, see Collecting Logging Data by Using Windows Azure Diagnostics (http://go.microsoft.com/fwlink/?LinkId=186765).
- Windows Azure Diagnostics must be configured to forward diagnostic data to a Windows Azure storage account. For more information about configuring Windows Azure Diagnostics, see Transferring Diagnostic Data to Windows Azure Storage (http://go.microsoft.com/fwlink/?LinkId=191347).

Key Configuration Steps to Use the Windows Azure Applications Monitoring Pack

To use the Windows Azure Applications management pack, follow these steps, which will discover the applications in your Azure subscription:

1. In the Operations console, at **Administration** -> **Run As Configuration** -> **Profiles**, select **Windows Azure Run As Profile Blob**, and click **Properties** from the Tasks pane.
2. On the Run As Accounts tab, click **Add**. In the Create Run As Account Wizard, select to create an account of the **Binary Authentication** type. Provide a name and click **Next**.
3. At the Provide account credentials page, browse to and import the .PFX certificate file (with private key) that corresponds to the Azure management certificate for your Azure subscription. Select the **More secure** method of credential delivery and click **Create**.
4. At Run As Configuration -> Profiles, select **Windows Azure Run As Profile Password**, and click **Properties** from the Tasks pane.
5. At the Run As Accounts tab, click **Add**. In the Create Run As Account Wizard, select to create an account of the **Basic Authentication** type. Provide a name and click **Next**.
6. At the Provide account credentials page, type any text for the user name (it is ignored) and in the password field, enter the password of the .PFX certificate file imported in step 3. Select the **More secure** method of credential delivery and click **Create**.
7. At Run As Configuration -> Accounts, select the Windows Azure Run As Profile Blob account specified in step 2, and click **Properties** from the Tasks pane.
8. On the Distribution tab, select **More secure** and Add the OpsMgr agent, gateway, or management server object in your management group that will be used for the proxy monitoring of Windows Azure applications. Click **OK**.
9. Repeat steps 7 and 8 for the Windows Azure Run As Profile Password account.
10. Navigate in the Operations console to **Authoring** -> **Management Pack Templates** -> **Windows Azure Application**. Run the Add Monitoring Wizard from the Tasks pane.
11. Give the monitor a name and select an appropriate management pack to which to save the customizations. On the Application Details page, enter the following information:
    - DNS prefix of the hosted service, such as MyApp.cloudapp.net.
    - Subscription ID, the GUID corresponding to your Azure subscription.
    - Select the Production or Staging environment, or both.
    - Select the Azure Certificate Blob Run As account (created in step 3).
    - Select the Azure Certificate Password Run As account (from step 6).

12. On the Proxy Agent page, select the OpsMgr agent, gateway, or management server object in your management group that will be used as the proxy agent for monitoring Windows Azure applications. Click **Create**.

Using the Windows Azure Applications Monitoring Pack

Your Windows Azure applications are automatically discovered after creating the Windows Azure Application discovery from the template in the Authoring space. Here are the features of the Windows Azure Applications monitoring pack:

- Availability monitoring of Windows Azure deployments, hosted services, roles, and role instances. Roles are Windows Azure Web, Worker, or VM roles. Figure A.6 shows the health model for monitoring the Windows Azure hosted service state.

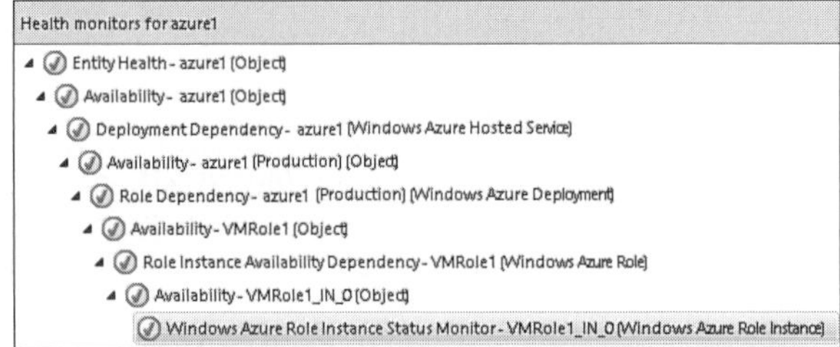

FIGURE A.6 Windows Azure hosted service state Health Explorer.

- Performance collection rules run every 5 minutes and collect performance data for each Windows Azure application that you discover:
  - ASP.NET Applications Requests/sec (Azure)
  - Network Interface Bytes Received/sec (Azure)
  - Network Interface Bytes Sent/sec (Azure)
  - Processor % Processor Time Total (Azure)
  - LogicalDisk Free Megabytes (Azure)
  - LogicalDisk % Free Space (Azure)
  - Memory Available Megabytes (Azure)
- Six rules fire alerts for issues such as database connection failure and policy module fault.

Grooming Data from Windows Azure Storage Services

Windows Azure diagnostics writes performance and event information to Azure storage, but does not delete it. This means that the tables in the Windows Azure storage account will continue to grow unless the data is groomed. The monitoring pack for Windows Azure Applications provides three rules that control data grooming:

- Windows Azure Role NT Event Log Grooming
- Windows Azure Role Performance Counter Grooming
- Windows Azure Role .NET Trace Grooming

These grooming rules are disabled by default. If you want OpsMgr to groom data from Windows Azure Storage Services periodically, use overrides to enable the rules. By default, rules you enable will run every 24 hours.

Windows Server Operating System

The Windows Server Operating System management packs are the fundamental building blocks on which most all other management packs depend and should be the first management packs imported after installing OpsMgr. In September 2012, Microsoft published the first release of a Windows Server Operating System management pack with support for Windows Server 2012. This is a highly evolved set of management packs with deep monitoring that is amazingly consistent across Windows OS versions.

Windows Server Operating System Management Packs Download

There are a number of management packs that are published for the Windows Server Operating System. The following management packs are essential for most OpsMgr 2012 management groups:

- Microsoft Windows Server Library
- Microsoft Windows Server 2012 Discovery
- Microsoft Windows Server 2012 Monitoring
- Microsoft Windows Server 2008 Discovery
- Microsoft Windows Server 2008 Monitoring
- Microsoft Windows Server Cluster Disks Monitoring
- Microsoft Windows Server Reports

Depending on your environment, the following additional management packs will be useful in your OpsMgr 2012 management group:

- Microsoft Windows Server 2008 R2 Monitoring BPA
- Microsoft Windows Server 2003
- Microsoft Windows Server 2000

Download and install the management pack(s) for Windows Server Operating System in one of two ways:

- Through the Operations console, navigate to **Administration** -> **Management Packs**. Right-click and choose **Download management packs**.
- Search for the Windows Server Operating System management pack from the Microsoft System Center Marketplace at http://systemcenter.pinpoint.microsoft.com.

Windows Server Operating System Management Pack Documentation

The management pack guide for this management pack is located at http://www.microsoft.com/en-us/download/details.aspx?id=9296.

Monitoring Features of the Windows Server Operating System Management Pack

For all versions of the Windows Server operating systems from Windows 2000 to Windows 2012, the management packs monitor availability and performance metrics:

- Availability Monitors for the Windows Server OS
    - **Key Operating System Services:** Required services are checked for status. For example running, not running, or paused.
    - **Storage:** Logical hard drives are checked for availability, sufficient free space, and integrity of the NTFS partition.
    - **Network:** Network adapters are checked for connection health, name and IP address conflicts.
- Performance Monitors for the Windows Server OS
    - **Processor:** System processor(s) performance is checked systemwide. Processors can optionally be monitored on a per processor basis.
    - **Memory:** Memory consisting of physical memory and virtual memory (also known as page files) is monitored using the following performance indicators:

      Available memory (in MB)

      Pages per second

      Page file percent usage
    - **Disks and Partitions:** Logical disks/partitions and physical disks are monitored, and performance data is collected for average disk seconds per read, disk seconds per write, and disk seconds per transfer. Monitoring is also provided for fragmentation of logical disks. Depending on the version of the operating system being monitored, either logical or physical monitoring is enabled by default.

- **Network Adapter:** Network adapters are monitored for the number of bytes received per second, the number of bytes sent per second, and the total bytes per second. In addition, the health state of the network adapter is evaluated and is set to Healthy if connected and Critical if disconnected.

Optional Configurations for the Windows Server Operating System Management Pack

You may want to enable one or more optional configurations after importing the Windows Server Operating System management packs. A design tenant of the management packs is that default Windows Server OS monitoring will not be too intrusive, noisy, or generate significantly more historical data than is necessary. However, you can "de-tune" the management packs to generate a practically infinite amount of data.

A 12-page appendix in the user guide to the System Center Monitoring Pack for Windows Server Operating System lists many dozens of monitors that are disabled by default. The authors recommend you consult the management pack guide for the detailed steps to override default monitoring in the following categories:

- **Physical Disks and Disk Partitions:** By default, Windows Server operating system management packs do not discover physical disk partitions, only logical disk partitions. To monitor physical disk drives, enable the Object Discoveries feature for any Windows Server physical disk object.

- **Logical and Physical Disks:** By default, Average Disk Seconds Per Transfer is enabled. However, Average Disk Seconds Per Read and Average Disk Seconds Per Write are not enabled by default.

- **Processors:** Windows Server 2012, Windows Server 2008, and Windows Server 2003 management packs can monitor individual instances of processors or all instances together. By default, the health of the processors is monitored as a total of all instances.

- **Network Adapters:** Percent Bandwidth Used Total is enabled by default. These counters are disabled by default: Percent Bandwidth Used Read, Percent Bandwidth Used Write, and Network Adapter Connection Health.

- **Memory Utilization:** A sample of available megabytes of memory is taken every 2 minutes, and three samples are taken to compute the threshold. This monitor is considered Healthy when available memory is above the threshold and Critical when it is below the threshold.

- **Probe Module: Is Feature Installed:** Checks whether a specified feature is installed on a computer running Windows Server 2008 or a later server operating system. This module can be used by developers who need to discover features installed.

- **Software Installation Failures:** The rule "A Software Update Installation Failed" is enabled by default for Windows 2000 Server and is disabled for Windows Server 2003 and Windows Server 2008. You can enable this rule for Windows Server 2003 and Windows Server 2008 by using overrides.

TIP: UPGRADING AN OPERATING SYSTEM: HOW TO PREVENT DISCOVERY PROBLEMS

As a best practice, before you upgrade the operating system on a monitored computer, uninstall the Operations Manager agent. After the upgrade, reinstall the Operations Manager agent. This is because a parent class that is not version-specific hosts the objects the management pack discovers, such as logical disks. When you upgrade the OS, the order in which discovery occurs can result in duplicate objects being discovered.

Windows Server Operating System Management Pack Reports

The Windows Server Operating System management packs include a large library of useful reports. Nearly identical view folders are visible in the OpsMgr Reporting pane for Windows Server 2003, Windows Server 2008, and Windows Server 2012. There is no report view folder for Windows Server 2000. Here are the reports:

- Disk Performance Analysis
- Memory Performance History (Available MB)
- Memory Performance History (Page Reads per Sec)
- Memory Performance History (Page Writes per Sec)
- Memory Performance History (Pages per Sec)
- Operating System Configuration
- Operating System Performance
- Operating System Storage Configuration
- Paging File Performance History (Percentage Usage)
- Performance History
- Performance History (Context Switches per Sec)
- Performance History (Percent Processor Time)
- Performance History (Processor Queue Length)
- Performance History Interrupt Time
- Physical Disk Performance History (Average Disk Queue Length)
- Pool Performance History (Non-Paged Bytes)
- Pool Performance History (Paged Bytes)

The following two reports are OS-neutral, are located in the Windows Server Operating System Reports folder, and can be targeted to any OpsMgr computer group as seen in Figure A.7:

- Performance By System
- Performance By Utilization

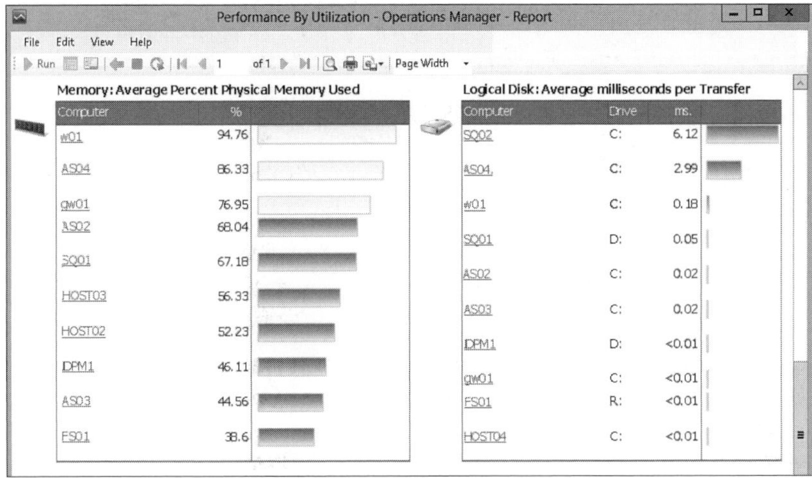

FIGURE A.7 The Performance by Utilization report, targeted to Windows Server 2012 computers.

APPENDIX B
Performance Counters

IN THIS APPENDIX

- Counters Maintained by the Monitored Computer
- Counters Maintained by the Management Server
- Counters Maintained by the OpsMgr Connector
- Counters Maintained by the ACS Collector

System Center Operations Manager (OpsMgr) 2012 collects a number of performance counters for the agent (monitored computer), management server, OpsMgr connector, and Audit Collection System (ACS) collector. These counters are created when the corresponding component is installed on a computer.

Counters Maintained by the Monitored Computer

Each managed agent maintains two sets of performance counters. Management servers maintain these counters as well.

- **Health service counters:** These are performance counters for the health service running on that computer (see Table B.1).
- **Health service management group counters:** These are performance counters relating to activity for the management group associated with that agent (see Table B.2). If the agent reports to multiple management groups (multi-homed), there will be multiple instances of the health service management group counters.

TABLE B.1 Health service counters

Counter*	Description
Active File Downloads	The number of file downloads to this management group that are currently active.
Active File Uploads	The number of file uploads from this management group that are currently active.
Data Batches Dropped	The total number of data batches that have been dropped.
Data Batches Dropped Rate	The rate at which data batches are being dropped.
Date Items Dropped	The total number of data items that have been dropped.
Data Items Dropped Rate	The rate at which data items are being dropped.
Malformed Data Items Dropped	The total number of malformed data items that have been dropped.
Malformed Data Items Dropped Rate	The rate at which malformed data items are being dropped.
Module Count	The number of modules running in the health service.
Send Queue Routes	The number of items in the send queue routing table.
Send Queue Virtual Queues	The number of items in the send queue virtual queues table.
Task Count	The number of tasks running in the health service.
Workflow count	The number of workflows running in the health service.

**There will be an instance of each of these per management group.*

TABLE B.2 Health service management groups counters

Counter*	Description
Active File Downloads	The number of file downloads to this management group that are currently active.
Active File Uploads	The number of file uploads from this management group that are currently active.
Average Bind Write Action Batch Size	The average amount of time in milliseconds it takes to process a batch of data.
Bind Data Source Average Batch Rate	The average number of items inserted per batch into the workflow that originated from a remote health service.
Bind Data Source Batch Post Rate	The rate at which batches that originated from a remote health service inserted into the workflow.
Bind Data Source Item Drop Rate	The rate at which items are dropped by the bind data source because the workflow cannot process them quickly enough.

Counter*	Description
Bind Data Source Item Incoming Rate	The rate at which items are received from another health service (System Center Management service).
Bind Data Source Item Post Rate	The rate at which items received from another health service are inserted into the workflow.
Bind Write Action Batch Insertion Rate	The rate at which batches are sent through the workflow destined for a remote health service.
Bind Write Action Multiple Item Batches	The number of batches sent through the workflow destined for a remote health service with more than one item in them.
Bind Write Action Single Item Batches	The number of batches sent through the workflow destined for a remote health service that have exactly one item in them.
Bind Write Action Zero Item Batches	The number of batches sent through the workflow destined for a remote health service with zero items in them (NULL Sets).
Incoming Management Data Rate	The rate at which management data is received by the health service.
Item Incoming Rate	The rate at which items are being received by the health service.
Max Send Queue Size	The maximum size of the send queue.
Send Queue % Used	Used space percentage of the send queue. One of the most important counters for a health service, as an increase in % used shows that items cannot be processed quickly enough, or there is a performance issue in flushing the queue to a management server, gateway server, or database. An increase could also indicate an agent problem with items that are stuck and require manual flushing. A warning alert is generated at 50% full and a critical alert at 60% full.
Send Queue Ack Timeout Rate (all send attempts)	The rate of items scheduled to re-send because they have not been encouraged and marked as not requiring guaranteed delivery.
Send Queue Incoming Acknowledgement Rate	The rate of incoming acknowledgements for items sent with guaranteed delivery.
Send Queue Insertion Rate	The number of items inserted into the queue.
Send Queue Insertion Rate (Guaranteed Delivery)	The number of items marked as guaranteed delivery inserted into the queue.
Send Queue Insertion Rate (Non-guaranteed Delivery)	The number of items marked as non-guaranteed delivery inserted into the queue.
Send Queue Item Expiration Rate	The rate at which items are being purged from the queue because they have not been sent within the queue expiration time.
Send Queue Items	The number of items in the send queue.

TABLE B.2 Continued

Counter*	Description
Send Queue Send Rate	The number of items sent from the queue.
Send Queue Send Rate (Guaranteed Delivery)	The number of items sent which are marked for guaranteed delivery. This only records items sent; it does not account for whether the items are acknowledged.
Send Queue Send Rate (Non-guaranteed Delivery)	The number of items sent which are not marked for guaranteed delivery.
Send Queue Size	The size of the send queue in bytes, not including any journaled data.

**There will be an instance of each of these per management group.*

Counters Maintained by the Management Server

In addition to the counters referenced in Tables B.1 and B.2, all management servers maintain performance counters for a number of items.

Here are the counters maintained on each management server:

- **OpsMgr SDK Service** (see Table B.3)
- **OpsMgr DB Write Action Caches** (see Table B.4)
- **OpsMgr DB Write Action Modules** (see Table B.5)
- **OpsMgr DW Synchronization Module** (see Table B.6)
- **OpsMgr DW Writer Module** (see Table B.7)
- **OpsMgr WF 4.0 Module** (see Table B.8)
- **SC Mgmt Config Delta Synchronization** (see Table B.9)
- **SC Mgmt Config Dirty Notification** (see Table B.10)
- **SC Mgmt Config Request** (see Table B.11)
- **SC Mgmt Config Request Queue** (see Table B.12)
- **SC Mgmt Config Snapshot Synchronization** (see Table B.13)
- **SC Mgmt Config Thread Count** (see Table B.14)

TABLE B.3 OpsMgr SDK Service counters

Counter*	Description
Client Connections	Number of current clients connected to the SDK Service

Counter*	Description
Client Connections Using Cache	Number of current clients connected to the SDK Service that are using the cache
Pending Client Type Cache Refresh Notifications	Number of currently executing type cache refresh threads in the SDK Service

**The SDK Service is also known as the System Center Data Access Service or DAS.*

TABLE B.4 OpsMgr DB Write Action caches

Counter*	Description
Cache Hit Ratio	Hit ratio for the cache
Cache Size	Number of entries in the cache

**These are collected for the managedentitycache and performancedatasourcecache instances.*

TABLE B.5 OpsMgr DB Write Action modules

Counter*	Description
Avg. Batch Size	Number of entries processed by the module on average
Avg. Processing Time	Amount of time it takes to process an incoming batch on average

**These are collected for a number of instances:*

- *alertwritemodule*
- *discoverywritemodule*
- *eventwritemodule*
- *performancesignaturewritemodule*
- *performancewritemodule*
- *sqlobwritemodule*
- *statechangewritemodule*

TABLE B.6 OpsMgr DW Synchronization module

Counter*	Description
Avg. Batch Processing Time, ms	Average batch processing time in ms
Avg. Batch Size	Average batch size
Batch Age, sec	Batch age in seconds
Batch Size	Batch size

TABLE B.6 Continued

Counter*	Description
Batches/sec	Batches per second
Data Items/sec	Data items per second
Errors/sec	Errors per second
Total Error Count	Total error count

**These are collected for a number of instances:*

- *config*
- *domainsnapshot*
- *healthserviceoutage*
- *maintenancemode*
- *managedentity*
- *relationship*
- *typemanagedentity*

TABLE B.7 OpsMgr DW Writer module

Counter*	Description
Avg. Batch Processing Time, ms	Average batch processing time in ms
Avg. Batch Size	Average batch size
Batches/sec	Batches per second
Data Items/sec	Data items per second
Dropped Batch Count	Dropped batch count
Dropped Data Item Count	Dropped data item count
Errors/sec	Errors per second
Total Error Count	Total error count

**These are collected for the alert, performance, state, and system.event.linkeddata instances.*

TABLE B.8 OpsMgr WF 4.0 module

Counter	Description
Active Workflows	Active workflows
Avg. Queue Wait Time, ms	Average queue wait time in ms
Workflows Queued	Number of workflows queued

TABLE B.9 SC Mgmt Config Delta synchronization

Counter*	Description
Avg. Batch Read Time, sec	Average data batch read time
Avg. Batch Write Time, sec	Average data batch write time

**These display statistics of delta data synchronization work items in the System Center Management Configuration service.*

TABLE B.10 SC Mgmt Config dirty notification

Counter*	Description
Avg. Dirty Notifications/sec	Average rate of dirty notifications per second
Dirty Notification Batch Size	Number of agents notified as dirty in the last batch

**These display statistics marked as dirty by the System Center Management Configuration service*

TABLE B.11 SC Mgmt Config request

Counter*	Description
Config Request - Avg. Time sec	Average processing time for configuration requests coming from agents
Config Request, Formatter - Avg. Time sec	Average processing time for formatter logic in configuration requests coming from agents
Config Request, Store - Avg. Time sec.	Average processing time for Configuration Store requests in configuration requests coming from agents
Config Requests - Avg. Processed/sec	Average rate of configuration requests processed per second
Config Requests - Failed/sec	Average rate of configuration requests failed per second
Config Requests - Failed Total	The number of configuration requests failed since service start
Management Pack Request - Avg. Time sec	Average processing time for management pack requests coming from agents
Management Pack Requests - Avg. Processed/sec	Average rate of management pack requests processed per second
Management Pack Requests - Failed/sec	Average rate of management pack requests failed per second
Management Pack Requests - Failed Total	The number of management pack requests failed since service start
Requests - Avg. Processed/sec	Average rate of requests processed per second

B

TABLE B.11 Continued

Counter*	Description
Requests - Failed/sec	Average rate of requests failed per second
Requests - Failed Total	The number of requests failed since service start

**These display statistics of requests to the System Center Management Configuration service*

TABLE B.12 SC Mgmt Config request queue

Counter*	Description
Config Request - Avg. Queue Wait Time/sec	Average time passed since configuration request was queued until it was served
Config Request - Queue Length	Queue length of configuration requests
Config Requests - Avg. Enqueued/sec	Average rate of configuration requests enqueued per second
Config Requests - Avg. Re-Enqueued/sec	Average rate of configuration requests re-enqueued per second
Management Pack Request - Avg. Queue Wait Time/sec.	Average time passed since management pack request was queued until it was served
Management Pack Request - Queue Length	Queue length of management pack requests
Management Pack Requests - Avg. Enqueued/sec	Average rate of management pack requests enqueued per second
Request - Queue Length	Queue length of all requests
Requests - Avg. Enqueued/sec	Average rate of requests enqueued per second

**These also display statistics of requests to the System Center Management Configuration service.*

TABLE B.13 SC Mgmt Config thread count

Counter*	Description
Avg. Batch Read Time, sec	Average data batch read time
Avg. Batch Write Time, sec	Average data batch write time

**This group of counters displays statistics of snapshot data synchronization work items in the System Center Management Configuration service.*

TABLE B.14 SC Mgmt Config snapshot synchronization

Counter*	Description
Agent Requests/Response Threads	Average rate of agent requests served by a single response thread
Maintenance Threads	The number of maintenance threads
Response Threads	The number of response threads serving configuration or management pack requests
Total Threads	The total number of active threads

**These counters display thread statistics of the System Center Management Configuration service.*

Counters Maintained by the OpsMgr Connector

The OpsMgr connector is located on management servers, database servers, and Web console servers. The connector is an interface to the OpsMgr System Center Data Access Service that allows applications to communicate synchronously with the management server pool. Counters used by the OpsMgr connector are listed in Table B.15.

TABLE B.15 OpsMgr connector counters

Counter	Description
Bytes Decrypted	The number of bytes decrypted by the connector per second. This may be more or less than the number of data bytes received by the connector due to compression.
Bytes Encrypted	The number of bytes encrypted by the connector per second. This may be more or less than the number of data bytes submitted for transmission due to compression.
Bytes Received	The total number of network bytes received by the OpsMgr connector per second. This may be more or less than the number of data bytes received due to compression and encryption.
Bytes Transmitted	The total number of network bytes that have been transmitted by the OpsMgr connector per second. This may be more or less than the number of data bytes submitted for transmission due to compression and encryption.
Data Bytes Received	The number of application data bytes received by the connector per second.
Data Bytes Transmitted	The number of application data bytes transmitted by the connector per second.
Fragmented Compression Packets	The number of compression packets by the connector that had to be reassembled per second. This can be caused by a number of factors including packet size, MTU of the network interface, quantity of traffic on the network, and/or the amount of load on the connector. Packet re-assembly can hurt performance and the ability of the server to scale.

TABLE B.15 Continued

Counter	Description
Fragmented Data Packets	The number of data packets received by the connector that had to be reassembled per second. This can be caused by a number of factors including the packet size, MTU of the network interface, quantity of traffic on the network, and/or the amount of load on the connector. Packet re-assembly can hurt performance and the ability of the server to scale.
Fragmented Encryption Packets	The number of encrypted packets received by the connector that had to be reassembled per second. This can be caused by a number of factors including packet size, MTU of the network interface, quantity of traffic on the network, the encryption algorithm used, and/or the amount of load on the connector. Packet re-assembly can hurt performance and the ability of the server to scale.
Fragmented Session Packets	The number of session packets received by the connector that had to be reassembled per second. This can be caused by a number of factors including packet size, the MTU of the network interface, quantity of traffic on the network, and/or the amount of load on the connector. Packet re-assembly can hurt performance and the ability of the server to scale.
Fragmented SSPI Packets	The number of SSPI negotiation packets received by the connector that had to be reassembled per second. This can be caused by a number of factors including packet size, MTU of the network interface, quantity of traffic on the network, and/or the amount of load on the connector. Packet re-assembly can hurt performance and the ability of the server to scale.
I/O Errors	The number of I/O errors encountered by the connector per second.
I/O Operations Timed Out	The number of I/O operations on the connector that timed out due to inactivity per second.
Open Connections	The number of TCP/IP connections currently open in the connector.
Server Listen Queue Length	The number of outstanding listen requests which are queued. If this drops to zero, the connector will not be able to accept incoming connections.

Counters Maintained by the ACS Collector

The ACS collector has two specific performance objects:

- **ACS Collector** (see Table B.16)
- **ACS Collector Client** (see Table B.17)

TABLE B.16 ACS collector counters

Counter	Description
Connected Clients	Number of clients currently connected.
Database Queue % Full	The ratio of the number of events currently in the database loader queue divided by the size of the database loader queue, expressed as a percentage.
Database Queue Backoff Threshold in %	The collector will not allow new connections while the database queue length is greater than this threshold.
Database Queue Disconnect Threshold in %	The collector will disconnect existing connections while the database queue length is greater than this threshold.
Database Queue Length	The number of events currently in the database loader queue.
DB Loader Event Inserts/sec	The number of records per second inserted into the dtEvent table.
DB Loaded Principal Inserts/sec	The number of records per second inserted into the dtPrincipal table.
DB Loader String Inserts/sec	The number of records per second inserted into the dtString table.
DB Principal Cache Hit %	The percentage of all principal handling requests that were handled by the string cache, avoiding a principal insert or lookup in the database.
DB Request Queue Length	The number of requests from the collector currently waiting to be serviced by the database. These requests are used during forwarder handshake and database maintenance and are not part of normal event handling.
DB String Cache Hit %	The percentage of all string handling requests that were handled by the string cache, avoiding a string insert or lookup in the database.
Event time in collector in milliseconds	The current time between event arrival at the collector and insertion in the database queues in milliseconds.
Incoming Events/sec	The total number of events per second arriving at the collector from all connected forwarders.
Interface Audit Insertions/sec	Interface Audit Insertions/sec.
Interface Queue Length	Length of internal queue to subscriber interface.
Registered Queries	Number of queries currently registered.

TABLE B.17 ACS collector client

Counter*	**Description**
Average time between event generation and collection in milliseconds	The average time between event generation time (creation timestamp) and collection time in milliseconds.
Incoming Audit Size	The total size of events per second arriving at the collector from a specific forwarder.
Incoming Audits/sec	The total number of events per second arriving at the collector from a specific forwarder.

**Instances of these appear for all forwarders.*

APPENDIX C
Registry Settings

IN THIS CHAPTER

- About the Registry
- Operations Manager-Related Registry Keys

The Windows registry is a hierarchical "database" that stores information about the operating system and applications on the local computer. The registry is organized in a tree format and can be viewed by using the registry editor program, regedit.exe.

About the Registry

Folders seen in the regedit utility represent keys. These folders are displayed in the left side or Navigation area in the registry editor window. There are five folders, or predefined keys:

- **HKEY_CURRENT USER (HKCU):** Contains the root of configuration information for the currently logged-on user. This information is referred to as a user's *profile*.
- **HKEY_USERS (HKU):** Contains the root of all user profiles on the computer. The `HKEY_CURRENT_USER` folder is actually a subkey of `HKEY_USERS`.
- **HKEY_LOCAL_MACHINE (HKLM):** Contains configuration information specific to the computer. This information can be used by any user.
- **HKEY_CLASSES_ROOT (HKCR):** A subset of information stored in `HKEY_LOCAL_MACHINE`. Information stored here ensures the correct program starts when you open a file using the Windows Explorer. It contains the linking between executable programs and the program extension used by data files on the system.
- **HKEY_CURRENT_CONFIG (HKCC):** Contains configuration data for the current hardware profile. The `HKCC\SYSTEM` subkey contains a subset of the information (the `CurrentControlSet`) that is a subkey of `HKEY_LOCAL_MACHINE\SYSTEM`.

Every computer has physical files stored on disk that hold the data you view using regedit. The physical files used by the registry are called *hives* and are loaded by Windows at system startup. The hive files are stored in the *%SystemRoot%*\system32\config folder of your system. Table C.1 shows the relationship between the hive files and their corresponding registry keys.

TABLE C.1 Hive files and corresponding registry keys

Hive File Name	Registry Key
Default	`HKEY_USERS\Default`
SAM	`HKEY_LOCAL_MACHINE\SAM`
Security	`HKEY_LOCAL_MACHINE\Security`
Software	`HKEY_LOCAL _MACHINE\Software`
System	`HKEY_LOCAL_MACHINE\System`

The hive for the current logged on user profile, `HKEY_CURRENT_USER`, is the ntuser.dat file stored within *%SystemDrive%*\documents and settings*<UserName>*. (The location of the file may vary based on the version of the Windows operating system installed on your computer.) Every time a new user logs on to a computer, a new hive is created for that user with a separate file for the user profile. This is called the *user profile hive*. A user's hive contains specific registry information pertaining to the user's application settings, desktop, environment, network connections, and printers. User profile hives are stored under the `HKEY_USERS` key.

Registry files have two formats: standard and latest:

- Standard format was used with Windows 2000 and is also supported by later versions of Windows for backward compatibility.
- Latest format is supported with all operating systems beginning with Windows XP. For versions of Windows supporting the latest format, these hives still use the standard format:
  - `HKEY_CURRENT_USER`
  - `HKEY_LOCAL_MACHINE\SAM`
  - `HKEY_LOCAL_MACHINE\Security`
  - `HKEY_USERS\.DEFAULT`

  All other hives use the latest format.

Most of the supporting files for the hives are in the *%Systemroot%*\system32\config folder and are updated each time a user logs on. The file name extensions in these folders, or in some cases the lack of an extension, indicate the type of data they contain. Table C.2 lists these extensions along with a description of the data in the file.

TABLE C.2 Description of file extensions used by hives

Extension	Description
None	A complete copy of the hive data.
.alt	A backup copy of the `HKEY\LOCAL\MACHINE\System` hive. Only the System key has an .alt file.
.log	A transaction log of changes to the keys and value entries in the hive.
.sav	A backup copy of a hive.

Incorrectly modifying the registry may render your system unusable, so you should always make a backup of the registry or its subkeys prior to making changes, as results may be unpredictable.

CAUTION: CHANGING DEFAULT SETTINGS

Exercise caution when changing the settings described in this appendix as some are not designed to be directly modified. Changing the registry may make your system unusable. In some cases, changes could be unsupported by Microsoft.

Operations Manager-Related Registry Keys

Keys located by System Center 2012 Operations Manager are located in quite a few places in both the software and system areas of the registry. The presence and content of these keys will vary based on the computer's role in the management group. Some of these areas have changed since OpsMgr 2007; others have not. The information is located in the following areas:

- `HKLM\Software\Microsoft\Microsoft Operations Manager\3.0`
- `HKLM\Software\Microsoft\System Center Operations Manager\12`
- `HKLM\System\CurrentControlSet\Services\`
- `HKLM\Software\ODBC`
- `HKLM\Software\Policies\Microsoft\`
- `HKCU\Software\Microsoft\Microsoft Operations Manager\3.0\`
- `HKLM\Software\Microsoft\SystemCertificates\Operations Manager`

These registry keys are discussed in the following sections of this appendix.

TIP: VALUES "0" AND "1" IN THE REGISTRY

Unless otherwise indicated, for all registry values, a setting of "0" designates no (or off) and a setting of "1" is yes (or on).

Agent Settings

In Operations Manager 2012, managed computers can be agent-managed or agentless managed. There are no registry settings for agentless managed systems on the management server or the agentless system; the data is stored in the BaseManagedEntity table in the operational database. Table C.3 lists registry settings for managed agents. Remember that OpsMgr servers are also agents, so you will find these registry keys on every agent-managed server including management servers and the root management server emulator.

TABLE C.3 Settings for a managed agent

Key Name	Name	Type	Data	Description
HKLM\Software\Microsoft\Microsoft Operations Manager\3.0\Agent Management Groups\<*ManagementGroup Name*>	AcceptIncoming Connections	REG_DWORD	0x0	Indicates if incoming connections are accepted. 0 unless agent is configured as a proxy; otherwise 1.
	IsServer	REG_DWORD	0x0	Indicates if system is management server. 0 on agent.
	RequestCompression	REG_DWORD	0x1	Indicates if compression is required. Default=1.
	RequireAuthentication	REG_DWORD	0x1	Indicates if authentication is required.
	RequireEncryption	REG_DWORD	0x1	Indicates if encryption is required.
	RequireValidation	REG_DWORD	0x1	Indicates if validation is required.

Key Name	Name	Type	Data	Description
	UseActiveDirectory	REG_DWORD	0x0	Indicates if Active Directory is used for agent assignment. Default=0.
HKLM\Software\Microsoft\Microsoft Operations Manager\3.0\Agent Management Groups\<*Management GroupName*>\Parent Health Services\0	AuthenticationName	REG_SZ	Management server name	Fully qualified name of management server (example: hannibal.odyssey.com).
	CanEstablishConnectionTo	REG_DWORD	0x1	
	MaxSendBytesPerSecond	REG_DWORD	0xf4240 (10000000)	Upper limit of the number of bytes sent per second (1,000,000 bytes by default from the agent).
	NetworkName	REG_SZ	Management server name	Fully qualified name of management server (example: hannibal.odyssey.com).
	NetworkTimeoutMilliseconds	REG_DWORD	0x ffffffff (4294967295)	Networking timeout, in milliseconds.
	Port	REG_DWORD	0x165b (5723)	Port used by agents to communicate with management server (5723 by default).
	Protocol	REG_SZ	tcp	

TABLE C.3

Key Name	Name	Type	Data	Description
	RetryAttempts	REG_DWORD	3	Number of retry attempts.
	RetryDelayMs	REG_DWORD	0x3e8 (1000)	Amount of time to retry delay (in milliseconds).
HKLM\Software\Microsoft\System Center Operations Manager\12\APMAgent	CollectorInstallPath	REG_SZ	Typically *%ProgramFiles%*\System Center Operations Manager\Agent\APMDOTNETCollector\	Installation path of APM .NET collector.
	InstallPath of Agent	REG_SZ	Typically *%ProgramFiles%*\System Center Operations Manager\Agent\V7.0.8560.0\ for RTM; Service Pack 1 would be \v7.0.9538.0\	Software installation path.
	PersistenceData	REG_BINARY		
HKLM\Software\Microsoft\System Center Operations Manager\12\Setup\Agent	InstallDirectory	REG_SZ	*%ProgramFiles%*\System Center Operations Manager\Agent\	Agent installation directory.

Key Name	Name	Type	Data	Description
HKLM\SYSTEM\CurrentControlSet\Services\HealthService\Parameters\Management Groups\<*ManagementGroup Name*>\	maximumQueueSizeKb	REG_DWORD	X3c00 (15360)	Agent queue size; can be changed on a per-agent basis.
HKLM\System\CurrentControlSet\Services\HealthService\Parameters\ConnectorManager	EnableADIntegration	REG_DWORD		Indicates status of Active Directory Integration. Value of 0 indicates it is turned off; value of 1 indicates it is turned on. The value can be changed on an agent, but do not manipulate this registry key on a management server.

Management Server Settings

An Operations Manager management group can have multiple management servers. Table C.4 include settings for these servers.

TABLE C.4 Management server settings

Key Name	Name	Type	Data	Description
HKLM\Software\Microsoft\Microsoft Operations Manager\3.0\Config Service	Config Service State	REG_SZ	C:\Program Files\System Center 2012\Operations Manager\Server\Config Service State	Current installed version.
HKLM\Software\Microsoft\Microsoft Operations Manager\3.0\Machine Settings	DefaultSDKServiceMachine	REG_SZ	Management server name	Fully qualified name of system running SDK, also known as the Data Access Service (example: Helios.odyssey.com).
HKLM\Software\Microsoft\Microsoft Operations Manager\3.0\Modules\Global\	AsyncProcessLimit	REG_DWORD		The number of concurrent command notifications. Default is 5 simultaneous command processes. To change the default, add this key.
HKLM\Software\Microsoft\Microsoft Operations Manager\3.0\Modules\Global\PowerShell	QueueMinutes	REG_DWORD	0x77 (119)	Defines how many minutes before a PowerShell script expires from the queue.
HKLM\Software\Microsoft\Microsoft Operations Manager\3.0\SDK Service	SDK Service State	REG_SZ	C:\Program Files\System Center 2012\Operations Manager\Server\SDK Service State\	
	Should Manage Memory	REG_SZ	false	
HKLM\Software\Microsoft\Microsoft Operations Manager\3.0\Server Management Groups<*ManagementGroup Name*>	Accept Incoming Connections	REG_DWORD	0x1	Indicates if incoming connections are accepted.

Key Name	Name	Type	Data	Description
	IsServer	REG_DWORD	0x1	0x1 indicates a management server.
	Port	REG_DWORD	0x165b (5723)	Port number used (5723 by default).
	RequestCompression	REG_DWORD	0x1	Indicates if compression is required.
	RequireAuthentication	REG_DWORD	0x1	Indicates if authentication is required.
	RequireEncryption	REG_DWORD	0x1	Indicates if encryption is required.
	RequireValidation	REG_DWORD	0x1	Indicates if validation is required.
	UseActiveDirectory	REG_DWORD	0x0	Indicates whether Active Directory Integration is implemented.
HKLM\Software\Microsoft\Microsoft Operations Manager\3.0\Setup	CurrentVersion	REG_SZ	7.0.8560.0 for RTM; Service Pack 1 would be 7.09538.0	Current installed version.
	DatabaseName	REG_SZ	OperationsManager	Name of operational database.
	Database ServerName	REG_SZ	example: thundercloud\sql_om	SQL Server name and instance for operational database.
	DataWarehouse DBName	REG_SZ	OperationsManagerDW	Name of data warehouse database.
	DataWarehouse DBServerName	REG_SZ	Example:whirlwind\sql_dw	SQL Server name and instance for data warehouse database.
	InstallDirectory	REG_SZ	Example: C:\Program Files\System Center\Operations Manager\Server	Installation folder.

TABLE C.4 Continued

Key Name	Name	Type	Data	Description
	InstalledOn	REG_SZ	Example: 10/16/2012-14:23:08	Installation data and time.
	ManagerServerPort	REG_SZ	5723	Port number used (5723 by default).
	Product	REG_SZ	System Center Operations Manager 2012 Server	Name of installed feature
	ServerVersion	REG_SZ	7.0.8560.0 for RTM, Service Pack 1 would be 7.0.9538.0	Software version of installed feature.
	UIVersion	REG_SZ	7.0.8560.0 for RTM, Service Pack 1 would be 7.0.9538.0	Software version of Operations console (this setting appears on any machine with an installed Operations console).

Operations Database Server Settings

There are no registry settings specific to the Operations Database server itself. Each management server has a registry entry pointing to the database server, at `HKLM\Software\Microsoft\Microsoft Operations Manager\3.0\Setup\DatabaseServerName`. If you move the operational database to another server, you will need to modify this value on each management server. Use the `ComputerName\Instance` format if using a named instance of SQL Server. For information on moving the operational database, see Chapter 12, "Backup and Recovery."

Data Warehouse Server Settings

There are no registry settings specific to the Data Warehouse server itself, also known as the Reporting Data Warehouse server. This is a change from OpsMgr 2007.

Each management server has a registry entry pointing to the database server, at `HKLM\Software\Microsoft\Microsoft Operations Manager\3.0\Setup\DataWarehouseDBServerName`. If you move the data warehouse database to another server, you will need to modify this value on each management server. Use the `ComputerName\Instance` format if using a named instance of SQL Server. Likewise, the Report Server has a registry setting specific to the data warehouse; if the data warehouse is moved, you will need to modify that value, specified in the next section. For information on moving the data warehouse database, see Chapter 12.

Report Server Settings

The Report Server feature is part of the SQL Server Reporting Services (SSRS) installation and is customized during Operations Manager setup. Operations Manager requires its own report server because it changes the security settings. This server feature contains the ReportServer and ReportServerTempDB databases. Table C.5 lists registry settings unique to this server.

TABLE C.5 Report server settings

Key Name	Name	Type	Data	Description
HKLM\Software\Microsoft\Microsoft Operations Manager\3.0\Reporting	DefaultSDKServiceMachine	REG_SZ	Example: Helios.odyssey.com	Location of the management server specified when installing reporting
	DWDBInstance	REG_SZ	Example: Whirlwind\SQL_DW	Location of data warehouse database (server\instance format)
	DWDBName	REG_SZ	OperationsManagerDW (default)	Name of datawarehouse database
	ReportingServerUrl	REG_SZ	Example: http://TEMPEST:80/ReportServer	URL and port of reporting server
	ReportRootFolderName	REG_SZ	/	Subfolder under ReportingServerUrl that is used as the Report root Folder
	SRSInstance	REG_SZ	Example: TEMPEST	Name of database server running SSRS
	Usingx86SQLOnx64	REG_SZ		Whether SQL Server is running 32-bit on a 64-bit machine

Audit Collection Services (ACS) Settings

Table C.6 includes the parameters stored in the registry for the ACS server, including the size of the ACS collector queue. Table C.7 lists the registry settings for the ACS forwarder.

There are no ACS-specific registry settings for the server hosting the ACS database (unless it is on the ACS server itself); the ODBC settings on the ACS server identify the database server and the name of the database.

TABLE C.6 Audit Collection Services - Server

Key Name	Name	Type	Data	Description
HKLM\System\CurrentControlSet\Services\AdtServer	DependOnService	REG_MULTI_SZ	Eventlog	
	Description	REG_SZ	Service for receiving audit events over the network and writing them to a database	
	DisplayName	REG_SZ	Operations Manager Audit Collection Service	
	ErrorControl	REG_DWORD	0x1	If the driver fails, produce warning but let startup continue.
	ImagePath	REG_EXPAND_SZ	*%SystemRoot%*\system32\Security\AdtServer\AdtServer.exe	Location of executable. Example: C:\WINDOWS\system32\Security\AdtServer\AdtServer.exe.
	ObjectName	REG_SZ	Credentials service is using	NT AUTHORITY\NetworkService.
	Start	REG_DWORD	0x2	When in the boot sequence the service should start. 0x2 indicates Autoload, meaning the service is always loaded and run.
	Type	REG_SZ	0x10	Defines the type of service or driver. 0x10 indicates a Win32 service that should be run as a stand-alone process.

C

Key Name	Name	Type	Data	Description
HKLM\System\CurrentControlSet\Services\AdtServer\Parameters	AdtAgentPort	REG_DWORD	0xcac5 (51909)	Port used by AdtAgent.
	BackOffThreshold	REG_DWORD	0x4b (75)	The percentage full the ACS collector queue can become before it denies new connections from the ACS forwarders.
	CertHash	REG_BINARY		
	ConfigFile	REG_SZ	*%SystemRoot%*\system32\Security\AdtServer\AcsConfig.xml	Configuration file Example: C:\WINDOWS\system32\Security\AdtServer\AcsConfig.xml.
	DBQueueQuery	REG_SZ	SELECT * FROM AdtsEvent WHERE NOT (HeaderUser='SYSTEM' OR Headeruser='LOCAL SERVICE' OR Headeruser='NETWORK SERVICE')	
	DefaultAssetValue	REG_DWORD	0xffffffff	
	DefaultGroup	REG_SZ	Default	
	DisconnectThreshold	REG_DWORD	0x5a (90)	The percentage full the ACS collector queue becomes before the ACS collector begins disconnecting ACS forwarders. 90% default.
	EventRetentionPeriod	REG_DWORD	0x150 (336)	Retention period, 336 days by default.

Key Name	Name	Type	Data	Description
	EventSchema	REG_DWORD	*%SystemRoot%*\system32\Security\AdtServer\EventSchema.xml	Location of Event Schema XML file.
	Heart Beat Interval	Reg_DWORD		Number of seconds since last communication before AdtServer increments the failed heartbeat count for an agent. Value 60 by default. Add this value to change from default of 60 seconds, valid values are from 0-864000.
	MaximumQueueLength	REG_DWORD	0x40000 (262144)	The maximum number of events that can queue in memory while waiting for the database (262144 by default). To change the default, this registry value must be created manually.
	ODBCConnection	REG_SZ	OpsMgrAC	Name of ODBC connection for Audit Collector database.
	ScriptFilePath	REG_SZ	*%SystemRoot%*\System32\Security\AdtServer\	Path to ACS script files.
HKLM\Software\ODBC\ODBC.INI\ODBC Data Sources	OpsMgrAC	REG_SZ	SQL Server	Type of ODBC data source used for Audit Collection database.
HKLM\Software\ODBC\ODBC.INI\OpsMgrAC	Database	REG_SZ	OperationsManagerAC	Name of Audit Collection Database, used with ODBC.
	Description	REG_SZ	Audit Collection Services	Database Description for ODBC.

C

TABLE C.6 Continued

Key Name	Name	Type	Data	Description
	Driver	REG_SZ	*%SystemRoot%*/System32\SQLSRV32.dll	Location of ODBC driver.
	Language	REG_SZ	Example: us_english	
	LastUser	REG_SZ	Exampl: ACS_SQL_login	
	Server	REG_SZ	Example: fireball.itchica.local	NetBIOS name of ACS database server.
	Trusted_Connection	REG_SZ	No	If a trusted connection is used.

TABLE C.7 Audit Collection Services - Forwarder

Key Name	Name	Type	Data	Description
HKLM\Software\Policies\Microsoft\AdtAgent\Parameters\	AdtServers	REG_MULTI_SZ	Example: hannibal.odyssey.com	List of collectors that the forwarder should attempt to connect to. Format: <*collector fqdn*>[:<*port*>[,<*priority*>[,<*asset value*>]]].
	EventLogLogging Level	REG_DWORD	0x2	The level of logging that the forwarder performs when logging events to the Application log. 0=errors 1=warnings+errors 2=informational+warnings+errors.

Key Name	Name	Type	Data	Description
	LocalConfig	REG_DWORD	0x1	If present and value is not 0, the forwarder does not use SRV resource records for locating collectors.
	NoCache	REG_DWORD	0x1	If present and value is not 0, the forwarder does not cache the last connector it used. Also does not use cache to preferentially connect to the collector.
	TraceFlags	REG_DWORD	x80084 (524420)	Create this manually to temporarily enable detailed logging on the forwarder. The log will be created at *%SystemRoot%*/Temp/AdtAgent.log.

Operations Manager Event Log Settings

Every monitored system has an Operations Manager Event log. Table C.8 documents the related registry settings.

TABLE C.8 Operations Manager event log

Key Name	Name	Type	Data	Description
HKLM\System\CurrentControlSet\Services\Eventlog\Operations Manager\	AutoBackupLogFiles	REG_DWORD	0x0	
	CustomSD	REG_SZ	O:BAG:SYD:(D;;0xf0007;;;AN)(D;;0xf0007;;;BG)(A;;0xf0007;;;SY)(A;;0x7;;;BA)(A;;0x7;;;SO)(A;;0x3;;;IU)(A;;0x3;;;SU)(A;;0x3;;;S-1-5-3)	
	MaxSize	REG_DWORD	0xf00000 (15728640)	
	RestrictGuestAccess	REG_DWORD	0x1	
	Retention	REG_DWORD	0x0	
	Sources	REG_MULTI_SZ	AdtServer Operations Manager Health Service Modules OpsMgr Connector HealthService Health Service Modules Ex AdtAgent OpsMgr Config Service OpsMgr Root Connector OpsMgr SDK Service OpsMgr SDK Client DataAccessLayer	Sources that write to the OpsMgr Event log. Each of these sources has a subkey located under `HKLM\System\CurrentControlSet\Services\Eventlog\Operations Manager\` with information specific to that data source. This includes the specific DLL(s) for the EventMessageFile.

Operations Manager Health Service

Settings for the Health Service are found on all systems other than those that are agentless managed. These settings are listed in Table C.9.

TABLE C.9 Health Service settings

Key Name	Name	Type	Data	Description
HKLM\System\CurrentControlSet\Services\HealthService\Parameters	Error Reports Enabled	REG_DWORD	0x0	
	Persistence Cache Maximum	REG_DWORD	Management Server:0x400006400 Agent:0x1900	Maximum cache size. Management Server:262144 decimal. Agent:6400.
	Persistence Checkpoint Depth Maximum	REG_DWORD	Management Server:0x1400000 Agent: 0xa00000	Management Server:20971520 decimal. Agent: 10485760 decimal.
	Persistence Initial Database Page Count	REG_DWORD	Management Server:0x9600 Agent:0x3200	Management Server:38400 decimal. Agent:12800.
	Persistence Maximum Sessions	REG_DWORD	Management Server:0x20 Agent:0x10	Management Server:32 decimal. Agent: 16 decimal
	Persistence Page Hint Cache Size	RE_DWORD	Management Server:0x40000 Agent:0x8000	Management Server:262144 decimal. Agent: 32768 decimal.
	Persistence Version Store Maximum	REG_DWORD	Management Server:0x2000 Agent:0x789	Management Server: 131072 decimal Agent:1920 decimal.
	Queue Error Reports	REG_DWORD	0x1	0 or 1.

C

TABLE C.9 Continued

Key Name	Name	Type	Data	Description
	Runtime CLR Version	REG_SZ	v4.0.30319	Found on Server only.
	Runtime Use Workstation GC	REG_DWORD	Management Server: 0x0 Agent: 0x1 (Agent)	0 or 1.
	Service Sizing	REG_DWORD	Management Server: 0x1 Agent: 0x0	0 or 1.
	State Directory	REG_SZ	*%ProgramFiles%*\System Center Operations Manager 2012\<*Server|Agent*>\Health Service State	
	UseBackground Priority	REG_DWORD	0x0	
HKLM\System \CurrentControlSet\Services\HealthService\Parameters\ConnectorManager\Approved AD Management groups				No values by default.
HKLM\System \CurrentControlSet\Services\HealthService\Parameters\Management Groups<*ManagementGroup Name*>	IsSourcedfromAD	REG_DWORD	0x1	If value is 1, indicates the agent is AD-integrated and gathers settings from the Service Connection Point. This is only present if the agent is AD-integrated.
	MaximumQueueSizeKb	REG_DWORD	0x19000	102400 decimal Agent maximum queue size.

Key Name	Name	Type	Data	Description
HKLM\System \ CurrentControlSet\ Services\HealthService\ Parameters\Management Groups<*ManagementGroup Name*>\AllowedSSIDs	RestrictSSIDs	REG_DWORD	0x0	
HKLM\System\ CurrentControlSet\Services\ HealthService\Parameters\ SecureStorageManager	(Default)	REG_BINARY	Private/private key pair	

C

Current Logged-on User

Operations console settings for the current logged-on user are listed in Table C.10. Most console settings are locally stored under `HKCU\Software\Microsoft\Microsoft Operations Manager\3.0\` and apply only to the user on that computer.

TABLE C.10 Console settings for the logged-on user

Key Name	Name	Type	Data	Description
HKCU\Software\Microsoft\Microsoft Operations Manager\3.0\Console	Various			Operations console settings which only affect the console for that user on that computer, include: Connection history with the names of management groups the console has connected to. Show or Hide Views selections. Whether the console is in a window or full screen; if in a window the size and position of the window. What the last navigation pane the console was open to when it was closed.
HKCU\Software\Microsoft\Microsoft Operations Manager\3.0\Console\CacheParameters	PollingInterval	REG_DWORD	0x1	Controls how often the Operations console polls. The default value (normal interval) is 1, 0 turns off polling. 2 doubles interval, meaning polling occurs half as often. Maximum value is 10; any number larger is treated as 10. Add this key to the registry to lessen polling occurrence.
HKEY_CURRENT_USER\Software\Microsoft\Microsoft Operations Manager\3.0\Console\DiagramViewParameters	MaxNodesThreshold	REG_WORD	(none)	Create to change when popup message appears (**The requested view will contain at least 50 objects and may require substantial time to render. Do you wish to continue?**) when opening a diagram view with a large number of objects. This appears by default when a diagram has 50 objects, which may be low for organizations with large distributed applications and appropriately scaled hardware.
HKCU\Software\Microsoft\Microsoft Operations Manager\3.0\User Settings	SDKServiceMachine	REG_SZ	Management server name	Fully Qualified Domain name of management server. Example: helios.odyssey.com.

Certificate Information

You can find information regarding certificates used by Operations Manager at HKLM\Software\Microsoft\SystemCertificates\Operations Manager.

This is binary data, which varies on each system.

APPENDIX D

Reference URLs

IN THIS CHAPTER

- General Resources
- Microsoft's OpsMgr Resources
- Blogs
- OpsMgr Shell
- PowerShell Information
- Cross Platform
- System Center
- Public Forums

This appendix includes a number of reference URLs associated with System Center 2012 Operations Manager (OpsMgr). URLs do change. Although the authors have made every effort to verify the references here as working links, there is no guarantee they will remain current. Sometimes the Wayback Machine (http://www.archive.org/index.php) can rescue you from dead or broken links. This site is an Internet archive, and it will take you back to an archived version of a site—sometimes.

These links are also available "live" at Pearson's InformIT website with the online content for this book at http://www.informit.com/store/system-center-2012-operations-manager-unleashed-9780672335914, under the Downloads tab. Look for Appendix D, "Reference URLs."

General Resources

A number of websites provide excellent resources for OpsMgr, as follows:

- A nice overview of System Center 2012 Operations Manager is in the February 2012 issue of *TechNet Magazine* at http://technet.microsoft.com/en-us/magazine/hh825624.aspx.
- Gartner Group placed Operations Manager 2007 R2 in the Leader's or "Magic" quadrant for IT Event Correlation and Analysis in December 2010 (this quadrant was retired in 2011; you can get the 2010 report at http://www.idgconnect.com/view_abstract/7198/gartner-magic-quadrant-it-event-correlation-analysis). OpsMgr 2012's application performance monitoring (APM) feature is in the Challenger's quadrant for Application

Performance Monitoring discussed at http://www.gartner.com/technology/reprints.do?ct=120820&id=1-1BRNFO0&st=sg and http://innetworktech.com/wp-content/uploads/2012/08/2012-Magic-Quadrant-for-Application-Performance-Monitoring.pdf.

- CRN names System Center 2012 to its annual Products of the Year list. See http://www.crn.com/slide-shows/components-peripherals/240144534/the-2012-products-of-the-year.htm?pgno=9.
- OpsMgr 2012 removes the root management server (RMS) feature. The RMS emulator is used to provide backward compatibility and support for legacy management packs. Read about the RMS emulator at
  - http://blogs.catapultsystems.com/cfuller/archive/2012/01/11/what-does-the-root-management-server-emulator-rmse-actually-do-in-opsmgr-scom.aspx
  - http://scug.be/blogs/christopher/archive/2012/01/09/scom-2012-move-rms-emulator-role.aspx
  - http://blogs.technet.com/b/momteam/archive/2011/08/22/topology-changes-in-system-center-2012-operations-manager-overview.aspx
- Kevin Greene presents an overview of APM at http://kevingreeneitblog.blogspot.com/2012/03/scom-2012-configuring-application.html. For additional readings on this feature, check out the following:
  - **System Center .NET application alerts versus events:** http://blogs.technet.com/b/shawngibbs/archive/2012/04/13/system-center-net-application-alerts-vs-events.aspx
  - **Custom APM rules for granular alerting:** http://blogs.technet.com/b/momteam/archive/2012/01/23/custom-apm-rules-for-granular-alerting.aspx
  - **Working with alerts:** http://blogs.technet.com/b/momteam/archive/2011/08/23/application-monitoring-working-with-alerts.aspx
  - **MMS 2012 – Digital MMS:** The Microsoft Management Summit (MMS) 2012 had many interesting sessions, follow the "Application Management" track for APM sessions at http://www.mms-2012.com/digitalmms.
  - **Microsoft TechNet—Monitoring .NET Applications:** Available at http://technet.microsoft.com/library/hh212856.aspx.
  - **VIAcode blog on Application Monitoring:** VIAcode Consulting LLC worked on the AVIcode product prior to its acquisition by Microsoft. After the acquisition, most of the employees relocated to Microsoft, although some stayed with VIAcode to continue working with Microsoft as contractors and consultants. The blog is located at http://viacode.com/blog.
- Here's another one on APM—Daniel Muscetta of the Operations Manager engineering team blogs about APM data trends at http://blogs.technet.com/b/momteam/archive/2012/06/18/event-to-alert-ratio-reviewing-problems-and-understanding-trends-for-apm-data-in-opsmgr-2012.aspx.

- Want to understand targeting? Check the article by Brian Wren at http://blogs.technet.com/ati/archive/2007/05/14/targeting-rules-and-monitors.aspx. Although written in the OpsMgr 2007 timeframe, it remains applicable for OpsMgr 2012. Steve Rachui discusses targeting as well at http://technet.microsoft.com/en-us/magazine/2008.11.targeting.aspx?pr=blog.
- The ReSearch This! management pack troubleshooting tool is hosted by System Center Central. It provides a way to quickly research OpsMgr alerts. You can download the management pack at http://www.systemcentercentral.com/PackCatalog/PackCatalogDetails/tabid/145/IndexID/21716/Default.aspx.
- Visio stencils for Operations Manager 2012 are available at http://blogs.catapultsystems.com/lrayl/archive/2012/11/13/system-center-2012-operations-manager-2012-stencil.aspx and http://www.systemcentercentral.com/Downloads/DownloadsDetails/tabid/144/IndexID/96587/Default.aspx.
- For a whitepaper on auditing using ACS and optimizing that experience with Secure Vantage, see http://www.securevantage.com/security-auditing-with-microsoft-system-center-bridging-the-gap/.
- Secure Vantage offers resources as free community downloads, available at http://www.securevantage.com/download/.
- Maarten Goet (System Center Data Center and Cloud Management MVP) has several ACS "deep dive" articles at System Center Central. Written in the OpsMgr 2007 timeframe, they are still applicable:
  - http://www.systemcentercentral.com/BlogDetails/tabid/143/IndexID/13052/Default.aspx
  - http://systemcentercentral.com/BlogDetails/tabid/143/indexid/13112/Default.aspx
- You can find an ACS disk and database planning calculator at http://www.systemcentercentral.com/Downloads/DownloadsDetails/tabid/144/IndexID/7425/Default.aspx. The calculator is also available through Appendix E, "Available Online." Microsoft's ACS sizing calculator is at http://blogs.technet.com/b/momteam/archive/2008/07/02/audit-collection-acs-database-and-disk-sizing-calculator-for-opsmgr-2007.aspx.
- Eric Fitzgerald (an original Microsoft ACS Program Manager) documents and demystifies ACS event transformation at http://blogs.msdn.com/ericfitz/archive/2008/02/27/acs-event-transformation-demystified.aspx.
- For information on configuring ACS to use certificate-based authentication, a good place to start is Clive Eastwood's article at http://blogs.technet.com/cliveeastwood/archive/2007/05/11/how-to-configure-audit-collection-system-acs-to-use-certificate-based-authenication.aspx.
- http://blogs.technet.com/b/neharris/archive/2011/03/22/acs-forwarders-and-high-availability-part-1.aspx discusses ACS high availability.

- Satya Vel discusses how to edit company knowledge using Word 2010 at http://blogs.technet.com/b/momteam/archive/2012/10/10/how-to-get-knowledge-editing-to-work-in-operations-manager-2012-with-office-2010.aspx.
- When creating company knowledge, one of the required pieces of software is the Visual Studio 2005 Tools for Office Second Edition Runtime. This is available at http://www.microsoft.com/downloads/details.aspx?FamilyID=F5539A90-DC41-4792-8EF8-F4DE62FF1E81&displaylang=en. (Microsoft Word is also required.)
- http://contoso.se/blog/?p=831 discusses using multiple gateway servers for automatic agent failover.
- Here are some additional resources regarding gateway servers:
  - http://technet.microsoft.com/en-us/library/hh212823.aspx discusses gateway server concepts.
  - Satya Vel gives 10 reasons to use a gateway server at http://blogs.technet.com/b/momteam/archive/2008/02/19/10-reasons-to-use-a-gateway-server.aspx.
- Read about chaining gateways at http://blogs.technet.com/b/momteam/archive/2009/12/08/how-to-link-multiple-gateway-servers-together.aspx.
- Mutual authentication takes one of two forms in Operations Manager—Kerberos or certificate authentication. http://www.systemcentercentral.com/BlogDetails/tabid/143/IndexID/32926/Default.aspx is Pete Zerger's master list of mutual authentication related errors. While written for OpsMgr 2007, there are only several new events in OpsMgr 2012, so it is still basically current.

  Pete also has a three-part series on PKI and gateway scenarios here, updated for Operations Manager 2012:
  - http://www.systemcentercentral.com/BlogDetails/tabid/143/indexid/19101/Default.aspx
  - http://www.systemcentercentral.com/BlogDetails/tabid/143/IndexID/19102/Default.aspx
  - http://www.systemcentercentral.com/BlogDetails/tabid/143/IndexID/31342/Default.aspx
- Walter Chomak, formerly of Microsoft Consulting Services, has updated his results on OpsMgr I/O considerations for System Center 2012 Operations Manager. Read about it at http://blog.mobieussystems.com/bid/183789/IO-Reference-Model-for-SCOM-2012.
- You will also want to read Satya Vel's article on network bandwidth utilization at http://blogs.technet.com/momteam/archive/2007/10/22/network-bandwidth-utilization-for-the-various-opsmgr-2007-roles.aspx. While written for OpsMgr 2007, the information is still applicable.
- A discussion of low-bandwidth scenarios is at http://blogs.technet.com/b/momteam/archive/2007/08/31/low-bandwidth-scenarios.aspx.

- Ready to dig into MP authoring? Check out Chapter 22, "Authoring Management Packs and Reports." As the chapter discusses, you can still use the OpsMgr 2007 R2 Authoring console for MP authoring. Read Pete Zerger's discussion of the OpsMgr 2007 R2 Authoring console at http://www.systemcentercentral.com/Details/tabid/147/IndexID/24878/Default.aspx. (You must be logged into System Center Central to download the article.)
- More information on management pack authoring is available at the AuthorMPs site at http://blogs.technet.com/b/authormps/ and Brian Wren's TechNet blog site at http://blogs.technet.com/b/mpauthor/.
- Check out the Management Pack University at http://74.52.12.162/~microsft/conference_agenda.php?cid=19; this contains some great videos developed in the OpsMgr 2007 timeframe.
- Tools for MP authors include the following:

  High-level comparison of the various options: http://www.code4ward.net/main/Blog/tabid/70/EntryId/152/System-Center-2012-Operations-Manager-Authoring-Options.aspx.

  System Center Operations Manager 2007 R2 Authoring Resource Kit: http://www.microsoft.com/downloads/details.aspx?FamilyID=9104af8b-ff87-45a1- 81cd-b73e6f6b51f0&displaylang=en.

  Tool for creating your own customized dashboards: http://blogs.technet.com/b/momteam/archive/2012/06/12/free-windows-server-2008-dashboards-for-opsmgr-2012-and-tool-to-help-create-your-own-customized-dashboards.aspx.

  OpsMgr Community Toolkit: A complete list of community-authored tools for OpsMgr is at http://systemcentercentral.com/tools. (Depending on when you view this site, some of the tools may only work with OpsMgr 2007.)
- Looking for community-authored management packs? For a complete list, see http://www.systemcentercentral.com/mps.
- http://www.systemcentercentral.com/tabid/63/tag/Pack_Catalog+MP_Catalog/Default.aspx is a collection of community-developed utilities and management packs.
- Brian Wren of Microsoft talks about programmatically creating groups at http://blogs.technet.com/brianwren/archive/2008/11/18/programmatically-creating-groups.aspx.
- Cameron Fuller writes about mass-creating computer groups with XML at http://blogs.catapultsystems.com/cfuller/archive/2012/11/28/blastfromthepast-mass-creating-groups-via-xml-in-opsmgr-aka-fun-with-xml.aspx.
- Read about how you can have explicit and dynamic members in a group at http://blogs.catapultsystems.com/cfuller/archive/2012/01/07/a-quick-question-about-groups-in-opsmgr-scom.aspx.

- Want to know how to combine a System.SnmpProbe and System.Performance. DeltaValueCondition module to calculate SNMP counter delta values? See Kris Bash's post at http://operatingquadrant.com/2009/10/14/scom-combining-a-system-snmp-probe-and-system-performance-deltavaluecondition-modules-to-calculate-snmp-counter-delta-values/.
- Looking for training? This is not an exhaustive list, but here are several places that offer courses on OpsMgr 2012:

  Information on InFront Consulting Group's training is at http://www.infrontconsulting.com/training.php. Course offerings include migration from OpsMgr 2007, helping operators use the console to work with alerts, and a boot camp.

  http://learning.microsoft.com/Manager/Catalog.aspx?nav=trainingtype%3aClassroom+Training&qry=system+center+2012 will get you a listing of Microsoft-developed training for System Center 2012.

  Training videos are available at http://technet.microsoft.com/en-us/opsmgr/bb498237.aspx. This page is updated as new material becomes available.

  http://technet.microsoft.com/en-us/video/ff832960?Category=System%20Center includes a list of assorted System Center videos.

  Other training videos and demos are available at http://www.microsoft.com/events/series/technetmms.aspx?tab=webcasts&id=42365.

  The Microsoft Virtual Academy provides an overview of Operations Manager 2012 at http://www.microsoftvirtualacademy.com/tracks/system-center-2012-operations-manager.

  Marnix Wolf, a contributor to this book, references various courses at http://thoughtsonopsmgr.blogspot.com/2012/01/system-center-2012-training-buffet-now.html.

  There is also http://www.kalliance.com/microsoft-it/scom12.htm.

  The System Center 2012 Private Cloud training videos are available for purchase at http://www.cbtplanet.com/it-training/microsoft/scom-2012.htm.

  Source Solutions offers a five-day course on OpsMgr 2012 implementation and administration. See http://www.sourcesolutionsco.com/current-courses/scom2012/ for information.
- *CIO Insight* documents the cost of downtime at http://www.cioinsight.com/c/a/Infrastructure/IT-Downtime-Carries-a-High-Pricetag-448122/.
- For a detailed guide about configuring SQL log shipping for OpsMgr, see http://social.technet.microsoft.com/wiki/contents/articles/11372.configure-sql-server-log-shipping-guide-for-the-system-center-operations-manager-2007-r22012-operational-database.aspx.

- Kevin Holman discusses recommended SQL maintenance for the OpsMgr databases at http://blogs.technet.com/b/kevinholman/archive/2008/04/12/what-sql-maintenance-should-i-perform-on-my-opsmgr-databases.aspx.
- http://blogs.msdn.com/steverac/archive/2007/12/13/scom-2007-operational-and-datawarehouse-grooming.aspx is a post by Steve Rachui discussing the `standarddatasetgroom` stored procedure in the data warehouse database to manually trigger grooming.
- An in-depth article on IOPS for the operational and data warehouse databases is at http://blogs.technet.com/b/momteam/archive/2008/06/24/performance-iops-for-the-db-and-dw-in-opsmgr-2007.aspx.
- To clean up clutter from the Monitoring pane of the Operations console, see Cameron Fuller's article at http://blogs.catapultsystems.com/cfuller/archive/2011/05/11/quicktricks-decluttering-the-monitoring-pane-view.aspx.
- Maintenance mode headaches? See Tim McFadden's GUI-based remote maintenance scheduler, available for download at http://www.scom2k7.com/scom-remote-maintenance-mode-scheduler-20.
- Tao Yang discusses his update of Steve Rachui's group maintenance mode script at http://blog.tyang.org/2012/11/22/group-maintenance-made-powershell-script-updated/. This update uses the OpsMgr software development kit (SDK) rather than the 2007 PowerShell snap-in, so the script works for both OpsMgr 2007 and 2012. For a PowerShell example of how to do this in 2012, see the "OpsMgr Shell" section.
- To enable the Windows Server 2008 physical disks counters, read Marnix Wolf's blog at http://thoughtsonopsmgr.blogspot.com/2010/04/where-are-my-counters-for-windows.html.
- If you're wondering how computer discovery works, see http://blogs.technet.com/b/momteam/archive/2007/12/10/how-does-computer-discovery-work-in-opsmgr-2007.aspx.
- To troubleshoot the discovery wizard, see the articles at http://thoughtsonopsmgr.blogspot.com/2010/08/discovery-wizard-is-running-for-ever.html and http://go.microsoft.com/fwlink/?LinkId=128940.
- To identify computers without an installed agent, see http://www.systemcentercentral.com/BlogDetails/tabid/143/IndexID/94221/Default.aspx, and then read about automating agent installation with PowerShell at http://www.systemcentercentral.com/BlogDetails/tabid/143/IndexID/94248/Default.aspx.
- Troubleshooting agent installation? Check these out:
    - **Troubleshooting installation of the System Center Operations Manager agent:** http://support.microsoft.com/kb/2566152
    - **Console-based agent deployment troubleshooting table:** http://www.systemcentercentral.com/BlogDetails/tabid/143/IndexId/60047/Default.aspx

- The OpsMgr 2012 agent has a new control panel applet that Kevin Holman discusses at http://blogs.technet.com/b/kevinholman/archive/2011/11/10/opsmgr-2012-new-feature-the-agent-control-panel-applet.aspx.
- Jonathan Almquist discusses when one should use Active Directory Integration in OpsMgr at http://blogs.technet.com/b/jonathanalmquist/archive/2010/06/14/ad-integration-considerations.aspx.
- How does Active Directory Integration work? See Steve Rachui's article at http://blogs.msdn.com/b/steverac/archive/2008/03/20/opsmgr-ad-integration-how-it-works.aspx.
- You should never close an alert on a monitor, unless it didn't auto close on its own. Read about this at http://blogs.catapultsystems.com/cfuller/archive/2011/04/15/opsmgr-never-close-an-alert-for-a-monitor-%E2%80%93-the-exception-to-the-%E2%80%9Crule-of-the-monitor%E2%80%9D.aspx.
- Want to use SharePoint to view Operations Manager data? http://technet.microsoft.com/en-us/library/hh212924.aspx#bkmk_howtodeploytheoperationsmanagerwebpart discusses how to deploy the Operations Manager web part. You will also want to check out http://www.scom2k7.com/how-to-view-scom-2012-dashboards-in-sharepoint-2010/, where Tim McFadden discusses how to view OpsMgr 2012 dashboards in SharePoint 2010. Cameron Fuller discusses benefits of using SharePoint with Operations Manager at http://blogs.catapultsystems.com/cfuller/archive/2012/08/16/the-top-5-benefits-of-combining-operations-manager-and-share-point-[scom-sysctr-sharepoint].aspx.
- For details on using web application availability monitoring to configure monitoring of web applications, see Marnix Wolf's article at http://thoughtsonopsmgr.blogspot.com/2012/06/how-to-use-web-application-availability.html, and the OpsMgr product team's article at http://blogs.technet.com/b/momteam/archive/2012/05/31/using-the-web-application-availability-monitoring-to-monitor-web-applications-health.aspx.
- Learn about dashboards from Dale Koetke at http://blogs.technet.com/b/momteam/archive/2011/09/27/introducing-operations-manager-2012-dashboards.aspx.
- How are OpsMgr dashboards different from reports? See http://blogs.technet.com/b/momteam/archive/2011/11/10/how-are-opsmgr-2012-dashboards-different-from-reports.aspx.
- The OpsMgr engineering team provides some Windows Server 2008 dashboards and a tool to help create your own customized dashboards at http://blogs.technet.com/b/momteam/archive/2012/06/12/free-windows-server-2008-dashboards-for-opsmgr-2012-and-tool-to-help-create-your-own-customized-dashboards.aspx.
- Several VMM dashboard views based on the new OpsMgr 2012 dashboard views were created by the *OpsMgr Unleashed* authoring team. These are described and are available for download from http://opsmgrunleashed.wordpress.com/2012/07/13/

free-opsmgr-2012-virtual-machine-manager-dashboards-from-the-opsmgr-unleashed-team-scom/. They are also available on the InformIT page for this book; see Appendix E for details.

- For examples of Live Maps and using them to display OpsMgr information, see
  - http://www.systemcentercentral.com/BlogDetails/tabid/143/IndexID/75218/Default.aspx
  - http://blogs.catapultsystems.com/cfuller/archive/2010/09/14/taking-distributed-applications-to-the-next-level-with-savision-live-maps-%E2%80%93-part-2.aspx
  - http://blogs.catapultsystems.com/cfuller/archive/2011/10/11/opsmgr-2012-savision-amp-dashboards.aspx
  - http://blogs.catapultsystems.com/cfuller/archive/2011/04/28/quicktricks-getting-the-url-for-a-savision-live-map.aspx
  - Savision has a gadget designed to provide state information, available as part of its Live Maps product at http://www.savision.com/resources/blog/sneak-preview-live-maps-vista-gadget
- Cameron Fuller writes about OpsMgr 2012 dashboards at http://www.windowsitpro.com/article/system-center/dashboards-operations-manager-2012-141491 and http://www.windowsitpro.com/article/systems-management/operations-manager-dashboards.
- For some useful SQL queries to use with OpsMgr, see http://blogs.technet.com/b/kevinholman/archive/2007/10/18/useful-operations-manager-2007-sql-queries.aspx and http://www.systemcentercentral.com/Downloads/DownloadsDetails/tabid/144/IndexID/86822/Default.aspx.
- Generating reports with data can be challenging. Read some tips at http://www.windowsitpro.com/article/microsoft-system-center-operations-manager-2007/10-system-center-operations-manager-reporting-tips-140603.
- For ideas on how to make AEM reports more useful, consult these resources:
  - http://contoso.se/blog/?p=537
  - http://blogs.technet.com/b/jimmyharper/archive/2009/02/21/aem-views-and-tables.aspx
- Read how to optimize SQL Server 2012 for private cloud at http://www.microsoft.com/sqlserver/en/us/solutions-technologies/hybrid-it/private-cloud.aspx.
- Michael Pearson has an excellent article discussing SQL Server Reporting Services (SSRS) Recovery Planning, available online from the SQL Server Central community at http://www.sqlservercentral.com/columnists/mpearson/recoveryplanningforsqlreportingservices.asp. You must register with SQLServerCentral to view the full article.

- For information on the types of SQL maintenance to perform on your OpsMgr databases, check Kevin Holman's posting at http://blogs.technet.com/kevinholman/archive/2008/04/12/what-sql-maintenance-should-i-perform-on-my-opsmgr-databases.aspx.
- Here's some information on setting up SQL Server clusters:
    - http://msdn.microsoft.com/en-us/library/ms179530.aspx.
    - http://blogs.technet.com/pfe-ireland/archive/2008/05/16/how-to-create-a-windows-server-2008-cluster-within-hyper-v-using-simulated-iscsi-storage.aspx discusses creating a virtual cluster on Windows 2008/Hyper-V.
- Coauthor Cameron Fuller wrote a (humorous) piece on the Clustering MP at http://www.systemcentercentral.com/BlogDetails/tabid/143/IndexId/51752/Default.aspx, emphasizing major steps to remember when working with clustered resources in OpsMgr.
- For a discussion of agent discovery hanging after enabling the SQL Broker Service, see Steve Rachui's posting at http://blogs.msdn.com/steverac/archive/2009/08/30/opsmgr-agent-discovery-hanging-after-enabling-broker-service.aspx.
- Have an interesting experience when trying to delete an agentless system? This happens if you first install agentless and then install as a managed agent without first deleting the agentless configuration. This information, written for OpsMgr 2007 but still applicable, is available at http://opsmgrunleashed.wordpress.com/2007/06/04/unable-to-delete-agentless-systems/.
- For information on debugging the infamous alert "Script or Executable Failed to Run," see http://blogs.catapultsystems.com/cfuller/archive/2012/11/28/blastfrom-thepast-debugging-the-script-or-executable-failed-to-run-alert.aspx.
- Steve Rachui has a two-part series on understanding monitors:
    - http://blogs.msdn.com/steverac/archive/2009/08/30/understanding-monitors-in-opsmgr-2007-part-i-unit-monitors.aspx
    - http://blogs.msdn.com/steverac/archive/2009/09/06/understanding-monitors-in-opsmgr-2007-part-ii-aggregate-monitors.aspx
- Trying to put systems into maintenance mode? Chapter 23, "PowerShell and Operations Manager," includes a PowerShell solution for this. Several individuals have also done some work to help you put computers into maintenance mode in batch. These were written during the OpsMgr 2007 timeframe, so require some tweaking for OpsMgr 2012.
    - Clive Eastwood's command-line tool, documented at http://blogs.technet.com/cliveeastwood/archive/2007/09/18/agentmm-a-command-line-tool-to-place-opsmgr-agents-into-maintenance-mode.aspx.
    - Andrzej Lipka enhances Clive's approach using the PsExec Tool. See http://blogs.technet.com/alipka/archive/2007/12/20/

opsmgr-2007-putting-computers-in-maintenance-mode-remotely.aspx. PsExec is available at http://technet.microsoft.com/en-us/sysinternals/bb897553.aspx.

- For tips on OLE DB queries, see
  - http://www.systemcentercentral.com/PackCatalog/PackCatalogDetails/tabid/145/IndexID/19773/Default.aspx
  - Kevin Holman provides an example of monitoring a non-Microsoft database at http://blogs.technet.com/b/kevinholman/archive/2012/03/19/opsmgr-how-to-monitor-non-microsoft-sql-databases-in-scom-an-example-using-postgre-sql.aspx
  - Maarten Damen provides an example of how to monitor an Oracle database with an OLE DB watcher at http://www.maartendamen.com/2010/09/monitor-an-oracle-database-with-a-scom-oledb-watcher/
- To learn about OpsMgr key performance indicators, read Cameron Fuller's article at http://www.windowsitpro.com/article/microsoft-system-center-operations-manager-2007/Operations-Manager-Key-Performance-Indicators-128969.
- Kevin Holman discusses self-tuning thresholds (STTs) and how they are created and tuned correctly at http://blogs.technet.com/b/kevinholman/archive/2008/03/19/self-tuning-thresholds-love-and-hate.aspx.
- Recalculating health does not work for more than 95% of all monitors in Operations Manager 2012. This is due to how on-demand recalculation works. To understand on-demand detection, read Boris Yanushpolsky's article at http://blogs.msdn.com/b/boris_yanushpolsky/archive/2008/06/03/on-demand-detection.aspx.
- Read about unit monitors at http://blogs.msdn.com/b/steverac/archive/2009/08/30/understanding-monitors-in-opsmgr-2007-part-i-unit-monitors.aspx. Steve also writes about aggregate rollup monitors; see http://blogs.msdn.com/b/steverac/archive/2009/09/06/understanding-monitors-in-opsmgr-2007-part-ii-aggregate-monitors.aspx.
- To find out if an alert was created by a rule or a monitor, see http://blogs.catapult-systems.com/cfuller/archive/2012/01/30/quicktrick-find-alerts-from-a-monitor-or-rule-in-opsmgr-2012-scom.aspx.
- If you can't get your reports to send email subscriptions, check out http://blogs.msdn.com/ketaanhs/archive/2005/09/05/461055.aspx on how to configure the PermittedHosts entry in the RSReportServer.config file.
- The Alert Forward management pack is available from http://www.systemcentercentral.com/tabid/145/indexId/11518/Default.aspx.
- Read about how to use custom groups to simplify the Operations console at http://opsmgrunleashed.wordpress.com/2009/08/28/how-to-use-customized-groups-to-simplify-the-opsmgr-console-for-server-owners-%E2%80%93-using-custom-groups-with-subscriptions-one-off-notifications/.

- To enable instant messaging in OpsMgr 2012, see http://opsmgrunleashed.wordpress.com/2012/02/24/enabling-instant-messaging-notifications-in-system-center-2012-operations-manager/.
- Check out http://thoughtsonopsmgr.blogspot.com/2010/06/sending-out-sms-messages-with-scom.html for the steps to get SMS functional. System Center Central also has a series of articles at http://www.systemcentercentral.com/tabid/143/IndexId/60339/Default.aspx.
- Kevin Holman discusses subscriptions in OpsMgr 2012 at http://blogs.technet.com/b/kevinholman/archive/2012/04/28/opsmgr-2012-configure-notifications.aspx.
- Want to create a web application synthetic transaction? For registry changes to use the web recorder on 64-bit Windows systems, see http://social.technet.microsoft.com/wiki/contents/articles/1307.scom-howto-use-the-webrecorder-on-windows-64bit.aspx.
- To troubleshoot web recorder issues, see http://blogs.technet.com/b/kevinholman/archive/2009/06/19/web-application-recorder-r2-the-recorder-bar-missing-in-ie.aspx and http://blogs.technet.com/b/kevinholman/archive/2008/11/15/recording-a-web-application-browser-session-driving-you-crazy.aspx.
- To learn about global service monitoring, newly available with SP 1, see http://blogs.technet.com/b/momteam/archive/2012/06/19/global-service-monitor-for-system-center-2012-observing-application-availability-from-an-outside-in-perspective.aspx.
- Interested in writing reports? Here are ways to get started:
    - **Building reports with Report Builder by Stefan Koell:** http://www.code-4ward.net/main/Blog/tabid/70/EntryId/81/How-to-use-Report-Builder-to-create-custom-reports-in-SCOM-2007.aspx.
    - **Building reports in SQL Server Business Intelligence Development Studio by Oskar Landman:** http://www.systemcentercentral.com/BlogDetails/tabid/143/IndexID/60805/Default.aspx.
    - **Building linked reports in OpsMgr 2007 R2 by Pete Zerger:** http://www.systemcentercentral.com/BlogDetails/tabid/143/IndexID/64107/Default.aspx.
    - **Reporting links for creating custom reports by Stefan Stranger:** http://blogs.technet.com/b/stefan_stranger/archive/2011/01/27/opsmgr-custom-reporting-links.aspx.
- David Wallis wrote an application allowing OpsMgr administrators to acknowledge and resolve alerts via email—download it at http://www.systemcentercentral.com/Downloads/DownloadsDetails/tabid/144/IndexID/44253/Default.aspx.
- http://www.systemcentercentral.com/Details/tabid/147/IndexID/35783/Default.aspx discusses using Process Monitor to identify which discovery and monitoring script is using more resources than expected.

- See http://social.technet.microsoft.com/wiki/contents/articles/6938.monitoring-and-modeling-shape-reference-for-visio-management-pack-designer.aspx for the monitoring and modeling shape reference for the Visio MP Designer.
- Kevin Holman documents custom information that can be added to alert descriptions and notifications at http://blogs.technet.com/b/kevinholman/archive/2007/12/12/adding-custom-information-to-alert-descriptions-and-notifications.aspx.
- To write reports on performance counters for large groups of servers, see http://www.bictt.com/blogs/bictt.php/2010/11/28/scom-reports-on-performance-counters-for-large-groups-of-servers.
- Here are some examples of how to query SQL and use the results in OpsMgr, including how to perform checks for a SQL full or differential backup and how to monitor the default management pack:
    - http://blogs.technet.com/b/stefan_stranger/archive/2009/02/02/opsmgr-sql-full-or-differential-backup-check.aspx
    - http://blogs.technet.com/b/jonathanalmquist/archive/2008/11/12/monitor-default-management-pack.aspx
- Read about how network monitoring works at http://blogs.technet.com/b/momteam/archive/sell/09/20/what-gets-monitored-with-system-center-operations-manager-2012-network-monitoring.aspx
- Wondering how to use a property bag? See http://blogs.msdn.com/mariussutara/archive/2008/01/24/momscriptapi-createtypedpropertybag-method.aspx and http://www.systemcentercentral.com/Downloads/DownloadsDetails/tabid/144/indexID/7803/Default.aspx. You may also want to check http://blogs.technet.com/b/momteam/archive/2009/02/13/mp-authoring-resources.aspx and http://blogs.technet.com/b/authormps/archive/2011/02/24/property-bags-and-multi-instance-monitoring.aspx.
- Management pack bundles are supported with OpsMgr 2012, first introduced with System Center Service Manager 2010. Information on how bundles work is at http://blogs.technet.com/b/servicemanager/archive/2009/09/04/introducing-management-pack-bundles.aspx.
- To extract files from an MP bundle, see Daniel Grandini's post at http://nocent-docent.wordpress.com/2012/02/28/opsmgr-2012-how-to-dump-management-pack-bundles/ and Stefan Stranger's discussion at http://blogs.technet.com/b/stefan_stranger/archive/2012/03/06/opsmgr-2012-how-to-dump-management-pack-bundles-small-improvement.aspx.
- Boris Yanushpolsky of the OpsMgr product team developed several utilities to assist with viewing management pack content. These have been updated for OpsMgr 2012 by Daniele Muscetta and can be downloaded from http://blogs.msdn.com/b/dmuscett/archive/2012/02/19/boris-s-tools-updated.aspx.

- Kevin Holman discusses collecting and monitoring information from WMI as performance data at http://blogs.technet.com/b/kevinholman/archive/2008/07/02/collecting-and-monitoring-information-from-wmi-as-performance-data.aspx.

Microsoft's OpsMgr Resources

The following list includes some general Microsoft resources available for OpsMgr 2012:

- A glossary of terms for OpsMgr 2012 is at http://technet.microsoft.com/en-us/library/hh710011.aspx.
- For links to OpsMgr 2012 product documentation and getting started, see http://technet.microsoft.com/en-us/systemcenter/hh285243.
- You can find the official support documentation for OpsMgr 2012 in the following locations:
  - **OpsMgr 2012 RTM:** http://technet.microsoft.com/en-us/library/jj656649.aspx
  - **OpsMgr 2012 Service Pack (SP) 1:** http://technet.microsoft.com/en-us/library/jj656654.aspx
- What's OpsMgr all about, anyway? Microsoft has published a key concepts document. This document, which includes a discussion of modeling, can be downloaded at http://www.microsoft.com/downloads/details.aspx?FamilyID=3a633532-1dde-49b6-930f-7df50b69b77b&DisplayLang=en.
- Microsoft has published a whitepaper on performance tuning guidelines for Windows Server 2008 R2 at http://msdn.microsoft.com/en-us/windows/hardware/gg463392. Guidelines for Windows Server 2012 are at msdn.microsoft.com/en-us/library/windows/hardware/jj248719.aspx.
- Documentation on deploying Operations Manager 2012 is at http://technet.microsoft.com/en-us/library/hh298609.aspx.
- Microsoft talks about mapping your requirements to an OpsMgr design at http://technet.microsoft.com/en-us/library/bb735402.aspx.
- The OpsMgr 2012 Operations Guide is at http://technet.microsoft.com/library/hh212887.aspx.
- http://technet.microsoft.com/en-us/library/hh872885 discusses operations associated with user role profiles.
- See http://technet.microsoft.com/en-us/library/jj628198.aspx for the list of SQL Server versions supported by OpsMgr 2012 Service Pack 1.
- Information about the different SQL Server 2012 editions is at http://www.microsoft.com/sqlserver/en/us/product-info/compare.aspx.
- Read about the differences between the three SQL Server recovery models at http://msdn.microsoft.com/en-us/library/ms189275.aspx.

- http://technet.microsoft.com/en-us/library/ms156421.aspx discusses moving the SSRS databases to another computer. You may also want to read about best practices for moving the SSRS databases in Chapter 12, "Backup and Recovery."
- For information on SQL Server best practices, see http://technet.microsoft.com/en-us/sqlserver/bb671430.aspx.
- The SQL Server 2008 R2 Best Practices Analyzer can be downloaded from http://www.microsoft.com/en-us/download/details.aspx?id=15289. The download page for the SQL Server 2012 version is at http://www.microsoft.com/en-us/download/details.aspx?id=29302.
- For a discussion on upgrading a distributed OpsMgr 2007 environment, see http://technet.microsoft.com/en-us/library/hh241304.
- The process flow diagram for upgrading Operations Manager is at http://technet.microsoft.com/en-us/systemcenter/hh204732.aspx.
- The SQL query to run against the operational database to clean up the Localizedtext table and the Publishmessage table after upgrade can be copied from http://technet.microsoft.com/en-us/library/8c2dbaf4-2966-45e3-a72d-5de90ff4f495#BKMK_VerifyUpgrade.
- Find out how to enable high availability for the Data Access Service at http://technet.microsoft.com/en-us/library/hh316108.aspx.
- For recommendations and best practices when creating overrides, see http://support.microsoft.com/kb/943239.
- Need to add or remove a management group? See the sample VBScript at http://msdn.microsoft.com/en-us/library/hh329017.aspx.
- The System Center 2012 Operations Manager SDK is at http://msdn.microsoft.com/en-us/library/hh329086.aspx.
- Management pack structure is discussed at http://technet.microsoft.com/en-us/library/hh457558.aspx.
- Microsoft's authoring documentation is available at http://technet.microsoft.com/en-us/library/hh457564.aspx.
- The OpsMgr 2012 Authoring guide is at http://technet.microsoft.com/en-us/library/hh457564.aspx.
- The Operations Manager Management Pack Development Kit is discussed at http://msdn.microsoft.com/en-us/library/jj130093.aspx. This provides the information necessary to build and design an OpsMgr management pack.
- Microsoft publishes a module types reference at http://msdn.microsoft.com/en-us/library/ee533869.aspx.
- To configure gateway server failover between management servers, see http://technet.microsoft.com/en-us/library/hh456445.aspx.

- Here are some articles on Audit Collection Services (ACS):
  - **Installing ACS:** http://technet.microsoft.com/en-us/library/hh284670.aspx, http://technet.microsoft.com/en-us/library/hh284665.aspx
  - **Collecting security events:** http://technet.microsoft.com/en-us/library/hh212908.aspx
  - **Deploying ACS and ACS Reporting:** http://technet.microsoft.com/en-us/library/hh298613.aspx
- ACS on UNIX and Linux is discussed at http://technet.microsoft.com/en-us/library/hh212908.aspx#bkmk_acsonunixandlinus.
- All console instances require Microsoft Report Viewer 2010 Redistributable Package, which you can download from http://www.microsoft.com/download/en/details.aspx?displaylang=en&id=6442.
- For information on connecting management groups in Operations Manager, see http://technet.microsoft.com/en-us/library/hh230698.aspx.
- The System Center 2012 Visio MP Designer is available at http://www.microsoft.com/en-us/download/details.aspx?id=30170. Installation instructions are at the TechNet Wiki, http://social.technet.microsoft.com/wiki/contents/articles/6936.installing-the-visio-management-pack-designer.aspx.
- The pattern reference for Visio Management Pack Designer is at http://social.technet.microsoft.com/wiki/contents/articles/6939.pattern-reference-for-visio-management-pack-designer.aspx.
- Download the System Center 2012 Visual Studio Authoring Extensions from http://www.microsoft.com/en-us/download/details.aspx?id=30169. You can find the installation instructions at the TechNet Wiki, http://social.technet.microsoft.com/wiki/contents/articles/5236.visual-studio-authoring-extensions-for-system-center-2012-operations-manager-en-us.aspx.
- Before you seal a management pack, you must create a key file. Jonathan Almquist documents the process for creating a key file at http://blogs.technet.com/b/jonathanalmquist/archive/2008/08/19/seal-a-management-pack.aspx. Sealing a management pack file using MPSeal is documented at http://technet.microsoft.com/en-us/library/hh457550.
- If you have a requirement to monitor VMware, check out Veeam's monitoring for System Center at http://www.veeam.com/vmware-microsoft-esx-monitoring.html.
- The .NET Framework SDK downloadable at http://www.microsoft.com/en-us/download/details.aspx?id=19988.
- The MOMScriptAPI object is documented at http://msdn.microsoft.com/en-us/library/bb437523.
- Microsoft's System Center Pack Catalog is located at the System Center Marketplace site at http://systemcenter.pinpoint.microsoft.com/.

- You can search the System Center Pack Catalog by component; Operations Manager content is at http://systemcenter.pinpoint.microsoft.com/en-US/applications/search/operations-manager-d11?q=.
- Find the Operations Manager management pack guides at http://go.microsoft.com/fwlink/?LinkId=85414.
- The TechNet jumping off page for Operations Manager is at http://technet.microsoft.com/en-us/library/hh205987.aspx.
- The Operations Manager Rule and Monitor Targeting Poster is available at http://download.microsoft.com/download/f/a/7/fa73e146-ab8a-4002-9311-bfe69a570d28/BestPractices_Rule_Monitor_REV_110607.pdf.
- The Microsoft Volume Licensing Brief is available for download at http://www.microsoft.com/en-us/server-cloud/buy/pricing-licensing.aspx. The System Center 2012 Licensing FAQ is available at http://download.microsoft.com/download/8/7/0/870B5D9B-ACF1-4192-BD0A-543AF551B7AE/System%20Center%202012%20Licensing%20FAQ.pdf.
- XML Notepad 2007 is an intuitive tool for browsing and editing XML documents. Read about it at http://msdn2.microsoft.com/en-us/library/aa905339.aspx and download the tool from http://www.microsoft.com/downloads/details.aspx?familyid=72d6aa49-787d-4118-ba5f-4f30fe913628&displaylang=en.
- How do multiple server resource pools actually work? See http://social.technet.microsoft.com/wiki/contents/articles/13920.how-do-multiple-servers-in-a-resource-pool-actually-work.aspx.
- Download OpsMgr component add-ons at http://www.microsoft.com/en-us/download/details.aspx?id=29270.
- Run As accounts for network monitoring are discussed at http://technet.microsoft.com/en-us/library/hh212920.aspx.
- Read about using the Power Consumption monitoring template at http://technet.microsoft.com/en-us/library/ee808918.aspx.
- Interested in learning more about the Microsoft Operations Framework? Check out version 4.0 of the MOF at http://go.microsoft.com/fwlink/?LinkId=50015. Details on the MOF Deliver phase are at http://technet.microsoft.com/en-us/library/cc543223.aspx and http://technet.microsoft.com/en-us/library/cc506047.aspx. You can read about the MOF Envision SMF at http://technet.microsoft.com/en-us/library/cc531013.aspx, and the Manage layer at http://technet.microsoft.com/en-us/library/cc506048.aspx.
- Information on the Infrastructure Optimization (IO) model is available at http://www.microsoft.com/technet/infrastructure.
- An IDC study about the IO model is at http://download.microsoft.com/download/a/4/4/a4474b0c-57d8-41a2-afe6-32037fa93ea6/IDC_windesktop_IO_whitepaper.pdf.

D

- If you want to learn about Service Modeling Language (SML), see http://www.w3.org/TR/sml/. For additional technical information on SML from Microsoft, visit http://technet.microsoft.com/en-us/library/bb725986.aspx.
- Read what's new in Operations Manager 2012 at http://technet.microsoft.com/en-US/library/jj656648.aspx. Changes for Service Pack 1 are documented at http://technet.microsoft.com/en-US/library/jj656650.aspx.
- System requirements for System Center 2012 Operations Manager are at http://technet.microsoft.com/en-us/library/hh205990.aspx. This includes information about the initial release as well as Service Pack 1.
- OpsMgr 2012 release notes are at http://technet.microsoft.com/en-us/library/hh561709.aspx. See http://technet.microsoft.com/en-US/library/jj656651.aspx for the Service Pack 1 release notes.
- You can download the Windows Server Operating System monitoring management pack at http://www.microsoft.com/en-us/download/details.aspx?id=9296.
- The OpsMgr 2007 resource kit is at the System Center Operations Manager TechCenter (http://go.microsoft.com/fwlink/?LinkId=94593). This is not yet updated for OpsMgr 2012.
- The Operations Manager 2012 Sizing Helper Tool is described at http://blogs.technet.com/b/momteam/archive/2012/04/02/operations-manager-2012-sizing-helper-tool.aspx and can be downloaded from http://blogs.technet.com/cfs-file.ashx/__key/communityserver-components-postattachments/00-03-48-96-45/System-Center-2012-Operations-Manager-Sizing-Helper-Tool-v1.xls.
- A discussion of applicable user roles for APM is at http://technet.microsoft.com/en-us/library/hh544002.
- APM grooming is discussed at http://technet.microsoft.com/en-us/library/jj159297.

Blogs

There has been an explosion of blogs with information regarding OpsMgr and System Center. Here are some blogs the authors have used. Some are more active than others, and new blogs seem to spring up overnight!

- A number of OpsMgr folks blog at System Center Central (http://www.systemcentercentral.com).
- The OpsMgr team has a blog at http://blogs.technet.com/b/momteam/. You can find older postings at http://blogs.technet.com/operationsmgr/ and http://blogs.technet.com/smsandmom/.
- If you're interested in keeping up with VMM, the VMM team has a blog at http://blogs.technet.com/scvmm/.
- http://www.contoso.se/blog/ is the System Center blog by Anders Bengtsson, now a Microsoft premier field engineer (PFE) and formerly an MVP.

- See a blog by Stefan Stranger (former MVP and now at Microsoft) at http://blogs.technet.com/stefan_stranger/.
- Kevin Sullivan's Management blog is at https://blogs.technet.com/kevinsul_blog/. (Kevin is a Technology Specialist at Microsoft focusing on management products.)
- http://blogs.technet.com/kevinholman is Kevin Holman's System Center blog. Kevin is the technical editor for this book.
- http://blogs.msdn.com/rslaten is a blog by Russ Slaten, a Microsoft Escalation Engineer supporting System Center products.
- http://blogs.msdn.com/steverac is Steve Rachui's manageability blog. Steve is a PFE at Microsoft, concentrating on OpsMgr and ConfigMgr.
- http://blogs.technet.com/mgoedtel/ is a blog by Matt Goedtel, a Microsoft MCS consultant focusing on Operations Manager.
- http://discussitnow.wordpress.com/ is by Blake Mengotto, a former MVP and self-described "MOM dude."
- http://blogs.msdn.com/eugenebykov/ is a great source of information on authoring OpsMgr reports by Eugene Bykov, an OpsMgr developer responsible for the reporting user interface.
- Veeam provides an extended generic report library (GRL) for analyzing the health and performance of infrastructure objects. Learn more at http://www.veeam.com/extended-generic-report-library.html.
- http://www.scom2k7.com/, by Timothy McFadden, is titled "Everything System Center 2012 Operations Manager."
- http://www.techlog.org/ is all about everything Microsoft, by Maarten Goet, Kenneth van Surksum, Steven van Loef, and Sander Klaassen in the Netherlands.
- http://blog.advisec.com/ is by Bjorn Axell, a System Center Datacenter and Cloud Management MVP currently working at Dell. Previous entries are at http://advisec.wordpress.com/.
- www.systemcenterguide.com is a System Center blog by Duncan McAlynn.
- Gordon McKenna's blog is available at http://wmug.co.uk/blogs/gordons_blog/default.aspx. Gordon is a System Center Datacenter and Cloud Management MVP, has worked with the Operations Manager software since its Mission Critical Software days, and is extremely knowledgeable on the product.
- Walter Chomak's blog on OpsMgr design and capacity planning while at Microsoft is at http://blogs.technet.com/wchomak/. He currently blogs at http://blog.mobieussystems.com.
- Ian Blyth, previously a Lead Technical Specialist in Microsoft UK, blogs at http://ianblythmanagement.wordpress.com/ on System Center Technologies.
- MVP Scott Moss blogs at http://om2012.wordpress.com/ and http://systemcentercentral.com/smoss.

- Jonathan Almquist, a contributor to this book, has blogs at http://blogs.technet.com/b/jonathanalmquist/ and http://scomskills.com/blog/.
- www.authoringfriday.com is MVP Oskar Landman's blog on authoring management packs and integration packs. Oskar is a contributor to this book.
- Contributor MVP Pete Zerger blogs at (and runs) http://www.systemcentercentral.com.
- http://thoughtsonopsmgr.blogspot.com is maintained by MVP Marnix Wolf, a contributor to this book.

Here are our own blogs:

- Our Operations Manager blogs are located at http://systemcentercentral.com/blogs/scomauthor and http://opsmgrunleashed.wordpress.com.
- http://blogs.catapultsystems.com/cfuller/ is where Cameron discusses his technical theories, ramblings, and rants. Cameron cross-publishes to System Center Central at http://www.systemcentercentral.com/CameronFuller.
- http://www.networkworld.com/community/meyler is a blog by Kerrie, with more general discussion topics, but concentrating on OpsMgr and Microsoft management.
- Check out http://www.techrepublic.com/topics/john+joyner for thoughts by John Joyner.
- http://www.systemcentercentral.com/tabid/150/tag/Blog+ByExample/Default.aspx is the OpsMgr by Example series on System Center Central, maintained by the *OpsMgr Unleashed* authors.

OpsMgr Shell

An extension to PowerShell, the Operations Manager Shell (known as the Command Shell prior to the OpsMgr 2007 R2 release), enables you to do most everything you would ever want to for OpsMgr in a batch or scripted mode. Here are some useful links:

- The PowerShell cmdlets for OpsMgr 2012 have been renamed. For more information about the new naming standards as well as cmdlet naming collisions, see http://blogs.msdn.com/b/powershell/archive/2009/09/20/what-s-up-with-command-prefixes.aspx.
- Stefan Stranger provides a handy cross reference between OpsMgr 2007 cmdlets and the new OpsMgr 2012 cmdlets at http://blogs.technet.com/b/stefan_stranger/archive/2011/11/26/everything-you-want-to-know-about-the-om12-cmdlets.aspx.
- http://www.systemcentercentral.com/BlogDetails/tabid/143/IndexID/94404/Default.aspx is an article about using PowerShell to create a Report Operator role.
- Scott Moss discusses using PowerShell for agent-based installation at http://om2012.wordpress.com/2011/12/07/om12-rc-deploying-agents-with-powershell.

- For information about configuring agent failover in PowerShell or a script to bulk-set this configuration for a group of servers, see http://www.teknoglot.se/code/powershell/opsmgr-2012-agent-failover-simple-script-with-wildcards-opsmgr-powershell/.
- http://blogs.msdn.com/scshell/ is about getting started with the OpsMgr Shell. Robert Sprague, a PowerShell guru on the OpsMgr team, maintains this site.
- http://www.systemcentercentral.com/BlogDetails/tabid/143/IndexID/93897/Default.aspx discusses using `Get_SCOMManagementPack` to bulk delete management packs, where the non-English management packs are deleted.
- An example of computer discovery and push install of the agent through PowerShell is demonstrated in a posting on automating agent discovery and deployment with PowerShell at http://www.systemcentercentral.com/BlogDetails/tabid/143/IndexID/94248/Default.aspx.
- Use PowerShell to get BeanSpy and PowerShell install scripts if your Java apps require manual discovery. The snippets are at http://www.systemcentercentral.com/BlogDetails/tabid/143/IndexID/94786/Default.aspx.
- See how to reset unit monitors in bulk with PowerShell at http://www.systemcentercentral.com/BlogDetails/tabid/143/IndexID/94705/Default.aspx.
- Finding computers without the Active Directory Helper Object (OOMADS) with PowerShell is discussed at http://www.systemcentercentral.com/BlogDetails/tabid/143/IndexID/94661/Default.aspx.
- System Center Central has a discussion on running a task in bulk using PowerShell at http://www.systemcentercentral.com/BlogDetails/tabid/143/IndexID/94493/Default.aspx.
- Read how to automate agent discovery and deployment with PowerShell at http://www.systemcentercentral.com/BlogDetails/tabid/143/IndexID/94248/Default.aspx, which includes a sample script.
- Use a PowerShell script to find servers experiencing the most heartbeat failures. http://www.systemcentercentral.com/BlogDetails/tabid/143/IndexID/94158/Default.aspx provides details.
- For examples of OpsMgr2007 PowerShell examples migrated to OpsMgr 2012, see the collection of updated single line PowerShell scripts (one-liners) at http://www.systemcentercentral.com/BlogDetails/tabid/143/IndexID/89870/Default.aspx.
- You can update agent failover settings in bulk as described in the article on updating agent failover settings from a spreadsheet with PowerShell at http://www.systemcentercentral.com/tabid/143/indexid/95393/default.aspx.
- To balance agents across multiple management servers, see a posting in the OpsMgr by Example series at http://www.systemcentercentral.com/BlogDetails/tabid/143/IndexID/96292/Default.aspx.

- Learn about OpsMgr 2012 group maintenance mode via PowerShell at http://www.systemcentercentral.com/BlogDetails/tabid/143/IndexID/94576/Default.aspx.
- Here's a four-part series on creating a two-state PowerShell script monitor using the OpsMgr 2007 R2 Authoring console by Stefan Koell (code4ward.net). The series comes with a sample MP you can use to check your work and see the intended end result (http://www.systemcentercentral.com/tabid/144/IndexId/50087/Default.aspx). (The PowerShell code, written for OpsMgr 2007, can be used with OpsMgr 2012 with some modifications. See Chapter 23 for further information.):
    - http://www.systemcentercentral.com/BlogDetails/tabid/143/IndexID/44971/Default.aspx
    - http://www.systemcentercentral.com/BlogDetails/tabid/143/IndexID/46908/Default.aspx
    - http://www.systemcentercentral.com/BlogDetails/tabid/143/IndexID/48469/Default.aspx
    - http://www.systemcentercentral.com/BlogDetails/tabid/143/IndexID/50085/Default.aspx
- Here's a posting on how to create a PowerShell task for OpsMgr using the Authoring console by Andreas Zuckerhut, at http://www.systemcentercentral.com/BlogDetails/tabid/143/IndexID/41687/Default.aspx.

PowerShell Information

You can find information on PowerShell itself at the following sites:

- The official PowerShell site is at http://www.microsoft.com/powershell.
- http://social.technet.microsoft.com/Forums/en-US/operationsmanagerextensibility/thread/a3d09372-1a93-418a-a93c-9bc9ddd075b9 is an unofficial PowerShell FAQ by former PowerShell MVP Marco Shaw. Marco updates this FAQ on an as-needed ("irregular") basis.
- The Microsoft TechNet social forum covering general PowerShell discussions is at http://social.technet.microsoft.com/Forums/en-US/winserverpowershell/threads.
- Marco Shaw maintains his own blog at http://marcoshaw.blogspot.com.
- You may want to check all the PowerShell webcasts by the Scripting Guys at http://www.microsoft.com/technet/scriptcenter/webcasts/ps.mspx.
- Direct from the PowerShell guy himself (Marc van Orsouw, PowerShell MVP), is located at http://thepowershellguy.com/blogs/posh/default.aspx.
- The Windows PowerShell team has its blog at http://blogs.msdn.com/powershell/.
- A self-training guide is available at http://blogs.technet.com/b/musings_of_a_technical_tam/archive/2012/06/04/windows-powershell-self-training-guide.aspx.

- If Windows PowerShell is new to you, check out this TechEd session at http://channel9.msdn.com/Events/TechEd/NorthAmerica/2012/WSV321-R. You may also want to check out Chapter 23 of this book if you haven't already.
- Here are resources that discuss using Microsoft's certificate creation tool, makecert.exe, to generate certificates to create self-signed PowerShell scripts:
  - Don Jones' *TechNet Magazine* article "Sign Here, Please," available at http://technet.microsoft.com/en-us/magazine/2008.04.powershell.aspx
  - Scott Hanselman's blog post Signing PowerShell scripts at http://www.hanselman.com/blog/SigningPowerShellScripts.aspx
- The Microsoft Scripting Guys provide a two-part series on signing PowerShell scripts with an enterprise PKI. See http://blogs.technet.com/b/heyscriptingguy/archive/2010/06/16/hey-scripting-guy-how-can-i-sign-windows-powershell-scripts-with-an-enterprise-windows-pki-part-1-of-2.aspx and http://blogs.technet.com/b/heyscriptingguy/archive/2010/06/17/hey-scripting-guy-how-can-i-sign-windows-powershell-scripts-with-an-enterprise-windows-pki-part-2-of-2.aspx.
- For information about the PowerShell pipeline, see http://technet.microsoft.com/en-us/magazine/2007.07.powershell.aspx by Don Jones. Don also created a pipeline input workbook that provides a good walkthrough of how the pipeline works, available at http://morelunches.com/files/powershell3/PipelineInput.pdf.
- Learn about variables in PowerShell at http://www.powershellpro.com/powershell-tutorial-introduction/variables-arrays-hashes/.
- Help with Windows PowerShell is available at http://social.technet.microsoft.com/Forums/en/ITCG/threads or http://powershellcommunity.org/Forums.aspx.
- Scheduling a PowerShell script through scheduled tasks is discussed at http://social.technet.microsoft.com/Forums/en-US/exchange2010/thread/0cad57bf-1113-4622-aac3-c3278fa97d72/.
- Find PowerShell script examples at http://www.microsoft.com/technet/scriptcenter/hubs/msh.mspx.
- PowerShell+ is a free PowerShell editing and debugging environment. You can get a free personal copy at http://www.powershell.com/downloads/psp1.zip.
- Even more about PowerShell and examples of some of the constructs are available in an article by Don Jones at http://www.microsoft.com/technet/technetmag/issues/2007/01/PowerShell/default.aspx.

Cross Platform

One of the most visible enhancements in the R2 version of OpsMgr 2007 was its integrated monitoring of cross platform environments, which continues to have improvements in OpsMgr 2012. Here are some references on cross platform monitoring:

- Cross platform security requirements are discussed at http://technet.microsoft.com/en-us/library/hh212926.aspx and http://technet.microsoft.com/en-us/library/hh212886.aspx. You will also want to read Scott Weisler's discussion at http://www.systemcentercentral.com/BlogDetails/tabid/143/indexId/94460/Default.aspx, also posted at http://opsmgrunleashed.wordpress.com/2012/07/07/cross-platform-discovery-settings/.
- For information on managing resource pools for UNIX and Linux systems, see http://technet.microsoft.com/en-us/library/hh287152.aspx.
- The monitoring pack and guides for UNIX and Linux systems can be downloaded from http://www.microsoft.com/en-us/download/details.aspx?id=29696. These are not available in the System Center catalog.
- To copy files to a UNIX or Linux system using SSH, see the instructions at http://www.garron.me/linux/scp-linux-mac-command-windows-copy-files-over-ssh.html.
- If you need to manually discover JEE application servers, see Chris Crammond's article at http://blogs.technet.com/b/random_happy_dev_thoughts/archive/2012/05/21/manually-discovering-jee-application-servers-with-scom-2012.aspx.
- Here are some articles specific to UNIX/Linux agent installation:
  - **Troubleshooting UNIX/Linux Agent Discovery in System Center 2012 - Operations Manager:** http://social.technet.microsoft.com/wiki/contents/articles/4966.aspx
  - **Installing sudo on Solaris:** http://sysinfo.bascomp.org/solaris/installing-sudo-on-solaris/
  - **Enable ssh root login in Solaris 10:** https://blogs.oracle.com/sunrise/entry/enable_ssh_root_login_in
- For information on configuring sudo, see http://social.technet.microsoft.com/wiki/contents/articles/7375.configuring-sudo-elevation-for-unix-and-linux-monitoring-with-system-center-2012-operations-manager.aspx.
- The wiki for UNIX/Linux agent deployment at http://social.technet.microsoft.com/wiki/contents/articles/4966.aspx.
- Kevin Holman's blog article on deploying UNIX/Linux agents using OpsMgr 2012 is at http://blogs.technet.com/b/kevinholman/archive/2012/03/18/deploying-unix-linux-agents-using-opsmgr-2012.aspx.
- For platforms not supported by the OpsMgr 2012 release, Microsoft has published the providers on CodePlex (http://scx.codeplex.com).

System Center

Here are some references and articles regarding other components of Microsoft's System Center:

- A great source of information for all things System Center-related including Operations Manager is System Center Central (http://www.systemcentercentral.com).
- The System Center Virtual User Group is dedicated to providing educational resources and collaboration between users of System Center technologies worldwide. Bi-monthly meetings present topics from industry experts, including Microsoft engineers. These sessions are recorded for your convenience. To join the user group, go to http://www.linkedin.com/groupRegistration?gid=101906.
- http://www.myITforum.com is a community of worldwide Information Technology (IT) professionals and a website established in 1999 by Rod Trent. myITforum includes topics on System Center and Information Technology.
- The Microsoft System Center website is at http://www.microsoft.com/en-us/server-cloud/system-center/.
- Microsoft's jumping off point for System Center technical resources starts at http://technet.microsoft.com/en-us/systemcenter/.
- The System Center Support page is at http://support.microsoft.com/ph/16340
- Read Network World's reviews of System Center at http://www.networkworld.com/reviews/2012/092412-microsoft-system-center-test-262332.html, http://www.networkworld.com/reviews/2012/071612-microsoft-system-center-260550.html, and http://www.networkworld.com/reviews/2012/092412-microsoft-system-center-test-how-262335.html.
- System Center is all about ITIL and MOF. Learn about the Information Technology Information Library (ITIL) 2011 update to ITIL v3 at http://www.itilnews.com/ITIL_v4_Simply_CSI_for_ITIL_v3.html.
- Get a jumpstart on Orchestrator runbooks at http://www.systemcentercentral.com/BlogDetails/tabid/143/IndexID/92651/Default.aspx.
- Virtual labs for System Center components are located at http://technet.microsoft.com/en-us/bb539977.aspx.
- Not officially in System Center, but definitely part of Microsoft's management story, is Windows Intune. Here are some links about Intune 4 ("Wave D"):
    - http://blogs.technet.com/b/server-cloud/archive/2012/09/10/system-center-2012-configuration-manager-sp1-beta-and-windows-intune-update.aspx
    - http://www.windowsitpro.com/article/cloud-computing2/microsoft-releases-windows-intune-4-145042
    - http://www.zdnet.com/microsoft-windows-intune-how-wave-d-changes-the-mobile-device-management-game-7000009027/
    - http://www.techlog.org/2012/12/31/configmgr-and-windows-intune-better-together/

- Read Network World's take on how System Center 2012 SP 1 helps customers manage their on-premises IT and Azure cloud services with a single set of tools at http://www.networkworld.com/news/2013/011513-microsoft-system-center-further-fuses-265852.html.
- Find out what's new in System Center 2012 SP 1 at http://technet.microsoft.com/library/jj649385.aspx.
- The Windows Server technical library is located at http://technet.microsoft.com/en-us/library/bb625087.aspx.
- Microsoft's *TechNet Magazine* is available online at http://technet.microsoft.com/en-us/magazine/default.aspx.
- Microsoft's Sysinternals website is at http://technet.microsoft.com/en-us/sysinternals/default.aspx.
- Windows IT Pro is an online publication including articles about System Center and other topics. See http://www.windowsitpro.com/ for information.

Public Forums

If you need an answer to a question, the first place to check is the Microsoft public forums. Here's a list of the current OpsMgr forums:

- **General:** http://social.technet.microsoft.com/Forums/en-US/operationsmanagergeneral/
- **Deployment:** http://social.technet.microsoft.com/Forums/en-US/operationsmanagerdeployment/
- **Management packs:** http://social.technet.microsoft.com/Forums/en-US/operationsmanagermgmtpacks/
- **Reporting:** http://social.technet.microsoft.com/Forums/en-US/operationsmanagerreporting/
- **Authoring:** http://social.technet.microsoft.com/Forums/en-US/operationsmanagerauthoring/
- **Extensibility (SDK, Connectors, and PowerShell):** http://social.technet.microsoft.com/Forums/en-US/operationsmanagerextensibility
- **AVIcode 5.7:** http://social.technet.microsoft.com/Forums/en-US/operationsmanageravicode/
- **UNIX and Linux:** http://social.technet.microsoft.com/Forums/en-US/operationsmanagerunixandlinux/
- **Application Performance Monitoring:** http://social.technet.microsoft.com/Forums/en-US/scomapm/

APPENDIX E
Available Online

IN THIS APPENDIX

Online content is available to provide add-on value to readers of *System Center 2012 Operations Manager Unleashed*. This material, organized by chapter, can be downloaded from http://www.informit.com/store/product.aspx?isbn=0672335913. This content is not available elsewhere. Note that the authors and publisher do not guarantee or provide technical support for the material.

Database Scripts

Chapter 12, "Backup and Recovery," discusses the Optimization_results.sql script to determine the optimization results of reindexing the data warehouse.

Chapter 12 also discusses the steps to move the operational database to a different SQL Server. During this process, error messages specific to Operations Manager are not moved as they are stored in the sys.messages Catalog View in the Master database. Running Fix_OM12DB_ErrorMsgs.SQL adds these messages to Master on the new server.

Chapter 16, "Network Monitoring," includes a number of SQL queries to assist with viewing monitoring workflows. These are

- Rules included in network monitoring management packs.sql
- Viewing out of box monitors.sql
- Network Monitoring Management packs rules enabled by default.sql
- Return rules targeting a specific type of device (Cisco).sql

PowerShell Failover Scripts

Chapter 9, "Complex Configurations," includes several PowerShell scripts:

- AgentFailOver.ps1 enables agent failover to another gateway server. Replace the NetBIOS names with NetBIOS names of your gateway servers and management server.
- ManagementServerFailOverForGateway.ps1 enables the gateway servers to fail over to another management server. Replace the fully qualified domain names (FQDNs) with FQDNs of your gateway server and management servers.

Chapter 23, "PowerShell and Operations Manager," gives a nice example of defining failover management servers, based on a script from Jimmy Harper. See Set-FailoverMS.ps1.

Cloning Notification Subscriptions

Chapter 23 also discusses copying subscriptions and references an article on cloning notification subscriptions at http://www.systemcentercentral.com/tabid/143/indexid/94855/default.aspx. A copy of the script in that article, CloneSub.ps1, is included with the online content for this book for your convenience.

Post Upgrade Cleanup Task

Chapter 6, "Upgrading to System Center 2012 Operations Manager," discusses the SCOM-2012-Post-Upgrade-SQL-Cleanup.sql script to use after upgrading the management group. This SQL query, run against the operational database, cleans up the Localizedtext table and the Publishmessage table. The script, available at http://technet.microsoft.com/en-us/library/8c2dbaf4-2966-45e3-a72d-5de90ff4f495#BKMK_VerifyUpgrade, is included as content for this book.

Discovery and Agent Activity

Chapter 8, "Installing and Configuring Agents," utilizes a number of scripts:

- **Computers in Active Directory without an OpsMgr Agent Installed.ps1:** Based on the OU or container you specify, this PowerShell script identifies computers in Active Directory that do not have an OpsMgr agent installed and stores that list of systems in a file.
- **Agent Discovery and Deployment with PowerShell.ps1:** This script automates agent installation based upon the file output from the Computers in Active Directory without an OpsMgr Agent Installed.ps1 script.
- **Uninstall Agents Based on Name.ps1:** This script disables the SCOMAgentProxy setting and uninstalls agents based upon a wildcard match of the DNSHostName field of the agent.

- **Set Primary and Failover Management Servers.ps1:** This useful script configures the primary and failover management servers for an agent.
- **Find Primary Management Server.ps1:** This script outputs the primary management server for an agent.
- **InstallOpsMgrAgent.cmd:** This can be used as a startup script in a group policy to deploy the OpsMgr agent.
- **PowerShell Based Agent Installation.ps1:** This is an example of how you could deploy an OpsMgr 2012 agent using PowerShell.

Creating a Report User Role

Chapter 10, "Security and Compliance," includes a parameter-driven PowerShell function to create a Report Operator role, CreateReportRole.ps1. This code was originally written for OpsMgr 2007 as a script; it has been modified to be a PowerShell function for OpsMgr 2012. It incorporates the OpsMgr 2007 PowerShell provider.

Obtaining SNMP Information

Chapter 16 discusses the SNMPUtil tool used to verify SNMP agent configuration. This tool was originally included with the Windows 2000 Resource Kit, which is no longer available on Microsoft's website. For your convenience, the authors include it as online content in a zip file.

ACS Database Sizing

Also discussed in Chapter 10 is ACS database sizing. The ACS DB Size Calculator.xlsx spreadsheet enables you to size the audit database, allowing for granular adjustments in security event logging options.

Virtual Machine Manager Dashboards

Chapter 11, "Dashboards, Trending, and Forecasting," steps through the process to create a dashboard management pack, Virtual.Machine.Manager.Dashboards.xml, for monitoring System Center Virtual Machine Manager. For your convenience, the authors include this as online content.

Backing Up Your Management Group

Chapter 12 discusses an approach to back up significant files and databases necessary to restore your management group. Backups.zip includes the scripts and instructions.

Authoring Files

Three zip files are included for Chapter 22, "Authoring Management Packs and Reports."

- **Authoring_reg files.zip:** This file contains registry files that prepare an OpsMgr 2012 agent to simulate all configurations for a car, adding several keys and values to the registry of the agent. Import the Unleashed.Car.Example.reg registry file (from the online content) into the registry by copying the file to the agent and double-clicking the .reg file.
- **Authoring_MP_Visio_Designer_Example.zip:** This contains the Visio diagram and management pack used to create the Visio Designer Management Pack. Additional information is in the ReadMe included in the zip file.
- **Authoring_VisualStudio_Example_and Key.zip:** Contains the Visual Studio projects to be opened and used in Visual Studio with the Visio Management Pack Extensions installed. The key file is used to seal the management packs. See the ReadMe for additional information.

Live Links

Reference URLs (see Appendix D, "Reference URLs") are provided as live links. These include more than 350 (clickable) hypertext links and references to materials and sites related to Operations Manager.

A disclaimer and unpleasant fact regarding live links: URLs change! Companies are subject to mergers and acquisitions, pages move and change on websites, and so on. Although these links were accurate in December 2012, it is possible some will change or be "dead" by the time you read this book. Sometimes the Wayback Machine (http://www.archive.org/index.php) can rescue you from dead or broken links. This site is an Internet archive, and it will take you back to an archived version of a site...sometimes.

Index

Symbols

A

B

C

D

E

F

G

H

I

J

K

L

M

N

O

P

Q

R

S

U

W

Safari
Books Online

FREE Online Edition

Your purchase of ***System Center 2012 Operations Manager Unleashed*** includes access to a free online edition for 45 days through the **Safari Books Online** subscription service. Nearly every Sams book is available online through **Safari Books Online**, along with thousands of books and videos from publishers such as Addison-Wesley Professional, Cisco Press, Exam Cram, IBM Press, O'Reilly Media, Prentice Hall, Que, and VMware Press.

Safari Books Online is a digital library providing searchable, on-demand access to thousands of technology, digital media, and professional development books and videos from leading publishers. With one monthly or yearly subscription price, you get unlimited access to learning tools and information on topics including mobile app and software development, tips and tricks on using your favorite gadgets, networking, project management, graphic design, and much more.

Activate your FREE Online Edition at informit.com/safarifree

STEP 1: Enter the coupon code: YMQSUWA.

STEP 2: New Safari users, complete the brief registration form. Safari subscribers, just log in.

If you have difficulty registering on Safari or accessing the online edition, please e-mail customer-service@safaribooksonline.com